The Nature of Mind

The Nature of Mind

Edited by

David M. Rosenthal

New York   Oxford
OXFORD UNIVERSITY PRESS
1991

Oxford University Press

Oxford   New York   Toronto
Delhi   Bombay   Calcutta   Madras   Karachi
Petaling Jaya   Singapore   Hong Kong   Tokyo
Nairobi   Dar es Salaam   Cape Town
Melbourne   Auckland

and associated companies in
Berlin   Ibadan

Published by Oxford University Press, Inc.,
200 Madison Avenue, New York, NY 10016

Oxford is a registered trademark of Oxford University Press

Library of Congress Cataloging-in-Publication Data
The Nature of mind / edited by David M. Rosenthal.
p.   cm.   Includes bibliographical references.
ISBN 0-19-504670-6. — ISBN 0-19-504671-4 (pbk.)
1. Philosophy of mind.   I. Rosenthal, David M.
BD418.3.N37   1990   89-48067
128′.2—dc20

5 7 9 8 6 4

Printed in the United States of America
on acid-free paper

For Joshua

Contents

II. Self and Other

Introduction   83

A. Knowing Other Minds

B. Privileged Access

C. The Theory Approach

III. Mind and Body

Introduction   161

A. The Topic-Neutral Approach

B. Functionalist Approaches

C. The Mental–Physical Contrast

D. Eliminative Materialism

IV. The Nature of Mind

Introduction   289

A. Thinking

B. Sensing

C. Consciousness, Self, and Personhood

V. Psychological Explanation

Introduction   479

A. The Computational Approach

B. Individualism

C. Scientific Versus Folk Psychology

The Nature of Mind

General Introduction

Few subjects excite more curiosity than the mind. Partly this is because mental phenomena are so basic to our own nature. We are creatures that think, experience, feel emotion, and make decisions. Understanding these things is central to our grasp of the kind of being we are. Our mental functioning is also important to what we are individually, since it is mainly in terms of the variations in our mental lives that we develop our sense of ourselves, and of each other, as individuals.

Another reason the mind captures our interest is that mental phenomena seem so different from everything else. The things around us normally have spatial characteristics, such as size, shape, and location. By contrast, it makes no sense to think of our experiences, desires, thoughts, and feelings as having size or shape, and it is even unclear whether we can assign bodily location to these things. Moreover, we know about mental states and processes differently from the way we know about everything else. Much of our knowledge about the mind is immediate, and seems even to have some sort of privileged status. Because mental states seem so different from everything else, it may strike us as unclear how they could possibly fit with the rest of reality. Indeed, it may even seem puzzling how mental states and processes could occur in a universe governed by physical laws and built up out of purely physical constituents. How to make sense of our own place in the physical universe will therefore seem problematic.

Mental phenomena also interest us because mental states play such a central role in the things that give meaning to our lives. Social interactions and interpersonal ties require us to understand each other's thoughts, feelings, and desires. Language, which expresses our thoughts and feelings, would itself be impossible without elaborate mental endowments. And we can understand the "higher" aspects of our lives, such as morality and aesthetic enjoyment, only if we have some grasp of the workings of the mind.

Despite our seemingly immediate grasp of mental states, it is often hard to put into words what we know about the mind. We seem to understand the mind readily enough from our own experience. What causes problems is articulating what we know objectively, that is, in terms that are independent of our own case. This raises a problem about how the study of mind should proceed. Are mental processes subject to scientific study, as other natural phenomena are? Or is the study of mind limited to our everyday, commonsense descriptions of mental states? If there can be a science of mind, what is its status relative to the other sciences?

The readings collected here reflect these concerns. Part I contains selections, some by historical figures, that discuss the general issue of how mind fits with the rest of reality. Part II focuses on how we know about mental states, in particular, the difference between how we know our own mental states and how we know about other people's. Part III asks how mental and bodily processes are related, and whether any acceptable model is possible of the relationship mind has to physical reality. Part IV takes up the question of how mental phenomena differ from the nonmental, and what distinguishes the main kinds of mental phenomena, such as thinking, sensing, and consciousness. Part V, finally, turns to various issues concerning the explanation of behavior by appeal to mental states and processes.

Each of these five parts is self-contained and can be studied without having read earlier selections. Moreover, individual selections from one part are often useful in connection with those of another. A brief introduction to each part sets out the issues and problems that motivate the selections and discusses the contribution each author makes toward understanding those issues and solving those problems. This general introduction provides a preliminary overview of these problems and issues and the connections among them. The five sections of the general introduction correspond to the five main parts of this anthology.

I.   Two Conceptions of Mind

It is an important feature of our commonsense conception of the mind that mental states and processes are unlike anything else. Our sense that the mental is unique stems in part from the way we know about the mind. To common sense it seems that simply being in various mental states is sufficient to tell us most of what we know about those mental states. When I am in pain, or believe something, my being in those states is by itself normally enough for me to know that I am. In this way, my knowing what I think or feel is automatic and immediate. We know what it is to think or feel just from our own thinking and feeling. Compared with this special, direct sort of knowledge, it may seem that we learn relatively little about mental states from their connections with other things. Once we know what it's like to think, feel, and experience, we know most, perhaps all, of what is important about those states, so much so that it may even seem that nothing more is necessary to grasp their nature.

Differences in how we know about things can often be explained by corresponding differences in the nature of those things. So it is natural to suppose that the character of mental states themselves makes this direct, automatic knowledge possible. Mental states must somehow lend themselves to being directly known. Moreover, because we know about nothing else in this special, immediate way, our sense is reinforced that mental processes are a singularity in nature, discontinuous from everything else.

But another aspect of our commonsense conception of mind suggests a rather different picture. Mental functioning as we know it is intimately bound up with biological makeup. We encounter mind and consciousness only in connection with human beings and other animals. The kind of sensory experiences creatures have varies to some extent with the kind of sense organs they have, just as their bodily behavior often depends partly on their mental processes.

And the ability to think and reason results from having certain especially well-developed brain structures. Human mental endowments, furthermore, are closest to those of creatures to which we are most closely related. Taken together, these ties between mind and biological makeup suggest a conception of mind as intimately connected with biological functioning, and hence as continuous with the rest of nature.

Our commonsense picture of mind therefore involves components that pull in opposite directions. According to one, mind is a singularity in nature, discontinuous with all other natural processes; the other points instead to a conception of mind as intimately bound to, and dependent on, various nonmental processes. It is far from obvious how these competing strands fit together. If mind is discontinuous with other natural processes, why does mental functioning depend so intimately on bodily endowment? On the other hand, how is direct, privileged knowledge of our own mental states possible if mind is continuous with biological function? Perhaps the most fundamental problem in understanding the mind is how to reconcile the conflict between these two aspects of our commonsense picture.

It is natural to try to solve this problem by taking one of the two components of our commonsense picture of mind to be fundamental, and then trying to explain the other on that basis. One might, for example, assume that mind is indeed a unique singularity in nature but try nonetheless to explain the manifest connections between mental and nonmental phenomena.

One can proceed equally well, of course, by taking as basic the continuities between mental and nonmental phenomena, and trying to explain the uniqueness of mental phenomena. But there is a tendency to favor theories that stress in some way the singularity of mental phenomena. One reason for this is that a theory that takes the uniqueness of mind as basic has a ready reply to the question why mental and nonmental processes seem so closely bound together. No matter how radically different mental and nonmental processes are in character, they still presumably interact causally. And that might suffice to account for whatever connections obtain between the two. The opposite approach may strike one as being a lot less promising. How can a theory that makes those continuities central effectively account for the ways mind strikes us as unique and singular?

The ways in which mind is unique, moreover, stand out more vividly than do the continuities between mental and nonmental processes. This is not surprising. What is distinctive about a phenomenon generally attracts more attention than do its continuities with other phenomena. A theory built around the uniqueness of mind thus automatically seems to do justice to what is most important. A theory that cannot explain this uniqueness may therefore strike one as less satisfactory than a theory that cannot account for continuities between mental and nonmental processes.

For these reasons, discussions of mind tend to favor theories that stress the distinctive singularity of mental phenomena, even when those theories downplay the ties mental phenomena have to biological functioning. Still, many have held that such an approach cannot do justice to the phenomenon of mind. For one thing, it is not obvious that causal interactions alone can capture the connections between mental and nonmental processes. More important, such theories seem to many to exaggerate just how much of a singularity mental phenomena are and, therefore, how hard it is for theories based on continuities with nonmental phenomena to explain that uniqueness.

Part I is devoted to the contrast between these two approaches. The writings in section A, by Descartes, Locke, and Reid, develop the idea of mind as a singularity in nature. The selections in section B, by Gilbert Ryle, P. F. Strawson, Gareth B. Matthews, and G.E.M. Anscombe urge instead that a correct view of the mind will emphasize the ways mental phenomena and nonmental phenomena are continuous in character. The general conflict between regarding mind as continuous with other natural phenomena and seeing it as utterly disparate from all nonmental reality leads to more specific problems about the mind. Each of parts II through V focuses on one such cluster of problems.

II. Self and Other

One cluster of problems, which is particularly accessible and also leads easily into other problems about the mind, concerns our knowledge of mental states. As noted above, the way we know about other people's mental states is plainly different from the way we know about our own. Since nothing seems to mediate between our mental states and the knowledge we have of those states, such knowledge seems both direct and automatic. It also seems to have some sort of privileged status, at least relative to our knowledge of other things. This privilege may not be absolute; it may not mean we are always correct about our own mental states, nor that what we know about them is all there is to know. But our apparently immediate and automatic access to our own mental states leads to a natural presumption that our beliefs about our own mental states are correct.

Knowing about the minds of others is, of course, nothing like this. It is often reasonably obvious what is going on in somebody else's mind. But even then, our knowledge is hardly automatic, much less infallible or exhaustive. We can be mistaken about others' mental states, and if I believe that you think or feel something and you say you do not, your word is generally authoritative, though perhaps not always.

In contrast to the automatic, direct access we have to our own thoughts and feelings, our access to those of others is mediated by their behavior. To know what you think and feel I must rely on how you look and act, and on what you say. No such thing is necessary to know our own mental states; we rarely, if ever, observe ourselves in order to find out what is on our minds. The way we know about others' mental states, therefore, resembles the way we come to know about ordinary physical objects and processes more than it resembles how we know about our own mental states.

This difference between how we know our own minds and how we know the minds of others leads to a number of problems. For one thing, these two ways of knowing about mental states suggest that there are two different ways in which mental states may be connected to behavior. If we have immediate, privileged access to our own mental states and are often authoritative about their occurrence and character, the connections mental states have with behavior will not be essential to their nature. If, on the other hand, behavioral cues allow us to tell reasonably often what others are thinking and feeling, the ties between mental states and particular patterns of behavior must be both strong and reliable. These connections will then result from, and reflect, the very nature of those states. That connection cannot be merely accidental, or contingent, if we generally have knowledge of what others think and feel.

Other, more specific problems arise as well. It is tempting to regard the special access we have to our own mental states as superior to any other sort of knowledge we could have about mind. In particular, such knowledge will very likely seem superior to knowledge that relies on the connections mental states have with behavior. This is not just because our direct access to our own mental states is less subject to error, but also because that direct access seems to reveal the very nature of mental states in a way that behavioral correlations cannot.

The more striking our knowledge of our own mental states is, the less impressive our knowledge of others' mental states seems by comparison. This raises yet another problem. If we regard ourselves as wholly authoritative about our own mental states, then perhaps others' beliefs about our mental states have the standing of mere conjecture. Only our direct knowledge of our own mental states would then count as real knowledge; we would never have genuine knowledge of the mental states of others. This conclusion is plainly unacceptable; we can and fairly frequently do know what others are thinking and feeling. The other-minds problem is the problem of how to reconcile the existence of such knowledge with the privileged status that seems to attach to knowledge of our own mental states. The selections in section A, by Bertrand Russell, Norman Malcolm, Stuart Hampshire, and Strawson, address these issues.

A complementary problem arises concerning knowledge of our own mental states. Knowing the mental states of others presupposes regular, reliable connections between those mental states and behavior. And unless such connections are essential to mental states, one could argue that they would be merely accidental; it would then be mere good fortune that we can sometimes tell what others are thinking and feeling.

If behavioral connections are essential to mental states, direct knowledge of one's own mental states cannot reveal what is essential to those states, or at least not all of what is essential to them. This calls into question the privileged status of such knowledge. A way of knowing something that does not reveal important aspects of its essential nature cannot be all that authoritative. Indeed, if we know about others' mental states by way of their connections with behavior and about our own mental states in some other way, perhaps there is room for doubt as to whether what we know about is the same in both cases.

Moreover, since we do not rely on behavioral evidence in knowing our own mental states, it is unclear what such knowledge does rely on. If our access to our own mental states is not based on something, does such access fall short of actual knowledge? The problem here is to explain how such knowledge is possible, and how it can have some sort of special status, if indeed it does. The selections in section B, by Sydney Shoemaker, D. M. Armstrong, and Richard Rorty address these issues.

A satisfactory account of these matters requires us to balance conflicting considerations. Knowing others' mental states requires strong ties between mental states and behavior, whereas knowing our own mental states presupposes that they are largely independent of behavior. A theory that takes account only of the need for strong ties to behavior risks reducing mental states to behavior; a theory that takes no account of behavioral ties is unable to explain much of what we know about mind. If we cannot somehow do justice to both competing demands, we must disarm the apparent conflict between them. One way to attempt this is to note ways in which the connections between mind and behavior resemble connections between ordinary, macroscopic objects and processes and the theoretical objects and processes postulated by the natural sciences. The final selections in this part, by Charles Chihara and J. A. Fodor and by Hilary Putnam, both adopt this strategy.

III. Mind and Body

Problems about special access and other minds concern how we know about mind, rather than the nature of mind itself. But how we know about things often depends to some extent on the nature of the things we know about. So problems about knowing the mind raise issues that bear directly on the nature of mental phenomena.

As already noted, problems about how we know the mind raise questions about the connection between mental states and bodily behavior. And how mind and behavior are connected presumably depends in part on the underlying nature of mental states. The most important issue about that underlying nature is whether mental states are in some way nonphysical, or are instead special kinds of physical states. If mental processes are in some way nonphysical, difficulties may arise in explaining the connection between mind and body and, in particular, the connection between mind and bodily behavior. By contrast, that connection will presumably be wholly unproblematic if mental states are simply special, distinctive kinds of bodily states. The issue of whether mental phenomena are in some way nonphysical is known as the mind–body problem.

Perhaps the main reason to regard mental states as nonphysical is that they seem utterly unlike any bodily or physical state of which we have any idea. If mental phenomena have nothing important in common with any physical objects or processes, perhaps the best explanation of that difference is that they simply are not physical in the first place.

This line of reasoning has strong roots in our commonsense picture of things. Thoughts, hopes, fears, and desires are always about things; if, for example, one thinks that it's raining, or hopes, fears, or desires that it is, one's mental state is about the rain. But it may well be unclear just how a physical state could be about anything. The difficulty seems even more acute when we turn to the qualitative character of sensations. How could any physical state have the characteristic feel of a pain, for example, or the color qualities distinctive of visual sensations? Indeed, how could could any physical process manifest consciousness? If no physical states can have such properties, mental phenomena must in some respect be nonphysical.

Qualitative character and being about something are the two main kinds of property that distinguish mental states. Part of what makes it difficult to see how any physical processes could have these properties is that they seem so unlike the properties we attribute to standard physical things. Indeed, the more obvious it is that a particular process or object is physical, the less its properties seem at all like those of mental states. Standard physical objects such as stones, trees, and planets and standard physical processes such as a stone's moving seem to have no properties that in any way resemble the qualitative character of sensations or the property of a thought's being about something.

If the dramatic differences between mental states and standard cases of physical objects and states tempt us not to count mental states as physical, compelling considerations point in the opposite direction. For one thing, it will be far more difficult to understand the connections mental processes have to bodily processes if mental processes are nonphysical. What mechanisms would explain the causal connections between mental and bodily processes if mental states were nonphysical? How could mental states arise in the course of the evolutionary development of life forms if they were nonphysical?

There is another reason, perhaps even more compelling, for thinking that mental states are, after all, special kinds of physical state. However much the uniqueness of mental phenomena may tempt us to regard those phenomena as nonphysical, it is by no means clear what it would mean for mental states to be nonphysical, above and beyond their simply being unique. And if we can give no clear sense to the idea that they are nonphysical, we must acquiesce in the hypothesis that they are physical.

One way to try to explain that idea would be in terms of Descartes's claim that mental processes occur in nonphysical substances, substances which have no spatial characteristics and exist independently of bodily objects. But few people would now accept that any such substances exist. More important, even that characterization of nonphysical substances is wholly negative, and offers no independent idea of what they would be like.

Another way to try to explain the idea that the mental is nonphysical is by analogy with abstract objects, such as numbers, sets, or other mathematical objects. Unlike physical objects, we cannot locate abstract entities in time or place, or characterize them in terms of standard physical properties such as color, size, and shape. Mental states seem in these ways to resemble abstract objects, they too lack spatial and temporal location, size, shape, and other standard physical properties. But abstract objects are also causally inert, whereas mental states plainly cause bodily behavior and causally result from bodily stimulations. So analogies with mathematical or theological objects are unlikely to help us understand what it would be for mental states to be nonphysical.

Despite the impressive advances of science in explaining and predicting natural processes, it remains open to suppose that human thought and action might forever evade the net of scientific explanation. Perhaps that possibility provides a way in which mental processes are nonphysical. It is reasonable to hold that all physical processes are susceptible to scientific explanation. So if mental processes are not, they are in that way not physical. But even this possibility gives us no independent idea of what being nonphysical amounts to.

It is noteworthy that the reasons we have both for thinking that mental states are nonphysical and for thinking that they are physical are all negative. We seem tempted to hold they are nonphysical only because they seem in no way to be like standard cases of physical objects and processes. This difficulty in saying just what it means for something to be nonphysical is a strong reason to conclude that mental states are physical.

It is widely agreed that this difficulty may well be insoluble; few today hold out hope for giving clear sense to the idea that mental processes are nonphysical. Most discussions of the issue tend accordingly to focus on whether the uniqueness of mental states rules out their being special kinds of physical states. Can physical processes have such characteristics as being about things or having a particular feel? And are these mental characteristics themselves physical characteristics?

Because of the difficulty in saying just what it is for something to be nonphysical, an account that represents mental states as nonphysical will strike many as merely labeling, rather than explaining, whatever it is that is special about mental phenomena. Such theories accordingly risk being uninformative. We can avoid these difficulties by adopting a theory on which physical processes can have mental properties, and those properties themselves turn out to be special kinds of physical properties. But such a theory may seem to lose the distinctive character of mental phenomena. If it does, the theory will seem not to be about mental states at all, but only about the mere physical accompaniments of those states. To settle whether those states are physical, therefore, we must determine whether an account of mental phenomena as special kinds of physical phenomena can do justice to the distinctive mental character of those phenomena.

The selections in section A, by J.J.C. Smart, Jerome Shaffer, Armstrong, and Keith Campbell, debate the question of whether physical processes can have mental characteristics, and whether those very mental characteristics might be special cases of physical characteristics. In section B, Putnam, David Lewis, and Ned Block take up the idea that we can characterize mental properties in terms of the pattern of causal connections mental states have with non-mental process and with each other. If so, some processes would be distinctively mental by virtue of having complex causal properties, which suitable physical processes might well have. Section C contains writings by Saul A. Kripke, Donald Davidson, and Jaegwon Kim which explore various complexities in the relation between mental and physical processes and characteristics. And in section D, Paul Feyerabend, Rorty, and W. V. Quine argue that, if mental states are not physical and physical processes cannot have mental characteristics, the correct conclusion to draw is that the commonsense category of mental phenomena is expendable.

IV.   The Nature of Mind

The question whether mental states are special kinds of physical states has to do with the underlying nature of those states. As just noted, the most promising way to settle that question is to tell whether the characteristics that make mental states unique and distinctive preclude their being physical. And we must also tell whether those very characteristics might themselves be physical characteristics.

It is clear enough in a general way what those characteristics are; they are properties such as sensory quality and the property of being about something. But to determine whether these mental properties might be special kinds of physical property, and whether the states that have such properties might be physical states, we need to know more than this. The main reason to reject the idea that mental states are physical states is that this might make it impossible to capture what is truly distinctive of mental phenomena. To evaluate this challenge, we must investigate the nature of these distinctive mental properties.

As noted earlier, mental characteristics fall into two broad categories. We describe many mental states—such as thinking, desiring, hoping, suspecting, doubting, wishing, intending, and wondering—by saying what they are about. We can further specify such mental states by a sentential clause that specifies what is thought, desired, hoped, doubted, and the like. For example, a person may think *that 2 + 2 = 4*, or hope *that so-and-so will win*, or doubt *that it's raining.* What the person thinks, hopes, or doubts is called propositional content; the properties of being about something and having propositional content are intentional properties of these mental states.

The other broad group of mental characteristics are sensory qualities. These include two subgroups. There are the properties in terms of which we distinguish among pains, aches, and other bodily feelings, and there are properties that belong to sensations of color, sound, and other sensations that figure in perception. Pains and aches, for example, may be sharp, burning, intense, dull, or faint. We also distinguish perceptual sensations in terms of various qualities; a visual sensation may be of something red or green, and an auditory sensation may be loud, deep, or ringing.

Sensations have no intentional properties. Pains and aches are not about anything, and have no propositional content. And even though we describe perceptual sensations as being of particular kinds *of* objects, described qualitatively, this does not mean they are about anything. A visual sensation *of* a red object is not *about* that object, as a thought about it is. Nor do bodily sensations have any propositional content. Similarly, mental states such as thinking, suspecting, doubting, and wondering have no sensory quality.

Other mental states do seem to exhibit both kinds of mental property. Emotions in particular, and perhaps some desires, typically have both intentional and sensory character. Being joyous, angry, or sad all have a distinctive feel. But we also say that somebody is angry, sad, or joyous that something is the case, or about a certain state of affairs. Many other mental phenomena, such as perceiving, remembering, imagining, also invite both sorts of description. But because the two kinds of mental characteristic are so different, it will be easiest to get clear about them if we focus primarily on states that have either intentional or qualitative character, but not both.

Understanding what these mental characteristics amount to is important partly to determine whether or not mental states are special kinds of physical states. But it is also important in its own right. To understand mental phenomena at all satisfactorily, we must know what it is for a thought or desire to be about something or have propositional content, and what it is for sensations and emotions to have sensory quality.

There are two main approaches to giving an account of these mental characteristics. According to one, any informative account of these characteristics will explain them in terms of some sort of nonmental phenomena. One example is to try to explain the intentional properties of such mental states as thinking, doubting, and wondering by reference to the corresponding characteristics manifested by speech acts, such as asserting and asking. Speech acts, like intentional states, are about things and have propositional content, and despite their close ties to those mental states, they are not themselves mental states. A second example would be to try somehow to explain what mental characteristics amount to in terms of the connections mental states have to behavior and sensory stimulation.

The other approach denies that any explanation along these lines is possible. According to that approach, no account of mental characteristics can succeed unless it relies on other mental properties. We cannot explain what it is for a mental state to be about something or to have some particular propositional content except by appeal to some other mental state's being about something and having propositional content. Nor can we say what is involved in a sensory state's having some particular qualitative character without appealing to other examples of sensory quality. Mental characteristics thus belong to closed families of properties, none of whose members can be explained except by reference to other members of the family. On this view, no account that relies solely on nonmental resources can capture the distinctive character of mind. Any such theory inevitably loses the very distinction between what is mental and what is not.

Because speech acts resemble mental states in being about things and having propositional content, an account of intentionality in terms of nonmental phenomena may seem promising. But it is far less clear that anything nonmental has properties that are at all like the qualitative character of sensory mental states. So there may be less hope for an account of qualitative character based on nonmental processes. In any case, it is plain that the question of whether we can understand mental characteristics in nonmental terms raises different issues in the sensory and intentional cases.

The readings in section A all focus on intentional character, and each raises issues about whether and, if so, how we can explain the intentionality of mental states in nonmental terms. Both Roderick M. Chisholm and Quine, despite other differences that divide them, insist we cannot. Wilfrid Sellars argues that we can do so by appealing to the intentionality of speech, while Fred I. Dretske advances an explanation in terms of information processing. Fodor, Daniel C. Dennett, and Davidson all discuss what the intentionality of mental states involves, and what a satisfactory account of it would look like.

Section B takes up qualitative character, examining whether one can explain sensory character in terms that break out of the family of qualitative phenomena. Chisholm and Frank Jackson both argue we cannot. Shoemaker attempts to explain the qualitative character of sensations in terms of thoughts about physical objects with corresponding perceivable qualities. Christopher Peacocke and Sellars approach the problem by tracing the connections that hold between those perceivable qualities and the qualities of sensory mental states.

Intentional and qualitative character are not the only issues an adequate characterization of mind must address. Another central topic is consciousness. We say that creatures are conscious if they are both awake and aware of things. But we also describe mental states themselves as conscious if one has unmediated, special access to it.

Related to these notions of consciousness is the idea of a center of consciousness, or self. Conscious states are connected by being states of a single conscious creature. These states in effect define a perspective or point of view, in terms of which we individuate selves. Still another crucial notion is that of being a person. Not every conscious being, or self, is a person; only those conscious beings whose mental lives are suitably elaborate and organized count as people.

Consciousness, self, and personhood are perhaps the most difficult mental phenomena to explain satisfactorily. As with intentionality and qualitative character, the question arises as to what resources are needed to explain these phenomena. Is any such explanation possible that does not make essential appeal to related mental phenomena? Can we explain them except in terms of each other, or cognate notions such as subjectivity and awareness?

Once again, opposing difficulties face any theory of consciousness, self, and personhood. An account that does not appeal to cognate concepts risks being unable to do justice to the mental phenomena in question. But theories that rely on cognate mental phenomena must operate within a closed family of phenomena, and so may in the end give wholly uninformative explanations. An acceptable characterization of mind must steer between these twin difficulties; it must do justice to mental phenomena, but avoid being uninformatively circular.

The selections in section C by Thomas Nagel, Ryle, Harry G. Frankfurt, Malcolm, and

David M. Rosenthal consider to what extent informative, noncircular accounts of these phenomena are possible. In addition, Frankfurt's article considers ways in which the concept of a person is connected with the nature of the will, and Robert M. Gordon's discussion of the emotions illustrates how it may be impossible to be in certain mental states without being in others.

V. Psychological Explanation

There are two main avenues to our knowledge about mental states and their intentional and sensory properties. One is introspection. We seem to know directly and authoritatively what the content of our thoughts is and what qualitative character our sensations have. And it is even tempting to think that our introspective access to mental states tells us something about what it is for such a state to have intentional and sensory properties.

The other avenue to knowledge about mind relies on the role mental states play in explaining behavior. We normally explain what people do by appealing to their thoughts, feelings, and desires. This puts a constraint on the nature of those states and of their distinguishing properties; these states and properties must be such as to make these explanations possible. Mental states are not only the objects of our introspective powers; they are also whatever states figure in psychological explanations.

The role of mental states in explaining behavior provides us with an important way to adjudicate among competing views about the nature of those states. Intentional and sensory characteristics are the distinguishing properties by reference to which we classify mental states, and psychological explanations make certain demands on how we can taxonomize mental states. Thus, we can assess the adequacy of a theory about these properties by asking whether it sorts mental states into types in the way required for psychological explanations to work. And more generally we can ask whether our theory squares with the way various mental states figure in these explanations.

We typically explain a person's behavior by appeal not to a single mental state, but to the interaction of several such states, for example, a belief and a desire. Moreover, being in one mental state often leads to our being in other specifiable mental states, in ways that are regular and predictable. For example, when we think and reason about things, we pass in predictable ways from one belief to another. Such reasoning may play an important role in determining our behavior. Myriad commonsense generalizations describe how intentional states interact, and how one leads to another. Any theory about psychological explanation must take account of these generalizations.

It is inviting at this point to invoke an analogy between mind and computer. Computers store, retrieve, and manipulate information, and it is convenient to describe that information in terms of propositional content. Moreover, processes in which one state leads to another are central not only to our mental functioning, but also to the way computational devices operate. When a computational device manipulates information, its states have systematic causal ties with one another, and with the input it accepts and the output it generates. So perhaps we can understand mental processes by describing them in computational terms.

This analogy is inviting in part because there is no mystery about how actual computers store, retrieve, and manipulate information; a computational model of mental processes may therefore help dispel whatever sense of mystery seems to surround those processes. Such a model is also appealing because it suggests collaborative efforts by researchers in such areas as psychology, linguistics, artificial intelligence, and philosophy. The selections in section A by Fodor, Dennett, John R. Searle, and Putnam examine the merits of this proposal.

It is crucial to psychological explanation that we know when two mental states are of the same type. But special problems arise about this in the case of intentional states, in particular, about whether they have the same content. Intentional states arguably must have stable causal connections with each other and with sensory input and behavioral output if we are to be able to explain behavior by reference to those states. This seems to be so for commonsense psychological explanations as well as the more precise explanations we could expect from a science of psychology. But the causal properties of a person's states, whether mental or not, presumably depend only on that person's internal makeup. It seems to follow that, for psychological explanation to be possible, the content of an intentional state can depend on nothing other than a person's individual makeup. Two physically indistinguishable people would perforce be in exactly the same intentional states.

But there are other considerations that conflict with this conclusion. It is a natural assumption that the language a person speaks influences to some extent what the content of that person's thoughts can be. Moreover, the content of one's thoughts may also depend in part on what external objects those thoughts happen to refer to. People with identical internal makeup would then differ in the content of their thoughts if their linguistic or physical environment diverged appropriately. Such environmental factors would then actually affect how we type people's intentional states.

This conflict about how to type intentional states is based on competing strands of our commonsense views about the mind. How, after all, could what one thinks depend on anything outside oneself? At the same time, doesn't the content of our thoughts depend in part on what those thoughts are about? And isn't that in part a function of how we interact with the world? These issues about typing intentional states are initially raised by Fodor in section A, and are pursued in depth in section B, by Tyler Burge, Brian Loar, and Robert Stalnaker.

Psychological explanation is crucial not only to our commonsense conception of mental phenomena but also to any scientific study of mind. This raises questions about the relationship between that commonsense conception and the view of mental phenomena that would emerge from such a scientific psychology. Physics gives us a picture of our physical environment different from that of commonsense; perhaps, as Stephen P. Stich argues in section C, the science of mind will diverge in important ways from commonsense folk psychology.

Physics, moreover, can force us to reject various commonsense presuppositions about the world. If common sense and science were dramatically at odds concerning the mind, perhaps a sufficiently well-established theory could even persuade us that our commonsense conception of mind cannot be sustained. Paul M. Churchland argues that this could well happen. Dennett, in the concluding selection, explores an alternative way to understand the connection between our scientific and commonsense views of the mind.

Bielefeld, West Germany

PART I
PROBLEMS ABOUT MIND

INTRODUCTION

Much of what we find puzzling about mental phenomena derives from the uneasy tension that exists between the way modern science represents physical reality and the special sense we have of ourselves as conscious beings. Since the time of Galileo, it has been accepted that the scientific laws that govern natural processes can be formulated in mathematical terms. As Galileo put it, the book of nature is written in mathematical language. Physics, of course, is the prime example of such a science. But chemistry and biology also aim at mathematically formulable laws, and it is widely hoped that these and other sciences are in some way or other reducible to physics.

Mental phenomena seem to resist any such treatment. It is hard to imagine how mathematically formulated laws could capture the feeling of a pain or an emotion, the quality of a visual or auditory perception, or the content of a thought or desire. How could any mathematically formulated science even begin to do justice to what it is like to experience something, or to be conscious?

These considerations create a sense of an unbridgeable gulf separating mental from physical phenomena. Physical processes are those which are subject to mathematically formulated laws; the mental is unique among natural phenomena in resisting such explanation. It is far from clear how this could be so unless mental and physical phenomena differ dramatically in nature.

The general lines of scientific thought, moreover, often influence our commonsense conceptions of things. So it has become a well-entrenched part of that commonsense picture that, because mental phenomena resist the sort of scientific treatment that works with everything else in nature, mind is unique and singular among natural processes.

At the same time, our mental lives intertwine so seamlessly in everyday experience with our bodily processes that it can be difficult to distinguish the mental from the bodily components of such experience. Actions, perceptions, and states of emotion all have both bodily and mental aspects, but it may seem to some extent arbitrary exactly where we draw the line between these two aspects. Moreover, mental phenomena never occur, so far as we know, except in highly organized bodily systems.

This raises a problem. If mind is so disparate from everything else, how can mental phenomena interweave so seamlessly with bodily processes? How can something so alien to physical reality interact with it so intimately? And given the gulf that seems to separate mind from matter, what relation does obtain between mind and the rest of reality?

A. Mind as Consciousness

Descartes was perhaps the first to try to come to terms systematically with the implications a mathematically formulated science has for our concept of mind. Physical reality, as he conceived it, has a single essential characteristic; it is extended, or occupies space. So everything essential to physical reality can be geometrically described, and physical reality is automatically susceptible to mathematical description and explanation.

By contrast, the essence of mind is to think. Descartes arrives at this conclusion as a corollary of his well-known argument that it is impossible to doubt that one exists, since that would mean doubting that one is doubting. No such considerations prevent one from doubting that one has a body. And, since doubting is a kind of thinking, the object whose existence one cannot doubt must be a thinking thing, and need have no bodily parts. The self is essentially a thing that thinks.

Descartes draws on this line of reasoning to develop a fairly full concept of mind. We know about the mind because we cannot doubt our own thinking. This suggests a view of mental activity on which our awareness of our own acts of thinking gives us knowledge far firmer than our knowledge about anything else. Moreover, no thinking takes place in our minds of which we are unaware. And since we know all our own thoughts and the essence of mind is thinking, there is nothing about the mind of which we are not directly aware. The mind is transparent to itself.

The way we know about mind has consequences about its nature. Because that knowledge is based solely on our inability to doubt our own thinking, thinking alone is essential to mind. Descartes concludes that all forms of mental activity are kinds of thinking. This idea is natural enough in the case of mental phenomena such as hoping, doubting, desiring, wondering, understanding, believing, and disbelieving. That is because we can always describe these mental phenomena in terms of some state of affairs. To hope, doubt, or believe is always to hope, doubt, or believe that something is the case. We refer generically to all such mental states as thinking.

But what about sensing and feeling? We must understand these, Descartes insists, as either forms of thinking or else not mental states at all. Seeing something red, insofar as it involves the mind, is just its seeming to one that a particular kind of object is there. Descartes counts seeing in this sense as a species of thinking. When seeing does not involve its seeming to one that things are a certain way, he regards it as just bodily stimulation, and therefore not mental at all.

This doctrine fits well with the idea that physical reality can be fully described in mathematical terms. We ordinarily think of physical objects as colored, and we think of sound as a physical process. The wave motions associated with color and sound are, of course, mathematically describable. But the qualities of color and sound themselves are not. We cannnot mathematically describe the qualitative character of, say, physical red or the sound of a trumpet.

One reaction to this difficulty is to deny that color or sound qualities actually exist in physical reality. This idea may seem reasonable, since no such qualities would exist in a world devoid of mental beings. Descartes in effect follows a variant of this strategy. One main reason to hold that physical objects and processes exhibit qualities such as color and sound is that we assume such physical qualities cause the corresponding qualities of our perceptual sensations. This line of reasoning fails, on Descartes's view, since sensing is just a kind of thinking, and involves no qualitative character.

The inability to doubt that one is doubting, and the related idea that the mind is transparent to itself, is important in another way. One can have access to everything in one's mind only if it is one and the same mind that thinks, doubts, and wonders various things. And because all those mental states are unified in a single center of consciousness, it seems to make no sense to think of dividing one's mind or consciousness into parts. But because the essence of body is that it is extended, body is essentially divisible. Descartes invokes this contrast to show that mind and body must be distinct objects. The object we ordinarily think of as a person is thus a compound of a mind and a human body with which it causally interacts.

If we know about mind from our knowledge of our own mental states, how do we ever learn about the minds of others, or even that others have minds? Because our bodies obey the laws of physics, we can predict and explain much of their behavior on the basis of those laws. But Descartes holds that some human behavior, most notably speech, cannot be so predicted or explained. Speech, moreover, expresses thinking; what we say is always something we think. Because we must explain speech by appeal to the mind, rather than to physical principles, we can infer that others have minds.

Descartes's reasoning here resembles that by means of which scientists establish the existence of theoretical entities, such as electrons. In each case, we infer from certain phenomena to the best explanation of those phenomena: in Descartes's case, from speech behavior to the thinking needed to explain it. This suggests that, although immediate access to one's own mental states is fundamental to Descartes's conception of the mental, mental states also have, on his conception, something like a theoretical dimension as well.

This line of reasoning also invites an astonishing conclusion. Because he holds that physical principles suffice to explain the behavior of animals that do not use language, Descartes concludes that such creatures lack mental lives altogether. This extravagant and unbelievable view is not a mere intellectual curiosity, but has actually influenced human treatment of nonhuman animals.

Many doubts can be raised about Descartes's conception of the self as an object distinct from one's body, and his casting the issues in terms of essential properties. Nonetheless, the concept of mind as transparent to itself and as engaged primarily in thinking continues today to exert a powerful influence on discussions about the mind.

Many features of Descartes's conception of the mind figure prominently in Locke's writings. In particular, Locke follows Descartes in taking the mind to be transparent to itself. Thinking unaccompanied by consciousness is impossible, and we know our own ideas infallibly and exhaustively.

Locke and Descartes diverge, however, in their treatment of sensing. Unlike Descartes, Locke recognizes sensing as something distinct from thought, and so does not try to reconstruct all mental states and processes as forms of thinking. He therefore needs a different reason from Descartes's to deny physical status to qualities such as color and sound, which resist description in mathematical terms.

Locke distinguishes these qualities sharply from qualities such as size, shape, and number, which do invite treatment in mathematical terms. He labels qualities such as figure and extension as primary qualities, and claims that our ideas of these qualities resemble the actual qualities of physical objects. But our ideas of secondary qualities, such as color and sound, do not resemble anything in external bodies. Rather, combinations of various primary qualities in bodies cause our ideas of secondary qualities such as color and sound. This allows Locke a conception of physical reality that is wholly explainable in mathematical terms.

Distinguishing these two groups of properties is not just a reaction to the new science, but has a basis in common sense. As Aristotle noted, we perceive qualities such as color and sound by only one sense modality; by contrast, we perceive such properties as shape and extension by both touch and sight. But interpreting this distinction in terms of whether ideas resemble what they represent is specially adapted to the conception of physical reality derived from the new science.

Locke is agnostic about whether, as Descartes insisted, we are compounds of bodies with distinct, nonphysical souls or instead are bodily objects with the abilities to think and sense. Like Descartes, he is convinced that there is nothing in the nature of matter that by itself could give rise to thought or sensation. But that does not imply that bodily objects cannot actually think and sense. Locke likens this possibility to cases in which motions produce various effects we could not have predicted. Nothing in the nature of such motions enables us to figure out that those effects will occur, even though they do. Similarly, nothing in the nature of matter enables us to see how a bodily system can think or sense, even though that may well be what happens.

Reid also operates with an essentially Cartesian concept of mind. He insists that consciousness accompanies all mental states, and holds that it is a mistake to extrapolate from our sensations to the characteristics of physical reality. But he takes issue with Locke's doctrine about primary and secondary qualities.

Locke had concluded that because no property of physical objects resembles our ideas of color and sound, the qualities of those ideas exist only in the mind and not in physical objects. Reid holds it is more natural to speak of both ideas and physical objects as having color, smell, and other such qualities, with the proviso that the colors and smells in the two cases constitute two wholly distinct kinds of quality. Although the two families of qualities do not resemble each other, the physical qualities cause the mental qualities in systematic ways.

This view is reinforced by noting that the same holds even for qualities such as size, shape, and motion. Physical size, shape, and motion can no more literally resemble any qualities of our ideas than the color and sound of our sensations can resemble any properties of physical objects. So the properties of size, shape, and motion that belong to our ideas must also be distinct from the properties of size, shape, and motion that belong to physical objects and processes.

B. Mind and Nature

The two central components of the Cartesian conception of mind are that mental phenomena are nonphysical and that the mind is transparent to itself. These ideas are related. Consciousness may well be the biggest obstacle to seeing how mental states could be special kinds of physical states. If thoughts or sensations exist that are not conscious, perhaps we can explain them in physical terms. But if the mind is transparent to itself, then all mental states without exception are conscious. This equivalence of mind and consciousness therefore supports the conviction that mental phenomena are in some way nonphysical.

Moreover, nothing about mental phenomena seems to permit description in mathematical terms. So the idea that the book of nature is written in mathematical language also makes the contrast between mental and physical seem impossible to bridge. The opposition between mental and physical therefore seems most uncompromising when, like Descartes, we both conceive of physical reality as wholly governed by mathematically formulable laws and also equate mind with consciousness.

Indeed, the idea that mind is transparent to itself seems actually to reflect a kind of mathematical model for the mind. It is natural to regard mathematical objects as immediately accessible to the intellect. Intellectual scrutiny would thus yield exhaustive and infallible knowledge of those objects. So if mind is transparent to itself, mental states would thus far be like mathematical entities. This analogy is reinforced by the idea that the objects of our thoughts and desires are abstract propositions, since abstract objects are generally held to be subject to unmediated mental apprehension.

But there is reason to doubt that mind and consciousness are equivalent. Little of what we know or believe is conscious at any particular moment, yet knowledge and beliefs are presumably stored in the mind. And desires and emotions often influence us even at times when we are unaware of them.

Perhaps even more important, thinking of physical reality in terms of the mathematically formulable laws of physics may well result in an inaccurate picture of how mind is related to the rest of reality. Most of our commonsense conceptions are alien to the framework of such a physics, even though the objects we describe in commonsense terms are plainly physical. This resistance of commonsense conceptions to redescription in mathematical terms is perhaps most dramatic with the phenomena of life, though these are indisputably physical processes. Biological processes are no more than vastly complex interactions among subatomic particles, but we would despair of trying to capture our commonsense understanding of life functions in terms of mathematical laws. So resistance to mathematical description does not show something to be nonphysical.

The sense of opposition between mind and matter may therefore be muted, and perhaps dispelled altogether, if we describe the world in commonsense terms when we formulate the problem about the place of mental phenomena in the rest of reality. This would require, among other things, that we pay special attention to the various distinctive levels of study intermediate between basic physics and conscious mind. And the biological might play an especially important role in helping to bridge the intuitive gulf between matter and mind, since biological processes are closely tied to many mental phenomena, such as perceiving and feeling. Descartes's stark opposition between mind and body goes hand in hand with his mechanical conception of life, and the attendant downgrading the status of sensing and feeling as mental phenomena.

The selections by Ryle, Strawson, and Matthews all challenge the Cartesian pictures of the place of mind in reality. Ryle argues that the distinction between mental and physical is not a distinction between two distinct kinds of entity or process, but between two ways of describing creatures with psychological abilities. It is therefore a conceptual mistake to hold that non-physical processes take place in the mind that interact with various bodily processes, a mistake that results from holding that psychological descriptions refer to processses in the very same way that bodily descriptions do. One therefore tries to model mental phenomena on physical processes, specifically, the mechanical processes of modern physics. To describe somebody in mental terms, Ryle urges, is actually no more than to say that the person does something, or might do it, in some special way, for example, intelligently or attentively.

On the Cartesian view, the mind, or self, is an independently existing, purely mental object. Strawson argues that such a conception allows no way to distinguish a single mind from more than one. And a concept of mind that allows us no way to do that, he concludes, is incoherent. Minds therefore cannot exist independently of people, in roughly the way a table's surface cannot exist without the table. We must conceive of people as having both physical and mental characteristics. Since the concept of a person is more basic than the concept of a mind, mental phenomena are states of people, not states of independent minds.

Matthews points out that, given the way we ordinarily think about things, nothing can think or be conscious unless it is alive. Descartes's theory of mind severs this commonsense tie between consciousness and life. And seeing mental and bodily function as independent, Matthews argues, goes hand in hand with conceiving of the mind as transparent to itself. As Matthews notes, this idea leads to seemingly intractable difficulties, which gives us good reason to reject the Cartesian framework and the independence it implies between consciousness and life.

Anscombe also holds that it is a person, conceived of as a living human body, which has thoughts and ideas. According to her, the fundamental Cartesian mistake is to insist that the function of the word 'I' is to refer to something. Referring requires having a conception of what kind of thing we refer to, and only a notion of a self defined by the Cartesian idea of self-consciousness could provide that for the word 'I'. If the word 'I' refers at all, therefore, we cannot avoid Descartes's conclusion that it refers to an independently existing self. But insuperable difficulties face that notion of a self as well as the idea that the world 'I' refers to something. Anscombe concludes that when I ostensibly think something about myself, say, that I am standing, my thought does not connect the predicate of standing with some subject. Rather, to have that thought is to have an unmediated conception of standing. It may well be, however, that this alternative construal faces difficulties of its own.

A. Mind as Consciousness

1

René Descartes

Selections

from *Meditations on First Philosophy*

SECOND MEDITATION

The Nature of the Human Mind, and How It Is Better Known Than the Body

So serious are the doubts into which I have been thrown as a result of yesterday's meditation that I can neither put them out of my mind nor see any way of resolving them. It feels as if I have fallen unexpectedly into a deep whirlpool which tumbles me around so that I can neither stand on the bottom nor swim up to the top. Nevertheless I will make an effort and once more attempt the same path which I started on yesterday. Anything which admits of the slightest doubt I will set aside just as if I had found it to be wholly false; and I will proceed in this way until I recognize something certain, or, if nothing else, until I at least recognize for certain that there is no certainty. Archimedes used to demand just one firm and immovable point in order to shift the entire earth; so I too can hope for great things if I manage to find just one thing, however slight, that is certain and unshakeable.

I will suppose then, that everything I see is spurious. I will believe that my memory tells me lies, and that none of the things that it reports ever happened. I have no senses. Body, shape, extension, movement and place are chimeras. So what remains true? Perhaps just the one fact that nothing is certain.

Yet apart from everything I have just listed, how do I know that there is not something else which does not allow even the slightest occasion for doubt? Is there not a God, or whatever I may call him, who puts into me[1] the thoughts I am now

having? But why do I think this, since I myself may perhaps be the author of these thoughts? In that case am not I, at least, something? But I have just said that I have no senses and no body. This is the sticking point: what follows from this? Am I not so bound up with a body and with senses that I cannot exist without them? But I have convinced myself that there is absolutely nothing in the world, no sky, no earth, no minds, no bodies. Does it now follow that I too do not exist? No: if I convinced myself of something[2] then I certainly existed. But there is a deceiver of supreme power and cunning who is deliberately and constantly deceiving me. In that case I too undoubtedly exist, if he is deceiving me; and let him deceive me as much as he can, he will never bring it about that I am nothing so long as I think that I am something. So after considering everything very thoroughly, I must finally conclude that this proposition, *I am, I exist*, is necessarily true whenever it is put forward by me or conceived in my mind.

But I do not yet have a sufficient understanding of what this 'I' is, that now necessarily exists. So I must be on my guard against carelessly taking something else to be this 'I', and so making a mistake in the very item of knowledge that I maintain is the most certain and evident of all. I will therefore go back and meditate on what I originally believed myself to be, before I embarked on this present train of thought. I will then subtract anything capable of being weakened, even minimally, by the arguments now introduced, so that what is left at the end may be exactly and only what is certain and unshakeable.

1. ' . . . puts into my mind' (French version).

2. ' . . . or thought anything at all' (French version).

From *The Philosophical Writings of Descartes*, by René Descartes, translated by John Cottingham, Robert Stoothoff, and Dugald Murdoch, 2 volumes. Cambridge: Cambridge University Press, 1985, volume II, pp. 16–23, 51–54, 56–61, and 171–72; volume I, pp. 195, 196, 204–5, and 216–19. Copyright © 1985 by Cambridge University Press. Reprinted with permission of the publisher.

What then did I formerly think I was? A man. But what is a man? Shall I say 'a rational animal'? No; for then I should have to inquire what an animal is, what rationality is, and in this way one question would lead me down the slope to other harder ones, and I do not now have the time to waste on subtleties of this kind. Instead I propose to concentrate on what came into my thoughts spontaneously and quite naturally whenever I used to consider what I was. Well, the first thought to come to mind was that I had a face, hands, arms and the whole mechanical structure of limbs which can be seen in a corpse, and which I called the body. The next thought was that I was nourished, that I moved about, and that I engaged in sense-perception and thinking; and these actions I attributed to the soul. But as to the nature of this soul, either I did not think about this or else I imagined it to be something tenuous, like a wind or fire or ether, which permeated my more solid parts. As to the body, however, I had no doubts about it, but thought I knew its nature distinctly. If I had tried to describe the mental conception I had of it, I would have expressed it as follows: by a body I understand whatever has determinable shape and a definable location and can occupy a space in such a way as to exclude any other body; it can be perceived by touch, sight, hearing, taste or smell, and can be moved in various ways, not by itself but by whatever else comes into contact with it. For, according to my judgement, the power of self-movement, like the power of sensation or of thought, was quite foreign to the nature of a body; indeed, it was a source of wonder to me that certain bodies were found to contain faculties of this kind.

But what shall I now say that I am, when I am supposing that there is some supremely powerful and, if it is permissible to say so, malicious deceiver, who is deliberately trying to trick me in every way he can? Can I now assert that I possess even the most insignificant of all the attributes which I have just said belong to the nature of a body? I scrutinize them, think about them, go over them again, but nothing suggests itself; it is tiresome and pointless to go through the list once more. But what about the attributes I assigned to the soul? Nutrition or movement? Since now I do not have a body, these are mere fabrications. Sense-perception? This surely does not occur without a body, and besides, when asleep I have appeared to perceive through the senses many things which I afterwards realized I did not perceive through the senses at all. Thinking? At last I have discovered it—thought; this alone is inseparable from me. I am, I exist—that is certain. But for how long? For as long as I am thinking. For it could be that were I totally to cease from thinking, I should

totally cease to exist. At present I am not admitting anything except what is necessarily true. I am, then, in the strict sense only a thing that thinks,[3] that is, I am a mind, or intelligence, or intellect, or reason—words whose meaning I have been ignorant of until now. But for all that I am a thing which is real and which truly exists. But what kind of a thing? As I have just said—a thinking thing.

What else am I? I will use my imagination.[4] I am not that structure of limbs which is called a human body. I am not even some thin vapour which permeates the limbs—a wind, fire, air, breath, or whatever I depict in my imagination; for these are things which I have supposed to be nothing. Let this supposition stand;[5] for all that I am still something. And yet may it not perhaps be the case that these very things which I am supposing to be nothing, because they are unknown to me, are in reality identical with the 'I' of which I am aware? I do not know, and for the moment I shall not argue the point, since I can make judgements only about things which are known to me. I know that I exist; the question is, what is this 'I' that I know? If the 'I' is understood strictly as we have been taking it, then it is quite certain that knowledge of it does not depend on things of whose existence I am as yet unaware; so it cannot depend on any of the things which I invent in my imagination. And this very word 'invent' shows me my mistake. It would indeed be a case of fictitious invention if I used my imagination to establish that I was something or other; for imagining is simply contemplating the shape or image of a corporeal thing. Yet now I know for certain both that I exist and at the same time that all such images and, in general, everything relating to the nature of body, could be mere dreams ⟨and chimeras⟩. Once this point has been grasped, to say 'I will use my imagination to get to know more distinctly what I am' would seem to be as silly as saying 'I am now awake, and see some truth; but since my vision is not yet clear enough, I will deliberately fall asleep so that my dreams may provide a truer and clearer representation.' I thus realize that none of the

---

3. The word 'only' is most naturally taken as going with 'a thing that thinks', and this interpretation is followed in the French version. When discussing this passage with Gassendi, however, Descartes suggests that he meant the 'only' to govern 'in the strict sense'.

4. ' . . . to see if I am not something more' (added in French version).

5. Lat. *maneat* ('let it stand'), first edition. The second edition has the indicative *manet*: 'The proposition still stands, *viz.* that I am nonetheless something.' The French version reads: 'without changing this supposition, I find that I am still certain that I am something'.

things that the imagination enables me to grasp is at all relevant to this knowledge of myself which I possess, and that the mind must therefore be most carefully diverted from such things[6] if it is to perceive its own nature as distinctly as possible.

But what then am I? A thing that thinks. What is that? A thing that doubts, understands, affirms, denies, is willing, is unwilling, and also imagines and has sensory perceptions.

This is a considerable list, if everything on it belongs to me. But does it? Is it not one and the same 'I' who is now doubting almost everything, who nonetheless understands some things, who affirms that this one thing is true, denies everything else, desires to know more, is unwilling to be deceived, imagines many things even involuntarily, and is aware of many things which apparently come from the senses? Are not all these things just as true as the fact that I exist, even if I am asleep all the time, and even if he who created me is doing all he can to deceive me? Which of all these activities is distinct from my thinking? Which of them can be said to be separate from myself? The fact that it is I who am doubting and understanding and willing is so evident that I see no way of making it any clearer. But it is also the case that the 'I' who imagines is the same 'I'. For even if, as I have supposed, none of the objects of imagination are real, the power of imagination is something which really exists and is part of my thinking. Lastly, it is also the same 'I' who has sensory perceptions, or is aware of bodily things as it were through the senses. For example, I am now seeing light, hearing a noise, feeling heat. But I am asleep, so all this is false. Yet I certainly *seem* to see, to hear, and to be warmed. This cannot be false; what is called 'having a sensory perception' is strictly just this, and in this restricted sense of the term it is simply thinking.

From all this I am beginning to have a rather better understanding of what I am. But it still appears—and I cannot stop thinking this—that the corporeal things of which images are formed in my thought, and which the senses investigate, are known with much more distinctness than this puzzling 'I' which cannot be pictured in the imagination. And yet it is surely surprising that I should have a more distinct grasp of things which I realize are doubtful, unknown and foreign to me, than I have of that which is true and known—my own self. But I see what it is: my mind enjoys wandering off and will not yet submit to being restrained within the bounds of truth. Very well then; just this once let us give it a completely free rein, so

that after a while, when it is time to tighten the reins, it may more readily submit to being curbed.

Let us consider the things which people commonly think they understand most distinctly of all; that is, the bodies which we touch and see. I do not mean bodies in general—for general perceptions are apt to be somewhat more confused—but one particular body. Let us take, for example, this piece of wax. It has just been taken from the honeycomb; it has not yet quite lost the taste of the honey; it retains some of the scent of the flowers from which it was gathered; its colour, shape and size are plain to see; it is hard, cold and can be handled without difficulty; if you rap it with your knuckle it makes a sound. In short, it has everything which appears necessary to enable a body to be known as distinctly as possible. But even as I speak, I put the wax by the fire, and look: the residual taste is eliminated, the smell goes away, the colour changes, the shape is lost, the size increases; it becomes liquid and hot; you can hardly touch it, and if you strike it, it no longer makes a sound. But does the same wax remain? It must be admitted that it does; no one denies it, no one thinks otherwise. So what was it in the wax that I understood with such distinctness? Evidently none of the features which I arrived at by means of the senses; for whatever came under taste, smell, sight, touch or hearing has now altered—yet the wax remains.

Perhaps the answer lies in the thought which now comes to my mind; namely, the wax was not after all the sweetness of the honey, or the fragrance of the flowers, or the whiteness, or the shape, or the sound, but was rather a body which presented itself to me in these various forms a little while ago, but which now exhibits different ones. But what exactly is it that I am now imagining? Let us concentrate, take away everything which does not belong to the wax, and see what is left: merely something extended, flexible and changeable. But what is meant here by 'flexible' and 'changeable'? Is it what I picture in my imagination: that this piece of wax is capable of changing from a round shape to a square shape, or from a square shape to a triangular shape? Not at all; for I can grasp that the wax is capable of countless changes of this kind, yet I am unable to run through this immeasurable number of changes in my imagination, from which it follows that it is not the faculty of imagination that gives me my grasp of the wax as flexible and changeable. And what is meant by 'extended'? Is the extension of the wax also unknown? For it increases if the wax melts, increases again if it boils, and is greater still if the heat is increased. I would not be making a correct judgement about the nature of wax unless I believed it capable of being extended in many more different

6. ' . . . from this manner of conceiving things' (French version).

ways than I will ever encompass in my imagination. I must therefore admit that the nature of this piece of wax is in no way revealed by my imagination, but is perceived by the mind alone. (I am speaking of this particular piece of wax; the point is even clearer with regard to wax in general.) But what is this wax which is perceived by the mind alone?[7] It is of course the same wax which I see, which I touch, which I picture in my imagination, in short the same wax which I thought it to be from the start. And yet, and here is the point, the perception I have of it[8] is a case not of vision or touch or imagination—nor has it ever been, despite previous appearances—but of purely mental scrutiny; and this can be imperfect and confused, as it was before, or clear and distinct as it is now, depending on how carefully I concentrate on what the wax consists in.

But as I reach this conclusion I am amazed at how ⟨weak and⟩ prone to error my mind is. For although I am thinking about these matters within myself, silently and without speaking, nonetheless the actual words bring me up short, and I am almost tricked by ordinary ways of talking. We say that we see the wax itself, if it is there before us, not that we judge it to be there from its colour or shape; and this might lead me to conclude without more ado that knowledge of the wax comes from what the eye sees, and not from the scrutiny of the mind alone. But then if I look out of the window and see men crossing the square, as I just happen to have done, I normally say that I see the men themselves, just as I say that I see the wax. Yet do I see any more than hats and coats which could conceal automatons? I *judge* that they are men. And so something which I thought I was seeing with my eyes is in fact grasped solely by the faculty of judgement which is in my mind.

However, one who wants to achieve knowledge above the ordinary level should feel ashamed at having taken ordinary ways of talking as a basis for doubt. So let us proceed, and consider on which occasion my perception of the nature of the wax was more perfect and evident. Was it when I first looked at it, and believed I knew it by my external senses, or at least by what they call the 'common' sense[9]—that is, the power of imagination? Or is my knowledge more perfect now, after a more careful investigation of the nature of the wax and of the means by which it is known? Any doubt on

this issue would clearly be foolish; for what distinctness was there in my earlier perception? Was there anything in it which an animal could not possess? But when I distinguish the wax from its outward forms—take the clothes off, as it were, and consider it naked—then although my judgement may still contain errors, at least my perception now requires a human mind.

But what am I to say about this mind, or about myself? (So far, remember, I am not admitting that there is anything else in me except a mind.) What, I ask, is this 'I' which seems to perceive the wax so distinctly? Surely my awareness of my own self is not merely much truer and more certain than my awareness of the wax, but also much more distinct and evident. For if I judge that the wax exists from the fact that I see it, clearly this same fact entails much more evidently that I myself also exist. It is possible that what I see is not really the wax; it is possible that I do not even have eyes with which to see anything. But when I see, or think I see (I am not here distinguishing the two), it is simply not possible that I who am now thinking am not something. By the same token, if I judge that the wax exists from the fact that I touch it, the same result follows, namely that I exist. If I judge that it exists from the fact that I imagine it, or for any other reason, exactly the same thing follows. And the result that I have grasped in the case of the wax may be applied to everything else located outside me. Moreover, if my perception of the wax seemed more distinct[10] after it was established not just by sight or touch but by many other considerations, it must be admitted that I now know myself even more distinctly. This is because every consideration whatsoever which contributes to my perception of the wax, or of any other body, cannot but establish even more effectively the nature of my own mind. But besides this, there is so much else in the mind itself which can serve to make my knowledge of it more distinct, that it scarcely seems worth going through the contributions made by considering bodily things.

I see that without any effort I have now finally got back to where I wanted. I now know that even bodies are not strictly perceived by the senses or the faculty of imagination but by the intellect alone, and that this perception derives not from their being touched or seen but from their being understood; and in view of this I know plainly that I can achieve an easier and more evident perception of my own mind than of anything else. But since the habit of holding on to old opinions cannot be set aside so quickly, I should like to stop

7. ' . . . which can only be conceived by the understanding or the mind' (French version).

8. ' . . . or rather the act whereby it is perceived' (added in French version).

9. [See last note in Meditation VI, below.]

10. The French version has 'more clear and distinct' and, at the end of this sentence, 'more evidently, distinctly and clearly'.

here and meditate for some time on this new knowledge I have gained, so as to fix it more deeply in my memory.

The Existence of Material Things, and the Real Distinction Between Mind and Body

* * * * *

To begin with, I will go back over all the things which I previously took to be perceived by the senses, and reckoned to be true; and I will go over my reasons for thinking this. Next, I will set out my reasons for subsequently calling these things into doubt. And finally I will consider what I should now believe about them.

First of all then, I perceived by my senses that I had a head, hands, feet and other limbs making up the body which I regarded as part of myself, or perhaps even as my whole self. I also perceived by my senses that this body was situated among many other bodies which could affect it in various favourable or unfavourable ways; and I gauged the favourable effects by a sensation of pleasure, and the unfavourable ones by a sensation of pain. In addition to pain and pleasure, I also had sensations within me of hunger, thirst, and other such appetites, and also of physical propensities towards cheerfulness, sadness, anger and similar emotions. And outside me, besides the extension, shapes and movements of bodies, I also had sensations of their hardness and heat, and of the other tactile qualities. In addition, I had sensations of light, colours, smells, tastes and sounds, the variety of which enabled me to distinguish the sky, the earth, the seas, and all other bodies, one from another. Considering the ideas of all these qualities which presented themselves to my thought, although the ideas were, strictly speaking, the only immediate objects of my sensory awareness, it was not unreasonable for me to think that the items which I was perceiving through the senses were things quite distinct from my thought, namely bodies which produced the ideas. For my experience was that these ideas came to me quite without my consent, so that I could not have sensory awareness of any object, even if I wanted to, unless it was present to my sense organs; and I could not avoid having sensory awareness of it when it was present. And since the ideas perceived by the senses were much more lively and vivid and even, in their own way, more distinct than any of those which I deliberately formed through meditating or which I found impressed on my memory, it seemed impossible that they should have come from within me; so the only alternative was that they came from other things. Since the sole source of my knowledge of these things was the ideas themselves, the supposition that the things resembled the ideas was bound to occur to me. In addition, I remembered that the use of my senses had come first, while the use of my reason came only later; and I saw that the ideas which I formed myself were less vivid than those which I perceived with the senses and were, for the most part, made up of elements of sensory ideas. In this way I easily convinced myself that I had nothing at all in the intellect which I had not previously had in sensation. As for the body which by some special right I called 'mine', my belief that this body, more than any other, belonged to me had some justification. For I could never be separated from it, as I could from other bodies; and I felt all my appetites and emotions in, and on account of, this body; and finally, I was aware of pain and pleasurable ticklings in parts of this body, but not in other bodies external to it. But why should that curious sensation of pain give rise to a particular distress of mind; or why should a certain kind of delight follow on a tickling sensation? Again, why should that curious tugging in the stomach which I call hunger tell me that I should eat, or a dryness of the throat tell me to drink, and so on? I was not able to give any explanation of all this, except that nature taught me so. For there is absolutely no connection (at least that I can understand) between the tugging sensation and the decision to take food, or between the sensation of something causing pain and the mental apprehension of distress that arises from that sensation. These and other judgements that I made concerning sensory objects, I was apparently taught to make by nature; for I had already made up my mind that this was how things were, before working out any arguments to prove it.

Later on, however, I had many experiences which gradually undermined all the faith I had had in the senses. Sometimes towers which had looked round from a distance appeared square from close up; and enormous statues standing on their pediments did not seem large when observed from the ground. In these and countless other such cases, I found that the judgements of the external senses were mistaken. And this applied not just to the external senses but to the internal senses as well. For what can be more internal than pain? And yet I had heard that those who had had a leg or an arm amputated sometimes still seemed to feel pain intermittently in the missing part of the body. So even in my own case it was apparently not quite certain that a particular limb was hurting, even if I felt pain in it. To these reasons for doubting, I recently added two very general ones. The first was that every sensory experience I have ever thought

I was having while awake I can also think of myself as sometimes having while asleep; and since I do not believe that what I seem to perceive in sleep comes from things located outside me, I did not see why I should be any more inclined to believe this of what I think I perceive while awake. The second reason for doubt was that since I did not know the author of my being (or at least was pretending not to), I saw nothing to rule out the possibility that my natural constitution made me prone to error even in matters which seemed to me most true. As for the reasons for my previous confident belief in the truth of the things perceived by the senses, I had no trouble in refuting them. For since I apparently had natural impulses towards many things which reason told me to avoid, I reckoned that a great deal of confidence should not be placed in what I was taught by nature. And despite the fact that the perceptions of the senses were not dependent on my will, I did not think that I should on that account infer that they proceeded from things distinct from myself, since I might perhaps have a faculty not yet known to me which produced them.

But now, when I am beginning to achieve a better knowledge of myself and the author of my being, although I do not think I should heedlessly accept everything I seem to have acquired from the senses, neither do I think that everything should be called into doubt.

First, I know that everything which I clearly and distinctly understand is capable of being created by God so as to correspond exactly with my understanding of it. Hence the fact that I can clearly and distinctly understand one thing apart from another is enough to make me certain that the two things are distinct, since they are capable of being separated, at least by God. The question of what kind of power is required to bring about such a separation does not affect the judgement that the two things are distinct. Thus, simply by knowing that I exist and seeing at the same time that absolutely nothing else belongs to my nature or essence except that I am a thinking thing, I can infer correctly that my essence consists solely in the fact that I am a thinking thing. It is true that I may have (or, to anticipate, that I certainly have) a body that is very closely joined to me. But nevertheless, on the one hand I have a clear and distinct idea of myself, in so far as I am simply a thinking, non-extended thing; and on the other hand I have a distinct idea of body,[1] in so far as

this is simply an extended, non-thinking thing. And accordingly, it is certain that I[2] am really distinct from my body, and can exist without it.

* * * * *

There is nothing that my own nature teaches me more vividly than that I have a body, and that when I feel pain there is something wrong with the body, and that when I am hungry or thirsty the body needs food and drink, and so on. So I should not doubt that there is some truth in this.

Nature also teaches me, by these sensations of pain, hunger, thirst and so on, that I am not merely present in my body as a sailor is present in a ship,[3] but that I am very closely joined and, as it were, intermingled with it, so that I and the body form a unit. If this were not so, I, who am nothing but a thinking thing, would not feel pain when the body was hurt, but would perceive the damage purely by the intellect, just as a sailor perceives by sight if anything in his ship is broken. Similarly, when the body needed food or drink, I should have an explicit understanding of the fact, instead of having confused sensations of hunger and thirst. For these sensations of hunger, thirst, pain and so on are nothing but confused modes of thinking which arise from the union and, as it were, intermingling of the mind with the body.

I am also taught by nature that various other bodies exist in the vicinity of my body, and that some of these are to be sought out and others avoided. And from the fact that I perceive by my senses a great variety of colours, sounds, smells and tastes, as well as differences in heat, hardness and the like, I am correct in inferring that the bodies which are the source of these various sensory perceptions possess differences corresponding to them, though perhaps not resembling them. Also, the fact that some of the perceptions are agreeable to me while others are disagreeable makes it quite certain that my body, or rather my whole self, in so far as I am a combination of body and mind, can be affected by the various beneficial or harmful bodies which surround it.

There are, however, many other things which I may appear to have been taught by nature, but which in reality I acquired not from nature but from a habit of making ill-considered judgements; and it is therefore quite possible that these are false. Cases in point are the belief that any space in which nothing is occurring to stimulate my senses must be empty; or that the heat in a body is something exactly resembling the idea of heat which is

---

1. The Latin term *corpus* as used here by Descartes is ambiguous as between 'body' (i.e. corporeal matter in general) and 'the body' (i.e. this particular body of mine). The French version preserves the ambiguity.

2. '. . . that is, my soul, by which I am what I am' (added in French version).

3. '. . . as a pilot in his ship' (French version).

in me; or that when a body is white or green, the selfsame whiteness or greenness which I perceive through my senses is present in the body; or that in a body which is bitter or sweet there is the selfsame taste which I experience, and so on; or, finally, that stars and towers and other distant bodies have the same size and shape which they present to my senses, and other examples of this kind. But to make sure that my perceptions in this matter are sufficiently distinct, I must more accurately define exactly what I mean when I say that I am taught something by nature. In this context I am taking nature to be something more limited than the totality of things bestowed on me by God. For this includes many things that belong to the mind alone—for example my perception that what is done cannot be undone, and all other things that are known by the natural light;[4] but at this stage I am not speaking of these matters. It also includes much that relates to the body alone, like the tendency to move in a downward direction, and so on; but I am not speaking of these matters either. My sole concern here is with what God has bestowed on me as a combination of mind and body. My nature, then, in this limited sense, does indeed teach me to avoid what induces a feeling of pain and to seek out what induces feelings of pleasure, and so on. But it does not appear to teach us to draw any conclusions from these sensory perceptions about things located outside us without waiting until the intellect has examined[5] the matter. For knowledge of the truth about such things seems to belong to the mind alone, not to the combination of mind and body. Hence, although a star has no greater effect on my eye than the flame of a small light, that does not mean that there is any real or positive inclination in me to believe that the star is no bigger than the light; I have simply made this judgement from childhood onwards without any rational basis. Similarly, although I feel heat when I go near a fire and feel pain when I go too near, there is no convincing argument for supposing that there is something in the fire which resembles the heat, any more than for supposing that there is something which resembles the pain. There is simply reason to suppose that there is something in the fire, whatever it may eventually turn out to be, which produces in us the feelings of heat or pain. And likewise, even though there is nothing in any given space that stimulates the senses, it does not follow that there is no body there. In these cases and many others I see that I have been in the habit of misusing the order of nature. For the proper purpose of the sensory percep-

tions given me by nature is simply to inform the mind of what is beneficial or harmful for the composite of which the mind is a part; and to this extent they are sufficiently clear and distinct. But I misuse them by treating them as reliable touchstones for immediate judgements about the essential nature of the bodies located outside us; yet this is an area where they provide only very obscure information.

I have already looked in sufficient detail at how, notwithstanding the goodness of God, it may happen that my judgements are false. But a further problem now comes to mind regarding those very things which nature presents to me as objects which I should seek out or avoid, and also regarding the internal sensations, where I seem to have detected errors[6]—e.g. when someone is tricked by the pleasant taste of some food into eating the poison concealed inside it. Yet in this case, what the man's nature urges him to go for is simply what is responsible for the pleasant taste, and not the poison, which his nature knows nothing about. The only inference that can be drawn from this is that his nature is not omniscient. And this is not surprising, since man is a limited thing, and so it is only fitting that his perfection should be limited.

And yet it is not unusual for us to go wrong even in cases where nature does urge us towards something. Those who are ill, for example, may desire food or drink that will shortly afterwards turn out to be bad for them. Perhaps it may be said that they go wrong because their nature is disordered, but this does not remove the difficulty. A sick man is no less one of God's creatures than a healthy one, and it seems no less a contradiction to suppose that he has received from God a nature which deceives him. Yet a clock constructed with wheels and weights observes all the laws of its nature just as closely when it is badly made and tells the wrong time as when it completely fulfils the wishes of the clockmaker. In the same way, I might consider the body of a man as a kind of machine equipped with and made up of bones, nerves, muscles, veins, blood and skin in such a way that, even if there were no mind in it, it would still perform all the same movements as it now does in those cases where movement is not under the control of the will or, consequently, of the mind.[7] I can easily see that if such a body suffers from dropsy, for example, and is affected by the dryness of the throat which normally produces in the mind the sensation of thirst, the resulting condition of the nerves

---

4. '. . . without any help from the body' (added in French version).

5. '. . . carefully and maturely examined' (French version).

6. '. . . and thus seem to have been directly deceived by my nature' (added in French version).

7. '. . . but occurs merely as a result of the disposition of the organs' (French version).

and other parts will dispose the body to take a drink, with the result that the disease will be aggravated. Yet this is just as natural as the body's being stimulated by a similar dryness of the throat to take a drink when there is no such illness and the drink is beneficial. Admittedly, when I consider the purpose of the clock, I may say that it is departing from its nature when it does not tell the right time; and similarly when I consider the mechanism of the human body, I may think that, in relation to the movements which normally occur in it, it too is deviating from its nature if the throat is dry at a time when drinking is not beneficial to its continued health. But I am well aware that 'nature' as I have just used it has a very different significance from 'nature' in the other sense. As I have just used it, 'nature' is simply a label which depends on my thought; it is quite extraneous to the things to which it is applied, and depends simply on my comparison between the idea of a sick man and a badly-made clock, and the idea of a healthy man and a well-made clock. But by 'nature' in the other sense I understand something which is really to be found in the things themselves; in this sense, therefore, the term contains something of the truth.

When we say, then, with respect to the body suffering from dropsy, that it has a disordered nature because it has a dry throat and yet does not need drink, the term 'nature' is here used merely as an extraneous label. However, with respect to the composite, that is, the mind united with this body, what is involved is not a mere label, but a true error of nature, namely that it is thirsty at a time when drink is going to cause it harm. It thus remains to inquire how it is that the goodness of God does not prevent nature, in this sense, from deceiving us.

The first observation I make at this point is that there is a great difference between the mind and the body, inasmuch as the body is by its very nature always divisible, while the mind is utterly indivisible. For when I consider the mind, or myself in so far as I am merely a thinking thing, I am unable to distinguish any parts within myself; I understand myself to be something quite single and complete. Although the whole mind seems to be united to the whole body, I recognize that if a foot or arm or any other part of the body is cut off, nothing has thereby been taken away from the mind. As for the faculties of willing, of understanding, of sensory perception and so on, these cannot be termed parts of the mind, since it is one and the same mind that wills, and understands and has sensory perceptions. By contrast, there is no corporeal or extended thing that I can think of which in my thought I cannot easily divide into parts;

and this very fact makes me understand that it is divisible. This one argument would be enough to show me that the mind is completely different from the body, even if I did not already know as much from other considerations.

My next observation is that the mind is not immediately affected by all parts of the body, but only by the brain, or perhaps just by one small part of the brain, namely the part which is said to contain the 'common' sense.[8] Every time this part of the brain is in a given state, it presents the same signals to the mind, even though the other parts of the body may be in a different condition at the time. This is established by countless observations, which there is no need to review here.

I observe, in addition, that the nature of the body is such that whenever any part of it is moved by another part which is some distance away, it can always be moved in the same fashion by any of the parts which lie in between, even if the more distant part does nothing. For example, in a cord ABCD, if one end D is pulled so that the other end A moves, the exact same movement could have been brought about if one of the intermediate points B or C had been pulled, and D had not moved at all. In similar fashion, when I feel a pain in my foot, physiology tells me that this happens by means of nerves distributed throughout the foot, and that these nerves are like cords which go from the foot right up to the brain. When the nerves are pulled in the foot, they in turn pull on inner parts of the brain to which they are attached, and produce a certain motion in them; and nature has laid it down that this motion should produce in the mind a sensation of pain, as occurring in the foot. But since these nerves, in passing from the foot to the brain, must pass through the calf, the thigh, the lumbar region, the back and the neck, it can happen that, even if it is not the part in the foot but one of the intermediate parts which is being pulled, the same motion will occur in the brain as occurs when the foot is hurt, and so it will necessarily come about that the mind feels the same sensation of pain. And we must suppose the same thing happens with regard to any other sensation.

My final observation is that any given movement occurring in the part of the brain that immediately affects the mind produces just one cor-

---

8. The supposed faculty which integrates the data from the five specialized senses (the notion goes back ultimately to Aristotle). 'The seat of the common sense must be very mobile, to receive all the impressions coming from the senses, but must be moveable only by the spirits which transmit these impressions. Only the *conarion* [pineal gland] fits these conditions' (letter to Mersenne, 21 April 1641).

responding sensation; and hence the best system that could be devised is that it should produce the one sensation which, of all possible sensations, is most especially and most frequently conducive to the preservation of the healthy man. And experience shows that the sensations which nature has given us are all of this kind; and so there is absolutely nothing to be found in them that does not bear witness to the power and goodness of God. For example, when the nerves in the foot are set in motion in a violent and unusual manner, this motion, by way of the spinal cord, reaches the inner parts of the brain, and there gives the mind its signal for having a certain sensation, namely the sensation of a pain as occurring in the foot. This stimulates the mind to do its best to get rid of the cause of the pain, which it takes to be harmful to the foot. It is true that God could have made the nature of man such that this particular motion in the brain indicated something else to the mind; it might, for example, have made the mind aware of the actual motion occurring in the brain, or in the foot, or in any of the intermediate regions; or it might have indicated something else entirely. But there is nothing else which would have been so conducive to the continued well-being of the body. In the same way, when we need drink, there arises a certain dryness in the throat; this sets in motion the nerves of the throat, which in turn move the inner parts of the brain. This motion produces in the mind a sensation of thirst, because the most

useful thing for us to know about the whole business is that we need drink in order to stay healthy. And so it is in the other cases.

It is quite clear from all this that, notwithstanding the immense goodness of God, the nature of man as a combination of mind and body is such that it is bound to mislead him from time to time. For there may be some occurrence, not in the foot but in one of the other areas through which the nerves travel in their route from the foot to the brain, or even in the brain itself; and if this cause produces the same motion which is generally produced by injury to the foot, then pain will be felt as if it were in the foot. This deception of the senses is natural, because a given motion in the brain must always produce the same sensation in the mind; and the origin of the motion in question is much more often going to be something which is hurting the foot, rather than something existing elsewhere. So it is reasonable that this motion should always indicate to the mind a pain in the foot rather than in any other part of the body. Again, dryness of the throat may sometimes arise not, as it normally does, from the fact that a drink is necessary to the health of the body, but from some quite opposite cause, as happens in the case of the man with dropsy. Yet it is much better that it should mislead on this occasion than that it should always mislead when the body is in good health. And the same goes for the other cases. . . .

from *Objections and Replies*

Author's Replies to the Fourth Set of Objections[1]

*   *   *   *   *

Reply to Part Two, Concerning God

*   *   *   *   *

As to the fact that there can be nothing in the mind, in so far as it is a thinking thing, of which it is not aware, this seems to me to be self-evident. For there is nothing that we can understand to be in the mind, regarded in this way, that is not a thought or dependent on a thought. If it were not a thought or dependent on a thought it would not belong to the mind *qua* thinking thing; and we

cannot have any thought of which we are not aware at the very moment when it is in us. In view of this I do not doubt that the mind begins to think as soon as it is implanted in the body of an infant, and that it is immediately aware of its thoughts, even though it does not remember this afterwards because the impressions of these thoughts do not remain in the memory.

But it must be noted that, although we are always actually aware of the acts or operations of our minds, we are not always aware of the mind's faculties or powers, except potentially. By this I mean that when we concentrate on employing one of our faculties, then immediately, if the faculty in question resides in our mind, we become actually aware of it, and hence we may deny that it is in the mind if we are not capable of becoming aware of it.

---

[1] Descartes addresses Mersenne, who acted as intermediary between him and Arnauld, author of the Fourth Set of Objections.

from *Principles of Philosophy*

PART ONE
The Principles of Human Knowledge

9. *What Is Meant by 'Thought'*

By the term 'thought', I understand everything which we are aware of as happening within us, in so far as we have awareness of it. Hence, *thinking* is to be identified here not merely with understanding, willing and imagining, but also with sensory awareness. For if I say 'I am seeing, or I am walking, therefore I exist', and take this as applying to vision or walking as bodily activities, then the conclusion is not absolutely certain. This is because, as often happens during sleep, it is possible for me to think I am seeing or walking, though my eyes are closed and I am not moving about; such thoughts might even be possible if I had no body at all. But if I take 'seeing' or 'walking' to apply to the actual sense or awareness of seeing or walking, then the conclusion is quite certain, since it relates to the mind, which alone has the sensation or thought that it is seeing or walking.

11. *How Our Mind Is Better Known Than Our Body*

In order to realize that the knowledge of our mind is not simply prior to and more certain than the knowledge of our body, but also more evident, we should notice something very well known by the natural light: nothingness possesses no attributes or qualities. It follows that, wherever we find some attributes or qualities, there is necessarily some thing or substance to be found for them to belong to; and the more attributes we discover in the same thing or substance, the clearer is our knowledge of that substance. Now we find more attributes in our mind than in anything else, as is manifest from the fact that whatever enables us to know anything else cannot but lead us to a much surer knowledge of our own mind. For example, if I judge that the earth exists from the fact that I touch it or see it, this very fact undoubtedly gives even greater support for the judgement that my mind exists. For it may perhaps be the case that I judge that I am touching the earth even though the earth does not exist at all; but it cannot be that, when I make this judgement, my mind which is making the judgement does not exist. And the same applies in other cases ⟨regarding all the things that come into our mind, namely that we who think of them exist, even if they are false or have no existence⟩.

32. *We Possess Only Two Modes of Thinking: The Perception of the Intellect and the Operation of the Will*

All the modes of thinking that we experience within ourselves can be brought under two general headings: perception, or the operation of the intellect, and volition, or the operation of the will. Sensory perception, imagination and pure understanding are simply various modes of perception; desire, aversion, assertion, denial and doubt are various modes of willing.

33. *We Fall into Error Only When We Make Judgements About Things Which We Have Not Sufficiently Perceived*

Now when we perceive something, so long as we do not make any assertion or denial about it, we clearly avoid error. And we equally avoid error when we confine our assertions or denials to what we clearly and distinctly perceive should be asserted or denied. Error arises only when, as often happens, we make a judgement about something even though we do not have an accurate perception of it.

34. *Making a Judgement Requires Not Only the Intellect But Also the Will*

In order to make a judgement, the intellect is of course required since, in the case of something which we do not in any way perceive, there is no judgement we can make. But the will is also required so that, once something is perceived in some manner, our assent may then be given. Now a judgement—some kind of judgement at least—can be made without the need for a complete and exhaustive perception of the thing in question; for we can assent to many things which we know only in a very obscure and confused manner.

34. *The Scope of the Will Is Wider Than That of the Intellect, and This Is the Cause of Error*

Moreover, the perception of the intellect extends only to the few objects presented to it, and is always extremely limited. The will, on the other hand, can in a certain sense be called infinite, since we observe without exception that its scope extends to anything that can possibly be an object of any other will—even the immeasurable will of God. So it is easy for us to extend our will beyond what we clearly perceive; and when we do this it is no wonder that we may happen to go wrong.

66. How Sensations, Emotions and Appetites May Be Clearly Known, Despite the Fact that We Are Frequently Wrong in Our Judgements Concerning Them

There remains sensations, emotions and appetites. These may be clearly perceived provided we take great care in our judgements concerning them to include no more than what is strictly contained in our perception—no more than that of which we have inner awareness. But this is a very difficult rule to observe, at least with regard to sensations. For all of us have, from our early childhood, judged that all the objects of our sense-perception are things existing outside our minds and closely resembling our sensations, i.e. the perceptions that we had of them. Thus, on seeing a colour, for example, we supposed we were seeing a thing located outside us which closely resembled the idea of colour that we experienced within us at the time. And this was something that, because of our habit of making such judgements, we thought we saw clearly and distinctly—so much so that we took it for something certain and indubitable.

67. We Frequently Make Mistakes, Even in Our Judgements Concerning Pain

The same thing happens with regard to everything else of which we have sensory awareness, even to pleasure and pain. For, although we do not suppose that these exist outside us, we generally regard them not as being in the mind alone, or in our perception, but as being in the hand or foot or in some other part of our body. But the fact that we feel a pain as it were in our foot does not make it certain that the pain exists outside our mind, in the foot, any more than the fact that we see light as it were in the sun, makes it certain the light exists outside us, in the sun. Both these beliefs are preconceived opinions of our early childhood, as will become clear below.

68. How to Distinguish What We Clearly Know in Such Matters from What Can Lead Us Astray

In order to distinguish what is clear in this connection from what is obscure, we must be very careful to note that pain and colour and so on are clearly and distinctly perceived when they are regarded merely as sensations or thoughts. But when they are judged to be real things existing outside our mind, there is no way of understanding what sort

of things they are. If someone says he sees colour in a body or feels pain in a limb, this amounts to saying that he sees or feels something there of which he is wholly ignorant, or, in other words, that he does not know what he is seeing or feeling. Admittedly, if he fails to pay sufficient attention, he may easily convince himself that he has some knowledge of what he sees or feels, because he may suppose that it is something similar to the sensation of colour or pain which he experiences within himself. But if he examines the nature of what is represented by the sensation of colour or pain—what is represented as existing in the coloured body or the painful part—he will realize that he is wholly ignorant of it.

69. We Know Size, Shape and So Forth in Quite a Different Way from the Way in Which We Know Colours, Pains and the Like

This will be especially clear if we consider the wide gap between our knowledge of those features of bodies which we clearly perceive, as stated earlier, and our knowledge of those features which must be referred to the senses, as I have just pointed out. To the former class belong the size of the bodies we see, their shape, motion, position, duration, number and so on (by 'motion' I mean local motion: philosophers have imagined that there are other kinds of motion distinct from local motion, thereby only making the nature of motion less intelligible to themselves).[1] To the latter class belong the colour in a body, as well as pain, smell, taste and so on. It is true that when we see a body we are just as certain of its existence in virtue of its having a visible colour as we are in virtue of its having a visible shape; but our knowledge of what it is for the body to have a shape is much clearer than our knowledge of what it is for it to be coloured.

70. There Are Two Ways of Making Judgements Concerning the Things That Can Be Perceived by the Senses: The First Enables Us to Avoid Error, While the Second Allows Us to Fall into Error

It is clear, then, that when we say that we perceive colours in objects, this is really just the same as saying that we perceive something in the objects whose nature we do not know, but which produces

1. By 'local motion' is meant, roughly, movement from place to place. Scholastic philosophers, following Aristotle, sometimes classified any alteration (e.g. a quantitative or a qualitative change) as a type of motion; various other distinctions, e.g. that between 'natural' and 'violent' motion, were also commonplace.

in us a certain very clear and vivid sensation which we call the sensation of colour. But the way in which we make our judgement can vary very widely. As long as we merely judge that there is in the objects (that is, in the things, whatever they may turn out to be, which are the source of our sensations) something whose nature we do not know, then we avoid error; indeed, we are actually guarding against error, since the recognition that we are ignorant of something makes us less liable to make any rash judgement about it. But it is quite different when we suppose that we perceive colours in objects. Of course, we do not really know what it is that we are calling a colour; and we cannot find any intelligible resemblance between the colour which we suppose to be in objects and that which we experience in our sensation. But this is something we do not take account of; and, what is more, there are many other features, such as size, shape and number which we clearly perceive to be actually or at least possibly present in objects in a way exactly corresponding to our sensory perception or understanding. And so we easily fall into the error of judging that what is called colour in objects is something exactly like the colour of which we have sensory awareness; and we make the mistake of thinking that we clearly perceive what we do not perceive at all.

71. *The Chief Cause of Error Arises from the Preconceived Opinions of Childhood*

It is here that the first and main cause of all our errors may be recognized. In our early childhood the mind was so closely tied to the body that it had no leisure for any thoughts except those by means of which it had sensory awareness of what was happening to the body. It did not refer these thoughts to anything outside itself, but merely felt pain when something harmful was happening to the body and felt pleasure when something beneficial occurred. And when nothing very beneficial or harmful was happening to the body, the mind had various sensations corresponding to the different areas where, and ways in which, the body was being stimulated, namely what we call the sensations of tastes, smells, sounds, heat, cold, light, colours and so on—sensations which do not represent anything located outside our thought.[2] At the same time the mind perceived sizes, shapes, motions and so on, which were presented to it not as sensations but as things, or modes of things, existing (or at least capable of existing) outside thought, although it was not yet aware of the difference between things and sensations. The next stage arose when the mechanism of the body, which is so constructed by nature that it has the ability to move in various ways by its own power, twisted around aimlessly in all directions in its random attempts to pursue the beneficial and avoid the harmful; at this point the mind that was attached to the body began to notice that the objects of this pursuit or avoidance had an existence outside itself. And it attributed to them not only sizes, shapes, motions and the like, which it perceived as things or modes of things, but also tastes, smells and so on, the sensations of which were, it realized, produced by the objects in question. Moreover, since the mind judged everything in terms of its utility to the body in which it was immersed, it assessed the amount of reality in each object by the extent to which it was affected by it. As a result, it supposed that there was more substance or corporeality in rocks and metals than in water or air, since it felt more hardness and heaviness in them. Indeed, it regarded the air as a mere nothing, so long as it felt no wind or cold or heat in it. And because the light coming from the stars appeared no brighter than that produced by the meagre glow of an oil lamp, it did not imagine any star as being any bigger than this. And because it did not observe that the earth turns on its axis or that its surface is curved to form a globe, it was rather inclined to suppose that the earth was immobile and its surface flat. Right from infancy our mind was swamped with a thousand such preconceived opinions; and in later childhood, forgetting that they were adopted without sufficient examination, it regarded them as known by the senses or implanted by nature, and accepted them as utterly true and evident.

---

2. '. . . but which vary accordingly to the different movements which pass from all parts of our body to the part of the brain to which our mind is closely joined and united' (added in French version).

from Letter to Elizabeth, 28 June 1643[1]

*   *   *   *   *

First of all then, I observe one great difference between these three kinds of notions. The soul can be conceived only by pure intellect; the body (i.e. extension, shape, and movement) can likewise be known by pure intellect, but much better by intellect aided by imagination; and finally what belongs to the union of the soul and the body can be known only obscurely by pure intellect or by intellect aided by imagination, but it can be known very clearly by the senses. That is why people who never philosophize and use only their senses have no doubt that the soul moves the body and that the body acts on the soul. They regard both of them as a single thing, that is to say, they conceive their union; because to conceive the union between two things is to conceive them as one single thing. Metaphysical thoughts, which exercise the pure intellect, help to familiarize us with the notion of the soul; and the study of mathematics, which exercises mainly the imagination in the consideration of shapes and movements, accustoms us to form distinct notions of bodies. But it is the ordinary course of life and conversation, and abstention from meditation and from the study of the things which exercise the imagination, that teaches us how to conceive the union of the soul and the body.

I am almost afraid that your Highness will think that I am not now speaking seriously; but that would go against the respect which I owe you and which I will never cease to show you. I can say with truth that the chief rule I have always observed in my studies, which I think has been the most useful to me in acquiring what knowledge I have, has been never to spend more than a few hours a day in the thoughts which occupy the imagination and a few hours a year on those which occupy the pure intellect. I have given all the rest of my time to the relaxation of the senses and the repose of the mind. And I include among the exercise of the imagination all serious conversations and anything which needs to be done with attention. This is why I have retired to the country. In the busiest city in the world I could still have as many hours to myself as I now employ in study, but I could not spend them so usefully if my mind was tired by the attention required by the bustle of life. I take the liberty of writing this to your Highness, so that she may see how genuine is my admiration for her devoting time to the meditations needed to appreciate the distinction between the mind and the body, despite all the business and care which attend people who combine great minds with high birth.

I think it is those meditations rather than thoughts requiring less attention that have made your Highness find obscurity in our notion of their union. It does not seem to me that the human mind is capable of conceiving at the same time the distinction and the union between body and soul, because for this it is necessary to conceive them as a single thing and at the same time to conceive them as two things; and this is absurd. This is why I made use earlier of an analogy with heaviness and other qualities which we commonly imagine to be united to certain bodies in the way that thought is united to ours. I supposed that your Highness still had in mind the arguments proving the distinction between the soul and the body, and I did not want to ask her to put them away in order to represent to herself the notion of the union which everyone has in himself without philosophizing. Everyone feels that he is a single person with both body and thought so related by nature that the thought can move the body and feel the things which happen to it. I did not worry about the fact that the analogy with heaviness was lame because such qualities are not real as people imagine them to be. This was because I thought that your Highness was already completely convinced that the soul is a substance distinct from the body.

Your Highness observes that it is easier to attribute matter and extension to the soul than to attribute to it the capacity to move and to be moved by the body without having matter. I beg her to feel free to attribute matter and extension to the soul because that is simply to conceive it as united to the body. And once she has formed a proper conception of this and experienced it in herself, it will be easy for her to consider that the matter attributed to the thought is not thought itself, and that the extension of the matter is of different nature from the extension of the thought, because the former is determined to a definite place, from which it excludes all other bodily extension, which is not the case with the latter. And so your Highness will easily be able to return to the knowledge of the distinction of soul and body in spite of having conceived their union. . . .

1. AT iii. 690; AM v. 322; in French; complete.

from *Discourse on the Method of Rightly Conducting One's Reason and Seeking the Truth in the Sciences* (AT VI)

* * * * *

Part Five

* * * * *

From the description of inanimate bodies and plants I went on to describe animals, and in particular men. But I did not yet have sufficient knowledge to speak of them in the same manner as I did of the other things—that is, by demonstrating effects from causes and showing from what seeds and in what manner nature must produce them. So I contented myself with supposing that God formed the body of a man exactly like our own both in the outward shape of its limbs and in the internal arrangement of its organs, using for its composition nothing but the matter that I had described. I supposed, too, that in the beginning God did not place in this body any rational soul or any other thing to serve as a vegetative or sensitive soul, but rather that he kindled in its heart one of those fires without light which I had already explained, and whose nature I understood to be no different from that of the fire which heats hay when it has been stored before it is dry, or which causes new wine to seethe when it is left to ferment from the crushed grapes. And when I looked to see what functions would occur in such a body I found precisely those which may occur in us without our thinking of them, and hence without any contribution from our soul (that is, from that part of us, distinct from the body, whose nature, as I have said previously, is simply to think). These functions are just the ones in which animals without reason may be said to resemble us. But I could find none of the functions which, depending on thought, are the only ones that belong to us as men; though I found all these later on, once I had supposed that God created a rational soul and joined it to this body in a particular way which I described.

* * * * *

I made special efforts to show that if any such machines had the organs and outward shape of a monkey or of some other animal that lacks reason, we should have no means of knowing that they did not possess entirely the same nature as these animals; whereas if any such machines bore a resemblance to our bodies and imitated our actions as closely as possible for all practical purposes, we should still have two very certain means of recognizing that they were not real men. The first is that they could never use words, or put together other signs, as we do in order to declare our thoughts to others. For we can certainly conceive of a machine so constructed that it utters words, and even utters words which correspond to bodily actions causing a change in its organs (e.g., if you touch it in one spot it asks what you want of it, if you touch it in another it cries out that you are hurting it, and so on). But it is not conceivable that such a machine should produce different arrangements of words so as to give an appropriately meaningful answer to whatever is said in its presence, as the dullest of men can do. Secondly, even though such machines might do some things as well as we do them, or perhaps even better, they would inevitably fail in others, which would reveal that they were acting not through understanding but only from the disposition of their organs. For whereas reason is a universal instrument which can be used in all kinds of situations, these organs need some particular disposition for each particular action; hence it is for all practical purposes impossible for a machine to have enough different organs to make it act in all the contingencies of life in the way in which our reason makes us act.

Now in just these two ways we can also know the difference between man and beast. For it is quite remarkable that there are no men so dull-witted or stupid—and this includes even madmen—that they are incapable of arranging various words together and forming an utterance from them in order to make their thoughts understood; whereas there is no other animal, however perfect and well-endowed it may be, that can do the like. This does not happen because they lack the necessary organs, for we see that magpies and parrots can utter words as we do, and yet they cannot speak as we do: that is, they cannot show that they are thinking what they are saying. On the other hand, men born deaf and dumb, and thus deprived of speech-organs as much as the beasts or even more so, normally invent their own signs to make themselves understood by those who, being regularly in their company, have the time to learn their language. This shows not merely that the beasts have less reason than men, but that they have no reason at all. For it patently requires very little reason to be able to speak; and since as much inequality can be observed among the animals of a given species as among human beings, and some animals are more easily trained than others, it would be incredible that a superior specimen of the monkey or parrot species should not be able to speak as well as the stupidest child—or at least as well as a child with a defective brain—if their souls were not completely different in nature from ours. And we must not confuse speech with the natural movements which express passions and which can be imitated by machines as well as by animals. Nor should we think, like some of the ancients, that the beasts speak, although we do not understand their language. For if that were true, then since they have many organs that correspond to ours, they could make themselves understood by us as well as by their fellows. It is also a very remarkable fact that although many animals show more skill than we do in some of their actions, yet the same animals show none at all in many others; so what they do better does not prove that they have any intelligence, for if it did then they would have more intelligence than any of us and would excel us in everything. It proves rather that they have no intelligence at all, and that it is nature which acts in them according to the disposition of their or-

gans. In the same way a clock, consisting only of wheels and springs, can count the hours and measure time more accurately than we can with all our wisdom.

After that, I described the rational soul, and showed that, unlike the other things of which I had spoken, it cannot be derived in any way from the potentiality of matter, but must be specially created.[1] And I showed how it is not sufficient for it to be lodged in the human body like a helmsman in his ship, except perhaps to move its limbs, but that it must be more closely joined and united with the body in order to have, besides this power of movement, feelings and appetites like ours and so constitute a real man. Here I dwelt a little upon the subject of the soul, because it is of the greatest importance. For after the error of those who deny God, which I believe I have already adequately refuted, there is none that leads weak minds further from the straight path of virtue than that of imagining that the souls of the beasts are of the same nature as ours, and hence that after this present life we have nothing to fear or to hope for, any more than flies and ants. But when we know how much the beasts differ from us, we understand much better the arguments which prove that our soul is of a nature entirely independent of the body, and consequently that it is not bound to die with it. And since we cannot see any other causes which destroy the soul, we are naturally led to conclude that it is immortal.

1. The section of the *Treatise on Man* referred to here has not survived.

from Letter to [the Marquess of Newcastle], 23 November 1646[1]

* * * * *

I cannot share the opinion of Montaigne and others who attribute understanding or thought to animals. I am not worried that people say that men have an absolute empire over all the other animals; because I agree that some of them are stronger than us, and believe that there may also be some who have an instinctive cunning capable of deceiv-

ing the shrewdest human beings. But I observe that they only imitate or surpass us in those of our actions which are not guided by our thoughts. It often happens that we walk or eat without thinking at all about what we are doing; and similarly, without using our reason, we reject things which are harmful for us, and parry the blows aimed at us. Indeed, even if we expressly willed not to put our hands in front of our head when we fall, we could not prevent ourselves. I think also that if we had no thought we would eat, as the animals do, with-

1. AT iv. 569; AM vii. 222; in French; extracts.

From *Descartes: Philosophical Letters,* translated by Anthony Kenny. Oxford: Oxford University Press, 1970, pp. 206–8, 243–45. Copyright © 1981 by Anthony Kenny. Reprinted with permission of Anthony Kenny.

out having to learn to; and it is said that those who walk in their sleep sometimes swim across streams in which they would drown if they were awake. As for the movements of our passions, even though in us they are accompanied with thought because we have the faculty of thinking, it is none the less very clear that they do not depend on thought, because they often occur in spite of us. Consequently they can also occur in animals, even more violently than they do in human beings, without our being able to conclude from that that they have thoughts.

In fact, none of our external actions can show anyone who examines them that our body is not just a self-moving machine but contains a soul with thoughts, with the exception of words, or other signs that are relevant to particular topics without expressing any passion. I say words or other signs, because deaf-mutes use signs as we use spoken words; and I say that these signs must be relevant, to exclude the speech of parrots, without excluding the speech of madmen, which is relevant to particular topics even though it does not follow reason. I add also that these words or signs must not express any passion, to rule out not only cries of joy or sadness and the like, but also whatever can be taught by training to animals. If you teach a magpie to say good-day to its mistress, when it sees her approach, this can only be by making the utterance of this word the expression of one of its passions. For instance it will be an expression of the hope of eating, if it has always been given a tit-bit when it says it. Similarly, all the things which dogs, horses, and monkeys are taught to perform are only expressions of their fear, their hope, or their joy; and consequently they can be performed without any thought. Now it seems to me very striking that the use of words, so defined, is something peculiar to human beings. Montaigne and Charron may have said that there is more difference between one human being and another than between a human being and an animal; but there has never been known an animal so perfect as to

use a sign to make other animals understand something which expressed no passion; and there is no human being so imperfect as not to do so, since even deaf-mutes invent special signs to express their thoughts. This seems to me a very strong argument to prove that the reason why animals do not speak as we do is not that they lack the organs but that they have no thoughts. It cannot be said that they speak to each other and that we cannot understand them; because since dogs and some other animals express their passions to us, they would express their thoughts also if they had any.

I know that animals do many things better than we do, but this does not surprise me. It can even be used to prove they act naturally and mechanically, like a clock which tells the time better than our judgement does. Doubtless when the swallows come in spring, they operate like clocks. The actions of honeybees are of the same nature, and the discipline of cranes in flight, and of apes in fighting, if it is true that they keep discipline. Their instinct to bury their dead is no stranger than that of dogs and cats who scratch the earth for the purpose of burying their excrement; they hardly ever actually bury it, which shows that they act only by instinct and without thinking. The most that one can say is that though the animals do not perform any action which shows us that they think, still, since the organs of their body are not very different from ours, it may be conjectured that there is attached to those organs some thoughts such as we experience in ourselves, but of a very much less perfect kind. To which I have nothing to reply except that if they thought as we do, they would have an immortal soul like us. This is unlikely, because there is no reason to believe it of some animals without believing it of all, and many of them such as oysters and sponges are too imperfect for this to be credible. But I am afraid of boring you with this discussion, and my only desire is to show you that I am, etc.

from Letter to More, 5 February 1649[1]

*   *   *   *   *

5. But there is no prejudice to which we are all more accustomed from our earliest years than the belief that dumb animals think. Our only reason for this belief is the fact that we see that many of

1. AT v. 267; AM viii. 121; in Latin; complete.

the organs of animals are not very different from ours in shape and movement. Since we believe that there is a single principle within us which causes these motions—namely the soul, which both moves the body and thinks—we do not doubt that some such soul is to be found in animals also. I came to realize, however, that there are two different principles causing our motions: one is purely mechanical and corporeal and depends solely on the force of the spirits and the construction of our organs, and can be called the corporeal soul; the other is the incorporeal mind, the soul which I have defined as a thinking substance. Thereupon I investigated more carefully whether the motions of animals originated from both these principles or from one only. I soon saw clearly that they could all originate from the corporeal and mechanical principle, and I thenceforward regarded it as certain and established that we cannot at all prove the presence of a thinking soul in animals. I am not disturbed by the astuteness and cunning of dogs and foxes, or all the things which animals do for the sake of food, sex, and fear; I claim that I can easily explain the origin of all of them from the constitution of their organs.

But though I regard it as established that we cannot prove there is any thought in animals, I do not think it is thereby proved that there is not, since the human mind does not reach into their hearts. But when I investigate what is most probable in this matter, I see no argument for animals having thoughts except the fact that since they have eyes, ears, tongues, and other sense-organs like ours, it seems likely that they have sensation like us; and since thought is included in our mode of sensation, similar thought seems to be attributable to them. This argument, which is very obvious, has taken possession of the minds of all men from their earliest age. But there are other arguments, stronger and more numerous, but not so obvious to everyone, which strongly urge the opposite. One is that it is more probable that worms and flies and caterpillars move mechanically than that they all have immortal souls.

It is certain that in the bodies of animals, as in ours, there are bones, nerves, muscles, animal spirits, and other organs so disposed that they can by themselves, without any thought, give rise to all the animal motions we observe. This is very clear in convulsive movements when the machine of the body moves despite the soul, and sometimes more violently and in a more varied manner than when it is moved by the will.

Second, it seems reasonable, since art copies nature, and men can make various automata which move without thought, that nature should produce its own automata, much more splendid than artificial ones. These natural automata are the animals. This is especially likely since we have no reason to believe that thought always accompanies the disposition of organs which we find in animals. It is much more wonderful that a mind should be found in every human body than that one should be lacking in every animal.

But in my opinion the main reason which suggests that the beasts lack thought is the following. Within a single species some of them are more perfect than others, as men are too. This can be seen in horses and dogs, some of whom learn what they are taught much better than others. Yet, although all animals easily communicate to us, by voice or bodily movement, their natural impulses of anger, fear, hunger and so on, it has never yet been observed that any brute animal reached the stage of using real speech, that is to say, of indicating by word or sign something pertaining to pure thought and not to natural impulse. Such speech is the only certain sign of thought hidden in a body. All men use it, however stupid and insane they may be, and though they may lack tongue and organs of voice; but no animals do. Consequently it can be taken as a real specific difference between men and dumb animals.

For brevity's sake I here omit the other reasons for denying thought to animals. Please note that I am speaking of thought, and not of life or sensation. I do not deny life to animals, since I regard it as consisting simply in the heat of the heart; and I do not deny sensation, in so far as it depends on a bodily organ. Thus my opinion is not so much cruel to animals as indulgent to men—at least to those who are not given to the superstitions of Pythagoras—since it absolves them from the suspicion of crime when they eat or kill animals. . . .

2

John Locke

from *Essay Concerning Human Understanding*

Book II, Chapter I, Of Ideas *in general, and their Original.*

§ 2. Let us then suppose the Mind to be, as we say, white Paper, void of all Characters, without any *Ideas;* How comes it to be furnished? Whence comes it by that vast store, which the busy and boundless Fancy of Man has painted on it, with an almost endless variety? Whence has it all the materials of Reason and Knowledge? To this I answer, in one word, From *Experience:* In that, all our Knowledge is founded; and from that it ultimately derives it self. Our Observation employ'd either about *external, sensible Objects; or about the internal Operations of our Minds, perceived and reflected on by our selves, is that, which supplies our Understandings with all the materials of thinking.* These two are the Fountains of Knowledge, from whence all the *Ideas* we have, or can naturally have, do spring.

§ 3. First, *Our Senses,* conversant about particular sensible Objects, do *convey into the Mind,* several distinct *Perceptions* of things, according to those various ways, wherein those Objects do affect them: And thus we come by those *Ideas,* we have of *Yellow, White, Heat, Cold, Soft, Hard, Bitter, Sweet,* and all those which we call sensible qualities, which when I say the senses convey into the mind, I mean, they from external Objects convey into the mind what produces there those *Perceptions.* This great Source, of most of the *Ideas* we have, depending wholly upon our Senses, and derived by them to the Understanding, I call *SENSATION.*

§ 2. *All* Ideas *come from Sensation or Reflection.*

§ 3. *The Objects of Sensation one Source of* Ideas.

§ 4. Secondly, The other Fountain, from which Experience furnisheth the Understanding with *Ideas,* is the *Perception of the Operations of our own Minds* within us, as it is employ'd about the *Ideas* it has got; which Operations, when the Soul comes to reflect on, and consider, do furnish the Understanding with another set of *Ideas,* which could not be had from things without: and such are, *Perception, Thinking, Doubting, Believing, Reasoning, Knowing, Willing,* and all the different actings of our own Minds; which we being conscious of, and observing in our selves, do from these receive into our Understandings, as distinct *Ideas,* as we do from Bodies affecting our Senses. This Source of *Ideas,* every Man has wholly in himself: And though it be not Sense, as having nothing to do with external Objects; yet it is very like it, and might properly enough be call'd internal Sense. But as I call the other *Sensation,* so I call this *REFLECTION,* the *Ideas* it affords being such only, as the Mind gets by reflecting on its own Operations within it self. By *REFLECTION* then, in the following part of this Discourse, I would be understood to mean, that notice which the Mind takes of its own Operations, and the manner of them, by reason whereof, there come to be *Ideas* of these Operations in the Understanding. These two, I say, *viz.* External, Material things, as the Objects of *SENSATION;* and the Operations of our own Minds within, as the Objects of *REFLECTION,* are, to me, the only Originals, from whence all our *Ideas* take their beginnings. The term *Operations* here, I use in a large sence, as comprehending not barely the Actions of the Mind about its *Ideas,* but some sort of Passions arising some-

§ 4. *The Operations of our Minds, the other Source of them.*

times from them, such as is the satisfaction or uneasiness arising from any thought.

§ 5. The Understanding seems to me, not to have the least glimmering of any *Ideas,* which it doth not receive from one of these two. *External Objects furnish the Mind with the* Ideas *of sensible, qualities,* which are all those different perceptions they produce in us: And the *Mind furnishes the Understanding with* Ideas *of its own Operations.*

These, when we have taken a full survey of them, and their several Modes, Combinations, and Relations, we shall find to contain all our whole stock of *Ideas;* and that we have nothing in our Minds, which did not come in, one of these two ways. Let any one examine his own Thoughts, and throughly search into his Understanding, and then let him tell me, Whether all the original *Ideas* he has there, are any other than of the Objects of his *Senses;* or of the Operations of his Mind, considered as Objects of his *Reflection:* and how great a mass of Knowledge soever he imagines to be lodged there, he will, upon taking a strict view, see, that he has *not any* Idea *in his Mind, but what one of these two have imprinted;* though, perhaps, with infinite variety compounded and enlarged by the Understanding, as we shall see hereafter.

§ 19. To suppose the Soul to think, and the Man not to perceive it, is, as has been said, to make two Persons in one Man: And if one considers well these Men's way of speaking, one should be led into a suspicion, that they do so. For they who tell us, that the Soul always thinks, do never, that I remember, say, That a Man always thinks. Can the Soul think, and not the Man? Or a Man think, and not be conscious of it? This, perhaps, would be suspected of *Fargon* in others. If they say, The Man thinks always, but is not always conscious of it; they may as well say, His Body is extended, without having parts. For 'tis altogether as intelligible to say, that a body is extended without parts, as that any thing *thinks without being conscious of it,* or perceiving, that it does so. They who talk thus, may, with as much reason, if it be necessary to their Hypothesis, say, That a Man is always hungry, but that he does not always feel it: Whereas hunger consists in that very sensation, as thinking consists in being conscious that one thinks. If they say, That a Man is always conscious to himself of thinking; I ask, How they know it? Consciousness is the perception of what passes in a Man's own mind. Can another Man perceive, that I am conscious of any thing, when I perceive

it not my self? No Man's Knowledge here, can go beyond his Experience. Wake a Man out of a sound sleep, and ask him, What he was that moment thinking on. If he himself be conscious of nothing he then thought on, he must be a notable Diviner of Thoughts, that can assure him, that he was thinking: May he not with more reason assure him, he was not asleep? This is something beyond Philosophy; and it cannot be less than Revelation, that discovers to another, Thoughts in my mind, when I can find none there my self: And they must needs have a penetrating sight, who can certainly see, that I think, when I cannot perceive it my self, and when I declare, that I do not; and yet can see, that Dogs or Elephants do not think, when they give all the demonstration of it imaginable, except only telling us, that they do so. This some may suspect to be a step beyond the *Rosecrucians;* it seeming easier to make ones self invisible to others, than to make another's thoughts visible to me, which are not visible to himself. But 'tis but defining the Soul to be a substance, that always thinks, and the business is done. If such a definition be of any Authority, I know not what it can serve for, but to make many Men suspect, That they have no Souls at all, since they find a good part of their Lives pass away without thinking. For no Definitions, that I know, no Suppositions of any Sect, are of force enough to destroy constant Experience; and, perhaps, 'tis the affectation of knowing beyond what we perceive, that makes so much useless dispute, and noise, in the World.

Chapter XXVII, Identity and Diversity

§ 9. This being premised to find wherein *personal Identity* consists, we must consider what *Person* stands for; which, I think, is a thinking intelligent Being, that has reason and reflection, and can consider it self as it self, the same thinking thing in different times and places; which it does only by that consciousness, which is inseparable from thinking, and as it seems to me essential to it: It being impossible for any one to perceive, without perceiving, that he does perceive. When we see, hear, smell, taste, feel, meditate, or will any thing, we know that we do so. Thus it is always as to our present Sensations and Perceptions: And by this every one is to himself, that which he calls *self:* It not being considered in this case, whether the same *self* be continued in the same, or divers Substances. For since consciousness always accompanies thinking, and 'tis that, that makes every one to be, what he calls *self;* and thereby distinguishes

§ 5. *All our* Ideas *are of the one or the other of these.*

§ 19. *That a Man should be busie in thinking, and yet not retain it the next moment, very improbable.*

§ 9. *Personal Identity.*

himself from all other thinking things, in this alone consists *personal Identity, i.e.* the sameness of a rational Being: And as far as this consciousness can be extended backwards to any past Action or Thought, so far reaches the Identity of that *Person;* it is the same *self* now it was then; and 'tis by the same *self* with this present one that now reflects on it, that that Action was done.

Book IV, Chapter VII, of Maxims

§ 4. For, *First,* the immediate perception of the agreement or disagreement of *Identity,* being founded in the Mind's having distinct *Ideas,* this affords us as many *self-evident* Propositions, as we have distinct *Ideas.* Every one that has any Knowledge at all, has, as the Foundation of it, various and distinct *Ideas:* And it is the first act of the Mind, (without which, it can never be capable of any Knowledge,) to know every one of its *Ideas* by it self, and distinguish it from others. Every one finds in himself, that he knows the *Ideas* he has; That he knows also, when any one is in his Understanding, and what it is; And that when more than one are there, he knows them distinctly and unconfusedly one from another. Which always being so, (it being impossible but that he should perceive what he perceives,) he can never be in doubt when any *Idea* is in his Mind, that it is there, and is that *Idea* it is; and that two distinct *Ideas,* when they are in his Mind, are there, and are not one and the same *Idea.*

* * * * *

Book II, Chapter VIII, *Some farther Considerations concerning our simple* Ideas.

§ 7. To discover the nature of our *Ideas* the better, and to discourse of them intelligibly, it will be convenient to distinguish them, as they are *Ideas* or Perceptions in our Minds; and as they are modifications of matter in the Bodies that cause such Perceptions in us: that so we *may not* think (as perhaps usually is done) that they are exactly the Images and *Resemblances* of something inherent in the subject; most of those of Sensation being in the Mind no more the likeness of something existing without us, than the Names, that stand for them, are the likeness of our *Ideas,* which yet upon hearing, they are apt to excite in us.

§ 8. Whatsoever the Mind perceives in it self, or is the immediate object of Perception, Thought, or

§ 4. First, As to Identity and Diversity, all Propositions are equally self-evident.

§§ 7, 8. Ideas *in the Mind, Qualities in Bodies.*

Understanding, that I call *Idea;* and the Power to produce any *Idea* in our mind, I call *Quality* of the Subject wherein that power is. Thus a Snow-ball having the power to produce in us the *Ideas* of *White, Cold,* and *Round,* the Powers to produce those *Ideas* in us, as they are in the Snow-ball, I call *Qualities;* and as they are Sensations, or Perceptions, in our Understandings, I call them *Ideas:* which *Ideas,* if I speak of sometimes, as in the things themselves, I would be understood to mean those Qualities in the Objects which produce them in us.

§ 9. Qualities thus considered in Bodies are, First such as are utterly inseparable from the Body, in what estate soever it be; such as in all the alterations and changes it suffers, all the force can be used upon it, it constantly keeps; and such as Sense constantly finds in every particle of Matter, which has bulk enough to be perceived, and the Mind finds inseparable from every particle of Matter, though less than to make it self singly be perceived by our Senses. *v.g.* Take a grain of Wheat, divide it into two parts, each part has still *Solidity, Extension, Figure,* and *Mobility;* divide it again, and it retains still the same qualities; and so divide it on, till the parts become insensible, they must retain still each of them all those qualities. For division (which is all that a Mill, or Pestel, or any other Body, does upon another, in reducing it to insensible parts) can never take away either Solidity, Extension, Figure, or Mobility from any Body, but only makes two, or more distinct separate masses of Matter, of that which was but one before, all which distinct masses, reckon'd as so many distinct Bodies, after division make a certain Number. These I call *original* or *primary Qualities* of Body, which I think we may observe to produce simple *Ideas* in us, *viz.* Solidity, Extension, Figure, Motion, or Rest, and Number.

§ 10. *2dly,* Such *Qualities,* which in truth are nothing in the Objects themselves, but Powers to produce various Sensations in us by their *primary Qualities, i.e.* by the Bulk, Figure, Texture, and Motion of their insensible parts, as Colours, Sounds, Tasts, *etc.* These I call *secondary Qualities.* To these might be added a third sort which are allowed to be barely Powers though they are as much real Qualities in the Subject, as those which I to comply with the common way of speaking call *Qualities,* but for distinction *secondary Qualities.* For the power in Fire to produce a new Colour, or consistency in Wax or Clay by its primary Qualities, is as much a quality in Fire, as the power it has to produce in me a new *Idea* or Sensation of warmth or burning, which I felt not before, by the

§§ 9, 10. *Primary and Secondary Qualities.*

same primary Qualities, *viz.* The Bulk, Texture, and Motion of its insensible parts.

§ 11. The next thing to be consider'd, is how *Bodies* produce *Ideas* in us, and that is manifestly *by impulse,* the only way which we can conceive Bodies operate in.

§ 12. If then external Objects be not united to our Minds, when they produce *Ideas* in it; and yet we perceive *these original Qualities* in such of them as singly fall under our Senses, 'tis evident, that some motion must be thence continued by our Nerves, or animal Spirits, by some parts of our Bodies, to the Brains or the seat of Sensation, there to *produce in our Minds the particular* Ideas *we have of them.* And since the Extension, Figure, Number, and Motion of Bodies of an observable bigness, may be perceived at a distance *by* the sight, 'tis evident some singly imperceptible Bodies must come from them to the Eyes, and thereby convey to the Brain some *Motion,* which produces these *Ideas,* which we have of them in us.

§ 13. After the same manner, that the *Ideas* of these original Qualities are produced in us, we may conceive, that the *Ideas of secondary Qualities* are also *produced, viz. by the operation of insensible particles on our Senses.* For it being manifest, that there are Bodies, and good store of Bodies, each whereof is so small, that we cannot, by any of our Senses, discover either their bulk, figure, or motion, as is evident in the Particles of the Air and Water, and other extremely smaller than those, perhaps, as much smaller than the Particles of Air, or Water, as the Particles of Air or Water, are smaller than Pease or Hail-stones. Let us suppose at present, that the different Motions and Figures, Bulk, and Number of such Particles, affecting the several Organs of our Senses, produce in us those different Sensations, which we have from the Colours and Smells of Bodies, *e.g.* that a Violet, by the impulse of such insensible particles of matter of peculiar figures, and bulks, and in different degrees and modifications of their Motions, causes the *Ideas* of the blue Colour, and sweet Scent of that Flower to be produced in our Minds. It being no more impossible, to conceive, that God should annex such *Ideas* to such Motions, with which they have no similitude; than that he should annex the *Idea* of Pain to the motion of a piece of Steel dividing our Flesh, with which that *Idea* hath no resemblance.

§ 14. What I have said concerning *Colours* and *Smells,* may be understood also of *Tastes* and *Sounds, and other the like sensible Qualities;* which, whatever reality we, by mistake, attribute to them, are in truth nothing in the Objects themselves, but Powers to produce various Sensations in us, and *depend on those primary Qualities, viz.* Bulk, Figure, Texture, and Motion of parts; as I have said.

§ 15. From whence I think it is easie to draw this Observation, That the *Ideas of primary Qualities* of Bodies, *are Resemblances* of them, and their Patterns do really exist in the Bodies themselves; but the *Ideas, produced* in us *by* these *Secondary Qualities, have no resemblance* of them at all. There is nothing like our *Ideas,* existing in the Bodies themselves. They are in the Bodies, we denominate from them, only a Power to produce those Sensations in us: And what is Sweet, Blue, or Warm in *Idea,* is but the certain Bulk, Figure, and Motion of the insensible Parts in the Bodies themselves, which we call so.

§ 23. The *Qualities* then that are in *Bodies* rightly considered, are of *Three sorts.*

First, The *Bulk, Figure, Number, Situation,* and *Motion, or Rest* of their solid Parts; those are in them, whether we perceive them or no; and when they are of that size, that we can discover them, we have by these an *Idea* of the thing, as it is in it self, as is plain in artificial things. These I call *primary Qualities.*

Secondly, The *Power* that is in any Body, *by* Reason of *its* insensible *primary Qualities,* to operate after a peculiar manner on any of our Senses, and thereby *produce in us the different Ideas* of several Colours, Sounds, Smells, Tastes, *etc.* These are usually called sensible Qualities.

Thirdly, The *Power* that is in any Body, *by* Reason of the particular Constitution of *its primary Qualities, to* make such a *change* in the *Bulk, Figure, Texture, and Motion of another Body,* as to make it operate on our Senses, differently from what it did before. Thus the Sun has a Power to make Wax white, and Fire to make Lead fluid. These are usually called Powers.

The First of these, as has been said, I think, may be properly called *real Original,* or *primary Qualities,* because they are in the things themselves, whether they are perceived or no: and upon their different Modifications it is, that the secondary Qualities depend.

The other two, are only Powers to act differently upon other things, which Powers result from the different Modifications of those primary Qualities.

§ 24. But though *these two later sorts of Qualities are Powers barely,* and nothing but Powers, relating to several other Bodies, and resulting from the different Modifications of the Original Qualities; yet they are generally otherwise thought of. For *the Second sort, viz.* The Powers to produce several *Ideas* in us by our Senses, *are looked upon as real Qualities, in the things* thus affecting us: But *the Third sort are call'd, and esteemed barely Powers. v.g.* the *Idea* of Heat, or Light, which we receive by our Eyes, or touch from thc Sun, arc commonly thought *real Qualities,* existing in the Sun, and something more than mere Powers in it. But when we consider the Sun, in reference to Wax, which it melts or blanches, we look upon the Whiteness and Softness produced in the Wax, not as Qualities in the Sun, but Effects produced by *Powers* in it: Whereas, if rightly considered, these Qualities of Light and Warmth, which are Perceptions in me when I am warmed, or enlightned by the Sun, are no otherwise in the Sun, than the changes made in the Wax, when it is blanched or melted, are in the Sun. They are all of them equally Powers in the Sun, depending on its primary Qualities; whereby it is able in the one case, so to alter the Bulk, Figure, Texture, or Motion of some of the insensible parts of my Eyes, or Hands, as thereby to produce in me the *Idea* of Light or Heat; and in the other, it is able so to alter the Bulk, Figure, Texture, or Motion of the insensible Parts of the Wax, as to make them fit to produce in me the distinct *Ideas* of White and Fluid.

§ 25. The Reason, *Why the one are ordinarily taken for real Qualities, and the other only for bare Powers,* seems to be, because the *Ideas* we have of distinct Colours, Sounds, *etc.* containing nothing at all in them, of Bulk, Figure, or Motion, we are not apt to think them the Effects of these primary Qualities, which appear not to our Senses to operate in their Production; and with which, they have not any apparent Congruity, or conceivable Connexion. Hence it is, that we are so forward to imagine, that those *Ideas* are the resemblances of something really existing in the Objects themselves: Since Sensation discovers nothing of Bulk, Figure, or Motion of parts in their Production; nor can Reason shew, how Bodies by their Bulk, Figure, and Motion, should produce in the Mind the *Ideas* of Blue, or Yellow, *etc.* But in the other Case, in the Operations of Bodies, changing the Qualities one of another, we plainly discover, that the Quality produced, hath commonly no resemblance with any thing in the thing producing it; wherefore we look on it as a bare Effect of Power.

For though receiving the *Idea* of Heat, or Light, from the Sun, we are apt to think, 'tis a Perception and Resemblance of such a Quality in the Sun: yet when we see Wax, or a fair Face, receive change of Colour from the Sun, we cannot imagine, that to be the Reception or Resemblance of any thing in the Sun it self. For our Senses, being able to observe a likeness, or unlikeness of sensible Qualities in two different external Objects, we forwardly enough conclude the Production of any sensible Quality in any Subject, to be an Effect of bare Power, and not the Communication of any Quality, which was really in the efficient, when we find no such sensible Quality in the thing that produced it. But our Senses, not being able to discover any unlikeness between the *Idea* produced in us, and the Quality of the Object producing it, we are apt to imagine, that our *Ideas* are resemblances of something in the Objects, and not the Effects of certain Powers, placed in the Modification of their primary Qualities, with which primary Qualities the *Ideas* produced in us have no resemblance.

§ 26. To conclude, beside those before mentioned *primary Qualities* in Bodies, *viz.* Bulk, Figure, Extension, Number, and Motion of their solid Parts; all the rest, whereby we take notice of Bodies, and distinguish them one from another, are nothing else, but several Powers in them, depending on those primary Qualities; whereby they are fitted, either by immediately operating on our Bodies, to produce several different *Ideas* in us; or else by operating on other Bodies, so to change their primary Qualities, as to render them capable of producing *Ideas* in us, different from what before they did. The former of these, I think, may be called *Secondary Qualities, immediately perceivable:* The latter, *Secondary Qualities, mediately perceivable.*

Book IV, Chapter III, *Of the Extent of Humane Knowledge.*

§ 6. From all which it is evident, that *the extent of our Knowledge* comes not only short of the reality of Things, but even of the extent of our own *Ideas.* Though our Knowledge be limited to our *Ideas,* and cannot exceed them either in extent, or perfection; and though these be very narrow bounds, in respect of the extent of Allbeing, and far short of what we may justly imagine to be in some even

---

§§ 24, 25. *The* 1st. *are Resemblances. The* 2d. *thought Resemblances, but are not. The* 3d. *neither are nor are thought so.*

§ 26. *Secondary Qualities two-fold; First, Immediately perceivable; Secondly, Mediately perceivable.*

§ 6. *Sixthly, Our Knowledge therefore narrower than our* Ideas.

created understandings, not tied down to the dull and narrow Information, is to be received from some few, and not very acute ways of Perception, such as are our Senses; yet it would be well with us, if our Knowledge were but as large as our *Ideas,* and there were not many Doubts and Enquiries concerning the *Ideas* we have, whereof we are not, nor I believe ever shall be in this World, resolved. Nevertheless, I do not question, but that Humane Knowledge, under the present Circumstances of our Beings and Constitutions may be carried much farther, than it hitherto has been, if Men would sincerely, and with freedom of Mind, employ all that Industry and Labour of Thought, in improving the means of discovering Truth, which they do for the colouring or support of Falshood, to maintain a System, Interest, or Party, they are once engaged in. But yet after all, I think I may, without Injury to humane Perfection, be confident, that our Knowledge would never reach to all we might desire to know concerning those *Ideas* we have; nor be able to surmount all the Difficulties, and resolve all the Questions might arise concerning any of them. We have the *Ideas* of a *Square,* a *Circle,* and *Equality;* and yet, perhaps, shall never be able to find a Circle equal to a Square, and certainly know that it is so. We have the *Ideas* of *Matter* and *Thinking,* but possibly shall never be able to know, whether any mere material Being thinks, or no; it being impossible for us, by the contemplation of our own *Ideas,* without revelation, to discover, whether Omnipotency has not given to some Systems of Matter fitly disposed, a power to perceive and think, or else joined and fixed to Matter so disposed, a thinking immaterial Substance: It being, in respect of our Notions, not much more remote from our Comprehension to conceive, that GOD can, if he pleases, superadd to Matter a Faculty of Thinking, than that he should superadd to it another Substance, with a Faculty of Thinking; since we know not wherein Thinking consists, nor to what sort of Substances the Almighty has been pleased to give that Power, which cannot be in any created Being, but merely by the good pleasure and Bounty of the Creator. For I see no contradiction in it, that the first eternal thinking Being should, if he pleased, give to certain Systems of created sensless matter, put together as he thinks fit, some degrees of sense, perception, and thought: Though, as I think, I have proved, *Lib.* 4. *c.* 10*th.* it is no less than a contradiction to suppose matter (which is evidently in its own nature void of sense and thought) should be that Eternal first thinking Being. What certainty of Knowledge can any one have that some perceptions, such as *v.g.* pleasure and pain, should not be in some bodies themselves, after a

certain manner modified and moved, as well as that they should be in an immaterial Substance, upon the Motion of the parts of Body: Body as far as we can conceive being able only to strike and affect body; and Motion, according to the utmost reach of our *Ideas,* being able to produce nothing but Motion, so that when we allow it to produce pleasure or pain, or the *Idea* of a Colour, or Sound, we are fain to quit our Reason, go beyond our *Ideas,* and attribute it wholly to the good Pleasure of our Maker. For since we must allow he has annexed Effects to Motion, which we can no way conceive Motion able to produce, what reason have we to conclude, that he could not order them as well to be produced in a Subject we cannot conceive capable of them, as well as in a Subject we cannot conceive the motion of Matter can any way operate upon?

* * * * *

Chapter X, Of our Knowledge of the Existence of a GOD

§ 9. There are but two sorts of Beings in the World, that Man knows or conceives.

First, Such as are purely material, without Sense, Perception, or Thought, as the clippings of our Beards, and paring of our Nails.

Secondly, Sensible, thinking, perceiving Beings, such as we find our selves to be, which if you please, we will hereafter call *cogitative and incogitative* Beings; which to our present purpose, if for nothing else, are, perhaps, better Terms, than material and immaterial.

§ 10. If then there must be something eternal, let us see what sort of Being it must be. And to that, it is very obvious to Reason, that it must necessarily be a *cogitative* Being. For it is as impossible to conceive, that ever bare incogitative Matter should produce a thinking intelligent Being, as that nothing should of it self produce Matter. Let us suppose any parcel of Matter eternal, great or small, we shall find it, in it self, able to produce nothing. For Example; let us suppose the Matter of the next Pebble, we meet with, eternal, closely united, and the parts firmly at rest together, if there were no other Being in the World, Must it not eternally remain so, a dead inactive Lump? Is it possible to conceive it can add Motion to it self, being purely Matter, or produce any thing? Matter then, by its own Strength, cannot produce in it self so much as Motion: the Motion it has, must also be from Eternity, or else be produced, and added to

§ 9. *Two sorts of Beings, Cogitative and Incogitative.*

§ 10. *Incogitative Being cannot produce a Cogitative.*

Matter by some other Being more powerful than Matter; Matter, as is evident, having not Power to produce Motion in it self. But let us suppose Motion eternal too; yet Matter, *incogitative Matter* and Motion, whatever changes it might produce of Figure and Bulk, *could never produce Thought:* Knowledge will still be as far beyond the Power of Motion and Matter to produce, as Matter is beyond the Power of *nothing,* or *nonentity* to produce. And I appeal to everyone's own Thoughts, whether he cannot as easily conceive Matter produced by *nothing,* as Thought to be produced by pure Matter, when before there was no such thing as Thought, or an intelligent Being existing. Divide Matter into as minute parts as you will, (which we are apt to imagine a sort of spiritualizing, or making a thinking thing of it,) vary the Figure and Motion of it, as much as you please, a Globe, Cube, Cone, Prism, Cylinder, *etc.* whose Diameters are but 1000000th part of a *Gry* (*a*) will operate no otherwise upon other Bodies of proportionable Bulk, than those of an inch or foot Diameter; and you may as rationally expect to produce Sense,

Thought, and Knowledge, by putting together in a certain Figure and Motion, gross Particles of Matter, as by those that are the very minutest, that do any where exist. They knock, impell, and resist one another, just as the greater do, and that is all they can do. So that if we will suppose nothing first, or eternal; *Matter* can never begin to be: If we suppose bare Matter, without Motion, eternal; *Motion* can never begin to be: If we suppose only Matter and Motion first, or eternal; *Thought* can never begin to be. For it is impossible to conceive that Matter either with or without Motion could have originally in and from it self Sense, Perception, and Knowledge, as is evident from hence, that then Sense, Perception, and Knowledge must be a property eternally inseparable from Matter and every Particle of it.

*   *   *   *   *

(*a*) *A Gry is ⅒ of a line, a line ⅒ of an inch, an inch ⅒ of a philosophical foot, a philosophical foot ½ of a pendulum, whose Diad-*

roms, in the latitude of 45 degrees, are each equal to one Second of time, or ¹⁄₆₀ of a minute. I have affectedly made use of this measure here, and the parts of it, under a decimal division with names to them; because, I think, it would be of general convenience, that this should be the common measure in the Commonwealth of Letters.

3

Thomas Reid

from *Essays on the Intellectual Powers of Man*

Essay I, Preliminary

Chapter V
Of the Proper Means of Knowing the Operations of the Mind.

Since we ought to pay no regard to hypotheses, and to be very suspicious of analogical reasoning, it may be asked, From what source must the knowledge of the mind and its faculties be drawn?

I answer, the chief and proper source of this branch of knowledge is accurate reflection upon the operations of our own minds. Of this source we shall speak more fully, after making some remarks upon two others that may be subservient to it. The first of them is attention to the structure of language.

The language of mankind is expressive of their thoughts, and of the various operations of their minds. The various operations of the understanding, will, and passions, which are common to mankind, have various forms of speech corresponding to them in all languages, which are the signs of them, and by which they are expressed: And a due attention to the signs may, in many cases, give considerable light to the things signified by them.

There are in all languages modes of speech, by which men signify their judgment, or give their testimony; by which they accept or refuse; by which they ask information or advice; by which they command, or threaten, or supplicate; by which they plight their faith in promises or contracts. If such operations were not common to mankind, we should not find in all languages forms of speech, by which they are expressed.

All languages, indeed, have their imperfections—they can never be adequate to all the varieties of human thought; and therefore things may be really distinct in their nature, and capable of being distinguished by the human mind, which are not distinguished in common language. We can only expect, in the structure of languages, those distinctions which all mankind in the common business of life have occasion to make.

There may be peculiarities in a particular language, of the causes of which we are ignorant, and from which, therefore, we can draw no conclusion. But whatever we find common to all languages, must have a common cause; must be owing to some common notion or sentiment of the human mind.

We gave some examples of this before, and shall here add another. All languages have a plural number in many of their nouns; from which we may infer that all men have notions, not of individual things only, but of attributes, or things which are common to many individuals; for no individual can have a plural number.

Another source of information in this subject, is a due attention to the course of human actions and conduct. The actions of men are effects; their sentiments, their passions, and their affections, are the causes of those effects; and we may, in many cases, form a judgment of the cause from the effect.

The behaviour of parents towards their children gives sufficient evidence even to those who never had children, that the parental affection is common to mankind. It is easy to see, from the general conduct of men, what are the natural objects of their esteem, their admiration, their love, their approbation, their resentment, and of all their other original dispositions. It is obvious, from the conduct of men in all ages, that man is by his

From *Essays on the Intellectual Powers of Man,* 8th edition. Edinburgh: James Thin, 1895; selections from Essays I, v and II, xvi, pp. 238–40, 310–11, 312–13.

nature a social animal; that he delights to associate with his species; to converse, and to exchange good offices with them.

Not only the actions, but even the opinions of men may sometimes give light into the frame of the human mind. The opinions of men may be considered as the effects of their intellectual powers, as their actions are the effects of their active principles. Even the prejudices and errors of mankind, when they are general, must have some cause no less general; the discovery of which will throw some light upon the frame of the human understanding.

I conceive this to be the principal use of the history of philosophy. When we trace the history of the various philosophical opinions that have sprung up among thinking men, we are led into a labyrinth of fanciful opinions, contradictions, and absurdities, intermixed with some truths; yet we may sometimes find a clue to lead us through the several windings of this labyrinth. We may find that point of view which presented things to the author of the system, in the light in which they appeared to him. This will often give a consistency to things seemingly contradictory, and some degree of probability to those that appeared most fanciful.

The history of philosophy, considered as a map of the intellectual operations of men of genius, must always be entertaining, and may sometimes give us views of the human understanding, which could not easily be had any other way.

I return to what I mentioned as the main source of information on this subject—attentive reflection upon the operations of our own minds.

All the notions we have of mind and of its operations, are, by Mr Locke, called *ideas of reflection*. A man may have as distinct notions of remembrance, of judgment, of will, of desire, as he has of any object whatever. Such notions, as Mr Locke justly observes, are got by the power of reflection. But what is this power of reflection? "It is," says the same author, "that power by which the mind turns its view inward, and observes its own actions and operations." He observes elsewhere, "That the understanding, like the eye, whilst it makes us see and perceive all other things, takes no notice of itself; and that it requires art and pains to set it at a distance, and make it its own object." Cicero hath expressed this sentiment most beautifully. Tusc. I. 28.

This power of the understanding to make its own operations its object, to attend to them, and examine them on all sides, is the power of reflection, by which alone we can have any distinct notion of the powers of our own or of other minds.

This reflection ought to be distinguished from consciousness, with which it is too often confounded, even by Mr Locke. All men are conscious of the operations of their own minds, at all times, while they are awake; but there are few who reflect upon them, or make them objects of thought.

From infancy, till we come to the years of understanding, we are employed solely about external objects. And, although the mind is conscious of its operations, it does not attend to them; its attention is turned solely to the external objects, about which those operations are employed. Thus, when a man is angry, he is conscious of his passion; but his attention is turned to the person who offended him, and the circumstances of the offence, while the passion of anger is not in the least the object of his attention.

I conceive this is sufficient to shew the difference between consciousness of the operations of our minds, and reflection upon them; and to shew that we may have the former without any degree of the latter. The difference between consciousness and reflection, is like to the difference between a superficial view of an object which presents itself to the eye while we are engaged about something else, and that attentive examination which we give to an object when we are wholly employed in surveying it. Attention is a voluntary act; it requires an active exertion to begin and to continue it, and it may be continued as long as we will; but consciousness is involuntary and of no continuance, changing with every thought.

The power of reflection upon the operations of their own minds, does not appear at all in children. Men must be come to some ripeness of understanding before they are capable of it. Of all the powers of the human mind, it seems to be the last that unfolds itself. Most men seem incapable of acquiring it in any considerable degree. Like all our other powers, it is greatly improved by exercise; and until a man has got the habit of attending to the operations of his own mind, he can never have clear and distinct notions of them, nor form any steady judgment concerning them. His opinions must be borrowed from others, his notions confused and indistinct, and he may easily be led to swallow very gross absurdities. To acquire this habit, is a work of time and labour, even in those who begin it early, and whose natural talents are tolerably fitted for it; but the difficulty will be daily diminishing, and the advantage of it is great. They will, thereby, be enabled to think with precision and accuracy on every subject, especially on those subjects that are more abstract. They will be able to judge for themselves in many important points, wherein others must blindly follow a leader.

Essay II, Of the Powers We Have by Means of Our External Senses

Chapter XVI.
Of Sensation.

Having finished what I intend, with regard to that act of mind which we call the perception of an external object, I proceed to consider another, which, by our constitution, is conjoined with perception, and not with perception only, but with many other acts of our minds; and that is sensation. To prevent repetition, I must refer the reader to the explication of this word given in Essay I., chap. i.

Almost all our perceptions have corresponding sensations which constantly accompany them, and, on that account, are very apt to be confounded with them. Neither ought we to expect that the sensation, and its corresponding perception, should be distinguished in common langauge, because the purposes of common life do not require it. Language is made to serve the purposes of ordinary conversation; and we have no reason to expect that it should make distinctions that are not of common use. Hence it happens, that a quality perceived, and the sensation corresponding to that perception, often go under the same name.

This makes the names of most of our sensations ambiguous, and this ambiguity hath very much perplexed philosophers. It will be necessary to give some instances, to illustrate the distinction between our sensations and the objects of perception.

When I smell a rose, there is in this operation both sensation and perception. The agreeable odour I feel, considered by itself, without relation to any external object, is merely a sensation. It affects the mind in a certain way; and this affection of the mind may be conceived, without a thought of the rose, or any other object. This sensation can be nothing else than it is felt to be. Its very essence consists in being felt: and when it is not felt, it is not. There is no difference beween the sensation and the feeling of it—they are one and the same thing. It is for this reason that we before observed that, in sensation, there is no object distinct from that act of the mind by which it is felt—and this holds true with regard to all sensations.

Let us next attend to the perception which we have in smelling a rose. Perception has always an external object; and the object of my perception, in this case, is that quality in the rose which I discern by the sense of smell. Observing that the agreeable sensation is raised when the rose is near, and ceases when it is removed, I am led, by my nature, to conclude some quality to be in the rose, which is the cause of this sensation. This quality in the rose is the object perceived; and that act of my mind by which I have the conviction and belief of this quality, is what in this case I call perception.

But it is here to be observed, that the sensation I feel, and the quality in the rose which I perceive, are both called by the same name. The smell of a rose is the name given to both: so that this name hath two meanings; and the distinguishing its different meanings removes all perplexity, and enables us to give clear and distinct answers to questions about which philosophers have held much dispute.

Thus, if it is asked, whether the smell be in the rose, or in the mind that feels it, the answer is obvious: That there are two different things signified by the smell of a rose; one of which is in the mind, and can be in nothing but in a sentient being; the other is truly and properly in the rose. The sensation which I feel is in my mind. The mind is the sentient being; and, as the rose is insentient, there can be no sensation, nor anything resembling sensation in it. But this sensation in my mind is occasioned by a certain quality in the rose, which is called by the same name with the sensation, not on account of any similitude, but because of their constant concomitancy.

All the names we have for smells, tastes, sounds, and for the various degrees of heat and cold, have a like ambiguity; and what has been said of the smell of a rose may be applied to them. They signify both a sensation, and a quality perceived by means of that sensation. The first is the sign, the last the thing signified. As both are conjoined by nature, and as the purposes of common life do not require them to be disjoined in our thoughts, they are both expressed by the same name: and this ambiguity is to be found in all languages, because the reason of it extends to all.

The same ambiguity is found in the names of such diseases as are indicated by a particular painful sensation: such as the toothache, the headache. The toothache signifies a painful sensation, which can only be in a sentient being; but it signifies also a disorder in the body, which has no similitude to a sensation, but is naturally connected with it.

Pressing my hand with force against the table, I feel pain, and I feel the table to be hard. The pain is a sensation of the mind, and there is nothing that resembles it in the table. The hardness is in the table, nor is there anything resembling it in the mind. Feeling is applied to both; but in a different sense; being a word common to the act of sensation, and to that of perceiving by the sense of touch.

I touch the table gently with my hand, and I

feel it to be smooth, hard, and cold. These are qualities of the table perceived by touch; but I perceive them by means of a sensation which indicates them. This sensation not being painful, I commonly give no attention to it. It carries my thought immediately to the thing signified by it, and is itself forgot, as if it had never been. But, by repeating it, and turning my attention to it, and abstracting my thought from the thing signified by it, I find it to be merely a sensation, and that it has no similitude to the hardness, smoothness, or coldness of the table, which are signified by it.

It is indeed difficult, at first, to disjoin things in our attention which have always been conjoined, and to make that an object of reflection which never was so before; but some pains and practice will overcome this difficulty in those who have got the habit of reflecting on the operations of their own minds.

Although the present subject leads us only to consider the sensations which we have by means of our external senses, yet it will serve to illustrate what has been said, and, I apprehend, is of importance in itself, to observe, that many operations of mind, to which we give one name, and which we always consider as one thing, are complex in their nature, and made up of several more simple ingredients; and of these ingredients sensation very often makes one. Of this we shall give some instances.

The appetite of hunger includes an uneasy sensation, and a desire of food. Sensation and desire are different acts of mind. The last, from its nature, must have an object; the first has no object. These two ingredients may always be separated in thought—perhaps they sometimes are, in reality; but hunger includes both.

Benevolence towards our fellow-creatures includes an agreeable feeling; but it includes also a desire of the happiness of others. The ancients commonly called it desire. Many moderns chuse rather to call it a feeling. Both are right: and they only err who exclude either of the ingredients. Whether these two ingredients are necessarily connected, is, perhaps, difficult for us to determine, there being many necessary connections which we do not perceive to be necessary; but we can disjoin them in thought. They are different acts of the mind.

An uneasy feeling, and a desire, are, in like manner, the ingredients of malevolent affections; such as malice, envy, revenge. The passion of fear includes an uneasy sensation or feeling, and an opinion of danger; and hope is made up of the contrary ingredients. When we hear of a heroic action, the sentiment which it raises in our mind, is made up of various ingredients. There is in it an agreeable feeling, a benevolent affection to the person, and a judgment or opinion of his merit.

If we thus analyse the various operations of our minds, we shall find that many of them which we consider as perfectly simple, because we have been accustomed to call them by one name, are compounded of more simple ingredients; and that sensation, or feeling, which is only a more refined kind of sensation, makes one ingredient, not only in the perception of external objects, but in most operations of the mind.

A small degree of reflection may satisfy us that the number and variety of our sensations and feelings is prodigious; for, to omit all those which accompany our appetites, passions, and affections, our moral sentiments and sentiments of taste, even our external senses, furnish a great variety of sensations, differing in kind, and almost in every kind an endless variety of degrees. Every variety we discern, with regard to taste, smell, sound, colour, heat, and cold, and in the tangible qualities of bodies, is indicated by a sensation corresponding to it.

The most general and the most important division of our sensations and feelings, is into the agreeable, the disagreeable, and the indifferent. Everything we call pleasure, happiness, or enjoyment, on the one hand; and, on the other, everything we call misery, pain, or uneasiness, is sensation or feeling; for no man can for the present be more happy or more miserable than he feels himself to be. He cannot be deceived with regard to the enjoyment or suffering of the present moment.

But I apprehend that, besides the sensations that are either agreeable or disagreeable, there is still a greater number that are indifferent. To these we give so little attention, that they have no name, and are immediately forgot, as if they had never been; and it requires attention to the operations of our minds to be convinced of their existence.

For this end we may observe, that, to a good ear, every human voice is distinguishable from all others. Some voices are pleasant, some disagreeable; but the far greater part can neither be said to be one nor the other. The same thing may be said of other sounds, and no less of tastes, smells, and colours; and, if we consider that our senses are in continual exercise while we are awake, that some sensation attends every object they present to us, and that familiar objects seldom raise any emotion, pleasant or painful, we shall see reason, besides the agreeable and disagreeable, to admit a third class of sensations that may be called indifferent.

The sensations that are indifferent, are far from being useless. They serve as signs to distinguish things that differ; and the information we have concerning things external, comes by their means. Thus, if a man had no ear to receive pleasure from the harmony or melody of sounds, he would still find the sense of hearing of great utility. Though sounds give him neither pleasure nor pain of themselves, they would give him much useful information; and the like may be said of the sensations we have by all the other senses.

As to the sensations and feelings that are agreeable or disagreeable, they differ much not only in degree, but in kind and in dignity. Some belong to the animal part of our nature, and are common to us with the brutes; others belong to the rational and moral part. The first are more properly called *sensations,* the last, *feelings.* The French word *sentiment* is common to both.

The intention of nature in them is for the most part obvious, and well deserving our notice. It has been beautifully illustrated by a very elegant French writer, in his *"Theorie des Sentiments Agreables."*

The Author of Nature, in the distribution of agreeable and painful feelings, hath wisely and benevolently consulted the good of the human species, and hath even shewn us, by the same means, what tenor of conduct we ought to hold. For, *first,* The painful sensations of the animal kind are admonitions to avoid what would hurt us; and the agreeable sensations of this kind invite us to those actions that are necessary to the preservation of the individual or of the kind. *Secondly,* By the same means, nature invites us to moderate bodily exercise, and admonishes us to avoid idleness and inactivity on the one hand, and excessive labour and fatigue on the other. *Thirdly,* The moderate exercise of all our rational powers gives pleasure. *Fourthly,* Every species of beauty is beheld with pleasure, and every species of deformity with disgust; and we shall find all that we call beautiful, to be something estimable or useful in itself, or a sign of something that is estimable or useful. *Fifthly,* The benevolent affections are all accompanied with an agreeable feeling, the malevolent with the contrary. And, *sixthly,* The highest, the noblest, and most durable pleasure is that of doing well, and acting the part that becomes us; and the most bitter and painful sentiment, the anguish and remorse of a guilty conscience. These observations, with regard to the economy of nature in the distribution of our painful and agreeable sensations and feelings, are illustrated by the author last mentioned, so elegantly and judiciously, that I shall not attempt to say anything upon them after him.

I shall conclude this chapter by observing that, as the confounding our sensations with that perception of external objects which is constantly conjoined with them, has been the occasion of most of the errors and false theories of philosophers with regard to the senses; so the distinguishing these operations seems to me to be the key that leads to a right understanding of both.

Sensation, taken by itself, implies neither the conception nor belief of any external object. It supposes a sentient being, and a certain manner in which that being is affected; but it supposes no more. Perception implies an immediate conviction and belief of something external—something different both from the mind that perceives, and from the act of perception. Things so different in their nature ought to be distinguished; but, by our constitution, they are always united. Every different perception is conjoined with a sensation that is proper to it. The one is the sign, the other the thing signified. They coalesce in our imagination. They are signified by one name, and are considered as one simple operation. The purposes of life do not require them to be distinguished.

It is the philosopher alone who has occasion to distinguish them, when he would analyse the operation compounded of them. But he has no suspicion that there is any composition in it; and to discover this requires a degree of reflection which has been too little practised even by philosophers.

In the old philosophy, sensation and perception were perfectly confounded. The sensible species coming from the object, and impressed upon the mind, was the whole; and you might call it sensation or perception as you pleased.

Des Cartes and Locke, attending more to the operations of their own minds, say, that the sensations by which we have notice of secondary qualities have no resemblance to anything that pertains to body; but they did not see that this might, with equal justice, be applied to the primary qualities. Mr Locke maintains, that the sensations we have from primary qualities are resemblances of those qualities. This shews how grossly the most ingenious men may err with regard to the operations of their minds. It must, indeed, be acknowledged, that it is much easier to have a distinct notion of the sensations that belong to secondary than of those that belong to the primary qualities. The reason of this will appear in the next chapter.

But, had Mr Locke attended with sufficient accuracy to the sensations which he was every day and every hour receiving from primary qualities, he would have seen that they can as little resemble any quality of an inanimated being as pain can resemble a cube or a circle.

What had escaped this ingenious philosopher, was clearly discerned by Bishop Berkeley. He had

a just notion of sensations, and saw that it was impossible that anything in an insentient being could
resemble them; a thing so evident in itself, that it
seems wonderful that it should have been so long
unknown.

But let us attend to the consequence of this discovery. Philosophers, as well as the vulgar, had
been accustomed to comprehend both sensation
and perception under one name, and to consider
them as one uncompounded operation. Philosophers, even more than the vulgar, gave the name
of sensation to the whole operation of the senses;
and all the notions we have of material things were
called ideas of sensation. This led Bishop Berkeley
to take one ingredient of a complex operation for
the whole; and, having clearly discovered the nature of sensation, taking it for granted that all that
the senses present to the mind is sensation, which
can have no resemblance to anything material, he
concluded that there is no material world.

If the senses furnished us with no materials of
thought but sensations, his conclusion must be
just; for no sensation can give us the conception of
material things, far less any argument to prove
their existence. But, if it is true that by our senses
we have not only a variety of sensations, but likewise a conception and an immediate natural conviction of external objects, he reasons from a false
supposition, and his arguments fall to the ground.

B. Mind and Nature

4

Gilbert Ryle

"Descartes' Myth"

I. The Official Doctrine

There is a doctrine about the nature and place of minds which is so prevalent among theorists and even among laymen that it deserves to be described as the official theory. Most philosophers, psychologists and religious teachers subscribe, with minor reservations, to its main articles and, although they admit certain theoretical difficulties in it, they tend to assume that these can be overcome without serious modifications being made to the architecture of the theory. It will be argued here that the central principles of the doctrine are unsound and conflict with the whole body of what we know about minds when we are not speculating about them.

The official doctrine, which hails chiefly from Descartes, is something like this. With the doubtful exceptions of idiots and infants in arms every human being has both a body and a mind. Some would prefer to say that every human being is both a body and a mind. His body and his mind are ordinarily harnessed together, but after the death of the body his mind may continue to exist and function.

Human bodies are in space and are subject to the mechanical laws which govern all other bodies in space. Bodily processes and states can be inspected by external observers. So a man's bodily life is as much a public affair as are the lives of animals and reptiles and even as the careers of trees, crystals and planets.

But minds are not in space, nor are their operations subject to mechanical laws. The workings of one mind are not witnessable by other observers; its career is private. Only I can take direct cognisance of the states and processes of my own mind.

A person therefore lives through two collateral histories, one consisting of what happens in and to his body, the other consisting of what happens in and to his mind. The first is public, the second private. The events in the first history are events in the physical world, those in the second are events in the mental world.

It has been disputed whether a person does or can directly monitor all or only some of the episodes of his own private history; but, according to the official doctrine, of at least some of these episodes he has direct and unchallengeable cognisance. In consciousness, self-consciousness and introspection he is directly and authentically apprised of the present states and operations of his mind. He may have great or small uncertainties about concurrent and adjacent episodes in the physical world, but he can have none about at least part of what is momentarily occupying his mind.

It is customary to express this bifurcation of his two lives and of his two worlds by saying that the things and events which belong to the physical world, including his own body, are external, while the workings of his own mind are internal. This antithesis of outer and inner is of course meant to be construed as a metaphor, since minds, not being in space, could not be described as being spatially inside anything else, or as having things going on spatially inside themselves. But relapses from this good intention are common and theorists are found speculating how stimuli, the physical sources of which are yards or miles outside a person's skin, can generate mental responses inside his skull, or how decisions framed inside his cranium can set going movements of his extremities.

Even when 'inner' and 'outer' are construed as metaphors, the problem how a person's mind and body influence one another is notoriously charged with theoretical difficulties. What the mind wills, the legs, arms and the tongue execute; what affects the ear and the eye has something to do with what the mind perceives; grimaces and smiles betray the mind's moods and bodily castigations lead, it is hoped, to moral improvement. But the actual transactions between the episodes of the private history and those of the public history remain mysterious, since by definition they can belong to neither series. They could not be reported among the happenings described in a person's autobiography of his inner life, but nor could they be reported among those described in some one else's biography of that person's overt career. They can be inspected neither by introspection nor by laboratory experiment. They are theoretical shuttle-cocks which are forever being bandied from the physiologist back to the psychologist and from the psychologist back to the physiologist.

Underlying this partly metaphorical representation of the bifurcation of a person's two lives there is a seemingly more profound and philosophical assumption. It is assumed that there are two different kinds of existence or status. What exists or happens may have the status of physical existence, or it may have the status of mental existence. Somewhat as the faces of coins are either heads or tails, or somewhat as living creatures are either male or female, so, it is supposed, some existing is physical existing, other existing is mental existing. It is a necessary feature of what has physical existence that it is in space and time, it is a necessary feature of what has mental existence that it is in time but not in space. What has physical existence is composed of matter, or else is a function of matter; what has mental existence consists of consciousness, or else is a function of consciousness.

There is thus a polar opposition between mind and matter, an opposition which is often brought out as follows. Material objects are situated in a common field, known as 'space', and what happens to one body in one part of space is mechanically connected with what happens to other bodies in other parts of space. But mental happenings occur in insulated fields, known as 'minds', and there is, apart maybe from telepathy, no direct causal connection between what happens in one mind and what happens in another. Only through the medium of the public physical world can the mind of one person make a difference to the mind of another. The mind is its own place and in his inner life each of us lives the life of a ghostly Robinson Crusoe. People can see, hear and jolt one another's bodies, but they are irremediably blind and deaf to the workings of one another's minds and inoperative upon them.

What sort of knowledge can be secured of the workings of a mind? On the one side, according to the official theory, a person has direct knowledge of the best imaginable kind of the workings of his own mind. Mental states and processes are (or are normally) conscious states and processes, and the consciousness which irradiates them can engender no illusions and leaves the door open for no doubts. A person's present thinkings, feelings and willings, his perceivings, rememberings and imaginings are intrinsically 'phosphorescent'; their existence and their nature are inevitably betrayed to their owner. The inner life is a stream of consciousness of such a sort that it would be absurd to suggest that the mind whose life is that stream might be unaware of what is passing down it.

True, the evidence adduced recently by Freud seems to show that there exist channels tributary to this stream, which run hidden from their owner. People are actuated by impulses the existence of which they vigorously disavow; some of their thoughts differ from the thoughts which they acknowledge; and some of the actions which they think they will to perform they do not really will. They are thoroughly gulled by some of their own hypocrisies and they successfully ignore facts about their mental lives which on the official theory ought to be patent to them. Holders of the official theory tend, however, to maintain that anyhow in normal circumstances a person must be directly and authentically seized of the present state and workings of his own mind.

Besides being currently supplied with these alleged immediate data of consciousness, a person is also generally supposed to be able to exercise from time to time a special kind of perception, namely inner perception, or introspection. He can take a (non-optical) 'look' at what is passing in his mind. Not only can he view and scrutinize a flower through his sense of sight and listen to and discriminate the notes of a bell through his sense of hearing; he can also reflectively or introspectively watch, without any bodily organ of sense, the current episodes of his inner life. This self-observation is also commonly supposed to be immune from illusion, confusion or doubt. A mind's reports of its own affairs have a certainty superior to the best that is possessed by its reports of matters in the physical world. Sense-perceptions can, but consciousness and introspection cannot, be mistaken or confused.

On the other side, one person has no direct access of any sort to the events of the inner life of another. He cannot do better than make problematic inferences from the observed behavior of the other persons's body to the states of mind which, by analogy from his own conduct, he supposes to be signalised by that behaviour. Direct access to the workings of a mind is the privilege of that mind itself; in default of such privileged access, the workings of one mind are inevitably occult to everyone else. For the supposed arguments from bodily movements similar to their own to mental workings similar to their own would lack any possibility of observational corroboration. Not unnaturally, therefore, an adherent of the official theory finds it difficult to resist this consequence of his premisses, that he had no good reason to believe that there do exist minds other than his own. Even if he prefers to believe that to other human bodies there are harnessed minds not unlike his own, he cannot claim to be able to discover their individual characteristics, or the particular things that they undergo and do. Absolute solitude is on this showing the ineluctable destiny of the soul. Only our bodies can meet.

As a necessary corollary of this general scheme there is implicitly prescribed a special way of construing our ordinary concepts of mental powers and operations. The verbs, nouns and adjectives, with which in ordinary life we describe the wits, characters and higher-grade performances of the people with whom we have do, are required to be construed as signifying special episodes in their secret histories, or else as signifying tendencies for such episodes to occur. When someone is described as knowing, believing or guessing something, as hoping, dreading, intending or shirking something, as designing this or being amused at that, these verbs are supposed to denote the occurrence of specific modifications in his (to us) occult stream of consciousness. Only his own privileged access to this stream in direct awareness and introspection could provide authentic testimony that these mental-conduct verbs were correctly or incorrectly applied. The onlooker, be he teacher, critic, biographer or friend, can never assure himself that his comments have any vestige of truth. Yet it was just because we do in fact all know how to make such comments, make them with general correctness and correct them when they turn out to be confused or mistaken, that philosophers found it necessary to construct their theories of the nature and place of minds. Finding mental-conduct concepts being regularly and effectively used, they properly sought to fix their logical geography. But the logical geography officially recommended would entail that there could be no regular or effective use of these mental-conduct concepts in our descriptions of, and prescriptions for, other people's minds.

2. The Absurdity of the Official Doctrine

Such in outline is the official theory. I shall often speak of it, with deliberate abusiveness, as 'the dogma of the Ghost in the Machine'. I hope to prove that it is entirely false, and false not in detail but in principle. It is not merely an assemblage of particular mistakes. It is one big mistake and a mistake of a special kind. It is, namely, a category-mistake. It represents the facts of mental life as if they belonged to one logical type or category (or range of types or categories), when they actually belong to another. The dogma is therefore a philosopher's myth. In attempting to explode the myth I shall probably be taken to be denying well-known facts about the mental life of human beings, and my plea that I aim at doing nothing more than rectify the logic of mental-conduct concepts will probably be disallowed as mere subterfuge.

I must first indicate what is meant by the phrase 'Category mistake'. This I do in a series of illustrations.

A foreigner visiting Oxford or Cambridge for the first time is shown a number of colleges, libraries, playing fields, museums, scientific departments and administrative offices. He then asks 'But where is the University? I have seen where the members of the Colleges live, where the Registrar works, where the scientists experiment and the rest. But I have not yet seen the University in which reside and work the members of your University.' It has then to be explained to him that the University is not another collateral institution, some ulterior counterpart to the colleges, laboratories and offices which he has seen. The University is just the way in which all that he has already seen is organized. When they are seen and when their co-ordination is understood, the University has been seen. His mistake lay in his innocent assumption that it was correct to speak of Christ Church, the Bodleian Library, the Ashmolean Museum *and* the University, to speak, that is, as if 'the University' stood for an extra member of the class of which these other units are members. He was mistakenly allocating the University to the same category as that to which the other institutions belong.

The same mistake would be made by a child witnessing the march-past of a division, who, having had pointed out to him such and such battalions, batteries, squadrons, etc., asked when the division was going to appear. He would be supposing that a division was a counterpart to the units already seen, partly similar to them and partly unlike them. He would be shown his mistake by being told that in watching the battalions, batteries and squadrons marching past he had been watching the division marching past. The march-past was not a parade of battalions, batteries, squadrons *and* a division; it was a parade of the battalions, batteries and squadrons *of* of a division.

One more illustration. A foreigner watching his first game of cricket learns what are the functions of the bowlers, the batsmen, the fielders, the umpires and the scorers. He then says 'But there is no one left on the field to contribute the famous element of team-spirit. I see who does the bowling, the batting and the wicket-keeping; but I do not see whose role it is to exercise *esprit de corps*.' Once more, it would have to be explained that he was looking for the wrong type of thing. Team-spirit is not another cricketing-operation supplementary to all of the other special tasks. It is, roughly, the keenness with which each of the special tasks is performed, and performing a task keenly is not performing two tasks. Certainly exhibiting team-spirit is not the same thing as bowling or catching, but nor is it a third thing such that we can say that the bowler first bowls *and* then exhibits team-spirit or that a fielder is at a given moment *either* catching *or* displaying *esprit de corps.*

These illustrations of category-mistakes have a common feature which must be noticed. The mistakes were made by people who did not know how to wield the concepts *University, division* and *team-spirit.* Their puzzles arose from inability to use certain items in the English vocabulary.

The theoretically interesting category-mistakes are those made by people who are perfectly competent to apply concepts, at least in the situations with which they are familiar, but are still liable in their abstract thinking to allocate those concepts to logical types to which they do not belong. An instance of a mistake of this sort would be the following story. A student of politics has learned the main differences between the British, the French and the American Constitutions, and has learned also the differences and connections between the Cabinet, Parliament, the various Ministries, the Judicature and the Church of England. But he still becomes embarrassed when asked questions about the connections between the Church of England, the Home Office and the British Constitution. For while the Church and the Home Office are institutions, the British Constitution is not another institution in the same sense of that noun. So inter-institutional relations which can be asserted or denied to hold between the Church and the Home Office cannot be asserted or denied to hold

between either of them and the British Constitution. 'The British Constitution' is not a term of the same logical type as 'the Home Office' and 'the Church of England'. In a partially similar way, John Doe may be a relative, a friend, an enemy or a stranger to Richard Roe; but he cannot be any of these things to the Average Taxpayer. He knows how to talk sense in certain sorts of discussions about the Average Taxpayer, but he is baffled to say why he could not come across him in the street as he can come across Richard Roe.

It is pertinent to our main subject to notice that, so long as the student of politics continues to think of the British Constitution as a counterpart to the other institutions, he will tend to describe it as a mysteriously occult institution; and so long as John Doe continues to think of the Average Taxpayer as a fellow-citizen, he will tend to think of him as an elusive insubstantial man, a ghost who is everywhere yet nowhere.

My destructive purpose is to show that a family of radical category-mistakes is the source of the double-life theory. The representation of a person as a ghost mysteriously ensconced in a machine derives from this argument. Because, as is true, a person's thinking, feeling and purposive doing cannot be described solely in the idioms of physics, chemistry and physiology, therefore they must be described in counterpart idioms. As the human body is a complex organised unit, so the human mind must be another complex organised unit, though one made of a different sort of stuff and with a different sort of structure. Or, again, as the human body, like any other parcel of matter, is a field of causes and effects, so the mind must be another field of causes and effects, though not (Heaven be praised) mechanical causes and effects.

3. The Origin of the Category-mistake

One of the chief intellectual origins of what I have yet to prove to be the Cartesian category-mistake seems to be this. When Galileo showed that his methods of scientific discovery were competent to provide a mechanical theory which should cover every occupant of space, Descartes found in himself two conflicting motives. As a man of scientific genius he could not but endorse the claims of mechanics, yet as a religious and moral man he could not accept, as Hobbes accepted, the discouraging rider to those claims, namely that human nature differs only in degree of complexity from clockwork. The mental could not be just a variety of the mechanical.

He and subsequent philosophers naturally but erroneously availed themselves of the following escape-route. Since mental-conduct words are not to be construed as signifying the occurrence of mechanical processes, they must be construed as signifying the occurrence of non-mechanical processes; since mechanical laws explain movements in space as the effects of other movements in space, other laws must explain some of the non-spatial workings of minds as the effects of other non-spatial workings of minds. The difference between the human behaviours which we describe as intelligent and those which we describe as unintelligent must be a difference in their causation; so, while some movements of human tongues and limbs are the effects of mechanical causes, others must be the effects of non-mechanical causes, i.e. some issue from movements of particles of matter, others from workings of the mind.

The differences between the physical and the mental were thus represented as differences inside the common framework of the categories of 'thing', 'stuff', 'attribute', 'state', 'process', 'change', 'cause' and 'effect'. Minds are things, but different sorts of things from bodies; mental processes are causes and effects, but different sorts of causes and effects from bodily movements. And so on. Somewhat as the foreigner expected the University to be an extra edifice, rather like a college but also considerably different, so the repudiators of mechanism represented minds as extra centres of causal processes, rather like machines but also considerably different from them. Their theory was a paramechanical hypothesis.

That this assumption was at the heart of the doctrine is shown by the fact that there was from the beginning felt to be a major theoretical difficulty in explaining how minds can influence and be influenced by bodies. How can a mental process, such as willing, cause spatial movements like the movements of the tongue? How can a physical change in the optic nerve have among its effects a mind's perception of a flash of light? This notorious crux by itself shows the logical mould into which Descartes pressed his theory of the mind. It was the self-same mould into which he and Galileo set their mechanics. Still unwittingly adhering to the grammar of mechanics, he tried to avert disaster by describing minds in what was merely an obverse vocabulary. The workings of minds had to be described by the mere negatives of the specific descriptions given to bodies; they are not in space, they are not motions, they are not modifications of matter, they are not accessible to public observation. Minds are not bits of clockwork, they are just bits of not-clockwork.

As thus represented, minds are not merely ghosts harnessed to machines, they are themselves just spectral machines. Though the human body is an engine, it is not quite an ordinary engine, since some of its workings are governed by another engine inside it—this interior governor-engine being one of a very special sort. It is invisible, inaudible and it has no size or weight. It cannot be taken to bits and the laws it obeys are not those known to ordinary engineers. Nothing is known of how it governs the bodily engine.

A second major crux points the same moral. Since, according to the doctrine, minds belong to the same category as bodies and since bodies are rigidly governed by mechanical laws, it seemed to many theorists to follow that minds must be similarly governed by rigid non-mechanical laws. The physical world is a deterministic system, so the mental world must be a deterministic system. Bodies cannot help the modifications that they undergo, so minds cannot help pursuing the careers fixed for them. *Responsibility, choice, merit* and *demerit* are therefore inapplicable concepts—unless the compromise solution is adopted of saying that the laws governing mental processes, unlike those governing physical processes, have the congenial attribute of being only rather rigid. The problem of the Freedom of the Will was the problem how to reconcile the hypothesis that minds are to be described in terms drawn from the categories of mechanics with the knowledge that higher-grade human conduct is not of a piece with the behaviour of machines.

It is an historical curiosity that it was not noticed that the entire argument was broken-backed. Theorists correctly assumed that any sane man could already recognise the differences between, say, rational and non-rational utterances or between purposive and automatic behaviour. Else there would have been nothing requiring to be salved from mechanism. Yet the explanation given presupposed that one person could in principle never recognise the difference between the rational and the irrational utterances issuing from other human bodies, since he could never get access to the postulated immaterial causes of some of their utterances. Save for the doubtful exception of himself, he could never tell the difference between a man and a Robot. It would have to be conceded, for example, that, for all that we can tell, the inner lives of persons who are classed as idiots or lunatics are as rational as those of anyone else. Perhaps only their overt behaviour is disappointing; that is to say, perhaps 'idiots' are not really idiotic, or 'lunatics' lunatic. Perhaps, too, some of those who are classed as sane are really idiots. According to the theory, external observers could never know how the overt behaviour of others is correlated with their mental powers and processes and so they could never know or even plausibly conjecture whether their applications of mental–conduct concepts to these people were correct or incorrect. It would then be hazardous or impossible for a man to claim sanity or logical consistency even for himself, since he would be debarred from comparing his own performances with those of others. In short, our characterisations of persons and their performances as intelligent, prudent and virtuous or as stupid, hypocritical and cowardly could never have been made, so the problem of providing a special causal hypothesis to serve as the basis of such diagnoses would never have arisen. The question, 'How do persons differ from machines?' arose just because everyone already knew how to apply mental-conduct concepts before the new causal hypothesis was introduced. This causal hypothesis could not therefore be the source of the criteria used in those applications. Nor, of course, has the causal hypothesis in any degree improved our handling of those criteria. We still distinguish good from bad arithmetic, politic from impolitic conduct and fertile from infertile imaginations in the ways in which Descartes himself distinguished them before and after he speculated how the applicability of these criteria was compatible with the principle of mechanical causation.

He had mistaken the logic of his problem. Instead of asking by what criteria intelligent behaviour is actually distinguished from non-intelligent behaviour, he asked 'Given that the principle of mechanical causation does not tell us the difference, what other causal principle will tell it us?' He realised that the problem was not one of mechanics and assumed that it must therefore be one of some counterpart to mechanics. Not unnaturally psychology is often cast for just this role.

When two terms belong to the same category, it is proper to construct conjunctive propositions embodying them. Thus a purchaser may say that he bought a left-hand glove and a right-hand glove, but not that he bought a left-hand glove, a right-hand glove and a pair of gloves. 'She came home in a flood of tears and a sedan-chair' is a well-known joke based on the absurdity of conjoining terms of different types. It would have been equally ridiculous to construct the disjunction 'She came home either in a flood of tears or else in a sedan-chair'. Now the dogma of the Ghost in the Machine does just this. It maintains that there exist both bodies and minds; that there occur physical processes and mental processes; that there are mechanical causes of corporeal movements and mental causes of corporeal movements. I shall argue that these and other analogous conjunctions are absurd; but, it must be noticed, the argument will not show that either of the illegitimately conjoined propositions is absurd in itself. I am not, for ex-

ample, denying that there occur mental processes. Doing long division is a mental process and so is making a joke. But I am saying that the phrase 'there occur mental processes' does not mean the same sort of thing as 'there occur physical processes', and, therefore, that it makes no sense to conjoin or disjoin the two.

If my argument is successful, there will follow some interesting consequences. First, the hallowed contrast between Mind and Matter will be dissipated, but dissipated not by either of the equally hallowed absorptions of Mind by Matter or of Matter by Mind, but in quite a different way. For the seeming contrast of the two will be shown to be as illegitimate as would be the contrast of 'she came home in a flood of tears' and 'she came home in a sedan-chair'. The belief that there is a polar opposition between Mind and Matter is the belief that they are terms of the same logical type.

It will also follow that both Idealism and Materialism are answers to an improper question. The 'reduction' of the material world to mental states and processes, as well as the 'reduction' of mental states and processes to physical states and processes, presuppose the legitimacy of the disjunction 'Either there exist minds or there exist bodies (but not both)'. It would be like saying, 'Either she bought a left-hand and a right-hand glove or she bought a pair of gloves (but not both)'.

It is perfectly proper to say, in one logical tone of voice, that there exist minds and to say, in another logical tone of voice, that there exist bodies. But these expressions do not indicate two different species of existence, for 'existence' is not a generic word like 'coloured' or 'sexed'. They indicate two different senses of 'exist', somewhat as 'rising' has different senses in 'the tide is rising', 'hopes are rising', and 'the average age of death is rising'. A man would be thought to be making a poor joke who said that three things are now rising, namely the tide, hopes and the average age of death. It would be just as good or bad a joke to say that there exist prime numbers and Wednesdays and public opinions and navies; or that there exist both minds and bodies. In the succeeding chapters I try to prove that the official theory does rest on a batch of category-mistakes by showing that logically absurd corollaries follow from it. The exhibition of these absurdities will have the constructive effect of bringing out part of the correct logic of mental-conduct concepts.

4. Historical Note

It would not be true to say that the official theory derives solely from Descartes' theories, or even

from a more widespread anxiety about the implications of seventeenth century mechanics. Scholastic and Reformation theology had schooled the
intellects of the scientists as well as of the laymen,
philosophers and clerics of that age. Stoic-Augus-
tinian theories of the will were embedded in the
Calvinist doctrines of sin and grace; Platonic and
Aristotelian theories of the intellect shaped the orthodox doctrines of the immortality of the soul.
Descartes was reformulating already prevalent
theological doctrines of the soul in the new syntax
of Galileo. The theologian's privacy of conscience
became the philosopher's privacy of consciousness, and what had been the bogy of Predestina-
tion reappeared as the bogy of Determinism.

It would also not be true to say that the two-
worlds myth did no theoretical good. Myths often
do a lot of theoretical good, while they are still
new. One benefit bestowed by the para-mechanical
myth was that it partly superannuated the then
prevalent para-political myth. Minds and their
Faculties had previously been described by analogies with political superiors and political subordi-
nates. The idioms used were those of ruling, obeying, collaborating and rebelling. They survived and
still survive in many ethical and some epistemological discussions. As, in physics, the new myth of
occult Forces was a scientific improvement on the
old myth of Final Causes, so, in anthropological
and psychological theory, the new myth of hidden
operations, impulses and agencies was an improvement on the old myth of dictations, defer-
ences and disobediences.

5

P. F. Strawson

"Self, Mind and Body"

One of the marks, though not a necessary mark, of a really great philosopher is to make a really great mistake: that is to say, to give a persuasive and lastingly influential form to one of those fundamental misconceptions to which the human intellect is prone when it concerns itself with the ultimate categories of thought. So to-day, more than three hundred years after the death of René Descartes, philosophers struggling with one of these fundamental misconceptions think of it under the name of Cartesian dualism. Not that they all think of the doctrine in question as a misconception. The doctrine has its defenders. Indeed if it did not represent a way of thinking about mind and body which has a powerful intellectual appeal, it would not be worth struggling against. There is little point in refuting errors which no one is inclined to make.

In this article I want to try to bring out the force of one way, which has received some attention in recent English philosophy, of demonstrating the, or a, central error in Cartesian dualism. First, we need a reasonably clear statement of the dualist position to work on.

It seems an obvious and uncontentious point that the sorts of things which we can truthfully say about ourselves and other human beings are very various, that they form a very mixed bag indeed. Thus we can and do ascribe to one and the same individual human being things as various as actions, intentions, sensations, thoughts, feelings, perceptions, memories, physical position, corporeal characteristics, skills or abilities, traits of character and so on. A person or human being, as a subject of discourse, typically collects predicates of all these kinds. Now a Cartesian dualist is one who holds that this way of talking about people, though convenient and perhaps essential for practical pur-

poses, tends to disguise rather than display the real nature of a human individual. We should first recognize, he thinks, that of these various predicates some refer directly to the states of consciousness of a person, some refer directly to his bodily condition and some refer in a more or less indirect and complicated way to both at once. But recognizing this is no more than a step in the right direction. It is not enough to acknowledge that a person has two sides to his nature and his history, a mental or conscious side and a material or corporeal side. For really the history of a human being is not the history of one two-sided thing, it is the history of two one-sided things. One of these things is a material object, a body; the other is an immaterial object, a soul or mind or spirit or individual consciousness. These are totally distinct kinds of thing, with totally distinct kinds of properties and states. None of the predicates which properly apply to bodies (like having a certain weight or size or colouring) properly apply to minds; and none of the predicates which properly apply to consciousnesses (like having a certain thought or experiencing a certain sensation) properly apply to bodies. During the lifetime of a human being, two of these things, one of each kind, are peculiarly intimately related; but the intimacy of their union does not count against or diminish the essential independence of their nature.

Now if the Cartesian were right in this, it seems that it should be possible in principle to lay down at least the general outlines of a new and more metaphysically revealing way of talking about people than that which we find practically convenient. This new way of talking would reflect, in a dualism of grammatical or linguistic subjects, the dualism of real or metaphysical subjects which the Carte-

From *Common Factor* 4 (Autumn 1966): 5–13. Copyright © 1966 by P. F. Strawson. Reprinted with permission of P. F. Strawson.

sian finds conjoined in the human individual. If we assembled all the statements which in our ordinary way of talking have the name of one man as their grammatical subject, and reconstructed them in a Cartesian grammar, then for each statement there would be three possibilities of reconstruction: either the grammatical subject of the new statement would be the designation of a body or a part of a body or it would be the designation of a mind or consciousness or the original statement would be analyzed into two separate statements, one of them about a mind and one of them about a body.

It might seem at first that the germs of an 'improved' or Cartesian style of speech about people were already present in our ordinary style of speech about people. For included in our ordinary style of speech is a lot of perfectly intelligible talk in which we explicitly ascribe predicates to people's bodies (or parts of them) and also a lot of perfectly intelligible talk in which we explicitly ascribe predicates to people's minds or even consciousnesses. So it might look as if our ordinary habits of thought and speech already contained an implicit, though incomplete, acknowledgement of the truth of Cartesianism.

However, it is clearly not enough for the Cartesian to point to our habit of talking about people's minds and bodies as well as about people, as if this were conclusive evidence for his thesis. The difference between the Cartesian and his opponent is a difference of view about the *relation* between the concept of a person on the one hand and the concept of a person's mind on the other. The anti-Cartesian holds that the concept of a person's mind has a secondary or dependent status. The fundamental concept, for him, is that of a human being, a man, a type of thing to which predicates of *all* those various classes I distinguished earlier can be ascribed. To talk about the mind of a man is just a way of talking about a man, in respect of certain sorts of things that are true of him. Just so we can talk of the *surfaces* of tables as well as of tables, of the *score* in a football match as well as of a football match. But we recognize that the concept of a surface is dependent on the concept of a material object, that the concept of a score is dependent on the concept of a game. Similarly, the anti-Cartesian holds, the concept of a mind or consciousness is dependent on the concept of a living person.

But the Cartesian cannot admit this dependence. He must hold that the notion of an individual consciousness or mind is perfectly intelligible apart from the notion of a person whose mind or individual consciousness it is. He cannot admit that the idea of a mind presupposes that of a person; he must hold, on the contrary, that a dualistic *reduction* or *analysis* of the idea of a person is in principle possible or intelligible.

Let us consider more carefully what would be necessary in order for a Cartesian reduction to be successfully carried through. We begin with statements of which the subjects are the designations of people and the predicates are of the various kinds already mentioned. The Cartesian thesis requires that these be replaceable in principle with sentences of which the subjects are either the designations of minds (consciousnesses) or the designations of bodies. Hence it seems to require too that the predicates of our original sentences should either be already equivalent to consciousness-predicates or to body-predicates or be capable of being analysed into a body-predicate component and a consciousness-predicate component. Moreover the Cartesian reduction-sentences, it seems, must be genuinely, and not merely apparently, reductive. Consider, for example, the statement that John is writing a letter. 'Writing a letter' seems to be one of those predicates which must be split up into a mental component and a bodily component, but it would seem unsatisfactory to try to isolate the mental component by means of some such a sentence as 'His mind was going through the mental processes involved in writing a letter'. For this leaves it open to the anti-Cartesian to say that the concept of such a mental process is dependent on the concept of writing a letter; and that writing a letter is essentially not something that a mind does or something that a body does, but something that a person does.

It seems, then, that there might be very considerable difficulties in effecting a genuine reduction of person-predicates to a mental component and a bodily component. And many of these difficulties are very clearly indicated in some work in recent British philosophy, notably in Professor Ryle's book, 'The Concept of Mind', and in Wittgenstein's posthumous 'Philosophical Investigations'. Yet I think that a convinced Cartesian might be comparatively unmoved by this kind of difficulty. He might agree that there were good reasons why our language was unequipped with, and perhaps was bound to remain unequipped with, the resources necessary for a genuine reduction of all such predicates as these to a mental component and a bodily component, and yet maintain that it was really quite obvious that all such activities as writing a letter really did involve both mental processes and bodily processes; and it would be hard to deny that on this point he was right in some sense, even if not in quite the sense he supposed.

What would move the Cartesian much more, I think, would be a clear demonstration that there was something wrong, not on the predicate side, but on the subject side, with the idea of a Cartesian reduction. We have already remarked that it is not sufficient for the Cartesian to appeal to the fact that we do intelligibly talk about people's minds and people's bodies. The anti-Cartesian thesis is not the thesis that there are no such things as minds, but that the concept of an individual mind or consciousness is only to be understood as logically derivative from the concept of an individual person. It is up to the Cartesian to show that this is not so, to show that we can make perfectly good sense of the idea of an individual mind without making that very idea dependent upon the idea of an individual person. Hence it is a *prima facie* awkwardness for the Cartesian that when we ordinarily talk about people's minds or consciousnesses, we do so by way of referring to the people whose minds or consciousnesses they are. Thus if we say 'Mary's consciousness was entirely occupied by the thought of how becoming her dress was', the grammatical subject of our statement is certainly the designation of an individual mind or consciousness. But we succeed in designating the consciousness only by way of designating Mary; and Mary, happily, is not simply a consciousness; she is not only *thinking* about the dress, she is *wearing* it.

It is easy enough for the Cartesian to meet this difficulty in a formal way: that is, to give examples of expressions designating consciousnesses which don't formally depend on designating people. One general form of substitute-designation might go something like this: 'The consciousness which stands in a peculiarly intimate relation with the body in such-and-such a place'. Another general form might run something like this: 'The mind which is at such-and-such a time occupied by such-and-such thoughts and feelings'. But we simply don't know whether, by the use of such forms, we achieve a reference to a mind which is genuinely independent of reference to a person, until we know the answer to a further and most important question: viz. what justifies us in using the little word 'the'—implying reference to a single one—before 'mind' or 'consciousness'.

It is here that we come—at last—to the central difficulty in Cartesianism. If we are to talk coherently about individual consciousnesses or minds, or about individual items of any kind whatever, there is one thing at least which we must know. We must know the difference between *one* such item and *two* such items. We must know, that is, on what principle such items are to be counted. And this means further—if they are supposed to be items capable of lasting through a period of time— that we must know how to identify the *same* item at different times. In general we have no idea what

a *so-and-so* is unless we have some idea what *a* so-and-so is. If we have no idea of how the notions of numerical identity and difference apply to individual consciousnesses then we really have no clear concept at all of such items.

Now the anti-Cartesian is able to satisfy this requirement for having a coherent concept of an individual mind or consciousness. Since he regards this concept as secondary to, or derivative from, that of an individual person, he can advance the following simple rule: *one* person, *one* consciousness; *same* person, *same* consciousness. His recipe for counting individual minds is to count people; for him the identification of a mind presents no greater (and no less) a problem than the identification of a person. He does not have to pretend that the question as to what the criteria of personal identity are is an easy or straightforward question. But he can properly point out that we have, and know how to use, adequate criteria for ordinary cases; and that we can perfectly intelligibly discuss how our criteria should be interpreted or adapted for any extraordinary cases which we might encounter or imagine.

But how does the matter stand on the Cartesian philosopher's view? It is essential to his view that the application of the notions of identity and numerability to souls (consciousnesses) should *not* be determined by their application to persons. (The determining must be the other way about.) But then how *is* the application of these notions to souls or consciousnesses to be determined? Suppose I were in debate with a Cartesian philosopher, say Professor X. If I were to suggest that when *the man,* Professor X, speaks, there are a thousand souls simultaneously thinking the thoughts his words express, having qualitatively indistinguishable experiences such as he, the man, would currently claim, how would he persuade me that there was only one such soul? (How would each indignant soul, once the doubt has entered, persuade itself of its uniqueness?) There is another, more familiar difficulty, about the identity of a soul from one time to another. If the concept of the identity of a soul or consciousness over time is not derivative from, dependent upon, the concept of the identity of a person over time, then how is it determined? What do we mean by 'the same consciousness' if not 'the same person's consciousness'? Some philosophers, like the British empiricist, Locke, used to suppose that an adequate account of the identity of a consciousness through time could be given in terms of memory alone; but the failure of such accounts is a commonplace of philosophical criticism which I will not repeat. Other philosophers refer, or used to refer, to a Pure Ego or soul-substance, as if this exempted them from having any idea what it *meant* to speak of *the same one* from one time to another. To them one may reply, in a rough paraphrase of Kant: if you're allowed to invoke that hypothesis whenever you like, without being required to elucidate the principle of its application, what is to prevent me from introducing a rival hypothesis, also unelucidated: wherever you say there's one continuing soul-substance, I say there's a whole series of them, each of which transmits its states and the consciousness of them to its successor, as motion might be transmitted from one to another of a whole series of elastic balls.

The dilemma is roughly, this. Either the concepts of identity and difference of individual human consciousnesses are derivative from the concepts of identity and difference of individual people (human beings, men and women) or they are not. If they are, then our ordinary style of talking about human beings is not even in principle reducible in the way in which the Cartesian must hold that it is. If they are not, if a Cartesian reduction is in principle possible, then it must also be possible to make *independently* intelligible what is meant by identity and difference of human consciousness. But there is not the slightest reason for thinking that this can be done.

What, then, is the source of the Cartesian delusion? Well, no doubt it has several sources. But I think a particularly important one is a certain experience of intense looking within, or introspective concentration, of which most of us are capable and which certainly seems to have been characteristic of Descartes' own meditations. One is tempted to say in such moments that one has direct experience of oneself as a conscious being. And this may be a harmless thing to say. But it may put us on the path of illusion. Let us see how it can do so.

The ordinary personal pronouns and possessives, including 'I' and 'my', are used in ordinary inter-personal communication for the purposes of personal reference. If the speaker says 'I', his or her hearers know what man or woman is meant. But when we reflect philosophically on the type of introspective experience I have just described, we can quite easily get into a kind of daze about the meaning of *'I'* and *'my'*. We can say to ourselves things like '*I* am aware of *myself* now' or 'This is how it is with *me* now' and say such things with the conviction of their expressing absolutely indubitable fact. And then perhaps we may begin to feel that we don't have to *explain* the notions of identity and the difference as applied to the soul, for we have *direct experience* of the individuality and identity of the soul, experience which might be expressed in remarks like these. And no doubt an experience of some kind *is* expressed in such a re-

mark. But, really, if we make this kind of *claim* about it (i.e. that it is direct experience of the individuality and identity of the human soul), then we are trying to have things both ways: we are trying to keep the immediacy and indubitability of the experience and at the same time to keep the ordinary referential force of 'I', the word that the individual *man* uses to refer to himself. We are tricking ourselves by simultaneously withdrawing the pronoun from the ordinary game and yet preserving the illusion that we're still using it to play the ordinary game. And it should be easy to see this, since Kant exposed the illusion; yet, as Kant also remarked, the illusion is powerful. Perhaps a way to get at it is this. All the immediacy and indubitability of experience which seem to go with the use of 'I' and 'me' in such remarks as I've just quoted could be preserved while re-expressing the remarks in some such form as '*This* is a conscious experience' or 'The soul having this experience is conscious of itself as having *this* experience'. Then it would be apparent where the limits of immediacy and indubitability fall; it would be apparent that there is nothing in the experience itself to rule out the suggestion that there might be a thousand exactly similar experiences occurring in association with the same body—hence a thousand souls simultaneously associated with that body—and equally nothing to rule out the suggestion that the, or each, soul having such an experience is just one evanescent member of such a temporal series as Kant spoke of—hence, perhaps, a thousand souls the next moment. If this suggestion is to be ruled out, it must be on grounds extraneous to the experience itself. But the fact that this is so is masked by the use of 'I' and 'me'—expressions which, even while they seem in this context to shake off, yet surreptitiously invoke, the ordinary criteria of distinctness and identity of persons. For when *a man* says 'I', then there speaks *one* identifiable man: he can be *distinguished as one* by ordinary criteria and *identified* by ordinary criteria as, perhaps, Professor X, the Cartesian.

The fact is that a Cartesian and an anti-Cartesian alike, and anyone else who wants to be taken seriously on the subject of the soul, wants his doctrine to have the consequence that a perfectly ordinary man, in the course of a perfectly ordinary life, has just one soul or consciousness which lasts him throughout. There is only one way of guaranteeing this consequence; and that is to allow that the notions of singularity and identity of souls or consciousnesses are conceptually dependent on those of singularity and identity of men or people. But if we allow this, we must reject a Cartesian conception of the soul.

The argument I have used to bring out a central

incoherence in the doctrine of Cartesian dualism are arguments of a partly logical, and partly epistemological, character. They turn essentially on the notions of the identity, and of the identification, of particular things. The importance of these notions, both in the present connexion and in others, has recently received a fair measure of acknowledgement in English philosophy. But, as my references to Kant have shown, these arguments are not essentially novelties, any more than is the recognition of the importance of these notions. The progress of philosophy, at least, is dialectical: we return to old insights in new and, we hope, improved forms.

6

Gareth B. Matthews

"Consciousness and Life"

In L. Frank Baum's story, *Ozma of Oz,* which is a sequel to Baum's much more famous story, *The Wonderful Wizard of Oz,* Dorothy and her companion come upon a wound-down mechanical man bearing a label on which are printed the following words:

Smith and Tinker's

Patent Double-Action, Extra-Responsive, Thought-Creating

Perfect-Talking

MECHANICAL MAN

Fitted with our Special Clock-Work Attachment

Thinks, Speaks, Acts, and Does Everything but Live

(*Ozma of Oz,* Chicago, 1907, p. 43)

As Dorothy and her companion are made to discover when they wind up this man ('Tik-Tok' is his name), he is indeed capable of doing all the things of which his label boasts—acting, speaking and even thinking. But as Tik-Tok himself insists, and no one in the story casts doubt on the matter, he is not alive.

Dorothy and her companion learn from the instructions that to make Tik-Tok think they are to wind under one of his arms, to make him talk they are to wind under the other, and to make him move about they are to wind in the middle of his back.

'Which shall we do first?' asks Dorothy. 'Wind up his think,' advises her companion. So she does. 'I don't see anything different,' says Dorothy after a moment's wait. 'Of course not,' explains her companion, 'He's just thinking; if you want to know *what* he's thinking, wind up his talk.' So Dorothy does. 'T-h-a-n-k y-o-u v-e-r-y m-u-c-h,' says Tik-Tok somewhat rustily.

Dorothy contrasts the case of Tik-Tok, who is incapable of living, with that of Nick Chopper, the much more famous tin man of the *The Wonderful Wizard of Oz.* In *Ozma of Oz* Dorothy puts the contrast this way:

Once . . . I knew a man made out of tin, who was a woodman named Nick Chopper. But he was live as we are, 'cause he was born a real man, and got his tin body a little at a time—first a leg and then a finger and then an ear—for the reason that he had so many accidents with his axe, and cut himself up in a very careless manner (p. 42).

Dorothy's account is slightly inaccurate, as checked against the original story. Nick did not, according to his own account of the matter in *The Wonderful Wizard of Oz,* lose parts of his original body through carelessness, but rather because of a wicked witch who cast a spell on his axe.

But the really important point is that Nick started out as a creature of flesh and bones and ended up as a creature of tin by the gradual, piece-by-piece replacement of each limb and gross segment of his body.

The story of Nick's life is a modern variant of the ancient tale of the ship of Theseus, the boards of which were replaced one plank at a time. The puzzle with Nick, as with the ship, is to say whether the original entity persists through the gradual replacement of each of its parts and, if it does not, to say just at what point in the proceedings it ceases to exist.

Nick's story adds two new and conceptually significant features to the old tale of the ship of Theseus. First, the replacement pieces are, in his case, of a different material from the parts they replace. Each time he gets a tin replacement for a fleshy original. Just how and why the material might be important to the question of persistence

From *Philosophy* LII, 199 (January 1977): 13–26. Copyright © 1977, The Royal Institute of Philosophy. Reprinted with permission of the Cambridge University Press and Gareth B. Matthews.

through time is not easy to say. To gain some appreciation for how 'not easy' it is one need only have a look at Aristotle's tortured efforts in *Metaphysics* Z 10 to say whether, and if so, in what way, matter might belong to the form or essence or definition of a thing. The issues involved in this question become more pressing as we today become more and more clever at replacing parts of human bodies with fabricated substitutes.

The second new feature in Nick's story of gradual transformation is the fact that *he* tells the story as the story of *his* life. He seems able to remember being the creature of flesh and bones on whose axe the wicked witch cast a spell. In the case of persons, memory has long been a favourite candidate for a criterion of identity.

None of these considerations applies to Tik-Tok. He seems to have been fashioned in a tinker's shop. He is not the product of the gradual transformation of a living thing. He seems to be, as his label suggests, quite incapable of living.

One might want to draw a distinction between thinking and consciousness, to allow, for example, that a computer might be capable of thought, but not of consciousness. In the story, however, no such distinction is drawn; Tik-Tok is treated as a conscious being. So, if the story is coherent, neither

(1) Tik-Tok thinks

nor even

(2) Tik-Tok is conscious

entails

(3) Tik-Tok is alive.

That is, if the story is coherent there is nothing incoherent or self-contradictory about the claim that, while (1) and (2) are true, (3) is false.

In a paper called 'Robots: Machines or Artificially Created Life?' Hilary Putnam reports, as follows, an (as he says) 'ingenious argument', which he attributes to Paul Ziff:

> Ziff wishes to show that it is false that [the robot] Oscar is conscious. He begins with the undoubted fact that if Oscar is not alive he cannot be conscious. Thus, given the semantical connection between 'alive' and 'conscious' in English, it is enough to show that Oscar is not *alive*. Now, Ziff argues, when we wish to tell whether or not something is alive, we do *not* go by its *behaviour*. Even if a thing looks like a flower, grows in my garden like a flower, etc., if I find upon taking it apart that it consists of gears and wheels and miniaturized furnaces and vacuum tubes and so on, I say 'What a clever mechanism', not 'What an unusual plant'. It is *structure*, not *behaviour* that determines whether or not something is alive;

and it is a violation of the semantical rules of our language to say of anything that is clearly a mechanism that it is 'alive'.[1]

I shall suppose that the talk of semantical rules at the end of this quotation can be expressed by saying that 'x is a mechanism' entails '~ (x is alive)'. It would then be Ziff's claim (as reported by Putnam) that

(4) Tik-Tok is a mechanism

which, one might say, is proclaimed on Tik-Tok's label, entails

(3') Tik-Tok is not alive

and (3') in turn entails

(2') Tik-Tok is not conscious.

If we assume again that neither Putnam or Ziff intends to make any crucial distinction between being conscious and thinking, we could as well say that (3') entails

(1') Tik-Tok does not think.

The upshot is that, according to Ziff, Tik-Tok's label would be self-contradictory.

For any of this to be at all plausible 'mechanism' must be understood in a rather hard-headed way, so that an expression such as 'the mechanisms of mind' would have to be metaphorical and so that in its literal use 'x is a mechanism' would entail that x operates on mechanical principles.

Ziff's reasoning (or anyway, the reasoning Putnam attributes to Ziff) is very traditional. One feels like saying that it is very Aristotelian. But there are good reasons for being cautious about saying that. For one thing, there seems not be a good equivalent in Aristotle's Greek for the word 'conscious' and its cognates.[2] This apparent lack is not trivial; it has, in part, to do with the very separation of consciousness from life and bodily function that is under discussion.

For another thing, one might be worried about whether Aristotle had a concept of mechanism like ours. Evidence that he did is, perhaps, to be found in his discussion of mechanical toys as models for animal movement in *De Motu Animalium* (701b1) and as models for reproduction in *De Generatione Animalium* (734b10).

Then there are those hesitations about whether thinking, even among mortal things, requires a body (at, e.g., 403a6, 408b18, 413a6, 413b24)—hesitations resolved, perhaps, by Aristotle's doctrine that thinking requires an image, a phantasm (431a16, 431b2, 432a8, 432a13).

Certainly Aristotle is willing to suppose that eternal things think; in *Metaphysics* Λ 7 he tells us that the prime mover does. But then it also lives—not in the way you and I do, but in a way appropriate to itself. So if Aristotle were to conclude that Tik-Tok thinks, there is reason to suppose he would also conclude that Tik-Tok lives.

The discussions of toys I referred to earlier suggest that Aristotle would not be willing to call Tik-Tok, or Ziff's mechanical flower, alive. So perhaps it is fair to connect Aristotle with Ziff's reasoning. With respect to astronomy and theology, Ziff and Aristotle might disagree about what things think and therefore about what things are alive; but perhaps they are quite close on the connection between thinking and living and the separation between being a mechanism and either thinking or living.

By contrast, explicitly drawn contrast, Descartes sought to break the conceptual connection between being conscious and being alive. Here is a revealing comment from Descartes' *Reply to Objections V:*

> . . . because probably men in the earliest times did not distinguish in us that principle in virtue of which we are nourished, grow, and perform all those operations which are common to us with the brutes apart from any thought, from that by which we think, they called both by the single name *soul* . . . But I, perceiving that the principle by which we are nourished is wholly distinct from that by means of which we think, have declared that the name *soul* when used for both is equivocal . . . I consider the mind not as part of the soul, but as the whole of that soul which thinks.[3]

Descartes makes clear elsewhere that he wants to give an account of something's being alive in terms of its having in it warm blood. Here is one such passage:

> . . . I would not wish to say that motion is the soul of brutes . . . I would prefer to say with the Bible (Deuteronomy, xii, 23, 'Only be sure that you eat not the blood; for the blood is the life; and you may not eat the life with the flesh') that blood is their soul; for blood is a fluid in rapid movement, and its more rarefied parts are called spirits. It is these which move the whole machine of the body as they flow from the arteries through the brain into the nerves and muscles.[4]

The mind, of course, has no blood in it (none, at least, in the relevant way, or perhaps in the relevant sense of 'in') and therefore is not alive. Yet the mind thinks, is conscious. Thus it does not follow from the fact that something is conscious that it is alive. Indeed, although the person made up of body and mind can presumably both be said to be alive and to be consious, Descartes understands the person to be alive because the body is alive and conscious because the mind is conscious.

There is another way in which Descartes opposed the Ziffian argument. Descartes understands the corporeal soul to be a purely mechanical principle. He thus refuses to accept the alleged distinction between mechanisms and living organisms. The following quotation from Descartes' *Treatise of Man* expresses clearly Descartes' thesis that the living human body is a machine and operates on mechanical principles no different from those on which clocks operate:

> I desire you to consider, further, that all the functions that I have attributed to this machine, such as [a] the digestion of food; [b] the beating of the heart and arteries; [c] the nourishment and growth of the members; [d] respiration; [e] waking and sleeping; [f] the reception by the external sense organs of light, sounds, smells, tastes, heat, and all other such qualities; [g] the imprinting of the ideas of these qualities in the organ of common sense and imagination; [h] the retention or imprint of these ideas in the memory; [i] the internal movements of the appetites and passions; and finally [j], the external movements of all the members that so properly follow both the actions of objects presented to the senses and the passions and impressions which are entailed in the memory—I desire you to consider, I say, that these functions imitate those of a real man as perfectly as possible and that they follow naturally in this machine entirely from the disposition of the organs—no more nor less than do the movements of a clock or other automaton, from the arrangement of its counterweights and wheels. Wherefore it is not necessary, on their account, to conceive of any vegetative or sensitive soul or any other principle of movement and life than its blood and its spirits, agitated by the heat of the fire which burns continually in its heart and which is of no other nature than all those fires that occur in inanimate bodies.[5]

Thus according to Descartes

(4) Tik-Tok is a mechanism

fails to entail either

(2') Tik-Tok is not conscious

or

(1') Tik-Tok does not think

both because it fails to entail

(3') Tik-Tok is not alive

and because (3') fails to entail (2'). In other words, Descartes rejected both a traditional connection and a traditional separation. The traditional connection he rejected is that between thinking, or being conscious, and living. He said that they do not really go together at all, except by a mysterious, divinely ordered coincidence. The traditional separation he rejected is the separation of living things and mechanisms; he said that living things are machines of a certain sort.[6] The separation, like the connection, is traditional, though it was not universally accepted, even in the ancient world. Thales, according to Aristotle (*De Anima* 405a19), ascribed soul to magnets. We do not know for sure that he also said magnets are alive. But there is every reason to suppose he accepted the ancient commonplace that whatever has soul is alive. If so, and if a magnet counts as a mechanism, then Thales is a precursor of Descartes in denying the separation between living things and mechanisms.

Still, the ancient world did not, in general, follow Thales in this line of thought. And Descartes certainly gives every evidence that he thought himself something of a radical in conceiving the living human body as a machine. In fact he was so nervous about his radicalism and apprehensive of censure from officialdom that he disguised his claim in the *Treatise of Man* by making it explicitly a claim about a *model* of human physiology. (In other contexts he was more forthright.[7])

As against Descartes, and in support of a somewhat Aristotelian position, Ziff claims that our language embodies a conceptual connection between being conscious and living and a conceptual incompatibility between being a mechanism and living. His claim is thus that our language remains resolutely anti-Cartesian on these matters.

Putnam, in his critique of the Ziffian argument, affirms the traditional connection between thinking and being alive. He speaks of 'the undoubted fact that if Oscar [the robot; we could substitute Tik-Tok, the Mechanical Man] is not alive he cannot be conscious' and of the 'semantical connection between "alive" and "conscious"'. But Putnam also shows some sympathy for Descartes' position in that he suspects the distinction between what is alive and what is mechanical is not clearcut. It might be, he reasons, that some thinking thing, though alive, is yet also mechanical. The sympathy is only very limited. Descartes' claim was not really that you could make a mechanical man that would be alive; his claim was that living bodies *are* machines.

To make out the possibility that some robot might be alive Putnam maintains that criteria for life are of two quite different sorts—structural criteria and behavioural criteria. With plants it is, he says, structural criteria that are most important. With animals, or at least with human, or humanlike, beings, behavioural criteria come into their own.

Crudely, Putnam's idea is this. Any robot with a programme that matched some reasonably good psychological theory of how people behave would thereby satisfy the behavioural criteria not only for being conscious but also for being alive. If it satisfied the *behavioural* criteria for life, but not the structural criteria, then so much the worse for the structural criteria in that case. It might, for all that, be alive.

What Ziff and Putnam call 'structural criteria' amount, I suppose, to some sort of biochemical definition of 'life'. By contrast the behavioural criteria would seem to belong to the family of functional criteria—digestion/absorption, growth, reproduction, self-motion, sensation/perception, and so on. It would be one thing to use two such basically different sets of criteria to get at roughly the same class of things. It is quite another thing to use one set of criteria for one group of putatively living things and another set for quite a different group. To do that would be, it seems, tantamount to admitting that 'living' means something quite different when it applies to plants, say, from what it means as applied to human beings or human-being-like mechanisms.

Perhaps Putnam thinks that the expressions 'living' and 'alive' are fundamentally equivocal in just such a way. I myself think that the concept of life is complex and rather unclear in a number of ways. But Putnam's talk of two sets of criteria suggests that there are really two different concepts that can be rather neatly marked off from each other, and that our single English word 'alive' equivocally expresses now the one concept and now the other. I, for one, would have to be convinced that that is so.

What I want to concentrate on, however, is not what Putnam contests, but what he concedes, namely, that as our language now stands 'x is conscious' does indeed entail 'x is alive'. Speaking of the corresponding French and Latin words of his day Descartes in effect agrees with Putnam. But what Descartes says is that we had better alter the language so that this entailment no longer holds. As Descartes wanted to use the Latin and French words we render with 'thinks' and 'is conscious' and their cognates there would be no entailment from 'x is conscious' to 'x is alive'. I want to consider now why Descartes thought we ought to talk in this way.

In *Meditation II* Descartes concludes that he is a thinking thing, 'a thing which doubts, understands, affirms, denies, wills, refuses, which also imagines and feels', and that he is *not* 'a collection of members which we call the human body'. Moreover, he presents this double conclusion as a deliberate rejection of the traditional concept of soul.[8]

In the following passage from *Meditation II* Descartes encapsulates the traditional concept of soul as animator in confessing that he once held a belief he now rejects:

> ... I considered that I was nourished, that I walked, that I felt, and that I thought, and I referred all these actions to the soul ... [9]

In these words one can recognize the traditional concept of soul as that whereby a human being is nourished, moves, perceives and thinks.

'But what am I', Descartes goes on to ask, 'now that I suppose there is a certain genius which is extremely powerful, and, if I may say so, malicious, who employs all his powers in deceiving me?'

This is a very peculiar question. Descartes does not ask, 'What do I *think* I am, now that I suppose such-and-such?' or 'What am I *justified* in thinking I am, now that I realize so-and-so?' He asks, 'What *am* I now that I suppose I might be deceived in all sorts of diabolical ways?' Descartes seems to suppose that what he is, what, as we might put it, actually belongs to him, is going to be something impervious to the most extravagant doubts he can conjure up. The assumption seems to be that what he is, what really and truly belongs to him, is something that he cannot doubt belongs to him. Descartes thus seems to accept this principle:

> (A) If I can doubt that x belongs to me, then x does not belong to me.

(A) looks at once too broad and too narrow to be a fundamental assumption. It looks too narrow in that it is restricted in its application to the person who enunciates it. (Or if we understand it as owned, so to speak, by Descartes, then we may be inclined to think of it as equivalent to

> (A$_d$) If Descartes can doubt that x belongs to him, then x does not belong to him

which is even narrower.) Surely if (A)—or (A$_d$)—is acceptable, it is because it instantiates some more general principle, such as

> (B) If x can doubt that y belongs to z, then y does not belong to z.

Or so one might reason.

(B), however, is unattractive in the extreme. From its universally quantified form one can conclude that everyone is infallible about everything.

Even (A) makes me infallible with respect to myself. Commentators have reached for this instead:

> (C) If I can doubt that x belongs to me, then x does not belong to my essence.

(C) of course follows from (A), and there is anyway independent evidence that Descartes accepted something like it. But in the passage under consideration Descartes simply asks, 'What am I?'—not 'What am I essentially?' or 'What is my essence?' As we shall see, there is a special reason for his wanting to accept (A), as well, perhaps, as something more like (C).

Let us return to the narrative in *Meditation II*. Am I then a soul, as souls are traditionally conceived? That is, am I that being whereby my body is nourished, moves, perceives and thinks? Well, replies Descartes, 'If it is so that I have no body it is also true that I can neither walk nor take nourishment'. So I can doubt whether either being able to walk or to take nourishment belongs to me. Thus by (A) above neither does belong to me.

Descartes moves on to perception, or sensation. 'But one cannot feel without a body', he reminds himself. Descartes then adds this curious remark:

> ... and besides I have thought I perceived many things during sleep that I recognized in my waking moments as not having been experienced at all.

What does Descartes suppose this remark relevant to?

His idea, I think, is this. There goes with the traditional concept of soul the idea that sensation and perception require a body. Consider, for example, this passage from Aristotle's *De Anima*:

> In most cases it seems that none of the affections, whether active or passive, can exist apart from the body. This applies to anger, courage, desire and sensation generally, though possibly thinking is an exception. But if this too is a kind of imagination, or at least is dependent upon imagination [the alternative Aristotle seems to opt for], even this cannot exist apart from the body.[10]

It is not just that anger, courage, desire and sensation generally, *as it happens,* turn out not to be manageable without a body. It is rather that a proper account of what these things are will bring in the physiology of anger, courage, desire and sensation. One could say that, using 'sense' (or 'perceive') in a traditional way,

> (5) X senses (perceives) something

entails

> (6) X has a bodily organ of sensation (perception)

and thus

> (7) X has a body (or is a body).

Descartes reasons that if I am going to use 'senses' and 'perceives' in this traditional way, I must say that sensation and perception do not belong to me, for I can doubt that I have a body at all and so I can doubt that I have bodily organs through which I might perceive or sense something. The remark about sleep is meant to give substance to this doubt.

A bit later on in *Meditation II* Descartes gives us a new meaning for 'sentire' ('sense' or 'perceive'). In that new meaning the objectionable entailment does not hold. Here is what he says:

> ... I am the same who feels, that is to say, who perceives certain things, *as by organs of sense,* since in truth I see light, I hear noise, I feel heat. But it will be said that these phenomena are false and that I am dreaming. Let it be so; still it is at least quite certain that it *seems to me* that I see light, that I hear noise and that I feel heat. This cannot be false, *properly speaking* it is what in me is called feeling ['*sentire*']; and used *in this precise sense* that is no other than thinking [or consciousness] (emphasis added).

This passage makes quite clear that Descartes thought of himself as recommending a way to use the terms for mental acts, or acts of consciousness. He wanted us to use them in such a way that the entailment from (5) to (6) and (7) will not hold—nor will the alleged entailment from (1), or (2), to (3).

In rejecting the traditional concept of soul and denying the traditional connection between consciousness and life Descartes does something much more interesting than simply isolating one function traditionally assigned to soul, namely, thinking, and supposing it to be independent of the rest. Instead he develops a new concept, consciousness, which includes thinking plus the 'inner part' (so to speak) of sensation and perception. Consciousness, conceived in Descartes' way, is the function of a self-transparent agent (the mind)—that is, of an agent whose acts and states are such that it cannot doubt that it has them.

The point is central. Let me have another try at stating it. In giving us the modern concept of mind Descartes does not simply isolate one accepted function of soul and say that a mind is something that does just that. Rather he divides up the functions of the soul in a new way and thinks about them in a new way. He supposed that a mind is a subject that performs a selection of soul-functions such that an entity cannot both perform one of those functions and also doubt that it is performing it. We must (so to speak) 'peel off' from seeing, hearing, tasting, etc., the *seeming* to see, to hear, to taste, etc., which is such that one cannot do that and also doubt that one is doing it. The mind is something that does all and only things of that self-revealing sort.

We can now see why Descartes accepts (A), and not just (C). One might accept (C) as an instantiation of this:

(D) If x can doubt that y belongs to z, then y does not belong to the essence of z.

Support for (D) could come from the idea that even in entertaining doubts about a thing (a case of thinking of the thing) one must know its essence, which knowledge in turn rules out doubting that y belongs to z when y belongs to the very essence of z.

The special reasons Descartes has for accepting (A) are very different. His idea is that there is a kind of entity, mind, which is self-transparent; for any act it performs and any state it is in, it cannot doubt that it performs that act or is in that state. Furthermore, he, Descartes, is (he supposes) an entity of that kind.

I shall not try to say anything about the vexed question of how Descartes knows he is an entity of that kind, if indeed he does know it, or about what his best argument for proving it might be.[11] For my immediate purpose it is enough to say that Descartes is convinced that he is an entity of such a kind and that others have found it easy to think of themselves as entites of that kind.

The idea that there are entities of this peculiarly self-transparent kind has found wide acceptance in modern thought. Its apparent acceptability underlies the plausibility of, to pick one interesting illustration, Richard Rorty's article, 'Incorrigibility as the Mark of the Mental' (*Journal of Philosophy* 67 (1970), pp. 399–424, especially pp. 408–421). In this article Rorty considers in turn each of the following candidates for a criterion to distinguish what is mental from what is physical: intentionality, purposiveness, non-spatiality, introspectability, privacy as incommunicability, privacy as special access, privacy as unsharability, and incorrigibility. Rorty gives persuasive reasons for saying of each of these except the last, namely, incorrigibility, that is unsatisfactory. Of special interest to him, and to us, is the problem of saying what 'intrinsic features . . . sensations and thought have in common' (p. 412) by virtue of which both sensations and thoughts count as something mental. It cannot be merely that they are soul functions, for on that basis, nutrition and locomotion should also count. As I have already suggested, the idea that they have something fundamental in common, something that they do not share with a traditional soul function, such as locomotion, is largely a Cartesian innovation.

In the end Rorty also finds problems with incorrigibility as a mark of the mental (the problems have to do with the fact that avowals of one's present beliefs, desires, moods, emotions, intentions, etc., are not really incorrigible—though they are, he says, '*almost* incorrigible' (pp. 419–420)). Rorty treats these problems as arising from *extending* the notion of the mental from thoughts and sensations to beliefs, desires, etc. It is not, I am afraid, historically true that the notion of the mental was first restricted to sensations and thoughts and then got extended to beliefs, desires, etc. Descartes clearly included beliefs, desires, emotions and intentions within the mental from the very first. Thus in *Meditation II* he says this:

> But what then am I? A thing which thinks. What is a thing which thinks? It is a thing which doubts, understands, affirms, desires, wills, refuses, which also imagines and feels.

The point is rather that Descartes was wrong in supposing that one cannot make mistakes about what one believes, desires, etc. Rorty's worry about whether first-person avowals of those things are truly incorrigible thus brings out a difficulty in the very concept of mind and the mental.

I have shifted rather naturally from talk of indubitability to talk of incorrigibility as a mark of the mental. Rorty gives a reason for preferring to speak of incorrigibility (p 418) but, as he implicitly allows, the difference is small; historically it is clear, I think, that indubitability first played this role.

Subjects of consciousness, according to Descartes, get yoked (albeit temporarily) to living bodies. A human being, as we normally conceive one, is then a mysterious union of mind and body. But each being, so conceived, has both an 'inside' and an 'outside'. The 'inside' is a mind or subject of consciousness, whose acts and states are indubitable to itself. The 'outside' is a body known to the mind or 'inside' only indirectly through quite dubitable inferences from sense impressions.

The picture of human beings as having, in this way, both an 'inside' and an 'outside' is so commonplace, so (as it may seem to us) commonsensical that we find it hard to realize how strikingly modern it is. But to appreciate its modernity one need only cast about for statements of it earlier than Descartes. One does find interesting anticipations of it in Augustine, but not much earlier, and not much between the time of Augustine and that of Descartes. Here is a relevant passage from Augustine's *Contra Academicos:*

> Do not assent to more than that you are convinced that it appears this way to you, and there is no deception; for I do not see how even an Academic can refute a man who says, 'I know that this looks white to me; I know that this sound pleases me; I know that this smells agreeable to me; I know that this tastes

sweet to me; I know that this feels cold to me'. . . . If I am relishing the taste of something, who would be so shameless as to say to me, 'Perhaps you are not tasting, but this is a dream'? Would I stop? Why tasting would give me pleasure even in a dream. Wherefore, no semblance to falsity can confuse what I have said I know (Bk 3, sec. II, chap. 26).

Just a little earlier on in the *Contra Academicos,* in chapter 25, Augustine suggests that one give the name 'world' to whatever impressions one has. Now, he announces triumphantly, this world exists and has whatever character it seems to have. No Academic sceptic can shake my incorrigible knowledge of my own inner world. Augustine's idea in *Contra Academicos* of an 'inner world', impervious to sceptical doubt, is Descartes' idea of the contents of one's mind or consciousness.

Given this Cartesian starting point it becomes a central problem—one familiar to all modern students of philosophy—to justify one's belief that there is also an 'outer world' and that this outer world contains living organisms, including, it may be hoped, a living organism that one can identify as one's own body. Thus on Descartes' way of thinking and speaking there is no essential connection between being conscious and being alive, or even between being conscious and having a living body.

If Tik-Tok can carry on an intelligent conversation, there is no good Cartesian reason why he should not be said to be conscious on a basis analogous to that on which you or I might be said to be conscious. He could be a mind in mysterious union with a machine; his machine differs from your machine and mine only in that its physical principle of action is a heavy spring, rather than warm blood.

Suppose the problems of a Cartesian philosophy of mind are in fact as intractable as many people now suppose them to be. When one realizes that these problems arise from a rather deliberate decision by Descartes and his followers to conceive and talk about perception and thinking in a new way, coupled with a deliberate effort to wipe out all suggestion of conceptual incompatibility between being a machine and being alive, it becomes appropriate to ask whether it is a good idea to acquiesce in Descartes' proposal. A full answer to that question would require that one examine the coherence, and, if it is coherent, the usefulness of the idea of a thing whose acts and states are indubitable to itself. But short of giving that full answer one can at least gain perspective on the question by reminding oneself that there is a way of conceiving and discussing these matters, well established in philosophical tradition, in which Tik-

Tok's label becomes, as no doubt Frank Baum intended that it should be, a conceptual joke.[12]

NOTES

1. 'Robots: Machines or Artificially Created Life?', *Journal of Philosophy* 61 (1964), 685–686; reprinted in Hilary Putnam, *Philosophical Papers* (Cambridge, 1975), Vol. 2, 402.

2. For helpful discussions of this question and the whole issue of how Aristotle's philosophy of mind bears on Cartesian ways of thinking see Charles Kahn, 'Sensation and Consciousness in Aristotle's Psychology', *Archiv für Geschichte der Philosophie* 48 (1966), 43–81, and especially Richard Sorabji, 'Body and Soul in Aristotle', *Philosophy* 49 (1974), 63–89.

3. Descartes, *The Philosophical Works,* Haldane and Ross (trans.), (Cambridge, 1931), Vol. 2, 210.

4. Letter to Buitendijck (1643), *Philosophical Letters,* A. Kenny (trans.), (Oxford, 1970), 146.

5. Descartes, *Treatise of Man,* T. S. Hall (trans.), (Cambridge, Mass., 1972), 112–113.

6. What Descartes actually says in the last passage quoted is that the human body is *exactly like* a machine of a certain sort. Elsewhere (e.g. in the passage from his *Description of the Body* quoted by T. S. Hall on pp. 114–115 of his edition of the *Treatise of Man*) he simply says it is a machine.

7. See previous note.

8. I am indebted to Professor G. E. M. Anscombe for making clear to me how explicit Descartes' concern with the traditional concept of soul is in *Meditation II.*

9. All translations from *Meditation II* are taken from *The Philosophical Works,* Haldane and Ross (trans.), (Cambridge, 1931), Vol. 1.

10. 403a6–10, W. S. Hett translation, Loeb edition.

11. Very helpful on these matters is G. E. M. Anscombe, 'The First Person', in *Mind and Language,* S. Guttenplan (ed.), (Oxford, 1975), 45–65.

12. Except for minor alterations the text of this article constitutes the third in a series of eight lectures given under the title, 'The Concept of Soul', in the Divinity School of Cambridge University in the Lent Term, 1976. I am indebted to Professor D. M. MacKinnon, to the other administrators of the Burney Fund and to the members of my wonderfully interdisciplinary audience for the opportunity to develop my ideas on the relevance of the traditional concept of soul to issues of contemporary concern.

7

G. E. M. Anscombe

"The First Person"

Descartes and St. Augustine share not only the argument *Cogito ergo sum*—in Augustine *Si fallor, sum*[1]—but also the corollary argument claiming to prove that *the mind* (Augustine) or, as Descartes puts it, *this I,* is not any kind of body. "I could suppose I had no body," wrote Descartes, "but not that I was not", and inferred that "this I" is not a body. Augustine says "The mind knows itself to think", and "it knows its own substance": hence "it is certain of being that alone, which alone it is certain of being."[2] Augustine is not here explicitly offering an argument in the first person, as Descartes is. The first-person character of Descartes's argument means that each person must administer it to himself in the first person; and the assent to St Augustine's various propositions will equally be made, if at all, by appropriating them in the first person. In these writers there is the assumption that when one says "I" or "the mind", one is naming something such that the knowledge of its existence, which is a knowledge of itself as thinking in all the various modes, determines what it is that is known to exist.

Saul Kripke has tried to reinstate Descartes's argument for his dualism. But he neglects its essentially first-person character, making it an argument about the non-identity of *Descartes* with his own body. Whatever else is said, it seems clear that the argument in Descartes depends on results of applying the method of doubt.[3] But by that method

1. *De Civitate Dei,* XI. 26.

2. *De Trinitate,* Book X.

3. *Principles of Philosophy,* I. LX contains Descartes's best statement, which is I think immune to the usual accusation of substitutional fallacy: "Each of us conceives of himself as a conscious

Descartes must have doubted the existence of the man Descartes: at any rate of that figure in the world of his time, that Frenchman, born of such-and-such a stock and christened René; but also, even of the man—unless a man isn't a sort of animal. *If,* then, the non-identity of himself with his own body follows from his starting-points, so equally does the non-identity of himself with the man Descartes. "I am not Descartes" was just as sound a conclusion for him to draw as "I am not a body." To cast the argument in the third person, replacing "I" by "Descartes", is to miss this. Descartes would have accepted the conclusion. That mundane, practical, everyday sense in which it would have been correct for him to say "I am Des-

being, and can in thought exclude from himself any other substance, whether conscious or extended; so from this mere fact it is certain that each of us, so regarded, is really distinct from every other conscious substance and from every corporeal substance. And even if we supposed that God had conjoined some corporeal substance to such a conscious substance so closely that they could not be more closely joined, and had thus compounded a unity out of the two, yet even so they remain really distinct" (*Philosophical Writings,* trans. G. E. M. Anscombe and P. T. Geach). Rendering Descartes's premise here as "I can conceive myself not to include or be my body", we come close to Kripke's version (but in the first person) "Possibly I am not *A*", where "*A*" means my body. But why can I so conceive myself if not because I can doubt the existence of my body?

But "doubting" here does not mean merely reflecting that I am ignorant of the existence of my body though not of myself. So understood, the argument would indeed involve the substitutional fallacy. "Doubting" means clearly understanding that the existence of my body is not guaranteed by something which is thoroughly understood, and is all I am sure of: the existence of myself. We see the importance of the premise supplied by St. Augustine "The mind knows its own existence."

From *Mind and Language: Wolfson College Lectures 1974,* edited by Samuel Guttenplan, Oxford: Oxford University Press, 1975, pp. 45–65.

cartes" was of no relevance to him in these arguments. That which is named by "I"—*that*, in *his* book, was not *Descartes.*

It may seem strange to say: "The non-identity of himself with Descartes was as valid a conclusion as the other" and not treat this as already a *reductio ad absurdum.* For is that phrase not equivalent to "the non-identity of *Descartes* with Descartes"?

No. It is not. For what is in question is not the ordinary reflexive pronoun, but a peculiar reflexive, which has to be explained in terms of "I". It is the reflexive called by grammarians the 'indirect reflexive' and there are languages (Greek, for example) in which there is a special form for it.[4]

"When John Smith spoke of James Robinson he was speaking of his brother, but he did not know this." That's a possible situation. So similarly is "When John Smith spoke of John Horatio Auberon Smith (named in a will perhaps) he was speaking of himself, but he did not know this." If so, then 'speaking of' or 'referring to' oneself is compatible with not knowing that the object one speaks of is oneself.

Yet we are inclined to think that "It's the word each one uses in speaking of himself" explains what "I" names, or explains "I" as a 'referring expression'. It cannot do so if "He speaks of himself" is compatible with ignorance and we are using the reflexive pronoun, in both cases, in the ordinary way.

Nor can we explain the matter, as we might suppose, by saying "'I' is the word each one uses when he knowingly and intentionally speaks of himself." For did not Smith knowingly and intentionally speak of Smith? Was not the person he intended to speak of—Smith? and so *was* not the person he intended to speak of—himself?

It may be said: "Not in the relevant sense. We all know you can't substitute every designation of the object he intended to speak of and keep the statement about his intention true." But that is not the answer unless the reflexive pronoun itself is a sufficient indication of the way the object is specified. And that is something the ordinary reflexive pronoun cannot be. Consider: "Smith realizes (fails to realize) the identity of an object he calls 'Smith' with himself." If the reflexive pronoun there is the ordinary one, then it specifies for us who frame or hear the sentence, an object whose

identity with the object he calls "Smith" Smith does or doesn't realize: namely the object designated by our subject word "Smith". But that does not tell us what identity Smith himself realizes (or fails to realize). For, as Frege held, there is no path back from reference to sense; any object has many ways of being specified, and in this case, through the peculiarity of the construction, we have succeeded in specifying an object (by means of the subject of our sentence) without specifying any conception under which *Smith's* mind is supposed to latch onto it. For we don't want to say "Smith does not realize the identity of Smith with Smith."

We only have to admit a failure of specification of the intended identiy, if we persist in treating the reflexive in "He doesn't realize the identity with himself" as the ordinary reflexive. In practice we have no difficulty at all. We know what we mean Smith doesn't realize. It is: "I am Smith." But if that is how we understand that reflexive, it is not the ordinary one. It is a special one which can be explained only in terms of the first person.

If that is right, the explanation of the word "I" as 'the word which each of us uses to speak of himself' is hardly an explanation!—At least, it is no explanation if that reflexive has in turn to be explained in terms of "I"; and if it is the ordinary reflexive, we are back at square one. We seem to need a sense to be specified for this quasiname "I". To repeat the Frege point: we haven't got this sense just by being told which object a man will be speaking of, whether he knows it or not, when he says "I". Of course that phrase "whether he knows it or not" seems highly absurd. His use of "I" surely guarantees that he does know it! But we have a right to ask *what* he knows; if "I" expresses a way its object is reached by him, what Frege called an "Art des Gegebenseins", we want to know what that way is and how it comes about that the only object reached in that way by anyone is identical with himself.

To say all this is to treat "I" as a sort of proper name. That's what gets us into this jam. Certainly "I" functions syntactically like a name. However, it has been observed not to be a proper name. Now this observation may strike us as obvious enough in a trivial sense. After all, we don't call it a proper noun but a personal *pro*noun. It is at any rate not an ordinary proper name. It could not have a lot of the characteristic use of a proper name. For if it is such, it is one that everyone has, and, worse still, one that each person uses only to refer to that person that he himself is. So it's no use for introducing people to one another, or for calling to someone,

4. ἑ, οὑ, οἱ. See Thucydides II. 13. The form is rare. Credit for discerning the indirect reflexive in English, which does not have a distinct form for it, belongs in the present day to H.-N. Castaneda in "The Logic of Self-Knowledge", *Nous,* I (1967), 9–22. But his presentation is excessively complicated and I believe it has not attracted enough attention to the substantive point.

or for summoning him. And while it might be used as a signature (like the signature of an aged and doddering parson that I heard of, on someone's marriage lines: Me, Vicar), one would be quite dependent on the other clues to the identity of the signatory. If this were the only name anyone had, the situation would be worse than it is for a bank in a Welsh village. These inconveniences are avoided, of course, because there are other more various proper names which people have as well. So the observation that "I" is not a proper name seems to reduce to the triviality that we perhaps would not *call* a word a proper name if everyone had it and used it only to speak of himself.—But is even that true? After all, all Sikhs seem to be called "Singh". So the real difference lies in that one point that each one uses the name "I" only to speak of himself. Is that a ground not to call it a proper name? Certainly to the eyes of our logicians it is a proper name. Are their eyes dim? Or is it really logically a proper name?

Let us ask: is it really true that "I" is only not called a proper name because everyone uses it only to refer to himself? Let us construct a clear case of just such a name. Imagine a society in which everyone is labelled with two names. One appears on their backs and at the top of their chests, and these names, which their bearers cannot see, are various: "B" to "Z" let us say. The other, "A", is stamped on the inside of their wrists, and is the same for everyone. In making reports on people's actions everyone uses the names on their chests or backs if he can see these names or is used to seeing them. Everyone also learns to respond to utterance of the name on his own chest and back in the sort of way and circumstances in which we tend to respond to utterance of our names. Reports on one's own actions, which one gives straight off from observation, are made using the name on the wrist. Such reports are made, not on the basis of observation alone, but also on that of inference and testimony or other information. B, for example, derives conclusions expressed by sentences with "A" as subject, from other people's statements using "B" as subject.

It may be asked: what is meant by "reports on one's own actions"? Let us lay it down that this means, for example, reports issuing from the mouth of B on the actions of B. That is to say: reports from the mouth of B saying that A did such-and-such are prima facie verified by ascertaining that B did it and are decisively falsified by finding that he did not.

Thus for each person there is one person of whom he has characteristically limited and also characteristically privileged views: except in mirrors he never sees the whole person, and can only get rather special veiws of what he does see. Some of these are specially good, others specially bad. Of course, a man B may sometimes make a mistake through seeing the name "A" on the wrist of another, and not realizing it is the wrist of a man whose other name is after all not inaccessible to B in the special way in which his own name ("B") is.

(It may help some people's imagination if we change the example: instead of these rather inhuman people, we suppose machines that are equipped with scanning devices, are marked with signs in the same way as the people in my story were marked with their names, and are programmed to translate what appears on the screens of their scanners into reports.)

In my story we have a specification of a sign as a name, the same for everyone, but used by each only to speak of himself. How does it compare with "I"?—The first thing to note is that our description does not include self-consciousness on the part of the people who use the name "A" as I have described it. They perhaps have no self-consciousness, though each one knows a lot about the object that he (in fact) is; and has a name, the same as everyone else has, which he uses in reports about the object that he (in fact) is.

This—that they have not self-consciousness—may, just for that reason, seem not to be true. B is conscious of, that is to say he observes, some of B's activities, that is to say his own. He uses the name "A", as does everyone else, to refer to himself. So he is conscious of himself. So he has self-consciousness.

But when we speak of self-consciousness we don't mean that. We mean something manifested by the use of "I" as opposed to "A".

Hence we must get to understand self-consciousness. Unsurprisingly, the term dates only from the seventeenth century and derives from philosophy. Getting into ordinary language, it alters, and by the nineteenth century acquires a sense which is pretty irrelevant to the philosophical notion: it comes to mean awkwardness from being troubled by the feeling of being an object of observation by other people. Such a change often happens to philosophical terms.—But this one also gets into psychology and psychiatry, and here its sense is not so far removed from the philosophical one.

The first explanation of self-consciousness that may occur to someone, and what the form of the expression suggests, is this: it is consciousness of a self. A self will be something that some things either have or are. If a thing has it it is something connected with the thing, in virtue of which the thing that has it is able to say, and mean, "I". It is what he calls "I". Being able to mean "I" is thus explained as having the right sort of thing to call "I". The fanciful use of the word, if someone should put a placard "I am only a waxwork" on a wax policeman, or in the label on the bottle in *Alice in Wonderland* "Drink me", is a pretence that the objects in question have (or are) selves. *The self* is not a Cartesian idea, but it may be tacked on to Cartesian Ego theory and is a more consequent development of it than Descartes's identification of 'this I' with his soul. If things are, rather than having, selves, then a self is something, for example a human being, in a special aspect, an aspect which he has as soon as he becomes a 'person'. "I" will then be the name used by each one only for himself (this is a direct reflexive) and precisely in that aspect.

On these views one would explain "self" in "self-consciousness" either by explaining what sort of object that accompanying self was, or by explaining what the aspect was. Given such explanation, one might have that special 'way of being given' of an object which is associated with the name one uses in speaking of it.

Now all this is strictly nonsensical. It is blown up out of a misconstrue of the reflexive pronoun. That it is nonsense comes out also in the following fact: it would be a question what guaranteed that one got hold of the right self, that is, that the self a man called "I" was always connected with *him,* or was always the man himself. Alternatively, if one said that "the self connected with a man" meant just the one he meant by "I" at any time, whatever self that was, it would be by a mere favour of fate that it had anything else to do with him.

But "self-consciousness" is not any such nonsense. It is something real, though as yet unexplained, which "I"-users have and which would be lacking to "*A*"-users, if their use of "*A*" was an adequate tool for their consciousness of themselves.

The expression "self-consciousness" can be respectably explained as 'consciousness that such-and-such holds of oneself'. Nor should we allow an argument running: since the occurrence of "oneself" is just like the occurrence of "himself" which left us perfectly well understanding what Smith failed to realize, the word "self" must itself connote the desired 'way of being given' that is associated with "I" as (logically speaking) a proper name. We must reject this argument because "oneself" is here nothing but the indirect reflexive: that is to say, the reflexive of indirect speech. Un-

derstanding indirect speech we know what the related direct speech is. That is all.

These considerations will lack appeal. The question was, what does "I" stand for? If that question is asked, and "I" is supposed to stand for its object as a proper name does, we need an account of a certain kind. The use of a name for an object is connected with a conception of that object. And so we are driven to look for something that, for each "I"-user, will be the conception related to the supposed name "I", as the conception of a city is to the names "London" and "Chicago", that of a river to "Thames" and "Nile", that of a man to "John" and "Pat". Such a conception is requisit if "I" is a name, and there is no conception that can claim to do the job except one suggested by 'self-consciousness'. That is why some philosophers have elaborated the notion of 'selves' (or 'persons' defined in terms of self-consciousness) and conducted investigations to see what such things may be. And just as we must be continuing our reference to the same city if we continue to use "London" with the same reference, so we must each of us be continuing our reference to the same self (or 'person') if we continue to use "I" with the same reference.

This led to an imaginative *tour de force* on the part of Locke: might not the thinking substance which thought the thought "I did it"—the genuine thought of agent-memory—nevertheless be a different thinking substance from the one that could have had the thought: "I am doing it" when the act was done? Thus he detached the identity of the self or 'person' from the identity even of the thinking being which does the actual thinking of the I-thoughts.

Considerations about reflexive pronouns are certainly not going to dam up the flood of inquiries about 'the self' or 'selves', so long as "I" is treated as a name and a correlative term is needed for its type of object. Nevertheless, these are embarrassing credentials for such inquiries. And a self *can* be thought of as what "I" stands for, or indicates, without taking "I" as a proper name. The reasons for considering it as a proper name were two: first, that to the logician's eye it is one, and second, that it seemed to be just like our "*A*" (which was clearly a proper name) except that it expressed 'self-consciousness'. So we tried to explain it as a proper name of a self. Now a lot of people who will have no objection to the talk of 'selves' will yet feel uneasy about calling "I" a proper name of a self or anything else. I assume it was made clear that the different reference in each mouth was not an objection (there is no objection to calling "*A*" a proper name), and so there is some other reason. The reason, I think, is that, so understood, a repeated use of "I" in connection with the same self would have to involve a reidentification of that self. For it is presumably always a use in the presence of its object! There is no objection to the topic of reidentification of selves—it is one of the main interests of the philosophers who write about selves—but this is not any part of the role of "I". The corresponding reidentification *was* involved in the use of "*A*", and that makes an additional difference between them.

So perhaps "I" is not a name but rather another kind of expression indicating 'singular reference'. The logician's conception of the proper name after all only required *this* feature. There are expressions which logically and syntactically function as proper names without being names. Possibly definite descriptions do, and certainly some pronouns. "I" is called a pronoun, so we will consider this first. Unluckily the category 'pronoun' tells us nothing, since a singular pronoun may even be a variable (as in "If anyone says that, *he* is a fool")—and hence not any kind of singular designation of an object. The suggestion of the word "pronoun" itself is not generally borne out by pronouns. Namely, that you get the same sense in a sentence if you replace the pronoun in it by a name, common or proper: what name in particular, it would be difficult to give a general rule for. Perhaps "pronoun" seemed an apt name just for the personal pronouns and especially for "I". But the sense of the lie "I am not E.A." is hardly retained in "E.A. is not E.A." So that suggestion is of little value.

Those singular pronouns called demonstratives ("this" and "that") are a clear example of non-names which function logically as names. For in true propositions containing them they provide reference to a distinctly identifiable subject-term (an object) of which something is predicated. Perhaps then, "I" is a kind of demonstrative.

Assimilation to a demonstrative will not—as would at one time have been thought—do away with the demand for a conception of the object indicated. For, even though someone may say just "this" or "that", we need to know the answer to the question "this *what?*" if we are to understand him; and he needs to know the answer if he is to be meaning anything.[5]

Thus a singular demonstrative, used correctly, does provide us with a proper logical subject so long as it does not lack a 'bearer' or 'referent', and so it conforms to the logician's requirement for a name. And the answer to the question "this what?" might be taken to be "this self", if it can be shewn that there are selves and that they are apparently what is spoken of by all these people saying "I". Thus would these philosophical inquiries about selves have a certain excuse.

It used to be thought that a singular demonstrative, "this" or "that", if used correctly, could not lack a referent. But this is not so, as comes out if we consider the requirement for an answer to "this what?". Someone comes with a box and says "This is all that is left of poor Jones." The answer to "this what?" is "this parcel of ashes"; but unknown to the speaker the box is empty. What "this" has to have, if used correctly, is something that it *latches on to* (as I will put it): in this example it is the box. In another example it might be an optical presentation. Thus I may ask "What's that figure standing in front of the rock, a man or a post?" and there may be no such object at all, but there is an appearance, a stain perhaps, or other marking of the rock face, which my "that" latches on to. The referent and what "this" latches on to may coincide, as when I say "this buzzing in my ears is dreadful", or, after listening to a speech, "That was splendid!" But they do not have to coincide, and the referent is the object of which the predicate is predicated where "this" or "that" is a subject.

There is no other pronoun but a demonstrative to which "I" could plausibly be assimilated as a singular term that provides a reference. Of course someone may say: "Why assimilate it at all? Each thing is what it is and not another thing! So "I" is a pronoun all right, but it is merely the pronoun that it is." But that is no good, because 'pronoun' is just a rag-bag category; one might as well say: "it is the word that it is." The problem is to describe its meaning. And, if its meaning involves the idea of reference, to see what 'reference' is here, and how accomplished. We are now supposing it is not accomplished as it is for a regular proper name; then, if "I" is not an abbreviation of a definite description, it must catch hold of its object in some

---

5. This point was not grasped in the days when people believed in pure ostensive definition without the ground's being prepared for it. Thus also in those days it was possible not to be so much impressed as we ought to be, by the fact that we can find no well-accounted-for term corresponding to "I" as "city" does to "London". It was possible to see that there was no 'sense' (in Frege's sense) for "I" as a proper name, but still to think that for each one of us "I" was the proper name of an 'object of acquaintance', a *this*. What *this* was could then be called "a self", and the word "self" would be felt to need no further justification. Thus, for example, McTaggart. See *The Nature of Existence*, Vol. II, ¶¶ 382, 386–7, 390–1, 394.

other way—and what way is there but the demonstrative?

But there is a contrast between "I" and the ordinary demonstrative. We saw that there may be reference–failure for "this", in that one may mean "this parcel of ashes" when there are no ashes. But "I"—if it makes a reference, if, that is, its mode of meaning is that it is supposed to make a reference—is secure against reference–failure. Just thinking "I . . ." guarantees not only the existence but the presence of its referent. It guarantees the existence *because* it guarantees the presence, which is presence to consciousness. But N.B., here "presence to consciousenss" means physical or real presence, not just that one is thinking of the thing. For if the thinking did not guarantee the presence, the existence of the referent could be doubted. For the same reason, if "I" is a name it cannot be an empty name. I's existence is existence in the thinking of the thought expressed by "I . . ." This of course is the point of the *cogito*—and, I will show, of the corollary argument too.

Whether "I" is a name or a demonstrative, there is the same need of a 'conception' through which it attaches to its object. Now what conception can be suggested, other than that of *thinking*, the thinking of the I-thought, which secures this guarantee against reference-failure? It may be very well to describe what selves are; but if I do not know that I am a self, then I cannot mean a self by "I".

To point this up, let me imagine a logician, for whom the syntactical character of "I" as a proper name is quite sufficient to guarantee it as such, and for whom the truth of propositions with it as subject is therefore enough to guarantee the existence of the object it names. He, of course, grants all that I have pointed out about the indirect reflexive. It cannot perturb him, so long as the 'way of being given' is of no concern to him. To him it is clear that "I", in my mouth, is just another name for E.A. "I" may have some curious characteristics; but they don't interest him. The reason is that "I" is a name governed by the following rule:

> If *X* makes assertions with "I" as subject, then those assertions will be true if and only if the predicates used thus assertively are true of *X*.
>
> This will be why Kripke—and others discussing Descartes—make the transition from Descartes's "I" to "Descartes".

Now first, this offers too swift a refutation of Descartes. In order to infer straight away that Descartes was wrong, we only need the information that Descartes asserted "I am not a body", together with the knowledge that he was a man: that is, an animal of a certain species; that is, a body living with a certain sort of life.

But there would and should come from Descartes's lips or pen a denial that, strictly speaking, *the man Descartes* made the assertion. The rule was sound enough. But the asserting subject must be the thinking subject. If you are a speaker who says "I", you do not find out what is saying "I". You do not for example look to see what apparatus the noise comes out of and assume that that is the sayer; or frame the hypothesis of something connected with it that is the sayer. If that were in question, you could doubt whether anything *was* saying "I". As, indeed, you can doubt whether anything is saying it out loud. (And sometimes *that* doubt is correct.)

Thus we need to press our logician about the 'guaranteed reference' of "I". In granting this, there are three degrees of it that he may assert. (1) He may say that of course the user of "I" must exist, otherwise he would not be using "I". As he *is* the referent, that is what 'guaranteed reference' amounts to. In respect of such guaranteed reference, he may add, there will be no difference between "I" and "*A*". But the question is, why "I" was said to *refer* to the "I"-user? Our logician held that "I" was logically a proper name—a singular term whose role is to make a reference—for two reasons: one, that "I" has the same syntactical place as such expressions, and the other, that it can be replaced *salva veritate* by a (more ordinary) name of *X* when it occurs in subject position in assertions made by *X*. In saying this, he no doubt thought himself committed to no views on the sense of "I" or what the "I"-user means by "I". But his second reason amounts to this: one who hears or reads a statement with "I" as subject needs to know whose statement it is if he wants to know of whom the predicate holds if the statement is true. Now, this requirement could be signalled by flashing a green light, say, in connection with the predicate, or perhaps adding a terminal '-O' to it. (I apologize to anyone who finds this suggestion altogether too fanciful, and beg him to suspend disbelief.) What would make such a signal or suffix ˙into a referring expression? The essential argument cannot be an argument back from syntax to reference, for such an argument would depend only on the form of sentence and would be absurd. (e.g. no one thinks that "it is raining" contains a referring expression, "it".) And so it seems that our logician cannot disclaim concern with the sense of "I", or at any rate with what the "I"-user must mean.

(2) So the "I"-user must intend to refer to

something, if "I" is a referring expression. And now there are two different things for "guaranteed reference" to mean here. It may mean (2a) guaranteed existence of the object meant by the user. That is to say, that object must exist, which he is taking something to be when he uses the expression in connection with it. Thus, if I suppose I know someone called "X" and I call something "X" with the intention of referring to that person, a guarantee of reference in this sense would be a guarantee that there is such a thing as X. The name "A" which I invented would have this sort of guaranteed reference. The "A"-user means to speak of a certain human being, one who falls under his observation in a rather special way. That person is himself, and so, given that he has grasped the use of "A", he cannot but be speaking of a real person.

If our logician takes this as an adequate account of the guaranteed reference of "I", then he will have to grant that there is a further sort of 'guaranteed reference', which "I" does *not* have. Guaranteed reference for that name "X" in this further sense (2b) would entail a guarantee, not just that there is such a thing as X, but also that what I take to be X *is* X. We saw that the "A"-user would not be immune to mistaken identification of someone else as 'A'. Will it also be so with "I"?

The suggestion seems absurd. It seems clear that if "I" is a 'referring expression' at all, it has both kinds of guaranteed reference. The object an "I"-user means by it must exist so long as he is using "I", nor can he take the wrong object to be the object he means by "I". (The bishop may take the lady's knee for his, but could he take the lady herself to be himself?)

Let us waive the question about the sense of "I" and ask *only* how reference to the right object could be guaranteed. (This is appropriate, because people surely have here the idea of a sort of pure direct reference in which one simply first means and then refers to an object before one.) It seems, then, that this reference could only be sure-fire if the referent of "I" were both freshly defined with each use of "I", and also remained in view so long as something was being taken to be *I*. Even so there is an assumption that something else does not surreptitiously take its place. Perhaps we should say: such an assumption is extremely safe for "I", and it would be altogether an excess of scepticism to doubt it! So we accept the assumption, and it seems to follow that what "I" stands for must be a Cartesian Ego.

For, let us suppose that it is some other object. A plausible one would be *this body*. And now imagine that I get into a state of 'sensory deprivation'. Sight is cut off, and I am locally anaesthe-tized everywhere, perhaps floated in a tank of tepid water; I am unable to speak, or to touch any part of my body with any other. Now I tell myself "I won't let this happen again!" If the object meant by "I" is this body, this human being, then in these circumstances it won't be present to my senses; and how else can it be 'present to' me? But have I lost what I mean by "I"? Is that not present to me? Am I reduced to, as it were, 'referring in absence'? I have not lost my 'self-consciousness'; nor can what I mean by "I" be an object no longer present to me. This both seems right in itself, and will be required by the 'guaranteed reference' that we are considering.

Like considerations will operate for other suggestions. Nothing but a Cartesian Ego will serve. Or, rather, a stretch of one. People have sometimes queried how Descartes could conclude to his RES *cogitans*.[6] But this is to forget that Descartes declares its essence to be nothing but thinking. The thinking that thinks this thought—that is what is guaranteed by "cogito".

Thus we discover that *if* "I" is a referring expression, then Descartes was right about what the referent was. His position has however, the intolerable difficulty of requiring an identification of the same referent in different "I"-thoughts. (This led Russell at one point to speak of 'short-term selves'.)

Our questions were a combined *reductio ad absurdum* of the idea of "I" as a word whose role is to 'make a singular reference'. I mean the questions how one is guaranteed to get the object right, whether one may safely assume no unnoticed substitution, whether one could refer to oneself 'in absence', and so on. The suggestion of getting the object right collapses into absurdity when we work it out and try to describe how getting hold of the wrong object may be excluded.

How, even, could one justify the assumption, if it is an assumption, that there is just one thinking which is this thinking of this thought that I am thinking, just one thinker? How do I know that 'I' is not ten thinkers thinking in unison? Or perhaps not quite succeeding. That might account for the confusion of thought which I sometimes feel.— Consider the reply "Legion, for we are many", given by the possessed man in the gospel. Perhaps we should take that solemnly, not as a grammatical joke.[7]—These considerations refute the 'defi-

---

6. A. J. Ayer for example. See *Language, Truth and Logic*, p. 142.

7. Ambrose Bierce has a pleasant entry under "I" in the *Devil's Dictionary:* "I is the first letter of the alphabet, the first word of the language, the first thought of the mind, the first object of the af-

nite description' account of "I". For the only serious candidate for such an account is "The sayer of this", where "sayer" implies "thinker".

Getting hold of the wrong object *is* excluded, and that makes us think that getting hold of the right object is guaranteed. But the reason is that there is no getting hold of an object at all. With names, or denoting expressions (in Russell's sense) there are two things to grasp: the kind of use, and what to apply them to from time to time. With "I" there is only the use.

If this is too hard to believe, if "I" *is* a 'referring expression', then Descartes was right. But now the troubles start. At first, it seems as if what "I" stands for ought to be the clearest and certainest thing— what anyone thinking of his own thinking and his own awareness of anything is most evidently aware of. It is most certain because, as Augustine said, it is involved in the knowledge of all mental acts or states by the one who has them. They could not be doubted. But the *I*, the 'mind', the 'self', was their subject, not their object, and looking for it as an object resulted, some people thought, in total failure. It was not to be found. It was rather as it were an area of darkness out of which light shone on everything else. So some racked their brains over what this invisible subject and the 'thinking of *it*' could be; others thought there was no such thing, there were just all the objects, and hence that "I", rather, was the name of the whole collection of perceptions. But that hardly fitted its grammar, and anyway—a problem which utterly stumped Hume—by what was *I* made into a unity? Others in effect treat selves as postulated objects for "I" to be names of in different people's mouths. Yet others denied that the self was invisible, and claimed that there is a unique feeling of oneself which is indescribable but very, very important, especially in psychology, in clinical psychology, and psychiatry.

With that thought: "The *I* was subject, not object, and hence invisible", we have an example of language itself being as it were possessed of an imagination, forcing its image upon us.

The dispute is self-perpetuating, endless, irresoluble, so long as we adhere to the initial assumption, made so far by all the parties to it: that "I" is a referring expression. So long as that is the as-

sumption you will get the deep division between those whose considerations show that they have not perceived the difficulty—for them "I" is in principle no different from my "*A*"; and those who do—or would—perceive the difference and are led to rave in consequence.

And this is the solution: "I" is neither a name nor another kind of expression whose logical role is to make a reference, *at all.*

Of course we must accept the rule "If *X* asserts something with 'I' as subject, his assertion will be true if and only if what he asserts is true of *X*." But if someone thinks that is a sufficient account of "I", we must say "No, it is not", for it does not make any difference between "I" and "*A*". The truth-condition of the whole sentence does not determine the meaning of the items within the sentence. Thus the rule does not justify the idea that "I", coming out of *X*'s mouth, is another name for *X*. Or for anything else, such as an asserting subject who is speaking through *X*.

But the rule does mean that the question "*Whose* assertion?" is all-important. And, for example, an interpreter might repeat the "I" of his principal in his translations. Herein resides the conceivability of the following: someone stands before me and says, "Try to believe this: when I say "I", that does not mean this human being who is making the noise. I am someone else who has borrowed this human being to speak through him." When I say "conceivability" I don't mean that such a communication might be the truth, but only that our imagination makes something of the idea. (Mediums, possession.)

If I am right in my general thesis, there is an important consequence—namely, that "I am E.A." is after all not an identity proposition. It is connected with an identity proposition, namely, "This thing here is E.A." But there is also the proposition "I am this thing here".

When a man does not know his identity, has, as we say, 'lost his memory', what he doesn't know is usually that *that* person he'd point to in pointing to himself (this is the direct reflexive) is, say, Smith, a man of such-and-such a background. He has neither lost the use of "I", nor is he usually at a loss what to point to as his body, or as the person he is; nor would he point to an unexpected body, to a stone, a horse, or another man, say. The last two of these three points may seem to be part of the first of them; but, as we have seen, it is possible at least for the imagination to make a division. Note that when I use the word "person" here, I use it in the sense in which it occurs in "offences against the person". At this point people will be-

---

fections. In grammar it is a pronoun of the first person and singular number. Its plural is said to be *We,* but how there can be more than one myself is doubtless clearer to the grammarians than it is to the author of this incomparable dictionary. Conception of two myselves is difficult, but fine. The frank yet graceful use of "I" distinguishes a good author from a bad; the latter carries it with the manner of a thief trying to cloak his loot."

tray how deeply they are infected by dualism, they will say: "You are using 'person' in the sense of 'body'"—and what *they* mean by "body" is something that is still there when someone is dead. But that is to misunderstand "offences against the person". None such can be committed against a corpse. 'The person' is a living human body.

There is a real question: with what object is my consciousness of action, posture, and movement, and are my intentions connected in such fashion that *that* object must be standing up if I have the thought that I am standing up and my thought is true? And there is an answer to that: it is this object here.

"I am this thing here" is, then, a real proposition, but not a proposition of identity. It means: this thing here is the thing, the person (in the 'offences against the person' sense) of whose action *this* idea of action is an idea, of whose movements *these* ideas of movement are ideas, of whose posture *this* ideas of posture is the idea. And also, of which *these* intended actions, if carried out, will be the actions.

I have from time to time such thoughts as "I am sitting", "I am writing", "I am going to stay still", "I twitched". There is the question: in happenings, events, etc. concerning what object are these verified or falsified? The answer is ordinarily easy to give because I can observe, and can point to, my body; I can also feel one part of it with another. "This body is my body" then means "My idea that I am standing up is verified by this body, if it is standing up." And so on. But observation does not show me which body is the one. Nothing shows me that.[8]

If I were in that condition of 'sensory deprivation', I could not have the thought "this object", "this body"—there would be nothing for "this" to latch on to. But that is not to say I could not still have the the ideas of actions, motion, etc, For these ideas are not extracts from sensory observation. If I do have them under sensory deprivation, I shall perhaps *believe* that there is such a body. But the possibility will perhaps strike me that there is none. That is, the possibility that there is then nothing that I am.

If "I" were a name, it would have to be a name for something with this sort of connection with this body, not an extra-ordinary name for this body. Not a name for this body because sensory deprivation and even loss of consciousness of pos-

ture, etc., is not loss of *I*. (That, at least, is how one would have to put it, treating "I" as a name.)

But "I" is not a name: these I-thoughts are examples of reflective consciousness of states, actions, motions, etc., not of an object I mean by "I", but of this body. These I-thoughts (allow me to pause and think some!) . . . are unmediated conceptions (knowledge or belief, true or false) of states, motions, etc., of this object here, about which I can find out (if I don't know it) that it is E.A. About which I did learn that it is a human being.

The I thoughts *now* that have *this* connection with E.A. are I–thoughts on the part of the same human being as the I-thoughts that had that connection twenty years ago. No problem of the continuity or reidentification of 'the *I*' can arise. There is no such thing. There is E.A., who, like other humans, has such thoughts as these. And who probably learned to have them through learning to say what she had done, was doing, etc.—an amazing feat of imitation.

Discontinutiy of 'self-feeling', dissociation from the self-feeling or self-image one had before, although one still has memories—such a thing is of course possible. And so perhaps is a loss of self-feeling altogether. What this 'self-feeling' is is no doubt of psychological interest. The more normal state is the absence of such discontinuity, dissociation, and loss. That absence can therefore be called the possession of 'self-feeling': I record my suspicion that this is identifiable rather by consideration of the abnormal than the normal case.

Self-knowledge is knowledge of the object that one is, of the human animal that one is. 'Introspection' is but one contributory method. It is a rather doubtful one, as it may consist rather in the elaboration of a self-image than in noting facts about oneself.

If the principle of human rational life in E.A. is a soul (which perhaps can survive E.A., perhaps again animate E.A.) *that* is not the reference of "I". Nor is it what I am. I am E.A. and shall exist only as long as E.A. exists. But, to repeat, "I am E.A." is not an identity proposition.

It will have been noticeable that the I-thoughts I've been considering have been only those relating to actions, postures, movements and intentions. Not, for example, such thoughts as "I have a headache", "I am thinking about thinking", "I see a variety of colours", "I hope, fear, love, envy, desire", and so on. My way is the opposite of Descartes's. These are the very propositions he would have considered, and the others were a difficulty for

8. Prof. Føllesdal and Mr. Guttenplan tell me that there is some likeness between what I say and what Spinoza says. I am grateful for the observation; but cannot say I understand Spinoza.

him. But what were most difficult for him are most easy for me.

Let me repeat what I said before. I have thoughts like "I am standing", "I jumped." It is, I said, a significant question: "In happenings, events, etc., concerning what object are these verified or falsified?"—and the answer was: "this one". The reason why I take only thoughts of actions, postures, movements, and intended actions is that only those thoughts both are unmediated, non-observational, and also arc descriptions (e.g. "standing") which are directly verifiable or falsifiable about the person of E.A. Anyone, including myself, can look and see whether that person is standing.

That question "In happenings, events, etc., concerning what object are these verified or falsified?" could indeed be raised about the other, the Cartesianly preferred, thoughts. I should contend that the true answer would be "If in any happenings, events, etc., then in ones concerning this object"—namely the person of E.A. But the description of the happenings, etc., would not be just the same as the description of the thought. I mean the thought "I am standing" is verified by the fact that this person here is *standing,* falsified if she is not. This identity of description is entirely missing for, say, the thought "I see a variety of colours." Of course you may say, if you like, that this is verified if this person here sees a variety of colours, but the question is, what is it for it to be so verified? The Cartesianly preferred thoughts all have this same character, of being far removed in their descriptions from the descriptions of the proceedings, etc., of a person in which they might be verified. And also, there might not be any. And also, even when there are any, the thoughts are not thoughts of such proceedings, as the thought of standing is the thought of a posture. I cannot offer an investigation of these questions here. I only want to indicate why I go after the particular "I"-thoughts that I do, in explaining the meaning of "I am E.A." This may suffice to show why I think the Cartesianly preferred thoughts are not the ones to investigate if one wants to understand "I" philosophically.

Suppose—as is possible—that there were no distinct first-person expression, no pronoun "I", not even any first-person inflection of verbs. Everyone uses his own name as we use "I". (Children sometimes do this.) Thus a man's own name takes the place of "I" in this supposed language. What then? Won't his own name still be a name? Surely it will! He will be using what is syntactically *and* semantically a name. That is, it is semantically a name in other people's mouths. But it will not be

so in his mouth, it will not signify like a name in his utterances.

If I used "E.A." like that, and had no first-person inflections of verbs and no such word as "I", I should be in a difficulty to frame the proposition corresponding to my present proposition: "I am E.A." The nearest I could get would be, for example, "E.A. is the object E.A." That is, "E.A. is the object referred to by people who identify something as E.A."

There is a mistake that it is very easy to make here. It is that of supposing that the difference of self-consciousness, the difference I have tried to bring before your minds as that between "I"-users and "A"–users, is a private experience. That there is this asymmetry about "I": for the hearer or reader it is in principle no different from "A"; for the speaker or thinker, the "I"-saying subject, it is different. Now this is not so: the difference between "I"-users and "A"-users would be perceptible to observers. To bring this out, consider the following story from William James. James, who insisted (rightly, if I am right) that consciousness is quite distinct from self-consciousness, reproduces an instructive letter from a friend: "We were driving . . . in a wagonette; the door flew open and X, alias 'Baldy', fell out on the road. We pulled up at once, and then he said 'Did anyone fall out?' or 'Who fell out?'—I don't exactly remember the words. When told that Baldy fell out he said 'Did Baldy fall out? Poor Baldy!'"[9]

If we met people who were A-users and had no other way of speaking of themselves, we would notice it quite quickly, just as his companions noticed what was wrong with Baldy. It was not that he used his own name. That came afterwards. What instigated someone to give information to him in the form "Baldy fell out" was, I suppose, that his behaviour already showed the lapse of self-consciousness, as James called it. He had just fallen out of the carriage, he was conscious, and he had the idea that someone had fallen out of the carriage—or he knew that someone had, but wondered who! That was the indication of how things were with him.

Even if they had spoken a language without the word "I", even if they had had one without any first-person inflexion,[10] but everybody used his own name in his expressions of self-consciousness, even so, Baldy's conduct would have had just the same significance. It wasn't that he used 'Baldy' and not "I" in what he said. It was that his thought

9. *Principles of Psychology,* Vol. II, p. 273n.

10. In Latin we have "ambulo" = "I walk". There is no subject-term. There is no need of one.

of the happening, falling out of the carriage, was one for which he looked for a subject, his grasp of it one which required a subject. And that could be explained even if we didn't have "I" or distinct first-person inflexions. He did not have what I will call 'unmediated agent-or-patient conceptions of actions, happenings, and states'. These conceptions are subjectless. That is, they do not involve the connection of what is understood by a predicate with a distinctly conceived subject. The (deeply rooted) grammatical illusion of a subject is what generates all the errors which we have been considering.

POST SCRIPTUM: My colleague Dr. J. Altham has pointed out to me a difficulty about the rule about "I" on page 55. How is one to extract the *predicate* for purposes of this rule in "I think John loves me"? The rule needs supplementation: where "I" or "me" occurs within an oblique context, the predicate is to be specified by replacing "I" or "me" by the indirect reflexive pronoun.

PART II:
SELF AND OTHER

INTRODUCTION

Having a mind is not a different sort of thing in one's own case from what it is in the case of others. Being conscious and being in various types of mental state are presumably the same things whether the person in question is oneself or somebody else.

But if having a mind is the same sort of thing for oneself and others, knowing about minds is quite different in the two cases. We know about our own mental states in a way plainly different from that by which we know about those of others, and the difference is such that our knowledge about ourselves is generally not only more detailed, but a lot more reliable than our knowledge of others. Knowing about our own mental states is connected with our being conscious creatures, and the asymmetry between knowing our own mental states and knowing other people's is therefore particularly vivid when we focus on what it is like to be a conscious being.

Ordinarily we take our knowledge of our own mental states for granted. This does not mean that such knowledge is in some way privileged, as Descartes and others have held. Our commonsense assumptions about these matters probably imply neither that we are always right about our own mental states, nor that we know everything there is to know about them. It is just that we do, in general, know what mental states we are in, and how we know this seems unproblematic. In this respect, knowing our own mental states is like having perceptual knowledge of our immediate environment. We have such knowledge, and normally no serious question arises about how we have it.

Because knowing the mental states of others is less automatic, questions arise about how we have such knowledge, questions that seem out of place in connection with knowing our own mental states. Though we often know what others think and feel, we also make mistakes about them, and we do so far more often than we do about ourselves. Indeed, our pronouncements concerning what we think and feel are generally taken as decisive, which has suggested to some that mistakes about our own mental states are not even possible.

This difference is reliability between knowledge about our own mental states and knowledge of other people's is related to differences in how we come to know about mental states in the two cases. To know about other people's mental states we must know what they do and how they act. No such mediation is necessary in our own case; so knowing our own mental states seems direct in a way that our knowledge of other people's does not.

A. Knowing Other Minds

Russell adopts the prereflective attitude just described, and assumes that no special difficulty exists about how we know about our own mental states. The only issue is how we know about other people's. His solution is that we know what others think and feel by by way of a tacit, unstated inference based on our own case. We know in our own case that particular kinds of mental states often cause distinctive bodily occurrences. So when we observe such a bodily occurrence in somebody else, it is natural to infer that it was caused by that person's being in the relevant mental state.

It is worth contrasting this reasoning with Descartes's. Descartes had based knowledge of other people's minds on the principle that nothing except thinking could explain other people's speech behavior. Russell, by contrast, reasons from causal connections between mental and bodily events, which we know obtain in our own case, to corresponding connections in the case of others. We know about other minds by analogy with ourselves.

This argument from analogy has considerable appeal. Many people, asked how it is possible to know what others think and feel, would answer along such lines. Nonetheless, this kind of inference faces serious problems.

Understanding a concept, Malcolm argues, involves the ability to apply it. We would not understand mental concepts, such as the concept of pain, unless we had some command over when those concepts correctly apply. So to understand what it means to say that somebody else is in pain requires that we know how to apply our concept of pain to others.

We plainly apply our concepts of mental states to other people on the basis of what they do and how they look and act. Malcolm therefore argues that our criteria for applying these concepts to others involve distinctive patterns of behavior. Our very understanding of what it is for others to be in pain, for example, presupposes knowing what patterns of behavior tell us that they are in pain. Accordingly, the connection between pain and these patterns of behavior is not merely contingent; rather, there is a conceptual connection between the two. These patterns of behavior do, however, figure in our applying these concepts to ourselves. Malcom concludes that we cannot learn what it is for others to be in those states from our own case.

The argument from analogy leads to a conclusion about the mental states of others. But we cannot infer that others are in the same kinds of states as we are unless we independently understand what it is for others to be in those states. According to Malcolm, this means knowing when to ascribe mental states to others. But, since knowing that is sufficient for us to know, in general at least, when others are in those states, the argument from analogy is superfluous. Our knowledge of other minds relies not on any such argument, but on conceptual connections that hold between people being in mental states and distinctive patterns of behavior.

This view makes knowing the mental states of others unproblematic, but it raises new difficulties about how mental concepts can apply in our own case. Behavior plays no role at all in determining whether most mental concepts apply in our own case. So, if we apply mental concepts on the basis of patterns of behavior, how can we apply those concepts to ourselves? The problem about other minds is replaced by a problem about our own.

Malcolm's answer is that, strictly speaking, we do not apply mental concepts to ourselves. When we say things like 'I am in pain', we are not so much applying the concept of pain as adopting an elaborate, socialized way to express a pain we feel. This explains why error about one's own pains seems impossible. Merely expressing a pain involves no cognitive claim; so there is nothing to be wrong about. Malcolm urges, therefore, that our use of terms for mental states in first-person sentences is different from our use of them in talking about others. The asymmetry between these two uses is the cost of the conceptual tie Malcolm posits between mental states and behavior.

Hampshire challenges this asymmetry. Statements about oneself, he notes, are always equivalent to statements about somebody other than the person speaking. If I say I'm in pain, and you say to me, "You're in pain," we both make the same statement, though I make it about myself and you made it about somebody distinct from you. There is no conceptual difference between statements about oneself and statements about others. Hampshire concludes that there can be no special problem about statements about the mental states of others, and hence no special problem about knowing other minds.

This reopens the possibility of arguing that we know about other minds by analogy, though the analogy Hampshire advances is more roundabout than Russell's. Each of us is often in a position to tell whether what others say about our mental states is correct. So we can often tell when others' inferences about our mental states are reliable. This gives us an independent basis on which to reason that when we make similar inferences about others they are often reliable. Hampshire's argument does not, as Malcom contends, beg the question about whether other people have mental states at all. That issue cannot even arise if the distinction between self and other is relative to context.

Like Malcolm, Strawson insists that we ascribe mental states to others on the basis of behavioral criteria. Otherwise we would have no independent way of correlating the mental states of others with the behavior that typically accompanies them. But he also insists that we do ascribe mental states to ourselves, even though behavioral criteria do not figure in those ascriptions. It is the difference between how we apply mental concepts to others and how we apply these concepts to ourselves that makes knowledge of other minds seem problematic.

Applying concepts for mental states presupposes being able to identify the things to which those mental concepts apply. Strawson argues that this requires these concepts must apply both to others on the basis of behavioral criteria, and to oneself, though on some other basis. Conceptual connections thus obtain both between mental states and patterns of behavior and between the application of mental concepts to oneself and to others.

B. Privileged Access

If behavioral criteria figure in how we know about others' mental states, but not our own, how can we know what mental states we are in? And does the way we know our own mental states support the idea that knowledge is somehow privileged?

Like Malcolm and Strawson, Shoemaker believes that we apply mental concepts to others on the basis of behavioral criteria. But that does not mean, he insists, that we use some other kind of criterion to apply those concepts to ourselves. Rather, he argues, there is no difference between believing that one is in a particular mental state and one's being in that state. So one cannot be mistaken about what mental states one is in, and sincere statements about those states are invariably true.

When we learn something by observation, we could always instead have learned it in some other way—say, by being told. But according to Shoemaker, being aware of our own mental states is in this respect unlike observing things. The only way we learn about our mental states is by being aware of them. It makes no sense, for example, to think of learning that one is in pain by somebody else's telling one, or by any other indirect means. Since one can learn that one is in pain only be being aware of the pain, evidence about whether one is in pain is idle. By the same token, when I say I am in some mental state, it is pointless to ask how I know. It is a conceptual truth that if I believe I am in pain, I am, and that if I am in pain, I am aware of the pain.

If we apply mental concepts to others on the basis of behavioral criteria, but not when we apply such concepts to ourselves, how is the application of these concepts to ourselves possible? Shoemaker claims it is just a fact about human beings that, without relying on criteria, we can learn to say what mental states we are in when the correct behavioral criteria are met.

Armstrong rejects the idea that being in a mental state and believing that one is are conceptually equivalent. If being in a mental state were conceptually the same as believing that one is, we could define one in terms of the other. And we cannot do so. For example, to define being in pain as believing one is in pain would be to define it in terms of itself. And if being in a mental state is distinct from its seeming that one is, we cannot preclude the possibility of being wrong about whether one is in the state. Our beliefs about our own mental states are accordingly not immune from error.

Is it possible to describe circumstances in which one would be wrong about one's own mental states? If not, perhaps no such error is possible after all. Armstrong envisages future brain science coming up with such powerful mind–brain correlations that we can tell what mental state somebody is in by direct inspection of the brain. If I then disagreed with the brain technician about my own mental state, we might reasonably conclude I was mistaken.

According to Rorty, it is not clear just what to make of such a case. Normally there are two ways we can be wrong about something. We may be factually wrong about what something is. But we may be right about what the thing is, but wrong about what to call it. When people report their mental states, we take it for granted that they are using the right words for those states. But there is no way to rule out the possibility that they are not. Because of this, the idea that such reports cannot be factually erroneous has no real force. Even if we assumed that people cannot make substantive factual errors about their own mental states, their reports would not be inviolate, since verbal error would still be possible.

Rorty also argues that, in reports about our own mental states, we have no way even to distinguish a mistaken use of words from a factual error. There is no difficulty in our rejecting a person's claim to be in some mental state if that claim does not conform to our criteria for when and how to apply the concept of the mental state in question. But there is no way to go further, and distinguish cases in which the person has misdescribed the state from cases in which the person is factually mistaken about what state it is. The difficulty of distinguishing factual error from misdescription in reports about mental states further undermines the idea that reports about our own mental states are factually infallible. It also helps explain why claims of infallibility are so appealing. If linguistic and factual errors are indistinguishable in these cases, we can always save factual infallibility by explaining any report that seems mistaken as due instead to linguistic error.

C. The Theory Approach

Various conceptual connections figure prominently in a number of the foregoing arguments. For example, it is crucial to Malcolm that patterns of behavior are tied conceptually to particular kinds of mental state. It is tempting to hold that some such conceptual connections must obtain. There are, of course, many nonconceptual, empirical correlations that mental states have to various things. But it is tempting to argue that we can never establish such empirical correlations unless we can identify what is correlated, in this case mental states, independently of the correlations to be established. And how can we identify mental states independently of empirical correlations except by relying on conceptual criteria for the occurrence of those states?

Chihara and Fodor contest this line of reasoning. There are, as they argue, correlations that neither are, nor rely on, conceptual connections. Cloud-chamber tracks indicate the presence of electrons. That cloud-chamber tracks do so is an empirical discovery, not a conceptual truth; so they cannot be conceptually tied to electrons. Nor do we depend on some other conceptual criteria to ensure that electrons are present. We rely instead on a theory that enables us to infer to the presence of electrons as the best explanation of those tracks.

Chihara and Fodor argue that the situation is similar with mental states. We do not rely on behavioral criteria that are conceptually tied to mental states to tell when those states occur. Rather, we explain people's behavior by appeal to mental states, tacitly invoking the complex causal interrelations that obtain among those states. We rely on patterns of behavior to tell when somebody else is in a mental state, but there is no conceptual tie between behavior and mental state. Learning about our own mental states, moreover, depends on learning about these interrelations. So there is no special difficulty about knowing the mental states of others, and no special privilege that attaches to knowing our own.

Putnam also invokes an analogy with scientific practice to argue that we need not rely on conceptual connections to tell when mental states occur. Before the discovery of the viral cause of diseases such as multiple sclerosis, we relied on symptoms to identify the disease. We could do so not because multiple sclerosis is conceptually tied to those symptoms, but because it causes them. It is plain that the disease is not conceptually tied to its normal symptoms, since we could imagine its occuring without them. The tie both to symptoms and to viral cause is empirical. We pick out multiple sclerosis without benefit of conceptual criteria as whatever normally causes typical symptoms.

Similarly, we pick out mental states such as pain as what causes particular patterns of behavior, even though no conceptual tie obtains between mental state and behavior. Just as with a disease, one can be in mental states without any standard behavior occurring, as with the people Putnam imagines who wholly conceal their pains. We know about mental states by knowing the network of connections they have with behavior and internal bodily processes, not by knowing conceptual connections. Reports about our own mental states seem authoritative only because we count as a pain, for example, anything we cannot distinguish from a pain.

A.   Knowing Other Minds

8

Bertrand Russell

"Analogy"

The postulates hitherto considered have been such as are required for knowledge of the physical world. Broadly speaking, they have led us to admit a certain degree of knowledge as to the space–time structure of the physical world, while leaving us completely agnostic as regards its qualitative character. But where other human beings are concerned, we feel that we know more than this; we are convinced that other people have thoughts and feelings that are qualitatively fairly similar to our own. We are not content to think that we know only the space–time structure of our friends' minds, or their capacity for initiating causal chains that end in sensations of our own. A philosopher might pretend to think that he knew only this, but let him get cross with his wife and you will see that he does not regard her as a mere spatio-temporal edifice of which he knows the logical properties but not a glimmer of the intrinsic character. We are therefore justified in inferring that his skepticism is professional rather than sincere.

The problem with which we are concerned is the following. We observe in ourselves such occurrences as remembering, reasoning, feeling pleasure, and feeling pain. We think that sticks and stones do not have these experiences, but that other people do. Most of us have no doubt that the higher animals feel pleasure and pain, though I was once assured by a fisherman that "Fish have no sense nor feeling." I failed to find out how he had acquired this knowledge. Most people would disagree with him, but would be doubtful about oysters and starfish. However this may be, common sense admits an increasing doubtfulness as we descend in the animal kingdom, but as regards human beings it admits no doubt.

It is clear that belief in the minds of others requires some postulate that is not required in physics, since physics can be content with a knowledge of structure. My present purpose is to suggest what this further postulate may be.

It is clear that we must appeal to something that may be vaguely called "analogy." The behavior of other people is in many ways analogous to our own, and we suppose that it must have analogous causes. What people say is what we should say if we had certain thoughts, and so we infer that they probably have these thoughts. They give us information which we can sometimes subsequently verify. They behave in ways in which we behave when we are pleased (or displeased) in circumstances in which we should be pleased (or displeased). We may talk over with a friend some incident which we have both experienced, and find that his reminiscences dovetail with our own; this is particularly convincing when he remembers something that we have forgotten but that he recalls to our thoughts. Or again: you set your boy a problem in arithmetic, and with luck he gets the right answer; this persuades you that he is capable of arithmetical reasoning. There are, in short, very many ways in which my responses to stimuli differ from those of "dead" matter, and in all these ways other people resemble me. As it is clear to me that the causal laws governing my behavior have to do with "thoughts," it is natural to infer that the same is true of the analogous behavior of my friends.

The inference with which we are at present concerned is not merely that which takes us beyond solipsism, by maintaining that sensations have causes about which *something* can be known. This kind of inference, which suffices for physics, has

From *Human Knowledge: Its Scope and Limits*, Part VI, chapter 8, "Analogy," London: George Allen & Unwin, 1948, pp. 482–86. Copyright © 1948 by Bertrand Russell. Renewed © 1975 by the Estate of Bertrand Russell. Reprinted with permission of Unwin Hyman, Ltd. and Simon & Schuster, Inc.

already been considered. We are concerned now with a much more specific kind of inference, the kind that is involved in our knowledge of the thoughts and feelings of others—assuming that we have such knowledge. It is of course obvious that such knowledge is more or less doubtful. There is not only the general argument that we may be dreaming; there is also the possibility of ingenious automata. There are calculating machines that do sums much better than our schoolboy sons; there are gramophone records that remember impeccably what So-and-so said on such-and-such an occasion; there are people in the cinema who, though copies of real people, are not themselves alive. There is no theoretical limit to what ingenuity could achieve in the way of producing the illusion of life where in fact life is absent.

But, you will say, in all such cases it was the thoughts of human beings that produced the ingenious mechanism. Yes, but how do you know this? And how do you know that the gramophone does *not* "think"?

There is, in the first place, a difference in the causal laws of observable behavior. If I say to a student, "Write me a paper on Descartes' reasons for believing in the existence of matter," I shall, if he is industrious, cause a certain response. A gramophone record might be so constructed as to respond to this stimulus, perhaps better then the student, but if so it would be incapable of telling me anything about any other philosopher, even if I threatened to refuse to give it a degree. One of the most notable peculiarities of human behavior is change of response to a given stimulus. An ingenious person could construct an automation which would always laugh at his jokes, however often it heard them; but a human being, after laughing a few times, will yawn, and end by saying, "How I laughed the first time I heard that joke."

But the difference in observable behavior between living and dead matter do not suffice to prove that there are "thoughts" connected with living bodies other than my own. It is probably possible theoretically to account for the behavior of living bodies by purely physical causal laws, and it is probably impossible to refute materialism by external observation alone. If we are to believe that there are thoughts and feelings other than our own, that must be in virtue of some inference in which our own thoughts and feelings are relevant, and such an inference must go beyond what is needed in physics.

I am, of course, not discussing the history of how we come to believe in other minds. We find ourselves believing in them when we first begin to reflect; the thought that Mother may be angry or pleased is one which rises in early infancy. What I

am discussing is the possibility of a postulate which shall establish a rational connection between this belief and data, e.g., between the belief "Mother is angry" and the hearing of a loud voice.

The abstract schema seems to be as follows. We know, from observation of ourselves, a causal law of the form "A causes B," where A is a "thought" and B a physical occurrence. We sometimes observe a B when we cannot observe any A; we then infer an unobserved A. For example: I know that when I say, "I'm thirsty," I say so, usually, because I am thirsty, and therefore, when I hear the sentence "I'm thirsty" at a time when I am not thirsty, I assume that someone else is thirsty. I assume this the more readily if I see before me a hot, drooping body which goes on to say, "I have walked twenty desert miles in this heat with never a drop to drink." It is evident that my confidence in the "inference" is increased by increased complexity in the datum and also by increased certainty of the causal law derived from subjective observation, provided the causal law is such as to account for the complexities of the datum.

It is clear that in so far as plurality of causes is to be suspected, the kind of inference we have been considering is not valid. We are supposed to know "A causes B," and also to know that B has occurred; if this is to justify us in inferring A, we must know that *only* A causes B. Or, if we are content to infer that A is probable, it will suffice if we can know that in most cases it is A that causes B. If you hear thunder without having seen lightning, you confidently infer that there was lightning, because you are convinced that the sort of noise you heard is seldom caused by anything except lightning. As this example shows, our principle is not only employed to establish the existence of other minds but is habitually assumed, though in a less concrete form, in physics. I say "a less concrete form" because unseen lightning is only abstractly similar to seen lightning, whereas we suppose the similarity of other minds to our own to be by no means purely abstract.

Complexity in the observed behavior of another person, when this can all be accounted for by a simple cause such as thirst, increases the probability of the inference by diminishing the probability of some other cause. I think that in ideally favorable circumstances the argument would be formally as follows:

From subjective observation I know that A, which is a thought or feeling, causes B, which is a bodily act, e.g., a statement. I know also that, whenever B is an act of my own body, A is its cause. I now observe an act of the kind B in a body not my own, and I am having no thought or feeling of the kind A. But I still believe, on the basis of self-observation, that only A can cause B; I there-fore infer that there was an A which caused B, though it was not an A that I could observe. On this ground I infer that other people's bodies are associated with minds, which resemble mine in proportion as their bodily behavior resembles my own.

In practice, the exactness and certainty of the above statement must be softened. We cannot be sure that, in our subjective experience, A is the only cause of B. And even if A is the only cause of B in our experience, how can we know that this holds outside our experience? It is not necessary that we should know this with any certainty; it is enough if it is highly probable. It is the assumption of probability in such cases that is our postulate. The postulate may therefore be stated as follows:

> If, whenever we can observe whether A and B are present or absent, we find that every case of B has an A as a causal antecedent, then it is probable that most B's have A's as causal antecedents, even in cases where observation does not enable us to know whether A is present or not.

This postulate, if accepted, justifies the infer-ence to other minds, as well as many other infer-ences that are made unreflectingly by common sense.

9

Norman Malcolm

"Knowledge of Other Minds"

I

I believe that the argument from analogy for the existence of other minds still enjoys more credit than it deserves, and my first aim in this paper will be to show that it leads nowhere. J. S. Mill is one of many who have accepted the argument and I take his statement of it as representative. He puts to himself the question, "By what evidence do I know, or by what considerations am I led to believe, that there exist other sentient creatures; that the walking and speaking figures which I see and hear, have sensations and thoughts, or in other words, possess Minds?" His answer is the following:

> I conclude that other human beings have feelings like me, because, first, they have bodies like me, which I know, in my own case, to be the antecedent condition of feelings; and because, secondly, they exhibit the acts, and other outward signs, which in my own case I know by experience to be caused by feelings. I am conscious in myself of a series of facts connected by an uniform sequence, of which the beginning is modifications of my body, the middle is feelings, the end is outward demeanor. In the case of other human beings I have the evidence of my senses for the first and last links of the series, but not for the intermediate link. I find, however, that the sequence between the first and last is as regular and constant in those other cases as it is in mine. In my own case I know that the first link produces the last through the intermediate link, and could not produce it without. Experience, therefore, obliges me to conclude that there must be an intermediate link; which must either be the same in others as in myself, or a different one: I must either believe them to be alive, or to be automatons: and by believing them to be alive, that is, by supposing the link to be of the same nature as in the case of which

I have experience, and which is in all other respects similar, I bring other human beings, as phenomena, under the same generalizations which I know by experience to be the true theory of my own existence.[1]

I shall pass by the possible objection that this would be very *weak* inductive reasoning, based as it is on the observation of a single instance. More interesting is the following point: Suppose this reasoning could yield a conclusion of the sort "It is probable that that human figure" (pointing at some person other than oneself) "has thoughts and feelings." Then there is a question as to whether this conclusion can *mean* anything to the philosopher who draws it, because there is a question as to whether the sentence "That human figure has thoughts and feelings" can mean anything to him. Why should this be a question? Because the assumption from which Mill starts is that he has *no criterion* for determining whether another "walking and speaking figure" does or does not have thoughts and feelings. If he had a criterion he could apply it, establishing with certainty that this or that human figure does or does not have feelings (for the only plausible criterion would lie in behavior and circumstances that are open to view), and there would be no call to resort to tenuous analogical reasoning that yields at best a probability. If Mill has no criterion for the existence of feelings other than his own then in that sense he does not understand the sentence "That human figure has feelings" and therefore does not understand the sentence "It is *probable* that that human figure has feelings."

There is a familiar inclination to make the following reply: "Although I have no criterion of verification still I *understand,* for example, the sen-

From *The Journal of Philosophy* LV, 23 (November 6, 1958): 969–78. Reprinted with permission of the editors and Norman Malcolm.

tence 'He has a pain.' For I understand the meaning of 'I have pain,' and 'He has a pain' means that he has the *same* thing I have when I have a pain." But this is a fruitless maneuver. If I do not know how to establish that "someone has a pain then I do not know how to establish that he has the *same* as I have when I have a pain.[2] You cannot improve my understanding of "He has a pain" by this recourse to the notion of "the same," unless you give me a criterion for saying that someone *has* the same as I have. If you can do this you will have no use for the argument from analogy: and if you cannot then you do not understand the supposed conclusion of that argument. A philosopher who purports to rely on the analogical argument cannot, I think, escape this dilemma.

There have been various attempts to repair the argument from analogy. Mr. Stuart Hampshire has argued[3] that its validity as a method of inference can be established in the following way: Others sometimes infer that I am feeling giddy from my behavior. Now I have direct, non-inferential knowledge, says Hampshire, of my own feelings. So I can check inferences made about me against the facts, checking thereby the accuracy of the "methods" of inference.

> All that is required for testing the validity of any method of factual inference is that each one of us should sometimes be in a position to confront the conclusions of the doubtful method of inference with what is known by him to be true independently of the method of inference in question. Each one of us is certainly in this position in respect of our common methods of inference about the feelings of persons other than ourselves, in virtue of the fact that each one of us is constantly able to compare the results of this type of inference with what he knows to be true directly and non-inferentially; each one of us is in the position to make this testing comparison, whenever he is the designated subject of a statement about feelings and sensations. I, Hampshire, know by what sort of signs I may be misled in inferring Jones' and Smith's feelings, because I have implicitly noticed (though probably not formulated) where Jones, Smith and others generally go wrong in inferring my feelings. [Pp. 4–5.]

Presumably I can also note when the inferences of others about my feelings do not go wrong. Having ascertained the reliability of some inference-procedures I can use them myself, in a guarded way, to draw conclusions about the feelings of others, with a modest but justified confidence in the truth of those conclusions.

My first comment is that Hampshire has apparently forgotten the purpose of the argument from analogy, which is to provide some probability that "the walking and speaking figures which I see

and hear, have sensations and thoughts" (Mill). For the reasoning that he describes involves the assumption that other human figures *do* have thoughts and sensations: for they are assumed to *make inferences* about me from *observations* of my behavior. But the philosophical problem of the existence of other minds *is* the problem of whether human figures other than oneself do, among other things, make observations, inferences, and assertions. Hampshire's supposed defense of the argument from analogy is an *ignoratio elenchi.*

If we struck from the reasoning described by Hampshire all assumption of thoughts and sensations in others we should be left with something roughly like this: "When my behavior is such and such there come from nearby human figures the sounds 'He feels giddy.' And generally I do feel giddy at the time. Therefore when another human figure exhibits the same behavior and I say 'He feels giddy,' it is probably that he does feel giddy." But the reference here to the sentence-like sounds coming from other human bodies is irrelevant, since I must not assume that those sounds express inferences. Thus the reasoning becomes simply the classical argument from analogy: "When my behavior is such and such I feel giddy; so probably when another human figure behaves the same way he feels the same way." This argument, again, is caught in the dilemma about the criterion of the *same.*

The version of analogical reasoning offered by Professor H. H. Price[4] is more interesting. He suggests that "one's evidence for the existence of other minds is derived primarily from the understanding of language" (p. 429). His idea is that if another body gives forth noises one understands, like "There's the bus," and if these noises give one new information, this "provides some evidence that the foreign body which uttered the noises is animated by a mind like one's own. . . . Suppose I am often in its neighborhood, and it repeatedly produces utterances which I can understand, and which I then proceed to verify for myself. And suppose that this happens in many different kinds of situation. I think that my evidence for believing that this body is animated by a mind like my own would then become very strong" (p. 430). The body from which these informative sounds proceed need not be a human body. "If the rustling of the leaves of an oak formed intelligible words conveying new information to me, and if gorse-bushes made intelligible gestures, I should have evidence that the oak or the gorse-bush was animated by an intelligence like my own" (p. 436). Even if the intelligible and informative sounds did not proceed from a body they would provide evidence for the existence of a (disembodied) mind (p. 435).

Although differing sharply from the classical analogical argument, the reasoning presented by Price is still analogical in form: I know by introspection that when certain combinations of sounds come from me they are "symbols in acts of spontaneous thinking"; therefore similar combinations of sounds, not produced by me, "probably function as instruments to an act of spontaneous thinking, which in this case is not my own" (p. 446). Price says that the reasoning also provides an *explanation* of the otherwise mysterious occurrence of sounds which I understand but did not produce. He anticipates the objection that the hypothesis is nonsensical because unverifiable. "The hypothesis is a perfectly conceivable one," he says, "in the sense that I know very well what the world would have to be like if the hypothesis were true—what sorts of entities there must be in it, and what sorts of events must occur in them. I know from introspection what acts of thinking and perceiving are, and I know what it is for such acts to be combined into the unity of a single mind ..." (pp. 446–447).

I wish to argue against Price that no amount of intelligible sounds coming from an oak tree or a kitchen table could create any probability that it has sensations and thoughts. The question to be asked is: What would show that a tree or table *understands* the sounds that come from it? We can imagine that useful warnings, true descriptions and predictions, even "replies" to questions, should emanate from a tree, so that it came to be of enormous value to its owner. How should we establish that it understood those sentences? Should we "question" it? Suppose that the tree "said" that there was a vixen in the neighborhood, and we "asked" it "What is a vixen?," and it "replied," "A vixen is a female fox." It might go on to do as well for "female" and "fox." This performance might incline us to say that the tree understood the words, in contrast to the possible case in which it answered "I don't know" or did not answer at all. But would it show that the tree understood the words in the same sense that a person could understand them? With a person such a performance would create a presumption that he could make correct *applications* of the word in question: but not so with a tree. To see this point think of the normal teaching of words (e.g., "spoon," "dog," "red") to a child and how one decides whether he understands them. At a primitive stage of teaching one does not require or expect definitions, but rather that the child should *pick out* reds from blues, dogs from cats, spoons from forks. This involves his looking, pointing, reaching for and going to the right things and not the wrong

ones. That a child says "red" when a red thing and "blue" when a blue thing is put before him, is indicative of a mastery of those words *only* in conjunction with the other activities of looking, pointing, trying to get, fetching and carrying. Try to suppose that he says the right words but looks at and reaches for the wrong things. Should we be tempted to say that he has mastered the use of those words? No, indeed. The disparity between words and behavior would make us say that he does not understand the words. In the case of a tree there could be no disparity between its words and its "behavior" because it is logically incapable of behavior of the relevant kind.

Since it has nothing like the human face and body it makes no sense to say of a tree, or an electronic computer, that it is looking or pointing at or fetching something. (Of course one can always *invent* a sense for these expressions.) Therefore it would make no sense to say that it did or did not understand the above words. Trees and computers cannot either pass or fail the tests that a child is put through. They cannot even take them. That an object was a source of intelligible sounds or other signs (no matter how sequential) would not be enough by itself to establish that it had thoughts or sensations. How informative sentences and valuable predictions could emanate from a gorsebush might be a grave scientific problem, but the explanation could never be that the gorsebush has a mind. Better no explanation that nonsense!

It might be thought that the above difficulty holds only for words whose meaning has a "perceptual content" and that if we imagined, for example, that our gorse-bush produced nothing but pure mathematical propositions we should be justified in attributing thought to it, although not sensation. But suppose there was a remarkable "calculating boy" who could give right answers to arithmetical problems but could not apply numerals to reality in empirical propositions, i.e., he could not *count* any objects. I believe that everyone would be reluctant to say that he *understood* the mathematical signs and truths that he produced. If he could count in the normal way there would not be this reluctance. And "counting in the normal way" involves looking, pointing, reaching, fetching, and so on. That is, it requires the human face and body, and human behavior—or something similar. Things which do not have the human form, or anything like it, not merely do not but *cannot* satisfy the criteria for thinking. I am trying to bring out part of what Wittgenstein meant when he said, "We only say of a human being and what is like one that it thinks" (*Investi-*

gations, § 360), and "The human body is the best picture of the human soul" (*ibid.*, p. 178).

I have not yet gone into the most fundamental error of the argument from analogy. It is present whether the argument is the classical one (the analogy between my body and other bodies) or Price's version (the analogy between my language and the noises and signs produced by other things). It is the mistaken assumption that *one learns from one's own case* what thinking, feeling, sensation are. Price gives expression to this assumption when he says: "I know from introspection what acts of thinking and perceiving are . . ." (*op. cit.*, p. 447). It is the most natural assumption for a philosopher to make and indeed seems at first to be the only possibility. Yet Wittgenstein has made us see that it leads first to solipsism and then to nonsense. I shall try to state as briefly as possible how it produces those results.

A philosopher who believes that one must learn what thinking, fear, or pain is "from one's own case," does not believe that the thing to be observed is one's behavior, but rather something "inward." He considers behavior to be related to the inward states and occurrences merely as an accompaniment or possibly an effect. He cannot regard behavior as a *criterion* of psychological phenomena: for if he did he would have no use for the analogical argument (as was said before) and also the priority given to "one's own case" would be pointless. He believes that he notes something in himself and he calls "thinking" or "fear" or "pain," and then he tries to infer the presence of the *same* in others. He should then deal with the question of what his criterion of the *same* in others is. This he cannot do because it is of the essence of his viewpoint to reject circumstances and behavior as a criterion of mental phenomena in others. And what else could serve as a criterion? He ought, therefore, to draw the conclusion that the notion of thinking, fear, or pain in others is in an important sense meaningless. He has no idea of what would count for or against it.[5] "That there should be thinking or pain other than my own is unintelligible," he ought to hold. This would be a rigorous solipsism, and a correct outcome of the assumption that one can know only from one's own case what the mental phenomena are. An equivalent way of putting it would be: "When I say 'I am in pain,' by 'pain' I mean a certain inward state. When I say '*He* is in pain,' by 'pain' I mean *behavior*. I cannot attribute pain to others *in the same sense* that I attribute it to myself."

Some philosophers before Wittgenstein may have been the solipsistic result of starting from "one's own case." But I believe he is the first to have shown how that starting point destroys itself. This may be presented as follows: One supposes that one inwardly picks out something as thinking or pain and thereafter identifies it whenever it presents itself in the soul. But the question to be pressed is, Does one make *correct* identifications? The proponent of the "private" identifications has nothing to say here. He feels sure that he identifies correctly the occurrences in his soul; but feeling sure is no guarantee of being right. Indeed he has no idea of what being *right* could mean. He does not know how to distinguish between actually making correct identifications and being under the impression that he does. (See *Investigations*, §258–9.) Suppose that he identified the emotion of anxiety as the sensation of pain? Neither he nor anyone else could know about this "mistake." Perhaps he makes a mistake *every* time! Perhaps all of us do! We ought to see now that we are talking nonsense. We do not know what a *mistake* would be. We have no standard, no examples, no customary practice, with which to compare our inner recognitions. The inward identification cannot hit the bull's-eye, or miss it either, because there is no bull's-eye. When we see that the ideas of correct and incorrect have no application to the supposed inner identification, the latter notion loses its appearance of sense. Its collapse brings down both solipsism and the argument from analogy.

II

This destruction of the argument from analogy also destroys the *problem* for which it was supposed to provide a solution. A philosopher feels himself in a difficulty about other minds because he assumes that first of all he is acquainted with mental phenomena "from his own case." What troubles him is how to make the transition from his own case to the case of others. When his thinking is freed of the illusion of the priority of his own case, then he is able to look at the familiar facts and to acknowledge that the circumstances, behavior, and utterances of others actually are his *criteria* (not merely his evidence) for the existence of their mental states. Previously this had seemed impossible.

But now he is in danger of flying to the opposite extreme of behaviorism, which errs by believing that through observation of one's own circumstances, behavior, and utterances one can find out that one is thinking or angry. The philosophy of "from one's own case" and behaviorism, though in a sense opposites, make the common assumption that the first-person, present-tense psychological statements are verified by self-observation. According to the "one's own case" philosophy the self-observation cannot be checked by others; according to behaviorism the self-observation would be by means of outward criteria that are available to all. The first position becomes unintelligible; the second is false for at least many kinds of psychological statements. We are forced to conclude that the first-person psychological statements are not (or hardly ever) verified by self-observation. It follows that they have no verification at all; for if they had a verification it would have to be by self-observation.

But if sentences like "My head aches" or "I wonder where she is" do not express observations then what do they do? What is the relation between my declaration that my head aches and the fact that my head aches, if the former is not the report of an observation? The perplexity about the existence of *other* minds has, as the result of criticism, turned into a perplexity about the meaning of one's own psychological sentences about oneself. At our starting point it was the sentence "*His* head aches" that posed a problem; but now it is the sentence "*My* head aches"that puzzles us.

One way in which this problem can be put is by the question, "How does *one know when to say* the words 'My head aches'?" The inclination to ask this question can be made acute by imagining a fantastic but not impossible case of a person who has survived to adult years without ever experiencing pain. He is given various sorts of injections to correct this condition, and on receiving one of these one day, he jumps and exclaims, "Now I feel pain!" One wants to ask, "How did he *recognize* the new sensation as a *pain?*"

Let us note that if the man gives an answer (e.g., "I knew it must be pain because of the way I jumped") then he proves by that very fact that he has not mastered the correct use of the words "I feel pain." They cannot be used to state a *conclusion*. In telling us *how* he did it he will convict himself of a misuse. Therefore the question "How did he recognize his sensation?" requests the impossible. The inclination to ask it is evidence of our inability to grasp the fact that the use of this psychological sentence has nothing to do with recognizing or identifying or observing a state of oneself.

The fact that this imagined case produces an especially strong temptation to ask the "How?" question shows that we have the idea that it must be more difficult to give the right name of one's sensation *the first time*. The implication would be that it is not so difficult *after* the first time. Why should this be? Are we thinking that then the man would have a paradigm of pain with which he could compare his sensations and so be in a position to know right off whether a certain sensation was or was not a pain? But the paradigm would be either something "outer" (behavior) or something "inner" (perhaps a memory impression of the sensation). If the former then he is misusing the first-person sentence. If the latter then the question of whether he compared *correctly* the present sensation with the inner paradigm of pain would be without sense. Thus the idea that the use of the first-person sentences can be governed by paradigms must be abandoned. It is another form of our insistent misconception of the first-person sentence as resting somehow on the identification of a psychological state.

These absurdities prove that we must conceive of the first-person psychological sentences in some entirely different light. Wittgenstein presents us with the suggestion (to which philosophers have not been sufficiently attentive) that the first-person sentences are to be thought of as similar to the natural non-verbal, behavioral expressions of psychological states. "My leg hurts," for example, is to be assimilated to crying, limping, holding one's leg. This is a bewildering comparison and one's first thought is that two sorts of things could not be more unlike. By saying the sentence one can make a *statement;* it has a *contradictory;* it is *true* or *false;* in saying it one *lies* or *tells the truth;* and so on. None of these things, exactly, can be said of crying, limping, holding one's leg. So how can there by any resemblance? But Wittgenstein knew this when he deliberately likened such a sentence to "the primitive, the natural, expressions" of pain, and said that it is "new pain-behavior" (*ibid.*, § 244). Although my limits prevent my attempting it here, I think this analogy ought to be explored. For it has at least two important merits: first, it breaks the hold on us of the question "How does one *know when to say* 'My leg hurts'?" for in the light of the analogy this will be as nonsensical as the question "How does one know when to cry, limp, or hold one's leg?"; second, it explains how the utterance of a first-person psychological sentence by another person can have *importance* for us, although not as an identification—for in the light of the analogy it will have the same importance as the natural behavior which serves as our pre-verbal criterion of the psychological states of others.

NOTES

1. J. S. Mill, *An Examination of Sir William Hamilton's Philosophy,* 6th edition (London, 1889), pp. 243–244.

2. "It is no explanation to say: the supposition that he has a pain is simply the supposition that he has the same as I. For *that* part of the grammar is quite clear to me: that is, that one will say that the stove has the same experience as I, *if* one says: it is in pain and I am in pain" (Wittgenstein, *Philosophical Investigations* (New York, 1953), §350).

3. "The Analogy of Feeling," *Mind*, January, 1952, pp. 1–12.

4. "Our Evidence for the Existence of Other Minds," *Philosophy*, Vol. 13, 1938, pp. 425–456.

5. One reason why philosophers have not commonly drawn this conclusion may be, as Wittgenstein acutely suggests, that they assume that they have "an infallible paradigm of identity in the identity of a thing with itself" (*Investigations*, § 215).

10

Stuart Hampshire

"The Analogy of Feeling"

1. I am concerned in this paper with only one source of one of the many puzzles associated with our knowledge of other minds. It is often said that statements about other people's feelings and sensations cannot be justified as being based upon inductive arguments of any ordinary pattern, that is, as being inferences from the observed to the unobserved of a familiar and accepted form; I shall argue that they can be so justified. I will not deny that such inferences are difficult; everyone has always known, apart altogether from philosophical theory, that they are difficult; but I will deny that they are *logically* peculiar or invalid, when considered simply as inductive arguments. I believe that modern philosophers have found something logically peculiar and problematical about our inferences to other minds, and have even denied the possibility of such inferences, at least in part because of an incomplete understanding of the functions of pronouns and of other contextual expressions in our language; in particular they have misunderstood the proper use of these expressions in combination with words like "know", "certain", "verify", "evidence". If I am right, it becomes easier to explain why what the solipsist wants to say cannot properly be said, why solipsism is a *linguistically* absurd thesis, and at the same time to explain why it is a thesis which tempts those who confuse epistemological distinctions with logical distinctions.

2. For reasons which will become clear later, I shall introduce two quasi-technical terms. As specimens of the type of sentence, the status of which, as normally used, is in dispute, I shall take the sentences, "I feel giddy", "you feel giddy", "he feels giddy", and so on through the other cases of the verb "feel". Any normal use of the sentence "I feel giddy" will be, in my invented terminology, a specimen of an autobiographical statement, where this phrase is simply shorthand for "a statement describing somebody's momentary feelings or sensations which is expressed in the first person singular". Any normal use of the sentences "he feels giddy", "you feel giddy", or "they feel giddy", will be specimens of heterobiographical statement—that is, statements describing somebody's feelings which are not expressed in the first person singular; "we feel giddy", as normally used, would be a statement which is partly autobiographical and partly heterobiographical in my sense. It may sometimes happen that someone chooses to tell the story of his own inner life, using not the first person singular, but the third person, or some fictitious or other name; it is actually possible to write one's own obituary notice, using the third person and including within it descriptions which are intended as descriptions of one's own feelings and sensations. But on such occasions the pronouns (or verb-cases for an inflected language) are misleadingly used, and deliberately so. The ordinary function of the word "I" (or of the corresponding verb-case in inflected languages) is to indicate explicitly that the author of the statement is also the designated subject of the statement; the exceptional, deliberately misleading uses mentioned above consciously take advantage of this fact. By "an autobiographical statement" I shall mean a statement describing someone's feelings or sensations which explicitly shows, in the actual form of its expression, that the author of the statement is also its designated subject. A statement, *e.g.* in a novel, about which we can argue, by reference to evidence external to the verbal form of the statement itself, whether it is, as a matter of fact, an

From *Mind* LXI, 241 (January 1952): 1–12. Reprinted with permission of the Oxford University Press and Stuart Hampshire.

autobiographical statement, will not therefore be an autobiographical statement in my artificial and restricted sense.

It has often been noticed that there are certain peculiarities about these first person singular statements about feelings and sensations, particularly when the main verb is in the present tense; these peculiarities have led some philosophers to characterise them as incorrigible statements and have led others to deny them the title of "statement" altogether; the peculiarities emerge in the use of words like "know", "believe", and "certain" in combination with these sentences, or rather in their lack of use. In respect of most statements, "I think that P is true but I may be mistaken" and "I have established that P is true beyond all reasonable doubt" are sentences having a normal use, whatever P may be; but there are no normal circumstances in which one would say "I think that I feel giddy but I may be mistaken" or "I have established beyond reasonable doubt that I feel giddy", and consequently there are no normal circumstances in which it would be in place to say "I am absolutely certain that I feel giddy". By contrast the sentences "you feel giddy" or "he feels giddy" do normally occur in statements of the form "I believe that he feels giddy but I am not certain" or "it is known that he feels giddy", and so on; but again, "he believes that he feels giddy" or "he is certain that he feels giddy" have no normal use. It is the corollary of this that the questions "how do you know?" or "what is your evidence?" are out of place in respect of statements about momentary feelings and sensations, when addressed to the author of the statement, if he is also explicitly shown to be the designated subject of it.

One inference which might be drawn from these facts is that heterobiographical statements about feelings can never be known to be true directly, where "known directly" means that no question arises of how the statement is known to be true and no question arises of any evidence being required to support the statement. But this, as it stands, would be a plainly false conclusion, since the person who is the designated subject of such a heterobiographical statement does generally know directly, without need of evidence, whether the statement made about him is true or false. The proper conclusion is only that the *author* of a heterobiographical statement of this kind can never know directly, in the sense indicated, whether the statement he has made is true or false; the author can always properly be asked how he knows, or on what grounds he believes, his heterobiographical statement to be true; he is required to produce his evidence. So the so-called asymmetry is not a matter of statements expressed in the first person singular, *as such,* being different in respect of the evidence which they require from statements expressed in the second or third person singular; both descriptions of feelings in the first person singular, and those in the second and third person, may be challenged either by reference to indirect evidence (*e.g.* "I am sure you are lying; you have obvious motives for lying, and you shown none of the symptoms which usually go with feeling giddy") or by a proper claim to direct knowledge (*e.g.* "I can tell you quite definitely that I do feel giddy, in spite of the evidence to the contrary").

This point is obvious, but it is apt to be dangerously slurred over when philosophers talk in general of "statements about other minds", and then go on to inquire into *the* methods appropriate to confirming or confuting such statements. They may be thought to mean by "statements about other minds" what I have called heterobiographical statements—that is, statements describing feelings and sensations which are not expressed in the first person singular; but the so-called problems of other minds, which is sometimes presented as a problem of how a *certain kind of statement* can be tested, does not attach to *a class of statements of any one particular form;* it arises equally for first person singular statements, if in this case the position of the audience is considered instead of that of the author. The problem of other minds is properly the problem of what tests and verifications are ever possible for anyone who is not in fact the designated subject of a statement about thoughts and feelings; it arises equally for any statement about feelings, whether the statement begins with the word "I" or with the word "you" or "we" or "they".

3. The commonsense answer to the question, so reformulated, seems obvious—indeed so obvious that simply to give it cannot possibly satisfy philosophers; something more is required to explain why it has been thought inadequate. The commonsense answer is: each one of us is sometimes the designated subject of an autobiographical statement and sometimes the subject of heterobiographical statements; each one of us sometimes makes, or is in a position to make, statements about feelings which are not inferential and do not require supporting evidence, and also makes, or is in a position to make, statements about feelings which are inferential and do require supporting evidence. All that is required for testing the validity of any method of factual inference is that each one of us should sometimes be in a position to confront the conclusions of the doubtful method of inference with what is known by him to be true independently of the method of inference in question. Each one of us is certainly in this position in

respect of our common methods of inference about the feelings of persons other than ourselves, in virtue of the fact that each one of us is constantly able to compare the results of this type of inference with what he knows to be true directly and non-inferentially; each one of us is in the position to make this testing comparison, whenever he is the designated subject of a statement about feelings and sensations. I, Hampshire, know by what sort of signs I may be misled in inferring Jones's and Smith's feelings, because I have implicitly noticed (though probably not formulated) where Jones, Smith and others generally go wrong in inferring my feelings. We all as children learn by experiment how to conceal and deceive, to pose and suppress; concurrently we are learning in this very process how to detect the poses and suppressions of others; we learn the signs and occasions of concealment at first-hand, and we are constantly revising our canons of duplicity as our own direct experience of its forms and occasions widens.

These are the commonsense considerations which seem at first glance to allow us to regard any heterobiographical statement, made by any one of us, as the conclusion of a valid inductive inference, the reliability of the method of inference used in any particular case being in principle testable by each one of us in confrontation with direct experience, that is, with non-inferential knowledge about the successes and failures of this particular method; and I think that, as is usual in these questions, the third glance will confirm the first. But before going further, it is worth noticing how the argument from analogy, as stated by philosophers, approaches what I have called the commonsense position, but also misrepresents and over-simplifies it. There is a sense of "analogy" in which it is true that I could justify my inference that Smith is now feeling giddy by an analogy between the particular method of inference "which I am now using and other uses of the same methods of" by other people in discussing my feelings and sensations; I know by direct experience how such feelings as giddiness are concealed and revealed; both I and Smith have been in a position to test the reliability of those methods of indirect inference about giddiness and cognate sensations which we from time to time use in talking about other people. The argument from analogy, as commonly stated by philosophers, only fails because the analogy has been looked for in the wrong place. What is required is not some simple analogy between my feelings and my external symptoms on the one hand and someone else's external symptoms, and so someone else's giddiness-feeling, on the other; what is needed, and is also available, is an *analogy between different uses of the same methods of argument by different people on different occasions.*

The inductive argument, the reliability of which is to be tested by each one of us, attaches both to the sentence "I feel giddy" and to the sentences "you feel giddy", "he feels giddy", etc.; it attaches to any sentence of the form "X feels giddy"; anyone hearing or using any sentence of this form, and anyone needing to test the statement conveyed on a particular occasion, can find such confirmation by looking for an analogy with occasions of its use when he was not in need of such inductive confirmation. To anyone entertaining a doubt about the justification of a particular method of inference about feelings and sensations, the reassuring analogy is between the different occasions of use of the sentence in question; for on some of these occasions the doubter, whoever he may be, was in a position to know non-inferentially that the method of inference now in question led to a correct or incorrect conclusion. Each of us is in a position to learn from his own experience that certain methods of inference to conclusions of the kind "X feels giddy" are generally successful. Of course, if I, Hampshire, have never felt giddy myself, or had any sensation which is even remotely like this one, I would to that extent be at a loss to know whether other people are speaking the truth when they describe autobiographically this utterly unknown kind of sensation. In certain extreme cases this total failure of testability, and therefore failure of communication, does in fact happen; in such cases I am in fact content to admit that I personally have no means of knowing whether what is said by others is pure invention or not; I simply do not know what they are talking about. But over the normal range of statements about feelings and sensations of which I am either the author or audience, I can generally point to occasions on which I was the subject of the particular statement in question and other people had to use the now questionable method of inference. Suppose that Smith and I each suspect the other of deceiving and of encouraging the other to use unreliable methods of inference. This again is a testable and empirical doubt, because we each of us know how we ourselves proceed when we are trying to deceive in this particular manner. We each base our devices of deception on our observations of other people's methods of inference about us. We each know that there is something in common to our different methods of deception, since we each sometimes know that we have failed to deceive and so we each know from our own experience how such deception may be detected. But no common psychological language could be established with beings, outwardly human and sensitive, who never tried openly and in words to infer our feelings and who never acknowledged in words our success in inferring theirs, using the one to guide them in the other in a circle of mutual correction. We would have no good inductive grounds for speculating about the feelings of utterly silent people, or of people who did not betray themselves in speculating about us. It is merely a matter of natural history, and not of logic, that total failures of communication and understanding do not occur more frequently, and that in fact we are each generally in a position to reassure ourselves about our methods of inference to the feelings of others by confrontation with the successes and failures of others in talking about us.

It has been necessary first to insist on the truism that all statements about feelings and sensations, including such statements expressed in the first person singular, are "statements about other minds" for some people, but not "statements about other minds" for other people; for it is precisely this feature of them which allows any one of us to test in direct experience the reliability of the numerous specific methods of inference which he uses when talking about the feelings of others. The importance of the truism can be brought out in the analogous case of "statements about the past"; philosophers have sometimes invented perplexities by writing as if we could pick out a class of statements as "statements about the past" and could then enquire how such statements can possibly be established as true by inductive argument; for how—it is asked—can we ever in principle confirm the validity of our inferences about the past? The mistakes which lead to this question are the same as in the "other minds" case. We cannot pick out a class of statements as statements about the past, unless we mean merely statements expressed in the past tenses. But the tenses, like the pronouns and cases of verbs, serve (among other functions) to relate a statement to the particular context or occasion of its utterance or of its consideration; clearly the *same* statement may be a statement about past, present or future, when considered, accepted or rejected by different people in different contexts; similarly, the *same* statement may be made either heterobiographically or autobiographically. A statement in the present tense, which is in this artificial sense a statement about the present, when verified and reaffirmed, may be reaffirmed as a statement about the past, and equally a statement about the future, when finally confirmed, may be reaffirmed as a statement about the present. *The very notion of confirmation involves this possibility of comparing the different contexts of utterance of the same statement.* It does not in general lie *within* the statement itself, or in its grammatical form of expression, that it is a statement about the mind of another, or that it is a statement

about the past; these are features of the circumstances of the utterance or consideration of the statement, features which are partially indicated (but not stated) by pronouns, by tenses and by other contextual expressions, whenever and by whomever the statement is asserted, re-asserted or denied. Strictly speaking, there can be no class of statements about the past, standing in hopeless need of confirmation, any more than there can be a class of past events; similarly there can be no class of minds which are other minds, or class of statements about them. This confusion of contextual idioms such as "other", "past" with class-terms has its roots in an unnoticed double use of the idioms, which must now be explained.

3. It is often suggested that the function of pronouns and other contextual expressions ("this", "that", "here", "now", etc.) is to designate or to refer uniquely to some person, thing, time, place, event, etc. Mr. Strawson (MIND, October, 1950) has suggested the appropriate label, "uniquely referring expressions"; certainly one of the ways in which pronouns and these other contextual expressions are used is in this uniquely referring way—that is, to indicate, in a particular context of utterance, a particular person, thing, event. But it is characteristic of the contextual expressions that they are not always or solely used to refer uniquely or to designate a particular person, thing, event; they also have an important *generalised* use, in which they make no reference to a particular individual and in which they can be interpreted without any reference whatever to any particular context of utterance. Consider the slogan, "do it *now*"; or "never put off till *to-morrow* what you can do *to-day*". In this use "now", "to-day", "to-morrow" do not refer uniquely, but have a force in some (but not all) ways like that of a variable, and might be expanded into "now, to whatever moment 'now' may refer", or "to-day, whatever day 'to-day' may refer to". Another example; "the future is quite uncertain"; as it stands, and without a context, this sentence is ambiguous, and might be used to make two quite different statements, or even two different kinds of statement; "the future" might be used in the uniquely referring way, so that we require to know the context of utterance in order to know what particular stretch of history is being referred to and described as uncertain; or "the future" might be used in the purely generalised way—"the future, at whatever point in history, is always uncertain". This familiar generalised, or quasivariable, use is transferred to philosophy when we talk of "statements about *the past*", "statements about the *other* side of the moon", and "statements about *other* minds". Confusion between the two kinds of use arises

when a transition is made within a single argument from the generalised to the uniquely referring use, or vice versa, without this transition being noticed; and just this is what generally happens in arguments about our knowledge of "other minds" and in formulations of the so-called *egocentric* predicament. The solipistic doubter will probably not put his question in the explicitly generalised form, but will ask: "How can *I* ever justify my inferences about what is going on in *your* mind, since *I* can have no independent means of checking *my* inferences about *your* feelings?" There may be a muddle in this: Does the "I" here mean "I, Hampshire"? Is it a lament about my, Hampshire's, peculiar isolation and the peculiar inscrutability of you, Smith? Or does the "I" mean "whoever 'I' refers to?" and the "you" "you, whoever 'you' may be?" If the latter is intended, and the pronoun is being used in the generalised way, the question becomes: "How can any one of us every justify any inference to the feelings of someone other than himself, since no one of us, whoever he may be, has any means of checking any inference to the feelings of anyone other than himself?" And to this generalised form of the question the common-sense answer again suggests itself: each and every one of us, whoever he may be, has the means of independently checking the reliability of the methods of inference which he uses, although, naturally, on those occasions when he needs to use any particular method of inference, he cannot be independently checking the inference on the same occasion. When I, Hampshire, check in my own experience the reliability of the various particular methods of inference which I use when talking about the feelings of others, the statements which I make at the conclusion of these checks are *ex-hypothesi* not themselves the conclusions of an inference; but they are none the less efficient as checks to my methods of inference. The solipsistic problem, cleared of these confusions, can now be re-stated: whenever anyone uses the sentence "I feel giddy", one person and one person only is in a position to know directly, and without need of inference, whether the statement conveyed is true; whenever anyone says "you feel giddy", or "he feels giddy", or "Smith feels giddy", one person and one person only is in a position to know without need of inference whether the statement is true; whenever anyone says, "we both feel giddy", or "they feel giddy", no one can ever know directly, and without need of inference, whether the conjoint statements conveyed are true. So the solipsist may correctly say that it is a distinguishing characteristic of statements about feelings, as opposed to statements about physical things, that at most one person can ever properly claim to know

directly, and without needing to give evidence or justification, whether such statements are true. But the solipsist originally wanted to separate, within the class of statement about minds, a class of statements about *other* minds, as being dubious and problematical, from autobiographical statements, which were held to be privileged and not dubious. It is this distinction which is untenable.

Suppose that, in talking about our feelings, we each solipsistically confined ourselves to statements which we may properly claim to know to be true directly and without appeal to evidence or to methods of inference; I, Hampshire, would be allowed to say "I feel giddy", and you, Smith, would be allowed to say "I feel giddy"; but, since all uses of other cases of the verb require problematical inference, we would never be allowed to assent to or dissent from each other's statements, or to place ourselves in the position of an audience discussing them. Under such conditions the pronouns and cases of the verb would have no further function, and all argument and the detection of lies would be excluded: our psychological language would simply serve to convey a set of undiscussable announcements. Communication in the ordinary sense upon such topics would have ceased; for communication essentially involves the use of sentences to convey statements by an author to an actual or potential audience, in such a way that all users of the language, in denying and confirming, may change from the position of audience to author in respect of any statement made. To compare the use of personal pronouns with the uses of tenses again: because those statements which refer to events long prior or subsequent to the moment of utterance are *pro tanto* relatively uncertain at the time they are made, it might be suggested that only statements in the present tense should be accepted as completely reliable. But unless we recognise the sense of "same statement" as something to be re-affirmed in different contexts, we remove the last possibility of correcting and denying statements, and with this we remove the possibility of all argument about them and testing of them, and also the possibility of expressing belief or disbelief; we therefore remove the essential conditions or point of statement-making; and this we would have done by failing to recognise the function of those devices which relate the same statement to the changing circumstances of its assertion. The formula often used, "I am in a position to judge of the truth of statements about my own feeling, but not about the feeling of others", has only succeeded in misleading, because of the two ways in which the expression "I" and "other" may be used, and the often unnoticed shift from one use to the other; it is this shift which suggests a solipsistic conclusion—*e.g.* that one mind only can be known with certainty to exist and one set of feelings and sensations known with certainty to have occurred. But of course no such conclusion about *one* mind follows from the argument when correctly stated. The proper truism is, "No one of us, whoever he may be, is in need of inference to assure himself of the truth of statements about his own feelings, but he can never assure himself directly, and without needing to appeal to evidence, of the truth of statements about the feelings, but he can never assure himself directly, and without needing to appeal to evidence, of the truth of statements about the feelings of others"; stated in this form, with a quasi-variable expression as the subject term, the truism cannot serve as a premise to any *solipsistic* conclusion.

4. The peculiarity of the word "know" and of its cognates—that the conditions of their proper use in combination with any type of statement vary with the indicated context of utterance—is not confined to discourse about minds and feelings; it applies over the whole range of application of words like "know", "certain", "verify", with whatever kind of statement they are combined. Whatever may be the topic under discussion, whether a claim to knowledge or certainty is or is not in place, must always depend upon who makes the claim, when, and under what conditions; it can never be solely a matter of the form of the statement itself or of its topic. Any empirical statement whatever is a matter of uncertain inference under some conditions of its use or consideration. There is no mystery in the fact that a statement which may be a matter of direct and certain knowledge for one person will always be a matter of uncertain inference for another, any more than there is mystery in the fact that the same statement which may

be known with certainty to be true at one time must be a matter of uncertain inference at other times. Philosophers (Plato, Descartes, Russell) have invented the mystery by writing as if being known to be true and being uncertain were intrinsic properties of statements, properties somehow adhering to them independently of the particular circumstances in which they were made or considered. It is proper and necessary that formal logicians, who study patterns of transformations of sentence-forms, should disregard those features of statements which relate them to a context of utterance; but philosophers' questions about use and meaning hinge on the different contexts in which words like "know" and "certain" may occur in combination with sentences of different forms and different topics.

5. *Conclusion.*—"Past", "Present", "Other", are not class terms but contextual terms, and there can be no class of events which are past events, and no class of minds which are other minds, and no class of statements which are statements about either of these. "Statements about other minds" is either an incomplete expression, requiring knowledge of the particular circumstance of its use in order that it should be intelligible—*e.g.* "minds other than mine, Hampshire's"; or the contextual expression may be used in the generalised sense and mean "statements about minds other than the author's, whoever the author may be"; if the latter is intended, then in raising the problem of other minds we are enquiring into the analogy which enables anyone to compare the situation in which he knows a statement about feelings to be true, independently of inference, with the situation in which he does not; and it is to this comparison that we refer when we talk of checking the reliability of any method of factual inference.

11

P. F. Strawson

"Persons"

I

In the *Tractatus* (5.631–5.641), Wittgenstein writes of the I which occurs in philosophy, of the philosophical idea of the subject of experiences. He says first: "The thinking, presenting subject—there is no such thing." Then, a little later: "*In an important sense* there is no subject." This is followed by: "The subject does not belong to the world, but is a limit of the world." And a little later comes the following paragraph: "There is [therefore] really a sense in which in philosophy we can talk non-psychologically of the I. The I occurs in philosophy through the fact that the 'world is my world.' The philosophical I is not the man, not the human body, or the human soul of which psychology treats, but the metaphysical subject, the limit—not a part of the world." These remarks are impressive, but also puzzling and obscure. Reading them, one might think: Well, let's settle for the human body and the human soul of which psychology treats, and which is a part of the world, and let the metaphysical subject go. But again we might think: No, when I talk of myself, I do after all talk of that which has all of my experiences, I do talk of the subject of my experiences—and yet also of something that is part of the world in that it, but not the world, comes to an end when I die. The limit of *my* world is not—and is not so thought of by me—the limit of *the* world. It may be difficult to explain the idea of something which is both a subject of experiences and a part of the world. But it is an idea we have: it should be an idea we can explain.

Let us think of some of the ways in which we ordinarily talk of ourselves, of some of the things which we ordinarily ascribe to ourselves. They are of many kinds. We ascribe to ourselves *actions and intentions* (I am doing, did, shall do this); *sensations* (I am warm, in pain); *thoughts and feelings* (I think, wonder, want this, am angry, disappointed, contented); *perceptions and memories* (I see this, hear the other, remember that). We ascribe to ourselves, in two senses, position: *location* (I am on the sofa) and *attitude* (I am lying down). And of course we ascribe to ourselves not only temporary conditions, states, and situations, like most of these, but also enduring characteristics, including such physical characteristics as height, coloring, shape, and weight. That is to say, among the things we ascribe to ourselves are things of a kind that we also ascribe to material bodies to which we would not dream of ascribing others of the things that we ascribe to ourselves. Now there seems nothing needing explanation in the fact that the particular height, coloring, and physical position which we ascribe to ourselves, should be ascribed to *something or other;* for that which one calls one's body is, at least, a body, a material thing. It can be picked out from others, identified by ordinary physical criteria and described in ordinary physical terms. But it can seem, and has seemed, to need explanation that one's states of consciousness, one's thoughts and sensations, are ascribed *to the very same thing* as that to which these physical characteristics, this physical situation, is ascribed. Why are one's states of consciousness ascribed to the very same thing as certain corporeal characteristics, a certain physical situation, etc.? And once this question is raised, another question follows it, viz.: Why are one's states of consciousness ascribed to (said to be of, or to belong to) anything at all? It is not to be supposed that the answers to these questions will be independent of one another.

It might indeed by thought that an answer to

From *Minnesota Studies in the Philosophy of Science*, volume II, Herbert Feigl, Michael Scriven, and Grover Maxwell, eds. Minneapolis: University of Minnesota Press, 1958, pp. 330–53. Reprinted with permission of the publisher.

both of them could be found in the unique role which each person's body plays in his experience, particularly his perceptual experience. All philosophers who have concerned themselves with these questions have referred to the uniqueness of this role. (Descartes was well enough aware of its uniqueness: "I am *not* lodged in my body like a pilot in a vessel.") In what does this uniqueness consist? Well, of course, in a great many facts. We may summarize some of these facts by saying that for each person there is one body which occupies a certain *causal* position in relation to that person's perceptual experience, a causal position which is in various ways unique in relation to each of the various kinds of perceptual experience he has; and—as a further consequence—that this body is also unique for him as an *object* of the various kinds of perceptual experience which he has. This complex uniqueness of the single body appears, moreover, to be a contingent matter, or rather a cluster of contingent matters; we can, or it seems that we can, imagine many peculiar combinations of dependence and independence of aspects of our perceptual experience on the physical states or situation of more than one body.

Now I must say, straightaway, that this cluster of apparently contingent facts about the unique role which each person's body plays in his experience does not seem to me to provide, *by itself,* an answer to our questions. Of course these facts explain *something.* They provide a very good reason why a subject of experience should have a *very special regard* for just one body, why he should think of it as unique and perhaps more important than any other. They explain—if I may be permitted to put it so—why I feel *peculiarly attached* to what in fact I call my own body; they even might be said to explain why, granted that I am going to speak of one body as *mine,* I should speak of this body (the body that I do speak of as mine) as mine. But they do not explain why I should have the concept of *myself* at all, why I should ascribe my thoughts and experiences to *anything.* Moreover, even if we were satisfied with some other explanation of why one's states of consciousness (thoughts and feelings and perceptions) were ascribed to *something,* and satisfied that the facts in question sufficed to explain why the "possession" of a particular body should be ascribed to the *same* thing (i.e., to explain why a particular body should be spoken of as standing in some special relation, called "being possessed by" to that thing), yet the facts in question still do not explain why we should, as we do, ascribe certain corporeal characteristics not simply to the body standing in this special relation to the thing "to which we ascribe thoughts, feelings, etc., but to the thing" itself to which we ascribe

thoughts, feelings, etc., but to the thing itself to which we ascribe those thoughts and feelings. (For we say "I am bald" as well as "I am cold," "I am lying on the hearthrug" as well as "I see a spider on the ceiling.") Briefly, the facts in question explain why a subject of experience should pick out one body from others, give it, perhaps, an honored name and ascribe to it whatever characteristics it has; but they do not explain why the experiences should be ascribed to any subject at all; and they do not explain why, if the experiences are to be ascribed to something, they and the corporeal characteristics which might be truly ascribed to the favored body, should be ascribed to the same thing. So the facts in question do not explain the use that we make of the word "I," or how any word has the use that word has. They do not explain the concept we have of a person.

II

A possible reaction at this point is to say that the concept we have is wrong or confused, or, if we make it a rule not to say that the concepts we have are confused, that the usage we have, whereby we ascribe, or seem to ascribe, such different kinds of predicate to one and the same thing, is confusing, that it conceals the true nature of the concepts involved, or something of this sort. This reaction can be found in two very important types of view about these matters. The first type of view is Cartesian, the view of Descartes and of others who think like him. Over the attribution of the second type of view I am more hesitant; but there is some evidence that it was held, at one period, by Wittgenstein and possibly also by Schlick. On both of these views, one of the questions we are considering, namely "Why do we ascribe our states of consciousness to the very same thing as certain corporeal characteristics, etc.?" is a question which does not arise, for on both views it is only a linguistic illusion that both kinds of predicate are properly ascribed to one and the same thing, that there is a common owner, or subject, of both types of predicate. And on the second of these views, the other question we are considering, namely "Why do we ascribe our states of consciousness to anything at all?" is also a question which does not arise; for on this view, it is only a linguistic illusion that one ascribes one's states of consciousness at all, that there is any proper subject of these apparent ascriptions, that states of consciousness belong to, or are states of, anything.

That Descartes held the first of these views is well enough known. When we speak of a person, we are really referring to one or both of two distinct substances (two substances of different types), each of which has its own appropriate type of states and properties; and none of the properties or states of either can be a property or state of the other. States of consciousness belong to one of these substances, and not to the other. I shall say no more about the Cartesian view at the moment—what I have to say about it will emerge later on—except to note again that while it escapes one of our questions, it does not escape, but indeed invites, the other: "Why are one's states of consciousness *ascribed* at all, to *any* subject?"

The second of these views I shall call the "no-ownership" or "no-subject" doctrine of the self. Whether or not anyone has explicitly held this view, it is worth reconstructing, or constructing, in outline.[1] For the errors into which it falls are instructive. The "no-ownership" theorist may be presumed to start his explanations with facts of the sort which illustrate the unique causal position of a certain material body in a person's experience. The theorist maintains that the uniqueness of this body is sufficient to give rise to the idea that one's experiences can be ascribed to some particular individual thing, can be said to be possessed by, or owned by, that thing. This idea, he thinks, though infelicitously and misleadingly expressed in terms of ownership, would have some validity, would make some sort of sense, so long as we thought of this individual thing, the possessor of the experiences, as the body itself. So long as we thought in this way, then to ascribe a particular state of consciousness to this body, this individual thing, would at least be to say something contingent, something that might be, or might have been, false. It might have been a misascription; for the experience in question might be, or might have been, causally dependent on the state of some other body; in the present admissible, though infelicitous, sense of "belong", it might have belonged to some other individual thing. But now, the theorist suggests, one becomes confused: one slides from this admissible, though infelicitous, sense in which one's experiences may be said to belong to, or be possessed by, some particular thing, to a wholly inadmissible and empty sense of these expressions; and in this new and inadmissible sense, the particular thing which is supposed to possess the experiences is not thought of as a body, but as something else, say an ego.

Suppose we call the first type of possession, which is really a certain kind of causal dependence, "having₁", and the second type of possession, "having₂"; and call the individual of the first type "B" and the supposed individual of the second type "E". Then the difference is that while it is genuinely a contingent matter that *all my experiences are had₁ by B,* it appears as a necessary truth that *all my experiences are had₂ by E.* But the belief in E and in having₂ is an illusion. Only those things whose ownership is logically transferable can be owned at all. So experiences are not owned by anything except in the dubious sense of being causally dependent on the state of a particular body. This is at least a genuine relationship to a thing, in that they might have stood in it to another thing. Since the whole function of E was to own experiences in a logically non-transferable sense of "own", and since experiences are not owned by anything in this sense, for there is no such sense of "own", E must be eliminated from the picture altogether. It only came in because of a confusion.

I think it must be clear that this account of the matter, though it contains *some* of the facts, is not coherent. It is not coherent, in that one who holds it is forced to make use of that sense of possession of which he denies the existence, in presenting his case for the denial. When he tries to state the contingent fact, which he thinks gives rise to the illusion of the "ego," he has to state it in some such form as "All *my* experiences are had₁ by (uniquely dependent on the state of) body B." For any attempt to eliminate the "my", or some other expression with a similar possessive force, would yield something that was not a contingent fact at all. The proposition that *all* experiences are causally dependent on the state of a single body B, for example, is just false. The theorist means to speak of all the experiences *had by a certain person* being contingently so dependent. And the theorist cannot consistently argue that "all the experiences of person P" *means the same thing* as "all experiences contingently dependent on a certain body B"; for then his proposition would not be contingent, as his theory requires, but analytic. He must mean to be speaking of some class of experiences of the members of which it is in fact contingently true that they are all dependent on body B. And the defining characteristic of this class is in fact that they are "*my* experiences" or "the experiences *of* some person," where the sense of "possession" is the one he calls into question.

This internal incoherence is a serious matter when it is a question of denying what prima facie is the case: that is, that one does genuinely ascribe one's states of consciousness to something, viz., oneself, and that this kind of ascription is precisely such as the theorist finds unsatisfactory, i.e., is such that it does not seem to make sense to suggest, for example, that the identical pain which was in fact one's own might have been another's. We do not have to seek far in order to understand the place of this logically non-transferable kind of ownership in our general scheme of thought. For if we think of the requirements of identifying reference, in speech, to *particular* states of consciousness, or private experiences, we see that such particulars cannot be thus identifyingly referred to except as the states or experiences *of* some identified *person*. States, or experiences, one might say, *owe* their identity as particulars to the identity of the person whose states or experiences they are. And from this it follows immediately that if they can be identified as particular states or experiences at all, they must be possessed or ascribable in just that way which the no-ownership theorist ridicules, i.e., in such a way that it is logically impossible that a particular state or experience in fact possessed by someone should have been possessed by anyone else. The requirements of identity rule out logical transferability of ownership. So the theorist could maintain his position only by denying that we could ever refer to particular states or experiences at all. And *this* position is ridiculous.

We may notice, even now, a possible connection between the no-ownership doctrine and the Cartesian position. The latter is, straightforwardly enough, a dualism of two subjects (two types of subject). The former could, a little paradoxically, be called a dualism too: a dualism of one subject (the body) and one non-subject. We might surmise that the second dualism, paradoxically so called, arises out of the first dualism, nonparadoxically so called; in other words, that if we try to think of that to which one's states of consciousness are ascribed as something utterly different from that to which certain corporeal characteristics are ascribed, then indeed it becomes difficult to see why states of consciousness should be ascribed, thought of as belonging to, anything at all. And when we think of this possibility, we may also think of another: viz., that both the Cartesian and the no-ownership theorist are profoundly wrong in holding, as each must, that there are two uses of "I" in one of which it denotes something which it does not denote in the other,

III

The no-ownership theorist fails to take account of all the facts. He takes account of some of them. He implies, correctly, that the unique position or role of a single body in one's experience is not a sufficient explanation of the fact that one's experiences, or states of consciousness, are ascribed to something which *has* them, with that peculiar nontransferable kind of possession which is here in question. It may be a necessary part of the explanation, but it is not, by itself, a sufficient explanation. The theorist, as we have seen, goes on to suggest that it is perhaps a sufficient explanation of something else: viz., of our confusedly and mistakenly *thinking* that states of consciousness are to be ascribed to something in this special way. And this suggestion, as we have seen, is incoherent: for it involves the denial that someone's states of consciousness are anyone's. We avoid the incoherence of this denial, while agreeing that the special role of a single body in someone's experience does not suffice to explain why that experience should be ascribed to anybody. The fact that there is this special role does not, by itself, give a sufficient reason why what we think of as a subject of experience should have any use for the conception of himself as such a subject.

When I say that the no-ownership theorist's account fails through not reckoning with all the facts, I have in mind a very simple but, in this question, a very central, thought: viz., that it is a necessary condition of one's ascribing states of consciousness, experiences, to oneself, in the way one does, that one should also ascribe them (or be prepared to ascribe them) to others who are not oneself.[2] This means not less than it says. It means, for example, that the ascribing phrases should be used in just the same sense when the subject is another, as when the subject is oneself. Of course the thought that this is so gives no trouble to the non-philosopher: the thought, for example, that "in pain" means the same whether one says "I am in pain" or "He is in pain." The dictionaries do not give two sets of meanings for every expression which describes a state of consciousness: a first-person meaning, and a second- and third-person meaning. But to the philosopher this thought has given trouble; indeed it has. How could the sense be the same when the method of verification was so different in the two cases—or, rather, when there was a method of verification in the one case (the case of others) and not, properly speaking, in the other case (the case of oneself)? Or, again, how can it be right to talk of ascribing in the case of oneself? For surely there can be a question of ascribing only if there is or could be a question of identifying that to which the ascription is made? And though there may be a question of identifying the one who is in pain when that one is another, how can there be such a question when that one is oneself? But this last query answers itself as soon as we remember that we speak primarily to others, for the information of others. In one sense, indeed, there is no question of my having to *tell who it is* who is in pain, when I am. In another sense I may have to *tell who it is*, i.e., to let others know who it is.

What I have just said explains, perhaps, how one may properly be said to ascribe states of consciousness to oneself, given that one ascribes them to others. But how is it that one can ascribe them to others? Well, one thing is certain: that *if* the things one ascribes states of consciousness to, in ascribing them to others, are thought of as a set of Cartesian egos to which *only* private experiences can, in correct logical grammar, be ascribed, *then* this question is unanswerable and this problem insoluble. If, in identifying the things to which states of consciousness are to be ascribed, private experiences are to be all one has to go on, then, just for the very same reason as that for which there is, from one's own point of view, no question of telling that a private experience is one's own, there is also no question of telling that a private experience is another's. All private experiences, all states of consciousness, will be mine, i.e., no one's. To put it briefly: one can ascribe states of consciousness to oneself only if one can ascribe them to others; one can ascribe them to others only if one can identify other subjects of experience; one cannot identify others if one can identify them *only* as subjects of experience, possessors of states of consciousness.

It might be objected that this way with Cartesianism is too short. After all, there is no difficulty about distinguishing bodies from one another, no difficulty about identifying bodies. And does not this give us an indirect way of identifying subjects of experience, while preserving the Cartesian mode? Can we not identify such a subject as, for example, "the subject that stands to that body in the same special relation as I stand to this one"; or, in other words, "the subject of those experiences which stand in the same unique causal relation to body N as *my* experiences stand to body M"? But this suggestion is useless. It requires me to have noted that *my* experiences stand in a special relation to body M, when it is just the right to speak of *my* experiences at all that is in question. (It requires me to have noted that *my* experiences stand in a special relation to body M; but it requires me to have noted this as a condition of being able to identify other subjects of experience, i.e., as a condition of having the idea of myself as a subject of experience, i.e., as a condition of thinking of any experience as *mine*.) So long as we persist in talking, in the mode of this explanation, of experiences on the one hand, and bodies on the other, the most I may be allowed to have noted is that experiences, *all* experiences, stand in a special relation to body M, that body M is unique in just this way, that this is what makes body M unique among bodies. (This "most" is, perhaps, too much—because of the presence of the word "experiences".) The proffered explanation runs: "Another subject of experience is distinguished and identified as the subject of those experiences which stand in the same unique causal relationship to body N as *my* experiences

stand to body M." And the objection is: "But what is the word 'my' doing in this explanation? (It could not get on without it.)"

What we have to acknowledge, in order to begin to free ourselves from these difficulties, is the *primitiveness* of the concept of a person. What I mean by the concept of a person is the concept of a type of entity such that *both* predicates ascribing states of consciousness and predicates ascribing corporeal characteristics, a physical situation, etc. are equally applicable to a single individual of that single type. And what I mean by saying that this concept is primitive can be put in a number of ways. One way is to return to those two questions I asked earlier: viz., (1) why are states of consciousness ascribed to anything at all? and (2) why are they ascribed to the very same thing as certain corporeal characteristics, a certain physical situation, etc.? I remarked at the beginning that it was not to be supposed that the answers to these questions were independent of each other. And now I shall say that they are connected in this way: that a necessary condition of states of consciousness being ascribed at all is that they should be ascribed to the *very same things* as certain corporeal characteristics, a certain physical situation, etc. That is to say, states of consciousness could not be ascribed at all, *unless* they were ascribed to persons, in the sense I have claimed for this word. We are tempted to think of a person as a sort of compound of two kinds of subject—a subject of experiences (a pure consciousness, an ego), on the one hand, and a subject of corporeal attributes on the other.

Many questions arise when we think in this way. But, in particular, when we ask ourselves how we come to frame, to get a use for, the concept of this compound of two subjects, the picture—if we are honest and careful—is apt to change from the picture of two subjects to the picture of one subject and one non-subject. For it becomes impossible to see how we could come by the idea of different, distinguishable, identifiable subjects of experiences—different consciousnesses—*if this idea is thought of as logically primitive,* as a logical ingredient in the compound idea of a person, the latter being composed of two subjects. For there could never by any question of assigning an experience, as such, to any subject other than oneself; and therefore never any question of assigning it to oneself either, never any question of ascribing it to a subject at all. So the concept of the pure individual consciousness—the pure ego—is a concept that cannot exist; or, at least, cannot exist as a primary concept in terms of which the concept of a person can be explained or analyzed. It can only exist, if at all, as a secondary, non-primitive concept, which itself is to be explained, analyzed, in terms of the concept of a person. It was the entity corresponding to this illusory primary concept of the pure consciousness, the ego-substance, for which Hume was seeking, or ironically pretending to seek, when he looked into himself, and complained that he could never discover himself without a perception and could never discover anything but the perception. More seriously—and this time there was no irony, but a confusion, a Nemesis of confusion for Hume—it was this entity of which Hume vainly sought for the principle of unity, confessing himself perplexed and defeated; sought vainly because there is no principle of unity where there is no principle of differentiation. It was this, too, to which Kant, more perspicacious here than Hume, accorded a purely formal ("analytic") unity: the unity of the "I think" that accompanies all my perceptions and therefore might just as well accompany none. And finally it is this, perhaps, of which Wittgenstein spoke when he said of the subject, first, that there is no such thing, and, second, that it is not a part of the world, but its limit.

So, then, the word "I" never refers to this, the pure subject. But this does not mean, as the no-ownership theorist must think and as Wittgenstein, at least at one period, seemed to think, that "I" in some cases does not refer at all. It refers, because I am a person among others. And the predicates which would, *per impossible,* belong to the pure subject if it could be referred to, belong properly to the person to which "I" does refer.

The concept of a person is logically prior to that of an individual consciousness. The concept of a person is not to be analyzed as that of an animated body or of an embodied anima. This is not to say that the concept of a pure individual consciousness might not have a logically secondary existence, if one thinks, or finds, it desirable. We speak of a dead person—a body—and in the same secondary way we might at least think of a disembodied person, retaining the logical benefit of individuality from having been a person.[3]

IV

It is important to realize the full extent of the acknowledgment one is making in acknowledging the logical primitiveness of the concept of a person. Let me rehearse briefly the stages of the argument. There would be no question of ascribing one's own states of consciousness, or experiences, to anything, unless one also ascribed states of consciousness, or experiences, to other individual entities of the same logical type as that thing to which one ascribes one's own states of consciousness. The condition of reckoning oneself as a subject of such predicates is that one should also reckon others as subjects of such predicates. The condition, in turn, of this being possible, is that one should be able to distinguish from one another (pick out, identify) different subjects of such predicates, i.e., different individuals of the type concerned. And the condition, in turn, of this being possible is that the individuals concerned, including oneself, should be of a certain unique type: of a type, namely, such that to each individual of that type there *must* be ascribed, or ascribable, *both* states of consciousness and corporeal characteristics. But this characterization of the type is still very opaque and does not at all clearly bring out what is involved. To bring this out, I must make a rough division, into two, of the kinds of predicates properly applied to individuals of this type. The first kind of predicate consists of those which are also properly applied to material bodies to which we would not dream of applying predicates ascribing states of consciousness. I will call this first kind M-predicates: and they include things like "weighs 10 stone", "is in the drawing room", and so on. The second kind consists of all the other predicates we apply to persons. These I shall call P-predicates. And P-predicates, of course, will be very various. They will include things like "is smiling", "is going for a walk", as well as things like "is in pain", "is thinking hard", "believes in God", and so on.

So far I have said that the concept of a person is to be understood as the concept of a type of entity such that *both* predicates ascribing states of consciousness *and* predicates ascribing corporeal characteristics, a physical situation, etc. are equally applicable to an individual entity of that type. And all I have said about the meaning of saying that this concept is primitive is that it is not to be analyzed in a certain way or ways. We are not, for example, to think of it as a secondary kind of entity in relation to two primary kinds, viz., a particular consciousness and a particular human body. I implied also that the Cartesian error is just a special case of a more general error, present in a different form in theories of the no-ownership type, of thinking of the designations, or apparent designations, of persons as *not* denoting precisely the same thing, or entity, for all kinds of predicate ascribed to the entity designated. That is, if we are to avoid the general form of this error we must *not* think of "I" or "Smith" as suffering from type-ambiguity. (If we want to locate type-ambiguity somewhere, we would do better to locate it in certain predicates like "is in the drawing room", "was hit by a stone", etc., and say they mean one thing when applied to material objects and another when applied to persons.)

This is all I have so far said or implied about

the meaning of saying that the concept of a person is primitive. What has to be brought out further is what the implications of saying this are as regards the logical character of those predicates in which we ascribe states of consciousness. And for this purpose we may well consider P-predicates in general. For though not all P-predicates are what we should call "predicates ascribing states of consciousness" (for example, "going for a walk" is not), they may be said to have this in common, that they imply the possession of consciousness on the part of that to which they are ascribed.

What then are the consequences of this view as regards the character of P-predicates? I think they are these. Clearly there is no sense in talking of identifiable individuals of a special type, a type, namely, such that they possess both M-predicates and P-predicates, unless there is in principle some way of telling, with regard to any individual of that type, and any P-predicate, whether that individual possesses that P-predicate. And, in the case of at least some P-predicates, the ways of telling must constitute in some sense logically adequate kinds of criteria for the ascription of the P-predicate. For suppose in no case did these ways of telling constitute logically adequate kinds of criteria. Then we should have to think of the relation between the ways of telling and what the P-predicate ascribes (or a part of what it ascribes) always in the following way: we should have to think of the ways of telling as *signs* of the presence, in the individual concerned, of this different thing (the state of consciousness). But then we could only know that the way of telling was a sign of the presence of the different thing ascribed by the P-predicate, by the observation of correlations between the two. But this observation we could each make only in one case, namely, our own. And now we are back in the position of the defender of Cartesianism, who thought our way with it was too short. For what, now, does "our own case" mean? There is no sense in the idea of ascribing states of consciousness to oneself, or at all, unless the ascriber already knows how to ascribe at least some states of consciousness to others. So he cannot (or cannot generally) argue "from his own case" to conclusions about how to do this; for unless he already knows how to do this, he has no conception of *his own case,* or any *case* (i.e., any subject of experiences). Instead, he just has evidence that pain, etc. may be expected when a certain body is affected in certain ways and not when others are.

The conclusion here is, of course, not new. What I have said is that one ascribes P-predicates to others on the strength of observation of their behavior; and that the behavior criteria one goes on are not just signs of the presence of what is meant by the P-predicate, but are criteria of a logically adequate kind for the ascription of the P-predicate. On behalf of this conclusion, however, I am claiming that it follows from a consideration of the conditions necessary for any ascription of states of consciousness to anything. The point is not that we must accept this conclusion in order to avoid skepticism, but that we must accept it in order to explain the existence of the conceptual scheme in terms of which the skeptical problem is stated. But once the conclusion is accepted, the skeptical problem does not arise. (And so with the generality of skeptical problems: their statement involves the pretended acceptance of a conceptual scheme and at the same time the silent repudiation of one of the conditions of its existence. This is why they are, in the terms in which they are stated, insoluble.) But this is only half the picture about P-predicates.

Now let us turn to the other half. For of course it is true, at least of some important classes of P-predicates, that when one ascribes them to oneself, one does not do so on the strength of observation of those behavior criteria on the strength of which one ascribes them to others. This is not true of all P-predicates. It is not, in general, true of those which carry assessments of character and capability: these, when self-ascribed, are in general ascribed on the same kind of basis as that on which they are ascribed to others. And of those P-predicates of which it is true that one does not generally ascribe them to oneself on the basis of the criteria on the strength of which one ascribes them to others, there are many of which it is also true that their ascription is liable to correction by the self-ascriber on this basis. But there remain many cases in which one has an entirely adequate basis for ascribing a P-predicate to oneself, and yet in which this basis is quite distinct from those on which one ascribes the predicate to another. (Thus one says, reporting a present state of mind or feeling: "I feel tired, am depressed, am in pain.") How can this fact be reconciled with the doctrine that the criteria on the strength of which one ascribes P-predicates to others are criteria of a logically adequate kind for this ascription?

The apparent difficulty of bringing about this reconciliation may tempt us in many directions. It may tempt us, for example, to deny that these self-ascriptions are really ascriptions at all; to *assimilate* first-person ascriptions of states of consciousness to those other forms of behavior which constitute criteria on the basis of which one person ascribes P-predicates to another. This device seems to avoid the difficulty; it is not, in all cases, entirely inappropriate. But it obscures the facts, and is needless. It is merely a sophisticated form of failure to recognize the special character of P-predicates (or at least of a crucial class of P-predicates). For just as there is not (in general) one primary process of learning, or teaching oneself, an inner private meaning for predicates of this class, then another process of learning to apply such predicates to others on the strength of a correlation, noted in one's own case, with certain forms of behavior, so—and equally—there is not (in general) one primary process of learning to apply such predicates to others on the strength of behavior criteria, and then another process of acquiring the secondary technique of exhibiting a new form of behavior, viz., first-person P-utterances. Both these pictures are refusals to acknowledge the unique logical character of the predicates concerned.

Suppose we write 'Px' as the general form of propositional function of such a predicate. Then according to the first picture, the expression which primarily replaces "x" in this form is "I", the first-person singular pronoun; its uses with other replacements are secondary, derivative, and shaky. According to the second picture, on the other hand, the primary replacements of "x" in this form are "he", "that person", etc., and its use with "I" is secondary, peculiar, not a true ascriptive use. But it is essential to the character of these predicates that they have both first- and third-person ascriptive uses, that they are both self-ascribable otherwise than on the basis of observation of the behavior of the subject of them, and other-ascribable on the basis of behavior criteria. To learn their use is to learn both aspects of their use. In order to *have* this type of concept, one must be both a self-ascriber and an other-ascriber of such predicates, and must see every other as a self-ascriber. And in order to *understand* this type of concept, one must acknowledge that there is a kind of predicate which is unambiguously and adequately ascribable *both* on the basis of observation of the subject of the predicate *and* not on this basis (independently of observation of the subject): the second case is the case where the ascriber is also the subject. If there were no concepts answering to the characterization I have just given, we should indeed have no philosophical problem about the soul; but equally we should not have *our* concept of a person.

To put the point—with a certain unavoidable crudity—in terms of one particular concept of this class, say, that of depression, we speak of behaving in a depressed way (of depressed behavior) and also of feeling depressed (of a feeling of depression). One is inclined to argue that feelings can be felt, but not observed, and behavior can be observed, but not felt, and that therefore there must be room here to drive in a logical wedge. But the concept of depression spans the place where one

wants to drive it in. We might say, in order for there to be such a concept as that of X's depression, the depression which X has, the concept must cover both what is felt, but not observed, by X and what may be observed, but not felt, by others than X (for all values of X). But it is perhaps better to say: X's depression *is* something, one and the same thing, which is felt but not observed by X and observed but not felt by others than X. (And, of course, what can be observed can also be faked or disguised.) To refuse to accept this is to refuse to accept the structure of the language in which we talk about depression. That is, in a sense, all right. One might give up talking; or devise, perhaps, a different structure in terms of which to soliloquize. What is not all right is simultaneously to pretend to accept that structure and to refuse to accept it; i.e., to couch one's rejection in the language of that structure.

It is in this light that we must see some of the familiar philosophical difficulties in the topic of the mind. For some of them spring from just such a failure to admit, or fully appreciate, the character which I have been claiming for at least some P-predicates. It is not seen that these predicates could not have either aspect of their use (the self-ascriptive and the non-self-ascriptive) without having the other aspect. Instead, one aspect of their use is taken as self-sufficient, which it could not be, and then the other aspect appears as problematical. And so we oscillate between philosophical skepticism and philosophical behaviorism. When we take the self-ascriptive aspect of the use of some P-predicate (say, "depressed") as primary, then a logical gap seems to open between the criteria on the strength of which we say that another is depressed, and the actual state of depression. What we do not realize is that if this logical gap is allowed to open, then it swallows not only his depression, but our depression as well. For if the logical gap exists, then depressed behavior, however much there is of it, is no more than a sign of depression. And it can become a sign of depression only because of an observed correlation between it and depression. But whose depression? Only mine, one is tempted to say. But if *only* mine, then *not* mine at all. The skeptical position customarily represents the crossing of the logical gap as at best a shaky inference. But the point is that not even the syntax of the premises of the inference exists if the gap exists.

If, on the other hand, we take the other-ascriptive uses of these predicates as self-sufficient, we may come to think that all there is in the meaning of these predicates, as predicates, is the criteria on the strength of which we ascribe them to others. Does this not follow from the denial of the logical gap? It does not follow. To think that it does is to forget the self-ascriptive use of these predicates, to forget that we have to do with a class of predicates to the meaning of which it is essential that they should be both self-ascribable and other-ascribable to the same individual, when self-ascriptions are not made on the observational basis on which other-ascriptions are made, but on another basis. It is not that these predicates have two kinds of meaning. Rather, it is essential to the single kind of meaning that they do have that both ways of ascribing them should be perfectly in order.

If one is playing a game of cards, the distinctive markings of a certain card constitute a logically adequate criterion for calling it, say, the Queen of Hearts; but, in calling it this, in the context of the game, one is also ascribing to it properties over and above the possession of those markings. The predicate gets its meaning from the whole structure of the game. So it is with the language which ascribes P-predicates. To say that the criteria on the strength of which we ascribe P-predicates to others are of a logically adequate kind for this ascription is not to say that all there is to the ascriptive meaning of these predicates is these criteria. To say this is to forget that they are P-predicates, to forget the rest of the language-structure to which they belong.

V

Now our perplexities may take a different form, the form of the question "But how can one ascribe to oneself, not on the basis of observation, *the very same thing* that others may have, on the basis of observation, a logically adequate reason for ascribing to one?" And this question may be absorbed in a wider one, which might be phrased: "How are P-predicates possible?" or "How is the concept of a person possible?" This is the question by which we replace those two earlier questions, viz.: "Why are states of consciousness ascribed at all, ascribed to anything?" and "Why are they ascribed to the very same thing as certain corporeal characteristics, etc.?" For the answer to these two initial questions is to be found nowhere else but in the admission of the primitiveness of the concept of a person, and hence of the unique character of P-predicates. So residual perplexities have to frame themselves in this new way. For when we have acknowledged the primitiveness of the concept of a person and, with it, the unique character of P-predicates, we may still want to ask what it is in the natural facts that makes it intelligible that we should have this concept, and to ask this in the hope of a non-trivial answer.[4] I do not pretend to be able to satisfy this demand at all fully. But I may mention two very

different things which might count as beginnings or fragments of an answer.

And, first, I think a beginning can be made by moving a certain class of P-predicates to a central position in the picture. They are predicates, roughly, which involve doing something, which clearly imply intention or a state of mind or at least consciousness in general, and which indicate a characteristic pattern, or range of patterns, of bodily movement, while not indicating at all precisely any very definite sensation or experience. I mean such things as "going for a walk", "furling a rope", "playing ball", "writing a letter". Such predicates have the interesting characteristic of many P-predicates that one does not, in general, ascribe them to oneself on the strength of observation, whereas one does ascribe them to others on the strength of observation. But, in the case of these predicates, one feels minimal reluctance to concede that what is ascribed in these two different ways is the same. And this is because of the marked dominance of a fairly definite pattern of bodily movement in what they ascribe, and the marked absence of any distinctive experience. They release us from the idea that the only things we can know about without observation, or inference, or both, are private experiences; we can know also, without telling by either of these means, about the present and future movements of a body. Yet bodily movements are certainly also things we can know about by observation and inference.

Among the things that we observe, as opposed to the things we know without observation, are the movements of bodies similar to that about which we have knowledge not based on observation. It is important that we understand such observed movements; they bear on and condition our own. And in fact we understand them, we interpret them, only by seeing them as elements in just such plans or schemes of action as those of which we know the present course and future development without observation of the relevant present movements. But this is to say that we see such movements (the observed movements of others) as *actions,* that we interpret them in terms of intention, that we see them as movements of individuals of a type to which also belongs that individual whose present and future movements we know about without observation; that we see others, as self-ascribers, not on the basis of observations, of what we ascribe to them on this basis.

Of course these remarks are not intended to suggest how the "problem of other minds" could be solved, or our beliefs about others given a general philosophical "justification." I have already argued that such a "solution" or "justification" is impossible, that the demand for it cannot be coherently stated. Nor are these remarks intended as a priori genetic psychology. They are simply intended to help to make it seem intelligible to us, at this stage in the history of the philosophy of this subject, that we have the conceptual scheme we have. What I am suggesting is that it is easier to understand how we can see each other (and ourselves) as persons, if we think first of the fact that we act, and act on each other, and act in accordance with a common human nature. "To see each other as persons" is a lot of things; but not a lot of separate and unconnected things. The class of P-predicates that I have moved into the center of the picture are not unconnectedly there, detached from others irrelevant to them. On the contrary, they are inextricably bound up with the others, interwoven with them. The topic of the mind does not divide into unconnected subjects.

I spoke just now of a common human nature. But there is also a sense in which a condition of the existence of the conceptual scheme we have is that human nature should not be common, should not be, that is, a community nature. Philosophers used to discuss the question of whether there was, or could be, such a thing as a "group mind." And for some the idea had a peculiar fascination, while to others it seemed utterly absurd and nonsensical and at the same time, curiously enough, pernicious. It is easy to see why these last found it pernicious: they found something horrible in the thought that people should cease to have toward individual persons the kind of attitudes that they did have, and instead have attitudes in some way analogous to those toward groups; and that they might cease to decide individual courses of action for themselves and instead merely participate in corporate activities. But their finding it pernicious showed that they understood the idea they claimed to be absurd only too well. The fact that we find it natural to individuate as persons the members of a certain class of what might also be individuated as organic bodies does not mean that such a conceptual scheme is inevitable for any class of beings not utterly unlike ourselves.

Might we not construct the idea of a special kind of social world in which the concept of an individual person has no employment, whereas an analogous concept for groups does have employment? Think, to begin with, of certain aspects of actual human existence. Think, for example, of two groups of human beings engaged in some competitive but corporate activity, such as battle, for which they have been exceedingly well trained. We may even suppose that orders are superfluous, though information is passed. It is easy to imagine that, while absorbed in such activity, the members of the groups make no references to individual persons at all, have no use for personal names or pronouns. They do, however, refer to the groups and apply to them predicates analogous to those predicates ascribing purposive activity which we normally apply to individual persons. They may, *in fact*, use in such circumstances the plural forms "we" and "they"; but these are not genuine plurals, they are plurals without a singular, such as we use in sentences like these: "We have taken the citadel," "We have lost the game." They may also refer to elements in the group, to members of the group, but exclusively in terms which get their sense from the parts played by these elements in the corporate activity. (Thus we sometimes refer to what are in fact persons as "stroke" or "tackle".)

When we think of such cases, we see that we ourselves, over a part of our social lives—not, I am thankful to say, a very large part—do operate conceptual schemes in which the idea of the individual person has no place, in which its place is taken, so to speak, by that of a group. But might we not think of communities or groups such that this part of the lives of their members was the dominant part—or was the whole? It sometimes happens, with groups of human beings, that, as *we* say, their members think, feel, and act "as one." The point I wish to make is that a condition for the existence, the use, of the concept of an individual person is that this should happen *only sometimes*.

It is absolutely useless to say, at this point: But all the same, even if this happened all the time, every member of the group would have an individual consciousness, would be an individual subject of experience. The point is, once more, that there is no sense in speaking of the individual consciousness just as such, of the individual subject of experience just as such: for there is no way of identifying such pure entities.[5] It is true, of course, that in suggesting this fantasy, I have taken our concept of an individual person as a starting point. It is this fact which makes the useless reaction a natural one. But suppose, instead, I had made the following suggestion: that each part of the human body, each organ and each member, had an individual consciousness, was a separate center of experiences. This, in the same way, but more obviously, would be a useless suggestion. Then imagine all the intermediate cases, for instance these. There is a class of moving natural objects, divided into groups, each group exhibiting the same characteristic pattern of activity. Within each group there are certain differentiations of appearance accompanying differentiations of function, and in particular there is one member of each group with a distinctive appearance. Cannot one imagine different sets of observations which might lead us, in the one case, to think of the particular member as the spokesman of the group, as its mouthpiece; and in the other case to think of them as its mouth, to think of the group as a single *scattered* body? The point is that as soon as we adopt the latter way of thinking then we want to drop the former; we are no longer influenced by the human analogy in its first form, but only in its second; and we no longer want to say: "Perhaps the members have consciousness." To understand the movement of our thought here, we need only remember the startling ambiguity of the phrase "a body and its members".

VI

I shall not pursue this attempt at explanation any further. What I have been mainly arguing for is that we should acknowledge the logical primitiveness of the concept of a person and, with this, the unique logical character of certain predicates. Once this is acknowledged, certain traditional philosophical problems are seen not to be problems at all. In particular, the problem that seems to have perplexed Hume[6] does not exist—the problem of the principle of unity, of identity, of the particular consciousness, of the particular subject of "perceptions" (experiences) considered as a primary particular. There is no such problem and no such principle. If there were such a principle, then each of us would have to apply it in order to decide whether any contemporary experience of his was his or someone else's; and there is no *sense* in this suggestion. (This is not to deny, of course, that one *person* may be unsure of his own identity in some way, may be unsure, for example, whether some particular action, or series of actions, had been performed by him. Then he uses the same methods (the same in principle) to resolve the doubt about himself as anyone else uses to resolve the same doubt about him. And these methods simply involve the application of the ordinary criteria for *personal* identity. There remains the question of what exactly these criteria are, what their relative weights are, etc.; but, once disentangled from spurious questions, this is one of the easier problems in philosophy.)

Where Hume erred, or seems to have erred, both Kant and Wittgenstein had the better insight. Perhaps neither always expressed it in the happiest way. For Kant's doctrine that the "analytic unity of consciousness" neither requires nor entails any principle of unity is not as clear as one could wish.

And Wittgenstein's remarks (at one time) to the effect that the data of consciousness are not owned, that "I" as used by Jones, in speaking of his own feelings, etc., does not refer to what "Jones" as used by another refers to, seem needlessly to flout the conceptual scheme we actually employ. It is needlessly paradoxical to deny, or seem to deny, that when Smith says "Jones has a pain" and Jones says "I have a pain," they are talking about the same entity and saying the same thing about it, needlessly paradoxical to deny that Jones can *confirm* that he has a pain. Instead of denying that self-ascribed states of consciousness are really ascribed at all, it is more in harmony with our actual ways of talking to say: For each user of the language, there is just one person in ascribing to whom states of consciousness he does not need to use the criteria of the observed behavior of that person (though he does not necessarily not do so); and that person is himself. This remark at least respects the structure of the conceptual scheme we employ, without precluding further examination of it.

NOTES

1. The evidence that Wittgenstein at one time held such a view is to be found in the third of Moore's articles in *Mind* on "Wittgenstein's Lectures in 1930–33" (*Mind,* 1955, especially pp. 13–14). He is reported to have held that the use of "I" was utterly different in the case of "I have a tooth-ache" or "I see a red patch" from its use in the case of "I've got a bad tooth" or "I've got a matchbox." He thought that there were two uses of "I" and that in one of them "I" was replaceable by "this body". So far the view might be Cartesian. But he also said that in the other use (the use exemplified by "I have a tooth-ache" as opposed to "I have a bad tooth"), the "I" *does not denote a possessor,* and that no ego is involved in thinking or in having tooth-ache; and referred with apparent approval to Lichtenberg's dictum that, instead of saying "I think," we (or Descartes!) ought to say "There is a thought," (i.e., "Es denkt").

The attribution of such a view to Schlick would have to rest on his article "Meaning and Verification," Pt. V (*Readings in Philosophical Analysis,* H. Feigl and W. Sellars, eds.). Like Wittgenstein, Schlick quotes Lichtenberg, and then goes on to say: "Thus we see that unless we choose to call our body the owner or bearer of the data [the data of immediate experience]—which seems to be a rather misleading expression—we have to say that the data have no owner or bearer." The full import of Schlick's article is, however, obscure to me, and it is quite likely that a false impression is given by the quotation of a single sentence. I shall say merely that I have drawn on Schlick's article in constructing the case of my hypothetical "no-subject" theorist; but shall not claim to be representing his views.

Lichtenberg's anti-Cartesian dictum is, as the subsequent argument will show, one that I endorse, if properly used. But it seems to have been repeated, without being understood, by many of Descartes' critics.

The evidence that Wittgenstein and Schlick ever held a "no-subject" view seems indecisive, since it is possible that the relevant remarks are intended as criticisms of a Cartesian view rather than as expositions of the true view.

2. I can imagine an objection to the unqualified form of this statement, an objection which might be put as follows. Surely the idea of a uniquely applicable predicate (a predicate which *in fact* belongs to only one individual) is not absurd. And, if it is not, then surely the most that can be claimed is that a necessary condition of one's ascribing predicates of a certain class to one individual (oneself) is that one should be prepared, or ready, on appropriate occasions, to ascribe them to other individuals, and hence that one should have a conception of what those appropriate occasions for ascribing them would be; but not, necessarily, that one should actually do so on any occasion.

The shortest way with the objection is to admit it, or at least to refrain from disputing it; for the lesser claim is all that the argument strictly requires, though it is slightly simpler to conduct it on the basis of the larger claim. But it is well to point out further that we are not speaking of a single predicate, or merely of some group or other of predicates, but of the whole of an enormous class of predicates such that the applicability of those predicates or their negations determines a major logical type or category of individuals. To insist, at this level, on the distinction between the lesser and the larger claims is to carry the distinction over from a level at which it is clearly correct to a level at which it may well appear idle or, possibly, senseless.

The main point here is a purely logical one: the idea of a predicate is correlative with that of a range of distinguishable individuals of which the predicate can be significantly, though not necessarily truly, affirmed.

3. A little further thought will show how limited this concession is. But I shall not discuss the question now.

4. A mean, in the hope of an answer which does not merely say: Well, there are people in the world.

5. More accurately: their identification is necessarily secondary to the identification of persons.

6. Cf. the Appendix to the *Treatise of Human Nature.*

B. Privileged Access

12

Sydney Shoemaker

from "How Is Self-Knowledge Possible?"

1. Underlying the theories about persons and personal identity that I have been criticizing is the idea that the criteria for the truth of statements about persons, and therefore the criteria that reveal the nature of persons and personal identity, must be criteria that we use in making these statements in the first person. If there are criteria for the truth of these statements, according to this idea, it must be directly on the basis of these criteria, i.e., because we have observed that they are satisfied, that we make the statements in the first person, and it must be because we are in a position to observe that the criteria are satisfied that we are entitled to make them or justified in making them. In at least some cases, it is supposed, the fact in which the truth of a psychological statement about a person consists must be one that the person making the statement can directly observe to hold. For statements like "I see an image" and "I have a toothache" are not inferred from anything (not even from "criterial evidence"), yet these statements are made with certainty and it seems unquestionable that we are justified in making them. Here, it seems, the fact in which the truth of the statement consists must be its *own* criterion, and must be observable by the person (and only the person) the statement is about.[1] In the case of first-person memory statements there is less inclination to say that one can literally observe the fact in which the truth of the statement consists. For such statements imply the persistence of a person (the speaker) through time, and there is, as we have seen, a tendency to think that no statement implying the persistence or continuance of something can be either an observation report or a memory report.[2] Such statements, one is inclined to say,

can only be known inferentially. Yet, just because they do imply the persistence of a person through time, it seems that such statements cannot be true unless criteria of identity are satisfied. But when one makes such statements about oneself one seems to know their truth in the most direct way possible; it certainly does not seem that in making a first-person memory statement one is drawing an inductive inference (e.g., is inferring that bodily criteria of identity are satisfied). So it seems that one must, in making them, have direct access to (must observe or remember observing) facts that are criterial evidence for their truth.

It is not difficult to see how this idea underlies the demand that the subject of awareness, if there is one, be an object of awareness, the denial that the persistence of a self implies the persistence of a subject, and the view that psychological facts about a person must be "analyzable" into facts that are directly observable by that person himself. But it also underlies the view that psychological facts are logically independent of bodily and behavioral facts, and that personal identity is logically distinct from bodily identity. For whatever one has to observe in order to be entitled to make present-tense psychological statements about oneself, one does not have to observe facts about one's body or behavior.[3] And whatever one has to observe in order to be entitled to make a past-tense statement about oneself on the basis of memory, one does not have to observe facts that are evidence for the truth of statements about the identity of one's body. But if there are facts that one must observe in order to make such statements, and if these facts are the criteria for the truth of the statements, then the criteria are not physical (bodily and behavioral) criteria. And if this is so, the relationships between physical and psychological facts, and between bodily identity and personal identity, can only be contingent relationships.

In my arguments in the last three chapters I have been attacking, for the most part indirectly, the idea expressed above, i.e., the idea that the criteria for the truth of first-person psychological statements must be criteria that we use in making first-person psychological statements. I now want to attack what seems to me the main source of this idea. One wants to say that we *know* such statements to be true when we assert them, or at least that we often or generally know them to be true; that we are *justified* in asserting them, or *entitled* to assert them; and that this can be explained only on the supposition that we make such statements because we observe, or know directly, that the criteria for their truth are satisfied—for it is clear that we do not make such statements on the basis of indirect inductive evidence. That we normally make such statements, believing them to be true, when in fact they *are* true seems inexplicable unless we make this supposition. When I say I am having a certain experience, I generally *am* having that experience, so apparently there must be something that *tells* me that I am entitled to say that I have it. And what tells me that I am entitled to make a first-person psychological statement cannot be a mere inductive indicator of the truth of the statement, for such statements are not inferred. Since we do not make first-person psychological statements on the basis of bodily and behavioral facts, and do not make first-person memory statements on the basis of criteria of bodily identity, it would seem that either we are not justified in making such statements at all, which seems absurd, or else that the criteria for the truth of such statements must consist in nonphysical facts.

Against the view just described I shall argue that our ability to know first-person psychological statements to be true, or the fact that we make them (for the most part) only when they are true, cannot possibly be explained on the supposition that we make them on the basis of criteria. A qualification must be made here. My contention is not that we never use criteria in making first-person psychological statements, but is rather that the criteria we do use (when we use any) are not criteria for saying that something is true of ourselves. Often a first-person statement contains or entails a statement that is not itself about the speaker. For example, the perceptual statement "I see that there is a eucalyptus tree on the hill" contains or entails the statement "There is a eucalyptus tree on the hill," and the memory statement "I remember that

there was a hurricane here last October" contains or entails the statement "There was a hurricane here last October." Now such statements may well be based on criteria, for instance (in the examples given), on the criteria for something's being a eucalyptus tree, or the criteria for something's being a hurricane. In such cases I shall say that the first-person statement is based on the criteria for the truth of a "nonpersonal component" of it. What I wish to attack is the view that a first-person statement, if known to be true or asserted with justification, must be based on the criteria for the truth of the *whole* statement, and not simply on the criteria for the truth of its nonpersonal components. It is the view that, for example, my statement "I see a eucalyptus tree on the hill" must be based on the criteria for its being true of *me* that *I see* a eucalyptus tree on the hill, and not simply on the criteria for its being true that there is a eucalyptus tree on the hill.

2. What I am here calling first-person psychological statements can be divided into two groups, those that are "corrigible" and those that are "incorrigible." Among the corrigible statements are perceptual statements of the ordinary sort—i.e., statements in which the reported object of perception is a material object or a publicly observable state of affairs—and memory statements. It is characteristic of these that a person can make such a statement sincerely, i.e., believing it to be true, when in fact the statement is false and could in principle be discovered to be false by other persons. Among the incorrigible statements are statements about "private" experiences and mental events, e.g., pain statements, statements about mental images, reports of thoughts, and so on. These are incorrigible in the sense that if a person sincerely asserts such a statement it does not make sense to suppose, and nothing could be accepted as showing, that he is mistaken, i.e., that what he says is false. While sincere first-person statements of the first sort can be discovered to be false by reference to the criteria for the truth of the statements, this is not so of statements of the second sort. That a statement of the second sort is a sincere assertion is itself a logically sufficient condition of its being true, and that such a statement has been asserted with apparent sincerity is itself criterial evidence that it is true. But our other criteria (our "nonverbal criteria") can show, or indicate, that such a statement is false and therefore not a sincere assertion (e.g., if someone says "No, it doesn't hurt a bit," but is biting his lip and grimacing); and they can show that a person does not understand the meanings of the words he is uttering, and that what sounds like an incorrigible psychological statement

is not really one (if, for example, a person characteristically utters the words "I am in pain" when anyone observing him would conclude from his behavior that he is exceptionally contented, and refuses to utter them when exhibiting what others would take to be manifestations of pain).

I suggested in Chapter Three that it is characteristic of a certain kind of statements, what I there called "first-person experience statements," that being entitled to assert such a statement does not consist in having established that the statement is true, i.e., in having good evidence that it is true or having observed that it is true, but consists *simply* in the statement's *being* true.[4] This can be said of both kinds of statements distinguished above. Corrigible first-person statements commonly have nonpersonal components, and if it is asked how a person is justified in asserting a nonpersonal component of such a statement the answer may be that he has established, that he observes or remembers observing, that the criteria for the truth of the component statement are satisfied. But if someone asks how a person is justified in saying, or what entitles him to say, that he perceives or remembers something, and is not asking how the person knows the truth of a nonpersonal component of his perceptual or memory statement, we can answer only that the person does perceive what he claims to perceive, or does remember what he claims to remember. *We* establish whether the person is justified in making such a statement by establishing whether the statement as a whole is true (i.e., if "*P*" is a nonpersonal component of his statement, whether he perceives, or remembers, that *P*, and not simply whether it is the case that *P*), and to establish this we must have bodily and behavioral criteria for the truth of the whole statement. But the person himself does not establish this at all; he establishes, perhaps, that the nonpersonal components of his statement are true, but he does not establish, and does not have to establish, that it is by observation, or by memory, that he knows them to be true. Likewise, turning to incorrigible statements, if anything can be said to justify a person in saying on a particular occasion that he is in pain, it is simply his being in pain, not his having evidence of this or his observing it to be so, that justifies him.

I think that there is a strong philosophical inclination to say that one cannot be justified in saying something in the way in which I have said that we are justified in making first-person psychological statements. One feels that if one simply utters certain statements when in fact they are true, but without having established that they are true, then it can only be an accident, a coincidence, that the

statements are true when one asserts them, and that one cannot be said to *know* their truth. There is perhaps a sense of "justified" in which a person can be said to be justified in making a statement only if he has observed or has good evidence that the statement is true. If the word "justified" is used in this sense then, on my view, we cannot be said to be justified in making first-person psychological statements (which is not to say that we are unjustified in making them[5]), though we can sometimes be justified in asserting the nonpersonal components of such statements. But there is a tendency to think that unless we are justified in this sense in making such statements, and make them because we observe the criteria for their truth to be satisfied, we cannot be in any sense entitled to make them. And what this mainly comes to, I think, is the idea that it is only by supposing that we are justified in this way in making such statements that it can be explained how it is that we commonly make them when they are true and seldom make them when they are false.

We must now consider the fact that is supposed to be explained by the supposition that we have criteria on the basis of which we make first-person psychological statements, namely, the fact that these statements, or the beliefs expressed in them, are generally true. We shall see, first in the case of the incorrigible statements and then in the case of the corrigible ones, that this fact cannot possibly be explained in this way. But we must also consider what sort of explanation can be given of this fact; we must consider how it is that the making of a first-person psychological statement, unlike the making of other empirical statements, can be justified simply by the fact that the statement is true (instead of by the fact that the speaker observes or has evidence that it is true), or, using the term "justified" in a narrower sense, how it is that such statements can be made without justification and nevertheless be generally true.

3. Concerning first-person statements of the kind that I have called "incorrigible," e.g., pain reports, we can say, not simply that such statements are *generally* true when asserted, but that they are *always* true when sincerely asserted. It is just the mark of an incorrigible statement that its being honestly asserted is a logically sufficient condition of its being true. Once we are clear about this, however, we should no longer be inclined to conclude from the "fact" that such statements are generally true that there is something, our observing that criteria of some kind are satisfied, that justifies us in asserting them. There is no difference between believing that one is in pain and being in pain, so

there can be no question of explaining how it "happens" that one believes that one is in pain only when in fact one is in pain.

But this matter needs to be pursued further, for there is a strong philosophical inclination to say the following: "I of course make no inference when I say 'I am in pain.' There would be an inference only if the fact with which I am acquainted when I say this, the fact on the basis of which I say it, were some fact other than the fact that I am in pain. But when I say 'I am in pain,' what I am acquainted with, or directly aware of, is just the pain itself, or just the fact of my being in pain. It is this direct awareness that justifies me in saying 'I am in pain.' If by 'criterion for saying that I am in pain' is meant something from which it can be inferred that I am in pain, then of course I use no criterion. But if by this is meant something that shows that I am in pain, then I do have a criterion; the pain, or the fact of my being in pain, is itself the criterion, for it shows me that I am in pain. It is just by being aware of the pain that I know I am in pain. And no one else can be shown that I am in pain in this way, for no one else can be directly aware of my pain in the way in which I can. My criterion, therefore, is a private one."

These remarks rest on a mistake. The mistake lies in the view that I know I am in pain *by* being "acquainted with" or "aware of" some entity or fact. This view is not so much false as senseless. We *seem* to explain my ability to know (or correctly assert) that I am in pain by saying that I have direct awareness of my pains, but we do not really do so. The illusion that we have an explanation here derives from the fact that our so-called awareness or consciousness of mental objects is regarded, illicitly, as a kind of perception or observation,[6] and from the fact that when words like "see," "perceive," and "observe" are used in their literal senses it is explanatory (sometimes) to say that one knows something to be the case *because* one sees, perceives, or observes it to be the case, or because one sees, perceives, or observes a certain entity. But if we consider how it is that statements like "I know there is a tree on the hill because I see one there" can be informative and explanatory, it becomes clear that the statement "I know I am in pain because I am aware of a pain" cannot be informative or explanatory in anything like the same way.

In the ordinary sense of "observe," what one knows to be the case because one observes it to be the case must be such that it would be possible for one to know it in other ways, i.e., on the basis of something other than direct observation; it must be something that one could believe to be the case even if one were not observing it to be the case; and it must be something that could be the case even if one were not observing it to be the case. In general, the question "How do you know that *P*?" and the expression "I know that *P* because . . ." have application only if there is more than one way in which one could know that *P*. If I say "I know that *P* because I observe that *P* (or because I observe X, of which '*P*' is a description)" I am, in effect, identifying one of the possible ways of knowing that *P* as the way in which I do in fact know it. An explanation of how one knows something, moreover, is always an attempt to justify one's knowledge claim. When I say "I know that *P* because . . . ," I do not present my knowledge that *P* as an accepted fact for which I am offering something like a causal explanation; I am trying to show *how* (not *why*) I know that *P*, and this involves trying to show *that* I know it (as opposed to merely believing it). The truth of my knowledge claim is something I am trying to show, not something I am taking for granted. Now, what sort of justification is one offering when one says "I know that *P* because I observe that *P*"? One is not citing one's knowledge of facts that are evidence that *P*. Rather, one is indicating that one is in a position to know that *P* without evidence. In so doing one indicates to others the appropriate way of appraising the validity of one's knowledge claim; one indicates that one's claim to know is not based, as it might have been, on knowledge of facts that are evidence that *P*, and hence that checking up on the validity of one's claim will consist, not in evaluating the evidence one offers in support of it (for one offers no evidence), but in determining whether one is in fact in a position to know the thing in question without evidence, i.e., whether one is in a position to observe that it is the case.

Being in a position to know that *P* without evidence is not simply believing that *P* without evidence when *P* is in fact the case. The fact that knowing something on the basis of observation involves being in a "position" to know it without evidence is closely related to the fact, emphasized in Chapter Five, that perception is always from a "point of view." Roughly speaking, to say that there is such a thing as knowing facts about an object *Y* without evidence is to say that there is a contingent relationship *R* such that for any normal person *X*, if we know that *X* stands in *R* to *Y* we are normally justified in concluding, on the basis of this knowledge, that *X* has true beliefs of a certain kind about *Y*. An example of the relationship *R* would be the relationship that holds between a person and an object when, in normal lighting conditions, there is no opaque object standing between the person and the object and the person is within a certain distance of the object and has his eyes open and turned in its direction. If we know that a person is so related to an object we can normally conclude that he has true beliefs concerning the visual properties of the object (its color, shape, and so on). By expanding on this account we can explain what it means to say that a person is in a position to know without evidence what is happening in a certain locality, in a position to know how one object is related spatially to another, and so on. In general, being in a position to know something without evidence can be said to consist in having a property, normally a relational property (standing in R to something), that one might not have had. Given that we know of the existence of such properties, there is an obvious sense in which we explain someone's ability to make true statements of a certain kind by saying that he has a property of the appropriate sort, for we know that *any* normal person who had that property would have that ability. There is an equally obvious sense in which the having of such a property can justify a person in making a statement, for it gives the statement, if it is of an appropriate kind, a high likelihood of being true. But such explanations and justifications can be given only where it is possible in principle to establish empirically whether a person does have the appropriate property, i.e., is in the appropriate position. For in giving such a justification for a statement of one's own one is not simply claiming that one's statement is justified, but is trying to show that it is, so it must be possible for others to see that it is (or that it is not). And we can find that a person is, or is not, in a position to know something without evidence; we can determine, for example, whether a person's eyes are open and directed toward a certain object, whether his fingers are touching a given thing, and so on.

It should now be evident that there is no such thing as being in a position to know without evidence (in the sense just explained) that one is in pain, and that "being aware of a pain" is not being in such a position. If being aware of a pain were observing a pain, and therefore involved being in such a position, it would have to be the case that it can be an open question, to be settled empirically, whether a person who is in pain and thinks that he is in pain is in fact aware of a pain; that it is possible for a person to be in pain without being aware of a pain; and that being aware of a pain is one of several possible ways of knowing that one is in pain. But none of these things is the case. More generally, if anything at all is to count as observing a pain (or observing that one is in pain), and therefore as being in a position to know with-

out evidence that one is in pain, it must be possible for it to be an open question, to be settled empirically, whether a person who is in pain and thinks that he is in pain is entitled to say without evidence that he is in pain, and it must be possible for a person to think that he is in pain without being entitled to say without evidence that he is in pain. And neither of these things is the case. We can say "It was raining, but Jones was not in a position to say that it was, for he had no evidence and was not in a position to observe that it was raining," but it would be absurd to say "Jones had a headache, but he was not entitled to say that he did, for he had no evidence and was not in a position to be aware (or to know without evidence) that he had a headache." Just because there is no such thing as my knowing *from* evidence that I am in pain there can be no such thing as my being in a special position to know *without* evidence that I am in pain. One can say "I know that Jones has a mustache now, but I've not seen it (Smith told me about it)," but it would be absurd to say "I know that I have a pain, but I am not aware of any pain (Smith tells me that I have one, and his information is usually reliable)." It is nonsense to speak of my knowing on inductive grounds, or on the basis of the testimony of others, that I am in pain. So if "I am aware of a pain (or that I have a pain)" were an answer to the question "How do you know that you have a pain?" it would be the *only possible* answer to that question. But if the question has only one possible answer, which must always be correct, it is at best a pointless question. And of course it is not a question that people (other than philosophers) ever raise. But it is not simply that we do not raise this question because we know in advance what the answer must be. There is no logical possibility of my being unjustified in thinking that I am in pain, so it is senseless to suppose that there is something other than (logically independent of) my thinking this that justifies me, and senseless (and not merely pointless) to ask what this justification is.

It may be objected that there is obviously such a thing as being in a special position to know that a certain person is in pain, namely, being that person. Certainly the following dialogue might occur. A: "Is the new patient still in pain?" B: "Yes he is." A: "How do you know?" B: "I am the new patient." But would this be a case of a person justifying his claim to know that he is in pain by saying, or indicating, that he is in a position to know this without evidence? What B is explaining is not his knowledge that he is in pain but rather his knowledge that the new patient is in pain. And he could be mistaken in claiming to know the latter (for he could be mistaken in thinking that he is the new patient), which he could not be in claiming to know the former. It makes sense to say that B might not have been the new patient, whereas it does not make sense to say that B might not have been himself, so the "fact" that B is himself provides no explanation of his knowledge that he is in pain. An explanation of how one knows something must assert that something that might not have been the case is in fact the case. If we explain someone's knowledge that P in terms of his having evidence that P, we explain it by saying that he has knowledge (of the evidence) that he might not have had. If we explain his knowledge by saying he observed that P we are saying he is (or was) in a position that he might not have been in. But where P is the statement "I am in pain," or any other incorrigible first-person statement, no such explanation can be given and none can sensibly be demanded.

4. Since sincere perceptual and memory statements, unlike sincere pain statements, can be false, it seems legitimate to ask how it happens that such statements are generally true. It is prima facie plausible to suppose that such statements are usually true because they are made on the basis of the criteria for their truth, and this of course implies that the criteria are nonphysical. I have already argued, in Chapter Three, that it is absurd to suppose that a person says he perceives something because he perceives himself perceiving it, or because he perceives some fact that is evidence that he perceives it, and in Chapter Four, that it is absurd to suppose that first-person memory statements are made on the basis of criteria of personal identity. From this it seems to me to follow that first-person perceptual and memory statements are *not* based on the criteria for their truth. Those arguments aside, however, what I shall now try to show is that it follows from the corrigibility of first-person perceptual and memory statements that the supposition that such statements are based on the criteria for their truth does not explain, but on the contrary makes utterly mysterious, the fact that such statements are generally true when sincerely asserted.

What distinguishes corrigible first-person psychological statements from incorrigible ones is just that sincere corrigible statements can be false and can in principle be discovered to be false by persons other than the speaker. If this were not true of first-person perceptual and memory statements, then these would be incorrigible rather than corrigible, and the argument of the preceding section would apply to them. There would in that case be no difference between perceiving something and merely seeming (to oneself) to perceive it, and no

difference between remembering something and merely seeming (to oneself) to remember it—just as in fact there is no difference between being in pain and merely seeming (to oneself) to be in pain.[7] And in that case, paradoxically, perceptual statements could not in any sense be said to be based on observation; if it were impossible for sincere perceptual statements to be false, it would be impossible for the "nonpersonal components" of such statements to be false, and there would be no such thing as being in a position to know a nonpersonal component of such a statement to be true. Certainly there could then be no question of explaining, either by the supposition that such statements are based on the criteria for their truth or in some other way, how it "happens" that such statements are generally true when sincerely asserted. But I think that it will be universally agreed that such statements are corrigible rather than incorrigible. So let us see what follows from this.

If first-person perceptual and memory statements are corrigible, then, as I have said, it must be possible for a sincere statement of this sort to be discovered to be false by persons other than the speaker. How is it that such statements would be discovered to be false? If a person says "I see a tree," we will know that his statement is false if we know that his eyes are not open and directed toward a tree. If a person says "I played tennis yesterday," we will know that his statement is false if we know that the body which utters this statement was not involved in a game of tennis on the previous day. If there were not bodily facts of this sort that would show such statements to be false, no sense could be given to the assertion that such statements can be false when sincerely asserted, and such statements would be incorrigible rather than corrigible. But what, given that such statements can be shown to be false in this way, is the cash value of saying that in fact such statements are generally true when sincerely asserted? Surely it is this, that in general such a statement is sincerely asserted when the facts about the speaker's body are not such that if others know these facts they would have to conclude that the statement is false. That is, it is generally the case that when a person claims to see an object of a certain kind his eyes are open and directed toward an object of that kind, and it is generally the case that when a person claims to remember a past event of a certain description he is identical, in accordance with physical criteria of identity, with someone who witnessed an event of that description in the past. This is not to say that the fact that a person's eyes are open and directed toward an object is sufficient to make it true that he sees that object, or that a fact of bodily identity can be sufficient to make it true that a certain person remembers a particular past event. But if a person's eyes are open and directed toward a certain object, and if *in addition* he sincerely claims to see that object, or an object of that kind, then there can be no doubt that he does see that object. Likewise, if a person was (is identical with in accordance with physical criteria of identity) a witness to a past event, and if *in addition* he sincerely claims to remember that event, or an event whose description is uniquely satisfied by that event, then there can be no doubt that he does remember that event.[8]

If this is correct, it follows from the corrigibility of first-person perceptual and memory statements that the fact that such statements are generally true when sincerely asserted consists in the fact that in general such statements are sincerely asserted (or believed) only when certain things are true of the body of the speaker. But how could *this* fact be explained by the supposition that such statements are asserted on the basis of the criteria for their truth? It might be explained in this way if it were true (1) that the bodily facts in question are (or are among) the criteria for the truth of the statements, and (2) that the statements are made on the basis of these bodily facts, i.e., because the speaker observes, or has established, that these facts hold. But (2) is clearly not the case, as everyone acknowledges. To suppose that the criteria for the truth of these first-person statements consist of facts that are logically independent of bodily facts, and that these statements are made on the basis of these nonphysical criteria, is to leave totally unexplained the fact that these statements are generally made only when certain bodily facts hold. This supposition therefore leaves totally unexplained the fact that sincere statements of this sort are generally true.

* * * * *

6. One reason why it is plausible to think it is a contingent fact, not a necessary one, that sincere and confident perceptual and memory statements are generally true is that there is a contingent fact, or a class of contingent facts, that is easily confused with it. It seems clear that it is only contingently true of me that I generally utter the words "I see a tree," in a confident and assertive manner, only when my eyes are open and directed toward a tree. And of any person it can only be contingently true, if it is true at all, that he generally utters that sentence under those conditions. Likewise, of any given person it can only be contingently true, if it is true at all, that after having eggs for breakfast he will respond to certain questions by uttering the sentence "I remember having eggs for breakfast

this morning," and that in general he utters this sentence, confidently and assertively, only when he has had eggs for breakfast. Much more generally, it is true, but is only contingently true, that sentences which in fact express perceptual and memory statements are most commonly uttered, confidently and assertively, in circumstances in which the statements expressed by them would be true.

It is not easy to state this contingent fact (or contingent facts of this kind) in a way that clearly distinguishes it (or them) from the necessary truth discussed in the preceding section, and the formulation above is not altogether satisfactory. To speak of a *person* is already to speak of a being that can be presumed to have the capability of remembering and perceiving, and to speak of a *sentence* is already to speak of something having an established meaning. Because of this, it is not altogether clear that even the facts stated above are purely contingent; it is not clear that an aboriginal in Borneo who happens to have uttered a set of sounds just like those I utter when I say "I see a tree" can be said to have uttered the *sentence* "I see a tree," and it is not clear that it makes sense to suppose that people might commonly utter that *sentence* in a confident and assertive manner without asserting the *statement* "I see a tree," i.e., without the speaker's saying that he sees a tree. But the contingent fact that I am interested in is about the making of certain sounds and gestures, not about the asserting of certain sentences. In the preceding paragraph I should have spoken, not of the *sentence* "I see a tree," but of the *sounds* "I see a tree," meaning by this the characteristic pattern of sounds made by English-speaking people when they utter the sentence "I see a tree." And it is better not to describe this as a fact about *persons.* I shall therefore state it as a fact about *human beings,* using the term "human being," in a technical sense, to mean "something that looks like, and has the physical characteristics (anatomical structure, chemical composition, and so forth) of a person." What might be regarded as essential attributes of persons, e.g., being able to remember some of their past actions, being capable of learning the use of language, and so forth, I shall regard as only contingent properties of human beings. My distinction between persons and human beings is similar to Locke's distinction between a person and a man. On Locke's use of the term "man," the identity of a man, as distinguished (possibly) from the identity of a person, is simply the identity of a human body. And I shall use the term "human being" in such a way that the identity of a human being is just the identity of a human body, something about which we can judge in exactly the way in which we judge concerning the identity of any material object.

I can now bring out more clearly the nature of the contingent truths stated above and their relation to the necessary truth that sincere and confident perceptual and memory statements are generally true. It is a *necessary* truth that *if* a group of human beings are persons, and do make perceptual and memory statements, there will exist correlations of a certain kind in their behavior—correlations between the uttering of certain sounds (or the making of certain gestures) and its being the case that the speaker's eyes are open and directed toward an object of a certain kind, and correlations between the uttering of certain other sounds (or the making of certain other gestures) and certain things having happened to the speaker in the past. But that such correlations do exist in the behavior of any group of human beings will be a *contingent* fact. If we should come across such a group of human beings for the first time, it would be just the existence of such contingent correlations that would show us that they do make perceptual and memory statements, and it would be this, among other things, that would show us that they are in fact persons. And of course there could be a group of human beings in whose behavior no such correlations could be found; such a group of human beings could not be said to speak a language in which perceptual and memory statements are made, even if they commonly uttered the sounds by which such statements are expressed in languages like English and Russian. It is just because the sounds "see" and "remember" are uttered by certain human beings (English-speaking people) in the circumstances in which they are uttered, i.e., because certain contingent generalizations are true of them, that they express the meanings they do.[12] If a group of human beings could not be taught, or trained, to utter some sounds (or to make some gestures) in such a way that correlations of the kind I have described would come to exist in their behavior, they could not be said to perceive or remember at all in the sense in which persons do, and could hardly be said to be persons at all.

Two points of importance can now be made. First, the necessary truth that perceptual and memory statements are generally true is best expressed in the conditional statement: "If perceptual and memory statements are made at all, most sincere and confident perceptual and memory statements are true." This conditional statement, because it is a conditional statement, does not describe anything that happens, and therefore does not report any happening or set of happenings for which an explanation can be demanded. On the other hand, the existence of contingent correlations of the sort discussed above *is* something for which an explanation can be demanded. But the explanation of the fact that these correlations exist is hardly to be found in any epistemological theory, e.g., in the supposition that first-person perceptual and memory statements are made on the basis of grounds or criteria. Strictly speaking, the fact to be explained is not the fact that statements of a certain kind are true, and is not a fact about the making of statements at all; what is to be explained is an empirical phenomenon, the fact that certain correlations exist in the behavior of human beings, and it is to the natural sciences (perhaps to physiology), not to epistemology, that we must turn if we want an explanation of it.

7. "What we have to mention in order to explain the significance, I mean the importance, of a concept, are often extremely general facts of nature: such facts as are hardly ever mentioned because of their extreme generality."[13] This remark of Wittgenstein's can be applied to the problems I have been discussing.

One general fact of nature, which is clearly of the kind Wittgenstein had in mind, is that different human beings respond in the same ways to the same training in the use of language. It is just a fact of nature that the gestures used in the teaching of linguistic expressions elicit similar responses in different human beings; for example, human beings react in a fairly uniform way to the gesture of pointing, and unless there were *some* gesture, the gesture of pointing or some other one, to which human beings *naturally* respond in a uniform way, i.e., without being trained to do so, the gesture of pointing could not play the role it does in ostensive teaching, and no other gesture could play that role. And as the result of being given a certain training different human beings will make similar linguistic responses in similar situations; i.e., if one human being utters certain sounds in one kind of situation and not in others, the same will generally be true of other human beings who have received the same training in the uttering of those sounds. If this were not so of at least some human beings, language would be impossible, and no sound could be said to express a meaning. What defines the *correct* response to the training in the use of a word (e.g., an ostensive definition together with the training which prepares human beings for being given ostensive definitions), and what also defines what is to count as the correct use of the word, is the *typical* response of those to whom the training is given. If the typical response of human beings to the ostensive teaching of the word "red" were different, both the correct response and the meaning of that word (or sound) would be different. And if there were no typical response at all, i.e., if every human being responded to the "training" in a different way, and it were impossible by further training to get human beings to respond in a uniform way, the sound "red" would not express a meaningful word at all, and the "training," i.e., the making of certain gestures and saying "Red!" would not be training.

Another general fact of nature, and a special case of the one described above, is that the uniform effect of a certain kind of training is a tendency, on the part of the human beings so trained, to utter certain sounds while exhibiting the behavioral manifestations of pain and not to utter them while exhibiting the behavioral manifestations of well-being and contentedness. Following a remark of Wittgenstein's, we might express this by saying that human beings can be taught "new pain-behavior."[14] If this were not so there could be no pain-*language,* e.g., there could be no word meaning what we mean by "pain."

Still another general fact of nature is that human beings are capable of being so trained in the use of language, or in the making of sounds and gestures, that as the result of their being given a certain training there will exist in their behavior correlations of the sort discussed in the preceding section, correlations that make it possible for the uttering of certain sounds by members of a group of human beings to be regarded as the making of first-person perceptual and memory statements. If human beings did not have this capacity, the concepts of perception and memory would not apply to them, except in the way in which they apply to nonhuman animals. The point here is not simply that if human beings did not have this capacity they would not generally make *true* perceptual and memory statements, though this is of course the case. It is rather that if they did not have this capacity they would not make perceptual and memory statements at all, could not be taught to make them, and could not be said to have beliefs that are expressible in such statements.

What human beings are capable of being trained to do is to utter certain expressions, or to make certain sounds, when, or only when, certain conditions are satisfied. The test of whether a human being has been so trained (e.g., has been trained to utter the sounds "I see" in the circumstances in which it would be correct for him to use the English *words* "I see") is simply whether he utters the sounds when, or only when, the appropriate conditions are in fact satisfied; it is not essential

that he should have *established* that those conditions are satisfied, and still less is it essential that he should utter the sounds because he has established this. Sometimes, to be sure, a human being can be taught to utter a sound in the following way: he is taught to determine whether certain conditions are satisfied and to utter the sound only if he finds that those conditions are satisfied. But it could not be the case that the use of linguistic expressions is always learned in this way. And, what is more important here, it *need* not be the case that the use of linguistic expressions is always learned in this way. Viewed simply as a natural phenomenon, the fact that as the result of a certain kind of training human beings utter certain sounds (e.g., the sounds "I see a tree") when certain conditions are satisfied (e.g., when the speaker's eyes are open and directed toward a tree), and utter them without establishing that the conditions are satisfied, is no more mysterious than the fact that a child who has been burnt in the past now shuns fire without first establishing that he has been burnt in the past. As a natural phenomenon this is simpler, and probably more easily explainable in causal terms, than the making of statements on the basis of grounds or criteria, i.e., the making of statements (and the uttering of the sounds which express statements) by a human being because he has established that certain conditions are satisfied. The former seems mysterious only when the existence of the conditions can be regarded as the criterion for the truth of a certain statement, and when the making of the sounds can be regarded as the asserting of that very statement. And then it seems mysterious because we have a faulty theory of knowledge, a faulty conception of how statements must be made if we are to be "entitled" to make them, and not because there is anything inexplicable about what actually happens.

I have already argued that first-person psychological statements of the sorts I have been concerned with cannot be made on the basis of the criteria for their truth, and that it is a necessary truth, not a contingent one, that such statements are generally true if they are made at all. If, after this has been shown, one is still inclined to ask how it is possible for us to make such statements on the right occasions without grounding them on the criteria for their truth, the only answer is that it is just a fact of nature that human beings can be so trained that they are able to make such statements; that the result of the training is precisely an ability to say certain things under certain conditions (these often being the conditions for the truth of what is said) without first ascertaining whether those conditions are satisfied; and that if human beings did not respond to training in this way there would be no such things as first-person psychological statements.

NOTES

1. Normally we would not say that someone who simply observes that *P* knows that *P* on the basis of criteria. Nor can we say this if knowing that *P* on the basis of criteria is equated with believing that *P* on the basis of adequate noninductive evidence that *P*, for a person who directly observes that *P* cannot naturally be said to know that *P* on the basis of *any* sort of *evidence*. But if we want to contrast knowing something on the basis of criteria with knowing something on the basis of inductive evidence, we might allow simply observing something to be the case as a special and limiting case of knowing something to be the case on the basis of criteria. Here the observed state of affairs might be said to be its own criterion. There is, of course, no sharp distinction between (1) observing that something is Φ and (2) observing that something has properties *X, Y,* and *Z,* and thereby knowing that it satisfies the criteria for being Φ.

2. See Chapter Four, Section 3.

3. In the case of some psychological states, e.g., being in love, angry, etc., it is possible for one to say "I am (have been) behaving in these ways, so I must be such and such (in love,

angry, etc.)." But this is not possible in the case of the sorts of psychological states we have been concerned with.

4. See Chapter Three, Section 9.

5. See Wittgenstein, *Investigations,* p. 99: "To use a word without justification does not mean to use it without right."

6. See Chapter Two, Section 8, where the sources of this idea are discussed.

7. For this reason the sentence "I seem to be in pain" is, if not senseless, without a role to play in our language.

8. This must be qualified. If we know that a person witnessed an event which he sincerely claims to remember, but know also that he has read about the event or heard it described by other persons, there can be a question whether he really does remember it. In such a case various considerations are relevant to the question whether he does remember the event; for example, whether in his description of the event he is able to go beyond what he read or was told, whether his confidence in the correctness of his description would be affected if we raised doubts about the reliability of those who told him about it, and so on. However, I do not believe that this qualification affects the point I am making.

12. These generalizations are of course very complicated, more so than I have indicated, for the words "see" and "remember" are often mentioned rather than used, and are often used, by actors and others, in utterances that are not assertions.

13. Wittgenstein, *Investigations,* p. 56.

14. *Ibid*, p. 80.

13

D. M. Armstrong

"Is Introspective Knowledge Incorrigible?"

I

By sense perception we can become aware of the current state of our physical environment, including our own body. It is very natural to say that, in similar fashion, we can become aware of the current events in our own minds. Instead of turning outward to physical events, the mind turns inward on itself and perceives a procession of mental events. Locke spoke of the faculty of reflection, Kant spoke of inner sense, modern philosophy often speaks of introspection. I believe this traditional view to be essentially correct.

But, it is often held, introspection differs from sense perception in one very important respect. Introspective reports of current mental events are alleged to be logically incorrigible or logically indubitable. If I make the sincere statement "I seem to be seeing something green now," then, it is alleged, it is *logically impossible* for me to be mistaken in my statement. I may be lying, of course, but then I will know that my statement is untrue. For, it is argued, if mistake were a possibility then it would make sense to say "*I think* I seem to be seeing something green now, *but perhaps I am wrong.*" But this is nonsense, it is said, and so introspection is logically incorrigible or logically indubitable. (In the rest of this paper I shall simply say "incorrigible" or "indubitable," and I shall use the two words interchangeably.)

Incorrigibility, or indubitability, must be distinguished from logical necessity. Whether or not the sincere statement "I seem to be seeing something green now" is incorrigible, it is certainly not logically necessary. This is most easily seen if we remember that a logically necessary truth is true in all possible worlds. Now we can certainly describe worlds where I do not seem to be seeing something green now. Contrariwise, it may be noted, a logically necessary statement need not be incorrigible. It is not true that we assent to any logically necessary statement as soon as we understand it. We may mistakenly think it is false. It took a long time to convince Hobbes that Pythagoras' theorem followed of necessity from Euclid's axioms. Those who have said that logically necessary statements were incorrigible or indubitable either were wrong or else meant something different by "incorrigible" or "indubitable." (I suspect they meant "logically necessary.")

But although incorrigibility is not the same thing as logical necessity, it can be defined in terms of logical necessity. For we can say that a statement is incorrigible if and only if it is logically necessary that, when the statement is sincerely made, it is true. A statement is incorrigible when sincerity *entails* truth.

Often associated with the doctrine that current introspective reports are incorrigible is the view that each of us has a *logically privileged access* to our own mental experiences. Behavioral and physiological evidence logically cannot prevail against our own evidence. If my statement that I feel a pain now is sincere, it automatically outweighs any other evidence about my hedonic state. It may seem that this is the doctrine of incorrigibility all over again, but this need not be so. In his 1959 British Academy lecture, "Privacy," A. J. Ayer conceded that introspective reports were not incorrigible, but went on to maintain the doctrine of logically privileged access. I could be wrong in thinking that I seem to be seeing something green now, but if I am wrong, correction could come only, if it came at all, from *me*.

In this paper I shall advance arguments to show that introspective knowledge cannot be incorrigi-

From *The Philosophical Review* LXXII, 4 (October 1963): 417–32. Reprinted with permission of the editors and D. M. Armstrong.

ble or indubitable, and also that we do not have a logically privileged access to our mental existence. I shall concentrate on the former because, as I shall show, once the doctrine of incorrigibility is refuted, Ayer's compromise quickly breaks down. By way of penance, I will add that one of the philosophers I am attacking is Armstrong (*Perception and the Physical World,* especially Chapter 4, and *Bodily Sensations,* especially Chapter 9).

Before I go on to advance arguments, however, I shall declare my interest in the question. I wish to defend the thesis, recently advanced by J. J. C. Smart and others, that mental states are, as a matter of contingent fact, states of the brain. Now if I accept the existence of introspection, as I also do, then I must conceive of both introspection and the objects of introspection as states of the brain. Introspection must be a self-scanning process in the brain. That it is logically possible that such a self-scanning process will yield wrong results is at once clear, nor is it possible to see how such a self-scanning process could yield a *logically* privileged access. So if introspection is incorrigible, or if we have logically privileged access to our own mental states, it seems that a materialist doctrine of mental states must be false. (A similar line of argument against Smart is developed by Kurt Baier in "Smart on Sensations," *Australasian Journal of Philosophy,* 40 [1962], 57–68.) I should hasten to add, however, that if my argument in this paper succeeds, I have done nothing positive to prove a materialist theory of mind. I shall therefore make no further mention of, and still less will I appeal to, this controversial doctrine of the nature of mind. What I say *here* may be true, even if that doctrine is false.

II

I shall open my case by advancing two closely connected arguments which do not strictly *disprove* the existence of incorrigible introspective knowledge, but which do cast the most serious doubt on its existence.

1. It seems clear that if there is incorrigible knowledge of our own mental states, then it cannot apply to the past, but only to the present. If I tell somebody about my mental experience yesterday, then it is quite clear that my report can be mistaken. What is more, although I am likely to be better able to say what those experiences were than anybody else, somebody else might be a better authority on them than I am. In order to see that this is so, consider the following imaginary case. Suppose I report (sincerely) that I was in pain a few seconds ago; but suppose also that my report is un-

truc. The fact that I was not in pain a few seconds ago might have been known at that time to a brain super-technician. Knowing the correlation between states of the brain and inner experiences, he was able to say with certainty that I was not in pain then. But then, using his art, he proceeded to interfere with the apparatus in the brain responsible for my memory of my past inner experiences. The result was that, in all sincerity, I made the false report that I was in pain a few seconds ago. Now here a case has been described in which not only am I wrong about the nature of my experiences a few seconds ago, but the brain technician is a better authority than I am as to what they really were.

But if we consider such a report as "I was in pain a few seconds ago," is it not a paradigm of an *empirically* indubitable statement? We can hardly imagine, in any concrete way, what it would be like to make a mistake about it. Only by describing a quite fantastic situation, as we did above, can we make the notion of a mistake intelligible. The mistake may be logically possible, but it is empirically impossible. Now what the upholder of the logical indubitability of current introspective reports has to maintain is that the logical character of our certainty *changes* as we move from the past to the present. Remember here that the experience does not even need to have occurred some seconds ago for error to be (logically) possible. Place the experience the merest fraction of a second in the past, and it is intelligible to say that error has occurred. Are we prepared to say that this fraction of a second changes the nature of our certainty and that error, from being empirically impossible, becomes logically impossible? Admittedly I have said nothing here which is a *strict* disproof of the thesis of indubitability, but the argument gives us the strongest grounds for *suspecting* the thesis.

2. I shall now advance a second, closely connected argument with the same aim of sowing strong suspicion. Instead of reporting "I was in pain just then" I report "I am in pain now." Now if we take the view that the latter is a piece of indubitable knowledge, to what period of time does the word "now" refer? Not to the time before I started speaking, for there I am depending on memory, which can be challenged. Not the time after I finish speaking, for then I depend on knowledge of the future, which can be challenged too. The time in question must therefore be the time during which the report is being made. But then it must be remembered that anything we say takes time to say. Suppose, then, that I am at the beginning of my report. My indubitable knowledge that I am in pain can surely embrace only the current instant: it cannot be logically indubitable that I will still be in pain by the time the sentence is fin-

ished. Suppose, again, that I am just finishing my sentence. Can I do better than *remember* what my state was when I began my sentence? So to what period of time does the "now" refer?

At this point it seems that the defender of indubitable introspective knowledge will have to introduce the notion of the "introspective instant." Let us consider first the more obvious notion of a "perceptual instant." Suppose a light is switched on and off very rapidly, so that we are *just,* and no more than just, able to follow every step in the cycle. We can say that, within this situation, the time that the light remains switched on or off is a "perceptual instant." It is the smallest unit of time visually discernible within that situation. In parallel fashion, the "introspective instant" would be the smallest unit of time discernible with respect to inner experiences. Now I think that the defender of indubitable introspective knowledge would have to say that our knowledge is indubitable only while it is knowledge of the current "introspective instant." During that instant we know indubitably what is going on in that instant, but past instants are only remembered and future instants only foreseen, so that doubt would be meaningful.

But the consequence of this is that the defender of incorrigibility will have to admit that it is in practice, if not in theory, impossible to make a *statement* of the required logical status about one's inner experiences. For, by the time one has finished speaking, the moment to which one was referring is in the past. Only if we could complete the statement within the "introspective instant" would it be beyond challenge. So what becomes of the alleged indubitability of the *statement* "I am in pain now" when I speak at ordinary speed? Is it in any different position from the *empirically* indubitable statements "I have a hand now" or "I was in pain a moment ago"? Special authority has to retreat from speech to the instant's awareness. And then we may well become skeptical whether there is any such logically privileged awareness. After all, the alleged indubitability was *established* by a consideration of *statements.* (See the second paragraph, above.)

3. Let us now go on, however, to consider arguments which, if valid, show that first-person reports of current experience *cannot* be indubitable. There is one important line of argument that derives from Wittgenstein. If introspective mistake is ruled out by logical necessity, then what sense can we attach to the notion of gaining knowledge by introspection? We can speak of gaining knowledge only in cases where it makes sense to speak of thinking wrongly that we have gained knowledge. In the words of the slogan: "If you can't be wrong,

you can't be right either." If failure is logically impossible, then talk of success is meaningless.

What I think is at bottom the same argument may be put in another way. Introspective apprehension or awareness, like all other apprehension, is an apprehension that the thing apprehended is *of a certain sort.* The apprehension involves *classifying* the experience, in however rudimentary a way; that is, it involves the application of *concepts.* Now, surely, the notions of classifying and misclassifying are co-ordinate notions; surely the one can apply only when it is meaningful to apply the other? We can apply a certain concept to our experience only if it is possible to withhold that concept. Yet, according to the doctrine of incorrigibility, the application of any concept except the concept we do apply is logically impossible. (Lying is no exception, for lying is uttering words *contra mentem.* In our minds, we are applying the right concept.)

4. My final argument against the indubitability of introspection runs as follows. (This argument was hit upon independently, at almost the same time, by J. J. C. Smart. See his reply to Baier in the *Australasian Journal of Philosophy, loc. cit.*) The acquiring of introspective knowledge must consist of the making of (sincere) reports of current mental occurrences, or else a nonverbal apprehension of these occurrences. In both cases the apprehension of the occurrence will have to be *distinct* from the occurrence that is apprehended. But if this is granted, then we can apply Hume's argument about "distinct existences." Wherever we have two distinct things, Hume points out, there we can always conceive of the one existing in the absence of the other. It follows that it is logically possible to have a sincere report of a current inner experience, or a nonverbal apprehension of that experience, without the experience existing. ("Apprehension," of course, is a success-word, and strictly it would be out of place here. But it would be possible for there to be something just like the apprehension, except that the object of the apprehension did not exist.) But this state of affairs would be the state in which we would be mistaken about our current inner mental state. Incidentally, this argument, if valid, would also prove that the experiences reported or apprehended might exist without being reported or apprehended, although they might not then be called "experiences." I shall return to this point at the end of the paper.

Now in the case of *reports* of mental states, it must surely be conceded that the report is perfectly distinct from the state reported on. Otherwise we are not *reporting.* But the point may not be readily conceded in the case of nonverbal apprehension.

To have a pain, it may be said, is to apprehend that we are in pain: to distinguish between the inner state and the apprehension of it is to be guilty of a false abstraction. And then it may be said that it is the presence of this apprehension—and so, *ipso facto,* this mental state—that makes a report of a current mental state a *sincere* report.

But, in fact, the apprehension of something must be distinct from the thing apprehended. For if not, we are faced with a flagrant circularity. Having a pain logically involves apprehension of—what? The pain itself! This is as bad as saying that to be a cat logically involves being the offspring of cats. It seems, therefore, that there must always be a distinction between *being* in a certain mental state and *being aware* that we are in that state. Hence there can be no indubitable introspective knowledge.

III

At this point, somebody may concede that it has been proved that no introspective awareness can be logically guaranteed to be free from mistake, but still maintain that we have a logically privileged access to our own inner states. It may be maintained, that is, that we are the logically ultimate authorities on our inner states, even while it is allowed that even we can be mistaken.

It seems clear, however, that this compromise is inadmissible. Once it has been admitted that I can be wrong about my current inner states, then we must allow the possibility that somebody else (for example, a brain technician) reaches a true belief about my inner state when I reach a false one. And then what reason is there to deny that the technician is a better authority on my mental state than I am? Indeed, once it is conceded that the apprehension of a mental state is something distinct from the mental state itself, is it not logically possible that others should have *direct* knowledge of my mental states, unmediated by observation of behavior or states of the brain? And if they are right where I am wrong, would they not be better authorities on my mental state than I am? So Ayer's compromise fails.

IV

I now consider objections that may be made to what has been said so far.

1. Somebody may object: "What would it be like to be mistaken about our current inner states? Only if you can *describe cases* where we would be inclined to say that introspective error had occurred will your position appear to have any plausibility."

Now there do seem to be cases where we are confused about the nature of our current experiences, and we could quite plausibly construe some of these as cases where error occurred. But these empirical cases are not very satisfactory for our purpose here, because it is not often plausible to regard them as involving *major* error about the nature of our mental experiences. So here it is better to consider imaginary cases. Consider again the case of a brain technician who has a perfect understanding of the correlation between states of my brain and inner experiences. Suppose, then, that I report, "I seem to be seeing something green," using the sentence as a phenomenological report on my visual experience. The brain technician is able to say from his knowledge of brain patterns that (i) I am not lying; (ii) my brain is in the appropriate state for some *other* experience; (iii) there are disturbances in the brain processes responsible for introspective awareness which would account for my mistake. On the evidence offered by the technician it ought to be concluded that I have made a mistake.

It may be objected to this example that there is no reason why we should side with the brain technician. If the brain technician and I disagree, should we not rather conclude that there is something wrong with brain theory? There is no doubt that this is a *possible* rejoinder, and that if brain theory were not well founded it would be the *rational* rejoinder; but why is it the rejoinder that we *must* accept? Any hypothesis whatever may be "protected" if we are prepared to make a sufficient number of *ad hoc* assumptions, but to protect a hypothesis indefinitely is not a rational attitude. The fact that we *could* cling to every deliverance of introspection even against the best-attested brain theory does nothing to show that it would be incorrect to side with the brain technician. In fact, I think it *would* be rational to side with him against the deliverance of introspection, provided that brain theory was well founded. This does not mean that we logically must accept the evidence of the brain technician. But there is no logically absolute need to accept the deliverance of introspection either.

It is true, of course, that the brain technician would have to build up his theory in the first place by accepting people's introspective reports and correlating them with brain states. But a well-established brain theory could still be used to cast doubt on some of these introspective reports. In the same way, our knowledge of the physical world is got by perception but this does not prevent us casting doubt on some perceptions.

Consider another case. I say perfectly sincerely, "I am in great pain." A little later I inquire why nobody gave me any assistance or sympathy when I shrieked out "I am in great pain" and exhibited every sign of distress. It is then proved to me that I said the words in a quiet, level voice while exhibiting every sign of relaxation. Might it not be reasonable to conclude that I was mistaken in thinking myself to be in pain? Perhaps other explanations are possible, but I cannot see why this explanation is not also possible.

It may be objected at this point that if extraordinary situations like the two I have just considered were to arise, we should not be so much convinced of introspective error as reduced to a state of total confusion. If evidence seems to suggest that I can be wrong in thinking I am in violent pain now, or that I seem to see something green, then the possibility of rational discourse has ceased. The conceptual reorganization necessary to accommodate such error would burst our system of thought.

I have some sympathy with this point, but I do not think that it does anything to prove the incorrigibility of current introspective reports. The discovery that I was under an illusion in thinking that I now have two hands or, still better, that I now have a head on my shoulders, would be an even greater shock to thought and the conceptual system. But surely it is clear that the statements "I have two hands now" or "I have a head" are not *logically* indubitable?

2. I pass on to consider another difficulty. It may be objected that if somebody denies that the report "I am in pain now" is indubitable, then he will be forced to admit indubitability at the next level. For if "I am in pain now" is not indubitable, then it must be admitted that "It seems to me that I am in pain now" *is* indubitable. But once indubitability is admitted anywhere (the objection goes on) there is no point in denying it to the original report?

It must be admitted, I think, that if we deny the indubitability of current introspective reports then we must say that a sentence like "It seems to me that I am in pain" has a clear and intelligible meaning. Indeed, it will have *two* possible uses. The phrase "It seems to me" might function simply as an *expression* of an inclination to assert the statement "I am in pain now." In that case no question of truth or falsity will arise, except about the report "I am in pain now," and so no question of indubitability will arise either. However, the whole sentence might also function as a phenomenological report on my belief in the truth of the

report "I am in pain now." But why need we say that this report of our belief in the truth of an introspective report is *indubitable?* It need be no more than *true.*[1]

When Descartes set out to examine his thoughts, to see if any were indubitable, he *presupposed* that he had these thoughts, for he could not examine his thoughts unless he had some to examine! But this did not make his statement "I am thinking now" a logically indubitable one. It was simply a logical presupposition of his starting point. In the same way, if it is *given* that I make the sincere report "I am in pain now," then that *presupposes* that I believe that I am in pain now. But that does not make the statement "I believe that I am in pain now" an indubitable one. It is simply a logical presupposition of the given starting point: a statement of what is in fact the case.

I suggest, then, that there is no *logical* objection to the introspective awareness of experiences, to the simultaneous introspective awareness of that awareness, and so on as far as we please. This will always involve an ultimate awareness that is not itself an *object* of awareness,[2] but it will not involve a logically guaranteed freedom from error at any point. How far such awareness goes *in fact* is an empirical question, to which the answer seems to be "Not very far." We can speak of awareness of awareness of awareness of awareness of awareness of . . . *X,* but no psychological reality seems to correspond to our words.

3. Now, however, it may be objected that if introspective reports about our current inner state are not indubitable, then they really lack any authority with us. For there is no way empirically available of checking whether I introspect correctly or not. Without such a check, and without indubitability, how can I claim *knowledge?* Yet in fact we are perfectly happy to talk of introspective *reports,* of *knowledge* gained by introspective *reports,* or of *knowledge* gained by introspection.

I do not believe that this objection is very serious. In the first place, there is some rough-and-ready check on introspective statements provided by observable behavior. If a man thinks that he currently experiences a spurt of hatred for another, he may later be inclined to withdraw this when he observes that his own *actions* are much more easily squared with the assumption that he fears the other, or that he loves him. In the second place, I see no reason why a faculty whose operation cannot be checked by other people, or by the same person with a different faculty, should not yield us knowledge. I think we *know* that, by and large, introspection yields us reliable information, just as sense perception does. And if I am asked to back up this claim by reasons, then I think little more can be said except that this is the place where reasons stop. After all, reasons always have to stop somewhere, sooner or later.

4. Here is the place to show that our theory of introspection solves the problem about how we teach children to speak about inner mental states, and how we, as children, learned to speak about such states.

Since it is simply an *empirical* fact that we have no direct awareness of other people's inner states, we can use the traditional inductive argument for their existence.[3] If a child cries, and has a splinter in his finger, I can assume on an inductive basis, ultimately based on my own case, that the child feels a pain in his finger. If his eyes are open, he has red spectacles on, and is looking at a white object, then I can assume that, in all likelihood, he is having sense impressions as of something red. I can therefore introduce such phrases as "pain in your finger" and "looks red *to you,* although it is not red." Further testing in similar situations will tell me whether or not the child has "caught on." Once I am fairly sure he has understood, I can then trust him, and he can trust himself, when he reports pain in the absence of any observed injury, or reports sense impressions as of something red in the absence of normal "red-look-producing conditions."

Once we realize that our mental experiences are not logically impervious to any apprehension except our own, then all Wittgenstein's difficulties about "private objects" are swept away. Suppose everybody had a beetle in a box, and nobody could, as a matter of empirical fact, observe the other man's beetle. Provided we could observe the outside of the boxes, and provided that these outsides exhibited characteristic marks of beetle-occupation (a correlation discovered in our own case), there would be no *special* difficulty in introducing the word "beetle" into the language.

5. Finally, it may be asked, if it is true that no introspective reports are indubitable, why did any philosophers so much as conceive the idea that these reports were in a specially privileged position? I will suggest two reasons.

In the first place (following Wittgenstein, but not following him the whole way), I think we must recognize that sentences like "I am in pain now," "It looks green to me now," "I want an apple now," and so forth, are not always used to make introspective reports. The sentence "I am in pain now" can be a substitute for a groan, a wince, or a cry for help. To say "It looks green to me now" is usually to express a tentative belief, or inclination to believe, that something in the physical environment is green. The sentence is not normally used to make a phenomenological report on our visual impressions. To say "I want an apple now" is normally to give expression to my desire for an apple; it is not to make an introspective report on my current desires.

Now in so far as these sentences have these noncognitive uses, so far it *makes no sense* to speak of cognitive error. This may be put in a misleading way by saying that it is logically impossible to be mistaken about such utterances. It is misleading because we are then tempted to think that here we have an utterance which, if uttered sincerely, embodies knowledge of a quite peculiar certainty.

So, when philosophers have considered sentences like "I am in pain now," they have been misled by their ambiguity. They have moved between their noncognitive use, where the question of intellectual mistake does not come up but equally there is no question of cognition, and their autobiographical use, where there is no doubt cognitive certainty but simply an *empirical* certainty. And so we persuade ourselves that such sentences express reports, but reports that have a special certainty and special authority. This confusion is made all the more easy because the utterance of such a sentence regularly *intertwines* both noncognitive and reporting functions. But, in truth, in so far as "I am in pain now" is a report, it is subject to the possibility of doubt, and so far as it is indubitable it is not a report at all.

In the second place, our unwillingness to admit that there can be error with respect to first-person reports of our current experiences may also reflect certain emotional attachments. We have a deep interest in *ourselves,* as opposed to other people and other things. This is the basis of the utterly natural fantasy "Nobody and nothing exists except myself." Not only do we have a special interest in ourselves, however, but we attach a quite peculiar importance to our own *experiences.* We feel that when we started experiencing, the world began; and when we stop experiencing, it will end. We feel that, whatever the world is really like, provided our experiences remain the same then *it does not matter.* (This is one of the psychological roots of phenomenalism.)

We also have a deep interest in the *present* state of the world as a whole, as opposed to its past or future. What happens now is more important than what happened in the past, or what will happen next. We have the feeling that, compared with the present, the past and the future are not so real, do not really exist. The biological reasons for this concentration of our interest on *ourselves* and on the *present* are of course perfectly obvious.

In the case of current inner experiences, our interest in our own experiences and our interest in the present *come together.* Our own current experiences are the things we are interested in above everything else. Perhaps this helps to explain our peculiar unwillingness to admit the possibility that we are mistaken about inner experiences at the instant of having them.

V

I will finish this paper by considering briefly whether our denial of the incorrigibility of current introspective reports forces us to admit the possibility of experiences that are *not* apprehended.

If we consider such phrases as "mental *experiences*" or "inner *experiences*" then it seems natural to say that these are the tautological accusatives of "inner sense," just as sights are the tautological accusatives of the sense of vision. If this is correct, or if it is adopted as a rule of language, then it makes no sense to speak of inner *experiences* of which we are not aware.

But this only postpones the real question. For we can now ask: "Are the happenings of which we are introspectively aware—such things as pains, sense impressions, mental images, and so forth—*necessarily* experiences, or can they exist when we are not aware of them?" And here, I think, we have to make a linguistic decision. We can legislate in favor of saying that having a pain, a sense impression, or an image *is* to have an experience, that is, something of which we must be aware. Or, perhaps more wisely, we can legislate in the other way.

For suppose that we decide that pains, sense impressions, images, and so forth must be apprehended; the logical possibility must still be admitted of inner happenings which resemble the having of pains, sense impressions, and so forth in *all* respects except that of being objects of introspective awareness. For if introspective awareness and its objects are "distinct existences," as we have argued, it must be possible for the objects to exist when the awareness does not exist.

Nor need we restrict ourselves to bare logical possibility, for there are plenty of empirical cases which can be naturally interpreted as involving the existence of inner states of which we are not aware. Consider the case of the patient who struggles and screams under nitrous oxide. Perhaps we do not

want to say that he is *in pain,* on the ground that he is not aware of being in pain. But he is exhibiting pain behavior, and it is at least a natural induction to say that this is caused by certain inner states which resemble the mental experience of being in pain, except for the fact that they are *not* experienced. To say that nothing but *mere* pain behavior can possibly be involved seems to be nothing but an exhibition that one is prisoner of a dogma.

Again, consider the interesting case of the chicken-sexer. He can, more or less accurately, say that a chicken will grow up to be a cock or a hen, but he does not know, and nobody else knows, what visual cues he is using. (Chicken-sexers are trained by being shown photos of chicks whose later career is known. They are told when they guess correctly, and they gradually come to guess better and better.) It is natural to say that female and male chicks give rise to different inner states resembling visual impressions in the chicken-sexer, and that these inner states are responsible for the sexer's choice, but yet that the sexer is not directly aware of these states. We may deny that these inner states are *sense impressions,* on the verbal ground that one must be aware of one's own sense impressions, but there is no reason why they should not have every property of sense impressions except that of being objects of awareness. And once we see this point, I do not think that we will be particularly zealous to keep words like "sense impression" solely for inner states that *are* apprehended.

I conclude that not only is it a mistake to say that introspective reports are indubitable or have a logically special authority, but also that the objects of introspective awareness can exist when we are not aware of them.

NOTES

1. I owe this point to Mr. J. E. McGechie.
2. This is the "systematic elusiveness" of the subject.
3. I believe, in fact, that a fuller account of the concept of a mental state than I can give here would show that our assurance of the existence of other minds is even better than that afforded by the inductive argument. But it is worth seeing that there is nothing wrong with the inductive argument.

14

Richard Rorty

from "Mind–Body Identity, Privacy, and Categories"

5. The "Privacy" Objection

The problem that the privacy of first-person sensation reports presents for the Identity Theory has recently been formulated in considerable detail by Baier.[1] In this section, I shall confine myself to a discussion of his criticism of Smart's initial reply to this argument. Smart holds that the fact that "the language of introspective reports has a different logic from the logic of material processes" is no objection to the Identity Theory, since we may expect that empirical inquiry can and will change this logic:

> It is obvious that until the brain-process theory is much improved and widely accepted there will be no *criteria* for saying 'Smith has an experience of such-and-such a sort' except Smith's introspective reports. So we have adopted a rule of language that (normally) what Smith says goes.[2]

Baier thinks that this reply "is simply a confusion of the privacy of the subject-matter and the availability of external evidence."[3] Baier's intuition is that the difference between a language stratum in which the fact that a report is sincerely made is sufficient warrant for its truth, and one in which this situation does not obtain, seems so great as to call for an explanation—and that the only explanation is that the two strata concern different subject-matters. Indeed Baier is content to let the mental-physical distinction stand or fall with the distinction between "private" subject-matters and "public" subject-matters, and he therefore assumes that to show that "introspective reports are necessarily about something private, and that being about something private is *incompatible with being*

about something public"[4] is to show, once and for all, that the Identity Theory involves a conceptual confusion. Baier, in short, is undertaking to show that "once private, always private."

He argues for his view as follows:

> To say that one day our physiological knowledge will increase to such an extent that we shall be able to make absolutely reliable encephalograph-based claims about people's experiences, is only to say that, if carefully checked, our encephalograph-based claims about 'experiences' will always be *correct,* i.e. will make the *same claims* as a *truthful* introspective report. If correct encephalograph-based claims about Smith's experiences contradict Smith's introspective reports, we shall be entitled to infer that he is *lying.* In that sense, what Smith says will no longer go. But we cannot of course infer that he is making a mistake, for that is nonsense. . . . *However good the evidence may be, such a physiological theory can never be used to show to the sufferer that he was mistaken in thinking that he had a pain, for such a mistake is inconceivable.* The sufferer's epistemological authority must therefore be better than the best physiological theory can ever be. Physiology can therefore never provide a person with more than *evidence* that someone else is having an experience of one sort or another. It can never lay down *criteria* for saying that someone is having an experience of a certain sort. Talk about brain-processes therefore must be about something other than talk about experiences. Hence, introspective reports and brain process talk cannot be merely different ways of talking about the same thing.[5]

Smart's own reply to this line of argument is to admit that

> No physiological evidence, say from a gadget attached to my skull, could make me withdraw the statement

From *The Review of Metaphysics* XIX, 1 (September 1965), § 5: 41–48. Reprinted with permission of the editor.

that I have a pain when as a matter of fact I feel a pain. For example, the gadget might show no suitable similarities of cerebral processes on the various occasions on which I felt a pain. . . . I must, I think, agree with Baier that if the sort of situation which we have just envisaged did in fact come about, then I should have to reject the brain process thesis, and would perhaps espouse dualism.[6]

But this is not the interesting case. The interesting case is the one in which suitable similarities are in fact found to occur—the same similarities in all subjects—until one day (long after all empirical generalizations about sensations *qua* sensations have been subsumed under physiological laws, and long after direct manipulation of the brain has become the exclusive method of relieving pain) somebody (call him Jones) thinks he has no pain, but the encephalograph says that the brain-process correlated with pain did occur. (Let us imagine that Jones himself is observing the gadget, and that the problem about whether he might have made a mistake is a problem for Jones; this eliminates the possibility of lying.) Now in most cases in which one's observation throws doubt on a correlation which is so central to current scientific explanations, one tries to eliminate the possibility of observational error. But in Baier's view it would be absurd for Jones to do this, for "a mistake is inconceivable." Actually, however, it is fairly clear what Jones' first move would be—he will begin to suspect that he does not know what pain is—i.e., that he is not using the word "pain" in the way in which his fellows use it.[7]

So now Jones looks about for independent verification of the hypothesis that he does not use "I am in pain" incorrectly. But here he runs up against the familiar difficulty about the vocabulary used in making introspective reports—the difficulty of distinguishing between "misuse of language" and "mistake in judgment", between (a) recognizing the state of affairs which obtains for what it is, but describing it wrongly because the words used in the description are not the right words, and (b) being able to describe it rightly once it is recognized for what it is, but not in fact recognizing it for what it is (in the way in which one deceived by an illusion does not recognize the situation for what it is). If we do not have a way of determining which of these situations obtains, we do not have a genuine contrast between misnaming and misjudging. To see that there is no genuine contrast in this case, suppose that Jones was not burned prior to the time that he hitches on the encephalograph, but now he is. When he is, the encephalograph says that the brain-process constantly correlated with pain-reports occurs in

Jones' brain. However, although he exhibits pain-behavior, Jones thinks that he does not feel pain. (But, now as in the past, he both exhibits pain-behavior and thinks that he feels pain when he is frozen, stuck, struck, racked, etc.) Now is it that he does not know that *pain* covers what you feel when you are burned as well as what you feel when you are stuck, struck, etc.? Or is it that he really does not feel pain when he is burned? Suppose we tell Jones that what he feels when he is burned is *also* called "pain." Suppose he then admits that he does feel *something,* but insists that what he feels is quite *different* from what he feels when he is stuck, struck, etc. Where does Jones go from here? Has he failed to learn the language properly, or is he correctly (indeed infallibly) reporting that he has different sensations than those normally had in the situation in question? (Compare the parallel question in the case of a man who uses "blue" in all the usual ways except that he refuses to grant that blue is a color—on the ground that it is so different from red, yellow, orange, violet, etc.)

The only device which would decide this question would be to establish a convention that anyone who sincerely denied that he felt a pain while exhibiting pain-behavior and being burned ipso facto did not understand how to use "pain." This denial would *prove* that he lacked such an understanding. But this would be a dangerous path to follow. For not to understand when to use the word "pain" in non-inferential reports is presumably to be unable to know which of one's sensations to call a "pain." And the denial that one felt pain in the circumstances mentioned would only prove such inability if one indeed *had* the sensation normally called a pain. So now we would have a public criterion, satisfaction of which would count as showing that the subject had such a sensation—i.e., that he felt a pain even though he did not think that he did. But if such a criterion exists, its application overrides any contradictory report that he may make—for such a report will be automatically disallowed by the fact that it constitutes a demonstration that he does not know what he is talking about. The dilemma is that either a report about one's sensations which violates a certain public criterion is a sufficient condition for saying that the reporter does not know how to use "pain" in the correct way, or there is no such criterion. If there is, the fact that one cannot be mistaken about pains does not entail that sincere reports of pain cannot be over-ridden. If there is not, then there is no way to answer the question formulated at the end of the last paragraph, and hence no way to eliminate the possibility that Jones may not know what pain is. Now since the a priori probability that he does not is a good deal higher than the a priori probability that the psycho-physiological theory of Jones' era is mistaken, this theory has little to fear from Jones. (Although it would have a great deal to fear from a sizable accumulation of cases like Jones'.)

To sum up this point, we may look back at the italicized sentence in the above quotation from Baier. We now see that the claim that "such a mistake is inconceivable" is an ellipsis for the claim that a mistake, made *by one who knows what pain is,* is inconceivable, for only this expanded form will entail that when Jones and the encephalograph disagree, Jones is always right. But when formulated in this way our infallibility about our pains can be seen to be empty. Being infallible about something would be useful only if we could draw the usual distinction between misnaming and misjudging, and, having ascertained that we were not misnaming, know that we were not misjudging. But where there are no criteria for misjudging (or to put it more accurately, where in the crucial cases the criteria for misjudging turn out to be the same as the criteria for misnaming) then to say that we are infallible is to pay ourselves an empty compliment. Our neighbors will not hesitate to ride roughshod over our reports of our sensations unless they are assured that we know our way around among them, and we cannot satisfy them on this point unless, up to a certain point, we tell the same sort of story about them as they do. The limits of permissible stories are flexible enough for us to be able to convince them occasionally that we have odd sensations, but not flexible enough for us to use these surprising sensations to break down, at one blow, well-confirmed scientific theories. As in the case of other infallible pronouncements, the price of retaining one's epistemological authority is a decent respect for the opinions of mankind.

Thus the common-sense remark that first-person reports always will be a better source of information about the occurrence of pains than any other source borrows its plausibility from the fact that we normally do not raise questions about a man's ability to use the word "pain" correctly. Once we *do* raise such questions seriously (as in the case of Jones), we realize that the question (1) "Does he know which sensations are called 'pains'?" and (2) "Is he a good judge of whether he is in pain or not?" are simply two ways of asking the same question: viz., "Can we fit his pain-reports into our scheme for explaining and predicting pains?" or, more bluntly, "Shall we disregard his pain-reports or not?" And once we see this we realize that if "always be a better source of information" means "will never be over-ridden on the sort of grounds on which presumed observational errors are over-ridden elsewhere in science," then our common-sensical remark is probably false. If "always be a better source of information" means merely "can only be over-ridden on the basis of a charge of misnaming, and never on the basis of a charge of misjudging," then our common-sensical remark turns out to depend upon a distinction that is not there.

This Wittgensteinian point that sensation-reports must conform to public criteria or else be disallowed may also be brought out in the following way. We determine whether to take a surprising first-person report of pain or its absence seriously (that is, whether to say that the sensation reported is something that science must try to explain) by seeing whether the reporter's overall pattern of pain-reporting is, by the usual behavioral and environmental criteria, normal. Now suppose that these public criteria (for "knowing how to use 'pain'") change as physiology and technology progress. Suppose, in particular, that we find it convenient to speed up the learning of contrastive observation predicates (such as "painful," "tickling," etc.) by supplying children with portable encephalographs-cum-teaching-machines which, when ever the appropriate brain-process occurs, murmur the appropriate term in their ears. Now "appropriate brain-process" will start out by meaning "brain-process constantly correlated with sincere utterances of 'I'm in pain' by people taught the use of 'pain' in the old rough-and-ready way." But soon it will come to mean, "the brain-process which we have always programmed the machine to respond to with a murmur of 'pain.'" (A meter is [now, but was not always] what matches the Standard Meter; intelligence is [now, but was not always] what intelligence tests test; pains will be [but are not now] what the Standard "Pain" Training Program calls "pain.") Given this situation, it would make sense to say things like "You say you are in pain, and I'm sure you are sincere, but you can see for yourself that your brain is not in the state to which you were trained to respond to with "Pain," so apparently the training did not work, and you do not yet understand what pain is." In such a situation, our "inability to be mistaken" about our pains would remain, but our "final epistemological authority" on the subject would be gone, for there would be a standard procedure for overriding our reports. Our inability to be mistaken is, after all, no more than our ability to have such hypothetical statements as "If you admit that I'm sincere and that I know the language, you have to accept what I say" accepted by our fellows. But this asset can only be converted into final epistemological authority if we can secure both admissions. Where a clear-cut public criterion *does* exist for "knowing the language," inability to be mistaken does not entail inability to be over-ridden.

Now Baier might say that if such criteria did exist, then we should no longer be talking about what we presently mean by "pains." I do not think that this needs to be conceded[8] but suppose that it is. Would this mean that there was now a subject-matter which was not being discussed—viz., the private subject-matter the existence of which Baier's argument was intended to demonstrate? That we once had contact with such a subject-matter, but lost it? These rhetorical questions are meant to suggest that Baier's explanation of the final epistemological authority of first-person reports of pains by the fact that this "logic" is "a function of this type of subject-matter" rather than, as Smart thinks, a convention—is an explanation of the obscure by the more obscure. More precisely, it will not be an explanation of the epistemological authority in question—but only an unenlightening redescription of it—unless Baier can give a meaning to the term "private subject-matter" other than "kind of thing which is reported in reports which cannot be over-ridden."

These considerations show the need for stepping back from Baier's argument and considering the criteria which he is using to demarcate distinct subject-matters.

NOTES

1. Kurt Baier, "Smart on Sensations," *Australasian Journal of Philosophy,* 40 (1962), pp. 57–68.

2. Smart, "Sensations and Brain Processes," p. 169.

3. Baier, p. 63.

4. Baier, p. 59.

5. Baier, pp. 64–65; italics added.

6. Smart, "Brain Processes and Incorrigibility—a Reply to Professor Baier," *Australasian Journal of Philosophy,* 40 (1962), p. 68.

7. This problem will remain, of course, even if Jones merely *thinks* about whether he is in pain, but does not say anything.

8. My reasons for thinking this concession unnecessary are the same as those presented in some recent articles by Hilary Putnam: cf. "Minds and Machines," *Dimensions of Mind,* ed. by S. Hook (New York, 1961), pp. 138–161, esp. pp. 153–160; "The Analytic and the Synthetic," *Minnesota Studies in the Philosophy of Science,* III, pp. 358–397; "Brains and Behavior," in *Analytical Philosophy,* II, ed. by R. J. Butler (Oxford, 1965).

C.   The Theory Approach

15

C. S. Chihara and J. A. Fodor

"Operationalism and Ordinary Language: A Critique of Wittgenstein"[1,2]

This paper explores some lines of argument in Wittgenstein's post-*Tractatus* writings in order to indicate the relations between Wittgenstein's philosophical psychology on the one hand and his philosophy of language, his epistemology, and his doctrines about the nature of philosophical analysis on the other. We shall hold that the later writings of Wittgenstein express a coherent doctrine in which an operationalistic analysis of confirmation and language supports a philosophical psychology of a type we shall call "logical behaviorism."

We shall also maintain that there are good grounds for rejecting the philosophical theory implicit in Wittgenstein's other works. In particular we shall first argue that Wittgenstein's position leads to some implausible conclusions concerning the nature of language and psychology; second, we shall maintain that the arguments Wittgenstein provides are inconclusive; and third, we shall try to sketch an alternative position which avoids many of the difficulties implicit in Wittgenstein's philosophy. In exposing and rejecting the operationalism which forms the framework of Wittgenstein's later writings, we do not, however, suppose that we have detracted in any way from the importance of the particular analyses of particular philosophical problems which form their primary content.

I

Among the philosophical problems Wittgenstein attempted to dissolve is the "problem of other minds." One aspect of this hoary problem is the question: What justification, if any, can be given for the claim that one can tell, on the basis of someone's behavior, that he is in a certain mental state? To this question, the sceptic answers: No good justification at all. Among the major motivations of the later Wittgenstein's treatment of philosophical psychology is that of showing that this answer rests on a misconception and is *logically* incoherent.

Characteristically, philosophic sceptics have argued in the following way. It is assumed as a premiss that there are no logical or conceptual relations between propositions about mental states and propositions about behavior in virtue of which propositions asserting that a person behaves in a certain way provide support, grounds, or justification for ascribing the mental states to that person. From this, the sceptic deduces that he has no compelling reason for supposing that any person other than himself is ever truly said to feel pains, draw inferences, have motives, etc. For, while his firsthand knowledge of the occurrence of such mental events is of necessity limited to his own case, it is entailed by the premiss just cited that application of mental predicates to others must depend upon logically fallible inferences. Furthermore, attempts to base such inferences on analogies and correlations fall short of convincing justifications.

Various replies have been made to this argument which do not directly depend upon contesting the truth of the premiss. For example, it is sometimes claimed that, at least in some cases, no *inference* from behavior to mental states is at issue in psychological ascriptions. Thus, we sometimes *see* that someone is in pain, and in these cases, we cannot be properly said to *infer* that he is in pain. However, the sceptic might maintain against this

From *American Philosophical Quarterly* II, 4 (October 1965): 281–95. Reprinted with permission of the editor.

argument that it begs the question. For the essential issue is whether anyone is *justified* in claiming to see that another is in pain. Now a physicist, looking at cloud-chamber tracks, may be justified in claiming to see that a charged particle has passed through the chamber. That is because in this case there is justification for the claim that certain sorts of tracks show the presence and motion of particles. The physicist can explain not only how he is able to detect particles, but also why the methods he uses are methods of detecting *particles.* Correspondingly, the sceptic can argue that what is required in the case of another's pain is some justification for the claim that, by observing a person's behavior, one can *see* that he is in *pain.*

Wittgenstein's way of dealing with the sceptic is to attack his premiss by trying to show that there do exist conceptual relations between statements about behavior and statements about mental events, processes, and states. Hence, Wittgenstein argues that in many cases our knowledge of the mental states of some person rests upon something other than an observed empirical correlation or an analogical argument, viz. a conceptual or linguistic connection.

To hold that the sceptical premiss is false is *ipso facto* to commit oneself to some version of *logical behaviorism* where by "logical behaviorism" we mean the doctrine that there are logical or conceptual relations of the sort denied by the sceptical premiss.[3] Which form of logical behaviorism one holds depends on the nature of the logical connection one claims obtains. The strongest form maintains that statements about mental states are translatable into statements about behavior. Wittgenstein, we shall argue, adopts a weaker version.

II

It is well known that Wittgenstein thought that philosophical problems generally arise out of misrepresentations and misinterpretations of ordinary language (PI, § 109, § 122, § 194). "Philosophy," he tells us, "is a fight against the fascination which forms of expression exert upon us" (BB, p. 27). Thus, Wittgenstein repeatedly warns us against being misled by superficial similarities between certain forms of expression (BB, p. 16) and tells us that, to avoid philosophical confusions, we must distinguish the "surface grammar" of sentences from their "depth grammar" (PI, § 11, § 664). For example, though the grammar of the sentence "*A* has a gold tooth" seems to differ in no essential respect from that of "*A* has a sore tooth," the apparent similarity masks important conceptual differ-

ences (BB, pp. 49, 53; PI, § 288–293). Overlooking these differences leads philosophers to suppose that there is a problem about our knowledge of other minds. It is the task of the Wittgensteinian philosopher to dissolve the problem by obtaining a clear view of the workings of pain language in this and other cases.

The Wittgensteinian method of philosophical therapy involves taking a certain view of language and of meaning. Throughout the *Investigations,* Wittgenstein emphasizes that "the speaking of language is part of an activity" (PI, § 23) and that if we are to see the radically different roles superficially similar expressions play, we must keep in mind the countless kinds of language-using activities or "language-games" in which we participate (BB, pp. 67–68).

It is clear that Wittgenstein thought that analyzing the meaning of a word involves exhibiting the role or use of the word in the various language-games in which it occurs. He even suggests that we "think of words as instruments characterized by their use . . ." (BB, p. 67).

This notion of analysis leads rather naturally to an operationalistic view of the meaning of certain sorts of predicates. For, in those cases where it makes sense to say of a predicate that one has determined that it applies, one of the central language-games that the fluent speaker has learned to play is that of making and reporting such determinations. Consider, for example, one of the language-games that imparts meaning to such words as "length," i.e., that of reporting the dimensions of physical objects. To describe this game, one would have to include an account of the procedures involved in measuring lengths; indeed, mastering (at least some of) those procedures would be an essential part of learning this game. "The meaning of the word 'length' is learnt among other things, by learning what it is to determine length" (PI, p. 225). As Wittgenstein comments about an analogous case, "Here the teaching of language is not explanation, but training" (PI, § 5). For Wittgenstein, "To understand a sentence means to understand a language." "To understand a language means to be master of a technique" (PI, § 199).

In short, part of being competent in the language-game played with "length" consists in the ability to arrive at the truth of such statements as "*x* is three feet long" by performing relevant operations with, e.g., rulers, range-finders, etc. A philosophic analysis of "length," insofar as it seeks to articulate the language-game played with that word, must thus refer to the operations which determine the applicability of length predicates. Finally, insofar as the meaning of the word is itself determined by the rules governing the language-games in which it occurs, a reference to these operations will be essential in characterizing the meaning of such predicates as "three feet long." It is in this manner that we are led to the view that the relevant operations for determining the applicability of a predicate are conceptually connected with the predicate.[4]

By parity of reasoning, we can see that to analyze such words as "pain," "motive," "dream," etc., will *inter alia* involve articulating the operations or observations in terms of which we determine that someone is in pain, or that he has such and such a motive, or that he has dreamed, etc. (PI, p. 224). But clearly, such determinations are ultimately made on the basis of the behavior of the individual to whom the predicates are applied (taking behavior in the broad sense in which it includes verbal reports). Hence, for Wittgenstein, reference to the characteristic features of pain behavior on the basis of which we determine that someone is in pain is essential to the philosophical analysis of the word "pain" just as reference to the operations by which we determine the applicability of such predicates as "three feet long" is essential to the philosophical analysis of the word "length." In both cases, the relations are conceptual and the rule of language which articulates them is in that sense a rule of logic.

III

But what, specifically, is this logical connection which, according to Wittgenstein, is supposed to obtain between pain behavior and pain? Obviously, the connection is not that of simple entailment. It is evident that Wittgenstein did not think that some proposition to the effect that a person is screaming, wincing, groaning, or moaning could entail the proposition that the person is in pain. We know that Wittgenstein used the term "criterion" to mark this special connection, but we are in need of an explanation of this term.

We have already remarked that one of the central ideas in Wittgenstein's philosophy is that of a "language-game." Apparently Wittgenstein was passing a field on which a football game was being played when the idea occurred to him that "in language we play *games* with *words*."[5] Since this analogy dominated so much of the later Wittgenstein's philosophical thinking, perhaps it would be well to begin the intricate task of explicating Wittgenstein's notion of criterion by considering some specific game.

Take basketball as an example. Since the object of the game is to score more points than one's opponents, there must be some way of telling if and

when a team scores. Now there are various ways of telling that, say, a field goal has been scored. One might simply keep one's eyes on the scoreboard and wait for two points to be registered. Sometimes one realizes that a field goal has been scored on the basis of the reactions of the crowd. But these are, at best, indirect ways of telling, for if we use them we are relying on someone else: the score-keeper or other spectators. Obviously, not every way of telling is, in that sense, indirect; and anyone who is at all familiar with the game knows that, generally, one *sees* that a field goal has been scored in seeing the ball shot or tipped through the hoop. And if a philosopher asks, "Why does the fact that the ball went through the basket show that a field goal has been scored?" a natural reply would be, "That is what the rules of the game say; that is the way the game is played." The ball going through the basket satisfies a *criterion* for scoring a field goal.

Notice that though the relation between a criterion and that of which it is a criterion is a logical or conceptual one, the fact that the ball goes through the hoop does not entail that a field goal has been scored. First, the ball must be "in play" for it to be possible to score a field goal by tossing the ball through the basket. Second, even if the ball drops through the hoop when "in play," it need not follow that a field goal has been scored, for the rules of basketball do not cover all imaginable situations. Suppose, for example, that a player takes a long two-handed shot and that the ball suddenly reverses its direction, and after soaring and dipping through the air like a swallow in flight, gracefully drops through the player's own basket only to change into a bat, which immediately entangles itself in the net. What do the rules say about that?

An analogous situation would arise, in the case of a "language-game," if what seemed to be a chair suddenly disappeared, reappeared, and, in general, behaved in a fantastic manner. Wittgenstein's comment on this type of situation is:

> Have you rules ready for such cases—rules saying whether one may use the word "chair" to include this kind of thing? But do we miss them when we use the word "chair"; and are we to say that we do not really attach any meaning to this word, because we are not equipped with rules for every possible application of it? (PI, § 80)

For Wittgenstein, a sign "is in order—if, under normal circumstances it fulfils its purpose." (PI, § 87).

> It is only in normal cases that the use of a word is clearly prescribed; we know, are in no doubt, what to say in this or that case. The more abnormal the case,

the more doubtful it becomes what we are to say. (PI, § 142)

Let us now try to make out Wittgenstein's distinction between *criterion* and *symptom,* again utilizing the example of basketball. Suppose that, while a game is in progress, a spectator leaves his seat. Though he is unable to see the playing court, he might realize that the home team had scored a field goal on the basis of a symptom—say, the distinctive roar of the crowd—which he had observed to be correlated with home-team field goals. This correlation, according to Wittgenstein, would have to be established *via* criteria, say, by noting the sound of the cheering when the home team shot the ball through the basket. Thus, a symptom is "a phenomenon of which experience has taught us that it coincided, in some way or other, with the phenomenon which is our defining criterion" (BB, p. 25). Though both symptoms and criteria are cited in answer to the question, "How do you know that so-and-so is the case?" (BB, p. 24), symptoms, unlike criteria, are discovered through experience or observation: that something is a symptom is not given by the rules of the "language-game" (not deducible from the rules alone). However, to say of a statement that it expresses a symptom is to say something about the relation between the statement and the rules, viz., that it is not derivable from them. Hence, Wittgenstein once claimed that "whereas 'When it rains the pavement gets wet' is not a grammatical statement at all, if we say 'The fact that the pavement is wet is a *symptom* that it has been raining' this statement is 'a matter of grammar'."[6] Furthermore, giving the criterion for (e.g.) another's having a toothache "is to give a grammatical explanation about the word 'toothache' and, in this sense, an explanation concerning the meaning of the word 'toothache'" (BB, p. 24). However, given that there is this important difference between criteria and symptoms, the fact remains that Wittgenstein considered both symptoms and criteria as "evidences" (BB, p. 51).

Other salient features of criteria can be illuminated by exploiting our illustrative example. Consider Wittgenstein's claim that "in different circumstances we apply different criteria for a person's reading" (PI, § 164). It is clear that in different circumstances we apply different criteria for a person's scoring a field goal. For example, the question whether a player scored a field goal may arise even though the ball went nowhere near the basket: in a "goal-tending" situation, the question will have to be decided on the basis of whether the ball had started its descent before the defensive player had deflected it. According to the rules it would be a decisive reason for not awarding a field goal that the ball had not reached its apogee when it was blocked.

One can now see that to claim that X is a criterion of Y is not to claim that the presence, occurrence, existence, etc., of X is a necessary condition of the applicability of 'Y', and it is not to claim that the presence, occurrence, existence, etc., of X is a sufficient condition of Y, although if X is a criterion of Y, it may be the case that X is a necessary or a sufficient condition of Y.

Again, consider the tendency of Wittgenstein, noted by Albritton,[7] to write as if X (a criterion of Y) just is Y or is what is called 'Y' in certain circumstances. We can understand a philosopher's wanting to say that shooting the ball through the basket in the appropriate situation just *is* scoring a field goal or is what we call "scoring a field goal."

Consider now the following passage from the *Investigations* (§ 376) which suggests a kind of test for "non-criterionhood":

When I say the ABC to myself, what is the criterion of my doing the same as someone else who silently repeats it to himself? It might be found that the same thing took place in my larynx and in his. (And similarly when we both think of the same thing, wish the same, and so on.) But then did we learn the use of the words: "to say such-and-such to oneself" by someone's pointing to a process in the larynx or the brain?

Obviously not. Hence, Wittgenstein suggests, something taking place in the larynx cannot be the criterion. The rationale behind this "test" seems to be this: For the teaching of a particular predicate 'Y' to be successful, the pupil must learn the rules for the use of 'Y' and hence must learn the criteria for 'Y' if there are such criteria. Thus, if the teaching could be entirely successful without one learning that X is something on the basis of which one tells that 'Y' applies, X cannot be a criterion of Y. For example, since a person could be taught what "field goal" means without learning that one can generally tell that the home team has scored a field goal by noting the roar of the home crowd, the roar of the home crowd cannot be a criterion of field goals.

Finally, let us examine the principle, which Wittgenstein appears to maintain, that any change of criteria of X involves changing the concept of X. In the *Investigations,* Wittgenstein makes the puzzling claim:

There is *one* thing of which one can say neither that it is one metre long, nor that it is not one metre long, and that is the standard metre in Paris.—But this is, of course, not to ascribe any extraordinary property to it, but only to mark its peculiar role in the language-game of measuring with a metre-rule.—Let us imagine samples of colour being preserved in Paris like the standard metre. We define: "Sepia" means the colour of the standard sepia which is there kept hermetically sealed. Then it will make no sense to say of this sample either that it is of this colour or that it is not. (PI, § 50)

Wittgenstein evidently is maintaining not only that the senses of the predicates "x is one meter long" and "x is sepia" are given by the operations which determine the applicability of the respective predicates (the operations of comparing objects in certain ways with the respective standards),[8] but also that these operations cannot be performed on the standards themselves and hence neither standard can be said to be an instance of either the *predicate* for which it is a standard or of its negation. (Cf., "A thing cannot be at the same time the measure and the thing measured" [RFM, I, § 40, notes].)

Wittgenstein would undoubtedly allow that we might introduce a new language-game in which "meter" is defined in terms of the wave length of the spectral line of the element krypton of atomic weight 86.[9] In this language-game, where such highly accurate and complex measuring devices as the interferometer are required, the standard meter does not have any privileged position: it, too, can be measured and "represented." In this language-game, the standard meter is or is not a meter. But here, Wittgenstein would evidently distinguish two senses of the term "meter." Obviously what is a meter in one language-game need not be a meter in the other. Thus, Wittgenstein's view seems to be that by introducing a new criterion for something's being a meter long, we have introduced a new language-game, a new sense of the term "meter," and a new concept of meter. Such a position is indicated by Wittgenstein's comment:

We can speak of measurements of time in which there is a different, and as we should say a greater, exactness than in the measurement of time by a pocket-watch; in which the words "to set the clock to the exact time" have a different, though related meaning. . . . (PI, § 88)

Returning to our basketball analogy, suppose that the National Collegiate Athletic Association ruled, that, henceforth, a player can score a field goal by pushing the ball *upward* through the basket. Obviously, this would involve changing the rules of basketball. And to some extent, by introducing this new criterion, the rules governing the use or "grammar" of the term "field goal" would be altered. To put it somewhat dramatically (in the Wittgensteinian style), a new *essence* of field goal would be created. (Cf. "The mathematician creates *essence*" [RFM, I, § 32].) For Wittgenstein, not

only is it the case that the criteria we use "give our words their common meanings" (BB, p. 57) and that to explain the criteria we use is to explain the meanings of words (BB, p. 24), but also it is the case that to introduce a new criterion of Y is to define a new concept of Y.[10]

In summary, we can roughly and schematically characterize Wittgenstein's notion of criterion in the following way: X is a criterion of Y in situations of type S if the very meaning or definition of 'Y' (or, as Wittgenstein might have put it, if the "grammatical" rules for the use of 'Y')[11] justify the claim that one can recognize, see, detect, or determine the applicability of 'Y' on the basis of X in *normal* situations of type S. Hence, if the above relation obtains between X and Y, and if someone admits that X but denies Y, the burden of proof is upon him to show that something is abnormal in the situation. In a normal situation, the problem of gathering evidence which justifies concluding Y from X simply does not arise.

IV

The following passage occurs in the *Blue Book* (p. 24):

When we learnt the use of the phrase "so-and-so has toothache" we were pointed out certain kinds of behavior of those who were said to have toothache. As an instance of these kinds of behavior let us take holding your cheek. Suppose that by observation I found that in certain cases whenever these first criteria told me a person had toothache, a red patch appeared on the person's cheek. Supposing I now said to someone "I see A has toothache, he's got a red patch on his cheek." He may ask me "How do you know A has toothache when you see a red patch?" I would then point out that certain phenomena had always coincided with the appearance of the red patch.

Now one may go on and ask: "How do you know that he has got toothache when he holds his cheek?" The answer to this might be, "I say, *he* has toothache when he holds his cheek because I hold my cheek when I have toothache." But what if we went on asking:—"And why do you suppose that toothache corresponds to his holding his cheek just because your toothache corresponds to your holding your cheek?" You will be at a loss to answer this question, and find that here we strike rock bottom, that is we have come down to conventions.

It would seem that, on Wittgenstein's view, empirical justification of the claim to see, recognize, or know that such and such is the case *on the basis of some observable feature or state of affairs,* would have to rest upon inductions from observed correlations, so that, if a person claims that Y is the case on the grounds that X is the case, in answer to the question "Why does the fact that X show that Y?" he would have to cite either conventions or observed correlations linking X and Y. Thus, Wittgenstein appears to be arguing that the possibility of ever inferring a person's toothache from his behavior requires the existence of a criterion of toothache that can sometimes be observed to obtain. A generalized form of this argument leads to the conclusion that "an 'inner process' stands in need of outward criteria" (PI, § 580).

As an illustration of Wittgenstein's reasoning, consider the following example: It appears to be the case that the measurement of the alcohol content of the blood affords a reasonably reliable index of intoxication. On the basis of this empirical information, we may sometimes justify the claim that X is intoxicated by showing that the alcohol content of his blood is higher than some specified percentage. But now consider the justification of the claim that blood-alcohol is in fact an index of intoxication. On Wittgenstein's view, the justification of *this* claim must rest ultimately upon correlating cases of intoxication with determinations of high blood-alcohol content. But, the observations required for this correlation could be made only if there exist independent techniques for identifying each of the correlated items. In any particular case, these independent techniques may themselves be based upon further empirical correlations; we might justify the claim that the blood-alcohol content is high by appealing to some previously established correlation between the presence of blood-alcohol and some test result. But ultimately according to Wittgenstein, we must come upon identifying techniques based not upon further empirical correlations, but rather upon definitions or conventions which determine criteria for applying the relevant predicates. This is why Wittgenstein can say that a symptom is "a phenomenon of which experience has taught us that it coincided, in some way or other with the phenomenon which is our defining criterion" (BB, p. 25).

A similar argument has recently been given by Sidney Shoemaker who writes:

If we know psychological facts about other persons at all, we know them on the basis of their behavior (including, of course, their verbal behavior). Sometimes we make psychological statements about other persons on the basis of bodily or behavioral facts that are only contingently related to the psychological facts for which we accept them as evidence. But we do this only because we have discovered, or think we have discovered, empirical correlations between physical (bodily and behavioral) facts of a certain kind and psychological facts of a certain kind. And if *all* relations between physical and psychological facts were

contingent, it would be impossible for us to discover such correlations.... Unless some relationships between physical and psychological states are not contingent, and can be known prior to the discovery of empirical correlations, we cannot have even indirect inductive evidence for the truth of psychological statements about other persons, and cannot know such statements to be true or even probably true.[12]

Malcolm argues in a similar manner in *Dreaming*.[13]

Of course, Wittgenstein did not claim that all predicates presuppose criteria of applicability. For example, Wittgenstein probably did not think that we, in general, see, tell, determine, or know that something is red on the basis of either a criterion or a symptom. The relevant difference between ascriptions of "red" and third-person ascriptions of "pain" is that we generally see, recognize, determine, or know that another is in pain on the basis of something which is not the pain itself (as for example, behavior and circumstances) whereas, if it made any sense at all to say we generally see, recognize, etc., that an object is red on the basis of something, what could this something be other than just the object's redness? But Wittgenstein's use of the term "criterion" seems to preclude redness being a criterion of redness. If someone asks "How do you know or tell that an object is red?" it would not, in general, do to answer "By its redness." (Cf. Wittgenstein's comment "How do I know that this color is red?—It would be an answer to say: 'I have learnt English'" [PI, § 381].) Evidently, some color predicates and, more generally, what are sometimes called "sense datum" predicates (those that can be known to apply—as some philosophers put it—*immediately*), do not fall within the domain of arguments of the above type. But the predicates with which we assign "inner states" to another person are not of this sort. One recognizes that another is in a certain mental state, Y, on the basis of something, say, X. Now it is assumed that X must be either a criterion or symptom of Y. If X is a symptom, X must be known to be correlated with Y, and we may then inquire into the way in which this correlation was established. Again, X must have been observed to be correlated with a criterion of Y or with a symptom, X_1, of Y. On the second alternative, we may inquire into the basis for holding that X_1 is a symptom of Y.... Such a chain may go on for any distance you like, but it cannot go on indefinitely. That is, at some point, we must come to a criterion of Y. But once this conclusion has been accepted, there appears to be no reasonable non-sceptical alternative to Wittgenstein's logical behaviorism, for if "inner" states require "outward" criteria, behavioral criteria are the only plausible candidates.

V

As a refutation of scepticism, the above argument certainly will not do; for, at best, it supports Wittgenstein's position only on the assumption that the sceptic is not right. That is, it demonstrates that there must be criteria for psychological predicates by assuming that such predicates are sometimes applied justifiably. A sceptic who accepts the argument of Section IV could maintain his position only by allowing that no one could have any idea of what would show or even indicate that another is in pain, having a dream, thinking, etc. In this section we shall show how Wittgenstein argues that that move would lead the sceptic to the absurd conclusion that it must be impossible to teach the meaning of these psychological predicates.

"What would it be like if human beings showed no outward signs of pain (did not groan, grimace, etc.)? Then it would be impossible to teach a child the use of the word 'toothache'" (PI, § 257). For just imagine trying to teach a child the meaning of the term "toothache," say, on the supposition that there is absolutely no way of telling whether the child—or anyone else for that matter—is actually in pain. How would one go about it, if one had no reason for believing that gross damage to the body causes pain or that crying out, wincing, and the like indicate pain? ("How could I even have come by the idea of another's experience if there is no possibility of any evidence for it?" [BB, p. 46; cf. also BB, p. 48].)

Again, what would show us that the child had grasped the teaching? If anything would, the argument of Section IV requires that there be a criterion of having succeeded in teaching the child. (As Wittgenstein says of an analogous case, "If I speak of communicating a feeling to someone else, mustn't I in order to understand what I say know what I shall call the criterion of having succeeded in communicating?" (BB, p. 185).) But the only plausible criterion of this would be that the child applied the psychological predicates correctly (cf. PI, § 146); and since the sceptical position implies that there is no way of knowing if the child correctly applies such predicates, it would seem to follow that nothing could show or indicate that the child had learned what these terms mean.

We now have a basis for explicating the sense of "logical" which is involved in the claim that scepticism is a logically incoherent doctrine. What Wittgenstein holds is not that "P and not-P" are strictly deducible from the sceptic's position, but rather that the sceptic's view presupposes a deviation from the rules for the use of key terms. In particular, Wittgenstein holds that if the sceptic were right, the preconditions for teaching the meaning of the mental predicates of our ordinary language could not be satisfied.[14]

We now see too the point to the insistence that the sceptic's position must incorporate an extraordinary and misleading use of mental predicates. The sceptic's view is logically incompatible with the operation of the ordinary language rules for the application of these terms, and these rules determine their meanings. (Cf. "What *we* do is to bring words back from their metaphysical to their everyday usage" [PI, § 116].) As Wittgenstein diagnoses the sceptic's view, the sceptic does not have in mind any criteria of third person ascriptions when he denies that he can know if anyone else has pains (cf. PI, § 272). The sceptic tempts us to picture the situation as involving "a barrier which doesn't allow one person to come closer to another's experience than to the point of observing his behavior"; but, according to Wittgenstein, "on looking closer we find that we can't apply the picture" (BB, p. 56); no clear meaning can be attached to the sceptic's claim: no sense can even be given the hypothesis that other people feel "pains," as the sceptic uses the term "pain." ("For how can I even make the hypothesis if it transcends all possible experience?" [BB, p. 48].) And if the sceptic says, "But if I suppose that someone has a pain, then I am simply supposing that he has just the same as I have so often had." Wittgenstein can reply:

> That gets us no further. It is as if I were to say: "You surely know what 'It is 5 o'clock here' means; so you also know what 'It's 5 o'clock on the sun' means. It means simply that it is just the same time there as it is here when it is 5 o'clock."—The explanation by means of *identity* does not work here. For I know well enough that one can call 5 o'clock here and 5 o'clock there "the same time," but what I do not know is in what cases one is to speak of its being the same time here and there. (PI, § 350)

Thus, we can see how Wittegenstein supports his logical behaviorism: the argument in Section IV purports to show that the only plausible alternative to Wittgenstein's philosophical psychology is radical scepticism; and the argument in the present section rules out this alternative. For Wittgenstein, then, "the person of whom we say 'he has pains' is, by the rules of the game, the person who cries, contorts his face, etc.," (BB, p. 68).

Undoubtedly, there is much that philosophers find comforting and attractive in Wittgenstein's philosophical psychology, but there are also difficulties in the doctrine which mar its attractiveness. To some of these difficulties, we shall now turn.

VI

In this section, we shall consider some consequences of applying the views just discussed to the analysis of dreaming, and we shall attempt to show that the conclusions to which these views lead are counter-intuitive.

According to Wittgenstein, we are to understand the concept of dreaming in terms of the language-games(s) in which "dream" plays a role and, in particular, in terms of the language-game of dream telling. For, to master the use of the word "dream" is precisely to learn what it is to find out that someone has dreamed, to tell what someone has dreamed, to report one's own dreams, and so on. Passages in the *Investigations* (e.g., PI, pp. 184, 222–223) indicate that, for Wittgenstein, a criterion of someone's having dreamed is the dream report. On this analysis, sceptical doubts about dreams arise when we fail to appreciate the logical bond between statements about dreams and statements about dream reports. The sceptic treats the dream report as, at best, an empirical correlate of the occurrence of a dream: a symptom that is, at any event, no more reliable than the memory of the subject who reports the dream. But, according to Wittgenstein, once we have understood the criterial relation between dream reporting and dreaming, we see that "the question whether the dreamer's memory deceives him when he reports the dream after waking cannot arise . . ." (PI, p. 222). (Compare: "Once we understand the rules for playing chess, the question whether a player has won when he has achieved check-mate cannot arise.")

The rules articulating the criteria for applying the word "dream" determine a logical relation between dreaming and reporting dreams. Moreover, the set of such rules fixes the language-game in which "dream" has its role and hence determines the meaning of the word.

It is important to notice that there are a number of *prima facie* objections to this analysis which, though perhaps not conclusive, supply grounds for questioning the doctrines which lead to it. Though we could perhaps learn to live with these objections were no other analyses available, when seen from the vantage point of an alternative theory they indicate deep troubles with Wittgenstein's views.

(1) Given that there exist no criteria for first-person applications of many psychological predictes ("pain," "wish," or the like) it is unclear how the first person aspects of the game played with these predicates are to be described. Wittgenstein does not appear to present a coherent account of the behavior of predicates whose applicability is not determined by criteria. On the other hand, the attempt to characterize "I dreamt" as criterion-governed leads immediately to absurdities. Thus, in Malcolm's *Dreaming* it is suggested that:

> If a man wakes up with the impressions of having seen and done various things, and if it is known that he did not see and do those things, then it is known that he dreamt them. . . . When he says "I dreamt so and so" he implies, first, that it seemed to him on waking up as if the so and so had occurred and second, that the so and so did not occur. (p. 66)

That this is an incredibly counter-intuitive analysis of our concept of dreaming hardly needs mentioning. We ask the reader to consider the following example: A person, from time to time, gets the strange feeling that, shortly before, he had seen and heard his father commanding him to come home. One morning he wakes with this feeling, knowing full well that his father is dead. Now we are asked by Malcolm to believe that the person *must have dreamt* that he saw and heard his father: supposedly, it would be logically absurd for the person to claim to have this feeling and deny that he had dreamt it!

(2) Wittgenstein's view appears to entail that no sense can be made of such statements as "Jones totally forgot the dream he had last night," since we seem to have no criteria for determining the truth of such a statement. (We have in mind the case in which Jones is totally unable to remember having dreamed and no behavioral manifestations of dreaming were exhibited.) It is sometimes denied that observations of what people ordinarily say are relevant to a description of ordinary language. But, insofar as statements about what we would say are susceptible to empirical disconfirmation, the claim that we would feel hesitation about saying that someone completely forgot his dream appears to be just false.[15]

(3) The Wittgensteinian method of counting concepts is certainly not an intuitive one. Consider Malcolm's analysis of dreaming again. Malcolm realizes that sometimes, on the basis of a person's behavior during sleep, we say that he had a dream, even though he is unable to recall a dream upon awaking. But, in such cases, Malcolm claims, "our words . . . have no clear sense" (*Dreaming*, p. 62). On the other hand, Malcolm admits that there is a *sense* of the term "nightmare" where behavior during sleep is the criterion. However, a different concept of dreaming is supposedly involved in this

case. An analogous situation is treated in the *Blue Book* (p. 63), where Wittgenstein writes:

> If a man tries to obey the order "Point to your eye," he may do many different things, and there are many different criteria which he will accept for having pointed to his eye. If these criteria, as they usually do, coincide, I may use them alternately and in different combinations to show me that I have touched my eye. If they don't coincide, I shall have to distinguish between different senses of the phrase "I touch my eye" or "I move my finger towards my eye."

Following this suggestion of Wittgenstein, Malcolm distinguishes not only different senses of the term "dream," but also different concepts of sleep—one based upon report, one based upon nonverbal behavior. But surely, this is an unnatural way of counting concepts. Compare Malcolm's two concepts of sleep with a case where it really does seem natural to say that a special concept of sleep has been employed, viz., where we say of a hibernating bear that it sleeps through the winter.

(4) As Malcolm points out, the language-game *now* played with "dream" seems to exhibit no criteria which would enable one to determine the precise duration of dreams. Hence, it would seem to follow (as Malcolm has noticed) that scientists who have attempted to answer such questions as, "How long do dreams last?" are involved in conceptual confusions rather than empirical determinations. For such questions cannot be answered without adopting criteria for ascribing the relevant properties to dreams. But since, on Wittgenstein's view, to adopt such new criteria for the use of a word is, to that extent, to change its meaning, it follows that the concept of "dream" that such researchers employ is not the ordinary concept and hence that the measurements they effect are not, strictly speaking, measurements of *dreams*.[16] The notion that adopting any test for dreaming which arrives at features of dreams not determinable from the dream report thereby alters the concept of a dream seems to run counter to our intuitions about the goals of psychological research. It is not immediately obvious that the psychologist who says he has found a method of measuring the duration of dreams *ipso facto* commits the fallacy of ambiguity.[17]

(5) Consider the fact that such measures as EEG, eye-movements and "dream-behavior" (murmuring, tossing, etc., during sleep) correlate reasonably reliably with one another and dream reports. The relation between, say, EEG and dream reports is clearly not criterial; no one holds that EEG is a criterion of dream reports. It would seem then that, on Wittgenstein's view, EEG provides us with, at best, a symptom of positive dream reports; and symptoms are supposedly discovered by observing co-occurrences. The difficulty, however, is that this makes it unclear how the expectation that such a correlation must obtain could have been a rational expectation even *before* the correlation was experimentally confirmed. One cannot have an inductive generalization over no observations; nor, in this case, was any higher level "covering law" used to infer the probability of a correlation between EEG and dream reports. Given Wittgenstein's analysis of the concept of dreaming, not only do the researches of psychologists into the nature of dreams appear mysterious, but even the expectations, based upon these researches, seem somewhat irrational.

The difficulties we have mentioned are not peculiar to the Wittgensteinian analysis of dreams. Most of them have counterparts in the analyses of sensation, perception, intention, etc. Whether or not these difficulties can be obviated, in some way, noticing them provides a motive for re-examining the deeper doctrines upon which Wittgensteinian analyses of psychological terms are based.

VIII

The Wittgensteinian argument of Section IV rests on the premiss that if we are justified in claiming that one can tell, recognize, see, or determine that 'Y' applies on the basis of the presence of X, then either X is a criterion of Y or observations have shown that X is correlated with Y. Wittgenstein does not present any justification for this premiss in his published writings. Evidently, some philosophers find it self-evident and hence in need of no justification. We, on the other hand, far from finding this premiss self-evident, believe it to be false. Consider: one standard instrument used in the detection of high-speed, charged particles is the Wilson cloud-chamber. According to present scientific theories, the formation of tiny, thin bands of fog on the glass surface of the instrument indicates the passage of charged particles through the chamber. It is obvious that the formation of these streaks is not a Wittgensteinian criterion of the presence and motion of these particles in the apparatus. That one can detect these charged particles and determine their paths by means of such devices is surely not, by any stretch of the imagination, a *conceptual* truth. C.T.R. Wilson did not learn what "path of a charged particle" means by having the cloud-chamber explained to him: he *discovered* the method, and the discovery was contingent upon recognizing the empirical fact that ions could act as centers of condensation in a supersaturated vapor. Hence, applying Wittgenstein's own test for non-criterionhood (see above), the formation of a cloud-chamber track cannot be a criterion of the presence and motion of charged particles.

It is equally clear that the basis for taking these streaks as indicators of the paths of the particles is not observed *correlations* between streaks and some criterion of motion of charged particles. (What criterion for determining the path of an electron could Wilson have used to establish such correlations?) Rather, scientists were able to give compelling explanations of the formation of the streaks on the hypothesis that high-velocity, charged particles were passing through the chamber; on this hypothesis, further predictions were made, tested, and confirmed; no other equally plausible explanation is available; and so forth.

Such cases suggest that Wittgenstein failed to consider all the possible types of answers to the question, "What is the justification for the claim that one can tell, recognize, or determine that *Y* applies on the basis of the presence of *X*?" For, where *Y* is the predicate "is the path of a high-velocity particle," *X* need not have the form of either a criterion or a correlate.

Wittgensteinians may be tempted to argue that cloud-chamber tracks really are criteria, or symptoms observed to be correlated with criteria, of the paths of charged particles. To obviate this type of counter, we wish to stress that the example just given is by no means idiosyncratic. The reader who is not satisfied with it will easily construct others from the history of science. What is at issue is the possibility of a type of justification which consists in neither the appeal to criteria nor the appeal to observed correlations. If the Wittgensteinian argument we have been considering is to be compelling, some grounds must be given for the exhaustiveness of these types of justification. This, it would seem, Wittgenstein has failed to do.

It is worth noticing that a plausible solution to the problem raised in VI.5 can be given if we consider experiments with dreams and EEG to be analogous to the cloud-chamber case. That is, we can see how it could be the case that the correlation of EEG with dream reports was anticipated prior to observation. The dream report was taken by the experimenters to be an indicator of a psychological event occurring prior to it. Given considerations about the relation of cortical to psychological events, and given also the theory of EEG, it was predicted that the EEG should provide an index of the occurrence of dreams. From the hypothesis that dream reports and EEG readings are both indices of the same psychological events, it could be deduced that they ought to be reliably correlated with one another, and this deduction in fact proved to be correct.

This situation is not at all unusual in the case of explanations based upon theoretical inferences to events underlying observable syndromes. As Meehl and Cronbach have pointed out, in such cases the validity of the "criterion" is often nearly as much at issue as the validity of the indices to be correlated with it.[18] The successful prediction of the correlation on the basis of the postulation of a common etiology is taken both as evidence for the existence of the cause and as indicating the validity of each of the correlates as an index of its presence.

In this kind of case, the justification of existential statements is thus identical neither with an appeal to criteria nor with an appeal to symptoms. Such justifications depend rather on appeals to the simplicity, plausibility, and predictive adequacy of an explanatory system as a whole, so that it is incorrect to say that relations between statements which are mediated by such explanations are either logical in Wittgenstein's sense or contingent in the sense in which this term suggests simple correlation.

It cannot be stressed too often that there exist patterns of justificatory argument which are not happily identified either with appeals to symptoms or with appeals to criteria, and which do not in any obvious way rest upon such appeals. In these arguments, existential claims about states, events, and processes which are *not* directly observable are susceptible of justification despite the fact that no *logical* relation obtains between the predicates ascribing such states and predicates whose applicability *can* be directly observed. There is a temptation to hold that in such cases there *must* be a criterion, that there must be some set of possible observations which would settle *for sure* whether the theoretical predicate applies. But we succumb to this temptation at the price of postulating stipulative definitions and conceptual alterations which fail to correspond to anything we can discover in the course of empirical arguments. The counter-intuitive features of philosophic analyses based on the assumption that there must be criteria are thus not the consequences of a profound methodological insight, but rather a projection of an inadequate philosophical theory of justification.

IX

It might be replied that the above examples do not constitute counter-instances to Wittgenstein's criterion-correlation premiss since Wittgenstein may have intended his principle to be applicable only in the case of ordinary language terms which, so it might seem, do not function within the framework of a theory. It is perhaps possible to have indicators that are neither criteria nor symptoms of such highly theoretical entities as electrons and positrons, but the terms used by ordinary people in everyday life are obviously (?) in a different category. (Notice that Wittgenstein considers "making scientific hypotheses and theories" a different "game" from such "language-games" as "describing an event" and "describing an immediate experience" [BB, pp. 67–68; Cf. PI, § 23].) Hence, Wittgenstein might argue, it is only in the case of ordinary language terms that the demand for criteria is necessary.

Once one perceives the presuppositions of Wittgenstein's demand for criteria, however, it becomes evident that alternatives to Wittgenstein's analyses of ordinary language mental terms should at least be explored. Perhaps, what we all learn in learning what such terms as "pain" and "dream" mean are not criterial connections which map these terms serverally onto characteristic patterns of behavior. We may instead form complex conceptual connections which interrelate a wide variety of mental states. It is to such a conceptual system that we appeal when we attempt to explain someone's behavior by reference to his motives, intentions, beliefs, desires, or sensations. In other words, in learning the language, we develop a number of intricately interrelated "mental concepts" which we use in dealing with, coming to terms with, understanding, explaining, interpreting, etc., the behavior of other human beings (as well as our own). In the course of acquiring these mental concepts we devleop a variety of beliefs involving them. Such beliefs result in a wide range of expectations about how people are likely to behave. Since only a portion of these beliefs are confirmed in the normal course, these beliefs and the conceptual systems which they articulate are both subject to correction and alteration as the consequence of our constant interaction with other people.

On this view, our success in accounting for the behavior on the basis of which mental predicates are applied might properly be thought of as supplying *evidence* for the existence of the mental processes we postulate. It does so by attesting to the adequacy of the conceptual system in terms of which the processes are understood. The behavior would be, in that sense, analogous to the cloud-chamber track on the basis of which we detect the presence and motion of charged particles. Correspondingly, the conceptual system is analogous to the physical *theory* in which the properties of these particles are formulated.

If something like this should be correct, it would be possible, at least in theory, to reconstruct and describe the conceptual system involved and then to obtain some confirmation that the putative system is in fact employed by English speakers. For example, confirmation might come *via* the usual methods of "reading off" the conceptual relation in the putative system and *matching them* against the linguistic intuitions of native speakers. Thus, given that a particular conceptual system is being employed, certain statements should strike native speakers as nonsensical, others should seem necessarily true, others should seem ambiguous, others empirically false, and so on, all of which would be testable.

To maintain that there are no criterial connections between pains and behavior does not commit us to holding that the fact that people often feel *pains* when they cry out is *just* a contingent fact (in the sense in which it is just a contingent fact that most of the books in my library are unread). The belief that other people feel pains is not gratuitous even on the view that there are no criteria of pains. On the contrary, it provides the only plausible explanation of the facts I know about the way that they behave in and *vis à vis* the sorts of situations I find painful. These facts are, of course, enormously complex. The "pain syndrome" includes not only correlations between varieties of overt behaviors but also more subtle relations between pain and motivations, utilities, desires, and so on. Moreover, I confidently expect that there must exist reliable members of this syndrome other than the ones with which I am currently familiar. I am in need of an explanation of the reliability and fruitfulness of this syndrome, an explanation which reference to the occurrence of pains supplies. Here, as elsewhere, an "outer" syndrome stands in need of an inner process.

Thus, it is at least conceivable that a non-Wittgensteinian account ought to be given of the way children learn the mental predicates. (It is, at any event, sufficient to notice that such an account *could* be given, that there exist alternatives to Wittgenstein's doctrine.) For example, if the concept of dreaming is *inter alia* that of an inner event which takes place during a definite stretch of "real" time, which causes such involuntary behavior as moaning and murmuring in one's sleep, tossing about, etc., and which is remembered when one correctly reports a dream, then there are a number of ways in which a child might be supposed to "get" this concept other than by learning criteria for the application of the word "dream." Perhaps it is true of many children that they learn what a dream is by being told that what they have just experienced was a dream. Perhaps it was also true of many children that, having grasped the notions of *imagining* and *sleep,* they learn what a dream is when they are told that dreaming is something like imagining in your sleep.

But does this imply that children learn what a dream is "from their own case?" If this is a logical rather than psychological question, the answer is "Not necessarily": a child who never dreamed, but who was very clever might arrive at an understanding of what dreams are just on the basis of the sort of theoretical inference we have described above. For our notion of a dream is that of a mental event having various properties that are required in order to explain the characteristic features of the dream-behavior syndrome. For example, dreams occur during sleep, have duration, sometimes cause people who are sleeping to murmur or to toss, can be described in visual, auditory, or tactile terms, are sometimes remembered and sometimes not, are sometimes reported and sometimes not, sometimes prove frightening, sometimes are interrupted before they are finished, etc. But if these are the sorts of facts that characterize our concept of dream, then there seems to be nothing which would, in principle, prevent a child who never dreamed from arriving at this notion.

A similar story might be told about how such sensation terms as "pain" are learned and about the learning of such quasi-dispositionals as "having a motive." In each case, since the features that we in fact attribute to these states, processes, or dispositions are just those features we know they must have if they are to fulfill their role in explanations of behavior, etiology, personality, etc., it would seem that there is nothing about them the child could not in principle learn by employing the pattern of inference we have described above, and hence nothing that he could in principle learn *only* by an analogy to his own case.

Now it might be argued that the alternative to Wittgenstein's position we have been sketching is highly implausible. For, if children do have to acquire the complicated conceptual system our theory requires to understand and use mental predicates, surely they would have to be taught this system. And the teaching would surely have to be terribly involved and complex. But as a matter of fact, children do not require any such teaching at all, and hence we should conclude that our alternative to Wittgenstein's criterion view is untenable.

The force of this argument, however, can to some extent be dispelled if we consider the child's acquisition of, e.g., the grammar of a natural langauge. It is clear that, by some process we are only now beginning to understand, a child, on the basis of a relatively short "exposure" to utterances in his language, develops capacities for producing and

understanding "novel" sentences (sentences which he has never previously heard or seen). The exercise of these capacities, so far as we can tell, "involve" the use of an intricate system of linguistic rules of very considerable generality and complexity.[19] That the child is not taught (in any ordinary sense) any such system of rules is undeniable. These capacities seem to develop naturally in the child in response to little more than contact with a relatively small number of sentences uttered in ordinary contexts in everyday life.[20] Granting for the moment that the apparent complexity of such systems of rules is not somehow an artifact of an unsatisfactory theory of language, the fact that the child develops these linguistic capacities shows that a corresponding "natural" development of a system of mental concepts may not, as a matter of brute fact, require the sort of explicit teaching a person needs to master, say, calculus or quantum physics.

X

It is easily seen that this unabashedly non-behavioristic view avoids each of the difficulties we raised regarding Wittgenstein's analyses of mental predicates. Thus, the asymmetry between first and third person uses of "dream" discussed in Section VI need not arise since there need be no criteria for "X dreamed," *whatever* value X takes: we do not have the special problem of characterizing the meaning of "I dreamed" since "dream" in this context means just what it means in third person contexts, viz., "a series of thoughts, images, or emotions occurring during sleep." Again, it is now clear why people find such remarks as "Jones totally forgot what and that he dreamed last night" perfectly sensible. It is even clear how such assertions might be confirmed. Suppose, for example, that there exists a neurological state α such that there is a very high correlation between the presence of α and such dream behavior as tossing in one's sleep, crying out in one's sleep, reporting dreams, and so on. Suppose, too that there exists some neurological state β such that whenever β occurs, experiences that the subject has had just prior to β are forgotten. Suppose, finally, that sometimes we observe sequences, α, β, and that such sequences are not followed by dream reports though the occurrences of α are accompanied by other characteristic dream behaviors. It seems clear that the reasonable thing to say in such a case is that the subject has dreamed and forgotten his dream. And since we have postulated no criterion for dreaming, but only a syndrome of dream behaviors each related to some inner psychological event, we need have no fear that, in saying what it is reasonable to say, we have changed the meaning of "dream." We leave it to the reader to verify that the other objections we raised against the Wittgensteinian analysis of "dream" also fail to apply to the present doctrine.

Thus, once we have abandoned the arguments for a criterial connection between statements about behavior and statements about psychological states, the question remains open whether applications of ordinary language psychological terms on the basis of observations of behavior ought not themselves be treated as theoretical inferences to underlying mental occurrences. The question whether such statements as "He moaned because he was in pain" function to explain behavior by relating it to an assumed mental event cannot be settled simply by reference to ordinary linguistic usage. Answering this question requires broadly empirical investigations into the nature of thought and concept formation in normal human beings. What is at issue is the question of the role of theory construction and theoretical inference in thought and argument outside pure science. Psychological investigations indicate that much everyday conceptualization depends on the exploitation of theories and explanatory models in terms of which experience is integrated and understood.[11] Such pre-scientific theories, far from being mere functionless "pictures," play an essential role in determining the sorts of perceptual and inductive expectations we form and the kind of arguments and explanations we accept. It thus seems *possible* that the correct view of the functioning of ordinary language mental predicates would assimilate applying them to the sorts of processes of theoretical inference operative in scientific psychological explanation. If this is correct, the primary difference between ordinary and scientific uses of psychological predicates would be just that the processes of inference which are made explicit in the latter case remain implicit in the former.

We can now see what should be said in reply to Wittgenstein's argument that the possibility of teaching a language rests upon the existence of criteria. Perhaps teaching a word would be impossible if it could not sometimes be determined that the student has mastered the use of the word. But this does not entail that there need be *criteria* for "*X* learned the word *w*." All that is required is that we must sometimes have good reasons for saying that the word has been mastered; and this condition is satisfied when, for example, the simplest and most plausible explanation available of the verbal behavior of the student is that he has learned the use of the word.

NOTES

1. This work was supported in part by the U.S. Army, Navy, and Air Force under Contract DA 36-039-AMC-03200(E); in part by the National Science Foundation (Grant GP-2495), the National Institutes of Health (Grant MH-04737-04), the National Aeronautics and Space Administration (Ns G-496), the U.S. Air Force (ESD Contract AF 19 (628)-2487), the National Institute of Mental Health (Grant MPM 17, 760); and, in addition, by a University of California Faculty Fellowship.

2. In making references to Part I of Ludwig Wittgenstein's *Philosophical Investigations* (New York, 1953), cited here as PI, we shall give section numbers, e.g. (PI, § 13), to Part II, we shall give page numbers, e.g. (PI, p. 220). In referring to his *The Blue and Brown Books* (New York, 1958), cited here as BB, we give page numbers. References to his *Remarks on the Foundations of Mathematics* (New York, 1956), cited here as RFM, will include both part and section numbers, e.g. (RFM, II, § 26).

3. Philosophers of Wittgensteinian persuasion have sometimes heatedly denied that the term "behaviorism" is correctly applied to the view that logical connections of the above sort exist. We do not feel that very much hangs on using the term "behaviorism" as we do, but we are prepared to give some justification for our terminology. "Behaviorism" is, in the first instance, a term applied to a school of psychologists whose interest was in placing constraints upon the conceptual equipment that might be employed in putative psychological explanations, but who were *not* particularly interested in the analysis of the mental vocabulary of ordinary language. The application of this label to a philosopher bent upon this latter task must therefore be, to some extent, analogical. Granted that there has been some tendency for the term "behaviorism" to be preempted, even in psychology, for the position held by such *radical* behaviorists as Watson and Skinner, who require that all psychological generalizations be defined over observables, insofar as C. L. Hull can be classifed as a behaviorist, there does seem to be grounds for our classification. Hull's view, as we understand it, is that mental predicates are in no sense "eliminable" in favor of behavioral predicates, but that it is a condition upon their coherent employment that they be severally related to behavioral predicates and that some of these relations be logical rather than empirical—a view that is strikingly similar to the one we attribute to Wittgenstein. Cf. C. F. Hull, *Principles of Behavior* (New York, 1943).

4. Cf. "Let us consider what we call an 'exact' explanation in contrast with this one. Perhaps something like drawing a chalk line round an area? Here it strikes us at once that the line has breadth. So a color-edge would be more exact. But has this exactness still got a function here: isn't the engine idling? And remember too that we have not yet defined what is to count as overstepping this exact boundary; *how, with what instruments, it is to be established*" (PI, § 88, italics ours). Cf., also RFM, I, § 5.

5. Norman Malcolm, *Ludwig Wittgenstein: a Memoir* (Oxford, 1958), p. 65.

6. G. E. Moore, "Wittgenstein's Lectures in 1930–33," *Philosophical Papers* (London, 1959), pp. 266–267.

7. Rogers Albritton, "On Wittgenstein's Use of the Term 'Criterion'," *Journal of Philosphy,* vol. 56 (1959), pp. 851–854.

8. Note Wittgenstein's suggestion that we can "give the phrase 'unconscious pain' sense by fixing experiential criteria for the case in which a man has pain and doesn't know it" (BB, p. 55). Cf., also: "If however we do use the expression 'the thought takes place in the head,' we have given this expression its meaning by describing the experience which would justify the *hypothesis* that the thought takes place in our heads, by describing the experience which we wish to call observing thought in our brain" (BB, p. 8).

9. Adopted by the eleventh General International Conference on Weights and Measures in the fall of 1960.

10. RFM, II, § 24; III, § 29; and I, Appendix I, § 15–16. See also C. S. Chihara "Mathematical Discovery and Concept Formation," *The Philosophical Review,* vol. 72 (1963), pp. 17–84.

11. Cf., "The person of whom we say 'he has pain' is, *by the rules of the game,* the person who cries, contorts his face, etc." (BB, p. 68, italics ours).

12. Sidney Shoemaker, *Self-knowledge and Self-identity* (Ithaca, 1963), pp. 167–168.

13. Norman Malcolm, *Dreaming* (London, 1959), pp. 60–61.

14. Cf., "'Before I judge that two images which I have are the same, I must recognize them as the same.' . . . Only if I can express my recognition in some other way, and if it is possible for someone else to teach me that 'same' is the correct word here" (PI, § 378).

15. Thus consider the following: "Up until the night I opened the door, I remembered my dreams. Soon after, I ceased to recall them. I still dreamed, but my waking consciousness concealed from itself what sleep revealed. If the recurrent nightmare of the iron fence awoke me, I recognized it. But if any other nightmare broke my sleep, I forgot what it was about by morning. And of all the other dreams I had during the night I remembered nothing" (Windham, D., "Myopia," *The New Yorker,* July 13, 1963).

16. In *Dreaming,* Malcolm gives a number of arguments, not be be found in Wittgenstein's published writings, for the position that psychologists attempting to discover methods of measuring the duration of dreams must be using the term "dream" in a misleading and extraordinary way. For a reply to these arguments, see C. S. Chihara "What Dreams are Made On" forthcoming in *Theoria.* See also H. Putnam's criticism of Malcolm,"Dreaming and 'Depth Grammar,'" *Analytical Philosophy,* ed. by R. J. Butler (Oxford, 1962), pp. 211–235.

17. The implausibility of this view is even more striking when Wittgenstein applies it in his philosophy of mathematics to arrive at the conclusion that every new theorem about a concept alters the concept or introduces a new concept. When the notion of conceptual change is allowed to degenerate this far, it is not easy to see that anything rides on the claim that a conceptual change has taken place. Cf. C. S. Chihara, "Mathematical Discovery and Concept Formation," *The Philosophical Review,* vol. 72 (1963), pp. 17–34.

18. P. M. Meehl and H. J. Cronbach, "Construct Validity in Psychological Tests," *Minnesota Studies in the Philosophy of Science,* vol. I, ed. by H. Feigl and M. Scriven (Minneapolis, 1956), pp. 174–204. We have followed Meehl and Cronbach's usage of the terms "reliability" and "validity" so that *reliability* is a measure of the correlation between criteria while *validity* is a measure of the correlation between a criterion and the construct whose presence it is supposed to indicate.

19. This point is suceptible of direct empirical ratification, for it can be demonstrated that in perceptual analysis, speech is analyzed into segments which correspond precisely to the segmentation assigned by a grammar.

20. Cf. N. Chomsky's "A Review of Skinner's *Verbal Behavior,*" reprinted in J. Fodor and J. Katz, *The Structure of Language* (Englewood Cliffs, 1964).

21. Among the many psychological studies relevant to this point, the following are of special importance: F. Bartlett, *Remembering, A Study in Experimental and Social Psychology* (Cambridge, 1932); J. Piaget, *The Child's Conception of the World* (London, 1928); J. Brunner, "On Perceptual Readiness," reprinted in *Readings in Perception,* ed. M. Wertheimer and D. Beardsley (Princeton, 1958), pp. 686–729.

16

Hilary Putnam

"Brains and Behaviour"[1]

Once upon a time there was a tough-minded philosopher who said, 'What is all this talk about "minds", "ideas", and "sensations"? Really—and I mean *really* in the real world—there is nothing to these so-called "mental" events and entities but certain processes in our all-too-material heads.'

And once upon a time there was a philosopher who retorted, 'What a masterpiece of confusion!' Even if, say, *pain* were perfectly correlated with any particular event in my brain (which I doubt) that event would obviously have certain properties—say, a certain numerical intensity measured in volts—which it would be *senseless* to ascribe to the feeling of pain. Thus, it is *two* things that are correlated, not *one*—and to call *two* things *one* thing is worse than being mistaken; it is utter contradiction.'

For a long time dualism and materialism appeared to exhaust the alternatives. Compromises were attempted ('double aspect' theories), but they never won many converts and practically no one found them intelligible. Then, in the mid-1930s, a seeming third possibility was discovered. This third possibility has been called *logical behaviourism*. To state the nature of this third possibility briefly, it is necessary to recall the treatment of the natural numbers (*i.e.,* zero, one, two, three . . .) in modern logic. Numbers are identified with *sets*, in various ways, depending on which authority one follows. For instance, Whitehead and Russell identified zero with the set of all empty sets, one with the set of all one-membered sets, two with the set of all two-membered sets, three with the set of all three-membered sets, and so on. (This has the appearance of circularity, but they were able to dispel this appearance by defining 'one-membered set', 'two-membered set', 'three-membered set', &c., without using 'one', 'two', 'three', &c.) In short, numbers are treated as *logical constructions out of sets.* The number theorist is doing set theory without knowing it, according to this interpretation.

What was novel about this was the idea of getting rid of certain philosophically unwanted or embarrassing entities (numbers) without failing to do justice to the appropriate body of discourse (number theory) by treating the entities in question as logical constructions. Russell was quick to hold up this 'success' as a model to all future philosophers. And certain of those future philosophers—the Vienna positivists, in their 'physicalist' phase (about 1930)—took Russell's advice so seriously as to produce the doctrine that we are calling *logical behaviourism*—the doctrine that, just as numbers are (allegedly) logical constructions out of *sets,* so *mental events* are logical constructions out of actual and possible *behaviour events.*

In the set theoretic case, the 'reduction' of number theory to the appropriate part of set theory was carried out in detail and with indisputable technical success. One may dispute the philosophical significance of the reduction, but one knows exactly what one is talking about when one disputes it. In the mind–body case, the reduction was never carried out in even *one* possible way, so that it is not possible to be clear on just *how* mental entities or events are to be (identified with) logical constructions out of behaviour events. But, broadly speaking, it is clear what the view implies: it implies that all talk about mental events is translatable into talk about actual or potential overt behaviour.

It is easy to see in what way this view differs from both dualism and classical materialism. The logical behaviourist agrees with the dualist that

From *Analytical Philosophy,* volume II, R. J. Butler, ed. Oxford: Basil Blackwell, 1968, pp. 1–19. Reprinted with permission of the publisher.

what goes on in our brains has no connection whatsoever with what we *mean* when we say that someone is in pain. He can even take over the dualist's entire stock of arguments against the materialist position. Yet, at the same time, he can be as 'tough-minded' as the materialist in denying that ordinary talk of 'pains', 'thoughts', and 'feelings' involves reference to 'Mind' as a Cartesian substance.

Thus it is not surprising that logical behaviourism attracted enormous attention—both pro and con—during the next thirty years. Without doubt, this alternative proved to be a fruitful one to inject into the debate. Here, however, my intention is not to talk about the fruitfulness of the investigations to which logical behaviourism has led, but to see if there was any upshot to those investigations. Can we, after thirty years, say anything about the rightness or wrongness of logical behaviourism? Or must we say that a third alternative has been added to the old two; that we cannot decide between three any more easily than we could decide between two; and that our discussion is thus half as difficult again as it was before?

One conclusion emerged very quickly from the discussion pro and con logical behaviourism: that the extreme thesis of logical behaviourism, as we just stated it (that all talk about 'mental events' is translatable into talk about overt behaviour) is false. But, in a sense, this is not very interesting. An extreme thesis may be false, although there is 'something to' the way of thinking that it represents. And the more interesting question is this: what, if anything, can be 'saved' of the way of thinking that logical behaviourism represents?

In the last thirty years, the original extreme thesis of logical behaviourism has gradually been weakened to something like this:

(1) That there exist entailments between mind-statements and behaviour-statements; entailments that are not, perhaps, analytic in the way in which 'All bachelors are unmarried' is analytic, but that nevertheless follow (in some sense) from the meanings of mind words. I shall call these *analytic entailments*.

(2) That these entailments may not provide an actual *translation* of 'mind talk' into 'behaviour talk' (this 'talk' talk was introduced by Gilbert Ryle in his *Concept of Mind*), but that this is true for such superficial reasons as the greater ambiguity of mind talk, as compared with the relatively greater specificity of overt behaviour talk.

I believe that, although no philosopher would to-day subscribe to the older version of logical behaviourism, a great many philosophers[2] would accept these two points, while admitting the unsatisfactory imprecision of the present statement of both of them. If these philosophers are right, then there is much work to be done (*e.g.,* the notion of 'analyticity' has to be made clear), but the direction of work is laid out for us for some time to come.

I wish that I could share this happy point of view—if only for the comforting conclusion that first-rate philosophical research, continued for some time, will eventually lead to a solution to the mind–body problem which is independent of troublesome empirical facts about brains, central causation of behaviour, evidence for and against nonphysical causation of at least some behaviour, and the soundness or unsoundness of psychical research and parapsychology. But the fact is that I come to bury logical behaviourism, not to praise it. I feel that the time has come for us to admit that logical behaviourism is a mistake, and that even the weakened forms of the logical behaviourist doctrine are incorrect. I cannot hope to establish this in so short a paper as this one[3]; but I hope to expose for your inspection at least the main lines of my thinking.

Logical Behaviourism

The logical behaviourist usually begins by pointing out what is perfectly true, that such words as 'pain' ('pain' will henceforth be our stock example of a mind word) are not taught by reference to standard examples in the way in which such words as 'red' are. One can point to a standard red thing, but one cannot point to a standard pain (that is, except by pointing to some piece of *behaviour*) and say: 'Compare the feeling you are having with this one (say, Jones's feeling at time t_1). If the two feelings have the identical *quality,* then your feeling is legitimately called a feeling of *pain.*' The difficulty, of course, is that I cannot have Jones's feeling at time t_1—unless I *am* Jones, and the time *is* t_1.

From this simple observation, certain things follow. For example, the account according to which the *intension* of the word 'pain' is a certain *quality* which 'I know from my own case' must be wrong. But this is not to refute dualism, since the dualist need not maintain that I know the intension of the English word 'pain' from my own case, but only that I experience the referent of the word.

What then is the intension of 'pain'? I am inclined to say that 'pain' is a cluster-concept. That is, the application of the word 'pain' is controlled by a whole cluster of criteria, *all of which can be regarded as synthetic.*[4] As a consequence, there is no satisfactory way of answering the question 'What does "pain" mean?' except by giving an exact synonym (*e.g.,* 'Schmerz'); but there are a million and one different ways of saying what pain is. One can, for example, say that pain is that feeling which is normally evinced by saying 'ouch', or by wincing, or in a variety of other ways (or often not evinced at all).

All this is compatible with logical behaviourism. The logical behaviourist would reply: 'Exactly. "Pain" is a cluster-concept—that is to say, it stands for *a cluster of phenomena.*' But that is not what I mean. Let us look at another kind of cluster-concept (cluster-concepts, of course, are not a homogeneous class): names of diseases.

We observe that, when a virus origin was discovered for polio, doctors said that certain cases in which all the symptoms of polio had been present, but in which the virus had been absent, had turned out not to be cases of polio at all. Similarly, if a virus should be discovered which normally (almost invariably) is the cause of what we presently call 'multiple sclerosis', the hypothesis that this virus is *the* cause of multiple sclerosis would not be falsified if, in some few exceptional circumstances, it was possible to have all the symptoms of multiple sclerosis for some other combination of reasons, or if this virus caused symptoms not presently recognized as symptoms of multiple sclerosis in some cases. These facts would certainly lead the lexicographer to *reject* the view that 'multiple sclerosis' means 'the simultaneous presence of such and such symptoms'. Rather he would say that 'multiple sclerosis' means 'that disease which is normally responsible for some or all of the following symptoms. . . .'

Of course, he does not have to say this. Some philosophers would prefer to say that 'polio' *used to mean* 'the simultaneous presence of such-and-such symptoms'. And they would say that the *decision* to accept the presence or absence of a virus as a criterion for the presence or absence of polio represented a *change of meaning.* But this runs strongly counter to our common sense. For example, doctors used to say 'I believe polio is caused by a virus'. On the 'change of meaning' account, those doctors were *wrong, not right.* Polio, *as the word was then used,* was not always caused by a virus; it is only what *we* call polio that is always caused by a virus. And if a doctor ever said (many did) 'I believe this may not be a case of polio', knowing that all of the text-book symptoms were present, that doctor must have been contradicting himself (even if we, to-day, would say that he was right) or, perhaps, 'making a disguised linguistic proposal'. Also, this account runs counter to good linguistic methodology. The definition we proposed a paragraph back—'multiple sclerosis' means 'the disease that is normally *responsible* for

the following symptoms. . . .'—has an exact analogue in the case of polio. This kind of definition leaves open the question whether there is a single cause or several. It is consonant with such a definition to speak of 'discovering a single origin for polio (or two or three or four)', to speak of 'discovering X did not have polio' (although he exhibited all the symptoms of polio), and to speak of 'discovering X did have polio' (although he exhibited *none* of the 'textbook symptoms'). And, finally, such a definition does not require us to say that any 'change of meaning' took place. Thus, this is surely the definition that a good lexicographer would adopt. But this entails *rejecting* the 'change of meaning' account as a philosopher's invention.[5]

Accepting that this is the correct account of the names of diseases, what follows? There *may* be analytic entailments connecting diseases and symptoms (although I shall argue against this). For example, it looks plausible to say that:

'Normally people who have multiple sclerosis have some or all of the following symptoms . . .'
is a necessary ('analytic') truth. But it does not follow that 'disease talk' is translatable into 'symptom talk'. Rather the contrary follows (as is already indicated by the presence of the word 'normally'): statements about multiple sclerosis are not translatable into statements about the symptoms of multiple sclerosis, not because disease talk is 'systematically ambiguous' and symptom talk is 'specific', but because *causes* are not logical constructions out of their *effects.*

In analogy with the foregoing, both the dualist and the materialist would want to argue that, although the meaning of 'pain' may be *explained* by reference to overt behaviour, what we mean by 'pain' is not the presence of a cluster of responses, but rather the presence of an event or condition that normally causes those responses. (Of course the pain is not the whole cause of the pain behaviour, but only a suitably invariant part of that cause,[6] but, similarly, the virus caused tissue damage is not the whole cause of the individual symptoms of polio in some individual case, but a suitably invariant part of the cause.) And they would want to argue further, that even if it *were* a necessary truth that

'Normally, when one says "ouch" one has a pain' or a necessary truth that

'Normally, when one has a pain one says "ouch"'
this would be an interesting observation about what 'pain' means, but it would shed no metaphysical light on what pain *is* (or *isn't*). And it certainly would not follow that 'pain talk' is translatable into 'response talk', or that the failure of translatability is only a matter of the 'systematic

ambiguity' of pain talk as opposed to the 'specificity' of response talk: quite the contrary. Just as before, *causes* (pains) are *not* logical constructions out of their *effects* (behaviour).

The traditional dualist would, however, want to go farther, and deny the *necessity* of the two propositions just listed. Moreover, the traditional dualist is right: there is nothing self-contradictory, as we shall see below, in talking of hypothetical worlds in which there are pains but *no* pain behaviour.

The analogy with names of diseases is still preserved at this point. Suppose I identify multiple sclerosis as the disease that normally produces certain symptoms. If it later turns out that a certain virus is the cause of multiple sclerosis, using this newly discoverd criterion I may then go on to find out that multiple sclerosis has quite different symptoms when, say, the average temperature is lower. I can then perfectly well talk of a hypothetical world (with lower temperature levels) in which multiple sclerosis does *not* normally produce the usual symptoms. It is true that if the *words* 'multiple sclerosis' are used in any world in such a way that the above lexical definition is a good one, *then* many victims of the disease must have had some or all of the following symptoms . . . And in the same way it is true that *if* the explanation suggested of the word 'pain' is a good one (*i.e.,* 'pain is the feeling that is normally being evinced when someone says "ouch", or winces, or screams, &c.'), *then* persons in pain must have at some time winced or screamed or said 'ouch'—but this does *not* imply that 'if someone ever had a pain, then someone must at some time have winced or screamed or said "ouch".' To conclude this would be to confuse preconditions for *talking* about pain as *we* talk about pain with preconditions for the existence of pain.

The analogy we have been developing is not an identity: linguistically speaking, mind words and names of diseases are different in a great many respects. In particular, *first person uses* are very different: a man may have a severe case of polio and not know it, even if he knows the word 'polio', but one cannot have a severe pain and not know it. At first blush, this may look like a point in favour of logical behaviourism. The logical behaviourist may say: it is because the premisses 'John says he has a pain', 'John knows English', and 'John is speaking in all sincerity',[7] *entail* 'John has a pain', that pain reports have this sort of special status. But even if this is right, it does not follow that logical behaviourism is correct unless *sincerity* is a 'logical construction out of overt behaviour'! A far more reasonable account is this: one can have a 'pink elephant hallucination', but one cannot have

a 'pain hallucination', or an 'absence of pain hallucination', simply because any situation that a person cannot discriminate from a situation in which he himself has a pain *counts* as a situation in which he has a pain, whereas a situation that a person cannot distinguish from one in which a pink elephant is present does not necessarily *count* as the presence of a pink elephant.

To sum up: I believe that pains are not clusters of responses, but that they are (normally, in our experience to date) the causes of certain clusters of responses. Moreover, although this is an empirical fact, it underlies the possibility of talking about pains in the particualr way in which we do. However, it does not rule out in any way the possibility of worlds in which (owing to a difference in the environmental and hereditary conditions) pains are not responsible for the usual responses, or even are not responsible for any responses at all.

Let us now engage in a little science fiction. Let us try to describe some worlds in which pains are related to responses (and also to causes) in quite a different way than they are in our world.

If we confine our attention to non-verbal responses by full grown persons, for a start, then matters are easy. Imagine a community of 'super-spartans' or 'super-stoics'—a community in which the adults have the ability to successfully suppress *all* involuntary pain behaviour. They may, on occasion, admit that they feel pain, but always in pleasant well-modulated voices—even if they are undergoing the agonies of the damned. They do *not* wince, scream, flinch, sob, grit their teeth, clench their fists, exhibit beads of sweat, or otherwise act like poeple in pain or people suppressing the unconditioned responses associated with pain. However, they do feel pain, and they dislike it (just as we do). They even admit that it takes a great effort of will to behave as they do. It is only that they have what they regard as important ideological reasons for behaving as they do, and they have, through years of training, learned to live up to their own exacting standards.

It may be contended that children and not fully mature members of this community will exhibit, to varying degrees, normal unconditioned pain behaviour, and that this is all that is necessary for the ascription of pain. On this view, the *sine qua non* for the significant ascription of pain to a species is that its immature members should exhibit unconditioned pain responses.

One might well stop to ask whether this statement has even a clear meaning. Supposing that there are Martians: do we have any criterion for something being an 'unconditioned pain response' for a Martian? Other things being equal, one *avoids* things with which one has had painful experiences: this would suggest that *avoidance* behaviour might be looked for as a universal unconditioned pain response. However, even if this were true, it would hardly be specific enough, since avoidance can also be an unconditioned response to many things that we do not associate with pain—to things that disgust us, or frighten us, or even merely bore us.

Let us put these difficulties aside, and see if we can devise an imaginary world in which there are not, even by lenient standards, any unconditioned pain responses. Specifically, let us take our 'super-spartans', and let us suppose that after millions of years they begin to have children who are born fully acculturated. They are born speaking the adult language, knowing the multiplication table, having opinions on political issues, and *inter alia* sharing the dominant spartan beliefs about the importance of not evincing pain (except by way of a verbal report, and even that in a tone of voice that suggests indifference). Then there would not *be* any 'unconditioned pain responses' in this community (although there might be unconditioned *desires* to make certain responses—desires which were, however, always suppressed by an effort of will). Yet there is a clear absurdity to the position that one cannot ascribe to these people a capacity for feeling pain.

To make this absurdity evident, let us imagine that we succeed in converting an adult 'super-spartan' to *our* ideology. Let us suppose that he begins to evince pain in the normal way. Yet he reports that the pains he is feeling are not more *intense* than are the ones he experienced prior to conversion—indeed, he may say that giving expression to them makes them *less* intense. In this case, the logical behaviourist would have to say that, through the medium of this one member, we had demonstrated the existence of unconditioned pain responses in the whole species, and hence that ascription of pain to the species is 'logically proper'. But this is to say that had this one man never lived, and had it been possible to demonstrate only indirectly (via the use of *theories*) that these beings feel pain, then pain ascriptions *would* have been improper.

We have so far been constructing worlds in which the relation of pain to its non-verbal *effects* is altered. What about the relation of pain to *causes?* This is even more easy for the imagination to modify. Can one not imagine a species who feel pain only when a magnetic field is present (although the magnetic field causes no detectable damage to their bodies or nervous systems)? If we now let the members of such a species become converts *to* 'super-spartanism', we can depict to ourselves a world in which pains, in our sense, are

clearly present, but in which they have neither the normal causes nor the normal effects (apart from verbal reports).

What about verbal reports? Some behaviourists have taken these as the characteristic form of pain behaviour. Of course, there is a difficulty here: If 'I am in pain' means 'I am disposed to utter this kind of verbal report' (to put matters crudely), then how do we tell that any particular report is 'this kind of verbal report'? The usual answer is in terms of the unconditioned pain responses and their assumed supplantation by the verbal reports in question. However, we have seen that there are no *logical* reasons for the existence of unconditioned pain responses in all species capable of feeling pain (there *may* be logical reasons for the existence of avoidance desires, but avoidance *desires* are not themselves behaviour any more than pains are).

Once again, let us be charitable to the extent of waving the first difficulty that comes to mind, and let us undertake the task of trying to imagine a world in which there are not even pain *reports*. I will call this world the 'X-world'. In the X-world we have to deal with 'super-super-spartans'. These have been super-spartans for so long, that they have begun to suppress even *talk* of pain. Of course, each individual X-worlder may have his private way of thinking about pain. He may even have the *word* 'pain' (as before, I assume that these beings are born fully acculturated). He may *think* to himself: 'This pain is intolerable. If it goes on one minute longer I shall scream. Oh No! I mustn't do that! That would disgrace my whole family . . .' But X-worlders do not even admit to *having* pains. They pretend not to know either the word or the phenomenon to which it refers. In short, if pains are 'logical constructs out of behaviour', then our X-worlders behave so as not to have pains!—Only, of course, they do have pains, and they know perfectly well that they have pains.

If this last fantasy is not, in some disguised way, self-contradictory, then logical behaviourism is simply a mistake. Not only is the second thesis of logical behaviourism—the existence of a near-translation of pain talk into behaviour talk—false, but so is even the first thesis—the existence of 'analytic entailments'. Pains *are* responsible for certain kinds of behaviour—but only in the context of our beliefs, desires, ideological attitudes, and so forth. From the statement 'X has a pain' by itself *no* behavioural statement follows—not even a behavioural statement with a 'normally' or a 'probably' in it.

In our concluding section we shall consider the logical behaviourist's stock of counter-moves to this sort of argument. If the logical behaviourist's positive views are inadequate owing to an oversimplified view of the nature of cluster words—amounting, in some instances, to an open denial that it is *possible* to have a word governed by a cluster of indicators, *all* of which are synthetic—his negative views are inadequate owing to an oversimplified view of empirical reasoning. It is unfortunately characteristic of modern philosophy that its problems should overlap three different areas—to speak roughly, the areas of linguistics, logic, and 'theory of theories' (scientific methodology)—and that many of its practitioners should try to get by with an inadequate knowledge of at least two out of the three.

Some Behaviourist Arguments

We have been talking of 'X-worlders' and 'super-spartans'. No one denies that, in *some* sense of the term, such fantasies are 'intelligible'. But 'intelligibility' can be a superficial thing. A fantasy may be 'intelligible', at least at the level of 'surface grammar', although we may come to see, on thinking about it for a while, that some absurdity is involved. Consider, for example, the supposition that last night, just on the stroke of midnight, all distances were instantaneously doubled. Of course, we did not notice the change, for *we* ourselves also doubled in size! This story may seem intelligible to us at first blush, at least as an amusing possibility. On reflection, however, we come to see that a logical contradiction is involved. For 'length' means nothing more nor less than a relation to a standard, and it is a contradiction to maintain that the length of everything doubled, while the relations to the standards remained unchanged.

What I have just said (speaking as a logical behaviourist might speak) is false, but not totally so. It is false (or at least the last part is false), because 'length' does *not* mean 'relation to a standard'. If it did (assuming a 'standard' has to be a macro-scopic material object, or anyway a material object), it would make no sense to speak of distances in a world in which there were only gravitational and electromagnetic fields, but no material objects. Also, it would make no sense to speak of the *standard* (whatever it might be) as having changed its length. Consequences so counter-intuitive have led many physicists (and even a few philosophers of physics) to view 'length' not as something operationally defined, but as a theoretical magnitude (like electrical charge), which can be measured in a virtual infinity of ways, but which is not explicitly and exactly definable in terms of any of the ways of measuring it. Some of these physicists—the 'unified field' theorists—would even say that, far from it being the case that 'length' (and hence

'space') depends on the existence of suitably related material bodies, material bodies are best viewed as local variations in the curvature of space—that is to say, local variations in the intensity of a certain magnitude (the tensor g_{ik}), one aspect of which we experience as 'length'.

Again, it is far from true that the hypothesis 'last night, on the stroke of midnight, everything doubled in length' has no testable consequences. For example, if last night everything did double in length, and the velocity of light did not also double, then this morning we would have experienced an apparent halving of the speed of light. Moreover, if g (the gravitational constant) did not double, then we would have experienced and apparent halving in the intensity of the gravitational field. And if h (Planck's constant) did not change, then. . . . In short, our world would have been bewilderingly different. And if we could survive at all, under so drastically altered conditions, no doubt some clever physicist would figure out what had happened.

I have gone into such detail just to make the point that in philosophy things are rarely so simple as they seem. The 'doubling universe' is a favourite classroom example of a 'pseudohypothesis'—yet it is the worst possible example if a 'clear case' is desired. In the first place, what is desired is a hypothesis with no testable consequences—yet *this* hypothesis, as it is always stated, *does* have testable consequences (perhaps some more complex hypothesis does not; but then we have to see this more complex hypothesis stated before we can be expected to discuss it). In the second place, the usual argument for the absurdity of this hypothesis rests on a simplistic theory of the meaning of 'length'—and a full discussion of *that* situation is hardly possible without bringing in considerations from unified field theory and quantum mechanics (the latter comes in in connection with the notion of a 'material standard'). But, the example aside, one can hardly challenge the point that a superficially coherent story may contain a hidden absurdity.

Or can one? Of course, a superficially coherent story may contain a hidden logical contradiction, but the whole point of the logical behaviourist's sneering reference to 'surface grammar' is that *linguistic coherence, meaningfulness of the individual terms,* and *logical consistency,* do not by themselves guarantee freedom from another kind of absurdity—there are 'depth absurdities' which can only be detected by more powerful techniques. It is fair to say that to-day, after thirty years of this sort of talk, we lack both a single *convincing* example of such a depth absurdity, and a technique of detection (or alleged technique of detection) which does not reduce to 'untestable, *therefore* nonsense'.

To come to the case at hand: the logical behaviourist is likely to say that our hypothesis about 'X-worlders' is untestable in principle (if there *were* 'X-worlders', by hypothesis we couldn't distinguish them from people who really didn't know what pain is); and *therefore* meaningless (apart from a certain 'surface significance' which is of no real interest). If the logical behaviourist has learned a little from 'ordinary language philosophy', he is likely to shy away from saying 'untestable, therefore *meaningless*', but he is still likely to say or at least think: 'untestable, therefore in *some* sense absurd'. I shall try to meet this 'argument' *not* by challenging the premiss, be it overt or covert, that 'untestable synthetic statement' is some kind of contradiction in terms (although I believe that premiss to be mistaken), but simply by showing that, on any but the most naive view of testability, our hypothesis *is* testable.

Of course, I could not do this if it were true that 'by hypothesis, we couldn't distinguish X-worlders from people who *really* didn't know what pain is'. But that isn't true—at any rate, it isn't true 'by hypothesis'. What is true by hypothesis is that we couldn't distinguish X-worlders from people who really didn't known what pain is *on the basis of overt behaviour alone*. But that still leaves many other ways in which we might determine what is going on 'inside' the X-worlders—in both the figurative and literal sense of 'inside'. For example, we might examine their *brains*.

It is a fact that when pain impulses are 'received' in the brain, suitable electrical detecting instruments record a characteristic 'spike' pattern. Let us express this briefly (and too simply) by saying that 'brain spikes' are one-to-one correlated with experiences of pain. If our X-worlders belong to the human species, then we can verify that they do feel pains, notwithstanding their claim that they don't have any idea what pain is, by applying our electrical instruments and detecting the tell-tale 'brain spikes'.

This reply to the logical behaviourist is far too simple to be convincing. 'It is true,' the logical behaviourist will object, 'that experiences of pain are one-to-one correlated with "brain spikes" in the case of normal human beings. But you don't know that the X-worlders are normal human beings, in this sense—in fact, you have every reason to suppose that they are *not* normal human beings.' This reply shows that no *mere* correlation, however carefully verified in the case of normal human beings, can be used to verify ascriptions of pain to X-worlders. Fortunately, we do not have to suppose that our knowledge will always be restricted to mere correlations, like the pain–'brain spike' correlation. At a more advanced level, considerations of simplicity and coherence can begin to play a rôle in a way in which they cannot when only crude observational regularities are available.

Let us suppose that we begin to detect waves of a new kind, emanating from human brains—call them 'V-waves'. Let us suppose we develop a way of 'decoding' V-waves so as to reveal people's unspoken thoughts. And, finally, let us suppose that our 'decoding' technique also works in the case of the V-waves emanating from the brains of X-worlders. How does this correlation differ from the pain–'brain spike' correlation?

Simply in this way: it is reasonable to say that 'spikes'—momentary peaks in the electrical intensity in certain parts of the brain—could have almost any cause. But waves which go over into coherent English (or any other language), under a relatively simple decoding scheme, could not have just any cause. The 'null hypothesis'—that this is just the operation of 'chance'—can be dismissed at once. And if, in the case of human beings, we verify that the decoded waves correspond to what we are in fact thinking, then the hypothesis that this same correlation holds in the case of X-worlders will be assigned an immensely high probability, simply because no other likely explanation readily suggests itself. But 'no other likely explanation readily suggests itself' isn't verification, the logical behaviourist may say. On the contrary. How, for example, have we verified that cadmium lines in the spectrographic analysis of sunlight indicate the presence of cadmium in the sun? Mimicking the logical behaviourist, we might say: 'We have verified that under normal circumstances, cadmium lines only occur when heated cadmium is present. But we don't know that circumstances on the sun are normal in this sense.' If we took this seriously, we would have to *heat cadmium on the sun* before we could say that the regularity upon which we base our spectrographic analysis of sunlight had been verified. In fact, we have verified the regularity under 'normal' circumstances, and we can *show* (deductively) that *if* many other laws, that have also been verified under 'normal' circumstances and *only* under 'normal' circumstances (*i.e.,* never on the surface of the sun), hold on the sun, *then* this regularity holds also under 'abnormal' circumstances. And if someone says, 'But perhaps *none* of the usual laws of physics hold on the sun', we reply that this is like supposing that a random process always produces coherent English. The fact is that the 'signals' (sunlight, radio waves, &c.) which we receive from the sun cohere with a vast body of theory. Perhaps there is some other explanation than that the sun obeys the usual laws of physics; but *no other likely explanation suggests itself.* This sort of reasoning *is* scientific verification; and if it is not reducible to simple Baconian induction—well, then, philosophers must learn to widen their notions of verification to embrace it.

The logical behaviourist might try to account for the decodability of the X-worlders' 'V–waves' into coherent English (or the appropriate natural language) without invoking the absurd 'null hypothesis'. He might suggest, for example, that the 'X-worlders' are having fun at our expense—they are able, say, to produce misleading V-waves at will. If the X-worlders have brains quite unlike ours, this may even have some plausibility. But once again, in an advanced state of knowledge, considerations of coherence and simplicty may quite conceivably 'verify' that this is false. For example, the X-worlders may have brains quite like ours, rather than unlike ours. And we may have built up enough theory to say how the brain of a human being should 'look' if that human being were pretending not to be in pain when he was, in fact, in pain. Now consider what the 'misleading V-waves' story requires: it requires that the X-worlders produce V-waves in quite a different way than we do, without specifying what that different way is. Moreover, it requires that this be the case, although the reverse hypothesis—that X-worlders' brains function *exactly* as human brains do—in fact, that they *are* human brains—fits all the data. Clearly, this story is in serious methodological difficulties, and any other 'counter-explanation' that the logical behaviourist tries to invoke will be in similar difficulties. In short, the logical behaviourist's argument reduces to this: 'You cannot verify "psycho-physical" correlations in the case of X-worlders (or at least, you can't verify ones having to do, directly or indirectly, with *pain*), because, by hypothesis, X-worlders won't tell you (or indicate behaviourally) when they are in pain. 'Indirect verification'—verification using theories which have been 'tested' only in the case of human beings—is not verification at all, because X-worlders *may* obey different laws than human beings. And it is not incumbent upon *me* (the logical behaviourist says) to suggest what those laws might be: it is incumbent upon *you* to rule out *all* other explanations.' And this is a silly argument. The scientist does not have to rule out all the ridiculous theories that someone *might* suggest; he only has to show that he has ruled out any reasonable alternative theories that one might put forward on the basis of present knowledge.

Granting, then, that we might discover a technique for 'reading' the unspoken thoughts of X-worlders: we would then be in the same position with respect to the X-worlders as we were with re-spect to the original 'super-spartans'. The super-spartans were quite willing to tell us (and each other) about their pains; and we could see that their pain talk was linguistically coherent and situationally appropriate (*e.g.,* a super-spartan will tell you that he feels intense pain when you touch him with a red hot poker). On this basis, we were quite willing to grant that the super-spartans did, indeed, feel pain—all the more readily, since the deviancy in their behaviour had a perfectly convincing ideological explanation. (Note again the rôle played here by considerations of coherence and simplicity). But the X-worlders also 'tell' us (and, perhaps, each other), exactly the same things, albeit *un*willingly (by the medium of the involuntarily produced 'V-waves'). Thus we have to say—at least, we have to say as long as the 'V–wave' theory has not broken down—that the X-worlders are what they, in fact, are—just 'super-super-spartans'.

Let us now consider a quite different argument that a logical behaviourist might use. 'You are assuming,' he might say, 'the following principle:

'If someone's brain is in the same state as that of a human being in pain (not just at the moment of the pain, but before and after for a sufficient interval), then he is in pain.

'Moreover, this principle is one which it would never be reasonable to give up (on your conception of "methodology"). Thus, you have turned it into a tautology. But observe what turning this principle into a tautology involves: it involves changing the meanning of "pain". What "pain" means for *you* is: the presence of pain, in the colloquial sense of the term, *or* the presence of a brain state identical with the brain state of someone who feels pain. Of course, in that sense we can verify that your "X-worlders" experience "pain"—but that is not the sense of "pain" at issue.'

The reply to this argument is that the premiss is simply false. It is just not true that, on my conception of verification, it would *never* be reasonable to give up the principle stated. To show this, I have to beg your pardons for engaging in a little more science fiction. Let us suppose that scientists discover yet another kind of waves—call them 'W–waves'. Let us suppose that W-waves do not emanate from human brains, but that they are detected emanating from the brains of X-worlders. And let us suppose that, once again, there exists a simple scheme for decoding W-waves into coherent English (or whatever language X-worlders speak), and that the 'decoded' waves 'read' like this: 'Ho, ho! are we fooling those Earthians! They think that the V-waves they detect represent our thoughts! If they only knew that instead of pretending not to have pains when we really have pains, we are really pretending to pretend not to have pains when we really do have pains when we really don't have pains!' Under these circumstances, we would 'doubt' (to put it mildly) that the same psycho-physical correlations held for normal humans and for X–worlders. Further investigations might lead us to quite a number of different hypotheses. For example, we might decide that X-worlders don't think with their brains at all—that the 'organ' of thought is not just the brain, in the case of X–worlders, but some larger structure—perhaps even a structure which is not 'physical' in the sense of consisting of elementary particles. The point is that what is necessarily true is not the principle stated two paragraphs back, but rather the principle:

> If someone (some organism) is in the same state as a human being in pain in all relevant respects, then he (that organism) is in pain.

—And *this* principle *is* a tautology by anybody's lights! The only *a priori* methodological restriction I am imposing here is this one:

> If some organism is in the same state as a human being in pain in all respects *known* to be relevant, and there is no reason to suppose that there exist *un*-known relevant respects, then don't postulate any.

—But this principle is not a 'tautology'; in fact, it is not a *statement* at all, but a methodological directive. And deciding to conform to this directive is not (as hardly needs to be said) changing the meaning of the word 'pain', or of *any* word.

There are two things that the logical behaviourist can do: he can claim that ascribing pains to X-worlders, or even super-spartans, involves a 'change of meaning',[8] or he can claim that ascribing pains to super-spartans, or at least to X-worlders, is 'untestable'. The first thing is a piece of unreasonable linguistics; the second, a piece of unreasonable scientific method. The two are, not surprisingly, mutually supporting: the unreasonable scientific method makes the unreasonable linguistics appear more reasonable. Similarly, the normal ways of thinking and talking are mutually supporting: reasonable linguistic field techniques are, needless to say, in agreement with reasonable conceptions of scientific method. Madmen sometimes have consistent delusional systems; so madness and sanity can both have a 'circular' aspect. I may not have succeeded, in this paper, in breaking the 'delusional system' of a committed logical behaviourist; but I hope to have convinced the uncommitted that that system need not be taken seriously. If we have to choose between 'circles', the circle of reason is to be preferred to any of the many circles of unreason.

NOTES

1. This paper was read as a part of the programme of The American Association for the Advancement of Science, Section L (History and Philosophy of Science), December 27th, 1961.

2. *E.g.,* these two points are fairly explicitly stated in Strawson's *Individuals.* Strawson has told me that he no longer subscribes to point (1), however.

3. An attempted fourth alternative—*i.e.,* an alternative to dualism, materialism, *and* behaviourism—is sketched in 'The Mental Life of Some Machines', which appeared in the Proceedings of the Wayne Symposium on the Philosophy of Mind. This fourth alternative is materialistic in the wide sense of being compatible with the view that organisms, including human beings, are physical systems consisting of elementary particles and obeying the laws of physics, but does not require that such 'states' as *pain* and *preference* be defined in a way which makes reference to either overt behaviour or physical-chemical constitution. The idea, briefly, is that predicates which apply to a system by virtue of its *functional organization* have just this characteristic: a given functional organization (*e.g.,* a given inductive logic, a given rational preference function) may realize itself in almost any kind of overt behaviour, depending upon the circumstances, and is capable of being 'built into' structures of many different logically possible physical (or even metaphysical) constitutions. Thus the statement that a creature prefers A to B does not tell us whether the creature has a carbon chemistry, or a silicon chemistry, or is even a disembodied mind, nor does it tell us how the creature would behave under any circumstances specifiable without reference to the creature's other preferences and beliefs, but it does not thereby become something 'mysterious'.

4. I mean not only that *each* criterion can be regarded as synthetic, but also that the cluster is *collectively* synthetic, in the sense that we are free in certain cases to say (for reason of inductive simplicity and theoretical economy) that the term applies although the whole cluster is missing. This is completely compatible with saying that the cluster serves to fix the meaning of the word. The point is that when we specify something by a cluster of indicators we assume that people will *use their brains.* That criteria may be over-ridden when good sense demands is the sort of thing we may regard as a 'convention associated with discourse' (Grice) rather than as something to be stipulated in connection with the individual words.

5. Cf. 'Dreaming and "Depth Grammar",' *Analytical Philosophy,* First Series.

6. Of course, 'the cause' is a highly ambiguous phrase. Even if it is correct in certain contexts to say that certain events in the brain are 'the cause' of my pain behaviour, it does *not* follow (as has sometimes been suggested) that my pain must be 'identical' with these neural events.

7. This is suggested in Wittgenstein's *Philosophical Investigations.*

8. This popular philosophical move is discussed in 'Dreaming and "Depth Grammar",' *Analytical Philosophy,* First Series.

PART III

MIND AND BODY

INTRODUCTION

It is natural to contrast mental states and processes with those which are merely bodily, or physical. This contrast between mental and bodily seems to be a basic part of our commonsense conception of mind. Indeed, it may even seem that without that opposition we would be unable to explain what it is for a phenomenon to be a mental phenomenon in the first place.

It is far from obvious, however, how we should understand this opposition. When we contrast mental with physical, do we rule out the possibility that mental states and processes are physical? Or do we leave that question open, and simply distinguish between mental states and those physical states which are not mental? If mental states are nonphysical, does that mean that they stand outside the physical order, and we cannot explain them in physical terms? If so, is psychology, which studies mental phenomena, a different sort of science from physics and chemistry? Or does the general opposition between mental and physical mean only that we have two different ways to describe creatures with psychological capacities, and not that mental phenomena stand outside the physical order? Why, then, do we have two ways of describing people, and how exactly do they differ? And if mental phenomena are just bodily phenomena, what is it about mental states that makes them special?

There are two traditional views about these issues. One view follows Descartes in maintaining that mental phenomena are not physical. The other, championed by Descartes's English contemporary Thomas Hobbes, claims instead that mental states are just particular physical states. Hobbes's argument for this was succinct. Plainly mental events and bodily motions interact causally; since only bodily motions can cause and be caused by other bodily motions, mental events must themselves be bodily. These two traditional theories still dominate discussion of the issues just raised.

A. The Topic-Neutral Approach

Perhaps the most widely discussed form of materialism is the mind–body identity thesis, which claims that all mental states are identical with bodily states, presumably states of the brain. On this view we have two distinct ways to describe mental states: in distinctively mental terms, and as bodily states of various kinds. But since the two kinds of description mean different things, the identity of mental with bodily states would not collapse the distinction between mental and physical. It is this version of mind–body materialism for which Smart argues.

For *a* and *b* to be identical is for them to have all their properties in common. According to the identity thesis every mental state, such as a sensation of red, is also physical state. Since states count as mental or physical in virtue of having properties that are mental or physical, mental states will have both mental and physical properties.

If a mental state such as a sensation of red is a physical state, how about the distinctively mental properties of that state? Are they also physical properties? One can argue that they are not. Perhaps the mental properties of these mental states must be irreducibly nonphysical if we are to be able to pick out mental states in distinctively mental terms. If so, the identity thesis implies that mental states are physical, but does not imply the distinct claim that their mental properties are physical as well. It would therefore sustain only a partial materialism.

Smart's reply is that when we describe mental states in ostensibly mental terms, our descriptions are actually noncommittal about whether the properties they ascribe to those states are mental properties or physical properties. Such descriptions pick out mental states not by reference to special mental properties, but by way of their resemblance to certain other states. Moreover, we need not specify how they are similar. For example, when I say I have a sensation of red, I say only that I am in some state that resembles, in some unspecified way, the state I am in when red objects visually stimulate me. As long as the respect of similarity remains unspecified, my description is neutral about whether the properties in virtue of which I pick the state out are mental or physical. My description is therefore "topic neutral," that is, neutral about the kind of property it ascribes. If the description seems nonphysical, that is because it is noncommittal about whether the property it ascribes is physical, and not because it ascribes some nonphysical property.

Shaffer argues that this reply is unsuccessful. We often notice that we are in some mental state without noticing any physical property of that state, any neurological event, or any external stimulus. This is possible, he contends, only if we notice the mental state by noticing some nonphysical property it has. He concludes that mental descriptions do ascribe nonphysical properties. This argument is not decisive. Smart would respond that we notice mental states by virtue of their similarity to other states, without noticing in what respect that resemblance obtains.

We typically describe sensory states in words we could also apply to the sensory situations that occasion them; sensations of red are typically caused by red physical objects. This lends plausibility to the idea that we describe sensory states solely in terms of similarity to what occurs in the presence of such stimuli.

Like Smart, Armstrong holds that mental descriptions are topic neutral. But rather than focus on sensory states, as Smart does, Armstrong takes intentional mental states, such as beliefs and desires, as central. And we do not describe such states so much in terms of situations that occasion them as in terms of the behavior they cause. Thoughts and desires in combination typically cause particular patterns of behavior. We often define concepts this way; for example, we define poisons in terms of the effects they produce. Similarly, Armstrong urges, mental states are states that characteristically cause and are caused by various patterns of behavior. This account, like Smart's, is topic neutral, and it arguably provides a fuller idea of what it is to be a mental state than an account based on unspecified similarity.

Campbell argues that even a casual account cannot capture the qualitative character of sensory states such as pains and sensations of red. A casual analysis cannot distinguish a case in which a person is in such qualitative states from a case of a being with no qualitative states which nonetheless behaves in all ways as if it does. So a casual account cannot say how those states seem to a person who is in them. According to Armstrong, however, the qualities in virtue of which sensory states differ from one another are not mental qualities but qualities of the relevant physical stimuli. To sustain this claim one would have to draw suitable connections between the ostensible mental qualities of sensory states and the qualities of the corresponding external stimuli.

In any case, the topic-neutral strategy cannot succeed. Topic-neutral descriptions are neutral as regards being mental or physical; mental descriptions plainly cannot be neutral in that way. Moreover, the topic-neutral strategy seems unnecessary to meet the objection about mental properties being nonphysical. Just as mental states may be a particular subgroup of physical states, mental properties of those states may themselves be a subgroup of physical properties. That would be sufficient to make describing mental states in terms of their mental properties different from picking them out by way of any other physical properties.

This conclusion does not conflict with the commonsense contrast between mental and physical. To be physical, in the present context, is simply not to be mental. Compare the contrast between physical and chemical processes; physical processes, in that context, are just those which are not chemical. It begs the question against materialism to assume that the mental is in any significant way nonphysical, even at the level of properties.

B. Functionalist Approaches

If mental states are a special subgroup of physical states, we can say how they are special by reference to their mental properties. But then we must go on to say what is distinctive about those properties. If these properties were nonphysical, that would certainly make them distinctive. Is there any other way to explain how these properties are special?

Armstrong's topic-neutral analyses characterize mental states in terms of their causal connections with behavior. Mental states have characteristic causal connections, however, not only with behavior, but with stimuli and other mental states as well. A person's desiring something, for example, is causally connected not only with behavior involved in pursuing that thing, but also with stimulations that indicate satisfaction of the desire, and with beliefs about the thing desired and the pleasure that comes from getting it. So perhaps what is distinctive of mental states is their membership in a system of states defined by these characteristic causal connections.

Mental states would then differ from everything else in virtue of belonging to such a system of states. There would thus be no special problem about the mental properties of these states. We characterize mental states as a group in terms of the whole system of causal interactions; but then we can describe each type of mental state by way of its causal role in this network of states. So the distinctive mental properties of each type of state would be its particular causal role.

It is important that these characteristic causal patterns include causal ties among various mental states. It is unlikely that we can specify any type of mental state in causal terms without referring to mental states of other types. Desiring, for example, has characteristic connections with behavior and sensory stimulation only given certain beliefs.

The view that mental states can be characterized in terms of such causal connections is functionalism. There is disagreement, however, about the implications of functionalism for mind–body materialism. Putnam contends that functionalism and materialism are competing views about what it is to be a particular type of mental state, that is, what mental states of the same type have in common. Distinct species exhibit huge anatomical and physiological differences. So when members of different species are in the same type of mental state, they will not generally be in the same type of physiological state. The same may well be so even within a particular species. So materialism cannot capture what mental states of the same type have in common. The functionalist answer, in terms of causal role, is far more likely to succeed.

But we need not see materialism as identifying types of mental state with physiological types. If we do not, functionalism may actually imply the identity thesis, as Lewis argues it does. Lewis takes our commonsense platitudes about mental states to constitute a kind of informal, folk scientific theory. Theoretical terms, he maintains, are defined functionally, by reference to causal roles; so mental states are whatever states occupy the causal roles specified by our aggregate commonsense psychological platitudes. It is empirically likely that certain neural states occupy those causal roles. So the mental states determined by our psychological platitudes are identical with the neural states we can expect to discover as occupants of the relevant causal roles. On this view, functionalism actually helps establish materialism.

Block argues that functionalism inevitably falls prey to one of two decisive difficulties. Either it attributes mental states to physical systems that have none, which Block calls liberalism, or it wrongly denies mental states of creatures that are physically unlike us, which Block labels chauvinism. A functionalist theory attributes mental states to any system that exemplifies the right functional pattern. So if a system such as the population of China, which plainly lacks mental states, satisfies the functional description of a human being for a period of time, a functionalist theory will attribute qualitative sensory states to that system. Moreover, functional descriptions claim to describe mental states in terms of causal ties to other mental states, and to behavioral output and sensory input. Describing these inputs and outputs in mental terms would make functionalism uninformative. But Block argues that physical descriptions of these inputs and outputs will either exclude creatures with mental states when their physical makeup is too different from ours or else include systems that plainly lack mentality altogether.

In a second selection, Lewis takes up another, related pair of difficulties for functionalism. Causal role determines what mental state one is in. In human beings the causal role of pain, for example, presumably picks out some kind of neural state. But suppose the neural organization in some human being was nonstandard, so that in that person that very kind of neural state had a different causal role. Being in pain would in that case coincide with being in the neural state that is standardly pain; functional role seems not to matter. In other cases, physiological state is irrelevant. The functional role distinctive of pain may well determine different physiological states in humans and other creatures. Since functional role determines what mental state one is in, pain would be different states in different creatures.

This last point causes no difficulty, since Lewis holds that the concept of a type of mental state is the concept of whatever occupies a particular causal role. Such concepts determine the states they do only contingently, in the way it is contingent that the concept of the first American president determines George Washington. This means that mental concepts can determine different states in different actual situations. Pain is whatever state has the relevant causal role in a particular species. But how then can it be that the human being with the nonstandard neural circuitry is in pain? Because that person belongs to a population in which the defining causal role determines a particular neural state, we can relativize pain to populations. Being in a particular mental state is being in a state that occupies the relevant causal role for the relevant population. Such a reply may well also work with the difficulties raised by Block.

C. The Mental–Physical Contrast

Can a functionalist account, which holds that the mental properties of mental states need not be nonphysical, capture the commonsense contrast between mental and physical? Kripke has powerfully argued for the view that we cannot do justice to that contrast unless we represent mental phenomena as nonphysical. Some terms refer to the things they do only contingently, such as 'the first Postmaster General'. Others determine what they refer to necessarily, since no situation is possible in which they would refer to anything else. When two terms that refer to the same thing both determine what they refer to necessarily, an identity statement involving the two terms is necessarily true. Kripke maintains that 'pain' and 'brain state B' both determine what they refer to necessarily; so if pain and some brain state B were identical at all, they would be necessarily identical. Since the tie between pains and brain states seems plainly contingent, they cannot be necessarily identical.

Our sense that an identity is contingent sometimes misleads us. Heat seems contingently identical with mean molecular kinetic energy, but only because we pick out heat by our sensation of heat, which is contingently tied to molecular kinetic energy. But Kripke contends that to be pain is necessarily to be felt as pain. If so, we pick out pain by the essential property of its being pain, and so have no basis for disregarding our sense that the tie between pain and brain state must be contingent. As Lewis notes, however, one need not hold, as Kripke does, that 'pain' determines the same state in all possible situations. Moreover, since we need not be aware of a pain at every moment, the relationship between pains and our awareness of them may indeed be contingent.

In any case, perhaps we need not represent the mental as nonphysical to capture the mental–physical contrast. Davidson and Kim both explore ways of doing so. According to Davidson, we can figure out what a person believes only relative to background assumptions about meaning and about the person's basic rationality. Relativity to these hypotheses precludes a unique determination of a person's beliefs. Since no such hypotheses figure in our determining when physical events occur, Davidson argues that there can be no lawlike correlations between mental and physical events.

For an event to figure in lawlike connections, it matters how we describe it. If there are no psychophysical laws, that means only that no laws connect physical events, described as such, with mental events, described as such. But mental and physical events do cause each other, and causation implies lawlike connections between cause and effect. Only if mental events can be described as physical events can they figure in laws connecting them with physical events. Every instance of a mental event is therefore identical with a physical event. The impossibility of psychophysical laws precludes correlating mental types with physical types. But that very impossibility also shows that every token of a mental state is identical with a token of a physical state. It is difficult, however, to evaluate Davidson's claim about psychophysical laws. For one thing, even if hypotheses about meaning and rationality prevent a unique determination of mental states, the admissible alternatives should be empirically equivalent. If so, our inability to choose among them may not rule out suitable laws.

If mental events figure in laws only when we describe them in physical terms, the physical has a certain primacy, relative to the mental. Kim explores an alternative model of the primacy of the physical. He defines a family of properties as supervening on another if, roughly, the properties in the first are determined by those in the second, and argues that mental properties supervene on physical properties. Such supervenience captures the idea that there is no mental difference without a physical difference, which underlies the main appeal of materialism.

Kim also argues that macroscopic objects and events supervene on events and objects at the micro level, which suggests useful analogies between the macroscopic, described in common-sense terms, and the mental. But on Kim's definition, supervening events do not, strictly speaking, cause each other. Rather, when one supervening event seems to cause another, each actually supervenes on events that are, in turn, causally related. It is unclear that this idea does justice to our sense that mental events are causally efficacious.

D. Eliminative Materialism

Standard materialism holds that mental states are special cases of physical states. So if making sense of the contrast between mental and physical requires us to assume the mental is nonphysical, standard materialism is wrong.

Even if mental phenomena are nonphysical, however, we might be able to salvage the basic materialist claim that nothing is nonphysical. Suppose we could explain and predict everything at least as successfully using no mental concepts as we can by using them. We might conclude that mental concepts are idle, and apply to nothing, that is, that nothing mental exists.

This view, advanced by Feyerabend and Rorty, and in a modified version by Quine, is known as eliminative materialism. Feyerabend argues that, since mental states have nonphysical properties, materialism can be sustained only by adopting a language devoid of mental terminology.

Rorty argues for a similar conclusion. Urging that 'mental' and 'physical' are incompatible terms, he argues that the only way to explain this incompatibility is to suppose that we can incorrigibly report our own mental states, but not anything else. He then considers a mythical people whose descriptions and explanations of things are as good as ours, who differ from us in no way except that they regard none of their reports as incorrigible. Since incorrigibility is the distinguishing mark of the mental, these people have no mental concepts or terminology; they regard nothing as mental. Since this lack does not, by hypothesis, impair their explanations and descriptions of things, Rorty concludes that our own mental terminology is idle. We could dispense with that terminology, in principle if not in practice, with no loss of descriptive or explanatory ability.

Feyerabend and Rorty both argue from the incompatibility of mental and physical, which begs the question against standard materialism. Rorty, for example, interprets his imaginary case as showing that, since his mythical people regard no reports as incorrigible, they have no concept of mind. But why not take this to show, instead, that they have a theory of mind different from Rorty's, a theory on which mental states are not incorrigible?

On that interpretation, Rorty's case would support not eliminative, but standard materialism. Indeed, the difference between the two views, as Quine notes, may well be idle—a difference only about whether or not one regards being mental and being physical as incompatible. Quine's own materialist argument, however, proceeds in eliminative terms. Since it is possible to learn about mental states only by way of publicly observable bodily occurrences, some bodily state must be associated with each mental state. So we would lose no descriptive or explanatory power if we talked just about those bodily states.

A. The Topic-Neutral Approach

17

J. J. C. Smart

"Sensations and Brain Processes"

This paper[1] takes its departure from arguments to be found in U. T. Place's "Is Consciousness a Brain Process?"[2] I have had the benefit of discussing Place's thesis in a good many universities in the United States and Australia, and I hope that the present paper answers objections to his thesis which Place has not considered and that it presents his thesis in a more nearly unobjectionable form. This paper is meant also to supplement the paper "The 'Mental' and the 'Physical,'" by H. Feigl,[3] which in part argues for a similar thesis to Place's.

Suppose that I report that I have at this moment a roundish, blurry-edged after-image which is yellowish towards its edge and is orange towards its center. What is it that I am reporting? One answer to this question might be that I am not reporting anything, that when I say that it looks to me as though there is a roundish yellowy-orange patch of light on the wall I am expressing some sort of *temptation,* the temptation to say that there *is* a roundish yellowy-orange patch on the wall (though I may know that there is not such a patch on the wall). This is perhaps Wittgenstein's view in the *Philosophical Investigations* (see §§ 367, 370). Similarly, when I "report" a pain, I am not really reporting anything (or, if you like, I am reporting in a queer sense of "reporting"), but am doing a sophisticated sort of wince. (See § 244. "The verbal expression of pain replaces crying and does not describe it." Nor does it describe anything else?)[4] I prefer most of the time to discuss an after-image rather than a pain, because the word "pain" brings in something which is irrelevant to my purpose: the notion of "distress." I think that "he is in pain" entails "he is in distress," that is, that he is in a certain agitation-condition.[5] Similarly, to say "I am in pain" may be to do more than "replace pain behavior": it may be partly to report something, though this something is quite nonmysterious, being an agitation-condition, and so susceptible of behavioristic analysis. The suggestion I wish if possible to avoid is a different one, namely that "I am in pain" is a genuine report, and that what it reports is an irreducibly psychical something. And similarly the suggestion I wish to resist is also that to say "I have a yellowish-orange after-image" is to report something irreducibly psychical.

Why do I wish to resist this suggestion? Mainly because of Occam's razor. It seems to me that science is increasingly giving us a viewpoint whereby organisms are able to be seen as physicochemical mechanisms:[6] it seems that even the behavior of man himself will one day be explicable in mechanistic terms. There does seem to be, so far as science is concerned, nothing in the world but increasingly complex arrangements of physical constituents. All except for one place: in consciousness. That is, for a full description of what is going on in a man you would have to mention not only the physical processes in his tissues, glands, nervous system, and so forth, but also his states of consciousness: his visual, auditory, and tactual sensations, his aches and pains. That these should be *correlated* with brain processes does not help, for to say that they are *correlated* is to say that they are something "over and above." You cannot correlate something with itself. You correlate footprints with burglars, but not Bill Sikes the burglar with Bill Sikes the burglar. So sensations, states of consciousness, do seem to be the one sort of thing left outside the physicalist picture, and for various reasons I just cannot believe that this can be so.

From *The Philosophy of Mind*, V. C. Chappell, ed. Englewood Cliffs: Prentice-Hall, Inc., 1962, New York: Dover, 1981, pp. 16–172. Copyright © 1962 by V. C. Chappell. Reprinted with permission of V. C. Chappell, J.J.C. Smart, and *The Philosophical Review*.

That everything should be explicable in terms of physics (together of course with descriptions of the ways in which the parts are put together—roughly, biology is to physics as radio-engineering is to electromagnetism) except the occurrence of sensations seems to me to be frankly unbelievable. Such sensations would be "nomological danglers," to use Feigl's expression.[7] It is not often realized how odd would be the laws whereby these nomological danglers would dangle. It is sometimes asked, "Why can't there by psychophysical laws which are of a novel sort, just as the laws of electricity and magnetism were novelties from the standpoint of Newtonian mechanics?" Certainly we are pretty sure in the future to come across new ultimate laws of a novel type, but I expect them to relate simple constituents: for example, whatever ultimate particles are then in vogue. I cannot believe that ultimate laws of nature could relate simple constituents to configurations consisting of perhaps billions of neurons (and goodness knows how many billion billions of ultimate particles) all put together for all the world as though their main purpose in life was to be a negative feedback mechanism of a complicated sort. Such ultimate laws would be like nothing so far known in science. They have a queer "smell" to them. I am just unable to believe in the nomological danglers themselves, or in the laws whereby they would dangle. If any philosophical arguments seemed to compel us to believe in such things, I would suspect a catch in the argument. In any case it is the object of this paper to show that there are no philosophical arguments which compel us to be dualists.

The above is largely a confession of faith, but it explains why I find Wittgenstein's position (as I construe it) so congenial. For on this view there are, in a sense, no sensations. A man is a vast arrangement of physical particles, but there are not, over and above this, sensations or states of consciousness. There are just behavioral facts about this vast mechanism, such as that it expresses a temptation (behavior disposition) to say "there is a yellowish-red patch on the wall" or that it goes through a sophisticated sort of wince, that is, says "I am in pain." Admittedly Wittgenstein says that though the sensation " is not a something," it is nevertheless "not a nothing either" (§304), but this need only mean that the word "ache" has a use. An ache is a thing, but only in the innocuous sense in which the plain man, in the first paragraph of Frege's *Foundations of Arithmetic,* answers the question "What is the number one?" by "a thing." It should be noted that when I assert that to say "I have a yellowish-orange after-image" is to express a temptation to assert the physical-object statement "There is a yellowish-orange patch on the wall," I mean that saying "I have a yellowish-orange after-image" is (partly) the exercise of the disposition[8] which is the temptation. It is not to *report* that I have the temptation, any more than is "I love you" normally a report that I love someone. Saying "I love you" is just part of the behavior which is the exercise of the disposition of loving someone.

Though for the reasons given above, I am very receptive to the above "expressive" account of sensation statements, I do not feel that it will quite do the trick. Maybe this is because I have not thought it out sufficiently, but it does seem to me as though, when a person says "I have an after-image," he *is* making a genuine report, and that when he says "I have a pain," he *is* doing more than "replace pain-behavior," and that "this more" is not just to say that he is in distress. I am not so sure, however, that to admit this is to admit that there are nonphysical correlates of brain processes. Why should not sensations just be brain processes of a certain sort? There are, of course, well-known (as well as lesser-known) philosophical objections to the view that reports of sensations are reports of brain-processes, but I shall try to argue that these arguments are by no means as cogent as is commonly thought to be the case.

Let me first try to state more accurately the thesis that sensations are brain-processes. It is not the thesis that, for example, "after-image" or "ache" means the same as "brain process of sort X" (where "X" is replaced by a description of a certain sort of brain process). It is that, in so far as "after-image" or "ache" is a report of a process, it is a report of a process that *happens to be* a brain process. It follows that the thesis does not claim that sensation statements can be *translated* into statements about brain processes.[9] Nor does it claim that the logic of a sensation statement is the same as that of a brain-process statement. All it claims is that in so far as a sensation statement is a report of something, that something is in fact a brain process. Sensations are nothing over and above brain processes. Nations are nothing "over and above" citizens, but this does not prevent the logic of nation statements being very different from the logic of citizen statements, nor does it insure the translatability of nation statements into citizen statements. (I do not, however, wish to assert that the relation of sensation statements to brain-process statements is very like that of nation statements to citizen statements. Nations do not just *happen to be* nothing over and above citizens, for example. I bring in the "nations" example merely to make a negative point: that the fact that the logic of A-statements is different from that of B-statements does not insure that A's are anything over and above B's.)

Remarks on Identity

When I say that a sensation is a brain process or that lightning is an electric discharge, I am using "is" in the sense of strict identity. (Just as in the—in this case necessary—proposition "7 is identical with the smallest prime number greater than 5.") When I say that a sensation is a brain process or that lightning is an electric discharge I do not mean just that the sensation is somehow spatially or temporally continuous with the brain process or that the lightning is just spatially or temporally continuous with the discharge. When on the other hand I say that the successful general is the same person as the small boy who stole the apples I mean only that the successful general I see before me is a time slice[10] of the same four-dimensional object of which the small boy stealing apples is an earlier time slice. However, the four-dimensional object which has the general-I-see-before-me for its late time slice is identical in the strict sense with the four-dimensional object which has the small-boy-stealing-apples for an early time slice. I distinguish these two senses of "is identical with" because I wish to make it clear that the brain-process doctrine asserts identity in the *strict* sense.

I shall now discuss various possible objections to the view that the processes reported in sensation statements are in fact processes in the brain. Most of us have met some of these objections in our first year as philosophy students. All the more reason to take a good look at them. Others of the objections will be more recondite and subtle.

Objection 1. Any illiterate peasant can talk perfectly well about his after-images, or how things look or feel to him, or about his aches and pains, and yet he may know nothing whatever about neurophysiology. A man may, like Aristotle, believe that the brain is an organ for cooling the body without any impairment of his ability to make true statements about his sensations. Hence the things we are talking about when we describe our sensations cannot be processes in the brain.

Reply. You might as well say that a nation of slugabeds, who never saw the Morning Star or knew of its existence, or who had never thought of the expression "the Morning Star," but who used the expression "the Evening Star" perfectly well, could not use this expression to refer to the same entity as we refer to (and describe as) "the Morning Star."[11]

You may object that the Morning Star is in a sense not the very same thing as the Evening Star, but only something spatiotemporally continuous with it. That is, you may say that the Morning Star is not the Evening Star in the strict sense of "identity" that I distinguished earlier.

There is, however, a more plausible example. Consider lightning.[12] Modern physical science tells us that lightning is a certain kind of electrical discharge due to ionization of clouds of water vapor in the atmosphere. This, it is now believed, is what the true nature of lightning is. Note that there are not two things: a flash of lightning and an electrical discharge. There is one thing, a flash of lightning, which is described scientifically as an electrical discharge to the earth from a cloud of ionized water molecules. The case is not at all like that of explaining a footprint by reference to a burglar. We say that what lightning really is, what its true nature as revealed by science is, is an electrical discharge. (It is not the true nature of a footprint to be a burglar.)

To forestall irrelevant objections, I should like to make it clear that by "lightning" I mean the publicly observable physical object, lightning, not a visual sense-datum of lightning. I say that the publicly observable physical object lightning is in fact the electrical discharge, not just a correlate of it. The sense-datum, or rather the having of the sense-datum, the "look" of lightning, may well in my view be a correlate of the electrical discharge. For in my view it is a brain state *caused* by the lightning. But we should no more confuse sensations of lightning with lightning than we confuse sensations of a table with the table.

In short, the reply to Objection 1 is that there can be contingent statements of the form "A is identical with B," and a person may well know that something is an A without knowing that it is a B. An illiterate peasant might well be able to talk about his sensations without knowing about his brain processes, just as he can talk about lightning though he knows nothing of electricity.

Objection 2. It is only a contingent fact (if it is a fact) that when we have a certain kind of sensation there is a certain kind of process in our brain. Indeed it is possible, though perhaps in the highest degree unlikely, that our present physiological theories will be as out of date as the ancient theory connecting mental processes with goings on in the heart. It follows that when we report a sensation we are not reporting a brain-process.

Reply. The objection certainly proves that when we say "I have an after-image" we cannot *mean* something of the form "I have such and such a brain-process." But this does not show that what we report (having an after-image) is not *in fact* a brain process. "I see lightning" does not *mean* "I see an electrical discharge." Indeed, it is logically possible (though highly unlikely) that the electrical discharge account of lightning might one day be given up. Again, "I see the Evening Star" does not *mean* the same as "I see the Morning Star," and yet "The Evening Star and the Morning Star are one and the same thing" is a contingent proposition. Possibly Objection 2 derives some of its apparent strength from a "Fido"—Fido theory of meaning. If the meaning of an expression were what the expression named, then of course it *would* follow from the fact that "sensation" and "brain-process" have different meanings that they cannot name one and the same thing.

Objection 3.[18] Even if Objections 1 and 2 do not prove that sensations are something over and above brain-processes, they do prove that the qualities of sensations are something over and above the qualities of brain-processes. That is, it may be possible to get out of asserting the existence of irreducibly psychic processes, but not out of asserting the existence of irreducibly psychic *properties.* For suppose we identify the Morning Star with the Evening Star. Then there must be some properties which logically imply that of being the Morning Star, and quite distinct properties which entail that of being the Evening Star. Again, there must be some properties (for example, that of being a yellow flash) which are logically distinct from those in the physicalist story.

Indeed, it might be thought that the objection succeeds at one jump. For consider the property of "being a yellow flash." It might seem that this property lies inevitably outside the physicalist framework within which I am trying to work (either by "yellow" being an objective emergent property of physical objects, or else by being a power to produce yellow sense-data, where "yellow," in this second instantiation of the word, refers to a purely phenomenal or introspectible quality). I must therefore disgress for a moment and indicate how I deal with secondary qualities. I shall concentrate on color.

First of all, let me introduce the concept of a normal percipient. One person is more a normal percipient than another if he can make color discriminations that the other cannot. For example, if A can pick a lettuce leaf out of a heap of cabbage leaves, whereas B cannot though he can pick a lettuce leaf out of a heap of beetroot leaves, then A is

more normal than B. (I am assuming that A and B are not given time to distinguish the leaves by their slight difference in shape, and so forth.) From the concept of "more normal than" it is easy to see how we can introduce the concept of "normal." Of course, Eskimos may make the finest discriminations at the blue end of the spectrum, Hottentots at the red end. In this case the concept of a normal percipient is a slightly idealized one, rather like that of "the mean sun" in astronomical chronology. There is no need to go into such subtleties now. I say that "This is red" means something roughly like "A normal percipient would not easily pick this out of a clump of geranium petals though he would pick it out of a clump of lettuce leaves." Of course it does not exactly mean this: a person might know the meaning of "red" without knowning anything about geraniums, or even about normal percipients. But the point is that a person can be *trained* to say "This is red" of objects which would not easily be picked out of geranium petals by a normal percipient, and so on. (Note that even a color-blind person can reasonably assert that something is red, though of course he needs to use another human being, not just himself, as his "color meter.") This account of secondary qualities explains their unimportance in physics. For obviously the discriminations and lack of discriminations made by a very complex neurophysiological mechanism are hardly likely to correspond to simple and nonarbitrary distinctions in nature.

I therefore elucidate colors as powers, in Locke's sense, to evoke certain sorts of discriminatory responses in human beings. They are also, of course, powers to cause sensations in human beings (an account still nearer Locke's). But these sensations, I am arguing, are identifiable with brain processes.

Now how do I get over the objection that a sensation can be identified with a brain process only if it has some phenomenal property, not possessed by brain processes, whereby one-half of the identification may be, so to speak, pinned down?

Reply. My suggestion is as follows. When a person says, "I see a yellowish-orange afterimage," he is saying something like this: "*There is something going on which is like what is going on when* I have my eyes open, am awake, and there is an orange illuminated in good light in front of me, that is, when I really see an orange." (And there is no reason why a person should not say the same thing when he is having a veridical sense-datum, so long as we construe "like" in the last sentence in such a sense that something can be like itself.) Notice that the italicized words, namely "there is something going on which is like what is going on when," are all quasilogical or topic-neutral words. This explains why the ancient Greek peasant's reports about his sensations can be neutral between dualistic metaphysics or my materialistic metaphysics. It explains how sensations can be brain-processes and yet how a man who reports them need know nothing about brain-processes. For he reports them only very abstractly as "something going on which is like what is going on when. . . ." Similarly, a person may say "someone is in the room," thus reporting truly that the doctor is in the room, even though he has never heard of doctors. (There are not two people in the room: "someone" *and* the doctor.) This account of sensation statements also explains the singular elusiveness of "raw feels"—why no one seems to be able to pin any properties on them.[14] Raw feels, in my view, are colorless for the very same reason that *something* is colorless. This does not mean that sensations do not have plenty of properties, for if they are brain-processes they certainly have lots of neurological properties. It only means that in speaking of them as being like or unlike one another we need not know or mention these properties.

This, then, is how I would reply to Objection 3. The strength of my reply depends on the possibility of our being able to report that one thing is like another without being able to state the respect in which it is like. I do not see why this should not be so. If we think cybernetically about the nervous system we can envisage it as able to respond to certain likenesses of its internal processes without being able to do more. It would be easier to build a machine which would tell us, say on a punched tape, whether or not two objects were similar, than it would be to build a machine which would report wherein the similarities consisted.

Objection 4. The after-image is not in physical space. The brain-process is. So the after-image is not a brain-process

Reply. This is an *ignoratio elenchi.* I am not arguing that the after-image is a brain-process, but that the experience of having an after-image is a brain-process. It is the *experience* which is reported in the introspective report. Similarly, if it is objected that the after-image is yellowy-orange, my reply is that it is the experience of seeing yellowy-orange that is being described, and this experience is not a yellowy-orange something. So to say that a brain-process cannot be yellowy-orange is not to say that a brain-process cannot in fact be the experience of having a yellowy-orange after-image. There is, in a sense, no such thing as an after-image or a sense-datum, though there is such a thing as

the experience of having an image, and this experience is described indirectly in material object language, not in phenomenal language, for there is no such thing.[15] We describe the experience by saying, in effect, that it is like the experience we have when, for example, we really see a yellowy-orange patch on the wall. Trees and wallpaper can be green, but not the experience of seeing or imagining a tree or wallpaper. (Or if they are described as green or yellow this can only be in a derived sense.)

Objection 5. It would make sense to say of a molecular movement in the brain that it is swift or slow, straight or circular, but it makes no sense to say this of the experience of seeing something yellow.

Reply. So far we have not given sense to talk of experiences as swift or slow, straight or circular. But I am not claiming that "experience" and "brain-process" mean the same or even that they have the same logic. "Somebody" and "the doctor" do not have the same logic, but this does not lead us to suppose that talking about somebody telephoning is talking about someone over and above, say, the doctor. The ordinary man when he reports an experience is reporting that something is going on, but he leaves it open as to what sort of thing is going on, whether in a material solid medium or perhaps in some sort of gaseous medium, or even perhaps in some sort of nonspatial medium (if this makes sense). All that I am saying is that "experience" and "brain-process" may in fact refer to the same thing, and if so we may easily adopt a convention (which is not a change in our present rules for the use of experience words but an addition to them) whereby it would make sense to talk of an experience in terms appropriate to physical processes.

Objection 6. Sensations are private, brain processes are *public.* If I sincerely say, "I see a yellowish-orange after-image," and I am not making a verbal mistake, then I cannot be wrong. But I can be wrong about a brain-process. The scientist looking into my brain might be having an illusion. Moreover, it makes sense to say that two or more people are observing the same brain-process but not that two or more people are reporting the same inner experience.

Reply. This shows that the language of introspective reports has a different logic from the language of material processes. It is obvious that until the brain-process theory is much improved and widely accepted there will be no *criteria* for saying "Smith has an experience of such-and-such a sort" *except* Smith's introspective reports. So we have adopted a rule of language that (normally) what Smith says goes.

Objection 7. I can imagine myself turned to stone and yet having images, aches, pains, and so on.

Reply. I can imagine that the electrical theory of lightning is false, that lightning is some sort of purely optical phenomenon. I can imagine that lightning is not an electrical discharge. I can imagine that the Evening Star is not the Morning Star. But it is. All the objection shows is that "experience" and "brain-process" do not have the same meaning. It does not show that an experience is not in fact a brain process.

This objection is perhaps much the same as one which can be summed up by the slogan: "What can be composed of nothing cannot be composed of anything."[16] The argument goes as follows: on the brain-process thesis the identity between the brain-process and the experience is a contingent one. So it is logically possible that there should be no brain-process, and no process of any other sort either (no heart process, no kidney process, no liver process). There would be the experience but no "corresponding" physiological process with which we might be able to identify it empirically.

I suspect that the objector is thinking of the experience as a ghostly entity. So it is composed of something, not of nothing, after all. On his view it is composed of ghost stuff, and on mine it is composed of brain stuff. Perhaps the counter-reply will be[17] that the experience is simple and uncompounded, and so it is not composed of anything after all. This seems to be a quibble, for, if it were taken seriously, the remark "What can be composed of nothing cannot be composed of anything" could be recast as an a priori argument against Democritus and atomism and for Descartes and infinite divisibility. And it seems odd that a question of this sort could be settled a priori. We must therefore construe the word "composed" in a very weak sense, which would allow us to say that even an indivisible atom is composed of something (namely, itself). The dualist cannot really say that an experience can be composed of nothing. For he holds that experiences are something over and above material processes, that is, that they are a sort of ghost stuff. (Or perhaps ripples in an underlying ghost stuff.) I say that the dualist's hypothesis is a perfectly intelligible one. But I say that experiences are not to be identified with ghost stuff but with brain stuff. This is another hypothesis, and in my view a very plausible one. The present argument cannot knock it down a priori.

Objection 8. The "beetle in the box" objection (see Wittgenstein, *Philosophical Investigations,* § 293). How could descriptions of experiences, if these are genuine reports, get a foothold in language? For any rule of language must have public criteria for its correct application.

Reply. The change from describing how things are to describing how we feel is just a change from uninhibitedly saying "this is so" to saying "this looks so." That is, when the naïve person might be tempted to say, "There is a patch of light on the wall which moves whenever I move my eyes" or "A pin is being stuck into me," we have learned how to resist this temptation and say "It *looks as though* there is a patch of light on the wallpaper" or "It *feels as though* someone were sticking a pin into me." The introspective account tells us about the individual's state of consciousness in the same way as does "I see a patch of light" or "I feel a pin being stuck into me": it differs from the corresponding perception statement in so far as it withdraws any claim about what is actually going on in the external world. From the point of view of the psychologist, the change from talking about the environment to talking about one's perceptual sensations is simply a matter of disinhibiting certain reactions. These are reactions which one normally suppresses because one has learned that in the prevailing circumstances they are unlikely to provide a good indication of the state of the environment.[18] To say that something looks green to me is simply to say that my experience is like the experience I get when I see something that really is green. In my reply to Objection 3, I pointed out the extreme openness or generality of statements which report experiences. This explains why there is no language or private qualities. (Just as "someone," unlike "the doctor," is a colorless word.)[19]

If it is asked what is the difference between those brain processes which, in my view, are experiences and those brain processes which are not, I can only reply that it is at present unknown. I have been tempted to conjecture that the difference may in part be that between perception and reception (in D. M. MacKay's terminology) and that the type of brain process which is an experience might be identifiable with MacKay's active "matching response."[20] This, however, cannot be the whole story, because sometimes I can perceive something unconsciously, as when I take a handkerchief out of a drawer without being aware that I am doing so. But at the very least, we can classify the brain processes which are experiences as those brain processes which are, or might have been, causal conditions of those pieces of verbal behavior which we call reports of immediate experience.

I have now considered a number of objections to the brain-process thesis. I wish now to conclude with some remarks on the logical status of the thesis itself. U. T. Place seems to hold that it is a straight-out scientific hypothesis.[21] If so, he is partly right and partly wrong. If the issue is between (say) a brain-process thesis and a heart thesis, or a liver thesis, or a kidney thesis, then the issue is a purely empirical one, and the verdict is overwhelmingly in favor of the brain. The right sorts of things don't go on in the heart, liver, or kidney, nor do these organs possess the right sort of complexity of structure. On the other hand, if the issue is between a brain-or-liver-or-kidney thesis (that is, some form of materialism) on the one hand and epiphenomenalism on the other hand, then the issue is not an empirical one. For there is no conceivable experiment which could decide between materialism and epiphenomenalism. This latter issue is not like the average straight-out empirical issue in science, but like the issue between the nineteenth-century English naturalist Philip Gosse[22] and the orthodox geologists and paleontologists of his day. According to Gosse, the earth was created about 4000 B.C. exactly as described in *Genesis*, with twisted rock strata, "evidence" of erosion, and so forth, and all sorts of fossils, all in their appropriate strata, just as if the usual evolutionist story had been true. Clearly this theory is in a sense irrefutable: no evidence can possibly tell against it. Let us ignore the theological setting in which Philip Gosse's hypothesis had been placed, thus ruling out objections of a theological kind, such as "what a queer God who would go to such elaborate lengths to deceive us." Let us suppose that it is held that the universe just *began* in 4004 B.C. with the initial conditions just everywhere as they were in 4004 B.C., and in particular that our own planet began with sediment in the rivers, eroded cliffs, fossils in the rocks, and so on. No scientist would ever entertain this as a serious hypothesis, consistent though it is with all possible evidence. The hypothesis offends against the principles of parsimony and simplicity. There would be far too many brute and inexplicable facts. Why are pterodactyl bones just as they are? No explanation in terms of the evolution of pterodactyls from earlier forms of life would any longer be possible. We would have millions of facts about the world as it was in 4004 B.C. that just have to be *accepted.*

The issue between the brain-process theory and epiphenomenalism seems to be of the above sort.

(Assuming that a behavioristic reduction of introspective reports is not possible.) If it be agreed that there are no cogent philosophical arguments which force us into accepting dualism, and if the brain process theory and dualism are equally consistent with the facts, then the principles of parsimony and simplicity seem to me to decide overwhelmingly in favor of the brain-process theory. As I pointed out earlier, dualism involves a large number of irreducible psychophysical laws (whereby the "nomological danglers" dangle) of a queer sort, that just have to be taken on trust, and are just as difficult to swallow as the irreducible facts about the paleontology of the earth with which we are faced on Philip Gosse's theory.

NOTES

1. This is a very slightly revised version of a paper which was first published in the *Philosophical Review*, LXVIII (1959), 141–156. Since that date there have been criticisms of my paper by J. T. Stevenson, *Philosophical Review*, LXIX (1960), 505–10, to which I have replied in *Philosophical Review*, LXX (1961), 406–7, and by G. Pitcher and by W. D. Joske, *Australasian Journal of Philosophy*, XXXVIII (1960), 150–60, to which I have replied in the same volume of that journal, pp. 252–54.

2. *British Journal of Psychology*, XLVII (1956), 44–50: reprinted in this volume, pp. 101–09 above. (Page references are to the reprint in this volume.)

3. *Minnesota Studies in the Philosphy of Science*, Vol. II (Minneapolis: University of Minnesota Press, 1958). pp. 370–497.

4. Some philosophers of my acquaintance, who have the advantage over me in having known Wittgenstein, would say that this interpretation of him is too behavioristic. However, it seems to me a very natural interpretation of his printed words, and whether or not it is Wittgenstein's real view it is certainly an interesting and important one. I wish to consider it here as a possible rival both to the "brain-process' thesis and to straight-out old-fashioned dualism.

5. See Ryle, *The Concept of Mind* (London: Hutchinson's University Library, 1949), p. 93.

6. On this point see Paul Oppenheim and Hilary Putnam, "Unity of Science as a Working Hypothesis," in *Minnesota Studies in the Philosophy of Science*, Vol. II (Minneapolis: University of Minnesota Press, 1958), pp. 3–36.

7. Feigl, *op. cit.*, p. 428. Feigl uses the expression "nomological danglers" for the laws whereby the entities dangle: I have used the expression to refer to the dangling entities themselves.

8. Wittgenstein did not like the word "disposition." I am using it to put in a nutshell (and perhaps inaccurately) the view which I am attributing to Wittgenstein. I should like to repeat that I do not wish to claim that my interpretation of Wittgenstein is correct. Some of those who knew him do not interpret him in this way. It is merely a view which I find myself extracting from his printed words and which I think is important and worth discussing for its own sake.

9. See Place, *op. cit.*, p. 102. and Feigl, *op. cit.*, p. 390, near top.

10. See J. H. Woodger, *Theory Construction,* International Encyclopedia of Unified Science, II, No. 5 (Chicago: University of Chicago Press, 1939), 38. I here permit myself to speak loosely. For warnings against possible ways of going wrong with this sort of talk, see my note "Spatialising Time," *Mind,* LXIV (1955), 239–41.

11. Cf. Feigl *op. cit.,* p. 439.

12. See Place *op. cit.,* p. 106; also Feigl, *op. cit.,* p. 438.

13. I think this objection was first put to me by Professor Max Black. I think it is the most subtle of any of those I have considered, and the one which I am least confident of having satisfactorily met.

14. See B. A. Farrell, "Experience," *Mind,* LIX (1950), 170–98; reprinted in *The Philosophy of Mind,* ed. V. C. Chappell (Englewood Cliffs: Prentice-Hall, Inc. 1962), pp. 23–48; see especially p. 27 of that volume [p. 174 of the original].

15. Dr. J. R. Smythies claims that a sense-datum language could be taught independently of the material object language ("A Note on the Fallacy of the 'Phenomenological Fallacy,'" *British Journal of Psychology,* XLVIII [1957], 141–44). I am not sure of this: there must be some public criteria for a person having got a rule wrong before we can teach him the rule. I suppose someone might *accidentally* learn color words by Dr. Smythies' procedure. I am not, of course, denying that we can learn a sense-datum language in the sense that we can learn to report our experience. Nor would Place deny it.

16. I owe this objection to Dr. C. B. Martin. I gather that he no longer wishes to maintain this objection, at any rate in its present form.

17. Martin did not make this reply, but one of his students did.

18. I owe this point to Place, in correspondence.

19. The "beetle in the box" objection is, *if it is sound,* an objection to *any* view, and in particular the Cartesian one, that introspective reports are genuine reports. So it is no objection to a weaker thesis that I would be concerned to uphold, namely, that if introspective reports of "experiences" are genuinely reports, then the things they are reports of are in fact brain processes.

20. See his article "Towards an Information-Flow Model of Human Behaviour," *British Journal of Psychology,* XLVII (1956), 30–43.

21. *Op. cit.* For a further discussion of this, in reply to the original version of the present paper, see Place's note "Materialism as a Scientific Hypothesis," *Philosophical Review,* LXIX (1960), 101–4.

22. See the entertaining account of Gosse's book *Omphalos* by Martin Gardner in *Fads and Fallacies in the Name of Science,* 2nd ed. (New York: Dover, 1957), pp. 124–27.

18

Jerome Shaffer

"Mental Events and the Brain"

When J. J. C. Smart propounded his version of the Identity Theory,[1] he confessed that he found the most powerful objection to his theory to be as follows. Even if we can establish the *de facto* identity of mental events and neural events, do we not still have to admit the existence of mental features (to pin down one side of the *de facto* identity)? Are we not then still committed to something irreducibly mental? If so, we have the "nomological danglers" which are incompatible with the thoroughgoing materialism Smart wishes to establish. Smart's attempt to deal with this objection has been criticized by me[2] and by others,[3] and Smart has replied to some of these criticisms.[4] I wish to reconsider this objection to Smart's theory, especially in the light of some recent criticisms[5] of my own paper.

On the Identity Theory, the having of an after-image, the feeling of a pain, or the occurrence of a thought is claimed to be identical, as a matter of empirical fact, with some event occurring in the brain. The two occurrences are held to be identical in the same sense that a flash of lightning is held to be identical with a particular sort of electrical discharge, i.e., not that the terms referring to them are synonymous but that the terms happen to pick out, refer to, or denote one and the same event.

Now there are serious problems concerning whether mental and brain events *could* be identical. I shall return to this issue at the end of this discussion. But assuming it could be shown that they are identical, there still is a problem here for Smart's materialism. For if it is an *empirical* identity, then how we identify mental events will have to be different from how we identify brain events; if they were identified in the same way, then they would not be logically independent. Now suppose we identified mental events by noticing the occurrence of some peculiarly *mental* feature. Then we

would still be left with some irreducibly nonphysical aspects, and this Smart would find objectionable.

So the new task, for Smart, is to give some account, in nonmentalistic terms, of what we report when we report the having of a thought or after-image or pain. According to Smart, all such reports are of the following form: there is now occurring an internal process, *x*, such that *x* is like what goes on when a particular physical stimulus affects me. Thus to report an orange after-image is to report "something going on which is like what is going on when I have my eyes open, am awake, and there is an orange illuminated in good light in front of me, that is, when I really seen an orange."[6] In this definition there appear only physicalistic terms and logical terms; there are no peculiarly mental terms in it. But there are no terms describing brain events either. So it can turn out to be the case that the "something going on" which is reported is factually identical with a particular brain event. Whatever will be found to be common to such situations will be, of course, for science to determine, if it can; that the common internal process is a brain process is merely an empirical conjecture. This is the way Smart replies to the charge that he is still left with an irreducibly mental feature.[7]

At the heart, then, of Smart's Identity Theory is the suggestion that mental events are definable as the concomitants or products of certain physical stimulus conditions or anything that is just like those concomitants or products. Now there are some very serious difficulties in this view. In the first place, I am inclined to think the definition could not be completed. Indefinitely many factors would be relevant in stating the causally sufficient conditions for, say, seeing an orange, to use the example of the after-image cited above. Any one of

From *The Journal of Philosophy* LX, 6 (March 14, 1963): 160–66. Reprinted with permission of the editors and Jerome A. Shaffer.

these could prevent the final brain event from occurring. We would have to mention "normal" conditions and "normal" subjects, or speak of "all other things being equal," and that would be to admit that we could not actually complete the translation. Secondly, even if the translation could be completed in theory, it would be so filled with complicated assertions about propagation of energy, media, nerves, etc., that it is unbelievable that such things would be part of what the ordinary man *means* when he reports a mental event (or even what the neurophysiologist means).

What leads Smart to think that mental events can be defined in terms of the stimulus conditions that are their causes? His reason is that "sensation talk must be learned by reference to some environmental stimulus situation or another."[8] But while this latter claim seems sensible enough, it does not follow that *what* is learned in some environmental stimulus situation is definable in terms of that environmental stimulus situation. We might learn what the expression, 'seeing stars', means by being hit on the head, but to know how the expression is learned is not to know the meaning; a blind man might know how the meaning of the expression is learned, but still not know the meaning. Smart's purported analyses of the meanings of mental terms are, at best, instructions for coming to learn the meanings of these terms, rules for the obtaining of examples to be used in ostensive definitions.

I have shown that Smart's account of the meaning of reports of sensations is defective. I now wish to give a general argument why no such materialistic maneuvering can succeed, showing that we cannot avoid admitting at the least the existence of *nonphysical properties or features,* even if we give up nonphysical *events* as a different class from physical *events.*

Let us take the case where a person reports the having of some mental event, the having of an after-image, a thought, or a sensation of pain. Now such a person has surely noticed that *something* has occurred, and he has surely noticed that this something has *some* features (or how could he report it was an after-image rather than a sensation of pain?). Now it seems to me obvious that, in many cases at least, the person does not notice any *physical* features—he does not notice that his brain is in some particular state, nor does he notice any external physical stimulus, nor any physical event between the stimulus and the neurological response. Yet he does notice *some* feature. Hence he must notice something other than a physical feature. The noticing of some nonphysical feature is the only way to explain how anything is noticed at all.

In my earlier discussion of Smart's views *(op. cit.),* I had put this point ambiguously by saying that we could have information about our own mental events without having information about our physical events. Cornman claims that I beg the question here against Identity Theory; he says, "If, as Smart believes, all mental states are indeed brain processes, then when we have information about mental states we thereby have information about brain processes" (Cornman, 488–89). I think Cornman is right here. That is why I now wish to put the point in terms of *noticing.* I may have noticed a person at a party, but from the fact that the person turns out to be the best dressed woman in America it does not follow that I noticed this feature of the person. Similarly, from the fact that the event I notice turns out to be a brain event (if the Identity Theory is correct) it does not follow that I noticed a neurological feature, nor a physical feature of any sort. Hence when I claim that a person may notice the occurrence of a mental event without noticing the occurrence of anything physical, I cannot be accused of begging the question against the Identity Theory.

If my argument is correct, Smart must conclude that when a person reports the having of some mental event, the person must have noticed the occurrence of some nonphysical feature. In some of Smart's recent replies, he suggests two ways he might try to avoid this conclusion. (1) He construes the reporter of a mental event to be noticing a similarity between two brain events, but says that the person may not notice the respect in which the events are similar.[9] My point is that it is most implausible to think that, at least in most cases of reporting mental events, the person notices anything at all about his brain. (2) He sometimes hints that the report of a mental event is merely a behavioral response and therefore not a case of noticing at all. Thus, at one point, in discussing how a person might report a similarity without being able to say in what respect they are similar, Smart says, "Thinking cybernetically it is indeed easier to envisage the nervous system as being able to react to likenesses of its internal processes without being able to issue descriptions of these likenesses."[10] And at another point, in trying to describe the difference between those brain events which are identical with mental events and those which are not, he says, "We can distinguish the ones which are sensations as those which can in suitable circumstances be the specific causal conditions of those behavior reactions which are sensation reports."[11] Although he admits to being "very receptive" to this view of the report as a mere expression or reaction, he cannot accept it.[12]

And surely he is right in rejecting it, for such a view cannot account for the obvious fact that 'I now have an orange after-image' can be used to make true or false statements and, therefore, can be used to make a genuine report.

If the above remarks are sound, then we must admit, at the very least, the existence of nonphysical properties or nonphysical features. Are they "irreducibly different" from physical properties, the "nomological danglers" that Smart is so fearful of? Not necessarily. Suppose we are able to discover psychological laws that govern mental phenomena. And suppose we are able to deduce these and other psychological laws from neurophysiological laws, via the empirically determined correspondences of the mental and neural. Furthermore, suppose we are able to predict the occurrence of further mental states not included in our original empirically determined correspondences on the basis of the occurrence of neural states. Will we not then be in a position to give a complete explanation of psychological phenomena and psychological laws in terms of the physical? And if we now adopt conventions that will allow us to speak of mental events as having location in the brain, then we will indeed have shown that psychology is reducible to physiology and the mental reducible to the physical. The properties would still be different properties, but they would no longer be *irreducibly* different.[13]

So far in this discussion I have assumed it could turn out that mental events and brain events are identical. I wish to consider this assumption now with respect to a recent criticism that has been made by Coburn *(op. cit.)*. I had argued that the Identity theory must be rejected on a priori grounds. If mental and brain events were identical, they would have to occur in the same place. But it makes no sense to say of some mental event, a thought for example, that it occurred in some particular part of the brain. Hence the identity cannot hold. However, I further suggested that we could adopt a convention for the locating of mental events in the brain which would rule out this a priori objection. The consequence of adopting this convention would be to change our concept of a mental event, but, I claimed, there was nothing in our present concept that ruled out the adoption of such a convention.

Coburn argues that such a convention could not be adopted. If we take mental events to be locatable in space, then they would be "'public' entities in the sense that no person would be in any better position essentially than any other for determining with certainty whether such an experience was occurring" (91). If Coburn is right in saying

that mental events would then become *"public"* in this sense, I would agree that a convention for locating them in space could not be adopted. But why should one think that they would become "public"? Coburn's reason is that "the idea that something should be going on in such and such a place and yet that one person should occupy an intrinsically privileged epistemological position vis-à-vis that occurrence is *prima facie* absurd" (91). But is that true? Mental events can occur at such and such a *time* and still be private. Why is *temporal* location possible but not *spatial* location? I see no absurdity in adopting such a convention.

As I pointed out in the paper Coburn discusses (820), mental events will have certain public aspects if we accept the Identity Theory. Brain events are public events, and if mental events are identical with them then there will be a respect in which mental events are public too. And conversely, of course, there will be a respect in which brain events are private. That is to say, there will be this class of events which will be known to occur either on the basis of neurological observations or by introspection. There will still be privileged access to these events, but there will also be public access to them. The event I know to have occurred on the basis of introspection will turn out to be one and the same as the event you know to have occurred by neurological observation. This is possible because one and the same event will have both physical and nonphysical features. Therefore there will be physiological criteria for its occurring; in addition the person concerned will be in a position to report its occurrence without appeal to these physiological criteria.

But suppose there is a conflict between neurological observation and introspection? Then we will have an *empirical* refutation of the Identity Theory.[14]

NOTES

1. "Sensations and Brain Processes," *The Philosophical Review*, 68 (1959).

2. "Could Mental States be Brain Processes?," *The Journal of Philosophy*, 58, 26 (Dec. 21, 1961), 813.

3. George Pitcher, "Sensations and Brain Processes: A Reply to Professor Smart," *Australasian Journal of Philosophy*, 38, 2 (August, 1960): 150; J. T. Stevenson, "Sensations and Brain Processes: A Reply to J. J. C. Smart," *The Philosophical Review*, 69, 4 (October, 1960): 505; Kurt Baier, "Smart on Sensations," *Australasian Journal of Philosophy*, 40, 1 (May, 1962): 56; James W. Cornman, "The Identity of Mind and Body," *The Journal of Philosophy*, 59, 18 (Aug. 30, 1962): 486.

4. "Sensations and Brain Processes: A Rejoinder to Dr. Pitcher and Mr. Joske," *Australasian Journal of Philosophy*, 38, 3 (December, 1960): 252; "Further Remarks on Sensations and Brain Processes," *The Philosophical Review*, 70 (1961): 406; "Brain Processes and Incorrigibility," *Australasian Journal of Philosophy*, 40, 1 (May, 1962): 68.

5. Cornman, *op. cit.*; Robert C. Coburn, "Shaffer on the Identity of Mental States and Brain Processes," *The Journal of Philosophy*, 60, 4 (Feb. 14, 1963): 89.

6. Smart, "Sensations and Brain Processes," 149.

7. This is clearly pointed out in Cornman's article (*op. cit.*, 489) as well as in some recent replies by Smart (cited above).

8. Smart, "Brain Processes and Incorrigibility," 69.

9. "Sensations and Brain Processes," 150; "Rejoinder to Dr. Pitcher and Mr. Joske," 253.

10. "Rejoinder to Dr. Pitcher and Mr. Joske," 253.

11. "Further Remarks," 407.

12. "Sensations and Brain Processes," 144.

13. This sort of empirical reduction is discussed at length by Ernest Nagel, *The Structure of Science*, chs. 11 and 12; cf. esp. p. 366.

19

D. M. Armstrong

"The Causal Theory of Mind"

Is Philosophy Just Conceptual Analysis?

What can philosophy contribute to solving the problem of the relation of mind to body? Twenty years ago, many English-speaking philosophers would have answered: "Nothing beyond an analysis of the various mental *concepts.*" If we seek knowledge of things, they thought, it is to science that we must turn. Philosophy can only cast light upon our concepts of those things.

This retreat from things to concepts was not undertaken lightly. Ever since the seventeenth century, the great intellectual fact of our culture has been the incredible expansion of knowledge both in the natural and in the rational sciences (mathematics, logic). Everyday life presents us with certain simple verities. But, it seems, through science and only through science can we build upon these verities, and with astonishing results.

The success of science created a crisis in philosophy. What was there for philosophy to do? Hume had already perceived the problem in some degree, and so surely did Kant, but it was not until the twentieth century, with the Vienna Circle and with Wittgenstein, that the difficulty began to weigh heavily. Wittgenstein took the view that philosophy could do no more than strive to undo the intellectual knots it itself had tied, so achieving intellectual release, and even a certain illumination, but no knowledge. A little later, and more optimistically, Ryle saw a positive, if reduced, role for philosophy in mapping the "logical geography" of our concepts: how they stood to each other and how they were to be analysed.

On the whole, Ryle's view proved more popular than Wittgenstein's. After all, it retained a spe-

cial, if much reduced, realm for philosophy where she might still be queen. There was better hope of continued employment for members of the profession!

Since that time, however, philosophers in the "analytic" tradition have swung back from Wittgensteinian and even Rylean pessimism to a more traditional conception of the proper role and tasks of philosophy. Many analytic philosophers now would accept the view that the central task of philosophy is to give an account, or at least play a part in giving an account, of the most general nature of things and of man. (I would include myself among that many.)

Why has this swing back occurred? Has the old urge of the philosopher to determine the nature of things by *a priori* reasoning proved too strong? To use Freudian terms, are we simply witnessing a return of what philosophers had repressed? I think not. One consideration that has had great influence was the realization that those who thought that they were abandoning ontological and other substantive questions for a mere investigation of concepts were in fact smuggling in views on the substantive questions. They did not acknowledge that they held these views, but the views were there; and far worse from their standpoint, the views imposed a form upon their answers to the conceptual questions.

For instance, in *The Concept of Mind* (1949), Gilbert Ryle, although he denied that he was a Behaviourist, seemed to be upholding an account of man and his mind that was extremely close to Behaviourism. Furthermore, it seemed in many cases that it was this view of the mind–body problem that led him to his particular analyses of particular

From D. M. Armstrong, *The Nature of Mind.* St. Lucia, Queensland: University of Queensland Press, 1980, pp. 16–31. Originally appeared in *Neue Hefte für Philosophie*, Heft 11, 1977, pp. 82–95. Reprinted with permission of the publisher and D. M. Armstrong.

mental concepts, rather than the other way around. Faced with examples like this, it began to appear that, since philosophers could not help holding views on substantive matters, and the views could not help affecting their analyses of concepts, the views had better be held and discussed explicitly instead of appearing in a distorted, because unacknowledged, form.

The swing back by analytic philosophers to first-order questions was also due to the growth of a more sophisticated understanding of the nature of scientific investigation. For a philosophical tradition that is oriented towards science, as, on the whole, Western philosophy is, the consideration of the *methods* of science must be an important topic. It was gradually realized that in the past scientific investigation had regularly been conceived in far too positivistic, sensationalistic and observationalistic a spirit. (The influence of Karl Popper has been of the greatest importance in this realization.) As the central role of speculation, theory and reasoning in scientific investigation began to be appreciated by more and more philosophers, the border-line between science and philosophy began to seem at least more fluid, and the hope arose again that philosophy might have something to contribute to first-order questions.

The philosopher has certain special skills. These include the stating and assessing of the worth of arguments, including the bringing to light and making explicit suppressed premisses of arguments, the detection of ambiguities and inconsistencies, and, perhaps especially, the analysis of concepts. But, I contend, these special skills do not entail that the *objective* of philosophy is to do these things. They are rather the special *means* by which philosophy attempts to achieve further objectives. Ryle was wrong in taking the analysis of concepts to be the end of philosophy. Rather, the analysis of concepts is a means by which the philosopher makes his contribution to great general questions, not about concepts, but about things.

In the particular case of the mind–body problem, the propositions the philosopher arrives at need not be of a special nature. They perhaps might have been arrived at by the psychologist, the neuro-physiologist, the biochemist or others, and, indeed, may be suggested to the philosopher by the results achieved or programmes proposed by those disciplines. But the way that the argument is marshalled by a philosopher will be a special way. Whether this special way has or has not any particular value in the search for truth is a matter to be decided in particular cases. There is no *a priori* reason for thinking that the special methods of philosophy will be able to make a contribution to the mind–body problem. But neither is there an *a priori* reason for assuming that the philosopher's contribution will be valueless.

The Concept of a Mental State

The philosophy of philosophy is perhaps a somewhat joyless and unrewarding subject for reflection. Let us now turn to the mind–body problem itself, hoping that what is to be said about this particular topic will confirm the general remarks about philosophy that have just been made.

If we consider the mind–body problem today, then it seems that we ought to take account of the following consideration. The present state of scientific knowledge makes it probable that we can give a purely physico-chemical account of man's body. It seems increasingly likely that the body and the brain of man are constituted and work according to exactly the same principles as those physical principles that govern other, non-organic, matter. The differences between a stone and a human body appear to lie solely in the extremely complex material set-up that is to be found in the living body and which is absent in the stone. Furthermore, there is rather strong evidence that it is the state of our brain that completely determines the state of our consciousness and our mental state generally.

All this is not beyond the realm of controversy, and it is easy to imagine evidence that would upset the picture. In particular, I think that it is just possible that evidence from psychical research might be forthcoming that a physico-chemical view of man's brain could not accommodate. But suppose that the physico-chemical view of the working of the brain is correct, as I take it to be. It will be very natural to conclude that mental states are not simply *determined* by corresponding states of the brain, but that they are actually *identical* with these brain-states, brain-states that involve nothing but physical properties.

The argument just outlined is quite a simple one, and it hardly demands philosophical skill to develop it or to appreciate its force! But although many contemporary thinkers would accept its conclusion, there are others, including many philosophers, who would not. To a great many thinkers it has seemed obvious *a priori* that mental states could not be physical states of the brain. Nobody would identify a number with a piece of rock: it is sufficiently obvious that the two entities fall under different categories. In the same way, it has been thought, a perception or a feeling of sorrow must be a different category of thing from an electro-chemical discharge in the central nervous system.

Here, it seems to me, is a question to which philosophers can expect to make a useful contribution. It is a question about mental concepts. Is our concept of a mental state such that it is an intelligible hypothesis that mental states are physical states of the brain? If the philosopher can show that it is an *intelligible* proposition (that is, a non-self-contradictory proposition) that mental states are physical states of the brain, then the scientific argument just given above can be taken at its face value as a strong reason for accepting the truth of the proposition.

My view is that the identification of mental states with physical states of the brain is a perfectly intelligible one, and that this becomes clear once we achieve a correct view of the analysis of the mental concepts. I admit that my analysis of the mental concepts was itself adopted because it permitted this identification, but such a procedure is commonplace in the construction of theories, and perfectly legitimate. In any case, whatever the motive for proposing the analysis, it is there to speak for itself, to be measured against competitors, and to be assessed as plausible or implausible independently of the identification it makes possible.

The problem of the identification may be put in a Kantian way: "How is it possible that mental states should be physical states of the brain?" The solution will take the form of proposing an *independently plausible* analysis of the concept of a mental state that will permit this identification. In this way, the philosopher makes the way smooth for a first-order doctrine, which, true or false, is a doctrine of the first importance: a purely physicalist view of man.

The analysis proposed may be called the Causal analysis of the mental concepts. According to this view, the concept of a mental state essentially involves, and is exhausted by, the concept of a state that is *apt to be the cause of certain effects or apt to be the effect of certain causes.*

An example of a causal concept is the concept of poison. The concept of poison is the concept of something that when introduced into an organism causes that organism to sicken and/or die.[1] This is but a rough analysis of the concept the structure of which is in fact somewhat more complex and subtle than this. If *A* pours molten lead down *B*'s throat, then he may cause *B* to die as a result, but he can hardly be said to have poisoned him. For a thing to be called a poison, it is necessary that it act in a certain *sort* of way: roughly, in a biological as opposed to a purely physical way. Again, a poison can be introduced into the system of an organism and that organism fail to die or even to sicken. This might occur if an antidote were administered promptly. Yet again, the poison may be present in insufficient quantities to do any damage. Other qualifications could be made.

But the essential point about the concept of poison is that it is the concept of *that, whatever it is, which produces certain effects.* This leaves open the possibility of the *scientific identification* of poisons, of discovering that a certain sort of substance, such as cyanide, is a poison, and discovering further what it is about the substance that makes it poisonous.

Poisons are accounted poisons in virtue of their active powers, but many sorts of things are accounted the sorts of thing they are by virtue of their *passive* powers. Thus brittle objects are accounted brittle because of the disposition they have to break and shatter when sharply struck. This leaves open the possibility of discovering empirically what sorts of thing are brittle and what it is about them that makes them brittle.

Now *if* the concepts of the various sorts of mental state are concepts of that which is, in various sorts of way, apt for causing certain effects and apt for being the effect of certain causes, then it would be a quite unpuzzling thing if mental states should turn out to be physical states of the brain.

The concept of a mental state is the concept of something that is, characteristically, the cause of certain effects and the effect of certain causes. What sort of effects and what sort of causes? The effects caused by the mental state will be certain patterns of behaviour of the person in that state. For instance, the desire for food is a state of a person or animal that characteristically brings about food-seeking and food-consuming behaviour by that person or animal. The causes of mental states will be objects and events in the person's environment. For instance, a sensation of green is the characteristic effect in a person of the action upon his eyes of a nearby green surface.

The general pattern of analysis is at its most obvious and plausible in the case of *purposes.* If a man's purpose is to go to the kitchen to get something to eat, it is completely natural to conceive of this purpose as a cause within him that brings about, or tends to bring about, that particular line of conduct. It is, furthermore, notorious that we are unable to characterize purposes *except* in terms of that which they tend to bring about. How can we distinguish the purpose to go to the kitchen to get something to eat from another purpose to go to the bedroom to lie down? Only by the different outcomes that the two purposes tend to bring about. This fact was an encouragement to Behaviourism. It is still more plausibly explained by saying that the concept of purpose is a causal concept. The further hypothesis that the two purposes are, in their own nature, different physical patterns in, or physical states of, the central nervous system is then a natural (although, of course, not logically inevitable) supplement to the causal analysis.

Simple models have great value in trying to grasp complex conceptions, but they are ladders that may need to be kicked away after we have mounted up by their means. It is vital to realize that the mental concepts have a far more complex logical structure than simple causal notions such as the concept of poison. The fact should occasion no surprise. In the case of poisons, the effect of which they are the cause is a gross and obvious phenomenon and the level of causal explanation involved in simply calling a substance "a poison" is crude and simple. But in the case of mental states, their effects are all those complexities of behaviour that mark off men and higher animals from the rest of the objects in the world. Furthermore, differences in such behaviour are elaborately correlated with differences in the mental causes operating. So it is only to be expected that the causal patterns invoked by the mental concepts should be extremely complex and sophisticated.

In the case of the notion of a purpose, for intance, it is plausible to assert that it is the notion of a cause within which drives, or tends to drive, the man or animal through a series of actions to a certain end-state. But this is not the whole story. A purpose is only a purpose if it works to bring about the behavioural effects *in a certain sort of way.* We may sum up this sort of way by saying that purposes are *information-sensitive* causes. By this is meant that purposes direct behaviour by utilizing *perceptions* and *beliefs,* perceptions and beliefs about the agent's current situation and the way it develops, and beliefs about the way the world works. For instance, it is part of what it is to be a purpose to achieve X that this cause will cease to operate, will be "switched off", if the agent perceives or otherwise comes to believe that X has been achieved.

At this point, we observe that an account is being given of that special species of cause that is a purpose in terms of *further* mental items: perceptions and beliefs. This means that if we are to give a purely causal analysis even of the concept of a purpose we also will have to give a purely causal analysis of perceptions and beliefs. We may think of man's behaviour as brought about by the joint operation of two sets of causes: first, his purposes and, second, his perceptions of and/or his beliefs about the world. But since perceptions and beliefs are quite different sorts of thing from purposes, a Causal analysis must assign quite different causal *roles* to these different things in the bringing about of behaviour.

I believe that this can be done by giving an account of perceptions and beliefs as *mappings* of the world. They are structures within us that model the world beyond the structure. This model is created in us by the world. Purposes may then be thought of as driving causes that utilize such mappings.

This is a mere thumb-nail, which requires much further development as well as qualification. One point that becomes clear when that development is given is that just as the concept of purpose cannot be elucidated without appealing to the concepts of perception and belief, so the latter cannot be eludicated without appealing to the concept of purpose. (This comes out, for instance, when we raise Hume's problem: what marks off beliefs from the mere entertaining of the same proposition? It seems that we can only mark off beliefs as those mappings in the light of which we are prepared to *act,* that is, which are potential servants of our purposes.) The logical dependence of purpose on perception and belief, and of perception and belief upon purpose, is not circularity in definition. What it shows is that the corresponding concepts *must be introduced together or not at all.* In itself, there is nothing very surprising in this. Correlative or mutually implicated concepts are common enough: for instance, the concepts of husband and wife or the concepts of soldier and army. No husbands without wives or wives without husbands. No soldiers without an army, no army without soldiers. But if the concepts of purpose, perception and belief are (i) correlative concepts and (ii) different species of purely causal concepts, then it is clear that they are far more complex in structure than a simple causal concept like poison. What falls under the mental concepts will be a complex and interlocking set of causal factors, which together are responsible for the "minded" behaviour of men and the higher animals.

The working out of the Causal theory of the mental concepts thus turns out to be an extremely complex business. Indeed when it is merely baldly stated, the Causal theory is, to use the phrase of Imre Lakatos, a *research programme* in conceptual analysis rather than a developed theory. I have tried to show that it is a hopeful programme by attempting, at least in outline, a Causal analysis of all the main mental concepts in *A Materialist Theory of the Mind* (1968); and I have supplemented the rather thin account given there of the concepts of belief, knowledge and inferring in *Belief, Truth and Knowledge* (1973).

Two examples of mental concepts where an especially complex and sophisticated type of Causal analysis is required are the notions of introspective awareness (one sense of the word "consciousness") and the having of mental imagery. Introspective awareness is analysable as a mental state that is a "perception" of mental states. It is a mapping of the causal factors themselves. The having of mental imagery is a sort of mental state that cannot be elucidated in *directly* causal terms, but only by resemblance to the corresponding perceptions, which *are* explicated in terms of their causal role.

Two advantages of the Causal theory may now be mentioned. First, it has often been remarked by philosophers and others that the realm of mind is a shadowy one, and that the nature of mental states is singularly elusive and hard to grasp. This has given aid and comfort to Dualist or Cartesian theories of mind, according to which minds are quite different sorts of thing from material objects. But if the Causal analysis is correct, the facts admit of another explanation. What Dualist philosophers have grasped in a confused way is that our direct acquaintance with mind, which occurs in introspective awareness, is an acquaintance with something that we are aware of only as something that is causally linked, directly or indirectly, with behaviour. In the case of our purposes and desires, for instance, we are often (though not invariably) introspectively aware of them. What we are aware of is the presence of factors within us that drive in a certain direction. We are not aware of the intrinsic nature of the factors. This emptiness or gap in our awareness is then interpreted by Dualists as immateriality. In fact, however, if the Causal analysis is correct, there is no warrant for this interpretation and, if the Physicalist identification of the nature of the causes is correct, the interpretation is actually false.

Second, the Causal analysis yields a still more spectacular verification. It shows promise of explaining a philosophically notorious feature of all or almost all mental states: their *intentionality*. This was the feature of mental states to which Brentano in particular drew attention, the fact that they may point towards certain objects or states of affairs, but that these objects and states of affairs need not exist. When a man strives, his striving has an objective, but that objective may never be achieved. When he believes, there is something he believes, but what he believes may not be the case. This capacity of mental states to "point" to what does not exist can seem very special. Brentano held that intentionality set the mind completely apart from matter.

Suppose, however, that we consider a concept like the concept of poison. Does it not provide us with a miniature and unsophisticated model for the intentionality of mental states? Poisons are substances apt to make organisms sicken and die when the poison is administered. So it may be said that this is what poisons "point" to. Nevertheless, poisons may fail of their effect. A poison does not fail to be a poison because an antidote neutralizes the customary effect of the poison.

May not the intentionality of mental states, therefore, be in principle a no more mysterious affair, although indefinitely more complex, than the death that lurks in the poison? As an intermediate case between poisons and mental states, consider the mechanisms involved in a homing rocket. Given a certain setting of its mechanism, the rocket may "point" towards a certain target in a way that is a simulacrum of the way in which purposes point towards their objectives. The mechanism will only bring the rocket to the target in "standard" circumstances: many factors can be conceived that would "defeat" the mechanism. For the mechanism to operate successfully, some device will be required by which the developing situation is "mapped" in the mechanism (i.e. what course the rocket is currently on, etc.) This mapping is an elementary analogue of perception, and so the course that is "mapped" in the mechanism may be thought of as a simulacrum of the perceptual intentional object. Through one circumstance or another (e.g. malfunction of the gyroscope) this mapping may be "incorrect".

It is no objection to this analogy that homing rockets are built by men with purposes, who deliberately stamp a crude model of their own purposes into the rocket. Homing rockets might have been natural products, and non-minded objects that operate in a similar but far more complex way are found in nature. The living cell is a case in point.

So the Causal analyses of the mental concepts show promise of explaining both the transparency and the intentionality of mental states. One problem quite frequently raised in connection with these analyses, however, is in what sense they can be called "analyses". The welter of complications in which the so-called analyses are involved make it sufficiently obvious that they do not consist of *synonymous translations* of statements in which mental terms figure. But, it has been objected, if synonymous translations of mental statements are unavailable, what precisely can be meant by speaking of "analyses of concepts"?

I am far from clear what should be said in reply to this objection. Clearly, however, it does depend upon taking all conceptual analyses as claims about the synonymy of sentences, and that seems to be too simple a view. Going back to the case of poison: it is surely not an empirical fact, to be learnt by experience, that poisons kill. It is at the centre of our notion of what poisons are that they have the power to bring about this effect. If they did not do that, they would not be properly called "poisons". But although this seems obvious enough, it is extremely difficult to give exact translations of sentences containing the word "poison" into other sentences that do not contain the word or any synonym. Even in this simple case, it is not at all clear that the task can actually be accomplished.

For this reason, I think that sentence translation (with synonymy) is too strict a demand to make upon a purported conceptual analysis. What more relaxed demand can we make and still have a conceptual analysis? I do not know. One thing that we clearly need further light upon here is the concept of a concept, and how concepts are tied to language. I incline to the view that the connection between concepts and language is much less close than many philosophers have assumed. Concepts are linked primarily with belief and thought, and belief and thought, I think, have a great degree of logical independence of language, however close the empirical connection may be in many cases. If this is so, then an analysis of concepts, although of course conducted *in* words, may not be an investigation *into* words. (A compromise proposal: analysis of concepts might be an investigation into some sort of "deep structure"—to use the currently hallowed phrase—which underlies the use of certain words and sentences.) I wish I were able to take the topic further.

The Problem of the Secondary Qualities

No discussion of the Causal theory of the mental concepts is complete that does not say something about the *secondary qualities*. If we consider such mental states as purpose and intentions, their "transparency" is a rather conspicuous feature. It is notorious that introspection cannot differentiate such states except in terms of their different objects. It is not so immediately obvious, however, that *perception* has this transparent character. Perception involves the existence of colour and of visual extension, touch of the whole obscure range of tactual properties, including tactual extension, hearing, taste and smell the experience of sounds, tastes and smells. These phenomenal qualities, it may be argued, endow different perceptions with different qualities. The lack of transparency is even more obvious in the case of bodily sensations. Pains, itches, tickles and tingles are mental states, even if mental states of no very high-grade sort, and they each seem to involve their own peculiar qualities. Again, associated with different emotions

it is quite plausible to claim to discern special emotion qualities. If perception, bodily sensation and emotions involve qualities, then this seems to falsify a purely Causal analysis of these mental states. They are not mere "that whiches" known only by their causal role.

However, it is not at all clear how strong is the line of argument sketched in the previous paragraph. We distinguish between the intention and what is intended, and in just the same way, we must distinguish between the perception and what is perceived. The intention is a mental state and so is the perception, but what is intended is not in general something mental and nor is what is perceived. What is intended may not come to pass, it is a merely intentional object, and the same may be said of what is perceived. Now in the case of the phenomenal qualities, it seems plausible to say that they are qualities not of the perception but rather of what is perceived. "Visual extension" is the shape, size, etc. that some object of visual perception is perceived to have (an object that need not exist). Colour seems to be a quality of that object. And similarly for the other phenomenal qualities. Even in the case of the bodily sensations, the qualities associated with the sensations do not *appear* to be qualities of mental states but instead to be qualities of portions of our bodies: more or less fleeting qualities that qualify the place where the sensation is located. Only in the case of the emotions does it seem natural to place the quality on the mental rather than the object side: but then it is not so clear whether there really *are* peculiar qualities associated with the emotions. The different patterns of bodily sensations associated with the different emotions may be sufficient to do phenomenological justice to the emotions.

For these reasons, it is not certain whether the phenomenal qualities pose any threat to the Causal analysis of the mental concepts. But what a subset of these qualities quite certainly does pose a threat to, is the doctrine that the Causal analysis of the mental concepts is a step towards: Materialism or Physicalism.

The qualities of colour, sound, heat and cold, taste and smell together with the qualities that appear to be involved in bodily sensations and those that may be involved in the case of the emotions, are an embarrassment to the modern Materialist. He seeks to give an account of the world and of man purely in terms of *physical* properties, that is to say in terms of the properties that the physicist appeals to in his explanations of phenomena. The Materialist is not committed to the *current* set of properties to which the physicist appeals, but he is committed to whatever set of properties the physicist in the end will appeal to. It is clear that such properties as colour, sound, taste and smell—the so-called "secondary qualities"—will never be properties to which the physicist will appeal.

It is, however, a plausible thesis that associated with different secondary qualities are properties that are respectable from a physicist's point of view. Physical surfaces *appear* to have colour. They not merely appear to, but undoubtedly do, emit light-waves, and the different mixtures of lengths of wave emitted are linked with differences in colour. In the same way, different sorts of sound are linked with different sorts of sound-wave and differences in heat with differences in the mean kinetic energy of the molecules composing the hot things. The Materialist's problem therefore would be very simply solved if the secondary qualities could be identified with these physically respectable properties. (The qualities associated with bodily sensations would be identified with different sorts of stimulation of bodily receptors. If there are unique qualities associated with the emotions, they would presumably be identified with some of the physical states of the brain linked with particular emotions.)

But now the Materialist philosopher faces a problem. Previously he asked: "How is it possible that mental states could be physical states of the brain?" This question was answered by the Causal theory of the mental concepts. Now he must ask: "How is it possible that secondary qualities could be purely physical properties of the objects they are qualities of?" A Causal analysis does not seem to be of any avail. To try to give an analysis of, say, the quality of being red in Causal terms would lead us to produce such analyses as "those properties of a physical surface, whatever they are, that characteristically produce *red sensations* in us." But this analysis simply shifts the problem unhelpfully from property of surface to property of sensation. Either the red sensations involve nothing but physically respectable properties or they involve something more. If they involve something more, Materialism fails. But if they are simply physical states of the brain, having nothing but physical properties, then the Materialist faces the problem: "How is it possible that red sensations should be physical states of the brain?" This question is no easier to answer than the original question about the redness of physical surfaces. (To give a Causal analysis of red sensations as the characteristic effects of the action of red surfaces is, of course, to move round in a circle.)

The great problem presented by the secondary qualities, such as redness, is that they are *unanalysable*. They have certain relations of resemblance and so on to each other, so they cannot be said to be completely simple. But they are simple in the sense that they resist any analysis. You cannot give any complete account of the concept of redness without involving the notion of redness itself. This has seemed to be, and still seems to many philosophers to be, an absolute bar to identifying redness with, say, certain patterns of emission of light-waves.

But I am not so sure. I think it can be maintained that although the secondary qualities *appear* to be simple, they are not in fact simple. Perhaps their simplicity is *epistemological* only, not ontological, a matter of our awareness of them rather than the way they are. The best model I can give for the situation is the sort of phenomena made familiar to us by the *Gestalt* psychologists. It is possible to grasp that certain things or situations have a certain special property, but be unable to analyse that property. For instance, it may be possible to perceive that certain people are all alike in some way without being able to make it clear to oneself what the likeness is. We are aware that all these people have a certain likeness to each other, but are unable to define or specify that likeness. Later psychological research may achieve a specification of the likeness, a specification that may come as a complete surprise to us. Perhaps, therefore, the secondary qualities are in fact complex, and perhaps they are complex characteristics of a sort demanded by Materialism, but we are unable to grasp their complexity in perception.

There are two divergences between the model just suggested and the case of the secondary qualities. First, in the case of grasping the indefinable likeness of people, we are under no temptation to think that the likeness is a likeness in some simple quality. The likeness is indefinable, but we are vaguely aware that it is complex. Second, once research has determined the concrete nature of the likeness, our attention can be drawn to, and we can observe individually, the features that determine the likeness.

But although the model suggested and the case of the secondary qualities undoubtedly exhibit these differences, I do not think that they show that the secondary qualities cannot be identified with respectable physical characteristics of objects. Why should not a complex property appear to be simple? There would seem to be no contradiction in adding such a condition to the model. It has the consequence that perception of the secondary qualities involves an element of illusion, but the consequence involves no contradiction. It is true also that in the case of the secondary qualities the illusion cannot be overcome within perception: it is impossible to see a coloured surface as a surface emitting certain light-waves. (Though one sometimes seems to *hear* a sound as a vibration of the air.) But while this means that the identification of colour and light-waves is a purely *theoretical* one, it still seems to be a possible one. And if the identification is a possible one, we have general scientific reasons to think it a *plausible* one.

The doctrine of mental states and of the secondary qualities briefly presented in this paper seems to me to show promise of meeting many of the traditional philosophical objectives to a Materialist or Physicalist account of the world. As I have emphasized, the philosopher is not professionally com-petent to argue the positive case for Materialism. There he must rely upon the evidence presented by the scientist, particularly the physicist. But at least he may neutralize the objections to Materialism advanced by his fellow philosophers.

NOTES

1. "Any substance which, when introduced into or absorbed by a living organism, destroys life or injures health." (*Shorter Oxford Dictionary,* 3rd edn., rev., 1978.)

20

Keith Campbell

from "Central State Materialism"

(i) The Causal Theory of the Mind

Some terms get their meaning by reference to the effects produced by what the terms denote. Take "poison", for example. No one understands what a poison is if he doesn't understand that drinking it is not a good idea. It is in terms of its deleterious effects upon human or animal health that we express what "poison" means. There is a conceptual connection between poisons and ill-health. Yet talk about poisons is not just talk about ill-health. It is talk about substances which can play a *causal role* in ill-health. A poisonous substance will, if swallowed in large enough doses, without any inhibitor, by a person who takes neither a neutralizer nor an emetic, and provided his metabolism is typical, adversely affect his health.

Arsenic is a substance quite separate from humans, healthy or otherwise. It is a poison whether swallowed or not. Yet although arsenic is something different from humans and health, when we describe it as poisonous we are adverting to its connection with illness and death. "A poison is apt to produce illness and death" is like "A furnace heats"; it is a statement specifying conditions under which a substance deserves the label "poison" ("furnace"). By contrast, "A poison tends to deteriorate if left standing" or "A furnace burns more fuel if the draft is forced" do not deal with what must be so if the label "poison" or "furnace" is deserved. We explain what a poison is by reference to health, but not to deterioration if left standing. "Poison", we can say, is an *essentially causal term*. Through this causal element, poisons and health are conceptually linked although they are different things.

Some terms apply to objects not in virtue of what the objects cause, but in virtue of what played a part in causing them; terms like that could be called *essentially effectual terms*. For example, "sedimentary rock" or "pig iron" can be explained only by reference to how such rock or such iron comes to be produced.

The Causal Theory of mind likens most mental descriptions to "poisonous", but appeals occasionally to the other pattern shown by "sedimentary rock".[1] A decision to go swimming, for example, is held to be a state of the person tending to cause going-swimming behavior, that is, behavior from the wide and vague collection: assembling swimming gear, asking others to come swimming, going to a beach, filling the pool, swimming, etc. As in the case of poisons, we must add qualifications when we say the appropriate effects will be produced. The decision will not issue in going-swimming behavior if I am paralyzed, or have an accident on the way, or change my mind, or am ordered by my superior officer to remain on duty. Nevertheless it is not just a matter of fact that your decisions to go swimming typically issue in your going swimming. The decision earns its title to the description "decision to go swimming" because it is a mental state which tends to have precisely that effect.

So too with, for example, "seeing a cricket ball". A man who sees a cricket ball is a man who is in a state which, if circumstances are favorable, has a characteristic range of effects: catching, dodging, striking the ball, warning people in its path, directing those searching for it, applauding the batsman, etc., etc. We can call effects in this range "cricket ball discriminating behavior," and say that seeing a cricket ball is a mental state which is both essentially effectual—it is produced by the ac-

From Keith Campbell, *Body and Mind*. New York: Doubleday and Co., Inc., 1984, pp. 77–85, 86–89, and 97–109. Reprinted with permission of the publisher and Keith Campbell.

tion of the cricket ball upon the eyes—and essentially causal—it is a condition of capacity for cricket ball-discriminating behavior. It is only a capacity for such behavior. The capacity is not necessarily exercised; the sight of a cricket ball may give rise to no discriminating behavior whatever.

A capacity is a disposition; the Behaviorists were right to emphasize how heavily dispositional much mental description is. The Causal Theory of mind appropriates that lesson of Behaviorism. Mental states are typically states with a causal role in disposing men to certain forms of behavior; so runs the Causal Theory.

An itch is a cause of scratching, a tickle of giggling, a pain of wincing. Emotions are causes of characteristic patterns of action: rage of shouting, jealousy of poisoning, envy of denigrating, joy of singing. Moods do not have dispositions to characteristic activities as effect, but are modifying causes: there is a recognizable style in the behavior of an anxious man no matter what he is doing; he behaves, as we say, anxiously, rather than indulges in any special sorts of action. On the Causal Theory of mind anxiety is an inner state which affects the manner in which he conducts himself. And the same goes for hope and desperation.

To describe a man as intelligent is not just to say with the Behaviorists that he is apt to turn in an intelligent performance, a performance in which more problems are solved more readily and more adequately than is typical for men. It is to say that an inner structure or condition of the man is an indispensable immediate causal factor in producing the intelligent performance, and that this inner condition is what is rightly called intelligence. "Intelligence" names not the performance-pattern but one part of its cause, the inner and therefore mental part.

Sometimes the connection of mental state to behavior is more indirect. In thinking, for example in deliberating upon what to do, mental states of belief and supposition lead not straight to behavior but to other mental states, inferred or concluded beliefs, which may then govern action at some much later time. And the opinions I form in deliberating may never be given a behavioral manifestation because situations in which they would be operative in controlling behavior never arise. Yet according to the Causal Theory, all mental states can, directly or through the mediation of other mental states, cause the person who has them to pursue one course rather than another in the conduct of his life.

Thus the Causal Theory of mind has two strands: that the various mental events and processes are postulated causes of segments of behavior belonging to various recognizable patterns, and

that the mental causes are given their names in virtue of their postulated connection with those behavior patterns. The first strand admits the view that the mind is something inner, separate, and standing behind behavior. It thus allows for the existence of definite, non-behavioral, non-dispositional mental episodes and states, and so avoids one chief problem of Behaviorism. It also allows (indeed insists) that mental states are causally efficacious in behavior, and so avoids the other chief problem.

The second strand, that mental terms get their meaning by reference to the behavioral effects of the mental states they denote, preserves the truth of Behaviorism that there is a conceptual connection of mind with behavior. But the connection between them is not that of referring to just the same facts.

The Causal Theory of mind views mental concepts as theoretical. The picture it paints is this: Men, confronted with the surprises of human (and animal) behavior in comparison with the activities of water, earth, and trees, have surmised that something inside them is causing their distinctive conduct. This something, of which little is known but its causal powers, is called a mind. And the mind is credited with as much complexity as there is complexity and difference in the characteristically human behavior of men. Talk about mental characteristics is talk in terms of a theory (the theory of minds) about what makes men tick.

Little is known, in this primitive stage of theorizing, about what a mind is: is the cause of behavior a demon in the breast, a soul dispersed throughout the body, a spirit without any spatial features, or a plastic box two inches behind the nose? It is a task of scientific theory-development to find out. The conceptual analysis of mental descriptions leads to *a* cause within the man, but leaves open what kind of cause it is. Defenders of the Causal Theory of mind liken "mind" to "gene". Men, struck by the surprising fact that for the most part cattle, sheep, sweet peas, and fruit flies reproduce offspring after their own kind, have surmised that something passed from parents to offspring is causally responsible for the offspring's development into a creature resembling its parents. There are as many genes as there are distinct hereditary characteristics. A gene is something which causes offspring to resemble parents in, say, eye color. Talk about genes is talk in terms of a theory (the theory of genes) about what makes children like their parents. It is talk in terms of *a* cause for the phenomenon of inheritance. Discovering what the cause actually is (a special DNA molecule in the cell nucleus) is a scientific triumph in theory development which no amount of reflection on statements of genetic theory will accomplish. The same holds for the mind.

(ii) The Significance of Mental Terms

The Causal Theory of mind requires an extension of the limits placed by positivism on the conditions under which terms are significant. Positivism restricts the content of a term to perceptual features in conditions to which it applies. A general positivism, provided it grants that bodily movements are perceptible, leads directly to Behaviorism about minds. By contrast, the causal account of minds depends upon an epistemology of postulation. The epistemology of postulation admits as significant terms which apply to postulated causes, which may be imperceptible, of perceptible features in the world. This extension not only allows the philosophy of mind to escape its Behaviorist fetters, it permits a much more satisfactory philosophy of micro-objects in scientific theory, and a much more realistic philosophy of God, of the past, and of what is hidden in the depths of the sea.

The argument to Behaviorism from positivist restrictions on the significance of mental terms has to my mind been successfully challenged by the more liberal epistemology of postulation. The way is open to explore less paradoxical accounts of what a mind is, and the Causal Theory is a very promising one of these. To give a sample of its promise: the mental causes of behavior may be causes of which we are not conscious; on this view the unconscious mind is not at all scandalous or impossible. Whether or not we have such a thing is just a question of psychological theory.

Again, the Causal Theory of mind allows that not all the properties of the mind must be mental ones. The mental properties are those relevant to the causation of behavior. But that which causes behavior can have a host of other properties as well, for example, warm or cool, moist or dry, which are not referred to in describing the mind as governing behavior. In breaking the idea that every property of the mind must be distinctively mental, the Causal Theory breaks one of the strongest prejudices supporting a Dualist bifurcation of the world.

Self-Awareness

The comparison of minds with genes reveals, however, a very great peculiarity of minds. Minds are supposed to be hypothetical, hidden, inner causes of behavior. Yet in our own case they may be inner, but are certainly not always hypothetical or hidden. Some mental episodes, mental states, and mental processes are given to us in self-awareness or by introspection. A fit of anger and a pang of remorse are not in our own case hypothetical events proposed to explain the experienced movements of our bodies. They are themselves items given to experience. They are given, of course, not to perception, but to the inner awareness whereby we know, without the use of sense organs, some of what is going on in our own minds. Such mental events are not theoretical; they belong to the data, not to its explanation.

Here the Causal Theory is given a subtle and ingenious turn. Why is there such difficulty in giving any full description of these mental episodes and conditions? Why do they prove so elusive to introspective research? Why are we so ignorant of their true nature and relations? The answer given is that we are aware of inner states only as causes more or less like each other. All I known, when I know I am having a fit of anger, is that a cause of throwing, gnashing, and abusing, directed at some person or group, has come to existence in me, that it is stronger or weaker than others, and that it is already producing bodily changes, for example, flushes, clenching, or shivering. In a slogan, we can say: Introspective knowledge is knowledge of causes. Introspective awareness is awareness only of the causal properties of an event or state. The awareness is in turn a mental state, and it also, insofar as it is mental, has causal properties. In this case, the causal properties give us a capacity for discriminative acts.

In its attempt to accommodate the facts of self-awareness, the Causal Theory of the mind thus exploits the transparent character of inner awareness, and the way that awareness continually points beyond the mental state to the associated action.

Inner knowledge is, according to the theory, direct knowledge of causal powers, which we have learned to recognize in the course of growing up. Whether there can be introspective knowledge of a mental state's causal powers without any associated knowledge of its intrinsic qualities is hard to say. Such knowledge is certainly unusual, but then introspective knowledge is unusual in all sorts of ways, so why not in this?

(iii) Central-State Materialism

The Causal Theory of mind sets up a scientific task: to find what in a man is causally responsible for those facets of his behavior which are "expressions" of mental conditions. When that task is complete we will have a full doctrine of what a mind is, and not just a causal schema which mentions some cause or other but does not fully specify it.

It is now universally accepted that in this connection the brain and its appendages are the bodily parts which matter most. If any bodily part is the thing whose events and processes are causes of behavior, the central nervous system is that thing. Central-State Materialism thus affirms the Causal Theory of mind and adds that behavior can be completely explained in terms of events in the central nervous system. The mind, the cause of behavior, turns out to be the brain.

One more step is required to reach Central-State Materialism. This step insists that the nervous system has no properties of a non-physical kind.[2] It insists that the only properties the nervous system has are the properties recognized in chemistry and physics, together with their derivatives. Without this step the doctrine is not a materialism but a theory which accords to the brain two different sorts of attributes, non-material as well as material ones. Such a view is compatible with the Causal Theory of mind whether or not the non-material properties are described in terms of their part in the causation of behavior. If they are, they would be mental properties of the mind. If they are not, they would belong to the mind but not be mental properties, like having a temperature of 98.4°F.

Central-State Materialism is thus the most uncompromisingly economical version of the Causal Theory of mind. It identifies the cause of behavior as a purely material object, the central nervous system as conceived in neurophysiology.

Central-State Materialism and the Mind–Body Problem

Central-State Materialism does not, like Behaviorism, deny that the mind is a thing. But it does deny that the mind is a spiritual thing. So Central-State Materialism solves the Mind–Body problem by denying the second of our four incompatible propositions.

More fully, the answer concerning the relation of mind to body is: the mind is part of the body. It is a special part, the part which controls behavior. That is, it is the part which governs the movement of the limbs under the influence both of its own states (e.g., purposes) and of sensorily gained information concerning the body's environment and attitude. The part which does this is the brain, whose connections are chiefly with sense organs, which affect it, and muscles and glands, which it affects.

Thus the Mind–Body problem resolves into one of scientific detail. In precisely what changes does the brain play a part, and what part does it play? Neurophysiology is the science which will furnish the full account of the relation of mind to body. The relation of mind to *matter* is already settled: a mind is a special arrangement of matter in an organism, which is another special arrangement of matter. It is not some different non-material sort of thing standing in mysterious relation to the matter which makes up living bodies.

Just as there is no specially philosophical problem of the relation of a bus to its engine, and no special Boat-Rudder problem or Pump-Refrigerator problem in philosophy, so there is no special Mind–Body problem beyond the scientific one of the causal interplay of elements in a system. Considered as a solution to the traditional problem of mind and body, Central-State Materialism is highly satisfactory.

As in the case of Behaviorism, the objections to Central-State Materialism lie not in its solution of the Mind–Body problem, but in its general doctrine as a philosophy of mind. Let us note first some problems which, like survival, are problems for materialism but not for the Causal Theory of mind on which it relies.

(iv)   The Causal Theory of Mind Examined

There are two strands in Central-State Materialism, the doctrine that the mind is the cause of behavior, and the doctrine that the central nervous system, being the cause of behavior, is the mind. Survival, freedom, and paranormal powers are threats to the second strand, but do not touch the first.

The Causal Theory of mind states that descriptions of mental events, states, and processes are descriptions of inner conditions insofar as they are, directly or indirectly, causally efficacious in the behavior of an organism. This is a simplified statement of the view. Some states, for example, having dream images, are described not as themselves causally efficacious, but as resembling other mental states, perceptual ones, which do have a real role in governing behavior. But images are exceptional; the simplified formula captures the heart of the mind. Whatever else the mind is, matter or spirit, electric or chemical, it is a field of causes, and all its distinctively mental properties prove to be causal ones.

There seems to me no doubt there is a conceptual connection, a connection of meaning, between mental and behavioral descriptions. It also seems plain enough that mental descriptions cannot in general be dissolved into statements of behavior and behavioral disposition without leaving something essential out. Further, we constantly employ mental categories in expounding the causes of human behavior. The Causal Theory of mind retains the vital conceptual link with behavior, gives to mind an independent existence as an inner something whose states are typically causes of that behavior, and so accounts for our natural employment of mental terms in causal explanations.

A doctrine with which it is hard to quarrel is that in our very understanding of what a mind is there proves to be an idea of the inner causation of behavior. The mental states, whether states of a spirit or states of a brain, will of course have many properties, of location, extent, physics, and chemistry (or mayhap spiritual machinery) in virtue of which they are causes. A state cannot be a cause and have *no* other properties; such a "pure cause" is just magic. But the Causal Theory of mind maintains that none of these other properties are mental. They do not enter into what we mean in any description of a state of mind as a state of mind. It is like a political description of an electorate. The electors are described by eligibility to vote, number, division into districts and wards, party affiliation, and so on. The electors are also men and women, short and tall, slim and stout. But sex and size do not enter into the political descriptions of these people. Similarly, only as causes of behavior do properties of inner states count as mental. The mental description, according to the Causal Theory of mind, encompasses only description as cause.

The crucial question, therefore, is: Is the mind, insofar as it is mental, nothing but a field of causes? Are the only genuinely mental properties of inner states causal properties, or similarities to states with causal powers?

Pains Again

In urging the deficiencies of Behaviorism, we argued that the theory could not cope satisfactorily with the fact that pains hurt. How does the Causal Theory of mind fare in dealing with this question?

Being in pain is a complex condition. Suppose my finger is burned, and is painful in consequence. In my mental state there are at least two components: awareness that my finger has been overheated, as a result of which it is still damaged, and a peremptory desire that this awareness should cease forthwith. In this present discussion, both the awareness and the desire must naturally be given a causal analysis.

"I am aware that my finger has been burned" is analyzed as "As a result of having been burned on the finger, I have entered a new inner state apt to produce behavior wherein I discriminate the burned finger from others which are not burned." In the discriminating behavior I not only favor the correct finger, I favor it in the burn-soothing way. That is, I give verbal and active expression to the belief that my finger has been burned.

So far so good. But the hurtfulness of the burn has not yet been captured. All that has so far been said would be true even if burns did not hurt but throbbed. Instead of the whole range of bodily sensations we in fact enjoy or endure, tingles, tickles, itches, searing pains, jabbing pains, aches, feelings of numbness, etc., suppose we only ever felt throbs. The frequency of the throbs could differentiate different bodily conditions. One throb per second in the finger would signal a burn, two a cut, three an itchy mosquito bite, three and a half a tickling feather, and so on. Then in our case of the burned finger, the whole of the above analysis of "I am aware that my finger has been burned" would be true, and the episode would not be one which hurt in the slightest.

Or again, suppose a being very like us except that instead of feeling a pain when he burns his finger or breaks his toe, he has no locatable sensations at all. He just spontaneously gains a new belief, it just "pops into his head" that he has burned his finger or broken his toe, as the case may be. Call this being an *imitation man*. His awareness of his own body would be like our awareness that the car we are driving in is getting a flat tire. Some change in our body, of which we are not conscious, has as a result that it just pops into our heads that the tire is going flat.

Awareness of the kind we have, that our finger is burned, ceases at the end of successful soothing operations. The bare belief of the imitation man that his finger has been burned could just disappear in the same way, as our belief that the tire is flat evaporates when we change the wheel.

The imitation man satisfies the analysis given above of "I am aware that I have burned my finger." But his pains do not hurt. There is nothing essentially hurtful, indeed no element which can be hurtful, in awareness of damage or malfunction as that awareness is analyzed by the Causal Theory. So the hurtfulness of pain must lie elsewhere.

Does it perhaps lie in the desire that the awareness should cease? Pains are unpleasant. We prefer not to have them. We often think that we prefer not to have them *because* they are hurtful. But perhaps this is a mistake. Perhaps their hurtfulness is precisely that we desire to be rid of them. Consider in the following how desire appears in a causal analysis.

"I desire to be rid of this condition of finger-burned awareness" is glossed as "I have entered an inner condition driving me toward (apt to produce) general expressions of pain, such as grimacing, together with whatever behavior I believe likely to minimize or eliminate another inner condition, my awareness of my burned finger." In everyone, this condition leads to wringing the hand and trying to cool it. In sophisticates like us, it leads further to searching out the burn cream, the analgesics, and even the doctor.

The strength of my drive to minimize awareness of my burned finger is the extent to which this purpose excludes or overrides all my other inner causes of behavior, and this varies directly with the intensity of the hurt. This is a point in favor of the idea that the desire is the hurtful element in pain. If conditions A and B increase and decrease together, then perhaps A and B are the same condition. If they vary inversely, or independently, then they must be different conditions.

Nevertheless, there seems to be something wrong with the idea that a desire, understood as a cause, could be the very thing which is hurtful. What is hurtful must be something felt, and we can see that a causally understood desire is not something felt by considering other cases.

An urgent desire, causally understood, is an inner condition which, temporarily suppressing other causes of behavior, generates a pattern of bodily activity. A condition of this kind can be induced by hypnotic suggestion. A subject can be given an urgent desire, which is to say, an overmastering drive toward one particular behavior pattern, and it is clear from this case that such an inner cause is not something which, as cause, can be felt. So it is not something which can hurt.

We can also see that the causal analyses of awareness and desire in pain fail to capture the hurtfulness of pains by considering the possibility of the transposition of pains. Suppose a man for whom burning pains and crushing pains were transposed, so that when his finger is burned he feels as we do when our finger is crushed, and vice versa. The causal analyses of the elements in pain make his situation and ours exactly alike. He is aware that his finger has been burned, and so are we. He is gripped by the purpose to minimize the inner condition of awareness, and so are we. He works this purpose out in grimacing, handwringing, cream-applying, etc., and so do we. On the causal analysis of mental states, his state and ours are identical. Yet he is being hurt in the feeling-crushed fashion, and we are not. Our mental states

are not identical. So the causal analysis leaves something out, something which distinguishes burning from crushing pains even where a transposition of pains makes their causal properties identical.

We might try to save the causal analysis by further complicating the picture of pain. Neither the awareness that my finger is burned, nor my desire to be rid of this awareness, is itself anything hurtful. But in pain I am not only aware through bodily sense of the condition of my finger; I am also aware, by introspection, that I am aware of my finger's condition. So we might suppose the element of the pain situation which involves suffering is this inner awareness.

Or alternatively, we could hold that the hurtful state is my introspective awareness of the desire that my bodily awareness of my burned finger should cease.

Neither of these strategies is successful. For the introspective awareness they invoke must itself be given a causal analysis. It is in its turn no more than the entering of a third new inner state enabling discriminative behavior—largely verbal behavior—toward the original states of bodily awareness and consequent desire. And once again, the description of this second, introspective, awareness as enabling discrimination leaves undescribed the hurtfulness which distinguishes us from the imitation man, who can perform this kind of introspection yet cannot suffer. So once again the hurtfulness of the burn in general, and its particular burning hurtfulness, elude a causal analysis of the mental concepts. Everything the causal doctrine can say about pains is true of the imitation man whose pains never hurt.

Although it is a very difficult matter, I believe the same general criticism holds in the case of the different perceptual states involved in seeing different colors, or smelling different smells, or, on the emotional side, undergoing different kinds of fear, fright, shock, and thrill. The causal doctrine covers well the description of mentality by one observing and explaining his fellow men. But the theory leaves out, to put it briefly, what waking life is like to him who is living it.

(v)   The Causal Theory of Mind Amended

The criticism leveled above at the Causal Theory of mind can be expressed in this way: The peculiarly "mental" features of mental states are not all of them causal properties respecting behavior or similarities to causal properties. There are, in addition, characteristics of some mental states which especially concern how those states seem to him who has them. Thus there are the burning, jabbing, throbbing, and aching sorts of pain; the salty, bitter, sweet, and avocado-like sorts of taste; the different experiences of seeing things as variously colored; the different feelings involved in different emotions.

Let us accept the existence of these additional, non-causal features of mental states, and let us call them *phenomenal* properties. What follows for Central-State Materialism from the existence of such phenomenal properties? The Causal Theory of mind is important for materialism because purely causal descriptions of a state are *ontically neutral.* That is to say, a purely causal description of a mental state begs no questions about what sort of state it is, claiming only that it is causally operative in producing an organism's behavior. So far as causal description goes, a mental state could be a state of a material thing, or a spiritual thing, or even a divine thing. The Causal Theory of mind leaves open, for scientific investigation to close, the question of what sort of thing a mind is. Philosophers who adopt the Causal Theory and go on to say scientific investigations indicate that the brain, a material thing, is the object whose states are causes of behavior are of course Central-State Materialists.

But Central-State Materialism is not automatically refuted if the Causal Theory is inadequate. If any property is ontically neutral, it is of course possible for a material object to have that property. So the mind can be an entirely material object even if mental states have phenomenal properties, provided the phenomenal properties are also ontically neutral. If phenomenal properties are ontically neutral, the Central-State Materialist is not embarrassed by their existence.

To see whether phenomenal properties are ontically neutral, let us return to the burning pain in my finger. The pain is a discrimination-enabling change in my mental state which sets up a desire for its own elimination. This change is in fact a change in the pattern and frequency of discharges of neurons in the cortex. But I am not aware of all this flurry of neuron firings *as a flurry of neuron firings.* Suppose, however, that I am aware of it as a condition which hurts. I do not grasp the brain-process clearly in its full reality, or in its reality at all. I grasp it, obscurely, in the guise of the painfulness of the pain. Nevertheless, it is this brain process, and not something else, which I grasp. To suffer is, on this account, to introspect rather clumsily a process which is itself material.

The phenomenal properties are not, on this view, properties of things as they actually are. They are how certain inner properties, which are both material and mental, appear to him who has them. They belong not to the reality, but to the appearance, of mental states.

Whatever belongs to appearance only is ontically neutral. It might have been some state of an indwelling spirit which, in suffering, I clumsily introspect. But it proves, so the argument runs, that the states set up in me by burning my finger, are brain states, and hurting is how these states seem to the organism enduring them.

The doctrine for hurting, that it is a merely apparent and not a real property, is then generalized to cover all phenomenal properties. So they are all ontically neutral. And as a result, even if we amend the Causal Theory and admit phenomenal properties, Central-State Materialism survives intact.

For a considerable time, I found this view very attractive. But I no longer think it acceptable. It is all very well to claim that hurtfulness is how activity of the C-fibers in the cortex appears, that the smell of onion is how the shape of onion molecules appears to a human with a normal nasal system, that scarlet is how a surface reflecting a certain pattern of photons appears to human vision. This deals with the pain, smell, or color apprehended and, relegating it to the category of appearance, renders it ontically neutral. But it leaves us with a set of *seemings,* acts of imperfect apprehension, in which the phenomenal properties are grasped. So we must ask the new question: Is it possible that things can *seem to be* in a certain way to a merely material system? Is there a way in which acts of imperfect apprehension can be seen to be ontically neutral?

Consider a camera. A green tree can certainly be within the field the camera can photograph. And with color film, the camera produces a negative from which a photograph of a green tree can be made. We can say if we wish, although it is stretching words a bit, that the tree appears to the camera, and even appears to the camera as green. A fancy camera is made which develops and prints its own film once exposed, and we could say of this camera that at exposure it enters an inner state apt for the production of green tree photographs. Especially if the developing process varies with the color of the tree, this is a simulacrum of green tree-perceiving behavior. And it is stretching words rather less to say that the tree appears as green to the fancy camera.

Even so, this is not the sort of *appearing to* that we are concerned with. We want to insist that the camera does not experience anything at all. For all its tricks, we do not think it makes a vast difference to the fancy camera whether its shutters are open or closed. We do not think this makes the world seem a very different place, for we do not think that to the camera the world seems to be any sort of place at all. With us it is different. Whether our eyelids are open or closed makes a great difference to how the world seems. It is this difference which is in question when we ask about the ontic neutrality of the awareness of phenomenal properties. Sensitivity to various environments and differential reaction to these environments do not suffice to account for the world's seeming thus and so.

Materialists sometimes argue at this point that the difference between an experiencing man and a non-experiencing self-developing camera lies in the simplicity of the one and the complexity of the other. The man is sensitive to a whole range of conditions whose variation makes no difference to the inner state of the camera. The man has memory, and purposes, and emotions, of which the camera is innocent. In the man, a whole host of feedback mechanisms monitor his activity. I do not find this appeal to complexity convincing. Think again of the imitation man, who duplicates all of a typical man's acquisition, processing, and retrieval of information, and all his activity, but for whom there are no phenomenal properties.

If the imitation man's finger is burned, he knows that something is going on in his finger. And he knows further that there is activity in him by which he knows this. The further activity is in fact activity of the C-fibers, but he does not know that that is what it is. He apprehends it imperfectly, as we do, but he does not apprehend it *by suffering,* as we do. He just knows it, as we just know when we are awake, for example, that whatever inner condition it is which marks off waking from sleep is present within us.

The imitation man can know sea and sky are alike in color, and even call them "blue". So can a blind man. Unlike a blind man, the imitation man can find it out for himself. When he looks at sea or sky he forms the belief that what he is looking at has the color which he has been taught to call "blue". Yet the imitation man does not see the sea and sky *as blue.* He is not able to enjoy their color, for they do not appear as colored to him. Similarly, he can tell when his finger is burned or crushed, and have a powerful drive to eliminate the condition by which he knows this. Yet he cannot suffer.

So far as I can see, imperfect apprehension can be kept ontically neutral only so long as it is analyzed solely in terms of what is known. So long as it is given that sort of account, the imitation man's imperfect apprehension is no different from ours. The difference is not in what is known but in how it is known. The materialist account of real men can find no place for the fact that our imperfect apprehension is by phenomenal property and not by, for example, beliefs just spontaneously arising.

I do not see how the ontically neutral descriptions available to the materialist can cover more than what is true of the imitation man. But I have not proved that this is impossible. Failing conclusive argument, we must just judge as best we can how adequate the materialist treatment of awareness by phenomenal properties can be.

NOTES

1. See, e.g., Armstrong, *op. cit.* [*A Materialist Theory of the Mind* (London: Routledge & Kegan Paul, 1968), pp. 32–34].

2. See Brian Medlin, "Ryle and the Materialist Hypothesis," in *The Identity Theory of Mind,* ed. C. F. Presley, Brisbane, 1967.

B. Functionalist Approaches

21

Hilary Putnam

"The Nature of Mental States"

The typical concerns of the Philosopher of Mind might be represented by three questions: (1) How do we know that other people have pains? (2) Are pains brain states? (3) What is the analysis of the concept *pain?* I do not wish to discuss questions (1) and (3) in this paper. I shall say something about question (2).[1]

I.   Identity Questions

"Is pain a brain state?" (Or, "Is the property of having a pain at time *t* a brain state?")[2] It is impossible to discuss this question sensibly without saying something about the peculiar rules which have grown up in the course of the development of "analytical philosophy"—rules which, far from leading to an end to all conceptual confusions, themselves represent considerable conceptual confusion. These rules—which are, of course, implicit rather than explicit in the practice of most analytical philosophers—are (1) that a statement of the form "being *A* is being B" (e.g., "being in pain is being in a certain brain state") can be *correct* only if it follows, in some sense, from the meaning of the terms *A* and *B;* and (2) that a statement of the form "being *A* is being *B*" can be philosophically *informative* only if it is in some sense reductive (e.g., "being in pain is having a certain unpleasant sensation" is not philosophically informative; "being in pain is having a certain behavior disposition" is, if true, philosophically informative). These rules are excellent rules if we still believe that the program of reductive analysis (in the style of the 1930's) can be carried out; if we don't, then they turn analytical philosophy into a mug's

game, at least so far as "is" questions are concerned.

In this paper I shall use the term 'property' as a blanket term for such things as being in pain, being in a particular brain state, having a particular behavior disposition and also for magnitudes such as temperature, etc.—i.e., for things which can naturally be represented by one-or-more-place predicates or functors. I shall use the term 'concept' for things which can be identified with synonymy-classes of expressions. Thus the concept *temperature* can be identified (I maintain) with the synonymy-class of the word 'temperature.'[3] (This is like saying that the number 2 can be identified with the class of all pairs. This is quite a different statement from the peculiar statement that 2 *is* the class of all pairs. I do not maintain that concepts *are* synonymy-classes, whatever that might mean, but that they can be identified with synonymy-classes, for the purpose of formalization of the relevant discourse.)

The question "What is the concept *temperature?*" is a very "funny" one. One might take it to mean "What is temperature? Please take my question as a conceptual one." In that case an answer might be (pretend for a moment 'heat' and 'temperature' are synonyms) "temperature is heat," or even "the concept of temperature is the same concept as the concept of heat." Or one might take it to mean "What are *concepts,* really? For example, what is 'the concept of temperature'?" In that case heaven knows what an "answer" would be. (Perhaps it would be the statement that concepts *can be identified with* synonymy-classes.)

Of course, the question "What is the property temperature?" is also "funny." And one way of in-

This work originally appeared as "Psychological Predicates" by Hilary Putnam in *Art, Mind, and Religion,* W. H. Capitan and D. D. Merrill, eds., pp. 37–48. Published in 1967 by the University of Pittsburgh Press. Reprinted with permission of the publisher. The title has been changed at the author's request.

terpreting it is to take it as a question about the concept of temperature. But this is not the way a physicist would take it.

The effect of saying that the property P_1 can be identical with the property P_2 only if the terms P_1, P_2 are in some suitable sense "synonyms" is, to all intents and purposes, to collapse the two notions of "property" and "concept" into a single notion. The view that concepts (intensions) *are* the same as properties has been explicitly advocated by Carnap (e.g., in *Meaning and Necessity*). This seems an unfortunate view, since "temperature is mean molecular kinetic energy" appears to be a perfectly good example of a true statement of identity of properties, whereas "the concept of temperature is the same concept as the concept of mean molecular kinetic energy" is simply false.

Many philosophers believe that the statement "pain is a brain state" violates some rules or norms of English. But the arguments offered are hardly convincing. For example, if the fact that I can know that I am in pain without knowing that I am in brain state S shows that pain cannot be brain state S, then, by exactly the same argument, the fact that I can know that the stove is hot without knowing that the mean molecular kinetic energy is high (or even that molecules exist) shows that it is *false* that temperature is mean molecular kinetic energy, physics to the contrary. In fact, all that immediately follows from the fact that I can know that I am in pain without knowing that I am in brain state S is that the concept of pain is not the same concept as the concept of being in brain state S. But either pain, or the state of being in pain, or some pain, or some pain state, might still be brain state S. After all, the concept of temperature is not the same concept as the concept of mean molecular kinetic energy. But temperature is mean molecular kinetic energy.

Some philosophers maintain that both 'pain is a brain state' and 'pain states are brain states' are unintelligible. The answer is to explain to these philosophers, as well as we can, given the vagueness of all scientific methodology, what sorts of considerations lead one to make an empirical reduction (i.e., to say such things as "water is H_2O," "light is electro-magnetic radiation," "temperature is mean molecular kinetic energy"). If, without giving reasons, he still maintains in the face of such examples that one cannot imagine parallel circumstances for the use of 'pains are brain states' (or, perhaps, 'pain states are brain states') one has grounds to regard him as perverse.

Some philosophers maintain that "P_1 is P_2" is something that can be true, when the 'is' involved is the 'is' of empirical reduction, only when the

properties P_1 and P_2 are (a) associated with a spatio-temporal region; and (b) the region is one and the same in both cases. Thus "temperature is mean molecular kinetic energy" is an admissible empirical reduction, since the temperature and the molecular energy are associated with the same space-time region, but "having a pain in my arm is being in a brain state" is not, since the spatial regions involved are different.

This argument does not appear very strong. Surely no one is going to be deterred from saying that mirror images are light reflected from an object and then from the surface of a mirror by the fact that an image can be "located" three feet *behind* the mirror! (Moreover, one can always find *some* common property of the reductions one is willing to allow—e.g., temperature is mean molecular kinetic energy—which is not a property of some one identification one wishes to disallow. This is not very impressive unless one has an argument to show that the very purposes of such identification depend upon the common property in question.)

Again, other philosophers have contended that all the predictions that can be derived from the conjunction of neurophysiological laws with such statements as "pain states are such-and-such brain states" can equally well be derived from the conjunction of the same neurophysiological laws with "being in pain is correlated with such-and-such brain states," and hence (sic!) there can be no methodological grounds for saying that pains (or pain states) *are* brain states, as opposed to saying that they are *correlated* (invariantly) with brain states. This argument, too, would show that light is only correlated with electromagnetic radiation. The mistake is in ignoring the fact that, although the theories in question may indeed lead to the same predictions, they open and exclude different *questions.* "Light is invariantly correlated with electromagnetic radiation" would leave open the questions "What is the light then, if it isn't the same as the electromagnetic radiation?" and "What makes the light accompany the electromagnetic radiation?"—questions which are excluded by saying that the light *is* the electromagnetic radiation. Similarly, the purpose of saying that pains are brain states is precisely to exclude from empirical meaningfulness the questions "What is the pain, then, if it isn't the same as the brain state?" and "What makes the pain accompany the brain state?" If there are grounds to suggest that these questions represent, so to speak, the wrong way to look at the matter, then those grounds are grounds for a theoretical identification of pains with brain states.

If all arguments to the contrary are unconvincing, shall we then conclude that it is meaningful (and perhaps true) to say either that pains are brain states or that pain states are brain states?

(1) It is perfectly meaningful (violates no "rule of English," involves no "extension of usage") to say "pains are brain states."

(2) It is not meaningful (involves a "changing of meaning" or "an extension of usage," etc.) to say "pains are brain states."

My own position is not expressed by either (1) or (2). It seems to me that the notions "change of meaning" and "extension of usage" are simply so ill-defined that one cannot in fact say *either* (1) or (2). I see no reason to believe that either the linguist, or the man-on-the-street, or the philosopher possesses today a notion of "change of meaning" applicable to such cases as the one we have been discussing. The *job* for which the notion of change of meaning was developed in the history of the language was just a *much* cruder job than this one.

But, if we don't assert either (1) or (2)—in other words, if we regard the "change of meaning" issue as a pseudo-issue in this case—then how are we to discuss the question with which we started? "Is pain a brain state?"

The answer is to allow statements of the form "pain is *A*," where 'pain' and '*A*' are in no sense synonyms, and to see whether any such statement can be found which might be acceptable on empirical and methodological grounds. This is what we shall now proceed to do.

II. Is Pain a Brain State?

We shall discuss "Is pain a brain state?," then. And we have agreed to waive the "change of meaning" issue.

Since I am discussing not what the concept of pain comes to, but what pain is, in a sense of 'is' which requires empirical theory construction (or, at least, empirical speculation), I shall not apologize for advancing an empirical hypothesis. Indeed, my strategy will be to argue that pain is *not* a brain state, not on *a priori* grounds, but on the grounds that another hypothesis is more plausible. The detailed development and verification of my hypothesis would be just as Utopian a task as the detailed development and verification of the brain-state hypothesis. But the putting-forward, not of detailed and scientifically "finished" hypotheses, but of schemata for hypotheses, has long been a function of philosophy. I shall, in short, argue that pain is not a brain state, in the sense of a physical-

chemical state of the brain (or even the whole nervous system), but another *kind* of state entirely. I propose the hypothesis that pain, or the state of being in pain, is a functional state of a whole organism.

To explain this it is necessary to introduce some technical notions. In previous papers I have explained the notion of a Turing Machine and discussed the use of this notion as a model for an organism. The notion of a Probabilistic Automation is defined similarly to a Turing Machine, except that the transitions between "states" are allowed to be with various probabilities rather than being "deterministic." (Of course, a Turing Machine is simply a special kind of Probabilistic Automaton, one with transition probabilities 0, 1.) I shall assume the notion of a Probabilistic Automaton has been generalized to allow for "sensory inputs" and "motor outputs"—that is, the Machine Table specifies, for every possible combination of a "state" and a complete set of "sensory inputs," an "instruction" which determines the probability of the next "state," and also the probabilities of the "motor outputs." (This replaces the idea of the Machine as printing on a tape.) I shall also assume that the physical realization of the sense organs responsible for the various inputs, and of the motor organs, is specified, but that the "states" and the "inputs" themselves are, as usual, specified only "implicitly"—i.e., by the set of transition probabilities given by the Machine Table.

Since an empirically given system can simultaneously be a "physical realization" of many different Probabilistic Automata, I introduce the notion of a *Description* of a system. A Description of *S* where *S* is a system, is any true statement to the effect that *S* possesses distinct states $S_1, S_2, \ldots, S_n$ which are related to one another and to the motor outputs and sensory inputs by the transition probabilities given in such-and-such a Machine Table. The Machine Table mentioned in the Description will then be called the Functional Organization of *S* relative to that Description, and the S_i such that *S* is in state S_i at a given time will be called the Total State of *S* (at that time) relative to that Description. It should be noted that knowing the Total State of a system relative to a Description involves knowing a good deal about how the system is likely to "behave," given various combinations of sensory inputs, but does *not* involve knowing the physical realization of the S_i as, e.g., physical-chemical states of the brain. The S_i, to repeat, are specified only *implicitly* by the Description—i.e., specified *only* by the set of transition probabilities given in the Machine Table.

The hypothesis that "being in pain is a functional state of the organism" may now be spelled out more exactly as follows:

(1) All organisms capable of feeling pain are Probabilistic Automata.

(2) Every organism capable of feeling pain possesses at least one Description of a certain kind (i.e., being capable of feeling pain *is* possessing an appropriate kind of Functional Organization).

(3) No organism capable of feeling pain possesses a decomposition into parts which separately possess Descriptions of the kind referred to in (2).

(4) For every Description of the kind referred to in (2), there exists a subset of the sensory inputs such that an organism with that Description is in pain when and only when some of its sensory inputs are in that subset.

This hypothesis is admittedly vague, though surely no vaguer than the brain-state hypothesis in its present form. For example, one would like to know more about the kind of Functional Organization that an organism must have to be capable of feeling pain, and more about the marks that distinguish the subset of the sensory inputs referred to in (4). With respect to the first question, one can probably say that the Functional Organization must include something that resembles a "preference function," or at least a preference partial ordering, and something that resembles an "inductive logic" (i.e., the Machine must be able to "learn from experience"). (The meaning of these conditions, for Automata models, is discussed in my paper "The Mental Life of Some Machines.") In addition, it seems natural to require that the Machine possess "pain sensors," i.e., sensory organs which normally signal damage to the Machine's body, or dangerous temperatures, pressures, etc., which transmit a special subset of the inputs, the subset referred to in (4). Finally, and with respect to the second question, we would want to require at least that the inputs in the distinguished subset have a high disvalue on the Machine's preference function or ordering (further conditions are discussed in "The Mental Life of Some Machines"). The purpose of condition (3) is to rule out such "organisms" (if they can count as such) as swarms of bees as single pain-feelers. The condition (1) is, obviously, redundant, and is only introduced for expository reasons. (It is, in fact, empty, since everything is a Probabilistic Automaton under *some* Description.)

I contend, in passing, that this hypothesis, in spite of its admitted vagueness, is far *less* vague than the "physical-chemical state" hypothesis is today, and far more susceptible to investigation of both a mathematical and an empirical kind. Indeed, to investigate this hypothesis is just to attempt to produce "mechanical" models of organisms—and isn't this, in a sense, just what psychology is about? The difficult step, of course, will be to pass from models of *specific* organisms to a *normal form* for the psychological description of organisms—for this is what is required to make (2) and (4) precise. But this too seems to be an inevitable part of the program of psychology.

I shall now compare the hypothesis just advanced with (a) the hypothesis that pain is a brain state, and (b) the hypothesis that pain is a behavior disposition.

III. Functional State Versus Brain State

It may, perhaps, be asked if I am not somewhat unfair in taking the brain-state theorist to be talking about *physical-chemical* states of the brain. But (a) these are the only sorts of states ever mentioned by brain-state theorists. (b) The brain-state theorist usually mentions (with a certain pride, slightly reminiscent of the Village Atheist) the incompatibility of his hypothesis with all forms of dualism and mentalism. This is natural if physical-chemical states of the brain are what is at issue. However, functional states of whole systems are something quite different. In particular, the functional-state hypothesis is *not* incompatible with dualism! Although it goes without saying that the hypothesis is "mechanistic" in its inspiration, it is a slightly remarkable fact that a system consisting of a body and a "soul," if such things there be, can perfectly well be a Probabilistic Automaton. (c) One argument advanced by Smart is that the brain-state theory assumes only "physical" properties, and Smart finds "non-physical" properties unintelligible. The Total States and the "inputs" defined above are, of course, neither mental nor physical *per se,* and I cannot imagine a functionalist advancing this argument. (d) If the brain-state theorist does mean (or at least allow) states other than physical-chemical states, then his hypothesis is completely empty, at least until he specifies *what* sort of "states" he *does* mean.

Taking the brain-state hypothesis in this way, then, what reasons are there to prefer the functional-state hypothesis over the brain-state hypothesis? Consider what the brain-state theorist has to do to make good his claims. He has to specify a physical-chemical state such that *any* organism (not just a mammal) is in pain if and only if (a) it possesses a brain of a suitable physical-chemical structure; and (b) its brain is in that physical-chemical state. This means that the physical-chemical state in question must be a possible state of a mammalian brain, a reptilian brain, a mollusc's brain (octopuses are mollusca, and certainly feel pain), etc. At the same time, it must *not* be a possible (physically possible) state of the brain of any physically possible creature that cannot feel pain. Even if such a state can be found, it must be nomologically certain that it will also be a state of the brain of any extra-terrestrial life that may be found that will be capable of feeling pain before we can even entertain the supposition that it may *be* pain.

It is not altogether impossible that such a state will be found. Even though octopus and mammal are examples of parallel (rather than sequential) evolution, for example, virtually identical structures (physically speaking) have evolved in the eye of the octopus and in the eye of the mammal, notwithstanding the fact that this organ has evolved from different kinds of cells in the two cases. Thus it is at least possible that parallel evolution, all over the universe, might *always* lead to *one and the same* physical "correlate" of pain. But this is certainly an ambitious hypothesis.

Finally, the hypothesis becomes still more ambitious when we realize that the brain state theorist is not just saying that *pain* is a brain state; he is, of course, concerned to maintain that *every* psychological state is a brain state. Thus if we can find even one psychological predicate which can clearly be applied to both a mammal and an octopus (say "hungry"), but whose physical-chemical "correlate" is different in the two cases, the brain-state theory has collapsed. It seems to me overwhelmingly probable that we can do this. Granted, in such a case the brain-state theorist can save himself by *ad hoc* assumptions (e.g., defining the disjunction of two states to be a single "physical-chemical state"), but this does not have to be taken seriously.

Turning now to the considerations *for* the functional-state theory, let us begin with the fact that we identify organisms as in pain, or hungry, or angry, or in heat, etc., on the basis of their *behavior.* But it is a truism that similarities in the behavior of two systems are at least a reason to suspect similarities in the functional organization of the two systems, and a much *weaker* reason to suspect similarities in the actual physical details. Moreover, we expect the various psychological states—at least the basic ones, such as hunger, thirst, aggression, etc.—to have more or less similar "transition probabilities" (within wide and ill-defined limits, to be sure) with each other and with behavior in the case of different species, because this is an artifact of the way in which we identify these states. Thus, we would not count an animal as

thirsty if its "unsatiated" behavior did not seem to be directed toward drinking and was not followed by "satiation for liquid." Thus any animal that we count as capable of these various states will at least *seem* to have a certain rough kind of functional organization. And, as already remarked, if the program of finding psychological laws that are not species-specific—i.e., of finding a normal form for psychological theories of different species—ever succeeds, then it will bring in its wake a delineation of the kind of functional organization that is necessary and sufficient for a given psychological state, as well as a precise definition of the notion "psychological state." In contrast, the brain-state theorist has to hope for the eventual development of neurophysiological laws that are species-independent, which seems much less reasonable than the hope that psychological laws (of a sufficiently general kind) may be species-independent, or, still weaker, that a species-independent *form* can be found in which psychological laws can be written.

IV. Functional State Versus Behavior-Disposition

The theory that being in pain is neither a brain state nor a functional state but a behavior disposition has one apparent advantage: it appears to agree with the way in which we verify that organisms are in pain. We do not in practice know anything about the brain state of an animal when we say that it is in pain; and we possess little if any knowledge of its functional organization, except in a crude intuitive way. In fact, however, this "advantage" is no advantage at all: for, although statements about how we verify that x is A may have a good deal to do with what the concept of being A comes to, they have precious little to do with what the property A *is.* To argue on the ground just mentioned that pain is neither a brain state nor a functional state is like arguing that heat is not mean molecular kinetic energy from the fact that ordinary people do not (they think) ascertain the mean molecular kinetic energy of something when they verify that it is hot or cold. It is not necessary that they should; what is necessary is that the marks that they take as indications of heat should in fact be explained by the mean molecular kinetic energy. And, similarly, it is necessary to our hypothesis that the marks that are taken as behavioral indications of pain should be explained by the fact that the organism is in a functional state of the appropriate kind, but not that speakers should *know* that this is so.

The difficulties with "behavior disposition" accounts are so well known that I shall do little more than recall them here. The difficulty—it appears to be more than "difficulty," in fact—of specifying the required behavior disposition except as "the disposition of X to behave as if X were in *pain*," is the chief one, of course. In contrast, we *can* specify the functional state with which we propose to identify pain, at least roughly, without using the notion of pain. Namely, the functional state we have in mind is the state of receiving sensory inputs which play a certain role in the Functional Organization of the organism. This role is characterized, at least partially, by the fact that the sense organs responsible for the inputs in question are organs whose function is to detect damage to the body, or dangerous extremes of temperature, pressure, etc., and by the fact that the "inputs" themselves, whatever their physical realization, represent a condition that the organism assigns a high disvalue to. As I stressed in "The Mental Life of Some Machines," this does *not* mean that the Machine will always *avoid* being in the condition in question ("pain"); it only means that the condition will be avoided unless not avoiding it is necessary to the attainment of some more highly valued goal. Since the behavior of the Machine (in this case, an oragnism) will depend not merely on the sensory inputs, but also on the Total State (i.e., on other values, beliefs, etc.), it seems hopeless to make any general statement about how an organism in such a condition *must* behave; but this does not mean that we must abandon hope of characterizing the condition. Indeed, we have just characterized it.[4]

Not only does the behavior-disposition theory seem hopelessly vague; if the "behavior" referred to is peripheral behavior, and the relevant stimuli are peripheral stimuli (e.g., we do not say anything about what the organism will do if its brain is operated upon), then the theory seems clearly false. For example, two animals with all motor nerves cut will have the same actual and potential "behavior" (viz., none to speak of); but if one has cut pain fibers and the other has uncut pain fibers, then one will feel pain and the other won't. Again, if one person has cut pain fibers, and another suppresses all pain responses deliberately due to some strong compulsion, then the actual and potential peripheral behavior may be the same, but one will feel pain and the other won't. (Some philosophers maintain that this last case is conceptually impossible, but the only evidence for this appears to be that *they* can't, or don't want to, conceive of it.)[5] If, instead of pain, we take some sensation the "bodily expression" of which is easier to suppress—say, a slight coolness in one's left little finger—the case becomes even clearer.

Finally, even if there *were* some behavior dis-

position invariantly correlated with pain (species-independently!), and specifiable without using the term 'pain,' it would still be more plausible to identify being in pain with some state whose presence *explains* this behavior disposition—the brain state or functional state—than with the behavior disposition itself. Such considerations of plausibility may be somewhat subjective; but if other things *were* equal (of course, they aren't) why shouldn't we allow considerations of plausibility to play the deciding role?

V. Methodological Considerations

So far we have considered only what might be called the "empirical" reasons for saying that being in pain is a functional state, rather than a brain state or a behavior disposition; viz., that it seems more likely that the functional state we described is invariantly "correlated" with pain, species-independently, than that there is either a physical-chemical state of the brain (must an organism have a *brain* to feel pain? perhaps some ganglia will do) or a behavior disposition so correlated. If this is correct, then it follows that the identification we proposed is at least a candidate for consideration. What of methodological considerations?

The methodological considerations are roughly similar in all cases of reduction, so no surprises need be expected here. First, identification of psychological states with functional states means that the laws of psychology can be derived from statements of the form "such-and-such organisms have such-and-such Descriptions" together with the identification statements ("being in pain is such-and-such a functional state," etc.). Secondly, the presence of the functional state (i.e., of inputs which play the role we have described in the Functional Organization of the organism) is not merely "correlated with" but actually explains the pain behavior on the part of the organism. Thirdly, the identification serves to exclude questions which (if a naturalistic view is correct) represent an altogether wrong way of looking at the matter, e.g., "What *is* pain if it isn't either the brain state or the functional state?" and "What causes the pain to be always accompanied by this sort of functional state?" In short, the identification is to be tentatively accepted as a theory which leads to both fruitful predictions and to fruitful *questions,* and which serves to discourage fruitless and empirically senseless questions, where by 'empirically senseless' I mean "senseless" not merely from the standpoint of verification, but from the standpoint of what there in fact *is.*

NOTES

1. I have discussed these and related topics in the following papers: "Minds and Machines," in *Dimensions of Mind,* ed. Sidney Hook, New York, 1960, pp. 148–179; "Brains and Behavior," in *Analytical Philosophy, second series,* ed. Ronald Butler, Oxford, 1965, pp. 1–20; and "The Mental Life of Some Machines," to appear in a volume edited by Hector Neri Castaneda, Detroit.

2. In this paper I wish to avoid the vexed question of the relation between *pains* and *pain states.* I only remark in passing that one common argument *against* identification of these two—viz., that a pain can be in one's arm but a state (of the organism) cannot be in one's arm—is easily seen to be fallacious.

3. There are some well-known remarks by Alonzo Church on this topic. Those remarks do not bear (as might at first be supposed) on the identification of concepts with synonymy-classes as such, but rather support the view that (in formal semantics) it is necessary to retain Frege's distinction between the normal and the "oblique" use of expressions. That is, even if we say that the concept of temperature *is* the synonymy-class of the word 'temperature,' we must not thereby be led into the error of supposing that 'the concept of temperature' is synonymous with 'the synonymy-class of the word "temperature"'—for then 'the concept of temperature' and 'der Begriff der Temperatur' would not be synonymous, which they are. Rather, we must say that 'the concept of temperature' *refers to* the synonymy-class of the word 'temperature' (on this particular reconstruction); but that class is *identified* not as "the synonymy class to which such-and-such a word belongs," but in another way (e.g., as the synonymy-class whose members have such-and-such a characteristic use).

4. In "The Mental Life of Some Machines" a further, and somewhat independent, characteristic of the pain inputs is discussed in terms of Automata models—namely the spontaneity of the inclination to withdraw the injured part, etc. This raises the question, which is discussed in that paper, of giving a functional analysis of the notion of a spontaneous inclination. Of course, still further characteristics come readily to mind—for example, that feelings of pain are (or seem to be) *located* in the parts of the body.

5. Cf. the discussion of "super-spartans" in "Brains and Behavior."

22

David Lewis

"Psychophysical and Theoretical Identifications"*

Psychophysical identity theorists often say that the identifications they anticipate between mental and neural states are essentially like various uncontroversial theoretical identifications: the identification of water with H_2O, of light with electromagnetic radiation, and so on. Such theoretical identifications are usually described as pieces of voluntary theorizing, as follows. Theoretical advances make it possible to simplify total science by positing bridge laws identifying some of the entities discussed in one theory with entities discussed in another theory. In the name of parsimony, we posit those bridge laws forthwith. Identifications are made, not found.

In 'An Argument for the Identity Theory',[1] I claimed that this was a bad picture of psychophysical identification, since a suitable physiological theory could *imply* psychophysical identities—not merely make it reasonable to posit them for the sake of parsimony. The implication was as follows:

Mental state M = the occupant of causal role R (by definition of M).
Neural state N = the occupant of causal role R (by the physiological theory).
∴ Mental state M = neural state N (by transitivity of =).

If the meanings of the names of mental states were really such as to provide the first premise, and if the advance of physiology were such as to provide the second premise, then the conclusion would follow. Physiology and the meanings of words would leave us no choice but to make the psychophysical identification.

In this sequel, I shall uphold the view that psychophysical identifications thus described would be like theoretical identifications, though they would not fit the usual account thereof. For the usual account, I claim, is wrong; theoretical identification *in general* are implied by the theories that make them possible—not posited independently. This follows from a general hypothesis about the meanings of theoretical terms: that they are definable functionally, by reference to causal roles.[2] Applied to common-sense psychology—folk science rather than professional science, but a theory nonetheless—we get the hypothesis of my previous paper[3] that a mental state M (say, an experience) is definable as the occupant of a certain causal role R—that is, as the state, of whatever sort, that is causally connected in specified ways to sensory stimuli, motor responses, and other mental states.

First, I consider an example of theoretical identification chosen to be remote from past philosophizing; then I give my general account of the meanings of theoretical terms and the nature of theoretical identifications; finally I return to the case of psychophysical identity.

I

We are assembled in the drawing room of the country house; the detective reconstructs the crime. That is, he proposes a *theory* designed to be the best explanation of phenomena we have observed: the death of Mr. Body, the blood on the wallpaper, the silence of the dog in the night, the clock seventeen minutes fast, and so on. He launches into his story:

X, Y and Z conspired to murder Mr. Body. Seventeen years ago, in the gold fields of Uganda, X was Body's

From *Australasian Journal of Philosophy* L, 3 (December 1972): 249–58. Reprinted with permission of the editor and David Lewis.

partner ... Last week, Y and Z conferred in a bar in Reading ... Tuesday night at 11:17, Y went to the attic and set a time bomb ... Seventeen minutes later, X met Z in the billiard room and gave him the lead pipe ... Just when the bomb went off in the attic, X fired three shots into the study through the French windows ...

And so it goes: a long story. Let us pretend that it is a single long conjunctive sentence.

The story contains the three names 'X', 'Y' and 'Z?'. The detective uses these new terms without explanation, as though we knew what they meant. But we do not. We never used them before, at least not in the senses they bear in the present context. All we know about their meanings is what we gradually gather from the story itself. Call these *theoretical terms* (*T-terms* for short) because they are introduced by a theory. Call the rest of the terms in the story *O-terms*. These are all the *other* terms except the T-terms; they are all the *old, original* terms we understood before the theory was proposed. We could call them our 'pre-theoretical' terms. But 'O' does *not* stand for 'observational'. Not all the O-terms are observational terms, whatever those may be. They are just any old terms. If part of the story was mathematical—if it included a calculation of the trajectory that took the second bullet to the chandelier without breaking the vase—then some of the O-terms will be mathematical. If the story says that something happened because of something else, then the O-terms will include the intensional connective 'because', or the operator 'it is a law that', or something of the sort.

Nor do the theoretical terms name some sort of peculiar theoretical, unobservable, semi-fictitious entities. The story makes plain that they name *people*. Not theoretical people, different somehow from ordinary, observational people—just people!

On my account, the detective plunged right into his story, using 'X', 'Y' and 'Z' as if they were names with understood denotation. It would have made little difference if he had started, instead, with initial existential quantifiers: 'There exist X, Y and Z such that ...' and then told the story. In that case, the terms 'X', 'Y' and 'Z' would have been bound variables rather than T-terms. But the story would have had the same explanatory power. The second version of the story, with the T-terms turned into variables bound by existential quantifiers, is the Ramsey sentence of the first. Bear in mind, as evidence for what is to come, how little difference the initial quantifiers seem to make to the detective's assertion.

Suppose that after we have heard the detective's story, we learn that it is true of a certain three people: Plum, Peacock and Mustard. If we put the

name 'Plum' in place of 'X', 'Peacock' in place of 'Y', and 'Mustard' in place of 'Z' throughout, we get a true story about the doings of those three people. We will say that Plum, Peacock and Mustard together *realize* (or are a *realization* of) the detective's theory.

We may also find out that the story is not true of any other triple.[4] Put in any three names that do not name Plum, Peacock and Mustard (in that order) and the story we get is false. We will say that Plum, Peacock and Mustard *uniquely realize* (are the *unique realization* of) the theory.

We might learn both of these facts. (The detective might have known them all along, but held them back to spring his trap; or he, like us, might learn them only after his story had been told.) And if we did, we would surely conclude that X, Y and Z in the story were Plum, Peacock and Mustard. I maintain that we would be compelled so to conclude, given the senses borne by the terms 'X', 'Y' and 'Z' in virtue of the way the detective introduced them in his theorizing, and given our information about Plum, Peacock and Mustard.

In telling his story, the detective set forth three roles and said that they were occupied by X, Y and Z. He must have specified the meanings of the three T-terms 'X', 'Y' and 'Z' thereby; for they had meanings afterwards, they had none before, and nothing else was done to give them meanings. They were introduced by an implicit functional definition, being reserved to name the occupants of the three roles. When we find out who are the occupants of the three roles, we find out who are X, Y and Z. Here is our theoretical identification.

In saying that the roles were occupied by X, Y and Z, the detective implied that they were occupied. That is, his theory implied its Ramsey sentence. That seems right; if we learnt that no triple realized the story, or even came close, we would have to conclude that the story was false. We would also have to deny that the names 'X', 'Y' and 'Z' named anything; for they were introduced as names for the occupants of roles that turned out to be unoccupied.

I also claim that the detective implied that the roles were uniquely occupied, when he reserved names for their occupants and proceeded as if those names had been given definite referents. Suppose we learnt that two different triples realized the theory: Plum, Peacock, Mustard; and Green, White, Scarlet. (Or the two different triples might overlap; Plum, Peacock, Mustard; and Green, Peacock, Scarlet.) I think we would be most inclined to say that the story was false, and that the names 'X', 'Y' and 'Z' did not name anything. They were introduced as names for the occupants of certain roles; but there is no such thing as *the* occupant of a doubly occupied role, so there is nothing suitable for them to name.

If, as I claim, the T-terms are definable as naming the first, second, and third components of the unique triple that realizes the story, then the T-terms can be treated like definite descriptions. If the story is uniquely realized, they name what they ought to name; if the story is unrealized or multiply realized, they are like improper descriptions. If too many triples realize the story, '*X*' is like 'the moon of Mars'; if too few triples—none—realize the story, '*X*' is like 'the moon of Venus'. Improper descriptions are not meaningless. Hilary Putnam has objected that on this sort of account of theoretical terms, the theoretical terms of a falsified theory come out meaningless.[5] But they do not, if theoretical terms of unrealized theories are like improper descriptions. 'The moon of Mars' and 'The moon of Venus' do not (in any normal way) name anything here in our actual world; but they are not meaningless, because we know very well what they name in certain alternative possible worlds. Similarly, we know what '*X*' names in any world where the detective's theory is true, whether or not our actual world is such a world.

A complication: what if the theorizing detective has made one little mistake? He should have said that *Y* went to the attic at 11:37, not 11:17. The story as told is unrealized, true of no one. But another story is realized, indeed uniquely realized: the story we get by deleting or correcting the little mistake. We can say that the story as told is *nearly realized,* has a unique *near-realization.* (The notion of a near-realization is hard to analyze, but easy to understand.) In this case the T-terms ought to name the components of the near-realization. More generally: they should name the components of the nearest realization of the theory, provided there is a unique nearest realization and it is near enough. Only if the story comes nowhere near to being realized, or if there are two equally near nearest realizations, should we resort to treating the T-terms like improper descriptions. But let us set aside this complication for the sake of simplicity, though we know well that scientific theories are often nearly realized but rarely realized, and that theoretical reduction is usually blended with revision of the reduced theory.

This completes our example. It may seem atypical; the T-terms are names, not predicates or functors. But that is of no importance. It is a popular exercise to recast a language so that its nonlogical vocabulary consists entirely of predicates; but it is just as easy to recast a language so that its nonlogical vocabulary consists entirely of names (provided that the logical vocabulary includes a cop-

ula). These names, of course, may purport to name individuals, sets, attributes, species, states, functions, relations, magnitudes, phenomena or what have you; but they are still names. Assume this done, so that we may replace all T-terms by variables of the same sort.

II

We now proceed to a general account of the functional definability of T-terms and the nature of theoretical identification. Suppose we have a new theory, *T*, introducing the new terms $t_1 \ldots t_n$. These are our T-terms. (let them be names.) Every other term in our vocabulary, therefore, is an O-term. The theory *T* is presented in a sentence called the *postulate* of *T*. Assume this is a single sentence, perhaps a long conjunction. It says of the entities—state, magnitudes, species, or whatever—named by the T-terms that they occupy certain *causal roles;* that they stand in specified causal (and other) relations to entities named by O-terms, and to one another. We write the postulate thus:[6]

$$T[t].$$

Replacing the T-terms uniformly by free variables $x_1 \ldots x_n$, we get a formula in which only O-terms appear:

$$T[x].$$

Any *n*-tuple of entities which satisfies this formula is a realization of the theory *T*. Prefixing existential quantifiers, we get the *Ramsey sentence* of *T*, which says that *T* has at least one realization:

$$\exists x \, T[x].$$

We can also write a *modified Ramsey sentence* which says that *T* has a unique realization:[7]

$$\exists_1 x \, T[x].$$

The Ramsey sentence has exactly the same O-content as the postulate of *T*; any sentence free of T-terms follows logically from one if and only if it follows from the other.[8] The modified Ramsey sentence has slightly more O-content. I claim that this surplus O-content does belong to the theory *T*—there are more theorems of *T* than follow logically from the postulate alone. For in presenting the postulate as if the T-terms has been well-defined thereby, the theorist has implicitly asserted that *T* is uniquely realized.

We can write the *Carnap sentence* of *T*: the conditional of the Ramsey sentence and the postulate, which says that if *T* is realized, then the T-terms name the components of some realization of T:

$$\exists x\ T[x] \supset T[t].$$

Carnap has suggested this sentence as a meaning postulate for T;[9] but if we want T-terms of unrealized or multiply realized theories to have the status of improper descriptions, our meaning postulates should instead be a *modified Carnap sentence,* this conditional with our modified Ramsey sentence as antecedent:

$$\exists_1 x\ T[x] \supset T[t],$$

together with another conditional to cover the remaining cases:[10]

$$\sim \exists_1 x\ T[x] \supset t = *.$$

This pair of meaning postulates is logically equivalent[11] to a sentence which explicitly defines the T-terms by means of O-terms:

$$t = \imath x\ T[x].$$

This is what I have called functional definition. The T-terms have been defined as the occupants of the causal roles specified by the theory T; as *the* entities, whatever those may be, that bear certain causal relations to one another and to the referents of the O-terms.

If I am right, T-terms are eliminable—we can always replace them by their definientia. Of course, this is not to say that theories are fictions, or that theories are uninterpreted formal abacuses, or that theoretical entities are unreal. Quite the opposite! Because we understand the O-terms, and we can define the T-terms from them, theories are fully meaningful; we have reason to think a good theory true; and if a theory is true, then whatever exists according to the theory really *does* exist.

I said that there are more theorems of T than follow logically from the postulate alone. More precisely: the theorems of T are just those sentences which follow from the postulate together with the corresponding functional definition of the T-terms. For that definition, I claim, is given implicitly when the postulate is presented as bestowing meanings on the T-terms introduced in it.

It may happen, after the introduction of the T-terms, that we come to believe of a certain n-tuple of entities, specified otherwise than as the entities that realize T, that they do realize T. That is, we may come to accept a sentence

$$T[r]$$

where $r_1 \ldots r_n$ are either O-terms or theoretical terms of some other theory, introduced into our language independently of $t_1 \ldots t_n$. This sentence,

which we may call a *weak reduction premise* for T, is free of T-terms. Our acceptance of it might have nothing to do with our previous acceptance of T. We might accept it as part of some new theory; or we might believe it as part of our miscellaneous, unsystematized general knowledge. Yet having accepted it, for whatever reason, we are logically compelled to make theoretical identifications. The reduction premise, together with the functional definition of the T-terms and the postulate of T, logically implies the identity:

$$t = r.$$

In other words, the postulate and the weak reduction premise definitionally imply the identities $t_i = r_i$.

Or we might somehow come to believe of a certain n-tuple of entities that they *uniquely* realize T; that is, to accept a sentence

$$\forall x(T[x] \equiv x = r)$$

where $r_1 \ldots r_n$ are as above. We may call this a *strong reduction premise* for T, since it definitionally implies the theoretical identifications by itself, without the aid of the postulate of T. The strong reduction premise logically implies the identity

$$r = \imath x\ T[x]$$

which, together with the functional definition of the T-terms, implies the identities $t_i = r_i$ by transitivity of identity.

These theoretical identifications are not voluntary posits, made in the name of parsimony; they are deductive inferences. According to their definitions, the T-terms name the occupants of the causal roles specified by the theory T. According to the weak reduction premise and T, or the strong reduction premise by itself, the occupants of those causal roles turn out to be the referents of $r_1 \ldots r_n$. Therefore, those are the entities named by the T-terms. That is how we inferred that X, Y and Z were Plum, Peacock and Mustard, and that, I suggest, is how we make theoretical identifications in general.

III

And that is how, someday, we will infer that[12] the mental states M_1, M_2, ... are the neural states N_1, N_2, ...

Think of common-sense psychology as a term-introducing scientific theory, though one invented long before there was any such institution as professional science. Collect all the platitudes you can think of regarding the causal relations of mental states, sensory stimuli, and motor responses. Perhaps we can think of them as having the form:

> When someone is in so-and-so combination of mental states and receives sensory stimuli of so-and-so kind, he tends with so-and-so probability to be caused thereby to go into so-and-so mental states and produce so-and-so motor responses.

Add also all the platitudes to the effect that one mental state falls under another—'toothache is a kind of pain', and the like. Perhaps there are platitudes of other forms as well. Include only platitudes which are common knowledge among us—everyone knows them, everyone knows that everyone else knows them, and so on. For the meanings of our words are common knowledge, and I am going to claim that names of mental states derive their meaning from these platitudes.

Form the conjunction of these platitudes; or better, form a cluster of them—a disjunction of all conjunctions of *most* of them. (That way it will not matter if a few are wrong.) This is the postulate of our term-introducing theory. The names of mental states are the T-terms.[13] The O-terms used to introduce them must be sufficient for speaking of stimuli and responses, and for speaking of causal relations among these and states of unspecified nature.

From the postulate, form the definition of the T-terms; it defines the mental states by reference to their causal relations to stimuli, responses, and each other. When we learn what sort of states occupy those causal roles definitive of the mental states, we will learn what states the mental states are—exactly as we found out who X was when we found out that Plum was the man who occupied a certain role, and exactly as we found out what light was when we found that electromagnetic radiation was the phenomenon that occupied a certain role.

Imagine our ancestors first speaking only of external things, stimuli, and responses—and perhaps producing what we, but not they, may call *Äusserungen* of mental states—until some genius invented the theory of mental states, with its newly introduced T-terms, to explain the regularities among stimuli and responses. But that did not happen. Our commonsense psychology was never a newly invented term-introducing scientific theory—not even of prehistoric folk-science. The story that mental terms were introduced as theoretical terms is a myth.

It is, in fact, Sellars' myth of our Rylean ancestors.[14] And though it is a myth, it may be a good myth or a bad one. It is a good myth if our names of mental states do in fact mean just what they would mean if the myth were true.[15] I adopt the working hypothesis that it is a good myth. This hypothesis can be tested, in principle, in whatever way any hypothesis about the conventional meanings of our words can be tested. I have not tested it; but I offer one item of evidence. Many philosophers have found Rylean behaviorism at least plausible; more have found watered down, 'criteriological' behaviorism plausible. There is a strong odor of analyticity about the platitudes of common-sense psychology. The myth explains the odor of analyticity and the plausibility of behaviorism. If the names of mental states are like theoretical terms, they name nothing unless the theory (the cluster of platitudes) is more or less true. Hence it is analytic that *either* pain, etc., do not exist *or* most of our platitudes about them are true. If this *seems* analytic to you, you should accept the myth, and be prepared for psychophysical identifications.

The hypothesis that names of mental states are like functionally defined theoretical terms solves a familiar problem about mental explanations. How can my behavior be explained by an explanans consisting of nothing but particular-fact premises about my present state of mind? Where are the covering laws? The solution is that the requisite covering laws are implied by the particular-fact premises. Ascriptions to me of various particular beliefs and desires, say, cannot be true if there are no such states as belief and desire; cannot be true, that is, unless the causal roles definitive of belief and desire are occupied. But these roles can only be occupied by states causally related in the proper lawful way to behavior.

Formally, suppose we have a mental explanation of behavior as follows.

$$\frac{C_1[t], C_2[t], \ldots}{E}$$

Here E describes the behavior to be explained; $C_1[t]$, $C_2[t]$, ... are particular-fact premises describing the agent's state of mind at the time. Various of the mental terms $t_1 \ldots t_n$ appear in these premises, in such a way that the premises would be false if the terms named nothing. Now let $L_1[t]$, $L_2[t]$, ... be the platitudinous purported causal laws whereby—according to the myth—the mental terms were introduced. Ignoring clustering for simplicity, we may take the term-introducing postulate to be the conjunction of these. Then our explanation may be rewritten:

$$\frac{\exists_1 x \left(\begin{array}{l} L_1[x] \ \& \ L_2[x] \ \& \ \ldots \ \& \\ C_1[x] \ \& \ C_2[x] \ \& \ \ldots \end{array} \right)}{E}$$

The new explanans is a definitional consequence of the original one. In the expanded version, however, laws appear explicitly alongside the particular-fact premises. We have, so to speak, an existential generalization of an ordinary covering-law explanation.[16]

The causal definability of mental terms has been thought to contradict the necessary infallibility of introspection.[17] Pain is one state; belief that one is in pain is another. (Confusingly, either of the two may be called 'awareness of pain'.) Why cannot I believe that I am in pain without being in pain—that is, without being in whatever state it is that occupies so-and-so causal role? Doubtless I am so built that this normally does not happen; but what makes it impossible?

I do not know whether introspection is (in some or all cases) infallible. But if it is, that is no difficulty for me. Here it is important that, on my version of causal definability, the mental terms stand or fall together. If common-sense psychology fails, all of them are alike denotationless.

Suppose that among the platitudes are some to the effect that introspection is reliable: 'belief that one is in pain never occurs unless pain occurs' or the like. Suppose further that these platitudes enter the term-introducing postulate as conjuncts, not as cluster members; and suppose that they are so important that an *n*-tuple that fails to satisfy them perfectly is not even a near-realization of common-sense psychology. (I neither endorse nor repudiate these suppositions.) Then the necessary infallibility of introspection is assured. Two states cannot be pain and belief that one is in pain, respectively (in the case of a given individual or species) if the second *ever* occurs without the first. The state that *usually* occupies the role of belief that one is in pain may, of course, occur without the state that *usually* occupies the role of pain; but in that case (under the suppositions above) the former no longer is the state of belief that one is in pain, and the latter no longer is pain. Indeed, the victim no longer is in any mental state whatever, since his states no longer realize (or nearly realize) common-sense psychology. Therefore it is impossible to believe that one is in pain and not be in pain.

NOTES

* Previous versions of this paper were presented at a conference on Philosophical Problems of Psychology held at Honolulu in March, 1968; at the annual meeting of the Australasian Association of Philosophy held at Brisbane in August, 1971; and at various university colloquia. This paper is expected to appear also in a volume edited by Chung-ying Cheng.

1. *Journal of Philosophy,* **63** (1966): 17–25.

2. See my 'How to Define Theoretical Terms', *Journal of Philosophy,* **67** (1970): 427–446.

3. Since advocated also by D. M. Armstrong, in *A Materialist Theory of the Mind* (New York: Humanities Press, 1968). He expresses it thus: 'The concept of a mental state is primarily the concept of a state of the person apt for bringing about a certain sort of behaviour [and secondarily also, in some cases] apt for being brought about by a certain sort of stimulus', p. 82.

4. The story itself might imply this. If, for instance, the story said '*X* saw *Y* give *Z* the candlestick while the three of them were alone in the billiard room at 9:17', then the story could not possibly be true of more than one triple.

5. 'What Theories are Not', in Nagel, Suppes and Tarski eds., *Logic, Methodology and Philosophy of Science* (Stanford University Press, 1962): 247.

6. Notation: boldface names and variables denote *n*-tuples; the corresponding subscripted names and variables denote components of *n*-tuples. For instance, t is $\langle t_1 \ldots t_n \rangle$. This notation is easily dispensable, and hence carries no ontic commitment to *n*-tuples.

7. That is, $\exists y \forall x (T[x] \equiv y = x)$. Note that $\exists_1 x_1 \ldots \exists_1 x_n$ $T[x]$ does not imply $\exists_1 x \, T[x]$, and does not say that T is uniquely realized.

8. On the assumptions reasonable for the postulate of a scientific theory—that the T-terms occur purely referentially in the postulate, and in such a way that the postulate is false if any of them are denotationless. We shall make these assumptions henceforth.

9. Most recently in *Philosophical Foundations of Physics* (New York: Basic Books, 1966): 265–274. Carnap, of course, has in mind the case in which the O-terms belong to an observation language.

10. $t = *$ means that each t_i is denotationless. Let $*$ be some chosen necessarily denotationless name; then $* $ is $\langle * \ldots *\rangle$ and $t = *$ is equivalent to the conjunction of all the identities $t_i = *$.

11. Given a theory of descriptions which makes an identity true whenever both its terms have the status of improper descriptions, false whenever one term has that status and the other does not. This might best be the theory of descriptions in Dana Scott, 'Existence and Description in Formal Logic', in R. Schoenman, ed., *Bertrand Russell: Philosopher of the Century* (London: Allen & Unwin, 1967).

12. In general, or in the case of a given species, or in the case of a given person. It might turn out that the causal roles definitive of mental states are occupied by different neural (or other) states in different organisms. See my discussion of Hilary Putnam 'Psychological Predicates' in *Journal of Philosophy,* **66**(1969): 23–25.

13. It may be objected that the number of mental states is infinite, or at least enormous; for instance, there are as many states of belief as there are propositons to be believed. But it would be better to say that there is one state of belief, and it is a relational state, relating people to propositions. (Similarly, centigrade temperature is a relational state, relating objects to numbers.) The platitudes involving belief would, of course, contain universally quantified proposition-variables. Likewise for other mental states with intentional objects.

14. Wilfrid Sellars, 'Empiricism and the Philosophy of Mind', in Feigl and Scriven, eds., *Minnesota Studies in the Philosophy of Science,* I (University of Minnesota Press, 1956): 309–320.

15. Two myths which cannot both be true together can nevertheless both be good together. Part of my myth says that names of color-sensations were T-terms, introduced using names of colors as O-terms. If this is a good myth, we should be able to define 'sensation of red' roughly as 'that state apt for being brought about by the presence of something red (before one's open eyes, in good light, etc.)'. A second myth says that names of colors were T-terms introduced using names of color-sensations as O-terms. If this second myth is good, we should be able to define 'red' roughly as 'that property of things apt for bringing about the sensation of red'. The two myths could not both be true, for which came first: names of color-sensations or of colors? But they could both be good. We could have a circle in which colors are correctly defined in terms of sensations and sensations are correctly defined in terms of colors. We could not discover the meanings *both* of names of colors and of names of color-sensations just by looking at the circle of correct definitions, but so what?

16. See 'How to Define Theoretical Terms': 440–441.

17. By Armstrong, in *A Materialist Theory of the Mind,* pp. 100–113. He finds independent grounds for denying the infallibility of introspection.

23

Ned Block

"Troubles with Functionalism"

1.0 Functionalism, Behaviorism, and Physicalism

The functionalist view of the nature of the mind is now widely accepted.[1] Like behaviorism and physicalism, functionalism seeks to answer the question "What are mental states?" I shall be concerned with identity thesis formulations of functionalism. They say, for example, that pain is a functional state, just as identity thesis formulations of physicalism say that pain is a physical state.

I shall begin by describing functionalism, and sketching the functionalist critique of behaviorism and physicalism. Then I shall argue that the troubles ascribed by functionalism to behaviorism and physicalism infect functionalism as well.

One characterization of functionalism that is probably vague enough to be acceptable to most functionalists is: each type of mental state is a state consisting of a disposition to act in certain ways *and to have certain mental states,* given certain sensory inputs and certain mental states. So put, functionalism can be seen as a new incarnation of behaviorism. Behaviorism identifies mental states with dispostions to act in certain ways in certain input situations. But as critics have pointed out (Chisholm, 1957; Geach, 1957; Putnam, 1963), desire for goal G cannot be identified with, say, the disposition to do A in input circumstances in which A leads to G, since, after all, the agent might not *know* that A leads to G and thus might not be disposed to do A. Functionalism replaces behaviorism's "sensory inputs" with "sensory inputs and mental states"; and functionalism replaces behaviorism's "dispostions to act" with "dispositions to act and have certain mental states." Functionalists want to individuate mental states causally, and since mental states have mental causes and effects as well as sensory causes and behavioral effects, functionalists individuate mental states partly in terms of causal relations to other mental states. One consequence of this difference between functionalism and behaviorism is that there are possible organisms that according to behaviorism, have mental states but, according to functionalism, do not have mental states.

So, necessary conditions for mentality that are postulated by functionalism are in one respect stronger than those postulated by behaviorism. According to behaviorism, it is necessary and sufficient for desiring that G that a system be characterized by a certain set (perhaps infinite) of input–output relations; that is, according to behaviorism, a system desires that G just in case a certain set of conditionals of the form 'It will emit O given I' are true of it. According to functionalism, however, a system might have these input–output relations, yet not desire that G; for according to functionalism, whether a system desires that G depends on whether it has internal states which have certain causal relations to other internal states (and to inputs and outputs). Since behaviorism makes no such "internal state" requirement, there are possible systems of which behaviorism affirms and functionalism denies that they have mental states.[2] One way of stating this is that, according to functionalism, behaviorism is guilty of *liberalism*—ascribing mental properties to things that do not in fact have them.

Despite the difference just sketched between functionalism and behaviorism, functionalists and

Revised and considerably abridged by the author from "Troubles with Functionalism," *Minnesota Studies in the Philosophy of Science,* volume IX, C. Wade Savage, ed. Minneapolis: University of Minnesota Press, 1978, pp. 261–325. Reprinted with permission of the publisher and Ned Block.

behavirorists need not be far apart in spirit.[3] Shoemaker (1975), for example, says, "On one construal of it, functionalism in the philosophy of mind is the doctrine that mental, or psychological, terms are, in principle, eliminable in a certain way" (pp. 306–7). Functionalists have tended to treat the mental-state terms in a functional characterization of a mental state quite differently from the input and output terms. Thus in the simplest Turing-machine version of the theory (Putnam, 1967; Block & Fodor, 1972), mental states are identified with the total Turing-machine states, which are themselves *implicitly* defined by a machine table that *explicitly* mentions inputs and outputs, described nonmentalistically.

In Lewis's version of functionalism, mental-state terms are defined by means of a modification of Ramsey's method, in a way that eliminates essential use of mental terminology from the definitions but does not eliminate input and output terminology. That is 'pain' is defined as synonymous with a definite description containing input and output terms but no mental terminology (see Lewis, 1972).

Furthermore, functionalism in both its machine and nonmachine versions has typically insisted that characterizations of mental states should contain descriptions of inputs and outputs in *physical* lanuage. Armstrong (1968), for example, says,

> We may distinguish between 'physical behaviour', which refers to any merely physical action or passion of the body, and 'behaviour proper' which implies relationship to the mind. . . . Now, if in our formula ["state of the person apt for bringing about a certain sort of behaviour"] 'behaviour' were to mean 'behaviour proper', then we would be giving an account of mental concepts in terms of a concept that already presupposes mentality, which would be circular. So it is clear that in our formula, 'behaviour' must mean 'physical behaviour'. (p. 84)

Therefore, functionalism can be said to "tack down" mental states only at the periphery—i.e., through physical, or at least nonmental, specification of inputs and outputs. One major thesis of this article is that, because of this feature, functionalism fails to avoid the sort of problem for which it rightly condemns behaviorism. Functionalism, too, is guilty of liberalism, for much the same reasons as behaviorism. Unlike behaviorism, however, functionalism can naturally be altered to avoid liberalism—but only at the cost of falling into an equally ignominious failing.

The failing I speak of is the one that functionalism shows *physicialism* to be guilty of. By 'physicialism', I mean the doctrine that pain, for example, is identical to a physical (or physiological) state.[4] As many philosophers have argued (notably Fodor, 1965, and Putnam, 1966; see also Block & Fodor, 1972), if functionalism is true, physicalism is probably false. The point is at its clearest with regard to Turing-machine versions of functionalism. Any given abstract Turing machine can be realized by a wide variety of physical devices; indeed, it is plausible that, given any putative correspondence between a Turing-machine state and a configurational physical (or physiological) state, there will be a possible realization of the Turing machine that will provide a counterexample to that correspondence. (See Kalke, 1969; Gendron, 1971; Mucciolo, 1974, for unconvincing arguments to the contrary; see also Kim, 1972.) Therefore, if pain is a functional state, it cannot, for example, be a brain state, because creatures without brains can realize the same Turing machine as creatures with brains.

I must emphasize that the functionalist argument against physicalism does not appeal merely to the fact that one abstract Turing machine can be realized by systems of different *material composition* (wood, metal, glass, etc.). To argue this way would be like arguing that temperature cannot be a microphysical magnitude because the same temperature can be had by objects with *different* microphysical structures (Kim, 1972). Objects with different microphysical structures, e.g., objects made of wood, metal, glass, etc., can have many interesting microphysical properties in common, such as molecular kinetic energy of the same average value. Rather, the functionalist argument against physicalism is that it is difficult to see how there *could be* a nontrivial first-order (see note 4) physical property in common to all and only the possible physical realizations of a given Turing-machine state. Try to think of a remotely plausible candidate! At the very least, the onus is on those who think such physical properties are conceivable to show us how to conceive of one.

One way of expressing this point is that, according to functionalism, physicalism is a *chauvinist* theory: it withholds mental properties from systems that in fact have them. In saying mental states are brain states, for example, physicialists unfairly exclude those poor brainless creatures who nonetheless have minds.

A second major point of this paper is that the very argument which functionalism uses to condemn physicalism can be applied equally well against functionalism; indeed, any version of functionalism that avoids liberalism falls, like physicalism, into chauvinism.

This article has three parts. The first argues that

functionalism is guilty of liberalism, the second that one way of modifying functionalism to avoid liberalism is to tie it more closely to empirical psychology, and the third that no version of functionalism can avoid both liberalism and chauvinism.

1.1 More About What Functionalism Is

One way of providing some order to the bewildering variety of functionalist theories is to distinguish between those that are couched in terms of a Turing machine and those that are not.

A Turing-machine table lists a finite set of machine-table states, $S_1 \ldots S_n$; inputs, $I_1 \ldots I_m$; and outputs, $O_1 \ldots O_p$. The table specifies a set of conditionals of the form: if the machine is in state S_i and receives input I_j, it emits output O_k and goes into state S_l. That is, given any state and input, the table specifies an output and a next state. Any system with a set of inputs, outputs, and states related in the way specified by the table is described by the table and is a realization of the abstract automaton specified by the table.

To have the power for computing any recursive function, a Turing machine must be able to control its input in certain ways. In standard formulations, the output of a Turing machine is regarded as having two components. It prints a symbol on a tape, then moves the tape, thus bringing a new symbol into the view of the input reader. For the Turing machine to have full power, the tape must be infinite in at least one direction and movable in both directions. If the machine has no control over the tape, it is a "finite transducer," a rather limited Turing machine. Finite transducers need not be regarded as having tape at all. Those who believe that machine functionalism is true must suppose that just what power automaton we are is a substantive empirical question. If we are "full power" Turing machines, the environment must constitute part of the tape.

Machine functionalists generally consider the machine in question as a probabilistic automaton—a machine whose table specifies conditionals of the following form: if the machine is in S_a and receives I_b, it has a probability p_1 of emitting O_1; p_2 of emitting $O_2 \ldots p_k$ of emitting O_k; r_1 of going into S_1; r_2 of going into $S_2 \ldots r_n$ of going into S_n. For simplicity, I shall usually consider a deterministic version of the theory.

One very simple version of machine functionalism (Block & Fodor, 1972) states that each system having mental states is described by at least one Turing-machine table of a specifiable sort and that each type of mental state of the system is identical to one of the machine-table states. Consider, for example, the Turing machine described in the table (cf. Nelson, 1975):

	S_1	S_2
nickel input	Emit no output Go to S_2	Emit a Coke Go to S_1
dime input	Emit a Coke Stay in S_1	Emit a Coke & a nickel Go to S_1

One can get a crude picture of the simple version of machine functionalism by considering the claim that S_1 = dime-desire, and S_2 = nickel-desire. Of course, no functionalist would claim that a Coke machine desires anything. Rather, the simple version of machine functionalism described above makes an analogous claim with respect to a much more complex hypothetical machine table. Notice that machine functionalism specifies inputs and outputs explicitly, internal states implicitly (Putnam [1967, p. 434] says: "The S_i, to repeat, are specified only *implicitly* by the description, i.e., specified *only* by the set of transition probabilities given in the machine table"). To be described by this machine table, a device must accept nickels and dimes as inputs and dispense nickels and Cokes as outputs. But the states S_1 and S_2 can have virtually any natures (even nonphysical natures), so long as those natures connect the states to each other and to the inputs and outputs specified in the machine table. All we are told about S_1 and S_2 are these relations; thus machine functionalism can be said to reduce mentality to input–output structures. This example should suggest the force of the functionalist argument against physicalism. Try to think of a first-order (see note 4) physical property that can be shared by all (and only) realizations of this machine table!

One can also categorize functionalists in terms of whether they regard functional identities as part of a priori psychology or empirical psychology. The a priori functionalists (e.g., Smart, Armstrong, Lewis, Shoemaker) are the heirs of the logical behaviorists. They tend to regard functional analyses as analyses of the meanings of mental terms, whereas the empirical functionalists (e.g., Fodor, Putnam, Harman) regard functional analyses as substantive scientific hypotheses. In what follows, I shall refer to the former view as 'Functionalism' and the latter as 'Psychofunctionalism'. (I shall use 'functionalism' with a lowercase 'f' as neutral between Functionalism and Psychofunctionalism. When distinguishing between Functionalism and Psychofunctionalism, I shall always use capitals.)

Functionalism and Psychofunctionalism and

the difference between them can be made clearer in terms of the notion of the Ramsey sentence of a psychological theory. Mental-state terms that appear in a pscyhological theory can be defined in various ways by means of the Ramsey sentence of the theory. All functional-state identity theories can be understood as defining a set of functional states (or functional properties) by means of the Ramsey sentence of a psychological theory—with one functional state corresponding to each mental state. The functional state corresponding to pain will be called the 'Ramsey functional correlate' of pain, with respect to the psychological theory. In terms of the notion of a Ramsey functional correlate with respect to a theory, the distinction between Functionalism and Psychofunctionalism can be defined as follows: Functionalism identifies mental state S and S's Ramsey functional correlate with respect to a *common-sense* psychological theory; Psychofunctionalism identifies S with S's Ramsey functional correlate with respect to a *scientific* psychological theory.

This difference between Functionalism and Psychofunctionalism gives rise to a difference in specifying inputs and outputs. Functionalists are restricted to specification of inputs and outputs that are plausibly part of common-sense knowledge; Psychofunctionalists are under no such restriction. Although both groups insist on physical—or at least nonmental—specification of inputs and outputs, Functionalists require externally observable classifications (e.g., inputs characterized in terms of objects present in the vicinity of the organism, outputs in terms of movements of body parts). Psychofunctionalists, on the other hand, have the option to specify inputs and outputs in terms of internal parameters, e.g., signals in input and output neurons.

Let T be a psychological theory of either common sense or scientific psychology. T may contain generalizations of the form: anyone who is in state w and receives input x emits output y, and goes into state z. Let us write T as

$$T(S_1 \ldots S_n, I_1 \ldots I_w, O_1 \ldots O_m)$$

where the Ss are mental states, the Is are inputs, and the Os are outputs. The 'S's are to be understood as mental-state *constants,* not variables, e.g., 'pain', and likewise for the 'I's and 'O's. Thus, one could also write T as

T(pain . . . , light of 400 nanometers entering

left eye . . . , left big toe moves

1 centimeter left . . .)

To get the Ramsey sentence of T, replace the mental state terms—*but not the input and output*

terms—by variables, and prefix an existential quantifier for each variable:

$$\exists F_1 \ldots \exists F_n T(F_1 \ldots F_n, I_1 \ldots I_k, O_1 \ldots O_m)$$

If 'F_{17}' is the variable that replaced the word 'pain' when the Ramsey sentence was formed, then we can define pain as follows in terms of the Ramsey sentence:

$$x \text{ is in pain} \leftrightarrow \exists F_1 \ldots \exists F_n T$$
$$[(F_1 \ldots F_n, I_1 \ldots I_k, O_1 \ldots O_m) \& x \text{ has } F_{17}]$$

The Ramsey functional correlate of pain is the property expressed by the predicate on the right hand side of this biconditional. Notice that this predicate contains input and output constants, but no mental constants, since the mental constants were replaced by variables. The Ramsey functional correlate for pain is defined in terms of inputs and outputs, but not in mental terms.

For example, let T be the theory that pain is caused by skin damage and causes worry and the emission of "Ouch", and worry, in turn, causes brow wrinkling. Then the Ramsey definition would be:

x is in pain ↔ There are 2 states (properties), the first of which is caused by skin damage and causes both the emission of "Ouch" and the second state, and the second state causes brow wrinkling, and x is in the first state.

The Ramsey functional correlate of pain with respect to this "theory" is the property of being in a state that is caused by skin damage and causes the emission of "ouch" and another state that in turn causes brow winkling. (Note that the words 'pain' and 'worry' have been replaced by variables, but the input and output terms remain.)

The Ramsey functional correlate of a state S is a state that has much in common with S. Specifically, S and its Ramsey functional correlate share the structural properties specified by the theory T. But, there are two reasons why it is natural to suppose that S and its Ramsey functional correlate will be distinct. First, the Ramsey functional correlate of S with respect to T can "include" at most those aspects of S that are captured by T; any aspects not captured by T will be left out. Second, the Ramsey functional correlate may even leave out some of what T does capture, for the Ramsey definition does not contain the "theoretical" vocabulary of T. The example theory of the last paragraph is true only of pain-feeling organisms—but trivially, in virtue of its use of the word 'pain'. However, the predicate that expresses T's Ramsey functional correlate does not contain this word (since it was replaced by a variable), and so can be true of things that don't feel pain. It would be easy to make a simple machine that has some artificial skin, a brow, a tape-recorded "ouch", and two states that satisfy the mentioned causal relations, but no pain.

The bold hypothesis of functionalism is that for *some* psychological theory, this natural supposition that a state and its Ramsey functional correlate are distinct is false. Functionalism says that there is a theory such that pain, for example, *is* its Ramsey functional correlate with respect to that theory.

One final preliminary point: I have given the misleading impression that functionalism identifies *all* mental states with functional states. Such a version of functionalism is obviously far too strong. Let X be a newly created cell-for-cell duplicate of you (which, of course, is functionally equivalent to you). Perhaps you remember being bar-mitzvahed. But X does not remember being bar-mitzvahed, since X never was bar-mitzvahed. Indeed, something can be functionally equivalent to you but fail to know what you know, or [verb], what you [verb], for a wide variety of "success" verbs. Worse still, if Putnam (1975b) is right in saying that "meanings are not in the head," systems functionally equivalent to you may, for similar reasons, fail to have many of your other propositional attitudes. Suppose you believe water is wet. According to plausible arguments advanced by Putnam and Kripke, a condition for the possibility of your believing water is wet is a certain kind of causal connection between you and water. Your "twin" on Twin Earth, who is connected in a similar way to XYZ rather than H_2O, would not believe water is wet.

If functionalism is to be defended, it must be construed as applying only to a subclass of mental states, those "narrow" mental states such that truth conditions for their application are in some sense "within the person." But even assuming that a notion of narrowness of psychological state can be satisfactorily formulated, the interest of functionalism may be diminished by this restriction. I mention this problem only to set it aside.

I shall take functionalism to be a doctrine about all "narrow" mental states.

1.2 Homunculi-Headed Robots

In this section I shall describe a class of devices that are *prima facie* embarrassments for all versions of functionalism in that they indicate functionalism is guilty of liberalism—classifying systems that lack mentality as having mentality.

Consider the simple version of machine func-

tionalism already described. It says that each system having mental states is described by at least one Turing-machine table of a certain kind, and each mental state of the system is identical to one of the machine-table states specified by the machine table. I shall consider inputs and outputs to be specified by descriptions of neural impulses in sense organs and motor-output neurons. This assumption should not be regarded as restricting what will be said to Psychofunctionalism rather than Functionalism. As already mentioned, every version of functionalism assumes *some* specification of inputs and outputs. A Functionalist specification would do as well for the purposes of what follows.

Imagine a body externally like a human body, say yours, but internally quite different. The neurons from sensory organs are connected to a bank of lights in a hallow cavity in the head. A set of buttons connects to the motor-output neurons. Inside the cavity resides a group of little men. Each has a very simple task: to implement a "square" of an adequate machine table that describes you. On one wall is a bulletin board on which is posted a state card, i.e., a card that bears a symbol designating one of the states specified in the machine table. Here is what the little men do: Suppose the posted card has a 'G' on it. This alerts the little men who implement G squares—'G-men' they call themselves. Suppose the light representing input I_{17} goes on. One of the G-men has the following as his sole task: when the card reads 'G' and the I_{17} light goes on, he presses output button O_{191} and changes the state card to 'M'. This G-man is called upon to exercise his task only rarely. In spite of the low level of intelligence required of each little man, the system as a whole manages to simulate you because the functional organization they have been trained to realize is yours. A Turing machine can be represented as a finite set of quadruples (or quintuples, if the output is divided into two parts): current state, current input, next state, next output. Each little man has the task corresponding to a single quadruple. Through the efforts of the little men, the system realizes the same (reasonably adequate) machine table as you do and is thus functionally equivalent to you.[5]

I shall describe a version of the homunculi-headed simulation, which has more chance of being nomologically possible. How many homunculi are required? Perhaps a billion are enough.

Suppose we convert the government of China to functionalism, and we convince its officials to realize a human mind for an hour. We provide each of the billion people in China (I chose China because it has a billion inhabitants) with a specially designed twoway radio that connects them in the appropriate way to other persons and to the artificial body mentioned in the previous example. We replace each of the little men with a citizen of China plus his radio. Instead of a bulletin board, we arrange to have letters displayed on a series of satellites placed so that they can be seen from anywhere in China.

The system of a billion people communicating with one another plus satellites plays the role of an external "brain" connected to the artificial body by radio. There is nothing absurd about a person being connected to his brain by radio. Perhaps the day will come when our brains will be periodically removed for cleaning and repairs. Imagine that this is done initially by treating neurons attaching the brain to the body with a chemical that allows them to stretch like rubber bands, thereby assuring that no brain-body connections are disrupted. Soon clever businessmen discover that they can attract more customers by replacing the stretched neurons with radio links so that brains can be cleaned without inconveniencing the customer by immobilizing his body.

It is not at all obvious that the China–body system is physically impossible. It could be functionally equivalent to you for a short time, say an hour.

"But," you may object, "how could something be functionally equivalent to me for *an hour?* Doesn't *my* functional organization determine, say, how I would react to doing nothing for a week but reading the *Reader's Digest?*" Remember that a machine table specifies a set of conditionals of the form: if the machine is in S_i and receives input I_j, it emits output O_k and goes into S_l. These conditionals are to be understood *subjunctively.* What gives a system a functional organization at a time is not just what it *does* at that time, but also the counterfactuals true of it at that time: what it *would* have done (and what its state transitions would have been) had it had a different input or been in a different state. If it is true of a system at time t that it *would* obey a given machine table no matter which of the states it is in and no matter which of the inputs it receives, then the system is described at t by the machine table (and realizes at t the abstract automaton specified by the table), even if it exists for only an instant. For the hour the Chinese system is "on," it *does* have a set of inputs, outputs, and states of which such subjunctive conditionals are true. This is what makes any computer realize the abstract automaton that it realizes.

Of course, there are signals the system would respond to that you would not respond to, e.g., massive radio interference or a flood of the Yangtze River. Such events might cause a malfunction, scotching the simulation, just as a bomb

in a computer can make it fail to realize the machine table it was built to realize. But just as the computer *without* the bomb *can* realize the machine table, the system consisting of the people and artificial body can realize the machine table so long as there are no catastrophic interferences, e.g., floods, etc.

"But," someone may object, "there is a difference between a bomb in a computer and a bomb in the Chinese system, for in the case of the latter (unlike the former), inputs as specified in the machine table can be the cause of the malfunction. Unusual neural activity in the sense organs of residents of Chungking Province caused by a bomb or by a flood of the Yangtze can cause the system to go haywire."

Reply: The person who says what system he or she is talking about gets to say what signals count as inputs and outputs. I count as inputs and outputs only neural activity in the artificial body connected by radio to the people of China. Neural signals in the people of Chungking count no more as inputs to this system than input tape jammed by a saboteur between the relay contacts in the innards of a computer count as an input to the computer.

Of course, the object consisting of the people of China + the artificial body has *other* Turing-machine descriptions under which neural signals in the inhabitants of Chungking *would* count as inputs. Such a new system (i.e., the object under such a new Turing-machine description) would not be functionally equivalent to you. Likewise, any commercial computer can be redescribed in a way that allows tape jammed into its innards to count as inputs. In describing an object as a Turing machine, one draws a line between the inside and the outside. (If we count only neural impulses as inputs and outputs, we draw that line inside the body; if we count only peripheral stimulations as inputs, we draw that line at the skin.) In describing the Chinese system as a Turing machine, I have drawn the line in such a way that it satisfies a certain type of functional description—one that you *also* satisfy, and one that, according to functionalism, justifies attributions of mentality. Functionalism does not claim that every mental system has a machine table of a sort that justifies attributions of mentality with respect to *every* specification of inputs and outputs, but rather, only with respect to *some* specification.

Objection: The Chinese system would work too slowly. The kind of events and processes with which we normally have contact would pass by far too quickly for the system to detect them. Thus, we would be unable to converse with it, play bridge with it, etc.

Reply: It is hard to see why the system's time

scale should matter. Is it really contradictory or nonsensical to suppose we could meet a race of intelligent beings with whom we could communicate only by devices such as time-lapse photography? When we observe these creatures, they seem almost inanimate. But when we view the time-lapse movies, we see them conversing with one another. Indeed, we find they are saying that the only way they can make any sense of us is by viewing movies greatly slowed down. To take time scale as all important seems crudely behavioristic.

What makes the homunculi-headed system (count the two systems as variants of a single system) just described a prima facie counterexample to (machine) functionalism is that there is prima facie doubt whether it has any mental states at all—especially whether it has what philosophers have variously called "qualitative states," "raw feels," or "immediate phenomenological qualities." (You ask: What is it that philosophers have called qualitative states? I answer, only half in jest: As Louis Armstrong said when asked what jazz is, "If you got to ask, you ain't never gonna get to know.") In Nagel's terms (1974), there is a prima facie doubt whether there is anything which it is like to be the homunculi-headed system.

The force of the prima facie counterexample can be made clearer as follows: Machine functionalism says that each mental state is identical to a machine–table state. For example, a particular qualitative state, Q, is identical to a machine–table state, S_q. But if there is nothing it is like to be the homunculi-headed system, it cannot be in Q even when it is in S_q. Thus, if there is prima facie doubt about the homunculi-headed system's mentality, there is prima facie doubt that Q = S_q, i.e., doubt that the kind of functionalism under consideration is true.[6] Call this argument the Absent Qualia Argument.

1.3   Putnam's Proposal

One way functionalists can try to deal with the problem posed by the homunculi-headed counterexamples is by the ad hoc device of stipulating them away. For example, a functionalist might stipulate that two systems cannot be functionally equivalent if one contains parts with functional organizations characteristic of sentient beings and the other does not. In his article hypothesizing that pain is a functional state, Putnam stipulated that "no organism capable of feeling pain possesses a decomposition into parts which separately possess Descriptions" (as the sort of Turing machine which can be in the functional state Putnam identifies with pain). The purpose of this condition is

"to rule out such 'organisms' (if they count as such) as swarms of bees as single pain feelers" (Putnam, 1967, pp. 434–435).

One way of filling out Putnam's requirement would be: a pain-feeling organism cannot possess a decomposition into parts *all* of which have a functional organization characteristic of sentient beings. But this would not rule out my homunculi-headed example, since it has nonsentient parts, such as the mechanical body and sense organs. It will not do to go to the opposite extreme and require that *no* proper parts be sentient. Otherwise pregnant women and people with sentient parasites will fail to count as pain feeling organisms. What seems to be important to examples like the homunculi-headed simulation I have described is that the sentient beings *play a crucial role* in giving the thing its functional organization. This suggests a version of Putnam's proposal which requires that a pain-feeling organism has a certain functional organization and that it has no parts which (1) themselves possess that sort of functional organization and also (2) play a crucial role in giving the whole system its functional organization.

Although this proposal involves the vague notion "crucial role," it is precise enough for us to see it will not do. Suppose there is a part of the universe that contains matter quite different from ours, matter that is infinitely divisible. In this part of the universe, there are intelligent creatures of many sizes, even humanlike creatures much smaller than our elementary particles. In an intergalactic expedition, these people discover the existence of our type of matter. For reasons known only to them, they decide to devote the next few hundred years to creating out of *their* matter substances with the chemical and physical characteristics (except at the subelementary particle level) of *our* elements. They build hordes of space ships of different varieties about the sizes of our electrons, protons, and other elementary particles, and fly the ships in such a way as to mimic the behavior of these elementary particles. The ships also contain generators to produce the type of radiation elementary particles give off. Each ship has a staff of experts on the nature of our elementary particles. They do this so as to produce huge (by our standards) masses of substances with the chemical and physical characteristics of oxygen, carbon, etc. Shortly after they accomplish this, you go off on an expedition to that part of the universe, and discover the "oxygen," "carbon," etc. Unaware of its real nature, you set up a colony, using these "elements" to grow plants for food, provide "air" to breathe, etc. Since one's molecules are constantly being exchanged with the environment, you and other colonizers come in (a period of a few years) to be composed mainly of the "matter" made of the tiny people in space ships. Would you be any less capable of feeling pain, thinking, etc. just because the matter of which you are composed contains (and depends on for its characteristics) beings who themselves have a functional organization characteristic of sentient creatures? I think not. The basic electrochemical mechanisms by which the synapse operates are now fairly well understood. As far as is known, changes that do not affect these electrochemical mechanisms do not affect the operation of the brain, and do not affect mentality. The electrochemical mechanisms in your synapses would be unaffected by the change in your matter.[7]

It is interesting to compare the elementary-particle-people example with the homunculi-headed examples the chapter started with. A natural first guess about the source of our intuition that the initially described homunculi-headed simulations lack mentality is that they have *too much* internal mental structure. The little men may be sometimes bored, sometimes excited. We may even imagine that they deliberate about the best way to realize the given functional organization and make changes intended to give them more leisure time. But the example of the elementary-particle people just described suggests this first guess is wrong. What seems important is *how* the mentality of the parts contributes to the functioning of the whole.

There is one very noticeable difference between the elementary-particle-people example and the earlier homunculus examples. In the former, the change in you as you become homunculus-infested is not one that makes any difference to your psychological processing (i.e., information processing) or neurological processing but only to your microphysics. No techniques proper to human psychology or neurophysiology would reveal any difference in you. However, the homunculi-headed simulations described in the beginning of the chapter are not things to which neurophysiological theories true of us apply, and *if they are construed as Functional* (rather than Psychofunctional) simulations, they need not be things to which psychological (information-processing) theories true of us apply. This difference suggests that our intuitions are in part controlled by the not unreasonable view that our mental states depend on our having the psychology and/or neurophysiology we have. So something that differs markedly from us in both regards (recall that it is a Functional rather than Psychofunctional simulation) should not be assumed to have mentality just on the ground that it has been designed to be Functionally equivalent to us.

1.4   Is the Prima Facie Doubt Merely Prima Facie?

The Absent Qualia Argument rested on an appeal to the intuition that the homunculi-headed simulations lacked mentality, or at least qualia. I said that this intuition gave rise to prima facie doubt that functionalism is true. But intuitions unsupported by principled argument are hardly to be considered bedrock. Indeed, intuitions incompatible with well-supported theory (e.g., the pre-Copernican intuition that the earth does not move) thankfully soon disappear. Even fields like linguistics whose data consist mainly in intuitions often reject such intuitions as that the following sentences are ungrammatical (on theoretical grounds):

The horse raced past the barn fell.

The boy the girl the cat bit scratched died.

These sentences are in fact grammatical though hard to process.[8]

Appeal to intuitions when judging possession of mentality, however, is *especially* suspicious. *No physical mechanism seems very intuitively plausible as a seat of qualia, least of all a brain.* Is a hunk of quivering gray stuff more intuitively appropriate as a seat of qualia than a covey of little men? If not, perhaps there is a prima facie doubt about the qualia of brain-headed systems too?

However, there is a very important difference between brain-headed and homunculi-headed systems. Since we know that *we are brain-headed systems,* and that *we* have qualia, we know that brain-headed systems can have qualia. So even though we have no theory of qualia which explains how this is *possible,* we have overwhelming reason to disregard whatever prima facie doubt there is about the qualia of brain-headed systems. Of course, this makes my argument partly *empirical*—it depends on knowledge of what makes us tick. But since this is knowledge we in fact possess, dependence on this knowledge should not be regarded as a defect.[9]

There is another difference between us meatheads and the homunculi-heads: they are systems designed to mimic us, but we are not designed to mimic anything (here I rely on another empirical fact). This fact forestalls any attempt to argue on the basis of an inference to the best explanation for the qualia of homunculi-heads. The best explanation of the homunculi-heads' screams and winces is not their pains, but that they were designed to mimic our screams and winces.

Some people seem to feel that the complex and

subtle behavior of the homunculi-heads (behavior just as complex and subtle—even as "sensitive" to features of the environment, human and nonhuman, as your behavior) is itself sufficient reason to disregard the prima facie doubt that homunculi-heads have qualia. But this is just crude behaviorism.

My case against Functionalism depends on the following principle: if a doctrine has an absurd conclusion which there is no independent reason to believe, and if there is no way of explaining away the absurdity or showing it to be misleading or irrelevant, and if there is no good reason to believe the doctrine that leads to the absurdity in the first place, then don't accept the doctrine. I claim that there is no independent reason to believe in the mentality of the homunculi-head, and I know of no way of explaining away the absurdity of the conclusion that it has mentality (though of course, my argument is vulnerable to the introduction of such an explanation). The issue, then, is whether there is any good reason to believe Functionalism. One argument for Functionalism is that it is the best solution available to the mind–body problem. I think this is a bad form of argument, but since I also think that Psychofunctionalism is preferable to Functionalism (for reasons to be mentioned below), I'll postpone consideration of this form of argument to the discussion of Psychofunctionalism.

The only other argument for Functionalism that I know of is that Functional identities can be shown to be true on the basis of analyses of the meanings of mental terminology. According to this argument, Functional identities are to be justified in the way one might try to justify the claim that the state of being a bachelor is identical to the state of being an unmarried man. A similar argument appeals to commonsense platitudes about mental states instead of truths of meaning. Lewis says that Functional characterizations of mental states are in the province of "common sense psychology—folk science, rather than professional science" (Lewis, 1972, p. 250). (See also Shoemaker, 1975, and Armstrong, 1968. Armstrong equivocates on the analyticity issue. See Armstrong, 1968, pp. 84–85, and p. 90.) And he goes on to insist that Functional characterizations should "include only platitudes which are common knowledge among us—everyone knows them, everyone knows that everyone else knows them, and so on" (Lewis, 1972, p. 256). I shall talk mainly about the "platitude" version of the argument. The analyticity version is vulnerable to essentially the same considerations, as well as Quinean doubts about analyticity.

I am willing to concede, for the sake of argument, that it is possible to define any given mental-state term in terms of platitudes concerning other mental-state terms, input terms, and output terms. But this does not commit me to the type of definition of mental terms in which all mental terminology has been eliminated via Ramsification or some other device. It is simply a fallacy to suppose that if each mental term is definable in terms of the others (plus inputs and outputs), then each mental term is definable non-mentalistically. To see this, consider the example given earlier. Indeed, let's simplify matters by ignoring the inputs and outputs. Let's define pain as the cause of worry, and worry as the effect of pain. Even a person so benighted as to accept this, needn't accept a definition of pain as *the cause of something,* or a definition of worry as *the effect of something.* Lewis claims that it is analytic that pain is the occupant of a certain causal role. Even if he is right about a causal role, specified in part mentalistically, one cannot conclude that it is analytic that pain is the occupant of any causal role, non-mentalistically specified.

I don't see any decent argument for Functionalism based on platitudes or analyticity. Further, the conception of Functionalism as based on platitudes leads to trouble with cases that platitudes have nothing to say about. Recall the example of brains being removed for cleaning and rejuvenation, the connections between one's brain and one's body being maintained by radio while one goes about one's business. The process takes a few days, and when it is completed, the brain is reinserted in the body. Occasionally it may happen that a person's body is destroyed by an accident while the brain is being cleaned and rejuvenated. If hooked up to input sense organs (but not output organs) such a brain would exhibit *none* of the usual platitudinous connections between behavior and clusters of inputs and mental states. If, as seems plausible, such a brain could have almost all the same (narrow) mental states as we have (and since such a state of affairs could become typical), Functionalism is wrong.

It is instructive to compare the way Psychofunctionalism attempts to handle brains in bottles. According to Psychofunctionalism, what is to count as a system's inputs and outputs is an empirical question. Counting neural impulses as inputs and outputs would avoid the problems just sketched, since the brains in bottles and paralytics could have the right neural impulses even without bodily movements. Objection: There could be paralysis that affects the nervous system, and thus affects the neural impulses, so the problem which arises for Functionalism arises for Psychofunctionalism as well. Reply: Nervous system diseases can actually *change mentality,* e.g., they can render victims incapable of having pain. So it might actually be true that a widespread nervous system disease that caused intermittent paralysis rendered people incapable of certain mental states.

According to plausible versions of Psychofunctionalism, the job of deciding what neural processes should count as inputs and outputs is in part a matter of deciding *what malfunctions count as changes in mentality and what malfunctions count as changes in peripheral input and output connections.* Psychofunctionalism has a resource that Functionalism does not have, since Psychofunctionalism allows us to *adjust the line we draw between the inside and the outside of the organism so as to avoid problems of the sort discussed.* All versions of Functionalism go wrong in attempting to draw this line on the basis of only common-sense knowledge; "analyticity" versions of Functionalism go especially wrong in attempting to draw the line a priori.

Objection: Sydney Shoemaker suggests (in correspondence) that problems having to do with brains in vats of the sort I mentioned, can be handled using his notion of a "paradigmatically embodied person" (see Shoemaker, 1976). Paradigmatic embodiment involves having functioning sensory apparatus and considerable voluntary control of bodily movements. Shoemaker's suggestion is that we start with a functional characterization of a paradigmatically embodied person, saying, inter alia, what it is for a physical state to realize a given mental state in a paradigmatically embodied person. Then, the functional characterization could be extended to nonparadigmatically embodied persons by saying that a physical structure that is not a part of a paradigmatically embodied person will count as realizing mental states, if, without changing its internal structure and the sorts of relationships that hold between its states, it could be incorporated into a larger physical system that would be the body of a paradigmatically embodied person in which the states in question played the functional roles definitive of mental states of a paradigmatically embodied person. Shoemaker suggests that a brain in a vat can be viewed from this perspective, as a limiting case of an amputee—amputation of everything but the brain. For the brain can (in principle) be incorporated into a system so as to form a paradigmatically embodied person without changing the internal structure and state relations of the brain.

Reply: Shoemaker's suggestion is very promising, but it saves functionalism only by retreating from Functionalism to Psychofunctionalism. Obviously, nothing in prescientific common-sense wisdom about mentality tells us what can or cannot be paradigmatically embodied *without changing its internal structure and state relations* (unless 'state relations' means 'Functional state relations', in which case the question is begged). Indeed, the scientific issues involved in answering this question may well be very similar to the scientific issues involved in the Psychofunctionalist question about the difference between defects in or damage to input–output devices, as opposed to defects in or damage to central mechanisms. That is, the scientific task of drawing the Psychofunctionalist line between the inside and the outside of an organism may be pretty much the same as Shoemaker's task of drawing the line between what can and what cannot be paradigmatically embodied without changing its internal structure and state relations.

I shall briefly raise two additional problems for Functionalism. The first might be called the Problem of Differentiation: there are mental states that are different, but that do not differ with respect to platitudes. Consider different tastes or smells that have typical causes and effects, but whose typical causes and effects are not known or are not known to very many people. For example, tannin in wine produces a particular taste immediately recognizable to wine drinkers. As far as I know, there is no standard name or description (except "tannic") associated with this taste. The causal antecedents and consequents of this taste are not widely known, there are no platitudes about its typical causes and effects. Moreover, there are sensations that not only have no standard names but whose causes and effects are not yet well understood by anyone. Let A and B be two such (different) sensations. Neither platitudes nor truths of meaning can distinguish between A and B. Since the Functional description of a mental state is determined by the platitudes true of that state, and since A and B do not differ with respect to platitudes, Functionalists would be committed to identifying A and B with the same Functional state, and thus they would be committed to the claim that A = B, which is ex hypothesi false.

A second difficulty for Functionalism is that platitudes are often wrong. Let us call this problem the Problem of Truth. Lewis suggests, by way of dealing with this problem, that we specify the causal relations among mental states, inputs and ouputs, not by means of the conjunction of all the platitudes, but rather by "a cluster of them—a disjunction of conjunctions of *most* of them (that way it will not matter if a few are wrong.)" This move may exacerbate the problem of Differentiation, however, since there may be pairs of different mental states that are alike with respect to *most* platitudes.

2.0 Psychofunctionalism

In criticizing Functionalism, I appealed to the following principle: if a doctrine has an absurd conclusion which there is no independent reason to believe, and if there is no way of explaining away the absurdity or showing it to be misleading or irrelevant, and if there is no good reason to believe the doctrine that leads to the absurdity in the first place, then don't accept the doctrine. I said that there was no independent reason to believe that the homunculi-headed Functional simulation has any mental states. However, there *is* an independent reason to believe that the homunculi-headed *Psycho*functional simulation has mental states, namely that a Psychofunctional simulation of you would be Psychofunctionally equivalent to you, so any psychological theory true of you would be true of it too. What better reason could there be to attribute to it whatever mental states are in the domain of psychology?

This point shows that any Psychofunctional simulation of you shares your *non*-qualitative mental states. However, in the next section, I shall argue that there is nonetheless some doubt that it shares your qualitative mental states.

There is another way in which Psychofunctionalism may seem to escape the type of argument that I applied to Functionalism. Assuming, as I argued earlier, that Psychofunctionalism is preferable to Functionalism, we could mount an "inference to the best explanation" argument for Psychofunctionalism: "What *else* could mental states be if not Psychofunctional states?" For example, Putnam (1967) hypothesizes that (Psycho)functionalism is true and then argues persuasively that (Psycho)functionalism is a better hypothesis than behaviorism or materialism.

But this is a very dubious use of "inference to the best explanation." For what guarantee do we have that *there is* an answer to the question "What are mental states?" of the sort behaviorists, materialists, and functionalists have wanted? Moreover, inference to the best explanation cannot be applied when none of the available explanations is any good. In order for inference to the best explanation to be applicable, two conditions have to be satisfied: we must have reason to believe an explanation is *possible,* and at least one of the available explanations must be *minimally adequate.* Imagine someone arguing for one of the proposed so-

lutions to Newcomb's Problem on the ground that despite its fatal flaw it is the best of the proposed solutions. That would be a joke. But is the argument for functionalism any better? Behaviorism, materialism, and functionalism are not theories of mentality in the way Mendel's theory is a theory of heredity. Behaviorism, materialism, and functionalism (and dualism as well) are attempts to solve a problem: the mind–body problem. Of course, this is a problem which can hardly be guaranteed to have a solution. Further, each of the proposed solutions to the mind–body problem has serious difficulties, difficulties I for one am inclined to regard as fatal.

Thus far, I have not argued against Psychofunctionalism as applied to non-qualitative mental states such as beliefs and desires. But there is a strong case to be made against it, namely that it falls afoul of *chauvinism.* After all, creatures who are very different from us in their mental mechanics can still think and believe.

I will discuss this issue in more detail in Section 3.0. Now I want to pursue Psychofunctionalism as applied to qualia.

2.1 Are Qualia Psychofunctional States?

I began this paper by describing a homunculi-headed device and claiming there is prima facie doubt about whether it has any mental states at all, especially whether it has qualitative mental states like pains, itches, and sensations of red. The special doubt about qualia can perhaps be explicated by thinking about *inverted* qualia rather than *absent* qualia. It makes sense, or seems to make sense, to suppose that objects we both call green look to me the way objects we both call red look to you. It seems that we could be functionally equivalent even though the sensation fire hydrants evoke in you is qualitatively the same as the sensation grass evokes in me. Imagine an inverting lens which when placed in the eye of a subject results in exclamations like "Red things now look the way green things used to look, and vice versa." Imagine further, a pair of identical twins one of whom has the lenses inserted at birth. The twins grow up normally, and at age 21 are functionally equivalent. This situation offers at least some evidence that each's spectrum is inverted relative to the other's. (See Shoemaker, 1975, note 17, for a convincing description of intrapersonal spectrum inversion.) However, it is very hard to see how to make sense of the analogue of spectrum inversion with respect to nonqualitative states. Imagine a pair of persons one of whom believes that p is true and that q is false, while the other believes that q is true and that p is false. Could these persons be functionally equivalent? It is hard to see how they could.[10] Indeed, it is hard to see how two persons could have only this difference in beliefs and yet there be no possible circumstance in which this belief difference would reveal itself in different behavior. Qualia seem to be supervenient on functional organization in a way that beliefs are not.

There is another reason to firmly distinguish between qualitative and nonqualitative mental states in talking about functionalist theories: Psychofunctionalism avoids Functionalism's problems with nonqualitative states, e.g., propositional attitudes like beliefs and desires. But Psychofunctionalism may be no more able to handle qualitative states than is Functionalism. The reason is that qualia may well not be in the domain of psychology.

To see this, let us try to imagine what a homunculi-headed realization of human psychology would be like. Current psychological theorizing seems directed toward the description of information-flow relations among psychological mechanisms. The aim seems to be to decompose such mechanisms into psychologically primitive mechanisms, "black boxes" whose internal structure is in the domain of physiology rather than in the domain of psychology. (See Fodor, 1968b, Dennett, 1975, and Cummins, 1975; interesting objections are raised in Nagel, 1969.) For example, a near-primitive mechanism might be one that matches two items in a representational system and determines if they are tokens of the same type. Or the primitive mechanisms might be like those in a digital computer, e.g., they might be (a) *add 1 to a given register,* and (b) *subtract 1 from a given register, or if the register contains 0, go to the nth (indicated) instruction.* (These operations can be combined to accomplish any digital computer operation; see Minsky, 1967, p. 206.) Consider a computer whose machine-language code contains only two instructions corresponding to (a) and (b). If you ask how it multiplies or solves differential equations or makes up payrolls, you can be answered by being shown a program couched in terms of the two machine-language instructions. But if you ask how it adds 1 to a given register, the appropriate answer is given by a wiring diagram, not a program. The machine is hard-wired to add 1. When the instruction corresponding to (a) appears in a certain register, the contents of another register "automatically" change in a certain way. The computational structure of a computer is determined by a set of primitive operations and the ways nonprimitive operations are built up from them. Thus it does not matter to the computa-

tional structure of the computer whether the primitive mechanisms are realized by tube circuits, transistor circuits, or relays. Likewise, it does not matter to the psychology of a mental system whether its primitive mechanisms are realized by one or another neurological mechanism. Call a system a "realization of human psychology" if every psychological theory true of us is true of it. Consider a realization of human psychology whose primitive psychological operations are accomplished by little men, in the manner of the homunculi-headed simulations discussed. So, perhaps one little man produces items from a list, one by one, another compares these items with other representations to determine whether they match, etc.

Now there is a good reason for supposing this system has some mental states. Propositional attitudes are an example. Perhaps psychological theory will identify remembering that P with having "stored" a sentencelike object which expresses the proposition that P (Fodor, 1975). Then if one of the little men has put a certain sentencelike object in "storage," we may have reason for regarding the system as remembering that P. But unless having qualia is just a matter of having certain information processing (at best a controversial proposal— see later discussion), there is no such theoretical reason for regarding the system as having qualia. In short, there is perhaps as much doubt about the qualia of this homunculi-headed system as there was about the qualia of the homunculi-headed Functional simulation discussed early in the chapter.

But the system we are discussing is ex hypothesi something of which any true psychological theory is true. *So any doubt that it has qualia is a doubt that qualia are in the domain of psychology.*

It may be objected: "The Kind of psychology you have in mind is *cognitive* psychology, i.e., psychology of thought processes; and it is no wonder that qualia are not in the domain of *cognitive* psychology!" But I *do not* have cognitive psychology in mind, and if it sounds that way, this is easily explained: nothing we know about the psychological processes underlying our conscious mental life has anything to do with qualia. What passes for the "psychology" of sensation or pain, for example, is (a) physiology, (b) psychophysics (i.e., study of the mathematical functions relating stimulus variables and sensation variables, e.g., the intensity of sound as a function of the amplitude of the sound waves), or (c) a grabbag of descriptive studies (see Melzack, 1973, Ch. 2). Of these, only psychophysics could be construed as being about qualia per se. And it is obvious that psychophysics touches only the *functional* aspect of sensation, not its qualitative character. Psychophysical experiments done on you would have the same results if done on any system Psychofunctionally equivalent to you, even if it had inverted or absent qualia. If experimental results would be unchanged whether or not the experimental subjects have inverted or absent qualia, they can hardly be expected to cast light on the nature of qualia.

Indeed, on the basis of the kind of conceptual apparatus now available in psychology, I do not see **how** psychology in anything like its present incarnation *could* explain qualia. We cannot now conceive how psychology could explain qualia, though we *can* conceive how psychology could explain believing, desiring, hoping, etc. (see Fodor, 1975). That something is currently inconceivable is not a good reason to think it is impossible. Concepts could be developed tomorrow that would make what is now inconceivable conceivable. But all we have to go on is what we know, and on the basis of what we have to go on, it looks as if qualia are not in the domain of psychology.

It is no objection to the suggestion that qualia are not psychological entities that qualia are the very paradigm of something in the domain of psychology. As has often been pointed out, it is in part an empirical question what is in the domain of any particular branch of science. The liquidity of water turns out not to be explainable by chemistry, but rather by subatomic physics. Branches of science have at any given time a set of phenomena they seek to explain. But it can be discovered that some phenomenon which seemed central to a branch of science is actually in the purview of a different branch.

The Absent Qualia Argument exploits the possibility that the Functional or Psychofunctional state Functionalists or Psychofunctionalists would want to identify with pain can occur without any quale occurring. It also seems to be conceivable that the latter occur without the former. Indeed, there are facts that lend plausibility to this view. After frontal lobotomies, patients typically report that they still have pains, though the pains no longer bother them (Melzack, 1973, p. 95). These patients show all the "sensory" signs of pain (e.g., recognizing pin pricks as sharp), but they often have little or no desire to avoid "painful" stimuli.

One view suggested by these observations is that each pain is actually a *composite* state whose components are a quale and a Functional or Psychofunctional state.[11] Or what amounts to much the same idea, each pain is a quale playing a certain Functional or Psychofunctional role. If this view is right, it helps to explain how people can have believed such different theories of the nature of pain and other sensations: they have emphasized one component at the expense of the other.

Proponents of behaviorism and functionalism have had one component in mind; proponents of private ostensive definition have had the other in mind. Both approaches err in trying to give one account of something that has two components of quite different natures.

3.0   Chauvinism vs. Liberalism

It is natural to understand the psychological theories Psychofunctionalism adverts to as theories of *human* psychology. On Psychofunctionalism, so understood, it is impossible for a system to have beliefs, desires, etc., except insofar as psychological theories true of us are true of it. Psychofunctionalism (so understood) stipulates that Psychofunctional equivalence to us is necessary for mentality.

But even if Psychofunctional equivalence to us is a condition on our *recognition of mentality,* what reason is there to think it is a condition on mentality itself? Could there not be a wide variety of possible psychological processes that can underlie mentality, of which we instantiate only one type? Suppose we meet Martians and find that they are roughly Functionally (but not Psychofunctionally) equivalent to us. When we get to know Martians, we find them about as different from us as humans we know. We develop extensive cultural and commercial intercourse with them. We study each other's science and philosophy journals, go to each other's movies, read each other's novels, etc. Then Martian and Earthian psychologists compare notes, only to find that in underlying psychology, Martians and Earthians are very different. They soon agree that the difference can be described as follows. Think of humans and Martians as if they were products of conscious design. In any such design project, there will be various options. Some capacities can be built in (innate), others learned. The brain can be designed to accomplish tasks using as much memory capacity as necessary in order to minimize use of computation capacity; or, on the other hand, the designer could choose to conserve memory space and rely mainly on computation capacity. Inferences can be accomplished by systems which use a few axioms and many rules of inference, or, on the other hand, few rules and many axioms. Now imagine that what Martian and Earthian psychologists find when they compare notes is that Martians and Earthians differ as if they were the end products of maximally different design choices (compatible with rough Functional equivalence in adults). Should we reject our assumpton that Martians can enjoy our films, believe their own apparent scientific results, etc.? Should they "reject" their "assumption" that we "enjoy" their novels, "learn" from their textbooks, etc.? Perhaps I have not provided enough information to answer this question. After all, there may be many ways of filling in the description of the Martian–human differences in which it would be reasonable to suppose there simply is no fact of the matter, or even to suppose that the Martians do not deserve mental ascriptions. But surely there are many ways of filling in the description of the Martian–Earthian difference I sketched on which it would be perfectly clear that even if Martians behave differently from us on subtle psychological experiments, they nonetheless think, desire, enjoy, etc. To suppose otherwise would be crude human chauvinism. (Remember theories are chauvinist insofar as they falsely *deny* that systems have mental properties and liberal insofar as they falsely *attribute* mental properties.)

An obvious suggestion of a way out of this difficulty is to identify mental states with Psychofunctional states, taking the domain of psychology to include *all creatures with mentality,* including Martians. The suggestion is that we define "Psychofunctionalism" in terms of "universal" or "cross-system" psychology, rather than the human psychology I assumed earlier. Universal psychology, however, is a suspect enterprise. For how are we to decide what systems should be included in the *domain* of universal psychology? One possible way of deciding what systems have mentality, and are thus in the domain of universal psychology, would be to use some *other* developed theory of mentality, e.g., behaviorism or Functionalism. But such a procedure would be at least as ill-justified as the other theory used. Further, if Psychofunctionalism must presuppose some other theory of mind, we might just as well accept the other theory of mind instead.

Perhaps universal psychology will avoid this "domain" problem in the same way other branches of science avoid it or seek to avoid it. Other branches of science start with tentative domains based on intuitive and prescientific versions of the concepts the sciences are supposed to explicate. They then attempt to develop natural kinds in a way which allows the formulations of lawlike generalizations which apply to all or most of the entities in the prescientific domains. In the case of many branches of science—including biological and social sciences such as genetics and linguistics—the prescientific domain turned out to be suitable for the articulation of lawlike generalizations.

Now it may be that we shall be able to develop universal psychology in much the same way we develop Earthian psychology. We decide on an intuitive and prescientific basis what creatures to include in its domain, and work to develop natural kinds of psychological theory which apply to all or at least most of them. Perhaps the study of a wide range of organisms found on different worlds will one day lead to theories that determine truth conditions for the attribution of mental states like belief, desire, etc., applicable to systems which are pretheoretically quite different from us. Indeed, such cross-world psychology will no doubt require a whole new range of mentalistic concepts. Perhaps there will be families of concepts corresponding to belief, desire, etc., that is, a family of belief-like concepts, desirelike concepts, etc. If so, the universal psychology we develop shall, no doubt, be somewhat dependent on which new organisms we discover first. Even if universal psychology is in fact possible, however, there will certainly be many possible organisms whose mental status is indeterminate.

On the other hand, it may be that universal psychology is *not* possible. Perhaps life in the universe is such that we shall simply have no basis for reasonable decisions about what systems are in the domain of psychology and what systems are not.

If universal psychology *is* possible, the problem I have been raising vanishes. Universal–Psychofunctionalism avoids the liberalism of Functionalism and the chauvinism of human–Psychofunctionalism. But the question of whether universal psychology is possible is surely one which we have no way of answering now.

Here is a summary of the argument so far:

(1) Functionalism has the bizarre consequence that a homunculi-headed simulation of you has qualia. This puts the burden of proof on the Functionalist to give us some reason for believing his doctrine. However, the one argument for Functionalism in the literature is no good, and so Functionalism shows no sign of meeting the burden of proof.

(2) Psychofunctional simulations of us share whatever states are in the domain of psychology, so the Psychofunctional homunculi-head does not cast doubt on psychofunctional theories of cognitive states, but only on Psychofunctionalist theories of qualia, there being a doubt as to whether qualia are in the domain of psychology.

(3) Psychofunctionalist theories of mental states that are in the domain of psychology, however, are hopelessly chauvinist.

So one version of functionalism has problems with liberalism, the other has problems with chauvinism. As to qualia, if they are in the domain of psychology, then Psychofunctionalism with respect to qualia is just as chauvinist as Psychofunctionalism with respect to belief. On the other hand, if qualia are not in the domain of psychology, the Psychofunctionalist homunculi-head can be used against Psychofunctionalism with respect to qualia. For the only thing that shields Psychofunctionalism with respect to mental state S from the homunculi-head argument is that if you have S, then any Psychofunctional simulation of you must have S, because the correct theory of S applies to it just as well as to you.

3.1 The Problem of the Inputs and the Outputs

I have been supposing all along (as Psychofunctionalists often do—see Putnam, 1967) that inputs and outputs can be specified by neural impulse descriptions. But this is a chauvinist claim, since it precludes organisms without neurons (e.g., machines) from having functional descriptions. How can one avoid chauvinism with respect to specification of inputs and outputs? One way would be to characterize the inputs and outputs *only as* inputs and outputs. So the functional description of a person might list outputs by number: output$_1$, output$_2$, ... Then a system could be functionally equivalent to you if it had a set of states, inputs, and outputs causally related to one another in the way yours are, no matter what the states, inputs, and outputs were like. Indeed, though this approach violates the demand of some functionalists that inputs and outputs be physically specified, other functionalists—those who insist only that input and output descriptions be *nonmental*—may have had something like this in mind. This version of functionalism does not "tack down" functional descriptions at the periphery with relatively specific descriptions of inputs and outputs; rather, this version of functionalism treats inputs and outputs just as all versions of functionalism treat internal states. That is, this version specifies states, inputs, and outputs only by requiring that they *be* states, inputs, and outputs.

The trouble with this version of functionalism is that it is wildly liberal. Economic systems have inputs and outputs, e.g., influx and outflux of credits and debits. And economic systems also have a rich variety of internal states, e.g., having a rate of increase of GNP equal to double the Prime Rate. It does not seem impossible that a wealthy sheik could gain control of the economy of a small country, e.g., Bolivia, and manipulate its financial system to make it functionally equivalent to a person, e.g., himself. If this seems implausible, remember that the economic states, inputs, and outputs designated by the sheik to correspond to his mental state, inputs, and outputs need not be "natural" economic magnitudes. Our hypothetical sheik could pick *any* economic magnitudes at all—e.g., the fifth time derivative of the balance of payments. His only constraint is that the magnitudes he picks be economic, that their having such and such values be inputs, outputs, and states, and that he be able to set up a financial structure which can be made to fit the intended formal mold. The mapping from psychological magnitudes to economic magnitudes could be as bizarre as the sheik requires.

This version of functionalism is far too liberal and must therefore be rejected. If there are any fixed points when discussing the mind–body problem, one of them is that the economy of Bolivia could not have mental states, no matter how it is distorted by powerful hobbyists. Obviously, we must be more specific in our descriptions of inputs and outputs. The question is: is there a description of inputs and outputs specific enough to avoid liberalism, yet general enough to avoid chauvinism? I doubt that there is.

Every proposal for a description of inputs and outputs I have seen or thought of is guilty of either liberalism or chauvinism. Though this paper has concentrated on liberalism, chauvinism is the more pervasive problem. Consider standard Functional and Psychofunctional descriptons. Functionalists tend to specify inputs and outputs in the manner of behaviorists: outputs in terms of movements of arms and legs, sound emitted and the like; inputs in terms of light and sound falling on the eyes and ears. Such descriptions are blatantly *species-specific*. Humans have arms and legs, but snakes do not—and whether or not snakes have mentality, one can easily imagine snakelike creatures that do. Indeed, one can imagine creatures with all manner of input–output devices, e.g., creatures that communicate and manipulate by emitting strong magnetic fields. Of course, one could formulate Functional descriptions for each such species, and somewhere in disjunctive heaven there is a disjunctive description which will handle all species that ever actually exist in the universe (the description may be infinitely long). But even an appeal to such suspicious entities as infinite disjunctions will not bail out Functionalism, since even the amended view will not tell us what there is in common to pain-feeling organisms in virtue of which they all have pain. And it will not allow the ascription of pain to some hypothetical (but nonexistent) pain-feeling creatures. Further, these are just the grounds on which functionalists typically acerbically reject the disjunctive theories sometimes advanced by desperate physicalists. If functionalists suddenly smile on wildly disjunctive states to save themselves from chauvinism, they will have no way of defending themselves from physicalism.

Standard Psychofunctional descriptions of inputs and outputs are also species-specific (e.g., in terms of neural activity) and hence chauvinist as well.

The chauvinism of standard input–output descriptions is not hard to explain. The variety of possible intelligent life is enormous. Given any fairly specific descriptions of inputs and outputs, any high-school-age science-fiction buff will be able to describe a sapient sentient being whose inputs and outputs fail to satisfy that description.

I shall argue that *any physical description* of inputs and outputs (recall that many functionalists have insisted on physical descriptions) yields a version of functionalism that is inevitably chauvinist or liberal. Imagine yourself so badly burned in a fire that your optimal way of communicating with the outside world is via modulations of your EEG pattern in Morse Code. You find that thinking an exciting thought produces a pattern that your audience agrees to interpret as a dot, and a dull thought produces a "dash." Indeed, this fantasy is not so far from reality. According to a recent newspaper article (*Boston Globe,* March 21, 1976), "at UCLA scientists are working on the use of EEG to control machines. . . . A subject puts electrodes on his scalp, and thinks an object through a maze." The "reverse" process is also presumably possible: others communicating with you in Morse Code by producing bursts of electrical activity that affect your brain (e.g., causing a long or short afterimage). Alternatively, if the cerebroscopes that philosophers often fancy become a reality, your thoughts will be readable directly from your brain. Again, the reverse process also seems possible. In these cases, *the brain itself becomes an essential part of one's input and output devices.* This possibility has embarrassing consequences for functionalists. You will recall that functionalists pointed out that physicalism is false because a single mental state can be realized by an indefinitely large variety of physical states that have no necessary and sufficient physical characterization.[12] But if this functionalist point against physicalism is right, *the same point applies to inputs and outputs,* since the physical realization of mental states can serve as an essential part of the input and output devices. That is, on any sense of 'physical' in which the functionalist criticism of physicalism is correct, *there will be no physical characterization that applies to all and only mental systems' inputs and outputs.* Hence, any attempt to formulate a functional description with physical characterizations of inputs and outputs will inevitably either exclude some systems with mentality or include some systems without mentality. Hence, *functionalists cannot avoid both chauvinism and liberalism.*

So physical specifications of inputs and outputs will not do. Moreover, mental or "action" terminology (e.g., "punching the offending person") can not be used either, since to use such specifications of inputs or outputs would be to give up the functionalist program of characterizing mentality in nonmental terms. On the other hand, as you will recall, characterizing inputs and outputs simply *as* inputs and outputs is inevitably liberal. I, for one, do not see how there can be a vocabulary for describing inputs and outputs that avoids both liberalism and chauvinism. I do not claim that this is a conclusive argument against functionalism. Rather, like the functionalist argument against physicalism, it is best construed as a burden-of-proof argument. The functionalist says to the physicalist: "It is very hard to see how there could be a single physical characterization of the internal states of all and only creatures with mentality." I say to the functionalist: "It is very hard to see how there could be a single physical characterization of the inputs and outputs of all and only creatures with mentality." In both cases, enough has been said to make it the responsibility of those who think there could be such characterizations to sketch how they could be possible.[13]

NOTES

1. See Fodor, 1965, 1968a; Lewis, 1966, 1972; Putnam, 1966, 1967, 1970, 1975a; Armstrong, 1968; Locke, 1968; perhaps Sellars, 1968; perhaps Dennett, 1969, 1978b; Nelson, 1969, 1975 (but see also Nelson, 1976); Pitcher, 1971; Smart, 1971; Block and Fodor, 1972; Harman, 1973; Lycan, 1974; Grice, 1975; Shoemaker, 1975; Wiggins, 1975; Field, 1978.

2. The converse is also true.

3. Indeed, if one defines 'behaviorism' as the view that mental terms can be defined in nonmental terns, then functionalism *is* a version of behaviorism.

4. State type, not state token. Throughout the chapter, I shall mean by 'physicalism' the doctrine that says each distinct type of mental state is identical to a distinct type of physical state; for example, pain (the universal) is a physical state. Token physicalism, on the other hand, is the (weaker) doctrine that each particular datable pain is a state of some physical type or other. Functionalism shows that type physicalism is false, but it does not show that token physicalism is false.

By 'physicalism', I mean *first-order* physicalism, the doctrine that, e.g., the property of being in pain is a first-order (in the Russell–Whitehead sense) physical property. (A first-order property is one whose definition does not require quantification over properties; a second-order property is one whose definition requires quantification over first-order properties—and not other properties.) The claim that being in pain is a second-order physical property is actually a (physicalist) form of functionalism. See Putnam, 1970.

5. The basic idea for this example derives from Putnam (1967). I am indebted to many conversations with Hartry Field on the topic. Putnam's attempt to defend functionalism from the problem posed by such examples is discussed in Section 1.4 of this essay.

6. Shoemaker, 1975, argues (in reply to Block & Fodor, 1972) that absent qualia are logically impossible, that is, that it is logically impossible that two systems be in the same functional state yet one's state have and the other's state lack qualitative content. If Shoemaker is right, it is wrong to doubt whether the homunculi-headed system has qualia. I criticize Shoemaker's argument in Block, 1980.

7. Since there is a difference between the role of the little people in producing your functional organization in the situation just described and the role of the homunculi in the homunculi-headed simulations this chapter began with, presumably Putnam's condition could be reformulated to rule out the latter without ruling out the former. But this would be a most ad hoc maneuver.

8. Compare the first sentence with 'The fish eaten in Boston stank.' The reason it is hard to process is that 'raced' is naturally read as active rather than passive. See Fodor, Bever, & Garrett, 1974, p. 360. For a discussion of why the second sentence is grammatical, see Fodor & Garrett, 1967; Bever, 1970; and Fodor, Bever, & Garrett, 1974.

9. We often fail to be able to conceive of how something is possible because we lack the relevant theoretical concepts. For example, before the discovery of the mechanism of genetic duplication, Haldane argued persuasively that no conceivable physical mechanism could do the job. He was right. But instead of urging that scientists should develop ideas that would allow us to conceive of such a physical mechanism, he concluded that a nonphysical mechanism was involved. (I owe the example to Richard Boyd.)

10. Suppose a man who has good color vision mistakenly uses 'red' to denote green and 'green' to denote red. That is, he simply confuses the two words. Since his confusion is purely linguistic, though he says of a green thing that it is red, he does not believe that it is red, any more than a foreigner who has confused 'ashcan' with 'sandwich' believes people eat ashcans for lunch. Let us say that the person who has confused 'red' and 'green' in this way is a victim of Word Switching.

Now consider a different ailment: having red/green inverting lenses placed in your eyes without your knowledge. Let us say a victim of this ailment is a victim of Stimulus Switching. Like the victim of Word Switching, the victim of Stimulus Switching applied 'red' to green things and vice versa. But the victim of Stimulus Switching does have false color beliefs. If you show him a green patch he says and believes that it is red.

Now suppose that a victim of Stimulus Switching suddenly becomes a victim of Word Switching as well. (Suppose as well that he is a lifelong resident of a remote Arctic village, and has no standing beliefs to the effect that grass is green, firehydrants are red, and so forth.) He speaks normally, applying 'green' to green patches and 'red' to red patches. Indeed, he is functionally normal. But his beliefs are just as abnormal as they were before he became a victim of Word Switching. Before he confused the words 'red' and 'green', he applied 'red' to a green patch, and mistakenly believed the patch to be red. Now he (correctly) says 'red', but his belief is still wrong.

So two people can be functionally the same, yet have incompatible beliefs. Hence, the inverted qualia problem infects belief as well as qualia (though presumably only qualitative belief). This fact should be of concern not only to those who hold functional state identity theories of belief, but also to those who are attracted by Harman-style accounts of meaning as functional role. Our double victim—of Word and Stimulus Switching—is a counterexample to such accounts. For his word 'green' plays the normal role in his reasoning and inference, yet since in saying of something that it "is green," he expresses his belief that it is red, he uses 'green' with an abnormal meaning. I am indebted to Sylvain Bromberger for discussion of this issue.

11. The quale might be identified with a physico-chemical state. This view would comport with a suggestion Hilary Putnam made in the late '60s in his philosophy of mind seminar. See also Ch. 5 of Gunderson, 1971.

12. Functionalists emphasize that there is no interesting physical condition that is necessary for mentality, because they are interested in refuting the sort of mental-state/brain-state thesis that physicalists have typically preferred. The functionalist point is that no brain state could be necessary for mentality, since a mental system need not even have a brain. Of course, there are uninteresting physical necessary conditions for something being a pain, such as being temporally located. What makes such necessary conditions uninteresting is that they are not sufficient.

13. I am indebted to Sylvain Bromberger, Hartry Field, Jerry Fodor, David Hills, Paul Horwich, Bill Lycan, Georges Rey, and David Rosenthal for their detailed comments on one or another earlier draft of this paper. Beginning in the fall of 1975, parts of earlier versions were read at Tufts University, Princeton University, the University of North Carolina at Greensboro, and the State University of New York at Binghamton.

REFERENCES

Armstrong, D. A materialist theory of mind. London: Routledge & Kegan Paul, 1968.

Bever, T. The cognitive basis for linguistic structures. In J. R. Hayes (Ed.), Cognition and the development of language. New York: Wiley, 1970.

Block, N. Are absent qualia impossible? Philosophical Review, 1980, 89(2).

Block, N. & Fodor, J. What psychological states are not. Philosophical Review, 1972, 81, 159–81.

Chisholm, Roderick. Perceiving. Ithaca: Cornell University Press, 1957.

Cummins, R. Functional analysis. Journal of Philosophy, 1975, 72, 741–64.

Davidson, D. Mental events. In L. Swanson & J. W. Foster (Eds.), Experience and theory. Amherst, University of Massachusetts Press, 1970.

Dennett, D. Content and consciousness. London: Routledge & Kegan Paul, 1969.

Dennett, D. Why the law of effect won't go away. *Journal for the Theory of Social Behavior,* 1975, 5, 169–87.

Dennett, D. Why a computer can't feel pain. In *Synthese,* 1978a, 38, 3.

Dennett, D. *Brainstorms.* Montgomery, Vt.: Bradford, 1978b.

Feldman, F. Kripke's argument against materialism. *Philosophical Studies,* 1973; 416–19.

Fodor, J. Explanations in psychology. In M. Black (Ed.), *Philosophy in America.* London: Routledge & Kegan Paul, 1965.

Fodor, J. The appeal to tacit knowledge in psychological explanation. *Journal of Philosophy,* 1968b, 65, 627–40.

Fodor, J. Special sciences. *Synthese,* 1974, 28, 97–115.

Fodor, J. *The language of thought.* New York: Crowell, 1975.

Fodor, J., Bever, T., & Garrett, M. *The psychology of language.* New York: McGraw-Hill, 1974.

Fodor, J. & Garrett, M. Some syntactic determinants of sentential complexity. *Perception and Psychophysics,* 1967, 2, 289–96.

Geach, P. *Mental acts.* London: Routledge & Kegan Paul, 1957.

Gendron, B. On the relation of neurological and psychological theories: A critique of the hardware thesis. In R. C. Buck and R. S. Cohen (Eds.), *Boston studies in the philosophy of science VIII.* Dordrecht: Reidel, 1971.

Grice, H. P. Method in philosophical psychology (from the banal to the bizarre). *Proceedings and Addresses of the American Philosophical Association,* 1975.

Gunderson, K. *Mentality and machines.* Garden City: Doubleday Anchor, 1971.

Harman, G. *Thought.* Princeton: Princeton University Press, 1973.

Hempel, C. Reduction: Ontological and linguistic facets. In S. Morgenbesser, P. Suppes & M. White (Eds.), *Essays in honor of Ernest Nagel.* New York: St. Martin's Press, 1970.

Kalke, W. What is wrong with Fodor and Putnam's functionalism? *Nous,* 1969, 3, 83–93.

Kim, J. Phenomenal properties, psychophysical laws, and the identity theory. *The Monist,* 1972, 56(2), 177–92.

Lewis, D. Psychophysical and theoretical identifications. *Australasian Journal of Philosophy,* 1972, 50(3), 249–58.

Locke, D. *Myself and others.* Oxford: Oxford University Press, 1968.

Melzack, R. *The puzzle of pain.* New York: Basic Books, 1973.

Minsky, M. *Computation.* Englewood Cliffs: Prentice-Hall, 1967.

Mucciolo, L. F. The identity thesis and neuropsychology. *Nous,* 1974, 8, 327–42.

Nagel, T. The boundaries of inner space. *Journal of Philosophy,* 1969, 66, 452–58.

Nagel, T. Armstrong on the mind. *Philosophical Review,* 1970, 79, 394–403.

Nagel, T. Review of Dennett's *Content and consciousness. Journal of Philosophy,* 1972, 50, 220–34.

Nagel, T. What is it like to be a bat? *Philosophical Review,* 1974, 83, 435–50.

Nelson, R. J. Behaviorism is false. *Journal of Philosophy,* 1969, 66, 417–52.

Nelson, R. J. Behaviorism, finite automata & stimulus response theory. *Theory and Decision,* 1975, 6, 249–67.

Nelson, R. J. Mechanism, functionalism, and the identity theory. *Journal of Philosophy,* 1976, 73, 364–86.

Oppenheim, P. and Putnam, H. Unity of science as a working hypothesis. In H. Feigl, M. Scriven & G. Maxwell (Eds.), *Minnesota studies in the philosophy of science II.* Minneapolis: University of Minnesota Press, 1958.

Pitcher, G. *A theory of perception.* Princeton: Princeton University Press, 1971.

Putnam, H. Brains and behavior. 1963. Reprinted as are all Putnam's articles referred to here (except "On properties") in *Mind, language and reality: Philosophical papers,* Vol. 2). London: Cambridge University Press, 1975.

Putnam, H. The mental life of some machines. 1966.

Putnam, H. The nature of mental states (originally published under the title *Psychological Predicates*). 1967.

Putnam, H. On properties. In *Mathematics, matter and method: Philosophical papers,* Vol. 1. London: Cambridge University Press, 1970.

Putnam, H. Philosophy and our mental life. 1975a.

Putnam, H. The meaning of 'meaning'. 1975b.

Rorty, R. Functionalism, machines and incorrigibility. *Journal of Philosophy,* 1972, 69, 203–20.

Scriven, M. *Primary philosophy.* New York: McGraw-Hill, 1966.

Sellars, W. Empiricism and the philosophy of mind. In H. Feigl & M. Scriven (Eds.), *Minnesota studies in philosophy of science I.* Minneapolis: University of Minnesota Press, 1956.

Sellars, W. *Science and metaphysics.* (Ch. 6). London: Routledge & Kegan Paul, 1968.

Shoemaker, S. Functionalism and qualia. *Philosophical studies,* 1975, 27, 271–315.

Shoemaker, S. Embodiment and behavior. In A. Rorty (Ed.), *The identities of persons.* Berkeley: University of California Press, 1976.

Shallice, T. Dual functions of consciousness. *Psychological Review,* 1972, 79, 383–93.

Smart, J.J.C. Reports of immediate experience. *Synthese,* 1971, 22, 346–59.

Wiggins, D. Identity, designation, essentialism, and physicalism. *Philosophia,* 1975, 5, 1–30.

24

David Lewis

"Mad Pain and Martian Pain"

I

There might be a strange man who sometimes feels pain, just as we do, but whose pain differs greatly from ours in its causes and effects. Our pain is typically caused by cuts, burns, pressure, and the like; his is caused by moderate exercise on an empty stomach. Our pain is generally distracting; his turns his mind to mathematics, facilitating concentration on that but distracting him from anything else. Intense pain has no tendency whatever to cause him to groan or writhe, but does cause him to cross his legs and snap his fingers. He is not in the least motivated to prevent pain or to get rid of it. In short, he feels pain but his pain does not at all occupy the typical causal role of pain. He would doubtless seem to us to be some sort of madman, and that is what I shall call him, though of course the sort of madness I have imagined may bear little resemblance to the real thing.

I said there might be such a madman. I don't know how to prove that something is possible, but my opinion that this is a possible case seems pretty firm. If I want a credible theory of mind, I need a theory that does not deny the possibility of mad pain. I needn't mind conceding that perhaps the madman is not in pain in *quite* the same sense that the rest of us are, but there had better be some straightforward sense in which he and we are both in pain.

Also, there might be a Martian who sometimes feel pain, just as we do, but whose pain differs greatly from ours in its physical realization. His hydraulic mind contains nothing like our neurons. Rather, there are varying amounts of fluid in many inflatable cavities, and the inflation of any one of these cavities opens some valves and closes others. His mental plumbing pervades most of his body—in fact, all but the heat exchanger inside his head. When you pinch his skin you cause no firing of C-fibers—he has none—but, rather, you cause the inflation of many smallish cavities in his feet. When these cavities are inflated, he is in pain. And the effects of his pain are fitting: his thought and activity are disrupted, he groans and writhes, he is strongly motivated to stop you from pinching him and to see to it that you never do again. In short, he feels pain but lacks the bodily states that either are pain or else accompany it in us.

There might be such a Martian; this opinion too seems pretty firm. A credible theory of mind had better not deny the possibility of Martian pain. I needn't mind conceding that perhaps the Martian is not in pain in *quite* the same sense that we Earthlings are, but there had better be some straightforward sense in which he and we are both in pain.

II

A credible theory of mind needs to make a place both for mad pain and for Martian pain. Prima facie, it seems hard for a materialist theory to pass this twofold test. As philosophers, we would like to characterize pain a priori. (We might settle for less, but let's start by asking for all we want.) As mate-

"Mad Pain and Martian Pain," from *Readings in the Philosophy of Psychology*, vol. I, Ned Block, ed. Cambridge, Mass.: Harvard University Press, 1980, pp. 216–22; "Knowing What It's Like," from David Lewis, *Philosophical Papers*, vol. I. New York: Oxford University Press, 1983, pp. 130–32; it appeared there as the postscript to "Mad Pain and Martian Pain." Reprinted with permission of David Lewis.

rialists, we want to characterize pain as a physical phenomenon. We can speak of the place of pain in the causal network from stimuli to inner states to behavior. And we can speak of the physical processes that go on when there is pain and that take their place in that causal network. We seem to have no other resources but these. But the lesson of mad pain is that pain is associated only contingently with its causal role, while the lesson of Martian pain is that pain is connected only contingently with its physical realization. How can we characterize pain a priori in terms of causal role and physical realization, and yet respect both kinds of contingency?

A simple identity theory straightforwardly solves the problem of mad pain. It goes just as straightforwardly wrong about Martian pain. A simple behaviorism or functionalism goes the other way: right about the Martian, wrong about the madman. The theories that fail our twofold test so decisively are altogether too simple. (Perhaps they are too simple ever to have had adherents.) It seems that a theory that can pass our test will have to be a mixed theory. It will have to be able to tell us that the madman and the Martian are both in pain, but for different reasons: the madman because he is in the right physical state, the Martian because he is in a state rightly situated in the causal network.

Certainly we can cook up a mixed theory. Here's an easy recipe: First, find a theory to take care of the common man and the madman, disregarding the Martian—presumably an identity theory. Second, find a theory to take care of the common man and the Martian, disregarding the madman—presumably some sort of behaviorism or functionalism. Then disjoin the two: say that to be in pain is to be in pain either according to the first theory or according to the second. Alternatively, claim ambiguity: say that to be in pain in one sense is to be in pain according to the first theory, to be in pain in another sense is to be in pain according to the second theory.

This strategy seems desperate. One wonders why we should have a disjunctive or ambiguous concept of pain, if common men who suffer pain are always in pain according to both disjuncts or both disambiguations. It detracts from the credibility of a theory that it posits a useless complexity in our concept of pain—useless in application to the common man, at least, and therefore useless almost always.

I don't object to the strategy of claiming ambiguity. As you'll see, I shall defend a version of it. But it's not plausible to cook up an ambiguity *ad hoc* to account for the compossibility of mad pain

and Martian pain. It would be better to find a widespread sort of ambiguity, a sort we would believe in no matter what we thought about pain, and show that it will solve our problem. That is my plan.

III

A dozen years or so ago, D. M. Armstrong and I (independently) proposed a materialist theory of mind that joins claims of type–type psychophysical identity with a behaviorist or functionalist way of characterizing mental states such as pain.[1] I believe our theory passes the twofold test. Positing no ambiguity without independent reason, it provides natural senses in which both madman and Martian are in pain. It wriggles through between Scylla and Charybdis.

Our view is that the concept of pain, or indeed of any other experience or mental state, is the concept of a state that occupies a certain causal role, a state with certain typical causes and effects. It is the concept of a state apt for being caused by certain stimuli and apt for causing certain behavior. Or, better, of a state apt for being caused in certain ways by stimuli plus other mental states and apt for combining with certain other mental states to jointly cause certain behavior. It is the concept of a member of a system of states that together more or less realize the pattern of causal generalizations set forth in commonsense psychology. (That system may be characterized as a whole and its members characterized afterward by reference to their place in it.)

If the concept of pain is the concept of a state that occupies a certain causal role, then whatever state does occupy that role is pain. If the state of having neurons hooked up in a certain way and firing in a certain pattern is the state properly apt for causing and being caused, as we materialists think, then that neural state is pain. But the concept of pain is not the concept of that neural state. ("The concept of . . ." is an intensional functor.) The concept of pain, unlike the concept of that neural state which in fact is pain, would have applied to some different state if the relevant causal relations had been different. Pain might have not been pain. The occupant of the role might have not occupied it. Some other state might have occupied it instead. Something that is not pain might have been pain.

This is not to say, of course, that it might have been that pain was not pain and nonpain was pain; that is, that it might have been that the occupant of the role did not occupy it and some nonoccupant did. Compare: "The winner might have lost" (true) versus "It might have been that the winner lost" (false). No wording is entirely unambiguous, but I trust my meaning is clear.

In short, the concept of pain as Armstrong and I understand it is a *nonrigid* concept. Likewise the word "pain" is a nonrigid designator. It is a contingent matter what state the concept and the word apply to. It depends on what causes what. The same goes for the rest of our concepts and ordinary names of mental states.

Some need hear no more. The notion that mental concepts and names are nonrigid, wherefore what *is* pain might not have been, seems to them just self–evidently false.[2] I cannot tell why they think so. Bracketing my own theoretical commitments, I think I would have no opinion one way or the other. It's not that I don't care about shaping theory to respect naive opinion as well as can be, but in this case I have no naive opinion to respect. If I am not speaking to your condition, so be it.

If pain is identical to a certain neural state, the identity is contingent. Whether it holds is one of the things that varies from one possible world to another. But take care. I do not say that here we have two states, pain and some neural state, that are contingently identical, identical at this world but different at another. Since I'm serious about the identity, we have not two states but one. This one state, this neural state which is pain, is not contingently identical to itself. It does not differ from itself at any world. Nothing does.[3] What's true is, rather, that the concept and name of pain contingently apply to some neural state at this world, but do not apply to it at another. Similarly, it is a contingent truth that Bruce is our cat, but it's wrong to say that Bruce and our cat are contingently identical. Our cat Bruce is necessarily self-identical. What is contingent is that the nonrigid concept of being our cat applies to Bruce rather than to some other cat, or none.

IV

Nonrigidity might begin at home. All actualities are possibilities, so the variety of possibilities includes the variety of actualities. Though some possibilities are thoroughly otherworldly, others may be found on planets within range of our telescopes. One such planet is Mars.

If a nonrigid concept or name applies to different states in different possible cases, it should be no surprise if it also applies to different states in different actual cases. Nonrigidity is to logical space

as other relatives are to ordinary space. If the word "pain" designates one state at our actual world and another at a possible world where our counterparts have a different internal structure, then also it may designate one state on Earth and another on Mars. Or, better, since Martians may come here and we may go to Mars, it may designate one state for Earthlings and another for Martians.

We may say that some state *occupies a causal role for a population.* We may say this whether the population is situated entirely at our actual world, or partly at our actual world and partly at other worlds, or entirely at other worlds. If the concept of pain is the concept of a state that occupies that role, then we may say that a state *is pain for a population.* Then we may say that a certain pattern of firing of neurons is pain for the population of actual Earthlings and some but not all of our other-worldly counterparts, whereas the inflation of certain cavities in the feet is pain for the population of actual Martians and some of their otherworldly counterparts. Human pain is the state that occupies the role of pain for humans. Martian pain is the state that occupies the same role for Martians.

A state occupies a causal role for a population, and the concept of occupant of that role applies to it, if and only if, with few exceptions, whenever a member of that population is in that state, his being in that state has the sort of causes and effects given by the role.

The thing to say about Martian pain is that the Martian is in pain because he is in a state that occupies the causal role of pain for Martians, whereas we are in pain because we are in a state that occupies the role of pain for us.

V

Now, what of the madman? He is in pain, but he is not in a state that occupies the causal role of pain for him. He is in a state that occupies that role for most of us, but he is an exception. The causal role of a pattern of firing of neurons depends on one's circuit diagram, and he is hooked up wrong.

His state does not occupy the role of pain for a population comprising himself and his fellow madmen. But it does occupy that role for a more salient population—mankind at large. He is a man, albeit an exceptional one, and a member of that larger population.

We have allowed for exceptions. I spoke of the definitive syndrome of *typical* causes and effects. Armstrong spoke of a state *apt* for having certain causes and effects; that does not mean that it has them invariably. Again, I spoke of a system of states that *comes near* to realizing commonsense psychology. A state may therefore occupy a role for mankind even if it does not at all occupy that role for some mad minority of mankind.

The thing to say about mad pain is that the madman is in pain because he is in the state that occupies the causal role of pain for the population comprising all mankind. He is an exceptional member of that population. The state that occupies the role for the population does not occupy it for him.

VI

We may say that *X* is in pain *simpliciter* if and only if *X* is in the state that occupies the causal role of pain for the *appropriate* population. But what is the appropriate population? Perhaps (1) it should be *us;* after all, it's our concept and our word. On the other hand, if it's *X* we're talking about, perhaps (2) it should be a population that *X* himself belongs to, and (3) it should preferably be one in which *X* is not exceptional. Either way, (4) an appropriate population should be a natural kind—a species, perhaps.

If *X* is you or I—human and unexceptional— all four considerations pull together. The appropriate population consists of mankind as it actually is, extending into other worlds only to an extent that does not make the actual majority exceptional.

Since the four criteria agree in the case of the common man, which is the case we usually have in mind, there is no reason why we should have made up our minds about their relative importance in cases of conflict. It should be no surprise if ambiguity and uncertainty arise in such cases. Still, some cases do seem reasonably clear.

If *X* is our Martian, we are inclined to say that he is in pain when the cavities in his feet are inflated; and so says the theory, provided that criterion (1) is outweighed by the other three, so that the appropriate population is taken to be the species of Martians to which *X* belongs.

If *X* is our madman, we are inclined to say that he is in pain when he is in the state that occupies the role of pain for the rest of us; and so says the theory, provided that criterion (3) is outweighed by the other three, so that the appropriate population is taken to be mankind.

We might also consider the case of a mad Martian, related to other Martians as the madman is to the rest of us. If *X* is a mad Martian, I would be inclined to say that he is in pain when the cavities in his feet are inflated; and so says our theory, pro-

vided that criteria (2) and (4) together outweigh either (1) or (3) by itself.

Other cases are less clear-cut. Since the balance is less definitely in favor of one population or another, we may perceive the relativity to population by feeling genuinely undecided. Suppose the state that plays the role of pain for us plays instead the role of thirst for a certain small subpopulation of mankind, and vice versa. When one of them has the state that is pain for us and thirst for him, there may be genuine and irresolvable indecision about whether to call him pained or thirsty—that is, whether to think of him as a madman or as a Martian. Criterion (1) suggests calling his state pain and regarding him as an exception; criteria (2) and (3) suggest shifting to a subpopulation and calling his state thirst. Criterion (4) could go either way, since mankind and the exceptional subpopulation may both be natural kinds. (Perhaps it is relevant to ask whether membership in the subpopulation is hereditary.)

The interchange of pain and thirst parallels the traditional problem of inverted spectra. I have suggested that there is no determinate fact of the matter about whether the victim of interchange undergoes pain or thirst. I think this conclusion accords well with the fact that there seems to be no persuasive solution one way or the other to the old problem of inverted spectra. I would say that there is a good sense in which the alleged victim of inverted spectra sees red when he looks at grass: he is in a state that occupies the role of seeing red for mankind in general. And there is an equally good sense in which he sees green: he is in a state that occupies the role of seeing green for him, and for a small subpopulation of which he is an unexceptional member and which has some claim to be regarded as a natural kind. You are right to say either, though not in the same breath. Need more be said?

To sum up. Armstrong and I claim to give a schema that, if filled in, would characterize pain and other states a priori. If the causal facts are right, then also we characterize pain as a physical phenomenon. By allowing for exceptional members of a population, we associate pain only contingently with its causal role. Therefore we do not deny the possibility of mad pain, provided there is not too much of it. By allowing for variation from one population to another (actual or merely possible) we associate pain only contingently with its physical realization. Therefore we do not deny the possibility of Martian pain. If different ways of filling in the relativity to population may be said to yield different senses of the word "pain," then we plead ambiguity. The madman is in pain in one sense, or relative to one population. The Martian is in pain in another sense, or relative to another population. (So is the mad Martian.)

But we do not posit ambiguity *ad hoc*. The requisite flexibility is explained simply by supposing that we have not bothered to make up our minds about semantic niceties that would make no difference to any commonplace case. The ambiguity that arises in cases of inverted spectra and the like is simply one instance of a commonplace kind of ambiguity—a kind that may arise whenever we have tacit relativity and criteria of selection that sometimes fail to choose a definite *relatum*. It is the same kind of ambiguity that arises if someone speaks of relevant studies without making clear whether he means relevance to current affairs, to spiritual well-being, to understanding, or what.

VII

We have a place for commonplace pain, mad pain, Martian pain, and even mad Martian pain. But one case remains problematic. What about pain in a being who is mad, alien, and unique? Have we made a place for that? It seems not. Since he is mad, we may suppose that his alleged state of pain does not occupy the proper causal role for him. Since he is alien, we may also suppose that it does not occupy the proper role for us. And since he is unique, it does not occupy the proper role for others of his species. What is left?

(One thing that might be left is the population consisting of him and his unactualized counterparts at other worlds. If he went mad as a result of some improbable accident, perhaps we can say that he is in pain because he is in the state that occupies the role for most of his alternative possible selves; the state that would have occupied the role for him if he had developed in a more probable way. To make the problem as hard as possible, I must suppose that this solution is unavailable. He did *not* narrowly escape being so constituted that his present state would have occupied the role of pain.)

I think we cannot and need not solve this problem. Our only recourse is to deny that the case is possible. To stipulate that the being in this example is in pain was illegitimate. That seems credible enough. Admittedly, I might have thought offhand that the case was possible. No wonder; it merely combines elements of other cases that are possible. But I am willing to change my mind. Unlike my opinions about the possibility of mad pain and Martian pain, my naive opinions about this case are not firm enough to carry much weight.

VIII

Finally, I would like to try to preempt an objection. I can hear it said that I have been strangely silent about the very center of my topic. *What is it like* to be the madman, the Martian, the mad Martian, the victim of interchange of pain and thirst, or the being who is mad, alien, and unique? What is the *phenomenal character* of his state? If it *feels* to him like pain, then it *is* pain, whatever its causal role or physical nature. If not, it isn't. It's that simple!

Yes. It would indeed be a mistake to consider whether a state is pain while ignoring what it is like to have it. Fortunately, I have not made that mistake. Indeed, it is an impossible mistake to make. It is like the impossible mistake of considering whether a number is composite while ignoring the question of what factors it has.

Pain is a feeling.[4] Surely that is uncontroversial. To have pain and to feel pain are one and the same. For a state to be pain and for it to feel painful are likewise one and the same. A theory of what it is for a state to be pain is inescapably a theory of what it is like to be in that state, of how that state feels, of the phenomenal character of that state. Far from ignoring questions of how states feel in the odd cases we have been considering, I have been discussing nothing else! Only if you believe on independent grounds that considerations of causal role and physical realization have no bearing on whether a state is pain should you say that they have no bearing on how that state feels.

NOTES

This paper was presented at a conference on mind-body identity held at Rice University in April 1978. I am grateful to many friends, and especially to Patricia Kitcher, for valuable discussions of the topic.

1. D. M. Armstrong, *A Materialist Theory of the Mind* (London: Routledge, 1968); "The Nature of Mind," in C. V. Borst, ed., *The Mind/Brain Identity Theory* (London: Macmillan, 1970), pp. 67–97; "The Causal Theory of the Mind," *Neue Heft für Philosophie*, no. 11 (Vendenhoek & Ruprecht, 1977), pp. 82–95. David Lewis, "An Argument for the Identity Theory," *Journal of Philosophy* 63 (1966): 17–25, reprinted with additions in David M. Rosenthal, ed., *Materialism and the Mind-Body Problem* (Englewood Cliffs, N.J.: Prentice-Hall, 1971), pp. 162–171; "Review of *Art, Mind, and Religion*," *Journal of Philosophy* 66 (1969): 22–27, particularly pp. 23–25; "Psychophysical and Theoretical Identifications," *Australasian Journal of Philosophy* 50 (1972): 249–258; "Radical Interpretation," *Synthese* 23 (1974): 331–344.

2. For instance, see Saul A. Kripke, "Naming and Ne-

cessity," in Gilbert Harman and Donald Davidson, eds., *Semantics of Natural Language* (Dordrecht: Reidel, 1972), pp. 253–355, 763–769, particularly pp. 335–336. Note that the sort of identity theory that Kripke opposes by argument, rather than by appeal to self–evidence, is not the sort that Armstrong and I propose.

3. The closest we can come is to have something at one

world with twin counterparts at another. See my "Counterpart Theory and Quantified Modal Logic," *Journal of Philosophy* 65 (1968): 113–126. That possibility is irrelevant to the present case.

4. Occurrent pain, that is. Maybe a disposition that sometimes but not always causes occurrent pain might also be called "pain."

Postscript: "Knowing What It's Like"

The most formidable challenge to any sort of materialism and functionalism comes from the friend of phenomenal qualia. He says we leave out the phenomenal aspect of mental life: we forget that pain is a feeling, that there is something it is like to hold one's hand in a flame, that we are aware of something when we suffer pain, that we can recognize that something when it comes again. . . . So far, our proper reply is the one sketched in Section VIII: we deny none of that! We say to the friend of qualia that, beneath his tendentious jargon, he is just talking about pain and various aspects of its functional role. We have already said what we take pain to be; and we do not doubt that part of its causal role is to give rise to judgments that one is in pain, and part is to enable one to recognize pain (the same realizer of the same role) when it comes again.

So far, so good. But if he persists, the friend of qualia can succeed in escaping out unwelcome agreement; and when he does, we must reverse our strategy. Suppose he makes his case as follows.[1]

> You have not tasted Vegemite (a celebrated yeast-based condiment). So you do not know what it is like to taste Vegemite. And you never will, unless you taste Vegemite. (Or unless the same experience, or counterfeit traces of it, are somehow produced in you by artificial means.) No amount of the information whereof materialists and functionalists speak will help you at all. But if you taste Vegemite, *then* you will know what it is like. So you will have gained a sort of information that the materialists and functionalists overlook entirely. Call this *phenomenal information.* By *qualia* I mean the special subject matter of this phenomenal information.

Now we must turn eliminative. We dare not grant that there is a sort of information we overlook; or, in other words, that there are possibilities exactly alike in the respects we know of, yet different in some other way. That would be defeat. Neither can we credibly claim that lessons in physics, physiology, . . . could teach the inexperienced what it is

like to taste Vegemite. Our proper answer, I think, is that knowing what it's like is not the possession of information at all. It isn't the elimination of any hitherto open possibilities. Rather, knowing what it's like is the possession of abilities: abilities to recognize, abilities to imagine, abilities to predict one's behavior by means of imaginative experiments. (Someone who knows what it's like to taste Vegemite can easily and reliably predict whether he would eat a second helping of Vegemite ice cream.) Lessons cannot impart these abilities—who would have thought that they could? There is a state of knowing what it's like, sure enough. And Vegemite has a special power to produce that state. But phenomenal information and its special subject matter do not exist.[2]

Imagine a smart data bank. It can be told things, it can store the information it is given, it can reason with it, it can answer questions on the basis of its stored information. Now imagine a pattern-recognizing device that works as follows. When exposed to a pattern it makes a sort of template, which it then applied to patterns presented to it in future. Now imagine one device with both faculties, rather like a clock radio. There is no reason to think that any such device must have a third faculty: a faculty of making templates for patterns it has never been exposed to, using its stored information about these patterns. If it has a full description about a pattern but no template for it, it lacks an ability but it doesn't lack information. (Rather, it lacks information in usable form.) When it is shown the pattern it makes a template and gains abilities, but it gains no information. We might be rather like that.

NOTES

1. This is the "knowledge argument" of Frank Jackson, "Epiphenomenal Qualia," *Philosophical Quarterly* 32 (1982):

127–36. It appears also, in less purified form, in Thomas Nagel, "What Is It like To Be a Bat?" *Philosophical Review* 83 (1974): 435–50, and in Paul Meehl, "The Compleat Autocerebroscopist," in Paul Feyerabend and Grover Maxwell, eds., *Mind, Matter, and Method: Essays in Philosophy and Science in Honor of Herbert Feigl* (Minneapolis: University of Minnesota Press, 1966).

2. This defense against the knowledge argument is presented in detail in Laurence Nemirow, *Functionalism and the Subjective Quality of Experience* (Ph.D. dissertation, Stanford University, 1979), chapter 2; and more briefly in his review of Thomas Nagel's *Mortal Questions, Philosophical Review* 89 (1980): 473–77.

C. The Mental–Physical Contrast

25

Saul A. Kripke

from *Naming and Necessity*

Lecture I: January 20, 1970

* * * * *

This table is composed of molecules. Might it not have been composed of molecules? Certainly it was a scientific discovery of great moment that it was composed of molecules (or atoms). But could anything be this very object and not be composed of molecules? Certainly there is some feeling that the answer to that must be 'no'. At any rate, it's hard to imagine under what circumstances you would have this very object and find that it is not composed of molecules. A quite different question is whether it is in fact composed of molecules in the actual world and how we know this. (I will go into more detail about these questions about essence later on.)

I wish at this point to introduce something which I need in the methodology of discussing the theory of names that I'm talking about. We need the notion of 'identity across possible worlds' as it's usually and, as I think, somewhat misleadingly called,[1] to explicate one distinction that I want to

---

1. Misleadingly, because the phrase suggests that there is a special problem of 'transworld identification', that we cannot trivially stipulate whom or what we are talking about when we imagine another possible world. The term 'possible world' may also mislead; perhaps it suggests the 'foreign country' picture. I have sometimes used 'counterfactual situation' in the test; Michael Slote has suggested that 'possible state (or history) of the world' might be less misleading than 'possible world'. It is better still, to avoid confusion, not to say, 'In some possible world, Humphrey would have won' but rather, simply, 'Humphrey might have won'. The apparatus of possible words has (I hope) been very useful as far as the set-theoretic model-theory of quantified modal logic is concerned, but has encouraged philosophical pseudo-problems and misleading pictures.

make now. What's the difference between asking whether it's necessary that 9 is greater than 7 or whether it's necessary that the number of planets is greater than 7? Why does one show anything more about essence than the other? The answer to this might be intuitively 'Well, look, the number of planets might have been different from what it in fact is. It doesn't make any sense, though, to say that nine might have been different from what it in fact is'. Let's use some terms quasi-technically. Let's call something a *rigid designator* if in every possible world it designates the same object, a *non-rigid* or *accidental designator* if that is not the case. Of course we don't require that the objects exist in all possible worlds. Certainly Nixon might not have existed if his parents had not gotten married, in the normal course of things. When we think of a property as essential to an object we usually mean that it is true of that object in any case where it would have existed. A rigid designator of a necessary existent can be called *strongly rigid.*

One of the intuitive theses I will maintain in these talks is that *names* are rigid designators. Certainly they seem to satisfy the intuitive test mentioned above: although someone other than the U.S. President in 1970 might have been the U.S. President in 1970 (e.g., Humphrey might have), no one other than Nixon might have been Nixon. In the same way, a designator rigidly designates a certain object if it designates that object wherever the object exists; if, in addition, the object is a necessary existent, the designator can be called *strongly rigid.* For example, 'the President of the U.S. in 1970' designates a certain man, Nixon; but someone else (e.g., Humphrey) might have been the President in 1970, and Nixon might not have; so this designator is not rigid.

Excerpted by permission of the author and publishers from Saul A. Kripke, *Naming and Necessity*. Cambridge, Mass.: Harvard University Press, pp. 47–50, 75–76, 97–100, 127–32, 140–55. Copyright © 1972, 1980 by Saul A. Kripke.

In these lectures, I will argue, intuitively, that proper names are rigid designators, for although the man (Nixon) might not have been the President, it is not the case that he might not have been Nixon (though he might not have been *called* 'Nixon'). Those who have argued that to make sense of the notion of rigid designator, we must antecedently make sense of 'criteria of transworld identity' have precisely reversed the cart and the horse; it is *because* we can refer (rigidly) to Nixon, and stipulate that we are speaking of what might have happened to *him* (under certain circumstances), that 'transworld identifications' are unproblematic in such cases.[2]

The tendency to demand purely qualitative descriptions of counterfactual situations has many sources. One, perhaps, is the confusion of the epistemological and the metaphysical, between a prioricity and necessity. If someone identifies necessity with a prioricity, and thinks that objects are named by means of uniquely identifying properties, he may think that it is the properties used to identify the object which, being known about it *a priori*, must be used to identify it in all possible worlds, to find out which object is Nixon. As against this, I repeat. (1) Generally, things aren't 'found out' about a counterfactual situation, they are stipulated; (2) possible worlds need not be given purely qualitatively, as if we were looking at them through a telescope. And we will see shortly that the properties an object has in every counterfactual world have nothing to do with properties used to identify it in the actual world.[3]

* * * * *

Lecture II: January 22, 1970

* * * * *

Similarly, even if we define what a meter is by reference to the standard meter stick, it will be a contingent truth and not a necessary one that that particular stick is one meter long. If it had been stretched, it would have been longer than one meter. And that is because we use the term 'one meter' rigidly to designate a certain length. Even though we fix what length we are designating by an accidental property of that length, just as in the case of the name of the man we may pick the man out by an accidental property of the man, still we

use the name to designate that man or that length in all possible worlds. The property we use need not be one which is regarded in any way as necessary or essential. In the case of a yard, the original way this property was picked out was, I think, the distance when the arm of King Henry I of England was outstretched from the tip of his finger to his nose. If this was the length of a yard, it nevertheless will not be a necessary truth that the distance between the tip of his finger and his nose should be a yard. Maybe an accident might have happened to foreshorten his arm; that would be possible. And the reason that it's not a necessary truth is not that there might be other criteria in a 'cluster concept' of yardhood. Even a man who strictly uses King Henry's arm as his one standard of length can say, counterfactually, that if certain things had happened to the King, the exact distance between the end of one of his fingers and his nose would not have been exactly a yard. He need not be using a cluster as long as he uses the term 'yard' to pick out a certain fixed reference to be that length in all possible worlds.

* * * * *

I think the next topic I shall want to talk about is that of statements of identity. Are these necessary or contingent? The matter has been in some dispute in recent philosophy. First, everyone agrees that descriptions can be used to make contingent identity statements. If it is true that the man who invented bifocals was the first Postmaster General of the United States—that these were one and the same—it's contingently true. That is, it might have been the case that one man invented bifocals and another was the first Postmaster General of the United States. So certainly when you make identity statements using descriptions—when you say 'the x such that φx and the x such that ψx are one and the same'—that can be a contingent fact. But philosophers have been interested also in the question of identity statements between names. When we say 'Hesperus is Phosphorus' or 'Cicero is Tully', is what we are saying necessary or contingent? Further, they've been interested in another type of identity statement, which comes from scientific theory. We identify, for example, light with electromagnetic radiation between certain limits of wavelengths, or with a stream of photons. We identify heat with the motion of molecules; sound with a certain sort of wave disturbance in the air; and so on. Concerning such statements the following thesis is commonly held. First, that these are obviously contingent identities: we've found out that light is a stream of photons, but of course it might not have been a stream of photons. Heat is in fact the motion of molecules; we found that out,

2. Of course I don't imply that language contains a name for every object. Demonstratives can be used as rigid designators, and free variables can be used as rigid designators of unspecified objects. Of course when we specify a counterfactual situation, we do not describe the whole possible world, but only the portion which interests us.

3. See Lecture I, p. 53 (on Nixon), and Lecture II, pp. 74–7.

but heat might not have been the motion of molecules. Secondly, many philosophers feel damned lucky that these examples are around. Now, why? These philosophers, whose views are expounded in a vast literature, hold to a thesis called 'the identity thesis' with respect to some psychological concepts. They think, say, that pain is just a certain material state of the brain or of the body, or what have you—say the stimulation of C-fibers. (It doesn't matter what.) Some people have then objected, 'Well, look, there's perhaps a *correlation* between pain and these states of the body; but this must just be a contingent correlation between two different things, because it was an empirical discovery that this correlation ever held. Therefore, by "pain" we must mean something different from this state of the body or brain; and, therefore, they must be two different things.'

Then it's said, 'Ah, but you see, this is wrong! Everyone knows that there can be contingent identities.' First, as in the bifocals and Postmaster General case, which I have mentioned before. Second, in the case, believed closer to the present paradigm, of theoretical identifications, such as light and a stream of photons, or water and a certain compound of hydrogen and oxygen. These are all contingent identities. They might have been false. It's no surprise, therefore, that it can be true as a matter of contingent fact and not of any necessity that feeling pain, or seeing red, is just a certain state of the human body. Such psychophysical identifications can be contingent facts just as the other identities are contingent facts. And of course there are widespread motivations—ideological, or just not wanting to have the 'nomological dangler' of mysterious connections not accounted for by the laws of physics, one to one correlations between two different kinds of thing, material states, and things of an entirely different kind, which lead people to want to believe this thesis.

I guess the main thing I'll talk about first is identity statements between names. But I hold the following about the general case. First, that characteristic theoretical identifications like 'Heat is the motion of molecules', are not contingent truths but necessary truths, and here of course I don't mean just physically necessary, but necessary in the highest degree—whatever that means. (Physical necessity, *might* turn out to be necessity in the highest degree. But that's a question which I don't wish to prejudge. At least for this sort of example, it might be that when something's physically necessary, it always is necessary *tout court*.) Second, that the way in which these have turned out to be necessary truths does not seem to me to be a way in which the mind–brain identities could turn out to be either necessary or contingently true. So this

analogy has to go. It's hard to see what to put in its place. It's hard to see therefore how to avoid concluding that the two are actually different.

* * * * *

Lecture III: January 29, 1970

* * * * *

According to the view I advocate, then, terms for natural kinds are much closer to proper names than is ordinarily supposed. The old term 'common name' is thus quite appropriate for predicates marking out species or natural kinds, such as 'cow' or 'tiger'. My considerations apply also, however, to certain mass terms for natural kinds, such as 'gold', 'water', and the like. It is interesting to compare my views to those of Mill. Mill counts both predicates like 'cow', definite descriptions, and proper names as names. He says of 'singular' names that they are connotative if they are definite descriptions but non-connotative if they are proper names. On the other hand, Mill says that *all* 'general' names are connotative; such a predicate as 'human being' is defined as the conjunction of certain properties which give necessary and sufficient conditions for humanity—rationality, animality, and certain physical features.[1] The modern logical tradition, as represented by Frege and Russell, seems to hold that Mill was wrong about singular names, but right about general names. More recent philosophy has followed suit, except that, in the case of both proper names and natural kind terms, it often replaces the notion of defining properties by that of a cluster of properties, only some of which need to be satisfied in each particular case. My own view, on the other hand, regards Mill as more-or-less right about 'singular' names, but wrong about 'general' names. *Perhaps* some 'general' names ('foolish', 'fat', 'yellow') express properties.[2] In a significant sense, such general names as 'cow' and 'tiger' do not, unless *being a cow* counts trivially as a property. Certainly 'cow'

---

1. Mill, *A System of Logic.*

2. I am not going to give any criterion for what I mean by a 'pure property', or Fregean intension. It is hard to find unquestionable examples of what is meant. Yellowness certainly expresses a manifest physical property of an object and, relative to the discussion of gold above, can be regarded as a property in the required sense. Actually, however, it is not without a certain referential element of its own, for on the present view yellowness is picked out and rigidly designated as that external physical property of the object which we sense by means of the *visual impression of yellowness.* It does in this respect resemble the natural kind terms. The phenomenological quality of the sensation itself, on the other hand, can be regarded as a *quale* in some pure sense. Perhaps I am rather vague about these questions, but further precision seems unnecessary here.

and 'tiger' are *not* short for the conjunction of properties a dictionary would take to define them, as Mill thought. Whether science can discover empirically that certain properties are *necessary* of cows, or of tigers, is another question, which I answer affirmatively.

Let's consider how this applies to the types of identity statements expressing scientific discoveries that I talked about before—say, that water is H_2O. It certainly represents a discovery that water is H_2O. We identified water originally by its characteristic feel, appearance and perhaps taste, (though the taste may usually be due to the impurities). If there were a substance, even actually, which had a completely different atomic structure from that of water, but resembled water in these respects, would we say that some water wasn't H_2O? I think not. We would say instead that just as there is a fool's gold there could be a fool's water; a substance which, though having the properties by which we originally identified water, would not in fact be water. And this, I think, applies not only to the actual world but even when we talk about counterfactual situations. If there had been a substance, which was a fool's water, it would then be fool's water and not water. On the other hand if this substance can take another form—such as the polywater allegedly discovered in the Soviet Union, with very different identifying marks from that of what we now call water—it is a form of water because it is the same substance, even though it doesn't have the appearances by which we originally identified water.

Let's consider the statement 'Light is a stream of photons' or 'Heat is the motion of molecules'. By referring to light, of course, I mean something which we have some of in this room. When I refer to heat, I refer not to an internal sensation that someone may have, but to an external phenomenon which we perceive through the sense of feeling; it produces a characteristic sensation which we call the sensation of heat. Heat *is* the motion of molecules. We have also discovered that increasing heat corresponds to increasing motion of molecules, or, strictly speaking, increasing average kinetic energy of molecules. So temperature is identified with mean molecular kinetic energy. However I won't talk about temperature because there is the question of how the actual scale is to be set. It might just be set in terms of the mean molecular kinetic energy.[3] But what represents an interesting phenomenological discovery is that

when it's hotter the molecules are moving faster. We have also discovered about light that light is a stream of photons; alternatively it is a form of electromagnetic radiation. Originally we identified light by the characteristic internal visual impressions it can produce in us, that make us able to see. Heat, on the other hand, we originally identified by the characteristic effect on one aspect of our nerve endings or our sense of touch.

Imagine a situation in which human beings were blind or their eyes didn't work. They were unaffected by light. Would that have been a situation in which light did not exist? It seems to me that it would not. It would have been a situation in which our eyes were not sensitive to light. Some creatures may have eyes not sensitive to light. Among such creatures are unfortunately some people, of course; they are called 'blind'. Even if all people had had awful vestigial growths and just couldn't see a thing, the light might have been around; but it would not have been able to affect people's eyes in the proper way. So it seems to me that such a situation would be a situation in which there was light, but people could not see it. So, though we may identify light by the characteristic visual impressions it produces in us, this seems to be a good example of fixing a reference. We fix what light is by the fact that it is whatever, out in the world, affects our eyes in a certain way. But now, talking about counterfactual situations in which let's say, people were blind, we would not then say that since, in such situations, nothing could affect their eyes, light would not exist; rather we would say that that would be a situation in which light—the thing we have identified as that which in fact enables us to see—existed but did not manage to help us see due to some defect in us.

Perhaps we can imagine that, by some miracle, sound waves somehow enabled some creature to see. I mean, they gave him visual impressions just as we have, maybe exactly the same color sense. We can also imagine the same creature to be completely *insensitive* to light (photons). Who knows what subtle undreamt of possibilities there may be? Would we say that in such a possible world, it was sound which was light, that these wave motions in the air were light? It seems to me that, given our concept of light, we should describe the situation differently. It would be a situation in which certain creatures, maybe even those who were called 'people' and inhabited this planet, were sensitive not to light but to sound waves, sensitive to them in exactly the same way that we are sensitive to light. If this is so, once we have found out what light is, when we talk about other possible worlds we are talking about *this* phenomenon in the world, and not using 'light' as a phrase *synon-*

---

3. Of course, there is the question of the relation of the statistical mechanical notion of temperature to, for example, the thermodynamic notion. I wish to leave such questions aside in this discussion.

ymous with 'whatever gives us the visual impression—whatever helps us to see'; for there might have been light and it not helped us to see; and even something else might have helped us to see. The way we identified light *fixed a reference.*

And similarly for other such phrases, such as 'heat'. Here heat is something which we have identified (and fixed the reference of its name) by its giving a certain sensation, which we call 'the sensation of heat'. We don't have a special name for this sensation other than as a sensation of heat. It's interesting that the language is this way. Whereas you might suppose it, from what I am saying, to have been the other way. At any rate, we identify heat and are able to sense it by the fact that it produces in us a sensation of heat. It might here be so important to the concept that its reference is fixed in this way, that if someone else detects heat by some sort of instrument, but is unable to feel it, we might want to say, if we like, that the concept of heat is not the same even though the referent is the same.

Nevertheless, the term 'heat' doesn't *mean* 'whatever gives people these sensations'. For first, people might not have been sensitive to heat, and yet the heat still have existed in the external world. Secondly, let us suppose that somehow light rays, because of some difference in their nerve endings, *did* give them these sensations. It would not then be heat but light which gave people the sensation which we call the sensation of heat.

Can we then imagine a possible world in which heat was not molecular motion? We can imagine, of course, having discovered that it was not. It seems to me that any case which someone will think of, which he thinks at first is a case in which heat—contrary to what is actually the case—would have been something other than molecular motion, would actually be a case in which some creatures with different nerve endings from ours inhabit this planet (maybe even we, if it's a contingent fact about us that we have this particular neural structure), and in which these creatures were sensitive to that something else, say light, in such a way that they felt the same thing that we feel when we feel heat. But this is not a situation in which, say, light would have been heat, or even in which a stream of photons would have been heat, but a situation in which a stream of photons would have produced the characteristic sensations which *we* call 'sensations of heat'.

Similarly for many other such identifications, say, that lightning is electricity. Flashes of lightning are flashes of electricity. Lightning is an electrical discharge. We can imagine, of course, I suppose, other ways in which the sky might be illuminated at night with the same sort of flash without any electrical discharge being present. Here too, I am inclined to say, when we imagine this, we imagine something with all the visual appearances of lightning but which is not, in fact, lightning. One could be told: this appeared to be lightning but it was not. I suppose this might even happen now. Someone might, by a clever sort of apparatus, produce some phenomenon in the sky which would fool people into thinking that there was lightning even though in fact no lightning was present. And you wouldn't say that that phenomenon, because it looks like lightning, was in fact lighting. It was a different phenomenon from lightning, which is the phenomenon of an electrical discharge; and this is not lighting but just something that deceives us into thinking that there is lightning.

* * * * *

Usually, when a proper name is passed from link to link, the way the reference of the name is fixed is of little importance to us. It matters not at all that different speakers may fix the reference of the name in different ways, provided that they give it the same referent. The situation is probably not very different for species names, though the temptation to think that the metallurgist has a different concept of gold from the man who has never seen any may be somewhat greater. The interesting fact is that the way the reference is fixed seems overwhelmingly important to us in the case of sensed phenomena: a blind man who uses the term 'light', even though he uses it as a rigid designator for the very same phenomenon as we, seems to us to have lost a great deal, perhaps enough for us to declare that he has a different concept. ('Concept' here is used non-technically!) The fact that we identify light in a certain way seems to us to be *crucial,* even though it is not necessary; the intimate connection may create an *illusion* of necessity. I think that this observation, together with the remarks on property-identity above, may well be essential to an understanding of the traditional disputes over primary and secondary qualities.[4]

4. To understand this dispute, it is especially important to realize that yellowness is not a dispositional property, although it is related to a disposition. Many philosophers for want of any other theory of the meaning of the term 'yellow', have been inclined to regard it as expressing a dispositional property. At the same time, I suspect many have been bothered by the 'gut feeling' that yellowness is a manifest property, just as much 'right out there' as hardness or spherical shape. The proper account, on the present conception is, of course, that the reference of 'yellowness' is fixed by the description 'that (manifest) property of objects which causes them, under normal circumstances, to be seen as yellow (i.e., to be sensed by certain visual impressions)'; 'yellow', of course, does not *mean* 'tends to produce such and such a sensation'; if we had had different neutral structures, if atmospheric conditions had been dif-

Let us return to the question of theoretical identification. Theoretical identities, according to the conception I advocate, are generally identities involving two rigid designators and therefore are examples of the necessary *a posteriori*. Now in spite of the arguments I gave before for the distinction between necessary and *a priori* truth, the notion of *a posteriori* necessary truth may still be somewhat puzzling. Someone may well be inclined to argue as follows: 'You have admitted that heat might have turned out not to have been molecular motion, and that gold might have turned out not to have been the element with the atomic number 79. For that matter, you also have acknowledged that Elizabeth II might have turned out not to be the daughter of George VI, or even to originate in the particular sperm and egg we had thought, and this table might have turned out to be made from ice made from water from the Thames. I gather that Hesperus might have turned out not to be Phosphorus. What then can you mean when you say that such eventualities are impossible? If Hesperus might have *turned out* not to be Phosphorus, then Hesperus might not have *been* Phosphorus. And similarly for the other cases: if the world could have *turned out* otherwise, it could have *been* otherwise. To deny this fact is to deny the self-evident modal principle that what is entailed by a possibility must itself be possible. Nor can you evade the difficulty by declaring the "might have" of "might have turned out otherwise" to be merely epistemic, in the way that "Fermat's Last Theorem might turn out to be true and might turn out to be false" merely expresses our present ignorance, and "Arithmetic might have turned out to be complete" signals our former ignorance. In these mathematical cases, we may have been ignorant, but it was in fact mathematically impossible for the answer to turn out other than it did. Not so in your favorite cases of essence and of identity between two rigid designators: it re-

---

ferent, if we had been blind, and so on, then yellow objects would have done no such thing. If one tries to revise the definition of 'yellow' to be, 'tends to produce such and such visual impressions under circumstances C', then one will find that the specification of the circumstances C either circularly involves yellowness or plainly makes the alleged definition into a scientific discovery rather than a synonymy. If we take the 'fixes a reference' view, then it is up to the physical scientist to identify the property so marked out in any more fundamental physical terms that he wishes.

Some philosophers have argued that such terms as 'sensation of yellow', 'sensation of heat', 'sensation of pain', and the like, could not be in the language unless they were identifiable in terms of external observable phenomena, such as heat, yellowness, and associated human behavior. I think that this question is independent of any view argued in the text.

ally is logically possible that gold should have turned out to be a compound, and this table might really have turned out not to be made of wood, let alone of a given particular block of wood. The contrast with the mathematical case could not be greater and would not be alleviated even if, as you suggest, there may be mathematical truths which it is impossible to know *a priori*.'

Perhaps anyone who has caught the spirit of my previous remarks can give my answer himself, but there is a clarification of my previous discussion which is relevant here. The objector is correct when he argues that if I hold that this table could not have been made of ice, then I must also hold that it could not have turned out to be made of ice; *it could have turned out that P entails that P could have been the case.* What, then, does the intuition that the table might have turned out to have been made of ice or of anything else, that it might even have turned out not to be made of molecules, amount to? I think that it means simply that there might have been *a table* looking and feeling just like this one and placed in this very position in the room, which was in fact made of ice. In other words, I (or some conscious being) could have been *qualitatively in the same epistemic situation* that in fact obtains, I could have the same sensory evidence that I in fact have, about *a table* which was made of ice. The situation is thus akin to the one which inspired the counterpart theorists; when I speak of the possibility of the table turning out to be made of various things, I am speaking loosely. *This* table itself could not have had an origin different from the one it in fact had, but in a situation qualitatively identical to this one with respect to all the evidence I had in advance, the room could have contained *a table made of ice* in place of this one. Something like counterpart theory is thus applicable to the situation, but it applies only because we are *not* interested in what might have been true of *this particular* table, but in what might or might not be true of *a table* given certain evidence. It is precisely because it is *not* true that this table might have been made of ice from the Thames that we must turn here to qualitative descriptions and counterparts. To apply these notions to genuine *de re* modalities is, from the present standpoint, perverse.

The general answer to the objector can be stated, then, as follows: Any necessary truth, whether *a priori* or *a posteriori*, could not have turned out otherwise. In the case of some necessary *a posteriori* truths, however, we can say that under appropriate qualitatively identical evidential situations, an appropriate corresponding qualitative statement might have been false. The loose and inaccurate statement that gold might have turned out to be a compound should be replaced (roughly) by the statement that it is logically possible that there should have been a compound with all the properties originally known to hold of gold. The inaccurate statement that Hesperus might have turned out not to be Phosphorus should be replaced by the true contingency mentioned earlier in these lectures: two distinct bodies might have occupied, in the morning and the evening, respectively, the very positions actually occupied by Hesperus–Phosphorus–Venus.[5] The reason the example of Fermat's Last Theorem gives a different impression is that here no analogue suggests itself, except for the extremely general statement that, in the absence of proof or disproof, it is possible for *a mathematical conjecture* to be either true or false.

I have not given any general paradigm for the appropriate corresponding qualitative contingent statement. Since we are concerned with how things might have turned out otherwise, our general paradigm is to redescribe both the prior evidence and the statement qualitatively and claim that they are only contingently related. In the case of identities, using two rigid designators, such as the Hesperus–Phosphorus case above, there is a simpler paradigm which is often usable to at least approximately the same effect. Let 'R_1' and 'R_2' be the two rigid designators which flank the identity sign. Then '$R_1 = R_2$' is necessary if true. The references of 'R_1' and 'R_2', respectively, may well be fixed by nonrigid designators 'D_1' and 'D_2', in the Hesperus and Phosphorus cases these have the form 'the heavenly body in such-and-such position in the sky in the evening (morning)'. Then although '$R_1 = R_2$' is necessary, '$D_1 = D_2$' may well be contingent, and this is often what leads to the erroneous view that '$R_1 = R_2$' might have turned out otherwise.

I finally turn to an all too cursory discussion of the application of the foregoing considerations to the identity thesis. Identity theorists have been concerned with several distinct types of identifications: of a person with his body, of a particular sensation (or event or state of having the sensation) with a particular brain state (Jones's pain at 06:00 was his C-fiber stimulation at that time), and of

types of mental states with the corresponding *types* of physical states (pain is the stimulation of C-fibers). Each of these, and other types of identifications in the literature, present analytical problems, rightly raised by Cartesian critics, which cannot be avoided by a simple appeal to an alleged confusion of synonymy with identity. I should mention that there is of course no obvious bar, at least (I say cautiously) none which should occur to any intelligent thinker on a first reflection just before bedtime, to advocacy of some identity theses while doubting or denying others. For example, some philosophers have accepted the identity of particular sensations with particular brain states while denying the possibility of identities between mental and physical *types*.[6] I will concern myself primarily with the type–type identities, and the philosophers in question will thus be immune to much of the discussion; but I will mention the other kinds of identities briefly.

Descartes, and others following him, argued that a person or mind is distinct from his body, since the mind could exist without the body. He might equally well have argued the same conclusion from the premise that the body could have existed without the mind.[7] Now the one response which I regard as plainly inadmissible is the re-

---

5. Some of the statements I myself make above may be loose and inaccurate in this sense. If I say, 'Gold *might* turn out not to be an element,' I speak correctly; 'might' here is *epistemic* and expresses the fact that the evidence does not justify *a priori* (Cartesian) certainty that gold is an element. I am also strictly correct when I say that the elementhood of gold was discovered *a posteriori*. If I say, 'Gold *might have* turned out not to be an element,' I seem to mean this metaphysically and my statement is subject to the correction noted in the text.

6. Thomas Nagel and Donald Davidson are notable examples. Their views are very interesting, and I wish I could discuss them in further detail. It is doubtful that such philosophers wish to call themselves 'materialists'. Davidson, in particular, bases his case for his version of the identity theory on the supposed *impossibility* of correlating psychological properties with physical ones.

The argument against token–token identification and the text *does* apply to these views.

7. Of course, the body *does* exist without the mind and presumably without the person, when the body is a corpse. This consideration, if accepted, would already show that a person and his body are distinct. (See David Wiggins, 'On Being at the Same Place at the Same Time', *Philosophical Review,* Vol. 77 (1968), pp. 90–5.) Similarly, it can be argued that a statue is not the hunk of matter of which it is composed. In the latter case, however, one might say instead that the former is 'nothing over and above' the latter; and the same device might be tried for the relation of the person and the body. The difficulties in the text would not then arise in the same form, but analogous difficulties would appear. A theory that a person is nothing over and above his body in the way that a statue is nothing over and above the matter of which it is composed, would have to hold that (necessarily) a person exists if and only if his body exists and has a certain additional physical organization. Such a thesis would be subject to modal difficulties similar to those besetting the ordinary identity thesis, and the same would apply to suggested analogues replacing the identification of mental states with physical states. A further discussion of this matter must be left for another place. Another view which I will not discuss, although I have little tendency to accept it and am not even certain that it has been set out with genuine clarity, is the so-called functional state view of psychological concepts.

sponse which cheerfully accepts the Cartesian premise while denying the Cartesian conclusion. Let 'Descartes' be a name, or rigid designator, of a certain person, and let 'B' be a rigid designator of his body. Then if Descartes were indeed identical to B, the supposed identity, being an identity between two rigid designators, would be necessary, and Descartes could not exist without B and B could not exist without Descartes. The case is not at all comparable to the alleged analogue, the identity of the first Postmaster General with the inventor of bifocals. True, this identity obtains despite the fact that there could have been a first Postmaster General even though bifocals had never been invented. The reason is that 'the inventor of bifocals' is not a rigid designator; a world in which no one invented bifocals is not *ipso facto* a world in which Franklin did not exist. The alleged analogy therefore collapses; a philosopher who wishes to refute the Cartesian conclusion must refute the Cartesian premise, and the latter task is not trivial.

Let 'A' name a particular pain sensation, and let 'B' name the corresponding brain state, or the brain state some identity theorist wishes to identify with A. *Prima facie*, it would seem that it is at least logically possible that B should have existed (Jones's brain could have been in exactly that state at the time in question) without Jones feeling any pain at all, and thus without the presence of A. Once again, the identity theorist cannot admit the possibility cheerfully and proceed from there; consistency, and the principle of the necessity of identities using rigid designators, disallows any such course. If A and B were identical, the identity would have to be necessary. The difficulty can hardly be evaded by arguing that although B could not exist without A, *being a pain* is merely a contingent property of A, and that therefore the presence of B without pain does not imply the presence of B without A. Can any case of essence be more obvious than the fact that *being a pain* is a necessary property of each pain? The identity theorist who wishes to adopt the strategy in question must even argue that *being a sensation* is a contingent property of A, for *prima facie* it would seem logically possible that B could exist without any sensation with which it might plausibly be identified. Consider a particular pain, or other sensation, that you once had. Do you find it at all plausible that *that very sensation* could have existed without being a sensation, the way a certain inventor (Franklin) could have existed without being an inventor?

I mention this strategy because it seems to me to be adopted by a large number of identity theorists. These theorists, believing as they do that the supposed identity of a brain state with the corre-

sponding mental state is to be analyzed on the paradigm of the contingent identity of Benjamin Franklin with the inventor of bifocals, realize that just as his contingent activity made Benjamin Franklin into the inventor of bifocals, so some contingent property of the brain state must make it into a pain. Generally they wish this property to be one statable in physical or at least 'topic-neutral' language, so that the materialist cannot be accused of positing irreducible nonphysical properties. A typical view is that *being a pain,* as a property of a physical state, is to be analyzed in terms of the 'causal role' of the state,[8] in terms of the characteristic stimuli (e.g., pinpricks) which cause it and the characteristic behavior it causes. I will not go into the details of such analyses, even though I usually find them faulty on specific grounds in addition to the general modal considerations I argue here. All I need to observe here is that the 'causal role' of the physical state is regarded by the theorists in question as a contingent property of the state, and thus it is supposed to be a contingent property of the state that it is a mental state at all, let alone that it is something as specific as a pain. To repeat, this notion seems to me self-evidently absurd. It amounts to the view that the *very pain I now have* could have existed without being a mental state at all.

I have not discussed the converse problem, which is closer to the original Cartesian consideration—namely, that just as it seems that the brain state could have existed without any pain, so it seems that the pain could have existed without the corresponding brain state. Note that *being a brain state* is evidently an essential property of B (the brain state). Indeed, even more is true: not only being a brain state, but even being a brain state of a specific type is an essential property of B. The configuration of brain cells whose presence at a given time constitutes the presence of B at that time is essential to B, and in its absence B would not have existed. Thus someone who wishes to claim that the brain state and the pain are identical must argue that the pain A could not have existed without a quite specific type of configuration of molecules. If $A = B$, then the identity of A with B is necessary, and any essential property of one must be an essential property of the other. Someone who wishes to maintain an identity thesis cannot simply *accept* the Cartesian intuitions that A can exist without B, that B can exist without A,

8. For example, David Armstrong, *A Materialist Theory of the Mind,* London and New York, 1968, see the discussion review by Thomas Nagel, *Philosophical Review* 79 (1970), pp. 394–403; and David Lewis, 'An Argument for the Identity Theory', *The Journal of Philosophy,* pp. 17–25.

that the correlative presence of anything with mental properties is merely contingent to *B*, and that the correlative presence of any specific physical properties is merely contingent to *A*. He must explain these intuitions away, showing how they are illusory. This task may not be impossible; we have seen above how some things which appear to be contingent turn out, on closer examination, to be necessary. The task, however, is obviously not child's play, and we shall see below how difficult it is.

The final kind of identity, the one which I said would get the closest attention, is the type–type sort of identity exemplified by the identification of pain with the stimulation of C-fibers. These identifications are supposed to be analogous with such scientific type–type identifications as the identity of heat with molecular motion, of water with hydrogen hydroxide, and the like. Let us consider, as an example, the analogy supposed to hold between the materialist identification and that of heat with molecular motion; both identifications identify two types of phenomena. The usual view holds that the identification of heat with molecular motion and of pain with the stimulation of C-fibers are both contingent. We have seen above that since 'heat' and 'molecular motion' are both rigid designators, the identification of the phenomena they name is necessary. What about 'pain' and 'C-fiber stimulation'? It should be clear from the previous discussion that 'pain' is a rigid designator of the type, or phenomenon, it designates: if something is a pain it is essentially so, and it seems absurd to suppose that pain could have been some phenomenon other than the one it is. The same holds for the term 'C-fiber stimulation', provided that 'C-fibers' is a rigid designator, as I will suppose here. (The supposition is somewhat risky, since I know virtually nothing about C-fibers, except that the stimulation of them is said to be correlated with pain.[9] The point is unimportant; if 'C-fibers' is not

a rigid designator, simply replace it by one which is, or suppose it used as a rigid designator in the present context.) Thus the identity of pain with the stimulation of C-fibers, if true, must be *necessary*.

So far the analogy between the identification of heat with molecular motion and pain with the stimulation of C-fibers has not failed; it has merely turned out to be the opposite of what is usually thought—both, if true, must be necessary. This means that the identity theorist is committed to the view that there could not be a C-fiber stimulation which was not a pain nor a pain which was not a C-fiber stimulation. These consequences are certainly surprising and counterintuitive, but let us not dismiss the identity theorist too quickly. Can he perhaps show that the apparent possibility of pain not having turned out to be C-fiber stimulation, or of there being an instance of one of the phenomena which is not an instance of the other, is an illusion of the same sort as the illusion that water might not have been hydrogen hydroxide, or that heat might not have been molecular motion? If so, he will have rebutted the Cartesian, not, as in the conventional analysis, by accepting his premise while exposing the fallacy of his argument, but rather by the reverse—while the Cartesian argument, given its premise of the contingency of the identification, is granted to yield its conclusion, the premise is to be exposed as superficially plausible but false.

Now I do not think it likely that the identity theorist will succeed in such an endeavor. I want to argue that, at least, the case cannot be interpreted as analogous to that of scientific identification of the usual sort, as exemplified by the identity of heat and molecular motion. What was the strategy used above to handle the apparent contingency of certain cases of the necessary *a posteriori*? The strategy was to argue that although the statement itself is necessary, someone could, *qualitatively* speaking, be in the same epistemic situation as the original, and in such a situation a *qualitatively* analogous statement could be false. In the case of identities between two rigid designators, the strategy can be approximated by a simpler one: Consider how the references of the designators are determined; if these coincide only contingently, it is this fact which gives the original statement its illusion of contingency. In the case of heat and molecular motion, the way these two paradigms work out is simple. When someone says, inaccurately, that heat might have turned out not to be molec-

9. I have been surprised to find that at least one able listener took my use of such terms as 'correlated with', 'corresponding to', and the like as already begging the question against the identity thesis. The identity thesis, so he said, is not the thesis that pains and brain states are correlated, but rather that they are identical. Thus my entire discussion presupposes the anti-materialist position that I set out to prove. Although I was surprised to hear an objection which concedes so little intelligence to the argument, I have tried especially to avoid the term 'correlated' which seems to give rise to the objection. Nevertheless, to obviate misunderstanding, I shall explain my usage. Assuming, at least *arguendo,* that scientific discoveries have turned out so as not to refute materialism from the beginning, both the dualist and the identity theorist agree that there is a correlation or correspondence between mental states and physical states. The dualist holds that the 'correlation' relation in question is irreflexive; the identity theorist holds that it is simply

a special case of the identity relation. Such terms as 'correlation' and 'correspondence' can be used neutrally without prejudging which side is correct.

ular motion, what is true in what he says is that someone could have sensed a phenomenon in the same way we sense heat, that is, feels it by means of its production of the sensation we call 'the sensation of heat' (call it 'S'), even though that phenomenon was not molecular motion. He means, additionally, that the planet might have been inhabited by creatues who did not get S when they were in the presence of molecular motion, though perhaps getting it in the presence of something else. Such creatures would be, in some qualitative sense, in the same epistemic situation as we are, they could use a rigid designator for the phenomenon that causes sensation S in them (the rigid designator could even be 'heat'), yet it would not be molecular motion (and therefore not heat!), which was causing the sensation.

Now can something be said analogously to explain away the feeling that the identity of pain and the stimulation of C-fibers, if it is a scientific discovery, could have turned out otherwise? I do not see that such an analogy is possible. In the case of the apparent possibility that molecular motion might have existed in the absence of heat, what seemed really possible is that molecular motion should have existed without being *felt as heat,* that is, it might have existed without producing the sensation S, the sensation of heat. In the appropriate sentient beings is it analogously possible that a stimulation of C-fibers should have existed without being felt as pain? If this is possible, then the stimulation of C-fibers can itself exist without pain, since for it to exist without being *felt as pain* is for it to exist without there *being any* pain. Such a situation would be in flat out contradiction with the supposed necessary identity of pain and the corresponding physical state, and the analogue holds for any physical state which might be identified with a corresponding mental state. The trouble is that the identity theorist does not hold that the physical state merely *produces* the mental state, rather he wishes the two to be identical and thus *a fortiori* necessarily co-occurrent. In the case of molecular motion and heat there is something, namely, the sensation of heat, which is an intermediary between the external phenomenon and the observer. In the mental–physical case no such intermediary is possible, since here the physical phenomenon is supposed to be identical with the internal phenomenon itself. Someone can be in the same epistemic situation as he would be if there were heat, even in the absence of heat, simply by feeling the sensation of heat; and even in the presence of heat, he can have the same evidence as he would have in the absence of heat simply by lacking the sensation S. No such possibility exists in the case of pain and other mental phenomena.

To be in the same epistemic situation that would obtain if one had a pain *is* to have a pain; to be in the same epistemic situation that would obtain in the absence of a pain *is* not to have a pain. The apparent contingency of the connection between the physical state and the corresponding brain state thus cannot be explained by some sort of qualitative analogue as in the case of heat.

We have just analyzed the situation in terms of the notion of a qualitatively identical epistemic situation. The trouble is that the notion of an epistemic situation qualitatively identical to one in which the observer had a sensation S simply *is* one in which the observer had that sensation. The same point can be made in terms of the notion of what picks out the reference of a rigid designator. In the case of the identity of heat with molecular motion the important consideration was that although 'heat' is a rigid designator, the reference of that designator was determined by an accidental property of the referent, namely the property of producing in us the sensation S. It is thus possible that a phenomenon should have been rigidly designated in the same way as a phenomenon of heat, with its reference also picked out by means of the sensation S, without that phenomenon being heat and therefore without its being molecular motion. Pain, on the other hand, is not picked out by one of its accidental properties; rather it is picked out by the property of being pain itself, by its immediate phenomenological quality. Thus pain, unlike heat, is not only rigidly designated by 'pain' but the reference of the designator is determined by an essential property of the referent. Thus it is not possible to say that although pain is necessarily identical with a certain physical state, a certain phenomenon can be picked out in the same way we pick out pain without being correlated with that physical state. If any phenomenon is picked out in exactly the same way that we pick out pain, then that phenomenon *is* pain.

Perhaps the same point can be made more vivid without such specific reference to the technical apparatus in these lectures. Suppose we imagine God creating the world; what does He need to do to make the identity of heat and molecular motion obtain? Here it would seem that all He needs to do is to create the heat, that is, the molecular motion itself. If the air molecules on this earth are sufficiently agitated, if there is a burning fire, then the earth will be hot even if there are no observers to see it. God created light (and thus created streams of photons, according to present scientific doctrine) before He created human and animal observers; and the same presumably holds for heat. How then does it appear to us that the identity of molecular motion with heat is a substantive scientific fact, that the mere creation of molecular motion still leaves God with the additional task of making molecular motion into heat? This feeling is indeed illusory, but what *is* a substantive task for the Deity is the task of making molecular motion felt as heat. To do this He must create some sentient beings to insure that the molecular motion produces the sensation *S* in them. Only after he has done this will there be beings who can learn that the sentence 'Heat is the motion of molecules' expresses an *a posteriori* truth in precisely the same way that we do.

What about the case of the stimulation of C-fibers? To create this phenomenon, it would seem that God need only create beings with C-fibers capable of the appropriate type of physical stimulation; whether the beings are conscious or not is irrelevant here. It would seem, though, that to make the C-fiber stimulation correspond to pain, or be felt as pain, God must do something in addition to the mere creation of the C-fiber stimulation; He must let the creatures feel the C-fiber stimulation as *pain,* and not as a tickle, or as warmth, or as nothing, as apparently would also have been within His powers. If these things in fact are within His powers, the relation between the pain God creates and the stimulation of C-fibers cannot be identity. For if so, the stimulation could exist without the pain; and since 'pain' and 'C-fiber stimulation' are rigid, this fact implies that the relation between the two phenomena is not that of identity. God had to do some work, in addition to making the man himself, to make a certain man be the inventor of bifocals; the man could well exist without inventing any such thing. The same cannot be said for pain; if the phenomenon exists at all, no further work should be required to make it into pain.

In sum, the correspondence between a brain state and a mental state seems to have a certain obvious element of contingency. We have seen that identity is not a relation which can hold contingently between objects. Therefore, if the identity thesis were correct, the element of contingency would not lie in the relation between the mental and physical states. It cannot lie, as in the case of heat and molecular motion, in the relation between the phenomenon (= heat = molecular motion) and the way it is felt or appears (sensation *S*), since in the case of mental phenomena there is no 'appearance' beyond the mental phenomenon itself.

Here I have been emphasizing the possibility, or apparent possibility, of a physical state without the corresponding mental state. The reverse possibility, the mental state (pain) without the physical state (C-fiber stimulation) also presents problems for the identity theorists which cannot be resolved by appeal to the analogy of heat and molecular motion.

I have discussed similar problems more briefly for views equating the self with the body, and particular mental events with particular physical events, without discussing possible countermoves in the same detail as in the type–type case. Suffice it to say that I suspect that the considerations given indicate that the theorist who wishes to identify various particular mental and physical events will have to face problems fairly similar to those of the type–type theorist; he too will be unable to appeal to the standard alleged analogues.

That the usual moves and analogies are not available to solve the problems of the identity theorist is, of course, no proof that no moves are available. I certainly cannot discuss all the possibilities here. I suspect, however, that the present considerations tell heavily against the usual forms of materialism. Materialism, I think, must hold that a physical description of the world is a *complete* description of it, that any mental facts are 'ontologically dependent' on physical facts in the straightforward sense of following from them by necessity. No identity theorist seems to me to have made a convincing argument against the intuitive view that this is not the case.[10]

10. Having expressed these doubts about the identity theory in the text, I should emphasize two things: first, identity theorists have presented positive arguments for their view, which I certainly have not answered here. Some of these arguments seem to me to be weak or based on ideological prejudices, but others strike me as highly compelling arguments which I am at present unable to answer convincingly. Second, rejection of the identity thesis does not imply acceptance of Cartesian dualism. In fact, my view above that a person could not have come from a different sperm and egg from the ones from which he actually originated implicitly suggests a rejection of the Cartesian picture. If we had a clear idea of the soul or the mind as an independent, subsistent, spiritual entity, why should it have to have any necessary connection with particular material objects such as a particular sperm or a particular egg? A convinced dualist may think that my views on sperms and eggs beg the question against Descartes. I would tend to argue the other way; the fact that it is hard to imagine me coming from a sperm and egg different from my actual origins seems to me to indicate that we have no such clear conception of a soul or self. In any event, Descartes' notion seems to have been rendered dubious ever since Hume's critique of the notion of a Cartesian self. I regard the mind–body problem as wide open and extremely confusing.

26

Donald Davidson

"Mental Events"

Mental events such as perceivings, rememberings, decisions, and actions resist capture in the nomological net of physical theory.[1] How can this fact be reconciled with the causal role of mental events in the physical world? Reconciling freedom with causal determinism is a special case of the problem if we suppose that causal determinism entails capture in, and freedom requires escape from, the nomological net. But the broader issue can remain alive even for someone who believes a correct analysis of free action reveals no conflict with determinism. *Autonomy* (freedom, self-rule) may or may not clash with determinism; *anomaly* (failure to fall under a law) is, it would seem, another matter.

I start from the assumption that both the causal dependence, and the anomalousness, of mental events are undeniable facts. My aim is therefore to explain, in the face of apparent difficulties, how this can be. I am in sympathy with Kant when he says,

> it is as impossible for the subtlest philosophy as for the commonest reasoning to argue freedom away. Philosophy must therefore assume that no true contradiction will be found between freedom and natural necessity in the same human actions, for it cannot give up the idea of nature any more than that of freedom. Hence even if we should never be able to conceive how freedom is possible, at least this apparent contradiction must be convincingly eradicated. For if the thought of freedom contradicts itself or nature . . . it would have to be surrendered in competition with natural necessity.[2]

Generalize human actions to mental events, substitute anomaly for freedom, and this is a description of my problem. And of course the connection is closer, since Kant believed freedom entails anomaly.

Now let me try to formulate a little more carefully the "apparent contradiction" about mental events that I want to discuss and finally dissipate. It may be seen as stemming from three principles.

The first principle asserts that at least some mental events interact causally with physical events. (We could call this the Principle of Causal Interaction.) Thus for example if someone sank the *Bismarck*, then various mental events such as perceivings, notings, calculations, judgments, decisions, intentional actions and changes of belief played a causal role in the sinking of the *Bismarck*. In particular, I would urge that the fact that someone sank the *Bismarck* entails that he moved his body in a way that was caused by mental events of certain sorts, and that this bodily movement in turn caused the *Bismarck* to sink.[3] Perception illustrates how causality may run from the physical to the mental: if a man perceives that a ship is approaching, then a ship approaching must have caused him to come to believe that a ship is approaching. (Nothing depends on accepting these as examples of causal interaction.)

Though perception and action provide the most obvious cases where mental and physical events interact causally, I think reasons could be given for the view that all mental events ultimately, perhaps through causal relations with other mental events, have causal intercourse with physical events. But if there are mental events that have no physical events as causes or effects, the argument will not touch them.

The second principle is that where there is causality, there must be a law: events related as cause and effect fall under strict deterministic laws. (We

From *Experience and Theory*, Lawrence Foster and J. W. Swanson, eds. Amherst: University of Massachusetts Press, 1970, pp. 79–101. Copyright © 1970 by The University of Massachusetts Press. Reprinted with permission.

may term this the Principle of the Nomological Character of Causality.) This principle, like the first, will be treated here as an assumption, though I shall say something by way of interpretation.[4]

The third principle is that there are no strict deterministic laws on the basis of which mental events can be predicted and explained (the Anomalism of the Mental).

The paradox I wish to discuss arises for someone who is inclined to accept these three assumptions or principles, and who thinks they are inconsistent with one another. The inconsistency is not, of course, formal unless more premises are added. Nevertheless it is natural to reason that the first two principles, that of causal interaction, and that of the nomological character of causality, together imply that at least some mental events can be predicted and explained on the basis of laws, while the principle of the anomalism of the mental denies this. Many philosophers have accepted, with or without argument, the view that the three principles do lead to a contradiction. It seems to me, however, that all three principles are true, so that what must be done is to explain away the appearance of contradiction; essentially the Kantian line.

The rest of this paper falls into three parts. The first part describes a version of the identity theory of the mental and the physical that shows how the three principles may be reconciled. The second part argues that there cannot be strict psychophysical laws; this is not quite the principle of the anomalism of the mental, but on reasonable assumptions entails it. The last part tries to show that from the fact that there can be no strict psychophysical laws, and our other two principles, we can infer the truth of a version of the identity theory, that is, a theory that identifies at least some mental events with physical events. It is clear that this "proof" of the identity theory will be at best conditional, since two of its premises are unsupported, and the argument for the third may be found less than conclusive. But even someone unpersuaded of the truth of the premises may be interested to learn how they may be reconciled and that they serve to establish a version of the identity theory of the mental. Finally, if the argument is a good one, it should lay to rest the view, common to many friends and some foes of identity theories, that support for such theories can come only from the discovery of psychophysical laws.

I

The three principles will be shown consistent with one another by describing a view of the mental and the physical that contains no inner contradiction and that entails the three principles. According to this view, mental events are identical with physical events. Events are taken to be unrepeatable, dated individuals such as the particular eruption of a volcano, the (first) birth or death of a person, the playing of the 1968 World Series, or the historic utterance of the words, "You may fire when ready, Gridley." We can easily frame identity statements about individual events; examples (true or false) might be:

The death of Scott = the death of the author of *Waverley;*
The assassination of the Archduke Ferdinand = the event that started the First World War;
The eruption of Vesuvius in A.D. 79 = the cause of the destruction of Pompeii.

The theory under discussion is silent about processes, states, and attributes if these differ from individual events.

What does it mean to say that an event is mental or physical? One natural answer is that an event is physical if it is describable in a purely physical vocabulary, mental if describable in mental terms. But if this is taken to suggest that an event is physical, say, if some physical predicate is true of it, then there is the following difficulty. Assume that the predicate 'x took place at Noosa Heads' belongs to the physical vocabulary; then so also must the predicate 'x did not take place at Noosa Heads' belong to the physical vocabulary. But the predicate 'x did or did not take place at Noosa Heads' is true of every event, whether mental or physical.[5] We might rule out predicates that are tautologically true of every event, but this will not help since every event is truly describable either by 'x took place at Noosa Heads' or by 'x did not take place at Noosa Heads.' A different approach is needed.[6]

We may call those verbs mental that express propositional attitudes like believing, intending, desiring, hoping, knowing, perceiving, noticing, remembering, and so on. Such verbs are characterized by the fact that they sometimes feature in sentences with subjects that refer to persons, and are completed by embedded sentences in which the usual rules of substitution appear to break down. This criterion is not precise, since I do not want to include these verbs when they occur in contexts that are fully extensional ('He knows Paris,' 'He perceives the moon' may be cases), nor exclude them whenever they are not followed by embedded sentences. An alternative characterization of the desired class of mental verbs might be that they are psychological verbs as used when they create apparently nonextensional contexts.

Let us call a description of the form 'the event that is M' or an open sentence of the form 'event x is M' a *mental description* or a *mental open sentence* if and only if the expression that replaces 'M' contains at least one mental verb essentially. (Essentially, so as to rule out cases where the description or open sentence is logically equivalent to one not containing mental vocabulary.) Now we may say that an event is mental if and only if it has a mental description, or (the description operator not being primitive) if there is a mental open sentence true of that event alone. Physical events are those picked out by descriptions or open sentences that contain only the physical vocabulary essentially. It is less important to characterize a physical vocabulary because relative to the mental it is, so to speak, recessive in determining whether a description is mental or physical. (There will be some comments presently on the nature of a physical vocabulary, but these comments will fall far short of providing a criterion.)

On the proposed test of the mental, the distinguishing feature of the mental is not that it is private, subjective, or immaterial, but that it exhibits what Brentano called intentionality. Thus intentional actions are clearly included in the realm of the mental along with thoughts, hopes, and regrets (or the events tied to these). What may seem doubtful is whether the criterion will include events that have often been considered paradigmatic of the mental. Is it obvious, for example, that feeling a pain or seeing an afterimage will count as mental? Sentences that report such events seem free from taint of nonextensionality, and the same should be true of reports of raw feels, sense data, and other uninterpreted sensations, if there are any.

However, the criterion actually covers not only the havings of pains and afterimages, but much more besides. Take some event one would intuitively accept as physical, let's say the collision of two stars in distant space. There must be a purely physical predicate 'Px' true of this collision, and of others, but true of only this one at the time it occurred. This particular time, though, may be pinpointed as the same time that Jones notices that a pencil starts to roll across his desk. The distant stellar collision is thus *the* event x such that Px and x is simultaneous with Jones' noticing that a pencil starts to roll across his desk. The collision has now been picked out by a mental description and must be counted as a mental event.

This strategy will probably work to show every event to be mental; we have obviously failed to capture the intuitive concept of the mental. It would be instructive to try to mend this trouble, but it is not necessary for present purposes. We can

afford Spinozistic extravagance with the mental since accidental inclusions can only strengthen the hypothesis that all mental events are identical with physical events. What would matter would be failure to include bona fide mental events, but of this there seems to be no danger.

I want to describe, and presently to argue for, a version of the identity theory that denies that there can be strict laws connecting the mental and the physical. The very possibility of such a theory is easily obscured by the way in which identity theories are commonly defended and attacked. Charles Taylor, for example, agrees with protagonists of identity theories that the sole "ground" for accepting such theories is the supposition that correlations or laws can be established linking events described as mental with events described as physical. He says, "It is easy to see why this is so: unless a given mental event is invariably accompanied by a given, say, brain process, there is no ground for even mooting a general identity between the two."[7] Taylor goes on (correctly, I think) to allow that there may be identity without correlating laws, but my present interest is in noticing the invitation to confusion in the statement just quoted. What can "a given mental event" mean here? Not a particular, dated event, for it would not make sense to speak of an individual event being "invariably accompanied" by another. Taylor is evidently thinking of events of a given *kind*. But if the only identities are of kinds of events, the identity theory presupposes correlating laws.

One finds the same tendency to build laws into the statement of the identity theory in these typical remarks:

> When I say that a sensation is a brain process or that lightning is an electrical discharge, I am using 'is' in the sense of strict identity . . . there are not two things: a flash of lightning and an electrical discharge. There is one thing, a flash of lightning, which is described scientifically as an electrical discharge to the earth from a cloud of ionized water molecules.[8]

The last sentence of this quotation is perhaps to be understood as saying that for every lightning flash there exists an electrical discharge to the earth from a cloud of ionized water molecules with which it is identical. Here we have an honest ontology of individual events and can make literal sense of identity. We can also see how there could be identities without correlating laws. It is possible, however, to have an ontology of events with the conditions of individuation specified in such a way that any identity implies a correlating law. Kim, for example, suggests that Fa and Gb "describe or refer to the same event" if and only if $a = b$ and the property of being F = the property of being G.

The identity of the properties in turn entails that $(x)(Fx \leftrightarrow Gx)$.[9] No wonder Kim says:

> If pain is identical with brain state B, there must be a concomitance between occurrences of pain and occurrences of brain state B. . . . Thus, a necessary condition of the pain–brain state B identity is that the two expressions 'being in pain' and 'being in brain state B' have the same extension. . . . There is no conceivable observation that would confirm or refute the identity but not the associated correlation.[10]

It may make the situation clearer to give a four-fold classification of theories of the relation between mental and physical events that emphasizes the independence of claims about laws and claims of identity. On the one hand there are those who assert, and those who deny, the existence of psychophysical laws; on the other hand there are those who say mental events are identical with physical and those who deny this. Theories are thus divided into four sorts: *Nomological monism,* which affirms that there are correlating laws and that the events correlated are one (materialists belong in this category); *nomological dualism,* which comprises various forms of parallelism, interactionism, and epiphenomenalism; *anomalous dualism,* which combines ontological dualism with the general failure of laws correlating the mental and the physical (Cartesianism). And finally there is *anomalous monism,* which classifies the position I wish to occupy.[11]

Anomalous monism resembles materialism in its claim that all events are physical, but rejects the thesis, usually considered essential to materialism, that mental phenomena can be given purely physical explanations. Anomalous monism shows an ontological bias only in that it allows the possibility that not all events are mental, while insisting that all events are physical. Such a bland monism, unbuttressed by correlating laws or conceptual economies, does not seem to merit the term "reductionism"; in any case it is not apt to inspire the nothing-but reflex ("Conceiving the *Art of the Fugue* was nothing but a complex neural event," and so forth.)

Although the position I describe denies there are psychophysical laws, it is consistent with the view that mental characteristics are in some sense dependent, or supervenient, on physical characteristics. Such supervenience might be taken to mean that there cannot be two events alike in all physical respects but differing in some mental respect, or that an object cannot alter in some mental respect without altering in some physical respect. Dependence or supervenience of this kind does not entail reducibility through law or definition: if it did, we could reduce moral properties to descriptive, and

this there is good reason to *believe* cannot be done; and we might be able to reduce truth in a formal system to syntactical properties, and this we *know* cannot in general be done.

This last example is in useful analogy with the sort of lawless monism under consideration. Think of the physical vocabulary as the entire vocabulary of some language L with resources adequate to express a certain amount of mathematics, and its own syntax. L′ is L augmented with the truth predicate 'true-in-L,' which is "mental." In L (and hence L′) it is possible to pick out, with a definite description or open sentence, each sentence in the extension of the truth predicate, but if L is consistent there exists no predicate of syntax (of the "physical" vocabulary), no matter how complex, that applies to all and only the true sentences of L. There can be no "psychophysical law" in the form of a biconditional, '(x) (x is true-in-L if and only if x is ϕ)' where 'ϕ' is replaced by a "physical" predicate (a predicate of L). Similarly, we can pick out each mental event using the physical vocabulary alone, but no purely physical predicate, no matter how complex, has, as a matter of law, the same extension as a mental predicate.

It should now be evident how anomalous monism reconciles the three original principles. Causality and identity are relations between individual events no matter how described. But laws are linguistic; and so events can instantiate laws, and hence be explained or predicted in the light of laws, only as those events are described in one or another way. The principle of causal interaction deals with events in extension and is therefore blind to the mental–physical dichotomy. The principle of the anomalism of the mental concerns events described as mental, for events are mental only as described. The principle of the nomological character of causality must be read carefully: it says that when events are related as cause and effect, they have descriptions that instantiate a law. It does not say that every true singular statement of causality instantiates a law.[12]

II

The analogy just bruited, between the place of the mental amid the physical, and the place of the semantical in a world of syntax, should not be strained. Tarski proved that a consistent language cannot (under some natural assumptions) contain an open sentence 'Fx' true of all and only the true sentences of that language. If our analogy were pressed, then we would expect a proof that there can be no physical open sentence 'Px' true of all and only the events having some mental property.

In fact, however, nothing I can say about the irreducibility of the mental deserves to be called a proof; and the kind of irreducibility is different. For if anomalous monism is correct, not only can every mental event be uniquely singled out using only physical concepts, but since the number of events that falls under each mental predicate may, for all we know, be finite, there may well exist a physical open sentence coextensive with each mental predicate, though to construct it might involve the tedium of a lengthy and uninstructive alternation. Indeed, even if finitude is not assumed, there seems no compelling reason to deny that there could be coextensive predicates, one mental and one physical.

The thesis is rather that the mental is nomologically irreducible: there may be *true* general statements relating the mental and the physical, statements that have the logical form of a law; but they are not *lawlike* (in a strong sense to be described). If by absurdly remote chance we were to stumble on a nonstochastic true psychophysical generalization, we would have no reason to believe it more than roughly true.

Do we, by declaring that there are no (strict) psychophysical laws, poach on the empirical preserves of science—a form of *hubris* against which philosophers are often warned? Of course, to judge a statement lawlike or illegal is not to decide its truth outright; relative to the acceptance of a general statement on the basis of instances, ruling it lawlike must be a priori. But such relative apriorism does not in itself justify philosophy, for in general the grounds for deciding to trust a statement on the basis of its instances will in turn be governed by theoretical and empirical concerns not to be distinguished from those of science. If the case of supposed laws linking the mental and the physical is different, it can only be because to allow the possibility of such laws would amount to changing the subject. By changing the subject I mean here: deciding not to accept the criterion of the mental in terms of the vocabulary of the propositional attitudes. This short answer cannot prevent further ramifications of the problem, however, for there is no clear line between changing the subject and changing what one says on an old subject, which is to admit, in the present context at least, that there is no clear line between philosophy and science. Where there are no fixed boundaries only the timid never risk trespass.

It will sharpen our appreciation of the anomological character of mental–physical generalizations to consider a related matter, the failure of definitional behaviorism. Why are we willing (as I assume we are) to abandon the attempt to give explicit definitions of mental concepts in terms of behavioral ones? Not, surely, just because all actual tries are conspicuously inadequate. Rather it is because we are persuaded, as we are in the case of so many other forms of definitional reductionism (naturalism in ethics, instrumentalism and operationalism in the sciences, the causal theory of meaning, phenomenalism, and so on—the catalogue of philosophy's defeats), that there is system in the failures. Suppose we try to say, not using any mental concepts, what it is for a man to believe there is life on Mars. One line we could take is this: when a certain sound is produced in the man's presence ("Is there life on Mars?") he produces another ("Yes"). But of course this shows he believes there is life on Mars only if he understands English, his production of the sound was intentional, and was a response to the sounds as meaning something in English; and so on. For each discovered deficiency, we add a new proviso. Yet no matter how we patch and fit the nonmental conditions, we always find the need for an additional condition (provided he *notices, understands,* etc.) that is mental in character.[13]

A striking feature of attempts at definitional reduction is how little seems to hinge on the question of synonymy between definiens and definiendum. Of course, by imagining counterexamples we do discredit claims of synonymy. But the pattern of failure prompts a stronger conclusion: if we were to find an open sentence couched in behavioral terms and exactly coextensive with some mental predicate, nothing could reasonably persuade us that we had found it. We know too much about thought and behavior to trust exact and universal statements linking them. Beliefs and desires issue in behavior only as modified and mediated by further beliefs and desires, attitudes and attendings, without limit. Clearly this holism of the mental realm is a clue both to the autonomy and to the anomalous character of the mental.

These remarks apropos definitional behaviorism provide at best hints of why we should not expect nomological connections between the mental and the physical. The central case invites further consideration.

Lawlike statements are general statements that support counterfactual and subjunctive claims, and are supported by their instances. There is (in my view) no nonquestion-begging criterion of the lawlike, which is not to say there are no reasons in particular cases for a judgment. Lawlikeness is a matter of degree, which is not to deny that there may be cases beyond debate. And within limits set by the conditions of communication, there is room for much variation between individuals in the pattern of statements to which various degrees of nomologicality are assigned. In all these respects, nomologicality is much like analyticity, as one might expect since both are linked to meaning.

'All emeralds are green' is lawlike in that its instances confirm it, but 'all emeralds are grue' is not, for 'grue' means 'observed before time t and green, otherwise blue,' and if our observations were all made before t and uniformly revealed green emeralds, this would not be a reason to expect other emeralds to be blue. Nelson Goodman has suggested that this shows that some predicates, 'grue' for example, are unsuited to laws (and thus a criterion of suitable predicates could lead to a criterion of the lawlike). But it seems to me the anomalous character of 'All emeralds are grue' shows only that the predicates 'is an emerald' and 'is grue' are not suited to one another: grueness is not an inductive property of emeralds. Grueness *is* however an inductive property of entities of other sorts, for instance of emerires. (Something is an emerire if it is examined before t and is an emerald, and otherwise is a sapphire.) Not only is 'All emerires are grue' entailed by the conjunction of the lawlike statements 'All emeralds are green' and 'All sapphires are blue,' but there is no reason, as far as I can see, to reject the deliverance of intuition, that it is itself lawlike.[14] Nomological statements bring together predicates that we know a priori are made for each other—know, that is, independently of knowing whether the evidence supports a connection between them. 'Blue,' 'red,' and 'green' are made for emeralds, sapphires, and roses; 'grue,' 'bleen,' and 'gred' are made for sapphalds, emerires, and emeroses.

The direction in which the discussion seems headed is this: mental and physical predicates are not made for one another. In point of lawlikeness, psychophysical statements are more like 'All emeralds are grue' than like 'All emeralds are green.'

Before this claim is plausible, it must be seriously modified. The fact that emeralds examined before t are grue not only is no reason to believe all emeralds are grue; it is not even a reason (if we know the time) to believe *any* unobserved emeralds are grue. But if an event of a certain mental sort has usually been accompanied by an event of a certain physical sort, this often is a good reason to expect other cases to follow suit roughly in proportion. The generalizations that embody such practical wisdom are assumed to be only roughly true, or they are explicitly stated in probabilistic terms, or they are insulated from counterexample by generous escape clauses. Their importance lies mainly in the support they lend singular causal claims and related explanations of particular events. The support derives from the fact that such a generalization, however crude and vague, may provide good reason to believe that underlying the

particular case there is a regularity that could be formulated sharply and without caveat.

In our daily traffic with events and actions that must be foreseen or understood, we perforce make use of the sketchy summary generalization, for we do not know a more accurate law, or if we do, we lack a description of the particular events in which we are interested that would show the relevance of the law. But there is an important distinction to be made within the category of the rude rule of thumb. On the one hand, there are generalizations whose positive instances give us reason to believe the generalization itself could be improved by adding further provisos and conditions stated in the same general vocabulary as the original generalization. Such a generalization points to the form and vocabulary of the finished law: we may say that it is a *homonomic* generalization. On the other hand there are generalizations which when instantiated may give us reason to believe there is a precise law at work, but one that can be stated only by shifting to a different vocabulary. We may call such generalizations *heteronomic.*

I suppose most of our practical lore (and science) is heteronomic. This is because a law can hope to be precise, explicit, and as exceptionless as possible only if it draws its concepts from a comprehensive closed theory. This ideal theory may or may not be deterministic, but it is if any true theory is. Within the physical sciences we do find homonomic generalizations, generalizations such that if the evidence supports them, we then have reason to believe they may be sharpened indefinitely by drawing upon further physical concepts: there is a theoretical asymptote of perfect coherence with all the evidence, perfect predictability (under the terms of the system), total explanation (again under the terms of the system). Or perhaps the ultimate theory is probabilistic, and the asymptote is less than perfection; but in that case there will be no better to be had.

Confidence that a statement is homonomic, correctible within its own conceptual domain, demands that it draw its concepts from a theory with strong constitutive elements. Here is the simplest possible illustration; if the lesson carries, it will be obvious that the simplification could be mended.

The measurement of length, weight, temperature, or time depends (among many other things, of course) on the existence in each case of a two-place relation that is transitive and asymmetric: warmer than, later than, heavier than, and so forth. Let us take the relation *longer than* as our example. The law or postulate of transitivity is this:

(L) $L(x,y)$ and $L(y,z) \rightarrow L(x,z)$

Unless this law (or some sophisticated variant) holds, we cannot easily make sense of the concept of length. There will be no way of assigning numbers to register even so much as ranking in length, let alone the more powerful demands of measurement on a ratio scale. And this remark goes not only for any three items directly involved in an intransitivity: it is easy to show (given a few more assumptions essential to measurement of length) that there is no consistent assignment of a ranking to any item unless (L) holds in full generality.

Clearly (L) alone cannot exhaust the import of 'longer than'—otherwise it would not differ from 'warmer than' or 'later than.' We must suppose there is some empirical content, however difficult to formulate in the available vocabulary, that distinguishes 'longer than' from the other two-place transitive predicates of measurement and on the basis of which we may assert that one thing is longer than another. Imagine this empirical content to be partly given by the predicate 'o(x,y)'. So we have this "meaning postulate":

$$(\text{M}) \quad \text{o}(x,y) \rightarrow \text{L}(x,y)$$

that partly interprets (L). But now (L) and (M) together yield an empirical theory of great strength, for together they entail that there do not exist three objects a, b, and c such that o(a,b), o(b,c), and o(c,a). Yet what is to prevent this happening if 'o(x,y)' is a predicate we can ever, with confidence, apply? Suppose we *think* we observe an intransitive triad; what do we say? We could count (L) false, but then we would have no application for the concept of length. We could say (M) gives a wrong test for length; but then it is unclear what we thought was the *content* of the idea of one thing being longer than another. Or we could say that the objects under observation are not, as the theory requires, *rigid* objects. It is a mistake to think we are forced to accept some one of these answers. Concepts such as that of length are sustained in equilibrium by a number of conceptual pressures, and theories of fundamental measurement are distorted if we force the decision, among such principles as (L) and (M): analytic or synthetic. It is better to say the whole set of axioms, laws, or postulates for the measurement of length is partly constitutive of the idea of a system of macroscopic, rigid, physical objects. I suggest that the existence of lawlike statements in physical science depends upon the existence of constitutive (or synthetic a priori) laws like those of the measurement of length within the same conceptual domain.

Just as we cannot intelligibly assign a length to any object unless a comprehensive theory holds of objects of that sort, we cannot intelligibly attribute any propositional attitude to an agent except within the framework of a viable theory of his beliefs, desires, intentions, and decisions.

There is no assigning beliefs to a person one by one on the basis of his verbal behavior, his choices, or other local signs no matter how plain and evident, for we make sense of particular beliefs only as they cohere with other beliefs, with preferences, with intentions, hopes, fears, expectations, and the rest. It is not merely, as with the measurement of length, that each case tests a theory and depends upon it, but that the content of a propositional attitude derives from its place in the pattern.

Crediting people with a large degree of consistency cannot be counted mere charity: it is unavoidable if we are to be in a position to accuse them meaningfully of error and some degree of irrationality. Global confusion, like universal mistake, is unthinkable, not because imagination boggles, but because too much confusion leaves nothing to be confused about and massive error erodes the background of true belief against which alone failure can be construed. To appreciate the limits to the kind and amount of blunder and bad thinking we can intelligibly pin on others is to see once more the inseparability of the question what concepts a person commands and the question what he does with those concepts in the way of belief, desire, and intention. To the extent that we fail to discover a coherent and plausible pattern in the attitudes and actions of others we simply forego the chance of treating them as persons.

The problem is not bypassed but given center stage by appeal to explicit speech behavior. For we could not begin to decode a man's sayings if we could not make out his attitudes towards his sentences, such as holding, wishing, or wanting them to be true. Beginning from these attitudes, we must work out a theory of what he means, thus simultaneously giving content to his attitudes and to his words. In our need to make him make sense, we will try for a theory that finds him consistent, a believer of truths, and a lover of the good (all by our own lights, it goes without saying). Life being what it is, there will be no simple theory that fully meets these demands. Many theories will effect a more or less acceptable compromise, and between these theories there may be no objective grounds for choice.

The heteronomic character of general statements linking the mental and the physical traces back to this central role of translation in the description of all propositional attitudes, and to the indeterminacy of translation.[15] There are no strict psychophysical laws because of the disparate commitments of the mental and physical schemes. It is a feature of physical reality that physical change can be explained by laws that connect it with other changes and conditions physically described. It is a feature of the mental that the attribution of mental phenomena must be responsible to the background of reasons, beliefs, and intentions of the individual. There cannot be tight connections between the realms if each is to retain allegiance to its proper source of evidence. The nomological irreducibility of the mental does not derive merely from the seamless nature of the world of thought, preference and intention, for such interdependence is common to physical theory, and is compatible with there being a single right way of interpreting a man's attitudes without relativization to a scheme of translation. Nor is the irreducibility due simply to the possibility of many equally eligible schemes, for this is compatible with an arbitrary choice of one scheme relative to which assignments of mental traits are made. The point is rather that when we use the concepts of belief, desire and the rest, we must stand prepared, as the evidence accumulates, to adjust our theory in the light of considerations of overall cogency: the constitutive ideal of rationality partly controls each phase in the evolution of what must be an evolving theory. An arbitrary choice of translation scheme would preclude such opportunistic tempering of theory; put differently, a right arbitrary choice of a translation manual would be of a manual acceptable in the light of all possible evidence, and this is a choice we cannot make. We must conclude, I think, that nomological slack between the mental and the physical is essential as long as we conceive of man as a rational animal.

III

The gist of the foregoing discussion, as well as its conclusion, will be familiar. That there is a categorial difference between the mental and the physical is a commonplace. It may seem odd that I say nothing of the supposed privacy of the mental, or the special authority an agent has with respect to his own propositional attitudes, but this appearance of novelty would fade if we were to investigate in more detail the grounds for accepting a scheme of translation. The step from the categorial difference between the mental and the physical to the impossibility of strict laws relating them is less common, but certainly not new. If there is a surprise, then, it will be to find the lawlessness of the mental serving to help establish the identity of the mental with that paradigm of the lawlike, the physical.

The reasoning is this. We are assuming, under the Principle of the Causal Dependence of the Mental, that some mental events at least are causes or effects of physical events; the argument applies only to these. A second Principle (of the Nomological Character of Causality) says that each true singular causal statement is backed by a strict law connecting events of kinds to which the events mentioned as cause and effect belong. Where there are rough, but homonomic, laws, there are laws drawing on concepts from the same conceptual domain and upon which there is no improving in point of precision and comprehensiveness. We urged in the last section that such laws occur in the physical sciences. Physical theory promises to provide a comprehensive closed system guaranteed to yield a standardized, unique description of every physical event couched in a vocabulary amenable to law.

It is not plausible that mental concepts alone can provide such a framework, simply because the mental does not, by our first principle, constitute a closed system. Too much happens to affect the mental that is not itself a systematic part of the mental. But if we combine this observation with the conclusion that no psychophysical statement is, or can be built into, a strict law, we have the Principle of the Anomalism of the Mental: there are no strict laws at all on the basis of which we can predict and explain mental phenomena.

The demonstration of identity follows easily. Suppose m, a mental event, caused p, a physical event; then under some description m and p instantiate a strict law. This law can only be physical, according to the previous paragraph. But if m falls under a physical law, it has a physical description; which is to say it is a physical event. An analogous argument works when a physical event causes a mental event. So every mental event that is causally related to a physical event is a physical event. In order to establish anomalous monism in full generality it would be sufficient to show that every mental event is cause or effect of some physical event; I shall not attempt this.

If one event causes another, there is a strict law which those events instantiate when properly described. But it is possible (and typical) to know of the singular causal relation without knowing the law or the relevant descriptions. Knowledge requires reasons, but these are available in the form of rough heteronomic generalizations, which are lawlike in that instances make it reasonable to expect other instances to follow suit without being lawlike in the sense of being indefinitely refinable. Applying these facts to knowledge of identities, we see that it is possible to know that a mental event is identical with some physical event without knowing which one (in the sense of being able to give it a unique physical description that brings it under a relevant law). Even if someone knew the entire physical history of the world, and every mental event were identical with a physical, it would not follow that he could predict or explain a single mental event (so described, of course).

Two features of mental events in their relation to the physical—causal dependence and nomological independence—combine, then, to dissolve what has often seemed a paradox, the efficacy of thought and purpose in the material world, and their freedom from law. When we portray events as perceivings, rememberings, decisions and actions, we necessarily locate them amid physical happenings through the relation of cause and effect; but that same mode of portrayal insulates mental events, as long as we do not change the idiom, from the strict laws that can in principle be called upon to explain and predict physical phenomena.

Mental events as a class cannot be explained by physical science; particular mental events can when we know particular identities. But the explanations of mental events in which we are typically interested relate them to other mental events and conditions. We explain a man's free actions, for example, by appeal to his desires, habits, knowledge and perceptions. Such accounts of intentional behavior operate in a conceptual framework removed from the direct reach of physical law by describing both cause and effect, reason and action, as aspects of a portrait of a human agent. The anomalism of the mental is thus a necessary condition for viewing action as autonomous. I conclude with a second passage from Kant:

> It is an indispensable problem of speculative philosophy to show that its illusion respecting the contradiction rests on this, that we think of man in a different sense and relation when we call him free, and when we regard him as subject to the laws of nature.... It must therefore show that not only can both of these very well co-exist, but that both must be thought *as necessarily united* in the same subject....[16]

NOTES

1. I was helped and influenced by Daniel Bennett, Sue Larson, and Richard Rorty, who are not responsible for the result. My research was supported by the National Science Foundation and the Center for Advanced Study in the Behavioral Sciences.

2. *Fundamental Principles of the Metaphysics of Morals,* trans. T. K. Abbott (London, 1909), pp. 75–76.

3. These claims are defended in my "Actions, Reasons and Causes," *The Journal of Philosophy,* LX (1963), pp. 685–

700 and in "Agency," a paper forthcoming in the proceedings of the November, 1968, colloquium on Agent, Action, and Reason at the University of Western Ontario, London, Canada [in *Agent, Action, and Reason,* edited by Robert Binkley, Richard Bronaugh, and Ausonio Marras (Oxford: Basil Blackwell, 1971), pp. 3–25].

4. In "Causal Relations," *The Journal of Philosophy,* LXIV (1967), pp. 691–703, I elaborate on the view of causality assumed here. The stipulation that the laws be deterministic is stronger than required by the reasoning, and will be relaxed.

5. The point depends on assuming that mental events may intelligibly be said to have a location; but it is an assumption that must be true if an identity theory is, and here I am not trying to prove the theory but to formulate it.

6. I am indebted to Lee Bowie for emphasizing this difficulty.

7. Charles Taylor, "Mind-Body Identity, a Side Issue?" *The Philosophical Review,* LXXVI (1967), p. 202.

8. J. J. C. Smart, "Sensations and Brain Processes," *The Philosophical Review,* LXVIII (1959), pp. 141–56. The quoted passages are on pp. 163–165 of the reprinted version in *The Philosophy of Mind,* ed. V. C. Chappell (Englewood Cliffs, N.J., 1962). For another example, see David K. Lewis, "An Argument for the Identity Theory," *The Journal of Philosophy,* LXIII (1966), pp. 17–25. Here the assumption is made explicit when Lewis takes events as universals (p. 17, footnotes 1 and 2). I do not suggest that Smart and Lewis are confused, only that their way of stating the identity theory tends to obscure the distinction between particular events and kinds of events on which the formulation of my theory depends.

9. Jaegwon Kim, "On the Psycho-Physical Identity Theory," *American Philosophical Quarterly,* III (1966), p. 231.

10. Ibid., pp. 227–28. Richard Brandt and Jaegwon Kim propose roughly the same criterion in "The Logic of the Identity Theory," *The Journal of Philosophy* LIV (1967), pp. 515–537. They remark that on their conception of event identity, the identity theory "makes a stronger claim than merely that there is a pervasive phenomenal-physical correlation" (p. 518). I do not discuss the stronger claim.

11. Anomalous monism is more or less explicitly recognized as a possible position by Herbert Feigl, "The 'Mental' and the 'Physical,'" in *Concepts, Theories and the Mind-Body Problem,* vol. II, *Minnesota Studies in the Philosophy of Science* (Minneapolis, 1958); Sydney Shoemaker, "Ziff's Other Minds," *The Journal of Philosophy,* LXII (1965), p. 589; David Randall Luce, "Mind-Body Identity and Psycho-Physical Correlation," *Philosophical Studies,* XVII (1966), pp. 1–7; Charles Taylor, op. cit., p. 207. Something like my position is tentatively accepted by Thomas Nagel, "Physicalism," *The Philosophical Review,* LXXIV (1965), pp. 339–356, and briefly endorsed by P. F. Strawson in *Freedom and the Will,* ed. D. F. Pears (London, 1963), pp. 63–67.

12. The point that substitutivity of identity fails in the context of explanation is made in connection with the present subject by Norman Malcolm, "Scientific Materialism and the Identity Theory," *Dialogue,* III (1964–65), pp. 123–124. See also my "Actions, Reasons and Causes," *The Journal of Philosophy,* LX (1963), pp. 696–699 and "The Individuation of Events" in *Essays in Honor of Carl G. Hempel,* ed. N. Rescher, et al. (Dordrecht, 1969).

13. The theme is developed in Roderick Chisholm, *Perceiving* (Ithaca, New York, 1957), chap. 11.

14. This view is accepted by Richard C. Jeffrey, "Goodman's Query," *The Journal of Philosophy,* LXII (1966), p. 286 ff., John R. Wallace, "Goodman, Logic, Induction," same journal and issue, p. 318, and John M. Vickers, "Characteristics of Projectible Predicates," *The Journal of Philosophy,* LXIV (1967), p. 285. On pp. 328–329 and 286–287 of these journal issues respectively Goodman disputes the lawlikeness of statements like "All emerires are grue." I cannot see, however, that he meets the point of my "Emeroses by Other Names," *The Journal of Philosophy,* LXIII (1966), pp. 778–780.

15. The influence of W. V. Quine's doctrine of the indeterminacy of translation, as in chap. 2 of *Word and Object* (Cambridge, Mass., 1960), is, I hope, obvious. In § 45 Quine develops the connection between translation and the propositional attitudes, and remarks that "Brentano's thesis of the irreducibility of intentional idioms is of a piece with the thesis of indeterminacy of translation" (p. 221).

16. Op. cit., p. 76.

27

Jaegwon Kim

"Epiphenomenal and Supervenient Causation"

1. Epiphenomenal Causation

Jonathan Edwards held the doctrine that ordinary material things do not persist through time but are at each moment created, and recreated, by God ex nihilo. He writes:

> If the existence of created *substance*, in each successive moment, be wholly the effect of God's immediate power, in *that* moment, without any dependence on prior existence, as much as the first creation out of *nothing*, then what exists at this moment, by this power, is a *new effect*, and simply and absolutely considered, not the same with any past existence, though it be like it, and follows it according to a certain established method.[1]

Thus, the present "time slice" of this table, although it is very much like the one preceding it, has no causal connection with it; for each slice is a wholly distinct creation by God. The temporal parts of this table are successive effects of an underlying persisting cause, God's creative activity. In arguing for this doctrine, Edwards offers the following striking analogy:

> The *images* of things in a glass, as we keep our eye upon them, seem to remain precisely the same, with a continuing, perfect identity. But it is known to be otherwise. Philosophers well know that these images are constantly *renewed*, by the impression and reflection of *new* rays of light; so that the image impressed by the former rays is constantly vanishing, and a *new* image impressed by *new* rays every moment, both on the glass and on the eye. . . . And the new images being put on *immediately* or *instantly*, do not make them the same, any more than if it were done with the intermission of an *hour* or a *day*. The image that exists at this moment is not at all *derived* from the image which existed at the last preceding moment. As

may be seen, because if the succession of new *rays* be intercepted, by something interposed between the object and the glass, the image immediately ceases; the *past existence* of the image has no influence to uphold it, so much as for a moment.[2]

Two successive mirror reflections of an object are not directly causally linked to each other; in particular, the earlier one is not a cause of the later one, even though the usual requirements of "Humean causation," including that of spatiotemporal contiguity, may be met. If all we ever observed were mirror images, like the shadows in Plato's cave, we might very well be misled into ascribing a cause–effect relation to the two images; but we know better, as Edwards says. The succession of images is only a reflection of the real causal process at the level of the objects reflected.

Edwards's example anticipates one that Wesley Salmon has recently used to illustrate the difference between "causal processes" and "pseudoprocesses":[3] consider a rotating spotlight, located at the center of a circular room, casting a spot of light on the wall. According to Salmon, a light ray traveling from the spotlight to the wall is a *causal process*, whereas the motion of the spot of light on the wall is only a *pseudoprocess*. Each spot of light on the wall is caused by a light ray traveling from the spotlight; however, it is not the cause of the spot of light appearing on the wall at an instant later. Two successive spots of light on the wall are related to each other as two successive mirror images are related. Both pairs mimic causal processes and are apt to be mistaken for such. Neither, however, is a process involving a real causal chain.

By "epiphenomenal causation" I have in mind *roughly* the sort of apparent causal relation in the examples of Edwards and Salmon. I say "roughly"

From *Midwest Studies in Philosophy*, vol. IX, Peter A. French, Theodore E. Uehling, Jr., and Howard K. Wettstein, eds. Minneapolis: University of Minnesota Press, 1984, pp. 257–70. Reprinted with permission of the publisher and Jaegwon Kim.

because, as will become clear later, they are somewhat less central cases of epiphenomenal causation, as this notion will be used in this paper; these examples are helpful, however, in the initial fixing of the concept that I have in mind. In any event, Edwards's contention was that *all* causal relations holding for material bodies, events, and processes are cases of epiphenomenal causation, the only true causation being limited to God's own creative actions. The world is constantly created anew by God; we may think that fire causes smoke, but it is only that God creates fire at one instant and then smoke an instant later. There is no direct causal connection between the fire and the smoke. The relation between them is one of epiphenomenal causation.

Another case of epiphenomenal causation, familiar in daily life, is the succession of symptoms associated with a disease: the symptoms are not mutually related in the cause–effect relationship, although to the medically naive they may appear to be so related. The appearance of a causal connection here merely points to the real causal process underlying the symptoms.

It should be clear that by saying that two events are related in an epiphenomenal causal relation I do not mean to suggest that the events themselves are "epiphenomena." The standard current use of this term comes from discussions of epiphenomenalism as a theory of the mind–body relation, and to call an event an "epiphenomenon" in this context is taken to mean that though it is a causal effect of other events, it has no causal potency of its own: it can be the cause of no other event, being the absolute terminal link of a causal chain. It is dubious that this notion of an epiphenomenon makes sense—for example, it is doubtful how such events could be known to exist.[4] In this paper I use the modifier "epiphenomenal" in "epiphenomenal causation" to qualify the causal relation, not the events standing in that relation.

One might object at this point that these examples of the so-called epiphenomenal causation are not cases of causation at all and that it is misleading to label them as such, because "epiphenomenal causation" sounds as though it is a *kind* of causal relation. In reply, I shall say two things: first, even though it is true that an earlier mirror image is not a cause of a later one, it is also true that there *is* a causal relation between the two—the two are successive effects of the same underlying causal process. To leave the matter where we have simply denied that the first is the cause of the second would be to ignore an important causal fact about the relation between the two events. Second, I shall argue that the central cases of epiphenomenal causation that will interest us will be seen to

involve "real" causal relations and that epiphenomenal causal relations of this kind are pervasively present all around us.

What is common to these cases and the earlier examples, such as Edwards's mirror images, which do not seem to involve real causal relations, is just this: they all involve at least *apparent* causal relations that are *grounded* in some underlying causal processes. These causal relations, whether only apparent or real, *are reducible to more fundamental causal relations.* If one takes the view that reducibility entails eliminability, there perhaps is no significant difference between the two types of cases. But then there also is the apparently opposed view: to be reduced is to be legitimatized. I believe in any case that my use of the term "epiphenomenon" is entirely consistent with the standard dictionary definition of "epiphenomenon" as "secondary symptom," "secondary phenomenon," or "something that happens in addition"; the idea that an epiphenomenon is causally inert is best taken as a philosophical doctrine of epiphenomenalism as a theory about the nature of the mental, not as something that merely arises out of the meaning of the term "epiphenomenon."

The principal claims that I want to defend in this paper are the following: that macrocausation should be viewed as a kind of epiphenomenal causation in the broad sense sketched above; that macrocausation as epiphenomenal causation should be explained as "supervenient causation" in the sense to be explained below; and that psychological causation, that is causation involving psychological events, is plausibly assimilated to macrocausation—that is, it is to be construed as supervenient epiphenomenal causation.

2. Macrocausation as Supervenient Causation

By "macrocausation" I have in mind causal relations involving macroevents and states, where a macroevent or state is understood as the exemplification of a macroproperty by an object at a time (this characterization can be generalized to macro*relations* in obvious ways). The micro–macro distinction is of course relative: temperature is macro relative to molecular motion; properties of molecules are macro relative to properties and relationships characterizing atoms and more basic particles, and so on. For our present discussion, however, the paradigmatic examples of macroobjects and properties are medium-sized material bodies around us and their observable properties. Thus, fire causing smoke would be a case of macrocausation; so is the rising temperature causing a metallic object to expand. All observable phenomena are macrophenomena in relation to the familiar theoretical objects of physics; hence, our first claim entails that all causal relations involving observable phenomena—all causal relations familiar from daily experience—are cases of epiphenomenal causation.

My defense of this claim is two-pronged. The first prong consists in a general argument to the effect that a certain familiar and plausible reductionist perspective requires us to view macrocausation as epiphenomenal causation. The second prong consists in the observation that modern theoretical science treats macrocausation as reducible epiphenomenal causation and that this has proved to be an extremely successful explanatory and predictive research strategy.

First, the general argument: philosophers have observed, in connection with the mind–body problem, that a thoroughgoing physicalism can no more readily tolerate the existence of irreducible psychological features or properties than irreducible psychological objects (e.g., Cartesian souls, visual images).[5] The thought behind this may be something like this: If F is an irreducible psychical feature, then its existence implies that something is F. (If F is never exemplified, being a mere "concept" of something psychical, the physicalist has nothing to worry about.) This means that there would be a physically irreducible event or state of this thing's being F, or a physically irreducible fact, namely the fact that the thing is F. So the world remains bifurcated: the physical domain and a distinct, irreducible psychical domain; and physical theory fails as a complete and comprehensive theory of the world. Moreover, we might want to inquire into the *cause* of something's being F. This gives rise to three possibilities, none of them palatable to the physicalist: first, the cause of the psychical event is a mystery not accessible to scientific inquiry; second, an autonomous psychical science emerges; third, physical theory provides a causal account of the psychical phenomena. The last possibility may be the worst, from the physicalist point of view: given the irreducibility of the psychical phenomena, this could only mean that physical theory would lose its *closed* character, by countenancing within its domain irreducibly nonphysical events and properties.

Parallel considerations should motivate the rejection of macrocausation as an irreducible feature of the world. It seems to be a fundamental methodological precept of theoretical physical science that we ought to formulate *microstructural theories* of objects and their properties—that is, to try to understand the behavior and properties of objects and processes in terms of the properties and relationships characterizing their microconstituents. The philosophical supposition that grounds this research strategy seems to be the belief that macroproperties are determined by, or supervenient upon, microproperties. This Democritean doctrine of mereological supervenience, or microdeterminism, forms the metaphysical backbone of the method of microreduction,[6] somewhat in the way that the principle of causal determinism constitutes the objective basis of the method of causal explanation. (I shall return to these themes below.)

In this global microdeterministic picture there is no place for irreducible macrocausal relations. We expect any causal relation between two macroevents (x's being F and y's being G, where F and G are macroproperties) to be micro-reductively explainable in terms of more fundamental causal processes, like any other facts involving macroproperties and events. If the causal relation is backed up by a law relating F and G, we would expect this macrolaw to be microreducible. A standard example: the rising temperature of a gas confined within a rigid chamber causes its pressure to rise. This macrocausal relation is subsumed under a macrolaw (the gas law), which in turn is microreduced by kinetic theory of gases. This explains, and reduces, the macrocausal relation. If the causal relation is at bottom just some sort of counterfactual dependency, then the macrocounterfactual "If x had not been F, y would not have been G" should be grounded in some lawlike connection involving microproperties associated with x and y in relation to F and G; or else, there should be some more basic counterfactual dependencies involving microconstituents of x and y that can explain the counterfactual dependency between F and G. It would be difficult to believe that this macrocounterfactual is a fundamental and irreducible fact about the world. At least, that should be our attitude if we accept the universal thesis of mereological supervenience and the validity of microreductive research strategy.

What is the general form of the reduction of a macrocausal relation to a microcausal process? The following model is attractively simple: if the macrocausal relation to be reduced is one from an instance of property F to an instance of property G, we need to correlate F with some microproperty m(F), and also G with m(G), and then show that m(F) and m(G) are appropriately causally connected. Showing the latter may take the form of exhibiting a precise law that connects the two microproperties, or a causal mechanism whereby an instance of F leads to an instance of G. How is the correlation between F and m(F) to be understood? The strongest claim defended by some philosophers is that F and m(F) are one and the same property.[7] The thought is that such property identities are necessary for the required microreduction to go through. Taking this identity approach, however, would force a reconstrual of the notions of microproperty and macroproperty; how could one and tne same property be both a microproperty and a macroproperty? But a more serious problem is this: in the given instance under consideration, the macroproperty may be "realized" or "grounded" in m(F), but in another instance F may be realized or grounded in a different microproperty m*(F), and there may be many other microproperties that can realize F, in that if anything has one of them, then necessarily it also exhibits F as a result. And it may well be that from the explanatory-causal point of view, the possibly infinite disjunction of these underlying microproperties could hardly be considered as a unitary property suitable as a reductive base.

The foregoing is a point often made in connection with the mind–body problem and used sometimes to support the "functionalist" view of the mental.[8] The multiple realizability of a state relative to a more basic level of analysis, or a richer descriptive vocabulary, appears to hold, with equal plausibility, for macrophysical characteristics in relation to microphysical properties and processes; perhaps this is a pervasive feature of mereological reduction. For these reasons, among others, I suggest the use of the concept of *supervenience,* which allows for the possibility of *alternative supervenience bases* for a given supervenient property, as particularly well suited for the purposes on hand. The core idea of supervenience as a relation between two families of properties is that the supervenient properties are in some sense *determined by,* or *dependent on,* the properties on which they supervene. More formally, *the supervenience of a family A of properties on another family B* can be explained as follows: necessarily, for any property F in A, if any object x has F, then there exists a property G in B such that x has G, and necessarily anything having G has F.[9] When properties F and G are related as specified in the definition, we may say that F is *supervenient* on G, and that G is a *supervenience base* of F. On this account, it is clear that a property in the supervenient family can have multiple supervenience bases: an object x has F, and for x the supervenience base of F is G; however, another object y that also has F does not have G, but rather has G*, as *its* supervenience base for F; and so on. Thus, if we think of macroproperties as supervenient on microproperties, the account allows for a given macroproperty F to be supervenient on a number of microproperties; that is, an object has a certain macroproperty (e.g., fragility) in virtue of having a certain microproperty (e.g., a

certain crystalline structure) on which the macroproperty supervenes; another object has the same macroproperty in virtue of having a different microproperty (another kind of crystalline structure); and so on.

The notion of *event supervenience* is easily explained on the basis of property supervenience: an event, x's having F, supervenes on the event, x's having G, just in case x has G and G is a supervenience base of F.

So the general schema for reducing a macrocausal relation between two events, x's having F and y's having G, where F and G are macroproperties, is this: x's having F supervenes on x's having m(F), y's having G supervenes on y's having m(G), where m(F) and m(G) are microproperties relative to F and G, and there is an appropriate causal connection between x's having m(F) and y's having m(G).

Any causal relation conforming to the pattern set forth above will be called a "supervenient causal relation." For the pattern can be taken to show the causal relation itself to be supervenient upon an underlying causal process through the supervenience of its relata upon the events involved in the underlying process.

I have left the causal relation between the two microevents unspecified; for it is not part of my present aim to advocate a particular analysis of causation. Generally, however, we would expect it to be mediated by laws, whether deterministic or statistical, and in favorable cases we may even have an account in terms of a mechanism by which one microstate evolves into another. But the kind of position I want to advocate here concerning macrocausation is largely independent of the particular views concerning the analysis of causation. Moreover, I do not wish to tie the fate of my general views about macrocausation too closely to the fate of my proposal regarding a proper construal of the relation between macroproperties and the microproperties on which they "depend." Although the use of mereological supervenience is an integral part of the total account being sketched here, the main points of the general picture of macrocausation I am advancing are independent of the question of what particular account is to be accepted for the macro–micro relation. What are these points? There are two: (1) macrocausal relations should be viewed as in general reducible to microcausal relations, and (2) the mechanism of the reduction involves identifying the microstates on which the macrostates in question depend, or with which they are correlated, and showing that a proper causal relation obtains for these microstates. Thus, to affirm (1) is to accept the view that macrocausation is to be viewed as epiphenomenal causation. To affirm that macrocausation is supervenient causation is to accept a particular account of the mechanism of reduction referred to in (2).

The sort of account I have given should be found attractive by those philosophers who believe that precise laws are rare—perhaps nonexistent—for macroproperties and states, at least those that are routinely referred to in ordinary causal talk, and that they must be "redescribed" at a more basic level before precise laws could be brought to bear on them.[10] My account in essence adds two things to this view: first, that *whether or not* there are macro-lawlike connections, macrocausal relations ought to be viewed as reducible to microcausal relations, and second, that what sanctions a given microredescription of a macrostate can be taken as a supervenience relation—that is to say, the relation between a macrodescription and a corresponding microredescription can be understood in terms of supervenience.

The broad metaphysical conviction that underlies these proposals is the belief that ultimately the world—at least, the physical world—is the way it is because the microworld is the way it is—because there are so many of just these sorts of microentities (elementary particles, atoms, or what not), and they behave in accordance with just these laws. As Terence Horgan has put it, worlds that are microphysically identical are one and the same world.[11] Even those who would reject this universal thesis of microdeterminism might find the following more restricted thesis plausible: worlds that are microphysically identical are one world from the physical point of view. This doctrine urges us to see macrocausal relations as emerging out of properties and relations holding for microentities, and this naturally leads to a search of microreductive accounts of macrocausal relations as well as other macroproperties, states, and facts. In fact, causal relations pervade our very conceptions of physical properties, states, and events (consider, for example, heat, magnetic, gene), and the reduction of causal relations, which often takes the form of exhibiting the micromechanisms underlying macrocausal relations, is probably the most important part of microreductive research. Causal relations that resist microreduction must be considered "causal danglers," which, like the notorious "nomological danglers," are an acute embarrassment to the physicalist view of the world.

There is ample evidence that the method of microreduction has been extremely successful in modern science, and it seems evident that much of the reduction that has been accomplished involves the reduction of macrocausal laws and relations.[12] The reduction of gas laws within kinetic theory of gases is of course a case in point; such examples are legion. Given our interest in identifying and understanding causal connections, it is not surprising that a predominant part of the reductive efforts in scientific research is directed toward the microreduction of macrocausal laws and relations. These last few remarks constitute the promised second prong of my defense of the claim that macrocausation ought to be viewed as epiphenomenal causation—and, more specifically, as supervenient causation.

3. Mereological Supervenience and Microdeterminism

The foregoing discussion moved fairly freely among such doctrines and concepts as microreduction, microexplanation, mereological supervenience, and microdeterminism, and I think it may be helpful to set forth their relationships more precisely. First of all, I am taking mereological supervenience and microdeterminism as a thesis concerning the objective features of the world—a metaphysical doctrine—roughly, as I said, to the effect that the macroworld is the way it is because the microworld is the way it is. The two doctrines can of course be sharpened and separated from each other. Mereological supervenience is usefully taken to be a general thesis affirming the supervenience of the characteristics of wholes on the properties and relationships characterizing their proper parts. Here, "characteristics" is understood to include relations, such as causal relations, among wholes. Mereological supervenience (in the sense of supervenience explained in the preceding section) requires that each (exemplified) macrocharacteristic be grounded in some specific microcharacteristics, and in this way it goes beyond the less specific thesis, earlier mentioned, that worlds that are microphysically identical are one and the same (physical) world. It may be convenient to reserve the term "microdeterminism" for this less specific thesis. It is plausible to think that under some reasonable assumptions, mereological supervenience as applied to the physical world entails microdeterminism; I am inclined to believe that, again under some reasonable assumptions, the converse entailment also holds.

In any event, it is useful to think of mereological supervenience and microdeterminism as constituting the metaphysical basis of the method of microreduction and microexplanation. By this I mean that the metaphysical doctrine rationalizes our microreductive proclivities by legitimatizing microreduction as a paradigm of scientific understanding and helping to explain why the microreductive method works as well as it does. Underlying this remark is the view that explanatory or reductive connections, as essentially epistemological connections, must themselves be grounded in the objective determinative connections holding for the events in the world. The root idea of causal determinism is the belief that the existence and properties of an event are determined by its temporally antecedent conditions. The metaphysical thesis of causal determinism can be thought of as the objective basis of the method of causal explanation—the method of seeking "laws of succession" and formulating explanations of events in terms of their antecedent conditions. Mereological supervenience views the world as determined along the part-whole dimension, whereas the causal determinism views it as determined along the temporal dimension; they respectively provide a metaphysical basis for the method of microreduction and that of causal explanation.

These are rather speculative and bald remarks; they are intended only to give a rough picture of the metaphysical terrain within which my more specific remarks concerning macrocausal relations can be located.

4. Mental Causation as Supervenient Causation

To say that the causal relation between two macroevents is a case of epiphenomenal causation is not to be understood to mean that the relation is illusory or unreal. In this respect, Jonathan Edwards's case of mirror images, Salmon's moving spot of light, and the case of successive symptoms of a disease differ from our central cases of macrocausal relations. For those cases, the causal relations are indeed only apparent: although the events are causally *related* in a broad sense, there is no direct causal relation *from* one event *to* the other—that is to say, one event is not the cause of the other. On the other hand, the causal relation between rising temperatures and increasing pressures of gases is no less "real" for being microreducible. To take microreducibility as impugning the reality of what is being reduced would make all of our observable world unreal. However, one reason for bundling the two types of cases together under "epiphenomenal causation" is the existence of another sense of "real" in which reduction does make what is reduced "less real," a sense in which modern physics is sometimes thought to have shown the unreality of ordinary material objects or a sense in which secondary qualities are sometimes thought to be "less real" than primary qualities. As I alluded earlier, reducibility is often taken to

imply eliminability; but this is a complex and unfruitful question to pursue here. There is, however, another more concrete reason for viewing these two kinds of cases under the same rubric; in both there is present an *apparent* causal relation that is explained, or explained away, at a more fundamental level. The difference between the two cases is this: macrocausal relations are *supervenient causal relations*—supervenient upon microcausal relations—whereas cases like Edwards's mirror images are not. This can be seen by reflecting on the fact that in a perfectly straightforward sense, mirror images, symptoms if a disease, and so on are causal effects of the underlying processes—they are not mereologically supervenient upon those processes. This is the theoretical difference between the two cases: some epiphenomenal causal relations are supervenient causal relations, and these are among the ones that are "real"; there are also cases of epiphenomenal causation that do not involve direct causal connections, and these include ones in which the events involved are successive causal effects of some underlying process.

What of causal relations involving mental events? Consider a typical case in which we would say a mental event causes a physical event: a sharp pain in my thumb causes a jerky withdrawal of my hand. It is hardly conceivable that the pain sensation qua mental event acts directly on the muscles of my arm, causing them to contract. I assume we have by now a fairly detailed story of what goes on at the physiological level when a limb movement takes place, and no amount of intuitive conviction or philosophical argument about the reality of psychophysical causation is going to preempt that story. If the pain is to play a causal role in the withdrawal of my hand, it must do so by somehow *making use of* the usual physiological causal path to this bodily event; it looks as though the causal path from the pain to the limb motion must *merge* with the physiological path at a certain point. There cannot be two independent, separate causal paths to the limb motion. But at what point does the mental causal path from the pain "merge" with the physiological path? If there is such a point, that must be where psychophysical causal action takes place. The trouble, of course, is that it is difficult to conceive the possibility of some nonphysical event causally influencing the course of physical processes.[13] Apart from the sheer impossibility of coherently imagining the details of what might have to be the case if some nonphysical agency is going to affect the course of purely physical events, there is a deeper problem that any such nonphysical intervention in a physical system would jeopardize the closed character of physical theory. It would force us to accept a conception of the physical in which to give a causal account of, say, the motion of a physical particle, it is sometimes necessary to go outside the physical system and appeal to some nonphysical agency and invoke some irreducible psychophysical law. Many will find this just not credible.

The difficulty of accounting for the possibility of psychophysical causation is simply resolved if one is willing to accept psychophysical identity: the pain *is* in fact a certain neural state, and the problem of accounting for the psychophysical causal relation is nothing but that of accounting for the causal relation between two physical states. On the other hand, if, for various reasons, one is averse to accepting a straightforward identity thesis, as many philosophers are, then the problem of accounting for psychophysical causation confronts us as a difficult problem, indeed.[14] The classical form of epiphenomenalism fails to provide a satisfactory solution, for it denies that mental-to-physical causal action ever takes place: mental phenomena are totally causally inert. And this is what many thinkers find so difficult to accept. If our reasons and desires have no causal efficacy at all in influencing our bodily actions, then perhaps no one has ever performed a single intentional action![15]

It seems to me that what is being advocated as "new" epiphenomenalism is not much help either. According to Keith Campbell, mental states are in fact brain states, but they have residual irreducible phenomenal properties as well; however, these phenomenal properties are causally impotent.[16] This position is akin to one of the two characterizations of epiphenomenalism offered by C. D. Broad some decades ago:

> Epiphenomenalism may be taken to assert one of two things. (a) That certain events which have physiological characteristics have *also* mental characteristics, and that no events which lack physiological characteristics have mental characteristics. That many events which have physiological characteristics are not known to have mental characteristics. And that an event which has mental characteristics never causes another event in virtue of its mental characteristics, but only in virtue of its physiological characteristics. Or (b) that no event has both mental and physiological characteristics; but that the complete cause of any event which has mental characteristics is an event or set of events which has physiological characteristics. And that no event which has mental characteristics is a cause-factor in the causation of any other event whatever, whether mental or physiological.[17]

The only significant difference between Broad's (a) and Campbell's epiphenomenalism seems to be that Broad's epiphenomenalism is formulated for all *mental* characteristics, presumably including intentional states such as belief and desire as well as phenomenal states, whereas Campbell is happy to take a straight physicalist approach with regard to mental states not involving phenomenal qualia. It is interesting to note that some versions of the currently popular "token identity" thesis are also strikingly similar to Broad's epiphenomenalism. Consider, for example, the influential "anomalous monism" of Donald Davidson.[18] According to this account, there are no type–type correlations between the mental and the physical; however, each individual mental event is in fact a physical event in the following sense: any event that has a mental description has also a physical description. Further, it is only under its physical description that a mental event can be seen to enter into a causal relation with a physical event (or any other event) by being subsumed under a causal law. If we read "mental characteristic" for "mental description" and "physiological characteristic" for "physical description," then something very much like Broad's (a) above emerges from Davidson's anomalous monism.

Broad's epiphenomenalism, however, did not satisfy philosophers who looked for a place for our commonsense conviction in the reality of psychophysical causation. Thus, William Kneale refers to "the great paradox of epiphenomenalism," which arises from "the suggestion that we are necessarily mistaken in all our ordinary thought about human action."[19] It seems to me that, for similar reasons, Davidson's anomalous monism fails to do full justice to psychophysical causation—that is, it fails to provide an account of psychophysical causation in which the mental *qua mental* has any real causal role to play. Consider Davidson's account: whether or not a given event has a mental description (optional reading: whether it has a mental characteristic) seems entirely irrelevant to what causal relations it enters into. Its causal powers are wholly determined by the physical description or characteristic that holds for it; for it is under its physical description that it may be subsumed under a causal law. And Davidson explicitly denies any possibility of a nomological connection between an event's mental description and its physical description that could bring the mental into the causal picture.[20]

The delicate task is to find an account that will give the mental a substantial enough causal role to let us avoid "the great paradox of epiphenomenalism" without infringing upon the closedness of physical causal systems. I suggest that we view psychophysical causal relations—in fact, all causal relations involving psychological events—as epiphenomenal supervenient causal relations. More specifically, when a mental event M causes a physical event P, this is so because M is supervenient upon a physical event, P*, and P* causes P. This latter may itself be a supervenient causal relation, but that is no matter: what is important is that, at some point, purely physical causal processes take over. Similarly, when mental event M causes another mental event M*, this is so because M supervenes on a physical state P, and similarly M* on P*, and P causes P*.

Thus, if a pain causes the sensation of fear an instant later, this account tells the following story: the pain is supervenient on a brain state, this brain state causes another appropriate brain state, and given this second brain state, the fear sensation must occur, for it is supervenient upon that brain state. I think this is a plausible picture that, among other things, nicely accounts for the temporal gaps and discontinuities in the series of causally related mental events. Returning to the case of a pain causing a hand to withdraw, we should note that, on the present account, no causal path from the pain "merges" with the physiological causal chain at any point. For there is no separate path from the pain to the limb withdrawal; there is only one causal path in this situation, namely the one from the neural state upon which the pain supervenes to the movement of the hand.

Does this proposal satisfy the desiderata we set for an adequate account of psychophysical causation? It would be foolish to pretend that the proposed account accords to the mental the full causal potency we accord to fundamental physical processes. On the other hand, it does not treat mental phenomena as causally inert epiphenomena; nor does it reduce mental causation to the status of a mere chimera. Mental causation does take place; it is only that it is epiphenomenal causation, that is, a causal relation that is reducible to, or explainable by, the causal processes taking place at a more basic physical level. And this, according to the present account, is also precisely what happens with macrophysical causation relations. *Epiphenomenal causal relations involving psychological events, therefore, are no less real or substantial than those involving macrophysical events. They are both supervenient causal relations.* It seems to me that this is sufficient to redeem the causal powers we ordinarily attribute to mental events. Does the account meet the other desideratum of respecting the closed character of physical theory? It evidently does; for supervenient epiphenomenal causation does not place the supervenient events at the level of the underlying causal processes to which it is reduced. Mental events do not become part of the fundamental physical causal chains any more than macrophysical events become part of the microphysical causal chains that underlie them.

One remaining question is whether psychological events do supervene on physical events and processes. If psychological states are conceived as some sort of inner theoretical states posited to explain the observable behavior of organisms, there is little doubt that they will be supervenient on physical states.[21] However, there are serious questions as to whether that is a satisfactory conception of the mental; and I believe these questions lead to a serious doubt as to whether *intentional* mental states, namely those with propositional content such as beliefs and desires, are determined wholly by the physical details of the organism or even by the total physical environment that includes the organism. However, this need not be taken as casting doubt on the account of psychological causation offered here; I think we may more appropriately take it as an occasion for reconsidering whether, and in what way, intentional psychological states enter into causal relations—especially with physical events. I think that the two questions, whether intentional psychological states are supervenient on the physical and whether they enter into *lawbased* causal relations with physical processes, are arguably equivalent questions. Psychophysical supervenience is a good deal more plausible, I believe, with regard to phenomenal mental states, and I am prepared to let the account of psychological causation proposed here stand for all psychological events and states that are physically supervenient.

NOTES

1. Jonathan Edwards, *Doctrine of Original Sin Defended* (1758), Part IV, Chap. II. The quotation is taken from *Jonathan Edwards,* edited by C. H. Faust and T. H. Johnson (New York, 1935), 335. I owe this interesting reference to Roderick M. Chisholm's discussion of Edwards's views in connection with the "Doctrine of Temporal Parts," in *Person and Object* (La Salle, Ill., 1976), 138ff.

2. Faust and Johnson, *Jonathan Edwards,* 336.

3. Wesley C. Salmon, "An 'At–At' Theory of Causal Influence," *Philosophy of Science* 44 (1977):215–24.

4. For a discussion of the issues see John Lachs, "Epiphenomenalism and the Notion of Cause," *Journal of Philosophy* 60 (1963):141–45.

5. For example, see J.J.C. Smart, "Sensations and Brain Processes," *Philosophical Review* 68 (1958):141–56.

6. The thesis of mereological supervenience itself need not carry a commitment to atomism.

7. There is a large literature on this and related issues concerning microreduction; see, e.g., Lawrence Sklar, "Types of Inter-Theoretic Reductions," *British Journal for the Philosophy of Science* 18 (1967):109–24; Robert L. Causey, *Unity of Science* (Dordrecht, 1977).

8. See, e.g., Hilary Putnam, "The Nature of Mental States," and Ned Block and J. A. Fodor, "What Psychological States Are Not," both in *Readings in Philosophy of Psychology* vol. 1, edited by Ned Block (Cambridge, Mass., 1980).

9. This corresponds to "strong supervenience" as characterized in my "Concepts of Supervenience" (forthcoming); for a general discussion of supervenience see also my "Supervenience and Nomological Incommensurables," *American Philosophical Quarterly* 15 (1978):149–56.

10. For an influential view of this kind see Donald Davidson, "Causal Relations," *Journal of Philosophy* 64 (1967):691–703.

11. See Terence Horgan, "Supervenience and Microphysics," *Pacific Philosophical Quarterly* 63 (1982):29–43; see also David Lewis, "New Work for a Theory of Universals" (forthcoming).

12. See the somewhat dated but still useful "Unity of Science as a Working Hypothesis" by Paul Oppenheim and Hilary Putnam, in *Minnesota Studies in the Philosophy of Science*, vol. 2, edited by Herbert Feigl et al. (Minneapolis, 1958).

13. For an effective description of the difficulty see Richard Taylor, *Metaphysics*, 3d ed. (Englewood Cliffs, N.J., 1983), chap. 3.

14. For some arguments against the identity thesis see Putnam, "Nature of Mental States"; Saul Kripke, *Naming and Necessity* (Cambridge, Mass., 1980), 144–55. For discus-sions of the problem of psychophysical causation see, e.g., J. L. Mackie, "Mind, Brain, and Causation," *Midwest Studies in Philosophy* 4 (1979):19–30; and my "Causality, Identity and Supervenience in the Mind-Body Problem," *Midwest Studies in Philosophy* 4 (1979):31–49.

15. See, e.g., Norman Malcolm, "The Conceivability of Mechanism," *Philosophical Review* 77 (1968):45–72.

16. *Body and Mind* (New York, 1970), chap. 6.

17. *The Mind and Its Place in Nature* (London, 1925), 472.

18. In "Mental Events" reprinted in Davidson, *Essays on Actions and Events* (New York, 1980).

19. William Kneale, "Broad on Mental Events and Epiphenomenalism," in *The Philosophy of C. D. Broad*, edited by P. A. Schilpp (New York, 1959), 453. See also Jerome A. Shaffer, *Philosophy of Mind* (Englewood Cliffs, N.J., 1968), 68–71; Taylor, *Metaphysics*, chap. 4.

20. See his "Mental Events" for an extended argument against psychophysical lawlike connections. I give an analysis, and a partial defense, of Davidson's argument in "Psychophysical Laws," in Ernest LePore and Brian McLaughlin, eds., *Actions and Events: Perspectives on the Philosophy of Donald Davidson* (Oxford: Basil Blackwell, 1985), pp. 369–386 [reference added by author].

21. For details see my "Psychophysical Supervenience," *Philosophical Studies* 41 (1982): 51–70.

D. Eliminative Materialism

28

Paul Feyerabend

"Mental Events and the Brain"

Shaffer's note (The *Journal of Philosophy*, 60, 6: 160) and the preceding discussion to which it refers show very clearly the dilemma of any identity hypothesis concerning mental events and brain processes. Such hypotheses are usually put forth by physiologically inclined thinkers who want also to be empiricists. Being physiologically inclined, they want to assert the *material* character of mental processes. Being empiricists, they want their assertion to be a testable statement about *mental* processes. They try to combine the two tendencies in an empirical statement of the form:

$$X \text{ is a mental process of kind A}$$
$$\equiv X \text{ is a central process of kind } \alpha \text{ (H)}$$

But this hypothesis backfires. It not only implies, as it is intended to imply, that mental events have physical features; it also seems to imply (if read from the right to the left) that some physical events, viz. central processes, have nonphysical features. It thereby replaces a dualism of events by a dualism of features. Moreover, this consequence seems to be the result of the way in which the physiologist has *formulated* his thesis. Even if he is a convinced monist he seems to be forced, by the very content of his thesis of monism, to acknowledge the correctness of a *dualistic* point of view.

For a dualist this predicament is proof of the untenability of monism. But surely he is too rash in drawing this conclusion! H implies dualism. Hence, dualism will be true *provided* H is true. However, if *monism* is correct, then H is false: there are then *no* mental processes in the usual (nonmaterialistic) sense. This shows that the discussion of the content of H regarded as an empirical hypothesis is not at all sufficient for deciding the issue between monism and dualism. It also shows *that the monist misstates his case when defending* H.

The proper procedure for him to adopt is to develop his theory without any recourse to existent terminology. If he wants to use H at all, he ought to use it for *redefining* 'mental process' (if he intends to perpetuate ancient terminology, that is). The empirical character of his theory is not endangered thereby. After all, a physiological theory of epilepsy does not become an empty tautology on account of the fact that it does not make use of the phrase—or of the notion—'possessed by the devil', 'devil' here occurring in its *theological* sense. There are enough independent predictions available, many more predictions in fact than the mentalist could ever provide—or would even be willing to provide (think only of the tremendous field of the physiology of perception).

However, so it is usually objected, unless a connection is established with previous language, we do not know what we are talking about, and we are therefore not able to formulate our observational results. This objection assumes that the terms of a general point of view and of a corresponding language can obtain meaning only by being related to the terms of some other point of view that is familiar and known by all. Now if that is indeed the case, then how did the latter point of view and the latter language ever obtain its familiarity? And if it could obtain its familiarity without help "from outside," as it obviously did, then there is no reason to assume that a different point of view cannot do equally well. (Besides, we learn the ordinary idiom when we are small children; is it assumed that a grown-up physiologist will be incapable of doing what a small child does quite well?) Moreover, observational results always have to be for-

From *The Journal of Philosophy* LX, 11 (May 23, 1963): 295–96. Reprinted with permission of the editors and Paul K. Feyerabend.

mulated with respect to a certain background of theory (with respect to a certain language-game, to use more fashionable terminology). There is no reason why physiology should not by itself be capable of forming such a background. We have to conclude, then, that the reasonableness—and the success—of a purely physiological approach to human beings is not at all dependent on the outcome of an analysis of H.

"Bridge-laws" such as H play a most important role within the current theory of explanation and reduction. If our comments above are correct, then it follows that these theories are inadequate as measures of the success of theory construction.

29

Richard Rorty

from "Persons Without Minds"

1. The Antipodeans

Far away, on the other side of our galaxy, there was a planet on which lived beings like ourselves—featherless bipeds who built houses and bombs, and wrote poems and computer programs. These beings did not know that they had minds. They had notions like "wanting to" and "intending to" and "believing that" and "feeling terrible" and "feeling marvelous." But they had no notion that these signified *mental* states—states of a peculiar and distinct sort—quite different from "sitting down," "having a cold," and "being sexually aroused." Although they used the notions of believing and knowing and wanting and being moody of their pets and their robots as well as of themselves, they did not regard pets or robots as included in what was meant when they said, "We all believe ..." or "We never do such things as. . . ." That is to say, they treated only members of their own species as *persons*. But they did not explain the difference between persons and nonpersons by such notions as "mind," "consciousness," "spirit," or anything of the sort. They did not *explain* it at all; they just treated it as the difference between "us" and everything else. They believed in immortality for themselves, and a few believed that this would be shared by the pets or the robots, or both. But this immortality did not involve the notion of a "soul" which separated from the body. It was a straightforward matter of bodily resurrection followed by mysterious and instantaneous motion to what they referred to as "a place about the heavens" for good people, and to a sort of cave, beneath the planet's surface, for the wicked. Their philosophers were concerned primarily with four topics: the nature of Being, proofs of the existence of a Benevolent and Omnipotent Being who would carry out arrangements for the resurrection, problems arising out of discourse about nonexistent objects, and the reconciliation of conflicting moral intuitions. But these philosophers had not formulated the problem of subject and object, nor that of mind and matter. There was a tradition of Pyrrhonian skepticism, but Locke's "veil of ideas" was unknown, since the notion of an "idea" or "perception" or "mental representation" was also unknown. Some of their philosophers predicted that the beliefs about immortality which had been central in earlier periods of history, and which were still held by all but the intelligentsia, would someday be replaced by a "positivistic" culture purged of all superstitions (but these philosophers made no mention of an intervening "metaphysical" stage).

In most respects, then, the language, life, technology, and philosophy of this race were much like ours. But there was one important difference. Neurology and biochemistry had been the first disciplines in which technological breakthroughs had been achieved, and a large part of the conversation of these people concerned the state of their nerves. When their infants veered toward hot stoves, mothers cried out, "He'll stimulate his C-fibers." When people were given clever visual illusions to look at, they said, "How odd! It makes neuronic bundle G-14 quiver, but when I look at it from the side I can see that it's not a red rectangle at all." Their knowledge of physiology was such that each well-formed sentence in the language which anybody bothered to form could easily be correlated with a readily identifiable neural state. This state occurred whenever someone uttered, or was tempted to utter, or heard, the sentence. This state also sometimes occurred in solitude and people reported such occasions with remarks like "I was suddenly in state S-296, so I put out the milk bottles." Sometimes they would say things like "It looked like an elephant, but then it struck me that elephants don't occur on this continent, so I realized that it must be a mastodon." But they would also sometimes say, in just the same circumstances, things like "I had G-412 together with F-11, but then I had S-147, so I realized that it must be a mastodon." They thought of mastodons and milk bottles as objects of beliefs and desires, and as causing certain neural processes. They viewed these neural processes as interacting causally with beliefs and desires—in just the same way as the mastodons and milk bottles did. Certain neural processes could be deliberately self-induced, and some people were more skillful than others in inducing certain neural states in themselves. Others were skilled at detecting certain special states which most people could not recognize in themselves.

In the middle of the twenty-first century, an expedition from Earth landed on this planet. The expedition included philosophers, as well as representatives of every other learned discipline. The philosophers thought that the most interesting thing about the natives was their lack of the concept of mind. They joked among themselves that they had landed among a bunch of materialists, and suggested the name Antipodea for the planet—in reference to an almost forgotten school of philosophers, centering in Australia and New Zealand, who in the previous century had attempted one of the many futile revolts against Cartesian dualism in the history of Terran philosophy. The name stuck, and so the new race of intelligent beings came to be known as Antipodeans. The Terran neurologists and biochemists were fascinated by the wealth of knowledge in their field which the Antipodeans exhibited. Since technical conversation on these subjects was conducted almost entirely in offhand references to neural states, the Terran experts eventually picked up the ability to report their own neural states (without conscious inference) instead of reporting their thoughts, perceptions, and raw feels. (The physiologies of the two species were, fortunately, almost identical.) Everything went swimmingly, except for the difficulties met by the philosophers.

The philosophers who had come on the expedition were, as usual, divided into two warring camps: the tender-minded ones who thought philosophy should aim at Significance, and the tough-minded philosophers who thought that it should aim at Truth. The philosophers of the first sort felt that there was no real problem about whether the Antipodeans had minds. They held that what was important in understanding other beings was a grasp of their mode of being-in-the-world. It became evident that, whatever *Existentiale* the Antipodeans were using, they certainly did not include any of those which, a century earlier, Heidegger had criticized as "subjectivist." The whole notion of "the epistemological subject," or the person as spirit, had no place in their self-descriptions, nor in their philosophies. Some of the tender-minded philosophers felt that this showed that the Antipodeans had not yet broken out of Nature into Spirit, or, more charitably, had not yet progressed from Consciousness to Self-Consciousness. These philosophers became town-criers of inwardness, attempting to bully the Antipodeans across an invisible line and into the Realm of Spirit. Others, however, felt that the Antipodeans exhibited the praiseworthy grasp of the union of πόλεμος and λόγος which was lost to Western Terran consciousness through Plato's assimilation of οὐσία to ἰδέα. The Antipodean failure to grasp the notion of mind, in the view of this set of philosophers, showed their closeness to Being and their freedom from the temptations to which Terran thought had long since succumbed. In the contest between these two views, equally tender-minded as both were, discussion tended to be inconclusive. The Antipodeans themselves were not much help, because they had so much trouble translating the background reading necessary to appreciate the problem—Plato's *Theaetetus,* Descartes's *Meditations,* Hume's *Treatise,* Kant's *Critique of Pure Reason,* Hegel's *Phenomenology,* Strawson's *Individuals,* etc.

The tough-minded philosophers, as usual, found a much more straightforward and clean-cut question to discuss. They did not care what the Antipodeans thought about themselves, but rather focused on the question: Do they in fact have minds? In their precise way, they narrowed this question down to: Do they in fact have sensations? It was thought that if it became clear whether they had, say, sensations of pain, as well as stimulated C-fibers, when touching hot stoves, everything else would be plain sailing. It was clear that the Antipodeans had the same behavioral dispositions toward hot stoves, muscle cramps, torture, and the like as humans. They loathed having their C-fibers stimulated. But the tough-minded philosophers asked themselves: Does their experience contain the same phenomenal properties as ours? Does the stimulation of C-fibers feel painful? Or does it feel some other, equally awful, way? Or does feeling not come into it at all? These philosophers were not surprised that the Antipodeans could offer noninferential reports of their own neural states, since it had been learned long since that psycho-physiologists could train human subjects to report alpha-rhythms, as well as various other physiologically describable cortical states. But they felt baffled by the question: Are some phenomenal properties being detected by an Antipodean who says, "It's my C-fibers again—you know, the ones that go off every time you get burned or hit or have a tooth pulled. It's just awful."?

It was suggested that the question could only be answered experimentally, and so they arranged with the neurologists that one of their number should be wired up to an Antipodean volunteer so as to switch currents back and forth between various regions of the two brains. This, it was thought, would also enable the philosophers to insure that the Antipodeans did not have an inverted spectrum, or anything else which might confuse the issue. As it turned out, however, the experiment produced no interesting results. The difficulty was that when the Antipodean speech center got an input from the C-fibers of the Earthling brain it always talked only about its C-fibers, whereas when the Earthling speech center was in control it always talked only about pain. When the Antipodean speech center was asked what the C-fibers felt like it said that it didn't quite get the notion of "feeling," but that stimulated C-fibers were, of course, terrible things to have. The same sort of thing happened for the questions about inverted spectra and other perceptual qualities. When asked to call off the colors on a chart, both speech centers called off the usual color-names in the same order. But the Antipodean speech center could also call off the various neuronic bundles activated by each patch on the chart (no matter which visual cortex it happened to be hooked up to). When the Earthling speech center was asked what the colors were like when transmitted to the Antipodean visual cortex, it said that they seemed just as usual.

This experiment seemed not to have helped. For it was still obscure whether the Antipodeans had pains. It was equally obscure whether they had one or two raw feels when indigo light streamed onto their retinas (one of indigo, and one of neural state C-692)—or whether they had no raw feels at all. The Antipodeans were repeatedly questioned about how they knew it was indigo. They replied that they could see that it was. When asked how they knew they were in C-692, they said they "just knew" it. When it was suggested to them that they might have unconsciously inferred that it was indigo on the basis of the C-692 feel, they seemed unable to understand what unconscious inference was, or what "feels" were. When it was suggested to them that they might have made the same in-

ference to the fact that they were in state C-692 on the basis of the raw feel of indigo, they were, of course, equally baffled. When they were asked whether the neural state appeared indigo, they replied that it did not—the *light* was indigo—and that the questioner must be making some sort of category mistake. When they were asked whether they could imagine having C-692 and not seeing indigo, they said they could not. When asked whether it was a conceptual truth or an empirical generalization that these two experiences went together, they replied that they were not sure how to tell the difference. When asked whether they could be wrong about whether they were seeing indigo, they replied that they of course could, but could not be wrong about whether they seemed to be seeing indigo. When asked whether they could be wrong about whether they were in state C-692, they replied in exactly the same way. Finally, skillful philosophical dialectic brought them to realize that what they could not imagine was seeming to see indigo and failing to seem to be in state C-692. But this result did not seem to help with the questions: "Raw feels?" "Two raw feels or one?" "Two referents or one referent under two descriptions?" Nor did any of this help with the question about the way in which stimulated C-fibers appeared to them. When they were asked whether they could be mistaken in thinking that their C-fibers were stimulated, they replied that of course they could—but that they could not imagine being mistaken about whether their C-fibers seemed to be stimulated.

At this point, it occurred to someone to ask whether they could detect the neural state which was the concomitant of "seeming to have their C-fibers stimulated." Antipodeans replied that there was, of course, the state T_{-435} which was the constant neural concomitant of the utterance of the sentence "My C-fibers seem to be stimulated," state T_{-497} which went with "It's just as if my C-fibers were being stimulated," state T_{-293} which went with "Stimulated C-fibers!" and various other neural states which were concomitants of various other roughly synonymous sentences—but that there was no further neural state which they were aware of in addition to these. Cases in which Antipodeans had T_{-435} but no stimulation of C-fibers included those in which, for example, they were strapped to what they were falsely informed was a torture machine, a switch was theatrically turned on, but nothing else was done.

Discussion among the philosophers now switched to the topic: Could the Antipodeans be mistaken about the T-series of neural states (the ones which were concomitants of understanding or uttering sentences)? Could they seem to be having T-$_{435}$ but not really be? Yes, the Antipodeans said, cerebroscopes indicated that sort of thing occasionally happened. Was there any explanation of the cases in which it happened—any pattern to them? No, there did not seem to be. It was just one of those odd things that turned up occasionally. Neurophysiology had not yet been able to find another sort of neural state, outside the T-series, which was a concomitant of such weird illusions, any more than for certain perceptual illusions, but perhaps it would someday.

This answer left the philosophers still in difficulties on the question of whether the Antipodeans had sensations of pain, or anything else. For there now seemed to be nothing which the Antipodeans were incorrigible about except how things seemed to them. But it was not clear that "how things seemed to them" was a matter of what raw feels they had, as opposed to what they were inclined to say. If they had the raw feel of painfulness, then they had minds. But a raw feel is (or has) a phenomenal property—one which you cannot have the illusion of having (because, so to speak, having the illusion of it is itself to have it). The difference between stimulated C-fibers and pains was that you could have the illusion of stimulated C-fibers (could have, e.g., T-$_{435}$) without having stimulated C-fibers, but could not have the illusion of pain without having pain. There was nothing which the Antipodeans could not be wrong about except how things seemed to them. But the fact that they could not "merely seem to have it seem to them that . . ." was of no interest in determining whether they had minds. The fact that "seems to seem . . ." is an expression without a use is a fact about the notion of "appearance," not a tip-off to the presence of "phenomenal properties." For the appearance–reality distinction is not based on a distinction between subjective representations and objective states of affairs; it is merely a matter of getting something wrong, having a false belief. So the Antipodeans' firm grasp of the former distinction did not help philosophers tell whether to ascribe the latter to them.

2. Phenomenal Properties

Coming back now to the present, what *should* we say about the Antipodeans? The first thing to do, presumably, is to look more closely at the notion of "phenomenal property," and in particular at the disanalogy between apprehending a physical phenomenon in a misleading way and apprehending a mental phenomenon in a misleading way.

Kripke's account of the distinction sums up the intuition on which defenders of dualism have usually relied, so we may begin a closer look by trying to apply his terminology:

> Someone can be in the same epistemic situation as he would be if there were heat, even in the absence of heat, simply by feeling the sensation of heat; and even in the presence of heat, he can have the same evidence as he would have in the absence of heat simply by lacking the sensation S. No such possibility exists in the case of pain or in other mental phenomena. To be in the same epistemic situation that would obtain if one had a pain *is* to have a pain; to be in the same epistemic situation that would obtain in the absence of a pain *is* not to have a pain. . . . The trouble is that the notion of an epistemic situation qualitatively identical to one in which the observer had a sensation S simply *is* one in which the observer had that sensation. The same point can be made in terms of the notion of what picks out the reference of a rigid designator [an expression which designates the same object in all the possible worlds in which it designates at all]. In the case of identity of heat with molecular motion the important consideration was that although "heat" is a rigid designator, the reference of that designator was determined by an accidental property of the referent, namely the property of producing in us the sensation S. . . . Pain, on the other hand, is not picked out by one of its accidental properties; rather it is picked out by the property of being pain itself, by its immediate phenomenological quality. Thus pain, unlike heat, is not only rigidly designated by "pain" but the reference of the designator is determined by an essential property of the referent. Thus it is not possible to say that although pain is necessarily identical with a certain physical state, a certain phenomenon can be picked out in the same way we pick out pain without being correlated with that physical state. If any phenomenon is picked out in exactly the same way that we pick out pain, then that phenomenon *is* pain.[1]

These considerations suggest that the real question is: Do the Antipodeans pick out mental phenomena by accidental properties? If we assume for the moment that they *do* have pains, could they perhaps miss the "immediate phenomenological quality" and note only the accidental feature of being constantly accompanied by stimulated C-fibers? Or, if they cannot exactly *miss* an immediate phenomenological quality, might they perhaps fail to have a name for it, and thus fail to pick out the entity that has the quality by an essential property? To put it another way, since the Antipodeans do *not* pick out pain "in exactly the same way that we pick out pain," can we conclude that whatever they have it is *not* pain? Is one's epistemic relation to one's raw feels necessary as well as sufficient to establish the existence of the raw feel in question?

Or should we say that actually they *do* pick out pain in exactly the way that we do—because when they say, "Ooh! Stimulated C-fibers!" they feel exactly what we feel when we say, "Pain!"? Actually, perhaps, they were feeling pain and calling that feeling "the state of seeming to have one's C-fibers stimulated," and they are in the same epistemic situation relative to seeming to have their C-fibers stimulated as we are in seeming to see something red, and to all other such incorrigible states.

It now looks as if what we need is some quite general criterion for deciding when two things are "really" the same thing described in two different ways. For there seems nothing distinctive about the present conundrum which makes it depend upon the peculiarities of the mental. If we agree that what counts in deciding whether the Antipodeans have raw feels is incorrigibility—the inability to have an illusion of . . .—the general problem about alternative descriptions will still prevent us from applying this criterion and thus resolving the issue. This problem is not one which is going to receive a neat, clear-cut, readily applicable solution. For nothing general will resolve every tension between saying,

> You're talking about X's all right, but practically everything you say about them is false

and saying instead,

> Since practically nothing you say is true of X's, you can't be talking about X's.

But let us put aside this difficulty for the moment (returning to it in chapter six) and consider the still more depressing point that anyone who even tried to state general criteria for assimilating or distinguishing referents of expressions would need some general ontological categories—some firm, if coarse, way of blocking things out—just to get started. It would help, in particular, to have a distinction between mental entities and physical entities. But the problem about the Antipodeans puts this whole distinction in doubt. To see why it does so, suppose that there are no criteria for "mental phenomenon" save Kripke's epistemic one.[2] This supposition identifies "the mental" with raw feels, passing thoughts, and mental images. It excludes such things as beliefs, moods, and the like (which, though indubitably "higher," are nonetheless not parts of our incorrigibly reportable inner life, and hence not such as to encourage the Cartesian kind of distinction between two ontological realms). The supposal amounts, in other words, to the claim that (1) it is sufficient for being a mental state that the thing in question be incorrigibly knowable by its possessor, and (2) we do not literally attribute any nonphysical states (e.g., beliefs)

to beings which fail to have some such incorrigibly knowable states. (This conforms to Antipodean practice, as well as to our intuition that dogs have nonphysical states simply by virtue of having pains, whereas computers do not, even by virtue of offering us novel and exciting truths.) On this supposition, then, there will be *nothing* to answer to the question "When they report that their C-fibers seem to be firing, are they reporting a feeling (perhaps the same feeling that we report by "pain!") or are they just making the noises which are triggered by their neurons being in certain states?" And if this is so, since the role played in our lives by reports of feelings is the same as the role played in Antipodean lives by reports of neurons, we face the further question: Are *we* reporting feelings or neurons when *we* use "pain"?

To see that this is a real issue, consider the implications of the identity of functional role. If it is the case that the Antipodeans have the entire range of culture that we do, if they are as intentional in their discourse and as self-consciously aesthetic in their choice of objects and persons as we, if their yearning for moral excellence and immortality is as great, they are likely to think our philosophers' interest in whether they have minds is a bit parochial. Why, they wonder, does it make such a difference? Why, they may ask us, do *we* think that we have these odd things called "feels" and "minds"? Now that they have taught us microneurology, cannot we see that talk of mental states was merely a place-holder for talk of neurons? Or, if we really do have some funny extra states besides the neurological ones, are they really all that important? Is the possession of such states really the basis for a distinction between ontological categories?

These last sets of questions illustrate how lightly the Antipodeans take the controversy which, among Terran philosophers, is the hard-fought issue between materialists and epiphenomenalists. Further, the success of Antipodean neurology, not only in the explanation and control of behavior but in supplying the vocabulary for the Antipodean self-image, shows that none of the other Terran theories about "the relation between mind and body" can even get a look-in. For parallelism and epiphenomenalism can only be differentiated on some non-Humean view of causation—some view according to which there is a causal mechanism to be discovered which will show which way causal lines run. But nobody, not even the most diehard Cartesian, imagines that when a molecule-by-molecule account of the neurons is before us (as, *ex hypothesi*, it is before the Antipodeans) there will still be a place to look for further causal mechanisms. (What would "looking" amount to?) So even if we abandon Hume, we are still in no position to be parallelist, except on some a priori ground according to which we "just know" that the mental is a self-contained causal realm. As for interactionism, the Antipodeans would not dream of denying that beliefs and desires, for example, interact causally with irradiations of the retina, movements of the arm, and so on. But they view talk of such an interaction not as yoking different ontological realms but as a handy (because brief) reference to function rather than to structure. (It is as philosophically unproblematic as a transaction between a government and an individual. No set of necessary and sufficient conditions stated in terms of just who did what to whom can be given for a remark about such a transaction, any more than for remarks about beliefs caused by radiations and movements caused by beliefs—but who would have thought they could?) Interaction would only be of interest if a neural discharge were swerved from its course by a raw feel, or drained of some of its power by a raw feel, or something of the sort. But the Antipodean neurologists have no need of such hypotheses.

If there is no way of explaining to the Antipodeans our problems and theories about mind and body—no way of making them see that this is the paradigm case of an ontological divide—we ought to be prepared to face up to the possibility that the "materialist" Antipodeans (as opposed to the more charitable "epiphenomenalist" ones) are right: we have just been reporting neurons when we thought we were reporting raw feels. It was just a happenstance of our cultural development that we got stuck so long with place-holders. It is as if, while perfecting many sublunary disciplines, we had never developed astronomy and had remained pre-Ptolemaic in our notions of what was above the moon. We would doubtless have many complicated things to say about holes in the black dome, movements of the dome as a whole, and the like—but once we were clued in we could redescribe what we had been reporting easily enough.

At this point, however, there is a familiar objection to be dealt with. It is expressed in such remarks as the following:

> . . . in the case of stabbing pains, it is not possible to hold that the micro-picture is the real picture, that perceptual appearances are only a coarse duplication, for in this case we are dealing with the perceptual appearances themselves, which cannot very well be a coarse duplicate of themselves.[3]

It is all very well to claim that hurtfulness is how activity of the C-fibers in the cortex appears, that the smell of onion is how the shape of onion molecules

appears to a human with a normal nasal system. . . . This deals with the pain, smell or color apprehended and, relegating it to the category of appearance, renders it ontically neutral. But it leaves us with a set of *seemings,* acts of imperfect apprehension, in which the phenomenal properties are grasped. So we must ask the new question: Is it possible that things can *seem to be* in a certain way to a merely material system? Is there a way in which acts of imperfect apprehension can be seen to be ontically neutral?

> . . . The materialist account of real men can find no place for the fact that our imperfect apprehension is by phenomenal property and not by, for example, beliefs just spontaneously arising.[4]

This objection common to Brandt and Campbell seems at first blush to be that one can only misdescribe things if one is not a "merely material system"—for such systems cannot have things appear to them differently from what they are. But this will not do as it stands, for, as I suggested earlier, the distinction between reality and appearance seems merely the distinction between getting things right and getting things wrong—a distinction which we have no trouble making for simple robots, servo-mechanisms, etc. To make the objection plausible we must say that "appearance" in the present context is a richer notion—one which has to be explicated by the notion of "phenomenal property." We must hold some principle like:

(P) Whenever we make an incorrigible report on a state of ourselves, there must be a property we are presented with which induces us to make the report.

But this principle, of course, enshrines the Cartesian notion that "nothing is closer to the mind than itself," and involves an entire epistemology and metaphysics, a specifically dualistic one.[5] So it is not surprising, once we have encapsulated this view in the notion of "phenomenal property," that "the materialist account . . . can find no place for the fact that our imperfect apprehension is by phenomenal property."

Still, we must ask whether there is some prephilosophical intuition which is preserved in (P) and which can be separated from the Cartesian picture. What exactly is the difference between misdescribing something like a star and misdescribing something like a pain? Why does the former seem obviously possible and the latter unimaginable? Perhaps the answer goes something like this. We expect the star to look the same even after we realize that it is a faraway ball of flame rather than a nearby hole, but the pain ought to feel different once we realize that it is a stimulated C-fiber, for the pain *is* a feeling, as the star is *not* a visual appearance. If we give this answer, however, we are still stuck with the notion of "feeling" and with the puzzle about whether the Antipodeans have any feelings. What, we must ask, is the difference between feeling a pain and simply reacting to a stimulated C-fiber with the vocable "pain," avoidance-behavior, and the like? And here we are inclined to say: no difference at all from the outside, but all the difference in the world from the inside. The difficulty is that there will never be any way in which we can explain this difference to the Antipodeans. The materialist Antipodeans think that we don't have any feelings, because they do not think there is such a thing as "feeling." The epiphenomenalist Antipodeans think that there may be such things, but cannot imagine why we make such a fuss about having them. The Terran philosophers who think that Antipodeans do have feelings but don't know it have reached the terminal stage of philosophizing mentioned by Wittgenstein: they just feel like uttering an inarticulate sound. They cannot even say to the Antipodeans that "it's different for us on the inside" because the Antipodeans do not understand the notion of "inner space"; they think "inside" means "inside the skull." *There,* they rightly remark, it *isn't* different. The Terran philosophers who think that the Antipodeans don't have feelings are in a better position only because they feel it beneath their dignity to argue with mindless beings about whether they have minds.

We seem to be getting nowhere with pursuing the objection offered by Brandt and Campbell. Let us try another tack. In the materialist view, every appearance of anything is going to be, in reality, a brain-state. So, it would seem, the materialist is going to have to say that the "coarse" duplicate of a brain-state (the way stimulated C-fibers feel) is going to be another brain-state. But, we may then say, let that other brain-state be the referent of "pain" rather than the stimulated C-fibers. Every time the materialist says "but that's just our description of a brain-state," his opponent will reply, "Okay, let's talk about the brain-state which is the 'act of imperfect apprehension' of the first brain-state."[6] And so the materialist seems to be pressed ever backward—with the mental cropping up again wherever error does. It is as if man's Glassy Essence, the Mirror of Nature, only became visible to itself when slightly clouded. A neural system can't have clouds but a mind can. So minds, we conclude, cannot be neural systems.

Consider now how the Antipodeans would view "acts of imperfect apprehension." They would see them not as cloudy portions of the Mirror of Nature but as a result of learning a second-rate language. The whole notion of incorrigibly knowable entities, as opposed to being incorrigible about how entities seem to be—the notion of "seemings" as themselves a kind of entity—strikes them as a deplorable way of speaking. The whole Terran vocabulary of "acts of apprehension," "cognitive states," "feelings," etc. strikes them as an unfortunate turn for a language to have taken. They see no way of getting us out of it except by proposing that we raise some of our children to speak Antipodean and see whether they don't do as well as a control group. The Antipodean materialists, in other words, see our notion of "mind and matter" as a reflection of an unfortunate linguistic development. The Antipodean epiphenomenalists are baffled by the question "What is the neural input to the Terrestrial speech center which produces pain reports as well as C-fiber reports?" Those Terrestrial philosophers who think that Antipodeans do have feelings think that the Antipodean language is "inadequate to reality." Those Terrestrial philosophers who think that the Antipodeans don't have feelings rest their case on a theory of language–development according to which the first things named are the things "better known to us"—raw feels—so that the absence of a name for feeling entails the absence of feeling.

To sharpen the issue a bit further, perhaps we may drop from consideration the Antipodean epiphenomenalists and the Terrestrial skeptics. The former's problem about the neurology of pain reports seems insoluble; if they are to continue charitably to ascribe states to Earthmen which are unknown to Antipodeans they will have to swallow a whole dualistic system, irrefutable by further empirical inquiry, in order to explain our linguistic behavior. As for the Terran skeptic's claim that the Antipodeans have no raw feels, this is based entirely on the a priori dictum that one cannot have a raw feel and lack a word for it. Neither intellectual position—the extreme charity of the Antipodean epiphenomenalist and the parochial distrust of the Terrestrial skeptic—is attractive. We are left with the Antipodean materialist saying "They think they have feelings but they don't" on the one hand and Terrestrial philosophers saying "They have feelings but don't know it" on the other hand. Is there a way out of this impasse, given that every empirical result (brain-switching, etc.) seems to weigh equally on both sides? Are there powerful philosophical methods which will cut through the problem and either settle it or offer some happy compromise?

3. Incorrigibility and Raw Feels

One philosophical method which will do no good at all is "analysis of meanings." Everybody understands everybody else's meanings very well indeed.

The problem is that one side thinks there are too many meanings around and the other side too few. In this respect the closest analogy one can find is the conflict between inspired theists and uninspired atheists. An inspired theist, let us say, is one who "just knows" that there are supernatural beings which play certain explanatory roles in accounting for natural phenomena. (They are not to be confused with natural theologians —who offer the supernatural as the best explanation of these phenomena.) Inspired theists have inherited their picture of the universe as divided into two great ontological realms—the supernatural and the natural—along with their language. The way they talk about things is inextricably tied up with—or at least strikes them as inextricably tied up with—references to the divine. The notion of the supernatural does not strike them as a "theory" any more than the notion of the mental strikes us as a "theory." When they encounter atheists they view them as people who don't know what's going on, although they admit that atheists seem able to predict and control natural phenomena very nicely indeed. ("Thank heaven," they say, "that we are not as those natural theologians are, or we too might lose touch with the real.") The atheists view these theists as having too many words in their language and too many meanings to bother about. Enthusiastic atheists explain to inspired theists that "all there *really* is is . . . ," and the theists reply that one should realize that there are more things in heaven and earth. . . . And so it goes. The philosophers on both sides may analyze meanings until they are blue in the face, but all such analyses are either "directional" and "reductive" (e.g., "noncognitive" analyses of religious discourse, which are the analogue of "expressive" theories of pain reports) or else simply describe alternative "forms of life," culminating in nothing more helpful than the announcement: "This language-game is played." The theists' game is essential to their self-image, just as the image of man's Glassy Essence is essential to the Western intellectual's, but neither has a larger context available in which to evaluate this image. Where, after all, would such a context come from?

Well, perhaps from philosophy. When experiment and "meaning analysis" fail, philosophers have traditionally turned to system-building—inventing a new context on the spot, so to speak. The usual strategy is to find a compromise which will enable both those who favor Occam's Razor (e.g., materialists, atheists) and those who cling to what they "just know" to be viewed indulgently as having achieved "alternate perspectives" on some larger reality which philosophy has just adumbrated. Thus some tender-minded philosophers

have risen above the "warfare between science and theology" and seen Bonaventure and Bohr as possessing different, noncompetitive "forms of consciousness." The question "consciousness of *what?*" is answered by something like "the world" or "the thing-in-itself" or "the sensible manifold" or "stimulations." It does not matter which of these is offered, since all are terms of art designed to name entities with no interesting features save placid neutrality. The analogue of this tactic amoung toughminded philosophers of mind is neutral monism, in which the mental and the physical are seen as two "aspects" of some underlying reality which need not be described further. Sometimes we are told that this reality is intuited (Bergson) or is identical with the raw material of sensation (Russell, Ayer), but sometimes it is simply postulated as the only means of avoiding epistemological skepticism (James, Dewey). In no case are we told anything about it save that "we just know what it's like" or that reason (i.e., the need to avoid philosophical dilemmas) requires it. Neutral monists like to suggest that philosophy has discovered, or should look for, an underlying substrate, in the same way in which the scientist has discovered molecules beneath elements, atoms beneath molecules, and so on. But in fact the "neutral stuff" which is neither mental nor physical is not found to have powers or properties of its own, but simply postulated and then forgotten about (or, what comes to the same thing, assigned the role of ineffable datum).[7] This tactic cannot help in coping with the question which the toughminded Terrestrial philosophers raised about the Antipodeans: Do they have raw feels or don't they?

The problem about the Antipodeans can be summarized as follows:

1. It is essential to raw feels that they be incorrigibly knowable

together with

2. There is nothing which the Antipodeans think themselves incorrigible about

seems to leave us either with

3. The Antipodeans do not have raw feels

or with

4. The Antipodeans do not know about their own incorrigible knowledge.

The trouble with (3) is that the Antipodeans have pretty much the behavior, physiology, and culture that we do. Further, we can train Antipodean infants to report raw feels, and take themselves to be incorrigible about them. These considerations seem to drive us toward (4). But (4) sounds silly, and needs at least to be softened to

4'. The Antipodeans do not know about their own capacity for incorrigible knowledge

which is a little odd but at least has a few parallels. (Compare "John XXIII had to be convinced by argument of his own infallibility upon succeeding to the papacy.") However, if we press (4'), the teachability of Antipodean infants seems to leave us up in the air between

5 The Antipodeans can be taught to recognize their own raw feels

and

5'. The Antipodeans can be taught, thanks to the presence of neural concomitants of raw feels, to simulate reports of raw feels without actually having any.

One might hope to resolve this new dilemma by finding a bilingual Antipodean. But the bilingual does not have "inside" knowledge about the meanings of the foreign expressions; he just has the same sort of theory which the lexicon-maker has. Consider an adult Antipodean who has come to speak English. He says, "I am in pain" or the Antipodean for "My C-fibers are firing," depending on which he's speaking. If a Terran interlocutor tells him that he really isn't in pain he points out that the remark is a deviant utterance, and claims privileged access. When Antipodean interlocutors show him that his C-fibers aren't in fact firing he says something like "That's funny; they certainly seem to be. That's why I told the Terrans I was in pain," or perhaps something like "That's funny; I'm certainly in what the Terrans call 'pain,' and that never happens except when my C-fibers are firing." It is hard to see that he would have any strong preference for either locution, and harder to see that philosophers could make anything out of a preference if he had one. Once again, we seem driven to the rhetorical question "But what does it *feel* like?"—to which the bilingual Antipodean replies, "It feels like pain." When asked, "Doesn't it also feel like C-fibers?" he explains that there is no concept of "feeling" in Antipodean, and so it would not occur to him to say that he *felt* his C-fibers firing, although of course he is aware of it whenever they do.

If this seems paradoxical, it is presumably because we think that "noninferential awareness" and "feeling" are pretty well synonymous. But pointing this out is no help. If we treat them as synonymous, then of course Antipodean *does* have the concept of a state called "feeling," but it still doesn't have the concept of "feelings" as inten-

tional objects of knowledge. Antipodean has the verb but not the noun, so to speak. An accommodating Antipodean can note that his language can express the notion of "state such that one cannot be mistaken in thinking one is in it"—namely, the state of it seeming to one that . . .—but still be puzzled about whether these states are the same things as the pains and other raw feels in which the Terrans are so interested. On the one hand, it seems all they *could* be talking about, for he remembers having learned to say "pain" when and only when his C-fibers seem to be firing. On the other hand, the Terrans insist that there is a difference between being in a state such that it seems to one that one is . . . and having a raw feel. The former state is an epistemic position toward something about which doubt is possible. The latter state automatically puts one in an epistemic position toward something about which doubt is impossible.

So the dilemma seems to boil down to this: We must affirm or deny

6. any report of how something seems to one is a report of a raw feel.

The only ground for affirming it seems to be that it is a corollary of the converse of (1), that is:

7. It is essential to whatever is incorrigibly knowable that it be a raw feel.

But (7) is just a form of the principle invoked by the Brandt-Campbell objection above, viz.:

(P) Whenever we make an incorrigible report on a state of ourselves, there must be a property which we are presented with which induces us to make the report

and in this principle everything turns on the notion "presented with"—a notion which harks straight back to the metaphors of the "Eye of the Mind," "presence to consciousness," and the like, which are in turn derived from the initial image of the Mirror of Nature—of knowledge as a set of immaterial representations. If we adopt this principle, then, oddly enough, we can no longer be skeptics: the Antipodeans automatically have raw feels. We *must* choose (5) over (5'). Since we do not contest that it seems to some Antipodean that his stomach is cramped or his C-fibers firing, and since we grant incorrigibility to such reports, we must grant that he has some raw feels which are the "basis" for his seems-statements and which he could be trained to report by learning an appropriate vocabulary. But this means, paradoxically enough, that a species of behaviorism is entailed by the very principle that incarnates the Cartesian image of the Eye of the Mind—the very image which has often been accused of leading to the "veil of ideas" and to solipsism. We should only be able to be skeptics and assert (5')—that simulation might be all the Antipodeans could do—by holding that when the Antipodeans made seems-statements they were not really meaning what we meant by them, and that the deviance, in Antipodean, of the expression "You may be mistaken in saying that it seems to you that your C-fibers are firing" does not suffice to show that the Antipodeans have any incorrigible knowledge. That is, we should have to reconstrue the behavior which we initially took to be exhibited, and base our skepticism about their raw feels on a more general skepticism about their possession of knowledge (or of some kinds of knowledge). But it is difficult to see how we could make skepticism about this plausible except on some antecedent conviction that they were mindless—a conviction which would a fortiori rule out raw feels. So skepticism here will have to be groundless and Pyrrhonian.[8] On the other hand, if we deny (6)—if we disengage seeming from the having of mental states and abandon the Cartesian pictures—then we have to face up to the possibility that we ourselves never had any feelings, any mental states, any minds, any Glassy Essence. This paradox seems so overwhelming as to drive us right back to (P) and the Mirror of Nature.

So the problem comes down to a choice among three troubling possibilities. We have to either share our Glassy Essence with any being which seems to speak a language containing seems-statements, or become Pyrrhonian skeptics, or else face up to the possibility that this essence was never ours. If we grant (7) above—the premise which makes being a raw feel essential to being an object of incorrigible knowledge—then we must admit either (a) that the Antipodean language, just by virtue of containing some incorrigible reports, is about raw feels, or (b) that we shall never know whether the Antipodeans speak a language just because we shall never know whether they have raw feels, or (c) that the whole issue about raw feels is a fake because the example of the Antipodeans shows that we never had any raw feels ourselves.

These three possibilities correspond roughly to three standard positions in the philosophy of mind—behaviorism, skepticism about other minds, and materialism. Rather than adopt any of these three, however, I suggest that we deny (7), and with it (P). That is, I suggest that we abandon the notion that we possess incorrigible knowledge by virtue of a special relation to a special kind of object called "mental objects." This suggestion is a corollary of Sellars's attack on the Myth of the Given. I shall present that attack in more detail in chapter four, but here I merely note that this myth

is the notion that such epistemic relations as "direct knowledge" or "incorrigible knowledge" or "certain knowledge" are to be understood on a causal, para-mechanical model, as a special relation between certain objects and the human mind which enables knowledge to take place more easily or naturally or quickly. If we think of incorrigible knowledge simply as a matter of social practice—of the absence of a normal rejoinder in normal conversation to a certain knowledge-claim—then no principle like (7) or (P) will seem plausible.

In the last two sections I have been treating "mental object" as if it were synonymous with "incorrigibly knowable object," and thus as if to have a mind were the same thing as having incorrigible knowledge. I have disregarded immateriality and the ability to abstract, which were discussed in chapter one, and intentionality, which will be discussed in chapter four. My excuse for pretending that the mind is nothing but a set of incorrigibly introspectible raw feels, and that its essence is this special epistemic status, is that the same pretense is current throughout the area called "philosophy of mind." This area of philosophy has come into existence in the thirty years since Ryle's *The Concept of Mind*. The effect of that book was to make issues about minds and bodies turn almost entirely on the cases which resisted Ryle's own logical behaviorist attempt to dissolve Cartesian dualism—namely, raw feels. Wittgenstein's discussion of sensations in *Philosophical Investigations* seemed to offer the same sort of attempt at dissolution. Thus many philosophers have taken it for granted that "the mind-body problem" was the question of whether raw feels could be viewed as dispositions to behave. Thus the only possibilities have seemed to be the ones I have just cited: (a) granting that Ryle and Wittgenstein were right, and that there are no mental objects, (b) saying that they were wrong, and that therefore Cartesian dualism stands intact, with skepticism about other minds a natural consequence, and (c) some form of mind-brain identity theory, according to which Ryle and Wittgenstein were wrong, but Descartes is not thereby vindicated.

The effect of setting up the issues in this way is to focus on pains, while paying less attention to the side of the mind which is, or should be, of more concern to epistemology—beliefs and intentions. (The balance has been somewhat redressed in recent years thanks to philosophers of mind who try to build bridges with empirical psychology. Their work will be discussed in chapter five.) But it is still the case that "the mind-body problem" is thought of primarily as a problem about pains, and the distinctive point about pains is just the one mentioned by Kripke—that there seems no such thing as an appearance–reality distinction in regard to our knowledge of them. In fact, as I have tried to show in chapter one, this is only one of several "mind–body problems," each of which has contributed to the fuzzy notion that there is something especially mysterious about man which makes him capable of knowing, or of certain special sorts of knowing.

For the remainder of this chapter, however, I shall try to support my claim that we should drop (P) and thus be neither dualists, skeptics, behaviorists, nor "identity-theorists." I do not know how to argue against (P) directly, since the claim that incorrigible knowledge is a matter of being presented with a phenomenal property is not so much a claim as an abbreviation for an entire theory—a whole set of terms and assumptions which center around the image of mind as mirroring nature, and which conspire to give sense to the Cartesian claim that the mind is naturally "given" to itself. It is this image itself which has to be set aside if we are to see through the seventeenth–century notion that we can understand and improve our knowing by understanding the workings of our mind. I hope to show the difference between setting it aside and adopting any of the positions which presuppose this image. So the remainder of this chapter is devoted to behaviorism, skepticism, and the mind-body identity theory, in an attempt to differentiate my position from each of these. In the concluding section of the chapter—"Materialism without Identity"—I attempt to say something more positive, but this attempt needs to be linked up with the discussion of other "mind–body problems" in chapter one in order to appear plausible.

4. Behaviorism

Behaviorism is the doctrine that talk of "inner states" is simply an abbreviated, and perhaps misleading, way of talking of dispositions to behave in certain ways. In its Rylean or "logical" form—with which I shall be concerned in what follows—its central doctrine is that there is a necessary connection between the truth of a report of a certain raw feel and a disposition to such-and-such behavior. One motive for holding this view is a distrust of what Ryle called "ghosts in machines," the Cartesian picture of people, and another is the desire to prevent the skeptic about other minds from raising the question of whether the person writhing on the floor has feels of the sort which the skeptic himself would have when he writhes. In the logical behaviorist view, reports of such feels are to be taken not to refer to nonphysical entities, and per-

haps not to any entities at all save to the writhing or the disposition to writhe.

This doctrine has been attacked on the ground that there seems no way to fill in a description of the requisite disposition to behave without giving infinitely long lists of possible movements and noises. It has also been attacked on the ground that whatever "necessity" there is in the area is not a matter of "meaning" but simply an expression of the fact that we customarily explain certain behavior by reference to certain inner states—so that the necessity is no more "linguistic" or "conceptual" than that which connects the redness of the stove to the fire within. Finally, it has been attacked as the sort of philosophical paradox which would only occur to a mind obsessed with instrumentalist or verificationist dogma—eager to reduce all unobservables to observables in order to avoid any risk of believing in something unreal.

All these criticisms are, I think, quite justified. The classic statements of logical behaviorism do indeed presuppose just the distinctions between observation and theory and between language and fact which philosophers would, as I shall argue in chapter four, do well to give up. But the feeling that the behaviorist is on to something remains. One point which he has going for him is that it seems absurd to suggest that we might someday, after years of fruitful conversation with the Antipodeans, have ground for saying, "Ah, no raw feels; so no minds; so no language, and not persons after all." The suggestion that we might find ourselves compelled to say that they had no raw feels makes us ask whether we can even imagine what such a compulsion could be like. It also makes us realize that even if we somehow were so compelled, we should almost certainly not draw the suggested inferences. On the contrary, we might begin to share the Antipodeans' bewilderment about why we had cared so much about this question. We should begin to appreciate the quizzical attitude which the Antipodeans adopt toward the whole topic—the same attitude with which the Polynesians viewed missionaries' preoccupation with the question "Are these descendants of Shem or of Ham?" The behaviorist's strong point is that the more one tries to answer them the more pointless the tough-minded philosopher's questions "Minds or no minds?" "Raw feels or no raw feels?" seem to become.

But this good point begins to go bad as soon as it is put as a thesis about "necessary connections" established by "analysis of meanings." Ryle's insight was frustrated by the positivistic epistemology he inherited. Instead of saying that incorrigible knowledge was just a matter of what practices of justification were adopted by one's peers (the position which I shall call "epistemological behaviorism" in chapter four), he was led to say that a certain type of behavior formed a necessary and sufficient condition for the ascription of raw feels, and that this was a fact about "our language." He then was confronted by a stubborn problem. The fact that our language licensed the inference to the presence of such feels made it difficult, without falling back on materialism, to deny that there really were ghostly entities to report. Thus the two motives behind logical behaviorism came into conflict, since the desire to find a "logical" barrier to skepticism about other minds seems to lead back toward dualism. For if we take the notion that a given linguistic practice, a given piece of behavior, is enough (*pace* the skeptic) to show the necessity of raw feels within, in whatever sense raw feels exist, then it seems necessary to say that our conversational experience with the Antipodeans entails that they have raw feels in whatever sense *we* have raw feels. That is, it seems necessary to adopt the following view:

> (P′) The ability to speak a language which includes incorrigible seems-statements entails the presence of raw feels in speakers of that language, in whatever sense raw feels are present in *us*.

It is easy to heap ridicule on the notion that we can discover the truth of such a claim by doing something called "analyzing meanings."[9] It seems easy to say (with the skeptic) that we might have the ability without the feels. But it is hard, as Wittgenstein and Bouwsma have made clear, actually to tell a coherent story about what we have imagined. Despite this, (P′) has a certain plausibility. The reason it is plausible is that it is, once again, a corollary of:

> (P) Whenever we make an incorrigible report on a state of ourselves, there must be a property with which we are presented which induces us to make this report—

a principle vital to the image of the Mirror of Nature. It is the picture according to which "appearance" is not just mistaken belief but mistaken belief generated by a particular mechanism (a misleading thing getting before the Eye of the Mind) which makes the connection between behavior and raw feel seem so necessary. It is the picture according to which three things are involved when a person gets something wrong (or, by extension, right): the person, the object he is talking about, and the inner representation of that object. Ryle thought that he had eschewed this picture, but that he was unable to do so is shown by his

attempt to show, paradoxically and fruitlessly, that there were no such things as incorrigible reports. Ryle was afraid that if there were any such reports, then something like (P) would have to be true in order to explain their existence. For he thought that if there were such a thing as an ability to make incorrigible noninferential reports on inner states, this would show that someone who knew nothing of behavior could know everything about inner states, and thus that Descartes was right after all. He rightly criticized the usual Cartesian account of introspection as a piece of "para-optics," but he did not have another account available and thus was forced into the impossible position of having to deny the phenomenon of privileged access altogether. He devoted the least convincing chapter of *The Concept of Mind* ("Self-Knowledge") to the paradoxical claim that "the sorts of things that I can find out about myself are the same as the sorts of things that I can find out about other people, and the methods of finding them out are much the same."[10] The result was that many philosophers who agreed that Ryle had shown that beliefs and desires were not inner states agreed also that he had left raw feels untouched, and thus that a choice still had to be made between dualism and materialism.[11]

To put Ryle's mistake in other words, he believed that if one could show a "necessary connection" between ascriptions of behavioral dispositions and ascriptions of inner states, then one would have shown that there were really no inner states. But this instrumentalist *non sequitur* can be avoided, as can (P), while preserving the antiskeptical point that the behavior of the Antipodeans is quite enough evidence to warrant the attribution to them of as much or as little of an inner life as we ourselves possess. The metaphysical inference which the behaviorist is tempted to make—the inference that there is no Glassy Essence within—is, in isolation, as implausible as any other instrumentalist claim. (Compare: "There are no positrons; there are just dispositions on the part of electrons to. . . ." "There are no electrons; there are just dispositions on the part of macroscopic objects to. . . ." "There are no physical objects; there are just dispositions on the part of sense-contents to. . . .") Stripped of its pretensions to rigor, the behaviorist position simply comes down to reminding us that the notion of raw feel only has a role in the context of a picture which connects certain sorts of behavior (introspective reports) with others (reports of physical objects) in terms of a certain image of what human beings (not just their minds) are like. The behaviorist is looking at the social role of the notion of "pain" and not attempting to burrow behind it to the ineffable phenomenological quality which pains have. The skeptic has to insist that it is this quality—which you only know of from your own experience—which counts. The reason why the behaviorist keeps edging himself into the paradoxical metaphysical position of denying that there are nondispositional mental causes for behavioral dispositions is put by Wittgenstein as follows:

> How does the philosophical problem about mental processes and states and about behaviorism arise?—The first step is the one that altogether escapes notice. We talk of processes and states and leave their nature undecided. Sometime perhaps we shall know more about them—we think. But that is just what commits us to a particular way of looking at the matter. For we have a definite concept of what it means to learn to know a process better. (The decisive movement in the conjuring-trick has been made, and it was the very one that we thought quite innocent.)[12]

Alan Donagan provides an admirable gloss on this passage, saying that

> the Cartesians . . . transformed the grammatical facts which we summed up in the proposition that sensation is non-dispositional and private into the grammatical fiction that sensations are states or processes in a private, and hence non-material, medium.

The behaviorists, on the other hand,

> whether moved by the barrenness of much introspectionist psychology, by the philosophical difficulties of Cartesianism, or by other considerations, began by denying that the private Cartesian processes in their nonmaterial medium exist at all.

Wittgenstein cleared up the matter, Donagan thinks, by allowing "that sensations are private non-dispositional accompaniments of the behavior by which they are naturally expressed," but refusing "to recognize those accompaniments as processes that can be named and investigated independently of the circumstances that produce them, and the behavior by which they are naturally expressed."[13]

I think that Donagan's pithy account of the common difficulty of behaviorists and dualistic skeptics about other minds is right, but that it can be clarified and carried one step further. The notion of a "private, . . . non-material medium" is obscure because it suggests that we have a notion of what it is like to have a Glassy Essence—a metaphysical grasp of what nonextended substance is like—which is independent of the epistemic criterion of the mental. If we neglect this notion and press Wittgenstein's phrase "a definite concept of what it means to learn to know a process better"

we can get a diagnosis of what Donagan calls the "opposite and complementary errors"[14] of behaviorism and Cartesianism which avoids reference to the metaphysical ("non-material," ghostly) nature of raw feels.

The basic epistemological premise which both schools share, and which forms their notion of "knowing better," is the doctrine of the Naturally Given, that is:

> Knowledge is either of the sort of entity naturally suited to be immediately present to consciousness, or of entities whose existence and properties are entailed by entities of the first sort (and which are thus "reducible" to those of the first sort).

The Cartesians thought that the only sorts of entities which were naturally suited to be directly present to consciousness were mental states. The behaviorists, at their epistemological best, thought that the only sort of entities directly present to consciousness were states of physical objects. The behaviorists prided themselves on escaping the notions of our Glassy Essence and the Inner Eye but they remained true to Cartesian epistemology in retaining the notion of an Eye of the Mind which got some things firsthand. Science, in this view, infers to other things entailed by "ground-floor" entities, and philosophy then reduces these other things back down again. The behaviorists gave up the notion that "nothing is better known to the mind than itself" but they kept the notion that some things were naturally knowable directly and others not, and the metaphysical corollary that only the first were "really real." This doctrine—that the most knowable was the most real—which George Pitcher has dubbed the "Platonic Principle,"[15] added to the principle of the Naturally Given, produced either an idealistic or panpsychist reduction of the physical to the mental, or a behaviorist or materialist reduction in the other direction. The choice between the two sorts of reduction depends, I think, not so much on difficulties in psychology or philosophy but on one's general notion of what wisdom is like, and thus of what philosophy is good for. Is it to emphasize the aspects of man reached by public methods of common conversation and scientific inquiry? Or rather a personal and inarticulate sense of "something far more deeply interfused"? This choice has little to do with philosophical argument or with the image of the Mirror of Nature. But the image—and particularly the metaphor of the Inner Eye—serves the purposes of both disputants equally well, which is why debate between them has been so lengthy and so inconclusive. Both have a clear sense of what is best known, and knowing a process means either knowing it *that* way, or else showing that it "really is nothing but" something else which *is* known that way.

If we look at the controversy between the behaviorist and the skeptic about other minds from the Antipodean point of view, the first thing we realize is there is no place for the "Naturally Given." There is, to be sure, a place for the notion of "direct knowledge." This is simply knowledge which is had without its possessor having gone through any conscious inference. But there is no suggestion that some entities are especially well suited to be known in this way. What we know noninferentially is a matter of what we happen to be familiar with. Some people (those who sit in front of cloud-chambers) are familiar with, and make noninferential reports of, elementary particles. Others are familiar with diseases of trees, and can report "another case of Dutch elm disease" without performing any inferences. All Antipodeans are familiar with the states of their nerves, and all Terrans with their raw feels. The Antipodeans do not suggest that there is something suspiciously metaphysical or ghostly about raw feels—they just do not see the point of talking about such things instead of talking about one's nerves. Nor, of course, does it help if the Terrans explain that though (putting aside the possibility of unconscious inference) perhaps anything *can* be known noninferentially it does not follow that anything except certain naturally suitable entities can be known *incorrigibly*. For the Antipodeans do not have the notion of *entities* known incorrigibly but only of *reports* (seems-statements) which are incorrigible and which may be about *any* sort of entity. They understand that the Terrans do have the former notion, but they are baffled why they think they need it, although they can see how, in ignorance of neurology, a lot of strange notions might have become current.

6.   Materialism Without Mind–Body Identity

Like the behaviorist and the skeptic about other minds, the materialist has a sound intuition which becomes paradoxical when stated in the vocabulary of the tradition to which it is a reaction. Encouraged by reflection on the Antipodeans, the materialist thinks it likely that reference to neurological microstructures and processes may replace reference to short-term mental states (sensations, thoughts, mental images) in the explanation of human behavior. (If he is wise, he does not think the same for beliefs, desires, and other long-term—and not incorrigibly knowable—mental states, but is content to view them as properties of persons

rather than of minds, in the manner of Ryle.) Not content with this plausible prediction, however, he wishes to say something metaphysical. The only thing to be said seems to be that "mental states are nothing but neural states." But this sounds paradoxical. So he tries various tactics to mitigate the paradox. One such tactic is to say that the nature of the mind has so far been misunderstood, and that once we understand it correctly we shall see that it is not paradoxical to say that it may turn out to be the nervous system. Behaviorism is one form of this tactic, and it is compatible with materialism in the sense that the claim:

> When we talk about mental events we are really talking about behavioral dispositions

though not comptabile with:

> When we talk about mental events we are really talking about neural events

is compatible with:

> There are, however, other things relevant to prediction and explanation of behavior than the systematic interrelationships of dispositions with events in the external world, and among these are the neural events which sometimes cause the onset of such dispositions.

It has been customary in recent discussions, however, to take behaviorism and materialism as two quite different ways—mild and violent, respectively—of modifying the seventeenth-century picture of the mind. In this spirit, materialists have fastened on those mental entities most recalcitrant to Ryle's dispositional analyses—the raw feels, the passing thoughts, the mental images—and tried to show that these are to be construed, roughly, as "whatever it is which *causes* the onset of certain behavior or behavioral dispositions." This so-called topic-neutral analysis of the mind (by, especially, J.J.C. Smart and David Armstrong) runs into trouble, however, over the intuitive distinction between "whatever mental state it is which causes the onset . . ." and "whatever physical state it is which causes the onset. . . ." To put it another way, the intuition that there is some difference between materialism and parallelism makes us feel that there is something misleading, or at least incomplete, in topic–neutral accounts of what makes the mental mental. Or, to put it still another way, if our notion of "mind" is what topic–neutral analyses say it is, it is very hard to explain the existence of a mind-body problem.[20] We may say that the lack of a fine-grained neurological account promoted the notion that there is something distinctive about the mind—that it must be something ghostly—but this tactic simply splits the traditional notion of the mental into two parts: the causal role and the Glassy Essence believed to play this causal role. Topic–neutral analyses obviously cannot capture, and do not want to capture, the latter. But it seems mere gerrymandering to split our concept of a "mental state" into the portion which is compatible with materialism and the portion which is not, and then say that only the former is "essential" to the concept.[21]

We can put the attempt at "topic–neutral" analyses in perspective by seeing it as one way to get around the following argument for dualism:

1. Some statements of the form "I just had a sensation of pain" are true
2. Sensations of pain are mental events
3. Neural processes are physical events
4. "Mental" and "physical" are incompatible predicates
5. No sensation of pain is a neural event
6. There are some nonphysical events

Ryleans, and some Wittgensteinians, taking mentality to consist in accessibility to privileged access, and indulging what Strawson calls "a hostility to privacy," deny (2). Panpsychists have denied (3).[22] "Reductive" materialists such as Smart and Armstrong, who offer "topic–neutral" analyses of mentalistic terms, challenge (4). "Eliminative" materialists like Feyerabend and Quine deny (1). This last position claims the advantage over the "reductive" version of not having to offer revisionary "analyses" of terms, and thus not having to get involved with dubious notions such as "meaning" and "analysis." It does not say that we have been misleadingly calling neural processes "sensations," but merely that there are no sensations. Nor does it say that the meaning of the term *sensation* can be analyzed in such a way as to produce such unexpected results as the denial of (4). It is fully "Quinean" and wholly anti-Rylean in the sense that it happily accepts all the things which the dualist would like to construe the man in the street as saying, and merely adds, "So much the worse for the man in the street."

This position seems to hold out hope of a sense in which the materialists' metaphysical claim "Mental states are nothing but neural states" can be cheaply bought. For now it can be defended without the need to do anything as laborious or as shady as "philosophical analysis." We can say that although in one sense there just are no sensations, in another sense what people *called* "sensations," viz., neural states, do indeed exist. The distinction of senses is no more sophisticated than when we say that the sky does not exist, but that there is something which people call the sky (the appearance of a blue dome as a result of refracted sunlight) which does exist (although, as the prevalence of the Brandt-Campbell objection discussed in section 2 shows, the analogy cannot be pressed so as to make a mental state the "appearance" of a neural state). So it looks as if the argument for dualism above can be handled by saying that all the dualist is entitled to is the following premise:

1′. Some statements of the form "I just had a sensation of pain" are as properly taken as true as "The sky is overcast" and "The sun is rising," but none of them *is* true.

If we substitute (1′) for (1) in the argument, then we will substitute the following for (2):

2′. If there were any sensations of pain, they would be mental events

and then draw the conclusion:

6′. The things which people have been calling "sensations" are physical (and, specifically, neural) events.

We can then conclude that although there are no mental events, the things which people have called mental events are physical events, even though "mental" and "physical" are as incompatible as "rising above the horizon" and "standing still."

This attempt at a cheap version of the identity of minds and brains will work well enough if we refrain from pressing questions about criteria of identity of reference, just as topic–neutral analyses will work well enough if we refrain from pressing questions about identity of meaning. I do not, however, think that there are criteria for the identity of either which are useful in philosophically controversial cases. So I do not think that "eliminative materialism" is a more plausible version of the thesis of mind–brain identity than "reductive materialism." When we try to make sense of any claim of the form "There aren't really any X's; what you have been talking about are nothing but Y's," it is always possible to object that (a) "X" refers to X's, and (b) we cannot refer to what does not exist. So to get around this standard criticism the eliminative materialist would have to say either that "sensation" does not refer to sensations, but to nothing at all, or that "refer" in the sense of "talk about" is not subject to (b). Either line is defensible, and I defend the second in discussing the notion of reference in connection with the so-called problem of conceptual change in chapter six below. But since I think that the reductive and eliminative versions of the identity theory are both merely awkward attempts to throw into current philosophical jargon our natural reaction to an encounter with the Antipodeans, I do not think that the difference between the two should be pressed. Rather, they should both be abandoned, and with them the notion of "mind–body identity." The proper reaction to the Antipodean story is to adopt a materialism which is not an identity theory in *any* sense, and which thus avoids the artificial notion that we must wait upon "an adequate theory of meaning (or reference)" before deciding issues in the philosophy of mind.[23]

This amounts to saying, once again, that the materialist should stop reacting to stories such as that about the Antipodeans by saying metaphysical things, and confine himself to such claims as "No predictive or explanatory or descriptive power would be lost if we had spoken Antipodean all our lives." It is pointless to ask whether the fact that cerebroscopes correct Antipodean reports of inner states shows that they are not *mental* states, or shows rather that mental states are really neural states. It is pointless not just because nobody has any idea how to resolve the issue, but because nothing turns on it. The suggestion that it *has* a clear-cut answer depends upon the pre-Quinean notion of "necessary and sufficient conditions built into our language" for the application of the terms "sensation," "mental," and the like, or upon some similar essentialism.[24] Only a philosopher with a lot invested in the notion of "ontological status" would need to worry about whether a corrigibly reportable pain was "really" a pain or rather a stimulated C-fiber.[25]

If we stop asking questions about what counts as "mental" and what does not, and instead recall that incorrigibility is all that is at issue in puzzles about the Antipodeans, then we can see the argument for dualism offered above as an overdramatized version of the following argument:

1. Some statements of the form "I just had a sensation of pain" are true
2′. Sensations of pain are incorrigibly reportable
3′. Neural events are not incorrigibly reportable
4′. Nothing can be both corrigibly and incorrigibly reportable
5. No sensation of pain is a neural event

Here the temptation to avoid (5) by denying (1) is much less great, for (4′) is more easily criticized than (4). It is hard to say that "mental" really means "something that might turn out to be physical," just as it is hard to say that "criminal behavior" really means "behavior which might turn out to be innocent." That is why detailed attempts at topic-neutral analysis in hopes of denying (4) seem foredoomed. But it is relatively easy to deny (4′) and say that something can be corrigibly reportable (by those who know neurology) and incorrigibly reportable (by those who don't), as easy as to say, "Something can be treated rather than punished (by those who understand psychology) and punished rather than treated (by those who don't)." For in both these latter examples we are talking about social practices rather than "intrinsic properties of the entities in question" or "the logic of our language." It is easy to imagine different social practices in regard to the same objects, actions, or events, depending upon the degree of intellectual and spiritual development of the culture in question ("higher" stages of development being, *pace* Hegel, those in which Spirit is less self-conscious). So by denying (4′) we seem to open the way for denying (5), and saying that "sensation" and "brain process" are just two ways of talking about the same thing.

Having earlier heaped scorn on both neutral monists and identity theorists, I may now seem to be edging into their camp. For the question now arises: Two ways of talking about *what?* Something mental or something physical? But here, I think, we have to resist our natural metaphysical urge, and *not* reply, "A third thing, of which both mentality and physicality are aspects." It would be better at this point to abandon argument and fall back on sarcasm, asking rhetorical questions like "What is this mental–physical contrast anyway? Whoever said that anything one mentioned had to fall into one or other of two (or half-a-dozen) ontological realms?" But this tactic seems disingenuous, since it seems obvious (once the psychology departments stop doing experiments with questionnaires and slide shows, and just do it all with cerebroscopes) that "the physical" has somehow triumphed.

But what did it triumph over? The mental? What was that? The practice of making incorrigible reports about certain of one's states? That seems too small a thing to count as an intellectual revolution. Perhaps, then, it triumphed over the sentimental intellectual's conviction that there was a private inner realm into which publicity, "scientific method," and society could not penetrate. But this is not right either. The secret in the poet's heart remains unknown to the secret police, despite their ability to predict his every thought, utterance, and movement by monitoring the cerebroscope which he must wear day and night. We can know which thoughts pass through a man's mind without understanding them. Our inviolable uniqueness lies in our poetic ability to say unique and obscure things, not in our ability to say obvious things to ourselves alone.

The real difficulty we encounter here is, once again, that we are trying to set aside the image of man as possessor of a Glassy Essence, suitable for mirroring nature with one hand, while holding on to it with the other. If we could ever drop the whole cluster of images which Antipodeans do not share with us, we would not be able to infer that matter had triumphed over spirit, science over privacy, or anything over anything else. These warring opposites are notions which do not make sense outside of a cluster of images inherited from the Terran seventeenth century. No one except philosophers, who are professionally obligated to take these images seriously, will be scandalized if people start saying, "The machine told me that it didn't really hurt—it only, very horribly, seemed to." Philosophers are too involved with notions like "ontological status" to take such developments lightly, but no other part of culture is. (Consider the fact that *only* philosophers remain perplexed about how one can have unconscious motives and desires.) Only the notion that philosophy should provide a permanent matrix of categories into which every possible empirical discovery and cultural development can be fitted without strain impels us to ask unanswerable questions like "Would this mean that there were no minds?" "Were we wrong about the nature of the mind?" "Were the Antipodeans right in saying, 'There never were any of those things you called "raw feels"'?"

Finally, the same overambitious conception of philosophy, stemming from the same set of seventeenth-century images, is responsible for materialists' fears that unless cerebral localization and "philosophical analysis" cooperate to "identify" the mind and the body, then "the unity of science"is endangered. If we follow Sellars in saying that science is the measure of all things, then we shall not worry about cerebral localization turning out to be a flop, much less about materialist "analyses" of our everyday mentalistic vocabulary succumbing to counter-examples. We shall not interpret either failure as showing that science has all the while been riding on two horses—one solid and one ghostly—which may start galloping off in opposite directions at any moment. Science's failure to figure out how the brain works will cause no more danger to science's "unity" than its failure to explain mononucleosis, or the migration of butterflies, or stockmarket cycles. Even if neurons turn out to "swerve"—to be buffeted by forces as yet unknown to science—Descartes would not be vindicated. To think otherwise is to commit the fallacy of *omne ignotum pro spectro*—taking everything one cannot understand to be a ghost, something known in advance to be beyond the reach of science, and which must therefore be despairingly handed over to philosophy.[26] If we do

not think of philosophy as supplying a permanent ontological frame for any possible scientific result (consisting, e.g., of categories like "mental" and "physical") we shall not think of science's failure as a vindication of Descartes, any more than we regard science's failure to explain the origin of the first living cell as a vindication of Aquinas. If the neurons do swerve, or if the brain works holistically rather than atomistically, this does not help show that we do, after all, have clear and distinct ideas of "the mental" and "the physical." These so-called ontological categories are simply the ways of packaging rather heterogenous notions, from rather diverse historical sources, which were convenient for Descartes's own purposes. But his purposes are not ours. Philosophers should not think of his artificial conglomerate as if it were a discovery of something preexistent—a discovery which because "intuitive" or "conceptual" or "categorial" sets permanent parameters for science and philosophy.

NOTES

1. Saul Kripke, "Naming and Necessity" in *Semantics of Natural Language,* ed. Donald Davidson and Gilbert Harman (Dordrecht, 1972), pp. 339–340. For criticism of Kripke's discussion of dualism and materialism, see Fred Feldman, "Kripke on the Identity Theory," and William Lycan, "Kripke and the Materialists," both in *Journal of Philosophy* 71 (1974), 665–689.

2. I defended a qualified form of this supposition in "Incorrigibility as the Mark of the Mental," *Journal of Philosophy* 67 (1970), 399–424. See also Jaegwon Kim, "Materialism and the Criteria of the Mental," *Synthese* 22 (1972), 323–345, esp. 336–341.

3. Richard Brandt, "Doubts about the Identity Theory," in *Dimensions of Mind,* ed. Sidney Hook (New York, 1961), p. 70.

4. Keith Campbell, *Body and Mind* (New York, 1960), pp. 106–107, 109.

5. George Pitcher has worked out an account of the linguistic behavior we display in reporting pains without using such a premise. Pitcher takes pains to be reports of damaged peripheral tissue, whereas the Antipodeans take them to be reports of states of the central nervous system. In his view, it is a mistake to think of the common-sense concept of pain as the concept of a mental particular. I would want to say that it *is* the concept of a mental particular, but claim that his analysis of the epistemological status of pains applies, *mutatis mutandis,* equally well wherever one stands on this question. See Pitcher, "Pain Perception," *Philosophical Review* 79 (1970), 368–393. Pitcher's general strategy is a defense of direct realism and is also found in his *A Theory of Perception* (Princeton, 1971) and in D. M. Armstrong, *Perception and the Physical World* (London and New York, 1961) and *A Materialist Theory of the Mind* (London and New York, 1968). This strategy seems to me essentially right, and enough

to show that the mental-particular view is optional. But I am dubious about Pitcher's and Armstrong's metaphilosophical stance, which would make this view a philosopher's misconstrual of what we believe, rather than a correct account of what we believe (but need not continue to believe).

6. I owe this way of putting the Brandt–Campbell point to Thomas Nagel.

7. Urging that philosophers need to do more than this, Cornelius Kampe has suggested that the mind–body identity theory will make sense only if we provide "a theoretical framework (or an ontology for the common idiom) of such a type as to provide a link for the two diverse phenomena whose identity is asserted." His motive for this revival of neutral monism is his belief that making sense of an identity theory requires that "the subjective–objective distinction must be abandoned, as must the privileged status of first-person introspective reports." Such a change, he says, would "drastically affect the logic of our language." I think Kampe is right that giving up the subjective–objective distinction would have such a drastic effect, but wrong in thinking that giving up privileged access would. As I think Sellars has shown, and as I have been arguing here, the subjective–objective distinction (the notion of "seems") can get along quite well without the notions of "mind," "phenomenal property," etc. (Cf. Kampe, "Mind–Body Identity: A Question of Intelligibility," *Philosophical Studies* 25 [1974], 63–67.)

8. I want to distinguish between "mere," or Pyrrhonian, skepticism and the specifically "Cartesian" form of skepticism which invokes the "veil of ideas" as a justification for a skeptical attitude. "Pyrrhonian" skepticism, as I shall use the term, merely says, "We can never be certain; so how can we ever know?" "Veil of ideas" skepticism, on the other hand, has something more specific to say, viz., "Given that we shall never have certainty about anything except the contents of our own minds, how can we ever justify an inference to a belief about anything else?" For a discussion of the intertwining of these two forms of skepticism, see Richard Popkin, *The History of Scepticism from Erasmus to Descartes* (New York, 1964).

9. For a sample of such ridicule, see Hilary Putnam, "Brains and Behavior" in *Mind, Language and Reality,* vol. II (Cambridge, 1975).

10. Gilbert Ryle, *The Concept of Mind* (New York, 1965), p. 155. The reference to "para-optics" is at p. 159.

11. Sellars's "Empiricism and the Philosophy of Mind" (in *Science, Perception and Reality* [London and New York, 1963]) took the first step beyond Ryle. Sellars showed that even though the fact that behavior is evidence for raw feels is "built into the very logic" of concepts of raw feels, this does not mean that there can be no raw feels, any more than the parallel point about macro-phenomena and microentities dictates the operationalist claims that there can be no microentities. Sellars there said what Ryle should have said in his chapter on "Self-Knowledge" but did not—viz., that introspective reporting was no more mysterious than any other noninferential report, and did not require the Myth of the Given (and thus did not require para-optics) for its explanation. Unfortunately, however, Sellars did not draw the conclusion that, as Armstrong was later to say, there was no such thing as "logically privileged access" but only "empirically privileged access" (Armstrong, *A Materialist Theory of the Mind* [London, 1968], p. 108). This point, which is vital to

the view I am presenting in this book, is suggested by everything Sellars says, but Quine's attack on the logical-empirical distinction was required to make it possible to get around the shibboleth of "logically necessary connections" which Ryle had built into the philosophy of mind. As I suggest in chapter four, Sellars has never quite been able to swallow Quineanism full strength, and his talk of "the very logic of these concepts" was unfortunately in the Rylean tradition.

12. Ludwig Wittgenstein, *Philosophical Investigations* (London and New York, 1953), pt. I, sec. 308.

13. All four quotations are from Alan Donagan, "Wittgenstein on Sensation," *Wittgenstein: The Philosophical Investigations: A Collection of Critical Essays,* ed. George Pitcher (New York, 1966), p. 350.

14 Ibid., p. 349.

15. Cf. Pitcher, *Theory of Perception,* p. 23 and Plato, *Republic* 478B: "So if the real is the object of knowledge, then the object of belief must be something other than the real."

20. See M. C. Bradley's "Critical Notice" of J.J.C. Smart's *Philosophy and Scientific Realism, Australasian Journal of Philosophy* 42 (1964), 262–283, on this point. My own "Incorrigibility as the Mark of the Mental," *Journal of Philosophy* 67 (1970), 399–424, begins with a discussion of this point, and was inspired by Bradley's review of Smart.

21. Doing so is the inverse of Kripke's Cartesian claim that the "immediate phenomenological quality" of pain is essential to it.

22. Hartshorne and Whitehead are perhaps the clearest examples in recent philosophy. I have argued against Whitehead's version of this doctrine in "The Subjectivist Principle and the Linguistic Turn" in *Alfred North Whitehead: Essays on His Philosophy,* ed. George Kline (Englewood Cliffs, N.J., 1963). A panpsychist view is also suggested by Thomas Nagel's proposal for an "objective phenomenology" which would "permit questions about the physical basis of experience to assume a more intelligible form" ("What Is It Like to Be a Bat?" *Philosophical Review* 83 [1974], 449). However, in both Hartshorne and Nagel, panpsychism tends to merge with neutral monism.

23. This is not to say that the controversies surrounding the reductive and eliminative forms of the identity theory have been pointless. On the contrary, I think that they have been very useful, and particularly so because of their interplay with questions in the philosophy of language. But I think that the upshot of this interplay has been, first, to bolster Quine's view that the notion of "sameness of meaning" cannot be invoked to solve philosophical problems where the notion of "coextensive" has failed and, second, to show that the sense of "really talking about" used in such discussions as that about materialism is not interestingly connected with the Fregean notion of reference (in which one cannot refer to what does not exist). (The latter point is argued in chapter six.) Having adopted an eliminative materialist position some years ago ("Mind–Body Identity, Privacy and Categories," *Review of Metaphysics* 19 [1965], 25–54), I am very grateful to the people whose criticisms of this article eventually led me to what I hope is a clearer understanding of the issues. I am especially indebted to publications by, or conversations with, Richard Bernstein, Eric Bush, David Coder, James Cornman, David Hiley, William Lycan, George Pappas, David Rosenthal, Steven Savitt, and Richard Sikora. The reader interested in following up the similarities and differences between re-

ductive and eliminative materialism might consult Cornman, *Materialism and Sensations* (New Haven, 1971), Lycan and Pappas, "What Is Eliminative Materialism?" *Australasian Journal of Philosophy* 50 (1972), 149–159, Bush, "Rorty Revisited," *Philosophical Studies* 25 (1974), 33–42, and Hiley, "Is 'Eliminative Materialism' Materialism?" *Philosophy and Phenomenological Research* 38 (1978), 325–337.

24. I injudiciously invoked such a notion in "Incorrigibility as the Mark of the Mental," cited in note 20 above. I there concluded that the development of due respect for cerebroscopes would mean the discovery that there had never been any mental events. But this is overdramatized, and tries to establish more of a difference between eliminative and reductive materialism than (as Lycan and Pappas have shown) there really is. I have been greatly helped to see the flaws in my earlier view by correspondence with David Coder concerning his "The Fundamental Error of Central State Materialism," *American Philosophical Quarterly* 10 (1973), 289–298, and with David Rosenthal concerning his "Mentality and Neutrality," *Journal of Philosophy* 73 (1976), 386–415.

25. But this is not to say that the Antipodeans would have no impact on philosophy. The disappearance of psychology as a discipline distinct from neurology, and similar cultural developments, might eventually free us from the image of the Mirror of Nature much more effectively than philosophers' identity theories. Outside of philosophy, there would be a bit of "blurring" in ordinary speech (a bit of "not knowing *what* to say" when the sincere introspector defied the cerebroscope), but common sense, language, and culture have survived worse muddles than this. Compare, for example, conversations between moralistic judges and psychiatrists who produce a case history to show that "criminal" is inappositely applied to the accused's behavior. Nobody but an overzealous philosopher would think that there was an essence of "crime" determined by looking at, for example, "our language" and capable of resolving judges' dilemmas.

26. This point can be made a bit more precisely by using Meehl and Sellars's distinction between "physical$_1$" ("an event or entity is physical$_1$ if it belongs in the space–time network") and "physical$_2$" ("an event or entity is physical$_2$ if it is definable in terms of theoretical primitives adequate to describe completely the actual states though not necessarily the potentialities of the universe before the appearance of life"). This distinction (drawn in "The Concept of Emergence," *Minnesota Studies in the Philosophy of Science*, I [1956], 252) can be multiplied to distinguish "physical$_1$" from appropriate senses of "physical$_n$" defined in terms of "the universe before the appearance of linguistic behavior" (" . . . of intentional action," "of beliefs and desires," etc.). For any such distinction, the point to be emphasized is that science's failure to explain something in terms of physical$_n$ (for n greater than I) entities does *nothing* to show that the explanation must be in terms of nonphysical$_1$ entities. The point is put to good use by Geoffrey Hellman and Frank Thompson in "Physicalism: Ontology, Determination and Reduction," *Journal of Philosophy* 72 (1975), 551–564 and "Physicalist Materialism," *Nous* 11 (1977), 309–346. Their version of "materialism without identity" should be compared with Davidson's in his "Mental Events" (discussed in chapter four below).

30

W. V. Quine

"States of Mind"*

Unless a case is to be made for disembodied spirits, we can argue that a dualism of mind and body is an idle redundancy. Corresponding to every mental state, however fleeting or however remotely intellectual, the dualist is bound to admit the existence of a bodily state that obtains when and only when the mental one obtains. The bodily state is trivially specifiable in the dualist's own terms, simply as the state of accompanying a mind that is in that mental state. Instead of ascribing the one state to the mind, then, we may equivalently ascribe the other to the body. The mind goes by the board, and will not be missed.

Not that we would continue to refer to the bodily state as the state of accompanying a mind in the mental state. That formulation was for the dualist's benefit, to show him that the bodily state was undeniable from his own point of view and specifiable in his own terms. For our part, we just appropriate the mentalistic terms themselves and construe them as referring to those bodily states. We even continue to speak of the states as mental. The only change is that we reckon mental states as states of the body rather than as states of another substance, the mind.

If this effortless physicalism smacks of trickery, we may do well to reflect on how we learn the mentalistic terms in the first place. All talk about one's mental life presupposes external reference. Introspect our mental states as we will, how do we know what to call them? How did we learn to call our anxieties anxieties, our dull aches dull aches, our joys joys and our awareness awareness? Why do we suppose that what we call joys and anxieties are what other people call by those names? How do we know what we are talking about? Clearly the answer is that such terms are applied in the light of publicly observable symptoms: bodily symptoms strictly of bodily states, and the mind is as may be. Someone observes my joyful or anxious expression, or perhaps observes my gratifying or threatening situation itself, or hears me tell about it. She then applies the word 'joy' or 'anxiety'. After another such lesson or two I find myself applying these words to some of my subsequent states in cases where no outward signs are to be observed beyond my report itself. Without the outward signs to begin with, mentalistic terms could not be learned at all. To apply these terms to the state of the body is just to put them back where they belonged to begin with.

I am not applying the terms to behavior. A mental state is not always manifested in behavior. Physically construed, it is a state of nerves. We can say which state it is, however, and tell one from another, without knowing the neural mechanism. We specify it with help of the mentalistic term, which in turn was learned on the strength of behavioral signs. Thus the net result, if we shortcut the mental bit, is that the behavior provides incomplete and sporadic symptoms whereby to identify and distinguish various complex states of nerves whereof the neural detail may still be a matter of conjecture; and it is these states that the mental terms may be seen as denoting.

Mental states, construed as states of nerves, are like diseases. A disease may be diagnosed in the light of observable signs though the guilty germ be still unknown to science. Incidentally, diagnosis depends heavily on symptoms reported by the patient; and such is the way, overwhelmingly, with the detection of mental states.

What now can we make of the difference between identifying the mental states with the states of nerves, as I just did, and repudiating them rather in favor of states of nerves? I see no differ-

From *The Journal of Philosophy* LXXXII, 1 (January 1985): 5–8. Reprinted with permission of the editor and W. V. Quine.

ence. In either case the states of nerves are retained, mental states in any other sense are repudiated, and the mental terms are thereupon appropriated to states of nerves. So I may as well persist in calling my proposed reduction of mind to body an identification of mental states with bodily ones, neural ones; a construing of the mental as neural.

There is no presumption that the mentalistic idioms would in general be translatable into the anatomical and biochemical terminology of neurology, even if all details of the neurological mechanisms were understood. Thus take belief. Assessed on its objective manifestations, belief is a very mixed bag. Lip service is our most convenient clue to belief, but is neither a necessary nor a sufficient condition. Acceptance of wagers is a firmer sign, and the accepted odds even afford a measure of the strength of the belief; but this test is available only if there is a prospect of subsequently finding the answer, acceptably to both parties, and settling the bet. Other behavior, such as searching or fleeing or standing expectantly, can serve tentatively as manifestations of one or another belief, but these manifestations vary drastically and unsystematically with the content of the belief to be ascribed. Other grounds for ascribing beliefs may be sought unsystematically by probing the subject's past for probable causes of his present state of mind, or by seeing how he will defend his purported belief when challenged.

The empirical content of ascriptions of belief is thus heterogeneous in the extreme, and the physiological mechanisms involved are no less so. The heterogeneity is cloaked under a linguistic uniformity: the connective 'believes that' followed by a subordinate sentence. The other idioms of propositional attitude have the same disarmingly uniform structure as the belief idiom, and it cloaks much the same heterogeneity in respect of empirical evidence and neural mechanism. Hence the insistence, from Brentano onward, on the need for an independent science of intension.[1] Even those of us who do not acquiesce in a metaphysical dualism of mind and body must take the best of what Davidson has called anomalous monism.[2]

The stubborn idioms of propositional attitude are as deeply rooted as the overtly physicalistic ones. One of them is almost coeval, it would seem, with observation sentences. Thus take the observation sentence 'It's raining'. Tom is learning it from Martha by ostension. Martha's business is to encourage Tom in uttering the sentence, or in assenting to it, when she sees that he is noticing appropriate phenomena, and to discourage him otherwise. Thus Tom's mastery of the physicalistic sentence 'It's raining' hinges on Martha's mastery, virtual if not literal, of the mentalistic sentence 'Tom perceives that it's raining'.

Observation sentences, learned ostensively, are where our command of language begins, and our learning them from our elders depends heavily on the ability of our elders to guess that we are getting the appropriate perception. the handing down of language is thus implemented by a continuing command, tacit at least, of the idiom 'x perceives that p' where 'p' ranges over observation sentences. This degree of implicit mastery of one idiom of propositional attitude would seem therefore to be nearly as old as language. The structure of this idiom, moreover—its embedding of a subordinate sentence—would have been clearly dictated by its primitive use in assessing children's acquisition of observation sentences. Analogical extension of the idiom to other than observation sentences would follow inevitably, and the development of parallel idioms for other propositional attitudes would then come naturally too, notwithstanding their opacity from a logical point of view. Naturalness is one thing, transparency another; familiarity one, clarity another.

NOTES

* This is an outgrowth of my piece in a colloquium of the American Philosophical Association, Detroit, 1980. Burton Dreben lately suggested some changes and urged publication. The key idea of the first half was briefly noted meanwhile in my *Theories and Things* (Cambridge, Mass.: Harvard, 1981), p. 18.

1. See Roderick Chisholm, *Perceiving* (Ithaca, N.Y.: Cornell, 1957), chapter 11.

2. Donald Davidson, *Action and Events* (New York: Oxford, 1980), pp. 214–225.

PART IV
THE NATURE OF MIND

INTRODUCTION

There are two main questions about the nature of mind. One is how mental phenomena differ from everything else; the other is how the various kinds of mental phenomena differ from one another.

It is natural to approach the first question by looking for a single property that is essential to all mental phenomena. But different kinds of mental phenomena are so disparate in character that it is far from obvious that they have anything interesting in common. What single property makes thoughts, feelings, sensations, emotions, and desires all mental? Perhaps all these states are nonphysical, though the negative character of this hypothesis suggests it is little more than a way to avoid having to give a substantive, informative characterization of those phenomena. Perhaps what they all have in common is consciousness, though it seems likely that many mental states and processes occur that are not conscious states and processes.

A general characterization of mind need not, however, rely on some single property that all mental phenomena share. Perhaps instead every mental state has one or another of a few basic mental characteristics, and these characteristics belong to nothing that is not mental. Adopting this strategy means using the characteristic differences among mental phenomena to construct an account of mind generally; we will answer the first question, how mental phenomena differ from everything else, by appeal to an answer to the second, how the various kinds of mental phenomena differ from one another.

The two natural candidates for such basic mental characteristics are intentional and sensory properties. A mental state has intentional properties if it is about something, or has propositional content. Examples of sensory character are the distinctive qualities in virtue of which bodily sensations such as pain and itches, or visual sensations of red and green, differ from one another. Many mental states have just one of these two kinds of property; thinking, for example, is intentional but has no sensory properties, whereas sensing has only qualitative properties. Some mental states, such as emotions and perceptions, seem to have both. But every kind of mental state seems to have either intentional propeties or sensory character.

These properties are therefore central to understanding both what distinguishes mind from everything else and how the various kinds of mental state differ from one another. And even if some mental states are not conscious, mental states are generally the sorts of things that could be conscious. So consciousness will also be important to questions about the nature of mind.

A. Thinking

Thinking is central to human mental functioning. Partly because of that, it is sometimes held that intentional properties are more basic to mind than sensory properties. Indeed, Descartes argued that all mental phenomena are actually kinds of thinking; he even claimed that sensing, at least insofar as it is a mental phenomenon, and not just bodily, was a kind of thinking. So it is tempting to try to delineate mental states as all and only those which have intentional character.

In the first selection, Chisholm tries in this spirit to draw the line between mental and non-mental by showing that when we ascribe mental states we use a special kind of sentence, a kind we need to use for no other purpose. A sentence is of this special sort if, for example, it contains an expression that purports to refer to something, and neither the sentence nor its denial implies either that that thing exists or that it does not. It is also of that special sort if it contains a referring expression, a, but even given that a is identical with b, the sentence does not imply another sentence exactly like it except for containing a in place of b. Borrowing the term 'intentional' for these and related forms of language, Chisholm claims that we need to use intentional language only when we describe mental phenomena.

Even apart from the existence of mental phenomena without intentional properties, this proposal faces two main difficulties. One is that intentional language is needed to describe phenomena, such as the meaning of linguistic expressions, that are ostensibly not mental. Chisholm argues this is not a counterexample, however, since we tacitly refer to people's mental processes when we talk about meaning. The other difficulty is that we can coin special terms that allow us to describe the mental without using intentional language. Chisholm states his thesis to take this into account; we cannot describe the mental without using either these terms or intentional language. Still, it is unlikely that there is any noncircular way to tell whether a term is of this special sort.

If we must use special kinds of language to describe mental phenomena, perhaps no single, uniform treatment of both mental and nonmental phenomena is possible; our accounts of mind and of nonmental processes may have to be independent. Moreover, perhaps the very way mental descriptions are distinctive actually shows that no sound treatment of mind is possible at all. Describing people's intentional states involves saying what the propositional content of those states is, that is, what the person believes, desires, and so forth. And Quine contends that there is so much looseness in how to specify the content of propositional attitudes that alternative ways of specifying it will often be equally good, making any precise account of intentional mental states impossible.

In a second selection, Quine distinguishes two ways in which we specify what somebody believes. If I believe someone is a spy, I may be described as believing of some particular individual that that person is a spy, or just as believing that somebody or other is a spy. In the first case we describe my believing as a relation between me and that person; in the second case the believing is not described as a relation at all. A similar contrast occurs even if I believe, say, that George is a spy; I may relationally believe of George that he is a spy, or I may just hold that the statement that George is a spy is true. In the second case it matters how we pick George out; even if he is the tallest man, I may not believe the tallest man is a spy. In the first case we abstract from the different ways of picking out that person; since my belief is a relation between George and me, how we pick him out does not matter there. The same contrast holds for other intentional mental states, or so called propositional attitudes.

Chisholm, in a second selection, develops a distinction we must draw within the case in which we describe belief and other intentional states as relations. Even if George believes of George that he is tall, he may or may not believe that he, himself, is tall; he will not in cases in which he does not know of himself that he is George. Chisholm proposes an explanation of this difference. Moreover, when George shaves George, it follows that he shaves himself; when George thinks about George, it does not follow that he thinks about himself, since he may not know he is George. Chisholm suggests that this difference may provide a more satisfactory mark of mental phenomena than that which he proposed earlier. He also argues that holding a propositional attitude of oneself is the most basic kind of intentional state, since we can explain other kinds of intentional states in terms of it, but not vice versa.

Fodor advances five conditions that he argues a theory of propositional attitudes must satisfy. It must fit with empirical findings. Moreover, it must represent propositional attitudes as relations between the person holding the attitude and what the attitude is held toward, for example, what the person believes. It must explain why the things we can say and think seem to be the same, and why the various kinds of speech acts correspond to the kinds of propositional attitude. It must explain why we cannot freely substitute terms that refer to the same thing in ascriptions of intentional states. And if somebody believes that it's raining, for example, what is believed must have enough internal structure to allow the belief state to interact appropriately with other intentional states about rain. These conditions strongly suggest that propositional attitudes are attitudes towards something that has linguistic structure. But that hypothesis runs afoul of various difficulties; Fodor concludes that propositional attitudes are attitudes not toward sentences in a spoken language but toward internal representations that have linguistic structure—representations that belong, in effect, to a language of thought.

One main reason for ascribing beliefs, desires, and other intentional states is to explain and predict behavior. Dennett argues that explaining behavior provides the key to understanding intentional states. He distinguishes three explanatory strategies, only one of which involves ascribing such states. The physical strategy predicts and explains solely on the basis of an object's physical makeup, and the design strategy invokes general facts about a particular thing's design, or about how it works. The intentional strategy, by contrast, relies on the assumption that the system under consideration operates as a rational agent.

Sometimes objective patterns exist about how a system operates that emerge only when we use the intentional strategy, patterns we would miss if we used just the design or physical strategy. It is in these cases that a system counts as having beliefs and desires. Since ascribing intentional states makes sense only against a background assumption of basic rationality, when a system is not fully rational we can expect some ineliminable slack about what its beliefs and desires are. It may well be that the intentional strategy works so well because the relevant system has internal representations. But something is an internal representation, Dennett argues, just in virtue of its playing a suitable role in regulating the behavior of an intentional system.

Thermometers carry information about ambient temperature because the relevant states of the thermometer depend on ambient temperature in a way determined by natural law. Laws of nature are sensitive to how we specify the relevant events; if some nomologically unrelated event were to occur for each ambient temperature, the thermometer carries information about temperature, and not the other event. So descriptions of both information and propositional mental states are alike in that substitutions are restricted in both cases. Dretske therefore proposes to reconstruct what it is to be an intentional state in terms of the concept of information. There is no mystery about the mental, since it is a special case of a common physical process; but special in what way? Because voltage and current flow are nomically related, galvanometers have just one set of states carrying information about these two distinct states of affairs. Dretske suggests that states such as belief are those special cases in which distinct states carry different, but nomically related information. But even a galvanometer does that to some extent, and it is unclear where the mental would begin on this continuum of increasingly fine-grained discriminative ability.

Whatever one's verdict about a language of thought, the intimate tie between thinking and speech may tempt one to hold, as Davidson does, that thinking depends somehow on the ability to speak. The fine-grained distinctions we make in ascribing propositional states mirror the differences among what can be said in spoken language, but that, he notes, is inconclusive. Davidson develops the idea that, to interpret someone's speech or attribute beliefs, we must optimize agreement between that person and us. It is crucial, he urges, that believing something presupposes understanding the difference between believing truly and believing erroneously, and that only language provides a context in which that distinction can take hold. Davidson's arguments show more convincingly, however, that we need the distinction between truth and error for the concept of belief than that we need it simply to have beliefs. And though language and its interpretation may well presuppose that distinction, the converse is less obvious.

Even if thinking can occur without language, language may still be central to understanding the kind of thinking that occurs in creatures that, like ourselves, have language. According to Sellars, we conceive of propositional mental states as states that explain our candid propensities to say things, in much the way that the entities postulated in scientific theories explain the behavior of commonsense objects. Sellars holds that we conceive of the microentities of physics partly by analogy with commonsense macroscopic objects; similarly, we conceive of propositional states in part by analogy with the speech episodes in which they sometimes culminate. Thinking is prior to speech insofar as mental acts explain the occurrence of speech acts; nonetheless, we develop the concept of thinking by building on the concept of speech. Since speech acts mean what they do in virtue of their functional role with respect to behavior, perception, and other speech acts, the content of thoughts also results from these causal ties.

B. Sensing

Just as we describe propositional mental states in terms like those used to characterize speech acts, so we describe sensory mental states using words we also apply to physical objects. We describe visual sensations, for example, in terms of their color and shape, though we also apply these concepts to physical objects. And we borrow words for physical objects like 'dull' and 'burning' to describe bodily sensations such as pain.

Chisholm argues that when we apply these color words, for example, to both physical objects and their appearance, the words mean different things in the two cases. A white physical object viewed under favorable conditions presents an appearance we also call white; white appearances cannot also do so, on pain of a vicious regress. Moreover, appearances cannot have the sorts of properties physical objects have, since appearances are not objects of any kind. For somebody to have an appearance is for that person to be in some sensory state, or to undergo some sensory process; for an appearance to be white is for that state or process to occur in a particular way. Since states and objects cannot have the same sorts of properties, the whiteness of an appearance cannot be the same as that of a physical object. Accordingly, whatever we can say in terms of appearances we can put more perspicuously by talking about the ways we are appeared to.

Jackson insists that we cannot eliminate talk about appearances in favor of talk about processes of appearing or ways in which one is appeared to. So we must regard sensations as mental objects. His most forceful argument is that, unless having a sensation is a relation to a mental object, rather than just being in some state, we cannot capture the difference between an afterimage that is red and green and two afterimages, one red and the other green. Jackson's argument rests on his assumption that a person can be in only one state at a time. Only then would talking about states imply the existence of fewer things than would talking about mental objects, which he assumes is the aim of talking in terms of states. But the advantage of mental states over mental objects is rather that states do not exist independently of the objects they are states of, whereas objects exist independently of one another. And even if one's total visual experience at a particular moment did constitute a single state, corresponding, say, to one's whole visual field, it would still have articulated parts that permit the right distinctions.

In a second selection, Jackson argues that the qualitative character of sensations cannot be physical. One could know everything about the physical nature of the world even if one had never had a sensation of red, but in that case one would not know what it is like to experience red. So to know that is to know something that is not physical. Jackson rejects Lewis's rejoinder (in section IIIB) that knowing what it is like to experience red is not having some kind of information, physical or otherwise, but is rather having certain abilities to recognize and imagine things. Knowing what an experience is like, Jackson insists, is not just knowing something about one's own experiences, but knowing it about other people's as well; and knowing about the experiences of others is plainly not an ability. But we have no reason to hold that knowing what other people's experiences are like is the having of some kind of information unless knowing what one's own experiences are like is. And that is what is in dispute.

Shoemaker argues that we can define the qualitative character of sensory states in terms of their functional connections with nonqualitative mental states. We can have introspective knowledge of qualitative states because these states tend to cause introspective beliefs about them; so part of the functional role of a qualitative state is causing these beliefs. Any state functionally identical to a qualitative state will therefore be introspectively as well as behaviorally indistinguishable from it, and so itself counts as a qualitative state. Moreover, perception is possible only because the similarities and differences in how things appear correspond to similarities and differences among perceptible objects. So we can define the qualitative similarities and differences among sensory states in terms of the tendency those states have to cause perceptual beliefs that perceived objects are similar or different. A qualitative shift in one's sensory states would thus be detectable, since it would result in different introspective and perceptual beliefs. The theoretical possibility of such a shift precludes functionally defining each kind of qualitative state, one by one; but the tie to perceptual beliefs allows us to define functionally the family of such states, as a group.

Peacocke argues that defining the qualitative character of a sensation of red in terms of beliefs about red physical objects would not capture changes in how things would look if the qualitative character of people's sensory states were to shift. Also, such a definition requires that we have independently defined what it is for a physical object to be red, and it is unlikely that that is possible. A sample of objects known independently of their color would not help, since a sample cannot itself determine the relevant property of the objects. But we can, instead, define the redness of physical objects in terms of a property, red', that belongs to regions of one's visual field. The concept of something's being red is part of the concept of something's looking red. Peacocke can allow this, since a state's being red' is different from some object's looking red. Having the concept of a physical object's being red does not presuppose that one have the concept of an experience, but only that one be sensitive to the presence of red' in one's visual field. So, even though red' must figure in any definition of the redness of physical objects, and not conversely, Peacocke suggests that one might not be able to have the concept of red' unless one had the concept of a physical object's being red.

Sellars advances a different conception of the relationship between the perceptible properties of physical objects and the corresponding properties of perceptual sensations. Although we can define neither sort of property in terms of the other, still we conceive of the various kinds of perceptual sensation by analogy with the corresponding perceptible properties of physical objects. The sensations that normally occur when we see physical objects that are red and triangular have properties analogous to the redness and triangularity of those objects. The two families of properties differ in type, since sensations are states of perceivers, and objects cannot have the same kinds of property as states. But because the properties of sensations resemble one another and differ in ways that correspond to the similarities and differences among the perceptible properties of physical objects, the two families of properties are analogous.

C. Consciousness, Self, and Personhood

The foregoing discussions focus mainly on what it is to have intentional or qualitative character, and largely bracket the way in which experiences and other mental states are forms of consciousness. Nagel argues that we must understand consciousness in terms of the point of view of a conscious creature. Having conscious experiences means that there is something that it is like to be a creature with those experiences. And we can understand what that is like only from the point of view of the relevant kind of sentient being. But an account of something is objective only insofar as it is independent of any particular points of view. Since consciousness is unavoidably tied to points of view, an objective description or explanation of it may well be impossible.

The points of view Nagel discusses are not unique to single individuals, but can be shared by relevantly similar individuals. So viewpoint presumably figures in characterizing conscious experiences because the qualitative properties of experience depend on the perceptual apparatus of the creature in question. But it is unclear why this dependence is not wholly objective.

We cannot always extrapolate to the kind of experiences a particular perceptual mechanism will produce; but that is no problem, since we cannot in general extrapolate to the macroscopic effects of novel physical processes. Sometimes we may be unable to tell at all what some creature's experience is like; but it is unclear why that should undermine the objectivity of an account we give of conscious experiences we do grasp, or of conscious experience in general.

Ryle, in the next section, argues that there is no real mystery about consciousness and self-consciousness. Being conscious of our mental processes resembles giving a mental commentary on those processes; the act of consciousness seems to elude us only because such mental commentary is never about itself.

The notion of a point of view is closely tied to the idea that a creature's conscious states are unified by belonging to a single center of consciousness. The concept of a person also seems to presuppose such an integration of conscious states. In a second selection, Nagel argues that this idea of the unity of a person may be illusory. Nagel reviews the loss of functional integration that can emerge with people in whom the connection between the cerebral hemispheres has been surgically severed, and argues that there is no right answer to the question how many minds they have. He concludes that the mental integration present in even normal human beings is more a matter of degree and less absolute than implied by our ordinary concept of a person.

Being a center of consciousness, or having a self, is not by itself sufficient to be a person; nonhuman animals generally also have mental lives. Frankfurt argues that the mental integration characteristic of people is due to an ability to form higher-order desires that some particular one of their first-order desires lead to action. Forming these higher order desires involves a kind of self-identification; one identifies oneself with one first-order desire rather than with another. Freedom of the will is also crucial to distinguishing people from other creatures with minds, and Frankfurt argues that higher-order desires also help explain that; one's will is free if one can will as one wants, that is, in conformity with one's higher-order desires.

Higher-order desires play an especially vivid role in the mental integration characteristic of people, but other higher-order mental states also help. And, although they are typically not about other mental states, emotions such as anger, fear, and joy also seem important to the unity and individuality distinctive of people. This is partly because emotions play a central role in determining personality and character traits. Moreover, the content of our emotions often involves interactions between oneself and others. The distinction between self and others is also central to understanding what is characteristic of the various kinds of emotion, such as anger, fear, and joy.

Gordon's argument about the ties emotions have to knowledge is a suggestive example of the way emotions interact with other mental processes. One cannot, he argues, be angry or delighted that some particular thing happened unless one knows it did, whereas fearing that it happened precludes such knowledge. Anger and delight can of course occur without knowledge; one can be angry because one thinks it happened. But we do not describe that as being angry that it happened. In such a case, moreover, its having happened is the content not of the anger, but only of the thought that caused the anger. Indeed, it is not clear how we might colloquially describe the content of that anger.

Granted that people are special among creatures with mental lives, just how does their mental functioning differ from our own? Malcolm approaches this question by distinguishing between thinking that something is so and having the thought that it is. Having a thought involves having the relevant propositional content consciously before one's mind, and one can do that, he claims, only if one can verbally express that content. By contrast, nonverbal behavior is enough to show that one thinks something is so. Malcolm concludes that a dog's behavior can indicate that it thinks something, even though dogs cannot have thoughts. Malcolm's useful distinction may not, however, sustain this result. Being able to express thoughts verbally is of course sufficient for having thoughts. But it may not also be necessary; perhaps nonverbal behavior can also express thoughts one has.

On Malcolm's distinction, having a thought means that the thought is conscious, whereas when one merely thinks something one's thinking is not conscious. Can mental states occur without being conscious? It is sometimes held that for a state to be a mental state at all is for it to be conscious. Rosenthal argues that this view makes it impossible to explain what it is for a state to be a conscious state; an explanation in terms of mental phenomena would then be circular, and no explanation that does not appeal to mental phenomena can work. Moreover, the arguments in favor of that view fail. But if mental states can occur without our being aware of them—mental states that are not conscious states—a noncircular explanation of consciousness is possible. Rosenthal develops such an account; a mental state is conscious if it is accompanied by a higher-order thought that one is in that mental state. This view turns out to do justice to our commonsense intuitions about what it is for mental states to be conscious. And it explains features of the consciousness of both sensory and intentional states which otherwise seem inexplicable.

A. Thinking

31

Roderick M. Chisholm

"Intentional Inexistence"

1. I have suggested that the locution "There is something that S *perceives* to be *f* " may be defined as meaning: there is something such that it is *f*, it appears to S in some way, S takes it to be *f*, and S has adequate evidence for so doing. And I have suggested that "S *takes* something to be *f* " may be defined by reference to what S assumes, or accepts. I have now said all that I can about the philosophic questions which the concepts of *adequate evidence* and of *appearing* involve. Let us finally turn, then, to the concept of *assuming, or accepting.* The principal philosophic questions which this concept involves may be formulated by reference to a thesis proposed by Franz Brentano.

Psychological phenomena, according to Brentano, are characterized "by what the scholastics of the Middle Ages referred to as the intentional (also the mental) inexistence of the object, and what we, although with not quite unambiguous expressions, would call relation to a content, direction upon an object (which is not here to be understood as a reality), or immanent objectivity."[1] This "intentional inexistence," Brentano added, is peculiar to what is psychical; things which are merely physical show nothing like it.

Assuming, or accepting, is one of the phenomena Brentano would have called intentional. I will first try to formulate Brentano's thesis somewhat more exactly; then I will ask whether it is true of assuming.

2. The phenomena most clearly illustrating the concept of "intentional inexistence" are what are sometimes called psychological attitudes; for example, desiring, hoping, wishing, seeking, believing, and assuming. When Brentano said that these attitudes "intentionally contain an object in themselves," he was referring to the fact that they can be truly said to "have objects" even though the objects which they can be said to have do not in fact exist. Diogenes could have looked for an honest man even if there hadn't been any honest men. The horse can desire to be fed even though he won't be fed. James could believe there are tigers in India, and *take* something there to be a tiger, even if there aren't any tigers in India.

But *physical*—or nonpsychological—phenomena, according to Brentano's thesis, cannot thus "intentionally contain objects in themselves." In order for Diogenes to sit in his tub, for example, there must be a tub for him to sit in; in order for the horse to eat his oats, there must be oats for him to eat; and in order for James to shoot a tiger, there must be a tiger there to shoot.

The statements used in these examples seem to have the form of relational statements. "Diogenes sits in his tub" is concerned with a relation between Diogenes and his tub. Syntactically, at least, "Diogenes looks for an honest man" is similar: Diogenes' quest seems to relate him in a certain way to honest men. But the relations described in this and in our other psychological statements, if they can properly be called "relations," are of a peculiar sort. They can hold even though one of their terms, if it can properly be called a "term," does not exist. It may seem, therefore, that one can be "intentionally related" to something which does not exist.[2]

These points can be put somewhat more precisely by referring to the language we have used. We may say that, in our language, the expressions "looks for," "expects," and "believes" occur in sentences which are intentional, or are used intentionally, whereas "sits in," "eats," and "shoots" do not. We can formulate a working criterion by means of which we can distinguish sentences that are intentional, or are used intentionally, in a certain language from sentences that are not. It is easy to see, I think, what this criterion would be like, if stated for ordinary English.

First, let us say that a simple declarative sentence is intentional if it uses a substantival expression—a name or a description—in such a way that neither the sentence nor its contradictory implies either that there is or that there isn't anything to which the substantival expression truly applies. "Diogenes looked for an honest man" is intentional by this criterion. Neither "Diogenes looked for an honest man" nor its contradictory—"Diogenes did *not* look for an honest man"—implies either that there are, or that there are not, any honest men. But "Diogenes sits in his tub" is not intentional by this criterion, for it implies that there *is* a tub in which he sits.

Secondly, let us say, of any noncompound sentence which contains a propositional clause, that it is intentional provided that neither the sentence nor its contradictory implies either that the propositional clause is true or that it is false. "James believes there are tigers in India" is intentional by this criterion, because neither it nor its contradictory implies either that there are, or that there are not, any tigers in India. "He succeeded in visiting India," since it implies that he did visit India, is not intentional. "He is able to visit India," although it does not imply that he will visit India, is also not intentional. For its contradictory—"He is not able to visit India"—implies that he does *not* visit India.

A third mark of intentionality may be described in this way. Suppose there are two names or descriptions which designate the same things and that *E* is a sentence obtained merely by separating these two names or descriptions by means of "is identical with" (or "are identical with" if the first word is plural). Suppose also that *A* is a sentence using one of those names or descriptions and that *B* is like *A* except that, where *A* uses the one, *B* uses the other. Let us say that *A* is intentional if the conjunction of *A* and *E* does not imply *B*.[3] We can now say of certain cognitive sentences—sentences using "know," "see," "perceive," and the like in one of the ways which have interested us here—that they, too, are intentional. Most of us knew in 1944 that Eisenhower was the one in command (*A*); but although he was (identical with) the man who was to succeed Truman (*E*), it is not true that we knew in 1944 that the man who was to succeed Truman was the one in command (*B*).

Let us say that a *compound* sentence is one compounded from two or more sentences by means of propositional connectives, such as "and," "or," "if–then," "although," "because," and the like. The three foregoing marks of intentionality apply to sentences which are *not* compound. We may now say that a compound declarative sentence is intentional if and only if one or more of its component sentences is intentional. Thus the antecedent of "If Parsifal sought the Holy Grail, he was a Christian" enables us to say that the whole statement is intentional.

When we use perception words propositionally, our sentences display the third of the above marks of intentionality. I may see that John is the man in the corner and John may be someone who is ill; but I do not now *see* that John is someone who is ill. Perception sentences, as we have seen, entail sentences about taking and assuming. And sentences about taking and assuming display the second of the above marks of intentionality. "He takes—and therefore assumes—those rocks to be the reef" does not imply that the rocks *are* the reef and it does not imply that they are not. And similarly for its contradiction: "He does not take—or assume—those rocks to be the reef."

We may now re-express Brentano's thesis—or a thesis resembling that of Brentano—by reference to intentional sentences. Let us say (1) that we do not need to use intentional sentences when we describe nonpsychological phenomena; we can express all of our beliefs about what is merely "physical" in sentences which are not intentional.[4] But (2) when we wish to describe perceiving, assuming, believing, knowing, wanting, hoping, and other such attitudes, then either (a) we must use sentences which are intentional or (b) we must use terms we do not need to use when we describe nonpsychological phenomena.

In describing nonpsychological phenomena, we do, on occasion, use sentences which are intentional by one or more of the above criteria. One may say, "This weapon, suitably placed, is capable of causing the destruction of Boston" and "The cash register knows that 7 and 5 are 12." But although these sentences are intentional according to our criteria, we can readily transform them into others which are not: "If this weapon were suitably placed, then Boston would be destroyed" and "If you press the key marked '7' and the one marked '5', the cash register will yield a slip marked '12.'"

It would be an easy matter, of course, to invent a psychological terminology enabling us to describe perceiving, taking, and assuming in sentences which are not intentional. Instead of saying, for example, that a man *takes* something to be a deer, we could say "His perceptual environment is deer-inclusive." But in so doing, we are using technical terms—"perceptual environment" and "deer-inclusive"—which, presumably, are not needed for the description of nonpsychological phenomena. And unless we can re-express the deer-sentence once again, this time as a nonintentional sentence containing no such technical terms, what we say about the man and the deer will conform to our present version of Brentano's thesis.

How would we go about showing that Brentano was wrong? I shall consider the three most likely methods. None of them seems to be satisfactory.

3. Some philosophers have tried to describe psychological attitudes in terms of *linguistic* behavior. In his inaugural lecture, *Thinking and Meaning,* Professor Ayer tried to define the locution "thinking of *x*" by reference to the use of symbol which designate *x*. A man is *thinking of* a unicorn, Ayer suggested, if (among other things) the man is disposed to use symbols which *designate* unicorns; he *believes* that there are unicorns if (among other things) he is disposed to utter sentences containing words which *designate* or *refer to* unicorns. And perhaps one might try to define "taking" and "assuming" in a similar way. But this type of definition leaves us with our problem.

When we talk about what is "designated" or "referred to" by words or sentences, our own sentences are intentional. When we affirm the sentence "In German, *Einhorn* designates, or refers to, unicorns," we do not imply that there are any unicorns and we do not imply that there are not; and similarly when we deny the sentence. If we think of words and sentences as classes of noises and marks, then we may say that words and sentences are "physical" (nonpsychological) phenomena. But we must not suppose the meaning of words and sentences to be a property which they have apart from their relations to the psychological attitudes of the people who *use* them.

For we know, as Schlick once put it, "that meaning does not inhere in a sentence where it might be discovered"; meaning "must be bestowed upon" the sentence.[6] Instead of saying, "In German, *Einhorn* designates, or refers to, unicorns," we could say, less misleadingly, "German-speaking people use the word *Einhorn* in order to designate, or refer to, unicorns." A word or sentence designates so-and-so only if people *use* it to designate so-and-so.

Or can we describe "linguistic behavior" by means of sentences which are not intentional? Can we define such locutions as "the word 'Q' designates so-and-so" in language which is not intentional? If we can do these things, and if, as Ayer suggested, we can define "believing," or "assuming," in terms of linguistic behavior, then we must

reject our version of Brentano's thesis. But I do not believe that we can do these things; I do not believe that we can define such locutions as "The word 'Q' designates so-and-so" or "The word 'Q' has such-and-such a *use*" in language which is not intentional.

Let us consider, briefly, the difficulties involved in one attempt to formulate such a definition.

Instead of saying, of a certain word or predicate "Q," that it designates or refers to so-and-so's, we may say that, if there were any so-and-so's, they would satisfy or fulfill the *intension* of the predicate "Q." But how are we to define "intension"? Professor Carnap once proposed a behavioristic definition of this use of "intension" which, if it were adequate, might enable us to formulate a behavioristic, nonintentional definition of "believe" and "assume." Although Carnap later conceded that his account was oversimplified, it is instructive, I think, to note the difficulties which stand in the way of defining "intension"—as well as "designates" and "refers to"—in nonintentional terms.[7]

Carnap had suggested that the "intension" of a predicate in a natural language may be defined in essentially this way: "The intension of a predicate 'Q' for a speaker X is the general condition which an object *y* must fulfill in order for X to be willing to ascribe the predicate 'Q' to *y*." Carnap did not define the term "ascribe" which appears in this definition, but from his general discussion we can see, I think, that he would have said something very much like this: "A person X ascribes 'Q' to an object *y*, provided that, in the presence of *y*, X gives an affirmative response to the question 'Q?'" (Let us assume that the expressions "is willing to," "in the presence of," "affirmative response," and "question" present no difficulties.)

Such a definition of "intension" is adequate only if it allows us to say of Karl, who speaks German, that an object *y* fulfills the intension of *Hund* for Karl if and only if *y* is a dog. Let us consider, then, a situation in which Karl mistakes something for a dog; he is in the presence of a fox, say, and takes it to be a dog. In this case, Karl would be willing to give an affirmative response to the question *"Hund?"* Hence the fox fulfills the condition which an object must fulfill for Karl to be willing to ascribe *"Hund"* to it. And therefore the definition is inadequate.

Perhaps we can assume that Karl is usually right when he takes something to be a dog. And perhaps, therefore, we can say this: "The intension of '*Hund*' for Karl is the general condition which, more often than not, an object *y* must fulfill in order for Karl to be willing to ascribe '*Hund*' to *y*." But if the occasion we have considered is the only one on which Karl has been in the presence of a fox, then, according to the present suggestion, we must say, falsely, that the fox does not fulfill the intension of Karl's word *"Fuchs."* Moreover, if Karl believes there are unicorns and, on the sole occasion when he thinks he sees one, mistakes a horse for a unicorn, then the present suggestion would require us to say, falsely, that the horse fulfills the intension, for Karl, of his word *"Einhorn."*

The obvious way to qualify Carnap's definition would be to reintroduce the term "believe" and say something of this sort: "The intension of a predicate 'Q' for a speaker X is the general condition which X must *believe* an object *y* to fulfill in order for X to be willing to ascribe the predicate 'Q' to *y*." And, in general, when we say, "People use such and such a word to refer to so-and-so," at least part of what we mean to say is that people use that word when they wish to express or convey something they *know* or *believe*—or *perceive* or *take*—with respect to so-and-so. But if we define "intension" and "designates" in terms of "believe" and "assume," we can no longer hope, of course, to define "believe" and "assume" in terms of "intension" or "designates."

4. The second way in which we might try to show that Brentano was wrong may be described by reference to a familiar conception of "sign behavior." Many philosophers and psychologists have suggested, in effect, that a man may be said to *perceive* an object *x*, or to *take* some object *x* to have a certain property *f*, provided only that there is something which *signifies x* to him, or which signifies to him that *x* is *f*. But what does "signify" mean?

We cannot be satisfied with the traditional descriptions of "sign behavior," for these, almost invariably, define such terms as "sign" by means of intentional concepts. We cannot say, for instance, that an object is a sign provided it causes someone to *believe*, or *expect*, or *think of* something; for sentences using "believe," "expect," and "think of" are clearly intentional. Nor can we say merely that an object is a sign provided it causes someone to be *set for*, or to be *ready for*, or to *behave appropriately to* something, for sentences using "set for," "ready for," and "behave appropriately to," despite their behavioristic overtones, are also intentional. Similar objections apply to such statements as "One object is a sign of another provided it *introduces the other object into the behavioral environment*, as contrasted with the physical environment, of some organism."

If we are to show that Brentano's thesis as applied to *sign* phenomena is mistaken, then we must not introduce any new technical terms into our analysis of sign behavior unless we can show that these terms apply also to nonpsychological situations.

Most attempts at nonintentional definitions of "sign" make use of the concept of *substitute stimulus*. If we use "referent" as short for "what is signified," we may say that, according to such definitions, the sign is described as a substitute for the referent. It is a substitute in the sense that, as stimulus, it has effects upon the subject which are similar to those the referent would have had. Such definitions usually take this form: V is a *sign* of R for a subject S if and only if V affects S in a manner similar to that in which R would have affected S.[8] The bell is a sign of food to the dog, because bell affects the dog's responses, or his dispositions to respond, in a way similar to that in which the food would have affected them.

This type of definition involves numerous difficulties of which we need mention but one—that of specifying the respect or degree of similarity which must obtain between the effects attributed to the sign and those attributed to the referent. This difficulty is involved in every version of the substitute–stimulus theory. Shall we say that, given the conditions in the above definition, V is a sign of R to a subject S provided only that those responses of S which are stimulated by V are similar in *some* respect to those which have been (or would be) stimulated by R? In other words, should we say that V is a sign of R provided that V has some of the effects which R has had or would had? This would have the unacceptable consequence that all stimuli signify each other, since any two stimuli have at least some effect in common. Every stimulus causes neural activity, for example; hence, to that extent at least, any two stimuli will have similar effects. Shall we say that V is a sign of R provided that V has *all* the effects which R would have had? If the bell is to have all the effects which the food would have had, then, as Morris notes, the dog must start to eat the bell.[9] Shall we say that V is a sign of R provided that V has the effects which *only* R would have had? If the sign has effects which only the referent can have, then the sign *is* the referent and only food can be a sign of food. The other methods of specifying the degree or respect of similarity required by the substitute-stimulus definition, so far as I can see, have equally unacceptable consequences.

Reichenbach, in his *Elements of Symbolic Logic*, has applied this type of analysis to the concept of taking; but the consequences are similar. To say of a subject S, according to Reichenbach, that S *takes* something to be a dog is to say: "There is a *z* which is a bodily state of S and which is such that, whenever S is sensibly stimulated by a dog, S is in this bodily state *z*."[10] In other words, there are certain bodily conditions which S must fulfill in order for S to be sensibly stimulated by a dog; and whenever S satisfies any of these conditions, then S is taking something to be a dog.

But among the many conditions one must fulfill if one is to be sensibly stimulated by a dog is that of being alive. Hence if we know that S is alive, we can say that S is taking something to be a dog. The difficulty is that the bodily state z, of Reichenbach's formula, is not specified strictly enough. And the problem is to find an acceptable modification.

In reply to this objection, Reichenbach suggested, in effect, that "S takes something to be a dog" means that S's bodily state has all those neural properties which it must have—which are "physically necessary" for it to have—whenever S is sensibly stimulated by a dog.[11] But this definition has the unacceptable consequence that, whenever S is sensibly stimulated by a dog, then S *takes* the thing to be a dog. Thus, although we can say that a man may be stimulated by a fox and yet take it to be a dog, we can never say that he may be stimulated by a dog and *not* take it to be a dog.[12]

Similar objections apply to definitions using such expressions as "dog responses," "responses specific to dogs," "responses appropriate to dogs," and the like. For the problem of specifying what a man's "dog responses" might be is essentially that of specifying the bodily state to which Reichenbach referred.

5. Of all intentional phenomena, expectation is one of the most simple and, I think, one which is most likely to be definable in terms which are not intentional. If we could define, in nonintentional terms, what it means to say of a man, or an animal, that he expects something—that he expects some state of affairs to come about—then, perhaps, we could define "believing" and "assuming," nonintentionally, in terms of this sense of "expecting." If we are to show that Brentano is wrong, our hope lies here, I think.

For every expectancy, there is some possible state of affairs which would *fulfill* or *satisfy* it, and another possible state of affairs which would *frustrate* or *disrupt* it. If I expect the car to stop, then, it would seem, I am in a state which would be fulfilled or satisfied if and only if the car were to stop—and which would be frustrated or disrupted if and only if the car were not to stop. Hence we might consider defining "expects" in this way:

"S *expects* E to occur" means that S is in a bodily state b such that either (i) b would be fulfilled if and only if E were to occur or (ii) b would be disrupted if and only if E were not to occur.

Our problem now becomes that of finding appropriate meanings for "fulfill" and "disrupt."

Perhaps there is a way of defining "fulfill" in terms of the psychological concept of *re-enforcement* and of defining "disrupt" in terms of *disequilibration, surprise,* or *shock.* And perhaps we can then provide an account of the dog and the bell and the food in terms which will show that this elementary situation is not intentional. It is possible that the dog, because of the sound of the bell, is in a state which is such that either (i) his state will be re-enforced if he receives food or (ii) it will be disequilibrated if he does not. And it is possible that this state can be specified in physiological terms. Whether this is so, of course, is a psychological question which no one, apparently, is yet in a position to answer. But even if it is so, there are difficulties in principle which appear when we try to apply this type of definition to human behavior.

If we apply "expects," as defined, to human behavior, then we must say that the appropriate fulfillments or disruptions must be caused by the occurrence, or nonoccurrence, of the "intentional object"—of *what* it is that is expected. But it is easy to think of situations which, antecedently, we should want to describe as instances of expectation, but in which the fulfillments or disruptions do not occur in the manner required. And to accommodate our definition to such cases, we must make qualifications which can be expressed only by reintroducing the intentional concepts we are trying to eliminate.

This difficulty may be illustrated as follows: Jones, let us suppose, *expects* to meet his aunt at the railroad station within twenty-five minutes. Our formulation, as applied to this situation, would yield: "Jones is in a bodily state which would be fulfilled if he were to meet his aunt at the station within twenty-five minutes or which would be disrupted if he were not to meet her there within that time." But what if he were to meet his aunt and yet *take* her to be someone else? Or if he were to meet someone else and yet *take* her to be his aunt? In such cases, the fulfillments and disruptions would not occur in the manner required by our definition.

If we introduce the intentional term "perceives" or "takes" into our definition of "expects," in order to say, in this instance, that Jones *perceives* his aunt, or *takes* someone to be his aunt, then, of course, we can no longer define "assume"—or "perceive" and "take"—in terms of "expects." It is worth noting, moreover, that even if we allow ourselves the intentional term "perceive" our definition will be inadequate. Suppose that Jones were to visit the bus terminal, believing it to be the railroad station, or that he were to visit the railroad station believing it to be the bus terminal. If he met his aunt at the railroad station, believing it to be the bus terminal, then, contrary to our formula, he may be frustrated or surprised, and, if he fails to meet her there, his state may be fulfilled. Hence we must add further qualifications about what he believes or doesn't believe.[13]

If his visit to the station is brief and if he is not concerned about his aunt, the requisite re-enforcement or frustration may still fail to occur. Shall we add ". . . provided he *looks for* his aunt"? But now we have an intentional expression again. And even if we allow him to look for her, the re-enforcement or frustration may fail to occur if he finds himself able to satisfy desires which are more compelling than that of finding his aunt.

We seem to be led back, then, to the intentional language with which we began. In attempting to apply our definition of "expects" to a situation in which "expects" is ordinarily applicable, we find that we must make certain qualifications and that these qualifications can be formulated only by using intentional terms. We have had to introduce qualifications wherein we speak of the subject *perceiving* or *taking* something to be the object expected; hence we cannot now define "perceive" and "assume" in terms of "expect." We have had to add that the subject has certain *beliefs* concerning the nature of the conditions under which he perceives, or fails to perceive, the object. And we have referred to what he is *looking for* and to his other possible *desires*.

It may be that some of the simple "expectancies" we attribute to infants or to animals can be described, nonintentionally, in terms of re-enforcement or frustration. And possibly, as Ogden and Richards intimated, someone may yet find a way of showing that believing, perceiving, and taking are somehow "theoretically analysable" into such expectancies.[14] But until such programs are carried out, there is, I believe, some justification for saying that Brentano's thesis does apply to the concept of *perceiving*.

NOTES

1. Franz Brentano, *Psychologie vom empirischen Standpunkte* (Leipzig, 1924), I, 124–125.

2. But the point of talking about "intentionality" is not that there is a peculiar type of "inexistent" object; it is rather that there is a type of psychological phenomenon which is unlike anything purely physical. In his later writings Brentano explicitly rejected the view that there are "inexistent objects"; see his *Psychologie,* II, 133 ff., and *Wahrheit und Evidenz* (Leipzig, 1930), pp. 87, 89.

3. This third mark is essentially the same as Frege's concept of "indirect reference." See Gottlob Frege, "Uber Sinn und Bedeutung," *Zeitschrift für Philosophie und philosophische Kritik,* n.s. C (1892), 25–50, especially 38; reprinted in Herbert Feigl and W. S. Sellars, eds., *Readings in Philosophical Analysis* (New York, 1949), and Peter Geach and Max Black, eds., *Philosophical Writings of Gottlob Frege* (Oxford, 1952).

4. There are sentences describing relations of comparison—for example, "Some lizards look like dragons"—which may constitute an exception to (1). If they are exceptions, then we may qualify (1) to read: "We do not need any intentional sentences, other than those describing relations of comparison, when we describe nonpsychological phenomena." This qualification would not affect any of the points to be made here.

5. A. J. Ayer, *Thinking and Meaning,* p. 13. Compare W. S. Sellars, "Mind, Meaning, and Behavior," *Philosophical Studies,* III (1952) 83–95; "A Semantical Solution of the Mind-Body Problem," *Methodos* (1953), pp. 45–85; and "Empiricism and the Philosophy of Mind," in Herbert Feigl and Michael Scriven, eds., *The Foundations of Science and the Concepts of Psychology and Psychoanalysis* (Minneapolis, 1956). See also Leonard Bloomfield, *Linguistic Aspects of Science* (Chicago, 1939), pp. 17–19.

6. Moritz Schlick, "Meaning and Verification," *Philosophical Review,* XLV (1936), 348; reprinted in Feigl and Sellars, eds., *Readings in Philosophical Analysis.* Compare this analogy, in "Meaning and Free Will," by John Hospers: "Sentences in themselves do not possess meaning; it is misleading to speak of 'the meaning of sentences' at all; meaning being conferred in every case by the speaker, the sentence's meaning is only like the light of the moon: without the sun to give it light, it would possess none. And for an analysis of the light we must go to the sun" (*Philosophy and Phenomenological Research,* X [1950], 308).

7. Carnap's definition appeared on p. 42 of "Meaning and Synonymy in Natural Languages," *Philosophical Studies,* IV (1955), 33–47. In "On Some Concepts of Pragmatics," *Philosophical Studies,* VI, 89–91, he conceded that "designates" should be defined in terms of "believes." The second article was written in reply to my "A Note on Carnap's Meaning Analysis," which appeared in the same issue (pp. 87–89).

8. Compare Charles E. Osgood, *Method and Theory in Experimental Psychology* (New York, 1953), p. 696: "A pattern of stimulation which is not the object is a sign of the object if it evokes in an organism a mediating reaction, this (a) being some fractional part of the total behavior elicited by the object and (b) producing distinctive self-stimulation that mediates responses which would not occur without the previous association of nonobject and object patterns of stimulation. All of these limiting conditions seem necessary. The mediation process must include part of the same behavior made to the object if the sign is to have its representing property." Some of the difficulties of the substitute stimulus concept [qualification (a) in this definition] are met by qualification (b), which implies that the subject must once have perceived the thing signified. But (b) introduces new difficulties. Since I have never seen the President of the United States, no announcement, according to this definition, could signify to me that the President is about to arrive.

9. See Charles Morris, *Signs, Language, and Behavior,* p.

12, and Max Black, "The Limitations of a Behavioristic Semiotic," *Philosophical Review,* LVI (1947), 258–272.

10. This is a paraphrase of what Hans Reichenbach formulated in special symbols on p. 275 of *Elements of Symbolic Logic* (New York, 1947).

11. Reichenbach suggests this modification in "On Observing and Perceiving," *Philosophical Studies,* II (1951), pp. 92–93. This paper was written in reply to my "Reichenbach on Observing and Perceiving" (*Philosophical Studies,* II, 45–48), which contains some of the above criticisms. In these papers, as well as in Reichenbach's original discussion, the word "perceive" was used in the way in which we have been using "take." Reichenbach used the term "immediate existence" in place of Brentano's "intentional inexistence"; see *Elements of Symbolic Logic,* p. 274.

12. This sort of modification may suggest itself: Consider those bodily states which are such that (i) S is in those states whenever he is sensibly stimulated by a dog and (ii) S cannot be in those states whenever he is *not* being stimulatd by a dog. Shall we say "S takes something to be a dog" means that S is in this particular class of states? If we define "taking" in this way, then, we must say that, in the present state of psychology and physiology, we have no way of knowing whether anyone ever *does* take anything to be a dog, much less whether people take things to be dogs on just those occasions on which we want to be able to *say* that they take things to be dogs.

13. R. B. Braithwaite in "Belief and Action" (*Aristotelian Society,* suppl. vol. XX [1946] p. 10) suggests that a man may be said to believe a proposition p provided this condition obtains: "If at a time when an occasion arises relevant to p, his springs of action are s, he will perform an action which is such that, if p is true, it will tend to fulfill s, and which is such that, if p is false, it will not tend to satisfy s." But the definition needs qualifications in order to exclude those people who, believing truly (p) that the water is deep at the base of Niagara Falls and wishing (s) to survive a trip over the falls, have yet acted in a way which has not tended to satisfy s. Moreover, if we are to use such a definition to show that Brentano was wrong, we must provide a nonintentional definition of the present use of "wish" or "spring of action." And, with Braithwaite's definition of "believe," it would be difficult to preserve the distinction which, apparently, we ought to make between *believing* a proposition and *acting upon* it (see Chapter One, Section 2). I have proposed detailed criticisms of a number of such definitions of "believe" in "Sentences about Believing," *Proceedings of the Aristotelian Society,* LVI (1955–1956), 125–148. Some of the difficulties involved in defining *purpose* nonintentionally are pointed out by Richard Taylor in "Comments on a Mechanistic Conception of Purpose," *Philosophy of Science,* XVII (1950), 310–317, and "Purposeful and Nonpurposeful Behavior: A Rejoinder," *ibid.,* 327–332.

14. C. K. Ogden and I. A. Richards, *The Meaning of Meaning,* 5th ed. (London, 1938), p. 71.

32

W. V. Quine

from "The Double Standard"

* * * * *

A reason for gravitating to indirect quotation as prime example of the propositional attitudes is that the quoted speaker's actual utterance exists as a standard with which to compare the variants, whereas in the case of believing, wishing, and the rest there is usually no such fixed point to work from. Not, of course, that this trait makes indirect quotation humanly dispensable. We tend, even if we hear a remark directly and not by hearsay, to forget its exact words and remember only enough to report by indirect quotation.[4] Hence the main utility of indirect quotation. And there is its utility also as a medium of translation. Indirect quotation is here to stay, and so, for similar and further reasons, are the other idioms of propositional attitude.

In general the underlying methodology of the idioms of propositional attitude contrasts strikingly with the spirit of objective science at its most representative. For consider again quotation, direct and indirect. When we quote a man's utterance directly we report it almost[5] as we might a bird call. However significant the utterance, direct quotation merely reports the physical incident and leaves any implications to us. On the other hand in indirect quotation we project ourselves into what, from his remarks and other indications, we imagine the speaker's state of mind to have been, and then we say what, in our language, is natural and relevant for us in the state thus feigned. An indirect quotation we can usually expect to rate only as better or worse, more or less faithful, and we cannot even hope for a strict standard of more and less; what is involved is evaluation, relative to special purposes, of an essentially dramatic act. Correspondingly for the other propositional attitudes, for all of them can be thought of as in-

volving something like quotation of one's own imagined verbal response to an imagined situation.

Casting our real selves thus in unreal roles, we do not generally know how much reality to hold constant. Quandaries arise. But despite them we find ourselves attributing beliefs, wishes, and strivings even to creatures lacking the power of speech, such is our dramatic virtuosity. We project ourselves even into what from his behavior we imagine a mouse's state of mind to have been, and dramatize it as a belief, wish, or striving, verbalized as seems relevant and natural to us in the state thus feigned.

In the strictest scientific spirit we can report all the behavior, verbal and otherwise, that may underlie our imputations of propositional attitudes, and we may go on to speculate as we please upon the causes and effects of this behavior; but, so long as we do not switch muses, the essentially dramatic idiom of propositional attitudes will find no place.

The Scholastic word 'intentional' was revived by Brentano in connection with the verbs of propositional attitude and related verbs of the sort studied in §32—'hunt', 'want', etc. The division between such idioms and the normally tractable ones is notable. We saw how it divides referential from non-referential occurrences of terms. Moreover it is intimately related to the division between behaviorism and mentalism,[6] between efficient cause and final cause, and between literal theory and dramatic portrayal.

The analysis in § 32 was such as to spare us any temptation to posit peculiar "intentional objects" of hunting, wanting, and the like. But there remains a thesis of Brentano's, illuminatingly developed of late by Chisholm,[7] that is directly relevant to our emerging doubts over the propositional attitudes and other intentional locutions. It is

From *Word and Object,* by W. V. Quine, Cambridge, Mass.: MIT Press, 1960, from chap. 6, § 45, pp. 218–21. Copyright © 1960 by the MIT Press. Reprinted with permission of the publisher.

roughly that there is no breaking out of the intentional vocabulary by explaining its members in other terms. Our present reflections are favorable to this thesis. Even indirect quotation, for all its tameness in comparison with other idioms of propositional attitude, and for all its concern with overt speech behavior, seems insusceptible to general reduction to behavioral terms; the best we can do with it is switch to direct quotation, and this adds information. And when we turn to belief sentences the difficulty is doubled. For, first there is trouble, e.g. over dumbness or mendacity, in explaining belief as disposition to assent to sentences at all; and second there remains, much as in the case of indirect quotation, the question what deviations to allow between the sentences actually assented to and the second-hand reports.

Chisholm counts the semantical terms 'meaning', 'denote', 'synonymous', and the like into the intentional vocabulary, and questions the extent to which such terms can be explained without the help of other semantical or intentional ones. Adapted to the example 'Gavagai' (Ch. II), the sort of difficulty he has in mind is this: we cannot equate 'Gavagai' and 'Rabbit' as outright responses to rabbits, for assent to these sentences is prompted not by the presence of rabbits but by their believed presence; and belief is intentional. Now we cleared this obstacle in § 8 by equating 'Gavagai' and 'Rabbit' on the basis of stimulations rather than rabbits. Stimulations, however deceptive, go by face value, and match up well enough from speaker to speaker to sustain the equation. There is the possibility that informants may lie to us, but one assumes that such deviations, where undetected as lies, are rare enough not to spoil a significant approximation of stimulus meanings.

But the predicament that Chisholm anticipates is still encountered when we turn from the stimulus synonymy of occasion sentences to the construing of terms. This is a step that requires analytical hypotheses, undetermined by verbal dispositions (§§ 12, 16); yet it is a step that the intentional vocabulary would represent as determinate. For, using the intentional words 'believe' and 'ascribe', one could say that a speaker's term is to be construed as 'rabbit' if and only if the speaker is disposed to ascribe it to all and only the objects that he believes to be rabbits. Evidently, then, the relativity to non-unique systems of analytical hypotheses invests not only translational synonymy but intentional notions generally. Brentano's thesis of the irreducibility of intentional idioms is of a piece with the thesis of indeterminacy of translation.

One may accept the Brentano thesis either as showing the indispensability of intentional idioms and the importance of an autonomous science of intention, or as showing the baselessness of intentional idioms and the emptiness of a science of intention. My attitude, unlike Brentano's, is the second. To accept intentional usage at face value is, we saw, to postulate translation relations as somehow objectively valid though indeterminate in principle relative to the totality of speech dispositions. Such postulation promises little gain in scientific insight if there is no better ground for it than that the supposed translation relations are presupposed by the vernacular of semantics and intention.

Not that I would forswear daily use of intentional idioms, or maintain that they are practically dispensable. But they call, I think, for bifurcation in canonical notation. Which turning to take depends on which of the various purposes of a canonical notation happens to be motivating us at the time. If we are limning the true and ultimate structure of reality, the canonical scheme for us is the austere scheme that knows no quotation but direct quotation and no propositional attitudes but only the physical constitution and behavior of organisms. (It would be pointless to exempt from this ban even those favored sentences of propositional attitude that can be explained in terms of stimulus synonymy; for when they can be thus paraphrased they are certainly dispensable.) If we are venturing to formulate the fundamental laws of a branch of science, however tentatively, this austere idiom is again likely to be the one that suits. But if our use of canonical notation is meant only to dissolve verbal perplexities or facilitate logical deductions, we are often well advised to tolerate the idioms of propositional attitude. Our purposes may then be well served by admitting the apparatus of propositional attitudes as of the end of § 44—hence minus the right to quantify over the attitudinal objects.[8]

NOTES

4. See Chisholm, *Perceiving* [Ithaca, N.Y.: Cornell University Press, 1957], p. 160.

5. This adverb allows for § 18.

6. See Chisholm, "Sentences about believing"; Bergmann, "Intentionality" [*Archivio di Filosofia* 1955, pp. 177–216] p. 211.

7. See Chisolm, *Perceiving*, Ch. 11, and his references to Brentano.

8. On the austere scheme, which Bergmann ("Intentionality") calls L_c, see further § 47. Its more liberal variant, accommodating intentional idioms, answers in spirit though not in detail to Bergmann's *L*. In his kindliness toward the intentional, Bergmann is nearer Brentano than I; but it is a difference not easily assessed, for we are agreed both that the intentional does not reduce and that it is at least in a practical way indispensable.

33

W. V. Quine

"Quantifiers and Propositional Attitudes"

I

The incorrectness of rendering 'Ctesias is hunting unicorns' in the fashion:

$$(\exists x)(x \text{ is a unicorn . Ctesias is hunting } x)$$

is conveniently attested by the non-existence of unicorns, but is not due simply to that zoological lacuna. It would be equally incorrect to render 'Ernest is hunting lions' as:

(1) $(\exists x)(x \text{ is a lion . Ernest is hunting } x)$,

where Ernest is a sportsman in Africa. The force of (1) is rather that there is some individual lion (or several) which Ernest is hunting; stray circus property, for example.

The contrast recurs in 'I want a sloop'. The version:

(2) $(\exists x)(x \text{ is a sloop . I want } x)$

is suitable insofar only as there may be said to be a certain sloop that I want. If what I seek is mere relief from slooplessness, then (2) gives the wrong idea.

The contrast is that between what may be called the *relational* sense of lion-hunting or sloop-wanting, viz., (1)–(2), and the likelier or *notional* sense. Appreciation of the difference is evinced in Latin and Romance languages by a distinction of mood in subordinate clauses; thus *'Procuro un perro que habla'* has the relational sense:

$$(\exists x)(x \text{ is a dog . } x \text{ talks . I seek } x)$$

as against the notional *'Procuro un perro que hable':*

I strive that $(\exists x)(x$ is a dog . x talks . I find x).

Pending considerations to the contrary in later pages, we may represent the contrast strikingly in terms of permutations of components. Thus (1) and (2) may be expanded (with some violence to both logic and grammar) as follows:

(3) $(\exists x)(x$ is a lion . Ernest strives that Ernest finds x),

(4) $(\exists x)(x$ is a sloop . I wish that I have x),

whereas 'Ernest is hunting lions' and 'I want a sloop' in their notional senses may be rendered rather thus:

(5)   Ernest strives that $(\exists x)(x$ is a lion . Ernest finds x),

(6)   I wish that $(\exists x)(x$ is a sloop . I have x).

The contrasting versions (3)–(6) have been wrought by so paraphrasing 'hunt' and 'want' as to uncover the locutions 'strive that' and 'wish that', expressive of what Russell has called *propositional attitudes.* Now of all examples of propositional attitudes, the first and foremost is *belief;* and, true to form, this example can be used to point up the contrast between relational and notional senses still better than (3)–(6) do. Consider the relational and notional senses of believing in spies:

(7) $(\exists x)(\text{Ralph believes that } x \text{ is a spy})$,

(8)   Ralph believes that $(\exists x)(x$ is a spy).

Both may perhaps be ambiguously phrased as 'Ralph believes that someone is a spy', but they may be unambiguously phrased respectively as 'There is someone whom Ralph believes to be a spy' and 'Ralph believes there are spies'. The difference is vast; indeed, if Ralph is like most of us, (8) is true and (7) false.

In moving over to propositional attitudes, as we did in (3)–(6), we gain not only the graphic structural contrast between (3)–(4) and (5)–(6) but also a certain generality. For we can now multiply examples of striving and wishing, unrelated to hunting and wanting. Thus we get the relational and notional senses of wishing for a president:

(9) $(\exists x)$(Witold wishes that x is president),

(10)   Witold wishes that $(\exists x)(x$ is president).

According to (9), Witold has his candidate; according to (10) he merely wishes the appropriate form of government were in force. Also we open other propositional attitudes to similar consideration—as witness (7)–(8).

However, the suggested formulations of the relational senses—viz., (3), (4), (7), and (9)—all involve quantifying into a propositional-attitude idiom from outside. This is a dubious business, as may be seen from the following example.

There is a certain man in a brown hat whom Ralph has glimpsed several times under questionable circumstances on which we need not enter here; suffice it to say that Ralph suspects he is a spy. Also there is a gray-haired man, vaguely known to Ralph as rather a pillar of the community, whom Ralph is not aware of having seen except once at the beach. Now Ralph does not know it, but the men are one and the same. Can we say of this *man* (Bernard J. Ortcutt, to give him a name) that Ralph believes him to be a spy? If so, we find ourselves accepting a conjunction of the type:

(11) w sincerely denies '. . .'. w believes that . . .

as true, with one and the same sentence in both blanks. For, Ralph is ready enough to say, in all sincerity, 'Bernard J. Ortcutt is no spy'. If, on the other hand, with a view to disallowing situations of the type (11), we rule simultaneously that

(12)   Ralph believes that the man in the brown hat
            is a spy,

(13)   Ralph does not believe that the man seen at
            the beach is a spy,

then we cease to affirm any relationship between Ralph and any man at all. Both of the component 'that'-clauses are indeed about the man Ortcutt; but the 'that' must be viewed in (12) and (13) as sealing those clauses off, thereby rendering (12) and (13) compatible because not, as wholes, about Ortcutt at all. It then becomes improper to quantify as in (7); 'believes that' becomes, in a word, referentially opaque.[1]

No question arises over (8); it exhibits only a quantification *within* the 'believes that' context,

not a quantification *into* it. What goes by the board, when we rule (12) and (13) both true, is just (7). Yet we are scarcely prepared to sacrifice the relational construction 'There is someone whom Ralph believes to be a spy', which (7) as against (8) was supposed to reproduce.

The obvious next move is to try to make the best of our dilemma by distinguishing two senses of belief: *belief*$_1$, which disallows (11), and *belief*$_2$, which tolerates (11) but makes sense of (7). For belief$_1$, accordingly, we sustain (12)–(13) and ban (7) as nonsense. For belief$_2$, on the other hand, we sustain (7); and for *this* sense of belief we must reject (13) and acquiesce in the conclusion that Ralph believes$_2$ that the man at the beach is a spy even though he *also* believes$_2$ (and believes$_1$) that the man at the beach is not a spy.

II

But there is a more suggestive treatment. Beginning with a single sense of belief, viz., belief$_1$ above, let us think of this at first as a relation between the believer and a certain *intension,* named by the 'that'-clause. Intensions are creatures of darkness, and I shall rejoice with the reader when they are exorcised, but first I want to make certain points with the help of them. Now intensions named thus by 'that'-clauses, without free variables, I shall speak of more specifically as intensions of degree 0, or propositions. In addition I shall (for the moment) recognize intensions of degree 1, or attributes. These are to be named by prefixing a variable to a sentence in which it occurs free; thus $z(z$ is a spy) is spyhood. Similarly we may specify intensions of higher degrees by prefixing multiple variables.

Now just as we have recognized a dyadic relation of belief between a believer and a proposition, thus:

(14)   Ralph believes that Ortcutt is a spy,

so we may recognize also a triadic relation of belief among a believer, an object, and an attribute, thus:

(15)   Ralph believes $z(z$ is a spy) of Ortcutt.

For reasons which will appear, this is to be viewed not as dyadic belief between Ralph and the proposition *that* Ortcutt has $z(z$ is a spy), but rather as an irreducibly triadic relation among the three things Ralph, $z(z$ is a spy), and Ortcutt. Similarly there is tetradic belief:

(16)   Tom believes $yz(y$ denounced z) of Cicero
            and Catiline,

and so on.

Now we can clap on a hard and fast rule against quantifying into propositional-attitude idioms; but we give it the form now of a rule against quantifying into names of intensions. Thus, though (7) as it stands becomes unallowable, we can meet the needs which prompted (7) by quantifying rather into the triadic belief construction, thus:

(17)   ($\exists x$)(Ralph believes $z(z$ is a spy) of x).

Here then, in place of (7), is our new way of saying that there is someone whom Ralph believes to be a spy.

Belief$_1$ was belief so construed that a proposition might be believed when an object was specified in it in one way, and yet not believed when the same object was specified in another way; witness (12)–(13). Hereafter we can adhere uniformly to this narrow sense of belief, both for the dyadic case and for triadic and higher; in each case the term which names the intension (whether proposition or attribute or intension of higher degree) is to be looked on as referentially opaque.

The situation (11) is thus excluded. At the same time the effect of belief$_2$ can be gained, simply by ascending from dyadic to triadic belief as in (15). For (15) does relate the men Ralph and Ortcutt precisely as belief$_2$ was intended to do. (15) does remain true of Ortcutt under any designation; and hence the legitimacy of (17).

Similarly, whereas from:

Tom believes that Cicero denounced Catiline

we cannot conclude:

Tom believes that Tully denounced Catiline,

on the other hand we can conclude from:

Tom believes $y(y$ denounced Catiline) of
Cicero

that

Tom believes $y(y$ denounced Catiline) of
Tully,

and also that

(18)   ($\exists x$)(Tom believes y (y denounced Catiline)
of x).

From (16), similarly, we may infer that

(19)   ($\exists w$)($\exists x$)(Tom believes $yz(y$ denounced z)
of w and x).

Such quantifications as:

($\exists x$)(Tom believes that x denounced
Catiline),

($\exists x$)(Tom believes $y(y$ denounced x) of
Cicero)

still count as nonsense, along with (7); but such legitimate purposes as these might have served are served by (17)–(19) and the like. Our names of intensions, and these only, are what count as referentially opaque.

Let us sum up our findings concerning the seven numbered statements about Ralph. (7) is now counted as nonsense, (8) as true, (12)–(13) as true, (14) as false, and (15) and (17) as true. Another that is true is:

(20)   Ralph believes that the man seen at the
beach is not a spy,

which of course must not be confused with (13).

The kind of exportation which leads from (14) to (15) should doubtless be viewed in general as implicative. [Correction: see Sleigh, p. 397.] Under the terms of our illustrative story, (14) happens to be false; but (20) is true, and it leads by exportation to:

(21)   Ralph believes $z(z$ is not a spy) of the man
seen at the beach.

The man at the beach, hence Ortcutt, does not receive reference in (20), because of referential opacity; but he does in (21), so we may conclude from (21) that

(22)   Ralph believes $z(z$ is not a spy) of Ortcutt.

Thus (15) and (22) both count as true. This is not, however, to charge Ralph with contradictory beliefs. Such a charge might reasonably be read into:

(23)   Ralph believes $z(z$ is a spy . z is not a spy)
of Ortcutt,

but this merely goes to show that it is undesirable to look upon (15) and (22) as implying (23).

It hardly needs be said that the barbarous usage illustrated in (15)–(19) and (21)–(23) is not urged as a practical reform. It is put forward by way of straightening out a theoretical difficulty, which, summed up, was as follows: Belief contexts are referentially opaque; therefore it is *prima facie* meaningless to quantify into them; how then to provide for those indispensable relational statements of belief, like 'There is someone whom Ralph believes to be a spy'?

Let it not be supposed that the theory which we have been examining is just a matter of allowing unbridled quantification into belief contexts after all, with a legalistic change of notation. On the contrary, the crucial choice recurs at each point: quantify if you will, but pay the price of accepting near-contraries like (15) and (22) at each point at which you choose to quantify. In other words: distinguish as you please between referential and non-referential positions, but keep track, so as to treat each kind appropriately. The notation of intensions, of degree one and higher, is in effect a device for inking in a boundary between referential and non-referential occurrences of terms.

III

Striving and wishing, like believing, are propositional attitudes and referentially opaque. (3) and (4) are objectionable in the same way as (7), and our recent treatment of belief can be repeated for these propositional attitudes. Thus, just as (7) gave way to (17), so (3) and (4) give way to:

(24) $(\exists x)(x$ is a lion . Ernest strives z(Ernest finds z) of x),

(25) $(\exists x)(x$ is a sloop . I wish z(I have z) of x),

a certain breach of idiom being allowed for the sake of analogy in the case of 'strives'.

These examples came from a study of hunting and wanting. Observing in (3)–(4) the quantification into opaque contexts, then, we might have retreated to (1)–(2) and forborne to paraphrase them into terms of striving and wishing. For (1)–(2) were quite straightforward renderings of lion-hunting and sloop-wanting in their relational senses; it was only the notional senses that really needed the breakdown into terms of striving and wishing, (5)–(6).

Actually, though, it would be myopic to leave the relational senses of lion-hunting and sloop-wanting at the unanalyzed stage (1)–(2). For, whether or not we choose to put these over into terms of wishing and striving, there are other relational cases of wishing and striving which require our consideration anyway—as witness (9). The untenable formulations (3)–(4) may indeed be either corrected as (24)–(25) or condensed back into (1)–(2); on the other hand we have no choice but to correct the untenable (9) on the pattern of (24)–(25), viz., as:

$(\exists x)$(Witold wishes y(y is president) of x).

The untenable versions (3)–(4) and (9) all had to do with wishing and striving in the relational sense. We see in contrast that (5)–(6) and (10), on the notional side of wishing and striving, are innocent of any illicit quantification into opaque contexts from outside. But now notice that exactly the same trouble begins also on the notional side, as soon as we try to say not just that Ernest hunts lions and I want a sloop, but that *someone* hunts lions or wants a sloop. This move carries us, ostensibly, from (5)–(6) to:

(26) $(\exists w)(w$ strives that $(\exists x)(x$ is a lion . w finds x)),

(27) $(\exists w)(w$ wishes that $(\exists x)(x$ is a sloop . w has x)),

and these do quantify unallowably into opaque contexts.

We know how, with help of the attribute apparatus, to put (26)–(27) in order; the pattern, indeed, is substantially before us in (24)–(25). Admissible versions are:

$(\exists w)(w$ strives y($\exists x)(x$ is a lion . y finds x) of w),

$(\exists w)(w$ wishes y($\exists x)(x$ is a sloop . y has x) of w),

or briefly:

(28) $(\exists w)(w$ strives y(y finds a lion) of w),

(29) $(\exists w)(w$ wishes y(y has a sloop) of w).

Such quantification of the subject of the propositional attitude can of course occur in belief as well; and, if the subject is mentioned in the belief itself, the above pattern is the one to use. Thus 'Someone believes he is Napoleon' must be rendered:

$(\exists w)(w$ believes y(y = Napoleon) of w).

For concreteness I have been discussing belief primarily, and two other propositional attitudes secondarily: striving and wishing. The treatment is, we see, closely parallel for the three; and it will pretty evidently carry over to other propositional attitudes as well—e.g., hope, fear, surprise. In all cases my concern is, or course, with a special technical aspect of the propositional attitudes: the problem of quantifying in.

IV

There are good reasons for being discontent with an analysis that leaves us with propositions, attributes, and the rest of the intensions. Intensions are less economical than extensions (truth values, classes, relations), in that they are more narrowly individuated. The principle of their individuation, moreover, is obscure.

Commonly logical equivalence is adopted as the principle of individuation of intensions. More explicitly: if S and S' are any two sentences with n (≥ 0) free variables, the same in each, then the respective intensions which we name by putting the

n variables (or 'that', if $n = 0$) before S and S' shall be one and the same intension if and only if S and S' are logically equivalent. But the relevant concept of logical equivalence raises serious questions in turn.[2] The intensions are at best a pretty obscure lot.

Yet it is evident enough that we cannot, in the foregoing treatment of propositional attitudes, drop the intensions in favor of the corresponding extensions. Thus, to take a trivial example, consider 'w is hunting unicorns'. On the analogy of (28), it becomes:

w strives $y(y$ finds a unicorn) of w.

Correspondingly for the hunting of griffins. Hence, if anyone w is to hunt unicorns without hunting griffins, the attributes

$y(y$ finds a unicorn),

$y(y$ finds a griffin)

must be distinct. But the corresponding classes are identical, being empty. So it is indeed the attributes, and not the classes, that were needed in our formulation. The same moral could be drawn, though less briefly, without appeal to empty cases.

But there is a way of dodging the intensions which merits serious consideration. Instead of speaking of intensions we can speak of sentences, naming these by quotation. Instead of:

w believes that . . .

we may say:

w believes-true '. . .'.

Instead of:

(30) w believes $y(. . . y . . .)$ of x

we may say:

(31) w believes '. . . y . . .' satisfied by x.

The words 'believes satisfied by' here, like 'believes of' before, would be viewed as an irreducibly triadic predicate. A similar shift can be made in the case of the other propositional attitudes, of course, and in the tetradic and higher cases.

This semantical reformulation is not, of course, intended to suggest that the subject of the propositional attitude speaks the language of the quotation, or any language. We may treat a mouse's fear of a cat as his fearing true a certain English sentence. This is unnatural without being therefore wrong. It is a little like describing a prehistoric ocean current as clockwise.

How, where, and on what grounds to draw a boundary between those who believe or wish or strive that p, and those who do not quite believe or

wish or strive that p, is undeniably a vague and obscure affair. However, if anyone does approve of speaking of belief of a proposition at all and of speaking of a proposition in turn as meant by a sentence, then certainly he cannot object to our semantical reformulation 'w believes-true S' on any special grounds of obscurity; for, 'w believes-true S' is explicitly definable in *his* terms as 'w believes the proposition meant by S.' Similarly for the semantical reformulation (31) of (30); similarly for the tetradic and higher cases; and similarly for wishing, striving, and other propositional attitudes.

Our semantical versions do involve a relativity to language, however, which must be made explicit. When we say that w believes-true S, we need to be able to say what language the sentence S is thought of as belonging to; not because w needs to understand S, but because S might by coincidence exist (as a linguistic form) with very different meanings in two languages.[3] Strictly, therefore, we should think of the dyadic 'believes-true S' as expanded to a triadic 'w believes-true S in L'; and correspondingly for (31) and its suite.

As noted two paragraphs back, the semantical form of expression:

(32) w believes-true '. . .' in L

can be explained in intensional terms, for persons who favor them, as:

(33) w believes the proposition meant by '. . .' in
                           L,

thus leaving no cause for protest on the score of relative clarity. Protest may still be heard, however, on a different score: (32) and (33), though equivalent to each other, are not strictly equivalent to the 'w believes that . . .' which is our real concern. For, it is argued, in order to infer (33) we need not only the information about w which 'w believes that . . .' provides, but also some extraneous information about the language L. Church[4] brings the point out by appeal to translations, substantially as follows. The respective statements:

w believes that there are unicorns,

w believes the proposition meant by 'There are unicorns' in English

go into German as:

(34) w glaubt, das es Einhörne gibt,

(35) w glaubt diejenige Aussage, die „There are unicorns" auf Englisch bedeutet,

and clearly (34) does not provide enough information to enable a German ignorant of English to infer (35).

The same reasoning can be used to show that 'There are unicorns' is not strictly or analytically equivalent to:

> 'There are unicorns' is true in English.

Nor, indeed, was Tarski's truth paradigm intended to assert analytic equivalence. Similarly, then, for (32) in relation to '*w* believes that . . .'; a systematic agreement in truth value can be claimed, and no more. This limitation will prove of little moment to persons who share my skepticism about analyticity.

What I find more disturbing about the semantical versions, such as (32), is the need of dragging in the language concept at all. What is a language? What degree of fixity is supposed? When do we have one language and not two? The propositional attitudes are dim affairs to begin with, and it is a pity to have to add obscurity to obscurity by bringing in language variables too. Only let it not be supposed that any clarity is gained by restituting the intensions.

NOTES

This paper appeared in the *Journal of Philosophy* (Volume 53, 1956), summing up some points which I had made in lectures at Harvard and Oxford from 1952 onward. It is reprinted here minus fifteen lines.

1. See *From a Logical Point of View*, pp. 142–159; also "Three grades of modal involvement," Essay 15 above, [In Quine's *The Ways of Paradox and Other Essays*, rev. ed.].

2. See my "Two dogmas"; also "Carnap and logical truth," which is Essay 12 above [in Quine's *The Ways of Paradox and Other Essays*, rev. ed.].

3. This point is made by Church, "On Carnap's analysis" [*Analysis* 10 (1950), pp. 97–99].

4. *Ibid.*, with an acknowledgment to Langford.

34

Roderick M. Chisholm

from *The First Person*

Chapter 3: The Problem of First-Person
Sentences

Belief *De Re*

What makes my belief about you, then, a belief
about *you?*

Let us look for the simplest answer possible. By
'the simplest answer', I mean, not only the answer
that is easiest to understand, but also the one that
involves the fewest philosophical commitments—
the fewest commitments about the nature of the
world and the fewest commitments about the faculties and potentialities of the thinking or referring
person.

What we are considering is what has come to
be known as *de re* belief. A believer may attribute
a property to another thing—and do so in such a
way that the other thing can be said to be the *object*
of his belief, to be *believed about* by him. I may
attribute to you, for example, the property of being
seated. In this case, we may say that I believe, *with
respect to you,* that you are seated. And this means
that *you* are such that you are believed by me to
be seated. To be believed by someone to be seated
may not be much of a property; it is a *denominatio
mere extrinsica.* But it *is* something that is true of
you and, under some circumstances, it could turn
out to be very important.

We are asking, then: What is it for me thus to
have a belief with respect to you? How is it that,
thus acting at a distance, I make you such that you
are believed by me to be seated?

There have been people who have been sceptical about the possibility of this kind of belief *de re.*
Some philosophers would say, of you, that you
cannot be believed about by me. According to

them, it cannot be a property of you—or of any
other thing—to be a thing which is such that it is
believed by some other thing to be seated. This denial of the possibility of belief *de re*—and of other
intentional attitudes *de re*—is obviously a kind of
scepticism, it may recall the doctrine philosophers
once expressed by saying: 'The mind cannot get
outside the circle of its own ideas', and one must
deal with it in the way in which one deals with
scepticism in general. I would propose that we do
not consider *that* question at the present time, for
we are assuming that you can be believed about by
me and I can be believed about by you.

In my book *Person and Object,* and elsewhere,
I had suggested that we could characterize *de re* belief in terms of *de dicto* belief. I had assumed, in
other words, that all believing is a matter of accepting some proposition or state of affairs. The
theory was essentially this: If I have a belief *(de re)*
with respect to you, then I accept *(de dicto)* a proposition or state of affairs which *implies something*
with respect to you. The theory presupposed, then,
that we be able to say what it is for a proposition
or state of affairs to 'imply something with respect
to you'. My idea was this: we may say that a proposition *implies* a property provided the proposition is necessarily such that if it is true then something has that property; now some of your
properties are identifying properties—they are
such that only one thing can have them at a time;
and so, if a proposition implies the conjunction of
one of your identifying properties with some other
property, then the proposition may be said to
imply, *with respect to you,* that you have that other
property. Hence the proposition 'implies something with respect to you'. This enables us to say
that, if I accept *(de dicto)* such a proposition, then

From *The First Person,* by Roderick M. Chisholm. Minneapolis: University of Minnesota Press, and Hassocks: The Harvester
Press, 1981, chaps. 3 and 4, pp. 13–40. Copyright © 1981 by the Royal Institute of Philosophy. Reprinted with permission of
the publishers and Roderick M. Chisholm.

I believe, with respect to you, that you have the property in question. The definition I had given was this:

> x believes that y has the property of being F = Df y has a property z such that only one thing can have z at a time, and x accepts a proposition implying the conjunction of z and the property of being F.

For example, if you are the tallest man and I accept the proposition that the tallest man is seated, than I accept a proposition which implies the conjunction of one of your identifying properties—that of being the tallest man—with the property of being seated. Hence the theory allows us to say that I believe, with respect to you, that you are seated.

This is a relatively simple theory of *de re* belief. It presupposes that believing is primarily propositional, and it is committed to the being of propositions as well as to the ability of persons to grasp and accept propositions. It also presupposes the being of properties and the ability to conceive both propositions and properties. I am confident that we must make these presuppositions, no matter what our theory of reference may be, but I think that the theory as I have spelled it out presupposes too much. For it has some strange consequences with respect to the nature of propositions and also with respect to the nature of the human mind.

A Difficulty with the Propositional Theory

I suggest that, to see the implausibility of the propositional theory of belief, we consider what the theory involves when it is applied to those beliefs that we have about *ourselves*. If I can be said to believe, with respect to you, that you are sitting, then, surely, I can also be said to believe, with respect to *me*, that I am standing. Given the propositional theory what would this latter imply?

It would imply that I accept a proposition which implies, with respect to me, that I am standing—hence that I accept a proposition which implies the conjunction of one of my identifying properties with the property of standing.

It may be tempting to say, then, that just as there are first-person sentences—for example, the English sentence 'I am standing'—there are also first-person propositions. The proposition that you accept when, say, you believe yourself to be standing would not be the same as the one I accept when I believe myself to be standing—even though we both use the first-person sentence 'I am standing'. Where my proposition implies one of my identifying properties, yours implies one of yours.

But *what* identifying properties do these propositions imply? If I say, without giving undue thought to myself, 'I am standing', *what* identifying property of me is involved in what I thus believe?

One may be tempted to reason this way: 'If there is an identifying property of me which is implied by the first-person proposition I would express by 'I am standing', then, it would seem, this property can be only the property of *being identical with me*. After all, what *other* property could it be? But if *being identical with me* is a property that I have, then it must be my individual essence or haecceity. For *being identical with me* would be a property that I necessarily have and one that no other thing can possibly have. It would therefore seem reasonable to conclude that I, at least, have an individual essence or haecceity'. Is this reasoning valid?

Some philosophers—for example, Frege and Husserl—have suggested that each of us has his own idea of himself, his own *Ich-Vorstellung* or individual concept. And some of the things that such philosophers have said suggest the following view: The word 'I', in the vocabulary of each person who uses it, has for its referent that person himself and has for its sense that person's *Ich-Vorstellung* or individual concept. The difference between my 'I'-propositions and yours would lie in the fact that mine imply my *Ich-Vorstellung* and not yours, and that yours imply your *Ich-Vorstellung* and not mine.[1]

Could we make a list of *Ich-Vorstellungen,* a list of individual concepts, as we might make a list of colours? We could make a list of colours and then go on to say: 'This first colour is the colour of that thing, this second colour is the colour of that other thing, and this third colour is the colour of that third thing.' But surely we cannot make a list of *Ich-Vorstellungen* in this way and go on to say: 'Here is the *Ich-Vorstellung* that that person expresses in his "I"-sentences, here is the one that that second person expresses in *his* "I"-sentences . . .

Brentano says that in those self-evident states of mind that present themselves to us we *never* grasp any properties that are individuating. According to him, any state of mine that I am readily able to grasp is one which, theoretically at least, can be exemplified in several different things at once.[2] Isn't this plausible?

It seems doubtful that I can ever be said thus to grasp my own individual essence or haecceity. If I were able to grasp it, shouldn't I also be able to single out its various marks? Perhaps I can single out *some* of the marks of my individual essence—if I have one. Thus it may include various universal essential properties (for example, being red or non-red, or being a musician if a violinist). And perhaps I can single out certain non-universal essential properties (for example, being an individual thing and being a person). But if I can grasp my individual essence, then I ought also to be able to single out in it those features that are unique to it. If *being identical with me* is my individual essence and *being identical with you* is yours, then, presumably, each analyses into personhood and something else as well—one something else in my case and another in yours—but I haven't the faintest idea what this something else might be.

The property, if there is one, which is intended by the expression 'being identical with me' would seem to be extraordinarily empty.

We have these two options, then, so far as individual essences are concerned. First, we could say that, although each of us has an individual essence, these individual essences involve certain properties that are 'unanalysable' and yet *also* such as to be restrictied to a single thing. But if *being identical with me* implies personhood, then it is at least *partially* analysable. Hence we would have to say that my individual essence contains an unanalysable part—and it is in that unanalysable part that the difference between my individual essence and yours is to be found.

The second possibility is to say that we have been too readily attracted to the assumption that each individual has an individual essence that he can grasp. This latter course seems to be to be the right one.

One may now be led to say: 'Then my first-person propositions must be interpreted in some other way'. But let us consider an even more far-reaching hypothesis. This is the hypothesis that, although there *are* such things as propositions, which can be expressed in certain types of well-formed sentence, and although there *are* first-person sentences, there are *no* such things as first-person propositions.

Let us also be prepared to accept the more general hypothesis, according to which the normal function of sentences containing demonstrative terms and proper names is *not* that of expressing propositions.

The Problem of the 'He, Himself' Locution

We were trying, then, to find a simple account of *de re* belief—of the way in which, for example, I could be said to make you my object and thus have a belief with respect to you. We had a relatively simple account of such belief, but it seemed to break down in application to beliefs about *oneself*—for example, in application to my belief that

I am standing. Let us now look at these cases somewhat more carefully, for they involve complications we have not yet considered. These complications pertain to what might be called 'the problem of the "he, himself " locution'.

The 'he, himself' locution may be illustrated by an example that Ernst Mach cites in the second edition of the *Analysis of Sensations.* He writes: 'Not long ago, after a trying railway journey by night, and much fatigued, I got into an omnibus, just as another gentleman appeared at the other end. "What shabby pedagogue is that, that has just entered?" thought I. It was myself; opposite me hung a large mirror. The physiognomy of my class, accordingly, was better known to me than my own.'[3] As Mach entered the bus, then, he believed with respect to Mach—and therefore with respect to himself—that he was a shabby pedagogue, but he did not believe *himself* to be a shabby pedagogue'. The experience might have made him say: '*That* man is a shabby pedagogue'. But—prior to his discovery of the mirror—it would not have led him to say: '*I* am a shabby pedagogue'.

Examples are readily multiplied. Elizabeth Anscombe[4] has noted that it is one thing for Descartes to doubt the identity of *Descartes* with Descartes and quite another thing for him to doubt the identity of *himself* with Descartes. She also cites this example:

> 'When John Smith spoke of James Robinson he was speaking of his brother, but he did not know this.' That's a possible situation. So similarly is 'When John Smith spoke of John Horatio Auberon Smith (named in a will perhaps) he was speaking of himself, but he did not know this'. If so, then 'speaking of' or 'referring to' oneself is compatible with not knowing that the object one speaks of is oneself.

Anscombe goes on to say that the expression: 'He doesn't realize the identity with himself' is not the 'ordinary' reflexive but 'a special one which can be explained only in terms of the first person'.

An abundance of other examples may be found in the writings of Peter Geach and Hector Castaneda, who brought this difficult problem before the attention of contemporary philosophy.[5]

To understand the 'he, himself' locution, let us consider its use in clauses expressing the objects of believing. We may contrast the three locutions:

(P) The tallest man accepts the proposition that the tallest man is wise.

(Q) There is an x such that x is identical with the tallest man and x is believed by x to be wise.

(S) The tallest man believes that he himself is wise.

An alternative formulation of S would be: 'That tallest man believes himself to be wise'.

The distinction between P and Q is familiar: P is an example of belief *de facto;* Q is an example of belief *de re;* and S is an example of the 'he, himself' locution in application to believing.

Let us consider, then, the logical relations among our three sentences. We may say:

(a) P does not imply Q;

(b) Q does not imply P;

(c) S does not imply P;

(d) P does not imply S;

(e) S implies Q;

(f) Q does not imply S.

Given our assumptions about *de re* belief, we may say that the only one of these assumptions that may seem problematic is the last one—that Q does not imply S. So, let us consider the conditions under which it might be the case that Q is true and S is false.

Assume, then, that S is false. In this case the tallest man cannot sincerely say: 'I believe that I am wise'. Suppose, however, that he reads the lines on his hand and takes them to be a sign of wisdom; he doesn't realize the hand is his; and he is unduly modest and entirely without conceit. He arrives at the belief, with respect to the man in question, that he is wise—just as I might arrive at the belief, with respect to you, that you are wise, and just as Mach had arrived at the belief, with respect to the man he was looking at, that that man was a shabby pedagogue. Hence, although the tallest man cannot sincerely say: 'I believe that I am wise', he can correctly express his conclusion by saying: 'Well, *that* person, at least, is wise'.

If we can say that P refers to a belief *de dicto* and Q to a belief *de re,* then we could say that the 'he, himself' locution, S, is an instance of belief *de re,* for S does imply Q.

The 'he, himself' locution, unlike the *de dicto* locution, implies the *de re* locution. Yet there is one respect in which the 'he, himself' locution is like belief *de dicto* and unlike belief *de re.* Using the 'he, himself' locution to contrast the three belief situations, we may note these things about what the believer can know: (i) If the tallest man believes *de re,* with respect to the tallest man, that he is wise, it may not be at all evident to him that he *does* thus believe with respect to the tallest man that he is wise (for he may have no idea that the man in question *is* the tallest man). (ii) If the tallest man believes *de dicto* that the tallest man is wise (that is to say, if the proposition that the tallest man is wise is one that he accepts), then it is *ipso*

facto evident to him that he believes that the tallest man is wise. And, finally, (iii) if he believes that *he, himself* is wise, then it is also *ipso facto* evident to him that he believes that he, himself is wise. This last point might encourage one to say that such believing is, after all, a matter of accepting first-person propositions, but we cannot take this course if we decide that there are no such propositions.

Why is it that the ordinary quantifier and variables don't seem to suffice in the case of the 'he, himself' locution? Does our sentence S express some element of subjectivity that escapes the ordinary notation of quantification—some kind of inner connection or intimacy that we don't encounter when we are not dealing with the relation of the psychological subject to itself?

Some Ways of Dealing with the Problem

At first consideration the problem may seem to admit of an easy solution. 'Can't we just say that if a person *x* believes *himself* to be wise, then *x* believes *x* to be wise and, moreover, *x* believes that he is *x*? In other words: 'There exists an *x* such that *x* believes *x* to be wise'' tells us this: "There exists an *x* such that *x* believes that *x* is wise and he is *x*".'

But this, of course, is only to transfer the problem. Our new problem will be: What is the relation between 'There exists an *x* such that *x* believes that *x* is wise and *he* is *x*' and 'There exists an *x* such that *x* believes that *x* is wise and *x* is *x*'? A similar objection applies to 'There exists an *x* such that *x* believes that *x* is wise and *x* knows that he is *x*'.

What of 'There exists an *x* such that *x* believes *x* to be wise and *x knows who x* is'? But the tallest man may well have known who he was, just as Mach, when he saw himself in the mirror, knew who he was. Hence *x* can be such that (i) he knows who *x* is, (ii) he believes *x* to be wise, and (iii) he does not believe himself to be wise.

What of 'There exists an *x* such that *x* believes *x* to be wise and *x* knows who it is that *x* believes to be wise'? Here, too, the two types of locution reappear: we must distinguish between '*x* knows who it is that *he* believes to be wise' and '*x* knows who it is that *x* believes to be wise'. And, once again, the two locutions are so related that the first implies the second, but not conversely.

Most recent philosophers who have considered the problem assume that the 'he, himself' locution can be explained only on the assumption that there are first-person propositions, and most such theorists are in agreement on two further points. Each theorist suggests that he can express his own first-person propositions by using the first-person pronoun, and each theorist seems to despair of being able to express any first-person proposition of any person other than himself.

Let us briefly consider four recent attempts to deal with the problem.

(i) There is Anscombe's theory, which she summarizes as follows: '"I am this thing here" is, then, a real proposition, but not a proposition of identity. It means: this thing here is the thing, the person ... of whose action *this* idea of action is an idea, of whose movements *these* ideas of movement are ideas, of whose posture *this* is the idea.'[6] She thus attempts to explicate *her* use of the first-person pronoun in terms of the demonstrative 'this'. It is clear that she cannot explicate *my* use of 'I' in this way, and I think she might concede that she cannot grasp my 'I'-propositions at all. Indeed, how would we report her view if we did not have access to direct quotation? We would have to say something like this: According to Professor Anscombe, the proposition she expresses by saying: 'I am this thing here' says that the thing to which *she* is calling attention is the person whose action *her* present idea of action is an idea . . . and so on.

It is fair to say, therefore, that she does not have a general theory about the indirect reflexive. That is to say, she does not present a theory which illuminates the logical relations among our three sentences, P, Q and S.

(ii) As noted above, I had previously defended the view that, for each person, that person's use of 'I' is such that he is its referent and his individual essence or haecceity is its sense. I said, in effect, that 'Jones believes that he himself is wise' tells us this: 'Jones has an individual essence *H*; he accepts a proposition which is certain for him and necessarily such that it is true if and only if whatever has *H* is wise.'[7] I, too, suggested that no one is able to grasp the 'I'-propositions of any other person.

This view is plausible only if it is plausible to suppose that there are 'I'-propositions. And, as we have seen, the most plausible version of the thesis that there are 'I'-propositions presupposes that there are individual essences and that each person can readily grasp his own; but we are now sceptical about these presuppositions.

(iii) Castaneda also assumes that there are first-person propositions. He tells us that, when a person uses an 'I'-sentence, then he is expressing a first-person proposition which 'is different from every third-person proposition about him, and, of course, different from any third-person proposition about anything else'.[8] Castaneda thus seems to suggest the view that he could never express *my* 'I'-

propositions, and I believe he would say that, strictly speaking, he could not even grasp them. He is led, moreover, to a special ontological view about first-person propositions. I had assumed, in the view set forth above, that first-person propositions are abstract objects which imply individual essences. Castaneda, however, is led to complicate the theory of propositions. He holds that first-person propositions, instead of being abstract objects, as propositions are commonly thought to be, are *contingent* things: 'the first-person propositions belonging to a person *X* have a contingent existence; they exist if and only if *X* exists'.[9]

One could go on to hold—but it is not clear whether Castaneda does this—that, for *every* contingent thing, there are contingent propositions that thus 'belong to' that thing—propositions which exist only if the thing exists. I believe that this view is intended by those philosophers who hold that, in addition to those propositions which are abstract objects, there are also contingent 'singular propositions', but we shall stay clear of these ontological complications.

(iv) Finally, making use of the concept of *de re* belief and the concept of empirical certainty, I once proposed a theory which does *not* presuppose that there are 'I'-propositions. Unfortunately, the theory is inadequate on other grounds.

I had said that a proposition is *empirically certain* for a given subject S provided that the proposition is one that is (a) contingent, (b) such that accepting it is more reasonable for S than withholding it, and (c) there is no contingent proposition *i* such that accepting *i* is more reasonable for S than accepting the proposition in question. Then I said:

> Propositions that are empirically certain, in this sense, will be propositions about what are traditionally called 'states of mind'—propositions about thinking, feeling, and believing. No proposition that is empirically certain for a given subject S will imply the existence of any person other than S. If I am not in pain, then the proposition *someone is in pain* cannot be empirically certain for me.[10]

I then went on to say that 'The tallest man believes that he himself is wise' could be put this way: 'It is empirically certain for the tallest man that there is someone who is believed to be wise'. The definition presupposed, as I said, that 'the proposition, *there is someone who is believed to be wise,* cannot be certain for any person unless that person can be said to believe that he, himself, is wise'. And then I was able to add:

> The referent of the first-person expression 'I' in English is the speaker himself and the function of En-

glish expressions of the form: 'I am F', is to express the fact that it is empirically certain for the speaker that there is someone who is believed to be F.

This approach, I now realize, is subject to the following epistemological difficulty: we may say generally that, for any proposition or state of affairs p, if p has some positive epistemic status (say, that of being certain) for a given subject S, then it is possible to formulate an epistemic principle stating the conditions under which p has such positive status for S. The principle will say that, if those conditions obtain, then p has that status for S. The conditions in question will be describable without the use of epistemic terms. In other words, the principle would refer to some state or property of the subject which is necessarily such that, if the subject is in that state or has that property, then it is certain for that subject that there is someone who is believed to be wise.[11] But what state or property could thus render it certain for a given subject that *there is someone who is believed to be wise?* The properties of *being believed to be wise* and of *being such that there is someone one believes to be wise* will not suffice, for obviously one could have either of these properties without thereby being certain that there is someone one believes to be wise. The only property that would yield the desired certainty is that of *believing oneself to be wise*—but that property leaves us with our problem.[12]

An Approach to the Problem

Let us use the term 'emphatic reflexive' for the 'he, himself' locution such as S, and let us use 'non-emphatic reflexive' for those locutions such as Q that do not imply the 'he, himself', or emphatic, reflexive. Thus 'There exists an x such that x believes himself to be wise' (S) will express an emphatic reflexive, and 'There exists an x such that x believes x to be wise' (Q) will express a non-emphatic reflexive.

Perhaps it will be agreed that the distinction between the two types of reflexive is one that holds only in intentional or psychological contexts. Now there are two ways of interpreting the significance of this distinction. In either case, we ask: 'Why is it that the non-emphatic reflexive (for example, Q) does not imply the corresponding emphatic reflexive (for example, S)?' But in the one case, we would trace the failure of implication to certain peculiarities of the emphatic reflexive. We would try to exhibit the emphatic reflexive as a special case of the nonemphatic reflexive. Whereas in the other case, we would proceed in the opposite direction: we would try to exhibit the nonemphatic reflexive

as a special case of the emphatic reflexive. If we take the second approach, we will deny that the emphatic reflexive presents us with any unique logical structure. We will say that the failure of implication is due, rather, to certain familiar facts about intentionality—as exhibited in the *non-emphatic* reflexive.

I suggest that, by exploring the possibility that the second approach is correct, we may arrive at a view enabling us to understand the logic of the two types of reflexive.

It will be instructive to remind ourselves of this fact: there are philosophers who (justifiably or unjustifiably) are not convinced of the validity of the distinction between the two types of reflexive; and what they are sceptical about is not the existence of the emphatic reflexive, but the existence of the non-emphatic reflexive—they doubt that there is a sense of 'There exists an x such that x believes x to be wise' that does *not* imply 'There exists an x such that x believes himself to be wise'. What is peculiar in the distinction, they might say, is the assumption that there is a reflexive which is *not* emphatic.

Consider, then, the possibility that, in the case of non-psychological reflexives, *all* reflexives are emphatic. In the case of motors, say, it will not matter whether we say: 'There is an x such that x refuels x' or: 'There is an x such that x refuels itself'; there is no non-emphatic reflexive here.

Indeed, we have here a kind of criterion of the psychological. If we can say: 'When the doctor treats the doctor, he thereby treats himself', then we are taking the verb, 'to treat' in a sense that is non-psychological or non-intentional. 'To treat' is here to be taken, wholly physicalistically, say as a matter of administering medicines and producing effects upon the patient. But if we can say: 'The doctor may treat the doctor without thereby treating *himself*', then we are taking the verb 'to treat' in a psychological or intentional sense. Treating, so interpreted, involves having certain beliefs and intentions that are directed upon the patient. If the doctor then treats the doctor and doesn't treat himself, then he is in the position Mach was in when he saw himself enter the bus. He is not only administering medicines and producing effects, but he also bears a certain intentional relation to himself. If we can specify what this relation is, then we may conclude that something psychological or intentional is involved when the non-emphatic reflexive holds and the emphatic reflexive fails.

So, instead of trying to understand the 'he, himself' locution as a special case of the ordinary *de re* locution, we shall try to understand the ordinary *de re* locution as a special case of the 'he, himself' locution.

If this, however, is the correct approach, then we have made a mistake in our formulation. We should have given S the ordinary quantification notation, and we should have exhibited Q as something that is obviously derivable from S. How are we to do this? We shall answer this question in the following chapter.

NOTES

1. Compare Frege, 'The Thought: A Logical Inquiry', *Mina*, LXV (1956), pp. 289–311, and Husserl, *Logical Investigations* (London: Routledge and Kegan Paul, 1970), pp. 315–16. I defended this view in Chapter One of *Person and Object: A Metaphysical Study* (London and La Salle, Ill., Allen and Unwin, Ltd., and the Open Court Publishing Company, 1976).

2. See Franz Brentano, *Psychology from an Empirical Standpoint* (London: Routledge & Kegan Paul, 1973), pp. 311–15; and *Kategorienlehre* (Hamburg: Felix Meiner Verlag, 1968), pp. 153–160.

3. Ernst Mach, *Analysis of Sensations* (Chicago: The Open Court Publishing Co., 1897), p. 4n. (Mach asked himself: 'Was steight doch da für ein herabgekommener Schulmeister ein?' Compare *Beiträge zur Analyse der Empfindungen* (Jena: Gustav Fischer, 1886), p. 34. I owe this reference to Michael Corrado.

4. Elizabeth Anscombe, 'The First Person', in S. Guttenplan, ed., *Mind and Language: Wolfson College Lectures 1974* (Oxford: The Clarendon Press, 1975), pp. 45–65.

5. Compare P. T. Geach, 'On Beliefs about Oneself' (1957), in *Logic Matters* (Oxford: Basil Blackwell, 1972), pp. 128–9. Compare the following by H. N. Castaneda: 'He: A Study in the Logic of Self-Consciousness', *Ratio*, Vol. 8 (1966), pp. 130–57; 'Indicators and Quasi-indicators, *American Philosophical Quarterly,* Vol. 4 (1967), pp. 85–100; 'On the Logic of Attributions of Self-Knowledge to Others', *The Journal of Philosophy,* Vol. 65 (1968), pp. 439–56, and 'On the Phenomeno-Logic of the I', *Akten des XIV. Internationalen Kongresses für Philosophie,* Vol. III (University of Vienna, 1969), pp. 260–6. See also John Perry, 'The Problem of the Essential Indexical', *Nous,* XIII (1979), pp. 3–21.

6. 'The First Person', p. 61.

7. *Person and Object,* p. 37.

8. H. N. Castaneda, *Thinking and Doing: The philosophical Foundations of Institutions* (Dordrecht: D. Reidel Publishing Company, 1975), p. 159.

9. 'On the Phenomeno–Logic of the I', p. 267.

10. See 'The Self and the World', in *Wittgenstein and His Impact on Contemporary Thought: Proceedings of the 2nd International Wittgenstein Symposium* (Vienna: Holder-Pichler-Tempsky, 1978), pp. 407–410. The quotations appear on p. 410.

11. Such principles will be discussed in detail in Chapters 7 and 8.

12. For a critical account of the relations between the two theories I had formerly held, compare Dieter Henrich, 'Zwei Theorein zur Verteidigung von Selbstbewusstsein', *Grazer Philosophische Studien,* VII (1979).

Chapter 4: Indirect Attribution

A Re-examination of Intentional Attitudes

Believing must be construed as a relation between a believer and *some* other thing; this much is essential to *any* theory of belief. What kind of thing, then? There are various possibilities: sentences, propositions or states of affairs, properties, individual things. The simplest conception, I suggest, is one which construes believing as a relation involving a believer and a property—a property which he may be said to attribute to himself. Then the various senses of believing may be understood by reference to this simple conception.

Analogous observations may be made with respect to other intentional attitudes—for example, desiring, knowing, hoping, intending. In each case, there is an elementary conception of the attitude in question in terms of which more familiar conceptions can be explicated. This elementary type of attitude, as we shall see, will enable us to understand the relation between the emphatic reflexive—the 'he, himself' locution—and the non-emphatic reflexive. It will throw light upon the nature of *de re* belief, as well as upon the use of proper names and such demonstratives as 'I', 'here' and 'this'.

I shall therefore suggest (1) that each of these intentional attitudes has a primary form which does not take a propositional object, and (2) that we may characterize the more familiar *de dicto* and *de re* forms of these attitudes in terms of the primary, non-propositional form.

I shall develop these points in their application to believing. But what I say may be applied, *mutatis mutandis,* to the other intentional attitudes.

Direct Attribution

Our basic doxastic locution may be spelled out as:

The property of being *F* is such that *x* directly attributes it to *y*.

The letter '*F*' is schematic and may be replaced by any predicative expression having a property as its sense; for simplicity we omit reference to a particular time. Our undefined formula contains the two variables, '*x*' and '*y*', but we shall also affirm the following principle about the nature of direct attribution:

P1 For every *x*, every *y* and every *z*, if *x* directly attributes *z* to *y*, then *x* is identical with *y*.

We shall also assume that the *content* of attribution is always a *property*—and hence a property in the purified sense we set forth in Chapter II.

P2 For every x, every y and every z, if x directly attributes z to y, then z is a property.

The 'he himself' locution of the indirect reflexive may now be introduced as an abbreviation of our undefined locution.

D1 x believes that he himself is F = Df. The property of being F is such that x directly attributes it to x.

Let us consider then, what is presupposed by our use of the concept of direct attribution.

We are assuming, Platonistically, that there *are* properties or attributes and that some of these properties or attributes are exemplified and some are not. Our basic locution, 'the property of being F is such that x directly attributes it to y', is intentional: the expression in the place of 'the property of being F' need not designate a property that is exemplified.

We presuppose two things about the abilities or faculties of believers. First, a believer can take himself as his intentional object; that is to say, he can direct his thoughts upon himself. And, secondly, in so doing, he grasps or conceives a certain property which he attributes to himself. We also presuppose that he is able to grasp or conceive propositions or states of affairs.

All other reference can be explicated in terms of such presuppositions. What we have said about attribution and believing may be extended to the other intentional attitudes and, indeed, to thought itself. Let us consider the latter briefly.

The expression 'entertaining' is sometimes taken to refer to the generic sense of thinking. Entertainment is then recognized as being an intentional attitude taking the same *objects* as believing, but not involving the doxastic commitment that is essential to believing. H. H. Price has described it this way: 'The entertaining of propositions is the most familiar of all intellectual phenomena. It enters into every form of thinking and into many of our conative and emotional attitudes as well. Indeed, one might be inclined to say that it is the basic intellectual phenomenon; so fundamental that it admits of no explanation or analysis, but on the contrary all other forms of thinking have to be explained in terms of it'.[1] Price here assumes that believing is essentially propositional.

But if the primary form of believing is the direct attribution of a property to oneself, then the primary form of 'entertainment' is analogous. It is that phenomenon which is *considering* oneself as having a certain property—or, alternatively put, thinking of oneself as having a certain property. If I am trying to make a decision as to which direction to travel in, I consider myself as travelling in one direction and then consider myself as travelling in another. I will be the *object* of such considering and the property I consider myself as having will be the *content*.

Our principle concern, in the present book, is with belief, or attribution.

Indirect Attribution

Let us now return to our general question about intentionality or indirect reference: How does one succeed in making *other* things one's intentional objects? In other words, how is it possible to refer to individuals other than oneself?

For example, how do I make you my intentional object? I would say that the answer is this: I make you my object by attributing a certain property to myself. The property is one which, in some sense, singles you out and thus makes you the object of an *indirect* attribution. What would it be, then, for one of my properties to single you out?

The answer involves two points:

(1) There is a certain relation R which is such that *you* are the thing to which I bear R. I shall say that such a relation is an *Identifying relation*— a relation by means of which the believer singles out the object of his indirect attribution. Thus you might be the person with whom I am talking, or the person I live across the street from, or the person I am sitting next to. (Note that, in saying that you are the thing that I bear the relation R to, I am not saying that I am *the* thing that bears R to you—or that you are the thing that bears R to me. If we use Russell's notation for descriptive functions, then, if I am x, you should be designated, not as 'the R of x', but as 'the thing that x bears R to'.)

(2) The property I directly attribute to myself may be said to imply that there is just one thing to which I bear R and that that thing has the property of being F. That is to say, the property is necessarily such that whatever has it bears R to just one thing and to a thing that is F.

When this situation obtains, I indirectly attribute to you the property of being F.

Suppose, for example, that I am talking with you and only with you, and that I believe with respect to you that you are wearing a hat. Then the property of being F—the property I indirectly attribute to you—would be that of wearing a hat; the identifying relation R that I bear to you and only to you would be that of talking with; and the property that I directly attribute to myself would be the property of talking with exactly one person and with a person wearing a hat. In thus indirectly attributing a property to you, I directly attribute a certain two-fold property to me. The first part of my direct attribution (that I bear the relation R to one and only one thing) will be correct; for I can attribute a property to you only if the identifying relation by means of which I attempt to single you out *is* a relation I bear to you and only to you. But the second part of the direct attribution (that the thing to which I bear R is a thing that is F) may or may not be correct. In either case, we may say: you are such that, *as* the person I am talking with, I indirectly attribute to you the property of wearing a hat.

More generally, whenever we have indirect attribution, then the believer attributes a property to the object, *as* the thing to which he bears a certain identifying relation. We may call the property thus attributed the *content* of the indirect attribution, and the thing to which the property is attributed the *object*. Thus the believer directly attributes to himself the property of bearing that identifying relation to a thing that exemplifies that content. Our definition of *indirect attribution,* then, is one that is suggestion by the proposed definition of *de re* belief mentioned at the beginning of the previous chapter. It is this:

> D2 y is such that, as the thing that x *bears R to,* x indirectly attributes to it the property of being F = Df x bears R to y and only to y; and x directly attributes to x a property which entails the property of bearing R to just one thing and to a thing that is F.

One property or relation may be said to *entail* another property or relation provided the first is necessarily such that (a) if it is exemplified then the second is exemplified and (b) whoever conceives it conceives the second.

Given the definition just formulated, we may introduce the following abbreviated locution:

> D3 y is such that x indirectly attributes to it the property of being F = Df. There is a relation R such that x indirectly attributes to y, as the thing to which x bears R, the property of being F.

According to this proposal, then, whenever a person indirectly attributes a property to a thing, he can specify a certain identifying relation R which is such that the thing in question is *the* thing to which he bears R. This is not difficult to do. Consider, for example, my beliefs about the present President of the United States. What relation R would be such that he is the thing to which I bear R? One would be that of living in the country where he is the President. Do we have here a *re-*

lation such that Mr Carter is the thing to which I bear that relation? Surely we do. The relation is that expressed by: 'x lives in a country where the President of that country is identical with y'.

Consider another example. What identifying relation is such that W. V. Quine is now the thing to which I bear that relation? It could be that of looking at my copy of a certain book that he wrote ('x is looking at his copy of the book *The Ways of Paradox,* which was written by y').

If there is a relation R such that you can be said to be the one to whom I bear R, and if there is a further relation S such that some third thing can be said to be the thing to which you bear S, then I may be in a position to attribute something indirectly to that third thing; and so on *ad indefinitum.* For example, if you are the one with whom I am talking, if there is an automobile which is the automobile that belongs to you, and if there is a person who is now driving that automobile, then I may be in a position to attribute something indirectly to that person—i.e. to the person who is driving the automobile that belongs to the person with whom I am talking. Or, again, if a certain house happens to be the thing at which I am looking, if Jack is the person who built the house, if Mary is the person who is married to Jack, then Mary will be the person who is married to the person who built the house at which I am looking, and I may, therefore, attribute a property to Mary.

Here, then, we have a procedure for answering the question of Wittgenstein's which we began: 'What makes my idea of him an idea of *him?*', and we can answer it without appealing to words or to terms that refer to him. A partial answer would be this: 'There is a certain relation I bear just to him; and I directly attribute to myself the property of bearing that relation to just one thing'. It is difficult to think of any answer that is simpler than this.

But to the question: 'What makes his *direct* attribution of a property to himself an attribution of a property to *him?*' there can be no answer at all, beyond that of 'He just does—and that is the end of the matter!' Do we have here, then, a difficulty that is unique to the present theory? It is important to see that *every* theory of reference and intentionality is such that, at some point, it must provide a similar answer: 'It just does'. Thus, according to the propositional theory of belief, I make *me* my object by making certain propositions my object. And how do I make those propositions my object? The answer must be that I do this directly—and not via some other thing which I have made my object.

The definition of indirect attribution that I have proposed here is similar, in fundamental respects, to a definition arrived at independently by

David Lewis. Lewis writes: 'A subject ascribes a property *X* to individual *Y* under description *D* if and only if (1) the subject bears the relation *Z* uniquely to *Y*, and (2) the subject self-ascribes the property of bearing relation *Z* uniquely to something which has the property *X*.' Lewis uses 'belief *de se*' for what I have called 'direct attribution'.

'Under a Description'

We can now make use of a locution similar to one that is a part of the active vocabulary of many contemporary philosophers: this is the 'under a description' locution. One could say, in connection with our example, that I indirectly attribute to you 'under the description, the person with whom I am talking' the property of wearing a hat. For this is to say only that I attribute this property to you *as* the person with whom I am talking. (It should be noted that I have not taken the 'under a description' locution as an undefined philosophical locution, but have defined it—in terms of what we have in D2 above.)

Suppose, then, that I indirectly attribute the property of wearing a hat to you under the description, the one with whom I am talking. It may well be that, 'under certain other descriptions' (say, as the one who robbed the bank where my savings are), I do not attribute this property to you—perhaps under that description I even attribute to you the property of *not* wearing a hat.

Indeed, it may be said more generally that, no matter how well I may be acquainted with you, it is possible that, although (1) I attribute a certain property to you under one of your descriptions, nevertheless (2) there is *another* description which is such that, under *that* description, I attribute the negation of the property in question to you.

Ordinarily, when we have occasion to say of one thing that it is thus believed about by some other thing, we do not specify the description under which the first thing is believed about by the second. But, I suggest, there always is such a description and it is usually made obvious by the context of the utterance. (Not many will misunderstand you if, in reporting a masquerade ball in Washington, you say: 'I thought the President's wife was the Secretary of the Treasury'.)

I can make you the object of my indirect attribution, then, whenever there is a description of you which is such that you can be believed about by me under that description. Shall we say, then, that you can be believed about by me whenever there is an identifying relation which is such that you are the thing to which I bear that relation?

We will answer this question when we discuss the problem of *de re* belief, in the final chapter.

Solution of the Problem of the 'He, Himself' Locution

Let us now return to the problem of the 'he, himself' locution which was set forth in the previous chapter. Consider once again the two sentences (S) 'The tallest man believes that he himself is wise' and (Q) 'There is an *x* such that *x* is identical with the tallest man and *x* is believed by *x* to be wise'. I had said that we should formulate S in the ordinary quantification notation and in a way that would illuminate the logical relation between S and Q. The notation should make clear, in particular, that although S implies Q, Q does not imply S.

I suggest, then, that what the sentences S and Q come to is the following:

S′ There is an *x* such that *x* is identical with the tallest man, and the property of being wise is such that *x* directly attributes it to *x*.

Q′ There is an *x* such that *x* is identical with the tallest man, and the property of being wise is one such that *x* directly or indirectly attributes it to *x*.

It is clear from our definitions that S′ implies Q′; and we have no reason to believe that Q′ implies S′. If this analysis is correct, we have made out the difference between what is asserted by the two sentences S and Q without modifying the theory of quantification or extending our ontology beyond individuals, properties and relations, and propositions or states of affairs.

Indeed, we may now affirm a more general thesis about intentionality. In application to believing, it is the thesis that one may attribute a property to oneself without *directly* attributing that property to oneself. *This* fact is the source of our philosophical perplexity.

Consider once again Ernst Mach and the omnibus. When Mach saw himself in the mirror without yet realizing that he was looking at himself, he attributed to himself the property of being a shabby-looking schoolmaster. But he did so *indirectly* and *not* directly.

Then there was the doctor who treated the doctor but didn't treat himself. I had said that the doctor who treats the doctor and doesn't treat himself does so in virtue of a certain intentional relation he bears to himself. We can now say what this relation is. It is that expressed by: '*x* indirectly but not directly endeavours to treat *x*'. (As we have noted, what we say about attribution has its analogues for other intentional attitudes—and hence for trying and undertaking.)

Again, as Elizabeth Anscombe noted, it was one thing for Descartes to doubt the identity of *Descartes* with Descartes, and another thing for

Descartes to doubt the identity of *himself* with Descartes. Possibly the first doubt was a doubt concerning an attribution that is not direct, or possibly the first doubt concerned a proposition—the proposition, say, that the philosopher called 'Descartes' is identical with the philosopher called 'Descartes'. But the second doubt, in any case, would have been a doubt pertaining to an attribution that is direct.

As for John Horatio Auberon Smith, when he spoke of himself without knowing that he was speaking of himself, he was expressing an attribution that was not direct and he had not made the corresponding direct attribution.

When, in Castaneda's example, the editor of *Soul* believes with respect to the editor of *Soul* that he is a millionaire, but does not believe that *he himself* is a millionaire, then the property of being a millionaire is one that he *indirectly* attributes to himself—i.e. to the editor of *Soul*.

Content and Object

'What is the *object* of direct attribution?' Using a traditional terminology we may say that, if something *x* believes something *y* to be wise, then *y* is the *object* of *x*'s belief and the property of being wise is the *content* of *x*'s belief. In the case of direct attribution as well as attribution generally, we shall say that the property attributed is the *content* of the attribution and that the thing *to* which the property is attributed is the *object* of the attribution. But there is no reason to suppose that there is still *another* thing, somehow involving both the individual thing and the property of being wise, which is properly called '*the object*' of direct attribution, this despite the fact that in such a case one can ask: 'And *what* is it that he believes?' For we have rejected the view that explicates attribution by reference to the acceptance of propositions.

I shall quote a statement of the distinction between *content* and *object* which A. N. Whitehead had made in the *Concept of Nature*. Whitehead had noted that a demonstrative phrase may function merely as a gesture without expressing any part of the content that the speaker wishes to convey and that descriptive phrases, which on some occasions may be used to express such content, may on other occasions be used purely demonstratively. He cites the following example:

Suppose that the expositor is in London, say in Regent's Park and in Bedford College, the great college which is situated in that park. He is speaking of the college hall and he says:
'This college building is commodious.'

The phrase 'this college building' is a demonstrative phrase. Now suppose the recipient answers:
'This is not a college building. It is the lion-house in the zoo.'
Then, provided that the expositor's original proposition has not been couched in elliptical phraseology, the expositor sticks to his original proposition when he replies,
'Anyhow, *it* is commodious.'
Note that the recipient's answer accepts the speculative demonstration of the phrase 'This college building'. He does not say: 'What do you mean?' He accepts the phrase as demonstrating an entity, but declares that same entity to be the lion-house in the zoo. In his reply, the expositor in his turn recognizes the success of his original gesture as a speculative demonstration, and waives the question of the suitability of its mode of suggestiveness with an 'anyhow'. But he is now in a position to repeat the original proposition with the aid of a demonstrative gesture robbed of any suggestiveness, suitable or unsuitable, by saying:
'*It* is commodious.'
The *'it'* of this final statement presupposes that thought has seized on the entity as a bare objective for consideration.[3]

According to what I have said, then, the *object* of direct attribution is always oneself. The object of *indirect* attribution is the thing to which one indirectly attributes a property. It may be oneself, but it need not be oneself. Moreover, indirect attribution may also have *multiple objects*. I may believe, with respect to two things, *x* and *y*, that *x* is larger than *y*. In this case, there will be two identifying relations, *R* and *S*, which are such that I bear *R* to *x* and only to *x* and I bear *S* to *y* and only to *y*. I will directly attribute to myself a property which is necessarily such that anything having it will be such that the thing to which it bears *R* is larger than the thing to which it bears *S*. The objects of indirect attribution may thus be multiplied *ad indefinitum*. In the final chapters we shall consider in more detail attribution involving a plurality of objects.

If, as I shall argue, all belief is reducible to direct attribution, there will be a sense in which we can say that the believing subject is the *primary object* of all belief, and analogously for the other intentional attitudes.

'But one cannot attribute anything to oneself unless one has an immediate apprehension of oneself—an apprehension enabling one to pick out the self from among all other things. And your view does not tell us *how* we thus succeed in picking out ourselves.'

The objection confuses direct and indirect attribution. For it presupposes that, in order to attribute a property to myself directly, I must be aware of the kind of identifying relation I bear to the subject of attribute when I attribute something to it indirectly.

Our view may throw some light upon the ancient doctrine according to which knowledge requires an identity between the knower and the object known. For we may say that the primary form of *reference* requires an identity between the one who refers and the thing to which he refers: one directly attributes a property to oneself. The primary object of knowing will be the knower and so, in one sense, the ancient doctrine is correct. But in knowing oneself, one may thereby indirectly attribute a property to something other than oneself.

Eternal Objects and Indirect Attribution

How does one refer to eternal objects—to such objects as properties, relations and states of affairs?

I have said that we presuppose two things about the abilities and faculties of believers. One is the ability to take onself as an intentional object, and the other is the ability to conceive certain eternal objects. The primary way, then, of referring to an eternal object is to *conceive* it.

What is it to have a *belief* about an eternal object—say, a belief about the property blue? If we look to our formula for indirect attribution, we will say that one has a belief about the property blue provided that one indirectly attributes some further property to the property blue—considered *as* the thing to which one bears a certain relation. What kind of relation, then, might I bear to the property blue and only to the property blue? There are many possible relations, all involving the conception of the property blue. The property blue may be the only property I'm now conceiving, or it may be the only colour property I'm now conceiving, or it may be the only property I'm contrasting with the property green. In short, I may bear certain *intentional* relations to the property blue and only to the property blue.

If now I *believe* with respect to the property blue that, say, it can be exemplified by many different things, then I'm making an indirect attribution of the following sort: the property blue, *as* the property that I'm now conceiving (or the colour property I'm now conceiving, or the property I'm now contrasting with the property green) is such that I indirectly attribute to it the property of being capable of exemplification in many different things.

States of affairs and propositions are analogous. For they, too, are things that can be objects of conception, and one way to have a belief about such a thing is to attribute a property to it, once again *as* the thing one is conceiving in a certain way.

Does belief about eternal objects involve more than such indirect attribution? We shall return to this question in the final chapter, when we consider the nature of *de re* belief.

De Dicto Belief

How shall we characterize *de dicto* belief—that type of believing which consists in the acceptance of propositions or states of affairs?

It is more natural to speak of accepting 'propositions' than it is to speak of accepting 'states of affairs'. For the present, however, we shall use the expressions 'proposition' and 'state of affairs' interchangeably. In the *Appendix,* we shall note the sense in which propositions may be said to constitute a sub-species of states of affairs.

I propose this definition of *de dicto* belief:

> D4 The state of affairs that p is accepted *(de dicto)* by x = Df. There is one and only one state of affairs which is the state of affairs that p; and either (a) x directly attributes to x the property of being such that p, or (b) x attributes to the state of affairs that p, as the thing he is conceiving in a certain way, the property of being true.

(In place of 'being true', we could also say 'obtaining'.) The letter '*p*' may here be replaced by any well-formed English indicative sentence, but we do not assume that every such sentence expresses a proposition or state of affairs. Hence our initial stipulation in the definiens above that there *is* the state of affairs that *p*.

The definition tells us, in effect, that there are two quite different conditions under which a person can be said to accept a proposition. The first condition is that wherein one attributes to oneself a certain universal property—that expressed by the locution, 'being such that *p*', and the second condition is that wherein one indirectly attributes to the state of affairs the property of obtaining (or being true). The first way of accepting a proposition is less sophisticated than the second since, unlike the second, it does not presuppose that the believer has the concept expressed by 'is true', or 'obtains'.

In reporting a person's *de dicto* belief, we do not need to use proper names, demonstratives or free variables in describing the content of his belief.

Let us now take note of an important fact about the logic of believing—more particularly, concerning the relation of direct attribution to belief *de dicto*. This fact constitutes a third principle about the logic of direct attribution.

> P3 For any subject *x*, if *x* directly attributes to *x* the property of being *F*, and if *x* considers there being something that is *F*, then the proposition that something is *F* will be accepted by *x*.

One may be said to 'consider there being something that is *F*' if one conceives the proposition. *There being something that is F*, or if one conceives the property of being such that there is something that is *F*.[4] Our principle P3 above should be interpreted as a necessary proposition pertaining to the nature of believing. It is necessary and *a priori* in just the sense in which such propositions as the following may be said to be necessary and *a priori:* for any subject *S*, if *S* accepts the proposition that it is raining and what is being sold on the market, then *x* accepts the proposition that wheat is being sold on the market.

One may ask concerning our principle: Why add the qualification: 'if *x* considers there being something that is *F*'? The answer is that it is possible for a person to believe himself, say to be walking without having made the generalization to what is expressed by 'Something is walking'. But our principle tells us that, if one believes oneself to be walking and also conceives the proposition that someone is walking, or conceives the property of being such that someone is walking, then one will also believe, *de dicto,* that someone is walking.

NOTES

1. H. H. Price, *Belief* (London: George Allen & Unwin, 1969), p. 192

2. David Lewis, 'Attitudes *De Dicto* and *De Se*', *Philosophical Review,* LXXXVIII (1979), pp. 513–43. Earlier versions of my definition may be found in 'The Indirect Reflexive', in *Intention and Intentionality: Essays in Honour of G. E. M. Anscombe,* eds. Cora Diamond and Jenny Teichman (Brighton: The Harvester Press, 1979), pp. 39–53; and in 'Objects and Persons: Revision and Replies', in *Grazer Philosophische Studien,* Vol. 7/8 (1979), pp. 317–88. I am indebted to Allen Renear for criticisms of an earlier version of my definition.

3. A. N. Whitehead, *The Concept of Nature* (Cambridge: The University Press, 1930), pp. 6–7. Compare the distinction between the 'referential' and the 'attributive' uses of definite descriptions, in Keith Donnellan, 'Reference and Definite Descriptions', in H. Feigl, W. Sellars and K. Lehrer, eds., *New Readings in Philosophical Analysis* (New York: Appleton-Century-Crofts, 1972), pp. 59–71; the paper first appeared in 1966.

4. From the fact that there is the proposition, *There being something that is F,* it does *not* follow that there is the property of being such that there is something that is *F*. Properties, we have said, are necessarily such that they can be exemplified. Hence if the proposition expressed by 'There are round squares' is an impossible proposition, there will be no property expressed by 'being such that there are round squares'.

35

J. A. Fodor

"Propositional Attitudes"

Some philosophers (Dewey, for example, and maybe Austin) hold that philosophy is what you do to a problem until it's clear enough to solve it by doing science. Others (Ryle, for example, and maybe Wittgenstein) hold that if a philosophical problem succumbs to empirical methods, that shows it wasn't *really* philosophical to begin with. Either way, the facts seem clear enough: questions first mooted by philosophers are sometimes co opted by people who do experiments. This seems to be happening now to the question: "what are propositional attitudes?" and cognitive psychology is the science of note.

One way to elucidate this situation is to examine theories that cognitive psychologists endorse, with an eye to explicating the account of propositional attitudes that the theories presuppose. That was my strategy in Fodor (1975). In this paper, however, I'll take another tack. I want to outline a number of a priori conditions which, on my view, a theory of propositional attitudes (PAs) ought to meet. I'll argue that, considered together, these conditions pretty clearly demand a treatment of PAs as relations between organisms and internal representations; precisely the view that the psychologists have independently arrived at. I'll thus be arguing that we have good reasons to endorse the psychologists' theory even aside from the empirical exigencies that drove them to it. I take it that this convergence between what's plausible a priori and what's demanded ex post facto is itself a reason for believing that the theory is probably true.

Three preliminary remarks: first, I'm not taking 'a priori' all that seriously. Some of the points I'll be making are, I suppose, strictly conceptual, but others are merely self-evident. What I've got is a

set of glaring facts about propositional attitudes. I don't doubt that we might rationally adopt an account of the attitudes which contravenes some, or maybe even all of them. But the independent evidence for such an account would have to be extremely persuasive or I, for one, would get the jitters. Second, practically everything I'll say about the attitudes has been said previously in the philosophical literature. All I've done is bring the stuff together. I do think, however, that the various constraints that I'll discuss illuminate each other; it is only when one attempts to satisfy them all at once that one sees how univocal their demands are. Finally, though I intend what I say to apply, mutatis mutandis, to PAs at large, I shall run the discussion pretty much exclusively on beliefs and wants. These seem to be the root cases for a systematic cognitive psychology; thus learning and perception are presumably to be treated as varieties of the fixation of belief, and the theory of action is presumably continuous with the theory of utility.[1]

Here, then, are my conditions, with comments.

I. Propositional attitudes should be analyzed as relations. In particular, the verb in a sentence like 'John believes it's raining' expresses a relation between John and something else, and a token of that sentence is true iff John stands in the belief-relation to that thing.[2] Equivalently, for these purposes, 'it's raining' is a term in 'John believes it's raining'.[3] I have three arguments for imposing condition 1, all of them inconclusive.

I-a) It's intuitively plausible. 'believes' looks like a two-place relation, and it would be nice if our theory of belief permitted us to save the appearances.

No doubt, appearances sometimes deceive. The "s" in 'Mary's sake' looks like expressing a relation

From *The Monist*, LXI, 4 (October 1978): 501–23. Reprinted with permission of the editor and Jerry A. Fodor.

(of possession) between Mary and a sake; but it doesn't, or so we're told. In fact, 'Mary's sake' doesn't look *very* relational, since *x's sake* would surely qualify as an idiom even if we had no ontological scruples to placate. There's something syntactically wrong with: ⌜Mary's sake is *F*er than Bill's⌝, 'Mary has a (little) sake', etc. For that matter, there's something syntactically wrong with 'a sake' *tout court*. Yet, we'd expect all such expressions to be well-formed if 'Mary's sake' contained a true possessive. 'Mary's sake' doesn't bear comparison with 'Mary's lamb'.

Still, there are some cases of *non*-idiomatic expressions which appear to be relational, but which, upon reflection, maybe aren't. 'Mary's voice' goes through the transformations even if 'Mary's sake' does not (Dennett, 1969). Yet there aren't, perhaps, such *things* as voices; and, if there aren't, 'Mary's voice' can't refer in virtue of a relation between Mary and one of them.[4] I think it is fair to view the "surface" grammar as ontologically misleading in *these* cases, but only because we know how to translate into more parsimonious forms. 'Mary has a good voice (bad voice; little voice; better voice than Bill's)' goes over, pretty much without residue, into 'Mary sings well (badly, weakly, less well than Bill)'. If, however, we were *un*able to provide (or, anyhow, to envision providing) the relevant translations, what right would we have to view such expressions as ontologically promiscuous? 'Bill believes it's raining' is not an idiom, and there is, so far as anybody knows, no way of translating sentences nominally about beliefs into sentences of reduced ontological load. (Behaviorists used to think such translations might be forthcoming, but they were wrong.) We must, then, either take the apparent ontological commitments seriously or admit to playing fast and loose.

I-b) Existential Generalization applies to the syntactic objects of verbs of propositional attitude; from 'John believes it's raining' we can infer 'John believes something' and 'there is something that John believes' (viz., that it's raining). *EG* may not be *criterial* for ontological commitment, but it is surely a straw in the wind.[5]

I-c) The only known alternative to the view that verbs of propositional attitude express relations is that they are (semantically) "fused" with their objects, and that view would seem to be hopeless.[6]

The fusion story is the proposal that sentences like 'John believes it's raining' ought really to be spelled 'John believes-it's-raining'; that the logical form of such sentences acknowledges a referring expression ('John') and a one-place predicate with no internal structure ('believes-it's-raining'). 'John believes it's raining' is thus an atomic sentence, similar *au fond* to 'John is purple'.

Talk about counter-intuitive! Moreover:

1. There are infinitely many (semantically distinct) sentences of the form *a believes complement*. If all such sentences are atomic, how is English learned? (Davidson, (1965)).
2. Different propositional attitudes are often "focused" on the same content; for example, one can both fear and believe that it will rain on Tuesday. But, on the fusion view, 'John fears that it will rain on Tuesday' has nothing in common with 'John believes that it will rain on Tuesday' save only the reference to John. In particular, it's an *accident* that the form of words 'it will rain on Tuesday' occurs in both.
3. Similarly, different beliefs can be related in such ways as the following: John thinks Sam is nice; Mary thinks Sam is nasty. Under ordinary English representation these beliefs overlap at the 'Sam' position, so the notation sustains the intuition that John and Mary disagree about Sam. But, if the fusion view is correct, 'John thinks Sam is nice' and 'Mary thinks Sam is nasty' have no more in common at the level of canonical notation than, say, 'John eats' and 'Mary swims'. Talk about imperspicuous! In respect of saving the intuitions, the recommended reconstruction does *worse* than the undisciplined orthography that we started with.[7] (For that matter, there's nothing in ⌜believes-that-*S*⌝ to suggest that it's about believing. Here too ⌜believes that *S*⌝ does much better.)
4. It could hardly be an accident that the declarative sentences of English constitute the (syntactic) objects of verbs like 'believe'. Whereas, on the fusion view it's *precisely* an accident; the complement of 'believes' in 'John believes it's raining' bears no more relation to the sentence 'It's raining' than, say, the word 'dog' bears to the first syllable of 'dogmatic'.
5. On the fusion view, it's a sheer accident that if 'John believes it's raining' is true, then what John believes is true iff 'it's raining' is true. But this, surely, is one accident too many. Surely the identity between the truth conditions on John's belief when he believes Fa, and those on the corresponding sentence ⌜a is F⌝ must be what connects the theory of sentence interpretation with the theory of PAs (and what explains our using 'it's rain-

ing', and not some other form of words, to specify *which* belief John has when he believes it's raining).

It's the mark of a bad theory that it makes the data look fortuitous. I conclude that the fusion story is not to be taken very seriously; that neither the philosophy of language nor the philosophy of mind is advanced just by proliferating hyphens. But the fusion story is (de facto) the only alternative to the view that 'believe' expresses a relation. Hence, first blush, we had better assume that 'believe' *does* express a relation and try to find an account of propositional attitudes which comports with that assumption.

II. A theory of PAs should explain the parallelism between verbs of PA and verbs of saying. ("Vendler's Condition").

Rather generally, the things we can be said to *believe* (want, hope, regret, etc.) are the very things that we can be said to *say* (assert, state, etc.). So, John can either belive or assert that it's about to blow; he can either hope that or inquire whether somebody has reefed the main; he can either doubt or demand that the crew should douse the Genny. Moreover, as Vendler (1972) has shown, there are interesting consequences of classifying verbs of PA (on the one hand) and verbs of saying (on the other) by reference to the syntax of their object complements. It turns out that the taxonomies thus engendered are isomorphic down to surprisingly fine levels of grain. Now, of course, this *could* be just an accident, as could the semantic and syntactic parallelisms between the complements of verbs of PA and free standing declaratives (see above). Certainly, it's a substantial inference from the syntactic similarities that Vendler observes to the conclusion he draws: that the object of assertion is identical with the object of belief. Suffice it for now to make the less ambitious point: we should prefer a theory which explains the facts to one which merely shrugs its shoulders; viz. a theory which satisfies Vendler's condition to a theory which does not.

III. A theory of propositional attitudes should account for their opacity ("Frege's Condition").

Thus far, I have stressed logico-syntactic analogies between the complements of belief clauses and the corresponding free-standing declaratives. However, it has been customary in the philosophical literature since Frege to stress one of their striking *dis*analogies: the former are, in general, opaque to inferential operations to which the latter are, in general, transparent. Since this aspect of the behavior of sentences that ascribe propositional attitudes has so dominated the philosophical discus-

sion, I shall make the point quite briefly here. Sentences containing verbs of PA are not, normally, truth functions of their complements. Moreover, contexts subordinated to verbs of PA are normally themselves non-truth functional, and *EG* and substitution of identicals may apply at syntactic positions in a free-standing declarative while failing at syntactically comparable positions in belief sentences. A theory of PAs should explain why all this is so.

It should be acknowledged that, however gross the inadequacies of the fusion view, it does at least provide an account of propositional attitudes which meets Frege's condition. If S doesn't so much as occur in ⌐John believes S⌐ it's hardly surprising that the one should fail to be a truth function of the other; similarly, if 'Mary' doesn't occur in 'Bill believes that John bit Mary', it's hardly surprising that the sentence doesn't behave the way it would if 'Mary' occurred referentially. The methodological moral is perhaps that Frege's condition under-constraints a theory of PAs; ideally, an acceptable account of opacity should follow from a theory that is independently plausible.

IV. The objects of propositional attitudes have logical form ("Aristotle's Condition").

Mental states (including, especially, token havings of propositional attitudes) interact causally. Such interactions constitute the mental processes which eventuate (inter alia) in the behaviors of organisms. Now, it is crucial to the whole program of explaining behavior by reference to mental states that the propositional attitudes belonging to these chains are typically *non*-arbitrarily related in respect of their content (taking the "content" of a propositional attitude, informally, to be whatever it is that the complement of the corresponding PA-ascribing sentence expresses).

This is not an a priori claim, though perhaps it is a transcendental one. For, though one can imagine the occurrence of causal chains of mental states which are not otherwise related (as, e.g., a thought that two is a prime number, causing a desire for tea, causing an intention to recite the alphabet backwards, causing an expectation of rain) and though such sequences doubtless actually occur (in dreams, say, and in madness) still if *all* our mental life were like this, it's hard to see what point ascriptions of contents to mental states would have. Even phenomenology presupposes some correspondence between the content of our beliefs and the content of our beliefs about our beliefs; else there would be no coherent introspections for phenomenologists to report.

The paradigm situation—the grist for the cognitivist's mill—is the one where propositional attitudes interact causally and do so *in virtue of* their content. And the paradigm of this paradigm is the practical syllogism. Since it is part of my point that the details matter not at all, I shall take liberties with Aristotle's text.

John believes that it will rain if he washes his car. John wants it to rain. So John acts in a manner intended to be a car-washing.

I take it that this might be a true, if informal, etiology of John's "car-washing behavior"; the car washing is an effect of the intention to car-wash, and the intention to car-wash is an effect of the causal interaction between John's beliefs and his utilities. Moreover, the etiological account might be counterfactual-supporting in at least the following sense: John wouldn't have car-washed had the content of his beliefs, utilities and intentions been other than they were. Or, if he did, he would have done so unintentionally, or for different reasons, or with other ends in view. To say that John's mental states interact causally *in virtue of* their content is, in part, to say that such counterfactuals hold.

If there are true, contingent counterfactuals which relate mental state *tokens* in virtue of their contents, that is presumably because there are true, contingent generalizations which relate mental state *types* in virtue of their contents. So, still following Aristotle at a distance, we can schematize etiologies like the one above to get the underlying generalization: if x believes that A is an action x can perform; and if x believes that a performance of A is sufficient to bring it about that Q; and if x wants it to be the case that Q; then x acts in a fashion intended to be a performance of A.

I am not, for present purposes, interested in whether this is a plausible decision theory; still less in whether it is the decision theory that Aristotle thought plausible. What interests me here is rather: (a) that any decision theory we can now contemplate will surely look rather like this one in that (b) it will entail generalizations about the causal relations among content-related beliefs, utilities and intentions; and (c) such generalizations will be specified by reference to the form of the propositional attitudes which instantiate them. (This remains true even if, as some philosophers suppose, an adequate decision theory is irremediably in need of ceteris paribus clauses to flesh out its generalizations. See, for example, Grice (1975).) So, in particular, we can't state the theory-relevant generalization that is instantiated by the relations among John's mental states unless we allow reference to beliefs of the form *if X then Y,* desires of the form *that Y;* intentions of the form *that X should come about;* and so forth. Viewed one way

(material mode) the recurrent schematic letters require identities of content among propositional attitudes. Viewed the other way (linguistically) they require formal identities among the complements of the PA-ascribing sentence which instantiate the generalizations of the theory that explains John's behavior. Either way, the form of the generalization determines how the theory relates to the events that it subsumes. There is nothing remarkable about this, of course, except that form is here being ascribed *inside* the scope of verbs of PA.

To summarize: our common-sense psychological generalizations relate mental states in virtue of their content, and canonical representation does what it can to reconstruct such content relations as relations of form. "Aristotle's condition" requires that our theory of propositional attitudes should rationalize this process by construing verbs of PA in a way that permits reference to the form of their objects. To do this is to legitimize the presuppositions of common-sense psychology and, for that matter, of real (viz. cognitive) psychology as well. (See Fodor, op. cit.).

In fact, we can state (and satisfy) Aristotle's condition in a still stronger version. Let anything be a *belief sentence* if it is of the form *a believes that S.* Define the *correspondent* of such a sentence as the formula which consists of S standing alone (i.e. the sentence# S#).[8] We remarked above that there is the following relation between the truth conditions on the belief that a belief sentence ascribes and the truth conditions on the correspondent of the belief sentence: the belief is true iff the correspondent is. This is, presumably, at least part of what is involved in viewing the correspondent of a belief sentence as *expressing* the ascribed belief.

It should not, therefore, be surprising to find that our intuitions about the form of the belief ascribed by a given belief sentence are determined by the logical form of its correspondent. So, intuitively, John's belief that Mary and Bill are leaving is a conjunctive belief (cf. the logical form of 'Mary and Bill are leaving'); John's belief that Alfred is a white swan is a singularly belief (cf. the logical form of 'Alfred is a white swan'); and so on. It is, of course, essential that we understand 'belief' *opaquely* in such examples; otherwise, the belief that P will have the logical form of any sentence equivalent to P. But this is as it should be: it is in virtue of its *opaque* content that John's belief that P plays its systematic role in John's mental life: e.g., in the determination of his actions and in the causation of his other mental states. Hence it is the opaque construal that operates in such patterns of explanation as the practical syllogism and its spiritual heirs.

We are now in position to state Aristotle's condition in its strongest (and final) version. A theory of propositional attitudes should legitimize the ascription of form to objects of propositional attitudes. In particular, it should explain why the form of a belief is identical to the logical form of the correspondent of a sentence which (opaquely) ascribes that belief.[9]

I digress: One may feel inclined to argue that the satisfaction of Aristotle's condition is incompatible with the satisfaction of Frege's condition; that the opacity of belief sentences shows the futility of assigning logical form to their objects. The argument might go as follows. Sentences have logical form in virtue of their behavior under logical transformations; the logical form of a sentence is that aspect of its structure in virtue of which it provides a domain for such transformations. But Frege shows us that the objects of verbs of propositional attitude are inferentially inert. Hence, it's a sort of charade to speak of the logical form of the objects of PAs; what's the force of saying that a sentence has the form $P \& Q$ if one must also say that simplification of conjunction does not apply?

Perhaps some such argument supplies the motive force of fusion theories. It is, in any event, misled. In particular, it muddles the distinction between what's entailed by what's believed, and what's entailed by believing what's believed. Less cryptically: if John believes that P & Q, then what John believes entails that P and what John believes entails that Q. This is surely incontestible; P & Q is what John believes, and P & Q entails P, Q. Full stop. It would thus be highly ill-advised to put Frege's condition as "P & Q is semantically inert when embedded to the context ⌜John believes . . .⌝"; for this makes it sound as though P & Q sometimes doesn't entail P: viz. when it's in the scope of "believes". (A parallel bad argument: P & Q sometimes doesn't entail P, viz. when it's in the scope of the operator 'not'.) What falls under Frege's condition, then, is not the sentence that expresses what John believes (viz. P & Q) but the sentence that expresses John's believing what he believes (viz. the sentence ⌜John believes that P & Q⌝). Note that the inertia of this latter sentence isn't an exception to simplification of conjunction since simplification of conjunction isn't defined for sentences of the form *a believes that P & Q;* only for sentences of the form *P & Q.*

"Still," one might say, "if the form of words ⌜P & Q⌝ is logically inert when embedded to the form of words ⌜John believes . . .⌝, what's the *point* of talking about the logical form of the complement of belief sentences?" This isn't an argument, of course, but it's a fair question. Answers: (a) because we may want to satisfy Aristotle's condition

(e.g., in order to be in a position to state the practical syllogism); (b) because we may want to compare beliefs in respect of their form (John's belief that (x) Fx→Gx is a generalization of Mary's belief that a is F and G; Sam's belief that P is incompatible with Bill's belief that not-P; etc.); (c) because we may wish to speak of the consequences of a belief, even while cheerfully admitting that the consequences of a belief may not themselves be objects of belief (viz. believed in). Indeed, we need the notion of the consequences of a belief if only in order to say that belief isn't closed under the consequence relation.

I cease to digress.

V. A theory of propositional attitudes should mesh with empirical accounts of mental processes.

We want a theory of PAs to say what (token) propositional attitudes *are;* or, at least, what the facts are in virtue of which PA ascriptions are true. It seems to me self-evident that no such theory could be acceptable unless it lent itself to explanations of the data—gross and commonsensical or subtle and experimental—about mental states and processes. This is not, of course, to require that a theory of PAs legitimize our current empirical psychology; only that it comport with some psychology or other that is independently warranted. I hear this as analogous to: the theory that water is H_2O couldn't be acceptable unless, taken together with appropriate empirical premises, it leads to explanations of the macro- and micro-properties of water. Hence, I hear it as undeniable.

I think, in fact, that the requirement that a theory of propositional attitudes should be empirically plausible can be made to do quite a lot of work; much more work than philosophers have usually realized. I'll return to this presently, when we have some theories in hand.

Those, then, are the conditions that I want a theory of propositional attitudes to meet. I shall argue that, taken together, they strongly suggest that propositional attitudes are relations between organisms and formulae in an internal language; between organisms and internal sentences, as it were. It's convenient, however, to give the arguments in two steps; first, to show that conditions I–V comport nicely with the view that the objects of PAs are sentences, and then to show that these sentences are plausibly internal.

I begin by anticipating a charge of false advertising. The arguments to be reviewed are explicitly non-demonstrative. All I claim for the internal language theory is that it works (a) surprisingly well, and (b) better than any of the available alternatives. The clincher comes at the end: even if we didn't need internal sentences for purposes of I–V, we'd need them to do our psychology. Another non-demonstrative argument, no doubt, but one I find terrifically persuasive.

Carnap's Theory

Carnap suggested, in *Meaning and Necessity* (1947), that PAs might be construed as relations between people and sentences they are disposed to utter; e.g., between people and sentences of English. What Carnap had primarily in mind was coping with the opacity problem, but it's striking and instructive that his proposal does pretty well with *all* the conditions I've enumerated. Consider:

I. If propositional attitudes are relations to sentences, then they are relations *tout court.* Moreover, assume that the relation ascribed by a sentence of the form *a believes* . . . holds between the individual denoted by 'a' and the correspondent of the complement clause. It is then immediately clear why the belief ascribed to *a* is true iff the correspondent is; the correspondent is the *object* of the belief (i.e., the correspondent is what's believed-true) if Carnap's story is right.

II. Vendler's condition is presumably satisfiable, though how the details go will depend on how we construe the objects of verbs of saying. A natural move for a neo-Carnapian to make would be to take 'John said that P' to be true in virtue of some relation between John and a token of the type P. Since, on this account, saying that P and believing that P involve relations to tokens of the very same sentence, it's hardly surprising that formulae which express the object of the *says-that* relation turn out to be logico-syntactically similar to formulae which express the object of the *believes-that* relation.

III. Frege's condition is satisfied; the opacity of belief is construed as a special case of the opacity of quotation. To put it slightly differently; 'John said "Bill bit Mary"' expresses a relation between John and a (quoted) sentence, so we're unsurprised by the fact that John may bear *that* relation to *that* sentence, while not bearing it to some arbitrarily similar but distinct sentence; e.g., to the sentence 'somebody bit Mary' or to the sentence 'Bill bit somebody', etc. But ditto, *mutatis mutandis,* if 'John believes Bill bit Mary' *also* expresses a relation between John and a quoted sentence.

IV. Aristotle's condition is satisfied in the strong form. The logical form of the object of a belief sentence is inherited from the logical form of the correspondent of the belief sentence. Of course it is, since on the Carnap view, the correspondent of the belief sentence *is* the object of the belief that it ascribes.

V. Whether you think that Carnap's theory can claim empirical plausibility depends on what you take the empirical facts about propositional attitudes to be and how ingenious you are in exploiting the theory to provide explanations of the facts. Here's one example of how such an explanation might go.

It's plausible to claim that there is a fairly general parallelism between the complexity of beliefs and the complexity of the sentences that express them. So, for example, I take it that 'the Second Punic War was fought under conditions which neither of the combatants could have desired or forseen' is a more complex sentence than, e.g., 'it's raining'; and, correspondingly, I take it that the thought that the Second Punic War was fought under conditions which neither of the combatants could have desired or forseen is a more complicated thought than the thought that it's raining. Carnap's theory explains this parallelism[10] since, according to the theory, what makes a belief ascription true is a relation between an organism and the correspondent of the belief-ascribing sentence. To hold the belief that the Second Punic War . . . , etc. is thus to be related to a more complex sentence than the one you are related to when you hold the belief that it's raining.

Some people need to count noses before they will admit to having one. In which case, see the discussion of "codability" in Brown and Lenneberg (1954) and Brown (1976). What the experiments showed is that the relative complexity of the descriptions which subjects supply for color chips predicts the relative difficulty that the subjects have in identifying the chips in a recognition–recall task. Brown and Lenneberg explain the finding along strictly (though inadvertently) Carnapian lines: complex descriptions correspond to complex memories because it's the description which the subject (opaquely) remembers when he (transparently) remembers the color of the chip.

We can now begin to see *one* of the ways in which Condition V is supposed to work. A theory of propositional attitudes specifies a construal of the objects of the attitudes. It tells for such a theory if it can be shown to mesh with an independently plausible story about the "cost accounting" for mental processes. A cost accounting function is just a (partial) ordering of mental states by their relative complexity. Such an ordering is, in turn, responsive to a variety of types of empirical data, both intuitive and experimental. Roughly, one has a "mesh" between an empirically warranted cost accounting and a theory of the objects of PAs when one can predict the relative complexity of a mental state (or process) from the relative complexity of whatever the theory assigns as its object (or domain). (So, if Carnap is right, then the relative complexity of beliefs should be predictable from the relative linguistic complexity of the correspondents of belief ascribing sentences, all other things being equal.)

There's a good deal more to be said about all this than I have space for here. Again, roughly: to require that the complexity of the putative objects of PAs predict the cost accounting for the attitudes is to impose empirical constraints on the *notation* of (canonical) belief-ascribing sentences. So, for example, we would clearly get different predictions about the relative complexity of beliefs if we take the object of a PA to be the correspondent of the belief ascribing sentence than if we take it to be, e.g., the correspondent transformed into disjunctive form. The fact that there are empirical consequences of the notation we use to specify the objects of PAs is, of course, part and parcel of the fact that we are construing the attitude ascriptions *opaquely;* it is precisely under opaque construal that we distinguish (e.g.,) the mental state of believing that P & Q from the mental state of believing that neither not-P nor not-Q.

In short, Carnap's theory fares rather well with conditions I–V; there's more to be said in its favor than one might gather from the muted enthusiasm which philosophers have generally accorded it. Nevertheless, I think the philosophical consensus is warranted; Carnap's theory won't do. Here are some of the reasons.

1. Carnap has a theory about the objects of the propositional attitudes (viz., they're sentences) and a theory about the character of the relation to those objects in virtue of which one has a belief, desire, etc. Now, the latter theory is blatantly behavioristic; on Carnap's view, to believe that so-and-so is to be disposed (under presumably specifiable conditions) to utter tokens of the correspondent of the belief-ascribing sentence. But, patently, beliefs aren't behavioral dispositions; a fortiori, they aren't dispositions to utter. Hence, something's wrong with at least part of Carnap's account of the attitudes.

I put this objection first because it's the easiest to meet. So far as I can see, nothing prevents Carnap from keeping his account of the *objects* of belief while scuttling the behavioristic analysis of the belief relation. This would leave him wanting an answer to such questions as: what relation to the sentence 'it's raining' is such that you believe that it's raining iff you and it are in that relation? In particular, he'd want some answer other than the behavioristic: "It's the relation of being disposed to utter tokens of that sentence when. . . ."

The natural solution would be for Carnap to turn functionalist; to hold that to believe it's raining is to have a token of 'it's raining' play a certain

role in the causation of your behavior and of your (other) mental states, said role eventually to be specified in the course of the detailed working out of empirical psychology . . . etc., etc. This is, perhaps, not much of a story, but it's fashionable. I know of nothing better, and it does have the virtue of explaining why propositional attitudes are opaque. Roughly, you wouldn't expect to be able to infer from 'tokens of the sentence S_1 have the causal role R' to 'tokens of the sentences S_2 have the causal role R' on the basis of any logical relation between S_1 and S_2 (except, of course, identity). More generally, so far as I can see, a functionalist account of the way quoted sentences figure in the having of PAs will serve as well as a disposition-to-utter account in coping with all of conditions I–V. From now on, I'll take this emendation for granted.

2. The natural way to read the Carnap theory is to take type identity of the correspondents of belief ascribing sentences as necessary and sufficient for type identity of the ascribed beliefs; and it's at least arguable that this cuts the PAs too thin. So, for example, one might plausibly hold that 'John believes Mary bit Bill' and 'John believes Bill was bitten by Mary' ascribe the same belief (see n. 9 above). In effect, this is the sinister side of the strategy of inheriting the opacity of belief from the opacity of quotation. The strategy fails whenever the identity conditions on beliefs are *different* from the identity conditions on sentences.

A way to cope would be to allow that the objects of beliefs are, in effect, *translation sets* of sentences; something like this seems to be the impetus for Carnap's doctrine of intentional isomorphism. In any event, the problems in this area are well-known. It may well be, for example, that the right way to characterize a translation relation for sentences is by referring to the communicative intentions of speaker/hearers of whatever language the sentences belong to. (S_1 translates S_2 iff the two sentences are both standardly used with the same communicative intentions.) But, of course, we can't both identify translations by reference to intentions and individuate propositional attitudes (including, n.b., intentions) by reference to translations. This problem holds quite independent of epistemological worries about the facticity of ascriptions of propositional attitudes, the determinacy or otherwise of translations, etc.; which suggests that it may be serious.

3. You can believe that it's raining even if you don't speak English. This is a variant of the thickness of slice problem just mentioned; it again suggests that the appropriate objects of belief are translation sets and raises the specters that haunt that treatment.

4. You can, surely, believe that it's raining even if you don't speak any language at all. To say this is to say that at least *some* human cognitive psychology generalizes to infra-human organisms; if it didn't, we would find the behavior of animals *utterly* bewildering, which, in fact, we don't.

Of course, relations are cheap; there must be *some* relation which a dog bears to 'it's raining' iff the dog believes that it's raining; albeit, perhaps, some not very interesting relation. So, why not choose *it* as the relation in virtue of which the belief-ascription holds of the dog? The problem is condition V. It would simply be a miracle if there were a relation between dogs and tokens of 'it's raining' such that any of the empirical facts about the propositional attitudinizing of dogs proved explicable in terms of that relation. (We can't, for example, choose any functional/causal relation because the behavior of dogs is surely not in any way caused by tokens of English sentences.) To put it generally if crudely, satisfying condition V depends on assuming that whatever the theory takes to be the object of a PA plays an appropriate role in the mental processes of the organism to which the attitude is ascribed. But English sentences play no role in the mental life of dogs. (Excepting, perhaps, such sentences as 'Down, Rover!' which, in any event, don't play the kind of role envisaged.)

5. We argued that the truth conditions on beliefs are inherited from the truth conditions on the correspondents of belief ascribing sentences, but this won't work if, for example, there are inexpressible beliefs. This problem is especially serious for behaviorist (or functionalist) accounts of the belief relation; to believe that P can't be a question of being disposed to utter (or of having one's behavior caused by) tokens of the sentence P if, as a matter of fact, there is no such sentence. Yet it is the appeal to quoted sentences which does the work in such theories: which allows them to satisfy I–V.

6. We remarked that there's a rough correspondence between the complexity of thoughts and the complexity of the sentences which express them, and that the (neo-) Carnapian theory provides for this; more generally, that the view that the objects of PAs are natural-language sentences might mesh reasonably well with an empirically defensible cost accounting for mental states and processes. Unfortunately this argument cuts both ways if we assume—as seems plausible—that the correspondence is no better than partial. Whenever it fails, there's prima facie evidence *against* the theory that sentences are the objects of propositional attitudes.

In fact, we can do rather better than appealing to intuitions here. For example: we noted above that the "codability" (viz., mean simplicity of descriptions in English) of colors predicts their recallability in a population of English-speakers, and that this comports with the view that what one remembers when one remembers a color is (at least sometimes) its description: i.e., with the view that descriptions are the objects of (at least some) propositional attitudes. It thus comes as a shock to find that codability *in English* also predicts recall for a Dani subject population. We can't explain this by assuming a correlation between codability-in-English and codability-in-Dani (i.e., by assuming that the colors that English speakers find easy to describe are the ones that Dani-speakers also find easy to describe) since, as it turns out, Dani has no vocabulary *at all* for chromatic variation; all such variation is *infinitely* uncodable in Dani. This comes close to being the paradox dreaded above: how could *English* sentences be the objects of the propositional attitudes of (monolingual) Dani? And, if they are not, how could a property defined over English sentences mesh with a theory of cost accounting for the mental processes of the Dani? It looks as though either: (a) some propositional attitudes are *not* relations to sentences, or (b) if they are—if English sentences are somehow the objects of Dani PAs—then sentences which constitute the objects of PAs need play no functional/causal role in the having of the attitudes. (For discussion of the cross-cultural results on codability, see Brown op. cit. For details of the original studies, see Heider (1972) and Berlin and Kay (1969).)

7. If (token) sentences of a natural language are the objects of propositional attitudes, how are (first) languages learned? On any theory of language learning we can now imagine that process must involve the collection of data, the formulation of hypotheses, the checking of the hypotheses against the data, and the decision about which of the hypotheses the data best confirm. That is, it must involve such mental states and processes as beliefs, expectation and perceptual integration. It's important to realize that *no* account of language learning which does not thus involve propositional attitudes and mental processes has ever been proposed by anyone, barring only behaviorists. And behaviorist accounts of language learning are, surely, not tenable. So, on pain of circularity, there must be *some* propositional attitudes which are not functional/causal relations to natural language sentences. I see no way out of this which isn't a worse option than rejecting the Carnap theory.

So, the situation looks discouraging. On the one hand, we have a number of plausible arguments in favor of accepting the Carnap story (viz., I–V) and, on the other, we have a number of equally plausible arguments in favor of not (viz. 1–

7). Never mind; for, at second blush, it seems we needn't accept the whole Carnap theory to satisfy I–V and we needn't reject the whole Carnap theory to avoid 1–7. Roughly, all that I–V require is the part of the story that says that the objects of PAs are *sentences* (hence have logical forms, truth conditions, etc.). Whereas what causes the trouble with 1–7 is only that part of the story which says that they are *natural language* sentences (hence raising problems about non-verbal organisms, first language learning, etc.). The recommended solution is thus to take the objects of PAs to be sentences of a *non*-natural language; in effect, formulae in an Internal Representational System.

The first point is to establish that this proposal does what it is supposed to: copes with I–V without running afoul of 1–7. In fact, I propose to do less than that since, so far as I can see, the details would be extremely complicated. Suffice it here to indicate the general strategy.

Conditions I and III are relatively easy to meet. I demands that propositional attitudes be relations, and so they are if they are relations to internal representations. III demands a construal of opacity. Carnap met this demand by reducing the opacity of belief to the opacity of quotation, and so do we: the only difference is that, whereas for Carnap, 'John believes it's raining' relates John to a sentence of English, for us it relates John to an internal formula.

Conditions II and IV stress logico/syntactic parallelism between the complements and the correspondents of belief-ascribing sentences; such relations are epitomized by the identity between the truth conditions on 'it's raining' and those on what is believed when it's believed that it's raining. (Neo-) Carnap explained these symmetries by taking the correspondents of belief ascriptions to be the objects of beliefs. The present alternative is spiritually similar but one step less direct: we assume that the correspondent of a belief-ascriber inherits its logico-semantic properties from the same internal formula which functions as the object of the belief ascribed.

There are three pieces in play: there are (a) *belief-ascribers* (like 'John believes it's raining'); (b) *complements* of belief ascribers (like ⌈it's raining⌉ in 'John believes it's raining'); and (c) *correspondents* of belief ascribers (like 'it's raining' standing free). The idea is to get all three to converge (though, of course, by different routes) on the same internal formula (call it 'F (it's raning)'[11]) thereby providing the groundwork for explaining the analogies that II and IV express.

To get this to work out right would be to supply detailed instructions for connecting the theory of PAs with the theory of sentence interpretation, and

I have misplaced mine. But the general idea is apparent. Belief ascribers are true in virtue of functional/causal (call them 'belief making') relations between organisms and tokens of internal formulae. Thus, in particular, 'John believes it's raining' is true in virtue of a belief-making relation between John and a token of F (it's raining). It is, of course, the complement of a belief-ascriber that determines *which* internal formula is involved in its truth conditions; in effect 'it's raining' in 'John believes it's raining' functions as an index which picks out F (it's raining) and not, for example, F (elephants have wings) as the internal formula that John is related to iff 'John believes it's raining' is true.

So, viewed along one vector, the complement of a belief-ascriber connects it with an internal formula. But, viewed along another vector, the complement of a belief ascriber connects it to its correspondent: if the correspondent of 'John believes it's raining' is 'it's raining', that is because the form of words 'it's raining' constitutes its complement. And now we can close the circle, since, of course, F (it's raining) is *also* semantically connected with the correspondent of 'John believes it's raining' viz., by the principle that 'it's raining' is the sentence that English speakers use when they are in the belief-making relation to a token of F (it's raining) and wish to use a sentence of English to say what it is that they believe.

There are various ways of thinking about the relation between internal formulae and the correspondents of belief-ascribers. One is to think of the conventions of a natural language as functioning to establish a pairing of its verbal forms with the internal formulae that mediate the propositional attitudes of its users; in particular, as pairing the internal objects of beliefs with the form of words that speaker/hearers use to express their beliefs. This is a natural way to view the situation if you think of a natural language as a system of conventional vehicles for the expression of thoughts (a view to which I know of no serious objections). So in the present case, the conventions of English pair: 'it's raining' with F (it's raining) (viz., with the object of the belief that it's raining); 'elephants have wings' with F (elephants have wings) viz., with the object of the belief that elephants have wings; and, generally, the object of each belief with the correspondent of some belief-ascribing sentence.[12]

Another option is to assume that F (it's raining) is distinguished by the fact that its tokens play a causal/functional role (not only as the object of the belief that it's raining, but also) in the production of linguistically regular utterances of 'it's raining'. Indeed, this option would plausibly be exercised in tandem with the one mentioned just above since it would be reasonable to construe "linguistically regular" utterances as the ones that are produced in light of the speaker's knowledge of the linguistic conventions. The basic idea, in any event, would be to implicate F (it's raining) as the object of the communicative intentions that utterances of 'it's raining' standardly function to express; hence, as among the mental causes of such utterances. I take it that, given this relation, it ought to be possible to work out detailed tactics for the satisfaction of conditions II and IV, but this is the bit I propose to leave to the ingenuity of the reader. What I want to emphasize here is the way the linguistic structure of the complement of a belief ascriber connects it with free declaratives (in one direction) and with internal formulae (in the other). Contrary to the fusion story, it's no accident that 'it's raining' occurs in 'John believes it's raining'. Rather, the availability of natural languages for saying *both* what one believes *and* that one believes it turns on the exploitation of this elegant symmetry.

What about condition V? I shall consider this in conjunction with 2–7, since what's noteworthy about the latter is that they all register *empirical* complaints against the Carnap account. For example, 3, 4 and 6 would be without force if only everybody, (viz., every subject of true propositional attitude ascriptions) talked English. 2 and 5 depend upon the empirical likelihood that English sentences fail to correspond one-to-one to objects of propositional attitudes. 7 would be met if only English were innate. Indeed, I suppose an ultra-hard-line-Neo-Carnapian might consider saving the bacon by claiming that—appearances to the contrary notwithstanding—English *is* innate, universal, just rich enough, etc. My point is that this is the right *kind* of move to make; all we have against it is its palpable untruth.

Whereas, it's part of the charm of the internal language story that, since practically nothing is known about the details of cognitive processes, we can make the corresponding assumptions about the internal representational system risking no more than gross implausibility at the very worst. So, let's assume—what we don't, at any event, *know* to be false—that the internal language is innate, that it's formulae correspond one-one with the contents of propositional attitudes (e.g., that 'John bit Mary' and 'Mary was bitten by John' correspond to the same "internal sentence"), and that it is *as* universal as human psychology; viz., that to the extent that an organism shares our mental processes, it also shares our system of internal representations. On these assumptions, everything works. It's no longer paradoxical, for example, that

codability *in English* predicts the relative complexity of the mental processes of the Dani; for, by assumption, it's not *really* the complexity of English sentences that predicts *our* cost accounting; we wouldn't expect *that* correspondence to be better than partial (see objection 6). What really predicts our cost accounting is the relative complexity of the internal representations that we use English sentences to express. And, again by assumption, the underlying system of internal representations is common to the Dani and to us. If you don't like this assumption, try and find some other hypothesis that accounts for the facts about the Dani.

Notice that to say that we can have our empirical assumptions isn't to say that we can have them for free. They carry a body of empirical commitments which, if untenable, will defeat the internal representation view. Imagine, for example, that cost accounting for English speakers proves utterly unrelated to cost accounting for (e.g.,) speakers of Latvian. (Imagine, in effect, that the Whorf-Sapir hypothesis turns out to be more or less true.) It's then hard to see how the system of internal representations could be universal. But if it's not universal, it's presumably not innate. And if it's not innate, it's not available to mediate the learning of first languages. And if it's not available to mediate the learning of first languages, we lose our means of coping with objection 7. There are plenty of ways in which we could find out that the theory's wrong if, in fact, it is.

Where we've gotten to is this: the general characteristics of propositional attitudes appear to demand sentence-like entities to be their objects. And broadly empirical conditions appear to preclude identifying these entities with sentences of *natural* languages; hence internal representations and private languages. How bad is it to have gotten here? I now want to argue that the present conclusion is independently required because it is presupposed by the best—indeed the only—psychology that we've got. Not just, as one philosopher has rather irresponsibly remarked, that "some psychologists like to talk that way," but that the best accounts of mental processes we have are quite unintelligible unless something like the internal representation story is true.

The long way of making this point is via a detailed discussion of such theories, but I've done that elsewhere and enough is enough. Suffice it here to consider a single example which is, however, prototypical. I claim again that the details don't matter; that one could make the same points by considering phenomena drawn from any area of congitive psychology which is sufficiently well worked out to warrant talk of a theory *in situ.*

So, consider a fragment of contemporary (psycho)linguistics; consider the explanation of the ambiguity of a sentence like 'they are flying planes' (hereinafter, frequently S). The conventional story goes as follows: the sentence is ambiguous because there are two ways of grouping the word sequence into phrases, two ways of "bracketing" it. One bracketing, corresponding to the reading of the sentence which answers 'what are those things?', goes: (they) (are) (flying planes). Viz., the sentence is copular, the main verb is 'are' and 'flying' is an adjectival modifier of 'planes'. Whereas, on the other bracketing, corresponding to the reading on which the sentence answers 'what are those guys doing?', the bracketing goes: (they) (are flying) (planes); viz. the sentence is transitive, the main verb is 'flying' and 'are' belongs to the auxiliary. I assume without argument that something like this is, or at least contributes to, the explanation of the ambiguity of S. The evidence for such treatments is overwhelming and there is, literally, no alternative theory in the field.

But what could it mean to speak of S as "having" two bracketings? I continue to tread the well-worn path: S has two bracketings in that there exists a function (call it G-proper) from (as it might be) the word 'sentence' onto precisely those bracketed word strings which constitute the sentences of English. And both '(they) (are) (flying planes)' and '(they) (are flying) (planes)' are in the range of that function. (Moreover, no other bracketing of that word sequence is in the range of G-proper . . . etc.)

Now, the trouble with this explanation, as it stands, is that it is either enthymemic or silly. For, one wants to ask, how *could* the mere, as it were Platonic, existence of G-proper account for the facts about the ambiguity of English sentences? Or, to put it another way, sure there is, Platonically, a function under which S gets two bracketings. But there is also, Platonically, a function G' under which it gets sixteen; and a function G'' under which it gets seven; and a function G''' under which it gets none. Since G', G'', and G''' are all, qua functions, just as good as G-proper, how could the mere *existence* of the latter explain the linguistic properties of S? (You may feel inclined to say: "Ah, but G-proper is the (or perhaps is *the*) grammar of English, and that distinguishes it from G', G'' and the rest." But this explanation takes one nowhere, since it invites the question: why does the grammar of English play a special role in the explanation of English sentences? Or, to put the same question minutely differently: call G' the schmamar of English. We now want to know how come it's the bracketing assigned by English grammar and not the bracketing assigned by English schmamar, which predicts the ambiguity of 'they are flying planes'?)

So far as I can see, there's only one way such questions can conceivably be answered; viz., by holding that G-proper (not only exists but) is the very system of (internal (what else?)) formulae that English speaker/hearers use to represent the sentences of their language. But, then, if we accept this, we are willy-nilly involved in talking of at least *some* mental processes (processes of understanding and producing sentences) as involving at least some relations to at least some internal representations. And, if we have to have internal representations anyhow, why not take them to be the objects of propositional attitudes, thereby placating I–V? I say "if we accept this"; but really we have no choice. For the account is well-evidenced, not demonstrably incoherent, and, again, it's the only one in the field. A working science is *ipso facto* in philosophical good repute.

So, by a series of non-demonstrative arguments: there are internal representations and propositional attitudes are relations that we bear to them. It remains to discuss two closely related objections.

Objection 1: Why not take the object of propositional attitudes to be *propositions?*

This suggestion has, no doubt, a ring of etymological plausibility; in fact, for all I know, it may be right. The mistake is in supposing it somehow conflicts with the present proposal.

I am taking seriously the idea that the system of internal representations constitutes a (computational) language. *Qua* language, it presumably has a syntax and a semantics; specifying the language involves saying what the properties are in virtue of which its formulae are well-formed, and what relation(s) obtain between the formulae and things in the (non-linguistic) world. I have no idea what an adequate semantics for a system of internal representations would look like; suffice it that, if propositions come in at all, they come in here. In particular, nothing stops us from specifying a semantics for the IRS by saying (inter alia) that some of its formulae express propositions. If we do say this, then we can make sense of the notion that propositional attitudes are relations to propositions; viz., they are *mediated* relations to propositions, with internal representations doing the mediating.

This is, quite generally, the way that representational theories of the mind work. So, in classical versions, thinking of John (construed opaquely) is a relation to an "idea"; viz., to an internal representation of John. But this is quite compatible with its also being (transparently) construable as a relation *to John.* In particular, when Smith is thinking of John, he (normally) stands in relation to John and does so *in virtue* of his standing in relation to an idea of John. Similarly, mutatis mutandis, if thinking that it will rain is standing in relation to a proposition, then, on the present account, you stand in that relation in virtue of your (functional/causal) relation to an internal formula which expresses the proposition. No doubt, the "expressing" bit is obscure; but that's a problem about propositions, not a problem about internal representations.

"Ah, but if you are going to allow propositions as the *mediate* objects of propositional attitudes, why bother with internal representations as their immediate objects? Why not just say: 'propositional attitudes are relations to propositions. Punkt!'" There's a small reason and a big reason. The small reason is that propositions don't have the right properties for our purposes. In particular, one anticipates problems of cost-accounting. Condition V, it will be remembered, permits us to choose among theories of PAs in virtue of the form of the entities they assign as objects of the attitudes. Now, the problem with propositions is that they are the sorts of things which, presumably, don't *have* forms. Propositions are sheer contents; they neutralize the lexico-syntactic differences between various ways of saying the same thing. That's what they're *for.* I say that this is a small problem but it looms prodigious if you hanker after a theory of the object of PAs which claims empirical repute. After all, it's not just cost-accounting which is supposed to be determined by formal aspects of the objects of PAs; it's *all* the mental processes and properties that cognitive psychology explains. That's what it *means* to speak of a *computational* psychology. Computational principles are ones that apply in virtue of the form of entities in their domain.

But my main reason for not saying "propositional attitudes are relations to propositions. Punkt." is that I don't understand it. I don't see how an organism can stand in an (interesting epistemic) relation to a proposition except by standing in a (causal/functional) relation to some token of a formula which expresses the proposition. I am aware that there is a philosophical tradition to the contrary. Plato says (I think) that there is a special intellectual faculty (theoria) wherewith one peers at abstract objects. Frege says that one *apprehends* (what I'm calling) propositions, but I can find no doctrine about what apprehension comes to beyond the remark (in "The Thought") that it's not sense perception because its objects are abstract and it's not introspection because its objects aren't

mental. (He also says that grasping a thought isn't much like grasping a hammer. To be sure. As for me, I want a mechanism for the relation between organisms and propositions, and the only one I can think of is mediation by internal representations.[13]

Objection 2: Surely it's *conceivable* that propositional attitudes are *not* relations to internal representations.

I think it is; the theory that propositional attitudes are relations to internal representations is a piece of empirical psychology, not an analysis. For, there might have been angels, or behaviorism might have been true, and then the internal representation story would have been false. The moral is, I think, that we ought to give up asking for analyses; psychology is all the philosophy of mind that we are likely to get.

But, moreover, it may be *empirically* possible that there should be creatures which have the same propositional attitudes we do (e.g., the same beliefs) but *not* the same system of internal representations; creatures which, as it were, share our epistemic states but not our psychology. Suppose, for example, it turns out that Martians, or porpoises, believe what we do but have a very different sort of cost accounting. We might then want to say that there are translation relations among systems of internal representation (viz., that formally distinct representations can express the same proposition). Whether we can make sense of saying this remains to be seen; we can barely think about the question prior to the elaboration of theories about how such systems are semantically interpreted; and as things now stand, we haven't got semantic theories for natural languages, to say nothing of languages of thought. Perhaps it goes without saying that it's no objection to a doctrine that it *may* run us into incoherencies. Or, rather, if it is an objection, there's an adequate reply: "Yes, but also it may not."

I'll end on the note just sounded. Contemporary cognitive psychology is, in effect, a revival of the representational theory of the mind. The favored treatment of PAs arises in this context. So, in particular, the mind is conceived of as an organ whose function is the manipulation of representations and these, in turn, provide the domain of mental processes and the (immediate) objects of mental states. That's what it is to see the mind as something like a computer. (Or rather, to put the horse back in front of the cart, that's what it is to see a computer as something like the mind. We give sense to the analogy by treating selected states of the machine as formulae and by specifying which semantic interpretations the formulae are to bear. It is in the context of such specifications that we speak of machine processes as computations and of machine states as intensional.)

If the representational theory of the mind is true, then we know what propositional attitudes are. But the net total of philosophical problems is surely not decreased thereby. We must now face what has always been *the* problem for representational theories to solve: what relates internal representations to the world? What is it for a system of internal representations to be semantically interpreted? I take it that this problem is now the main content of the philosophy of mind.[14]

NOTES

1. I shall have nothing at all to say about knowing, discovering, recognizing, or any other of the "factive" attitudes. The justification for this restriction is worth discussing, but not here.

2. I haven't space to discuss here the idea that 'John believes' should be construed as an operator on 'it's raining'. Suffice it (a) that it's going to be hard to square that account with such observations as I-b below; and (b) that it seems quite implausible for such sentences as 'John believes what Mary said' (and what Mary said might *be* that it's raining). In general, the objects of propositional attitude verbs exhibit the syntax of object noun phrases, which is just what the operator account would not predict.

3. I assume that this is approximately correct: given a sentence of the syntactic from NP$_1$ (V (NP$_2$) VP, V expresses a relation iff NP$_1$ and NP$_2$ refer. So, for present purposes, the question whether 'believes' expresses a relation in 'John believes it's raining' comes down to the question whether there are such things as objects of beliefs. I shan't, therefore, bother to distinguish among these various ways of putting the question in the discussion which follows.

4. Of course, it might refer in virtue of a relation between Mary and something other than a voice. 'John is taller than the average man' isn't true in virtue of a relation between John and the average man ('the average man' doesn't refer). But the sentence is relational for all that. It's for this sort of reason that such principles as the one announced in n3 hold only to a first approximation.

5. NB., verbs of propositional attitude are transparent, in this sense, only when their objects are *complements;* one can't infer 'there is something Ponce de Leon sought' from 'Ponce de Leon sought the Fountain of Youth'. It may, however, be worth translating 'seek' to 'try to find' to save the generalization. This would give us: 'Ponce de Leon tried to find the Fountain of Youth', which does, I suppose, entail that there is something that Ponce de Leon tried (viz., tried to do; viz., to find the Fountain of Youth).

Also, to say that *EG* applies *to* the complement of verbs of PA is, of course, not to say that it applies *in* the complement of verbs of PA. 'John wants to marry Marie of Rumania' implies that there is something that John wants (viz., to marry Marie of Rumania); it notoriously does *not* imply that there is someone whom John wants to marry (see III below).

6. Fusion has been contemplated as a remedy for untransparency in several philosophical contexts; see Goodman (1968); Dennett (1969); Nagel (1965). Nb., 'contemplated', not 'embraced'.

7. 3 is not a point about *EG*. On the fusion view, there's no representation of the fact that 'the belief that Sam is nice' is about Sam even when 'belief' and 'about' are both construed *opaquely*.

8. Defining 'correspondent' gets complicated where verbs of PA take *transformed* sentences as their objects, but the technicalities needn't concern us here. Suffice it that we want the correspondent of 'John wants to leave' to be 'John leaves'; the correspondent of 'John objects to Mary and Bill being elected' to be 'Mary and Bill are elected', etc.

9. I am assuming that two sentences with correspondents of *different* logico-syntactic form cannot assign the same (opaque) belief, and someone might wish to challenge this; consider 'John believes that Mary bit Bill' and 'John believes that Bill was bitten by Mary'. This sort of objection is serious and will be accommodated later on.

10. In speaking of Carnap's theory, I don't wish to imply that Carnap would endorse the uses to which I'm putting it; quite the contrary, I should imagine.

11. Where *F* might be thought of as a function from (e.g., English) sentences onto internal formulae.

12. Assuming, as we may but now needn't do, that all beliefs are expressible in English. It is, of course, a consequence of the present view that all the beliefs we can entertain are expressible in the internal code.

13. The notion that the apprehension of propositions is mediated by linguistic objects is not entirely foreign even to the Platonistic tradition. Church says: " . . . the preference of (say) seeing over *understanding* as a method of observation seems to me capricious. For just as an opaque body may be seen, so a concept may be understood or grasped . . . In both cases the observation is not direct but through intermediaries . . . linguistic expressions in the case of the concept." (1951a) see also the discussion in Dummett (1973, pp. 156–57).

14. All of the following helped: Professors Ned Block, Noam Chomsky, Dan Dennett, Hartrey Field, Janet Dean Fodor, Keith Lehrer and Brian Loar. Many thanks.

REFERENCES

Berlin, B. and Kay, P. *Basic Color Terms.* Berkeley, California: University of California Press, 1969.

Brown, R. Reference—in memorial tribute to Eric Lenneberg. *Cognition,* 1976, *4,* 125–53.

Brown, R. and Lenneberg, E. A study in language and cognition. *J. Abnormal and Social Psychol.,* 1954, No. 49, 454–62.

Carnap, R. *Meaning and Necessity.* Chicago: Phoenix Books, University of Chicago Press, 1947.

Church A. "The need for abstract entities in semantic analysis." In *Contributions to the Analysis and Synthesis of Knowledge,* Proceedings of the American Academy of Arts and Sciences, 1951, No. 80, pp. 100–12.

Davidson, D. "Theories of meaning and learnable languages". In *Logic, Methodology and Philosophy of Science,* Proceedings of the 1964 International Congress, Y. Bar-Hillel (ed.). Amsterdam, 1965, pp. 383–94.

Dennett, D. *Content and Consciousness.* New York: Rout-
    ledge and Kegan Paul, 1969.
Dummett, M. *Frege.* London: Buckworth & Co., 1973.
Fodor, J. A. *The Language of Thought.* New York: Thomas
    Y. Crowell Co., 1975.
Goodman, N. *Languages of Art.* New York: Bobbs-Merrill,
    1968.
Grice, H. P. "Method in philosophical psychology". *Proceed-*
*ings and Addresses of the American Philosophical Asso-
    ciation,* 1975, Vol. XLVIII, pp. 23–53.
Heider, E. Universals in color naming and memory. *J. Exp.
    Psychol.,* 1972, No. 93, 10–20.
Nagel, T. Physicalism. *The Philosophical Review,* 1965, *74,*
    339–56.
Vendler, Z. *Res Cogitans.* Ithaca, New York: Cornell Uni-
    versity Press, 1972.

36

Daniel C. Dennett

"True Believers: The Intentional Strategy and Why It Works"

DEATH SPEAKS

There was a merchant in Baghdad who sent his servant to market to buy provisions and in a little while the servant came back, white and trembling, and said, Master, just now when I was in the market-place I was jostled by a woman in the crowd and when I turned I saw it was Death that jostled me. She looked at me and made a threatening gesture; now, lend me your horse, and I will ride away from this city and avoid my fate. I will go to Samarra and there Death will not find me. The merchant lent him his horse, and the servant mounted it, and he dug his spurs in its flanks and as fast as the horse could gallop he went. Then the merchant went down to the market-place and he saw me standing in the crowd, and he came to me and said, why did you make a threatening gesture to my servant when you saw him this morning? That was not a threatening gesture, I said, it was only a start of surprise. I was astonished to see him in Baghdad, for I had an appointment with him tonight in Samarra.

W. Somerset Maugham

In the social sciences, talk about *belief* is ubiquitous. Since social scientists are typically self-conscious about their methods, there is also a lot of talk about *talk about belief*. And since belief is a genuinely curious and perplexing phenomenon, showing many different faces to the world, there is abundant controversy. Sometimes belief attribution appears to be a dark, risky, and imponderable business—especially when exotic, and more particularly religious or superstitious, beliefs are in the limelight. These are not the only troublesome cases; we also court argument and scepticism when we attribute beliefs to non-human animals, or to infants, or to computers or robots. Or when the beliefs we feel constrained to attribute to an apparently healthy, adult member of our own society are contradictory, or even just wildly false. A biologist colleague of mine was once called on the telephone by a man in a bar who wanted him to settle a bet. The man asked: 'Are rabbits birds?' 'No' said the biologist. 'Damn!' said the man as he hung up. Now could he *really* have believed that rabbits were birds? Could anyone really and truly be attributed that belief? Perhaps, but it would take a bit of a story to bring us to accept it.

In all of these cases belief attribution appears beset with subjectivity, infected with cultural relativism, prone to 'indeterminacy of radical translation'—clearly an enterprise demanding special talents: the art of phenomenological analysis, hermeneutics, empathy, *Verstehen,* and all that. On other occasions, normal occasions, when familiar beliefs are the topic, belief attribution looks as easy as speaking prose, and as objective and reliable as counting beans in a dish. Particularly when these straightforward cases are before us, it is quite plausible to suppose that *in principle* (if not yet in practice) it would be possible to confirm these simple, objective belief attributions by *finding something inside the believer's head*—by finding the beliefs themselves, in effect. 'Look', someone might say, 'You either believe there's milk in the fridge or you don't believe there's milk in the fridge' (you might have no opinion, in the latter case). But if you do believe this, that's a perfectly objective fact about you, and it must come down in the end to your brain's being in some particular physical state. If we knew more about physiologi-

From *Scientific Explanations: Papers based on Herbert Spencer Lectures Given in the University of Oxford,* A. F. Heath, ed. Oxford: Oxford University Press, 1975, pp. 53–75. Copyright © 1981 by Oxford University Press. Reprinted with permission of Oxford University Press.

cal psychology we could in principle determine the facts about your brain state, and thereby determine whether or not you believe there is milk in the fridge, even if you were determined to be silent, or disingenuous on the topic. In principle, on this view physiological psychology could trump the results—or non-results—of any 'black box' method in the social sciences that divines beliefs (and other mental features) by behavioural, cultural, social, historical, *external* criteria.

These differing reflections congeal into two opposing views on the nature of belief attribution, and hence on the nature of belief. The latter, a variety of *realism,* likens the question of whether a person has a particular belief to the question of whether a person is infected with a particular virus—a perfectly objective internal matter of fact about which an observer can often make educated guesses of great reliability. The former, which we could call *interpretationism* if we absolutely had to give it a name, likens the question of whether a person has a particular belief to the question of whether a person is immoral, or has style, or talent, or would make a good wife. Faced with such questions, we preface our answers with 'Well, it all depends on what you're interested in', or make some similar acknowledgment of the relativity of the issue. 'It's a matter of interpretation', we say. These two opposing views, so baldly stated, do not fairly represent any serious theorists' positions, but they do express views that are typically seen as mutually exclusive and exhaustive; the theorist must be friendly with one and only one of these themes.

I think this is a mistake. My thesis will be that while belief is a perfectly objective phenomenon (that apparently makes me a realist), it can be discerned only from the point of view of one who adopts a certain *predictive strategy,* and its existence can be confirmed only by an assessment of the success of that strategy (that apparently makes me an interpretationist).

First I will describe the strategy, which I call the intentional strategy, or adopting the intentional stance. To a first approximation, the intentional strategy consists of treating the object whose behaviour you want to predict as a rational agent with beliefs and desires and other mental states exhibiting what Brentano and others call *intentionality.* The strategy has often been described before, but I shall try to put this very familiar material in a new light, by showing *how* it works, and by showing *how well* it works.

Then I will argue that any object—or as I shall say, any *system*—whose behaviour is well predicted by this strategy is in the fullest sense of the word a believer. *What it is* to be a true believer is to be an *intentional system,* a system whose behav-

iour is reliably and voluminously predictable via the intentional strategy. I have argued for this position before,[1] and my arguments have so far garnered few converts and many presumed counterexamples. I shall try again here, harder, and shall also deal with several compelling objections.

The Intentional Strategy and How It Works

There are many strategies, some good, some bad. Here is a strategy, for instance, for predicting the future behaviour of a person: determine the date and hour of the person's birth, and then feed this modest datum into one or another astrological algorithm for generating predictions of the person's prospects. This strategy is deplorably popular. Its popularity is deplorable only because we have such good reasons for believing that *it does not work.*[2] When astrological predictions come true, this is sheer luck, or the result of such vagueness or ambiguity in the prophecy that almost any eventuality can be construed to confirm it. But suppose the astrological strategy did in fact work well on some people. We could call those people *astrological systems*—systems whose behaviour was, as a matter of fact, predictable by the astrological strategy. If there were such people, such astrological systems, we would be more interested than most of us in fact are in *how the astrological strategy works*—that is, we would be interested in the rules, principles, or methods of astrology. We could find out how the strategy works by asking astrologers, reading their books, and observing them in action. But we would also be curious about *why* it worked. We might find that astrologers had no useful opinions about this latter question—they either had no theory of why it worked, or their theories were pure hokum. Having a good strategy is one thing; knowing why it works is another.

So far as we know, however, the class of astrological systems is empty, so the astrological strategy is of interest only as a social curiosity. Other strategies have better credentials. Consider the physical strategy, or physical stance: if you want to predict the behaviour of a system, determine its physical constitution (perhaps all the way down to the micro-physical level) and the physical nature of the impingements upon it, and use your knowledge of the laws of physics to predict the outcome for any input. This is the grand and impractical strategy of Laplace for predicting the entire future of everything in the universe, but it has more modest, local, actually usable versions. The chemist or physicist in the laboratory can use this strategy to predict the behaviour of exotic materials, but equally the cook in the kitchen can predict the effect of leaving the pot on the burner too long. The strategy is not always practically available, but that it will always work *in principle* is a dogma of the physical sciences. (I ignore the minor complications raised by the sub-atomic indeterminacies of quantum physics.)

Sometimes, in any event, it is more effective to switch from the physical stance to what I call the design stance, where one ignores the actual (possibly messy) details of the physical constitution of an object, and, on the assumption that it has a certain design, predicts that it will behave *as it is designed to behave* under various circumstances. For instance, most users of computers have not the foggiest idea what physical principles are responsible for the computer's highly reliable, and hence predictable, behaviour. But if they have a good idea of what the computer is designed to do (a description of its operation at any one of the many possible levels of abstraction), they can predict its behaviour with great accuracy and reliability, subject to disconfirmation only in cases of physical malfunction. Less dramatically, almost anyone can predict when an alarm clock will sound on the basis of the most casual inspection of its exterior. (One does not know or care to know whether it is spring wound, battery driven, sunlight powered, made of brass wheels and jewel bearings or silicon chips — one just assumes that it is designed so that the alarm will sound when it is set to sound, and it is set to sound where it appears to be set to sound, and the clock will keep on running until that time and beyond, and is designed to run more or less accurately, and so forth. For more accurate and detailed design stance predictions of the alarm clock, one must descend to a less abstract level of description of its design; for instance, to the level at which gears are described, but their material is not specified.

Only the designed behaviour of a system is predictable from the design stance, of course. If you want to predict the behaviour of an alarm clock when it is pumped full of liquid helium, revert to the physical stance. Not just artefacts, but also many biological objects (plants and animals, kidneys and hearts, stamens and pistils) behave in ways that can be predicted from the design stance. They are not just physical systems but designed systems.

Sometimes even the design stance is practically inaccessible, and then there is yet another stance or strategy one can adopt: the intentional stance. Here is how it works: first you decide to treat the object whose behaviour is to be predicted as a rational agent; then you figure out what beliefs that agent ought to have, given its place in the world and its purpose. Then you figure out what desires it ought to have, on the same considerations, and finally you predict that this rational agent will act to further its goals in the light of its beliefs. A little practical reasoning from the chosen set of beliefs and desires will in many—but not all—instances yield a decision about what the agent ought to do; that is what you predict the agent *will* do.

The strategy becomes clearer with a little elaboration. Consider first how we go about populating each other's heads with beliefs. A few truisms: sheltered people tend to be ignorant; if you expose someone to something he comes to know all about it. In general, it seems, we come to believe all the truths about the parts of the world around us we are put in a position to learn about. *Exposure to x,* that is, sensory confrontation with *x* over some suitable period of time, is the *normally sufficient* condition for knowing (or having true beliefs) about *x*. As we say, we come to *know all about* the things around us. Such exposure is only *normally* sufficient for knowledge, but this is not the large escape hatch it might appear; our threshold for accepting abnormal ignorance in the face of exposure is quite high. 'I didn't know the gun was loaded', said by one who was observed to be present, sighted, and awake during the loading, meets with a variety of utter scepticism that only the most outlandish supporting tale could overwhelm.

Of course we do not come to learn or remember all the truths our sensory histories avail us. In spite of the phrase 'know all about', what we come to know, normally, are only all the *relevant* truths our sensory histories avail us. I do not typically come to know the ratio of spectacle-wearing people to trousered people in a room I inhabit, though if this interested me, it would be readily learnable. It is not just that some facts about my environment are below my thresholds of discrimination or beyond the integration and holding-power of my memory (such as the height in inches of all the people present), but that many perfectly detectable, graspable, memorable facts are of no interest to me, and hence do not come to be believed by me. So one rule for attributing beliefs in the intentional strategy is this: attribute as beliefs all the truths relevant to the system's interests (or desires) that the system's experience to date has made available. This rule leads to attributing somewhat too much—since we all are somewhat forgetful, even of important things. It also fails to capture the false beliefs we are all known to have. But the attribution of false belief, *any* false belief, requires a special genealogy, which will be seen to consist in the main in true beliefs. Two paradigm cases: S believes (falsely) that *p,* because S believes (truly) that Jones told him that *p,* that Jones is pretty clever, that Jones did not intend to deceive him, . . . etc.

Second case: S believes (falsely) that there is a snake on the barstool, because S believes (truly) that he seems to see a snake on the barstool, is himself sitting in a bar not a yard from the barstool he sees, and so forth. The falsehood has to start somewhere; the seed may be sown in hallucination, illusion, a normal variety of simple misperception, memory deterioration, or deliberate fraud, for instance, but the false beliefs that are reaped grow in a culture medium of true beliefs.

Then there are the arcane and sophisticated beliefs, true and false, that are so often at the focus of attention in discussions of belief attribution. They do not arise directly, goodness knows, from exposure to mundane things and events, but their attribution requires tracing out a lineage of mainly good argument or reasoning from the bulk of beliefs already attributed. An implication of the intentional strategy, then, is that true believers mainly believe truths. If anyone could devise an agreed-upon method of individuating and counting beliefs (which I doubt very much), we would see that all but the smallest portion (say, less than 10 per cent) of a person's beliefs were attributable under our first rule.[3]

Note that this rule is a derived rule, an elaboration and further specification of the fundamental rule: attribute those beliefs the system *ought to have.* Note also that the rule interacts with the attribution of desires. How do we attribute the desires (preferences, goals, interests) on whose basis we will shape the list of beliefs? We attribute the desires the system *ought to have.* That is the fundamental rule. It dictates, on a first pass, that we attribute the familiar list of highest, or most basic, desires to people: survival, absence of pain, food, comfort, procreation, entertainment. Citing any one of these desires typically terminates the 'Why?' game of reason giving. One is not supposed to need an ulterior motive for desiring comfort or pleasure or the prolongation of one's existence. Derived rules of desire attribution interact with belief attributions. Trivially, we have the rule: attribute desires for those things a system believes to be good for it. Somewhat more informatively, attribute desires for those things a system believes to be best means to other ends it desires. The attribution of bizarre and detrimental desires thus requires, like the attribution of false beliefs, special stories.

The interaction between belief and desire becomes trickier when we consider what desires we attribute on the basis of verbal behaviour. The capacity to *express* desires in language opens the floodgates of desire attribution. 'I want a two-egg mushroom omelette, some French bread and butter, and a half bottle of lightly chilled white Burgundy.' How could one begin to attribute a desire for anything so specific in the absence of such verbal declaration? How, indeed, could a creature come to *contract* such a specific desire without the aid of language? Language *enables* us to formulate highly specific desires, but it also *forces* us on occasion to commit ourselves to desires altogether more stringent in their conditions of satisfaction than anything we would otherwise have any reason to endeavour to satisfy. Since in order to get what you want you often have to say what you want, and since you often cannot say what you want without saying something more specific than you antecedently mean, you often end up giving others evidence—the very best of evidence, your unextorted word—that you desire things or states of affairs far more particular than would satisfy you—or better, than would have satisfied you, for once you have declared, being a man of your word, you acquire an interest in satisfying exactly the desire you declared and no other.

'I'd like some baked beans, please.'

'Yes sir, How many?'

You might well object to having such a specification of desire demanded of you, but in fact we are all socialized to accede to similar requirements in daily life—to the point of not noticing it, and certainly not feeling oppressed by it. I dwell on this because it has a parallel in the realm of belief, where our linguistic environment is forever forcing us to give—or concede—precise verbal expression to convictions that lack the hard edges verbalization endows them with.[4] By concentrating on the *results* of this social force, while ignoring its distorting effect, one can easily be misled into thinking that it is *obvious* that beliefs and desires are rather like *sentences stored in the head.* Being language-using creatures, it is inevitable that we should often come to believe that some particular, actually formulated, spelled and punctuated sentence *is true,* and that on other occasions we should come to want such a sentence to *come true,* but these are special cases of belief and desire, and as such may not be reliable models for the whole domain.

That is enough, on this occasion, about the principles of belief and desire attribution to be found in the intentional strategy. What about the rationality one attributes to an intentional system? One starts with the ideal of perfect rationality and revises downwards as circumstances dictate. That is, one starts with the assumption that people believe all the implications of their beliefs, and believe no contradictory pairs of beliefs. This does not create a practical problem of clutter (infinitely many implications, for instance), for one is interested only in ensuring that the system one is predicting is rational enough to get to the particular implications that are relevant to its behavioural predicament of the moment. Instances of irrationality, or of finitely powerful capacities of inference, raise particularly knotty problems of interpretation, which I will set aside on this occasion.[5]

For I want to turn from the description of the strategy to the question of its use. Do people actually use this strategy? Yes, all the time. There may someday be other strategies for attributing belief and desire and for predicting behaviour, but this is the only one we all know now. And when does it work? It works with people almost all the time. Why would it *not* be a good idea to allow individual Oxford colleges to create and grant academic degrees whenever they saw fit? The answer is a long story, but very easy to generate. And there would be widespread agreement about the major points. We have no difficulty thinking of the reasons people would then have for acting in such ways as to give others reasons for acting in such ways as to give others reasons for . . . creating a circumstance we would not want. Our use of the intentional strategy is so habitual and effortless that the role it plays in shaping our expectations about people is easily overlooked. The strategy also works on most other mammals most of the time. For instance, you can use it to design better traps to catch those mammals, by reasoning about what the creature knows or believes about various things, what it prefers, what it wants to avoid. The strategy works on birds, and on fish, and on reptiles, and on insects and spiders, and even on such lowly and unenterprising creatures as clams (once a clam believes there is danger about, it will not relax its grip on its closed shell until it is convinced that the danger has passed). It also works on some artefacts: the chess-playing computer will not take your knight because it knows that there is a line of ensuing play that would lead to losing its rook, and it does not want that to happen. More modestly, the thermostat will turn off the boiler as soon as it comes to believe the room has reached the desired temperature.

The strategy even works for plants. In a locale with late spring storms you should plant apple varieties that are particularly *cautious* about *concluding* that it is spring—which is when they *want* to blossom, of course. It even works for such inanimate and apparently undesigned phenomena as lightning. An electrician once explained to me how he worked out how to protect my underground water pump from lightning damage: lightning, he said, always wants to find the best way to ground—or earth, as you say in England—but sometimes it gets tricked into taking second-best paths. You can protect the pump by making another, better path more *obvious* to the lightning.

True Believers as Intentional Systems

Now clearly this is a motley assortment of 'serious' belief attributions, dubious belief attributions, pedagogically useful metaphors, *façons de parler,* and perhaps worse: outright frauds. The next task would seem to be distinguishing those intentional systems that *really* have beliefs and desires from those we may find it handy to treat *as if* they had beliefs and desires. But that would be a Sisyphean labour, or else would be terminated by fiat. A better understanding of the phenomenon of belief begins with the observation that even in the worst of these cases, even when we are surest that the strategy works *for the wrong reasons,* it is nevertheless true that it does work, at least a little bit. This is an interesting fact, which distinguishes this class of objects, the class of *intentional systems,* from the class of objects for which the strategy never works. But is this so? Does our definition of an intentional system exclude any objects at all? For instance, it seems the lectern in this lecture room can be construed as an intentional system, fully rational, and believing that it is currently located at the centre of the civilized world (as some of you may also think); and desiring above all else to remain at that centre. What should such a rational agent so equipped with belief and desire do? Stay put, clearly, which is just what the lectern does. I predict the lectern's behaviour, accurately, from the intentional stance, so is it an intentional system? If it is, anything at all is.

What should disqualify the lectern? For one thing, the strategy does not recommend itself in this case, for we get no predictive power from it that we did not antecedently have. We already knew what the lectern was going to do—namely nothing—and tailored the beliefs and desires to fit in a quite unprincipled way. In the case of people, or animals, or computers, however, the situation is different. In these cases often the only strategy that is at all practical is the intentional strategy; it gives us predictive power we can get by no other method. But, it will be urged, this is no difference in nature, but merely a difference that reflects upon our limited capacities as scientists. The Laplacean omniscient physicist could predict the behaviour of a computer—or of a live human body, assuming it to be ultimately governed by the laws of physics—without any need for the risky, short-cut methods of either the design or intentional strategies. For people of limited mechanical aptitude, the intentional interpretation of a simple thermostat is a handy and largely innocuous crutch, but the engineers among us can quite fully grasp its internal operation without the aid of this anthropomorphizing. It may be true that the cleverest engineers find it practically impossible to maintain a clear conception of more complex systems, such as a time-sharing computer system or remote-controlled space probe, without lapsing into an intentional stance (and viewing these devices as asking and telling, trying and avoiding, wanting and believing), but this is just a more advanced case of human epistemic frailty. We would not want to classify these artefacts with the true believers—ourselves—on such variable and parochial grounds, would we? Would it not be intolerable to hold that some artefact, or creature, or person was a believer from the point of view of one observer, but not a believer at all from the point of view of another, cleverer observer? That would be a particularly radical version of interpretationism, and some have thought I espoused it in urging that belief be viewed in terms of the success of the intentional strategy. I must confess that my presentation of the view has sometimes invited that reading, but I now want to discourage it. The decision to adopt the intentional stance is free, but the facts about the success or failure of the stance, were one to adopt it, are perfectly objective.

Once the intentional strategy is in place, it is an extraordinarily powerful tool in prediction—a fact that is largely concealed by our typical concentration on the cases in which it yields dubious or unreliable results. Consider, for instance, predicting moves in a chess game. What makes chess an interesting game, one can see, is the *un*-predictability of one's opponent's moves, except in those cases where moves are 'forced'—where there is *clearly* one best move—typically the least of the available evils. But this unpredictability is put in context when one recognizes that in the typical chess situation there are very many perfectly legal and hence available moves, but only a few—perhaps half a dozen—with anything to be said for them, and hence only a few high probability moves according to the intentional strategy. Even where the intentional strategy fails to distinguish a single move with a highest probability, it can dramatically reduce the number of live options.

The same feature is apparent when the intentional strategy is applied to 'real world' cases. It is notoriously unable to predict the exact purchase and sell decisions of stock traders, for instance, or the exact sequence of words a politician will utter when making a scheduled speech, but one's confidence can be very high indeed about slightly less specific predictions: that the particular trader *will not buy utilities today,* or that the politician *will side with the unions against his party,* for example. This inability to predict fine-grained descriptions of actions, looked at another way, is a source of strength for the intentional strategy, for it is this

neutrality with regard to details of implementation that permits one to exploit the intentional strategy in complex cases, for instance, in *chaining predictions.*[6] Suppose the U.S. Secretary of State were to announce he was a paid agent of the KGB. What an unparalleled event! How unpredictable its consequences! Yet in fact we can predict dozens of not terribly interesting but perfectly salient consequences, and consequences of consequences. The President would confer with the rest of the Cabinet, which would support his decision to relieve the Secretary of State of his duties pending the results of various investigations, psychiatric and political, and all this would be reported at a news conference to people who would write stories that would be commented upon in editorials that would be read by people who would write letters to the editors, and so forth. None of that is daring prognostication, but note that it describes an arc of causation in space–time that could not be predicted under *any* description by any imaginable practical extension of physics or biology.

The power of the intentional strategy can be seen even more sharply with the aid of an objection first raised by Robert Nozick some years ago. Suppose, he suggested, some beings of vastly superior intelligence—from Mars, let us say—were to descend upon us, and suppose that we were to them as simple thermostats are to clever engineers. Suppose, that is, that they did not *need* the intentional stance—or even the design stance—to predict our behaviour in all its detail. They can be supposed to be Laplacean super-physicists, capable of comprehending the activity on Wall Street, for instance, at the micro-physical level. Where we see brokers and buildings and sell orders and bids, they see vast congeries of sub-atomic particles milling about—and they are such good physicists that they can predict days in advance what ink marks will appear each day on the paper tape labelled 'Closing Dow Jones Industrial Average'. They can predict the individual behaviours of all the various moving bodies they observe without ever treating any of them as intentional systems. Would we be right then to say that from *their* point of view we really were not believers at all (any more than a simple thermostat is)? If so, then our status as believers is nothing objective, but rather something in the eye of the beholder—provided the beholder shares our intellectual limitations.

Our imagined Martians might be able to predict the future of the human race by Laplacean methods, but if they did not also see us as intentional systems, they would be *missing something* perfectly objective: the *patterns* in human behaviour that are describable from the intentional stance, and only from that stance, and which support generalizations and predictions. Take a particular instance in which the Martians observe a stock broker deciding to place an order for 500 shares of General Motors. They predict the exact motions of his fingers as he dials the phone, and the exact vibrations of his vocal cords as he intones his order. But if the Martians do not see that indefinitely many *different* patterns of finger motions and vocal cord vibrations—even the motions of indefinitely many different individuals—could have been substituted for the actual particulars without perturbing the subsequent operation of the market, then they have failed to see a real pattern in the world they are observing. Just as there are indefinitely many ways of *being a spark plug*— and one has not understood what an internal combustion engine is unless one realizes that a variety of different devices can be screwed into these sockets without affecting the performance of the engine—so there are indefinitely many ways of *ordering 500 shares of General Motors,* and there are societal sockets in which one of these ways will produce just about the same effect as any other. There are also societal pivot points, as it were, where which way people go depends on whether they *believe that p,* or *desire A,* and does not depend on any of the other infinitely many ways they may be alike or different.

Suppose, pursuing our Martian fantasy a little further, that one of the Maritans were to engage in a predicting contest with an Earthling. The Earthling and the Martian observe (and observe each other observing) a particular bit of local physical transaction. From the Earthling's point of view, this is what is observed. The telephone rings in Mrs Gardner's kitchen. She answers, and this is what she says: 'Oh, hello dear. You're coming home early? Within the hour? And bringing the boss to dinner? Pick up a bottle of wine on the way home, then, and drive carefully.' On the basis of this observation, our Earthling predicts that a large metallic vehicle with rubber tyres will come to a stop in the drive within one hour, disgorging two human beings one of whom will be holding a paper bag containing a bottle containing an alcoholic fluid. The prediction is a bit risky, perhaps, but a good bet on all counts. The Martian makes the same prediction, but has to avail himself of much more information about an extraordinary number of interactions of which, so far as he can tell, the Earthling is entirely ignorant. For instance, the deceleration of the vehicle at intersection A, five miles from the house, without which there would have been a collision with another vehicle—whose collision course had been labouriously calculated over some hundreds of metres by the Martian. The Earthling's performance would look

like magic! How did the Earthling know that the human being who got out of the car and got the bottle in the shop would get back in? The coming true of the Earthling's prediction, after all the vagaries, intersections, and branches in the paths charted by the Martian, would seem to anyone bereft of the intentional strategy as marvellous and inexplicable as the fatalistic inevitability of the appointment in Samarra. Fatalists—for instance, astrologers—believe that there is a pattern in human affairs that is inexorable, that will impose itself *come what may,* that is, no matter how the victims scheme and second-guess, no matter how they twist and turn in their chains. These fatalists are wrong, but they are *almost* right. There *are* patterns in human affairs that impose themselves, not quite inexorably but with great vigour, absorbing physical perturbations and variations that might as well be considered random; these are the patterns that we characterize in terms of the beliefs, desires, and intentions of rational agents.

No doubt you will have noticed, and been distracted by, a serious flaw in our thought experiment: the Martian is presumed to treat his Earthling opponent as an intelligent being like himself, with whom communication is possible, a being with whom one can make a wager, against whom one can compete. In short, a being with beliefs (such as the belief he expressed in his prediction) and desires (such as the desire to win the prediction contest). So if the Martian sees the pattern in one Earthling, how can he fail to see it in the others? As a bit of narrative, our example could be strengthened by supposing that our Earthling cleverly learned Martian (which is transmitted by X-ray modulation) and disguised himself as a Martian, counting on the species-chauvinism of these otherwise brilliant aliens to permit him to pass as an intentional system while not giving away the secret of his fellow human beings. This addition might get us over a bad twist in the tale, but might obscure the moral to be drawn: namely, the unavoidability of the intentional stance with regard to oneself and one's fellow intelligent beings. This unavoidability is itself interest relative; it is perfectly possible to adopt a physical stance, for instance, with regard to an intelligent being, oneself included, but not to the exclusion of maintaining at the same time an intentional stance with regard to oneself at a minimum, and one's fellows *if* one intends, for instance, to learn what they know (a point that has been powerfully made by Stuart Hampshire in a number of writings). We can perhaps suppose our superintelligent Martians fail to recognize *us* as intentional systems, but we cannot suppose them to lack the requisite concepts.[7] If they observe, theorize, predict, communicate, they view *themselves* as intentional systems.[8] Where there are intelligent beings the patterns must be there to be described, whether or not we care to see them.

It is important to recognize the objective reality of the intentional patterns discernible in the activities of intelligent creatures, but also important to recognize the incompleteness and imperfections in the patterns. The objective fact is that the intentional strategy *works as well as it does,* which is not perfectly. No one is perfectly rational, perfectly unforgetful, all-observant, or invulnerable to fatigue, malfunction, or design imperfection. This leads inevitably to circumstances beyond the power of the intentional strategy to describe, in much the same way that physical damage to an artefact, such as a telephone or an automobile, may render it indescribable by the normal design terminology for that artefact. How do you draw the schematic wiring diagram of an audio amplifier that has been partially melted, or how do you characterize the programme state of a malfunctioning computer? In cases of even the mildest and most familiar cognitive pathology—where people seem to hold contradictory beliefs, or to be deceiving themselves, for instance—the canons of interpretation of the intentional strategy fail to yield clear, stable verdicts about which beliefs and desires to attribute to a person.

Now a *strong* realist position on beliefs and desires would claim that in these cases the person in question really does have some particular beliefs and desires which the intentional strategy, as I have described it, is simply unable to divine. On the milder sort of realism I am advocating, there is no fact of the matter of exactly which beliefs and desires a person has in these degenerate cases, but this is not a surrender to relativism or subjectivism, for *when* and *why* there is no fact of the matter is itself a matter of objective fact. On this view one can even acknowledge the *interest relativity* of belief attributions, and grant that given the different interests of different cultures, for instance, the beliefs and desires one culture would attribute to a member might be quite different from the beliefs and desires another culture would attribute to that very same person. But supposing that were so in a particular case, there would be the further facts about *how well* each of the rival intentional strategies worked for predicting the behaviour of that person. We can be sure in advance that no intentional interpretation of an individual will work to perfection, and it may be that two rival schemes are about equally good, and better than any others we can devise. That this is the case is itself something about which there can be a fact of the matter. The objective presence of one pattern (with what-

ever imperfections) does not rule out the objective presence of another pattern (with whatever imperfections).

The bogey of radically different interpretations with equal warrant from the intentional stragegy is theoretically important—one might better say metaphysically important—but practically negligible once one restricts one's attention to the largest and most complex intentional systems we know: human beings.[9]

Until now I have been stressing our kinship to clams and thermostats, in order to emphasize a view of the logical status of belief attribution, but the time has come to acknowledge the obvious differences, and say what can be made of them. The perverse claim remains: *all there is* to being a true believer is being a system whose behaviour is reliably predictable via the intentional strategy, and hence *all there is* to really and truly believing that p (for any proposition p) is being an intentional system for which p occurs as a belief in the best (most predictive) interpretation. But once we turn our attention to the truly interesting and versatile intentional systems, we see that this apparently shallow and instrumentalistic criterion of belief puts a severe constraint on the internal constitution of a genuine believer, and thus yields a robust version of the belief after all.

Consider the lowly thermostat, as degenerate a case of an intentional system as could conceivably hold our attention for more than a moment. Going along with the gag we might agree to grant it the capacity for about half a dozen different beliefs and fewer desires—it can believe the room is too cold or too hot, that the boiler is on or off, and that if it wants the room warmer it should turn on the boiler, and so forth. But surely this is imputing too much to the thermostat; it has no concept of heat or of a boiler, for instance. So suppose we *deinterpret* its beliefs and desires: it can believe that A is too F or G, and if it wants the A to be more F it should do K, and so forth. After all, by attaching the thermostatic control mechanism to different input and output devices, it could be made to regulate the amount of water in a tank, or the speed of a train, for instance. Its attachment to a heat-sensitive 'transducer' and a boiler is too impoverished a link to the world to grant any rich semantics to its belief-like states.

But suppose we then enrich these modes of attachment. Suppose we give it more than one way of learning about the temperature, for instance. We give it an eye of sorts that can distinguish huddled, shivering occupants of the room, and an ear so that it can be told how cold it is. We give it some facts about geography so that it can conclude that it is probably in a cold place if it learns that its spatio-temporal location is Winnipeg in December. Of course giving it a visual system that is multi-purpose and general—not a mere shivering-object detector—will require vast complications of its inner structure. Suppose we also give our system more behavioural versatility: it chooses the boiler fuel, purchases it from the cheapest and most reliable dealer, checks the weather stripping and so forth. This adds another dimension of internal complexity; it gives individual belief-like states *more to do,* in effect, by providing more and different occasions for their derivation or deduction from other states, and by providing more and different occasions for them to serve as premises for further reasoning. The cumulative effect of enriching these connections between the device and the world in which it resides is to enrich the semantics of its dummy predicates, *F* and *G* and the rest. The more of this we add, the less amenable our device becomes to serving as the control structure of anything other than a room temperature maintenance system. A more formal way of saying this is that the class of indistinguishably satisfactory models of the formal system embodied in its internal states gets smaller and smaller as we add such complexities; the more we add, the richer or more demanding or specific the semantics of the system, until eventually we reach systems for which a *unique* semantic interpretation is *practially* (but never in *principle*) dictated.[10] At that point we say this device (or animal, or person) has beliefs *about heat,* and *about this very room,* and so forth, not only because of the system's *actual* location in, and operations on, the world, but because we cannot imagine another niche in which it could be placed *where it would work.*

Our original simple thermostat had a state we called a belief about a particular boiler, to the effect that it was on or off. Why about *that* boiler? Well, what *other* boiler would you want to say it was about? The belief is about the boiler because it is *fastened* to the boiler.[11] Given the actual, if minimal, causal link to the world that happened to be in effect, we could endow a state of the device with *meaning* (of a sort) and *truth conditions,* but it was altogether too easy to substitute a different minimal link and completely change the meaning (in this impoverished sense) of that internal state. But as systems become perceptually richer and behaviourally more versatile, it becomes harder and harder to make substitutions in the actual links of the system to the world without changing the organization of the system itself. If you change its environment, it will *notice,* in effect, and make a change in its internal state in response. There comes to be a two-way constraint of growing specificity between the device and the environment.

Fix the device in any one state and it demands a *very* specific environment in which to operate properly (you can no longer switch it easily from regulating temperature to regulating speed or anything else); but at the same time, if you do not *fix* the state it is in, but just plonk it down in a changed environment, its sensory attachments will be sensitive and discriminative enough to respond appropriately to the change, driving the system into a new state, in which it will operate effectively in the new environment. There is a familiar way of alluding to this tight relationship that can exist between the organization of a system and its environment: you say that the organism continuously *mirrors* the environment, or that there is a *representation* of the environment in—or implicit in—the organiztion of the system.

It is not that we attribute (or should attribute) beliefs and desires only to things in which we find internal representations, but rather that when we discover some object for which the intentional strategy works, we endeavor to interpret some of its internal states or processes as internal representations. What makes some internal feature of a thing a representation could only be its role in regulating the behaviour of an intentional system.

Now the reason for stressing our kinship with the thermostat should be clear. There is no magic moment in the transition from a single thermostat to a system that *really* has an internal representation of the world around it. The thermostat has a minimally demanding representation of the world, fancier thermostats have more demanding representations of the world, fancier robots for helping around the house would have still more demanding representations of the world. Finally you reach us. We are so multifariously and intricately connected to the world that almost no substitution is possible—though it is clearly imaginable in a thought experiment. Hilary Putnam imagines the planet Twin Earth, which is just like Earth right down to the scuff marks on the shoes of the Twin Earth replica of your neighbour, but which differs from Earth in some property that is entirely beneath the thresholds of your capacities to discriminate. (What they call water on Twin Earth has a different chemical analysis.) Were *you* to be whisked instantaneously to Twin Earth and exchanged for your Twin Earth replica, you would never be the wiser—just like the simple control system that cannot tell whether it is regulating temperature, speed, or volume of water in a tank. It is easy to devise radically different Twin Earths for something as simple and sensorily deprived as a thermostat, but your internal organization puts a much more stringent demand on substitution. Your Twin Earth and Earth must be virtual repli-

↗ holisme contenu
dans des états mentaux

cas or you will change state dramatically on arrival.

So which boiler are *your* beliefs about, when you believe the boiler is on? Why, the boiler in your cellar (rather than its twin on Twin Earth, for instance). What *other* boiler would your beliefs be about? The *completion* of the semantic interpretation of your beliefs, fixing the *referents* of your beliefs, requires, as in the case of the thermostat, facts about your actual embedding in the world. The principles, and problems, of interpretation that we discover when we attribute beliefs to people are the *same* principles and problems we discover when we look at the ludicrous, but blessedly simple, problem of attributing beliefs to a thermostat. The differences are of degree, but nevertheless of such great degree that understanding the internal organization of a simple intentional system gives one very little basis for understanding the internal organization of a complex intentional system, such as a human being.

Why Does the Intentional Strategy Work?

When we turn to the question of *why* the intentional strategy works as well as it does, we find that the question is ambiguous, admitting of two very different sorts of answers. If the intentional system is a simple thermostat, one answer is simply this: the intentional stragegy works because the thermostat is well designed; it was designed to be a system that could be easily and reliably comprehended and manipulated from this stance. That is true, but not very informative, if what we are after are the actual features of its design that explain its performance. Fortunately, however, in the case of a simple thermostat those features are easily discovered and understood, so the other answer to our *why* question, which is really an answer about *how the machinery works,* is readily available.

If the intentional system in question is a person, there is also an ambiguity in our question. The first answer to the question of why the intentional strategy works is that evolution has designed human beings to be rational, to believe what they ought to believe and want what they ought to want. The fact that we are products of a long and demanding evolutionary process guarantees that using the intentional strategy on us is a safe bet. This answer has the virtues of truth and brevity, and on this occasion the additional virtue of being an answer Herbert Spencer would applaud, but it is also strikingly uninformative. The more difficult version of the question asks, in effect, how the machinery which Nature has provided us works. And we cannot yet give a good answer to that question.

We just do not know. We do know how the *strategy* works, and we know the easy answer to the question of why it works, but knowing these does not help us much with the hard answer.

It is not that there is any dearth of doctrine, however. A Skinnerian behaviourist, for instance, would say that the strategy works because its imputations of beliefs and desires are shorthand, in effect, for as yet unimaginably complex descriptions of the effects of prior histories of response and reinforcement. To say that someone wants some ice cream is to say that in the past the ingestion of ice cream has been reinforced in him by the results, creating a propensity under certain background conditions (also too complex to describe) to engage in ice-cream-acquiring behaviour. In the absence of detailed knowledge of those historical facts we can nevertheless make shrewd guesses on inductive grounds; these guesses are embodied in our intentional stance claims. Even if all this were true, it would tell us very little about the way such propensities were regulated by the internal machinery.

A currently more popular explanation is that the account of how the strategy works and the account of how the mechanism works will (roughly) *coincide:* for each predictively attributable belief, there will be a functionally salient internal state of the machinery, decomposable into functional parts in just about the same way the sentence expressing the belief is decomposable into parts—that is, words or terms. The inferences we attribute to rational creatures will be mirrored by physical, causal processes in the hardware; the *logical* form of the propositions believed will be copied in the *structural* form of the states in correspondence with them. This is the hypothesis that there is a *language of thought* coded in our brains, and our brains will eventually be understood as symbol manipulating systems in at least rough analogy with computers. Many different versions of this view are currently being explored, in the new research programme called cognitive science, and provided one allows great latitude for attenuation of the basic, bold claim, I think some version of it will prove correct.

But I do not believe that this is *obvious.* Those who think that it is obvious, or inevitable, that such a theory will prove true (and there are many who do), are confusing two different empirical claims. The first is that intentional stance description yields an objective, real pattern in the world— the pattern our imaginary Martians missed. This is an empirical claim, but one that is confirmed beyond scepticism. The second is that this real pattern is *produced by* another real pattern roughly isomorphic to it within the brains of intelligent creatures. Doubting the existence of the second real pattern is not doubting the existence of the first. There *are* reasons for believing in the second pattern, but they are not overwhelming. The best simple account I can give of the reasons is as follows.

As we ascend the scale of complexity from simple thermostat, through sophisticated robot, to human being, we discover that our efforts to design systems with the requisite behaviour increasingly run foul of the problem of *combinatorial explosion*. Increasing some parameter by, say, 10 per cent—10 per cent more inputs, or more degrees of freedom in the behaviour to be controlled, or more words to be recognized, or whatever—tends to increase the internal complexity of the system being designed by orders of magnitude. Things get out of hand very fast and, for instance, can lead to computer programs that will swamp the largest, fastest machines. Now somehow the brain has solved the problem of combinatorial explosion. It is a gigantic network of billions of cells, but still finite, compact, reliable, and swift, and capable of learning new behaviours, vocabularies, theories, almost without limit. Some elegant, *generative*, indefinitely extendable principles of representation must be responsible. We have only one model of such a representation system: a human language. So the argument for a language of thought comes down to this: what else could it be? We have so far been unable to imagine any plausible alternative in any detail. That is a good enough reason, I think, for recommending as a matter of scientific tactics that we pursue the hypothesis in its various forms as far as we can.[12] But we will engage in that exploration more circumspectly, and fruitfully, if we bear in mind that its inevitable rightness is far from assured. One does not well understand even a true empirical hypothesis so long as one is under the misapprehension that it is necessarily true.[13]

NOTES

1. Intentional systems. *Journal of Philosophy* (1971). Conditions of personhood. In *The identies of persons* (ed. A. Rorty). University of California Press (1975). Both reprinted in *Brainstorms* Montgomery, Vt., Bradford (1978). Three kinds of intentional psychology. In *Mind, psychology and reductionism* (ed. R. A. Healey). Cambridge University Press (1981).

2. *Pace* Paul Feyerabend, whose latest book, *Science in a free society,* New Left Books, London (1978), is heroically open-minded about astrology.

3. The idea that most of anyone's beliefs *must* be true seems obvious to some people. Support for the idea can be found in works by Quine, Putnam, Shoemaker, Davidson, and myself. Other people find the idea equally incredible—so probably each side is calling a different phenomenon belief. Once one makes the distinction between belief and opinion (in my technical sense—see How to change your mind. In *Brainstorms* Chapter 16), according to which opinions are linguistically infected, relatively sophisticated cognitive states—*roughly,* states of betting on the truth of a particular, formulated sentence, one can see the near triviality of the claim that most beliefs are true. A few reflections on peripheral matters should bring it out. Consider Democritus, who had a systematic, all-embracing, but (let us say, for the sake of argument) entirely false physics. He had things *all* wrong, though his views held together and had a sort of systematic utility. But even if *every claim* that scholarship permits us to attribute to Democritus (either explicit or implitic in his writings) is false, these represent a vanishingly small fraction of his *beliefs*, which include both the vast numbers of humdrum standing beliefs he must have had (about which house he lived in, what to look for in a good pair of sandals, and so forth), and also those occasional beliefs that came and went by the millions as his perceptual experience changed.

But, it may be urged, this isolation of his humdrum beliefs from his science relies on an insupportable distinction between truths of observation and truths of theory; all Democritus' beliefs are theory-laden, and since his theory is false, they are false. The reply is as follows: Granted that all observation beliefs are theory laden, why should we choose Democritus' *explicit,* sophisticated theory (couched in his *opinions*) as the theory with which to burden his quotidian observations? Note that the least theoretical compatriot of Democritus also had myriads of theory-laden observation beliefs—and was, in one sense, none the wiser for it. Why should we not suppose their observations are laden with the same theory? If Democritus forgot his theory, or changed his mind, his observational beliefs would be *largely* untouched. To the extent that his sophisticated theory played a discernible role in his routine behaviour and expectations and so forth, it would be quite appropriate to couch his humdrum beliefs in terms of the sophisticated theory, but this will not yield a *mainly false* catalogue of beliefs, since so few of his beliefs will be affected. (The effect of theory on observation is nevertheless often underrated. See Paul Churchland, *Scientific realism and the plasticity of mind,* Cambridge University Press (1979), for dramatic and convincing examples of the tight relationship that can sometimes exist between theory and experience. (The discussion in this note was distilled from a useful conversation with Paul and Patricia Churchland and Michael Stack.)

4. See my *Content and consciousness* pp. 184–5, Routledge & Kegan Paul, London (1969), and How to change your mind, in *Brainstorms.*

5. See *Brainstorms,* and Three kinds of intentional psychology. See also C. Cherniak, Minimal rationality *Mind,* (1981) and my response to Stephen Stich's Headaches. In *Philosophical books,* (1980).

6. See On giving libertarians what they say they want, in *Brainstorms.*

7. A member of the audience in Oxford pointed out that if the Martian included the Earthling in his physical stance purview (a possibility I had not explicitly excluded), he would not be surprised by the Earthling's prediction. He would indeed have predicted exactly the pattern of X-ray modulations produced by the Earthling speaking Martian. True, but as the Martian wrote down the results of his calculations, his pre-

diction of the Earthling's prediction would appear, word by Martian word, as on a Ouija board, and what would be baffling to the Martian was how this chunk of mechanism, the Earthling predictor dressed up like a Martian, was able to yield this *true* sentence of Martian when it was so informationally isolated from the events the Martian needed to know of in order to make his own prediction about the arriving automobile.

8. Might there not be intelligent beings who had no use for communicating, predicting, observing . . . ? There might be marvellous, nifty, invulnerable entities lacking these modes of action, but I cannot see what would lead us to call them *intelligent.*

9. John McCarthy's analogy to cryptography nicely makes this point. The larger the corpus of cipher text, the less chance there is of dual, systematically unrelated decipherings. For a very useful discussion of the principles and presuppositions of the intentional stance applied to machines—explicitly including thermostats—see McCarthy's Ascribing mental qualities to machines. In *Philosophical perspectives on artificial intelligence* (ed. Martin Ringle). Humanities Press (1979).

10. Patrick Hayes explores this application of Tarskian model theory to the semantics of mental representation in "The naive physics manifesto" (forthcoming) [in Donald Michie, ed. *Expert Systems in the Micro-electronic Age* (Edinburgh: Edinburgh University Press, 1979, pp. 242–70.

11. This idea is the ancestor in effect of the species of different ideas lumped together under the rubric of *de re* belief. If one builds from this idea towards its scions one can see better the difficulties with them, and how to repair them.

12. The fact that all *language of thought* models of mental representation so far proposed fall victim to combinatorial explosion in one way or another should temper one's enthusiasm for engaging in what Fodor aptly calls 'the only game in town'.

13. This paper was written during a Fellowship at the Center for Advanced Study in the Behavioural Sciences. I am grateful for financial support provided by the National Endowment for the Humanities, the National Science Foundation (BNS 78-24671), and the Alfred P. Sloan Foundation.

Postscript: "Reflections: Real Patterns, Deeper Facts, and Empty Questions"

Several of the themes that receive a brisk treatment in "True Believers" expand into central topics in subsequent chapters. Perhaps the major source of disquiet about my position over the years has been its delicate balancing act on the matter of the observer-relativity of attributions of belief and other intentional states. On my view, is belief attribution (or meaning) in the eye of the beholder? Do I think there are *objective truths* about what people believe, or do I claim that all attrubutions are just *useful fictions?* My discussion of Nozick's objection attempts to place my view firmly on the knife-edge between the intolerable extremes of simple realism and simple relativism, but this has not been recognized as a stable and attractive option by many others in the field, and my critics have persistently tried to show that my position tumbles into one abyss or the other.

My view is, I insist, a *sort* of realism, since I maintain that the patterns the Martians miss are really, objectively there to be noticed or overlooked. How could the Martians, who "know everything" about the physical events in our world, miss these patterns? What could it mean to say

that some patterns, while objectively there, are visible only from one point of view? An elegant two-dimensional microworld provides a clear instance: John Horton Conway's Game of Life (Gardner 1970), a simple yet extraordinarily rich source of insights that should become a part of everyone's imaginative resources as a versatile testbed for thought experiments about the relation of levels in science.

Imagine a huge piece of graph paper. The intersections (not the squares) of this grid are the only places—called cells—in the Life microworld, and at any instant each cell is either ON or OFF. Each cell has eight neighbors: the four adjacent cells north, south, east and west of it, and the four nearest diagonal cells (northeast, southeast, southwest, northwest). Time in the Life world is also discrete, not continuous; it advances in ticks, and the state of the world changes between each tick according to the following rule:

Each cell, in order to determine what to do in the next instant, counts how many of its eight neighbors is ON at the present instant. If the answer is exactly two, the

Postscript: From *The Intentional Stance,* by Daniel C. Dennett, Cambridge, Mass.: MIT Press/Bradford Books, 1987, pp. 37–42. Reprinted with permission of the publisher and Daniel C. Dennett.

cell stays in its present state (ON or OFF) in the next instant. If the answer is exactly three, the cell is ON in the next instant whatever its current state. Under all other conditions, the cell is OFF.

The entire, deterministic physics of the Life world is captured in that single unexceptioned law. (While this is the fundamental law of the "physics" of the Life world, it helps at first to conceive this curious physics in biological terms: think of cells going ON as births, cells going OFF as deaths, and succeeding instants as generations. Either overcrowding or isolation causes death; birth occurs only under propitious circumstances.) By the scrupulous application of the law, one can predict with perfect accuracy the next instant of any configuration of ON and OFF cells, and the instant after that, and so forth. So the Life world is a fine Laplacean playpen: a simplified deterministic world in which we finite creatures can adopt the physical stance and predict the future with supreme confidence. Many computer simulations of the Life world exist, in which one can set up configurations on the screen and then watch them evolve according to the rule. In the best simulations, one can change the scale of both time and space, alternating between close-up and bird's-eye view.

One soon discovers that some simple configurations are more interesting than others. There are things that blink back and forth between two configurations, things that grow and then disintegrate, "glider guns" that emit "gliders"—configurations that reproduce themselves translated a few cells over, gradually gliding across the two-dimensional landscape—puffer trains, strafing machines, eaters, antibodies, space rakes. Once one understands the behavior of these configurations, one can adopt the design stance and ask oneself how to design larger assemblages of these objects that will perform more complicated tasks. One of the triumphs of the design stance in the Life world is a universal Turing machine—a configuration whose behavior can be interpreted as the state-switching, symbol-reading, and symbol-writing of a simple computer, which can be "programmed" to compute any computable function. (For more on Turing machines, see "The Abilities of Men and Machines" in *Brainstorms,* and Dennett 1985a.)

Anyone who hypothesizes that some configuration in the Life world is such a Turing machine can predict its future state with precision, efficiency, and a modicum of risk. Adopt the "Turing machine stance" and, ignoring both the physics of the Life world and the design details of the machine, just calculate the function being computed by the Turing machine; then translate the function's output back into the symbol system of the Life world machine. That configuration of ONs and OFFs will soon appear, you can predict, provided that no stray gliders or other noisy debris collide with the Turing machine and destroy it or cause it to malfunction.

Is the pattern that enables you to make this prediction "real"? So long as it lasts it is, and if the pattern includes "armor" to insulate the machine from noise, the pattern may survive for quite some time. The pattern *may* owe its existence to the intentions (clear-sighted or confused) of the machine's designer, but its reality in any interesting sense—its longevity or robustness—is strictly independent of historical facts about its origin.

Whether one can see the pattern is another matter. In one sense it would be visible to anyone who watched the unfolding of the particular configurations on the Life plane. One of the delights of the Life world is that nothing is hidden in it; there is no backstage. But it takes a big leap of insight to see this unfolding *as* the computation of a Turing machine. Ascending to the point of view from which this level of explanation and prediction is readily visible is optional, and might be difficult for many.

I claim that the intentional stance provides a vantage point for discerning similarly useful patterns. These patterns are objective—they are *there* to be detected—but from our point of view they are not *out there* entirely independent of us, since they are patterns composed partly of our own "subjective" reactions to what is out there; they are the patterns made to order for our narcissistic concerns (Akins 1986). It is easy for us, constituted as we are, to perceive the patterns that are visible from the intentional stance—and only from that stance.[1] Martians might find it extremely difficult, but they can aspire to know the regularities that are second nature to us just as we can aspire to know the world of the spider or the fish.

So I am a sort of realist. I decline the invitation to join Rorty's (1979, 1982) radical perspectivalism (Dennett 1982a). But I also maintain that when these objective patterns fall short of perfection, as they always must, there will be uninterpretable gaps; it is always possible in principle for rival intentional stance interpretations of those patterns to tie for first place, so that no further fact could settle what the intentional system in question *really* believed.

This idea is not new. It is a quite direct extension of Quine's (1960) thesis of the indeterminacy of radical translation, applied to the "translation" of not only the patterns in subjects' dispositions to engage in external behavior (Quine's "stimulus meanings"), but also the further patterns in dispositions to "behave" internally. As Quine says, "radical translation begins at home" (1969, p. 46), and the implications of his thesis extend beyond his peripheralism or behaviorism.

> The metaphor of the black box, often so useful, can be misleading here. The problem is not one of hidden facts, such as might be uncovered by learning more about the brain physiology of thought processes. To expect a distinctive physical mechanism behind every genuinely distinct mental state is one thing; to expect a distinctive mechanism for every purported distinction that can be phrased in traditional mentalistic language is another. The question whether . . . the foreigner *really* believes *A* or believes rather *B*, is a question whose very significance I would put in doubt. This is what I am getting at in arguing the indeterminacy of translation. (Quine 1970, pp. 180–81)

My argument in "Brain Writing and Mind Reading" (1975) enlarged on this theme, exposing the error of those who had hoped to *find something in the head* to settle the cases Quine's peripheralism left indeterminate: exactly the same considerations applied to the translation of any "language of thought" one might discover once one abandoned behaviorism for cognitive science. Another Quinian[2] who has defended this position with regard to belief is Davidson (1974a):

> Indeterminacy of meaning or translation does not represent a failure to capture significant distinctions; it marks the fact that certain apparent distinctions are not significant. If there is indeterminacy, it is because when all the evidence is in, alternative ways of stating the facts remain open. (p. 322)

More recently another application of the idea of indeterminacy has been ably defended by Parfit (1984), who has argued that the principles we (should) rely on to determine questions of *personal identity* will also inevitably leave open the possibility in principle of puzzling indeterminate cases. This is extraordinarily hard for many people to accept.

> Most of us are inclined to believe that, in any conceivable case, the question "Am I about to die?" must have an answer. And we are inclined to believe that this answer must be either, and quite simply, Yes or No. Any future person must either be me, or someone else. These beliefs I call the view that *our identity must be determinate.* (p. 214)

We are just as strongly attracted to the view that *the contents of our thoughts or beliefs must be determinate* and resist the suggestion that the question "Do I believe there is milk in the fridge?" could fail to have a determinate answer, yes or no.

Parfit shows that there are other cases in which we rest content without an answer to such questions.

> Suppose that a certain club exists for several years, holding regular meetings. The meetings then cease. Some years later, some of the members of this club form a club with the same name, and the same rules. We ask: "Have these people reconvened the *very same* club? Or have they merely started up *another* club, which is exactly similar?" There might be an answer to this question. The original club might have had a rule explaining how, after such a period of non-existence, it could be reconvened. Or it might have had a rule preventing this. But suppose that there is no such rule, and no legal facts, supporting either answer to our question. And suppose that the people involved, if they asked our question, would not give it an answer. There would then be no answer to our question. The claim "This is the same club" would be *neither true nor false.*
>   Though there is no answer to our question, there may be nothing that we do not know. . . . When this is true of some question, I call this question *empty.* (p. 213)

We recognize that in the case of the club's existence, and in similar cases, there is no "deeper fact" that would settle the matter, but in the case of personal identity, the supposition that there is—must be—just such a deeper fact dies hard. Not surprisingly, this is one of the brute convictions that Nagel (1986) cannot abandon:

> Why isn't it enough to identify myself as a person in the weaker sense in which this is the subject of mental predicates but not a separately existing thing—more like a nation than a Cartesian ego?
>   I don't really have an answer to this, except the question-begging answer . . . (p. 45)

I make the analogous case for what we might call belief identity or belief determinacy. In chapter 8, "Evolution, Error, and Intentionality,"* I show how Searle, Fodor, Dretske, Kripke, and Burge (among others) all are tempted to search for this deeper fact, and how their search is forlorn. I claim, in other words, that some of the most vigorously disputed questions about belief attribution are, in Parfit's sense, empty questions.

How is this persistent illusion created? In the reflections on "Making Sense of Ourselves,"* I describe a false contrast (between our beliefs and those of lower animals) that creates the mistaken conviction that our own beliefs and other mental states must have determinate content.

Another *leitmotif* that gets its first play in "True Believers" is the comparison between Put-

---

* [all in *The Intentional Stance* (see fn. 2).]

nam's Twin Earth thought experiment and various simpler environmental dislocations or exchanges—of thermostats, in this instance. The theme is developed more fully in chapter 5, "Beyond Belief," and in the example of the "two-bitser" in chapter 8.*

Finally, the attenuated and conditional endorsement of the idea of a language of thought at the end of "True Believers" is further elaborated in chapter 5 and in chapter 6, "Styles of Mental Representation," and the reflections following it.*

NOTES

1. Anscombe spoke darkly of "an order which is there whenever actions are done with intentions" (1957, p. 80) but did not say *where* in the world this order was to be discerned. In the brain? In behavior? For years I could not make sense of this, but now I see what she may have intended and why she was so coy in her description (and location) of the order. It is as hard to say where the intentional order is as it is to say where the intentional patterns are in the Life world. If you "look at" the world in the right way, the patterns are obvious. If you look at (or describe) the world in any other way, they are, in general, invisible.

2. Some non-Quinians have maintained versions of this idea. Wheeler (1986) insightfully shows that Derrida can be seen to "provide important, if dangerous, supplementary arguments and considerations" to those that have been advanced by Davidson and other Quinians. As Wheeler notes:

For Quineans, of course, it is obvious already that speech and thought are brain-writing, some kind of tokenings which are as much subject to interpretation as any other. . . . Still, there seems in non-Quinean circles to be a covert belief that somehow inner speech is directly expressive of thought. (p. 492)

This covert belief is exposed to attack in chapter 8. ["Evolution, Error, and Intentionality," in *The Intentional Stance* (Cambridge, MA: MIT/Bradford, 1987), pp. 287–321.]

BIBLIOGRAPHY

Akins, K. A. (1986). "On Piranhas, Narcissism, and Mental Representation," CCM-86-2, Center for Cognitive Studies, Tufts University.

Anscombe, E. (1957). *Intention.* Oxford: Blackwell.

Davidson, D. (1974a). "Belief and the Basis of Meaning," *Synthese,* 27, pp. 309–23.

Dennett, D. C. (1975). "Brain Writing and Mind Reading," in K. Gunderson, ed., *Language, Mind, and Meaning.* Minnesota Studies in Philosophy of Science, VII. Minneapolis: University of Minnesota Press.

Dennett, D. C. (1978a). *Brainstorms: Philosophical Essays on Mind and Psychology.* Montgomery, VT: Bradford Books.

Dennett, D. C. (1982a). "Comment on Rorty," *Synthese,* 53, pp. 349–56.

Dennett, D. C. (1985a). "Can Machines Think?" in M. Shafto, ed., *How We Know.* San Francisco: Harper and Row.

Gardner, M. (1970). "Mathematical Games," *Scientific American,* 223, no. 4, pp. 120–23.

Nagel, T. (1986). *The View From Nowhere.* Oxford: Oxford University Press.

Parfit, D. (1984). *Reasons and Persons.* Oxford: Oxford University Press.

Quine, W. V. O. (1960). *Word and Object.* Cambridge, MA: The MIT Press.

Quine, W. V. O. (1969). "Propositional Objects," in *Ontological Relativity and Other Essays.* New York: Columbia University Press, pp. 139–60.

Quine, W. V. O. (1970). "On the Reasons for Indeterminacy of Translation," *Journal of Philosophy,* LXVII, pp. 178–83.

Rorty, R. (1979). *Philosophy and the Mirror of Nature.* Princeton: Princeton University Press.

Rorty, R. (1982). "Contemporary Philosophy of Mind," *Synthese,* 53, pp. 323–48.

Wheeler, S. C. (1986). "Indeterminacy of French Interpretation: Derrida and Davidson," in E. Lepore, ed., *Truth and Interpretation: Perspectives on the Philosophy of Donald Davidson.* Oxford: Basil Blackwell.

37

Fred I. Dretske

"The Intentionality of Cognitive States"

To know, perceive, or remember is to know, per-ceive, or remember *something.* Subtleties aside, this something may be either a thing or a fact.[1] We remember a party, see a game, and know a person; but we also remember that the party was a bore, see that the game has started, and know that Hilda is a grouch.

It may be, as some have argued, that we cannot know, remember, or perceive a thing without knowing, remembering, or perceiving some fact about that thing. According to this view, what we know, perceive, and remember is always proposi-tional in character. To describe someone as know-ing a person, thing, or event is just to describe the person as knowing some relevant facts about the item in question without disclosing, by one's man-ner of description, *what facts* it is that are known.

I do not intend to quarrel with this view. I think it mistaken, but I do not have the time to argue the point here. My objectives are more limited. I mean to discuss our *propositional* attitudes and, in par-ticular, those propositional attitudes that involve the possession of knowledge. I mean, that is, to dis-cuss those mental states whose expression calls for a factive nominal, a that-clause, as complement to the verb, and moreover, whose expression implies that the subject of that state *knows* what is ex-pressed by that factive nominal. I am concerned with knowing, seeing, and remembering that your dog is lame, *not* with knowing, seeing and remembering your (lame) dog. I shall call such states *cognitive* states. The *belief* that your dog is lame is not, on this characterization, a cognitive state.

1. Intentional States

If I know that the train is moving and you know that its wheels are turning, it does not follow that I know what you know just because the train never moves without its wheels turning. More generally, if all (and only) Fs are G, one can nonetheless know that something is F without knowing that it is G. Extensionally equivalent predicate expres-sions, when applied to the same object, do not (necessarily) express the same cognitive content. Furthermore, if Tom is my uncle, one cannot infer (with a possible exception to be mentioned later) that if S knows that Tom is getting married, he thereby knows that my uncle is getting married. The content of a cognitive state, and hence the cognitive state itself, depends (for its identity) on something beyond the extension or reference of the terms we use to express the content. I shall say, therefore, that a description of a cognitive state is non–extensional.

Any state of affairs having a propositional con-tent whose expression is non–extensional I shall call an *intentional* state. On this characterization our cognitive states are all intentional states. The truth of the statement "S knows that *a* if *F*" does not depend, simply, on the extension or reference of the terms '*a*' and '*F*'. This statement therefore describes an intentional state of S. I think that this use of the word 'intentional' is in reasonably close agreement with current philosophical usage—even if it does not capture all that Brentano intended in speaking of intentionality as the mark of the men-tal.

Intentional states (and, therefore, cognitive

From *Midwest Studies in Philosophy,* vol. V, Peter A. French, Theodore E. Uehling, Jr., and Howard K. Wettstein, eds. Minne-apolis: University of Minnesota Press, 1980, pp. 281–94. Reprinted with permission of the publisher.

states) appear to have something like *meanings* (propositions) as their object (content), as that *on which* the mind is directed. I say things appear this way since virtually any change in meaning (in the terms used to express the content) generates a different content and, thus, a different intentional state.

A materialist confronts the task of explaining, or explaining away, this intentional feature of cognitive states. Some account must be given of how a purely physical system could occupy states having a content of this sort. Or, failing this, some explanation must be given of why we systematically delude ourselves into thinking that *we occupy* states of this sort. What follows is a crude blueprint, an attempt to sketch, along realistic lines, an explanation for how purely physical systems *could* (because even the simplest mechanical systems *do*) occupy intentional states of the appropriate kind. The distinctive character of our cognitive states lies, not in their intentionality (for even the humble thermometer occupies intentional states), but in their *degree* of intentionality.

2. Behavior and Meaning

Central state materialists find themselves tugged in two directions: *inward* as the locus of our mental states; and *outward* as the locus for whatever meaning or content these central states might have. The result of this tension is often a curious blend of behaviorism with psychological realism. Our psychological states are genuine *inner* states (to be distinguished from the behavior they help to produce), but everything that makes them psychological (in contrast, say, to gastronomical or *just* neurological) is borrowed, so to speak, from the sort of behavior they help to determine. The flower of mentality has its roots inside, but all the blossoms are outside. It is behaviorism with a displaced reference. Some call it functionalism.

The approach to intentionality is typical. The output, or some of the output, of language-using creatures has a semantic dimension (a meaning) that neatly parallels that kind of content we (as materialists) want to attribute to the system's internal physical states in describing its cognitive processes. Why not let the internal states "borrow" this content?[2] This, of course, would make our attributions of content to the internal states themselves (in our ordinary descriptions of people knowing and remembering things) a bit of a fiction. The internal states would not literally have this content. Nevertheless, this is the best that can be done with the confused ontology of ordinary language. The idea, roughly, is that if S utters the

words, "The sun is shining," and if his utterance of these words is causally explicable in terms of a central neural state, then this central state acquires the content: The sun is shining. It, so to speak, shares in the glory of meaning this. By virtue of this borrowed content, the central state acquires the status of a *belief*: the belief that the sun is shining. Harnessing this account of belief with a causal theory of knowledge, one then goes on the say that if this state is brought about (in the right way) by a shining sun, then it constitutes S's *knowledge* that the sun is shining. The verbal output provides the "pattern" for assigning semantic properties (meaning or content) to those internal, neurological states that produced it. The intentional structure of our cognitive states is merely a reflection of the semantic properties of the output they produce.

What about creatures that do not have a language? One option is to simply deny that they (dogs, cats, birds) know or believe anything at all—at least nothing expressible in *our* language. My dog does not know (believe, think) that I am leaving. He just *acts* that way. My preparations to leave may *cause* him to act that way. It may even be true to say that the dog sees me getting ready to leave (and his seeing me getting ready to leave is why he is getting so excited), but he does not *see that* I am getting ready to leave. He has no internal state with this content because he exhibits no output with precisely this meaning (a meaning, it should be noted, that contrasts with "My master is putting on his coat and moving toward the door").[3]

Another option in the case of creatures without language is to appeal to other, non-verbal, behavior as the source of cognitive content. Food is to be eaten. Predators are to be avoided. It is the appropriateness of these responses to one thing rather than another, just as it is (given the ordinary meanings of the words) the appropriateness of the utterance "The sun is shining" to one state of affairs (a shining sun) rather than another, that confers on the internal source of this behavior the derived content "This is food" or "That is a predator (or dangerous)."[4] Roughly speaking, if the dog eats it, he must think it is food. But thinking it is food is an explanatory artifact—nothing more or less than being in a state (whatever neural state this is) that prompts the dog to salivate, chew, swallow, etc. Once again, the intentional character of the internal state, its having a content expressible as "This is food," is only a reflection of the properties of the consequent behavior. The dog knows or believes that there is food in front of him, he occupies a physical state having this content or meaning, *only* because the state prompts the dog to exhibit behavior appropriate to food. If the dog has no response that is appropriate to X (e.g., to daisies *qua* daisies), then he is incapable of believing or knowing that anything is an X.

This behavioristically inspired approach to the analysis of intentional structure has a certain degree of plausibility. Nevertheless, it always stumbles on the circularity inherent in analyzing cognitive content in terms of something (verbal behavior, appropriateness of response) that lacks the relevant properties (meaning, appropriateness) unless the internal source of that behavior is *already,* and *independently* of its producing that output, conceived of as having a determinate content. The appropriateness of what we do depends on what we know and believe (not to mention what we desire and intend). There is nothing inappropriate about my saying, "The sun is shining" at midnight if I sincerely believe the sun is shining. At least there is nothing inappropriate about it in any sense of 'appropriate' that tells us something about what I know or believe. Is it inappropriate for the hen *not* to run from the fox? This depends. It depends, among other things, on whether the hen *recognizes* the fox, on whether she *wants* to protect her chicks, on what her *purposes* are. Independently of these factors, the hen's behavior is neither appropriate nor inappropriate. To describe the hen, for example, as engaging in diversionary tactics (to protect her chicks) is already to describe her behavior in a way that presupposes an intentional structure for the internal source of that behavior. The appropriateness of response, then, insofar as this is relevant to what the organism believes and intends,[5] is a property the response acquires only in virtue of its production by internal states having a content.

This is particularly obvious with verbal behavior. If what I *say* is to have a content of the sort required, then it cannot be understood as merely the *sounds* I make. It must be understood as the meaning, the semantic content, of these sounds. But this, I submit, is circular.[6] Until we have a system, or community of systems, with beliefs and intentions, the output does not have the requisite *semantic* structure (meaning). Internal states cannot acquire their meaning from the output they produce because until the internal states have a content, they cannot produce a relevantly meaningful output. Replacing a door bell by a device (tape recorder, etc.) that announced "Someone is at the door" whenever the door button is pushed brings one no closer to a system with internal states having content. The output of such a device may be said to *mean* that someone is at the door, but this is either Grice's *natural* meaning (in which case the ringing bell means the same thing) or it is a meaning *we* assign it in virtue of the acoustic pattern's significance in *our* system of communication. In the latter case the output may be said to mean something in the relevant *linguistic* sense, but this is a meaning it derives from its occurrence in an appropriate community of fully intentional systems (speakers of the language). Output or behavior has nothing relevant to give except where the gift is not needed.

3.   The Intentional Structure of Information

The problem of intentionality loses some of its mystery if we think of simple communication systems. If we approach the problem in this way, it soon becomes clear that intentionality, rather than being a "mark of the mental," is a pervasive feature of *all* reality—mental and physical. Even the humble thermometer occupies intentional states. What is distinctive, and hence problematic, about our cognitive states is not the fact that they have a content, not the fact that this content has intentional characteristics (for this is true as well of the thermometer), but the fact that they have a *higher order* intentionality.

To see why this is so, consider a simple information processing device. The fundamental idea of Communication Theory is that the amount of information transmitted between two points is a function of the degree of nomic or lawful dependence between the events occurring in these two locations. The mathematical details are not really important for our purposes. What is important is that the quantity of information arriving at R (the receiver) from S (source) depends on the set of conditional probabilities relating events at R and S. If there is only a chance correlation between what occurs at S and what occurs at R, then no information passes between them. From this extreme we pass through a continuum of possible gradations until we reach a situation in which the flow of information between S and R is optimal: a noiseless (or equivocation free) channel between S and R. For this condition to exist, a certain set of conditional probabilities must obtain. Every conditional probability must be either 0 or 1—strict nomic dependence between the events occurring at S and R.[7]

It is important to emphasize that the conditional probabilities governing the flow of information are *nomic* or *lawful* in character. It is not enough that the type of event at the receiver should correspond, one-to-one, to the type of event occurring at the source. It is essential to the transmission of information that this correspondence have its basis in a lawful dependence, statistical or deterministic, between the events at S and R. For me to communicate, telephathically, with you it is not enough to have thoughts occurring to you that correspond exactly to what I am thinking. For genuine communication to occur, for you to receive information from me, it is essential that there be a lawful dependence between what I am thinking and what you think I am thinking.

If we conceive of information in this way, a thermometer may be said to carry information about its environment to the extent to which its state (e.g., the height of the mercury column) depends, lawfully, on the ambient temperature. And a pressure gauge carries information about, say, altitude.

With only these rudiments of Communication Theory in hand, we are in a position to appreciate an important fact about the transmission, receipt, and processing of information. Information has an intentional structure that it derives from the *nomic* relationships on which it depends. Since a nomic relation between properties (magnitudes) F and G is an intentional relationship, information, understood as the measure of this mutual dependency, inherits this structure. If F is lawfully related to G, and 'G' is extensionally equivalent to 'H', F is not necessarily related in a lawful way to H. If it is a natural law that things having the property F have the property G, it does not follow that there is a law relating the property F to the property H just because, as a matter of fact, everything that is G is also H (and vice versa). To use a well-known example, drunks may have liver problems and these problems may have their basis in a nomic relationship between excessive alcoholic intake and the condition of the liver. But we cannot infer from this fact that there is a nomic connection between sitting on park bench B and liver trouble just because all, and only, drunks sit (have sat, are sitting, and will sit) on park bench B. To reach this conclusion we would first have to be assured that there was some *lawful* regularity between sitting on the bench and being a drunk. This, though, is an assurance not provided by being told, simply, that there is an extensional equivalence between 'is a drunk' and 'sits on park bench B'.

It is obvious that there is a vast network of lawful relationships existing between the properties and magnitudes of our physical universe. Some of these we know. Others we do not. It is this kind of nomic dependence that underlies and supports our assertion of subjunctive conditionals of the form: "The metal would not have expanded unless it was heated"; "If the capacitor had discharged, it would have moved the galvanometer needle"; and "The pressure would not increase unless we were losing altitude." It is also obvious, except perhaps to a few philosophers, that statements describing the lawful relations between properties and magnitudes give expression to something more than an *extensional* relationship between these properties or magnitudes. To assert that it is a *law* that all Fs are G is to assert something stronger than that nothing is (was or will be) F that is not G.

It is not my purpose in this paper to analyze this feature of natural laws. Sufficient unto my purpose is the fact that laws *have* this feature. This, I think, is undeniable. How it is to be explained is another matter.

Since, therefore, the amount of information transmitted from one point to another depends on the system of nomic regularities that prevail between the events at these points, the information reaching the receiver about the events occurring at the source has the very same intentional character as do the underlying regularities. Even when 'F' and 'G' are extensionally equivalent, one can receive the information that something is F without receiving the information that something is G. One can receive information about property F (e.g., x is F) without receiving information about property G (e.g., x is G) even though nothing is F that is not G. This is possible because the signal one receives may have properties that depend, lawfully, on x's being F without depending, lawfully, on x's being G. And in such a case the signal carries information about the one property that it does not carry about the other.

Any physical system, then, whose internal states are lawfully dependent, in some statistically significant way, on the value of an external magnitude (in the way of properly connected measuring instrument is sensitive to the value of the quantity it is designed to measure) qualifies as an intentional system. It occupies states having a content that can be expressed only in non-extensional ways. A device that measures the value of F, and hence occupies a state with the content "F is increasing," does not (necessarily) occupy a state with the content "G is increasing" even though G always increases when F increases.

What this suggests, of course, is that the intentionality of our cognitive states has its source in the intentionality of informational structures. S can know that x is F without knowing that x is G (despite the extensional equivalence of 'F' and 'G') *because* S can receive information to the effect that x is F without receiving information to the effect that x is G. And if we assume, as it seems plausible to assume, that S cannot know that x is G unless he receives *some* quantity of information to the effect that x is G, then we have a tidy explanation for the intentionality of epistemic contexts. One cannot substitute co-referential expressions, *salva veritate,* in the context "S knows that . . . " because knowledge requires information and statements describing the information S has received are themselves non-extensional. And this intentionality derives, in turn, from the non-extensionality of statements describing *nomic* dependencies. Cognitive states exhibit an intentional structure because they are, fundamentally, nomically dependent states.

I have, so far, concentrated on the predicate term in those clauses we use to give expression to what is known. Despite extensional equivalence, S's knowing that x is F is different than S's knowing that x is G, and this difference is to be explained by the difference between receiving information to the effect that x is F and receiving information to the effect that x is G. It may be thought, however, that the parallel between knowledge and information collapses when we examine the subject term, the 'x', in these expressions. Someone can know that the blonde, standing in the corner, is angry without knowing that my sister is angry despite the fact that the blonde is my sister. That is to say, the context "S knows that . . ." is opaque, not only with respect to the embedded predicate expressions, but also with respect to the embedded subject terms. How is this feature of our epistemic descriptions to be explained?

As it turns out, it can be explained quite easily. I would not have raised the point (not, at least, at this time) unless it could be. A signal can carry the information that A is F without carrying the information that it is, in fact, A which is F. S can receive information that a woman (who happens to be my sister) is angry without receiving the information that she (the angry woman) is my sister. A thermometer, immersed in water, can tell us what the temperature of the water is, but it does not thereby tell us *what it is* that has that temperature. When partial information of this kind is received, we can explain why S does not know that my sister is angry even though the person he knows to be angry is my sister. He does not know it because, although he received the information that she (my sister) was angry, he did not (or may not have) received the information that she was my sister.

4.   Higher Levels of Intentionality

It seems, then, that the intentionality associated with out cognitive states can be viewed as a manifestation of an underlying network of nomic regularities. If, therefore, the lawful dependence of one magnitude on another is part of the physicist's picture of reality, then intentionality is also part of that picture. Hence, to the extent to which the

mentality of our cognitive states resides in their intentional structure, knowledge, perception, and memory are perfectly "natural" phenomena. There is nothing unique about them.

It may seem, however, that I have gone too far. In my efforts to naturalize the mental, have I not succeeded, only, in mentalizing the natural? For if the intentional structure of our cognitive states can be understood in terms of their information-carrying status (where the latter is understood, merely, as their nomic dependence on the condition defining the content of the cognitive state), then not only will living organisms perceive, know, and remember, but such simple devices as galvanometers, television sets, and pressure gauges will also qualify for cognitive attributes. For they also receive, process, and store information of the kind *now* under discussion, and their outputs are variously regulated by this information. Hence, they occupy intentional states of the same kind. Of course, they do not behave in interestingly diverse ways; they do not exhibit what we think of as intelligent behavior; they do not *learn.* But since behavior has already been rejected as the source of intentional structure, their dull, predictable responses to information-bearing stimuli should be irrelevant. According to the present line of argument, simple information-processing devices, mechanical artifacts, should have internal states possessing a content of the same sort that living organisms have when they know or perceive that something is the case.

The danger here is real. If galvanometers occupy intentional states, the conclusion to be drawn is not that galvanometers know things, but that knowledge is not *simply* a matter of occupying an intentional state, a state with a content corresponding to what is known when something is known.

Let me clarify this by contrasting the intentional state of a galvanometer (a device for detecting and measuring electrical current flow) and a genuine cognitive state—the state *we* are in when we know, for example, that there is a current flow between points A and B. Despite the fact that galvanometers receive, process, and display (for the convenience of someone using the instrument) information about affairs external to them, they do not occupy cognitive states. The reason they do not is not because their internal states (the amount of torque, say, on the mobile armature to which a pointer is affixed) fail to have a content, a content to which we can give expression with the sentence "There is a current flow between points A and B." The instrument's internal states certainly *have* this content. If they did not, *we* could never *learn* that there was a current flow between A and B by using the instrument. We get this information *from* the instrument, we depend on it to deliver, transmit, something with this content. This is only to say that such instruments are designed so that their output (hence the internal states responsible for that output) depends, nomically, on the amount of electrical current flowing between points to which their probes are affixed.

No, the reason the galvanometer does not know anything is because those states of the instrument that do carry information, and hence possess a content, carry *too much* information, have *too much* content, to qualify as genuine cognitive states. A galvanometer, and every other simple information-processing device of the sort now in question, is so constituted that it cannot distinguish between pieces of information that, from a cognitive standpoint, are different. If there is, as we know there is, a law that relates current flow to voltage differences (current will flow between points A and B only if there is a voltage difference between points A and B), then the galvanometer is incapable of representing one state of affairs without representing the other. It cannot carry the information (hence have the content) that there is a current flow between A and B without carrying the information (hence having the content) that there is a voltage difference between A and B. This is a consequence of the fact that nomic dependence is a transitive relation: if the position of the instrument's pointer depends on there being a current flow between A and B, and the latter depends on there being a voltage difference between A and B, then the pointer's position depends on there being a voltage difference between A and B. The swing of the pointer carries *both* pieces of information. Both pieces of information qualify as the pointer position's *content*.[8] But there is more. The movement of the pointer also carries information about the intensity of the magnetic field created by the current flow, the amount of increased tension in the instrument's restraining spring, and so on. *All* this information is embodied in the behavior of the pointer. There is, as it were, no way for the galvanometer to "know" that there is a current flow without "knowing" that there is a voltage difference, a magnetic field, an increased tension in the restraining spring, and so forth. All of these are part of the pointer's *informational content*. We, the users of the instrument, may be interested only in one magnitude, but the instrument itself is absolutely undiscriminating with respect to these contents.

This is why the galvanometer cannot know anything—even about those things about which it carries information. Its internal states, although they have a content of sorts, a content whose expression is non-extensional, do not have an exclusive *semantic* content of the sort characterizing genuine cognitive states. What is known when something is known differs, not only from extensionally equivalent pieces of information, but from nomically equivalent pieces of information. Knowledge that there is a current flow between points A and B is *different* than knowledge that there is a voltage difference between A and B despite the nomic inseparability of current flow from voltage differences. This is a distinction the galvanometer cannot make. It is insensitive to such cognitive differences. Hence the intentional states of a galvanometer do not qualify as cognitive states. They are intentional (as this was defined) but they are not *intentional enough*.

The point can perhaps be put more simply in the following way. If there is a natural law to the effect that every F is G, then no information-processing system (man included) can occupy a state having the informational content that something is F without, thereby, occupying a state (the same state) having the informational content that something is G. Every internal state that represents x as being F automatically represents x as being G. This is not question of unsophisticated filtering techniques. *No* filter can make a structure depend on x's being F without making it depend on x's being G if, as we are assuming, x's being F itself depends on x's being G. Therefore, if a system is to be capable of knowing that x is F without knowing that x is G, and I take this *possibility* to be part of what it means to say that S knows that x is F (where 'F' and 'G', though differing in meaning, specify properties that are nomically dependent), this system must be endowed with the resources for representing nomically related states of affairs in different ways. The system must be given the wherewithal to represent x's being F without representing x's being G even though it cannot carry the one piece of information without carrying the other. For this to occur, the *cognitive* content of the system's internal states must be a function, not only of the information they are designed (or were evolved) to carry, but of *the manner* in which this information is represented or coded.

How is this possible? This is not the place to develop a full account of the matter, but perhaps the following, extremely oversimplified, example will help illustrate a promising avenue of development. Think of an organism that is sensitive to hydrocloric acid (HCl). This is the *only* acid to which it is sensitive. Some kind of receptor system is responsible for picking up and delivering the information that the organism is in the presence of HCl. We put the organism in a solution of HCl and it reacts appropriately (i.e., the way it always reacts in the presence of HCl). Assuming that the organism's response is controlled by some internal nervous state, what can we say about the content of this internal state? If we think merely in terms of the information carried by the organism's internal states, any state having the content "This is HCl" will also have the content "This is an acid." The neural state may be said to carry the information (hence have the content) that HCl is present, but the very same state that carries this information also carries the information (hence has the content) that an acid is present. Such an organism resembles our galvanometer in its inability to distinguish between cognitively different contents. These contents are different (*cognitively* different) because one can know that something is an acid without knowing that it is HCl—perhaps (on some accounts of these matters) even know that something is HCl without knowing it is an acid. The organism we have described does not have internal states that exhibit this kind of difference in content. Hence it does not know that it is in the presence of HCl nor does it know that it is in the presence of an acid. It does not know anything.

Compare the organism just described to one that is sensitive to a variety of different acids—exhibiting the same response to all. Let us suppose, however, that occasionally, in the presence of HCl (but no other acid) it exhibits a unique response. If we assume, once again, that there are different types of neural states responsible for different types of response, then we can begin to see the crude beginning of genuine cognition. For when we place this organism in HCl, there are *two different ways* it can code the information (or represent the fact) that it is in the presence of an acid. If it responds in the way it does to acids in general, then the associated neural state is *one way* it has of representing the acidity of its surroundings. If it responds in the unique way to HCl, then the associated neural state is *another way* it has of representing the acidity of its surroundings. Both internal states carry the information that an acid is present (recall: no state that carries the information that x is HCl can fail to carry the information that x is acid), but the coding of this information is different in the two cases.

Suppose, then, we understand a structure's cognitive content to be determined not solely by the information it carries but by the way it codes or represents this information. We now have a basis for distinguishing internal structures in a way that approximates the way we distinguish cognitive states. We have, in other words, a more satisfactory model of that higher order intentionality characteristic of cognitive content. When placed in

HCl, the second organism described can occupy either one of two distinct states: one having the (cognitive) content: This is HCl; and the other having the (cognitive) content: This is an acid. It senses, so to speak, HCl (this information gets in), but this (sensory) information is capable of generating either one of two different cognitive states—either the "belief" that it is HCl or the "belief" that it is an acid. Although no structure can carry the information that x is HCl without carrying the information that x is an acid, a system that is sufficiently rich in the kind of information it can receive can nonetheless *extract* one of these pieces of information without extracting the other. It does so by having different structure types for encoding the incoming information: one structure type "meaning" that x is HCl, the other "meaning" that it is an acid.

On this account of things, the difference between a system that knows that something is F and a system that merely receives, processes, and has its output controlled by the information that x is F is that the former has, while the latter lacks, a representational or coding system that is sufficiently rich to distinguish between something's being F and its being G where nothing can be F without being G. This capacity for differentially encoding the various pieces of information arriving in a given signal is a capacity a system has (or can develop) in virtue of its capacity for receiving information about x's being G without receiving information about x's being F (either because x is not F or because, though it is F, the signal fails to carry this more specific piece of information). If the only way an organism can receive the information that x is an acid is through the information that x is HCl, then it cannot possibly develop a way of coding information about acidity that is different from the way it encodes information about *this specific kind* of acid. It cannot, as it were, acquire the concept *acidity*. Hence its internal states will never reflect the cognitive differences between *this is HCl* and *this is an acid*. This is why our galvanometer can never distinguish between voltage and current flow; it has no way of obtaining information about voltage differences except through information about current flow—hence no way of representing voltage differences in a way that is different from the way it represents current flow.

For a system to know what it is described as knowing, for it to occupy cognitive states with an appropriate content, it must have an informational receiving and coding capacity that is at least as rich in its representational powers as the language we use to express what is known. If it does not, then the language we use to describe what it knows cuts the intentional pie into slices that are too thin for the system to handle. It does not have a representational system rich enough to reflect the kind of distinctions (between various *cognitive* contents) required. Many simple information-processing devices can receive, process, and transmit the information they are required to have in order to know things. In fact, we often rely on them as conduits for the information that *we* require in order to know things. The cognitive inadequacy of these devices lies not in their information-processing capabilities but in their failure to have (and inability to develop) a *singular way* of representing the individual components of information embodied in the signals they do receive. They exhibit intentionality, but they do not exhibit it at the level required for cognitive systems.

5. Conclusions and Excuses

So much remains to be said that I hesitate to claim much, or anything, for what has been said. What I have tried to do is to indicate how a materialist might go about analyzing cognitive structure in a way that preserved a number of realistic intuitions about the nature of our propositional (more specifically, cognitive) attitudes. The resulting picture, assuming it could be fleshed out, yields a view of our cognitive states that (1) makes them internal states; (2) gives them a content exhibiting a significant degree of intentionality; and (3) makes the content of these states independent of the particular way the states themselves happen to be manifested in overt behavior (you do not *have* to eat it just because you believe it is food—even when you happen to be hungry).

Now the excuses. I have not discussed—indeed, I have carefully avoided—the notion of *belief.* I have restricted my attention to states whose contents were *true* (since cognitive states involve knowledge and knowledge implies truth). This was a convenient restriction since it allowed me to characterize a cognitive state's content in terms of the situation (condition, state of affairs) on which it was nomically dependent (about which it carried information). But beliefs can be false; there need be no *facts* corresponding to the belief's content in the way there must be for cognitive states. How, then, can we understand a belief's content in informational terms? A belief, or the internal structure that is to qualify as a belief, need not have any *informational* content.

This is a problem, but not, I think, an insuperable problem. A story must be told about the way certain types of structures develop (during learn-ing) as information-bearing structures and, hence, acquire an (information-carrying) role—a role which they sometimes fail to play. This, though, is another story.

I have talked, rather glibly, about levels or grades of intentionality. I have suggested that we can, with simple mechanical models, simulate a system with internal states having a considerable degree of intentionality. But there are still higher levels of intentionality, and our cognitive states exhibit these higher levels. To construct an adequate model of *cognitive* content, we need structures that can distinguish not only between nomically related situations but between *analytically* (or, if you do not like that word, *logically*) related contents. Since knowing that P can be distinguished from knowing that Q even when P entails Q (sometimes at least), the problem is to develop the above analysis of cognitive content in such a way as to reflect this higher grade of intentionality.

There are other problems, but I prefer to dwell on what I have done. What I have done, I think, is to focus the problem of intentionality in a slightly different way—a way that lends itself more readily to reductionistic efforts. The problem is not: how do we build systems that exhibit intentional characteristics? For we already have such systems in the simple mechanical appliances to be found in our kitchens and workshops. Rather, the problem is: how can such physical systems be endowed with a rich enough information-handling capacity so that they can achieve the degree of intentionality characteristic of our cognitive states? This is a problem, I concede, but not a problem of *kind* (building intentional systems out of extensionally describable systems). It is a matter of *degree.* And if I am not mistaken, this is just the kind of difference in degree that work in artificial intelligence is progressively narrowing.

NOTES

1. We also use interrogative nominals (know who he is, see where he is going) and infinitive clauses (remember to buy a present) as complements to these verbs. For the purpose of this paper I shall assume that when these constructions are used to describe what someone knows, sees, or remembers, they imply something of the form: S knows *that* . . . For example, if S knows where she is, then S must know that she is, say, in the closet. I shall not be concerned with knowing *how* to do things.

2. Wilfrid Sellars's "Empiricism and the Philosophy of Mind," *The Foundations of Science and the Concepts of Psychology and Psychoanalysis,* vol. I in Minnesota Studies in the Philosophy of Science, ed. Herbert Feigl and Michael Scriven (Minneapolis, 1956), is an early example of this type of approach.

3. I take this to be Donald Davidson's motive for refusing to credit dogs, say, with intentional cognitive states: their output is compatible with a variety of different intentionally characterized inner states and this underdetermination is not merely epistemological. This, at least, is the way I interpreted some of his arguments in a series of lectures delivered in Madison, Wisconsin.

4. This seems to be Daniel Dennett's approach in *Content and Consciousness* (London, 1969).

5. There are, of course, senses of 'appropriate' in which a response can be characterized as appropriate independently of the subject's beliefs and intentions. But these senses of 'appropriate' tell us correspondingly little about what the subject believes or intends and are, therefore, poor candidates for analyzing the content of internal states that produce the response.

6. Dennett puts the point nicely in contrasting the way we treat human snores (mere sounds having a cuase but no meaning) and vocal emissions that have a semantic interpretation. "Once one makes the decision to treat these sounds as utterances with a semantic interpretation on the other hand, one is committed to an intentionalistic interpretation of their etiology, for one has decided to view the sounds as the products of communicative intentions, as the expressions of beliefs, or as lies, as requests, questions, commands and so forth." "Two Approaches to Mental Images," in *Brainstorms* (Hanover, N.H., 1978), p. 180.

7. The type of information I am here describing is the type associated with Claude Shannon and Warren Weaver's *The Mathematical Theory of Communication* (Urbana, Ill., 1949). The Mathematical Theory of Communication has had a checkered career in psychology, and most investigators now tend to disparage its usefulness for semantic or cognitive studies. I think this is a mistake. The present article should help indicate why I think this is so. I exploit this theory—or, better, the principles underlying it—to a much greater extent in *Knowledge and the Flow of Information* (unpublished) [Cambridge, Mass.: MIT Press/Bradford Books, 1981] from which the present article is derived.

8. This is why one can use a properly constructed galvanometer to measure voltage as well as, or instead of, current flow. Indeed, one can measure *any* magnitude (e.g., pressure, depth, speed) variations which can be converted, by an appropriate transducer, into electrical form. All that is needed is a suitable calibration of the scale along which the pointer moves.

38

Donald Davidson

"Thought and Talk"

What is the connection between thought and language? The dependence of speaking on thinking is evident, for to speak is to express thoughts. This dependence is manifest in endless further ways. Someone who utters the sentence 'The candle is out' as a sentence of English must intend to utter words that are true if and only if an indicated candle is out at the time of utterance, and he must believe that by making the sounds he does he is uttering words that are true only under those circumstances. These intentions and beliefs are not apt to be dwelt on by the fluent speaker. But though they may not normally command attention, their absence would be enough to show he was not speaking English, and the absence of any analogous thoughts would show he was not speaking at all.

The issue is on the other side: can there be thought without speech? A first and natural reaction is that there can be. There is the familiar, irksome experience of not being able to find the words to express one's ideas. On occasion one may decide that the editorial writer has put a point better than one could oneself. And there is Norman Malcolm's dog who, having chased a squirrel into the woods, barks up the wrong tree. It is hard not to credit the dog with the belief that the squirrel is in that tree.

A definite, if feebler, intuition tilts the other way. It is possible to wonder whether the speaker who can't find the right words has a clear idea. Attributions of intentions and beliefs to dogs smack of anthropomorphism. A primitive behaviourism, baffled by the privacy of unspoken thoughts, may take comfort in the view that thinking is really 'talking to oneself'—silent speech.

Beneath the surface of these opposed tendencies run strong, if turgid, currents, which may help to explain why philosophers have, for the most part, preferred taking a stand on the issue to producing an agrument. Whatever the reason, the question of the relationship between thought and speech seems seldom to have been asked for its own sake. The usual assumption is that one or the other, speech or thought, is by comparison easy to understand, and therefore the more obscure one (whichever that is) may be illuminated by analysing or explaining it in terms of the other.

The assumption is, I think, false: neither language nor thinking can be fully explained in terms of the other, and neither has conceptual priority. The two are, indeed, linked, in the sense that each requires the other in order to be understood; but the linkage is not so complete that either suffices, even when reasonably reinforced, to explicate the other. To make good this claim what is chiefly needed is to show how thought depends on speech, and this is the thesis I want to refine, and then to argue for.

We attribute a thought to a creature whenever we assertively employ a positive sentence the main verb of which is psychological—in English, 'believes', 'knows', 'hopes', 'desires', 'thinks', 'fears', 'is interested' are examples—followed by a sentence and preceded by the name or description of the creature. (A 'that' may optionally or necessarily follow the verb.) Some such sentences attribute states, others report events or processes: 'believes', 'thinks', and 'wants' report states, while 'came to believe', 'forgot', 'concluded', 'noticed', 'is proving' report events or processes. Sentences that can be used to attribute a thought exhibit what is often called, or analysed as, semantic intensionality, which means that the attribution may be changed

From *Mind and Language: Wolfson College Lectures 1974*, Samuel Guttenplan, ed. Oxford: Oxford University Press, 1975, pp. 7–23. Copyright © 1975 by Oxford University Press. Reprinted with permission of Oxford University Press.

from true to false, or false to true, by substitutions in the contained sentences that would not alter the truth value of that sentence in isolation.

I do not take for granted that if a creature has a thought, then we can, with resources of the kind just sketched, correctly attribute that thought to him. But thoughts so attributable at least constitute a good sample of the totality.

It is doubtful whether the various sorts of thought can be reduced to one, or even to a few: desire, knowledge, belief, fear, interest, to name some important cases, are probably logically independent to the extent that none can be defined using the others, even along with such further notions as truth and cause. Nevertheless, belief is central to all kinds of thought. If someone is glad that, or notices that, or remembers that, or knows that, the gun is loaded, then he must believe that the gun is loaded. Even to wonder whether the gun is loaded, or to speculate on the possibility that the gun is loaded, requires the belief, for example, that a gun is a weapon, that it is a more or less enduring physical object, and so on. There are good reasons for not insisting on any particular list of beliefs that are needed if a creature is to wonder whether a gun is loaded. Nevertheless, it is necessary that there be endless interlocked beliefs. The system of such beliefs identifies a thought by locating it in a logical and epistemic space.

Having a thought requires that there be a background of beliefs, but having a particular thought does not depend on the state of belief with respect to that very thought. If I consider going to a certain concert, I know I will be put to a degree of trouble and expense, and I have more complicated beliefs about the enjoyment I will experience. I will enjoy hearing Beethoven's Grosse Fuge, say, but only provided the performance achieves a reasonable standard, and I am able to remain attentive. I have the thought of going to the concert, but until I decide whether to go, I have no fixed belief that I will go; until that time, I merely entertain the thought.

We may say, summarizing the last two paragraphs, that a thought is defined by a system of beliefs, but is itself autonomous with respect to belief.

We usually think that having a language consists largely in being able to speak, but in what follows speaking will play only an indirect part. What is essential to my argument is the idea of an interpreter, someone who understands the utterances of another. The considerations to be put forward imply, I think, that a speaker must himself be an interpreter of others, but I shall not try to demonstrate that an interpreter must be a speaker, though there may be good reason to hold this. Perhaps it

is worth pointing out that the notion of a language, or of two people speaking the same language does not seem to be needed here. Two speakers could interpret each other's utterances without there being, in any ordinary sense, a common language. (I do not want to deny that in other contexts the notion of a shared language may be very important.)

The chief thesis of this paper is that a creature cannot have thoughts unless it is an interpreter of the speech of another. This thesis does not imply the possibility of reduction, behaviouristic or otherwise, of thoughts to speech; indeed the thesis imputes no priority to language, epistemological or conceptual. The claim also falls short of similar claims in that it allows that there may be thoughts for which the speaker cannot find words, or for which there are no words.

Someone who can interpret an utterance of the English sentence 'The gun is loaded' must have many beliefs, and these beliefs must be much like the beliefs someone must have if he entertains the thought that the gun is loaded. The interpreter must, we may suppose, believe that a gun is a weapon, and that it is a more or less enduring physical object. There is probably no definite list of things that must be believed by someone who understands the sentence 'The gun is loaded,' but it is necessary that there be endless interlocked beliefs.

An interpreter knows the conditions under which utterances of sentences are true, and often knows that certain sentences are true, others must be. For example, an interpreter of English knows that if 'The gun is loaded and the door is locked' is true, then 'The door is locked' is true. The sentences of a language have a location in the logical space created by the pattern of such relationships. Obviously the pattern of relations between sentences is very much like the pattern of relations between thoughts. This fact has encouraged the view that it is redundant to take both patterns as basic. If thoughts are primary, a language seems to serve no purpose but to express or convey thoughts; while if we take speech as primary, it is tempting to analyse thoughts as speech dispositions: as Sellars puts it, ' . . . thinking at the distinctly human level . . . is essentially verbal activity'.[1] But clearly the parallel between the structure of thoughts and the structure of sentences provides no argument for the primacy of either, and only a presumption in favour of their interdependence.

We have been talking freely of thoughts, beliefs,

1. Wilfrid Sellars, 'Conceptual Change', in *Conceptual Change,* ed. G. Pearce and P. Maynard, Dordrecht, 1973, p. 82.

meanings, and interpretations; or rather, freely using sentences that contain these words. But of course it is not clear what entities, or sorts of entities, there must be to make systematic sense of such sentences. However, talk apparently of thoughts and sayings does belong to a familiar mode of explanation of human behaviour and must be considered an organized department of common sense that may as well be called a theory. One way of examining the relation between thought and language is by inspecting the theory implicit in this sort of explanation.

Part of the theory deals with the teleological explanation of action. We wonder why a man raises his arm; an explanation might be that he wanted to attract the attention of a friend. This explanation would fail if the arm-raiser didn't believe that by raising his arm he would attract the attention of his friend, so the complete explanation of his raising his arm, or at any rate a more complete explanation, is that he wanted to attract the attention of his friend *and* believed that by raising his arm he would attract his friend's attention. Explanation of this familiar kind has some features worth emphasizing. It explains what is relatively apparent—an arm-raising—by appeal to factors that are far more problematical: desires and beliefs. But if we were to ask for evidence that the explanation is correct, this evidence would in the end consist of more data concerning the sort of event being explained, namely further behaviour which is explained by the postulated beliefs and desires. Adverting to beliefs and desires to explain action is therefore a way of fitting an action into a pattern of behaviour made coherent by the theory. This does not mean, of course, that beliefs are nothing but patterns of behaviour, or that the relevant patterns can be defined without using the concepts of belief and desire. Nevertheless, there is a clear sense in which attributions of belief and desire, and hence teleological explanations of belief and desire, are supervenient on behaviour more broadly described.

A characteristic of teleological explanation not shared by explanation generally is the way in which it appeals to the concept of *reason*. The belief and desire that explain an action must be such that anyone who had that belief and desire would have a reason to act in that way. What's more, the descriptions we provide of desire and belief must, in teleological explanation, exhibit the rationality of the action in the light of the content of the belief and the object of the desire.

The cogency of a teleological explanation rests, as remarked, on its ability to discover a coherent pattern in the behaviour of an agent. Coherence here includes the idea of rationality both in the

sense that the action to be explained must be reasonable in the light of the assigned desires and beliefs, but also in the sense that the assigned desires and beliefs must fit with one another. The methodological presumption of rationality does not make it impossible to attribute irrational thoughts and actions to an agent, but it does impose a burden on such attributions. We weaken the intelligibility of attributions of thoughts of any kind to the extent that we fail to uncover a consistent pattern of beliefs and, finally, of actions, for it is only against a background of such a pattern that we can identify thoughts. If we see a man pulling on both ends of a piece of string, we may decide he is fighting against himself, that he wants to move the string in incompatible directions. Such an explanation would require elaborate backing. No problem arises if the explanation is that he wants to break the string.

From the point of view of someone giving teleological explanations of the actions of another, it clearly makes no sense to assign priority either to desires or to beliefs. Both are essential to the explanation of behaviour, and neither is more directly open to observation than the other. This creates a problem, for it means that behaviour, which is the main evidential basis for attributions of belief and desire, is reckoned the result of two forces less open to public observation. Thus where one constellation of beliefs and desires will rationalize an action, it is always possible to find a quite different constellation that will do as well. Even a generous sample of actions threatens to leave open an unacceptably large number of alternative explanations.

Fortunately a more refined theory is available, one still firmly based on common sense: the theory of preference, or decision-making, under uncertainty. The theory was first made precise by Frank Ramsey, though he viewed it as a matter of providing a foundation for the concept of probability rather than as a piece of philosophical psychology.[2] Ramsey's theory works by quantifying strength of preference and degree of belief in such a way as to make sense of the natural idea that in choosing a course of action we consider not only how desirable various outcomes are, but also how apt available courses of action are to produce those outcomes. The theory does not assume that we can judge degrees of belief or make numerical comparisons of value directly. Rather it postulates a reasonable pattern of preferences between courses of

2. Frank Ramsey, 'Truth and Probability', in *Foundations of Mathematics and Other Essays*, ed. R. B. Braithwaite, London, 1931.

action, and shows how to construct a system of quantified beliefs and desires to explain the choices. Given the idealized conditions postulated by the theory, Ramsey's method makes it possible to identify the relevant beliefs and desires uniquely. Instead of talking of postulation, we might put the matter this way: to the extent that we can see the actions of an agent as falling into a consistent (rational) pattern of a certain sort, we can explain those actions in terms of a system of quantified beliefs and desires.

We shall come back to decision theory presently; now it is time to turn to the question of how speech is interpreted. The immediate aim of a theory of interpretation is to give the meaning of an arbitrary utterance by a member of a language community. Central to interpretation, I have argued, is a theory of truth that satisfies Tarski's Convention T (modified in certain ways to apply to a natural language). Such a theory yields, for every utterance of every sentence of the language, a theorem of the form: 'An utterance of sentence s by a speaker x at time t is true if and only if ————.' Here 's' is to be replaced by a description of a sentence, and the blank by a statement of the conditions under which an utterance of the sentence is true relative to the parameters of speaker and time. In order to interpret a particular utterance it is neither necessary nor sufficient to know the entire theory: it is enough to know what the theory says the truth conditions are for the utterance, and to know that those conditions are entailed by a theory of the required sort. On the other hand, to belong to a speech community—to be an interpreter of the speech of others—one does need to know much of a whole theory, in effect, and to know that it is a theory of the right kind.[3]

A theory of interpretation, like a theory of action, allows us to redescribe certain events in a revealing way. Just as a theory of action can answer the question of what an agent is doing when he has raised his arm by redescribing the act as one of trying to catch his friend's attention, so a method of interpretation can lead to redescribing the utterance of certain sounds as an act of saying that snow is white. At this point, however, the analogy breaks down. For decision theory can also explain actions, while it is not at all clear how a theory of interpretation can explain a speaker's uttering the words 'Snow is white.' But this is, after all, to be expected, for uttering words is an action, and so must draw for its teleological explanation on beliefs and desires. Interpretation is not irrelevant to

the teleological explanation of speech, since to explain why someone said something we need to know, among other things, his own interpretation of what he said, that is, what he believes his words mean in the circumstances under which he speaks. Naturally this will involve some of his beliefs about how others will interpret his words.

The interlocking of the theory of action with interpretation will emerge in another way if we ask how a method if interpretation is tested. In the end, the answer must be that it helps bring order into our understanding of behaviour. But at an intermediary stage, we can see that the attitude of *holding true* or *accepting as true,* as directed towards sentences, must play a central role in giving form to a theory. On the one hand, most uses of language tell us directly, or shed light on the question, whether a speaker holds a sentence to be true. If a speaker's purpose is to give information, or to make an honest assertion, then normally the speaker believes he is uttering a sentence true under the circumstances. If he utters a command, we may usually take this as showing that he holds a certain sentence (closely related to the sentence uttered) to be false; similarly for many cases of deceit. When a question is asked, it generally indicates that the questioner does not know whether a certain sentence is true; and so on. In order to infer from such evidence that a speaker holds a sentence true we need to know much about his desires and beliefs, but we do not have to know what his words mean.

On the other hand, knowledge of the circumstances under which someone holds sentences true is central to interpretation. We saw in the case of thoughts that although most thoughts are not beliefs, it is the pattern of belief that allows us to identify any thought; analogously, in the case of language, although most utterances are not concerned with truth, it is the pattern of sentences held true that gives sentences their meaning.

The attitude of holding a sentence to be true (under specified conditions) relates belief and interpretation in a fundamental way. We can know that a speaker holds a sentence to be true without knowing what he means by it or what belief it expresses for him. But if we know he holds the sentence true *and* we know how to interpret it, then we can make a correct attribution of belief. Symmetrically, if we know what belief a sentence held true expresses, we know how to interpret it. The methodological problem of interpretation is to see how, given the stentences a man accepts as true under given circumstances, to work out what his beliefs are and what his words mean. The situation is again similar to the situation in decision theory

3. There is further discussion of these issues in my 'Radical Interpretation', *Dialectica* (Vol. 27, Nos. 3–4, 1973).

where, given a man's preferences between alternative courses of action, we can discern both his beliefs and his desires. Of course it should not be thought that a theory of interpretation will stand alone, for as we noticed, there is no chance of telling when a sentence is held true without being able to attribute desires and being able to describe actions as having complex intentions. This observation does not deprive the theory of interpretation of interest, but assigns it a place within a more comprehensive theory of action and thought.[4]

It is still unclear whether interpretation is required for a theory of action, which is the question we set ourselves to answer. What is certain is that all the standard ways of testing theories of decision or preference under uncertainty rely on the use of language. It is relatively simple to eliminate the necessity for verbal responses on the part of the subject: he can be taken to have expressed a preference by taking action, by moving directly to achieve his end, rather than by saying what he wants. But this cannot settle the question of what he has chosen. A man who takes an apple rather than a pear when offered both may be expressing a preference for what is on his left rather than his right, what is red rather than yellow, what is seen first, or judged more expensive. Repeated tests may make some readings of his actions more plausible than others, but the problem will remain how to tell what he judges to be a repetition of the same alternative. Tests that involve uncertain events—choices between gambles—are even harder to present without using words. The psychologist, sceptical of his ability to be certain how a subject is interpreting his instructions, must add a theory of verbal interpretation to the theory to be tested. If we think of all choices as revealing a preference that one sentence rather than another be true, the resulting total theory should provide an interpretation of sentences, and at the same time assign beliefs and desires, both of the latter conceived as relating the agent to sentences or utterances. This composite theory would explain all behaviour, verbal and otherwise.

All this strongly suggests that the attribution of desires and beliefs (and other thoughts) must go hand in hand with the interpretation of speech, that neither the theory of decision nor of interpretation can be successfully developed without the other. But it remains to say, in more convincing

detail, why the attribution of thought depends on the interpretation of speech. The general, and not very informative, reason is that without speech we cannot make the fine distinctions between thoughts that are essential to the explanations we can sometimes confidently supply. Our manner of attributing attitudes ensures that all the expressive power of language can be used to make such distinctions. One can believe that Scott is not the author of *Waverley* while not doubting that Scott is Scott; one can want to be the discoverer of a creature with a heart without wanting to be the discoverer of a creature with a kidney. One can intend to bite into the apple in the hand without intending to bite into the only apple with a worm in it; and so forth. The intensionality we make so much of in the attribution of thoughts is very hard to make much of when speech is not present. The dog, we say, knows that its master is home. But does it know that Mr. Smith (who is his master), or that the president of the bank (who is that same master), is home? We have no real idea how to settle, or make sense of, these questions. It is much harder to say, when speech is not present, how to distinguish universal thoughts from conjunctions of thoughts, or how to attribute conditional thoughts, or thoughts with, so to speak, mixed quantification ('He hopes that everyone is loved by someone').

These considerations will probably be less persuasive to dog lovers than to others, but in any case they do not constitute an argument. At best what we have shown, or claimed, is that unless there is behaviour that can be interpreted as speech, the evidence will not be adequate to justify the fine distinctions we are used to making in the attribution of thoughts. If we persist in attributing desires, beliefs, or other attitudes under these conditions, our attributions and consequent explanations of actions will be seriously underdetermined in that many alternative systems of attribution, many alternative explanations, will be equally justified by the available data. Perhaps this is all we can say against the attribution of thoughts to dumb creatures; but I do not think so.

Before going on I want to consider a possible objection to the general line I have been pursuing. Suppose we grant, the objector says, that very complex behaviour not observed in infants and elephants is necessary if we are to find application for the full apparatus available for the attribution of thoughts. Still, it may be said, the sketch of how interpretation works does not show that this complexity must be viewed as connected with language. The reason is that the sketch makes too much depend on the special attitude of being

---

4. The interlocking of decision theory and radical interpretation is explored also in my 'Psychology as Philosophy', in *Philosophy of Psychology*, ed. S. C. Brown, London, 1974, pp. 41–52; and in my 'Belief and the Basis of Meaning', *Synthese* (vol. 27, 1974, pp. 309–24).

thought true. The most direct evidence for the existence of this attitude is honest assertion. But then it would seem that we could treat as speech the behaviour of creatures that never did anything with language except make honest assertions. Some philosophers do dream of such dreary tribes; but would we be right to say they had a language? What has been lost to view is what may be called *the autonomy of meaning*. Once a sentence is understood, an utterance of it may be used to serve almost any extra-linguistic purpose. An instrument that could be put to only one use would lack autonomy of meaning; this amounts to saying it should not be counted as a language. So the complexity of behaviour needed to give full scope to attributions of thought need not, after all, be exactly the same complexity that allows, or requires, interpretation as a language.

I agree with the hypothetical objector that autonomy of meaning is essential to language; indeed it is largely this that explains why linguistic meaning cannot be defined or analysed on the basis of the extralinguistic intentions and beliefs. But the objector fails to distinguish between a language that *could* be used for only one purpose and one that *is* used for only one purpose. An instrument that could be used for only one purpose would not be language. But honest assertion alone might yield a theory of interpretation, and so a language that, though capable of more, might never be put to further uses. (As a practical matter, the event is unthinkable. Someone who knows under what conditions his sentences are socially true cannot fail to grasp, and avail himself of, the possibilities in dishonest assertion—or in joking, story-telling, goading, exaggerating, insulting, and all the rest of the jolly crew.)

A method of interpretation tells us that for speakers of English an utterance of 'It is raining' by a speaker x at time t is true if and only if it is raining (near x) at t. To be armed with this information, and to know that others know it, is to know what an utterance means independently of knowing the purposes that prompted it. The autonomy of meaning also helps to explain how it is possible, by the use of language, to attribute thoughts. Suppose someone utters assertively the sentence 'Snow is white.' Knowing the conditions under which such an utterance is true I can add, if I please, 'I believe that too,' thus attributing a belief to myself. In this case we may both have asserted that snow is white, but sameness of force is not necessary to the self-attribution. The other may say with a sneer, expressing disbelief, 'Snow is white'—and I may again attribute a belief to myself by saying, 'But *I* believe that.' It can work as well in another way: if I can take advantage of an

utterance of someone else's to attribute a belief to myself, I can use an utterance of my own to attribute a belief to someone else. First I utter a sentence, perhaps 'Snow is white,' and then I add 'He believes that.' The first utterance may or may not be an assertion; in any case, it does not attribute a belief to anyone (though if it is an assertion, then I do *represent* myself as believing that snow is white). But if my remark 'He believes that' is an assertion, I have attributed a belief to someone else. Finally, there is no bar to my attributing a belief to myself by saying first, 'Snow is white' and then adding, 'I believe that.'

In all these examples, I take the word 'that' to refer demonstratively to an utterance, whether it is an utterance by the speaker of the 'that' or by another speaker. The 'that' cannot refer to a sentence, both because, as Church has pointed out in similar cases, the reference would then have to be relativized to a language, since a sentence may have different meanings in different languages;[5] but also, and more obviously, because the same sentence may have different truth values in the same language.

What demonstrative reference to utterances does in the sort of case just considered it can do as well when the surface structure is altered to something like 'I believe that snow is white' or 'He believes that snow is white.' In these instances also I think we should view the 'that' as a demonstrative, now referring ahead to an utterance on the verge of production. Thus the logical form of standard attributions of attitude is that of two utterances paratactically joined. There is no connective, though the first utterance contains a reference to the second. (Similar remarks go, of course, for inscriptions of sentences.)

I have discussed this analysis of verbal attributions of attitude elsewhere, and there is no need to repeat the arguments and explanations here.[6] It is an analysis with its own difficulties, especially when it comes to analysing quantification into the contained sentence, but I think these difficulties can be overcome while preserving the appealing features of the idea. Here I want to stress a point that connects the paratactic analysis of attribution of attitude with our present theme. The propsoed analysis directly relates the autonomous feature of meaning with our ability to describe and attribute thoughts, since it is only because the interpretation of a sentence is independent of its use that the ut-

5. Alonzo Church, 'On Carnap's Analysis of Statements of Assertion and Belief', *Analysis*, X (1950), 97–9.

6. See 'On Saying That', in *Words and Objections: Essays on the Work of W. V. Quine*, eds. D. Davidson and J. Hintikka, Dordrecht, 1969, pp. 158–74.

terance of a sentence can serve in the description of the attitudes of others. If my analysis is right, we can dispense with the unlikely (but common) view that a sentence bracketed into a 'that'-clause needs an entirely different interpretation from the one that works for it in other contexts. Since sentences are not names or descriptions in ordinary contexts, we can in particular reject the assumption that the attitudes have objects such as propositions which 'that'-clauses might be held to name or describe. There should be no temptation to call the utterance to which reference is made according to the paratactic analysis the object of the attributed attitude.

Here a facile solution to our problem about the relation between thoughts and speech suggests itself. One way to view the paratactic analysis, a way proposed by Quine in *Word and Object,* is this: when a speaker attributes an attitude to a person, what he does is ape or mimic an actual or possible speech act of that person.[7] Indirect discourse is the best example, and assertion is another good one. Suppose I say, 'Herodotus asserted that the Nile rises in the Mountains of the Moon.' My second utterance—my just past utterance of 'The Nile rises in the Mountains of the Moon'—must, if my attribution to Herodotus is correct, bear a certain relationship to an utterance of Herodotus'; it must, in some appropriate sense, be a translation of it. Since, assuming still that the attribution is correct, Herodotus and I are *samesayers,* my utterance mimicked his. Not with respect to force, of course, since I didn't assert anything about the Nile. The sameness is with respect to the content of our utterances. If we turn to other attitudes, the situation is more complicated, for there is typically no utterance to ape. If I affirm 'Jones believes that snow is white,' my utterance of 'Snow is white' may have no actual utterance of Jones's to imitate. Still, we could take the line that what I affirm is that Jones would be honestly speaking his mind were he to utter a sentence translating mine. Given some delicate assumptions about the conditions under which such a subjunctive conditional is true, we could conclude that only someone with a language could have a thought, since to have a thought would be to have a disposition to utter certain sentences with appropriate force under given circumstances.

We could take this line, but unfortunately there seems no clear reason why we have to. We set out to find an argument to show that only creatures with speech have thoughts. What has just been outlined is not an argument, but a proposal, and a

proposal we need not accept. The paratactic analysis of the logical form of attributions of attitude can get along without the mimic-theory of utterance. When I say, 'Jones believes that snow is white' I describe Jones's state of mind directly: it is indeed the state of mind someone is in who could honestly assert 'Snow is white' if he spoke English, but that may be a state a languageless creature could also be in.

In order to make my final main point, I must return to an aspect of interpretation so far neglected. I remarked that the attitude of holding true, directed to sentences under specified circumstances, is the basis for interpretation, but I did not say how it can serve this function. The difficulty, it will be remembered, is that a sentence is held true because of two factors: what the holder takes the sentence to mean, and what he believes. In order to sort things out, what is needed is a method for holding one factor steady while the other is studied.

Membership in a language community depends on the ability to interpret the utterances of members of the group, and a method is at hand if one has, and knows one has, a theory which provides truth conditions, more or less in Tarski's style, for all sentences (relativized, as always, to time and speaker). The theory is correct as long as it entails, by finitely stated means, theorems of the familiar form: '"It is raining" is true for a speaker x at time t if and only if it is raining (near x) at t. The evidential basis for such a theory concerns sentences held true, facts like the following: '"It is raining" is held true by Smith at 8 a.m. on 26 August and it did rain near Smith at that time.' It would be possible to generate a correct theory simply by considering sentences to be true when held true, provided (1) there was a theory which satisfied the formal constraints and was consistent in this way with the evidence, and (2) all speakers held a sentence to be true just when that sentence was true—provided, that is, all beliefs, at least as far as they could be expressed, were correct.

But of course it cannot be assumed that speakers never have false beliefs. Error is what gives belief its point. We can, however, take it as given that *most* beliefs are correct. The reason for this is that a belief is identified by its location in a pattern of beliefs; it is this pattern that determines the subject matter of the belief, what the belief is about. Before some object in, or aspect of, the world can become part of the subject matter of a belief (true or false) there must be endless true beliefs about the subject matter. False beliefs tend to undermine the identification of the subject matter; to undermine, therefore, the validity of a description of the belief as being about that subject. And so, in turn, false

7. W. V. Quine, *Word and Object,* Cambridge, Mass., 1960, p. 219.

beliefs undermine the claim that a connected belief is false. To take an example, how clear are we that the ancients—some ancients—believed that the earth was flat? *This* earth? Well, this earth of ours is part of the solar system, a system partly identified by the fact that it is a gaggle of large, cool, solid bodies circling around a very large, hot star. If someone believes *none* of this about the earth, is it certain that it is the earth that he is thinking about? An answer is not called for. The point is made if this kind of consideration of related beliefs can shake one's confidence that the ancients believed the earth was flat. It isn't that any one false belief necessarily destroys our ability to identify further beliefs, but that the intelligibility of such identifications must depend on a background of largely unmentioned and unquestioned true beliefs. To put it another way: the more things a believer is right about, the sharper his errors are. Too much mistake simply blurs the focus.

What makes interpretation possible, then, is the fact that we can dismiss *a priori* the chance of massive error. A theory of interpretation cannot be correct that makes a man assent to very many false sentences: it must generally be the case that a sentence is true when a speaker holds it to be. So far as it goes, it is in favour of a method of interpretation that it counts a sentence true just when speakers hold it to be true. But of course, the speaker may be wrong; and so may the interpreter. So in the end what must be counted in favour of a method of interpretation is that it puts the interpreter in general agreement with the speaker: according to the method, the speaker holds a sentence true under specified conditions, and these conditions obtain, in the opinion of the interpreter, just when the speaker holds the sentence to be true.

No simple theory can put a speaker and interpreter in perfect agreement, and so a workable theory must from time to time assume error on the part of one or the other. The basic methodological precept is, therefore, that a good theory of interpretation maximizes agreement. Or, given that sentences are infinite in number, and given further considerations to come, a better word might be *optimize.*

Some disagreements are more destructive of understanding than others, and a sophisticated theory must naturally take this into account. Disagreement about theoretical matters may (in some cases) be more tolerable than disagreement about what is more evident; disagreement about how things look or appear is less tolerable than disagreement about how they are; disagreement about the truth of attributions of certain attitudes

to a speaker by that same speaker may not be tolerable at all, or barely. It is impossible to simplify the considerations that are relevant, for everything we know or believe about the way evidence supports belief can be put to work in deciding where the theory can best allow error, and what errors are least destructive of understanding. The methodology of interpretation is, in this respect, nothing but epistemology seen in the mirror of meaning.

The interpreter who assumes his method can be made to work for a language community will strive for a theory that optimizes agreement throughout the community. Since easy communication has survival value, he may expect usage within a community to favour simple common theories of interpretation.

If this account of radical interpretation is right, at least in broad outline, then we should acknowledge that the concepts of objective truth, and of error, necessarily emerge in the context of interpretation. The distinction between a sentence being held true and being in fact true is essential to the existence of an interpersonal system of communication, and when in individual cases there is a difference, it must be counted as error. Since the attitude of holding true is the same, whether the sentence is true or not, it corresponds directly to belief. The concept of belief thus stands ready to take up the slack between objective truth and the held true, and we come to understand it just in this connection.

We have the idea of belief only from the role of belief in the interpretation of language, for as a private attitude it is not intelligible except as an adjustment to the public norm provided by language. It follows that a creature must be a member of a speech community if it is to have the concept of belief. And given the dependence of other attitudes on belief, we can say more generally that only a creature that can interpret speech can have the concept of a thought.

Can a creature have a belief if it does not have the concept of belief? It seems to me it cannot, and for this reason. Someone cannot have a belief unless he understands the possibility of being mistaken, and this requires grasping the contrast between truth and error—true belief and false belief. But this contrast, I have argued, can emerge only in the context of interpretation, which alone forces us to the idea of an objective, public truth.

It is often wrongly thought that the semantical concept of truth is redundant, that there is no difference between asserting that a sentence *s* is true, and using *s* to make an assertion. What may be right is a redundancy theory of belief, that to believe that *p* is not to be distinguished from the belief that p is true. This notion of truth is not the semantical notion: language is not directly in the picture. But it is only just out of the picture; it is part of the frame. For the notion of a true belief depends on the notion of a true utterance, and this in turn there cannot be without shared language. As Ulysses was made to put it by a member of our speech community:

> ... no man is the lord of anything,
> Though in and of him there be much consisting,
> Till he communicate his parts to others;
> Nor doth he of himself know them for aught
> Till he behold them formed in th'applause
> Where they're extended.
>
> (*Troilus and Cressida*, III. iii. 115–20.)

39

Wilfrid Sellars

from "The Structure of Knowledge"
Lecture II: Minds

I

1. In my first lecture, I was exploring the nature of our perceptual knowledge of such elementary facts as that there is a pink ice cube in front of one or that there is a red book on the shelf. I emphasized that I was 'bracketing', that is, suspending commitment to, the stratum of concepts introduced by micro-physical theory and considering perception as it might have been considered by an epistemologist who lived in the days when atomic theory was but a gleam in the Democritean eye. In short, the model with which I was working was essentially an Aristotelian one, though I was not concerned with problems of historical exegesis.

2. I was emphasizing that in this model material things are colored in a sense which is not to be *explicated* in terms of a hypothetical reference to sensations of color. I asked you to contemplate a pink ice cube and urged the implausibility of the suggestion that to see it to be pink is to see it to have the power to cause normal observers in standard conditions to have sensations of pink or to sense pinkly. Indeed, I argued that the concept of the sensation of the pink cube is a theoretical concept, an element in a theoretical explanation, not only of how people can seem to see pink ice cubes, when no pink transparent material object is before their eyes, but how the veridical perception itself differs from a purely conceptual awareness of the pink ice cube.

3. I concluded by suggesting that the most satisfactory form of this theoretical account makes it a version of the 'adverbial' theory of sensing. According to this version, the theoretical concepts of

manners of sensing are formed by analogy with concepts pertaining to the common and proper sensible attributes of physical objects as conceived in the Manifest Image of the world. Thus, the color manners of sensing form a family of incompatibles, where the incompatibilities involved are to be understood in terms of the incompatibilities within the family of ordinary physical color attributes. And, correspondingly, the shape manners of sensing would exhibit, as do physical shapes, the abstract structure of a pure geometrical system.

4. Thus, sensing a pink cube is a manner of sensing which is conceived by analogy (a transcategorial analogy!) with a pink physical cube and which, though normally caused by the presence of a pink and cubical transparent object in front of a normal perceiver's eyes, can also be brought about in abnormal circumstances by, say, a grey object illuminated by pink light or by a pink rhomboidal object viewed through a distorting medium, or in hallucination by, for example, a probing of a certain region of the brain with an electrode, or by the taking of an hallucinogenic drug after much talk of pink ice cubes.

5. I distinguished between the propositional and the non-propositional components of the visual experience. I characterized the former as a thinking that something is the case, where the thinking is construed as the occurrence, in the mind, of a sentence in Mentalese or, to use the traditional term, 'inner speech'. I said relatively little about Mentalese, save to emphasize the positive analogy between it and overt verbal behavior. I concentrated on the non-propositional aspect of visual experiences and was concerned to show that

unless supplemented by theory construction, the phenomenology of perception takes us no further than the idea that *somehow, something* which is in *some* sense pink and cubical is present to the perceiver when, rather than *merely thinking* that there is a pink ice cube in a certain place, he sees, or seems to see, a pink ice cube in that place.

6. In this lecture I want to explore the topic of thinking as 'inner speech' (Mentalese) and lay the groundwork for discussion of the implications of the scientific revolution for this concept. Unless one takes a purely instrumental view of scientific objects, both sensing and thinking must be correctly located in a context of neurophysiological activity. The traditional mind–body problem has two dimensions which have often been run together—or, at least, not carefully distinguished: (1) What is the relation of sensations to physical states of the body? (2) What is the relation of conceptual states (thinkings, inner speech) to physical states of the body? It should not be assumed that these two dimensions of the mind–body problem admit of the same type of solution.

II

7. How is the postulated analogy between Mentalese and overt linguistic behavior to be understood? To begin with, we must simplify our own model by abstracting from those features of language by virtue of which it is an instrument for influencing people. As Austin has emphasized, we can *do* things with words. We can inform or misinform, we can communicate our beliefs, we can make promises, etc., etc. Illocutionary and perlocutionary acts are *actions*. Like all actions, they are sometimes deliberate, sometimes unintended, sometimes thoughtless.

8. But though I am going to abstract from these features of linguistic behavior, I am not going to remove *all* reference to linguistic action from the positive analogy, for some thought processes *are* actions—that is, are the sort of things that can be *undertaken,* that one can decide to do—and, consequently, a place must be left in our model for linguistic actions proper. Roughly, I am excluding only those linguistic actions which are other-oriented and involve language as a means of communicating with, making commitments to, and influencing our fellowmen.

9. The simplified model which I propose to work with can be called 'Verbal Behaviorism'. It is not intended as an adequate account of thinking; it is, indeed, radically oversimplified. But I believe that it will prove a useful tool which will help us

understand some of the features of thinking, and of our awareness of ourselves as thinking beings, which have been a source of puzzlement since the very dawn of philosophy.

10. According to this model, 'thinking that-*p*', where this means 'having the thought occur to one that-*p*', has as its *primary* sense saying '*p*' and a derivative sense in which it stands for a short-term proximate propensity to say '*p*'. Propensities tend to be actualized (a logical point about the term). When they are not, we speak of them as, for example, 'blocked'. For the purposes of the *VB* model, the relevant inhibiting factor which keeps the saying that-*p* from being actualized is that of not being in a thinking-out-loud frame of mind. One might use the model of a general 'on–off' switch which gets into the 'wiring diagram' when the child learns to keep his thoughts to himself.

11. Notice that I am treating that-clauses as quoted expressions; thus;

The thought that 2 plus 2 = 4 occurred to Jones

becomes, in the Verbal Behaviorist model,

Jones said (or had a short-term proximate disposition to say) '2 plus 2 = 4'.

I shall shortly take into account the fact that non-English-speaking people are not precluded from thinking that 2 plus 2 = 4. But our initial model will be provincial.

12. Picking up some themes from the above discussion of linguistic *action,* it is essential to note that just as thinking that-*p*, in the sense of having the thought occur to one that-*p*, is not a mental *performance,* something that one does or could do voluntarily, so, in the *VB* model, saying '*p*' is not to be construed as an illocutionary act. It is to be construed, as I have elsewhere put it, as candidly *thinking-out-loud-that-p* and is not to be confused with asserting (to someone) that-*p*, telling someone that-*p*, or any of the verbal performances so lovingly collected by Austin.

13. Of course, in any ordinary sense, saying '*p*' is a performance, because the phrase permits the utterance to which it applies to be either a spontaneous thinking-out-loud-that-*p* or a deliberate use of words to achieve a purpose. I, on the other hand, am using the expression '*S* says *p*' in a *contrived* sense in which these options are closed and the utterance specifically construed as a spontaneous or candid thinking-out-loud.

14. We can imagine a child to learn a rudimentary language in terms of which he can perceive, draw inferences, and act. In doing so, he begins by uttering noises which *sound like* words and sentences and ends by uttering noises which *are* words and sentences. We might use quoted words

to describe what he is doing at both stages, but in the earlier stage we are classifying his utterances as *sounds* and only by courtesy and anticipation as *words*.

15. Only when the child has got the hang of how the sounds function in the language can he be properly characterized as saying 'this is a book', or 'it is not raining', or 'lightning, so shortly thunder', or 'you spanked me, so you don't love me'.

16. To say what a person says, or, more generally, to say what a kind of utterance says, is to give a functional classification of the utterance. This functional classification involves a special (illustrating) use of the expressions classified, or of synonyms—where allowance must be made for degrees of synonymy or likeness of meaning—of these expressions with which the addressee is familiar.

17. Some functional relationships are purely intra-linguistic (syntactical) and are correlated with the formation and transformation rules. Others concern language as a response to sensory stimulation by environmental objects—thus, candidly saying, or having the short–term propensity to say, 'lo! this table is red'. Still others concern the connection of practical thinking with behavior. All these dimensions of functioning recur at the meta-linguistic level in the language in which we respond to verbal behavior, draw inferences about verbal behavior, and engage in practical thinking about verbal behavior—i.e., practical thinking-out-loud (or propensities to think-out-loud) about thinking-out-loud (or propensities to think-out-loud).

18. Thus, when we characterize a person's utterances by using a quotation, we are implying that the utterance is an instance of certain specific ways of functioning. For example, it would be absurd to say

Tom said (as contrasted with 'uttered the noises') 'it is not raining' but has no propensity to avoid saying 'it is raining and not raining'.

19. In particular, to characterize a person's utterance by quoting sentences containing logical words is to imply that the corresponding sounds function properly in the Verbal Behavior in question, and is to imply that the uniformities characteristic of these ways of functioning are present in his sayings and proximate dispositions to say.

20. The functioning which gives the utterances of one who has learned a language their meaning *can* exist merely at the level of uniformities, as in the case of the fledgling speaker. Those who train him, thus, his parents, think about these function-

ings and attempt to ensure that his verbal behavior exemplifies them. In this respect, the trainer operates not only at the level of the trainee, thinking thoughts about things, but also at that higher level which is thinking thoughts about the functions by virtue of which first-level language has the meaning it does. In traditional terms, the trainer knows the *rules* which govern the *correct* functioning of language. The language learner begins by *conforming* to these rules without grasping them himself.

21. Only subsequently does the language learner become a full-fledged member of the linguistic community who thinks thoughts (theoretical and practical) not only about non-linguistic items but about *linguistic* items, i.e., from the point of view of our simple *VB* model, about first-level thoughts. He has then developed from being the object of training and criticism by others to the stage at which he can train and criticize other language users, and even himself. Indeed, he has now reached the level at which he can formulate new and sophisticated standards in terms of which to reshape his language and develop new modes of thought.

22. Notice that on the *VB* model of thinking, we can distinguish clearly between the *functional* role of utterances and the *phonemic* description of the linguistic materials which embody or are the 'vehicles' of these functions.

23. It is a most significant fact that the classical conception of thought as 'inner speech' (Mentalese) draws no such clear distinction between the conceptual *functions* of the Mentalese symbols and the materials which serve as the *vehicle* of these functions. Yet, if the analogy between thinking, classically construed, and overt linguistic behavior is to be a reasonably positive one, the idea that there must be inner-linguistic *vehicles* (materials) would seem to be a reasonable one. It is often thought that imagery is the vehicle of Mentalese— but there doesn't seem to be enough imagery to go round. And, indeed, the idea of imageless thought is by no means incoherent. What might the vehicle be?

III

24. To our *VB* model there are, in addition to the objections, considered yesterday, to any attempts to construe thinking on the model of language, three familiar objections which must be given more attention:

(1) Surely, it will be said, thinking that-*p* isn't just saying that-*p*—even candidly saying that-*p* as you

have characterized it. For thinking-out-loud that-*p* involves knowing the meaning of what one says, and surely this is no matter of producing sound!

Answer: There is all the difference in the world between parroting words and thinking-out-loud in terms of words. But the difference is not that the latter involves a non-linguistic "knowing the meaning" of what one utters; rather it is that the utterances which one makes cohere with each other and with the context in which they occur in a way which is absent in mere parroting. Furthermore, the relevant sense of 'knowing the meaning of words' (which is a form of what Ryle has called *knowing how*) must be carefully distinguished from knowing the meaning of words in the sense of being able to talk about them as a lexicographer might—thus, defining them. Mastery of the language involves the latter as well as the former ability. Indeed they are both forms of *know how,* but at different levels—the one at the 'object language' level, the other at the 'metalanguage' level.

25. I turn now to a second objection:

(2) Surely, it will be objected, we are often thinking when we are not saying anything. Our thoughts succeed one another with lightning rapidity. How can this be reconciled with the *VB* model?

Answer: It must be remembered that according to *VB,* thinking that-*p* is saying or having a short-term proximate propensity to say '*p*'. To grasp how rapidly short-term propensities can shift, one need only think of the electromagnet in a doorbell and consider how rapidly it acquires and loses the propensity to attract the clapper.

26. A third objection runs as follows:

(3) Thinking, as was pointed out above, does not seem to occur in words. We are often conscious that we are thinking, for example, about a certain problem, without 'any words going through our mind'.

Answer: Only a very naive person would think of the flammability of gasoline as a hidden or inner flame, or of the propensity of an electron to jump from one orbit to another as hidden jumping. Thus, the Verbal Behaviorist would point out that the short-term propensity to say "I've just missed the bus" should not be construed as an 'inner' or 'hidden' saying "I've just missed the bus." Thus, the Verbal Behaviorist believes himself in a position to account for the classical conception of thoughts as analogous to linguistic activity but as, nevertheless, involving no actual equivalents of the

words "in the mind." He sees the classical theory as an attempt to blend into one coherent picture items belonging to the radically different categories of act and propensity.

27. Above all, the *VB* model makes it clear how we know about thoughts. For in their primary mode of being, thoughts are publicly observable episodes: *people saying things.*

28. Thus, we can know what we think, in the primary sense, by literally hearing ourselves think. When we hear ourselves say (in a candid frame of mind) "I've just missed my bus," we are literally hearing the thought occur to us that we have just missed the bus.

29. And in hearing this, we would be thinking the higher-order thought:

The thought has just occurred to me that I have missed my bus.

And this higher-order thought would be an auditory perceptual response to one's actual thinking-out-loud "I've just missed the bus."

30. But what of those cases in which we know what we think, although we are not thinking-out-loud? The answer clearly does not consist in pointing out that thoughts in this sense are propensities to think-out-loud and that the propensities of things can be known by induction.

31. We know, for example, that acid turns litmus paper red by observing the relevant sequence in a number of cases and drawing a general conclusion from these observations.

32. And in more complicated cases we can, for example, know that our dog has the propensity to go and get his leash, because he, for example, sees us start to put on our rubber boots. And, in the most relevant type of case, people who know us very well are often able to predict what we are likely to think, given what is happening to us in the circumstances in which they see us.

33. Yet in reply to all this, the expostulation is surely justified that our own knowledge of what we are thinking (when we are *not* thinking-out-loud) is not *inductive,* is not an inference from our overt behavior, in the circumstances in which we find ourselves, to the existence of a certain propensity.

34. Yet the fact that we are able to learn the propensities of others (and ourselves) by inductive inference is the first step in the answer. But before developing it, we must consider how the account of perceptual experience sketched yesterday afternoon appears in the light of *VB.*

35. Thus, consider the case where

Jones sees there to be a red apple in front of him.

According to the account offered in the first lecture, this experience contains as its conceptual core the thought (which Jones is caused to have)

Here is a red apple.

36. In terms of our *VB* model, this becomes:

Jones thinks-out-loud: Lo! Here is a red apple.

37. Now to say that this visual thinking-out-loud that something is the case is epistemically *justified* or *reasonable* or has authority is clearly *not* to say that Jones has correctly inferred from certain premises, which he has good reason to believe, that there is a red apple in front of him. For we are dealing with a *paradigm* case of non-inferential belief. *The authority of the thinking accrues to it in quite a different way. It can be traced to the fact that Jones has learned how to use the relevant words in perceptual situations.*

38. It is for this reason that, when Jones candidly says, in response to visual stimulation,

Lo! Here is a red apple,

it is *likely to be true* that there is a red apple in front of him. I say *likely* to be true, because we all know of various ways in which things can go wrong. Jones is in front of a mirror; the supposed apple is a piece of wax; the illumination is abnormal and the object is really purple; or, there is nothing in front of him, but he has taken LSD, and people have been pounding his ears about red apples.

39. If we were to overhear him, and if we had reason to believe that none of these countervailing situations obtain, *we* would be justified in reasoning as follows,

Jones has thought-out-loud 'Lo! Here is a red apple'
(no countervailing conditions obtain);
So, there is good reason to believe that there is a red apple in front of him.

Note that although this is an *inferential* justification of *our* belief that there is a red apple in front of Jones, it is a special kind of inference. It has the form:

The thought that–*p* occurs to Jones in a certain context and manner;
So, it is reasonable to believe that–*p*.

The same proposition, that–*p,* is mentioned in both the premise and the conclusion. But the first mention concerns the fact of its occurrence *as a propositional event* in a context to which the basic features of language learning are relevant. From this premise, the inference is drawn that the proposition in question is one which it is reasonable to believe.

40. We looked at the above example from the standpoint of an external observer. Let us now look at it from the standpoint of Jones himself. As we saw in the preceding lecture, to be fully a master of his language, *Jones must know these same facts about what is involved in learning to use perceptual sentences in perceptual contexts.* Thus, Jones too must know that other specifiable[1] things being equal, the fact that a person says 'Lo! Here is a red apple' is good reason to believe that he is indeed in the presence of a red apple. Thus, Jones, *too,* can reason:

I just thought-out-loud 'Lo! Here is a red apple'
(no countervailing conditions obtain);
So, there is good reason to believe that there is a red apple in front of me.

41. Of course, the conclusion of this reasoning is not the *thinking* involved in his original perceptual experience. Like all justification arguments, it is a higher-order thinking. He did not originally *infer* that there is a red apple in front of him. *Now,* however, he is inferring from the character and context of his experience that it is veridical and that there is good reason to believe that there is indeed a red apple in front of him.

42. I wish now to argue that *VB* not only throws light on non-inferential perceptual knowledge but also gives us a strategy for coping with the problems posed by the existence of non-inferential knowledge of what we are thinking when we are *not* (candidly) thinking out loud.

43. The first step in the argument consists in pointing out that part of the process of learning to use a language is learning to make autobiographical statements. And not only autobiographical statements in general, but autobiographical statements about what one is thinking.

44. Now in the case of perception, non-inferential knowledge on the *VB* model, as we just saw, involves reliably *responding* to physical objects in standard conditions with the appropriate perceptual sentences; thus:

Lo! There is a red book over there,
Lo! Here is a pink ice cube,

in response to a red book or a pink ice cube, where the *reliability* of the response is a function of the way in which language is learned.

45. Now the more we know about a person, the better we are able to judge what (in the circumstances as we see them to be) he would be likely to say (think-out-loud)—if he were in a thinking-out-loud frame of mind. It is obviously difficult to be accurate about this, particularly when we are deal-

ing with sophisticated minds. But even here the difficulty is one in *practice* rather than of *principle*. And when it is children in the initial stage of learning a language who are the subjects, the difficulty in *practice* is substantially less than it becomes subsequently when they have learned to lie, deceive, and conceal their thoughts.

46. Can we not, as children, be trained by those who know us intimately (our parents), and who therefore know *(ceteris paribus)* what our short-term verbal propensities are (i.e., what we are thinking), to *respond* reliably to our own short-term propensities to say that-*p*, as well as to respond to our actual sayings of '*p*'?

47. And can not this ability be generalized in such a way that we can reliably respond to new propensities, i.e., to thoughts other than those in terms of which we have been trained? And would not the fact that such responses are *reliable* constitute the core of the explanation of non-inferential knowledge of what one is thinking (in the proximate propensity sense), as the existence of reliable verbal responses to perceptible things is the core of the explication of non-inferential perceptual knowledge?

48. Many have thought that to explicate the concept of non-inferential knowledge of 'what is going on in one's mind at the present moment', one must return to the Cartesian framework. From the point of view sketched in this lecture, the essential feature of the latter framework is that it denies that 'thinking-out-loud' makes sense save as analyzable into 'thinking *occurrent non-verbal thoughts* and giving them expression in one's verbal behavior'. In short, the Cartesian argues that the concept of thinking-out-loud *includes* the concept of thoughts as Cartesian inner episodes. According to the *VB* position, on the other hand, the concept of thinking-out-loud stands on its own feet as the *primary* concept pertaining to thought, so that if a concept *like* the Cartesian concept of thought *episodes* which are *not* propensities to think-out-loud does turn out to be needed in giving a full account of "what thinking is," those who are inclined to accept something like the *VB* position would argue that it is a concept built on a *VB* foundation and is in some sense a derivative or secondary concept. As a useful parallel, consider the case of micro-physics. Macro-objects, we say, if we are scientific realists, are *really* systems of micro-physical particles. Yet our concepts of these particles are built—not on direct observation—but on a foundation of knowledge at the perceptual level. In short, though *VB* argues that even if there is a sense in which Cartesian thoughts are prior in the order of being to thinking-out-loud, the latter is prior in the order of knowing.

IV

49. There are many delicate issues in this neighborhood, some of which can be left to slumber. Nevertheless, I introduced *VB* as a simple model, and while I have been polishing and defending it, it was introduced in order to be transcended. It correctly represents a basic stratum in our conception of what thinking is, but it is only a part of a larger picture, to which I now turn.

50. In the case of the dispositions and propensities of material things, we distinguish between the propensities and dispositions themselves, which are iffy states definable in terms of test conditions and empirically ascertainable results, on the one hand, and the *explanation* of these dispositions and propensities, which theoretical physics has made available, on the other.

51. Consider the case of our repeatedly magnetized soft iron. The repeated onslaughts and flights of the iffy property of being such that if iron filings are present, then they cling is, from the theoretical point of view, accompanied by certain actual physical processes which are induced by the current and other physical processes which replace them when the current is discontinued.[2]

52. Can we not regard classical theories of mental acts construed as *pure occurrents* (as contrasted with short-term propensities to think-out-loud) as *theories* in a sense which is analogous to micro-physical theories? Indeed, cannot we regard our common-sense conception of thought processes as such a theory? Such a theory would be designed to *explain* propensities to think-out-loud[3] as micro-physical theory is designed to explain the powers and propensities which we know things to have at the perceptual level, sophisticated by laboratory techniques.

53. The theory of 'inner speech' or Mentalese would construe these postulated thought episodes or occurrences as items which have a strong positive analogy with the thinkings-out-loud to which the *VB* calls attention. And it is interesting to note that when we refer to the thoughts which are occurring in a person's mind, we find it quite natural to quote them—even though they are not overt sayings. Yet the negative analogy must not be neglected. They are not thought of as waggings of an inner tongue. Nor, as we have seen, is the vehicle of Mentalese to be construed as imagery.

54. I shall not elaborate the theory, for this is done by classical philosophies of mind. The points I am interested in making are points *about* the theory rather than *in* it.

55. Perhaps the most important point is that what the theory postulates in the way of new entities are *processes* and *acts* rather than *individu-*

als. In this sense, it remains within the manifest image. Persons remain the basic individuals of the system. We have simply enlarged our conception of what persons do, as compared with the *VB* model with which we began. In addition to sayings and short-term propensities to say, we now conceive persons to be characterized by purely occurrent episodes of thinking in this analogically introduced sense. We might be tempted to refer to them as 'inner' episodes. But the spatial metaphor is misleading. They are primarily 'in' the person as *states* of the person. To be sure, they are not *perceptible,* but neither is solubility, and solubility is not in any more interesting sense 'in' the salt. It is only when we come to think that some particular part of the body (e.g., the heart or the brain) is the locus of these activities that the term 'inner' acquires richer meaning. And this is what begins to happen when the scientific revolution makes its impact on our conception of the world. But before I turn to this and other topics, let me sum up the picture of man and the world which I have been developing.

56. I introduced the manifest image of man-in-the-world as, essentially, an image which has been purged of the scientific objects postulated by physical science. The basic *individuals* which it countenances are certain merely material things, living things other than persons (about which I have had little to say), and persons.

57. The *attributes* which it ascribes to material things include, in the first instance, the proper and common sensibles. But it also allows in its universal discourse attributes which are definable in terms of sensible attributes, and of which the most interesting are the powers and propensities of material things to change in certain perceptible ways when subject to influences which are themselves definable in terms of perceptible qualities and relations.

58. Then there are persons. These individuals have perceptible characteristics and behave in perceptible ways. The behavior on which we have concentrated is the use of language. We restricted ourselves to that use of language which we called thinking-out-loud, and we developed a *VB* model according to which the meaningfulness of verbal behavior is to be found in the coherence which it exhibits, not only within speech itself, but in its relation to the contexts in which it occurs and the actions to which it leads. Here again, dispositions and propensities pertaining to perceptible traits of individuals were taken into account—in particular, the shifting short-term propensities to say things which, according to the *VB* model, are thinkings in a secondary sense of this term.

59. But notice that this austere conception of the person has been enriched in two important respects without introducing new individuals. Thus, *sensings* were introduced as theoretical states involved in the explanation, for example, of how it could seem to a person that there is a pink ice cube in front of him when in point of fact there is not. In both the veridical perception of a pink ice cube and a perceptual experience which *would* be veridical *if* there were such an object in front of one, the person senses a-pink-cubely, or, in more familiar terms, has a sensation of a pink cube (where 'of a pink cube' is to be construed depth-grammar-wise as an adjective) so that the expression might be parsed 'an of-a-pink-cube sensation'.

60. Again we began our account of thinking with a *VB* model but proceeded to sketch an account of mental acts as theoretical states or processes which provide some underpinning for the concept of Mentalese propositional episodes in terms of which the argument for sense impressions was couched.

61. Notice, however, that I have continued to abstract from the impact of the revolution in the physical sciences on the problem 'what is a person?' My appeal to micro-physics has been limited to suggesting that 'classical' thoughts as pure mental episodes can be interpreted as standing to *propensities to say* as micro-physical processes stand to the physical propensities of the familiar material things around us.

62. The *enriched* image of man-in-the-world, which includes sensings and Mentalese thinkings, but no individuals other than common-sense material things, living things other than persons, and persons, is what I have called the Manifest Image of man-in-the-world. Its coherence as a conceptual framework must be fully savored before one turns to the problem of assessing the impact on this Image of the scientific revolution.

63. An understandable consequence of the impact of the conceptual revolution in the physical sciences on the problem of the nature of the person was the resurgence of dualism—a dualism, however, arising from neither religious nor ethical considerations, nor from abstruse philosophical puzzles concerning the nature of knowledge, but rather from the attempt to think through the implications of science. The passage of time has intensified the problem of understanding the unity of the person (though not, of course, for those who take an instrumentalist stance toward scientific theories). The more sophisticated we get, the more intricate our puzzlement. We now await the flowering of neurophysiology, the science which is inheriting the glamor of molecular genetics.

64. The one thing we can be sure of is that we will be confronted with new ways of looking at

such 'familiar' facts as that neurons 'fire' and electro-chemical impulses are transmitted through networks and around circuits in the central nervous system. Science has already presented us with new and subtle categories. I suspect that newer and still more subtle categories will be needed to solve the problem of the place of persons in the scientific image of the world. The philosopher can attempt to see the future as in a glass darkly, but essentially his role must be the (by no means unfamiliar) one of a midwife.

65. Part of this midwifery will consist in submitting existing categories to critical examination, as Berkeley, Mach, and Poincaré, to name but three, did in the case of Newtonian mechanics. Part will consist in conceptual experimentation on a cooperative basis which will parallel the free thinking in logic, mathematics, and, dare I say, ontology which provided the context in which relativity was born. Nevertheless, an essential part of the philosopher's role in the concerted attempt to understand how a person is *really* related to what his body *really* is, is to clarify what, in outline, we already know *thinking* and *sensing* to be; and it is to this task that I've addressed myself in these first two lectures.

NOTES

1. Which is not to say that there are no cases in which we would not know what to say—e.g., electrode hallucinations.

2. A careful formulation would distinguish between the iffy truths at the theoretical level which are correlated with the original iffy truths, and the non-iffy processes of a theoretical character which are nomologically tied to these theoretical iffy truths.

3. And it is important to note that we all grant that there is such a thing as thinking-out-loud—though Cartesians give an account of it which presupposes the concept of non-verbal conceptual episodes.

B.　Sensing

40

Roderick M. Chisholm

from "The Status of Appearances"

The Problem of Democritus

When a man sees an external thing, say, a tree, his perception is the result of a complex physiological and psychological process. Light reflected from the thing stimulates the rod cells and cone cells in his eyes; in consequence of this stimulation, there is a further effect within the brain which, in turn, produces a visual sensation. Perception by means of the other sense organs is similar. In each case, the sensation (also referred to as the "sense impression," "appearance," "idea," or "sense datum") would seem to depend for its existence upon the state of the perceiving subject. Or to proceed somewhat more cautiously, the ways in which the things that we perceive *appear* to us when we perceive them depend in part upon our own psychological and physiological condition. This fact has led to some of the most puzzling questions of the theory of knowledge.

Democritus took it to imply not only that we do not perceive what it is that we think we perceive, but also that external things are not at all what we tend to believe that they are. The appearances of things, he said, "change with the condition of our body and the influences coming toward it or resisting it."[1] The question as to whether any particular thing will appear white, black, yellow, red, sweet, or bitter, he noted, cannot be answered merely by reference to the nature of the thing; one must also refer to the nature of the person or animal who is perceiving the thing. And from these premises, which are undeniable, Democritus then went on to infer (1) that no one ever *perceives* any external thing to be white, black, yellow, red, sweet, or bitter, and also (2), that no unperceived external thing *is*, in fact, white, black, yellow, red, sweet, or bitter.

The same premises have also been used to support other, equally extreme, conclusions. Oversimplifying slightly, we may say that Democritus reasoned in this way: "The wine that tastes sweet to me tastes sour to you; therefore, I do not perceive that it is sweet and you do not perceive that it is sour, and the wine itself is neither sweet nor sour." Protagoras, however, reasoned in a somewhat different way: "The wine that tastes sweet to me tastes sour to you; hence, I perceive that it is sweet and you perceive that it is sour; and therefore, one cannot say absolutely either that the wine is sweet or that the wine is sour; one can only say relativistically that whereas it is true for me that the wine is sweet, it is true for you that the wine is sour."[2] And some of the American New Realists, in defense of the view that "things *are* just what they *seem,*" drew still another conclusion: "The wine that tastes sweet to me tastes sour to you; therefore, one must say (absolutely and not relativistically) that there are contradictions in nature; one must say of the wine not only that it is both sweet and not sweet, but also that it is both sour and not sour."[3]

Variants of these arguments may be found not only in writings on popular science ("Physics and psychology teach us that the world is not at all like what we perceive"), but also in the works of distinguished psychologists and philosophers. Some philosophers, in order to avoid such extreme conclusions, have been led to question the premises. It has been suggested, for example, that the appearances of things may only *appear* to change with the condition of our body.[4] It has also been suggested that things may not actually appear in different ways—that it is a mistake to suppose that by altering either our perceptual apparatus or the conditions of observation, we can produce anything that

Roderick M. Chisholm, *Theory of Knowledge,* 1st ed. © 1966, from chapter 6, pp. 91–98. Reprinted with permission of Prentice-Hall, Inc., Englewood Cliffs, N.J.

might properly be called a change in the way in which a physical thing appears.[5] But such extreme measures are not at all necessary. We can accept the premises that Democritus used and, at the same time, reject his conclusions, for the conclusions do not follow from the premises. This would also hold true for the other versions of the argument.

Aristotle's Solution

Referring to Democritus, Aristotle wrote: "The earlier students of nature were mistaken in their view that without sight there was no white or black, without taste no savour. This statement of theirs is partly true, partly false. 'Sense' and 'the sensible object' are ambiguous terms; i.e., they may denote either potentialities or actualities. The statement is true of the latter, false of the former. This ambiguity they wholly failed to notice."[6]

In suggesting that the terms "white" and "black" are ambiguous, Aristotle is taking note of the fact that in certain uses, these terms are intended to refer to ways of appearing and that in other uses they are intended to refer to certain properties or dispositions of physical things—those properties or dispositions in virtue of which the things appear in the ways in which they do appear. If a physical thing *is* white, if it has the properties or dispositions to which Aristotle referred, then it is such that, when it is viewed by an ordinary observer under favorable lighting conditions, it will appear white to that observer. The physicist can tell us in detail just what the conditions are that a thing must satisfy if it is to have this property; that is to say, he can tell us just what characteristics a physical surface must have if it is to appear white to a normal observer in ordinary light. Let us say of such terms as "white," "black," "yellow," "red," "bitter," and "sweet," that when they are used to refer to these properties or dispositions, they have a *dispositional* use, and that when they are used to refer to ways of appearing, to ways in which things may appear, they have a *sensible* use. Aristotle is telling us, then, that the statement "Without sight, there is no white or black, without taste, no savour" is true if the terms "white," "black," and "savour" have a sensible use, and false if they have a dispositional use. Democritus, therefore, seems to have committed the fallacy of equivocation: Having established that the statement is true when it is taken in the first of these two ways, he goes on to infer fallaciously that it is also true when it is taken in the second.

And it is clear that in the passages referred to, Democritus does not establish his thesis about perception—his thesis that no one ever *perceives* any object to be white, black, yellow, red, bitter, or sweet. For the only argument that he presents in favor of this thesis is the fallacious argument in favor of his thesis concerning the nature of physical things.

Similar objections apply to the other versions of the argument. In each of the three versions considered, the terms "sweet" and "sour" have their sensible use in the premise ("The wine that tastes sweet to me tastes sour to you") and their dispositional use in the conclusion.

Sense-Datum Fallacies

The deceptive character of all three versions of the argument might be said to lie in the fact that certain truths about appearances are mistaken for truths about the things that present those appearances. From the fact that a thing's *appearing* white depends upon the condition of the perceiver, one infers mistakenly that the thing's *being* white is also something that depends upon the condition of the perceiver.

It is also possible to err in the other direction. One may make the mistake of supposing, with respect to certain truths about the things that appear to us, that they are also truths that hold of the appearances that those things present.

One such mistake, very frequently made, is that of supposing that if we perceive a physical thing, then we also *perceive* its appearances—that we see its visual appearances, hear its auditory appearances, feel its tactual appearances. But this is to misconceive the nature of perception. We perceive a thing when the thing as stimulus object has acted upon our sense organs, thereby causing us to be appeared to. The appearances of things, however, are not stimulus objects that affect our sense organs and therefore they are not themselves anything that we perceive. We do not see, hear, or feel the appearances of things.

Another such mistake may be more pernicious. From the fact that a physical thing *appears* white, for example, one might infer mistakenly that the thing presents an appearance which *is* white, and hence, that there are certain physical things and certain appearances which are alike in color. If this inference were sound, one could also say that, under favorable conditions of observation, the appearances of things have the same color as do the things themselves, in which case appearances could be said to *resemble* their objects in important respects. Thus, Lucretius suggested that when a man perceives a tree, a *simulacrum*—a small physical object having the characteristics that the tree is seen to have—is produced inside the head.[7] Subsequent philosophers have said that the appearance may "picture" or even "duplicate" the thing that appears.[8] And why *not* say that if a physical thing appears white, then it presents an appearance which *is* white?

For one thing, it is clear that the inference from "Something appears *F*" to "Something presents an appearance that *is F*" is not in general valid. For there are adjectives which are such that, if we replace "*F*" by any of those adjectives, then "Something appears *F*" will be true and "Something presents an appearance which is *F*" will be false. From "The man appears tubercular," we may not infer "The man presents an appearance which is tubercular," and from "The books appear worn and dusty and more than two hundred years old," we may not infer "The books present appearances which are worn and dusty and more than two hundred years old."

Moreover, there is an absurdity inherent in saying that an appearance and a physical thing may have the same color. If we say of a physical thing that it is white, we are saying that the thing is such that, when it is viewed by a normal observer under favorable conditions, then it will appear white. Suppose, then, that "It will appear white" does imply "It will present an appearance which is white," where "is white" has the sense that it has when it is applied to a physical thing. In such a case, a white, physical thing would be something such that, when it is viewed by a normal observer under favorable conditions, it will present an appearance which is such that, when *it*—the appearance—is viewed under favorable conditions, then it will present a (second-order) appearance which is white; the (second-order) appearance will therefore be such that, when it is viewed under favorable conditions, then it will present a (third-order) appearance which is such that . . . and so on, *ad indefinitum.*

If we thus assimilate appearances to substances or concrete things, we multiply entities—and problems—beyond necessity. We find ourselves confronted, for example, with such strange questions as: If the appearance can be white in the sense in which a rose can be white, does it also have a certain weight, an inside, and a backside? Could it be that the backside of the white appearance, the side that (somehow) faces away, is green, or blue, or yellow?

But what is the appearance if it is not a substance or concrete thing?

The Adverbial Theory

When we say "The appearance of the thing is white," our language suggests that we are attributing a certain property to a substance. But we could just as well have said "The thing appears white," using the verb "appears" instead of the substantive "appearance." And in "The thing appears white," as already noted, the word "white" functions as an adverb.[9] Ordinarily, the point of an adverb is not to attribute a property to a substance, but to attribute a property to another property ("He is exceptionally tall") or to attribute a property to an event, process, or state of affairs ("He is walking slowly"). We might say, then, that the word "white," in what we have called its sensible use, tells us something about that state of affairs which is an object's appearing; it tells us something about the *way* in which the object appears, just as "slowly" may tell us something about the way in which an object moves.

We have noted, however, that a man may be presented with a "white appearance" when no object is appearing (say, when he is thinking about a possible white object). Hence, if we are to speak more strictly, we should not say that "white," in its sensible use, always refers to the way in which an object appears; it refers, rather, to the way in which one is *appeared to*—whether or not an object appears. Or if we introduce an active verb such as "sensing" or "experiencing" as a synonym for the passive "is appeared to," we could say that "white," in its sensible use, refers to the way in which a man may sense or experience.

No longer needing such expressions as "white appearance," we need not countenance the question as to whether the white appearance has a certain weight, or a backside, or an inside. And thus, we need not wonder whether the backside of a white appearance might be green, or blue, or yellow. We need not ask whether appearances might exist unsensed—whether, in Bertrand Russell's terms, there are "unsensed sensibilia."[10] And we need not ask whether appearances might be identical with parts of the external physical things that we perceive—whether the white appearance that we sense might be identical with the surface of the white object that we see. For in saying "He is appeared to white," or "He senses whitely," we are not committed to saying that there *is* a thing—an appearance—of which the word "white," in its sensible use, designates a property. We are saying, rather, that there is a certain state or process—that of being appeared to, or sensing, or experiencing—and we are using the adjective "white," or the adverb "whitely," to describe more specifically the way in which that process occurs.

The Phenomenological Problem

One may feel, however, that this "adverbial" theory leaves something out. Even if the appearance is not a *simulacrum* of the object that appears, the relation between the appearance and the object may seem to be more intimate than the "adverbial" theory, as we have it so far, would allow. The problem of saying just what this relationship is may be called the phenomenological problem of appearances. The facts are familiar to everyone, but it is difficult to describe them without either overestimating or underestimating the role of appearances and without drawing unwarranted philosophical conclusions. The principal facts, I believe, are four.

(1) We perceive the object to have the characteristics we do perceive it to have, partly *because* of the way in which it appears to us. If the objects that we now perceive happened to appear in certain ways *other* than those in which they are now appearing, then we would not be perceiving them to be the objects that we are now perceiving them to be. It does not follow from these facts, however, that to perceive something to be, say, a tree, is to "make a causal inference" or "to frame the hypothesis" that a tree is one of the causes of the way in which one is being appeared to. Perceiving no more consists in deducing the causes of appearing, than reading consists in deducing the causes of ink marks.

(2) As we emphasized earlier, the appearance of a physical object—the way of being appeared to which the object as stimulus serves to cause—plays a fundamental role in the context of *justification*. If I ask myself Socratically what my justification is for thinking that it is a *tree* that I see, and if I continue my self-examination in the way we at tempted to describe in Chapter 2, I will reach a point at which I will justify my claim about the tree by appeal to a proposition about the way in which I am appeared to.

(3) A point of a rather different sort follows from one of the familiar features of perception. Whenever we *see* a physical object, then we also see certain parts of that object and fail to see certain other parts of that object. (But from the fact that we fail to perceive certain parts of the object, it does not follow that we fail to perceive the object. Verbs of perception are like "to be located in" and unlike "to contain." If one object contains another, then it contains every part of the other;

hence, New Hampshire contains every part of Jaffrey. But one object may be located in another without being located in every part of the other; what is in New Hampshire need not also be in Jaffrey.[11]) As the use of a microscope may suggest, every part that we see has parts of its own that we do not see. Similar remarks apply to perception by means of any of the other senses: Whenever we perceive an object by means of any one of the senses, there are certain parts of that object that we perceive and certain other parts of it that we do not perceive. With reference to these facts, we may now make our third point concerning the relation between perceiving and being appeared to: Whenever we perceive an object, then the object appears to us in a certain way; each of the parts that we perceive also appears to us in a certain way; and those parts that we do not perceive do not appear to us in any way.

(4) Using, for the moment, the terminology of "appearances," we may also say that the appearances of the parts of the object are included in the appearances of the whole. If, for example, a man is looking at a hen, then we may say of the hen itself, and of those parts of the hen that the man happens to see, that each of these objects presents an appearance. We can say of the hen that it is a whole in which these various parts (among others) are contained; we can also say of the appearance of the hen, that it, too, is a whole in which the appearances of the various parts are contained. Indeed we might say of the appearance of each part, that it is a part of the appearance of the whole. The appearance of the outer part of the tip of one of the feathers is a part of the appearance of the feather; the appearance of the feather is a part of the appearance of the wing; the appearance of the wing is a part of the appearance of the side of the hen; and the appearance of the side of the hen is a part of the appearance of the hen. And these facts, it must be conceded, are difficult to formulate, either in the terminology of "appearing" or in the terminology of "sensing" or "being appeared to."

If we use the terminology of "appearing," we might express the facts in question as follows: "The way in which a thing appears to a man includes ways in which some, but not all, of its parts appear, and the way in which any part of a thing appears is included in the way in which the whole appears." If we use the terminology of "being appeared to," we might say: "The way in which a man is appeared to by a thing includes ways in which he is appeared to by some, but not all, of the parts of the thing, and the way in which he is appeared to by any part of the thing is included in the way in which he is appeared to by the thing."

And if we use the terminology of "sensing," then we shall have to replace the "by" by some other preposition or phrase—possibly, "with respect to"—and say: "The way in which a man senses with respect to a thing includes ways in which he senses with respect to some, but not all, of the parts of the thing, and the way in which he senses with respect to any part of the thing is included in the way in which he senses with respect to the thing." It is clear that the terminology of "appearances," whatever its theoretical limitations, has a practical advantage at this point. But if I am not mistaken, the facts of the matter can be put in the terminology of "being appeared to."

*   *   *   *   *

NOTES

1. Fragment quoted from Milton Nahm, *Selections from Early Greek Philosophy* (New York: Appleton-Century-Crofts, 1934), p. 209; cf. pp. 173–87, 194–95.

2. See the discussion of Protagoras' view in Plato's *Theaetetus*, p. 145.

3. Cf. E. B. Holt, Ralph Barton Perry, and others, *The New Realism* (New York: The Macmillan Company, 1912), pp. 2, 365. For a more detailed discussion of New Realism and the views to which it led, see Roderick M. Chisholm, *Realism and the Background of Phenomenology* (New York: Free Press of Glencoe, Inc., 1960), and Roderick M. Chisholm, "Theory of Knowledge," in *Philosophy* (Englewood Cliffs: Prentice-Hall, Inc., 1964; Humanistic Scholarship in America, The Princeton Studies), by Roderick M. Chisholm, Herbert Feigl, William K. Frankena, John Passmore, and Manley Thompson.

4. Cf. G. E. Moore, *Philosophical Studies* (London: Routledge & Kegan Paul, Ltd., 1922), p. 245.

5. This suggestion seems to be presupposed by passages in J. L. Austin's *Sense and Sensibilia* (New York: Oxford University Press, Inc., 1962). Cf. the criticism of this book in Roderick Firth's "Austin and the Argument from Illusion," *Philosophical Review,* LXXIII (1964), 372–82.

6. *De Anima,* Book III, Chap. 2, p. 426a; see also *Metaphysics,* Book IV, Chap. 5. 1010b.

7. *On the Nature of Things,* Book IV.

8. "No man doubts that when he brings to mind the look of a dog he owned when a boy, there is something of a canine sort immediately present to and therefore compresent with his consciousness, but that it is quite certainly not that dog in the flesh." A. O. Lovejoy, *The Revolt against Dualism* (New York: W. W. Norton & Company, Inc., 1930), p. 305. This view has been called "the representative theory of perception." But it would seem advisable to avoid such expressions (along with "realism," "direct realism," "indirect realism," "critical realism," and the like), since they have come to be used in many different and conflicting ways by people who write about philosophy.

9. The point is developed in detail by C. J. Ducasse, *Nature, Mind and Death* (La Salle, Ill.: Open Court Publishing Co., 1949), Chap. 13. This general view of appearing is suggested by Thomas Reid, in his *Essays on the Intellectual Powers of Man,* Essay I, Sec. 12, and by G. F. Stout, in "Are Presentations Mental or Physical?" *Proceedings of the Aristotelian Society,* n.s., Vol. IX (1909).

10. See the essay "The Relation of Sense-Data to Physics," in Russell's *Mysticism and Logic* (New York: W. W. Norton & Company, Inc., 1929); this book was first published in 1918.

11. C. D. Broad once argued that, inasmuch as we do not see every part of the bell on any of those occasions on which, as we like to think, we see a bell, therefore, strictly speaking, we never see a bell at all; see his *Mind and Its Place in Nature* (New York: Harcourt, Brace & World, Inc., 1925), pp. 149–50. This is like saying that, since the butcher doesn't cut every part of the roast, therefore, strictly speaking, he doesn't cut the roast at all.

41

Frank Jackson

"The Existence of Mental Objects"

I

The mental objects I will be concerned with in this paper are such things as pains, itches and throbs—that is, the bodily sensations; and such things as after-images and mirages—that is, the visual hallucinations. There is a very widespread view that, while there may be things like the *having* of bodily sensations and the *experiencing* of after-images, there are, strictly speaking, no such things as bodily sensations and after-images. What exists includes the experiencing of pains and after-images, but not the pains and after-images themselves.

I will argue that there are considerable problems facing this denial of mental objects, and to this extent support that there are mental objects and the associated act-object account of having sensations and after-images. (The view that sensations and images exist, is just that. It is not that they exist *independently* of sentient creatures. It is an open question whether everything (that exists) exists independently, one to be settled by looking at cases—including ours of sensations and images.)

II

We talk as if there were mental objects: "*There is* a pain in my foot," "*This* after-image is brighter than *that* one," and so on.

This settles nothing as it stands. We once talked as if there were demons, and we now often talk about the average family or the next waltz; yet there are no demons, average families or waltzes. These three examples illustrate three ways to show that there are no *A*s. We were wrong about de-mons, because certain statements we took to be true turned out false (epilepsy is *not* caused by demons). There is no average family because statements that appear to be about this family can be given a reductive style of analysis in terms of the many non-average families that there are. The case with waltzes is different. No doubt, "The waltz is about to start" can be given a reductive analysis in which "waltz" does not appear. But it is sufficient to observe that "The waltz is about to start" can be construed as "People are about to start waltz-ing." We don't need a full-scale analysis of waltz-ing, we only need to know enough about the meaning of "waltz" to know that statements pu-tatively about waltzes can be, and are best, re-cast as about people waltzing.

Likewise, there are three ways we might seek to show that there are no mental objects: by showing that all statements of the form "*S* has a pain (itch, after-image, etc.)" are false; by producing a reduc-tive analysis of such statements, for example, of a behaviourist or topic-neutral kind, which elimi-nates the relevant psychological terms; or, finally, by offering a partial analysis (a recasting which bet-ter displays logical form) of these psychological statements, and which, while not eliminating all mentalist vocabulary, shows that these statements are not really about mental objects.

Of the first strategy, I will just say that I am sure it is mistaken, but do not know how to prove that it is. For I do not know of any premises which are more obvious than that it is sometimes true that we are in pain, having a red after-image, and so on, from which a proof might be constructed. The sec-ond strategy has been much discussed in connec-tion with the translation versions of materialism advanced by J.J.C. Smart and D. M. Armstrong. I

From *American Philosophical Quarterly*, XIII, 1 (January 1976): 33–40. Reprinted with permission of the editor.

don't find the analyses they give of psychological statements plausible for reasons that are familiar and which will be taken as read.

I will concentrate on the third strategy in this paper. I am sure the popularity of the denial of mental objects is due to the belief that it can be sustained by a relatively simple recasting of visual image and sensation statements without recourse to either a wholesale rejection of their truth or a full-scale, reductive analysis.

III

With one exception, our discussion of the third strategy applies equally to bodily sensations and visual images. The exception arises from Bruce Aune's suggestion that sensations can be regarded as relations between persons and their bodies. His ground for this is that "'I have a pain *in my arm*' . . . may be rephrased as, 'My arm pains me' or 'My arm hurts'."[1] But it is impossible for a relation to hold in the absence of its relata. Hence, if sensation statements essentially related persons to parts of their body, they could not be true in the absence of appropriate parts of the body. But the phantom limb phenomenon shows that they can be; and a statement that I have a pain "in a phantom limb" cannot be regarded by Aune as relating me to my phantom limb, because either phantom limbs don't exist or else they are a species of mental object (part of the "body-image"). Moreover, even if—as has sometimes been maintained—a pain in my phantom limb is really in my stump, the statement cannot be rephrased as "My stump pains me," because this is the translation of a quite different statement according to the view in question, namely "I have a pain in my stump."

IV

I now turn to examples to strategy three which are equally applicable to sensations and images. I will start by talking in terms of the sensation case and switch later, for variety, to the image case.

The following passage from Thomas Nagel's paper, "Physicalism," makes a convenient starting point.

> . . . we may regard the ascription of properties to a sensation simply as part of the specification of a psychological state's being ascribed to the person. When we assert that a person has a sensation of a certain description B, this is not to be taken as asserting that there exist an x and a y such that x is a person and y is a sensation and $B(y)$ and x has y. Rather we are to

take it as asserting the existence of only one thing, x, such that x is a person, and moreover $C(x)$, where C is the attribute "has a sensation of description B."[2]

Nagel's general idea is to switch from predicates on or descriptions of sensations, to predicates on or descriptions of persons: strictly, nothing is painful, but many things are persons with painful sensations. But how does the switch he recommends dispose of sensations?

Every description of my brother can be transposed to a description of me without meaning loss: "My brother is tall," for instance, goes to "I have a tall brother." But the possibility of switching from "is tall" as a predicate on my brother to "has a tall brother" as a predicate on me is irrelevant to the question of my brother's existence. What matters is how we ought to understand the predicate "has a tall brother"; the answer in this case being that it is to be understood as formed from a relation by filling an argument place with a singular term. Likewise, what is crucial for whether sensations exist, is not just that a statement like "My pain is severe" can be rendered as "I have a severe pain"; but whether or not it can be so rendered with the predicate "has a severe pain" understood other than as containing "a pain" functioning as a singular term filling an argument place in the relation "x has y."

V

Can we, then, view the semantic structure of "has a painful sensation" and the like so as not to commit ourselves to there being painful sensations?

The simplest such view would be the view which sees nothing; the view, that is, that sensation predicates on persons have no semantic structure at all; they have meaning only as wholes; a view we might express by writing "has-a-painful-sensation" or "hasapainfulsensation."

This is holism gone mad. It is perfectly obvious, for example, that the meanings of "has a burning pain" and "has a burning itch" are related, and that this relation is a function of the common term "burning": if they did not have this term is common, the relation would not be the same. But to concede that the appearance of "burning" in *both* is semantically significant is to concede that its appearance in *either* is, which is to concede that the predicates are semantically structured.

Given the unacceptibility of this no-structure theory, what theories are open to one who denies that there are mental objects? Just two seem to have either currency or plausibility: the first I will call the state theory, the second the adverbial theory.

VI

Those who deny that there are mental objects commonly make considerable use of terms like "state" and "condition." For instance, Nagel urges that to say that a person has a pain "describes a *condition* of one entity, the person," and again "we may regard the ascription of properties to a sensation simply as part of the specification of a psychological *state's* being ascribed to the person."[3]

This suggests a state theory of the following kind. "I have a throbbing, painful sensation in my knee" does not relate me to my sensation, saying of it that it is throbbing, painful and in my knee; rather it is about me and a state (or condition) of mine: it says that I am in a throbbing, painful, in my knee sensation-state. The sensing, not the sensation has the properties.

Does this really achieve anything? On the act-object theory, "I have a painful sensation" is explicated as "$(\exists x)$[I have x & x is painful & x is a sensation]," while on the state theory we get "$(\exists x)$[I am in x & x is a sensation state & x is painful]." The gain appears to be verbal rather than ontological.

The state theorist has some sort of reply if he distinguishes *unitary* states from *relational* states. A unitary state of a person is a state of that person not essentially involving anything over and above that person. My being happy, to take a psychological example, and my being warm, to take a physical example, are both unitary states of mine. There is a natural, if philosophically difficult, sense in which my being happy or being warm at some time are not things over and above and distinct from me at that time. This is essentially linked to the connection between the counting principles for persons and their unitary states: for a given person at a time, there cannot be more than one unitary state of a given kind. For instance, there cannot be more cases of persons being warm (happy) in a room than there are persons. If this were not so, if there might be two unitary states of a given kind for one person at one time, there would be no sense to the claim that such states were, in some substantial sense, nothing over and above the one subject in these states. Therefore, if the state theorist insists that the sensation states—the sensings—are unitary, rather than relational states like being happy *at* or being warmed *by,* it appears he has a theory distinct from the act-object theory.

He also has a theory exposed to two serious objections. I will call the first, the many property objection, and the second, the complement objection.

VII

The many property objection arises from the fact that we ascribe many things to our sensations: a sensation may be painful *and* burning *and* in the foot. How can a state theorist handle this?

The state theorist transcribes "I have an F sensation" as "I am in an F sensation-state." Hence, the obvious account for him to give of "I have a sensation which is F and G" is "I am in a sensation-state which is F and G."

This account faces a decisive difficulty. Suppose I have a sensation which is F and a sensation which is G, then, on the state theory, I am in a sensation-state which is F and in one which is G. But there may be at a given time be only one such unitary state for a given person; therefore, I am in a sensation-state which is F and G. But the latter is the preferred account of "I have a sensation which is F and G." Hence, we have "I have a sensation which is F and sensation which is G" entailing "I have a sensation which is F and G," which is quite wrong. For I may have one sensation which is F and, at the same time, another which is G. That is, having, for example, a burning, painful sensation is being conflated with having a burning sensation and a painful sensation.

The state theorist must, therefore, give a different account of statements that a particular sensation is F and G and. . . . It turns out that the various possibilities are essentially the same as those that arise in the discussion of the corresponding objection to the adverbial theory, so I will postpone the matter until then.

VIII

The complement objection to the state theory is a special case of a general way of showing that some term does not qualify a given thing, the way which proceeds by showing that if the term did, so might its complement.

The view that truth is a property of sentence *types* may be refuted by noting that "is true" and its complement "is not true" may apply to one and the same sentence type depending on the meanings given to the constituent terms of that type. A second example is the view that "school-age" in "I have a school-age child" qualifies having a child rather than the child; that is, that being of school-age is, strictly, a property of having children rather than of children. But "I have a school-age child" and "I have a non-school-age child" are both true. And nothing, including the having of children, can be both *F* and non-*F,* hence it is the children which are or are not of school-age.

Likewise, it may be the case that "I have a painful sensation" and "I have a non-painful sensation" are both true at the one time, hence we cannot construe being painful or not as a characteristic of the having of the pain rather than the pain. For if we did, we would have a state being both *F* and non-*F*. As with the first objection, the possible replies are essentially the same as those to the corresponding objection to the adverbial theory, and will thus be discussed then.

(A digression: the possibility of having different kinds of sensations at the one time also seems to me to undermine Descartes' suggestion that we view sensations on the model of impressions in wax: "I allow only so much difference between the soul and its ideas as there is between a piece of wax and the various shapes it can assume."[4] But it is impossible for one thing to be two different shapes at the same time; hence the analogy fails at a crucial point.)

IX

The most widely canvassed theory which denies that there are mental objects is the so-called adverbial theory.[5] Our discussion will be couched principally in terms of visual images (after-images, for example) rather than bodily sensations.

This theory utilises the fact that after-images, sensations, and the like, cannot exist when not sensed by some person (sentient creature), in order to reconstrue statements which purport to be about sensations, after-images and so on, as being about the way or mode in which some person is sensing. Thus, "I have a red after-image" becomes "I sense red-ly," and "I have a pain" becomes "I sense painfully." A parallel is often drawn with the elimination of talk about smiles in favour of talk about the manner of smiling; as in the recasting of "Mary wore a seductive smile" as "Mary smiled seductively."

My two objections parallel the two brought against the state theory.

X

Our statements about visual images are not just to the effect that an image is red, or square, or whatever; they are also to the effect that an image is red

and square *and.* . . . As with the state theory, I will refer to this as the many property problem.

Adverbial theorists have been rather reticent about how they handle this problem. It is clear that their view is that to have an image which is *F*, is to sense *F*-ly—the attribute, *F*, goes to the mode or manner, *F*-ly. But it is not clear just what account would be offered of having an image which is *F* and *G*. Do both of the (in their view, apparent) attributes go to separate modes, so that to have an image which is *F* and *G* is analysed as sensing *F*-ly and *G*-ly; or do we have a new, compound mode, *F*-*G*-ly? It seems to me that both of these answers, and the variants on them, face substantial difficulties.

Suppose having an *F*, *G* image is analysed as sensing *F*-ly and *G*-ly.[6] This conjunctive style of answer has the advantage of explaining the entailment from "I have a red, square image" to "I have a red image"; for it will correspond to the entailment from "I sense red-ly and square-ly" to "I sense red-ly."

But if it is adopted, it will be impossible for the adverbial theorist to distinguish the two very different states of affairs of having a red, square afterimage at the same time as having a green, round one, from that of having a green, square afterimage at the same time as having a red, round one; because both will have to be accounted the same, namely, as sensing red-ly and round-ly and square-ly and green-ly. In essence, the point is that we must be able to distinguish the statements: "I have an *F* and a *G* image," and "I have an *F*, *G* image."

In discussion it has been suggested to me that the adverbial theorist might have recourse to the point that when I have a red, square after-image at the same time as a green, round one, they must (as we say) be in different places in my visual field: the red one will be, for instance, to the left of the green one. But how can this help the adverbial theorist? For "I have a red after-image to the left of a green one" raises the same problem; namely, that it cannot be analysed conjunctively as "I sense red-ly and to-the-left-ly and green-ly"; for that is equivalent to "I sense green-ly and to-the-left-ly and red-ly" which would be the analysis of "I have a green after-image to the left of a red one."

Perhaps the thought is that "red" and "square" when applied to images are *incomplete,* they demand supplication with a term indicating location in a visual field. But this can't be right. I can know perfectly well what saying someone has a red or a square after-image means without having any idea at all of its location. Moreover, it is evidently not possible to give an exhaustive list, $p_1, \ldots, p_n$ of all the parts of a person's visual field that might be occupied by one of his after-images. So that "I have a red after-image" cannot be analysed as "I sense red-p_1-ly or ... or red-p_n-ly." The best that can be done is "$(\exists x)[x$ is a part of my visual field and I sense red-x-ly]," which—leaving aside the question of interpreting quantification into adverbial modification—commits the adverbial theorist to the existence of a species of mental object, namely, parts of visual fields, and so undermines the whole rationale behind his theory.

XI

An alternative approach would be to translate "I have an F, G image" as "I sense F-ly G-ly," and model the latter on "He wrote astonishingly slowly": "F-ly" being taken to modify "G-ly" rather than "sense," just as "astonishingly" modifies "slowly" rather than "spoke" in the model.

But the two essential features of "He wrote astonishingly slowly" are, first, that it is evidently not equivalent to "He wrote slowly astonishingly," and, second, that it does not entail "He wrote astonishingly": it is these two feature which lead us to distinguish it sharply from "He wrote astonishingly and slowly."

The adverbial theorist, however, cannot attribute either feature to his translations. He must allow that "I sense red-ly square-ly" is equivalent to "I sense square-ly red-ly," for they are, respectively, his translations of the evidently equivalent "I have a red, square image" and "I have a square, red image." He must also allow that "I sense red-ly square-ly" entails "I sense red-ly," for "I have a red, square image" entails "I have a red image." Having a red, square image is a special case of having a red image, while writing astonishingly slowly is not a special case of writing astonishingly (just as writing very quickly is not a special case of writing very).

XII

When talking of having a red, triangular sense-impression, Wilfrid Sellars talks of sensing red-triangular-ly.[7] The hypenation suggests an interpretation according to which red-triangular-ly is not a mode of sensing having red-ly as a component; it is, rather, a quite new mode of sensing; and so, the meaning of "red-triangular-ly" is not to be viewed as being built out of independently semantically significant components like "red" and "triangular"; and likewise for "green-square-ly," etc.[8]

Put thus, this view obviously faces the difficulty just considered. Having a red, triangular after-image is a special case of having a red after-image,

hence any adverbial theorist must treat sensing red-triangular-ly as a special case of sensing red-ly. But sensing red-triangular-ly fails to have sensing red-ly as even a component on this view.

It might, however, be refined. In discussions of the step from "This is a horse's head" to "This is a head," it is sometimes suggested that the latter should be read as "This is a head of something." In similar vein, it might be suggested that "I have a red image" should be expanded to "I have a red image of some shape," and consequently its adverbial translation should be expanded to "I sense red-some-shape-ly." On this view, red-ly isn't a mode of sensing at all. The modes of sensing are red-triangular-ly, green-round-ly, and so on; and sensing red-ly is to be understood as sensing red-square-ly or red-round-ly or red- ... -ly.

There are two serious difficulties facing this suggestion (apart from that of giving a precise construal of the dots). The first is that the modification appears to undermine the adverbial theorist's claim to be offering a philosophically perspicuous account of after-images. When I have a red, square after-image, the redness and the squareness appear as discriminable elements in my experience; and hence elements that it is desirable to have reflected in distinct elements of any offered analysis. But, on the modification in question, having a red, square after-image is accounted as sensing red-square-ly, where the hyphenation indicates that this mode of sensing is not to be further broken up into distinct elements. Indeed, on this view, someone who remarks on the common feature in having red, square after-image and having a red, round after-image is making a plain mistake. But, far from being a plain mistake, the remark looks like an evident truth.

The second objection derives from the point that there are indefinitely many things that may be said about one's images. An after-image may be red, red and square, red and square and fuzzy at the edges, red and square and fuzzy at the edges and to the left of a blue after-image, and so on. Now consider how the adverbial theory should handle "I have a red, square, fuzzy after-image." It cannot analyse this as "I sense red-square-ly and fuzzy-ly," for the same reason the conjunctive account had to be rejected. In brief, such a treatment would conflate "I have a red, square, fuzzy after-image" with "I have a red, square after-image and a fuzzy after-image." Should the theory then abandon the view that red-square-ly is a fundamental mode of sensing, and adopt the view that red-square-fuzzy-ly is a fundamental mode of sensing? On this further modification, "I have a red, square fuzzy after-image" would go to "I sense red-square-fuzzy-ly"; and "I have a red, square after-image" would be analysed as, roughly, "I sense red-square-fuzzy-ly or I sense red-square-sharply." Thus, on this further modification, red-square-ly, green-round-ly, and so on, are no longer modes of sensing; rather red-square-fuzzy-ly, green-round-sharp-ly, and so on, will be the various ways of sensing.

However, in view of the point this objection started with, this process of modification will continue without end. For any n that the adverbial theorist offers an analysis of "I have an $F_1, \ldots, F_n$ after-image" as "I sense F_1- ... -F_n-ly," he can be challenged for his analysis of "I have an $F_1, \ldots, F_{n+1}$ after-image"; and so, for the reasons above, be forced to abandon F_1-...-F_n-ly in favour of F_1-...-F_n-F_{n+1}-ly as a basic mode of sensing. This means that the adverbial theorist cannot ever give even a single example of a basic mode of sensing, and thus cannot ever complete even one of his adverbial analyses; and even if he could, would, moreover, end up with a theory no better than the no-structure one rejected earlier.

I suspect that some adverbial theorists who have written down expressions like "red-square-ly," have meant by the hyphenation no more than that mode of sensing associated with what we normally, and in their view misleadingly, call having a red, square after-image. But this is not to give us a theory we can oppose to the act-object theory, it is merely to express the hope that such a theory may be forth-coming. It is not to argue or show that we can do without mental objects, it is just to say that we can; for the central question of how to interpret the hyphenation is left unanswered except for a reference to the very theory being denied.

XIII

My second objection to the adverbial theory is the complement objection transferred from the state theory to the adverbial. Just as it is not possible for something to be F and non-F at the same time, it is not possible for a person at a given time to V both F-ly and non-F-ly. I can sing badly easily enough, but I cannot sing both well and badly at the same time; I can run quickly, but not both quickly and slowly; and I can inspect carefully, but not both carefully and carelessly; and so on and so forth.

Therefore, to have an image which is F cannot be to sense F-ly; for it is manifestly possible to have an image which is F at the same time as one which is non-F: I may have a red and a green after-image at the same time, or a square and a round one at

the same time; while it is not possible to sense F-ly and non-F-ly at the same time.

The only reply which appears to have any real plausibility here is to urge that, though one cannot V both F-ly and non-F-ly at a given time, one can V F-ly with respect to A and V non-F-ly with respect to B: I can, during a concerto, listen happily to the strings and unhappily to the piano. And that when I have a red and a non-red after-image together, I am sensing red-ly with respect to one thing and non-red-ly with respect to another. But what are these things with respect to which I am sensing, for there need, of course, be no appropriate physical thing in the offing? It is hard to see what they could be other than the mental objects of the act-object theory.

XIV

Two matters in conclusion.

(i) Terence Parsons claims that

(1) John wrote painstakingly and illegibly.

and

(2) John wrote painstakingly and John wrote illegibly.

are not equivalent because—though (1) entails (2)—(2) does not entail (1). He gives two cases which he claims show (2) may be true when (1) is false:

... if there were two separate past occasions on which John wrote, on one of which he wrote painstakingly, and on the other of which he wrote illegibly, but no past occasion on which he did both at once. ... Also if on one and the same occasion he wrote painstakingly with one hand and illegibly with the other.[9]

This might appear to threaten my arguments in two ways. First, in my discussion of the conjunctive reply in §10 I was clearly working under the general assumption that there is no significant distinction between a statement like (1) and the corresponding statement like (2). Second, Parson's second case where (2) may be true while (1) is false, could easily be modified to threaten the principle that one cannot V F-ly and non-F-ly at the same time, and so my discussion of complementation *vis a vis* the adverbial theory. The modification would be to consider a case where John wrote illegibly with his left hand while writing legibly with his right; would he then be writing legibly and illegibly at the same time?

The threat, however, is more apparent than real. This is obvious in the first case Parsons gives, because it involves considering *different* times of writing; and our discussion of the conjunctive reply involved just *one* time—we noted the possibility of having different visual images at the *same* time. In short, it is sufficient for us if "John is writing painstakingly and illegibly" is equivalent to "John is writing painstakingly and John is writing illegibly," and the first case does not threaten this equivalence.

With the second case we must remember that we are dealing with something that can be judged both overall and in a particular aspect. Normally, when we say that Jones wrote illegibly, we mean that overall the writing was illegible, not that every word was illegible (likewise, a speech may be impressive without every part of it being impressive). In this sense, "Jones wrote illegibly with one hand (his left, say)," does not entail that Jones wrote illegibly, for most of the writing may have been with his right hand in elegant copperplate; and similarly for "painstakingly." And in this sense Parsons will be right that it is possible that Jones wrote painstakingly with one hand and illegibly with the other without (1) being true, but equally this is possible without (2) being true, so the case fails to establish that (2) may be true without (1) being true.

On the other hand, if we take "Jones wrote illegibly" to count as true if any part or aspect of Jones' writing was illegible, and likewise for "painstakingly"; then if Jones wrote painstakingly with one hand and illegibly with the other, (2) must be true, but so will (1); and so there is still no case for denying that (2) entails (1).

Parallel remarks apply to the possibility of writing illegibly and legibly. It is not, in the overall sense, possible to write, on a given occasion, both legibly and illegibly (though it is possible to write in manner which deserves neither epithet). It is possible that one aspect of one's writing be legible and *another* be illegible. But we noted in §13 that the possibility of *V*-ing *F*-ly with respect to *A* while *V*-ing non-*F*-ly with respect to *B* is of no use to the adverbial theory; for the only plausible candidates for *A* and *B* in the sensing case are mental objects.

In general, whether or not one agrees with my discussion of (1) and (2), there is little comfort for the adverbial theorist in Parson's remarks. The case for distinguishing (1) and (2) rests heavily on there being something *more* involved than just the person (John's hand as well as John); and the adverbial theorist's aim is to effect an ontic reduction to the person alone in his account of sensing.

(ii) The second matter concerns the "predicate modifier" formal semantics for adverbs given by Parsons. By contrast with Davidson's event-predi-

cate treatment,[10] these semantics view adverbs as functions on predicates; and it might be thought that they could be appealed to by the adverbial theorist to elucidate "green-triangular-ly" and so on in a way which acknowledged structure without facing the problems of the conjunctive treatment.

The "predicate-modifier" theorist must, however, see a certain *intensionality* in *all* adverbs. "*X* senses" and "*x* breathes" are (we may suppose) co-extensional. But John doesn't breathe slowly if and only if he senses slowly, and the adverbial theorist won't allow that he breathes red-ly when he senses red-ly. Without going into the details,[11] this means that possible worlds (and beings) other than the actual must be invoked in predicate-modifier semantics. Hence, they achieve nothing for the adverbial theory. Perhaps (perhaps) we need possibilia for the elucidation of modal statements, but "I have a pain" and "I have a red image" are statements about the actual world, if any are. Moreover, appeal to possibilia would make a mockery of any claim of the adverbial theory to greater ontological economy than the act-object theory.[12]

NOTES

1. *Knowledge, Mind, and Nature* (New York, 1967), p. 130.

2. *The Philosophical Review*, vol. 74 (1965), p. 342.

3. *Ibid.*, p. 342. My emphasis.

4. *Descartes Philosophical Writings*, tr. by Elizabeth Anscombe and P. T. Geach (Nelson, 1954), p. 288.

5. Advanced in, e.g., C. J. Ducasse, *Nature, Mind, and Death* (Illinois, 1951); R. M. Chisholm, *Perceiving* (Ithaca, 1957); Aune, *op. cit.*

6. This is the obvious reading of Ducasse, *op. cit.*, ch. 13, §22.

7. In, e.g., *Science and Metaphysics* (London, 1968). Sellars ties his view to a topic-neutral analysis of the kind I have said (without arguing) is implausible.

8. Such a view is explicitly advanced by George Pitcher, "Minds and Ideas in Berkeley," *American Philosophical Quarterly*, vol. 6 (1969), pp. 198–207.

9. "Some Problems Concerning the Logic of Grammatical Modifiers," *Synthese*, vol. 21 (1970), p. 131.

10. In "The Logical Form of Action Sentences," *Logic of Action and Preference*, ed. by Nicholas Rescher (Pittsburgh, 1967). Adoption of this treatment would make the adverbial and state theories virtually indistinguishable.

11. But see David Lewis, "General Semantics," *Synthese*, vol. 22 (1970), esp. p. 28.

12. I am much indebted to Tim Oakley, Tom Richards and Barry Taylor for convincing me of the inadequacies of an earlier treatment of §10, 11, 12 titled "On The Adverbial Analysis of Visual Experience," *Metaphilosophy*, vol. 6 (1975), and to Keith Campbell and Chris Mortensen for comments on earlier drafts of this paper.

42

Frank Jackson

"What Mary Didn't Know"*

Mary is confined to a black-and-white room, is educated through black-and-white books and through lectures relayed on black-and-white television. In this way she learns everything there is to know about the physical nature of the world. She knows all the physical facts about us and our environment, in a wide sense of 'physical' which includes everything in *completed* physics, chemistry, and neurophysiology, and all there is to know about the causal and relational facts consequent upon all this, including of course functional roles. If physicalism is true, she knows all there is to know. For to suppose otherwise is to suppose that there is more to know than every physical fact, and that is just what physicalism denies.

Physicalism is not the noncontroversial thesis that the actual world is largely physical, but the challenging thesis that it is entirely physical. This is why physicalists must hold that complete physical knowledge is complete knowledge simpliciter. For suppose it is not complete: then our world must differ from a world, $W(P)$, for which it is complete, and the difference must be in nonphysical facts; for our world and $W(P)$ agree in all matters physical. Hence, physicialism would be false at our world [though contingently so, for it would be true at $W(P)$].[1]

It seems, however, that Mary does not know all there is to know. For when she is let out of the black-and-white room or given a color television, she will learn what it is like to see something red, say. This is rightly described as *learning*—she will not say "ho, hum." Hence, physicalism is false. This is the knowledge argument against physicalism in one of its manifestations.[2] This note is a reply to three objections to it mounted by Paul M. Churchland.[†]

1. Three Clarifications

The knowledge argument does not rest on the dubious claim that logically you cannot imagine what sensing red is like unless you have sensed red. Powers of imagination are not to the point. The contention about Mary is not that, despite her fantastic grasp of neurophysiology and everything else physical, she *could not imagine* what it is like to sense red; it is that, as a matter of fact, she *would not know*. But if physicalism is true, she would know; and no great powers of imagination would be called for. Imagination is a faculty that those who *lack* knowledge need to fall back on.

Secondly, the intensionality of knowledge is not to the point. The argument does not rest on assuming falsely that, if S knows that a is F and if $a = b$, then S knows that b is F. It is concerned with the nature of Mary's total body of knowledge before she is released: is it complete, or do some facts escape it? What is to the point is that S may know that a is F and *know* that $a = b$, yet arguably not know that b is F, by virtue of not being sufficiently logically alert to follow the consequences through. If Mary's lack of knowledge were at all like this, there would be no threat to physicalism in it. But it is very hard to believe that her lack of knowledge could be remedied merely by her explicitly following through enough logical consequences of her vast physical knowledge. Endowing

* I am much indebted to discussions with David Lewis and with Robert Pargetter.

† "Reduction, Qualia, and the Direct Introspection of Brain States," this JOURNAL, LXXXII, 1 (January 1985):8–28. Unless otherwise stated, future page references are to this paper.

From *The Journal of Philosophy* LXXXIII, 5 (May 1986):291–95. Reprinted with permission of the editors and Frank C. Jackson.

her with great logical acumen and persistence is not in itself enough to fill in the gaps in her knowledge. On being let out, she will not say "I could have worked all this out before by making some more purely logical inferences."

Thirdly, the knowledge Mary lacked which is of particular point for the knowledge argument against physicalism is *knowledge about the experiences of others,* not about her own. When she is let out, she has new experiences, color experiences she has never had before. It is not, therefore, an objection to physicalism that she learns *something* on being let out. Before she was let out, she could not have known facts about her experience of red, for there were no such facts to know. That physicalist and nonphysicalist alike can agree on. After she is let out, things change; and physicalism can happily admit that she learns this; after all, some physical things will change, for instance, her brain states and their functional roles. The trouble for physicalism is that, after Mary sees her first ripe tomato, she will realize how impoverished her conception of the mental life of *others* has been *all along.* She will realize that there was, all the time she was carrying out her laborious investigations into the neurophysiologies of others and into the functional roles of their internal states, something about these people she was quite unaware of. All along their experiences (or many of them, those got from tomatoes, the sky, . . .) had a feature conspicuous to them but until now hidden from her (in fact, not in logic). But she knew all the physical facts about them all along; hence, what she did not know until her release is not a physical fact about their experiences. But it is a fact about them. That is the trouble for physicalism.

II.   Churchland's Three Objections

(i) Churchland's first objection is that the knowledge argument contains a defect that "is simplicity itself" (23). The argument equivocates on the sense of 'knows about'. How so? Churchland suggests that the following is "a conveniently tightened version" of the knowledge argument:

(1) Mary knows everything there is to know about brain states and their properties.

(2) It is not the case that Mary knows everything there is to know about sensations and their properties.

Therefore, by Leibniz's law,

(3) Sensations and their properties ≠ brain states and their properties (23).

Churchland observes, plausibly enough, that the type or kind of knowledge involved in premise 1 is distinct from the kind of knowledge involved in premise 2. We might follow his lead and tag the first 'knowledge by description', and the second 'knowledge by acquaintance'; but, whatever the tags, he is right that the displayed argument involves a highly dubious use of Leibniz's law.

My reply is that the displayed argument may be convenient, but it is not accurate. It is not the knowledge argument. Take, for instance, premise 1. The whole thrust of the knowledge argument is that Mary (before her release) does *not* know everything there is to know about brain states and their properties, because she does not know about certain qualia associated with them. What is complete, according to the argument, is her knowledge of matters physical. A convenient and accurate way of displaying the argument is:

(1)′ Mary (before her release) knows everything physical there is to know about other people.

(2)′ Mary (before her release) does not know everything there is to know about other people (because she *learns* something about them on her release).

Therefore,

(3)′ There are truths about other people (and herself) which escape the physicalist story.

What is immediately to the point is not the kind, manner, or type of knowledge Mary has, but *what* she knows. What she knows beforehand is ex hypothesi everything physical there is to know, but is it everything there is to know? That is the crucial question.

There is, though, a relevant challenge involving questions about kinds of knowledge. It concerns the *support* for premise 2′. The case for premise 2′ is that Mary learns something on her release, she acquires knowledge, and that entails that her knowledge beforehand (*what* she knew, never mind whether by description, acquaintance, or whatever) was incomplete. The challenge, mounted by David Lewis and Laurence Nemirow, is that on her release Mary does *not* learn something or acquire knowledge in the relevant sense. What Mary acquires when she is released is a certain representational or imaginative ability; it is knowledge how rather than knowledge that. Hence, a physicalist can admit that Mary acquires something very significant of a knowledge kind—which can hardly be denied—without admitting that this shows that her earlier factual knowledge is defective. She knew all *that* there was to know about the experiences of others beforehand, but lacked an ability until after her release.[3]

Now it is certainly true that Mary will acquire abilities of various kinds after her release. She will, for instance, be able to imagine what seeing red is like, be able to remember what it is like, and be able to understand why her friends regarded her as so deprived (something which, until her release, had always mystified her). But is it plausible that that is *all* she will acquire? Suppose she received a lecture on skepticism about other minds while she was incarcerated. On her release she sees a ripe tomato in normal conditions, and so has a sensation of red. Her first reaction is to say that she now knows more about the kind of experiences others have when looking at ripe tomatoes. She then remembers the lecture and starts to worry. Does she really know more about what their experiences are like, or is she indulging in a wild generalization from one case? In the end she decides she does know, and that skepticism is mistaken (even if, like so many of us, she is not sure how to demonstrate its errors). What was she to-ing and fro-ing about—her abilities? Surely not; her representational abilities were a known constant throughout. What else then was she agonizing about than whether or not she had gained factual knowledge of others? There would be nothing to agonize about if ability was *all* she acquired on her release.

I grant that I have no *proof* that Mary acquires on her release, as well as abilities, factual knowledge about the experiences of others—and not just because I have no disproof of skepticism. My claim is that the knowledge argument is a valid argument from highly plausible, though admittedly not demonstrable, premises to the conclusion that physicalism is false. And that, after all, is about as good an objection as one could expect in this area of philosophy.

(ii) Churchland's second objection (24/5) is that there must be something wrong with the argument, for it proves too much. Suppose Mary received a special series of lectures over her black-and-white television from a full-blown dualist, explaining the "laws" governing the behavior of "ectoplasm" and telling her about qualia. This would not affect the plausibility of the claim that on her release she learns something. So if the argument works against physicalism, it works against dualism too.

My reply is that lectures about qualia over black-and-white television do not tell Mary all there is to know about qualia. They may tell her some things about qualia, for instance, that they do not appear in the physicalist's story, and that the quale we use 'yellow' for is nearly as different

from the one we use 'blue' for as is white from black. But why should it be supposed that they tell her everything about qualia? On the other hand, it is plausible that lectures over black-and-white television might in principle tell Mary everything in the physicalist's story. You do not need color television to learn physics or functionalist psychology. To obtain a good argument against dualism (attribute dualism; ectoplasm is a bit of fun), the premise in the knowledge argument that Mary has the full story according to physicalism before her release, has to be replaced by a premise that she has the full story according to dualism. The former is plausible; the latter is not. Hence, there is no "parity of reasons" trouble for dualists who use the knowledge argument.

(iii) Churchland's third objection is that the knowledge argument claims "that Mary could not even *imagine* what the relevant experience would be like, despite her exhaustive neuroscientific knowledge, and hence must still be missing certain crucial information" (25), a claim he goes on to argue against.

But, as we emphasized earlier, the knowledge argument claims that Mary would not know what the relevant experience is like. What she could imagine is another matter. If her knowledge is defective, despite being all there is to know according to physicalism, then physicalism is false, whatever her powers of imagination.

NOTES

1. The claim here is not that, if physicalism is true, only what is expressed in explicitly physical language is an item of knowledge. It is that, if physicalism is true, then if you know everything expressed or expressible in explicitly physical language, you know everything. *Pace* Terence Horgan, "Jackson on Physical Information and Qualia," *Philosophical Quarterly,* XXXIV, 135 (April 1984):147–152.

2. Namely, that in my "Epiphenomenal Qualia," *ibid.,* XXXII, 127 (April 1982): 127–136. See also Thomas Nagel, "What Is It Like to Be a Bat?", *Philosophical Review,* LXXXIII, 4 (October 1974): 435–450, and Howard Robinson, *Matter and Sense* (New York: Cambridge, 1982).

3. See Laurence Nemirow, review of Thomas Nagel, *Mortal Questions, Philosophical Review,* LXXXIX, 3 (July 1980):473–477, and David Lewis, "Postscript to 'Mad Pain and Martian Pain'," *Philosophical Papers,* vol. 1 (New York: Oxford, 1983). Churchland mentions both Nemirow and Lewis, and it may be that he intended his objection to be essentially the one I have just given. However, he says quite explicitly (bottom of p. 23) that his objection does not need an "ability" analysis of the relevant knowledge.

43

Sydney Shoemaker

"Functionalism and Qualia"

1

In their recent paper 'What Psychological States are Not,' N. J. Block and J. A. Fodor raise a number of objections to the 'functional state identity theory' (FSIT), which says that "for any organism that satisfies psychological predicates at all, there exists a unique best *description* such that each psychological state of the organism is identical with one of its machine states relative to that description."[1] FSIT is a version of 'functionalism', which they characterize as the more general doctrine that "the type-identity conditions for psychological states refer only to their relations to inputs, outputs, and one another."[2] Most of the objections Block and Fodor raise they take to be objections only to FSIT, and not to functionalism more broadly construed. I shall not be concerned with these objections here. But they raise one objection which, they say, "might be taken to show that psychological states cannot be functionally defined *at all* and that they cannot be put into correspondence with *any* properties definable over abstract automata."[3] Briefly put, the objection is that the way of 'type-identifying' psychological states proposed by FSIT, and by functionalism generally, "fails to accommodate a feature of at least some such states that is critical for determining their type: namely their 'qualitative' character."[4]

Block and Fodor devote only a couple of pages to this objection, and raise it in a fairly tentative way; so it is quite likely that the length of my discussion of it here is disproportionate to the importance they put on it. But they have given a concise and vivid formulation to an objection which is felt, and voiced in conversation, more often than it is expressed in print, and which seems to me to raise fundamental issues. Other philosophers have raised much the same objection by saying that functionalism (or behaviorism, or materialism, or 'causal' theories of the mind—the objection has been made against all of these) cannot account for the 'raw feel' component of mental states, or for their 'internal', or 'phenomenological', character. My primary concern here is not with whether this objection is fatal to FSIT; if I understand that theory correctly, it is sufficiently refuted by the other objections Block and Fodor raise against it. But as they characterize functionalism 'in the broad sense', it is, while vague, a view which many philosophers, myself included, find attractive; and it seems to me worth considering whether it can be defended against this objection.

I shall follow Block and Fodor in speaking of mental states (or rather, of some mental states) as having 'qualitative character(s)' or 'qualitative content'. I hope that it will emerge in the ensuing discussion that this does not commit me to anything which a clear headed opponent of 'private objects', or of 'private language', should find objectionable.

2

Block and Fodor develop their objection in two stages. The first of these they call the 'inverted qualia argument', and the second can be called the 'absent qualia argument'.

Because they are unpersuaded by the familiar

From *Philosophical Studies* XXVII, 5 (May 1975): 292–315. Copyright © 1975 by D. Reidel Publishing Company. Reprinted with permission of Kluwer Academic Publishers. The article is reprinted here, slightly revised by the author, in a version that first appeared in *Readings in the Philosophy of Psychology*, vol. I, Ned Block, ed. Cambridge, MA: Harvard University Press, 1980, pp. 251–67, with permission of the publisher.

'verificationist' arguments against the conceptual coherence of the 'inverted spectrum hypothesis', Block and Fodor are inclined to think that cases of 'inverted qualia' may be possible. They take it that there would be qualia inversion (presumably an extreme case of it) if it were true that "every person does, in fact, have slightly different qualia (or, better still, grossly different qualia) when in whatever machine table state is alleged to be identical to pain."[5] The possibility of this is incompatible with functionalism on the plausible assumption that "nothing would be a token of the type 'pain state' unless it felt like a pain, . . . even if it were connected to all of the other psychological states of the organism in whatever ways pains are."[6]

Block and Fodor do not regard the possibility of qualia inversion as constituting by itself a decisive objection to functionalism, for they think that it may be open to the functionalist to deny the *prima facie* plausible assumption that pains must be qualitatively similar (and, presumably, the related assumption that anything qualitatively identical to a pain is itself a pain).[7] If qualia inversion actually occurred in the case of pain (i.e., if a state functionally identical to a pain differed from it in qualitative character), then, they say, "it might be reasonable to say that the character of an organism's qualia is irrelevant to whether it is in pain or (equivalently) that pains feel quite different to different organisms."[8] Such a view is not in fact unheard of. According to Don Locke, "A sensation's being a pain sensation is not a matter of how it feels, but a matter of its being of the sort caused by bodily damage and leading to pain behavior."[9] And Alan Donagan has attributed to Wittgenstein the view that "you and I correctly say that we have the same sensation, say toothache, if we both have something frightful that we would naturally express by holding and rubbing our jaws, by certain kinds of grimace, and the like. Whether the internal character of what is expressed in these ways is the same for you as for me is irrelevant to the meaning of the word 'toothache'."[10]

But while Block and Fodor do not dismiss this response to the inverted qualia argument as obviously mistaken, they see it as possibly opening the door to an argument much more damaging to functionalism, namely the *absent* qualia argument. Their thought may be that once it is admitted that a given functional state can exist without having a given 'qualitative content', it will be difficult to deny the possibility that it might exist without having any qualitative content (or character) at all. At any rate, they go on to say that

> For all that we know, it may be nomologically possible for two psychological states to be functionally

identical (that is, to be identically connected with inputs, outputs, and successor states), even if only one of the states has a qualitative content. In this case, FSIT would require us to say that an organism might be in pain even though it is feeling *nothing at all,* and this consequence seems totally unacceptable.[11]

And if cases of 'absent qualia' are possible, i.e., if a state can be functionally identical to a state having a qualitative character without itself having a qualitative content, then not only FSIT, but also functionalism in the broad sense, would seem to be untenable.

3

If mental states can be alike or different in 'qualitative character', we should be able to speak of a class of states, call them 'qualitative states', whose 'type-identity conditions' could be specified in terms of the notion of qualitative (or 'phenomenological') similarity. For each determinate qualitative character a state can have, there is (i.e., we can define) a determinate qualitative state which a person has just in case he has a state having precisely that qualitative character. For example, there is a qualitative state someone has just in case he has a sensation that feels the way my most recent headache felt. Now, qualitative states will themselves be 'mental' or 'psychological' states. And this calls into question the suggestion by Block and Fodor that a functionalist could deal with the 'inverted qualia argument' by maintaining that "the character of an organism's qualia is irrelevant to whether it is in pain." If mental states include qualitative states, what such a functionalist says about pain could not be said about mental states generally, since it would be self-contradictory to say that the character of an organism's qualia is irrelevant to what qualitative states it has. And of course, if qualitative states themselves could be functionally defined, then the possibility of qualia inversion would pose no difficulty for functionalism, and the functionalist would have no need to make the counterintuitive denial that the character of an organism's qualia is relevant to whether it is in pain. But if, as Block and Fodor apparently assume, qualitative states cannot be functionally defined, then there is one class of mental states, namely the qualitative states themselves, that cannot be functionally defined.

This raises questions which I shall return to in later sections, namely (a) in what sense are qualitative states not functionally definable (or, in what sense are they not functionally definable if qualia inversion is possible), and (b) is their being functionally undefinable (in whatever sense they are) seriously damaging to functionalism? As we shall see in the remainder of the present section, this question is also raised by a consideration of the alleged possibility of 'absent qualia'.

We can establish the impossibility of cases of 'absent qualia' if we can show that if a state is functionally identical to a state having qualitative content then it must itself have qualitative content. One might try to do this by construing the notion of functional identity in such a way that qualitative states are included among the 'other psychological states' by relation to which, along with input and output, the 'type-identity' of a given psychological state is to be defined. Thus one might argue that if a given psychological state has a certain qualitative character, this involves its standing in some determinate relationship to some particular qualitative state (namely the qualitative state a person is in just in case he is in a state having that qualitative character), and that any state functionally identical to it must stand in the same relationship to that qualitative state, and so must have the same qualitative character.[12] But this argument is not very convincing. One objection to it is that since qualitative states cannot themselves be functionally defined (assuming the possibility of *inverted* qualia), it is illegitimate to include them among the psychological states by reference to which other psychological states are functionally defined, or in terms of which 'functional identity' is defined. I shall return to this objection later, since it is also a *prima facie* objection against the more plausible argument I shall present next. Another objection is that the relationship which a state has to a qualitative state, in having the 'qualitative character' corresponding to that qualitative state, is not anything like a causal relationship and so is not the sort of relationship in terms of which a psychological state can be functionally defined. But the argument I shall present next is not open to this objection, and does seem to me to show that on any plausible construal of the notion of functional identity a state cannot be functionally identical to a state having qualitative character without itself having qualitative character.

One important way in which pains are related to other psychological states is that they give rise, under appropriate circumstances, to introspective awareness of themselves as having certain qualitative characters, i.e., as feeling certain ways. I shall assume that the meaning of this can be partially unpacked by saying that being in pain typically gives rise, given appropriate circumstances, to what I shall call a 'qualitative belief', i.e., a belief to the effect that one feels a certain way (or, more abstractly, that one is in a state having a certain qualitative character, or, in still other terms, that

one has a certain qualitative state). Any state functionally identical to a pain state will share with the pain state not only (1) its tendency to influence overt behavior in certain ways, and (2) its tendency to produce in the person the belief that there is something organically wrong with him (e.g., that he has been cut or burnt), but also (3) its tendency to produce qualitative beliefs in the person, i.e., to make him think that he has a pain having a certain qualitative character (one that he dislikes). According to the 'absent qualia argument', such a state may nevertheless lack qualitative character, and so fail to be a pain. Let us consider whether this is plausible.

Supposing such cases of 'absent qualia' are possible, how might we detect such a case if it occurred? And with what right does each of us reject the suggestion that perhaps his own case is such a case, and that he himself is devoid of states having qualitative character? Indeed, with what right do we reject the suggestion that perhaps no one ever has any feelings (or other states having qualitative character) at all? It is, of course, a familiar idea that behavior provides inconclusive evidence as to what qualitative character, if any, a man's mental states have. But what usually underlies this is the idea that the man himself has a more 'direct' access to this qualitative character than behavior can possibly provide, namely introspection. And introspection, whatever else it is, is the link between a man's mental states and his beliefs about (or his knowledge or awareness of) those states. So one way of putting our question is to ask whether anything could be evidence (for anyone) that someone was not in pain, given that it follows from the states he is in, plus the psychological laws that are true of him (the laws which describe the relationships of his states to one another and to input and output), that the totality of possible behavioral evidence *plus* the totality of possible introspective evidence points unambiguously to the conclusion that he is in pain? I do not see how anything could be. To be sure, we can imagine (perhaps) that 'cerebroscopes' reveal that the person is not in some neurophysiological state that we ourselves are always in when we are (so we think) in pain. But this simply raises the question, on what basis can we say that *we* have genuine pain (i.e., a state having a qualitative character as well as playing the appropriate functional role in its relationships to input, output, and other psychological states)? Here it seems that if the behavioral and introspective evidence are not enough, nothing could be enough. But if they are enough in the case of us, they are enough in the case of our hypothetical man. In any event, if we are given that a man's state is functionally identical with a state that in us is pain, it is hard to see how a physiological difference between him and us could be any evidence at all that his states lack qualitative character; for if anything can be evidence for us about his psychological state, the evidence that his state is functionally equivalent to ours is *ipso facto* evidence that any physiological difference between us and him is irrelevant to whether, although not to how, the state of pain is realized in him.

To hold that it is logically possible (or, worse, nomologically possible) that a state lacking qualitative character should be functionally identical to a state having qualitative character is to make qualitative character irrelevant both to what we can take ourselves to know in knowing about the mental states of others and also to what we can take ourselves to know in knowing about our own mental states. There could (on this view) be no possible physical effects of any state from which we could argue by an 'inference to the best explanation' that it has qualitative character; for if there were, we could give at least a partial functional characterization of the having of qualitative character by saying that it tends to give rise, in such and such circumstances, to those physical effects, and could not allow that a state lacking qualitative character could be functionally identical to a state having it. And for reasons already given, if cases of 'absent qualia' were possible, qualitative character would be necessarily inaccessible to introspection. If qualitative character were something that is irrelevant in this way to all knowledge of minds, self-knowledge as well as knowledge of others, it would not be at all 'unacceptable', but would instead be just good sense, to deny that pains must have qualitative character. But of course it is absurd to suppose that ordinary people are talking about something that is in principle unknowable by anyone when they talk about how they feel, or about how things look, smell, sound, etc. to them. (Indeed, just as a causal theory of knowledge would imply that states or features that are independent of the causal powers of the things they characterize would be in principle unknowable, so a causal theory of reference would imply that such states and features are in principle unnamable and inaccessible to reference.) And if, to return to sanity, we take qualitative character to be something that can be known in the ways we take human feelings to be knowable (at a minimum, if it can be known introspectively), then it is not possible, not even logically possible, for a state that lacks qualitative character to be functionally identical to a state that has it.

This is not a 'verificationist' argument. It does not assume any general connection between meaningfulness and verifiability (or knowability). What it does assume is that if there is to be any reason for supposing (as the 'absent qualia argument' does) that it is essential to pain and other mental states that they have 'qualitative character', then we must take 'qualitative character' to refer to something which is knowable in at least some of the ways in which we take pains (our own and those of others) to be knowable. It also assumes that if there could be a feature of some mental state that was entirely independent of the causal powers of the state (i.e., was such that its presence or absence would make no difference to the state's tendencies to bring about other states, and so forth), and so was irrelevant to its 'functional identity', then such a feature would be totally unknowable (if you like, this assumes a causal theory of knowledge).

Against this argument, as against an earlier one, it may be objected that the other psychological states by relation to which (along with inputs and outputs) a given psychological state is functionally defined must not include any states that cannot themselves be functionally defined. For, it may be said, the states I have called 'qualitative beliefs' can no more be functionally defined than can qualitative states themselves. The most important relationship of these states to other states would appear to be their relationship to the qualitative states that characteristically give rise to them, yet (so the argument goes) the latter cannot be functionally defined and so cannot legitimately be referred to in functional definitions of the former. Moreover (remembering that the possibility of cases of *inverted* qualia is not here being questioned), it seems plausible to suppose that if two people differed in the qualitative character of their pains, but in such a way that the difference would not be revealed in any possible behavior, then they would also differ in their qualitative beliefs, and this latter difference too would be such that its existence could not be revealed in any possible behavior. And if this is possible, there seems as much reason to deny that qualitative beliefs are capable of functional definition as there is to deny that qualitative states are capable of functional definition.

This objection does not touch one important point implicit in my argument, namely that we cannot deny, without being committed to an intolerable skepticism about the pains of others, that someone's saying that he feels a sharp pain is good evidence that he has some qualitative state or other, and is so because someone's saying this is, normally, an *effect* of his having a state having qualitative character—and this by itself strongly suggests that if a mental state of one person has qualitative character, and if an otherwise similar state of another person lacks qualitative character, then the states differ in the ways they tend to influence behavior ('output') and hence differ functionally. Still, the possibility of 'inverted qualia' does seem to imply that qualitative states, and hence qualitative beliefs, cannot be functionally defined. To see whether this is compatible with functionalism, and whether it undercuts the argument given above, we need to consider in what sense it is true that qualitative states (and qualitative beliefs) are not functionally definable, and what limits there are on the ways in which reference to mental states that are not functionally definable can enter into functional definitions of other mental states.

In order to consider these questions I wish to change examples, and shift our consideration from the case of pain to that of visual experience. There are two reasons why such a shift is desirable. First, the possibility of 'spectrum inversion' (one person's experience of colors differing systematically, in its qualitative or phenomenological character, from another person's experience of the same colors) seems to me far less problematical than the possibility of 'qualia inversion' in the case of pain (pain feeling radically different to different persons). Second, and related to this, it is much easier to distinguish seeing blue (for example) from its qualitative character than it is to distinguish pain from its qualitative character, and accordingly much easier to consider how reference to qualitative states might enter into a functional account of seeing colors than it is to consider how reference to such states might enter into a functional account of pain.

4

If I see something, it looks somehow to me, and the way it looks resembles and differs from, in varying degrees and various respects, the ways other things look to me or have looked to me on other occasions. It is because similarities and differences between these 'ways of being appeared to' correlate in systematic ways with similarities and differences between seen objects that we are able to see these objects and the properties of them in virtue of which the similarities and differences obtain.[13] Being appeared to in a certain way, e.g., things looking to one the way things now look to me as I stare out my window, I take to be a qualitative state. So seeing essentially involves the occurrence of qualitative states. Moreover, reference

to these qualitative states enters into what looks very much like a functional account of seeing. For it would seem that what it means to say that someone sees something to be blue is something like the following:

> S sees something to be blue if and only if (1) S has a repertoire of qualitative states which includes a set of states K which are associated with the colors of objects in such a way that (a) visual stimulation by an object of a certain color under 'standard conditions' produces in the person the associated qualitative state, and (b) the degrees of 'qualitative' or 'phenomenological' similarity between the states in K correspond to the degrees of similarity between the associated colors, and (2) person S (a) is at present in the qualitative state associated with the color blue, (b) is so as the result of visual stimulation by something blue and (c) believes, because of (a) and (b), that there is something blue before him.[14]

I must now qualify the assertion that 'being appeared to' in a certain way is a qualitative state. If asked to describe how he is appeared to, or, more naturally, how things look to him, a man might say, among other things, that a certain object looks blue to him, or that it looks to him as if he were seeing something blue, or (if he is a philosopher who speaks the 'language of appearing') that he is 'appeared blue-to'. And it is natural to make it a condition of someone's being appeared-blue-to that he be in the qualitative state that is, in him at that time, associated with visual stimulation by blue things; that is, it is natural to give an analysis of 'S is appeared-blue-to' which is the same as the above analysis of 'S sees something to be blue' except that clauses (b) and (c) of condition (2) are deleted. But if we do this, then being appeared-blue-to will not itself be a qualitative state. Or at any rate, this will be so if spectrum inversion is possible. We might sum up the situation by saying that being appeared-blue-to is, on the proposed analysis, a functional state whose functional characterization requires it always to have some qualitative character (or other) but does not require it to have the same qualitative character in different persons (assuming the possibility of intersubjective spectrum inversion) or in the same person at different times (assuming the possibility of intrasubjective spectrum inversion). But this raises again the question of whether qualitative states are themselves functionally definable and, if they are not, whether they can legitimately be referred to in functional characterizations of other mental states.

The expression 'appeared-blue-to' could, I think, have a use in which it would stand for a qualitative state. I could 'fix the reference' of this expression by stipulating that it refers to (or, since it is a predicate rather than a singular term, that it predicates or ascribes) that qualitative state which is at the present time (April, 1974) associated in me with the seeing of blue things.[15] Understanding the expression in this way, if I underwent spectrum inversion tomorrow it would cease to be the case that I am normally appeared-blue–to when I see blue things, and might become the case that I am normally appeared-yellow–to on such occasions.[16] (By contrast, in the 'functional' sense of 'appeared-blue–to' sketched above, it could be true before and after intrasubjective spectrum inversion that I am normally appeared-blue–to when I see blue things, although of course being appeared-blue–to would have the qualitative character at the later time which another visual state, say, being appeared-yellow–to, had at the earlier time.) I do not think that there would be much utility in having expressions that were, in this way, 'rigid designators' (or 'rigid predicators') of visual qualia. On the other hand, I see no reason in principle why we could not have them. But if we did have them, they could not be functionally defined. Such terms would have to be introduced by Kripkean 'reference fixing' or (what is a special case of this) ostensive definition. To be sure, there is the theoretical possibility of giving a verbal definition of one of these expressions by making use of other expressions of the same sort; just as I might define 'blue' by means of a description of the form 'the color that is not yellow, or red, or green . . . etc.', so I might define 'being appeared-blue–to' as equivalent to a description of the form 'the color qualia which is neither being appeared-yellow–to, nor being appeared-red–to, nor being appeared-green–to, . . . etc.' But this is of very little interest, since it is obviously impossible that names (or predicates) for all visual qualia should be defined in this way without circularity. So, assuming that talk of defining functional states is equivalent to talk of defining names or 'rigid designators' for qualitative states, there seems to be a good sense in which qualitative states cannot be functionally defined.

But what seems to force us to this conclusion is the seeming possibility of spectrum inversion. I think that what (if anything) forces us to admit the possibility of spectrum inversion is the seeming conceivability and detectability of *intra*subjective spectrum inversion. And if we reflect on the latter, we will see, I believe, that while we cannot functionally define particular qualitative states, there is a sense in which we can functionally define the *class* of qualitative states—we can functionally define the identity conditions for members of this class, for we can functionally define the relationships of qualitative (phenomenological) similarity

and difference. This is what I shall argue in the following section.

5

Taken one way, the claim that spectrum inversion is possible implies a claim that may, for all I know, be empirically false, namely that there is a way of mapping determinate shades of color onto determinate shades of color which is such that (1) every determinate shade (including 'muddy' and unsaturated colors as well as the pure spectral colors) is mapped onto some determinate shade, (2) at least some of the shades are mapped onto shades other than themselves, (3) the mapping preserves, for any normally sighted person, all of the 'distance' and 'betweenness' relationships between the colors (so that if shades a, b and c are mapped onto shades d, e and f, respectively, then a normally sighted person will make the same judgments of comparative similarity about a in relation to b and c as about d in relation to e and f), and (4) the mapping preserves all of our intuitions, except those that are empirically conditioned by knowledge of the mixing properties of pigments and the like, about which shades are 'pure' colors and which have other colors 'in' them (so that, for example, if shades a and b are mapped onto shades of orange and red, respectively, we will be inclined to say that a is less pure than b and perhaps that it has b in it). But even if our color experience is not in fact such that a mapping of this sort is possible, it seems to me conceivable that it might have been—and that is what matters for our present philosophical purposes.[17] For example, I think we know well enough what it would be like to see the world nonchromatically, i.e., in black, white, and the various shades of grey—for we frequently do see it in this way in photographs, moving pictures, and television. And there is an obvious mapping of the nonchromatic shades onto each other which satisfies the conditions for inversion. In the discussion that follows I shall assume, for convenience, that such a mapping is possible for the full range of colors—but I do not think that anything essential turns on whether this assumption is correct.

Supposing that there is such a mapping (and, a further assumption of convenience, that there is only one), let us call the shade onto which each shade is mapped the 'inverse' of that shade. We will have *inter*subjective spectrum inversion if the way each shade of color looks to one person is the way its inverse looks to another person, or, in other words, if for each shade of color the qualitative state associated in one person with the seeing of that shade is associated in another person with the seeing of the inverse of that shade. And we will have *intra*subjective spectrum inversion if there is a change in the way the various shades of color look to someone, each coming to look the way its inverse previously looked.

What strikes us most about spectrum inversion is that if it can occur *inter*subjectively there would appear to be no way of telling whether the color experience of two persons is the same or whether their color spectra are inverted relative to each other. The systematic difference between experiences in which intersubjective spectrum inversion would consist would of course not be open to anyone's introspection. And there would appear to be no way in which these differences could manifest themselves in behavior—the hypothesis that your spectrum is inverted relative to mine and the hypothesis that our color experience is the same seem to give rise to the same predictions about our behavior. Here, of course, we have in mind the hypothetical case in which the various colors have always looked one way to one person and a different way to another person. And the situation seems very different when we consider the case of *intra* subjective spectrum inversion. In the first place, it seems that such a change would reveal itself to the introspection, or introspection *cum* memory, of the person in whom it occurred. But if this is so, other persons could learn of it through that person's reports. Moreover, and this is less often noticed, there is non-verbal behavior, as well as verbal behavior, that could indicate such a change. If an animal has been trained to respond in specific ways to objects of certain colors, and then begins, spontaneously, to respond in those ways to things of the inverse colors, and if it shows surprise that its responses are no longer rewarded in the accustomed ways, this will surely be some evidence that it has undergone spectrum inversion. In the case of a person we could have a combination of this sort of evidence and the evidence of the person's testimony.[18]

If we did not think that we could have these kinds of evidence of intrasubjective spectrum inversion, I think we would have no reason at all for thinking that spectrum inversion of any sort, intrasubjective or intersubjective, is even logically possible. To claim that spectrum inversion is possible but that it is undetectable even in the intrasubjective case would be to sever the connection we suppose to hold between qualitative states and introspective awareness of them (between them and the qualitative beliefs to which they give rise), and also their connections to perceptual beliefs about the world and, *via* these beliefs, to behavior. No doubt

one could so *define* the term 'qualitative state' as to make it inessential to qualitative states that they have these sorts of connections. But then it would not be in virtue of similarities and differences between 'qualitative states' (in that defined sense) that things look similar and different to people, and the hypothesis that people differ radically in what 'qualitative states' they have when they see things of various colors would be of no philosophical interest, and would not be the 'inverted spectrum hypothesis' as usually understood. Indeed, the supposition that intrasubjective spectrum inversion could occur, but would be undetectable, is incoherent in much the same way as the 'absent qualia hypothesis', i.e., the supposition that states 'functionally identical' to states having qualitative content might themselves lack qualitative content. Neither supposition makes sense unless the crucial notions in them are implicitly defined, or redefined, so as to make the supposition empty or uninteresting.

But what, then, are we supposing about qualitative states, and about the relationships of qualitative or phenomenological similarity and difference between these states, in supposing that intrapersonal spectrum inversion *would* be detectable? In what follows I shall speak of token qualitative states as 'experiences', and will say that experiences are 'co-conscious' if they are conscious to a person at the same time, where an experience counts as conscious to a person when he correctly remembers it as well as when he is actually having it. One thing we are supposing, if we take intrasubjective spectrum inversion to be detectable in the ways I have indicated, is that when experiences are co-conscious the similarities between them tend to give rise to belief in the existence of objective similarities in the physical world, namely similarities between objects in whose perception the experiences occurred, and differences between them tend to give rise to belief in the existence of objective differences in the world. And these beliefs, in turn, give rise (in combination with the person's wants and other mental states) to overt behavior which is appropriate to them. This explains how there can be non-verbal behavior that is evidence of spectrum inversion; the behavior will be the manifestation of mistaken beliefs about things which result from the fact that in cases of intrasubjective spectrum inversion, things of the same color will produce qualitatively different experiences after the inversion than they did before, while things of each color will produce, after the inversion, experiences qualitatively like those produced by things of a different color before the inversion.

But even if, for some reason, a victim of spectrum inversion were not led to have and act on mistaken beliefs about objective similarities and dissimilarities in this way, we could still have evidence that his spectrum had inverted—for he could tell us that it had. And in supposing that *he* can know of the spectrum inversion in such a case, and so be in a position to inform us of it, we are supposing something further about the relationships of qualitative similarity and difference, namely that when they hold between co–conscious experiences, this tends to give rise to introspective awareness of the holding of these very relationships, i.e., it tends to give rise to correct "qualitative beliefs" to the effect that these relationships hold.

Philosophers who talk of mental states as having behavioral 'criteria' have sometimes said that the criterion of experiences being similar is their subject's sincerely reporting, or being disposed to report, that they are.[19] If we recast this view in functionalist terms, it comes out as the view that what constitutes experiences being qualitatively similar is, in part anyhow, that they give rise, or tend to give rise, to their subject's having a qualitative belief to the effect that such a similarity holds, and, in virtue of this belief, a disposition to make verbal reports to this effect. But as a functional *definition* of qualitative similarity this would of course be circular. If we are trying to explain what it means for experiences to be similar, we cannot take as already understood, and as available for use in our explanation, the notion of believing experiences to be similar.

But no such circularity would be involved in functionally defining the notions of qualitative similarity and difference in terms of the first sort of relationship I mentioned, namely between, on the one hand, a person's experiences being qualitatively similar or different in certain ways, and, on the other, his believing in the existence of certain sorts of objective similarities or differences in the world, and, ultimately, his behaving in certain ways. I believe that a case can be made, although I shall not attempt to make it here, for saying that the tendency of sensory experiences to give rise to introspective awareness of themselves, and of their similarities and differences, is, for creatures having the conceptual capacities of humans, an inevitable by-product of their tendency to give rise to perceptual awareness of objects in the world, and of similarities and differences between these objects. And my suggestion is that what makes a relationship between experiences the relationship of qualitative (phenomenological) similarity is precisely its playing a certain 'functional' role in the perceptual awareness of objective similarities, namely its tending to produce perceptual beliefs to the effect that such similarities hold. Likewise, what makes a relationship between experiences the relationship of qualitative difference is its playing a corresponding role in the perceptual awareness of objective differences.[20]

This suggestion is, of course, vague and sketchy. But all that I have to maintain here is that the claim that we can give a functional account of qualitative similarity and difference along these lines is no less plausible than the claim that such mental states as belief and desire can be functionally defined. For my aim is not the ambitious one of showing that functionalism provides a fully satisfactory philosophy of mind; it is the much more modest one of showing that the fact that some mental states have 'qualitative character' need not pose any special difficulties for a functionalist. And an important step toward showing the latter is to show that the notions of qualitative similarity and difference are as plausible candidates for functional definition as other mental notions. I conceded earlier that there is a sense in which particular qualitative states cannot be functionally defined. But it will be remembered that what distinguishes qualitative states from other sorts of mental states is that their 'type-identity conditions' are to be given in terms of the notion of qualitative similarity. At the beginning of our discussion, specifying identity conditions in such terms seemed to contrast sharply with specifying them in functional terms. But this contrast becomes blurred if, as I have suggested, the notion of qualitative similarity can itself be defined in functional terms. And if the latter is so, and hence the identity conditions for qualitative states can be specified in functional terms, it seems not inappropriate to say, as I did earlier, that while particular qualitative states cannot be functionally defined, the *class* of qualitative states can be functionally defined.

6

Now let us return to the question of whether it is legitimate to make reference to qualitative states in giving functional definitions of other sorts of mental states.

On one construal of it, functionalism in the philosophy of mind is the doctrine that mental, or psychological, terms are, in principle, eliminable in a certain way. If, to simplify matters, we take our mental vocabulary to consist of names for mental states and relationships (rather than predicates ascribing such states and relationships), the claim will be that these names can be treated as synonymous with definite descriptions, each such description being formulable, in principle, without the use of any of the mental vocabulary. Mental states will indeed be quantified over, and in some cases identifyingly referred to, in these definite descriptions; but when they are, they will be characterized and identified, not in explicitly mentalistic terms, but in terms of their causal and other 'topic neutral' relations to one another and to physical inputs and outputs.[21]

Now what I have already said implies that names of qualitative states (if we had them) could not be defined as equivalent to such definite descriptions—on the assumption, of course, that 'qualia inversion' is possible. If the causal role played by a given qualitative state (in conjunction with other mental states) in mediating connections between input and output could be played by another qualitative state, and if that qualitative state could play a different role, then it is not essential to the state that it plays that causal role and it cannot be part of the meaning, or sense, of a term that rigidly designates it that the state so designated is *the* state that plays such a causal role. Moreover, since such a term could not be eliminated in this way in favor of a definite description, it could not occur within the definite description which functionally defines the name of some other mental state—assuming that the aim of such functionalist definitions is to eliminate mental terminology in favor of physical and topic neutral terminology.

But there is nothing in this to imply that qualitative states cannot be among the states quantified over in the definite descriptions that define other sorts of mental states. And it seems that it would be quantification over such states, rather than reference to particular states of this kind, that would be needed in the defining of other mental states. If spectrum inversion is possible, we do not want to make the occurrence of any particular qualitative state a necessary condition of seeing (or seeming to see) something blue, but we do want to require that at any given time in the history of a person there is some qualitative state or other that is (at that time) standardly involved in his seeing (or seeming to see) blue things. The specification of the roles of the qualitative states in the seeing of blue things will no doubt invoke the notions of qualitative similarity and difference; but this causes no difficulties for a functionalist if, as I have suggested, these notions can themselves be functionally defined.

There would appear, however, to be some mental states (other than qualitative states) that cannot be functionally defined in the strong sense here under consideration, namely in such a way that there is no essential (uneliminable) use of mental terminology in the *definiens*. For consider the

states I have called 'qualitative beliefs', i.e., beliefs about qualitative states and in particular beliefs to the effect that one is (oneself) in a particular qualitative state. Qualitative beliefs can be divided into two groups, those in whose propositional content there is reference to particular qualitative states, and those in whose propositional content there is quantification over qualitative states but no reference to particular qualitative states. So far as I can see, qualitative beliefs of the second sort provide no special difficulties for the functionalist; if other sorts of beliefs can be functionally defined, so can these. But qualitative beliefs of the first sort do seem to resist functional definition. Consider the belief I would express if I said 'I am in the state of being appeared-blue-to', using the phrase 'state of being appeared-blue-to' to rigidly designate a particular qualitative state. If we tried to characterize this state of believing functionally, i.e., in terms of its relationships to other mental states and to input and output, it would seem that we would have to make reference in our characterization to the qualitative state the belief is about—we would have to say that the state of believing that one is appeared-blue to is typically the result of the state of being appeared-blue-to. If so, it is impossible to define such states (qualitative beliefs of the first sort) without making essential use of mental terms.

But this constitutes no obstacle to our functionally defining other sorts of mental states. For while we may want to include in our functional characterizations of some kinds of mental states that they give rise to qualitative beliefs of the first sort (i.e., those in whose propositional content there is reference to particular qualitative states), this need not involve our making identifying reference to beliefs of this sort in our functional characterizations; all that this need involve is quantifying over such beliefs. Thus, for example, we can build it into our functional characterization of pain that being in pain typically results in some qualitative belief to the effect that one has some specific qualitative state, without saying of any specific qualitative state that being in pain tends to give rise to a belief about it. And if quantifying over qualitative states is permissible in giving functional definitions, I see no reason why quantifying over functional beliefs should not be permissible as well.

Now let us return briefly to my argument in section 3 against the possibility of cases of 'absent qualia'. In that argument I pointed out that it is characteristic of pains to give rise to introspective awareness of themselves as having particular qualitative characters, and so to give rise to 'qualitative beliefs', and I used this to argue that any state functionally identical to a state having qualitative character (e.g., a pain) must itself have qualitative character. The objection was raised to this argument that since qualitative beliefs, like qualitative states, cannot be functionally defined, they cannot legitimately enter into a functional account of the 'type-identity conditions' for other mental states. We can now answer this objection. No doubt pains give rise to qualitative beliefs of the sort that (so I am allowing) cannot be functionally defined, i.e., beliefs to the effect that one is having some specific qualitative state. But they also give rise to beliefs to the effect that one is in pain—and if (as the 'absent qualia argument' apparently assumes) pain is necessarily a state having qualitative character, then the belief that one is in pain presumably involves (at least in the case of a reflective person) the belief that one is in a state having some qualitative character or other. And while the latter belief is a qualitative belief, its propositional content quantifies over qualitative states rather than involving reference to particular qualitative states. No reason has been given why qualitative beliefs of this sort should not be regarded as functionally definable. And if they are functionally definable, there is no reason why the tendency of other states to give rise to such beliefs should not be part of what constitutes the functional identity of those other states. And this is all the argument of section 3 requires.

7

Over the last few decades, much of the controversy in the philosophy of mind has involved a battle between two seemingly conflicting sets of intuitions. On the one hand there is the intuition that mental states are somehow logically, or conceptually, connected with physical states of affairs, in particular the behaviors that are taken to manifest them. This intuition has found expression in a succession of different philosophical positions—logical behaviorism, the 'criteriological' views inspired by Wittgenstein, and, most recently, functional or causal analyses of mental states (these usually being combined with some form of materialism or physicalism).[22] On the other hand there is the intuition that connections between mental states and behavior are, at bottom, contingent; that under the most 'intrinsic' descriptions of mental states, it is a contingent fact that they are related as they are to behavior and to other sorts of physical states. And a common expression of this view has been the claim that spectrum inversion and other sorts of 'qualia inversion' are logically possible; for to say that these are logically possible is apparently to say that what intrinsic, internal character these mental

states have, their 'qualitative content', is logically irrelevant to their being related as they are to their bodily causes and behavioral manifestations. I have conceded that there is a substantial element of truth in this view. For I have allowed that spectrum inversion is a possibility, and have allowed that this implies that at least some qualitative states (and qualitative beliefs) cannot be functionally defined. But I believe that there is a substantial element of truth in the other view as well. I think that where the other view—the view that mental states are 'logically' or 'conceptually' connected with behavior—has its greatest plausibility is in its application to such states as desire and belief, and I think that these states do not have 'qualitative character' in the sense that here concerns us, although they may sometimes be accompanied by qualitative states. But as I have tried to show, even qualitative states can be accommodated within the framework of a functional, or causal, analysis of mental states. While it may be of the essence of qualitative states that they are 'ineffable' in the sense that one cannot say in general terms, or at any rate in general terms that do not include names of qualitative states, what it is for a person to be in a particular qualitative state, this does not prevent us from giving a functional account of what it is for a state to be a qualitative state, and of what the identity conditions for qualitative states are. Thus it may be possible to reconcile these firmly entrenched, and seemingly conflicting, intuitions about the contingency or otherwise of relations between mental states and the physical world.

There are a number of issues that would have to be investigated before it could be claimed that this attempted reconciliation is successful. The account of qualitative similarity and difference that I have suggested was tailored to the case of perceptual experiences, and it needs to be considered whether it can be plausibly applied to sensations like pains. What its application to the case of pain may require is the acceptance of the view of pains as somatic sense impressions, i.e., impressions (which need not be veridical) of bodily injuries and the like.[23] Also, this account of qualitative similarity and difference is tailored to the case in which the experiences being compared are experiences of one and the same person, and it needs to be considered whether it gives sense, and the right sort of sense, to intersubjective comparisons of experiences. This would involve, among other things, a consideration of whether it is possible for experiences of different persons to be 'co-conscious' in the sense defined earlier; and I think this reduces to the question of whether it is possible for there to be 'fusion' between persons of the sort envisaged in some recent discussions of personal identity, i.e., a merging of two persons into a single person (or single subject of consciousness) who then remembers, and is able to compare, the experiences the persons had prior to the fusion. (It is worth noting that if fusion is possible, then it is not after all the case that no possible behavior would reveal whether the color experience of two persons was the same or whether their color spectra were inverted relative to each other; for were the persons to fuse, the behavior of the resulting person could presumably settle this question.) But these are all complex issues, and I shall not attempt to discuss them here.[24]

NOTES

1. N. J. Block and J. A. Fodor, 'What Psychological States are Not', *The Philosophical Review* 81 (1972), p. 165.

2. *Op. cit.*, p. 173.

3. *Op. cit.*, pp. 173–174.

4. *Op. cit.*, p. 172.

5. *Op. cit.*, p. 173.

6. *Op. cit.*, p. 172. It is worth noting that this assumption, or one very much like it, plays a crucial role in Saul Kripke's recent arguments against the psychophysical identity theory; Kripke expresses it by saying that pain "is not picked out by one of its accidental properties; rather it is picked out by the property of being pain itself, by its immediate phenomenological quality. Thus pain . . . is not rigidly designated by 'pain' but the reference of the designator is determined by an essential property of the referent"; 'Naming and Necessity', in D. Davidson and H. Harman (eds.) *Semantics of Natural Language* (D. Reidel Publ. Co., Dordrecht-Holland, 1972, p. 340).

7. Block and Fodor mention another way, besides that mentioned in the text, in which a functionalist might try to meet the inverted qualia argument; he might maintain that "though inverted qualia, *if they occurred*, would provide counterexamples to his theory, as a matter of nomological fact it is impossible that functionally identical psychological states should be qualitatively distinct" (p. 172). The thought here must be that the mere logical, or conceptual, possibility of qualia inversion is not incompatible with functionalism. It would seem, however, that if the actual occurrence of inverted qualia would provide counterexamples to functionalism (as the envisioned reply concedes), then the mere logical possibility of inverted qualia is incompatible with functionalism; pain cannot be *identical* with a given functional state if there is a possible world, even a logically but not nomologically possible world, in which the functional state exists without pain existing, or *vice versa*. (On the general claim about identity here being invoked, namely that if *a* and *b* are identical they must be identical in any logically possible world in which either exists, see Kripke's 'Naming and Necessity', already cited, and his 'Identity and Necessity', in Milton K. Munitz, (ed.), *Identity and Individuation*, New York, 1971.

8. Block and Fodor, *op. cit.*, p. 173.

9. Don Locke, *Myself and Others*, Oxford, 1968, p. 101.

10. Alan Donagan, 'Wittgenstein on Sensations,' in G. Pitcher (ed.), *Wittgenstein: The Philosophical Investigations*, Garden City, New York, 1966.

11. Block and Fodor, *loc. cit.*

12. Just what is the relationship that a state must have to a qualitative state in order to have the qualitative character corresponding to that state? It cannot be, in the cases that concern us, the relationship of identity (that would permit only qualitative states to have qualitative character, and would not permit us to speak of the qualitative character of states whose 'type-identity' conditions are given in functional terms). And presumably it must be something stronger than the relationship 'is accompanied by', or 'is coinstantiated with'. The best I can do is to say that a particular token of a state *S* had the qualitative character corresponding to qualitative state *Q* if on the occasion in question the tokening (instantiation) of *S* essentially involved the tokening (instantiation) of *Q*. Possibly, but I am not sure of this, we could strengthen this, and make it less vague, by saying that on such occasions the token of *S* is a token of *Q*.

13. The 'being appeared to' terminology I take from Roderick Chisholm; see his "'Appear', 'Take', and 'Evident'", in R. J. Swartz (ed.), *Perceiving, Sensing and Knowing*, Garden City, New York, 1965, especially p. 480, footnote 6. One is 'appeared to' both in cases of veridical perception and in cases of illusion and hallucination, and can be appeared to in the same ways in all of these sorts of cases. The technical locution 'appeared-blue-to' is used in the text as an abbreviation for the locution 'sees or seems to see something blue' (on a 'nonepistemic' understanding of that locution).

14. As an analysis this will not quite do. I can see something to be blue even though it looks green (i.e., even if my visual qualitative state is that associated with green), if I have been 'tipped off' that in these circumstances blue things look green.

15. I take the notion of 'reference fixing' and the notion of a 'rigid designator' employed below, from Saul Kripke; see his 'Naming and Necessity', pp. 269–275 and *passim*. The use of a definite description 'the *x* such that *Fx*' to 'fix the reference' of a term *T* contrasts with defining *T* as equivalent in meaning to, i.e., as an abbreviation of, the definite description; in the former case, but not in the latter, the statement 'if *T* exists, then *T* is the *x* such that *Fx*' will be contingently rather than necessarily true. An expression is a rigid designator if it designates the same object in all possible worlds (or in all possible worlds in which it designates anything). According to Kripke, ordinary names are rigid designators, while many definite descriptions are not. When a definite description is used to introduce a name (and hence a rigid designator), it is used to 'fix its reference' rather than to 'define' it or give its 'meaning'.

16. My distinction between the 'functional' sense of 'appeared-blue-to' and a (possible) sense in which it rigidly designates (or, better, rigidly predicates) a qualitative state is similar to Chisholm's distinction between the 'comparative' and 'noncomparative' senses of expressions like 'looks blue'. See his *Perceiving: A Philosophical Study*, Ithaca, 1957, Chapter Four.

17. In a book which came to my attention after this

paper was written (*Form and Content*, Oxford, Basil Blackwell, 1973), Bernard Harrison presents empirical evidence against the possibility of what I am calling spectrum inversion. He also tries to show on a priori grounds—and here I find him much less convincing—that "the linguistic and conceptual machinery which governs colour naming works in such a way that any difference in the perceived content of the colour presentations seen by different speakers must show itself in differences in the way in which they apply colour names, or in the privileges of occurrence in sentential contexts which colour names display in their discourse" (p. 133).

18. Sometimes it is suggested that if someone reported having undergone spectrum inversion, the most reasonable thing for us to conclude would be that something had gone awry with his grasp of the color vocabulary. This overlooks the fact that such a report could be backed up by behavioral evidence of a non-verbal sort. And I think we can imagine a series of events that would leave us no alternative but to conclude that spectrum inversion had occurred. Let us represent the color spectrum by a vertical line, and let us, arbitrarily, divide the line into six equal segments, labeling these from top to bottom with the first six letters of the alphabet. And now consider the case of George. At time t_1 George's color experience, and his use of color words, was perfectly normal. But at time t_2 he tells us that a remarkable change has occurred; while most things look to him just as they used to, or look different only in ways that might be expected (e.g., if there is painting being done), a sizable minority of objects look to him very different than they did before, and he knows, from consulting other persons and from spectroscopic evidence, that in fact these objects have not undergone any significant change in color. George describes the change by saying that if he now looks at what we would regard as a normal spectrum, it looks the way a spectrum would have looked at t_1 if the end segments, A and F, had been interchanged and rotated one hundred and eighty degrees, the positions of the other segments remaining unchanged. According to this, the structure of George's color experience at t_2 is different from its structure at t_1. And since the putative change involves a change in structure, our evidence that it occurred need not be limited to George's testimony. George's claim will be supported by his recognitional and discriminatory behavior if, as we will suppose, he finds it easy to discriminate certain shades of color, for example those on either side of the boundary between segments A and B of the spectrum, which he formerly found it difficult to discriminate (and which the rest of us still find it difficult to discriminate), and sometimes finds it difficult to discriminate between different shades, for example if one is near the bottom boundary of segment A and the other is near the bottom boundary of segment E, which he formerly found it easy to discriminate (and which the rest of us still find it easy to discriminate). To continue the story, at time t_3 George tells us that another such change has occurred and added itself, as it were, to the first one; this time it is as if segments B and E of the spectrum had been interchanged and rotated. Again we can suppose that there is behavioral evidence to substantiate his claim. Finally, at time t_4 he tells us that still another such change has occurred; this time it is as if segments C and D had been interchanged and rotated. And again there is the substantiating behavioral evidence. But at t_4, unlike at t_2 and t_3, George's judgments of color similarity and difference will coincide with ours and with those he made

at t_1 (allowing, of course, for whatever objective changes in color may have occurred in the interim); at t_4 the 'structure' of George's color experience will be the same as it was at t_1. Yet George reports that his color experience is systematically different from what it was at t_1; each color looks the way its inverse looked previously. And this claim of George's seems to be supported by the behavioral evidence that supported his claims that there were changes in his color experience between t_1 and t_2, between t_2 and t_3, and between t_3 and t_4; for these partial changes add up to a total spectrum inversion.

19. See, for example, Carl Ginet, "How Words Mean Kinds of Sensations," *The Philosophical Review* 77, 1 (January, 1968), p. 9.

20. Further arguments for this view are presented in my "Phenomenal Similarity," *Critica* 7, 20 (October, 1975), 2–34.

21. This account of what functional definition would amount to, and the elaboration of it that follows, is based loosely on David Lewis' account in 'Psychophysical and Theoretical Identification', *Australasian Journal of Philosophy* 50 (December, 1972), pp. 249–258.

Starting with the 'theory' which consists of the set of 'platitudes' about relations of mental states to one another and to input and output which it is plausible to regard as analytic or quasi-analytic, we can define the mental terms in that theory (supposing them, for simplicity, to be names of mental states) in the following way. We first write the theory as a single conjunctive sentence. We then replace each of the mental terms in the theory with a different variable, forming an open sentence. We then prefix quantifiers which transform the open sentence into the 'modified Ramsey sentence' of the theory, which says (in effect) that there exists a unique n-tuplet of states satisfying the open sentence. We are now in a position to define any of the mental terms that occurred in the original theory. Supposing that T_i is the term we wish to define, and y_i is the variable we replaced it with in forming the modified Ramsey sentence, we can turn the modified Ramsey sentence into a definite description by (1) adding to the open sentence within the scope of the initial quantifiers the conjunct '$y_i = x$,' where 'x' is a variable that does not occur in the modified Ramsey sentence, and (2) prefixing the whole sentence with a definite description operator binding 'x'. What we then get is something of the form: (the x)(E!y_1) ... (E!y_i) ... (E!y_n)(...... y_i ...... & $y_i = x$). In this description there will occur no mental terms. And we can define T_i as being synonymous with this description. [*Editor's note:* In this anthology, the ordinary "E" is used instead of the backward "E" as the existential quantifier.]

I should emphasize that what I am characterizing here is only one version of functionalism. Many philosophers who would regard themselves as functionalists would disavow any intention of giving, or providing a recipe for giving, any sort of meaning analysis of psychological terms.

22. Some advocates of causal or functional theories of the mind, especially those who would not accept the characterization of functionalism in section 6 and footnote 21, would object to being put in this company. But others have clearly seen their accounts as incorporating what is correct in, or as explaining the intuitions which make plausible, behavioristic and criteriological views. See, for example, David Lewis, *op. cit.*, p. 257, David Armstrong, *A Materialist Theory of the Mind*, London, 1968, p. 92, and Alvin Goldman,

A Theory of Human Action, Englewood Cliffs, N.J., 1970, p. 112.

23. Such a view has in fact been advanced by D. M. Armstrong and by George Pitcher. See Armstrong, *op. cit.,* p. 313ff., and Pitcher's 'Pain Perception', *The Philosophical Review* 79 (1970), pp. 368–393.

24. I have benefited from discussions on this topic with Jonathan Bennett and Keith Lehrer, and am grateful to Bennett, and to N. J. Block, for criticisms of an earlier version of the paper. The paper was written while I was a Fellow at the Center for Advanced Study in the Behavioral Sciences, in Stanford, California, and I would like to express my gratitude to that institution.

44

Christopher Peacocke

"Colour Concepts and Colour Experiences"*

What is the relation between the concept of an object's being red on the one hand and experiences as of red objects on the other? That is the recalcitrant question to which this paper is addressed.[1]

The question contains the term of art "concept". This term will be used here correlatively at the level of properties as the phrase "mode of presentation" is used at the level of objects by Frege. Thus if the thought that an object presented in a given way is ϕ has potentially a different cognitive significance from the thought that it is ψ, then ϕ and ψ are different concepts. Our recalcitrant question concerns the realm of thought, informativeness and cognitive significance, rather than the realm of reference.

Why has the question, and similarly its analogue for any other secondary quality, proved so recalcitrant? The reason is that there exists an apparently straightforward dilemma about the relation between being red and experiences as of red things, i.e., experiences in which something looks red. There are arguments for saying that each must be more fundamental than the other. Someone does not have the concept of being red unless he knows what it is like to have a visual experience as of a red object; and the occurrence of such an experience is just an experience in which something looks red. The connection here is specifically with visual experience. Consider these two biconditionals:

> A perceptible object is red iff it looks red in standard circumstances

and

> A perceptible object is square iff it looks square in standard circumstances.

Both seem to be true, but they are not of the same status. For

> A perceptible object is square iff it feels square in standard circumstances

is as acceptable as the visual version in the case of squareness; whereas "feels red" makes no sense. Again, the congenitally blind can understand "is square". For these familiar reasons, visual experience seems to occupy a special position in an explanation of what it is for something to be red that no particular sense modality occupies in an explanation of what it is for something to be square. The point is not just that squareness is accessible to more than one sense: rather, what it is for something to have the property of being square cannot be explained in sensory terms at all. (Other differences are consequential on this.) These points are precisely what we should expect if looking red is conceptually more fundamental than being red. Yet on the other hand the expression "looks red" is not semantically unstructured. Its sense is determined by that of its constituents. If one does not understand those constituents, one does not fully understand the compound; and conversely, with a general understanding of the "looks" construction and of some predicate ϕ for which "looks ϕ" makes sense, one can understand the compound without the need for additional information. Equally on the side of thought rather than language, being red is precisely how an experience as of something red presents that thing as being: the remark is platitudinous. So from this angle it appears that looking red could not be more fundamental than being red. How is this dilemma to be resolved?[2]

From *Synthese* LVIII, 3 (March 1984):365–81. Copyright © 1984 by D. Reidel Publishing Company. Reprinted with permission of Kluwer Academic Publishers.

If colour is a coherent notion at all, it seems there are three possible types of response to this problem. These types are defined by the relations that they take to hold between the concept of being red on the one hand and concepts of experience on the other:

(i) The concept of being red is philosophically prior to that of looking red and to other experiential concepts. This is true not just in the uncontroversial sense that the phrase "looks red" contains "red" as a semantic constituent.[3] On this first type of view it is true also in the more substantial sense that an account of what makes an experience an experience as of something red must ultimately make use of the concept applicable to physical objects of being red, where this concept is not to be explained in terms of properties of experiences. This we will label "the antiexperientialist option".

(ii) Neither being red nor any relevant family of concepts true of experiences ("experiential concepts") is prior to the other: both have to be characterized simultaneously by means of their relations to one another and to other notions. This is the no-priority view.

(iii) The concept of being red has to be explained in terms of experiential concepts: this can be done in a way not undermined by the fact that "looks red" semantically contains "red" and without any circular use of the concept of being red. This might be called "the pure experientialist view"—"pure" because the no-priority view is a partially experiential view. But for brevity we will call a view of this third type simply "the experientialist view".

These three positions exhaust the possibilities only for a given notion of priority. I have written, very loosely, of the relation "more fundamental than", "conceptually prior to", and "philosophically prior to". To be more precise, my topic here is a priority of definability. We can say that concept A is definitionally prior to concept B iff B can be defined illuminatingly in a given respect in terms of A: the fixed relation of priority with which we are concerned is definitional priority, and the respect in which we want to be illuminated is what it is to have the concept of being red. There are other notions of priority in the offing: I will return to one of them later.

I take first the anti-experientialist view. One form such a view might take has been developed by Shoemaker: he holds, by implication, that the fact that an experience is as of something red consists in the fact that it would, in the absence of countervailing beliefs, give rise to the belief that the presented object *is* red.[4] Alternatively, such an anti-experientialist might try to characterize such experiences as those playing a certain role in an ex-

periandally-based ability to discriminate red from non-red things. In either case, the property of being red is employed in the account of what it is for an experience to be as of something red.

What, then, can the anti-experientialist say about the property of being red? His view collapses into the third option, that taken by the experientialist, if he attempts to explain redness in turn by appeal to the properties of experiences. One cannot assess the anti-experientialist's view, and neither can he establish the special connection with visual experience, until he gives some positive account of colour properties of objects.

One response that is not immediately circular is to say that the predicate "red" in fact picks out either a dispositional property of objects to reflect light of a certain sort, or picks out the categorical ground of this disposition. This is Armstrong's view, later adopted by Smart.[5] Such a view may have a relatively sophisticated structure. It may be said that after being introduced to certain sample objects as being within the extension of "red" one goes on to act in accordance with the definition that "red" picks out that state S of these objects which causes human observers to be in some experiential state which tends to give rise to the belief that some object has S, or tends to give rise to an ability to discriminate things with the property S. Such methods of introducing "red" are not formally illegitimate and avoid circularity, provided that the states quantified over can be characterized in terms other than "states which produce experiences of such-and-such kind". For instance, in verifying that some physical state T conforms to this more sophisticated definition, one has to check that T is possessed by the initial sample objects and that it produces in humans the belief that some object has T, or produces an ability to discriminate objects with the property T. The objections at this point are not those of circularity.

Told only that a word refers only to a certain object, we are not in a position to know what way of thinking of the object that word is used to express. Similarly, we can draw a distinction between physical properties themselves and ways of thinking of them; and the move we are envisaging the anti-experientialist as making gives an account of which physical property the word "red" picks out, but gives no account of a way of thinking of that property the word expresses. We just said cautiously on behalf of the anti-experientialist that "red" picks out that state S of some initial sample of objects which causes human beings to be in some experiential state which tends to give rise to the belief that some object has S, or tends to give rise to the ability to discriminate things with the property S. But someone would equally be "acting in accordance with" such a specification if he employed some instrument which is sensitive to the reflectance properties of surfaces, and which gives this information in auditory form through a small loudspeaker. He may come to use this device unreflectively, and have beliefs about the properties of surfaces, beliefs which are caused by the auditory experience produced by the instrument, and which are not based on inference. Yet this person, if blind, need not have the concept of being red; and he does not fully understand "red" if he knows only that the word picks out the property he knows to be instantiated when he uses the instrument. This way of developing the anti-experientialist view lacks any component which would explain why possession of the concept and full understanding of the word is so closely tied to visual experience.

Since the anti-experientialist has an account only of the property "red" picks out but does not have any account of the way an understander is required to think of that property, the only propositional attitude and more generally psychological contexts containing "red" that he can explain are those in which it occurs transparently: contexts that say that someone believes of the property that such-and-such object has it, or of the property that it falls under so-and-so higher order condition. This leads to a difficulty in carrying out the anti-experientialist's programme of explaining the property of looking red in terms of being red, even when we confine our attention to visual experience.

Suppose that initially surfaces with a given physical reflectance property R look red, and those with a given physical reflectance property G look green. Then at a certain time, perhaps because of some effect on people's brains, things with R look green, and things with G look red. This is a case of universal intrasubjective change; it is detectable, and, we suppose, actually detected. The most difficult problem for our anti-experientialist is not whether in these circumstances things with R are no longer red—a question on which intuitions vary—but what account of "looks red" he can give which squares with the possibility of the case: for as the case is described, it is not in dispute that objects which have R no longer *look* red after the change (whether or not they really are red). How can the anti-experientialist secure this consequence?

The anti-experientialist may reply that immediately after the change experiences of a kind that before the change were produced by objects with R still tend to produce after the change the belief of the property R that the presented object has it. Such a belief, after the change, is false: but the anti-experientialist can argue that the case is analogous to those considered in discussions of proper names. If someone just like Quine kidnaps Quine early on in Quine's life and starts to act Quine's role, we will falsely believe this man to be Quine; in acquiring beliefs about him we also acquire beliefs that Quine is thus-and-so. The problem is rather that if the imposter continues long enough, the beliefs expressed in utterances of "Quine is thus-and-so" come to concern the imposter, so similarly in the anti-experientialist's account of the colour example: after a time it is correct to say that experiences in which something looks red tend to produce the belief that the presented object has physical property G, the one which before the change produced experiences as of green objects. In whatever sense Armstrong, for instance, would say that before the change experiences as of something red tend to produce beliefs (in a transparent sense) about physical property R, a long time after that change in that same sense such experiences will tend to produce beliefs about the different physical property G. For exactly the same relations hold between experiences in which things look red and the physical property G at a much later time as held before the change between such experiences and physical property R. This remains true if the change in the effects of R and G went unnoticed. (The same general point can also be made if the account of looking red in terms of red speaks of abilities to discriminate objects with property R.) But then the anti-experientialist account delivers the wrong answer on the question of the qualitative similarity of two experiences, one e before the change and another e' a sufficiently long time afterwards. e and e' may both be as of something red, but e tends to produce the belief of the presented object that it has physical property R (by Armstrongian standards), while e' tends to produce the belief that it has physical property G. It does not help to try to appeal to what would be the case if experience of the kind of e and e' occurred simultaneously to someone: for the *kinds* here will have to include determinate specifications of the experienced colour, and that is what we were asking the anti-experientialist to explain, and not just take for granted.

At this point the anti-experientialist may be tempted to argue that he can admit the possibility of intrasubjective inversion of the colour experiences produced by a given type of physical surface in fixed lighting conditions. He may argue that this possibility is allowed for in the fact that different central brain states may be produced by looking at such a physical surface at different times. But of course brain states may alter while experience remains the same: a change of brain state produced by the surface is not sufficient for a change in colour experience. To make this account work, our anti-experientialist needs to distinguish just those changes in brain state which produce or are correlated with change in the colour the object looks: and he cannot legitimately do so in explaining "looks red". The problem here is one of meaning or significance. We have a conception of colour experience on which such a change of brain state is not constitutively sufficient for change in colour experience (which is not to say that it may not in some circumstances be good evidence for it). A general principle is applicable here. Suppose one can conceive of evidence which counts in favour of a hypothesis: that does not suffice to show the hypothesis to be significant if it is also true that our conception of what it is for that hypothesis to be true allows that either the evidence could obtain and the hypothesis be false, or vice versa. The rationale for this principle is obvious: if either the hypothesis or the evidence can obtain independently of the other obtaining, then to cite possible evidence does not exhaust the content of the hypothesis. We could call this general principle the Principle of Significance. It is not itself intrinsically a verificationist principle; rather, it functions as a constraint, a condition of adequacy, on any substantive general theories of meaning together with views about the content of particular sentences.[6] The Principle gets a grip here because the anti-experientialist was citing as possible evidence for intrasubjective inversion altered brain states, which are not, as we ordinarily conceive it, sufficient for such inversion.[7]

The anti-experientialist may complain that too much is being asked of him. "Why", he may ask, "cannot the concept of being red have the priority I claim for it whilst that concept is not further explicable? To someone who does not possess it, one can convey it only by suitable training (or brain surgery)." The problem with such a position is that it still does not account for the special features of the ability such training or brain surgery induces. No one has the concept of redness unless his exercises of that concept stand in quite special relations to his visual experience: it is hard to see how the anti-experientialist can explain why this is so without moving, by bringing in experience, from the first position to the second or third of the possibilities we described. The difficulty seems endemic to the anti-experientialist view.

The second option was a no-priority view. A no-priority view must offer more than the observation that 'Red things in standard circumstances look red' and 'Being red cannot be eliminated from an account of what it is for an experience to be as of something red' are both constitutively true. For corresponding claims are true of being square, and yet being square does not have the special relationship with visual experience that being red does. It is a virtue of the pure experientialist view, the third option, that it is not left as a mysterious, inexplicable necessary truth that one cannot experience objects as red in modalities other than the visual: the impossibility is rather a simple consequence of an account of what it is for an object to be red which mentions specifically a feature special to visual experience. A no-priority theorist must explain the special relationship with visual experience.

A different no-priority theorist, one aware of this requirement, might try to explain both "red" and "looks red" in terms of the type of experience that is present when a certain experientially-based ability is exercised: something looks red to someone when this ability would be exercised with a particular result, and it is really red when it would be exercised with that result in standard circumstances. Now what would the ability be? One cannot say that the ability on the basis of visual experience to discriminate red from non-red things. The occurrence of "red" in his description of the ability would prevent the resulting claim from being described as a no-priority view. But we ought to consider a bold modification of this idea, one on which we try to characterize the ability extensionally. We say that someone has a *reactive recognitional ability* (RRA) for a class A of objects in a given period (with respect to given physical circumstances) if and only if when trained to act in a particular way when he has a visual experience caused by objects in some sample subset of A, he goes on to act in the same way on the basis of the visual experience caused in him in the given physical circumstances by the remaining members of A, all in that period. An RRA is something one has in relation to a class, and so long as there is a class of red objects, one can speak of the existence of an RRA for a given class, and in terms of it explain "looks red" and "red" without initially using "red" and "looks red". Presumably the idea would be that there is a class with respect to which we have an RRA, a class such that when an object causes us (after training) to give on the basis of the visual experience it causes in us a positive response to it, we say it looks red: and it is red if it meets a similar condition in some standard specified circumstances. So the idea of this particular no-priority theory would be that both "red" and "looks red" are explained by reference to an RRA, and in such a way that certain connections—as that a red object looks red in standard conditions, etc.—are preserved between them.

This is a tempting theory, but the problems

seem insuperable. If the properties of being purple and being shiny were coextensive, the corresponding RRA's would be identical, since they are identified by classes. The account needs to be thickened to distinguish between looking purple and looking shiny. This could not be done by appealing to counterfactual circumstances in which the responses for "purple" and "shiny" would come apart. This is not because they would not come apart—they would—but because the antecedents of the counterfactuals specifying the circumstances in which they come apart would either contain colour predicates or mention of the physical grounds of looking a particular colour. If they contained colour predicates, the account would be circular, while the physical grounds of looking red may alter.[8]

There is also a second problem. The definition of a RRA requires the ability to learn to produce a new response to red objects when conditioned anew. But the ability to learn new responses seems distinct from the enjoyment of colour experience, and may be absent in a creature though it does enjoy such experiences. It would be too weak to require only that in some circumstances the creature gives the same experientially based response to precisely the things in a certain class; for in some circumstances the response may not be to the colour of the object.

This does not exhaust the plausible no-priority theories. In particular, there is a form of no-priority view which tries to take on board the considerations in favour of the third option, that of the experientialist, and then goes on to claim that these considerations can all be accommodated within the no-priority view. We will be able to formulate this properly only after developing that third option, taken by the experientialist.

The experientialist can say that when a normal human sees a red object in daylight, there is a certain property possessed by the region of his visual field in which that object is presented to him. This property we can label "red'": the canonical form is that region r of the visual field is red in token experience e. Being purely a property of the visual field, rather than a property the experience has in virtue of representing the world as being a certain way, red' does not require the possession of any particular concepts by the subject in whose experiences it is instantiated. It is true, of course, that we have picked out the property red' of experiences by using the ordinary notion of redness; but it does not follow that someone could not manifest a sensitivity to the red'-ness of his experiences without already possessing the concept of redness. The experientialist may now say this: in mastering the predicate "red" of objects, one comes to be dis-

posed to apply it to an object when the region of one's visual field in which it is presented is red' and circumstances are apparently normal (and when one has indirect evidence that it would meet this condition were it so presented). The experientialist will say that this explains the inclination we feel initially to explain "red" in terms of "looks red". He will say that what is correct is to explain red in terms of red': since normally when something looks red, the region of the visual field in which it is presented is red', he will say that the inclination is not surprising. Since for him the property red' of experiences and a sensitivity of one's judgments to its presence are the fundamental notions, rather than that of looking red, this experientialist does not need to deny the obvious fact that "red" is a semantically significant constituent of "looks red".

The experientialist is not committed to the consequence that anyone who can exercise the concept of redness also has to have the sophisticated concept of experience. All this experientialist requires for the possession of the concept of redness is a certain pattern of sensitivity in the subject's judgements to the occurrence of red' experiences: this sensitivity can exist in a subject who does not himself possess the concept of experience. This experientialist can then agree with the letter of Wittgenstein's claims in these passages:

> 315. Why doesn't one teach a child the language-game "It looks red to me" from the first? Because it is not yet able to understand the rather fine distinction between seeming and being?

> 316. The red visual impression is a new *concept.*

> 317. The language-game that we teach him then is "It looks to me . . . , it looks to you . . ." In the first language-game a person does not occur as perceiving subject.

> 318. You give the language-game a new joint. Which does not mean, however, that now it is always used.[9]

It is important to note that the experientialist is operating with three, and not two, notions: that of being red', that of looking red, and that of being red. The second of these is not in any simple way definable in terms of the first. However plausible it may seem at first blush, it is not true that anything which looks ϕ must be presented in a region of the visual field which is ϕ'. If one looks through a sheet of red glass at an array which includes a sheet of white paper, the sheet will be represented in the experience itself as being really white: anyone who has such an experience will, taking his experience at face value, be disposed to judge that the sheet really *is* white, and "white" here refers to the property of physical objects. It should be emphasized that this is not a matter of conscious inference: the surface of the paper is *seen* as white.[10] In such a case, it would be wrong to insist that the region of the visual field in which the paper is presented is white' and wrong to insist that it is red'. We have here a new kind of experience, and any extension of these primed properties from the cases where the conditions of viewing are more normal seems partly stipulative. Certainly to insist that in this case the region of the visual field is obviously white' seems to rely tacitly on the representational content of the experience in determining the application of the primed predicates: and since this representational content contains the concept of being white, the experientialist cannot on pain of circularity use such applications of primed properties in explaining colour predicates. The experientialist should, rather, agree that something can look ϕ without being presented in a ϕ' region of the visual field, and explain how this can be so as follows. Insofar as he is prepared to offer a definition of "x is red", it would be along these lines: "x is disposed in normal circumstances to cause the region of the visual field in which it is presented to be red' in normal humans". Now this concept of being red may enter the representational content of a subject's experiences. That it may so enter is an instance of a general phenomenon of concepts entering the representational content of experience. In possessing, for instance, the concept of complacency, one has the concept of a person who is unconcerned about something when there are available to him good reasons for concern: this is a trait that manifests itself in the man's thoughts. But one can also *see* a face or a gesture as complacent, and one can hear an utterance as complacent. The experientialist should say that the property red' stands to being red as the components of an account of being complacent stand to being complacent; while the property of an experience of representing something as red stands to being red in certain respects as the property of representing a gesture as complacent stands to being complacent. One must, then, beware of pinning an overly simple account of the property of representing something as red on the experientialist. In normal circumstances (and—unlike complacency—constitutively so) a thing presented in a red' region of the visual field is indeed seen as being red; but this is not the only way something can be seen as red, and the experientialist can acknowledge the fact.

We noted earlier that not all views of the no-priority type had yet been discussed. What we considered earlier were no-priority views which claimed that being red and looking red have to be simultaneously explained. It now appears that a much stronger type of no-priority view would be one on which the concepts which have to be intro-duced simultaneously are not those of being red and looking red, but rather those of being red and of being red'. Red objects are ones that in normal viewing conditions are presented in red' regions of the visual field: and red' is that property of regions of the visual field instantiated in regions in which red objects are presented in normal circumstances. Such a no-priority view can take over much of what we have already attributed to the experientialist, including the threefold distinction between red, looking red and red'.

But can these relations between red and red' really sustain the claim that we have here a no-priority view? We said that the sense in which the definition of being red in terms of red' was relevant to possession of the concept of redness is not that anyone who possesses it must be able to supply that definition, but rather that it captures a sensitivity to red' experiences which must be present in judgements that a presented object is red. Is it equally true that if someone possesses the concept red', there must be some appropriate sensitivity of his judgements involving *it* to the presence of redness, as opposed to other properties? One way to see that this is implausible is to consider a community the members of which not only often see things in normal daylight, but also often see them under ultraviolet light (perhaps at night). They might use "red$_{UV}$" as a predicate true of objects which are presented in a red' region of the visual field when seen under ultraviolet light. Now we can ask: is it true that anyone who possesses the concept red' must have a special sensitivity of his judgments involving *it* to the presence of redness as opposed to red$_{UV}$-ness? This seems to have no plausibility: if someone learns that red' is that property of the visual field instantiated by regions in which red$_{UV}$ objects are presented in ultraviolet light, he can fully understand "red'". Indeed anything that tells him what that experiential property is, whether or not it mentions redness, will suffice to give him understanding. This seems to undermine the status of the view under consideration as a no-priority view: though one can indeed give definitions of each of "red" and "red'" in terms of the other, a sensitivity to red'-ness is essential in grasping the concept of redness, whereas a sensitivity to redness is not essential to grasping the concept of red'-ness in the same way. The result seems to be a priority of red'-ness, an experientialist rather than a no-priority conclusion.[11]

An objector might agree that it is false that red rather than red$_{UV}$ has to be used to explain red'; but he may nevertheless say that what is definitionally prior to both red and red$_{UV}$ is a certain *character*, in a suitable generalization of Kaplan's notion.[12] Different utterances of "I" may refer to different persons, but there is a single uniform rule for determining which person is referred to at any given context of utterance. The objector's point may be that we should adapt Kaplan's notion by replacing "context of utterance" with "condition of perception taken as standard". We could then say this: words differing as "red" and "red$_{UV}$" differ may refer to different properties, but there is a single uniform rule for determining which property such a word refers to if any given condition of perception is taken as standard. Thus in a certain sense the characters of our "red" and their "red$_{UV}$" are one and the same, and it is this character which is prior to red'.

This view would indeed circumvent the objection. But the difficulty for it lies in stating what the common character of "red" and "red$_{UV}$" is. What is the common rule which, applied to different conditions of perception taken as standard, gives the different properties of being red and of being red$_{UV}$? The objector can hardly say that for given conditions of perception the rule picks out the property of looking *red* under those conditions: for that brings back all the old problems. But if the objector were to say that the rule should advert to the property of being presented in a red' region of the visual field, he has not shown red to be definitionally prior to red'.

There are other types of priority than the definitional. We can say that a concept A is *cognitively prior* to B if no one could possess the concept B without possessing the concept A. In the simplest case, this will be because a property thought of by way of the concept B has to be thought of as the property bearing certain relations to concept A. One should not assume that definitional priority and cognitive priority must coincide. It may be that in some cases one concept is definitionally prior to a second, while that second concept is cognitively prior to the first. This may be the case where the first concept is red' and the second is that of being red.

If concept A is definitionally prior to concept B because a thinker has to use that definition in thought when he employs the concept A, and if one concept can be cognitively prior to another only because the latter has to be defined in terms of the former, then it might be that definitional and cognitive priority have to coincide. But in the case of red' and red, the first antecedent of this conditional is false. A definition of an object's being red as its disposition to present itself in a red' region of the visual field under certain conditions is good not because it captures the way everyone must think of being red; rather, as we said, the judgements of one who has the concept of being red is responsive to experience and evidence in ex-

actly the same ways as would be the judgements of one who explicitly used this definition. If one wishes to maintain that red' is definitionally prior to red, but cognitively posterior to it, then the fact that one can have an experience in which a region of one's visual field is red' without having the concept red' is crucial in avoiding circularity in the account of mastery of the concept of being red.

The reasons which might be given for saying that red is cognitively prior to red' are subjects for other work.[13] It might, for example, be held that a necessary condition of possessing a conception of other minds according to which others can have red' experiences in exactly the same sense as one can oneself is that red' experiences, one's own and others, are alike thought of as experiences which bear certain relations to the property of objects, perceivable by oneself and others, of *being* red. (Such a reason would, if correct, have an a priori status, as required by the characterization of cognitive priority.) What matters for the present is just the possibility of such a position. For if it is possible, one must be careful before drawing any anti-experientialist conclusions from considerations of priority, and correspondingly careful in ascribing the anti-experientialist view to others. For someone's insistence that red is prior to red' may be an expression of cognitive priority. Such a theorist may not be rejecting definitional priority in the reverse direction. If he is not, then it would be wrong to ascribe to him anti-experientialist views. Indeed, it may well be that Wittgenstein should be regarded as holding just such a combination of views. In a passage already displayed, he insists that "red" has to be learned before certain concepts of experience; while elsewhere he seems to hold at least that seeming to be a certain colour cannot be left out of an account of what it is to have that colour:

97. Don't we just *call* brown the table which under certain circumstances appears brown to the normal-sighted? We could certainly conceive of someone to whom things seemed sometimes this colour and sometimes that, independently of the colour they are.

98. That it seems so to men is their criterion for its *being* so.

99. Being and seeming may, of course, be independent of one another in exceptional cases, but that doesn't make them logically independent; the language-game does not reside in the exception.[14]

If Wittgenstein did or would have believed in the cognitive priority of red over red', but was nevertheless not an anti-experientialist, then according to the arguments I have been endorsing, his position was consistent.

The experientialist view also has consequences for the explanation of experience. In the case of primary qualities, it is legitimate, and arguably mandatory in normal cases, to explain someone's experience of an object as square by the fact that it really is square (or by something entailed by its being square). But on the experientialist view one could not explain in a central case an object's looking red to someone by citing the fact that it really is red—at least, not if this explanation were intended to leave open the question of whether there is any primary quality ground of redness. Genuine explanations cannot have a *virtus dormitiva* character. On the particular experientialist theory I suggested, for something to be red is for it to produce experiences of a certain kind, red' experiences, in standard circumstances. In central cases—those by reference to which possession of the concept of redness was analyzed—for a thing to look red to someone is for it to produce red experiences. So on the experientialist option, the conditional "If circumstances are standard, in a central case if an object is red, then it looks red" is *a priori*: it reduces to a logical truth of the form $\forall x((Sx \mathbin{\&} (Sx \supset Rx)) \supset Rx)$. An expression might of course be introduced as an abbreviating ("descriptive") name for whatever physical state (if any) is the ground of objects' producing red' experiences. It is not clear, and perhaps not determinate, whether "red" is used in this way in English, but if it were what would make it legitimate to say "It's red" in explanation of something's producing red experiences in standard conditions would be the existence of some other, physical, characterization of the object that produces red' experiences.[15]

NOTES

* I have been helped by the comments of Rogers Albritton, Philippa Foot, John McDowell, and Colin McGinn on an ancestor of this paper written in 1980, and by Crispin Wright on a more recent version. This paper was written before, and the proofs corrected after, the final version of my *Sense and Content*, Oxford University Press, Oxford, 1983. Where it differs from, or is more elaborate than, the treatment of colour concepts in *Sense and Content*, the paper supercedes the book. The book does, however, contain more elaboration of the idea of a sensational property, of which red' is but one instance.

1. This question is intimately related to another, also touched on by Wittgenstein, viz., 'What is the nature of the relation of qualitative sameness of two experiences of different subjects, or of one subject at different times?' An answer to that question is partly constrained by the correct answer to the question of this paper.

The present paper is the first half of another, too long for inclusion in this special issue. The second half of the longer paper is concerned with sameness of experience between subjects and over time: I aim to publish that second part as soon as other pressures permit.

The reader whose primary interest is the interpretation of Wittgenstein should be warned that, wanting to take into account the views of more recent writers on our question, I have adopted a more eclectic framework for the discussion than Wittgensteinian exegesis alone would dictate.

2. There is a passage in *The Concept of Mind*, Penguin, London, 1963 in which Ryle brings out the dilemma, but curiously leaves it untreated: " . . . when I describe a common object as green or bitter . . . I am saying that it would look or taste so-and-so to anyone who was in a condition and position to see or taste properly. . . It must be noticed that the formula "it would look so-and-so to anyone" cannot be paraphrased by "it would look *green* to anyone", for to say that something looks green is to say that it looks as if it would if it were green and conditions were normal." Having denied that this paraphrase is correct, Ryle is left explaining "green" by a definition which takes the phrase "looks so-and-so" as an unexplained primitive: this unacceptable price is what he pays to avoid the threatened circularity.

3. For emphasis on the importance of this relatively uncontroversial point, see Anscombe, 'The Intensionality of Sensation' in R. Butler (ed.), *Analytical Philosophy* (Second Series), Blackwell, Oxford, 1968, p. 172 and W. Sellars, 'Empiricism and the Philosophy of Mind' in his *Science, Perception and Reality*, Routledge, London, 1963, p. 141ff. Sellar's later explanation (p. 147) of why, as he puts it, it is a necessary truth that something is red iff it looks red to standard observers in standard circumstances is that standard conditions are just conditions in which things look as they are. This may be true, but it applies to any predicate F for which "looks F" has some application: it does not explain why the concept of being red has a closer connection with visual experience than does the concept of being square.

4. Shoemaker, 'Functionalism and Qualia', *Philosophical Studies* **27**, 1975, 291–315.

5. D. M. Armstrong, *A Materialist Theory of the Mind*, Routledge, London, 1968; J. J. C. Smart, 'On Some Criticisms of a Physicalist Theory of Colour', in Chung-yin-Chen (ed.), *Philosophical Aspects of the Mind-Body Problem*, University of Hawaii, Honolulu, 1975.

6. The principle should also be accepted by criterial theorists of meaning, in the sense in which "criterion" is understood by, for instance, P. M. S. Hacker in *Insight and Illusion*, Oxford University Press, Oxford, 1972. Such a theorist would not (or should) not admit the possibility that someone in pain yet none of the criteria, however far one investigates possible defeating conditions, indicate that he is.

7. These remarks apply to Shoemaker, 'Phenomenal Similarity', *Critica* **20**, 1975, p. 267. They could also be applied *mutatis mutandis* to his remark in 'Functionalism and Qualia' that if two persons could fuse into a single subject of consciousness, "the behaviour of the resulting person could presumably settle [the question of whether their colour spectra were inverted relative to each other]"—N. Block (ed.), *Readings in the Philosophy of Psychology* (Reprint), Vol. 1, Harvard University Press, Cambridge, 1980, p. 264.

8. Extensionality also produces other problems: it is difficult to give a satisfactory account of how an object that is in fact red might not have been.

9. Block (ed.), *Remarks on the Philosophy of Psychology,* Vol. 2.

10. The red of a pane of red glass is a transparent film colour (Flächenfarbe) rather than a surface colour in the sense of psychologists of colour perception. The *locus classicus* is D. Katz, *The World of Colour,* Kegan Paul, London, 1935, p. 17ff. In seeing a snowman through a pane of red glass, one sees the pane as having a transparent film colour red and the snowman as having the *surface* colour white behind it. A red snowman by contrast would have the surface colour red. If the pane of glass is thick, the colour red may appear as a volume colour—one that is presented as occupying a volume of space. (See Katz, or again J. Beck, *Surface Colour Perception,* Cornell University Press, Ithaca, 1972, p. 20.) Anyone who doubts these points should look at a white surface through a coloured transparent bottle, or consult Plate 1 of Beck's book.

11. This point does not depend upon taking "red" and "red'" as natural kind terms. The view for which I am arguing is that for an object to be red is for it to be presented in a red' region of the visual field in certain conditions (external and internal to a perceiver). In the case of red and red$_{UV}$ these conditions are different, and so the properties of being red and of being red$_{UV}$ are different in at least one sense. There is no commitment in saying that an object is red$_{UV}$ to how it would look in normal daylight.

12. David Kaplan, 'On the Logic of Demonstratives', *Journal of Philosophical Logic* **8,** 1978, 81–98.

13. I have discussed some of them in 'Consciousness and Other Minds', *Proceedings of the Aristotelian Society,* Supp. Vol. 1984.

14. Ludwig Wittgenstein, *Remarks on Colour* (trans. L. McAlister and M. Schättle), Blackwell, London, 1977, p. 29e.

15. In *Form and Content,* Blackwell, Oxford, 1973, Bernard Harrison argues that colours are not "natural nameables". These last are objects which are "defined as distinct objects of reference . . . independently of linguistic convention". The experientialist does treat colours as natural nameables under this definition: the fact that something is a natural nameable in Harrison's sense does not exclude the possibility that an account of the nature of the object may have to make reference to human experience.

Harrison's own model of colour-naming is as follows: we fix a set of shades as name-bases, and apply the colour word associated with that name-base to any shade which more closely resembles that name-base than any other. He takes this to justify his view that colours are not natural nameables: yet it seems clear that the experientially caused actions of a nonlinguistic creature could manifest sensitivity to exactly the colour distinctions which are determined by Harrison's model of colour-naming as applied to, say, English.

45

Wilfrid Sellars

from "Phenomenalism"

VI. Sense Impressions Again

From the point of view we have now reached, sense impressions can, *as a first approximation,* be construed as entities postulated by a theory (at first common-sensical, then more and more refined) the aim of which is to explain such general truths as that when people look in mirrors in front of which there is a red object, there seems to them to be a red object 'behind the mirror', and other facts of this kind.

The significance of the phrase 'as a first approximation' will come out in a moment. But before I make any other moves, I must emphasize that the following argument presupposes that the 'calculational device' interpretation of theoretical entities is mistaken.[1] As I see it, to have good reason for holding a theory is *ipso facto* to have good reason for holding that the entities postulated by the theory exist. Thus, when I say that, as a first approximation, sense impressions can be construed as theoretical entities, I am not implying that sense impressions do not 'really' exist. Indeed, I should argue, not only do they really exist (since the theory is a good one), we can *directly* know (not merely infer by using the theory) on particular occasions that we are having sense impressions of such and such kinds. This ability directly to know that one is having a sense impression of a certain kind, however, presupposes the inter-subjective logical space of sense impressions as an explanation of such perceptual phenomena as those referred to in the first paragraph of this section. This fact about the logic of sense impressions also finds

its expression in the fact that the training of people to respond conceptually to states of themselves which are not publicly observable requires that trainer and trainee alike (they may be identical) share *both* the intersubjective framework of public objects and the intersubjective theory of private episodes, autobiographical sentences of which (in the present tense) are to acquire the additional role of *Konstatierungen* by becoming symptoms (through conditioning) of inner episodes and recognized as such.[2]

The crucial move in understanding the logic of sense impressions talk, however, is a reprise of a point made early in the chapter when, in the course of discussing the 'of-ness' of sense impressions, it was pointed out that if

(a) S has an impression of a red triangle

had the sense of

(b) S is in that state brought about in normal circumstances by the influence of red and triangular physical objects on the eyes

then the truth of (*a*) would not entail the existence of anything red and triangular.[3] Even if, as will become clear, this account of the meaning of (*a*) won't do as it stands, the logical point that (*a*) has the form

S is in a state of kind ϕ, i.e. ϕ (S)

rather than

(S) R (*y*)

remains true when it has been corrected.

What, then, is a visual impression (e.g. of a red triangle), if it is not simply that state of a perceiver which is normally brought about by the influence of a red and triangular physical object on the eye? The answer is implicit in the above characterization of the framework of sense impressions as a 'theory' certain sentences of which have been enriched by a reporting role. For even where a theoretical state of affairs can be given a definite description (in Russell's sense) in terms of the phenomena it is introduced to explain, this definite description cannot exhaust the sense of the relevant theoretical expression. If it did, the theory would be no theory at all, but at most the claim that a theory can be found. Clearly what gives sense to the primitive expressions of a formalized theory are in the first place the postulates which connect theoretical states of affairs with one another and in the second place the correspondence rules which connect the deductive system with the phenomena to be explained. Thus, to grasp the sense of the phrase 'impression of a red triangle', we must see how this phrase functions in the 'postulates' of the framework of sense impressions.

Here we run up against the obvious fact that the framework of sense impressions is *not* a formalized theory. Its 'postulates' are formulated in terms of analogies the force and limitations of which must be tickled out piecemeal by exploring the logic of sample uses of the framework. Such an explanation, which, if it were not for the danger of terminological confusion, might be called the phenomenology of sense impressions, is an arduous and time-consuming task which lies beyond the scope of this discussion. In any case, my concern is with broad issues of philosophical strategy, and even a large-scale map of the jungle of perceptual epistemology can bring decisive clarification. I shall therefore limit myself to a summary statement of what I take to be the outcome of such an exploration.

One item stands out above all others. Analysis reveals a *second* way in which the sense of 'impression of a red triangle' is related to the sense of 'red and triangular physical object'. The first has already been characterized by relating 'S has an impression of a red triangle' to 'S is in that state, etc.' The second consists in the fact that visual impressions of red triangles are conceived as items which are analogous *in certain respects* to physical objects which are red and triangular on the facing side.[4] Here it is essential to note that the analogy is between sense impressions and physical objects and not between sense impressions and *perceptions of* physical objects. Failure to appreciate this fact reinforces the temptation to construe impressions as *cognitive* and *conceptual* which arises from

the misassimilation of the 'of-ness' of sensation to the 'of-ness' of thought.[5] It is also essential to note that the analogy is a trans-category analogy, for it is an analogy between a state and a physical thing. Failure to appreciate this fact reinforces the temptation to construe

S has an impression of a red triangle

as having the form 'xRy', where y is a strange kind of particular[6] analogous in certain respects to the facing side of a red and triangular physical object.

With these warnings out of the way, we can turn our attention to the positive analogy. It has two parts:

(a) Impressions of red, blue, yellow, etc., triangles are implied to resemble-and-differ in a way which is formally analogous to that in which physical objects which are triangular and (red or blue or yellow, etc.) on the facing side resemble-and-differ; and similarly *mutatis mutandis* in the case of other shapes.

(b) Impressions of red triangles, circles, squares, etc., are implied to resemble-and-differ in a way which is formally analogous to that in which physical objects which are red and (triangular or circular or square, etc.), on the facing side resemble-and-differ; and similarly *mutatis mutandis* in the case of other colours.

In effect, these analogies have the force of postulates implicitly defining two families of predicates, 'ϕ_1'...'ϕ_n' and 'ψ_1'...'ψ_n', applicable to sense impressions, one of which has a logical space analogous to that of colours, the other a logical space analogous to that of the spatial properties of physical things.

In addition to these analogies, the framework of sense impressions involves a causal hypothesis, the general character of which can be indicated by saying that the fact that blue objects appear in certain circumstances to be green, and that in certain circumstances there appear to be red and triangular objects in front of people when there is no object there at all, are explained by postulating that in these circumstances impressions are brought about of the kinds which are normally brought about by blue objects (in the first case) and by red and triangular objects (in the second).

It has sometimes been suggested that the basic mode of existence of colours is 'adverbial', i.e. that the basic mode of existence of blue is expressed by the context 'S senses bluely'. This suggestion is typically developed into the idea that physical blue is the power to cause normal perceivers to sense bluely. From our standpoint this suggestion, although it contains an important insight, puts the cart before the horse and misconstrues as basic a 'colour' concept which is derived by analogy from colour concepts pertaining to physical objects. The violence done by this construction is reflected both by its paradoxical ring, and the reluctance of its sponsors to extend the same interpretation of the way in which shapes are involved in the impressions of sense.

The sound core of the adverbial interpretation of perceptible qualities consists in the fact that verbal nouns relating to inner episodes presuppose the corresponding verbs. Thus:

x has a circular$_s$ impression

(where 'circular$_s$' is the analogical predicate corresponding to 'circular$_p$') would, from the standpoint of a rational reconstruction, presuppose the form

x is impressed circularly$_s$

or, in the active voice,

x senses circularly$_s$

Notice that these analogical adverbs are not adverbs of manner comparable to 'quickly', 'clearly' etc. They combine with 'senses' or 'is impressed' to constitute the verb, thus 'senses-circularly$_s$', and 'is-impressed-circularly$_s$'.

NOTES

1. I argue this point in Chapter 4 [The Language of Theories," in Sellars' *Science, Perception and Reality*].

2. A fuller treatment of this topic would tie it in with the discussion of trans-level inference in the preceding section. Furthermore, since the 'theory' of sense-impressions presupposes not only the framework of public physical objects, but also that of perceivers and perceptual episodes, it is clear that an adequate account of the logical status of sense impressions and our knowledge of them presupposes an account of such private episodes as seeing or seeming to see that there is a red and triangular physical object in front of one. There is a discussion of these topics in Chapter 5 [Empiricism and the Philosophy of Mind," in Sellars' *Science, Perception and Reality*].

3. Though, as was also pointed out, if the locution 'a red and triangular sense content exists' were introduced as the equivalent of 'Someone has a sensation of a red triangle' then we could say that the truth of (a) entails the existence of something red and triangular. But what he would be saying would be exciting only if misunderstood.

4. That only one side is relevant to the analogy accounts for the fact tht the red triangle of an impression of a red triangle has no back side.

5. The correct interpretation of the 'of-ness' of thought does resemble, in an important respect the 'of-ness' of sense impressions as analysed above. To oversimplify, a thought *of* p turns out to have the form a though of the ·p· kind, where the latter are episodes which whatever their character as scientific objects, play a role analogous to that played in English by tokens of 'p'. This similarity, however, highlights rather than obscures the essential difference between the intentionality of thought and the seudo-intentionality of sense impressions.

6. See the previous footnote but one.

from "Being and Being Known"

*   *   *   *   *

19. The first thing to note is that the expressions by which we refer to and characterize sensations do show a remarkable analogy to the expressions by which we refer to and characterize items belonging to the intentional or cognitive order. Thus we speak of

a sensation of a white triangular thing

and this shows a striking grammatical similarity to the language by which we refer to and characterize thoughts; thus we speak of

a thought of a white triangular thing.

And since we are construing the latter as an act of the intellect which signifies a white triangular thing by virtue of being a token of the mental phrase ·(such and such a) white triangular thing· , there is

a strong temptation to construe the former as an act of sense which signifies a white triangular thing by virtue of being a token of the mental (sensitive) phrase ·(this) white triangular thing·.*

20. But it is doubtful if this temptation would be strong enough to carry the day if it weren't for the considerations which generate the idea that the natures *white* and *triangular* inform the act of sense in an *immaterial* way. For this amounts to the idea that the sense in act is *isomorphic* in the *immaterial* mode with the object of sense, and I shall be arguing subsequently (a) that there is a sense in which sensations *are* isomorphic with objects of sense, (b) that sensations are not white and triangular in the way in which *material* objects are

* I shall form the names of mental words by putting the corresponding English expressions within dot quotes. [This footnote occurs in paragraph 8, which is omitted from this selection.]

white and triangular, and (c), in § 56 below, that there are plausible, if mistaken, considerations which point to an equation of intentionality with isomorphism in the immaterial mode, considerations which are the very source of the latter conception.

21. Now it certainly must be granted that the sensation of a white triangular thing is neither white nor triangular (nor, for that matter, a thing) in the way in which its external cause is a white triangular thing. And, I believe, it must also be granted that unless the sensation of a white triangular thing were *in some way* isomorphic with its external cause, knowledge of the physical world would be impossible. Finally, I believe, it must be granted that whiteness and triangularity are *somehow* involved in the form or species of the act of sense. It is, unfortunately, only too easy to suppose that these admissions add up to the Thomistic theory of sensation. It is therefore important to see that all of these theses can be accounted for in a radically different way which involves no attribution of intentionality to sense.

22. According to this alternative account, our concept of a sensation of a white triangular thing is the concept of a state of the perceiving organism which

(a) is of a kind which is normally brought about by white and triangular objects,
(b) is of a kind which differs systematically from those states which are normally brought about by objects of other colors and shapes,
(c) is of a kind which is brought about in abnormal circumstances by objects of other colors and shapes, and hence contributes to the explanation of the fact that objects viewed in abnormal circumstances seem to be other than they are.

23. Thus although the sensation is not literally white and triangular, it is of a kind which can be called white and triangular *in a derivative sense of these predicates.* In Thomistic terminology, the act of sense which is a sensation *of* a white triangular thing must indeed, have a form or species *qua* act, but this form or species does not consist of the *white* and *triangular* appropriate to material things though immaterially received; it consists of *white* and *triangular* in a different sense of these terms. By this I do not, of course, mean that 'white' as in 'a white sensation' and 'white' as in 'a white elephant' are mere homonyms. They have different but related meanings, as, in a different way, do 'healthy' as in 'healthy food' and the same word as

in 'healthy man'. Thus, instead of saying that the act of sense is informed *immaterially* by the natures *white* and *triangular* in the primary sense of these terms, we can simply say that the act of sense is informed by the natures *white* and *triangular* in the derivative sense characterized in paragraph 22 above.

24. This can also be put by saying that the concepts of the various kinds of sensation are concepts formed by analogy. The Thomistic tradition makes significant use of the idea that certain of our concepts are analogical concepts; and contemporary philosophies of science stress the role of analogy in the conceptual structures of scientific theory. What is, perhaps, new in the account I am proposing is the idea that direct self-knowledge may essentially involve analogical concepts, i.e. that the concepts in terms of which we have what is often called 'reflexive knowledge' of our mental acts are analogical extensions of concepts pertaining to the public or intersubjective world of things and persons.

25. This thesis certainly runs counter to the Cartesian interpretation of the reflexive awareness of a mental act as an adequate (i.e., among other things, non-analogical) grasp of the act as being of a certain determinate kind or species. But, I think we must say, so much the worse for Descartes. It is a serious mistake to suppose that merely by virtue of having sensations we experience sensations *as* sensations (do animals experience sensations as being sensations?), and that from this experience, by an act of so-called abstraction, the intellect can acquire a non-analogical understanding of what it is to be a sensation. I shall shortly be arguing that the same situation obtains in the case of our concepts of intellectual acts, which I shall also construe as analogical concepts the *fundamentum* of which are concepts pertaining to meaningful speech.

26. I suggested a moment ago that the concept of a sensation of a white triangular thing is the concept of an act which is white and triangular in a derivative sense of these terms. It is, to repeat, a white and triangular act *not* by being immaterially white and triangular in the sense of 'white' and 'triangular' appropriate to material things, but by simply being white and triangular in a derivative sense.[1] Let me now remind you that on the ac-

---

1. It is perhaps worth noting that the above account of the derivation omits an essential step, in that the expression 'white and triangular sensation' presupposes the expression 'sensing whitely and triangularly' so that the introduction of the adverbs 'whitely' and 'triangularly' would be the basic analogical move.

count I am proposing, the analogy between the two *whites* and the two *triangulars* involved the idea that the various species of visual sensation form a family of resemblances and differences which corresponds to the family of resemblances and differences which is the system of sensible qualities in the basic sense, the sense which pertains to material things. It is in this way that the isomorphism of acts of sense and material things is to be understood. The place of *derivative white* and *derivative triangular* in the system of the species of sense acts is isomorphic in the *structural* sense (explained by contemporary relation theory) with the place of *basic white* and *basic triangular* in the system of the perceptible qualities of material things.

*   *   *   *   *

C. Consciousness, Self, and Personhood

46

Thomas Nagel

"What Is It Like to Be a Bat?"

Consciousness is what makes the mind–body problem really intractable. Perhaps that is why current discussions of the problem give it little attention or get it obviously wrong. The recent wave of reductionist euphoria has produced several analyses of mental phenomena and mental concepts designed to explain the possibility of some variety of materialism, psychophysical identification, or reduction.[1] But the problems dealt with are those common to this type of reduction and other types, and what makes the mind–body problem unique, and unlike the water–H_2O problem or the Turing machine–IBM machine problem or the lightning–electrical discharge problem or the gene–DNA problem or the oak tree–hydrocarbon problem, is ignored.

Every reductionist has his favorite analogy from modern science. It is most unlikely that any of these unrelated examples of successful reduction will shed light on the relation of mind to brain. But philosophers share the general human weakness for explanations of what is incomprehensible in terms suited for what is familiar and well understood, though entirely different. This has led to the acceptance of implausible accounts of the mental largely because they would permit familiar kinds of reduction. I shall try to explain why the usual examples do not help us to understand the relation between mind and body—why, indeed, we have at present no conception of what an explanation of the physical nature of a mental phenomenon would be. Without consciousness the mind–body problem would be much less interesting. With consciousness it seems hopeless. The most important and characteristic feature of conscious mental phenomena is very poorly understood. Most reductionist theories do not even try to explain it. And careful examination will show that no currently available concept of reduction is applicable to it. Perhaps a new theoretical form can be devised for the purpose, but such a solution, if it exists, lies in the distant intellectual future.

Conscious experience is a widespread phenomenon. It occurs at many levels of animal life, though we cannot be sure of its presence in the simpler organisms, and it is very difficult to say in general what provides evidence of it. (Some extremists have been prepared to deny it even of mammals other than man.) No doubt it occurs in countless forms totally unimaginable to us, on other planets in other solar systems throughout the universe. But no matter how the form may vary, the fact that an organism has conscious experience *at all* means, basically, that there is something it is like to *be* that organism. There may be further implications about the form of the experience; there may even (though I doubt it) be implications about the behavior of the organism. But fundamentally an organism has conscious mental states if and only if there is something that it is like to *be* that organism—something it is like *for* the organism.

We may call this the subjective character of experience. It is not captured by any of the familiar, recently devised reductive analyses of the mental, for all of them are logically compatible with its absence. It is not analyzable in terms of any explanatory system of functional states, or intentional states, since these could be ascribed to robots or automata that behaved like people though they experienced nothing.[2] It is not analyzable in terms of the causal role of experiences in relation to typical human behavior—for similar reasons.[3] I do not deny that conscious mental states and events cause behavior, nor that they may be given functional characterizations. I deny only that this kind of

From *The Philosophical Review* LXXXIII, 4 (October 1974): 435–50. Reprinted with permission of the editors and Thomas Nagel.

thing exhausts their analysis. Any reductionist program has to to be based on an analysis of what is to be reduced. If the analysis leaves something out, the problem will be falsely posed. It is useless to base the defense of materialism on any analysis of mental phenomena that fails to deal explicitly with their subjective character. For there is no reason to suppose that a reduction which seems plausible when no attempt is made to account for consciousness can be extended to include consciousness. Without some idea, therefore, of what the subjective character of experience is, we cannot know what is required of a physicalist theory.

While an account of the physical basis of mind must explain many things, this appears to be the most difficult. It is impossible to exclude the phenomenological features of experience from a reduction in the same way that one excludes the phenomenal features of an ordinary substance from a physical or chemical reduction of it—namely, by explaining them as effects on the minds of human observers.[4] If physicalism is to be defended, the phenomenological features must themselves be given a physical account. But when we examine their subjective character it seems that such a result is impossible. The reason is that every subjective phenomenon is essentially connected with a single point of view, and it seems inevitable that an objective, physical theory will abandon that point of view.

Let me first try to state the issue somewhat more fully than by referring to the relation between the subjective and the objective, or between the *pour-soi* and the *en-soi*. This is far from easy. Facts about what it is like to be an X are very peculiar, so peculiar that some may be inclined to doubt their reality, or the significance of claims about them. To illustrate the connection between subjectivity and a point of view, and to make evident the importance of subjective features, it will help to explore the matter in relation to an example that brings out clearly the divergence between the two types of conception, subjective and objective.

I assume we all believe that bats have experience. After all, they are mammals, and there is no more doubt that they have experience than that mice or pigeons or whales have experience. I have chosen bats instead of wasps or flounders because if one travels too far down the phylogenetic tree, people gradually shed their faith that there is experience there at all. Bats, although more closely related to us than those other species, nevertheless present a range of activity and a sensory apparatus so different from ours that the problem I want to pose is exceptionally vivid (though it certainly could be raised with other species). Even without

the benefit of philosophical reflection, anyone who has spent some time in an enclosed space with an excited bat knows what it is to encounter a fundamentally *alien* form of life.

I have said that the essence of the belief that bats have experience is that there is something that it is like to be a bat. Now we know that most bats (the microchiroptera, to be precise) perceive the external world primarily by sonar, or echolocation, detecting the reflections, from objects within range, of their own rapid, subtly modulated, high-frequency shrieks. Their brains are designed to correlate the outgoing impulses with the subsequent echoes, and the information thus acquired enables bats to make precise discriminations of distance, size, shape, motion, and texture comparable to those we make by vision. But bat sonar, though clearly a form of perception, is not similar in its operation to any sense that we possess, and their is no reason to suppose that it is subjectively like anything we can experience or imagine. This appears to create difficulties for the notion of what it is like to be a bat. We must consider whether any method will permit us to extrapolate to the inner life of the bat from our own case,[5] and if not, what alternative methods there may be for understanding the notion.

Our own experience provides the basic material for our imagination, whose range is therefore limited. It will not help to try to imagine that one has webbing on one's arms, which enables one to fly around at dusk and dawn catching insects in one's mouth; that one has very poor vision, and perceives the surrounding world by a system of reflected high-frequency sound signals, and that one spends the day hanging upside down by one's feet in an attic. In so far as I can imagine this (which is not very far), it tells me only what it would be like for *me* to behave as a bat behaves. But that is not the question. I want to know what it is like for a *bat* to be a bat. Yet if I try to imagine this, I am restricted to the resources of my own mind, and those resources are inadequate to the task. I cannot perform it either by imagining additions to my present experience, or by imagining segments gradually subtracted from it, or by imagining some combination of additions, subtractions, and modifications.

To the extent that I could look and behave like a wasp or a bat without changing my fundamental structure, my experiences would not be anything like the experiences of those animals. On the other hand, it is doubtful that any meaning can be attached to the supposition that I should possess the internal neurophysiological constitution of a bat. Even if I could by gradual degrees be transformed into a bat, nothing in my present constitution enables me to imagine what the experiences of such a future stage of myself thus metamorphosed would be like. The best evidence would come from the experiences of bats, if we only knew what they were like.

So if extrapolation from our own case is involved in the idea of what it is like to be a bat, the extrapolation must be incompletable. We cannot form more than a schematic conception of what it *is* like. For example, we may ascribe general *types* of experience on the basis of the animal's structure and behavior. Thus we describe bat sonar as a form of three-dimensional forward perception; we believe that bats feel some versions of pain, fear, hunger, and lust, and that they have other, more familiar types of perception besides sonar. But we believe that these experiences also have in each case a specific subjective character, which it is beyond our ability to conceive. And if there is conscious life elsewhere in the universe, it is likely that some of it will not be describable even in the most general experiential terms available to us.[6] (The problem is not confined to exotic cases, however, for it exists between one person and another. The subjective character of the experience of a person deaf and blind from birth is not accessible to me, for example, nor presumably is mine to him. This does not prevent us each from believing that the other's experience has such a subjective character.)

If anyone is inclined to deny that we can believe in the existence of facts like this whose exact nature we cannot possibly conceive, he should reflect that in contemplating the bats we are in much the same position that intelligent bats or Martians[7] would occupy if they tried to form a conception of what it was like to be us. The structure of their own minds might make it impossible for them to succeed, but we know they would be wrong to conclude that there is not anything precise that it is like to be us: that only certain general types of mental state could be ascribed to us (perhaps perception and appetite would be concepts common to us both; perhaps not). We know they would be wrong to draw such a skeptical conclusion because we know what it is like to be us. And we know that while it includes an enormous amount of variation and complexity, and while we do not possess the vocabulary to describe it adequately, its subjective character is highly specific, and in some respects describable in terms that can be understood only by creatures like us. The fact that we cannot expect ever to accommodate in our language a detailed description of Martian or bat phenomenology should not lead us to dismiss as meaningless the claim that bats and Martians have experiences fully comparable in richness of detail to our own. It would be fine if someone were to develop con-

cepts and a theory that enabled us to think about those things; but such an understanding may be permanently denied to us by the limits of our nature. And to deny the reality or logical significance of what we can never describe or understand is the crudest form of cognitive dissonance.

This brings us to the edge of a topic that requires much more discussion than I can give it here: namely, the relation between facts on the one hand and conceptual schemes or systems of representation on the other. My realism about the subjective domain in all its forms implies a belief in the existence of facts beyond the reach of human concepts. Certainly it is possible for a human being to believe that there are facts which humans never *will* possess the requisite concepts to represent or comprehend. Indeed, it would be foolish to doubt this, given the finiteness of humanity's expectations. After all, there would have been transfinite numbers even if everyone had been wiped out by the Black Death before Cantor discovered them. But one might also believe that there are facts which *could* not ever be represented or comprehended by human beings, even if the species lasted forever—simply because our structure does not permit us to operate with concepts of the requisite type. This impossibility might even be observed by other beings, but it is not clear that the existence of such beings, or the possibility of their existence, is a precondition of the significance of the hypothesis that there are humanly inaccessible facts. (After all, the nature of beings with access to humanly inaccessible facts is presumably itself a humanly inaccessible fact.) Reflection on what it is like to be a bat seems to lead us, therefore, to the conclusion that there are facts that do not consist in the truth of propositions expressible in a human language. We can be compelled to recognize the existence of such facts without being able to state or comprehend them.

I shall not pursue this subject, however. Its bearing on the topic before us (namely, the mind–body problem) is that it enables us to make a general observation about the subjective character of experience. Whatever may be the status of facts about what it is like to be a human being, or a bat, or a Martian, these appear to be facts that embody a particular point of view.

I am not adverting here to the alleged privacy of experience to its possessor. The point of view in question is not one accessible only to a single individual. Rather it is a *type*. It is often possible to take up a point of view other than one's own, so the comprehension of such facts is not limited to one's own case. There is a sense in which phenomenological facts are perfectly objective: one person can know or say of another what the quality of the other's experience is. They are subjective, however, in the sense that even this objective ascription of experience is possible only for someone sufficiently similar to the object of ascription to be able to adopt his point of view—to understand the ascription in the first person as well as in the third, so to speak. The more different from oneself the other experiencer is, the less success one can expect with this enterprise. In our own case we occupy the relevant point of view, but we will have as much difficulty understanding our own experience properly if we approach it from another point of view as we would if we tried to understand the experience of another species without taking up *its* point of view.[8]

This bears directly on the mind–body problem. For if the facts of experience—facts about what it is like *for* the experiencing organism—are accessible only from one point of view, then it is a mystery how the true character of experiences could be revealed in the physical operation of that organism. The latter is a domain of objective facts *par excellence*—the kind that can be observed and understood from many points of view and by individuals with differing perceptual systems. There are no comparable imaginative obstacles to the acquisition of knowledge about bat neurophysiology by human scientists, and intelligent bats or Martians might learn more about the human brain than we ever will.

This is not by itself an argument against reduction. A Martian scientist with no understanding of visual perception could understand the rainbow, or lightning, or clouds as physical phenomena, though he would never be able to understand the human concepts of rainbow, lightning, or cloud, or the place these things occupy in our phenomenal world. The objective nature of the things picked out by these concepts could be apprehended by him because, although the concepts themselves are connected with a particular point of view and a particular visual phenomenology, the things apprehended from that point of view are not: they are observable from the point of view but external to it; hence they can be comprehended from other points of view also, either by the same organisms or by others. Lightning has an objective character that is not exhausted by its visual appearance, and this can be investigated by a Martian without vision. To be precise, it has a *more* objective character than is revealed in its visual appearance. In speaking of the move from subjective to objective characterization, I wish to remain noncommittal about the existence of an end point, the completely objective intrinsic nature of the thing, which one might or might not be able to reach. It may be more accurate to think of objectivity as a direction

in which the understanding can travel. And in understanding a phenomenon like lightning, it is legitimate to go as far away as one can from a strictly human viewpoint.[9]

In the case of experience, on the other hand, the connection with a particular point of view seems much closer. It is difficult to understand what could be meant by the *objective* character of an experience, apart from the particular point of view from which its subject apprehends it. After all, what would be left of what it was like to be a bat if own removed the viewpoint of the bat? But if experience does not have, in addition to its subjective character, an objective nature that can be apprehended from many different points of view, then how can it be supposed that a Martian investigating my brain might be observing physical processes which were my mental processes (as he might observe physical processes which were bolts of lightning), only from a different point of view? How, for that matter, could a human physiologist observe them from another point of view?[10]

We appear to be faced with a general difficulty about psychophysical reduction. In other areas the process of reduction is a move in the direction of greater objectivity, toward a more accurate view of the real nature of things. This is accomplished by reducing our dependence on individual or species specific points of view toward the object of investigation. We describe it not in terms of the impressions it makes on our senses, but in terms of its more general effects and of properties detectable by means other than the human senses. The less it depends on a specifically human viewpoint, the more objective is our description. It is possible to follow this path because although the concepts and ideas we employ in thinking about the external world are initially applied from a point of view that involves our perceptual apparatus, they are used by us to refer to things beyond themselves—toward which we *have* the phenomenal point of view. Therefore we can abandon it in favor of another, and still be thinking about the same things.

Experience itself, however, does not seem to fit the pattern. The idea of moving from appearance to reality seems to make no sense here. What is the analogue in this case to pursuing a more objective understanding of the same phenomena by abandoning the initial subjective viewpoint toward them in favor of another that is more objective but concerns the same thing? Certainly it *appears* unlikely that we will get closer to the real nature of human experience by leaving behind the particularity of our human point of view and striving for a description in terms accessible to beings that could not imagine what it was like to be us. If the subjective character of experience is fully comprehensible only from one point of view, then any shift to greater objectivity—that is, less attachment to a specific viewpoint—does not take us nearer to the real nature of the phenomenon: it takes us farther away from it.

In a sense, the seeds of this objection to the reducibility of experience are already detectable in successful cases of reduction; for in discovering sound to be, in reality, a wave phenomenon in air or other media, we leave behind one viewpoint to take up another, and the auditory, human or animal viewpoint that we leave behind remains unreduced. Members of radically different species may both understand the same physical events in objective terms, and this does not require that they understand the phenomenal forms in which those events appear to the senses of members of the other species. Thus it is a condition of their referring to a common reality that their more particular viewpoints are not part of the common reality that they both apprehend. The reduction can succeed only if the species-specific viewpoint is omitted from what is to be reduced.

But while we are right to leave this point of view aside in seeking a fuller understanding of the external world, we cannot ignore it permanently, since it is the essence of the internal world, and not merely a point of view on it. Most of the neobehaviorism of recent philosophical psychology results from the effort to substitute an objective concept of mind for the real thing, in order to have nothing left over which cannot be reduced. If we acknowledge that a physical theory of mind must account for the subjective character of experience, we must admit that no presently available conception gives us a clue how this could be done. The problem is unique. If mental processes are indeed physical processes, then there is something it is like, intrinsically,[11] to undergo certain physical processes. What it is for such a thing to be the case remains a mystery.

What moral should be drawn from these reflections, and what should be done next? It would be a mistake to conclude that physicalism must be false. Nothing is proved by the inadequacy of physicalist hypotheses that assume a faulty objective analysis of mind. It would be truer to say that physicalism is a position we cannot understand because we do not at present have any conception of how it might be true. Perhaps it will be thought unreasonable to require such a conception as a condition of understanding. After all, it might be said, the meaning of physicalism is clear enough: mental states are states of the body; mental events are physical events. We do not know *which* physical states and events they are, but that should not prevent us from understanding the hypothesis.

What could be clearer than the words "is" and "are"?

But I believe it is precisely this apparent clarity of the word "is" that is deceptive. Usually, when we are told that X is Y we know *how* it is supposed to be true, but that depends on a conceptual or theoretical background and is not conveyed by the "is" alone. We know how both "X" and "Y" refer, and the kinds of things to which they refer, and we have a rough idea how the two referential paths might converge on a single thing, be it an object, a person, a process, an event, or whatever. But when the two terms of the identification are very disparate it may not be so clear how it could be true. We may not have even a rough idea of how the two referential paths could converge, or what kind of things they might converge on, and a theoretical framework may have to be supplied to enable us to understand this. Without the framework, an air of mysticism surrounds the identification.

This explains the magical flavor of popular presentations of fundamental scientific discoveries, given out as propositions to which one must subscribe without really understanding them. For example, people are now told at an early age that all matter is really energy. But despite the fact that they know what "is" means, most of them never form a conception of what makes this claim true, because they lack the theoretical background.

At the present time the status of physicalism is similar to that which the hypothesis that matter is energy would have had if uttered by a pre-Socratic philosopher. We do not have the beginnings of a conception of how it might be true. In order to understand the hypothesis that a mental event is a physical event, we require more than an understanding of the word "is." The idea of how a mental and a physical term might refer to the same thing is lacking, and the usual analogies with theoretical identification in other fields fail to supply it. They fail because if we construe the reference of mental terms to physical events on the usual model, we either get a reappearance of separate subjective events as the effects through which mental reference to physical events is secured, or else we get a false account of how mental terms refer (for example, a causal behaviorist one).

Strangely enough, we may have evidence for the truth of something we cannot really understand. Suppose a caterpillar is locked in a sterile safe by someone unfamiliar with insect metamorphosis, and weeks later the safe is reopened, revealing a butterfly. If the person knows that the safe has been shut the whole time, he has reason to believe that the butterfly is or was once the caterpillar, without having any idea in what sense this might be so. (One possibility is that the caterpillar contained a tiny winged parasite that devoured it and grew into the butterfly.)

It is conceivable that we are in such a position with regard to physicalism. Donald Davidson has argued that if mental events have physical causes and effects, they must have physical descriptions. He holds that we have reason to believe this even though we do not—and in fact *could* not—have a general psychophysical theory.[12] His argument applies to intentional mental events, but I think we also have some reason to believe that sensations are physical processes, without being in a position to understand how. Davidson's position is that certain physical events have irreducibly mental properties, and perhaps some view describable in this way is correct. But nothing of which we can now form a conception corresponds to it; nor have we any idea what a theory would be like that enabled us to conceive of it.[13]

Very little work has been done on the basic question (from which mention of the brain can be entirely omitted) whether any sense can be made of experiences' having an objective character at all. Does it make sense, in other words, to ask what my experiences are *really* like, as opposed to how they appear to me? We cannot genuinely understand the hypothesis that their nature is captured in a physical description unless we understand the more fundamental idea that they *have* an objective nature (or that objective processes can have a subjective nature).[14]

I should like to close with a speculative proposal. It may be possible to approach the gap between subjective and objective from another direction. Setting aside temporarily the relation between the mind and the brain, we can pursue a more objective understanding of the mental in its own right. At present we are completely unequipped to think about the subjective character of experience without relying on the imagination—without taking up the point of view of the experiential subject. This should be regarded as a challenge to form new concepts and devise a new method—an objective phenomenology not dependent on empathy or the imagination. Though presumably it would not capture everything, its goal would be to describe, at least in part, the subjective character of experiences in a form comprehensible to beings incapable of having those experiences.

We would have to develop such a phenomenology to describe the sonar experiences of bats; but it would also be possible to begin with humans. One might try, for example, to develop concepts that could be used to explain to a person blind from birth what it was like to see. One would reach a blank wall eventually, but it should be possible to devise a method of expressing in objective terms much more than we can at present, and with much greater precision. The loose intermodal analogies—for example, "Red is like the sound of a trumpet"—which crop up in discussions of this subject are of little use. That should be clear to anyone who has both heard a trumpet and seen red. But structural features of perception might be more accessible to objective description, even though something would be left out. And concepts alternative to those we learn in the first person may enable us to arrive at a kind of understanding even of our own experience which is denied us by the very ease of description and lack of distance that subjective concepts afford.

Apart from its own interest, a phenomenology that is in this sense objective may permit questions about the physical[15] basis of experience to assume a more intelligible form. Aspects of subjective experience that admitted this kind of objective description might be better candidates for objective explanations of a more familiar sort. But whether or not this guess is correct, it seems unlikely that any physical theory of mind can be contemplated until more thought has been given to the general problem of subjective and objective. Otherwise we cannot even pose the mind–body problem without sidestepping it.[16]

NOTES

1. Examples are J. J. C. Smart, *Philosophy and Scientific Realism* (London, 1963); David K. Lewis, "An Argument for the Identity Theory," *Journal of Philosophy*, LXIII (1966), reprinted with addenda in David M. Rosenthal, *Materialism & the Mind-Body Problem* (Englewood Cliffs, N.J., 1971); Hilary Putnam, "Psychological Predicates" in Capitan and Merrill, *Art, Mind, & Religion* (Pittsburgh, 1967), reprinted in Rosenthal, *op. cit.*, as "The Nature of Mental States"; D. M. Armstrong, *A Materialist Theory of the Mind* (London, 1968); D. C. Dennett, *Content and Consciousness* (London, 1969). I have expressed earlier doubts in "Armstrong on the Mind," *Philosophical Review*, LXXIX (1970), 394–403; "Brain Bisection and the Unity of Consciousness," *Synthèse*, 22 (1971); and a review of Dennett, *Journal of Philosophy*, LXIX (1972). See also Saul Kripke, "Naming and Necessity" in Davidson and Harman, *Semantics of Natural Language* (Dordrecht, 1972), esp. pp. 334–342; and M. T. Thornton, "Ostensive Terms and Materialism," *The Monist*, 56 (1972).

2. Perhaps there could not actually be such robots. Perhaps anything complex enough to behave like a person would have experiences. But that, if true, is a fact which cannot be discovered merely by analyzing the concept of experience.

3. It is not equivalent to that about which we are incorrigible, both because we are not incorrigible about experience and because experience is present in animals lacking language and thought, who have no beliefs at all about their experiences.

4. Cf. Richard Rorty, "Mind-Body Identity, Privacy, and Categories," *The Review of Metaphysics*, XIX (1965), esp. 37–38.

5. By "our own case" I do not mean just "my own case," but rather the mentalistic ideas that we apply unproblematically to ourselves and other human beings.

6. Therefore the analogical form of the English expression "what it is *like*" is misleading. It does not mean "what (in our experience) it *resembles*," but rather "how it is for the subject himself."

7. Any intelligent extraterrestrial beings totally different from us.

8. It may be easier than I suppose to transcend inter-species barriers with the aid of the imagination. For example, blind people are able to detect objects near them by a form of sonar, using vocal clicks or taps of a cane. Perhaps if one knew what that was like, one could by extension imagine roughly what it was like to possess the much more refined sonar of a bat. The distance between oneself and other persons and other species can fall anywhere on a continuum. Even for other persons the understanding of what it is like to be them is only partial, and when one moves to species very different from oneself, a lesser degree of partial understanding may still be available. The imagination is remarkably flexible. My point, however, is not that we cannot *know* what it is like to be a bat. I am not raising that epistemological problem. My point is rather that even to form a *conception* of what it is like to be a bat (and a fortiori to know what it is like to be a bat) one must take up the bat's point of view. If one can take it up roughly, or partially, then one's conception will also be rough or partial. Or so it seems in our present state of understanding.

9. The problem I am going to raise can therefore be posed even if the distinction between more subjective and more objective descriptions or viewpoints can itself be made only within a larger human point of view. I do not accept this kind of conceptual relativism, but it need not be refuted to make the point that psychophysical reduction cannot be accommodated by the subjective-to-objective model familiar from other cases.

10. The problem is not just that when I look at the "Mona Lisa," my visual experience has a certain quality, no trace of which is to be found by someone looking into my brain. For even if he did observe there a tiny image of the "Mona Lisa," he would have no reason to identify it with the experience.

11. The relation would therefore not be a contingent one, like that of a cause and its distinct effect. It would be necessarily true that a certain physical state felt a certain way. Saul Kripke *(op. cit.)* argues that causal behaviorist and related analyses of the mental fail because they construe, e.g., "pain" as a merely contingent name of pains. The subjective character of an experience ("its immediate phenomenological quality" Kripke calls it [p. 340]) is the essential property left out by such analyses, and the one in virtue of which it is, necessarily, the experience it is. My view is closely related to his. Like Kripke, I find the hypothesis that a certain brain state should *necessarily* have a certain subjective character incomprehensible without further explanation. No such explanation emerges from theories which view the mind–brain relation as contingent, but perhaps there are other alternatives, not yet discovered.

A theory that explained how the mind–brain relation was

necessary would still leave us with Kripke's problem of explaining why it nevertheless appears contingent. That difficulty seems to me surmountable, in the following way. We may imagine something by representing it to ourselves either perceptually, sympathetically, or symbolically. I shall not try to say how symbolic imagination works, but part of what happens in the other two cases is this. To imagine something perceptually, we put ourselves in a conscious state resembling the state we would be in if we perceived it. To imagine something sympathetically, we put ourselves in a conscious state resembling the thing itself. (This method can be used only to imagine mental events and states—our own or another's.) When we try to imagine a mental state occurring without its associated brain state, we first sympathetically imagine the occurrence of the mental state: that is, we put ourselves into a state that resembles it mentally. At the same time, we attempt to perceptually imagine the non-occurrence of the associated physical state, by putting ourselves into another state unconnected with the first: one resembling that which we would be in if we perceived the non-occurrence of the physical state. Where the imagination of physical features is perceptual and the imagination of mental features is sympathetic, it appears to us that we can imagine any experience occurring without its associated brain state, and vice versa. The relation between them will appear contingent even if it is necessary, because of the independence of the disparate types of imagination.

(Solipsism, incidentally, results if one misinterprets sympathetic imagination as if it worked like perceptual imagination: it then seems impossible to imagine any experience that is not one's own.)

12. See "Mental Events" in Foster and Swanson, *Experience and Theory* (Amherst, 1970); though I don't understand the argument against psychophysical laws.

13. Similar remarks apply to my paper "Physicalism," *Philosophical Review* LXXIV (1965), 339–356, reprinted with postscript in John O'Connor, *Modern Materialism* (New York, 1969).

14. This question also lies at the heart of the problem of other minds, whose close connection with the mind–body problem is often overlooked. If one understood how subjective experience could have an objective nature, one would understand the existence of subjects other than oneself.

15. I have not defined the term "physical." Obviously it does not apply just to what can be described by the concepts of contemporary physics, since we expect further developments. Some may think there is nothing to prevent mental phenomena from eventually being recognized as physical in their own right. But whatever else may be said of the physical, it has to be objective. So if our idea of the physical ever expands to include mental phenomena, it will have to assign them an objective character—whether or not this is done by analyzing them in terms of other phenomena already regarded as physical. It seems to me more likely, however, that mental–physical relations will eventually be expressed in a theory whose fundamental terms cannot be placed clearly in either category.

16. I have read versions of this paper to a number of audiences, and am indebted to many people for their comments.

47

Gilbert Ryle

from "Self-Knowledge"

(6) The Self

Not only theorists but also quite unsophisticated people, including young children, find perplexities in the notion of 'I'. Children sometimes puzzle their heads with such questions as, 'What would it be like if I became you and you became me?' and 'Where was I before I began?' Theologians have been exercised over the question 'What is it in an individual which is saved or damned?', and philosophers have speculated whether 'I' denotes a peculiar and separate substance and in what consists my indivisible and continuing identity. Not all such puzzles arise from the unwitting adoption of the para-mechanical hypothesis, and I propose in this section to try to do justice to one particular family of such enigmas, the expounding and solving of which may be of some general theoretical interest.

The enigmas that I have in mind all turn on what I shall call the 'systematic elusiveness' of the concept of 'I'. When a child, like Kim, having no theoretical commitments or equipment, first asks himself, 'Who or What am I?' he does not ask it from a desire to know his own surname, age, sex, nationality or position in the form. He knows all his ordinary personalia. He feels that there is something else in the background for which his 'I' stands, a something which has still to be described after all his ordinary personalia have been listed. He also feels, very vaguely, that whatever it is that his 'I' stands for, it is something very important and quite unique, unique in the sense that neither it, nor anything like it, belongs to anyone else. There *could* only be one of it. Pronouns like 'you', 'she' and 'we' feel quite unmystifying, while 'I'

feels mystifying. And it feels mystifying, anyhow in part, because the more the child tries to put his finger on what 'I' stands for, the less does he succeed in doing so. He can catch only its coat-tails; it itself is always and obdurately a pace ahead of its coat-tails. Like the shadow of one's own head, it will not wait to be jumped on. And yet it is never very far ahead; indeed, sometimes it seems not to be ahead of the pursuer at all. It evades capture by lodging itself inside the very muscles of the pursuer. It is too near even to be within arm's reach.

Theorists have found themselves mocked in a similar way by the concept of 'I'. Even Hume confesses that, when he has tried to sketch all the items of his experience, he has found nothing there to answer to the word 'I', and yet he is not satisfied that there does not remain something more and something important, without which his sketch fails to describe his experience.

Other epistemologists have felt similar qualms. Should I, or should I not, put my knowing self down on my list of the sorts of things that I can have knowledge of? If I say 'no', it seems to reduce my knowing self to a theoretically infertile mystery, yet if I say 'yes', it seems to reduce the fishing-net to one of the fishes which it itself catches. It seems hazardous either to allow or to deny that the judge can be put into the dock.

* * * * *

In considering specifically human behaviour—behaviour, that is, which is unachieved by animals, infants and idiots—we should for several reasons notice the fact that some sorts of actions are in one way or another concerned with, or are operations upon, other actions. When one person retaliates

Excerpted by permission of the publisher from Gilbert Ryle, *The Concept of Mind*. London: Hutchinson and Company, Ltd., 1949, from chap. 6, from §§6–7, pp. 186–87, 191, and 195–98. Copyright © 1949 by Century Hutchinson Publishing Group, Ltd.

upon another, scoffs at him, replies to him or plays hide-and-seek with him, his actions have to do, in one way or another, with certain actions on the part of the other; in a sense to be specified later, the performance of the former involves the thought of the latter. An action on the part of one agent could not be one of spying or applauding, unless it had to do with the actions of another agent; nor could I behave as a customer, unless you or someone else behaved as a seller. One man must give evidence if another is to cross-examine him; some people must be on the stage, if others are to be dramatic critics. It will sometimes be convenient to use the title 'higher order actions' to denote those the descriptions of which involve the oblique mention of other actions.

* * * * *

(7) The Systematic Elusiveness of 'I'

We are now in a position to account for the systematic elusiveness of the notion of 'I', and the partial non-parallelism between it and the notion of 'you' or 'he'. To concern oneself about oneself in any way, theoretical or practical, is to perform a higher order act, just as it is to concern oneself about anybody else. To try, for example, to describe what one has just done, or is now doing, is to comment upon a step which is not itself, save *per accidens,* one of commenting. But the operation which is the commenting is not, and cannot be, the step on which that commentary is being made. Nor can an act of ridiculing be its own butt. A higher order action cannot be the action upon which it is performed. So my commentary on my performances must always be silent about one performance, namely itself, and this performance can be the target only of another commentary. Self-commentary, self-ridicule and self-admonition are logically condemned to eternal penultimacy. Yet nothing that is left out of any particular commentary or admonition is privileged thereby to escape comment or admonition for ever. On the contrary it may be the target of the very next comment or rebuke.

The point may be illustrated in this way. A singing-master might criticise the accents or notes of a pupil by mimicking with exaggerations each word that the pupil sang; and if the pupil sang slowly enough, the master could parody each word sung by the pupil before the next came to be uttered. But then, in a mood of humility, the singing-master tries to criticise his own singing in the same way, and more than that to mimic with exaggerations each word that he utters, including those that he utters in self-parody. It is at once clear, first, that he can never get beyond the very earliest word of

his song and, second, that at any given moment he has uttered one noise which has yet to be mimicked—and it makes no difference how rapidly he chases his notes with mimicries of them. He can, in principle, never catch more than the coat-tails of the object of his pursuit, since a word cannot be a parody of itself. None the less, there is no word that he sings which remains unparodied; he is always a day late for the fair, but every day he reaches the place of yesterday's fair. He never succeeds in jumping on to the shadow of his own head, yet he is never more than one jump behind.

An ordinary reviewer may review a book, while a second order reviewer criticises reviews of the book. But the second order review is not a criticism of itself. It can only be criticised in a further third order review. Given complete editorial patience, any review of any order could be published, though at no stage would all the reviews have received critical notices. Nor can every act of a diarist be the topic of a record in his diary; for the last entry made in his diary still demands that the making of it should in its turn be chronicled.

This, I think, explains the feeling that my last year's self, or my yesterday's self, could in principle be exhaustively described and accounted for, and that my past or present self could be exhaustively described and accounted for by me, but that my today's self perpetually slips out of any hold of it that I try to take. It also explains the apparent non-parallelism between the notion of 'I' and that of 'you', without construing the elusive residuum as any kind of ultimate mystery.

There is another thing which it explains. When people consider the problems of the Freedom of the Will and try to imagine their own careers as analogous to those of clocks or water-courses, they tend to boggle at the idea that their own immediate future is already unalterably fixed and predictable. It seems absurd to suppose that what I am just about to think, feel or do is already preappointed, though people are apt to find no such absurdity in the supposition that the futures of other people are so preappointed. The so-called 'feeling of spontaneity' is closely connected with this inability to imagine that what I am going to think or do can already be anticipated. On the other hand, when I consider what I thought and did yesterday, there seems to be no absurdity in supposing that that could have been forecast, before I did it. It is only while I am actually trying to predict my own next move that the task feels like that of a swimmer trying to overtake the waves that he sends ahead of himself.

The solution is as before. A prediction of a deed or a thought is a higher order operation, the performance of which cannot be among the things considered in making the prediction. Yet as the state of mind in which I am just before I do something may make some difference to what I do, it follows that I must overlook at least one of the data relevant to my prediction. Similarly, I can give you the fullest possible advice what to do, but I must omit one piece of counsel, since I cannot in the same breath advise you how to take that advice. There is therefore no paradox in saying that while normally I am not at all surprised to find myself doing or thinking what I do, yet when I try most carefully to anticipate what I shall do or think, then the outcome is likely to falsify my expectation. My process of pre-envisaging may divert the course of my ensuing behaviour in a direction and degree of which my prognosis cannot take account. One thing that I cannot prepare myself for is the next thought that I am going to think.

The fact that my immediate future is in this way systematically elusive to me has, of course, no tendency to prove that my career is in principle unpredictable to prophets other than myself, or even that it is inexplicable to myself after the heat of the action. I can point to any other thing with my index-finger, and other people can point at this finger. But it cannot be the object at which it itself is pointing. Nor can a missile be its own target, though anything else may be thrown at it.

This general conclusion that any performance can be the concern of a higher order performance, but cannot be the concern of itself, is connected with what was said earlier about the special functioning of index words, such as 'now', 'you' and 'I'. An 'I' sentence indicates whom in particular it is about by being itself uttered or written by someone in particular. 'I' indicates the person who utters it. So, when a person utters an 'I' sentence, his utterance of it may be part of a higher order performance, namely one, perhaps of self-reporting, self-exhortation or self-commiseration, and this performance itself is not dealt with in the opera-

tion which it itself is. Even if the person is, for special speculative purposes, momentarily concentrating on the Problem of the Self, he has failed and knows that he has failed to catch more than the flying coat-tails of that which he was pursuing. His quarry was the hunter.

To conclude, there is nothing mysterious or occult about the range of higher order acts and attitudes, which are apt to be inadequately covered by the umbrella-title 'self-consciousness'. They are the same in kind as the higher order acts and attitudes exhibited in the dealings of people with one other. Indeed the former are only a special application of the latter and are learned first from them. If I perform the third order operation of commenting on a second order act of laughing at myself for a piece of manual awkwardness, I shall indeed use the first personal pronoun in two different ways. I say to myself, or to the company, 'I was laughing at myself for being butter-fingered'. But so far from this showing that there are two 'Mes' in my skin, not to speak, yet, of the third one which is still commenting on them, it shows only that I am applying the public two-pronoun idiom in which we talk of her laughing at him; and I am applying this linguistic idiom, because I am applying the method of inter-personal transaction which the idiom is ordinarily employed to describe.

Before concluding this chapter, it is worth mentioning that there is one influential difference between the first personal pronoun and all the rest. 'I', in my use of it, always indicates me and only indicates me. 'You', 'she' and 'they' indicate different people at different times. 'I' is like my own shadow; I can never get away from it, as I can get away from your shadow. There is no mystery about this constancy, but I mention it because it seems to endow 'I' with a mystifying uniqueness and adhesiveness. 'Now' has something of the same besetting feeling.

48

Thomas Nagel

"Brain Bisection and the Unity of Consciousness"

I

There has been considerable optimism recently, among philosophers and neuroscientists, concerning the prospect for major discoveries about the neurophysiological basis of mind. The support for this optimism has been extremely abstract and general. I wish to present some grounds for pessimism. That type of self-understanding may encounter limits which have not been generally foreseen: the personal, mentalist idea of human beings may resist the sort of coordination with an understanding of humans as physical systems, that would be necessary to yield anything describable as an understanding of the physical basis of mind. I shall not consider what alternatives will be open to us if we should encounter such limits. I shall try to present grounds for believing that the limits may exist—grounds derived from extensive data now available about the interaction between the two halves of the cerebral cortex, and about what happens when they are disconnected. The feature of the mentalist conception of persons which may be recalcitrant to integration with these data is not a trivial or peripheral one, that might easily be abandoned. It is the idea of a *single* person, a single subject of experience and action, that is in difficulties. The difficulties may be surmountable in ways I have not foreseen. On the other hand, this may be only the first of many dead ends that will emerge as we seek a physiological understanding of the mind.

To seek the physical basis or realization of features of the phenomenal world is in many areas a profitable first line of inquiry, and it is the line encouraged, for the case of mental phenomena, by those who look forward to some variety of empir-

ical reduction of mind to brain, through an identity theory, a functionalist theory, or some other device. When physical reductionism is attempted for a phenomenal feature of the external world, the results are sometimes very successful, and can be pushed to deeper and deeper levels. If, on the other hand, they are not entirely successful, and certain features of the phenomenal picture remain unexplained by a physical reduction, then we can set those features aside as *purely* phenomenal, and postpone our understanding of them to the time when our knowledge of the physical basis of mind and perception will have advanced sufficiently to supply it. (An example of this might be the moon illusion, or other sensory illusions which have no discoverable basis in the objects perceived.)

However, if we encounter the same kind of difficulty in exploring the physical basis of the phenomena of the mind itself, we cannot adopt the same line of retreat. That is, if a phenomenal feature of mind is left unaccounted for by the physical theory, we cannot postpone the understanding of it to the time when we study the mind itself—for that is exactly what we are supposed to be doing. To defer to an understanding of the basis of mind which lies beyond the study of the physical realization of certain aspects of it is to admit the irreducibility of the mental to the physical. A clearcut version of this admission would be some kind of dualism. But if one is reluctant to take such a route, then it is not clear what one should do about central features of the mentalistic idea of persons which resist assimilation to an understanding of human beings as physical system. It may be true of some of these features that we can neither find an objective basis for them, nor give them up. It may be impossible for us to abandon certain ways of conceiving and representing ourselves, no matter how little support they get from scientific research. This, I suspect, is true of the idea of the unity of a person: an idea whose validity may be called into question with the help of recent discoveries about the functional duality of the cerebral cortex. It will be useful to present those results here in outline.

II

The higher connections between the two cerebral hemispheres have been severed in men, monkeys, and cats, and the results have led some investigators to speak of the creation of two separate centers of consciousness in a single body. The facts are as follows.[1]

By and large, the left cerebral hemisphere is associated with the right side of the body and the right hemisphere with the left side. Tactual stimuli from one side are transmitted to the opposite hemisphere—with the exception of the head and neck, which are connected to both sides. In addition, the left half of each retina, i.e. that which scans the right half of the visual field, sends impulses to the left hemisphere, and impulses from the left half of the visual field are transmitted by the right half of each retina to the right hemisphere. Auditory impulses from each ear are to some degree transmitted to both hemispheres. Smells, on the other hand, are transmitted ipsilaterally: the left nostril transmits to the left hemisphere and the right nostril to the right. Finally, the left hemisphere usually controls the production of speech.

Both hemispheres are linked to the spinal column and peripheral nerves through a common brain stem, but they also communicate directly with one another, by a large transverse band of nerve fibres called the corpus callosum, plus some smaller pathways. These direct cerebral commissures play an essential role in the ordinary integration of function between the hemisphere of normal persons. It is one of the striking features of the subject that this fact remained unknown, at least in the English-speaking world, until the late 1950's, even though a number of patients had had their cerebral commissures surgically severed in operations for the treatment of epilepsy a decade earlier. No significant behavioral or mental effects on these patients could be observed, and it was conjectured that the corpus callosum had no function whatever, except perhaps to keep the hemispheres from sagging.

Then R. E. Myers and R. W. Sperry introduced a technique for dealing with the two hemispheres separately.[2] They sectioned the optic chiasma of cats, so that each eye sent direct information (information about the opposite half of the visual field) only to one side of the brain. It was then possible to train the cats in simple tasks using one eye, and to see what happened when one made them use the other eye instead. In cats whose callosum was intact, there was very good transfer of learning. But in some cats, they severed the corpus callosum as well as the optic chiasma; and in these cases nothing was transmitted from one side to the other. In fact the two severed sides could be taught conflicting discriminations simultaneously, by giving the two eyes opposite stimuli during a single course of reinforcement. Nevertheless this capacity for independent function did not result in serious deficits of behavior. Unless inputs to the two hemispheres were artificially segregated, the animal seemed normal; (though if a split-brain monkey gets hold of a peanut with both hands, the result is sometimes a tug of war.)

Instead of summarizing all the data, I shall concentrate on the human cases, a reconsideration of which was prompted by the findings with cats and monkeys.[3] In the brain-splitting operation for epilepsy, the optic chiasma is left intact, so one cannot get at the two hemispheres separately just through the two eyes. The solution to the problem

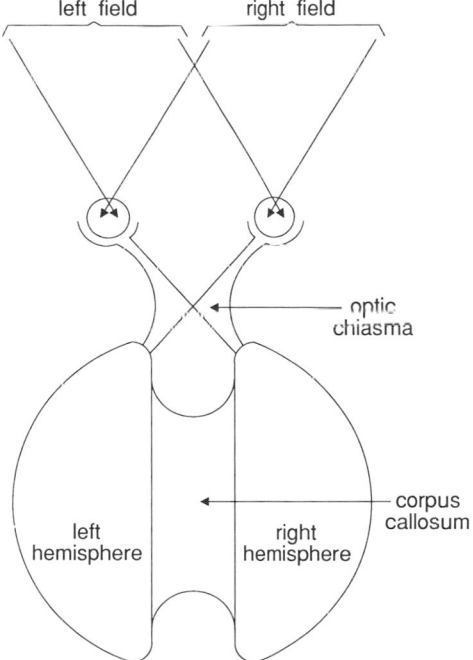

Fig. 1. A very schematic top view of the eyes and cerebral cortex.

of controlling visual input is to flash signals on a screen, on one or other side of the midpoint of the patient's gaze, long enough to be perceived but not long enough to permit an eye movement which would bring the signal to the opposite half visual field and hence to the opposite side of the brain. This is known as tachistoscopic stimulation. Tactile inputs through the hands are for the most part very efficiently segragated, and so are smells through the two nostrils. Some success has even been achieved recently in segregating auditory input, since each ear seems to signal more powerfully to the contralateral than to the ipsilateral hemisphere. As for output, the clearest distinction is provided by speech, which is exclusively the product of the left hemisphere.[4] Writing is a less clear case: it can occasionally be produced in rudimentary form by the right hemisphere, using the left hand. In general, motor control is contralateral, i.e. by the opposite hemisphere, but a certain amount of ipsilateral control sometimes occurs, particularly on the part of the left hemisphere.

The results are as follows. What is flashed to the right half of the visual field, or felt unseen by the right hand, can be reported verbally. What is flashed to the left half field or felt by the left hand cannot be reported, though if the word 'hat' is flashed on the left, the left hand will retrieve a hat from a group of concealed objects if the person is told to pick out what he has seen. At the same time he will insist verbally that he saw nothing. Or, if two different words are flashed to the two half fields (e.g. 'pencil' and 'toothbrush') and the individual is told to retrieve the corresponding object from beneath a screen, with both hands, then the hands will search the collection of objects independently, the right hand picking up the pencil and discarding it while the left hand searches for it, and the left hand similarly rejecting the toothbrush which the right had lights upon with satisfaction.

If a concealed object is placed in the left hand and the person is asked to guess what it is, wrong guesses will elicit an annoyed frown, since the right hemisphere, which receives the tactile information, also hears the answers. If the speaking hemisphere should guess correctly, the result is a smile. A smell fed to the right nostril (which stimulates the right hemisphere) will elicit a verbal denial that the subject smells anything, but if asked to point with the left hand at a corresponding object he will succeed in picking out e.g. a clove of garlic, protesting all the while that he smells absolutely nothing, so how can he possibly point to what he smells. If the smell is an unpleasant one like that of rotten eggs, these denials will be accompanied by wrinklings of the nose and mouth, and guttural exclamations of disgust.[5]

One particularly poignant example of conflict between the hemispheres is as follows. A pipe is placed out of sight in the patient's left hand, and he is then asked to write with his left hand what he was holding. Very laboriously and heavily, the left hand writes the letters P and I. Then suddenly the writing speeds up and becomes lighter, the I is converted to an E, and the word is completed as PENCIL. Evidently the left hemisphere has made a guess based on the appearance of the first two letters, and has interfered, with ipsilateral control. But then the right hemisphere takes over control of the hand again, heavily crosses out the letters ENCIL, and draws a crude picture of a pipe.[6]

There are many more data. The split brain patient cannot tell whether shapes flashed to the two half visual fields or held out of sight in the two hands are the same or different—even if he is asked to indicate the answer by nodding or shaking his head (responses available to both hemispheres). The subject cannot distinguish a continuous from a discontinuous line flashed across both halves of the visual field, if the break comes in the middle. Nor can he tell whether two lines meet at an angle, if the joint is in the middle. Nor can he tell whether two spots in opposite half-fields are the same or different in color—though he can do all these things if the images to be compared fall within a single half field. On the whole the right hemisphere does better at spatial relations tests, but is almost incapable of calculation. It appears susceptible to emotion, however. For example, if a photograph of a naked woman is flashed to the left half field of a male patient, he will grin broadly and perhaps blush, without being able to say what has pleased him, though he may say "Wow, that's quite a machine you've got there".

All this is combined with what appears to be complete normalcy in ordinary activities, when no segregation of input to the two hemispheres has been artificially created. Both sides fall asleep and wake up at the same time. The patients can play the piano, button their shirts, swim, and perform well in other activites requiring bilateral coordination. Moreover they do not report any sensation of division or reduction of the visual field. The most notable deviation in ordinary behavior was in a patient whose left hand appeared to be somewhat hostile to the patient's wife. But by and large the hemispheres cooperate admirably, and it requires subtle experimental techniques to get them to operate separately. If one is not careful, they will give each other peripheral cues, transmitting information by audible, visible, or otherwise sensorily perceptible signals which compensate for the lack of a direct commissural link. (One form of communication is particularly difficult to prevent, because it is so direct: both hemispheres can move the neck and facial muscles, and both can feel them move; so a response produced in the face or head by the right hemisphere can be detected by the left, and there is some evidence that they send signals to one another via this medium.)[7]

III

What one naturally wants to know about these patients is how many minds they have. This immediately raises questions about the sense in which an ordinary person can be said to have one mind, and what the conditions are under which diverse experiences and activities can be ascribed to the same mind. We must have some idea what an ordinary person is one of in order to understand what we want to know whether there is *one or two* of, when we try to describe these extraordinary patients.

However, instead of beginning with an analysis of the unity of the mind, I am going to proceed by attempting to apply the ordinary, unanalyzed conception directly in the interpretation of these data, asking whether the patients have one mind, or two, or some more exotic configuration. My conclusion will be that the ordinary conception of a single, countable mind cannot be applied to them at all, and that there is no number of such minds that they possess, though they certainly engage in mental activity. A clearer understanding of the idea of an individual mind should emerge in the course of this discussion but the difficulties which stand in the way of its application to the split-brain cases will provide ground for more general doubts. The concept may not be applicable to ordinary human beings either, for it embodies too simple a conception of the way in which human beings function.

Nevertheless I shall employ the notion of an individual mind in discussing the cases initially, for I wish to consider systematically how they might be understood in terms of countable minds, and to argue that they cannot be. After having done this, I shall turn to ordinary people like you and me.

There appear to be five interpretations of the experimental data which utilize the concept of an individual mind.

(1) The patients have one fairly normal mind associated with the left hemisphere, and the responses emanating from the nonverbal right hemisphere are the responses of an automaton, and are not produced by conscious mental processes.

(2) The patients have only one mind, associated with the left hemisphere, but there also occur (associated with the right hemisphere) isolated conscious mental phenomena, not integrated into a mind at all, though they can perhaps be ascribed to the organism.

(3) The patients have two minds, one which can talk and one which can't.

(4) They have one mind, whose contents derive from both hemispheres and are rather peculiar and dissociated.

(5) They have one normal mind most of the time, while the hemispheres are functioning in parallel, but two minds are elicited by the experimental situations which yield the interesting results. (Perhaps the single mind splits in two and reconvenes after the experiment is over.)

I shall argue that each of these interpretations is unacceptable for one reason or another.

IV

Let me first discuss hypotheses (1) and (2), which have in common the refusal to ascribe the activities of the right hemisphere to a mind, and then go on to treat hypotheses (3), (4), and (5), all of which associate a mind with the activities of the right hemisphere, though they differ on what mind it is.

The only support for hypothesis (1), which refuses to ascribe consciousness to the activities of the right hemisphere at all, is the fact that the subject consistently denies awareness of the activities of that hemisphere. But to take this as proof that the activities of the right hemisphere are unconscious is to beg the question, since the capacity to give testimony is the exclusive ability of the left hemisphere, and of course the left hemisphere is not conscious of what is going on in the right. If on the other hand we consider the manifestations of the right hemisphere itself, there seems no reason in principle to regard verbalizability as a *necessary* condition of consciousness. There may be other grounds for the ascription of conscious mental states that are sufficient even without verbalization. And in fact, what the right hemisphere can do on its own is too elaborate, too intentionally directed and too psychologically intelligible to be regarded merely as a collection of unconscious automatic responses.

The right hemisphere is not very intelligent and it cannot talk; but it is able to respond to complex visual and auditory stimuli, including language, and it can control the performance of discriminatory and manipulative tasks requiring close attention—such as the spelling out of simple words with plastic letters. It can integrate auditory, visual, and tactile stimuli in order to follow the experimenter's instructions, and it can take certain aptitude tests. There is no doubt that if a person were deprived of his left hemisphere entirely, so that the only capacities remaining to him were those of the right, we should not on that account say that he had been converted into an automaton. Though speechless, he would remain conscious and active, with a diminished visual field and partial paralysis on the right side from which he would eventually recover to some extent. In view of this, it would seem arbitrary to deny that the activities of the right hemisphere are conscious, just because they occur side by side with those of the left hemisphere, about whose consciousness there is no question.

I do not wish to claim that the line between conscious and unconscious mental activity is a sharp one. It is even possible that the distinction is partly relative, in the sense that a given item of mental activity may be assignable to consciousness or not, depending on what other mental activities of the same person are going on at the same time, and whether it is connected with them in a suitable way. Even if this is true, however, the activities of the right hemisphere in split-brain patients do not fall into the category of events whose inclusion in consciousness depends on what else is going on in the patient's mind. Their determinants include a full range of psychological factors, and they demand alertness. It is clear that attention, even concentration is demanded for the tasks of the concealed left hand and tachistoscopically stimulated left visual field. The subjects do not take their experimental tests in a dreamy fashion: they are obviously in contact with reality. The left hemisphere occasionally complains about being asked to perform tasks which the right hemisphere can perform, because it does not know what is going on when the right hemisphere controls the response. But the right hemisphere displays enough awareness of what it is doing to justify the attribution of conscious control in the absence of verbal testimony. If the patients did not deny any awareness of those activities, no doubts about their consciousness would arise at all.

The considerations that make the first hypothesis untenable also serve to refute hypothesis (2), which suggests that the activities of the right hemisphere are conscious without belonging to a mind at all. There may be problems about the intelligibility of this proposal, but we need not consider them here, because it is rendered implausible by the high degree of organization and intermodal coherence of the right hemisphere's mental activities. They are not free-floating, and they are not organized in a fragmentary way. The right hemisphere follows instructions, integrates tactile, auditory

and visual stimuli, and does most of the things a good mind should do. The data present us not merely with slivers of purposive behavior, but with a system capable of learning, reacting emotionally, following instructions, and carrying out tasks which require the integration of diverse psychological determinants. It seems clear that the right hemisphere's activities are not unconscious, and that they belong to something having a characteristically mental structure: a subject of experience and action.

V

Let me now turn to the three hypotheses according to which the conscious mental activities of the right hemisphere are ascribed to a mind. They have to be considered together, because the fundamental difficulty about each of them lies in the impossibility of deciding among them. The question, then, is whether the patients have two minds, one mind, or a mind that occasionally splits in two.

There is much to recommend the view that they have two minds, i.e. that the activities of the right hemisphere belong to a mind of their own.[8] Each side of the brain seems to produce its own perceptions, beliefs, and actions, which are connected with one another in the usual way, but not to those of the opposite side. The two halves of the cortex share a common body, which they control through a common midbrain and spinal cord. But their higher functions are independent not only physically but psychologically. Functions of the right hemisphere are inaccessible not only to speech but to any direct combination with corresponding functions of the left hemisphere—i.e. with functions of a type that the right hemisphere finds easy on its home ground, like shape or color discrimination.

One piece of testimony by the patient's left hemispheres may appear to argue against two minds. They report no diminution of the visual field, and little absence of sensation on the left side. Sperry dismisses this evidence on the ground that it is comparable to the testimony of victims of scotoma (partial destruction of the retina), that they notice no gaps in their visual field—although these gaps can be discovered by others observing their perceptual deficiencies. But we need not assume that an elaborate confabulatory mechanism is at work in the left hemisphere to account for such testimony. It is perfectly possible that although there are two minds, the mind associated with each hemisphere receives, through the common brain stem, a certain amount of crude ipsilateral stimulation, so that the speaking mind has a rudimentary and undifferentiated appendage to the left side of its visual field, and vice versa for the right hemisphere.[9]

The real difficulties for the two-minds hypothesis coincide with the reasons for thinking we are dealing with one mind—namely the highly integrated character of the patients' relations to the world in ordinary circumstances. When they are not in the experimental situation, their startling behavioral dissociation disappears, and they function normally. There is little doubt that information from the two sides of their brains can be pooled to yield integrated behavioral control. And although this is not accomplished by the usual methods, it is not clear that this settles the question against assigning the integrative functions to a single mind. After all, if the patient is permitted to touch things with both hands and smell them with both nostrils, he arrives at a unified idea of what is going on around him and what he is doing, without revealing any left–right inconsistencies in his behavior or attitudes. It seems strange to suggest that we are not in a position to ascribe all those experiences to the same person, just because of some peculiarities about how the integration is achieved. The people who *know* these patients find it natural to relate to them as single individuals.

Nevertheless, if we ascribe the integration to a single mind, we must also ascribe the experimentally evoked dissociation to that mind, and that is not easy. The experimental situation reveals a variety of dissociation or conflict that is unusual not only because of the simplicity of its anatomical basis, but because such a wide *range* of functions is split into two noncommunicating branches. It is not as though two conflicting volitional centers shared a common perceptual and reasoning apparatus. The split is much deeper than that. The one-mind hypothesis must therefore assert that the contents of the individual's single consciousness are produced by two independent control systems in the two hemispheres, each having a fairly complete mental structure. If this dual control were accomplished during experimental situations by temporal alternation, it would be intelligible, though mysterious. But that is not the hypothesis, and the hypothesis as it stands does not supply us with understanding. For in these patients there appear to be things happening *simultaneously* which cannot fit into a single mind: simultaneous attention to two incompatible tasks, for example, without interaction between the purposes of the left and right hands.

This makes it difficult to conceive what it is like to *be* one of these people. Lack of interaction at the level of a preconscious control system would be comprehensible. But lack of interaction in the domain of visual experience and conscious intention threatens assumptions about the unity of consciousness which are basic to our understanding of another individual as a person. These assumptions are associated with our conception of ourselves, which to a considerable extent constrains our understanding of others. And it is just these assumptions, I believe, that make it impossible to arrive at an interpretation of the cases under discussion in terms of a countable number of minds.

Roughly, we assume that a single mind has sufficiently immediate access to its conscious states so that, for elements of experience or other mental events occurring simultaneously or in close temporal proximity, the mind which is their subject can also experience the simpler *relations* between them if it attends to the matter. Thus, we assume that when a single person has two visual impressions, he can usually also experience the sameness or difference of their coloration, shape, size, the relation of their position and movement within his visual field, and so forth. The same can be said of cross-modal connections. The experiences of a single person are thought to take place in an *experientially* connected domain, so that the relations among experiences can be substantially captured in experiences of those relations.[10]

Split-brain patients fail dramatically to conform to these assumptions in experimental situations, and they fail over the simplest matters. Moreover the dissociation holds between two classes of conscious states each characterized by significant *internal* coherence: normal assumptions about the unity of consciousness hold intra-hemispherically, although the requisite comparisons cannot be made across the interhemispheric gap.

These considerations lead us back to the hypothesis that the patients have two minds each. It at least has the advantage of enabling us to understand what it is like to *be* these individuals, so long as we do not try to imagine what it is like to be both of them at the same time. Yet the way to a comfortable acceptance of this conclusion is blocked by the compelling behavioral integration which the patients display in ordinary life, in comparison to which the dissociated symptoms evoked by the experimental situation seem peripheral and atypical. We are faced with diametrically conflicting bodies of evidence, in a case which does not admit of arbitrary decision. There is a powerful inclination to feel that there must be *some* whole number of minds in those heads, but the data prevent us from deciding how many.

This dilemma makes hypothesis (5) initially attractive, especially since the data which yield the conflict are to some extent gathered at different times. But the suggestion that a second mind is brought into existence only during experimental situations loses plausibility on reflection. First, it is entirely ad hoc: it proposes to explain one change in terms of another without suggesting any explanation of the second. There is nothing about the experimental situation that might be expected to produce a fundamental internal change in the patient. In fact it produces no anatomical changes and merely elicits a noteworthy set of symptoms. So unusual an event as a mind's popping in and out of existence would have to be explained by something more than its explanatory convenience.

But secondly, the behavioral evidence would not even be explained by this hypothesis, simply because the patients' integrated responses and their dissociated responses are not clearly separated in time. During the time of the experiments the patient is functioning largely as if he were a single individual: in his posture, in following instructions about where to focus his eyes, in the whole range of trivial behavioral control involved in situating himself in relation to the experimenter and the experimental apparatus. The two halves of his brain cooperate completely except in regard to those very special inputs that reach them separately and differently. For these reasons hypothesis (5) does not seem to be a real option; if two minds are operating in the experimental situation, they must be operating largely in harmony although partly at odds. And if there are two minds then, why can there not be two minds operating essentially in parallel the rest of the time?

Nevertheless the psychological integration displayed by the patients in ordinary life is so complete that I do not believe it is possible to accept that conclusion, nor any conclusion involving the ascription to them of a whole number of minds. These cases fall midway between ordinary persons with intact brains (between whose cerebral hemispheres there is also cooperation, though it works largely via the corpus callosum), and pairs of individuals engaged in a performance requiring exact behavioral coordination, like using a two-handed saw, or playing a duet. In the latter type of case we have two minds which communicate by subtle peripheral cues; in the former we have a single mind. Nothing taken from either of those cases can compel us to assimilate the split-brain patient to one or the other of them. If we decided that they definitely had two minds, then it would be problematical why we didn't conclude on anatomical grounds that everyone has two minds, but that we don't notice it except in these odd cases because most pairs of minds in a single body run in perfect parallel due to the direct communication between the hemispheres which provide their anatomical bases. The two minds each of us has running in harness would be much the same except that one could talk and the other couldn't. But it is clear that this line of argument will get us nowhere. For if the idea of a single mind applies to anyone it applies to ordinary individuals with intact brains, and if it does not apply to them it ought to be scrapped, in which case there is no point in asking whether those with split brains have one mind or two.[11]

VI

If I am right, and there is no whole number of individual minds that these patients can be said to have, then the attribution of conscious, significant mental activity does not require the existence of a single mental subject. This is extremely puzzling in itself, for it runs counter to our need to construe the mental states we ascribe to others on the model of our own. Something in the ordinary conception of a person, or in the ordinary conception of experience, leads to the demand for an account of these cases which the same conception makes it impossible to provide. This may seem a problem not worth worrying about very much. It is not so surprising that, having begun with a phenomenon which is radically different from anything else previously known, we should come to the conclusion that it cannot be adequately described in ordinary terms. However, I believe that consideration of these very unusual cases should cause us to be skeptical about the concept of a single subject of consciousness as it applies to ourselves.

The fundamental problem in trying to understand these cases in mentalistic terms is that we take ourselves as paradigms of psychological unity, and are then unable to project ourselves into their mental lives, either once or twice. But in thus using ourselves as the touchstone of whether another organism can be said to house an individual subject of experience or not, we are subtly ignoring the possiblity that our own unity may be nothing absolute, but merely another case of integration, more or less effective, in the control system of a complex organism. This system speaks in the first person singular through our mouths, and that makes it understandable that we should think of its unity as in some sense numerically absolute, rather than relative and a function of the integration of its contents.

But this is quite genuinely an illusion. The illusion consists in projecting inward to the center of the mind the very subject whose unity we are trying to explain: the individual person with all his complexities. The ultimate account of the unity of what we call a single mind consists of an enumeration of the types of functional integration that typify it. We know that these can be eroded in different ways, and to different degrees. The belief that even in their complete version they can be explained by the presence of a numerically single subject is an illusion. Either this subject contains the mental life, in which case it is complex and its unity must be accounted for in terms of the unified operation of its components and functions, or else it is an extensionless point, in which case it explains nothing.

An intact brain contains two cerebral hemispheres each of which possesses perceptual, memory, and control systems adequate to run the body without the assistance of the other. They cooperate in directing it with the aid of a constant two-way internal communication system. Memories, perceptions, desires and so forth therefore have duplicate physical bases on both sides of the brain, not just on account of similarities of initial input, but because of subsequent exchange. The cooperation of the undetached hemispheres in controlling the body is more efficient and direct than the cooperation of a pair of detached hemispheres, but it is cooperation nonetheless. Even if we analyze the idea of unity in terms of functional integration, therefore, the unity of our own consciousness may be less clear than we had supposed. The natural conception of a single person controlled by a mind possessing a single visual field, individual faculties for each of the other senses, unitary systems of memory, desire, belief, and so forth, may come into conflict with the physiological facts when it is applied to ourselves.

The concept of a person might possibly survive an application to cases which require us to speak of two or more persons in one body, but it seems strongly committed to some form of whole number countablity. Since even this seems open to doubt, it is possible that the ordinary, simple idea of a single person will come to seem quaint some day, when the complexities of the human control system become clearer and we become less certain that there is anything very important that we are *one* of. But it is also possible that we shall be unable to abandon the idea no matter what we discover.[12]

NOTES

1. The literature on split brains is sizeable. An excellent recent survey is Michael S. Gazzaniga, *The Bisected Brain*, New York, Appleton-Century-Crofts, 1970. Its nine-page list of references is not intended to be a complete bibliography of the subject, however. Gazzaniga has also written a brief popular exposition: 'The Split Brain in Man', *Scientific American* **217** (1967), p. 24. The best general treatment for philosophical purposes is to be found in several papers by R. W. Sperry, the leading investigator in the field: 'The Great Cerebral Commissure', *Scientific American* **210** (1964), p. 42; 'Brain Bisection and Mechanisms of Consciousness' in *Brain and Conscious Experience,* ed. by Eccles, J. C., Berlin, Springer-Verlag, 1966; 'Mental Unity Following Surgical Disconnections of the Cerebral Hemispheres', *The Harvey Lectures*, Series **62**, New York, Academic Press, 1968, p. 293; 'Hemisphere Deconnection and Unity in Conscious Awareness', *American Psychologist* **23** (1968), p. 723. Several interesting papers are to be found in *Functions of the Corpus Callosum: Ciba Foundation Study Group No. 20,* ed. by G. Ettlinger, London, J. and A. Churchill, 1965.

2. Myers and Sperry, 'Interocular Transfer of a Visual Form Discrimination Habit in Cats after Section of the Optic Chiasm and Corpus Callosum', *Anatomical Record* **115** (1953), p. 351; Myers, 'Interocular Transfer of Pattern Discrimination in Cats Following Section of Crossed Optic Fibers', *Journal of Comparative and Physiological Psychology* **48** (1955), p. 470.

3. The first publication of these results was M. S. Gazzaniga, J. E. Bogen, and R. W. Sperry, 'Some Functional Effects of Sectioning the Cerebral Commissures in Man', *Proceedings of the National Academy of Sciences* **48** (1962), Part 2, p. 1765. Interestingly the same year saw publication of a paper proposing the interpretation of a case of human brain *damage* along similar lines, suggested by the earlier findings with animals. Cf. N. Geschwind and E. Kaplan, 'A Human Cerebral Deconnection Syndrome', *Neurology* **12** (1962), p. 675. Also of interest is Geschwind's long two-part survey of the field, which takes up some philosophical questions explicitly: 'Disconnextion Syndromes in Animals and Man', *Brain* **88** (1965) 247–94, 585–644. Parts of it are reprinted, with other material, in *Boston Studies in the Philosophy of Science*, Vol. IV (1969). See also his paper 'The Organization of Language and the Brain', *Science* **170** (1970), p. 940.

4. There are individual exceptions to this, as there are to most generalizations about cerebral function: left-handed people tend to have bilateral linguistic control, and it is common in early childhood. All the subjects of these experiments, however, were right-handed, and displayed left cerebral dominance.

5. H. W. Gordon and R. W. Sperry, 'Lateralization of Olfactory Perception in the Surgically Separated Hemispheres of Man', *Neuropsychologia* **7** (1969), p. 111. One patient, however, was able to say in these circumstances that he smelled something unpleasant, without being able to describe it further.

6. Reported in Jerre Levy, *Information Processing and Higher Psychological Functions in the Disconnected Hemispheres of Human Commissurotomy Patients* (unpublished doctoral dissertation, California Institute of Technology, 1969).

7. Moreover, the condition of radical disconnection may not be stable: there may be a tendency toward the formation of new interhemispheric pathways through the brain stem, with the lapse of time. This is supported partly by observation of commissurotomy patients, but more importantly by cases of agenesis of the callosum. People who have grown up without one have learned to manage without it; their performance

on the tests is much closer to normal than that of recently operated patients. (Cf. Saul and Sperry, 'Absence of Commissurotomy Symptoms with Agenesis of the Corpus Callosum', *Neurology* **18** (1968).) This fact is very important, but for the present I shall put it aside to concentrate on the immediate results of disconnection.

8. It is Sperry's view. He puts it as follows: "Instead of the normally unified single stream of consciousness, these patients behave in many ways as if they have two independent streams of conscious awareness, one in each hemisphere, each of which is cut off from and out of contact with the mental experiences of the other. In other words, each hemisphere seems to have its own separate and private sensations; its own perceptions; its own concepts; and its own impulses to act, with related volitional, cognitive, and learning experiences. Following the surgery, each hemisphere also has thereafter its own separate chain of memories that are rendered inaccessible to the recall process of the other." (*American Psychologist* **23**, *op. cit.*, p. 724.

9. There is some direct evidence for such primitive ipsilateral inputs, both visual and tactile; cf. Gazzaniga, *The Bisected Brain,* Chapter 3.

10. The two can of course diverge, and this fact underlies the classic philosophical problem of inverted spectra, which is only distantly related to the subject of this paper. Type of relation can hold between elements in the experience of a single person that cannot hold between elements of the experience of distinct persons: looking similar in color, for example. Insofar as our concept of similarity of experience in the case of a single person is dependent on his experience of similarity, the concept is not applicable between persons.

11. In case anyone is inclined to embrace the conclusion that we all have two minds, let me suggest that the trouble will not end here. For the mental operations of a single hemisphere, such as vision, hearing, speech, writing, verbal comprehension, etc. can to a great extent be separated from one another by suitable cortical deconnections; why then should we not regard *each* hemisphere as inhabited by several cooperating minds with specialized capacities? Where is one to stop? If the decision on the number of minds associated with a brain is largely arbitrary, the original point of the question has disappeared.

12. My research was supported in part by the National Science Foundation.

49

Harry G. Frankfurt

"Freedom of the Will and the Concept of a Person"

What philosophers have lately come to accept as analysis of the concept of a person is not actually analysis of *that* concept at all. Strawson, whose usage represents the current standard, identifies the concept of a person as "the concept of a type of entity such that *both* predicates ascribing states of consciousness *and* predicates ascribing corporeal characteristics . . . are equally applicable to a single individual of that single type."[1] But there are many entities besides persons that have both mental and physical properties. As it happens—though it seems extraordinary that this should be so—there is no common English word for the type of entity Strawson has in mind, a type that includes not only human beings but animals of various lesser species as well. Still, this hardly justifies the misappropriation of a valuable philosophical term.

Whether the members of some animal species are persons is surely not to be settled merely by determining whether it is correct to apply to them, in addition to predicates ascribing corporeal characteristics, predicates that ascribe states of consciousness. It does violence to our language to endorse the application of the term 'person' to those numerous creatures which do have both psychological and material properties but which are manifestly not persons in any normal sense of the word. This misuse of language is doubtless innocent of any theoretical error. But although the offense is "merely verbal," it does significant harm. For it gratuitously diminishes our philosophical vocabulary, and it increases the likelihood that we will overlook the important area of inquiry with which the term 'person' is most naturally associated. It might have been expected that no problem would be of more central and persistent concern to philosophers than that of understanding what we ourselves essentially are. Yet this problem is so generally neglected that it has been possible to make off with its very name almost without being noticed and, evidently, without evoking any widespread feeling of loss.

There is a sense in which the word 'person' is merely the singular form of 'people' and in which both terms connote no more than membership in a certain biological species. In those senses of the word which are of greater philosophical interest, however, the criteria for being a person do not serve primarily to distinguish the members of our own species from the members of other species. Rather, they are designed to capture those attributes which are the subject of our most humane concern with ourselves and the source of what we regard as most important and most problematical in our lives. Now these attributes would be of equal significance to us even if they were not in fact peculiar and common to the members of our own species. What interests us most in the human condition would not interest us less if it were also a feature of the condition of other creatures as well.

Our concept of ourselves as persons is not to be understood, therefore, as a concept of attributes that are necessarily species-specific. It is conceptually possible that members of novel or even of familiar nonhuman species should be persons; and it is also conceptually possible that some members of the human species are not persons. We do in fact assume, on the other hand, that no member of another species is a person. Accordingly, there is a presumption that what is essential to persons is a set of characteristics that we generally suppose—whether rightly or wrongly—to be uniquely human.

It is my view that one essential difference be-

From *The Journal of Philosophy* LXVIII, 1 (January 14, 1971): 5–20. Reprinted with permission of the editors and Harry G. Frankfurt.

tween persons and other creatures is to be found in the structure of a person's will. Human beings are not alone in having desires and motives, or in making choices. They share these things with the members of certain other species, some of whom even appear to engage in deliberation and to make decisions based upon prior thought. It seems to be peculiarly characteristic of humans, however, that they are able to form what I shall call "second-order desires" or "desires of the second order."

Besides wanting and choosing and being moved *to do* this or that, men may also want to have (or not to have) certain desires and motives. They are capable of wanting to be different, in their preferences and purposes, from what they are. Many animals appear to have the capacity for what I shall call "first-order desires" or "desires of the first order," which are simply desires to do or not to do one thing or another. No animal other than man, however, appears to have the capacity for reflective self-evaluation that is manifested in the formation of second-order desires.[2]

I

The concept designated by the verb 'to want' is extraordinarily elusive. A statement of the form "*A* wants to *X*"—taken by itself, apart from a context that serves to amplify or to specify its meaning—conveys remarkably little information. Such a statement may be consistent, for example, with each of the following statements: (a) the prospect of doing *X* elicits no sensation or introspectible emotional response in *A*; (b) *A* is unaware that he wants to *X*; (c) *A* believes that he does not want to *X*; (d) *A* wants to refrain from *X*-ing; (e) *A* wants to *Y* and believes that it is impossible for him both to *Y* and to *X*; (f) *A* does not "really" want to *X*; (g) *A* would rather die than *X*; and so on. It is therefore hardly sufficient to formulate the distinction between first-order and second-order desires, as I have done, by suggesting merely that someone has a first-order desire when he wants to do or not to do such-and-such, and that he has a second-order desire when he wants to have or not to have a certain desire of the first order.

As I shall understand them, statements of the form "*A* wants to *X*" cover a rather broad range of possibilities.[3] They may be true even when statements like (a) through (g) are true: when *A* is unaware of any feelings concerning *X*-ing, when he is unaware that he wants to *X*, when he deceives himself about what he wants and believes falsely that he does not want to *X*, when he also has other desires that conflict with his desire to *X*, or when he is ambivalent. The desires in question may be

conscious or unconscious, they need not be univocal, and *A* may be mistaken about them. There is a further source of uncertainty with regard to statements that identify someone's desires, however, and here it is important for my purposes to be less permissive.

Consider first those statements of the form "*A* wants to *X*" which identify first-order desires—that is, statements in which the term 'to *X*' refers to an action. A statement of this kind does not, by itself, indicate the relative strenght of *A*'s desire to *X*. It does not make it clear whether this desire is at all likely to play a decisive role in what *A* actually does or tries to do. For it may correctly be said that *A* wants to *X* even when his desire to *X* is only one among his desires and when it is far from being paramount among them. Thus, it may be true that *A* wants to *X* when he strongly prefers to do something else instead; and it may be true that he wants to *X* despite the fact that, when he acts, it is not the desire to *X* that motivates him to do what he does. On the other hand, someone who states that *A* wants to *X* may mean to convey that it is this desire that is motivating or moving *A* to do what he is actually doing or that *A* will in fact be moved by this desire (unless he changes his mind) when he acts.

It is only when it is used in the second of these ways that, given the special usage of 'will' that I propose to adopt, the statement identifies *A*'s will. To identify an agent's will is either to identify the desire (or desires) by which he is motivated in some action he performs or to identify the desire (or desires) by which he will or would be motivated when or if he acts. An agent's will, then, is identical with one or more of his first-order desires. But the notion of the will, as I am employing it, is not coextensive with the notion of first-order desires. It is not the notion of something that merely inclines an agent in some degree to act in a certain way. Rather, it is the notion of an *effective* desire—one that moves (or will or would move) a person all the way to action. Thus the notion of the will is not coextensive with the notion of what an agent intends to do. For even though someone may have a settled intention to do *X*, he may nonetheless do something else instead of doing *X* because, despite his intention, his desire to do *X* proves to be weaker or less effective than some conflicting desire.

Now consider those statements of the form "*A* wants to *X*" which identify second-order desires—that is, statements in which the term 'to *X*' refers to a desire of the first order. There are also two kinds of situation in which it may be true that *A* wants to want to *X*. In the first place, it might be true of *A* that he wants to have a desire to *X* despite the fact that he has a univocal desire, altogether free of conflict and ambivalence, to refrain from *X*-ing. Someone might want to have a certain desire, in other words, but univocally want that desire to be unsatisfied.

Suppose that a physician engaged in psychotherapy with narcotics addicts believes that his ability to help his patients would be enhanced if he understood better what it is like for them to desire the drug to which they are addicted. Suppose that he is led in this way to want to have a desire for the drug. If it is a genuine desire that he wants, then what he wants is not merely to feel the sensations that addicts characteristically feel when they are gripped by their desires for the drug. What the physician wants, insofar as he wants to have a desire, is to be inclined or moved to some extent to take the drug.

It is entirely possible, however, that, although he wants to be moved by a desire to take the drug, he does not want this desire to be effective. He may not want it to move him all the way to action. He need not be interested in finding out what it is like to take the drug. And insofar as he now wants only to *want* to take it, and not to *take* it, there is nothing in what he now wants that would be satisfied by the drug itself. He may now have, in fact, an altogether univocal desire *not* to take the drug; and he may prudently arrange to make it impossible for him to satisfy the desire he would have if his desire to want the drug should in time be satisfied.

It would thus be incorrect to infer, from the fact that the physician now wants to desire to take the drug, that he already does desire to take it. His second-order desire to be moved to take the drug does not entail that he has a first-order desire to take it. If the drug were now to be administered to him, this might satisfy no desire that is implicit in his desire to want to take it. While he wants to want to take the drug, he may have *no* desire to take it; it may be that *all* he wants is to taste the desire for it. That is, his desire to have a certain desire that he does not have may not be a desire that his will should be at all different than it is.

Someone who wants only in this truncated way to want to *X* stands at the margin of preciosity, and the fact that he wants to want to *X* is not pertinent to the identification of his will. There is, however, a second kind of situation that may be described by '*A* wants to want to *X*'; and when the statement is used to describe a situation of this second kind, then it does pertain to what *A* wants his will to be. In such cases the statement means that *A* wants the desire to *X* to be the desire that moves him effectively to act. It is not merely that he wants the desire to *X* to be among the desires by which, to one degree or another, he is moved or inclined to act.

He wants this desire to be effective—that is, to provide the motive in what he actually does. Now when the statement that *A* wants to want to *X* is used in this way, it does entail that *A* already has a desire to *X*. It could not be true both that *A* wants the desire to *X* to move him into action and that he does not want to *X*. It is only if he does want to *X* that he can coherently want the desire to *X* not merely to be one of his desires but, more decisively, to be his will.[4]

Suppose a man wants to be motivated in what he does by the desire to concentrate on his work. It is necessarily true, if this supposition is correct, that he already wants to concentrate on his work. This desire is now among his desires. But the question of whether or not his second-order desire is fulfilled does not turn merely on whether the desire he wants is one of his desires. It turns on whether this desire is, as he wants it to be, his effective desire or will. If, when the chips are down, it is his desire to concentrate on his work that moves him to do what he does, then what he wants at that time is indeed (in the relevant sense) what he wants to want. If it is some other desire that actually moves him when he acts, on the other hand, then what he wants at that time is not (in the relevant sense) what he wants to want. This will be so despite the fact that the desire to concentrate on his work continues to be among his desires.

II

Someone has a desire of the second order either when he wants simply to have a certain desire or when he wants a certain desire to be his will. In situations of the latter kind, I shall call his second-order desires "second-order volitions" or "volitions of the second order." Now it is having second-order volitions, and not having second-order desires generally, that I regard as essential to being a person. It is logically possible, however unlikely, that there should be an agent with second-order desire, but with no volitions of the second order. Such a creature, in my view, would not be a person. I shall use the term 'wanton' to refer to agents who have first-order desires but who are not persons because, whether or not they have desires of the second order, they have no second-order volitions.[5]

The essential characteristic of a wanton is that he does not care about his will. His desires move him to do certain things, without its being true of him either that he wants to be moved by those desires or that he prefers to be moved by other desires. The class of wantons includes all nonhuman animals that have desires and all very young children. Perhaps it also includes some adult human beings as well. In any case, adult humans may be more or less wanton; they may act wantonly, in response to first-order desires concerning which they have no volitions of the second order, more or less frequently.

The fact that a wanton has no second-order volitions does not mean that each of his first-order desires is translated heedlessly and at once into action. He may have no opportunity to act in accordance with some of his desires. Moreover, the translation of his desires into action may be delayed or precluded either by conflicting desires of the first order or by the intervention of deliberation. For a wanton may possess and employ rational faculties of a high order. Nothing in the concept of a wanton implies that he cannot reason or that he cannot deliberate concerning how to do what he wants to do. What distinguishes the rational wanton from other rational agents is that he is not concerned with the desirability of his desires themselves. He ignores the question of what his will is to be. Not only does he pursue whatever course of action he is most strongly inclined to pursue, but he does not care which of his inclinations is the strongest.

Thus a rational creature, who reflects upon the suitability to his desires of one course of action or another, may nonetheless be a wanton. In maintaining that the essence of being a person lies not in reason but in will, I am far from suggesting that a creature without reason may be a person. For it is only in virtue of his rational capacities that a person is capable of becoming critically aware of his own will and of forming volitions of the second order. The structure of a person's will presupposes, accordingly, that he is a rational being.

The distinction between a person and a wanton may be illustrated by the difference between two narcotics addicts. Let us suppose that the physiological condition accounting for the addiction is the same in both men, and that both succumb inevitably to their periodic desires for the drug to which they are addicted. One of the addicts hates his addiction and always struggles desperately, although to no avail, against its thrust. He tries everything that he thinks might enable him to overcome his desires for the drug. But these desires are too powerful for him to withstand, and invariably, in the end, they conquer him. He is an unwilling addict, helplessly violated by his own desires.

The unwilling addict has conflicting first-order desires: he wants to take the drug, and he also wants to refrain from taking it. In addition to these first-order desires, however, he has a volition of the second order. He is not a neutral with regard to the conflict between his desire to take the drug and his desire to refrain from taking it. It is the latter desire, and not the former, that he wants to constitute his will; it is the latter desire, rather than the former, that he wants to be effective and to provide the purpose that he will seek to realize in what he actually does.

The other addict is a wanton. His actions reflect the economy of his first-order desires, without his being concerned whether the desires that move him to act are desires by which he wants to be moved to act. If he encounters problems in obtaining the drug or in administering it to himself, his reponses to his urges to take it may involve deliberation. But it never occurs to him to consider whether he wants the relations among his desires to result in his having the will he has. The wanton addict may be an animal, and thus incapable of being concerned about his will. In any event he is, in respect of his wanton lack of concern, no different from an animal.

The second of these addicts may suffer a first-order conflict similar to the first-order conflict suffered by the first. Whether he is human or not, the wanton may (perhaps due to conditioning) both want to take the drug and want to refrain from taking it. Unlike the unwilling addict, however, he does not prefer that one of his conflicting desires should be paramount over the other; he does not prefer that one first-order desire rather than the other should constitute his will. It would be misleading to say that he is neutral as to the conflict between his desires, since this would suggest that he regards them as equally acceptable. Since he has no identity apart from his first-order desires, it is true neither that he prefers one to the other nor that he prefers not to take sides.

It makes a difference to the unwilling addict, who is a person, which of his conflicting first-order desires wins out. Both desires are his, to be sure; and whether he finally takes the drug or finally succeeds in refraining from taking it, he acts to satisfy what is in a literal sense his own desire. In either case he does something he himself wants to do, and he does it not because of some external influence whose aim happens to coincide with his own but because of his desire to do it. The unwilling addict identifies himself, however, through the formation of a second-order volition, with one rather than with the other of his conflicting first-order desires. He makes one of them more truly his own and, in so doing, he withdraws himself from the other. It is in virtue of this identification and withdrawal, accomplished through the formation of a second-order volition, that the unwilling addict may meaningfully make the analytically puzzling statements that the force moving him to take the drug is a force other than his own, and that it is not of his own free will but rather against his will that this force moves him to take it.

The wanton addict cannot or does not care which of his conflicting first-order desires wins out. His lack of concern is not due to his inability to find a convincing basis for preference. It is due either to his lack of the capacity for reflection or to his mindless indifference to the enterprise of evaluating his own desires and motives.[6] There is only one issue in the struggle to which his first-order conflict may lead: whether the one or the other of his conflicting desires is the stronger. Since he is moved by both desires, he will not be altogether satisfied by what he does no matter which of them is effective. But it makes no difference *to him* whether his craving or his aversion gets the upper hand. He has no stake in the conflict between them and so, unlike the unwilling addict, he can neither win nor lose the struggle in which he is engaged. When a *person* acts, the desire by which he is moved is either the will he wants or a will he wants to be without. When a *wanton* acts, it is neither.

III

There is a very close relationship between the capacity for forming second-order volitions and another capacity that is essential to persons—one that has often been considered a distinguishing mark of the human condition. It is only because a person has volitions of the second order that he is capable both of enjoying and of lacking freedom of the will. The concept of a person is not only, then, the concept of a type of entity that has both first-order desires and volitions of the second order. It can also be construed as the concept of a type of entity for whom the freedom of its will may be a problem. This concept excludes all wantons, both infrahuman and human, since they fail to satisfy an essential condition for the enjoyment of freedom of the will. And it excludes those suprahuman beings, if any, whose wills are necessarily free.

Just what kind of freedom is the freedom of the will? This question calls for an identification of the special area of human experience to which the concept of freedom of the will, as distinct from the concepts of other sorts of freedom, is particularly germane. In dealing with it, my aim will be primarily to locate the problem with which a person is most immediately concerned when he is concerned with the freedom of his will.

According to one familiar philosophical tradition, being free is fundamentally a matter of doing what one wants to do. Now the notion of an agent who does what he wants to do is by no means an

altogether clear one: both the doing and the wanting, and the appropriate relation between them as well, require elucidation. But although its focus needs to be sharpened and its formulation refined, I believe that this notion does capture at least part of what is implicit in the idea of an agent who *acts* freely. It misses entirely, however, the peculiar content of the quite different idea of an agent whose *will* is free.

We do not suppose that animals enjoy freedom of the will, although we recognize that an animal may be free to run in whatever direction it wants. Thus, having the freedom to do what one wants to do is not a sufficient condition of having a free will. It is not a necessary condition either. For to deprive someone of his freedom of action is not necessarily to undermine the freedom of his will. When an agent is aware that there are certain things he is not free to do, this doubtless affects his desires and limits the range of choices he can make. But suppose that someone, without being aware of it, has in fact lost or been deprived of his freedom of action. Even though he is no longer free to do what he wants to do, his will may remain as free as it was before. Despite the fact that he is not free to translate his desires into actions or to act according to the determinations of his will, he may still form those desires and make those determinations as freely as if his freedom of action had not been impaired.

When we ask whether a person's will is free we are not asking whether he is in a position to translate his first-order desires into actions. That is the question of whether he is free to do as he pleases. The question of the freedom of his will does not concern the relation between what he does and what he wants to do. Rather, it concerns his desires themselves. But what question about them is it?

It seems to me both natural and useful to construe the question of whether a person's will is free in close analogy to the question of whether an agent enjoys freedom of action. Now freedom of action is (roughly, at least) the freedom to do what one wants to do. Analogously, then, the statement that a person enjoys freedom of the will means (also roughly) that he is free to want what he wants to want. More precisely, it means that he is free to will what he wants to will, or to have the will he wants. Just as the question about the freedom of an agent's action has to do with whether it is the action he wants to perform, so the question about the freedom of his will has to do with whether it is the will he wants to have.

It is in securing the conformity of his will to his second-order volitions, then, that a person exercises freedom of the will. And it is in the descrepancy between his will and his second-order volitions, or in his awareness that their coincidence is not his own doing but only a happy chance, that a person who does not have this freedom feels its lack. The unwilling addict's will is not free. This is shown by the fact that it is not the will he wants. It is also true, though in a different way, that the will of the wanton addict is not free. The wanton addict neither has the will he wants nor has a will that differs from the will he wants. Since he has no volitions of the second order, the freedom of his will cannot be a problem for him. He lacks it, so to speak, by default.

People are generally far more complicated than my sketchy account of the structure of a person's will may suggest. There is as much opportunity for ambivalence, conflict, and self-deception with regard to desires of the second order, for example, as there is with regard to first-order desires. If there is an unresolved conflict among someone's second-order desires, then he is in danger of having no second-order volition; for unless this conflict is resolved, he has no preference concerning which of his first-order desires is to be his will. This condition, if it is so severe that it prevents him from identifying himself in a sufficiently decisive way with *any* of his conflicting first-order desires, destroys him as a person. For it either tends to paralyze his will and to keep him from acting at all, or it tends to remove him from his will so that his will operates without his participation. In both cases he becomes, like the unwilling addict though in a different way, a helpless bystander to the forces that move him.

Another complexity is that a person may have, especially if his second-order desires are in conflict, desires and volitions of a higher order than the second. There is no theoretical limit to the length of the series of desires of higher and higher orders; nothing except common sense and, perhaps, a saving fatigue prevents an individual from obsessively refusing to identify himself with any of his desires until he forms a desire of the next higher order. The tendency to generate such a series of acts of forming desires, which would be a case of humanization run wild, also leads toward the destruction of a person.

It is possible, however, to terminate such a series of acts without cutting it off arbitrarily. When a person identifies himself *decisively* with one of his first-order desires, this commitment "resounds" throughout the potentially endless array of higher orders. Consider a person who, without reservation or conflict, wants to be motivated by the desire to concentrate on his work. The fact that his second-order volition to be moved by this desire is a decisive one means that there is no room

for questions concerning the pertinence of desires or volitions of higher orders. Suppose the person is asked whether he wants to want to want to concentrate on his work. He can properly insist that this question concerning a third-order desire does not arise. It would be a mistake to claim that, because he has not considered whether he wants the second-order volition he has formed, he is indifferent to the question of whether it is with this volition or with some other that he wants his will to accord. The decisiveness of the commitment he has made means that he has decided that no further question about his second-order volition, at any higher order, remains to be asked. It is relatively unimportant whether we explain this by saying that this commitment implicitly generates an endless series of confirming desires of higher orders, or by saying that the commitment is tantamount to a dissolution of the pointedness of all questions concerning higher orders of desire.

Examples such as the one concerning the unwilling addict may suggest that volitions of the second order, or of higher orders, must be formed deliberately and that a person characteristically struggles to ensure that they are satisfied. But the conformity of a person's will to his higher-order volitions may be far more thoughtless and spontaneous than this. Some people are naturally moved by kindness when they want to be kind, and by nastiness when they want to be nasty, without any explicit forethought and without any need for energetic self-control. Others are moved by nastiness when they want to be kind and by kindness when they intend to be nasty, equally without forethought and without active resistance to these violations of their higher-order desires. The enjoyment of freedom comes easily to some. Others must struggle to achieve it.

IV

My theory concerning the freedom of the will accounts easily for our disinclination to allow that this freedom is enjoyed by the members of any species inferior to our own. It also satisfies another condition that must be met by any such theory, by making it apparent why the freedom of the will should be regarded as desirable. The enjoyment of a free will means the satisfaction of certain desires—desires of the second or of higher orders—whereas its absence means their frustration. The satisfactions at stake are those which accrue to a person of whom it may be said that his will is his own. The corresponding frustrations are those suffered by a person of whom it may be said that he is estranged from himself, or that he finds himself a helpless or a passive bystander to the forces that move him.

A person who is free to do what he wants to do may yet not be in a position to have the will he wants. Suppose, however, that he enjoys both freedom of action and freedom of the will. Then he is not only free to do what he wants to do; he is also free to want what he wants to want. It seems to me that he has, in that case, all the freedom it is possible to desire or to conceive. There are other good things in life, and he may not possess some of them. But there is nothing in the way of freedom that he lacks.

It is far from clear that certain other theories of the freedom of the will meet these elementary but essential conditions: that it be understandable why we desire this freedom and why we refuse to ascribe it to animals. Consider, for example, Roderick Chisholm's quaint version of the doctrine that human freedom entails an absence of causal determination.[7] Whenever a person performs a free action, according to Chisholm, it's a miracle. The motion of a person's hand, when the person moves it, is the outcome of a series of physical causes; but some event in this series, "and presumably one of those that took place within the brain, was caused by the agent and not by any other events" (18). A free agent has, therefore, "a prerogative which some would attribute only to God: each of us, when we act, is a prime mover unmoved" (23).

This account fails to provide any basis for doubting that animals of subhuman species enjoy the freedom it defines. Chisholm says nothing that makes it seem less likely that a rabbit performs a miracle when it moves its leg than that a man does so when he moves his hand. But why, in any case, should anyone *care* whether he can interrupt the natural order of causes in the way Chisholm describes? Chisholm offers no reason for believing that there is a discernible difference between the experience of a man who miraculously initiates a series of causes when he moves his hand and a man who moves his hand without any such breach of the normal causal sequence. There appears to be no concrete basis for preferring to be involved in the one state of affairs rather than in the other.[8]

It is generally supposed that, in addition to satisfying the two conditions I have mentioned, a satisfactory theory of the freedom of the will necessarily provides an analysis of one of the conditions of moral responsibility. The most common recent approach to the problem of understanding the freedom of the will has been, indeed, to inquire what is entailed by the assumption that someone is morally responsible for what he has done. In my view, however, the relation between moral responsibility and the freedom of the will has been very widely misunderstood. It is not true that a person is morally responsible for what he has done only if his will was free when he did it. He may be morally responsible for having done it even though his will was not free at all.

A person's will is free only if he is free to have the will he wants. This means that, with regard to any of his first-order desires, he is free either to make that desire his will or to make some other first-order desire his will instead. Whatever his will, then, the will of the person whose will is free could have been otherwise; he could have done otherwise than to constitute his will as he did. It is a vexed question just how 'he could have done otherwise' is to be understood in contexts such as this one. But although this question is important to the theory of freedom, it has no bearing on the theory of moral responsibility. For the assumption that a person is morally responsible for what he has done does not entail that the person was in a position to have whatever will he wanted.

This assumption *does* entail that the person did what he did freely, or that he did it of his own free will. It is a mistake, however, to believe that someone acts freely only when he is free to do whatever he wants or that he acts of his own free will only if his will is free. Suppose that a person has done what he wanted to do, that he did it because he wanted to do it, and that the will by which he was moved when he did it was his will because it was the will he wanted. Then he did it freely and of his own free will. Even supposing that he could have done otherwise, he would not have done otherwise; and even supposing that he could have had a different will, he would not have wanted his will to differ from what it was. Moreover, since the will that moved him when he acted was his will because he wanted it to be, he cannot claim that his will was forced upon him or that he was a passive bystander to its constitution. Under these conditions, it is quite irrelevant to the evaluation of his moral responsiblity to inquire whether the alternatives that he opted against were actually available to him.[9]

In illustration, consider a third kind of addict. Suppose that his addiction has the same physiological basis and the same irresistible thrust as the addictions of the unwilling and wanton addicts, but that he is altogether delighted with his condition. He is a willing addict, who would not have things any other way. If the grip of his addiction should somehow weaken, he would do whatever he could to reinstate it; if his desire for the drug should begin to fade, he would take steps to renew its intensity.

The willing addict's will is not free, for his desire to take the drug will be effective regardless of whether or not he wants this desire to constitute his will. But when he takes the drug, he takes it freely and of his own free will. I am inclined to understand his situation as involving the overdetermination of his first-order desire to take the drug. This desire is his effective desire because he is physiologically addicted. But it is his effective desire also because he wants it to be. His will is outside his control, but, by his second-order desire that his desire for the drug should be effective, he has made this will his own. Given that it is therefore not only because of his addiction that his desire for the drug is effective, he may be morally responsible for taking the drug.

My conception of the freedom of the will appears to be neutral with regard to the problem of determinism. It seems conceivable that it should be causally determined that a person is free to want what he wants to want. If this is conceivable, then it might be causally determined that a person enjoys a free will. There is no more than an innocuous appearance of paradox in the proposition that it is determined, ineluctably and by forces beyond their control, that certain people have free wills and that others do not. There is no incoherence in the proposition that some agency other than a person's own is responsible (even *morally* responsible) for the fact that he enjoys or fails to enjoy freedom of the will. It is possible that a person should be morally responsible for what he does of his own free will and that some other person should also be morally responsible for his having done it.[10]

On the other hand, it seems conceivable that it should come about by chance that a person is free to have the will he wants. If this is conceivable, then it might be a matter of chance that certain people enjoy freedom of the will and that certain others do not. Perhaps it is also conceivable, as a number of philosophers believe, for states of affairs to come about in a way other than by chance or as the outcome of a sequence of natural causes. If it is indeed conceivable for the relevant states of affairs to come about in some third way, then it is also possible that a person should in that third way come to enjoy the freedom of the will.

NOTES

1. P. F. Strawson, *Individuals* (London: Methuen, 1959), pp. 101–102. Ayer's usage of 'person' is similar: "it is characteristic of persons in this sense that besides having various physical properties . . . they are also credited with various forms of consciousness" [A. J. Ayer, *The Concept of a Person* (New York: St. Martin's, 1963), p. 82]. What concerns Strawson and Ayer is the problem of understanding the relation between mind and body, rather than the quite different problem of understanding what it is to be a creature that not only has a mind and a body but is also a person.

2. For the sake of simplicity, I shall deal only with what someone wants or desires, neglecting related phenomena such as choices and decision. I propose to use the verbs 'to want' and 'to desire' interchangeably, although they are by no means perfect synonyms. My motive in forsaking the established nuances of these words arises from the fact that the verb 'to want', which suits my purposes better so far as its meaning is concerned, does not lend itself so readily to the formation of nouns as does the verb 'to desire'. It is perhaps acceptable, albeit graceless, to speak in the plural of someone's "wants." But to speak in the singular of someone's "want" would be an abomination.

3. What I say in this paragraph applies not only to cases in which 'to X' refers to a possible action or inaction. It also applies to cases in which 'to X' refers to a first-order desire and in which the statement that 'A wants to X' is therefore a shortened version of a statement—"A wants to want to X"— that identifies a desire of the second order.

4. It is not so clear that the entailment relation described here holds in certain kinds of cases, which I think may fairly be regarded as nonstandard, where the essential difference between the standard and the nonstandard cases lies in the kind of description by which the first-order desire in question is identified. Thus, suppose that A admires B so fulsomely that, even though he does not know what B wants to do, he wants to be effectively moved by whatever desire effectively moves B; without knowing what B's will is, in other words, A wants his own will to be the same. It certainly does not follow that A already has, among his desires, a desire like the one that constitutes B's will. I shall not pursue here the questions of whether there are genuine counterexamples to the claim made in the text or of how, if there are, that claim should be altered.

5. Creatures with second-order desires but no second-order volitions differ significantly from brute animals, and, for some purposes, it would be desirable to regard them as persons. My usage, which withholds the designation 'person' from them, is thus somewhat arbitrary. I adopt it largely because it facilitates the formulation of some of the points I wish to make. Hereafter, whenever I consider statements of the form "A wants to want to X," I shall have in mind statements identifying second-order volitions and not statements indentifying second-order desires that are not second-order volitions.

6. In speaking of the evaluation of his own desires and motives as being characteristic of a person, I do not mean to suggest that a person's second-order volitions necessarily manifest a *moral* stance on his part toward his first-order desires. It may not be from the point of view of morality that the person evaluates his first-order desires. Moreover, a person may be capricious and irresponsible in forming his second-order volitions and give no serious consideration to what is at stake. Second-order volitions express evaluations only in the sense that they are preferences. There is no essential restriction on the kind of basis, if any, upon which they are formed.

7. "Freedom and Action," in K. Lehrer, ed., *Freedom and Determination* (New York: Random House, 1966), pp. 11–44.

8. I am not suggesting that the alleged difference between these two states of affairs is unverifiable. On the contrary, physiologists might well be able to show that Chisholm's conditions for a free action are not satisfied, by establishing that there is no relevant brain event for which a sufficient physical cause cannot be found.

9. For another discussion of the considerations that cast doubt on the principle that a person is morally responsible for what he has done only if he could have done otherwise, see my "Alternate Possibilities and Moral Responsibility," *The Journal of Philosophy,* LXVI, 23 (Dec. 4, 1969): 829–839.

10. There is a difference between being *fully* responsible and being *solely* responsible. Suppose that the willing addict has been made an addict by the deliberate and calculated work of another. Then it may be that both the addict and this other person are fully responsible for the addict's taking the drug, while neither of them is solely responsible for it. That there is a distinction between full moral responsibility and sole moral responsibility is apparent in the following example. A certain light can be turned on or off by flicking either of two switches, and each of these switches is simultaneously flicked to the "on" position by a different person, neither of whom is aware of the other. Neither person is solely responsible for the light's going on, nor do they share the responsibility in the sense that each is partially responsible; rather, each of them is fully responsible.

50

Robert M. Gordon

"Emotions and Knowledge"*

In philosophy as in psychology, there is growing emphasis on the cognitive basis of emotions. Philosophers in particular tend to agree now that there is a connection between the way one's emotion is to be described and the nature of the beliefs or the knowledge on which it is based. It appears that, unless one knows or believes certain things, one cannot experience certain emotions at all. Most philosophers who have studied the emotions would probably agree, for example, that a person so starry-eyed that he never believes any act or social arrangement to be unjust, could never experience indignation. They would agree, too, that a man who neither knew nor believed that Faulkner won the Nobel Prize could neither be indignant nor disappointed nor delighted that Faulkner won the Prize.

I want to show in this brief paper that it is often what a person *knows,* as opposed to what he merely *believes,* that determines how his emotion is to be described.

I

Let me build from the ashes of a familiar but unsatisfactory distinction. "Backward-looking" emotions are said to be directed toward things, persons, or states of affairs that exist presently or have existed in the past; "forwarding-looking" emotions are said to be directed toward future possibilities. Most emotions are backward-looking; hope, fear,

and terror are among the forward-looking emotions. Some support for this distinction seems to come from the tense preferences of emotions with "propositional objects." Contrast 'He hopes that the next two presidents will be Democrats' with 'He hopes that the last two presidents were Democrats'. What is said in the first sentence could be true of many people; but it is hard to imagine someone hoping that the last two presidents were Democrats. The same holds when 'hopes' is replaced by 'fears' or 'is worried'. But when other emotion words are substituted, precisely the reverse holds: it would be strange to be told of someone who was glad or unhappy that the next two presidents will be Democrats.

As defined above, the distinction is unsatisfactory. No emotions are exclusively backward-looking, and no emotions are exclusively forward-looking. We can readily imagine someone hoping or being afraid, say, that a certain train arrived late (past tense), just as we can readily imagine someone being glad or unhappy that the train will arrive late (future tense). We are left with two questions. Why are some emotions generally forward-looking and others generally backward-looking? And why are the train examples among the exceptions to this general dichotomy?

It is possible that a passenger on a train, wishing to finish reading a novel before his trip is over, hopes that the train will arrive late; while, at the same time, the conductor, wishing to avoid congestion at the terminal, is glad that the train will arrive late. What is not possible is that the same person, at one and the same time, both hopes that the train will arrive late and is glad that it will. The same person cannot at the same time be glad or unhappy that *p, and* hope or be afraid that *p.* (If this is not obvious, it will become so.) There is

* Several people have given me their helpful comments on this paper. I must especially thank my colleagues Bruce Freed and Peter Unger, who have, in ways obvious and unobvious, influenced my thinking in this and other matters.

From *The Journal of Philosophy* LXVI, 13 (July 3, 1969): 408–13. Reprinted with permission of the editors and Robert M. Gordon.

some condition, apparently, that always holds when someone is glad or unhappy that p, and never holds when someone hopes or is afraid that p. What we shall discover is that a person is glad or unhappy that p only if he *knows* that p, and that a person hopes or is afraid that p only if he *does not know* that p. This explains why it is hard to imagine people being glad or unhappy that the next two presidents will be Democrats, but easy to imagine people being glad or unhappy that the train will arrive late: for it is hard to imagine people *foreknowing* that the next two presidents will be Democrats, but easy to imagine people foreknowing that some particular train will arrive late. We can also see why it is hard to imagine people hoping or being afraid that the last two presidents were Democrats, but easy to imagine people hoping or being afraid that the train arrived late: for it is hard to imagine people (Americans, at least) not knowing that the last two presidents were Democrats, but easy to imagine people not knowing that some particular train arrived late.

What we find is that any "emotion that p" either requires knowledge that p or is incompatible with knowledge that p. A person emotes that p only if knows that p, for any of the following replacements for 'emotes':

is amazed	is disgusted	is proud
is amused	is embarrassed	is resentful
is angry	is excited	is sorry
is annoyed	is furious	is surprised
is ashamed	is glad	is thankful
is astonished	is horrified	is unhappy
is delighted	is indignant	is upset
is disappointed	is pleased	*feels* ashamed (etc.)

On the other hand, a person emotes that p only if he does *not* know that p, for any of the following:[1]

is afraid	hopes	is terrified
fears	is hopeful	is worried
is frightened		

Only a few "emotions that p," perhaps just those on the second list, are knowledge-precluders. All the rest, of which the first list is a sample, are knowledge-requirers.

II

It is reasonably clear that a person is amazed (etc.) that p only if he knows *or believes* that p. Of course, if my neighbors' quarreling produces a noise that upsets or annoys me, I am upset or an-

noyed *by* their quarreling, whether or not I know or believe that they are quarreling. In such a case, however, I am not upset by or about *the fact* that my neighbors are quarreling; neither am I upset that they are quarreling.

More precisely, a person is amazed (etc.) that p only if he knows or has a *true* belief that p. There may be people today who fear or are worried that there are Martian space-ships circling the earth. There may be some who confidently believe that there are. But it would be unnerving to hear: "Yes, and some people are quite upset that there are Martian space-ships circling the earth." Or: "I have a crazy friend who is glad that there are Martians flying around up there." For, no one, crazy or not, is upset or glad that p, unless p. This is not, of course, to deny that there are people of whom we should say: "He is upset because he thinks there are Martian space-ships circling the earth." (In a novel or a psychiatric case study, where we want the reader to know how things seem to a certain person S, we may speak as if whatever S confidently believes to be true S *knew* to be true. There we may even say: "He is upset that there are Martian space-ships circling the earth.")

Finally, it is knowledge that is required, rather than merely knowledge or true belief.[2] First note that, on either view, the following story would be inconsistent:

As John's new Bulova had been running slow, he returned it to the shop for repair. On receiving it back and putting it on his wrist, John inadvertently set the hands one hour too early. At the end of the day, John discovered that his watch was exactly one hour behind. Naturally, *he was annoyed that his new Bulova was still running slow.*

But suppose that not one mistake had been made, but two: suppose that the repairman had inadvertently switched John's watch with an older Bulova belonging to a doctor from Tanzania, and consequently returned to each man the other's watch. Then John, thinking the Tanzanian's watch to be his own, put it on his wrist and set the hands—again incorrectly, as above. Later, he discovered the watch to be exactly an hour behind. "Naturally," our amended story concludes, "he was annoyed that his new Bulova was still running slow."

Suppose that what is required were, not knowledge, but either knowledge or true belief. Then, paradoxically, our amended story would be consistent! For it is possible that John's new Bulova, now gracing the wrist of the doctor from Tanzania, perhaps thousands of miles away, happens to be running slow: in which case John has; by a mere coincidence, a true belief that his new Bulova is still running slow. If we added that *this* watch, too, was keeping correct time, only then would we make the story inconsistent. All of which is plainly counterintuitive. If John believes that his new Bulova is still running slow, only because he believes the watch on his own wrist—which in fact is neither his watch, nor new, nor running slow—to be running slow, then it is both false that John *knows* that his new Bulova is still running slow, and false that John *is annoyed* that his new Bulova is still running slow. A person is annoyed that *p*, only if he knows that *p*. The same holds for any of the emotions on the first list, above.

As I have said, the knowledge requirement explains why it is implausible that anyone might be pleased or glad or unhappy or upset that the next two presidents will be Democrats; for, although true beliefs abound in such matters, it is implausible that anyone might have foreknowledge of such matters. On the other hand, since it is plausible that some people might know in advance that a certain train will arrive late, it is plausible that some might be pleased or glad or unhappy or upset that the train will arrive late.

Finally, the knowledge requirement explains why the same person cannot be pleased or annoyed or upset that *p* and at the same time be worried or terrified that *p*. For it is apparent that a person hopes that *p* or is worried, afraid, or terrified that *p*, only if he does not at the same time know that *p*. A man is on a train scheduled to arrive in Chicago at 3 o'clock. He wants to finish reading a novel before the train arrives. He knows that at 2:45 the train is still an hour away from Chicago, at best: he may be *glad* that the train will arrive late, but he cannot *hope* that it will. It is true that a person who knows that he will be hanged may be afraid or terrified because he knows this: but he is not afraid or terrified *that he will be hanged.*

III

In saying that the dichotomy between knowledge-requiring and knowledge-precluding emotions that *p* is exhaustive, I do not think I am legislating: anything that might plausibly be considered an *emotion* that *p* will fit under one or the other heading. If this is so, then I have specified one condition that must be satisfied by anything that is truly an *emotion* that *p*. I have obviously not given a sufficient condition. No one remembers that *p* or sees that *p* or recognizes that *p* unless he knows that *p*: yet these are not knowledge-requiring *emotions*.

(Similarly, conjecturing that *p* and suspecting that *p*, though they preclude knowing that *p*, do not seem to be knowledge-precluding *emotions*.) One way in which remembering, seeing, and recognizing appear to differ from the knowledge-requiring emotions is this: whereas the former are, roughly, *ways* of knowing or of coming to know, the latter are merely *based* on knowledge. In the absence of an account of what it is for an emotion to be "based on" knowledge, however, I do not think that this is very enlightening.

One final suggestion may help to explain *why* our descriptions of emotions respond in the way they do to the difference between knowing and merely believing. There is some reason to think that, in the case of the knowledge-*requiring* emotions, the "object" of the emotion is necessarily a cause, or a causal condition, of the emotion. Thus, where John was annoyed that his new Bulova was still running slow, it would follow that his annoyance was caused by, among other conditions, his watch's running slow. For one thing, the way we speak of emotions suggests this: we use 'annoyed that' and 'annoyed because' almost interchangeably. (Note that this is not true of 'afraid that' and 'afraid because'. It holds *only* for knowledge-requiring emotions that *p*.) But if John's annoyance had been based on a mere *belief* that his new Bulova was still running slow, this could hardly be plausible. Even true belief would not be enough. In the amended story above, though John's emotion was based on a true belief about his new Bulova, there was obviously no causal connection at all between his state of mind, as he stood glaring at the watch on his wrist, and the state of his Tanzania-bound new Bulova. But had his annoyance been based on the *knowledge* that his new Bulova was still running slow, such a connection would have to have existed: this, or something fairly close to it, is what we are led to think by several recent analyses of knowing that *p*.[3] Emotions that require knowledge as their basis are based, ultimately, on the way things are, rather than the way they are taken to be; they orginate, we might say, in our common world. This would be enough to explain why our descriptions of emotions are sensitive to the difference between knowing and merely believing.

NOTES

1. Perhaps this is merely because one is afraid (etc.) that *p* only if one is not *sure* that *p*. It is worth adding that, when 'I am afraid that . . .' is used, in the first person, to make a

disturbing revelation to someone, it does not seem to carry either implication; or the implication is neutralized by the context.

2. The decision to go this extra step was urged upon me by Peter Unger. Here, and elsewhere, my inclinations had been toward patchword compromises; mainly it was Mr. Unger who dissuaded me from these.

3. I refer to the following three papers, all published in *The Journal of Philosophy*: Alvin I. Goldman, "A Causal Theory of Knowing," and Brian Skyrms, "The Explication of 'X Knows that p'," both in LXIV, 12 (June 22, 1967): 357, 373, and Peter Unger, "An Analysis of Factual Knowledge," LXV, 6 (Mar. 21, 1968): 157; and to an unpublished paper by Fred I. Dretske, entitled "Conclusive Reasons."

51

Norman Malcom

"Thoughtless Brutes"*

I

When readers of Descartes first come upon his theme that animals are automatons, lacking consciousness, they are astonished. As Zeno Vendler says in his recent book, *Res Cogitans,* "the notorious doctrine of the automatism of brutes" is "perhaps the most counterintuitive item" in Descartes' philosophy.[1] Descartes himself had no concern for the "counterintuitive" character of his thesis. He declares that the belief that animals "act by an interior principle like the one within ourselves, that is to say, by means of a soul which has feeling and passions like ours," is an outstanding example of prejudice. One cannot, he says, present the reasons against this belief "without exposing oneself to the ridicule of children and feeble minds."[2]

The doctrine of the automatism of animals was a topic of much controversy for a century and a half after Descartes' death. It was even claimed by some opponents of the doctrine that the Cartesians were deliberately brutal to animals. La Fontaine said of the philosophers and logicians of Port-Royal:

> They administered beatings to dogs with perfect indifference, and made fun of those who pitied the creatures, as if they had felt pain. They said that the animals were clocks; that the cries they emitted when struck, were only the noise of a little spring that had been touched, but that the whole body was without feeling.[3]

Decartes himself remarks on this point that "my opinion is not so much cruel to animals as indul-

* Presidential Address delivered before the Sixty-ninth Annual Eastern Meeting of the American Philosophical Association in Boston, December 28, 1972.

gent to men . . . since it absolves them from the suspicion of crime when they eat or kill animals."[4]

It is worth noting that in a letter to Henry More, Descartes says that it cannot be *proved* that there is no "thought in animals," because "the human mind does not reach into their hearts."[5] This is a surprising remark, considering his view that thoughts are noncorporeal and nonspatial. Why does he speak as if the issue were one of what is *inside* the animals? Was it a metaphor? The reference to "hearts" *(corda)* is certainly metaphorical. But the idea that our minds cannot look into the animals to determine whether or not any thoughts are there, does not seem to be *just* metaphor, since it is offered as an *explanation* (*quia:* because) of why we cannot *prove* that animals do not think. In this same letter Descartes sets forth his "main reason" for holding that animals are without thought—namely, that they do not use "real speech." "Such speech," he says, "is the only certain sign of thought hidden in a body."[6] In another letter to More he expresses himself in the same way, saying that only speech shows thought hidden in a body *(in corpore latentem).*[7] Previously I quoted a passage in which he spoke of the soul as being an "interior" principle. My impression is that although Descartes' formal position is that soul (or mind), and thought, are completely nonspatial and so could not be inside or outside of anything, nevertheless he was actually much influenced by the common metaphysical picture of thought as occurring *inside* a person—of thought as being something *inner.*

In maintaining that animals do not think, Descartes certainly meant that they do not reflect or meditate; but did he also mean that they do not have feelings, sensations, or any kind of consciousness? We know from Meditation II that to feel

From *Proceedings and Addresses of the American Philosophical Association,* 1972–73, XLVI (November 1973): 5–20. Reprinted with permission of the American Philosophical Association and Norman Malcolm.

(sentire) is to think *(cogitare)*.[8] Thus if animals don't think they don't feel. In his *Passions of the Soul* Descartes states that nothing ought to be attributed to the soul except thoughts, and that these are of two kinds, actions and passions.[9] Since passions are thoughts, and animals don't have thoughts, therefore they don't have passions, such as fear or anger.

On the other hand, in one of the letters to More, Descartes says that he does *not* deny "sensation" to animals, "in so far as it depends on a bodily organ."[10] In a letter to the Marquess of Newcastle he says that dogs, horses and monkeys sometimes "express passions" such as fear, hope and joy.[11] Yet, in still another letter, he says that animals do not have "real feeling" or "real passion" *(vray sentiment, vray passion)*.[12]

In order to see how these apparent contradictions are to be removed, we need a clear understanding of what Descartes means by a "thought." In an important and difficult passage in Meditation III he says:

> Some of my thoughts are, as it were, images of things; the name of "idea" belongs properly to those alone: as when I think of a man, or a chimaera, or heaven, or an angel, or God. But other thoughts have other forms besides: as when I will, when I fear, and when I affirm, when I deny, I do indeed always apprehend something as the object of my thought, yet in the thought I add something else to the idea of that thing; and some of these thoughts are called volitions or affections, and others judgments.[13]

Descartes is saying, I believe, that in every instance of thinking there is, first and foremost, an *idea*. By an "idea" he means a *representation:* this is why he calls it an "image." It is the first form of "thought." As he is using the term "idea" in this passage, an idea would appear to be what is usually meant by a "proposition," or a "propositional content," since ideas he says can be affirmed or denied. The idea of God, for example, might be expressed by the sentence, "There is a Supremely Perfect Being," or by the nominalized phrase, "the existence of a Supremely Perfect Being." In either case, what was expressed could be affirmed or denied.

The second form of "thought" of which Descartes speaks in this passage, is not propositional content, but is some "attitude" taken toward propositional content—for example, an attitude of affirming, or denying, or wanting, or fearing, or hoping. One could affirm or deny that a Supremely Perfect Being exists, or want this to be so, or hope or fear that it is so. The kernel of every mental operation is a proposition, *i.e.,* an idea, *i.e.,* a thought in the *first* sense. A thought in the *second* sense is

what nowadays is variously called a "propositional attitude," or a "mental frame."[14]

This conception of what is involved in all "mental operations" has been popular with philosophers. Bertrand Russell subscribed to it in *The Analysis of Mind.* According to him a propositional content could be expressed by the phrase, "an egg for breakfast." A person might take different attitudes toward this content: expect it, remember it, merely "entertain" it, desire it, or feel aversion to it.[15] C. I. Lewis had the same conception. The propositional content expressed by the phrase, "Mary making pies now," can be the object of different "moods of entertainment": it can be asserted, denied, questioned, postulated, approved, and so on.[16]

The passage from Meditation III, previously cited, reveals how Descartes conceived of what might be called "the mental side" of an emotion such as fear. "When I fear," he says, I apprehend something (that is, I "take in" some particular propositional content—for example, that there is a danger confronting me). Then I apply to this propositional content the mental frame or attitude of fearing. If I met a lion in the jungle I would have, according to Descartes, two forms of thought. The first would be a representation, *i.e.,* a propositional content, such as might be expressed by the sentence, "The lion may attack me." The second form of thought might be the mental frame of fear. The union of these two forms of thought might be expressed by the sentence, "I fear that the lion may attack me."

What else would be involved in my perception and fear of the lion? There would be something purely physical: the physical stimulation of my sensory organs; some physiological changes in heart, brain, nerves, glands; and some avoidance behavior, *e.g.,* running. On Descartes' view the connection between the sensory stimulation and the behavior would be entirely mechanical, unless there was an intervention of the will to prevent the behavior. As Anthony Kenny says:

> In its essentials the theory is that the physiological processes involved in the perception of a fearful object, set in motion, by purely mechanical causation, a further physiological process which issues in the behavior characteristic of fear.[17]

In one of his letters to More, Descartes says:

> Even in us all the motions of the members which accompany our passions are caused not by the soul but simply by the machinery of the body.[18]

If a dog met a lion in the jungle his reaction might appear to be like mine. The sensory stimulation, the physiological processes, and the resulting behavior

havior could be quite similar. But for the dog there would be no propositional content and no propositional attitude. There would be no "thought," in either sense of the word, and therefore nothing of the "mental" aspect of fear. When confronted by a fearful object the dog responds purely as a machine. Descartes gives examples of our own human behavior that he regards as machine performances:

> If someone quickly thrusts his hand against our eyes as if to strike us, even though we know him to be our friend, that he only does it in fun, and that he will take great care not to hurt us, we have, all the same, trouble in preventing ourselves from closing them; and this shows that it is not by the intervention of our soul that they close . . . ; but it is because the machine of our body is so formed that the movement of this hand towards our eyes excites another movement in our brain which conducts the animal spirits into the muscles which cause the eyelids to close.[19]

It becomes clear why Descartes said, on the one hand, that animals have feeling and passion but, on the other hand, that they do not have "real" feeling and passion. The propositional representations and attitudes, that are produced in people by sensory stimulations and physiological processes, do not occur in the "lower" animals. For the same reason the animals do not have *sensation* in the full sense. Descartes wrote to More that "thought is included in our mode of sensation."[20] He meant the human mode of sensation. If every human sensation includes thought, and if thought is propositional content together with propositional attitude, then at the center of every sensation of ours there is a proposition. Animals do not have propositional thoughts and therefore do not have sensations in the human mode.

In first reading Descartes it surprises one that he should include emotion, feeling and sensation under "thinking." But this would be a natural employment of the word "thinking," *given* his conception of the propositional nature of human emotion, feeling and sensation.

In the *Reply to Objections VI* Descartes distinguishes between three "grades" of sensation:

> To the first (grade) belongs the immediate affection of the bodily organ by external objects; and this can be nothing else than the motion of the particles of the sensory organs and the change of figure and position due to that motion. The second (grade) comprises the immediate mental results, due to the mind's union with the corporeal organ affected; such are the perceptions of pain, of pleasurable stimulation, of thirst, of hunger, of colours, of sound, savour, odour, cold, heat, and the like . . . Finally the third (grade) contains all those judgments which, on the occasion of motions occurring in the corporeal organ, we have

from our earliest years been accustomed to pass about things external to us.[21]

The first grade of sensation is shared by animals and people. It is the only sense in which animals have sensation. The second grade involves perceptions *(perceptiones)* of pain, heat, cold, sound, and so on. On Descartes' view this grade of sensation involves propositional content, and so is *thinking.* Presumably the propositional content of a sensation of heat in the second grade, would be expressed by the sentence, "It seems to me that I feel heat." In Meditation II he presents such an occurrence as its seeming to him that he feels heat as an example of what is properly called sensation or feeling *(sentire);* and he declares that it is "nothing other than thinking"*(cogitare).*[22] I suppose that the propositional content of a sensation of pain would be "I feel pain." In a letter to Mersenne, Descartes actually says that "pain exists only in the understanding" *(la douleur n'est que dan l'entendement),* and that animals don't have pain.[23] It appears that in order to have a pain one must apprehend and affirm a proposition. In the *Principles,* Descartes says that my sensation *(sensu)* of seeing or of walking is "my consciously seeming to see or to walk": this "refers only to my mind, which alone is concerned with my feeling or thinking that I see and I walk."[24] Descartes' third grade of sensation is called "thinking" because it consists of "customary judgments" about the material world—for example, that there is a source of heat nearby; that it is the burn on my arm that is giving me pain; that I am walking.

How does Descartes conceive the relation between thought and consciousness? He says:

> By the word "thought" I understand all those things that are in us consciously, in so far as we are conscious of them.[25]

In other words, something is a thought of mine if and only if I am conscious of it, and only to the extent I am conscious of it. Since animals have no thought they have no consciousness of anything.

Although Zeno Vendler's interpretations of Descartes are admirable, here I want to pick a slight quarrel with him. He seems to think that Descartes' identification of "thoughts" with "all those things that are in us consciously," led him into the mistake of regarding sensations as thoughts, since we are conscious of sensations. According to Vendler our actual concept of thought is restricted to mental acts and states that have propositional content. He believes that Descartes "never succeeded in catching this distinction"— that is, the distinction between mental states that have propositional content and those that do not. Vendler says that "instead of the specific distinction between the propositional and the nonpropositional, all he (Descartes) sees is a difference of degree between the clear and the confused."[26]

According to my understanding, however, Descartes was precisely insisting that when we mean by "sensation" something other than mere physiological processes, then sensation does have propositional content. Indeed, I suggest that for Descartes the distinction between the "mental" and the "physical" is *defined* by the presence or absence of propositional content. In the *Passions* he says that "there is nothing in us that we ought to attribute to our soul excepting our thoughts," and he adds, as we previously noted, that thoughts are of two sorts, actions and passions.[27] Actions are volitions *(volontez)*. According to the analysis of Meditation III, a volition consists of an *idea, i.e.,* a propositional content, together with the attitude or mental frame of willing that content. Similarly, a passion is a propositional content, plus the attitude of fearing, or hoping, and so on. Thus *everything* properly attributed to soul or mind is propositional.

As Vendler notes, bodily sensations are regarded by Descartes as "confused modes of thought." Descartes says:

> For all these sensations of hunger, thirst, pain, etc., are in truth none other than certain confused modes of thought which are produced by the union and apparent intermingling of mind and body.[28]

What is the nature of the "confusion" in this mode of thought? According to Descartes it is a *conceptual* confusion. We have a natural inclination to assume that when we feel pain in our foot, there actually is a sensation in our foot—as if a *sensation* could be located *in one's foot!* We can, however, purge ourselves of that confusion. We can arrive at a clear understanding of what a pain is. Descartes says that "we have a clear or distinct knowledge of pain, colour, and other things of the sort when we consider them simply as sensations or thoughts" *(sensus sive cogitationes)*.[29] When I succeed in regarding a pain of mine as nothing else than a sensation, that is to say, as a *thought*, I shall be freed of my former conceptual blunder—since I cannot suppose that there is *a thought in my foot!*

Probably I shall regard *in-my-foot* as a quality of the sensation (just as *throbbing* can be a quality of a sensation). Certainly I shall not regard "in-my-foot" as specifying a physical location of my sensation! Regardless, however, of whether or not I attain to that stage of supposed conceptual clarity the fact is, according to Descartes, that the pain-in-my-foot is a thought! It consists of a propositional content (which might be expressed by the phrase, "My having an in-my-foot pain"), plus the mental frame of affirming, joined (no doubt) by the mental frame of dislike. If I wince, cry out, or limp, this has nothing to do with the sensation as such, but is solely a performance of my bodily machine.

According to my understanding of Descartes, he explicitly and consciously adopted the position that there is a propositional kernel in every feeling, desire, voluntary act, emotion, and sensation. This is why he could hold that his essential nature consists solely in being a thinking thing.[30] It was *not* because he employed *cogitare* and *penser* in an eccentrically broad way that he listed imagining, sensation and emotion under "thinking." It was because he believed that every "mental operation" consists in taking an attitude towards a proposition.

In my opinion this is an absurdly overintellectualized view of the life of man. It helps us to understand, however, why Descartes thought that animals are automatons. They are devoid of mind, of all consciousness and awareness, of real feeling and sensation, because they do not "apprehend," "entertain," "contemplate," or, in plain language, think of, *propositions.*

II

In real life we commonly employ the verb "think" in respect to animals. We say, "Towser thinks he is going to be fed," just as naturally as we say, "Towser wants to be fed." Suppose our dog is chasing the neighbor's cat. The latter runs full tilt toward an oak tree, but suddenly swerves at the last moment and disappears up a nearby maple. The dog doesn't see this maneuver and on arriving at the oak tree he rears up on his hind legs, paws the trunk as if trying to scale it, and barks excitedly into the branches above. We who observe the whole episode from a window say, "He thinks that the cat went up that oak tree." We say "thinks" because he is barking up the wrong tree. If the cat *had* gone up the oak tree and if the dog's performance had been the same, we could have said, "He knows that the cat went up the oak." But let us stay with "thinks." A million examples could be produced in which it would be a correct way of speaking to say of an animal, something of the form, "He thinks that *p*." Clearly there is an error in Descartes' contention that animals do not think.

Let us, however, take note of a distinction. In commenting later on the incident of the dog and the cat we could, without any qualms, say of our dog, "He thought that the cat went up the oak tree." We should, in contrast, feel reluctant and embarrassed to say, "He had the thought that the cat went up the oak tree." In referring to an animal, it is natural enough to say, "He thought that *p*," but not, "He had the thought that *p*." It would sound funny to say of a dog, monkey or dolphin, that the thought that *p* occurred to him, or struck him, or went through his mind. All of us are familiar with the sort of evidence on the basis of which we predicate of animals (or rather, of *some* animals) that they think that so-and-so; but we are not familiar with any basis for attributing *thoughts* to them.

Apparently Descartes did not catch this distinction between "to think" and "to have thoughts." In his first letter to Henry More, he says it is a prejudice to suppose that "dumb animals think" *(bruta animantia cogitare);* and then he goes on to give his reasons for holding that "beasts lack thought" *(bestias cogitatione destitutas esse).*[31] He is treating "to think" and "to have thoughts" as if they are equivalent: but we have seen that they are not.[32]

One way of stating the interest of this distinction is to say that although we apply the word "think" to animals, using it as a transitive verb taking a propositional phrase as its object, we do not thereby imply that the animal *formulated* or *thought of* a proposition, or had a proposition "before its mind." In saying something about the animal, we employ a verb that, grammatically, takes a propositional expression as object, without meaning that as a matter of psychological fact the animal thought of a proposition.

The next point to see is that we employ the verb "think" in the same way in regard to *people.* On the basis of circumstances and behavior we say that a man "thought that *p*," without implying that he thought of *p* or formulated *p*, or that *p* occurred to him or was in his thoughts. For example, suppose a friend of mine and I are engrossed in an exciting conversation. We are about to drive off in his car. While holding up his end of the conversation he fumbles in his pocket for the car keys. I, knowing that they are in the glove compartment, say to myself, "He thinks the keys are in his pocket." I do not imply that he said to himself, or thought to himself, "The keys are in my pocket." Grammatical form is no index of psychological reality.

I am aware that the example of my friend fumbling in his pocket and, even more so, the example of the dog clawing the tree, produce philosophical discomfort. How can it be correct to say that my friend "thinks" the keys are in his pocket, when he isn't having any thoughts about the keys? How can

it be correct to say that the dog "thinks" the cat went up the oak tree, in face of the fact that a dog cannot rightly be said to have thoughts about anything? There is a half-hearted inclination to *deny* that it is really correct to say those things. Here I simply appeal to ordinary language. It is clearly right to use "thinks" in both cases.

The next move to relieve the discomfort is more interesting. There is an inclination to suppose that what we *mean* when we say, as in my example, "He thinks the keys are in his pocket", is "He *acts as if* he had the thought 'The keys are in my pocket'". Likewise, the dog *acts as if* he had the thought "That confounded cat went up this tree".

This is an interesting move because it reveals a tendency to regard *having thoughts* as the prototype or the paradigm of *thinking.* Other uses of "thinks" are felt to be derivative from, or parasitic on, this prototype. If those uses somehow refer to, or converge on, the prototype, they are intelligible; otherwise not.

I believe this idea is mistaken. There is nothing that deserves to be regarded as *the* paradigm or prototype of thinking. There are many paradigms of thinking, no one of which holds a central place in the application of the word. Just as there is nothing that is *the* prototype of *furniture.* There are different kinds of furniture, and different forms of thinking, none being furniture or thinking *par excellence.* There are connections between the different forms of thinking: but this does not mean that there is an essential nature of thinking, or that the forms of thinking converge towards a center. There is no reason to believe that the concept of thinking has that kind of unity.

Just why there is an especially strong urge to select the phenomenon of having thoughts as being that which lies at the center, is a fascinating problem into which I cannot venture on the present occasion. I limit myself to remarking that there is no warrant for believing that there is *a center,* occupied by anything.

Let us return to the observation that the formula, "He thought that *p*", does not entail the formula, "The thought that *p* occurred to him". The same holds for a host of propositional verbs. You and I notice, for example, that Robinson is walking in a gingerly way, and you ask why? I reply, "Because he realizes that the path is slippery." I do not imply that the proposition, "This path is slippery," crossed his mind. Another example: I wave at a man across the quad. Later on I may say to someone, "I saw Kaspar today." It may be true that I recognized Kaspar, or recognized that the man across the quad was Kaspar, but not true that I thought to myself, "That is Kaspar." Turning from propositional verbs to emotions and sensations, it is plainly false that whenever a man is angry he thinks of the proposition, "I am angry"; or that whenever he feels a pain in his leg the thought, "I have a pain in my leg," occurs to him. Descartes was wrong in holding that "our mode of sensation includes thought." Human sensation does not always, or even characteristically, include thought.

Noting these facts should help us to see that the gap between ourselves and at least the higher of the lower animals is not as great as Descartes supposed. His distorted view of the matter was in part due to his doctrine that human mental phenomena are always propositional. His claim that his essential nature is thinking is actually the claim that his essential nature consists in *thinking of propositions*. When we see the enormity of this exaggeration of the propositional in human life, our unwillingness to ascribe propositional thinking to animals ought no longer to make us refuse to attribute to them a panoply of forms of feeling, of perception, of realization, of recognition, that are, more often than not, nonpropositional in the human case. Their nonpropositional character does *not* mark them as something less than real forms of consciousness.

III

Still, there is a gap, as is revealed by our reluctance to attribute thoughts to animals. Once I owned an Airedale dog who hated a bath, and it came about in the course of time that whenever he saw preparations for a bath underway he would go into hiding. I have no hesitation in saying that he "realized" he was going to be given a bath; or in saying that he had "learned from experience" that certain preparations were followed by a bath. (Whether or not this adds up to his being "rational" I won't try to say.) But certainly I would not attribute to him the thought, "Here we go again! Another of those horrible baths."

In this regard I would take a stronger position than Descartes did. He said it could not be *proved* either that animals do or that they do not have thoughts "hidden in their bodies," thus conceding it to be *possible* that they do have thoughts after all. But the idea that we cannot determine whether dogs have thoughts *in* them is a dreadful confusion. Suppose we did know everything that is hidden in their bodies: How could we tell which of these things were thoughts?

The notion that dogs may have hidden thoughts is a red herring. The relevant question is whether they *express* thoughts. I think the answer

is clearly in the negative. Let us go back to Robinson who is walking on a slippery path. Just from his gingerly movements we know he is aware that the footing is slippery; but we cannot determine from this character of his movements whether the thought, "This path is slippery," has occurred to him. In the case of a person we can often find out whether the thought that *p* crossed his mind, either by overhearing him *say* that *p*, or by his subsequently *testifying* that the thought that *p* occurred to him. With animals we don't have either recourse. The possession of language makes the whole difference. If a dog on that slippery path moved in an equally gingerly way, we could say with propriety that the dog is aware that the path is slippery. What further thing could we do to find out whether the thought, "This path is slippery," occurred to it, or crossed its mind? An undertaking of trying to find out whether the dog did or didn't have that thought is not anything we understand.

Descartes' notion was that speech is the only "sign" of the presence of thought. This suggests, as I have said, that just conceivably animals may have thoughts of which they give no sign. This implies a looseness of connection between thought and the linguistic expression of thought, that is deeply disturbing. It conveys the picture of two kinds of processes, sometimes running more or less parallel, one consisting of the linguistic expression of thoughts, the other consisting of the thoughts themselves. This picture, if taken seriously, ought to create an uncertainty as to whether *people* have thoughts. If thoughts are states or processes that linguistic utterances are supposed to match, then how can one be sure that the right matchings are made, or any matchings at all, not only in the case of other people, but in one's own case too? The relationship between language and thought must be closer than that; so close that it is really senseless to conjecture that people may *not* have thoughts, and also really senseless to conjecture that animals *may* have thoughts.

Thoughts cannot, of course, be identified with sentences: they are not linguistic entities. Nor can thoughts be identified with the uttering of sentences. Nor can they be identified with behavioral propensities. Nor with physiological events. Nor can they be identified with a flow of bodily sensations and images. What are they then?

This is a strange question. Why should we even be moved to ask what thoughts are, in general? Given a certain context we often know what particular thought a particular man had. For example, McCarthy always takes the 7:30 bus to work, but this morning he was late and missed it. On returning to the house he says to his wife, "This may cause me to lose my job." We know what his thought was. What can be said, other than that his thought was that he might lose his job? What makes us suppose there might be some other kind of answer? It is only from the vantage, or disadvantage, of a philosophical theory, such as a monolithic behaviorism, or a monolithic materialism, that it can seem to us that another sort of answer is in the offing.

We need to avoid identifying thoughts with their linguistic expression. At the same time we should reject the suggestion that it is *possible* that language-less creatures should have thoughts. The case is somewhat analogous to the fact that mirror images are not identical with mirrors, yet it is impossible that there should be mirror images without mirrors. The analogy fails in the following respect: It is possible that a person should have had a certain thought at time *t*, even though no linguistic expression of that thought occurred at *t*. Whereas it is impossible that a mirror image should exist at *t* unless a mirroring surface existed at *t*. But this disanalogy does not argue an independence of thought from language: for it is meaningful to suppose that a person might have had a thought to which he gave no expression, only because this person speaks or spoke a language in which there is an institution of testifying to previously unexpressed thoughts.

I agree, therefore, with the Cartesians that thoughts cannot be attributed to animals that are without language. But I come here, not to praise men for their thoughts, but to defend animals from their Cartesian and Neo-Cartesian detractors. These philosophers say that animals do not have "minds." People quarrel profoundly over the question of whether cats are more or less intelligent than dogs. Could cats be more intelligent than dogs but still not have minds? Of some animals we can say that they are frightened, joyous, affectionate,—that they want, seek, pursue, hide, lie in wait, play, tease, defend; that they see, hear, smell, like, dislike, avoid; that they remember, recognize, realize and think. Despite all this and more, don't they have minds? It is hard to get a grip on the question.

Descartes say that a mind is something that thinks: in this case both I and my dog *are* minds, for both of us may think that the cat went up the oak tree. I have tried to show, however, that Descartes mistakenly equates thinking with having thoughts.[33] His view is that a "mind" is something that has thoughts. Now, *I* have thoughts, but my poor doggy has none. So *I* am a mind but he is not. The latter-day Cartesian, Zeno Vendler, says that "To have a mind is to have thoughts."[34] If this is true, then my dog neither is nor has a mind. But we should understand what this comes to—just

that he doesn't have thoughts; which in turn comes to just this, that he doesn't have a language. We can appreciate, however, that despite this the dog isn't so badly off, since a great range of feelings, sensations, wants, perceptions, and realizings, can be accurately attributed to him.

What about consciousness? A dog, like a man, can be knocked unconscious. But if a dog runs around, barks, and picks a fight with another dog, isn't he conscious? We saw that Descartes ties consciousness exclusively to thoughts. Although Vendler believes Descartes was mistaken in regarding animals as automatons, he inclines to interpret consciousness in the same narrow way that Descartes did, namely, as consisting solely in having thoughts. Vendler says:

> If . . . consciousness be defined as the totality of one's thoughts (at a given moment), then sensations and feelings do not enter consciousness until by noticing or being aware of them one forms or entertains a perceptual judgment. If this is true, then we must agree with Descartes that animals, strictly speaking, cannot be conscious of their sensations and other experiences.[35]

But isn't there a great deal of human consciousness that doesn't involve thoughts or propositional content? I stop my car at an intersection because the light is red. I was aware of the red light and was also aware that the light was red. Did I think to myself, "That light is red"? Probably not. Or suppose that as you pass an acquaintance he says "Hello" to you, and you respond in kind. Did you think to yourself, "He said, 'Hello'"? Suppose you did not. Would it be true, therefore, that you were not conscious of his greeting? Of course not.

There are many forms of human response that manifest consciousness of objects, situations and events; and animals share in some of these forms of consciousness. Descartes says that this belief is due to a pervasive prejudice. I think the shoe is on the other foot. It is the prejudice of philosophers that only propositional thoughts belong to consciousness, that stands in the way of our perceiving the continuity of consciousness between human and animal life.

NOTES

1. Zeno Vendler, *Res Cogitans,* Ithaca 1972, p. 152.

2. Anthony Kenny (ed.), *Descartes; Philosophical Letters,* Oxford 1970 (hereafter, *DL*), p. 53: C. Adam and P. Tannery (eds.), *Oeuvres de Descartes* (hereafter, *AT*), Vol. 2, 39. See also *DL*, 243: *AT* 5, 276.

3. L. C. Rosenfield, *From Beast-Machine to Man-Machine,* New York 1941, p. 54.

4. *DL* 245: *AT 5*, 278.

5. *DL* 244: *AT 5*, 276–277 (quia mens humans illorum corda non pervadit).

6. *DL* 245: *AT 5*, 278 (Haec enim loquela unicum est cogitationis in corpore latentis signum certum).

7. *DL* 251: *AT 5*, 345.

8. E. Haldane and G. Ross (eds.), *Philosophical Works of Descartes* (hereafter, *HR*) *1*, 153: *AT 7*, 28.

9. *Passions* I, 17: *HR 1*, 340: *AT 11*, 342.

10. *DL* 245: *AT 5*, 278.

11. *DL* 206–207: *AT 4*, 574–575.

12. *DL* 54: *AT 2*, 41.

13. *HR 1*, 159: *AT 7*, 37.

14. "Mental frame" is Vendler's phrase: *op. cit.,* p. 167.

15. B. Russell, *The Analysis of Mind*, New York 1921, p. 243.

16. C. I. Lewis, *An Analysis of Knowledge and Valuation,* La Salle, 1946, pp. 48–55.

17. Anthony Kenny, *Action, Emotion and Will*, New York 1963, p. 8.

18. *DL* 251: *AT 5*, 345.

19. *Passions,* I, 13: *HR 1*, 338: *AT 11*, 338–339. "Animal spirits" are minute bodies that move at high speed.

20. *DL* 244: *AT 5*, 277 (in nostro sentiendi modo cogitatio includitur).

21. *HR 2*, 251: *AT 7*, 436–437.

22. *HR 1*, 153; *AT 7, 29*,

23. *AT 3*, 85.

24. *Principles* I, 9: *HR 1*, 222: *AT 8*, 7–8.

25. *Principles* I, 9: *HR 1*, 222: *AT 8*, 7. (Cogitationis nomine, intellego illa omnia, quae nobis consciis in nobis sunt, quatenus eorum in nobis conscientia est.)

26. Vendler, *op. cit.,* p. 155.

27. *Passions,* I, 17: *HR 1*, 350: *AT 11*, 342.

28. Meditation VI: *HR 1*, 192: *AT 7*, 81.

29. *Principles* I, 68: *HR 1*, 248: *AT 8*, 33. See also *Principles* I, 67.

30. Meditation VI: *HR 1*, 190: *AT 7*, 78.

31. *DL* 243, 244: *AT 5*, 276, 278.

32. Vendler points out (*op. cit.,* pp. 198–199) that Descartes sometimes uses *cogitare* as a transitive, propositional verb—that is, as meaning "to think that *p*." One of several examples Vendler cites is *cogitem me videre,* which can be translated as "I think I see" or "I think that I see" (*HR 1*, 156: *AT 7*, 33).

33. This Cartesian view is so commonly held that some philosophers regard it as a *truism.* For example, in the most recent number of *Mind,* Justus Hartnack says: "It may be maintained, *although a bit trivally,* that thinking consists of thoughts. Thinking is the stream of thoughts" ("On Thinking", *Mind,* Oct. 1972, p. 550; my italics). Hartnack also takes a Cartesian position in declaring that "there can be no thoughts and no thinking if there is no language" (ibid., p. 551). I am urging that once we acknowledge the distinction between thinking and having thoughts, then we can see that if there were no language thinking could occur, but no one could have thoughts

34. Vendler, *op. cit.,* p. 187.

35. *Ibid,* p. 162

52

David M. Rosenthal

"Two Concepts of Consciousness"

No mental phenomenon is more central than consciousness to an adequate understanding of the mind. Nor does any mental phenomenon seem more stubbornly to resist theoretical treatment.

Consciousness is so basic to the way we think about the mind that it can be tempting to suppose that no mental states exist that are not conscious states. Indeed, it may even seem mysterious what sort of thing a mental state might be if it is not a conscious state. On this way of looking at things, if any mental states do lack consciousness, they are exceptional cases that call for special explanation or qualification. Perhaps dispositional or cognitive states exist that are not conscious, but nonetheless count as mental states. But if so, such states would be derivatively mental, owing their mental status solely to their connection with conscious states. And perhaps it makes sense to postulate nonconscious versions of ordinary mental states, as some psychological theories do. But if consciousness is central to mentality in the way this picture insists, any such states are at best degenerate examples of mentality, and thus peripheral to our concept of mind.

This picture is both inviting and familiar. But there are other features of the way we normally think about mind which result in a rather different conception of the relation between consciousness and mentality. We often know, without being told, what another person is thinking or feeling. And we sometimes know this even when that person actually is not aware, at least at first, of having those feelings or thoughts. There is nothing anomalous or puzzling about such cases. Even if it is only seldom that we know the mental states of others better than they do, when we do, the mental states in question are not degenerate or derivative examples

of mentality. Moreover, conscious states are simply mental states we are conscious of being in. So when we are aware that somebody thinks or feels something that that person is initially unaware of thinking or feeling, those thoughts and feelings are at first mental states that are not also conscious states. These considerations suggest a way of looking at things on which we have no more reason to identify being a mental state with being a conscious state than we have to identify physical objects with physical objects that somebody sees. Consciousness is a feature of many mental states but, on this picture, it is not necessary or even central to a state's being a mental state. Consciousness seems central to mentality only because it is so basic to how we know our own mental states. But how we know about things is often an unreliable guide to their nature.

These two alternative pictures of the connection between consciousness and mentality have different implications about what sort of explanation is possible of what it is for a mental state to be a conscious state. If we take the view that consciousness is not a necessary feature of mental states, then we cannot define mental states as conscious states. Accordingly, we must seek some other account of what makes a state a mental state. But once we have an account of mentality that does not appeal to consciousness, we can then try to explain what conscious states are by building upon that very account of mentality. In particular, it then makes sense to try to formulate nontrivial necessary and sufficient conditions for a mental state to be a conscious state. On this conception of mentality and consciousness, it is open for us to proceed sequentially in this way, first defining mentality and then consciousness.

From *Philosophical Studies* 94, 3 (May 1986): 329–59. Copyright © 1986 by D. Reidel Publishing Company. Reprinted, with slight revisions by the author, with permission of Kluwer Academic Publishers.

No such procedure, however, is possible if instead we adopt the view that being a mental state is at bottom the same as being a conscious state. For we cannot then explain what makes conscious states conscious by appeal to a prior account of mentality, since on that view mentality presupposes consciousness itself. Any attempt to explain consciousness by formulating necessary and sufficient conditions for a mental state to be conscious will thus automatically fail. If consciousness is already built into mentality, any such explanation will be uninformative. If not, then, on the present view, the conception of mind on which our explanation of consciousness is based will unavoidably be radically defective. It is plain that there is no third way; nothing that is not mental can help to explain consciousness. So, if consciousness is essential to mentality, no informative, nontrivial explanation of consciousness is possible at all. Moreover, since we cannot then proceed sequentially, explaining mentality first and then consciousness, the gulf that seems to separate mind and consciousness from the rest of reality will appear impossible to bridge. Thomas Nagel succinctly expresses this view when he writes that "[c]onsciousness is what makes the mind–body problem really intractable."[1]

Although it seems effectively to preclude our giving any informative explanation of consciousness, the view that consciousness is essential to all mental states does have apparent advantages. For one thing, that view, which has strong affinities with the Cartesian view of mind, fits well with many of our common-sense intuitions about the mental. And perhaps that view even does greater justice to those intuitions than a view of the mind on which not all mental states are conscious. These two competing pictures of mind and consciousness seem to present us, therefore, with a difficult choice. We can opt to save our presystematic intuitions at the cost of being unable to explain consciousness. Or we can hold open the possibility of giving a satisfactory explanation, but risk being less faithful to our common-sense intuitions about what mental states are.

One reaction to this quandary is simply to accept the more Cartesian of the two pictures, and accept that an illuminating explanation of consciousness will simply prove impossible. This traditional response is now hard to credit. Mind and consciousness are continuous with other natural phenomena of which we can give impressively powerful explanations. And it is difficult to believe that a singularity in nature could exist that would utterly and permanently resist all attempts to explain it. For these reasons, some more recent writers have chosen, instead, simply to abandon common-sense intuitions about mind when they conflict with our explanatory goals. Physics does not aspire to reconstruct all our presystematic intuitions about the things around us. Why, proponents of this eliminativist approach ask, should the science of mind proceed differently?[2]

But we should, wherever possible, seek to explain our common-sense intuitions rather than just explain them away. And we should hesitate to jettison our presystematic conceptions of things, whether mental or physical, unless efforts to do justice to them have decisively failed. Indeed, even physical theories must square as much as possible with our common-sense picture of physical reality. In what follows, I argue that we need embrace neither the Cartesian nor the eliminativist stance toward the consciousness of mental states. Instead, we can both be faithful to our presystematic intuitions about consciousness and mind and, at the same time, construct useful, informative explanations of those phenomena. In section I, I develop the two pictures sketched above. In particular, I articulate the two different definitions of mentality itself that comprise the core of those two pictures. I then use the non-Cartesian concept of mind and consciousness to construct a systematic and theoretically satisfying explanation of what it is for a mental state to be conscious—an explanation, that is, of what it is that distinguishes conscious from nonconscious mental states. I show further how the definition of mentality central to each of the two pictures determines a distinct conception of consciousness, and how the Cartesian concept of consciousness makes any informative explanation of consciousness impossible. In sections II and III, then, I go on to argue that the non-Cartesian explanation can save the phenomenological appearances and explain the data of consciousness as well as the more familiar Cartesian picture. And I argue there that the standard considerations that favor the Cartesian view are baseless. And in section IV I conclude with some observations about consciousness and our knowledge of the mental, and about the actual significance of the insights that underlie the Cartesian picture.

I

All mental states, of whatever sort, exhibit properties of one of two types: intentional properties and phenomenal, or sensory, properties. Something has an intentional property if it has propositional content, or if it is about something. Sensory properties, by contrast, are less homogeneous. Examples are the redness of a visual sensation and the sharp painful quality of certain bodily sensations. Some mental states may have both intentional and phenomenal properties. But whatever else is true of mental states, it is plain that we would not count a state as a mental state at all unless it had some intentional property or some phenomenal property.

Something close to the converse holds as well. For one thing, only mental states can have phenomenal properties. Although we use words such as 'red' and 'round' to refer to properties of physical objects as well as to properties of mental states, we refer to different properties in the two cases. The introspectible redness of a visual sensation is not the same property as the perceptible redness of a tomato, for example, since each can occur in the absence of the other. Moreover, mental states are not objects at all, and therefore cannot have the same properties of shape and color that physical objects have. Indeed, we do not even use quality words the same way when we talk about mental states and about physical objects. We speak interchangeably about red sensations and sensations of red, but it makes no nonmetaphorical sense to talk about tomatoes of red. Similar considerations apply to properties that are special to bodily sensations. Knives and aches may both be dull, but the dullness of a knife, unlike that of an ache, has to do with the shape of its edge. Phenomenal properties, properly so called, are unique to mental states.[3]

Things are slightly less straightforward with intentional properties, since items other than mental states can exhibit in intentionality. Speech acts and works of art, for example, can be about things and can have propositional content. But except for mental states themselves, nothing has intentional properties other than those modes and products of behavior which express intentional mental states. So it is reasonable to hold that these modes and products of behavior derive their intentionality from the mental states they express. As Roderick M. Chisholm puts it, "thoughts are a 'source of intentionality'—i.e., nothing would be intentional were it not for the fact that thoughts are intentional."[4] So, even though intentional properties belong to things other than mental states, they do so only derivatively. Accordingly, all mental states have intentional or sensory properties, and sensory properties belong only to mental states and intentional properties nonderivatively to mental states alone. We thus have a compelling basis for defining mental states as just those states which have either intentionality or phenomenal quality.

There are, however, objections to this way of delineating the distinctively mental which seem to favor a mark of the mental based on consciousness instead. For one thing, a mark of the mental that relies solely on intentional and phenomenal properties may seem to underplay the special access we have to our own mental states. Even if all mental states do exhibit intentional or sensory features, one might urge that the more revealing mark of the mental would somehow appeal, instead, to that special access. On such a mark, what is essential to mental states would not be intentional or sensory character, but consciousness itself. Moreover, if we take the possession of either sensory or intentional properties to be definitive of the mental, we must then explain why we regard this disjunctive mark as determining the mental. Why do we construe as a single category the class of states that have one or the other of these two kinds of properties? It does not help to note that that some mental states, for example, perceptual states, have both sorts of characteristic. Despite the existence of such mongrel cases, it seems unlikely that pure phenomenal states, such as pains, have anything interesting in common with pure intentional states, such as beliefs. And we can avoid this difficulty if, instead, we take consciousness to be what makes a state a mental state. Finally, the characteristically mental differences among kinds of mental states are all differences in what intentional or sensory properties those states have. So those properties may seem to figure more naturally in an account of how we distinguish among types of mental state than in an account of how mental states differ from everything else. These various considerations all suggest that an account of mind in terms of consciousness may be preferable to an account that appeals to intentionality and phenomenal character.

Moreover, defining mentality in terms of consciousness need not involve any circularity. We can say what it is to be a conscious state in a way that does not explicitly mention being mental. A state is conscious if whoever is in it is to some degree aware of being in it in a way that does not rely on inference, as that is ordinarily conceived, or on some sort of sensory input. Conscious states are simply those states to which we have noninferential and nonsensory access.

People do, of course, have many more beliefs and preferences, at any given time, than occur in their stream of consciousness. And the nonconscious beliefs and preferences must always have intentional properties. But this need not be decisive against taking consciousness as our mark of the mental. For we can construe beliefs and preferences as actual mental states only when they are conscious. On other occasions we could regard them to be merely dispositions for actual mental states to occur; in those cases, we can say, one is simply disposed to have occurrent thoughts and desires.

Consciousness is intuitively far more crucial for sensory states than for intentional states. This disparity is something we must explain if we take consciousness as the mark of all mental states. Construing nonconscious beliefs and preferences not as actual mental states but as mere dispositions to be in such states helps us give a suitable explanation. Sensory states normally result from short-term stimulations; so we have little reason to talk about our being disposed to be in particular types of sensory state. By constrast, we are often disposed to be in intentional states of various kinds. Since we are typically not conscious of being thus disposed, the tie between consciousness and mentality may at first sight seem less strong with intentional than with sensory states. But that tie may apply equally to both sorts of state if we count only nondispositional states as mental states, properly speaking. For when we focus on short-term, episodic intentional states, the common-sense intuition that mental states must be conscious is no less compelling than it is in the case of phenomenal states.

The two marks of the mental just sketched are independent of each other, and both lay claim to long and well-established histories. Thus writers with Cartesian leanings have generally favored some mark based on consciousness, while those in a more naturalist, Aristotelian tradition have tended to rely instead on some such mark as intentionality or sensory character. For it is a roughly Aristotelian idea that the mental is somehow dependent on highly organized forms of life, in something like the way in which life itself emerges in highly organized forms of material existence. And this idea suggests that one should try to delimit the mental in terms of the various distinctively mental kinds of functioning and, thus, by reference to the intentional and phenomenal characteristics of mental states. To the Aristotelian, such a mark has the advantage of inviting one to conceive of the mental as continuous with other natural phenomena. Thus Aristotle's own account of psychological phenomena gives great prominence to sense perception, thereby stressing the continuity between the mental and the biological.

The Cartesian tradition, by contrast, conceives of the mental as one of the two jointly exhaustive categories of existence, standing in stark opposition to everything physical. And on this view it is tempting to select some single essential feature, such as consciousness, to be the mark of the mental. For this kind of mark will stress the sharp contrast between mental and physical, and play down the differences among types of mental states compared to how different all mental states are from everything else. In this spirit, Descartes takes non-perceptual, propositional states to be the paradigm of the mental and, notoriously, has great difficulty in explaining how perception can involve both mental and bodily states.

Although both marks of the mental have enjoyed widespread acceptance, it is crucial which mark we adopt if our goal is to give an explanation of consciousness. Conscious states are simply mental states we are conscious of being in. And, in general, our being conscious of something is just a matter of our having a thought of some sort about it. Accordingly, it is natural to identify a mental state's being conscious with one's having a roughly contemporaneous thought that one is in that mental state. When a mental state is conscious, one's awareness of it is, intuitively, immediate in some way. So we can stipulate that the contemporaneous thought one has is not mediated by any inference or perceptual input. We are then in a position to advance a useful, informative explanation of what makes conscious states conscious. Since a mental state is conscious if it is accompanied by a suitable higher-order thought, we can explain a mental state's being conscious by hypothesizing that the mental state itself causes that higher-order thought to occur.

At first sight it may seem that counterexamples to this explanation are rife. Although we are usually, when awake, in some conscious mental state or other, we rarely notice having any higher-order thoughts of the sort this explanation postulates. Typically, mental states occur in our stream of consciousness without our also having any evident thought that we are in those states. But such cases are not counterexamples unless we presuppose, contrary to the present explanation, that all mental states are conscious states. For otherwise, there will be no reason to assume that the higher-order thoughts that our explanation posits would, in general, be conscious thoughts. On this explanation, a mental state is conscious if one has a suitable second-order thought. So that second-order thought would itself be a conscious thought only if one also had a third-order thought that one had the second-order thought. And it begs the question against that account to assume that these higher-order thoughts are usually, or even often, conscious thoughts. If a mental state's being conscious does consist in one's having a suitable higher-order thought, there is no reason to expect that this thought would ordinarily be a conscious thought. Indeed, we would expect, instead, that the third-order thoughts that confer consciousness on such second-order thoughts would be relatively rare; it is hard to hold in mind a thought about a thought that is in turn about a thought. So the present account correctly predicts that we would seldom be aware of our second-order thoughts, and this actually helps confirm the account.

It is important to distinguish a mental state's being conscious from our being introspectively aware of that state. Higher-order thoughts are sometimes invoked to explain introspection, which is a special case of consciousness.[5] But introspection is a more complex phenomenon than the ordinary consciousness of mental states. Intuitively, a mental state's being conscious means just that it occurs in our stream of consciousness. Introspection, by contrast, involves consciously and deliberately paying attention to our contemporaneous mental states. As Ryle remarks "introspection is an attentive operation and one which is only occasionally performed, whereas consciousness is supposed to be a constant element of all mental processes."[6] Normally when mental states occur in one's stream of consciousness, one is unaware of having any higher-order thought about them. But when we are reflectively or introspectively aware of a mental state, we are aware not only of being in that mental state; we are also aware that we are aware of being in it. The Cartesian picture of mind and consciousness thus tacitly conflates a mental state's being conscious with our being introspectively aware of it. For on that picture the consciousness of a mental state is inseparable from that mental state. So reflective awareness, which is being aware both of a mental state and of one's awareness of that state, will be inseparable from awareness of the state which is not thus reflective. Here our common-sense intuitions diverge from the Cartesian view that consciousness is essential to mental states, since the two kinds of awareness plainly do differ.

Introspection is consciously and deliberately paying attention to mental states that are in our stream of consciousness. So, whatever else one holds about consciousness, it is natural to explain introspection as one's having a conscious higher-order thought that one is in the mental state that one is introspectively aware of. So, if these higher-order thoughts all had to be conscious, we could invoke them only to explain introspective consciousness. For only when we are introspectively aware of a mental state are we also aware of our higher-order thoughts. But higher-order thoughts are not automatically conscious, any more than other mental states are. They are conscious only when we have a yet higher-order thought that we have such a thought. So there is no difficulty about using higher-order thoughts to explain not only reflective or introspective awareness, but also what it is for a mental state just to be in our stream of consciousness without our also consciously focusing on it. Introspective awareness of a particular mental state is having a thought that one is in that mental state, and also a thought that one has that thought. Having a conscious mental state without introspectively focusing on it is having the second-order thought without the third-order thought. It may seem slightly odd that each of these hierarchies of conscious mental states has a nonconscious thought at its top. But whatever air of paradox there seems to be here is dispelled by the common-sense truism that we cannot be conscious of everything at once.

One might urge against the present account that higher-order thoughts are unnecessary to explain the consciousness of mental states. Intuitively, a mental state is conscious if it is introspectible. And one might conclude from this that, to explain such consciousness, we need not posit actual higher-order thoughts, but only dispositions to have such thoughts. A mental state is conscious, on this suggestion, if one is disposed to think that one is in that state.[7] But there are several difficulties with such a dispositional account. For one thing, the consciousness of mental states is phenomenologically something occurrent. Since consciousness does not appear to be dispositional, it is ad hoc simply to posit a disposition that comes and goes as needed. We cannot, of course, save all the phenomenological appearances, but we should prefer to do so when we can. Moreover, it is unclear what explanatory work a disposition to have a higher-order thought would do, except when one actually had that thought, and the disposition would then be superfluous.

In any case, the present account readily enables us to explain the intuition that a state's being conscious means that it is introspectible. To introspect a mental state is to have a conscious thought about that state. So introspection is having a thought about some mental state one is in and, also, a yet higher-order thought that makes the first thought conscious. It is a feature of our experience that, when a mental state is conscious, we can readily come to have a conscious thought about that mental state. On the present account, we do not come to have a new thought about that mental state; we simply come to be conscious of a thought we already had, albeit nonconsciously. Higher-order thoughts are mental states we can become aware of more or less at will. A state's being conscious therefore amounts to its being introspectible. Only if being unaware of a higher-order thought meant that one simply did not have that thought would we have reason to try to make do with dispositions, rather than the actual thoughts themselves.

On the present account, conscious mental states are mental states that cause the occurrence of higher-order thoughts that one is in those mental states. And, since those higher-order thoughts are distinct from the mental states that are conscious, those thoughts can presumably occur even when the mental states that the higher-order thoughts purport to be about do not exist. But such occurrences would not constitute an objection to this account. It is reasonable to suppose that such false higher-order thoughts would be both rare and pathological. Nor would they be undetectable if they did occur. We can determine the presence of nonconscious mental states by way of their causal connections with behavior and stimuli, and with other mental states, both conscious and not. Similarly, we can detect the absence of mental states by virtue of the causal connections they would have with such other events.

By itself, the present account of consciousness does not imply a materialist or naturalist theory of mind. Indeed, the account is compatible with even a thoroughgoing Cartesian dualism of substances. But it does square nicely with materialist views. For the account holds that what makes conscious mental states conscious is their causing higher-order thoughts that one is in those mental states. And the materialist can reasonably maintain that this causal pattern is due to suitable neural connections.

Moreover, the materialist can argue that intentional and sensory properties are themselves simply special sorts of physical properties. For one thing, arguments that these mental properties are not physical properties usually rely on the unstated, and question-begging assumption that anything mental is automatically nonphysical. Independent support for this supposition is seldom attempted. Even more important, however, the characteristics that are supposed to show that intentional or sensory properties are not physical turn out, on scrutiny, to be characteristics that various indisputably physical properties also exhibit.[8] So even if no developed, satisfactory account of these properties is presently at hand, there is no reason to doubt that accurate accounts will be forthcoming that are compatible with a thoroughgoing naturalist view of mind. Together with the present explanation of the consciousness of mental states, this should make possible a reasonably comprehensive naturalist theory of mind.

It is a welcome benefit of the present account that it is hospitable to naturalist theories, but this is not its main strength. Rather, its principal advantage is just that it enables us to explain what it is for a mental state to be a conscious state. The present explanation, moreover, has precise empirical consequences that one could reasonably hope to test. For it implies not only that conscious mental states are accompanied by distinct higher-order thoughts, but also that some causal mechanism exists that connects conscious mental states to the corresponding higher-order thoughts.

Such an explanation is possible only if we adopt the non-Cartesian view that intentional and sensory character are jointly the mark of the mental. If, instead, we were to follow the Cartesian tradition in regarding consciousness itself as the key to mentality, no account of consciousness in terms of higher-order thoughts could succeed. For then one would have to deny that a mental state could occur without its being conscious. As Descartes put it, "no thought can exist in us of which we are not conscious at the very moment it exists in us."[9] But, if all mental states are conscious, and a higher-order thought exists for every conscious mental state, serious, insurmountable difficulties immediately ensue. For one thing, there would be denumerably many distinct higher-order thoughts corresponding to every conscious mental state. No mental state could be conscious without being accompanied by a higher-order thought. But that thought would itself have to be conscious, and so a yet higher-order thought would be necessary. This regress would never halt. It strains credulity to suppose that human beings can have infinitely many conscious thoughts at a particular time. And even if we could, it is hardly sensible to explain a mental state's being conscious by way of such an infinite series.

Even more damaging consequences follow for an account in terms of higher-order thoughts if all mental states are conscious states. As noted above, we are not normally aware of the higher-order thoughts that, on such an account, make mental states conscious. But, if all mental states were conscious, we would be aware of any higher-order thoughts that we have. So we could not explain why we typically seem not to have such thoughts by saying that they are simply not conscious thoughts. By requiring that all mental states be conscious states, the Cartesian conception of mentality rules out our explaining consciousness by reference to higher-order thoughts.

If consciousness were what makes a state a mental state, therefore, any account that represents that consciousness as being due to a connection that conscious mental states have with some other mental state would be radically misguided. For that other mental state would then itself have to be conscious, and we would have to invoke yet another mental state to explain its being conscious. A vicious regress would thus be unavoidable. So long as we hold that all mental states are conscious, we can prevent that regress only by maintaining that the consciousness of a mental state is not a relation that state bears to some other mental state, but rather an intrinsic property. Moreover, if consciousness is what makes mental states mental, it will be viciously circular to explain that consciousness in terms of a relation that conscious mental states bear to other mental states, since those other mental states would themselves then have to be conscious. It is plain that we cannot explain or analyze consciousness at all unless we can do so in terms of some sort of mental phenomenon. So, if consciousness is what makes a state a mental state, consciousness will not only be an intrinsic, nonrelational property of all mental states; it will be unanalyzable as well. It will, as Russell disparagingly put it, be "a pervading quality of psychical phenomena."[10] Indeed, if being mental means being conscious, we can invoke no mental phenomenon whatever to explain what it is for a state to be a conscious state. Since no nonmental phenomenon can help, it seems plain that, on the Cartesian concept of mentality, no informative explanation is possible of what it is for a mental state to be conscious.

Since consciousness is a matter of our noninferential and nonsensory knowledge of our mental states, it is tempting to describe the issue in terms of such notions as incorrigibility, infallibility, and privacy.[11] But the foregoing obstacles to explaining consciousness do not derive from any such epistemic matters. Rather, they result simply from the Cartesian idea that all mental states are conscious states.

On the Cartesian concept of mentality and consciousness, consciousness is essential to mental states. It is therefore a nonrelational property of those states that is very likely unanalyzable as well. That this conception prevents us from explaining consciousness in any useful way is the most compelling reason we can have for adopting, instead, a non-Cartesian mark of the mental. But there are other reasons as well to prefer a non-Cartesian mark. For one thing, it is impossible to conceive of a mental state, whether or not it is conscious, that lacks both intentional and sensory properties. So, even though it may not always be easy to imagine one's being in a mental state that is not conscious, intentional and sensory properties are evidently more central to our concept of a mental state than consciousness is. So, even though the characteristically mental differences among mental states are, as noted earlier, a function of their intentional and sensory properties, those properties are not only important for explaining how we distinguish among the various types of mental state. They are also necessary for explaining how mental states differ from everything nonmental.

The Cartesian might concede that we can have

no notion of a mental state that has neither intentional nor phenomenal character, but go on to insist that we also can have no idea of what it would be like to be in a nonconscious mental state even if it does have intentional or sensory properties. But knowing what it would be like to be in such a state is not relevant here. Knowing what it is like to be in a state is knowing what it is like to be aware of being in that state. So, if the state in question is not a conscious mental state, there will be no such thing as what it is like to be in it, at least in the relevant sense of that idiom. This does not show, however, that intentional and phenomenal states cannot lack consciousness. Conscious states resemble and differ in respect of their intentional or phenomenal features. Accordingly, nonconscious mental states will simply be states that resemble and differ from one another in exactly these ways, but without one's being noninferentially aware of their existence and character.

Indeed, it is indisputable that inner states that resemble and differ in just these ways do occur outside our stream of consciousness. Many sorts of mental state, such as beliefs, desires, hopes, expectations, aspirations, various emotions, and arguably even some bodily feelings such as aches, often occur in us without our noticing their presence. And the only thing that makes these states the kinds of states they are is the intentional and phenomenal properties they have. So we must explain what it is for these states to be mental not by reference to consciousness, but by appeal to their having phenomenal or intentional character. As noted above, we can deny that some of these mental phenomena are properly speaking mental states at all, and instead construe them as mere dispositions for mental states to occur. But states of these sorts often have a strong effect on our actual behavior, and even influence the course and content of our stream of consciousness. These mental phenomena must presumably be nondispositional states at least on those occasions when they exercise such causal influence. So the only reason to regard them as mere dispositions would be a question-begging concern to sustain the theory that all mental states are conscious states.

Perhaps the Cartesian will counter that, even if nonconscious intentional states are unproblematic, the idea that a mental state could have sensory character and yet not be conscious is simply unintelligible. For it may seem that the very idea of a nonconscious state with sensory qualities is, in effect, a contradiction in terms. What seems to make intelligible the idea of a mental state's having phenomenal qualities at all is our immediate awareness of how such states feel, or what they are like for those who are in them. This issue will receive extended consideration in section III. For now, however, it is enough to note that, even if we understand what it is for a state to have sensory quality only because we are familiar with cases in which we are conscious of being in such states, it hardly follows that nonconscious sensory states cannot occur. That we understand a kind of phenomenon by way of a particular kind of case does not show that cases of other sorts are impossible.

II

On the Cartesian view, consciousness is definitive of the mental. This concept of mentality implies that consciousness cannot be a relational characteristic of mental states, and that it may well be inexplicable as well. The difficulty in explaining consciousness on that view actually results from the Cartesian strategy for dealing with mental phenomena. The main strength of the Cartesian picture is that it closely matches our presystematic, common-sense intuitions. But it achieves this close match by building those intuitions into our very concepts of mind and consciousness. And this automatically trivializes any explanation we might then give of them. We cannot very well give non-question-begging accounts of intuitions that we incorporate definitionally into our very concepts. Explanations based on the Cartesian conceptions of mind and consciousness thus rely heavily, and ineliminably, on interdefinition of such terms as 'mind', 'consciousness', 'subjectivity', and 'self'. Such interdefinition may be useful in marking out a range of interconnected phenomena, but it cannot do much to help explain the phenomena thus delineated.

On the non-Cartesian concept, by contrast, consciousness is not essential to mental states, and thus consciousness may well be an extrinsic characteristic of whatever mental states have it. The Cartesian achieves its close match with common sense at the cost of ruling out any useful explanation. No such trade-off is necessary on the non-Cartesian picture. The non-Cartesian has no trouble in giving a theoretically satisfying explanation of consciousness. And it is possible to show that this account enables us to save the phenomenological appearances at least roughly as well as the Cartesian can. Moreover, objections to an account cast in terms of higher-order thoughts can be convincingly met. In this section and the next I consider some of the most pressing of these objections, and also argue that such an account does do justice to the phenomenological data. In the present section

I take up various general questions about the adequacy of the non-Cartesian account; in section III I address issues that pertain specifically to sensory qualities and to subjectivity.

One especially notable feature of our presystematic view of consciousness which the Cartesian conception seems to capture perspicuously is the close connection between being in a conscious state and being conscious of oneself. An account in terms of higher-order thoughts has no trouble here. If a mental state's being conscious consists of having a higher-order thought that one is in that mental state, being in a conscious state will imply having a thought about oneself. But being conscious of oneself is simply having a thought about oneself. So being in a conscious mental state is automatically sufficient for one to be conscious of oneself.

Any reasonable account of consciousness will presumably insist on this connection. But the Cartesian can say little that is informative about why the connection should hold. An account that appeals to higher-order thoughts has no such difficulty. Moreover, there is a well-motivated reason why the higher-order thought that the non-Cartesian invokes must be a thought about oneself. To confer consciousness of a particular mental state, the higher-order thought must be about that very mental state. And the only way for a thought to be about a particular mental state is for it to be about somebody's being in that state. Otherwise, the thought would just be about that type of mental state, and not about the particular token of it. So, in the case at hand, the higher-order thought must be a thought that one is, oneself, in that mental state.[12]

Having a thought that one is, oneself, in a particular mental state does not by itself presuppose any prior conception of the self, or of some sort of unity of consciousness. Rather, the present view allows us to explain these conceptions as themselves actually arising from our being in conscious mental states. For we can construe the second-order thoughts as each being a thought to the effect that whatever individual has this very thought is also in the target mental state. And, if a fair number of these thoughts are conscious thoughts, it is plausible to suppose that a sense of the unity of consciousness will, in time, emerge.

If one held the Cartesian view that all mental states are conscious, invoking higher-order thoughts would issue in the vicious regress noted in section I. So, if one is tempted by both these moves, one might try to adjust things in order to avoid that outcome. The most promising way to do so would be simply to insist that the higher-order thoughts in virtue of which we are conscious of conscious mental states are actually part of those conscious states themselves. Every conscious mental state would then be, in part, about itself, and our knowledge that we are in such states would be due to that self-reference. Metaphorically, we would then conclude that a mental state's knowing itself is, in Ryle's apt metaphors, a matter of its being "self-intimating" (158) or "self-luminous" (159).[13]

This line of reasoning is particularly inviting, since it suggests that the Cartesian can, after all, give some nontrivial explanation of the consciousness of mental states. Conscious mental states are conscious, on this account, because they are about themselves. And this self-reference is intrinsic; it does not result from some connection those states have with other mental states. But anything that would support the view that conscious mental states are conscious because they know, or are in part about, themselves would provide equally good evidence that consciousness is due to an accompanying higher-order thought. Moreover, we have no nonarbitrary way to tell when one mental state is a part of another. Accordingly, there is no reason to uphold the idea that our awareness of conscious states is a part of those states other than a desire to sustain the Cartesian contention that all mental states are conscious states. Moreover, if conscious states have parts in this way, the question arises whether all the parts of such states must be conscious, or only some. If all, then the awareness of the mental state will have to be conscious. A regress would thus arise that is exactly parallel to that which arose when we construed the awareness of conscious mental states as due to a distinct higher-order thought. The only advantage of an account on which that awareness is a part of the conscious mental state is if the awareness is a nonconscious part of the conscious state. This reinforces the conclusion that there is no nonarbitrary way to distinguish this view from an account in terms of higher-order thoughts. And it undercuts the idea that the Cartesian can formulate an informative explanation of consciousness along these lines. Since the Cartesian explanation would work only if the part of each conscious state that makes it conscious were itself conscious, the regress is unavoidable.

One reason that consciousness seems intrinsic to our sensory states is that it is difficult to isolate that consciousness as a distinct component of our mental experience. When we try to focus on the consciousness of a particular sensory state, we typically end up picking out only the sensory state we are conscious of, instead. As Moore usefully put it, consciousness is "transparent," or "diaphanous."[14] Since efforts to pick out consciousness itself issue instead in the states we are conscious of, it is tempting to conclude that the consciousness is actually part of those states. But the present account gives a better explanation of the diaphanous character of consciousness. We normally focus on the sensory state and not on our consciousness of it only because that consciousness consists in our having a higher-order thought, and that thought is usually not itself a conscious thought.

There is a strong intuitive sense that the consciousness of mental states is somehow reflexive, or self-referential. But we need not invoke the idea that conscious states are conscious of themselves to explain this intuition. For a mental state to be conscious, the corresponding higher-order thought must be a thought about oneself, that is, a thought about the mental being that is in that conscious state. So, as noted above, we can construe that thought as being, in part, about itself. For it is reasonable to regard the content of the thought as being that whatever individual has this very thought is also in the specified mental state. The sense that something is reflexive about the consciousness of mental states is thus not due to the conscious state's being directed upon itself, as is often supposed. Rather, it is the higher-order thought that confers such consciousness that is actually self-directed.

The foregoing objections have all challenged whether an account based on higher-order thoughts can do justice to various ways we think about consciousness. But one might also question whether higher-order thoughts are enough to make mental states conscious. Here a difficulty seems to arise about mental states that are repressed. By hypothesis such states are not conscious. But it might seem that mental states can be repressed even if one has higher-order thoughts about them. Higher-order thoughts could not then be what makes mental states conscious. A person who has a repressed feeling may nonetheless take pleasure, albeit unconscious pleasure, from having that repressed feeling. But to take pleasure in something we must presumably think that it is so. So that person will have a higher-order thought about the repressed feeling.[15] Moreover, it appears intuitively that the feeling cannot remain unconscious unless the pleasure taken in it also does. And this suggests that, contrary to the present account, a higher-order thought can confer consciousness only if that thought is itself already conscious.

But genuine counterexamples along these lines are not all that easy to come up with. Despite the foregoing suggestion, one can take pleasure in something without having any actual thought about it. I cannot, of course, take pleasure in something I disbelieve or doubt,[16] but that does not imply the actual occurrence of a thought that it is so. Indeed, we frequently form no actual thought about the things in which we take pleasure. Sometimes, by 'thought', we mean only to speak of propositional contents, as when I talk about some thought you put forth. Taking pleasure is a propositional mental state; so taking pleasure in something does involve a thought about it, in the sense of a proposition. But it hardly follows that one also has a thought, in the sense of a particular kind of mental state. Having a thought in that sense is the holding of an assertive mental attitude, which need not occur when one takes pleasure in something. So, in the foregoing example, we have no reason to suppose that the person would actually have any higher-order thought about the repressed feeling.

The difference between taking pleasure in a mental state and having an actual thought about it is crucial for the present account of consciousness. It is natural to hold that being aware of something means having a thought about it, not taking pleasure in it. And one can take pleasure in something without knowing what it is that gives one pleasure. One may have no idea why one feels good, or be mistaken about why. One may even be unaware of feeling good at all if one is sufficiently distracted or other factors interfere. So taking pleasure in something is compatible with being unaware of that thing. Such considerations also apply to putative counterexamples based on other sorts of higher-order mental states. For example, repressed feelings are, presumably, always accompanied by higher-order desires not to be in them. But desires that something not be so do not, in general, imply any awareness that it is.

Conceiving of nonconscious mental states on the model of the repressed cases is doubly misleading. For one thing, it ignores factors that in such cases presumably block consciousness. Moreover, it conceals a tacit Cartesian premise. For it suggests that consciousness is the norm: unless exceptional pressures intervene, a mental state will automatically be conscious. Consciousness is to be presupposed unless some external factor prevents it. Thus, on this model, we can explain the forces that interfere with consciousness, but consciousness itself may very likely be inexplicable.[17]

III

Whatever one holds about intentional states, it may seem altogether unacceptable to try to explain the consciousness of sensory states by way of higher-order thoughts. Consciousness seems virtually inseparable from sensory qualities, in a way that does not seem so for intentional properties. Indeed, as noted at the end of section I, it may seem almost contradictory to speak of sensory states' lacking consciousness. This intimate tie between sensory quality and consciousness seems to hold for all sensory states, but appears strongest with somatic sensations, such as pain. Saul A. Kripke succinctly captures this intuition when he insists that "[f]or a sensation to be *felt* as pain is for it to *be* pain"[18] and, conversely, that "for [something] to exist without being *felt as pain* is for it to exist without there *being any* pain."[19] And, more generally, Kripke seems to insist that for something to be a sensation of any sort it must be felt in a particular way (*NN* p. 146).

Since consciousness seems more closely tied to sensations than to intentional states, it is tempting to consider a restricted form of the Cartesian view, on which all sensations are conscious but not all intentional states are.[20] This restricted thesis would still allow one to explain consciousness in terms of higher-order thoughts; no regress would arise, because then those thoughts could themselves be nonconscious. But the Cartesian view holds not only that all mental states are conscious, but also that consciousness is an intrinsic property of mental states. And if it is, an explanation in terms of higher-order thoughts is impossible, and all the problems about giving an informative explanation of consciousness will arise. So even if not all mental states are conscious, it is important to see whether consciousness is intrinsic to those which are.

We can, however, explain our tendency to associate consciousness and sensory qualities without having to suppose that consciousness is intrinsic to sensory states, or even that all sensory states are conscious. We are chiefly concerned to know what bodily sensations we and others have because they are highly useful indicators of bodily and general well being. People cannot tell us about their nonconscious sensations, and bodily sensations usually have negligible effect on behavior unless they are conscious. So nonconscious sensations are not much use as cues to such well being, and we thus have little, if any, interest in pains or other somatic sensations, except when they are conscious.

Things are different with other sorts of mental states, even perceptual sensations. It is often useful to know somebody's thoughts, emotions, and perceptual sensations, even when that person is unaware of them. Moreover, when mental states are not conscious, our interest in knowing about them is greatest with propositional states, less with emotions, less still with perceptual sensations, and far the least with somatic sensations. Strikingly, our sense that consciousness is intrinsic to mental states increases accordingly. The less useful it is to know about a particular kind of mental state even when the person is unaware of it, the more compelling is our intuition that that kind of mental state must be conscious. This correlation is telling evidence that, even in the case of pains and other somatic sensations, the idea that being mental entails being conscious is just a reflection of our usual interests, and not a matter of the meanings of our words or of the nature of the mental itself.

Some of our idiomatic ways of describing somatic sensations do entail consciousness. Something's hurting, for example, implies awareness of the hurt. And perhaps one cannot correctly say that somebody is in pain unless that person knows it. Phrases such as 'what a sensation is like' and 'how a sensation feels' reinforce this impression, since they refer both to a sensory quality and to our awareness of it, and seem thus to yoke the two together. But when one is in pain or when something hurts, we not only are in a sensory state, but are also aware that we are. And our idiomatic descriptions of these situations have no bearing on whether that very kind of sensory state may sometimes occur without one's being aware of it. Perhaps we would then withhold from such states the epithet 'pain'. But those states would still resemble and differ from other nonconscious states in just those ways in which conscious pains resemble and differ from other conscious sensory states. And that is what it is for a state to have sensory qualities. The intuitive simplicity of those qualities might tempt one to hold that consciousness also is simple and, hence, an intrinsic characteristic of sensory states. But it is question begging to suppose that the apparent simplicity of sensory qualities tells us anything about the nature of our consciousness of them.

Examples of sensory states that sometimes occur without consciousness are not hard to come by. When a headache lasts several hours, one is seldom aware of it for that entire time. Distractions occur, and one pays attention to other things, or just forgets for a bit. But we do not conclude that each headache literally ceases to exist when it temporarily stops being part of our stream of consciousness, and that such a person has only a sequence of discontinuous, brief headaches. Rather, when that happens, our headache is literally a nonconscious ache.[21] The same holds even more vividly for mild pains and minor bodily discomforts. So, to insist that nonconscious states are just not mental states, or that they cannot have sensory qualities, is not, as Kripke seems to urge (e.g., *NN* 152–3), the elucidation of decisive and defensible presystematic intuitions, but only the tacit expression of the Cartesian definition of mind.

Indeed, an account in terms of higher-order thoughts actually helps explain the phenomenological appearances. If a sensory state's being conscious is its being accompanied by a suitable higher-order thought, that thought will be about the very quality we are conscious of. It will be a thought that one is in a state that has that quality. So it will indeed be impossible to describe that consciousness without mentioning the quality. An account in terms of higher-order thoughts actually helps explain why the qualities of our conscious experiences seem inseparable from our consciousness of them.

Moreover, we typically come to make more fine-grained discriminations as we master more subtle concepts pertaining to various distinct sensory qualities. Experiences from wine tasting to hearing music illustrate this process vividly. An account in term of higher-order thoughts explains the bearing these concepts have on our very awareness of sensory differences. If consciousness is intrinsic to sensory states, the relevance of concepts remains mysterious. The Cartesian might just deny that sensory differences exist when we are unaware of them. But it will be even more difficult to explain how learning new concepts can actually cause sensory qualities to arise that previously did not exist.

Perhaps the strongest objection to an account in terms of higher-order thoughts is that there are creatures with conscious sensations whose ability to have any thoughts at all may be in doubt. Infants and most nonhuman animals presumably have a relatively rudimentary ability to think, but plainly do have conscious sensations. But one need not have much ability to think to be able to have a thought that one is in a particular sensation. Infants and nonhuman animals can discriminate among external objects, and master regularities pertaining to them. So most of these beings can presumably form thoughts about such objects, albeit primitive thoughts that are very likely not conscious. No more is needed to have thoughts about one's more salient sensory experiences. Infants and nonhuman animals doubtless lack the concepts required for drawing many distinctions among their sensory states. But, as just noted, one can be aware of sensory states and yet unaware of many of the sensory qualities in virtue of which those states differ.

The common tendency to link the ability to think with the ability to express thoughts in speech may account for the doubt we can fall into about whether infants and nonhuman animals can think at all. But the capacity for speech is hardly necessary for thinking. It is often reasonable to interpret nonlinguistic behavior, of other people and of non-language-using creatures alike, in terms of the propositional content and mental attitude we take it to express. Such behavior is convincing evidence of the occurrence of intentional states.

Forming higher-order thoughts about one's own propositional mental states takes a lot more than having such thoughts about one's sensations. For one thing, the concept of a mental state with propositional content is more complex than the concept of a sensory experience. And picking out particular intentional states demands an elaborate system of concepts, whereas referring to salient sensory experiences does not. An account in terms of higher-order thoughts fits well with these points. Infants and most nonhuman species lack the ability to have the more complex higher-order thoughts needed to make intentional states conscious, though they presumably can form higher-order thoughts about their sensory states. And, though these beings plainly have conscious sensations, we have little reason to suppose that their intentional states are also conscious. Indeed, these considerations help explain why we associate consciousness so much more strongly with sensory than with intentional states. Consciousness of sensory states arises far more readily, since higher-order thoughts about them are far easier to have.

Some animal species, however, lack the ability to think at all. And this may seem to support Nagel's contention that conscious "experience is present in animals lacking language and thought" (167, n. 3). But being a conscious creature does not entail being in conscious mental states. For an organism to be conscious means only that it is awake, and mentally responsive to sensory stimuli (cf. Ryle, pp. 156–7). To be mentally responsive does require that one be in mental states. And to be mentally responsive to sensory stimuli may even mean that one is in some way conscious of the objects or events that are providing such stimulation. But a creature can be in mental states without being in conscious mental states, and can be conscious of external or bodily events without also being aware of its own mental states.

Conscious experiences, as Nagel has stressed, manifest a certain subjectivity. We each experience our sensory states in a way nobody else does, and from a point of view nobody else shares. It is notoriously difficult to articulate these differences. But we understand their occurrence reasonably well, and it is far from clear that such subjectivity causes any problem for the present account.

One way differences arise in sensory experiences is from variations in sense organs, or other aspects of physical makeup. Experiences also vary from individual to individual because of such factors as background and previous experience.

When these factors diverge markedly, aspects of our sensory experiences may as well. When the individuals belong to distinct species, this effect may be quite dramatic. But hard as it is to pin down precisely what these differences amount to, they do not bear specifically on the consciousness of the experiences in question. Rather, the variations are due to differences in the mental context in which the experiences occur, or, when biological endowment is at issue, they are actual differences in the sensory qualities of those experiences. Nagel holds that "the subjective character of experience" is a matter of what "it is like to *be* a particular organism—[what] it is like *for* that organism" (p. 166). But the present account can accommodate this idea. What it is like to be a particular conscious individual is a matter of the sensory qualities of that individual's conscious experiences, and the mental context in which those experiences occur. The consciousness of those experiences, by contrast, is simply that individual's being aware of having the experiences.[22]

According to Nagel, "[a]ny reductionist program has to be based on an analysis of what is to be reduced. If the analysis leaves something out, the problem will be falsely posed" (p. 167). Indeed, no account that is even "logically compatible with" the absence of consciousness could, Nagel contends, be correct (p. 166; cf. "Panpsychism," p. 189). And the present account is reductionist, since it seeks to explain conscious mental states ultimately in terms of mental states that are not conscious. But that account aims only at explaining consciousness, and not also at conceptual analysis. And satisfactory explanations do not, *pace* Nagel, require full analyses of the relevant concepts. Explanation, in science and everyday context alike, must generally proceed without benefit of complete conceptual analyses.

Nagel's language is strongly evocative of that sense we have of ourselves which can make it appear difficult to see how, as conscious selves, we could find ourselves located among the physical furniture of the universe. When we focus on ourselves in this way, there seems to be nothing more basic to our nature than consciousness itself. If nothing were more basic to us than consciousness, there would be nothing more basic in terms of which we could explain consciousness. All we could do then is try to make consciousness more comprehensible by eliciting a sense of the phenomenon in a variety of different ways. Analyzing concepts would be central to any such project, and Nagel's demand for conceptual analysis would then make sense. But consciousness could be essential to our nature only if all mental states are conscious states. If a fair number of our mental states are not conscious, we cannot define our mental natures in terms of consciousness, and there will be nonconscious mental phenomena in terms of which we can explain consciousness itself.

The puzzled cognitive disorientation that can result from reflecting on the gulf that seems to separate physical reality from consciousness makes any noncircular explanation of consciousness seem inadequate. How could any explanation of consciousness in terms of nonconscious phenomena help us to understand how consciousness can exist in the physical universe, or how physical beings like ourselves can have conscious states? But no other explanation can do better with these quandaries so long as an unbridgeable gulf seems to divide the conscious from the merely physical. To understand how consciousness can occur in physical things, we must dissolve the intuitive force of that gulf. And we can do so only by explaining the consciousness of mental states in terms of mental states that are not conscious. For the stark discontinuity between conscious mental states and physical reality does not also arise when we consider only nonconscious mental states. And once we have explained consciousness by reference to nonconscious mental states, we may well be able to explain nonconscious mental states in terms of phenomena that are not mental at all.

IV

The central place consciousness has in our conception of the mental is doubtless due in large measure to the way we know about mind in general, and in particular about our own mental states. We get most of that knowledge, directly or indirectly, from introspection. And we have introspective access to mental states only when they are conscious. Since our chief source of knowledge about the mind tells us only about conscious mental states, it is natural to infer that consciousness is an important feature of mental phenomena.

But stronger claims are sometimes made about the epistemic status of introspection. Introspection may seem particularly well adapted to its subject matter, since most of our knowledge of mind derives from introspection, and all introspective knowledge is about mind. This close fit may tempt some to hold that introspection is a privileged source of knowledge that is somehow immune from error. If so, perhaps introspection reveals the essential nature of mental states. And, since introspection tells us only about conscious mental states, perhaps consciousness is itself a part of that essential nature. But inviting as these Cartesian conclusions may be, they are without foundation.

Introspection is simply the having of conscious thoughts that one is in particular mental states. Those thoughts can by themselves no more reveal the essences of those states than having a conscious perceptual thought that a table is in front of one can reveal the essence of the table. Nor can we infer anything from the close fit between introspection and its subject matter. Sight is equally well adapted to knowing about colored physical objects. But there are other ways to know about those objects. And even though sight informs us only about illuminated objects, we can hardly conclude that only illuminated objects are colored.

Introspective apprehension seems to differ, however, from perceptual knowledge in a way that undermines this analogy. Perception is never entirely direct. Some causal process always mediates, even in ostensibly direct perception, between our perceptual experience and what we perceive. Introspection, by contrast, may seem wholly unmediated. And if it is, there would be no way for error or distortion to enter the introspective process. There would thus be no difference between how our mental states appear to us and how they really are. Mental states would have no nonintrospectible nature, and introspection would be an infallible and exhaustive source of knowledge about the mind. Nagel evidently endorses this view when he claims that "[t]he idea of moving from appearance to reality seems to make no sense" in the case of conscious experiences (174). Kripke too seems to hold that introspection is different from perception in this way. Thus he writes:

> although we can say that we pick out [physical] heat contingently by the contingent property that it affects us in such and such a way, we cannot similarly say that we pick out pain contingently by the fact that it affects us in such and such a way ("IN" p. 161; cf. *NN* pp. 150–2).

We could not, Kripke contends, have been aware of our pains in a way different from the way we actually are.

Introspection is the reflective awareness of our mental states. So, the only way introspective apprehension of those states might be entirely unmediated would be for consciousness to be a part, or at least an intrinsic property, of such states. For nothing could then come between a mental state and our being conscious of it, nor between our being thus conscious and our also having reflective consciousness. But as noted in section II, that view is indefensible. Accordingly, consciousness must be a relational property, for example, the property of being accompanied by higher-order thoughts. And some causal process must therefore mediate between mental states and our awareness of them—in Kripke's example, between a pain and "the fact that it affects us in such and such a way." And, since mental states might have been connected causally to different high-order thoughts, we might have been aware of mental states differently from the way we are. The appearance of mental states will not, therefore, automatically coincide with their reality. Indeed, since how mental states appear is a matter of our introspective awareness of them, their appearance and reality could be the same only if our consciousness of mental states were a part or an intrinsic property of those states.

These considerations notwithstanding, we do rely heavily on introspection in picking out and describing mental states. And introspection tells us about nothing except conscious mental states. So even though consciousness is not what distinguishes mental states from everything else, it is reasonable to hold that it is by reference to a range of conscious states that we fix the extension of the term 'mental'. Similarly, even though the various kinds of mental state can all occur nonconsciously, it is also reasonable to suppose that we fix the extensions of our terms for the different kinds of mental state by way of the conscious cases. As Kripke and Hilary Putnam have stressed, what fixes the extension of a general term can turn out to be distinct from what is essential to the items in that extension.[23] And, just as the way we know about things is not, in general, a reliable guide to their nature, so the way we pick out things is not, either. So, even if we fix the extensions of terms for mental states by way of the conscious instances, we could still discover that the states so determined are not all conscious, and that what is actually essential to all such states is just their sensory or intentional properties.

The idea that we fix mental extensions by way of the conscious cases plainly supports the non-Cartesian picture. But it also helps explain why consciousness seems so crucial to our mental concepts. And it even enables us to explain why we group sensory and intentional states together as mental states, despite its seeming that they have little intrinsic in common. We do so because in both cases we fix extensions by way of states to which we have noninferential and nonobservational access.

Kripke contends that what fixes the reference of terms for sensory states cannot diverge from what is essential to those states (NN pp. 149–54; "IN" pp. 157–61). Thus, he insists, "[i]f any phenomenon is picked out in exactly the same way that we pick out pain, then that phenomenon is pain."[24] But what fixes the extension of 'pain' must coincide with what is essential to pains only if it is necessary that pains affect us in the way they do. And this would be necessary only if consciousness were intrinsic to them. It therefore begs the question to base the Cartesian picture on an insistence that what fixes the extensions of mental terms cannot diverge from the essences of mental states. Kripke offers no independent support for that insistence.

Relative to what we now know about other natural phenomena, we still have strikingly scant understanding of the nature of the mental. So introspection looms large as a source of information, just as sense perception was a more central source of knowledge about physical reality before the flourishing of the relevant systematic sciences. But, since not all knowledge about mind is derived from introspection, we have no more reason to suppose that mental states have no nonintrospectible nature than that the nature of physical objects is wholly perceptible. Nor, therefore, have we any reason to hold that the essences of mental states must be what fixes the extensions of mental terms. It is reasonable to conclude that whatever temptation we have to accord absolute epistemic authority to introspection derives solely from our relative ignorance about the mind. Only because we now know so little about mental processes does it make sense to suppose that, in the case of mental states, appearance and reality coincide. Accordingly, we have no reason to continue to favor that picture, or to reject an explanation of consciousness based on higher-order thoughts.[25]

NOTES

1. 'What is it like to be a bat?', The Philosophical Review, LXXXIII, 4 (October 1974): 435–50; reprinted in Nagel's Mortal Questions (Cambridge and New York: Cambridge University Press, 1979); 165–180, p. 165. Page references to Nagel will be to Mortal Questions and, unless otherwise indicated, to that article.

2. Richard Rorty and Paul M. Churchland, among others, have championed this view; see Rorty's Philosophy and the Mirror of Nature (Princeton: Princeton University Press, 1979), Part I, and Churchland's Scientific Realism and the Plasticity of Mind (Cambridge: Cambridge University Press, 1979).

3. In a review of Frank Jackson's Perception [The Journal of Philosophy, LXXXII, 1 (January 1985): 28–41] I argue in detail that words for such qualities have this double use. On this point see also G. E. Moore, 'A reply to my critics', in The Philosophy of G. E. Moore ed. Paul Arthur Schilpp (LaSalle, Illinois: Open Court, 1942): 535–677, pp. 665–8; and Thomas Reid, Essays on the Intellectual Powers of Man, ed. Baruch A. Brody (Cambridge, MA: The M.I.T. Press, 1969), II, xvi, p. 244.

4. 'Chisholm-Sellars correspondence on intentionality', in Minnesota Studies in the Philosophy of Science, II, ed. Herbert Feigl, Michael Scriven, and Grover Maxwell (Minneap-

olis: University of Minnesota Press, 1958): 521–39, p. 533. In 'Intentionality,' *Midwest Studies in Philosophy,* X (1985), I argue that this claim is defensible if it is construed in strictly causal terms.

5. See, e.g., David M. Armstrong, *A Materialist Theory of the Mind* (New York: Humanities Press, 1968), pp. 92–115 and 323–7 and 'What is consciousness?', in Armstrong's *The Nature of Mind and Other Essays* (Ithaca, NY: Cornell University Press, 1980): 55–67, pp. 59–61; David Lewis, 'An argument for the identity theory,' *The Journal of Philosophy,* LXIII, 1 (January 6, 1969): 17–25, p. 21 and "Psychophysical and Theoretical Identifications," *Australasian Journal of Philosophy,* 50, 3 (December 1972): 249–58, p. 258; and Wilfrid Sellars, "Empiricism and the Philosophy of Mind," in Sellars' *Science, Perception and Reality* (London: Routledge & Kegan Paul and New York: Humanities Press, 1963): 127–96, pp. 188–9 and 194–5.

6. Gilbert Ryle, *The Concept of Mind* (London: Hutchinson and Company, 1949), p. 164.

7. Allen Hazen has urged this line especially forcefully, in correspondence. Also, see Kant's claim that the representation 'I think' must be able to accompany all other representations (*K.d.R.V.,* B131–2; cf. B406, though Kant insists that the representation 'I think' is a nonempirical (B132) or transcendental (B401, A343) representation.

8. For a detailed argument to this effect, see my 'Mentality and neutrality,' *The Journal of Philosophy,* LXXIII, 13 (July 15, 1976): 386–415, sec. I.

9. Fourth Replies, *Oeuvres de Descartes,* ed. Charles Adam and Paul Tannery (Paris, J. Vrin, 1964–75) [henceforth "AT"] VII, 246 [see *The Philosophical Works of Descartes,* ed. Elizabeth S. Haldane and G.R.T. Ross (Cambridge: Cambridge University Press, 1931) (henceforth "HR") II, 115]. See also the *Geometrical Exposition of the Second Replies:* "the word 'thought' applies to all that exists in us in such a way that we are immediately conscious of it" [AT VII, 160 (see HR II, 52)], and elsewhere, e.g.: *First Replies,* AT VII, 107 (HR II, 13), Letter to Mersenne, AT III, 273 [see Descartes: *Philosophical Letters,* ed. Anthony Kenny (Oxford: Oxford University Press, 1970), p. 90], *Fourth Replies,* AT VII, 232 (HR II, 105) and AT VII, 246 (HR II, 115), and *Principles* I, ix, AT VIII–1, 7 (HR I, 222).

10. Bertrand Russell, *The Analysis of Mind* (London: George Allen & Unwin Ltd. and New York: Humanities Press, 1921), p. 9.

11. See, e.g., Rorty's argument "that incorrigibility is the best candidate" for a satisfactory mark of the "sorts of entities [that] make up the content of the stream of consciousness" ["Incorrigibility as the Mark of the Mental," *The Journal of Philosophy,* LXVII, 12 (June 25, 1970): 399–424, pp. 406–7; cf. also Rorty's *Philosophy and the Mirror of Nature,* e.g., pp. 88–96, and Part I, *passim.*

12. As Hector-Neri Castaneda and G.E.M. Anscombe have pointed out, believing something of oneself must involve the mental analogue of the indirect reflexive construction, represented here by 'oneself' [Castaneda: 'On the Logic of Attributions of Self-Knowledge to Others,' *The Journal of Philosophy,* LXV, 15 (August 8, 1968): 439–56 and elsewhere; Anscombe: 'The first person,' in *Mind and Language,* ed. Samuel Guttenplan (Oxford: Oxford University Press), 1975: 45–65]. Even when George believes that somebody who turns out to be George is *F* is may not be true that George believes that he, himself, is *F*. For example, George

may truly believe somebody is *F* while wrongly believing that that person is not George, himself. Or he may not even believe of himself that he is George. Unlike token-reflexive constructions, these terms involve anaphora. But the clauses that contain them are grammatical transforms of sentences that do contain genuine token reflexives.

13. See Franz Brentano, *Psychology from an Empirical Standpoint,* tr. Antos C. Rancurello et al. (London: Routledge & Kegan Paul and New York: Humanities Press, 1973), pp. 129–30.

14. G. E. Moore, 'The Refutation of Idealism', in his *Philosophical Studies* (London: Routledge & Kegan Paul, 1922): 1–30, pp. 20 and 25.

15. I am grateful to Georges Rey and Eric Wefald for independently raising this point.

16. On this point, see Robert M. Gordon's illuminating 'Emotions and knowledge,' *The Journal of Philosophy,* LXVI, 13, (July 3, 1969): 408–13 and 'The aboutness of emotions,' *American Philosophical Quarterly,* 11, 1 (January 1974): 27–36.

17. It is noteworthy that this very attitude appear even in Freud's own writings. Freud does, indeed, "energetically den[y] the equation between what is psychical and what is conscious" ['Some elementary lessons in psycho-analysis,' in *The Complete Psychological Works of Sigmund Freud,* tr. and ed. James Strachey (London: The Hogarth Press, 1966–74) (henceforth *"Works"*), XXIII: 279–86]. And he understood that to do so one must define the mental in terms of phenomenal and intentional character; thus he insisted that "all the categories which we employ to describe conscious mental acts . . . can be applied" equally well to unconscious mental states ('The Unconscious,' *Works,* XIV: 166–215, p. 168). Moreover, he maintained that "[t]he psychical, whatever its nature may be, is itself unconscious" ('Some elementary lessons,' p. 283), and so, "[l]ike the physical, the psychical is not necessarily in reality what it appears to us to be" ("The Unconscious," p. 171; Cf. 'Some elementary lessons', p. 282 and *The Interpretation of Dreams, Works,* V, p. 613). But despite all this, Freud operated with a surprisingly Cartesian concept of consciousness. Consciousness, he wrote, is a "unique, indescribable" quality of mental states ('Some elementary lessons,' p. 282), and "the fact of consciousness" "defies all explanation or description" (*An Outline of Psycho-Analysis, Works,* XXIII: 141–208, p. 157). In thus regarding consciousness as unanalyzable, Freud seems to have uncritically accepted the core of the Cartesian doctrine he strove to discredit. (To dissociate the present account from Freud's views I eschew here the colloquial 'unconscious mental state' in favor of the somewhat awkward term 'nonconscious'.)

18. 'Identity and necessity,' in *Identity and Individuation,* ed. Milton K. Munitz (New York: New York University Press, 1971): 135–64 [henceforth "IN"], p. 163, n. 18; emphasis original here and elsewhere.

19. *Naming and Necessity* (Cambridge, MA: Harvard University Press, 1980) [henceforth *"NN"*] p. 151. Compare Reid, *Essays,* II, xvi, p. 243: "When [a sensation] is not felt, it is not. There is no difference between the sensation and the feeling of it; they are one and the same thing.

20. Even Freud does not hold that feelings can strictly speaking be unconscious, though he sees no difficulty about unconscious intentional states (*The Ego and the Id, Works,* XIX: 3–68, pp. 22–3; cf. *An Outline,* p. 197).

21. Thus it is a parody for Wittgenstein to suppose that

all we could mean by an unconscious toothache, e.g., is "a certain state of decay in a tooth, not accompanied by what we commonly call toothache" [*The Blue and Brown Books* (Oxford: Basil Blackwell, 1958), p. 22].

22. On difficulties in Nagel's discussion and, especially, his notion of a point of view, see my 'Reductionism and knowledge,' in *How Many Questions?*, ed. Leigh S. Cauman, Issac Levi, Charles Parsons, and Robert Schwartz (Indianapolis: Hacket Publishing Company, 1983): 276–300.

23. *NN* 54–9, "IN" 156–61, and Putnam, 'The meaning of "meaning",' in Putnam's *Philosophical Papers,* vol. 2 (Cambridge: Cambridge University Press, 1975): 215–71, pp. 223–35.

24. *NN* 153; cf. "IN" 162–3. Again, cf. Reid, *Essays,* II, xvi, p. 243: A "sensation can be nothing else than it is felt to be. Its very essence consists in being felt." Cf. also J.J.C. Smart: "[t]o say that a process is an ache is simply to classify it with other processes that are felt to be similar" ['Materialism,' *The Journal of Philosophy,* LX, 22 (October 24, 1963): 651–62, p. 655. It is striking that this Cartesian claim about our mental concepts should be shared by theorists who, in other respects, diverge as sharply and as thoroughly as do Smart and Kripke. That it is so shared suggests that this claim may underlie much of what is, in different ways, unintuitive about each of those theories.

25. I am greatly indebted to many friends and colleagues for comments on earlier versions of this paper, most especially to Margaret Atherton, Adam Morton, and Robert Schwartz.

PART V
PSYCHOLOGICAL EXPLANATION

INTRODUCTION

No feature of mental states is more important than their central role in explaining behavior. Knowing what somebody wants, thinks, and feels often enables us to predict and understand what that person will do. And because of that, we can often infer what a person's mental states must be by determining what thoughts, desires, and feelings would explain the person's behavior.

This role in explaining behavior sheds light on the nature of mental states; whatever else mental states may be, they are the sorts of things that figure in such explanations. Moreover, this explanatory role suggests a useful test for any theory of mind. This is especially clear for theories of the intentional and sensory properties of mental states. Psychological explanations place certain constraints on how we classify mental states. Since we taxonomize mental states into types on the basis of their intentional and sensory properties, a theory of these properties will be acceptable only if the way it classifies mental states squares with the demands imposed by such explanations.

Psychological explanations presuppose causal interactions that mental states have with behavior, sensory stimulations, and other mental states. This has led some to propose defining intentional and sensory properties in terms of these causal interactions. But whatever our verdict about such functionalist theories, any satisfactory account of these properties must capture the role played by various types of mental states in psychological explanations of behavior.

Intentional states such as belief and desire are central to explanations of behavior. So the explanatory role of mental states will be particularly informative about the nature of intentional properties; the selections in this section therefore all focus on intentional states. Mental processes, in which one intentional state leads to another, are important in psychological explanation, and the nature of these processes may well have implications about intentional properties. An issue also arises about how to classify intentional states, whether to do so solely on the basis of what is going on inside a person, or partly by reference to external factors. Finally, there are questions about the relationship between commonsense psychological explanation and explanations we can expect from a scientific psychology.

A. The Computational Approach

As just noted, intentional states are crucial to explaining behavior. If I believe some apples are over there and I want to have one, my belief and desire explain my going and getting one. Fodor counts a theory of mind as representational if it treats one's being in an intentional state as one's bearing a relation to a mental representation. The content of one's propositional state is due to the representation to which one is related, and the attitude held toward that content, such as believing, hoping, doubting, and the like, is a matter of what relation one bears to the representation.

A mental process such as reasoning involves a succession of representations. These representations presumably succeed one another by virtue of their causal connections; causally indistinguishable representations will play the same role in mental processes. Fodor argues that these causal connections do not depend on any semantic properties of those representations, that is, on their content or their relation to what they represent. A theory that satisfies this constraint, and explains mental processes solely in terms of the nonsemantic properties of the relevant representations, counts as computational. Such a theory, by ignoring environmental factors in explaining mental processes, adheres to a kind of methodological solipsism.

Intentional states with the same content seem to play the same role in mental processes, and similarly for intentional states with different content; so the nonsemantic properties of those states will reflect their semantic properties. Fodor emphasizes that content is relevant to explaining behavior only insofar as it reflects how the agent takes things to be, regardless of how they actually are. The conception of content that matters here is therefore independent of whatever objects a representation happens to be about. This satisfies the constraints a computational theory imposes, on which a representation's role in mental processes is independent of external objects.

One can argue, however, that the content of an intentional state is not independent of what object that state is about. Imagine, following Putnam ("The Meaning of 'Meaning'": 139–44), a planet whose makeup and inhabitants are macroscopically indistinguishable from those of the earth. They are also indistinguishable at the molecular level, except that wherever the earth has water, the other planet has stuff with a different chemical composition but macroscopically indiscernible from water. My double's representations are therefore nonsemantically identical to mine; moreover, there is no difference in how the two of us take things to be. Still, since whenever my representations are about water, my double's are about the other stuff, it is unintuitive to regard those representations as having the same content. In a commentary and reply, Stich and Fodor take up this issue, and also discuss whether content will play any role in psychological explanation if computational states are typed nonsemantically.

Fodor holds that the semantic properties of representations depend on causal connections between representations and the objects they represent. So a purely computational theory will not address those semantic properties. Moreover, he argues that no theoretical treatment of these properties will be forthcoming. Since causal connections presuppose scientific laws, he urges that such a theory would require precise scientific descriptions of the objects representations are about, and these are generally unavailable. But commonsense descriptions of the objects we think about may well sustain whatever causal connections are needed for such a theory.

It is natural to think of representations as being neurally coded somehow; if so, they would have different neural realizations, and thus differ nonsemantically. Dennett raises difficulties for this idea. Since we believe indefinitely many things, only our core beliefs could be neurally coded; the rest would have to be derived on particular occasions by some neural mechanism. But to determine what beliefs to derive, Dennett argues, that mechanism would need its own store of beliefs. But we would then need another mechanism to determine the consequences of those beliefs, which yields a vicious regress. Moreover, beliefs can be a lot less determinate in content than anything expressible in language; so it is unlikely that beliefs generally are encoded in sentential form. And if each belief were neurally coded, one could induce a new belief by altering a person's neural states. But since a state of a person counts as a belief only if its content fits reasonably well with that of a person's other beliefs, neural states cannot code beliefs individually, one by one.

Searle argues that implementing a computer program cannot by itself produce intentional states. He considers a person who, knowing no Chinese, is enclosed in a room and receives and transmits Chinese characters of specified shapes, in conformity with a program that happens to simulate the behavior of somebody fluent in Chinese. No matter how effective the simulation, the person would still understand no Chinese. This is so even if the person fully internalizes the program and executes its instructions automatically. Our brains do produce intentional states, and in doing so they instantiate any number of programs. But since instantiating those programs in the fashion of Searle's case would not produce intentional states, implementing a program cannot by itself do so. Searle concludes that instantiating a program cannot produce understanding, or other intentional states. He also maintains that implementing a program does not even contribute to producing intentional states, but it is less clear that his case shows that. Fodor and Searle take up one version of this issue in the first of two interchanges.

Putnam imagines a language in which some single word means *silver* in one dialect and *aluminum* in another, but young speakers of each dialect encounter the relevant metal in identical circumstances. Even though this word refers to and means different things in the two dialects, Putnam argues that these young speakers would have computationally indistinguishable mental representations corresponding to that word. So a computational treatment could not capture everything about the content of one's representations; we would need in addition some way to interpret these representations, much as we interpret words in a language. Putnam also argues that meaning and content depend both on what the word or representation refers to and on various social factors. We can interpret words and representations only in the light of how well our interpretation makes sense of the speaker's purposes, beliefs, and behavior; we must occasionally even construe statements nonliterally so as to make sense of somebody's overall speech and behavior. So we cannot interpret a person's propositional attitudes one by one but must interpret them against a background of all the person's beliefs and desires. Since a computational theory cannot help in this task, Putnam concludes it cannot capture the role of propositional attitudes in explaining behavior.

B. Individualism

What intentional states refer to depends in part on what is in the environment. So, if the content of an intentional state depends partly on what that state refers to, what objects exist in a person's environment will affect the content of that person's intentional states. A person's individual makeup, then, does not by itself determine that content; two people could be physically indistinguishable and yet be in intentional states with different content.

Even apart from what occurs in the physical environment, Burge argues that social factors also influence the content of one's intentional states. Consider a person with fairly standard views about arthritis, except for believing wrongly that arthritis can occur outside the joints. That person may well still have many propositional attitudes whose content involves arthritis.

Imagine now that this person belongs not to our linguistic community, but to a community that actually applies the term 'arthritis' more broadly, to include rheumatoid ailments outside the joints. Everything else is the same; there is no difference in the person's individual makeup or past linguistic experience, no nonlinguistic difference in the physical environment, and so forth. People regard their words as meaning pretty much what the words of others in their linguistic comunity mean; the content of their thoughts tends to follow suit. The content of one's thoughts depends partly on the linguistic community one is responsible to. So this imaginary community has no word for what we call arthritis. And when our person now uses the word 'arthritis' to express various thoughts and beliefs, the content of those states does not involve what we call arthritis. Since a change in linguistic context can change the content of one's thoughts, Burge concludes that such content depends partly on one's social environment. Computational and functional theories do not capture this social component.

Loar maintains that content is what individuates propositional mental states for purposes of commonsense psychological explanation. And linguistic environment makes no difference to how one's beliefs, say, figure in such explanations, nor to how they interact with my other propositional attitudes. If Loar is right, the shift in linguistic environment Burge imagines could not affect the content of one's beliefs.

Loar does concede, however, that we cannot use our word 'arthritis' to describe the beliefs of somebody in Burge's imaginary community. We, in our community, cannot describe a person in the imaginary community as believing, say, that arthritis is painful. This creates a problem. We typically describe what people think by means of 'that' clauses; we say they think *that* it's raining, or *that* snow is white. But Loar argues that these descriptions do not always capture similarities and differences in the content of our thoughts. In particular, two beliefs can have the same content even when they cannot be described by means of the same 'that' clause. And if 'that' clauses do not always reflect similarities and differences of content, linguistic environment could affect which 'that' clauses we can use to describe a person's beliefs, while leaving unchanged the content of those beliefs.

Even if social or environmental factors do affect content as we ordinarily conceive of it, one could still try to define a kind of content—"narrow" content, in terminology derived from Putnam—that depends only on a person's internal makeup. Content that does depend partly on external factors is wide content. One could then insist that, although wide content cannot figure in psychological explanations, narrow content is ideally suited to do so.

Stalnaker argues not only that we ordinarily individuate content in terms of external factors, but that it is unlikely that we can define any kind of content solely in terms of internal makeup. Proponents of a narrow analogue of ordinary content have not shown how in general to tell when the narrow content of beliefs are the same, nor even that there is anything we can individuate internally that is suitably like ordinary content. Moreover, descriptions of the content of a person's intentional states do not characterize how the person takes the world to be in absolute terms, but only relative to a range of relevant possibilities.

But there is no difficulty, Stalnaker argues, about using ordinary wide content in psychological explanations. A problem would arise only if externally individuated states were causally irrelevant to a person's behavior. But many externally individuated states of things are relevant to how those things behave. Mosquito bites help explain behavior even though we individuate them by reference to their causes; similarly, externally individuated intentional states can help explain behavior.

C.   Scientific Versus Folk Psychology

Scientific theories often posit objects other than those which figure in our everyday descriptions of things, for example, the molecules of chemistry and the fields and particles of physics. Other sciences, such as geology, proceed wholly or in large measure in terms of commonsense, macroscopic objects. Many theorists hold that a scientific psychology will take the second path. Such a psychology would follow folk psychology in appealing to the very kinds of intentional states in terms of which we formulate commonsense explanations of behavior, and describe the content of those states in just the way that folk psychology does.

Stich raises doubts about whether psychological explanations will actually proceed in this way. He assumes that for psychological states to be relevant to psychological explanations, physically identical organisms must be in exactly the same psychological states. Seeing and knowing involve relations to external objects, which physical replicas need not share. But such cases do not refute Stich's asumption, since they consist of an external relation plus an internal psychological state, and only the internal state pertains to psychological explanation. A problem also arises, however, about believing. If physical replicas are located in different times and places, their beliefs about their present time or current location would be about different things, and so diverge in content. Many other beliefs of physical replicas would also have different content. Since replicas would not share these beliefs, Stich's assumption prevents their playing any role in psychological explanation. And even if believing consists of internal states plus external relations, Stich urges that the internal state would neither represent nor refer to anything, and so would not be relevantly like a belief. He concludes that psychological explanation will probably invoke no states that are at all like those of folk psychology

Churchland, by contrast, argues that folk psychology has the character of a scientific theory. But as a theory it is so radically defective that, like other defective theories, it may well be replaced by a more advanced scientific theory. Folk psychology is a theory, he argues, because so regarding it provides the best explanation of a number of traditional problems about mind. But, he insists, folk psychology fails to address many important phenomena within its scope, has not developed for two millennia, and uses concepts apparently incommensurable to those of the sciences with which one might expect it to connect. To dispel the sense that it is inconceivable that a more sophisticated scientific theory might replace folk psychology, Churchland concludes by speculatively sketching three ways in which this could happen. Churchland also assures us that much that folk psychology gives us would be reconstituted within the new theory. But, if so, the new theory might well in effect contain much of folk psychology within it, and folk psychology would not have been replaced so much as revised and enhanced.

The eliminativist arguments of Stich and Churchland appeal to the promise of folk psychology in explaining behavior, and its standing as a theory. These arguments in effect extend the familiar idea that when everyday concepts do not figure in a fully developed scientific account of reality, they do not strictly speaking apply to anything. Such eliminativist arguments therefore differ from those of Feyerabend and Rorty in Part III, which rely instead on the implications of folk psychology about whether mental states could be special kinds of physical states.

Dennett argues that folk psychology and scientific psychology are not in competition. Folk psychology attributes beliefs and desires by calculating what the subject would ideally believe and desire, relative to limitations such as perceptual capacity. In this respect folk psychology presupposes rather than explains rationality. Folk psychological beliefs and desires resemble centers of gravity; both are abstractions from states of things used to calculate behavior of those things. So even though they are not themselves causally efficacious states of things, they are both real. Folk psychology does sometimes describe beliefs as causing behavior. But even then, he argues, such beliefs are typically abstractions like centers of gravity, not actual states.

We can clarify things, Dennett urges, by separating the abstract and causal strands of folk psychology into two distinct theories. Intentional system theory attributes interdependent groups of abstract beliefs and desires to whole systems, under the assumption of rationality. Such a theory thus models the competence of those systems. Actual organisms, whose behavior is governed by their actual causal properties, can only approximate that competence, much as a hand calculator only approximates arithmetic competence. Subpersonal cognitive psychology explains how actual organisms do this. As with a calculator, the parts of the competence model typically will not correspond to parts of the mechanism that approximates that competence. Similarly, the abstract beliefs of intentional system theory will not generally match the actual states of an organism. So folk psychology may well reduce to intentional system theory, but not to subpersonal cognitive psychology.

A.   The Computational Approach

53

J. A. Fodor

"Methodological Solipsism Considered as a Research Strategy in Cognitive Psychology"[1]

Plus commentary by Stephen P. Stich, and Fodor's response

. . . to form the idea of an object and to form an idea simply is the same thing; the reference of the idea to an object being an extraneous denomination, of which in itself it bears no mark or character.

Hume's *Treatise,* Book I

Your standard contemporary cognitive psychologist—your thoroughly modern mentalist—is disposed to reason as follows. To think (e.g.) that Marvin is melancholy is to represent Marvin in a certain way; viz., as being melancholy (and not, for example, as being maudlin, morose, moody, or merely moping and dyspeptic). But surely we cannot represent Marvin as being melancholy except as we are in some or other relation to a representation of Marvin; and not just to *any* representation of Marvin, but, in particular, to a representation the content of which is *that* Marvin is melancholy; a representation which, as it were, expresses the proposition that Marvin is melancholy. So, a fortiori, at least some mental states/processes are or involve at least some relations to at least some representations. Perhaps, then, this is the *typical* feature of such mental states/processes as cognitive psychology studies; perhaps all such states can be viewed as relations to representations and all such processes as operations defined on representations.

This is, prima facie, an appealing proposal since it gives the psychologist two degrees of freedom to play with and they seem, intuitively, to be the right two. On the one hand, mental states are distinguished by the *content* of the associated representations, so we can allow for the difference between thinking that Marvin is melancholy and thinking that Sam is (or that Albert isn't, or that it sometimes snows in Cincinnati); and, on the other hand, mental states are distinguished by the *relation* that the subject bears to the associated representation (so we can allow for the difference between thinking, hoping, supposing, doubting and pretending that Marvin is melancholy). It's hard to believe that a serious psychology could make do with fewer (or less refined) distinctions than these, and it's hard to believe that a psychology that makes these distinctions could avoid taking the notion of mental representation seriously. Moreover, the burden of argument is clearly upon anyone who claims that we need *more* degrees of freedom than just these two: the least hypothesis that is remotely plausible is that a mental state is (type) individuated by specifying a relation and a representation such that the subject bears the one to the other.[2]

I'll say that any psychology that takes this line is a version of the REPRESENTATIONAL THEORY OF THE MIND. I think that it's reasonable to adopt some such theory as a sort of working hypothesis, if only because there aren't any alternatives which seem to be even remotely plausible and because empirical research carried out within this framework has, thus far, proved interesting and fruitful.[3]

However, my present concern is neither to attack nor to defend this view, but rather to distinguish it from something other—and stronger—that modern cognitive psychologists *also* hold. I shall put this stronger doctrine as the view that mental states and process are COMPUTATIONAL. Much of what is characteristic of cognitive psychology is a consequence of adherence to this stronger view. What I want to do in this paper is to say something about what this stronger view is, something about why I think it's plausible, and, most of all, something about the ways in which it shapes the cognitive psychology we have.

I take it that computational processes are both *symbolic* and *formal.* They are symbolic because they are defined over representations, and they are formal because they apply to representations, in virtue of (roughly) the *syntax* of the representations. It's the second of these conditions that makes the claim that mental processes are computational stronger than the representational theory of the mind. Most of this paper will be a meditation upon the consequences of assuming that mental processes are formal processes.

I'd better cash the parenthetical "roughly." To say that an operation is formal isn't the same as saying that it is syntactic since we could have formal processes defined over representations which don't, in any obvious sense, *have* a syntax. Rotating an image would be a timely example. What makes syntactic operations a species of formal operations is that being syntactic is a way of *not* being semantic. Formal operations are the ones that are specified without reference to such semantic properties of representations as, for example, truth, reference and meaning. Since we don't know how to complete this list (since, that is, we don't know what semantic properties there are), I see no responsible way of saying what, in general, formality amounts to. The notion of formality will thus have to remain intuitive and metaphoric, at least for present purposes: formal operations apply in terms of the, as it were, "shapes" of the objects in their domains.[4]

To require that mental processes be computational (viz., formal-syntactic) is thus to require something not very clear. Still, the requirement has some clear consequences, and they are striking and tendentious. Consider that we started by assuming that the *content* of representations is a (type) individuating feature of mental states. So far as the *representational* theory of the mind is concerned, it's possibly the *only* thing that distinguishes Peter's thought that Sam is silly from his thought that Sally is depressed. But, now, if the *computational* theory of the mind is true (and if, as we may assume, content is a semantic notion par excellence) it follows that content alone cannot distinguish thoughts. More exactly, the computational theory of the mind requires that two thoughts can be distinct in content only if they can be identified with relations to formally distinct representations. More generally: fix the subject and the relation, and then mental states can be (type) distinct only if the representations which constitute their objects are formally distinct.

Again, consider that accepting a formality condition upon mental states implies a drastic narrowing of the ordinary ontology of the mental; all sorts of states which look, prima facie, to be mental states in good standing are going to turn out to be none of the psychologist's business if the formality condition is endorsed. This point is one that philosophers have made in a number of contexts, and usually in a deprecating tone of voice. Take, for example, knowing that such-and-such, and assume that you can't know what's not the case. Since, on that assumption, knowledge is involved with truth, and since truth is a semantic notion, it's going to follow that there can't be a psychology of *knowledge* (even if it is consonant with the formality condition to hope for a psychology of *belief*). Similarly, it's a way of making a point of Ryle's to say that, strictly speaking, there can't be a psychology of perception if the formality condition is to be complied with. Seeing is an achievement; you can't see what's not there. From the point of view of the representational theory of the mind, this means that seeing involves relations between mental representations *and their referents;* hence, semantic relations within the meaning of the act.

I hope that such examples suggest (what, in fact, I think is true) that even if the formality condition isn't very clear, it is quite certainly very strong. In fact, I think it's not all *that* anachronistic to see it as the central issue which divides the two main traditions in the history of psychology: "Rational psychology" on the one hand, and "Naturalism" on the other. Since this is a mildly eccentric way of cutting the pie, I'm going to permit myself a semihistorical excursus before returning to the main business of the paper.

Descartes argued that there is an important sense in which how the world is makes no difference to one's mental states. Here is a well-known passage from the *Meditations:*

> At this moment it does indeed seem to me that it is with eyes awake that I am looking at this paper; that this head which I move is not asleep, that it is deliberately and of set purpose that I extend my hand and perceive it. . . . But in thinking over this I remind myself that on many occasions I have been deceived by

similar illusions, and in dwelling on this reflection I see so manifestly that there are no certain indications by which we may clearly distinguish wakefulness from sleep that I am lost in astonishment. And my astonishment is such that it is almost capable of persuading me that I now dream. (Decartes 1931)

At least three sorts of reactions to this kind of argument are distinguishable in the philosophical literature. First, there's a long tradition, including both Rationalists and Empiricists, which takes it as axiomatic that one's experiences (and, a fortiori, one's beliefs) might have been just as they are even if the world had been quite different from the way that it is. See, for example, the passage from Hume which serves as an epigraph to this paper. Second, there's a vaguely Wittgensteinian mood in which one argues that it's just *false* that one's mental states might have been what they are had the world been relevantly different. For example, if there had been a dagger there, Macbeth would have been *seeing,* not just hallucinating. And what could be more different than that? If the Cartesian feels that this reply misses the point, he is at least under an obligation to say precisely which point it misses; in precisely *which* respects the way the world is is irrelevant to the character of one's beliefs, experiences, etc. Finally there's a tradition which argues that—epistemology to one side—it is at best a strategic mistake to attempt to develop a psychology which individuates mental states without reference to their environmental causes and effects (e.g., which counts the state that Macbeth *was* in as type-identical to the state he would have been in had the dagger been supplied). I have in mind the tradition which includes the American Naturalists (notably Pierce and Dewey), all the learning theorists, and such contemporary representatives as Quine in philosophy and Gibson in psychology. The recurrent theme here is that psychology is a branch of biology, hence that one must view the organism as embedded in a physical environment. The psychologist's job is to trace those organism/environment interactions which constitute its behavior. A passage from William James (1890, p. 6) will serve to give the feel of the thing:

On the whole, few recent formulas have done more service of a rough sort in psychology than the Spencerian one that the essence of mental life and of bodily life are one, namely, 'the adjustment of inner to outer relations.' Such a formula is vagueness incarnate; but because it takes into account the fact that minds inhabit environments which act on them and on which they in turn react; because; in short, it takes mind in the midst of all its concrete relations, it is immensely more fertile than the old-fashioned 'rational psychology' which treated the soul as a detached existent, sufficient unto itself, and assumed to consider only its nature and its properties.

A number of adventitious intrusions have served to muddy the issues in this long-standing dispute. On the one hand, it may well be that Descartes was relying on a specifically introspectionist construal of the claim that the individuation of mental states is independent of their environmental causes. That is, Descartes' point may have been that (a) mental states are (type) identical if and only if (iff) they are introspectively indistinguishable, and (b) introspection cannot distinguish (e.g.) perception from hallucination, or knowledge from belief. On the other hand, the naturalist, in point of historical fact, is often a behaviorist as well. He wants to argue not only that mental states are individuated by reference to organism/environment relations, but also that such relations constitute the mental. In the context of the present discussion, he is arguing for the abandonment not just of the formality condition, but of the notion of mental representation as well.

If, however, we take the computational theory of the mind as what's central to the issue, we can reconstruct the debate between rational psychologists and naturalists in a way that does justice to both their points; in particular, in a way that frees the discussion from involvement with introspectionism on the one side and behaviorism on the other.

Insofar as we think of mental processes as computational (hence as formal operations defined on representations) it will be natural to take the mind to be, inter alia, a kind of computer. That is, we will think of the mind as carrying out whatever symbol manipulations are constitutive of the hypothesized computational processes. To a first approximation, we may thus construe mental operations as pretty directly analogous to those of a Turing machine. There is, for example, a working memory (corresponding to a tape) and there are capacities for scanning and altering the contents of the memory (corresponding to the operations of reading and writing on the tape). If we want to extend the computational metaphor by providing access to information about the environment, we can think of the computer as having access to "oracles" which serve, on occasion, to enter information in the memory. On the intended interpretation of this model, these oracles are analogs to the senses. In particular, they are assumed to be transducers, in that what they write on the tape is determined solely by the ambient environmental energies that impinge upon them. (For elaboration of this sort of account, see Putnam [1960]; it is, of course, widely familiar from discussions in the field of artificial intelligence.)

I'm not endorsing this model, but simply presenting it as a natural extension of the computational picture of the mind. Its present interest is that we can use it to see how the formality condition connects with the Cartesian claim that the character of mental processes is somehow independent of their environmental causes and effects. The point is that, so long as we are thinking of mental processes as purely computational, the bearing of environmental information upon such processes is exhausted by the formal character of whatever the oracles write on the tape. In particular, it doesn't matter to such processes whether what the oracles write is *true;* whether, for example, they really are transducers faithfully mirroring the state of the environment, or merely the output end of a typewriter manipulated by a Cartesian demon bent on deceiving the machine. I'm saying, in effect, that the formality condition, viewed in this context, is tantamount to a sort of methodological solipsism. If mental processes are formal, then they have access only to the formal properties of such representations of the environment as the senses provide. Hence, they have no access to the *semantic* properties of such representations, including the property of being true, of having referents, or, indeed, the property of being representations *of the environment.*

That some such methodological solipsism really is implicated in much current psychological practice is best seen by examining what researchers actually do. Consider, for example, the well-known work of Professor Terry Winograd. Winograd was primarily interested in the computer simulation of certain processes involved in the handling of verbal information; asking and answering questions, drawing inferences, following instructions and the like. The form of his theory was a program for a computer which "lives in" and operates upon a simple world of blocklike geometric objects (see Winograd 1971). Many of the capacities that the device exercises vis-à-vis its environment seem impressively intelligent. It can arrange the blocks to order, it can issue "perceptual" reports of the present state of its environment and "memory" reports of its past states, it can devise simple plans for achieving desired environmental configurations, and it can discuss its undertakings (more or less in English) with whoever is running the program.

The interesting point for purposes, however, is that the machine environment which is the nominal object of these actions and conversations actually isn't there. What actually happens is that the programmer so arranges the memory states of the machine that the available data are whatever they would be *if* there were objects for the machine to perceive and manipulanda for it to operate upon. In effect, the machine lives in an entirely notional world; all its beliefs are false. Of course, it doesn't matter to the machine that its beliefs are false since falsity is a semantic property and, qua computer, the device satisfies the formality condition; viz., it has access only to formal (nonsemantic) properties of the representations that it manipulates. In effect, the device is in precisely the situation that Descartes dreads; it's a mere computer which dreams that it's a robot.

I hope that this discussion suggests how acceptance of the computational theory of the mind leads to a sort of methodological solipsism as a part of the research strategy of contemporary cognitive psychology. In particular, I hope it's clear how you get that consequence from the formality condition alone, without so much as raising the introspection issue. I stress this point because it seems to me that there has been considerable confusion about it among the psychologists themselves. People who do machine simulation, in particular, very often advertise themselves as working on the question how thought (or language) is related to the world. My present point is that, whatever else they're doing, they certainly aren't doing *that.* The very assumption that defines their field—viz., that they study mental processes *qua* formal operations on symbols—guarantees that their studies won't answer the question how the symbols so manipulated are semantically interpreted. You can, for example, build a machine that answers baseball questions in the sense that (e.g.) if you type in "Who had the most wins by a National League pitcher since Dizzy Dean?" it will type out "Robin Roberts, who won 28." But you delude yourself if you think that a machine which in this sense answers baseball questions, is thereby answering questions *about* baseball (or that the machine has somehow referred to Robin Roberts). If the *programmer* chooses to interpret the machine inscription "Robin Roberts won 28" as a statement about Robin Roberts (e.g., as the statement that he won 28), that's all well and good, but it's no business of the machine's. The machine has no access to that interpretation, and its computations are in no way affected by it. The machine doesn't know what it's talking about, it doesn't care; *about* is a semantic relation.[5]

This brings us to a point where, having done some sort of justice to the Cartesian's insight, we can also do some sort of justice to the naturalist's. For, after all, mental processes are supposed to be operations on representations, and it is in the nature of representations to represent. We have seen that a psychology which embraces the formality condition is thereby debarred from raising questions about the semantic properties of mental representations; yet surely such questions ought *somewhere* to be raised. The computer which prints out "RR won 28" is not thereby referring to RR. But, surely, when I think: *RR won 28*, I *am* thinking about RR, and if not in virtue of having performed some formal operations on some representations, then presumably in virtue of something else. It's perhaps borrowing the least tendentious fragment of causal theories of reference to assume that what fixes the interpretation of my mental representations of RR is something about the way that he and I are embedded in the world; perhaps not a causal chain stretching between us, but anyhow *some* facts about how he and I are causally situated; *Dasein,* as you might say. Only a *naturalistic* psychology will do to specify these facts, because here we are explicitly in the realm of organism/environment transactions.

We are on the verge of a bland and ecumenical conclusion: that there is room both for a computational psychology—viewed as a theory of formal processes defined over mental representations— *and* a naturalistic psychology, viewed as a theory of the (presumably causal) relations between representations and the world which fix the semantic interpretations of the former. I think that, in principle, this is the right way to look at things. In practice, however, I think that it's misleading. So far as I can see, it's overwhelmingly likely that computational psychology is the only one that we are going to get. I want to argue for this conclusion in two steps. First, I'll argue for what I've till now only assumed: that we must *at least* have a psychology which accepts the formality condition. Then I'll argue that there's good reason to suppose that that's the most that we can have; that a naturalistic psychology isn't a practical possibility and isn't likely to become one.

The first move, then, is to give reasons for believing that at least *some* part of psychology should honor the formality condition. Here too the argument proceeds in two steps. I'll argue first that it is typically under an *opaque* construal that attributions of propositional attitudes to organisms enter into explanations of their behavior; and second that the formality condition is intimately involved with the explanation of propositional attitudes so construed: roughly, that it's reasonable to believe that we can get such explanations only within computational theories. *Caveat emptor:* the arguments under review are, in large part, nondemon-

strative. In particular, they will assume the perfectibility in principle of the kinds of psychological theories now being developed, and it is entirely possible that this is an assumption contrary to fact.

Thesis: when we articulate the generalizations in virtue of which behavior is contingent upon mental states, it is typically an opaque construal of the mental state attributions that does the work; for example, it's a construal under which believing that *a is F* is logically independent from believing that *b is F,* even in the case where a = b. It will be convenient to speak not only of opaque construals of propositional attitude ascriptions, but also of *opaque taxonomies* of mental state types; e.g., of taxonomies which, inter alia, count the belief that the Morning Star rises in the east as type distinct from the belief that the Evening Star does. (Correspondingly, *transparent* taxonomies are such as, inter alia, would count these beliefs as type-identical). So, the claim is that mental states are typically opaquely taxonomized for purposes of psychological theory.[6]

The point doesn't depend upon the examples, so I'll stick to the most informal sorts of cases. Suppose I know that John wants to meet the girl who lives next door, and suppose I know that this is true when "wants to" is construed opaquely. Then, given even rough-and-ready generalizations about how people's behaviors are contingent upon their utilities, I can make some reasonable predictions (guesses) about what John is likely to do: he's likely to say (viz., utter), "I want to meet the girl who lives next door." He's likely to call upon his neighbor. He's likely (at a minimum, and all things being equal) to exhibit next-door-directed behavior. None of this is frightfully exciting, but it's all I need for present purposes, and what more would you expect from folk psychology?

On the other hand, suppose that all I know is that John wants to meet the girl next door where "wants to" is construed transparently; i.e., all I know is that it's true of the girl next door that John wants to meet her. Then there is little or nothing that I can predict about how John is likely to proceed. And this is *not* just because rough and ready psychological generalizations want *ceteris paribus* clauses to fill them in; it's also for the deeper reason that I can't infer from what I know about John to any relevant description of the mental causes of his behavior. For example, I have no reason to predict that John will say such things as "I want to meet the girl who lives next door" since, let John be as cooperative and as truthful as you like, and let him be utterly a native speaker, still, he *may* believe that the girl he wants to meet languishes in Latvia. In which case, "I want to meet the girl who lives next door" is the last thing it will occur to him to say. (The contestant wants to say "suspender," for "suspender" is the magic word. Consider what we can predict about his probable verbal behavior if we take this (a) opaquely and (b) transparently. And, of course, the same sorts of points apply, mutatis mutandis, to the prediction of *non*verbal behavior.)

Ontologically, transparent readings are stronger than opaque ones; for example, the former license existential inferences which the latter do not. But psychologically opaque readings are stronger than transparent ones; they tell us more about the character of the mental causes of behavior. The representational theory of mind offers an explanation of this anomaly. Opaque ascriptions are true in virtue of the way that the agent represents the objects of his wants (intentions, beliefs, etc.) *to himself.* And, by assumption, such representations function in the causation of the behaviors that the agent produces. So, for example, to say that it's true *opaquely* that Oedipus did such-and-such because he wanted to marry Jocasta, is to say something like (though not, perhaps, *very* like; see Fodor [forthcoming]): "Oedipus said to himself, 'I want to marry Jocasta,' and his so saying was among the causes of his behavior." Whereas to say (only) that it's true transparently that O. wanted to marry J. is to say no more than that among the causes of his behavior was O.'s saying to himself "I want to marry . . ." where the blank was filled by *some* expression that denotes J.[7] But now, what O. *does,* how he in the proprietary sense behaves, will depend on which description he (literally) had in mind.[8] If it's "Jocasta," courtship behavior follows *ceteris paribus.* Whereas, if it's "my Mum," we have the situation towards the end of the play and Oedipus at Colonus eventually ensues.

I dearly wish that I could leave this topic here, because it would be very convenient to be able to say, without qualification, what I strongly implied above: the opaque readings of propositional attitude ascriptions tell us how people represent the objects of their propositional attitudes. What one would like to say, in particular, is that if two people are identically related to formally identical mental representations, then they are in opaquely type-identical mental states. This would be convenient because it yields a succinct and gratifying characterization of what a computational cognitive psychology is about: such a psychology studies propositional attitudes opaquely taxonomized.

I think, in fact, that this is *roughly* the right thing to say since what I think is *exactly* right is that the construal of propositional attitudes which such a psychology renders is nontransparent. (It's nontransparency that's crucial in all the examples

we have been considering.) The trouble is that nontransparency isn't quite the same notion as opacity, as we shall now see.

The question before us is: "What are the relations between the pretheoretic notion of type identity of mental states opaquely construed and the notion of type identity of mental states that you get from a theory which strictly honors the formality condition?" And the answer is: complicated. For one thing, it's not clear that we have *a* pretheoretic notion of the opaque reading of a propositional attitude ascription: I doubt that the two standard tests for opacity (failure of existential generalization and failure of substitutivity of identicals) even pick out the same class of cases. But what's more important are the following considerations. While it's notorious that extensionally identical thoughts may be opaquely type distinct (e.g., thoughts about the Morning Star and thoughts about the Evening Star) there are nevertheless some semantic conditions on opaque type identification. In particular:

(a) there are some cases of formally distinct but co-extensive token thoughts which count as tokens of the same (opaque) type (and hence as identical in content at least on one way of individuating contents); and

(b) *non*coextensive thoughts are ipso facto, type-distinct (and differ in content, at least on one way of individuating contents).

Cases of type (a): 1. I think I'm sick and you think I'm sick. What's running through my head is "I'm sick"; what's running through your head is "he's sick." But we are both having thoughts of the same (opaque) type (and hence of the same content).

2. You think: "that one looks edible"; I think: "this one looks edible." Our thoughts are opaquely type-identical if we are thinking about the same one.

It connects with the existence of such cases that pronouns and demonstratives are typically (perhaps invariably) construed as referring, even when they occur in what are otherwise opaque constructions. So, for example, it seems to me that I can't report Macbeth's hallucination by saying: "Macbeth thinks that's a dagger" if Macbeth is staring at nothing at all. Which is to say that "that's a dagger" doesn't report Macbeth's mental state even though "that's a dagger" may be precisely what is running through Macbeth's head (precisely the representation his relation to which is constitutive of his belief).

Cases of type (b): 1. Suppose that Sam feels faint and Misha knows he does. Then what's running through Misha's head may be "he feels faint." Suppose too that Misha feels faint and Alfred knows he does. Then what's running through Alfred's head, too, may be "he feels faint." I have no, or rather no univocal, inclination to say, in this case, that Alfred and Misha are having type identical thoughts even though the principle of type individuation is, by assumption, opaque and even though Alfred and Misha have the same things running through their heads. But if this is right, then formal identity of mental representations cannot be sufficient for type identity of opaquely taxonomized mental states.[9] (There is an interesting discussion of this sort of case in Geach [1957] . Geach says that Aquinas says that there is no "intelligible difference" between Alfred's thought and Misha's. I don't know whether this means that they are having the same thought or that they aren't).

2. Suppose that there are two Lake Eries (two bodies of water so-called). Consider two tokens of the thought "Lake Erie is wet," one of which is, intuitively speaking about the Lake Erie in North America and one of which is about the other one. Here again, I'm inclined to say that the aboriginal, uncorrupted pretheoretical notion of type-wise same thought wants these to be tokens of *different* thoughts and takes these thoughts to differ in content. (Though in this case, as in the others, I think there's also a countervailing inclination to say that they count as type-identical—and as identical in content—for some relevant purposes and in some relevant respects. How like aboriginal, uncorrupted, pretheoretical intuition!)

I think, in short, that the intuitive opaque taxonomy is actually what you might call "semitransparent." On the one hand, certain conditions on coreference are in force (Misha's belief that he's ill is type distinct from Sam's belief that *he's* ill and my thought *this is edible* may be type identical to your thought *that is edible*.) On the other hand, you don't get free substitution of coreferring expressions (beliefs about the Morning Star are type-distinct from beliefs about the Evening Star) and existential generalization doesn't go through for beliefs about Santa Claus.

Apparently, then, the notion of same mental state that we get from a theory which honors the formality condition is related to, but not identical to, the notion of same mental state that unreconstructed intuition provides for opaque construals. And it would certainly be reasonable to ask whether we actually need both. I think the answer is probably: yes, if we want to capture *all* the intuitions. For if we restrict ourselves to either one of the taxonomies, we get consequences that we don't like. On the one hand, if we taxonomize *purely* formally, we get identity of belief compatible with difference of truth value. (Misha's belief

that he's ill will be type-identical to Sam's belief that *he's* ill, but one may be true while the other is false.) On the other hand, if we taxonomize solely according to the pretheoretic criteria, we get trouble with the idea that people act out of their beliefs and desires. We need, in particular, some taxonomy according to which Sam and Misha have the *same* belief in order to explain why it is that they exhibit the same behaviors. It is, after all, *part* of the pretheoretic notion of belief that difference in belief ought *ceteris paribus* to show up in behavior *somewhere;* ("ceteris paribus" means "given relevant identities among other mental states"). Whereas, it's possible to construct cases where differences like the one between Misha's belief and Sam's can't show up in behavior even in principle (see note 9). What we have, in short, is a tension between a partially semantic taxonomy and an entirely functional one, and the recommended solution is to use both.

Having said all this, I now propose largely to ignore it and use the term "opaque taxonomy" for principles of type individuation according to which Misha and Sam are in the same mental state when each believes himself to be ill. When I need to distinguish this sense of opaque taxonomy from the pretheoretic one, I'll talk about *full* opacity and fully opaque type identification.

My claim has been that, in doing our psychology, we want to attribute mental states fully opaquely because it's the fully opaque reading which tells us what the agent has in mind, and it's what the agent has in mind that causes his behavior. I now need to say something about how, precisely, all this is supposed to constitute an argument for the formality condition.

Point one: it's just as well that it's the fully opaque construal of mental states that we need since, patently, that's the only one that the formality condition permits us. This is because the formality condition prohibits taxonomizing psychological states by reference to the semantic properties of mental representations and, at bottom, transparency is a semantic (viz., nonformal; viz., nonsyntactic) notion. The point is sufficiently obvious: if we count the belief that the Evening Star is F as (type) identical to the belief that the Morning Star is F, that must be because of the coreference of such expressions as "the Morning Star" and "the Evening Star." But coreference is a semantic property, and not one which could conceivably have a formal doppleganger; it's inconceivable, in particular, that there should be a system of mental representations such that, in the general case, coreferring expressions are formally identical in that system. (This might be true for God's mind, but not, surely, for anybody else's [and not for God's either unless he is an Extensionalist; which I doubt.]) So if we want transparent taxonomies of mental states, we will have to give up the formality condition. So it's a good thing for the computational theory of the mind that it's not transparent taxonomies that we want.

What's harder to argue for (but might, nevertheless, be true) is point two: that the formality condition *can* be honored by a theory which taxonomizes mental states according to their content. For, barring caveats previously reviewed, it may be that mental states are distinct in content only if they are relations to formally distinct mental representations; in effect, that aspects of content can be reconstructed as aspects of form, at least insofar as appeals to content figure in accounts of the mental causation of behavior. The main thing to be said in favor of this speculation is that it allows us to explain, within the context of the representational theory of mind, how beliefs of different content *can* have different behavioral effects, even when the beliefs are transparently type-identical. The form of explanation goes: it's because different content implies formally distinct internal representations (via the formality condition) and formally distinct internal representations can be functionally different; can differ in their causal role. Whereas, to put it mildly, it's hard to see how internal representations could differ in causal role *unless* they differed in form.

To summarize: transparent taxonomy is patently incompatible with the formality condition; whereas taxonomy in respect of content *may* be compatible with the formality condition, plus or minus a bit. That taxonomy in respect of content *is* compatible with the formality condition, plus or minus a bit, is perhaps *the* basic idea of modern cognitive theory. The representational theory of mind and the computational theory of mind merge here for, on the one hand, it's claimed that psychological states differ in content only if they are relations to type-distinct mental representations; and, on the other, it's claimed that only formal properties of mental representations contribute to their type individuation for the purposes of theories of mind/body interaction. Or, to put it the other way 'round, it's allowed that mental representations affect behavior in virtue of their content, but it's maintained that mental representations are distinct in content only if they are also distinct in form. The first clause is required to make it plausible that mental states are relations to mental representations and the second is required to make it plausible that mental processes are computations. (Computations just *are* processes in which representations have their causal consequences in virtue of their form.) By thus exploiting

the notions of content and computation *together*, a cognitive theory seeks to connect the *intensional* properties of mental states with their *causal* properties vis-à-vis behavior. Which is, of course, exactly what a theory of the mind ought to do.

As must be evident from the preceding, I'm partial to programmatic arguments: ones that seek to infer the probity of a conceptual apparatus from the fact that it plays a role in some prima facie plausible research enterprise. So, in particular, I've argued that a taxonomy of mental states which honors the formality condition seems to be required by theories of the mental causation of behavior, and that that's a reason for taking such taxonomies very seriously.

But there lurks, within the general tradition of representational theories of mind, a deeper intuition: that it is not only *advisable* but actually *mandatory* to assume that mental processes have access only to formal (nonsemantic) properties of mental representations; that the contrary view is not only empirically fruitless but also conceptually unsound. I find myself in sympathy with this intuition, though I'm uncertain precisely how the arguments ought to go. What follows is just a sketch.

I'll begin with a version that I *don't* like, an epistemological version:

> Look, it makes no *sense* to suppose that mental operations could apply to mental representations in virtue of (e.g.) the truth or falsity of the latter. For, consider: truth value is a matter of correspondence to the way the world is. To determine the truth value of a belief would therefore involve what I'll call 'directly comparing' the belief with the world; i.e., comparing it with the way the world *is*, not just with the way the world is represented as being. And the representational theory of mind says that we have access to the world only *via* the ways in which we represent it. There is, as it were, nothing that corresponds to looking around (behind? through? what's the right metaphor?) one's beliefs to catch a glimpse of the things they represent. Mental processes can, in short, compare representations; but they can't compare representations with what they're representations of. Hence mental processes can't have access to the truth value of representations or, mutatis mutandis, to whether they denote. Hence the formality condition.

This line of argument could, certainly, be made a good deal more precise. It has been in, for example, some of the recent work of Nelson Goodman (see especially Goodman 1978). For present purposes, however, I'm content to leave it *impre*cise so long as it sounds familiar. For I suspect that all versions of the argument suffer from a common deficiency: they assume that you can't run a *correspondence* theory of truth together with a *coherence* theory of evidence. Whereas I see nothing compelling in the interference from "truth is a matter of the correspondence of a belief with the way the world is" to "*ascertaining* truth is a matter of 'directly comparing' a belief with the way the world is." Perhaps we ascertain the truth of our beliefs by comparing them with one another, appealing to inference to the best explanation whenever we need to do so.

Anyhow, it would be nice to have a *non*epistemological defence of the formality condition; one which saves the intuition that there's something conceptually wrong with its denial but doesn't acquire the skeptical/relativistic commitments with which the traditional epistemic versions of the argument have been encumbered. Here goes:

Suppose, just for convenience, that mental processes are algorithms. So, we have rules for the transformation of mental representations, and we have the mental representations that constitute their ranges and domains. Think of the rules as being like hypothetical imperatives; they have antecedents which specify conditions on mental representations, and they have consequents which specify what is to happen if the antecedents are satisfied. And now consider rules (a) and (b):

(a) Iff it's the case that P, do such and such.

(b) Iff you believe it's the case that P, do such and such.

Notice, to begin with, that the compliance conditions on these injunctions are quite different. In particular, in the case where P is *false but believed true*, compliance with (b) consists in doing such and such, whereas compliance with (a) consists in *not* doing it. But despite this difference in compliance conditions, there's something *very* peculiar (perhaps *pragmatically* peculiar, whatever precisely that may mean) about supposing that an organism might have different ways of going about attempting to comply with (a) and (b). The peculiarity is patent in (c). To borrow a joke from Professor Robert Jagger, (c) is a little like the advice: "buy low, sell high." One knows just what it would be *like* to comply with either, but somehow knowing that doesn't help much.

(c) Do such and such iff it's the case that P, *whether or not* you believe that it's the case that P.[10]

The idea is this: when one has done what one can to establish that the belief that P is warranted, one has done what one can to establish that the antecedent of (a) is satisfied. And, conversely, when one has done what one can do to establish that the antecedent of (a) is satisfied, one has done what one can to establish the warrant of the belief that P. Now, I suppose that the following is at least close to being true: to have the belief that P is to have the belief that the belief that P is warranted; and conversely, to have the belief that the belief that P is warranted is to have the belief that P. And the upshot of *this* is just the formality condition all over again. Given that mental operations have access to the fact that P is believed (and hence that the belief that P is believed to be warranted, and hence that the belief that the belief that P is warranted is believed to be warranted, . . . etc.) there's nothing further left to do; there is nothing that corresponds to the notion of a mental operation which one undertakes to perform just in case one's belief that P is *true*.

This isn't, by the way, any form of skepticism, as can be seen from the following: there's nothing wrong with Jones having one mental operation which he undertakes to perform iff it's the case that P and another *quite different* mental operation which he undertakes to perform iff *Smith* ($\neq$ Jones) believes that it's the case that P. (Cf. "I promise . . . though I don't intend to . . ." vs. "I promise . . . though Smith doesn't intend to . . . ") There's a first person/third person asymmetry here, but it doesn't impugn the semantic distinction between "P is true" and "P is believed true." The suggestion is that it's the tacit recognition of this pragmatic asymmetry that accounts for the traditional hunch that you can't both identify mental operations with transformations on mental representations and at the same time flout the formality condition; that the representational theory of mind and the computational theory of mind are somehow conjoint options.

So much, then, for the formality condition and the psychological tradition which accepts it. What about Naturalism? The first point is that none of the arguments *for* a rational psychology is, in and of itself, an argument *against* a Naturalistic psychology. As I remarked above, to deny that mental operations have access to the semantic properties of mental representations is *not* to deny that mental representations *have* semantic properties. On the contrary, beliefs are *just* the kinds of things which exhibit truth and denotation, and the Naturalist proposes to make science out of the organism/environment relations which (presumably) fix these properties. Why, indeed, should he not?

This all *seems* very reasonable. Nevertheless, I now wish to argue that a computational psychology is the only one that we are likely to get; that qua research strategy, the attempt to construct a *naturalistic* psychology is very likely to prove fruitless. I think that the basis for such an argument is already to be found in the literature, where it takes the form of a (possibly inadvertent) reductio ad absurdum of the contrary view.

Consider, to begin with, a distinction that Professor Hilary Putnam introduces in "The Meaning of Meaning" (1975) between what he calls "psychological states in the wide sense" and "psychological states in the narrow sense." A psychological state in the *narrow* sense is one the ascription of which does not "(presuppose) the existence of any individual other than the subject to whom that state is ascribed" (p. 10). All others are psychological states in the wide sense. So, for example, *x's jealousy of y* is a schema for expressions which denote psychological states in the wide sense since such expressions presuppose the existence, not only of the *x*s who are in the states, but also of the *y*s who are its objects. Putnam remarks that methodological solipsism (the phrase, by the way, is his) can be viewed as the requirement that only psychological states in the narrow sense are allowed as constructs in psychological theories.

Whereas, it's perhaps Putnam's main point that there are at least *some* scientific purposes (e.g., semantics and accounts of intertheoretical reference) which demand the wide construal. Here, rephrased slightly, is the sort of example that Putnam finds persuasive.

There is a planet (call it "Yon") where things are very much like here. In particular, by a cosmic accident, some of the people on Yon speak a dialect indistinguishable from English and live in an urban conglomerate indistinguishable from the Greater Boston Area. Still more, for every one of our Greater Bostonians, there is a doppelganger on Yon who has precisely the same neurological structure down to and including microparticles. We can assume that, so long as we're construing "psychological state" narrowly, this latter condition guarantees type identity of our psychological states with theirs.

However, Putnam argues, it doesn't guarantee that there is a corresponding identity of psychological states, hither and Yon, if we construe "psychological state" *widely*. Suppose that there is this difference between Yon and Earth; whereas, over here, the stuff we call "water" has the atomic structure H_2O, it turns out that the stuff that they call "water" over there has the atomic structure XYZ ($\neq H_2O$). And now, consider the mental state *thinking about water*. The idea is that, so long as we construe that state widely, it's one that we, but not our doppelgangers, can reasonably aspire to. For, construed widely, one is thinking about water only if it is water that one is thinking about. But it's water that one's thinking about only if it is H_2O that one's thinking about; water *is* H_2O. But since, by assumption, they never think about H_2O over Yon, it follows that there's at least one wide psy-

chological state that we're often in and they never are, however neurophysiologically like us they are, and however much our narrow psychological states converge with theirs.

Moreover, if we try to say what they speak about, refer to, mention, etc.; if, in short, we try to supply a semantics for their dialect, we will have to mention XYZ, not H_2O. Hence it would be wrong, at least on Putnam's intuitions, to say that they have a word for *water*. A fortiori, the chemists who work in what they call "M.I.T." don't have theories about *water,* even though what runs through their heads when they talk about XYZ may be identical to what runs through our heads when we talk about H_2O. The situation is analogous to the one that arises for demonstratives and token reflexives, as Putnam insightfully points out.

Well, what are we to make of this? Is it an argument against methodological solipsism? And, if so, it is a *good* argument against methodological solipsism?

To begin with, Putnam's distinction between psychological states in the narrow and wide sense looks to be very intimately related to the traditional distinction between psychological state ascriptions opaquely and transparently construed. I'm a bit wary about this since what Putnam *says* about wide ascriptions is only that they "presuppose the existence" of objects other than the ascribee; and, of course *a believes Fb and b exists* does not entail *b is such that a believes F of him,* or even *∃x (a believes Fx).* Moreover, the failure of such entailments is notoriously important in discussions of quantifying in. For all that, however, I don't *think* that it's Putnam's intention to exploit the difference between the existential generalization test for transparency and the presupposition of existence test for wideness. On the contrary, the burden of Putnam's argument seems to be precisely that "John believes (widely) that water is F" is true only if water (viz., H_2O) is such that John believes it's F. It's thus unclear to me why Putnam gives the weaker condition on wideness when it appears to be the stronger one that does the work.[11]

But whatever the case may be with the wide sense of belief, it's pretty clear that the narrow sense must be (what I've been calling) fully opaque. (This is because only full opacity allows type identity of beliefs that have different truth conditions [Sam's belief that he's ill with Misha's belief that *he* is; Yon beliefs about XYZ with hither beliefs about H_2O.]) I want to emphasize this correspondence between narrowness and full opacity and not just in aid of terminological parsimony. Putnam sometimes writes as though he takes the methodological commitment to a psychology of narrow mental states to be a sort of vulgar prejudice: "Making this assumption is, of course, adopting a *restrictive program*—a program which deliberately limits the scope and nature of psychology to fit certain mentalistic preconceptions or, in some cases, to fit an idealistic reconstruction of knowledge and the world" (p. 137). But, in light of what we've said so far, it should be clear that this is a methodology with malice aforethought. Narrow psychological states are those individuated in light of the formality condition; viz., without reference to such semantic properties as truth and reference. And honoring the formality condition is part and parcel of the attempt to provide a theory which explains (a) how the belief that the Morning Star is F could be different from the belief that the Evening Star is F despite the well-known astronomical facts; and (b) how the behavioral effects of believing that the Morning Star is F could be different from those of believing that the Evening Star is F, astronomy once again apparently to the contrary notwithstanding. Putnam is, of course, dubious about this whole project: ". . . The three centuries of failure of mentalistic psychology is tremendous evidence against this procedure, in my opinion" (p. 137). I suppose this is intended to include everybody from Locke and Kant to Freud and Chomsky. I should have such failures.

So much for background. I now need an argument to show that a naturalistic psychology (a psychology of mental states transparently individuated; hence, presumably, a psychology of mental states in the wide sense) is, for practical purposes, out of the question. So far as I can see, however, Putnam has given that argument. For, consider: a naturalistic psychology is a theory of organism/environment transactions. So, to stick to Putnam's example, a naturalistic psychology would have to find some stuff S and some relation R, such that one's narrow thought that water is wet is a thought about S in virtue of the fact that one bears R to S. Well, *which* stuff? The natural thing to say would be: "Water, of course." Notice, however, that if Putnam is right, it may not even be *true* that the narrow thought that water is wet is a thought about water; it *won't* be true of tokens of that thought which occur on Yon. Whether the narrow thought that water is wet is about water depends on whether it's about H_2O; and whether it's about H_2O depends on "how science turns out"—viz., on what chemistry is true. (Similarly, mutatis mutandis, "water" refers to water is *not*, on this view, a truth of any branch of linguistics; it's chemists who tell us what it is that "water" refers to.) Surely, however, characterizing the objects of thought is

methodologically prior to characterizing the causal chains that link thoughts to their objects. But the theory which characterizes the objects of thought is the theory of *everything;* it's all of science. Hence, the methodological moral of Putnam's analysis seems to be: the naturalistic psychologists will inherit the Earth, but only after everybody else is finished with it. No doubt it's alright to have a research strategy that says "wait awhile." But who wants to wait *forever?*

This sort of argument isn't novel. Indeed, it was anticipated by Bloomfield (1933). Bloomfield argues that, for all practical purposes, you can't do semantics. The reason that you can't is that to do semantics you have to be able to say, for example, what "salt" refers to. But what "salt" refers to is NaCl, and that's a bit of chemistry, not linguistics:

The situations which prompt people to utter speech include every object and happening in their universe. In order to give a scientifically accurate definition of meaning for every form of a language, we would have to have a scientifically accurate knowledge of everything in the speaker's world. The actual extent of human knowledge is very small compared to this. We can define the meaning of a speech-form accurately when this meaning has to do with some matter of which we possess scientific knowledge. We can define the names of minerals, as when we say that the ordinary meaning of the English word *salt* is 'sodium chloride (NaCl),' and we can define the names of plants or animals by means of the technical terms of botany or zoology, but we have no precise way of defining words like *love* or *hate,* which concern situations that have not been accurately classified. . . . The statement of meanings is therefore the weak point in language-study, and will remain so until knowledge advances very far beyond its present state. (pp. 139–140)

It seems to me as though Putnam ought to endorse all of this *including the moral:* the distinction between wanting a naturalistic semantics (psychology) and not wanting any is real but academic.[12]

The argument just given depends, however, on accepting Putnam's analysis of his example. But suppose that one's intuitions run the other way. Then one is at liberty to argue like this:

1. They do too have water over Yon; all Putnam's example shows is that there could be two kinds of water, our kind (= H_2O) and their kind (= XYZ).
2. Hence, Yon tokens of the thought that water is wet are thoughts about water after all.
3. Hence, the way chemistry turns out is irrelevant to whether thoughts about water are about water.

4. Hence, the naturalistic psychology of thought need not wait upon the sciences of the objects of thought.
5. Hence, a naturalistic psychology may be in the cards after all.

Since the premises of this sort of reply may be tempting (since, indeed, they may be *true*) it's worth presenting a version of the argument which doesn't depend on intuitions about what XYZ is.

A naturalistic psychology would specify the relations that hold between an organism and an object in its environment when the one is thinking about the other. Now, think how such a theory would have to go. Since it would have to define its generalizations over mental states on the one hand and environmental entities on the other, it will need, in particular, some canonical way of referring to the latter. Well, *which* way? If one assumes that what makes my thought about Robin Roberts a thought *about Robin Roberts* is some causal connection between the two of us, then we'll need a description of RR such that the causal connection obtains in virtue of his satisfying that description. And *that* means, presumably, that we'll need a description under which the relation between him and me instantiates a law.

Generally, then, a naturalistic psychology would attempt to specify environmental objects in a vocabulary such that environment/organism relations are law-instantiating when so described. But here's the depressing consequence again: we have no access to such a vocabulary prior to the elaboration (completion?) of the nonpsychological sciences. "What Granny likes with her herring" isn't, for example, a description under which salt is law-instantiating; nor, presumably, is "salt." What we need is something like "NaCl," and descriptions like "NaCl" are available only *after* we've done our chemistry. What this comes down to is that, at a minimum, "*x*'s being F causally explains . . ." can be true only when "F" expresses nomologically necessary properties of the *x*s. Heaven knows it's hard to say what *that* means, but it presumably rules out both "Salt's being what Granny likes with herring . . ." and "Salt's being salt . . ."; the former for want of being necessary, and the latter for want of being nomological. I take it, moreover, that Bloomfield is right when he says (a) that we don't know relevant nomologically necessary properties of most of the things we can refer to (think about) and (b) that it isn't the linguist's (psychologist's) job to find them out.

Here's still another way to put this sort of argument. The way Bloomfield states his case invites the question: "Why *should* a semanticist want a definition of 'salt' that's 'scientifically accurate' in your sense? Why wouldn't a 'nominal' definition do?" There is, I think, some point to such a query. For example, as Hartry Field has pointed out (1972), it wouldn't make much difference to the way that truth-conditional semantics goes if we were to say only " 'salt' refers to whatever it refers to." All we need for this sort of semantics is some way or other of referring to the extension of "salt"; we don't, in particular, need a "scientifically accurate" way. It's therefore pertinent to do what Bloomfield notably does not: distinguish between the goals of *semantics* and those of a naturalistic psychology of language. The latter, by assumption, purports to explicate the organism/environment transactions in virtue of which relations like reference hold. It therefore requires, at a minimum, lawlike generalizations of the (approximate) form: *X's utterance of 'salt' refers to salt iff X bears relation R to ———.* Since this whole thing *is* supposed to be lawlike, what goes in for "   " must be a projectible characterization of the extension of "salt." But, in general, we discover which descriptions are projectible only *a posteriori;* in light of how the sciences (including the nonpsychological sciences) turn out. We are back where we started. Looked at this way, the moral is that we can do (certain kinds of) semantics if we have a way of referring to the extenson of "salt." But we can't do the naturalistic psychology of reference unless we have some way of saying what salt *is;* which of its properties determine its causal relations.

It's important to emphasize that these sorts of arguments do *not* apply against the research program embodied in "Rational psychology"; viz., to the program which envisions a psychology that honors the formality condition. The problem we've been facing is: under what description does the object of thought enter into scientific generalizations about the relations between thoughts and their objects? It looks as though the naturalist is going to have to say: under a description that's law instantiating; e.g., under physical description. Whereas the rational psychologist has a quite different answer. What *he* wants is *whatever description the organism has in mind* when it thinks about the object of thought, construing "thinks about" fully opaquely. So, for a theory of psychological states narrowly construed, we want such descriptions of Venus as, e.g., "the Morning Star," "the Evening Star," "Venus," etc., for it's these sorts of descriptions which we presumably entertain when we think that the Morning Star is *F*. In particular, it's our relation to these sorts of descriptions that determines what psychological state type we're in insofar as the goal in taxonomizing psychological states is explaining how they affect behavior.

A final point under the general head: the hopelessness of naturalistic psychology. Practicing naturalistic psychologists have been at least dimly aware all along of the sort of bind that they're in. So, for example, the "physical specification of the stimulus" is just about invariably announced as a requirement upon adequate formulations of S-R generalizations. We can now see why. Suppose, wildly contrary to fact, that there exists a human population (e.g., English speakers) in which pencils are, in the technical sense of the notion, discriminative stimuli controlling the verbal response "pencil." The point is that, even if some such generalization were true, it wouldn't be among those enunciated by a naturalistic psychology; the generalizations of naturalistic psychology are presumably supposed to be nomological, and there aren't any *laws* about pencils *qua* pencils. That is: expressions like "pencil" presumably occur in no true, lawlike sentences. Of course, there presumably is *some* description in virtue of which pencils fall under the organism/environment laws of a naturalistic psychology, and everybody (except, possibly, Gibson) has always assumed that those descriptions are, approximately, physical descriptions. Hence, the naturalist's demand, perfectly warranted by his lights, that the stimulus should be physically specified.

But though their theory has been consistent, their practice has uniformly not. In practice, and barring the elaborately circumscribed cases that psychophysics studies, the requirement that the stimulus be physically specified has been ignored by just about *all* practitioners. And, indeed, they were well advised to ignore it; how else could they get on with their job? If they really had to wait for the physicists to determine the description(s) under which pencils are law-instantiators, how would the psychology of pencils get off the ground?

So far as I can see, there are really only two ways out of this dilemma:

1. We can fudge, the way that learning theorists usually do. That is, we can "read" the description of the stimulus from the character of the organism's response. In point of historical fact, this has led to a kind of naturalistic psychology which is merely a solemn paraphrase of what everybody's grandmother knows: e.g., to saying "pencils are discriminative stimuli for the utterance of 'pencil'" where Granny would have said "pencil" refers to pencils. I take it that Chomsky's review of *Verbal Behavior* (1959) demonstrated, once and for all, the fatuity of this course. What *would* be interesting—what would have surprised Grandmother—is a generalization of the form Δ *is the discriminative stimulus for utterances of "pencil"* where Δ is a description which picks out pencils in some projectible vocabulary (e.g., in the vocabulary of physics). Does anybody suppose that such descriptions are likely to be forthcoming in, say, the *next* three hundred years?

2. The other choice is to try for a computational psychology; which is, of course, the burden of my plaint. On this view, what we can reasonably hope for is a theory of mental states fully opaquely type-individuated. We can try to say what the mental representation is, and what the relation to a mental representation is, such that one believes that the Morning Star is F in virtue of bearing the latter to the former. And we can try to say how that representation, or that relation, or both, differ from the representation and the relation constitutive of believing that the Evening Star is F. A naturalistic psychology, by contrast, remains a sort of ideal of pure reason; there must *be* such a psychology since, presumably, we do sometimes think of Venus and, presumably, we do so in virtue of a causal relation between it and us. But there's no practical hope of making science out of this relation. And, of course, for methodology, practical hope is *everything*.

One final point, and then I'm through. Methodological solipsism isn't, of course, solipsism *tout court*. It's not part of the enterprise to assert, or even suggest, that you and I are actually in the situation of Winograd's computer. Heaven only knows what relation between me and Robin Roberts makes it possible for me to think of him (refer to him, etc.), and I've been doubting the practical possibility of a science whose generalizations that relation instantiates. But I *don't* doubt that there *is* such a relation or that I do sometimes think of him. Still more: I have reasons not to doubt it; precisely the sorts of reasons I'd supply if I were asked to justify my knowledge claims about his pitching record. In short: it's true that Roberts won twenty-eight, and it's true that I know that he did, and nothing in the preceding tends to impugn these truths. (Or, contrariwise, if he didn't and I'm mistaken, then the reasons for my mistake are philosophically boring; they're biographical, not epistemological or ontological). My point, then, is *of course* not that solipsism is true; it's just that truth, reference and the rest of the semantic notions aren't psychological categories. What they are is: they're modes of *Dasein*. I don't know what *Dasein* is, but I'm sure that there's lots of it around, and I'm sure that you and I and Cincinnati have all got it. What more do you want?

NOTES

1. I've had a lot of help with this one. I'm particularly indebted to: Professors Ned Block, Sylvain Bromberger, Janet Dean Fodor, Keith Gundersen, Robert Richardson, Judith Thomson; and to Mr. Israel Krakowski.

2. I shall speak of "type identity" (distinctness) of mental states to pick out the sense of "same mental state" in which, for example, John and Mary are in the same mental state if both believe that water flows. Correspondingly, I shall use the notion of "token identity" (distinctness) of mental state to pick out the sense of "same mental state" in which it's necessary that if x and y are in the same mental state, then $x = y$.

3. For extensive discussion, see Fodor (1975; forthcoming).

4. This is *not*, notice, the same as saying "formal operations are the ones that apply mechanically"; in this latter sense, *formality* means something like *explicitness*. There's no particular reason for using "formal" to mean both "syntactic" and "explicit," though the ambiguity abounds in the literature.

5. Some fairly deep methodological issues in Artifical Intelligence are involved here. See Fodor (1978) where this surface is lightly scratched.

6. I'm told by some of my friends that this paragraph could be read as suggesting that there are *two kinds* of beliefs: opaque ones and transparent ones. That is not, of course, the way that it is intended to be read. The idea is rather that there are two kinds of conditions that we can place on determinations that a pair of belief tokens count as tokens of the same belief type. According to one set of conditions (corresponding to transparent taxonomy) a belief that the Morning Star is such and such counts as the same belief as a belief that the Evening Star is such and such; whereas, according to the other set of conditions (corresponding to opaque taxonomy), it does not.

7. I'm leaving it open that it may be to say still less than this (e.g., because of problems about reference under false descriptions). For purposes of the present discussion, I don't need to run a line of the truth conditions for transparent propositional attitude ascriptions. Thank Heaven, since I do not have one.

8. It's worth emphasizing that the sense of "behavior" *is* proprietary, and that that's pretty much what you would expect. Not every true description of an act can be such that a theory of the mental causation of behavior will explain the act under that description. (In being rude to Darcy, Elizabeth is insulting the man whom she will eventually marry. A theory of the mental causation of her behavior might have access to the former description, but not, surely, to the latter.)

Many philosophers—especially since Wittgenstein—have emphasized the ways in which the description of behavior may depend upon its context, and it is a frequent charge against modern versions of Rational psychology that they typically ignore such characterizations. So they do, but so what? You can't have explanations of everything under every description, and it's a question for empirical determination which descriptions of behavior reveal its systematicity vis-à-vis its causes. The Rational psychologist is prepared to bet that—to put it *very* approximately—behavior will prove to be systematic under some of the descriptions under which it is intentional.

At a minimum, the present claim goes like this: there is a way of taxonomizing behaviors and a way of taxonomizing mental states such that, given these taxonomies, theories of the mental causation of behavior will be forthcoming. And that way of taxonomizing mental states construes them non-transparently.

9. One might try saying: what counts for opaque type individuation is what's *in* your head, not just what's running through it. So, for example, though Alfred and Misha are both thinking "he feels faint," nevertheless different counterfactuals are true of them: Misha would cash his pronoun as: "he, Sam" whereas Alfred would cash *his* pronoun as: "he, Misha." The problem would then be to decide *which* such counterfactuals are relevant since, if we count all of them, it's going to turn out that there are few, if any, cases of distinct organisms having type-identical thoughts.

I won't, in any event, pursue this proposal since it seems clear that it won't, in principle, cope with all the relevant cases. Two people would be having different thoughts when each is thinking "I'm ill" even if *everything* in their heads were the same.

10. I'm assuming, for convenience that all the Ps are such that either they or their denials are believed. This saves having to relativize to time (e.g., having (b) and (c) read ". . . you believe or come to believe . . .").

11. I blush to admit that I had missed some of these complexities until Sylvain Bromberger kindly rubbed my nose in them.

12. It may be that Putnam *does* accept this moral. For example, the upshot of the discussion around p. 153 of his article appears to be that a Greek semanticist prior to Archimedes *could* not (in practice) have given a correct account of what (the Greek equivalent of) "gold" means; viz., because the theory needed to specify the extension of the term was simply not available. Presumably *we* are in that situation vis-à-vis the objects of many of *our* thoughts and the meanings of many of our terms; and, presumably, we will continue to do so into the indefinite future. But, then, what's the point of defining psychology (semantics) so that there can't be any?

Open Peer Commentary

* * * * *

"Paying the Price for Methodological Solipsism"

STEPHEN P. STICH

As I read it, the central thesis of Fodor's paper is this: "it is overwhelmingly likely that computational psychology is the only one that we are going to get." Though I would add a quibble here and a caveat there, I think Fodor's central thesis is right. But I fear that Fodor will find me an unwelcome ally. For while I agree that methodological solipsism is the right strategy to pursue in psychology, I don't think that Fodor has faced up to the price that must be paid for pursuing it. That price, I shall argue, is the abandonment of the representational theory of the mind.

The representational theory of the mind, as Fodor characterizes it, holds that "a mental state is (type) individuated by specifying a relation and a representation such that the subject bears the one to the other." And representations are individuated by their contents. However, methodologial solipsism requires that we taxonomize mental states by invoking the formality condition; a pair of mental states will count as type-distinct for the methodological solipsist only if they are formally distinct. Now it is my contention that two results ensue when we type mental states in the method-ological solipsist's way. First, most computational (or formal) mental state types will have tokens (either actual or possible) whose contents are radically different from one another, as judged by our "aboriginal, uncorrupted, pretheoretic intuition." Second, there will be some computational mental state types whose tokens can be assigned no content at all by our aboriginal intuition, though these "contentless" computational states will serve the purposes of the computational theory of mind fully as well as their contentful cousins. If I can make a case for both of these claims, I think we could reasonably conclude that the taxonomy of mental states imposed by the methodological so-lipsist's formality condition yields state *types* to which *no content can be assigned*. But a state with-out a content is no *representation* at all. So if the methodological solipsist is right, the representa-tional theory of the mind is wrong.

My first claim, that a computational taxonomy yields state types whose tokens differ in content, is one that Fodor grudgingly concedes. He does not contend that taxonomy of mental states in respect of content is compatible with the formality con-dition, but rather that "taxonomy in respect of content *may* be compatible with the formality condition, *plus or minus a bit*" (last emphasis mine). But what Fodor sees as a bit I see as the tip of an iceberg. To make valid the lack of fit between formal taxonomies and content taxonomies, con-sider the yarn about hither and Yon. Our Fodor here on Earth no doubt believes that Jimmy Carter is from Georgia. And, ex hypothesi, Fodor's dop-pelganger on Yon has a belief which he would ex-press just as hither Fodor would, by saying "Jimmy Carter is from Georgia." But surely our pretheoretic intuition counts these as beliefs with radically different contents. They are beliefs about different men. And what is believed about these dif-ferent men is different as well. Were hither Fodor to believe that our Jimmy Carter was from Yon Georgia, we might well begin to fear for his sanity. So it looks as though a computational taxonomy forces us to treat as type-identical a pair of belief tokens which aboriginal intuition takes to repre-sent quite different states of affairs, and thus to have quite different contents. Nor is this an iso-lated example. Generalizing in one direction, we may consider the beliefs of yet another Fodor-compute-alike, this one on the faroff planet of Elsewhere. Elsewhere Fodor, like his earthly dop-pelganger, sometimes sincerely says "Jimmy Car-ter is from Georgia." But the belief *he* is expressing is yet a third one about yet a third man. General-izing in another dimension, it is obvious that the same story can be told, *mutantis mutandis,* con-cerning almost any belief about persons, places, times, and so forth. What is more, if we share Put-nam's view on natural kind terms we may add be-liefs about natural kinds to this list as well. In fact, there seems to be relatively few examples of a be-lief token whose computational (or formal) equiv-alence class does *not* include members with intui-tively different content. Plus or minus a bit, indeed! (For a more leisurely exposition of the ar-gument of this paragraph, see Stich 1978.)

So much for my first claim, let me turn now to the second. The claim is that the computational theory of mind will find no reason to discriminate against formally individuated state types to which intuition can assign no content at all. Since the editor insists that commentaries be short, I will have to run the argument in a fast and dirty version. (For slow and dirty versions, see Stich 1979, and forthcoming.) The central premise of my argument is an observation that has been made by a number of writers in a number of ways (cf. Quine 1960, Dennett 1969 [ch. 10], Davidson 1975). The observation is this: as a person acquires more and more beliefs which we take to be exotic, it becomes increasingly difficult to specify the content of his beliefs in any intuitively plausible way. Varying explanations have been offered for this phenomenon, and I have my own line to peddle. But there is no room here for a sales pitch. So let us take it simply as a brute fact: the odder the beliefs, the harder it is to assign them a content.

Now to establish the conclusion I am after, we need only conjure the case of a subject whose beliefs are so exotic from our point of view that we simply cannot assign content to them. There are obvious science fiction illustrations of such subjects. We could, for example, start with a robot who is a computational copy of Fodor and gradually fiddle with his store of beliefs. As the changes become greater and greater, we will loose our grip on what it is that the robot believes. There will simply be no way for our aboriginal intuition to assign content to the robot's beliefs. But the assignment of content does no work in a computational theory. So our old computational theory of (Fodor and) the robot, along with an updated account of the symbols stored in the robot's memory, will do just as well at predicting and explaining the robot's behavior. I am inclined to think that there are many non-science-fiction illustrations of the same point. People from exotic cultures and animals are the two most intriguing examples, though both would surely be controversial. If I am right about any of these examples it establishes yet another radical difference between an intuitive, content-based taxonomy of mental states and a taxonomy that accords with the methodological solipsist's formality condition. The formality condition finds distinctions aplenty amongst the computational states of the robot, the Neanderthal and the frog. But to pretheoretic intuition, they all have the same content, that is, none.

There is a certain irony in the fact that a thoroughgoing acceptance of the computational paradigm entails a rejection of the representational theory of the mind. For as Fodor rightly suggests, much of the impetus for computational theories can be traced to a hope that they would do justice to the insights of the representational theory while rebuilding them on firmer foundations. But in science as well as in philosophy it is a venerable tradition to kick away your ladder after you have climbed it.

from "Author's Response"

J. A. FODOR

Stich. Stich's first argument—anticipated in my paper—seems to me to overplay its hand. First off: I take it that intuition is in fact divided on whether or not we have identity of content in these sorts of cases, and that what's dividing it is precisely whether we are feeling the pull of truth theory (*Carter is from Georgia* will differ in truth value depending on where it's uttered) or the pull of psychological theory (the two token beliefs will be indistinguishable in functional role). But, as I remarked in my target article, there is simply nothing to stop us from taxonomizing in different ways for purposes of different theoretical enterprises.

And second off: suppose that, for purposes of doing our psychology, we had to decide identity and difference of content in *highly* counterintuitive ways. That wouldn't be a serious objection to an (independently valued) account unless it could be shown that the way it assigns content is somehow incoherent. And Stich hasn't shown this or even tried to.

The second argument is, I think, considerably more interesting. One could put it like this: you could consistently accept the propriety of explanations of behavior which advert to the causal role of *functionally individuated mental states* while refusing to accept *ascriptions of content to such states*. Indeed, you would perhaps be well advised to do so if you were doing the psychology of creatures with sufficiently exotic views. (Though just what it would mean *simultaneously* to suppose a creature's views to be exotic *and* deny that its mental states have contents is, perhaps, a little unclear.) So, the point would be: given this possibility, what justifies *ever* ascribing content to functionally individuated mental states?

I think the answer is that there are generalizations that we would miss—would be unable to state—were we to fail to make such assignments; generalizations about the ways in which mental states are related *in respect of their contents.* Here is one such generalization, dredged from the very depths of the theory of fixation of belief (i.e., of learning theory): beliefs whose content is that all the *x*s are *F* are often caused by beliefs whose content is that some or other *x* is *F*. There are many other such generalizations: logic can be viewed as (inter alia) formulating a number of them (as **Rey** points out), and so can decision theory, linguistics, and, in fact, every other area of cognitive psychology that has looked remotely like working. I think, in fact, that the following is probably true: we know of *no* generalizations *that are worth reporting* about relations among mental states *except* such generalizations as relate them in respect of their content.

Rather than give up such generalizations under the pressure of outlandish examples, one might take the view that there are (or could be) some organisms of which we are unable to do the psychology; either because they have no psychology (their mental states satisfy functional ascriptions but not ascriptions of content) or because *their* beliefs boggle *our* minds: we can't imagine what it would be like to be that different from us. This will strike philosophical initiates as the crudest sort of metaphysical Realism. Absolutely.

REFERENCES

Chomsky, N. (1959) Review of Skinner's *Verbal Behavior. Language,* 35:26–58.

Davidson, D. (1975) Thought and talk. In: Guttenplan, S. (ed.), *Mind and language.* Oxford: Oxford Univ. Press.

Dennett, D. C. (1969) *Content and consciousness.* London: Routledge and Kegan Paul.

Descartes, R. (1931) *Meditations on first philosophy,* trans. E. S. Haldane and G.R.T. Ross. Cambridge: Cambridge Univ. Press.

Field, H. (1972) Tarski's theory of truth. *Journal of Philosophy* 69:347–375.

Fodor, J. A. (1975) *The language of thought.* New York: Thomas Y. Crowell.

——— (1978) Tom Swift and his procedural grandmother. *Cognition* 6:229–247.

——— (1979) Propositional attitudes. *The Monist* (special issue on philosophy and cognitive psychology), forthcoming.

Geach, P. (1957) *Mental acts.* London: Routledge & Kegan Paul.

Goodman, N. (1978) *Ways of world making.* Indianapolis: Hackett.

James, W. (1890) *Principles of psychology,* vol. I. (repr., New York: Dover, 1950) New York: Henry Holt.

Putnam, H. (1960) Minds and machines. In: Hook, S. (ed.), *Dimensions of mind.* New York: New York Univ. Press.

——— (1975) The meaning of meaning. In: Gundersen, K. (ed.), *Minnesota studies in the philosophy of science. 7. Language, mind and knowledge.* Minneapolis: Univ. of Minnesota Press.

Quine, W.V.O. (1960) *Word and object.* Cambridge, Mass.: MIT Press.

Stich, S. P. (1978) Autonomous psychology and the belief-desire thesis. *The Monist* 61:4.

——— (1979) Do animals have beliefs? *Australasian Journal of Philosophy* 57:1.

——— (forthcoming) On the ascription of content. In: Woodfield, A. (ed.), Mental representation and intentional content.

Winograd, T. (1972) *Understanding natural language.* New York: Academic Press.

54

Daniel C. Dennett

"Brain Writing and Mind Reading"

What are we to make of the popular notion that our brains are somehow libraries of our thoughts and beliefs? Is it *in principle* possible that brain scientists might one day know enough about the workings of our brains to be able to "crack the cerebral code" and read our minds? Philosophers have often rather uncritically conceded that it *is* possible in principle, usually in the context of making some point about privacy or subjectivity.[1] I read Anscombe to deny the possibility. In *Intention*[2] she seems to be arguing that the *only* information about a person that can be brought to bear in a determination of his beliefs or intentions is information about his past and future actions and experiences; a person's beliefs and intentions are whatever they must be to render his behavioral biography coherent, and neurological data could not possibly shed light on this. This is often plausible. Suppose Jack Ruby had tried to defend himself in court by claiming he didn't know (or believe) the gun was loaded. Given even the little we know about his biography, could we even make sense of a neurologist who claimed that he had scientific evidence to confirm Ruby's disclaimer? But in other cases the view is implausible. Sometimes one's biography seems completely compatible with two different ascriptions of belief, so that the Anscombean test of biographical coherence yields no answer. Sam the reputable art critic extols, buys, and promotes mediocre paintings by his son. Two different hypotheses are advanced: (a) Sam does not believe the paintings are any good, but out of

loyalty and love he does this to help his son, or (b) Sam's love for his son has blinded him to the faults of the paintings, and he actually believes they are good. Presumably if (a) were true Sam would deny it to his grave, so his future biography will look the same in either case, and his past history of bigheartedness, we can suppose, fits both hypotheses equally well. I think many of our intuitions support the view that Sam really and objectively had one belief and not the other, and it goes against the grain to accept the Anscombean position that in the absence of telltale behavioral biography there is simply nowhere else to look. Couldn't the brain scientist (in principle) work out the details of Sam's belief mechanisms, discover the *system* the brain uses to store beliefs, and then, using correlations between brain states and Sam's *manifest* beliefs as his Rosetta Stone, extrapolate to Sam's covert beliefs? Having deciphered the brain writing, he could read Sam's mind. (Of course, if we could establish this practice for Sam the art critic, we would have to reopen the case of Jack Ruby, but perhaps, just perhaps, we could then devise a scenario in which neurologists were able to confirm that Ruby was the victim of a series of unlikely but explainable beliefs—as revealed by his "cerebroscope.")

I admit to finding the brain-writing hypothesis tempting,[3] but suspect that it is not coherent at all. I have been so far unable to concoct a proof that it is incoherent, but will raise instead a series of difficulties that seem insuperable to me. First, though, it would be useful to ask just why the view is plausible at all. Why, for instance, is the brain-writing hypothesis more tempting than the hypothesis that on the lining of one's stomach there is a decipherable record of all the meals one has

AUTHOR'S NOTE: Earlier drafts of this paper were read at the University of Maine, Tufts University, and the University of Cincinnati Colloquium on Brain and Mind, November 1971.

From *Minnesota Studies in the Philosophy of Science,* vol. VII, Keith Gunderson, ed. Minneapolis: University of Minnesota Press, 1975, pp. 403–15. Reprinted with permission of the publisher. Postscript: From Daniel C. Dennett, *Brainstorms,* Cambridge Mass.: MIT Press/Bradford Books, 1978, p. 50. Reprinted with permission of Daniel C. Dennett.

ever eaten? Gilbert Harman offers the first few steps of an answer:

> We know that people have beliefs and desires, that beliefs and desires influence action, that interaction with the environment can give rise to new beliefs, and that needs and drives can give rise to desires. Adequate psychological theories must reflect this knowledge and add to it. So adequate models must have states that correspond to beliefs, desires and thoughts such that these states function in the model as psychological states function in the person modeled, and such that they are representational in the way psychological states are representational. Where there is such representation, there is a system of representation; and that system may be identified with the inner language in which a person thinks.
>
> This reduces the claim that there is an inner language, which one thinks in, to the trivial assertion that psychological states have a representational character.[4]

The first point, then, is that human behavior has proven to be of such a nature that the only satisfactory theories will be those in which inner *representations* play a role (though not necessarily a role that is not climinable at another level of theory). Diehard peripheralist behaviorists may still wish to deny this, but that is of concern to historians of science, not us. It is Harman's next point that strikes me as controversial: where there is representation there is system, and this system *may be identified with* a person's inner language. Are all representations bound up in systems? Is *any* system of representations like a language? Enough like a language to make this identification more useful than misleading? Or is Harman's claim rather that whatever sorts of representations there may be, the sorts we need for human psychology must be organized in a system, and this system must be more like the system of a language than not? Assuming Harman's claim survives these questions, we still would not have an argument for the full-fledged brain-writing hypothesis; two more steps are needed. First, we need the claim that these psychological models with their language-style representations must be realized in brainware, not ectoplasm or other ghostly stuff.[5] This ought to be uncontroversial; though psychologists may ignore the details of realization while elaborating and even testing their models, the model-making is ultimately bound by the restriction that any function proposed in a model must be physiologically or mechanically realizable one way or another. Second, it must be claimed that it will be possible to determine the details of such realizations from an empirical examination of the brainware and its causal role in behavior. This second point raises some interesting questions. Could the

functional organization of the brain be so inscrutable from the point of view of the neurophysiologist or other physical scientist that no fixing of the representational role of any part were possible? Could the brain use a system that no outsider could detect? In such a case what would it mean to say the brain used a system? I am not sure how one would go about giving direct answers to these questions, but light can be shed on them, I think, by setting up a crude brain-writing theory and refining it as best we can to meet objections.

Again Harman gives us the first step:

> In a simple model, there might be two places in which representations are stored. Representations of things believed would be stored in one place; representations of things desired in the other. Interaction with the environment would produce new representations that would be stored as beliefs. Needs for food, love, etc., would produce representations to be stored as desires. Inferences could produce changes in both the set of beliefs and the set of desires. (*Ibid.,* p. 34)

No doubt we would also want to distinguish more or less permanent storage (belief and desire) from the more fleeting or occurrent *display* of representations (in perception, during problem solving, sudden thoughts, etc.). In any case we already have enough to set some conditions on the brain-writing hypothesis. Some formulations of it are forbidden us on pain of triviality. For instance, claiming that there is brain writing, but that each representation is written in a different language, is just an oblique way of asserting that there is no brain writing. I think the following six conditions will serve to distinguish genuine brain-writing hypotheses from masqueraders.

(1) The system of representations must have a generative grammar. That is, the system must be such that if you understand the system and know the finite vocabulary you can generate the representations—the sentences of brain writing—you haven't yet examined. Otherwise the language will be unlearnable.[6] Only if there were a generative grammar could the investigator get himself into a position to extrapolate from manifest beliefs and desires to covert beliefs and desires. There need not be a single generative grammar covering all representations, however. Just so long as there is a finite number of different "languages" and "multilingual" functional elements to serve as interpreters, the learnability condition will be met.

(2) Syntactical differences and similarities of the language must be reflected in physical differences and similarities in the brain. That is, the tokens of a syntactical type must be physically distinguishable by finite test from the tokens of other syntactical types. That does not mean that all to-

kens of a type must be physically similar. What physical feature is peculiar to spoken and written tokens of the word "cat"? There must simply be a finite number of physical sorts of token of each type. Tokens and "strings" of tokens may of course align themselves in physical dimensions other than those of natural language. For instance, lexical items might be individuated not by shape but by spatial location, and ordering in the strings might be accomplished not by a sequence in space or time but by degree of electric potential.

(3) Tokens must be physically salient. This is a "practical" point. Tokens might bear physical similarities, but similarities so complex, so diffuse and multidimensional that no general *detection* mechanism could be devised; no frequency filters, stereo-locators, litmus papers, or simple combination of these could be built into a token detector. If tokens turned out not to be physically salient—and this is rather plausible in the light of current research—the brain-writing hypothesis would fail for the relatively humdrum reason that brain writing was illegible. It is worth mentioning only to distinguish it from more important obstacles to the hypothesis.

(4) The representation store must meet Anscombe's condition of biographical coherence. The sentences yielded by our neurocryptographer's radical translation must match well with the subject's manifest beliefs and desires, and with common knowledge. If too many unlikely beliefs or obvious untruths appear in the belief store, we will decide that we have hit upon something strange and marvelous—like finding the Lord's Prayer written in freckles on a man's back—but not his belief store. To give a more plausible example, we might discover that certain features of brain activity could be interpreted as a code yielding detailed and accurate information about the relative tensions of the eye muscles, the orientation of the eyeball, the convexity of the lens, etc., and this might give us great insight into the way the brain controlled the perceptual process, but since a man does not ordinarily have any beliefs about these internal matters, this would not be, except indirectly, a key to his belief store.[7]

(5) There must be a reader or playback mechanism. It must be demonstrated that the physical system in which the brain writing is accomplished is functionally connected in the appropriate ways to the causes of bodily action, and so forth. Of course, if we were to find the cortex written all over with sentences expressing the subject's manifest beliefs, we would be convinced this was no coincidence, but until the operation of the mechanisms that utilized the writing was discovered we would not have a theory. (A person who discovered such

a marvel would be roughly in the same evidential position as a clairvoyant, who (we can imagine) might be able to predict with uncanny accuracy what a person would say, etc., and yet could not be supposed to have any authority—in a court of law, for instance—about a person's beliefs.)

(6) The belief store must be—in the main—consistent. If our translation manual yields sentences like "My brother is an only child" and pairs of sentences like "All dogs are vicious" and "My dog is sweet-tempered" one of several things must be wrong. If the subject declines to assert or assent to these anomalous sentences we will discredit the translation manual (cf. Quine on radical translation); if the man does issue forth with these sentences we will conclude that we have discovered a pathological condition, and our brain-writing system will be viewed as a sort of assent-inducing tumor.[8]

A more graphic way of looking at this point is to ask whether the neurocryptographer could do a bit of tinkering and thereby *insert* a belief in his subject. That is, if he can *read* brain writing he ought to be able to *write* brain writing. Let us suppose we are going to insert in Tom the false belief: "I have an older brother living in Cleveland." Now can the neurocryptographer translate this into brain writing and do a bit of rewiring? Let us suppose he can do any rewiring, as much and as delicate as you wish. This rewiring will either impair Tom's basic rationality or not. Consider the two outcomes. Tom is sitting in a bar and a friend asks "Do you have any brothers or sisters?" Tom says, "Yes, I have an older brother living in Cleveland." "What's his name?" Now what is going to happen? Tom may say "Name? Whose name? Oh, my gosh, what was I saying? I don't have an older brother!" Or he may say, "I don't know his name," and when pressed he will deny all knowledge of this brother, assert things like "I am an only child and have an older brother living in Cleveland." In neither case has our neurocryptographer succeeded in wiring in a new belief. This does not show that wiring in beliefs is impossible, or that brain writing is impossible, but just that one could only wire in one belief by wiring in (indefinitely?) many other cohering beliefs so that neither biographical nor logical coherence is lost.[9]

Now suppose we have a brain-writing theory that meets all of these conditions: we have a storage facility functionally tied to behavior that is somehow administered to preserve logical and biographical coherence, and the mode of storage involves elements having physically salient syntactical parts for which we have a generative grammar. This system is going to take up some room. How much room do we need? Marvin Minsky has an optimistic answer: "One can't find a hundred things that he knows a thousand things about. . . . I therefore feel that a machine will quite critically need to acquire the order of a hundred thousand elements of knowledge in order to behave with reasonable sensibility in ordinary situations. A million, if properly organized, should be enough for a very great intelligence."[10] If Minsky's estimate were realistic, the brain, with its ten billion neurons or trillions of molecules would be up to the task, no doubt. But surely his figure is much too low. For in addition to all the relatively *difficult* facts I have mastered, such as that New York is larger than Boston and salt is sodium chloride, there are all the easy ones we tend to overlook, like New York is not on the moon, or in Venezuela, salt is not sugar, or green, or oily, salt is good on potatoes, on eggs, tweed coats are not made of salt, a grain of salt is smaller than an elephant. . . . Surely I can think of more than a thousand things I know or believe about salt, and salt is not one of a hundred, but one of thousands upon thousands of things I can do this with. Then there is my knowledge of arithmetic; two plus two is four, twenty plus twenty is forty. . . . My beliefs are apparently infinite, which means their storage, however miniaturized, will take up more room than there is in the brain. The objection, of course, seems to point to its own solution: it must be that I *potentially* believe indefinitely many things, but I *generate* all but, say, Minsky's hundred thousand by the activity of an extrapolator-deducer mechanism attached to the core library. So let us attach such a mechanism to our model and see what it looks like.

It has the capacity to extract axioms from the core when the situation demands it and deduce further consequences. If it is to do this, it will need to have an information store of its own, containing information about what items it would be appropriate at any time to retrieve from the core, and, for instance, the metalinguistic information it needs to analyze the contradiction in "all cats are black" and "my cat is brown." Now perhaps it does this by storing the information that what is black is not brown, or maybe *that* information is in the core storage, and the metalinguistic information stored in the extrapolator-deducer mechanism is to the effect that the core element, "what is black is not brown," is relevant to an analysis of the contradiction. Now how will the extrapolator-deducer mechanism store its information? In its own core library of brain-writing sentences? If it has a core library, it will also need an extrapolator-deducer mechanism to act as librarian, and what of *its* information store? Recalling Lewis Carroll's argument in "What the Tortoise Said to Achil-

les,"[11] we can see that the extrapolator-deducer will be hamstrung by a vicious regress if it must always rely on linguistically stored beliefs which it must retrieve and analyze about what can be deduced from what. This a priori point has been "empirically discovered" in the field by more than one frustrated model-builder. As one teams sums it up: ". . . a memory that merely stores *propositions* leads to technological, or organic, monstrosities and frustrates, rather than facilitates inductive operations."[12]

The conclusion is that writing—for instance, brain writing—is a dependent form of information storage. The brain must store at least some of its information in a manner not capturable by a brain-writing model. Could it do without brain writing altogether? I think we can get closer to an answer to this by further refining our basic model of belief.

Representations apparently play roles at many different levels in the operation of the brain. I have already mentioned the possibility of codes representing information about the tension of eye muscles and so forth, and these representations do not fall into the class of our beliefs. At another level there is the information "we use" to accomplish depth perception. Psychophysicists ascribe to us such activities as *analyzing* depth cues and *arriving at conclusions* about distance based on *information we have* about texture gradients, binocular interaction, and so forth. Yet it is nothing conscious that I do in order to perceive depth, and if you ask me what beliefs I have about texture gradients I draw a blank. Closer to home, a child can demonstrate his understanding of addition by reeling off sums without being able to formulate or understand propositions about the commutativity of addition. His performance indicates that he has caught on to commutativity, but should we say that among his beliefs is the belief that addition is commutative? To give one more case, while driving down a familiar road I suddenly am struck by the thought that its aspect has changed—somebody has painted his shutters or a tree has blown down, or something. Do I have a *belief* about how it used to be that grounds my current judgment that it has changed? If so, it is a belief to which I can give no expression and about which I am quite in the dark. Somehow, though, the information is there to be used.

Suppose we partition our information store into the part that is verbally retrievable and the part that is not. I would not want to claim that this separates our beliefs from everything else. Far from it. Our preanalytical notion of belief would permit young children and dumb animals to have beliefs, which must be verbally irretrievable. Perhaps, though, a strong case can be made out that at least our verbally retrievable beliefs are stored in brain writing. The picture that emerges is not, I think, implausible: there are on the one hand those representations that are available for our conscious, personal use and apprehension, and on the other hand those that operate behind the scenes to keep us together. If any representations are stored in brain writing, the former will be, for they are in intimate relation to our natural languages. Included in this group will be the bits of factual knowledge we pick up by asking questions and reading books, especially the facts that only language-users could apprehend, such as the fact that Thanksgiving is always on Thursday. With regard to this group of representations Minsky's figure of a hundred thousand looks more realistic, provided we have an extrapolator-deducer mechanism.[13]

If ever it seems that we are *storing sentences*, it is when we are picking up facts in this verbal manner, but are these things we pick up our beliefs? Sometimes we salt away a sentence because we like the sound of it, or because we will later be rewarded for producing it on demand, or just because it has a sort of staying power in our imagination. In Chekhov's *Three Sisters*, Tchebutykin, reading a journal, mutters: "Balzac was married in Berditchev," and then repeats it, saying he must make a note of it. Then Irina dreamily repeats it: "Balzac was married in Berditchev." Did they acquire a belief on that occasion? Whether *they* did or not, the sentence has stuck in *my* mind, and yet I wouldn't say it was one of my beliefs. I deliberately have not looked it up in the encyclopedia; probably it's true—why would Chekhov insert a distracting falsehood, for mischief? No doubt if someone offered me a thousand dollars if I could tell him where Balzac was married, I'd say Berditchev (wherever that is), but it would be wrong for him to conclude that this was a belief of mine.

If brain writing served only for such storage of words and sentences that we pick up for various reasons, at least we could all breathe a lot easier about the prospects of evil scientists reading our every seditious thought and turning us over to the authorities. Imagine the Loyalty Commissar asking the neurocryptographer if the man in the cerebroscope is a true patriot. "Let's see," says the scientist, "Here is the sentence we've been looking for: 'I pledge allegiance to the flag . . .'" Would finding the sentence, "America's the greatest land of all," satsify the Commissar? I think not.

The matter of verbally retrievable beliefs is in any case more complicated than the picture we've just been examining. Whereas if I am asked who won the Super Bowl in 1969 it does seem a bit as if I am searching for a ready-made sentence to utter in response, in other cases this sort of account does not ring true at all. Suppose I am watching the shell game, intent on which shell the little pea is under. At any moment it seems to be true that I have a belief about where the pea is, and can tell you if you ask, but it does not seem plausible that this is accomplished by a rapid writing and erasing of successive sentences: "now it's left, now it's center, now right" and the flashing on and off of the negation sign in front of "it's under the center shell." For one thing, if asked to give you my perceptual beliefs of a moment I may have to work a bit to formulate them, yet the perceptual representation was what it was before I was asked. The representationality—or intentionality—of something (e.g., a belief or perception) is compatible with its being vague or indeterminate in some respects.[14] The effort of retrieval is often an effort to formulate a sentence that is an approximation of a belief, and we are often distressed at the hard edge of determinacy our verbal output substitutes for the fuzziness of our convictions.

The answer we formulate, the judgment we find an expression for when asked for our belief, is determinate and individuated, because it consists of a specific string of words in our natural language, whether we then speak it aloud or not. *These* representations, not the beliefs to which we have verbal access but the occurrent, datable judgments themselves, have the syntactic parts we have been looking for, and about these the brain-writing hypothesis looks much more workable. Not only are judgments determinate; they are, as Harman has pointed out, lexically and syntactically unambiguous.[15] If it occurs to me that our mothers bore us, I know for sure whether I am thinking of birth or ennui. So it is proper to view a judgment not as a sentence simpliciter but as a deep structure or sentence under an analysis. Judgments, unlike beliefs, occur one at a time; we have at any moment indefinitely many beliefs, but can be thinking just one thought. We saw that the brain-writing hypothesis with regard to storage of beliefs did not really effect any economies of design, because however systematic and efficient one's grammar is, one still needs infinite space to store infinitely many tokens, but with regard to representation of judgments the situation is different. A finite mechanism incorporating a generative grammar would be an efficient means of representing, one at a time, any of an infinite set of propositions.

The interesting thing abut judgments is that although each of us is authoritative about the *content* of his judgments and although each of us is authoritative about his sincerity or lack of sincerity in giving outward verbal expression of a judgment, we are not in a privileged position when it comes to the question of whether our judgments are reliable indicators of our beliefs.[16] Normally there is harmony between our judgments and our behavior, and hence between our judgments and our beliefs, but when we are afflicted by Sartre's *mauvaise foi,* our sincerest judgments can be lies about our beliefs. I may judge to myself that a man is innocent, while believing him guilty.

This suggests that even if we were to discover a brain-writing system that represented our judgments, the mind reading that could be accomplished by exploiting the discovery would not uncover our beliefs. To return to the case of Sam the art critic, if our neurocryptographer were able to determine that Sam's last *judgment* on his deathbed was "My consolation is that I fathered a great artist," we could still hold that the issue between the warring hypotheses was undecided, for this judgment may be a self-deception. But at this point I think we are entitled to question the intuition that inspired the search for brain writing in the first place. If discovering a man's judgments still left the matter of belief ascription undecided, and if in fact either ascription of belief will account for, explain, predict Sam's behavior as well as the other, are we so sure that Sam determinately had one belief or the other? Are we sure there is a difference between his really and truly believing his son is a good artist, and his deceiving himself out of love while knowing the truth in his heart of hearts? If there were brain writing, of course, there would have to be a physical difference between these two cases, but now, what reasons do we have for supposing there is brain writing?

We are thrown back on our conviction that the brain must be an organ that *represents,* but I hope it is no longer obvious that the brain must represent in sentences. In fact we know that at least some of the representation must be accomplished in some more fundamental way. Must there be a system for such representation? I cannot yet see that there must. In particular, I cannot yet see that there must be a *learnable* system, in Davidson's sense, for it is not clear to me that the brain must—or can—learn (the way a child learns a language) its own ways of representing. Certainly information can be transmitted by means of unlearnable languages. Consider a string of nine light bulbs in a row; there are 512 different patterns of lit and unlit bulbs possible in this array, and so we can use the array to transmit the natural numbers from 0 to 511. There are all sorts of systems one might use to assign patterns to numbers. An obvious and efficient one would be binary notations: 000000001 is 1, 000000010 is 2, and so forth. Once a person knows the system he can generate the numbers he hasn't yet observed, but suppose

instead of using this or any other system, the patterns are assigned numbers randomly; a random assignment will carry the information just as well; the outsider will simply not be in a position to predict the balance of the assignments, having learned some of them. Can the brain "use" information carried by unlearnable systems? At some levels of "coding" it obviously does—where the "codes" carry very specific and limited information. In general can the brain get along without learnable representation systems? Until we can say a lot more about what it is for a system to use representations, I for one cannot see how to answer this question. If the answer is no, then there must be brain writing, but how it overcomes the difficulties I have raised here is beyond me. If the answer is yes, then the only way translation of representation can be accomplished is "sentence by sentence," assigning meaning to representations by determining their functional role in the behavior of the whole system. But where competing translations are behaviorally indistinguishable, the content of the representation will be indeterminate.

NOTES

1. See, in another context, A. I. Melden's use of the notion in *Free Action* (New York: Humanities, 1961), pp. 211–215.

2. G.E.M. Anscombe, *Intention* (2nd ed.; Oxford: Blackwell, 1963).

3. I claimed it was a distinct possibility with regard to intentions in "Features of Intentional Actions," *Philosophy and Phenomenological Research,* 29 (1968):232–244.

4. "Language Learning," *Nous,* 4 (1970):35. See also his "Three Levels of Meaning," *Journal of Philosophy,* 65 (1968):590–602, esp. p. 598.

5. Cf. Wilfrid Sellars, "Notes on Intentionality," *Journal of Philosophy,* 61(1964):663, where he discusses mental acts as tokens expressing propositions, and claims that all tokens must be *sorts* of tokens and must have a determinate factual character, and proposes identifying them with neurophysiological episodes.

6. See Donald Davidson, "Theories of Meaning and Learnable Languages," in Y. Bar-Hillel, ed., *Logic, Methodology, and Philosophy of Science* (Amsterdam: North-Holland, 1965), pp. 383–394.

7. Discovering such a code is not establishing that the information the code carries for the scientist is also carried for the person or even for his brain. D. H. Perkel and T. H. Bullock, in "Neural Coding" (in F. Schmitt, T. Melnechuk, et al., eds., *Neurosciences Research Symposium Summaries,* vol. 3 [Cambridge, Mass.: M.I.T. Press, 1969]), discuss the discovery of a code "carrying" phasic information about wing position in the locust; it is accurately coded, but the "insect apparently makes no use of this information." (Blocking this input and substituting random input produces no loss of flying rhythm, ability, etc.)

8. This condition of rationality has some slack in it. We do permit some small level of inconsistency, but large-scale illogicality must be indicative of either a defect in the subject so serious as to disqualify him as a believer at all, or a defect in our translation hypotheses. See my "Intentional Systems," *Journal of Philosophy,* 68(1971):87–106.

9. I examine this case more fully in "Mechanism and Responsibility," in Ted Honderich, ed., *Essays on Freedom of Action* (London: Routledge and Kegan Paul, 1973), pp. 157–184. Joan Straumanis has pointed out to me that there is some experimental evidence that suggests that another outcome of the rewiring experiment could be that Tom spontaneously and unconsciously fabricates a web of cohering beliefs to "protect" the inserted belief and his others from each other (a sort of pearl-in-the-oyster effect).

10. M. L. Minsky, ed., *Semantic Information Processing* (Cambridge, Mass.: M.I.T. Press, 1968), p. 26.

11. *Mind* (1895), reprinted in I. M. Copi and J. A. Gould, eds., *Readings on Logic* (New York: Macmillan, 1964). Harman offers a similar argument in "Psychological

Aspects of the Theory of Syntax," *Journal of Philosohy,* 64(1967):75–87.

12. H. von Foerster, A. Inselberg, and P. Weston, "Memory and Inductive Inference," in H. L. Oestreicher and D. R. Moore, eds., *Cybernetic Problems in Bionics* (New York: Gordon and Breach, 1968).

13. Minsky's anthology, *Semantic Information Processing,* is a collection of several brilliant attempts to provide working models for just such question-answering, extrapolating systems. It is a gold mine of philosophically tantalizing suggestions and problems.

14. See G.E.M. Anscombe, "The Intentionality of Sensation: A Grammatical Feature," in R. J. Butler, ed., *Analytical Philosophy, Second Series* (Oxford: Blackwell, 1965).

15. "Language Learning."

16. See John Vickers, "Judgment and Belief," in K. Lambert, ed., *The Logical Way of Doing Things* (New Haven, Conn.: Yale University Press, 1969), and A. W. Collins, "Unconscious Belief," *Journal of Philosophy,* 66(1969):667–680.

Postscript, 1978

In the seven years since this essay was written many books and articles have appeared dealing with the nature of mental representation. Compared with the models discussed today, the model described here is naive, but the conclusions I draw from it can still be drawn from today's sophisticated models, though less obviously. It has become clearer in recent years that strictly "propositional" data-structures lack the powers required to serve as models of the fundamental "mental representations", but few uncontroversial assertions can be made about the structure or function of non-propositional or quasi-propositional representations. The trade-off between storing information in "compiled" or "propositional" or "coded" form, and storing it "tacitly" in the organization of the representational system, has been fruitfully explored by people in artificial intelligence and cognitive psychology. Discussions of these developments are found in Chapters 6, 7 and 9 [in Dennett's *Brainstorms:* "A Cure for the Common Code," "Artificial Intelligence as Philosophy and as Psychology," and "Toward a Cognitive Theory of Consciousness"].

55

John R. Searle

"Minds, Brains, and Programs"

Plus commentary by J. A. Fodor, and Searle's response

What psychological and philosophical significance should we attach to recent efforts at computer simulations of human cognitive capacities? In answering this question, I find it useful to distinguish what I will call "strong" AI from "weak" or "cautious" AI (Artificial Intelligence). According to weak AI, the principal value of the computer in the study of the mind is that it gives us a very powerful tool. For example, it enables us to formulate and test hypotheses in a more rigorous and precise fashion. But according to strong AI, the computer is not merely a tool in the study of the mind; rather, the appropriately programmed computer really *is* a mind, in the sense that computers given the right programs can be literally said to *understand* and have other cognitive states. In strong AI, because the programmed computer has cognitive states, the programs are not mere tools that enable us to test psychological explanations; rather, the programs are themselves the explanations.

I have no objection to the claims of weak AI, at least as far as this article is concerned. My discussion here will be directed at the claims I have defined as those of strong AI, specifically the claim that the appropriately programmed computer literally has cognitive states and that the programs thereby explain human cognition. When I hereafter refer to AI, I have in mind the strong version, as expressed by these two claims.

I will consider the work of Roger Schank and his colleagues at Yale (Schank & Abelson 1977), because I am more familiar with it than I am with

any other similar claims, and because it provides a very clear example of the sort of work I wish to examine. But nothing that follows depends upon the details of Schank's programs. The same arguments would apply to Winograd's SHRDLU (Winograd 1973), Weizenbaum's ELIZA (Weizenbaum 1965), and indeed any Turing machine simulation of human mental phenomena.

Very briefly, and leaving out the various details, one can describe Schank's program as follows: the aim of the program is to simulate the human ability to understand stories. It is characteristic of human beings' story-understanding capacity that they can answer questions about the story even though the information that they give was never explicitly stated in the story. Thus, for example, suppose you are given the following story: "A man went into a restaurant and ordered a hamburger. When the hamburger arrived it was burned to a crisp, and the man stormed out of the restaurant angrily, without paying for the hamburger or leaving a tip." Now, if you are asked "Did the man eat the hamburger?" you will presumably answer, "No, he did not." Similarly, if you are given the following story: "A man went into a restaurant and ordered a hamburger; when the hamburger came he was very pleased with it; and as he left the restaurant he gave the waitress a large tip before paying his bill," and you are asked the question, "Did the man eat the hamburger?", you will presumably answer, "Yes, he ate the hamburger." Now Schank's machines can similarly answer

"Minds, Brains, and Programs," "Intrinsic Intentionality and Observer-Relative Ascriptions of Intentionality," and "Fodor," by John R. Searle, and "Searle on What Only Brains Can Do," by J. A. Fodor, from *The Behavioral and Brain Sciences* III, 3 (September 1980): 417–24, 431–32 (Fodor), 451–52, and 454. Copyright © 1980 by Cambridge University Press. Reprinted with permission of the editor, Cambridge University Press, John R. Searle, and Jerry A. Fodor. Fodor's "After-thoughts: Yin and Yang in the Chinese Room" and Searle's "Yin and Yang Strike Out" appear here for the first time.

questions about restaurants in this fashion. To do this, they have a "representation" of the sort of information that human beings have about restaurants, which enables them to answer such questions as those above, given these sorts of stories. When the machine is given the story and then asked the question, the machine will print out answers of the sort that we would expect human beings to give if told similar stories. Partisans of strong AI claim that in this question and answer sequence the machine is not only simulating a human ability but also

1. that the machine can literally be said to *understand* the story and provide the answers to questions, and
2. that what the machine and its program do *explains* the human ability to understand the story and answer questions about it.

Both claims seem to me to be totally unsupported by Schank's[1] work, as I will attempt to show in what follows.

One way to test any theory of the mind is to ask oneself what it would be like if my mind actually worked on the principles that the theory says all minds work on. Let us apply this test to the Schank program with the following *Gedankenexperiment.* Suppose that I'm locked in a room and given a large batch of Chinese writing. Suppose furthermore (as is indeed the case) that I know no Chinese, either written or spoken, and that I'm not even confident that I could recognize Chinese writing as Chinese writing distinct from, say, Japanese writing or meaningless squiggles. To me, Chinese writing is just so many meaningless squiggles. Now suppose further that after this first batch of Chinese writing I am given a second batch of Chinese script together with a set of rules for correlating the second batch with the first batch. The rules are in English, and I understand these rules as well as any other native speaker of English. They enable me to correlate one set of formal symbols with another set of formal symbols, and all that "formal" means here is that I can identify the symbols entirely by their shapes. Now suppose also that I am given a third batch of Chinese symbols together with some instructions, again in English, that enable me to correlate elements of this third batch with the first two batches, and these rules instruct me how to give back certain Chinese symbols with certain sorts of shapes in response to certain sorts of shapes given me in the third batch. Unknown to me, the people who are giving me all of these symbols call the first batch "a script," they call the second batch a "story," and they call the third batch "questions." Furthermore, they call the symbols I give them back in response to the third batch "an-

swers to the questions," and the set of rules in English that they gave me, they call "the program." Now just to complicate the story a little, imagine that these people also give me stories in English, which I understand, and they then ask me questions in English about these stories, and I give them back answers in English. Suppose also that after a while I get so good at following the instructions for manipulating the Chinese symbols and the programmers get so good at writing the programs that from the external point of view—that is, from the point of view of somebody outside the room in which I am locked—my answers to the questions are absolutely indistinguishable from those of native Chinese speakers. Nobody just looking at my answers can tell that I don't speak a word of Chinese. Let us also suppose that my answers to the English questions are, as they no doubt would be, indistinguishable from those of other native English speakers, for the simple reason that I am a native English speaker. From the external point of view—from the point of view of someone reading my "answers"—the answers to the Chinese questions and the English questions are equally good. But in the Chinese case, unlike the English case, I produce the answers by manipulating uninterpreted formal symbols. As far as the Chinese is concerned, I simply behave like a computer; I perform computational operations on formally specified elements. For the purposes of the Chinese, I am simply an instantiation of the computer program.

Now the claims made by strong AI are that the programmed computer understands the stories and that the program in some sense explains human understanding. But we are now in a position to examine these claims in light of our thought experiment.

1. As regards the first claim, it seems to me quite obvious in the example that I do not understand a word of the Chinese stories. I have inputs and outputs that are indistinguishable from those of the native Chinese speaker, and I can have any formal program you like, but I still understand nothing. For the same reasons, Schank's computer understands nothing of any stories, whether in Chinese, English, or whatever, since in the Chinese case the computer is me, and in cases where the computer is not me, the computer has nothing more than I have in the case where I understand nothing.

2. As regards the second claim, that the program explains human understanding, we can see that the computer and its program do not provide sufficient conditions of understanding since the computer and the program are functioning, and there is no understanding. But does it even provide

a necessary condition or a significant contribution to understanding? One of the claims made by the supporters of strong AI is that when I understand a story in English, what I am doing is exactly the same—or perhaps more of the same—as what I was doing in manipulating the Chinese symbols. It is simply more formal symbol manipulation that distinguishes the case in English, where I do understand, from the case in Chinese, where I don't. I have not demonstrated that this claim is false, but it would certainly appear an incredible claim in the example. Such plausibility as the claim has derives from the supposition that we can construct a program that will have the same inputs and outputs as native speakers, and in addition we assume that speakers have some level of description where they are also instantiations of a program. On the basis of these two assumptions we assume that even if Schank's program isn't the whole story about understanding, it may be part of the story. Well, I suppose that is an empirical possibility, but not the slightest reason has so far been given to believe that it is true, since what is suggested—though certainly not demonstrated—by the example is that the computer program is simply irrelevant to my understanding of the story. In the Chinese case I have everything that artificial intelligence can put into me by way of a program, and I understand nothing; in the English case I understand everything, and there is so far no reason at all to suppose that my understanding has anything to do with computer programs, that is, with computational operations on purely formally specified elements. As long as the program is defined in terms of computational operations on purely formally defined elements, what the example suggests is that these by themselves have no interesting connection with understanding. They are certainly not sufficient conditions, and not the slightest reason has been given to suppose that they are necessary conditions or even that they make a significant contribution to understanding. Notice that the force of the argument is not simply that different machines can have the same input and output while operating on different formal principles—that is not the point at all. Rather, whatever purely formal principles you put into the computer, they will not be sufficient for understanding, since a human will be able to follow the formal principles without understanding anything. No reason whatever has been offered to suppose that such principles are necessary or even contributory, since no reason has been given to suppose that when I understand English I am operating with any formal program at all.

Well, then, what is it that I have in the case of the English sentences that I do not have in the case of the Chinese sentences? The obvious answer is that I know what the former mean, while I haven't the faintest idea what the latter mean. But in what does this consist and why couldn't we give it to a machine, whatever it is? I will return to this question later, but first I want to continue with the example.

I have had the occasions to present this example to several workers in artificial intelligence, and, interestingly, they do not seem to agree on what the proper reply to it is. I get a surprising variety of replies, and in what follows I will consider the most common of these (specified along with their geographic origins).

But first I want to block some common misunderstandings about "understanding": in many of these discussions one finds a lot of fancy footwork about the word "understanding." My critics point out that there are many different degrees of understanding; that "understanding" is not a simple two-place predicate; that there are even different kinds and levels of understanding, and often the law of excluded middle doesn't even apply in a straightforward way to statements of the form "x understands y"; that in many cases it is a matter for decision and not a simple matter of fact whether x understands y; and so on. To all of these points I want to say: of course, of course. But they have nothing to do with the points at issue. There are clear cases in which "understanding" literally applies and clear cases in which it does not apply; and these two sorts of cases are all I need for this argument.[2] I understand stories in English; to a lesser degree I can understand stories in French; to a still lesser degree, stories in German; and in Chinese, not at all. My car and my adding machine, on the other hand, understand nothing: they are not in that line of business. We often attribute "understanding" and other cognitive predicates by metaphor and analogy to cars, adding machines, and other artifacts, but nothing is proved by such attributions. We say, "The door knows when to open because of its photoelectric cell," "The adding machine knows how (understands how, is able) to do addition and subtraction but not division," and "The thermostat perceives changes in the temperature." The reason we make these attributions is quite interesting, and it has to do with the fact that in artifacts we extend our own intentionality,[3] our tools are extensions of our purposes, and so we find it natural to make metaphorical attributions of intentionality to them; but I take it no philosophical ice is cut by such examples. The sense in which an automatic door "understands instructions" from its photoelectric cell is not at all the sense in which I understand English. If the sense in which Schank's programmed computers understand stories is supposed to be the metaphorical sense in which the door understands, and not the sense in which I understand English, the issue would not be worth discussing. But Newell and Simon (1963) write that the kind of cognition they claim for computers is exactly the same as for human beings. I like the straightforwardness of this claim, and it is the sort of claim I will be considering. I will argue that in the literal sense the programmed computer understands what the car and the adding machine understand, namely, exactly nothing. The computer understanding is not just (like my understanding of German) partial or incomplete; it is zero.

Now to the replies:

I. The systems reply (Berkeley). "While it is true that the individual person who is locked in the room does not understand the story, the fact is that he is merely part of a whole system, and the system does understand the story. The person has a large ledger in front of him in which are written the rules, he has a lot of scratch paper and pencils for doing calculations, he has 'data banks' of sets of Chinese symbols. Now, understanding is not being ascribed to the mere individual; rather it is being ascribed to this whole system of which he is a part."

My response to the systems theory is quite simple: let the individual internalize all of these elements of the system. He memorizes the rules in the ledger and the data banks of Chinese symbols, and he does all the calculations in his head. The individual then incorporates the entire system. There isn't anything at all to the system that he does not encompass. We can even get rid of the room and suppose he works outdoors. All the same, he understands nothing of the Chinese, and a fortiori neither does the system, because there isn't anything in the system that isn't in him. If he doesn't understand, then there is no way the system could understand because the system is just a part of him.

Actually I feel somewhat embarrassed to give even this answer to the systems theory because the theory seems to me so unplausible to start with. The idea is that while a person doesn't understand Chinese, somehow the *conjunction* of that person and bits of paper might understand Chinese. It is not easy for me to imagine how someone who was not in the grip of an ideology would find the idea at all plausible. Still, I think many people who are committed to the ideology of strong AI will in the end be inclined to say something very much like this; so let us pursue it a bit further. According to one version of this view, while the man in the internalized systems example doesn't understand Chinese in the sense that a native Chinese speaker does (because, for example, he doesn't know that the story refers to restaurants and hamburgers, etc.), still "the man as a formal symbol manipulation system" *really does understand Chinese.* The subsystem of the man that is the formal symbol manipulation system for Chinese should not be confused with the subsystem for English.

So there are really two subsystems in the man; one understands English, the other Chinese, and "it's just that the two systems have little to do with each other." But, I want to reply, not only do they have little to do with each other, they are not even remotely alike. The subsystem that understands English (assuming we allow ourselves to talk in this jargon of "subsystems" for a moment) knows that the stories are about restaurants and eating hamburgers, he knows that he is being asked questions about restaurants and that he is answering questions as best he can by making various inferences from the content of the story, and so on. But the Chinese system knows none of this. Whereas the English subsystem knows that "hamburgers" refers to hamburgers, the Chinese subsystem knows only that "squiggle squiggle" is followed by "squoggle squoggle." All he knows is that various formal symbols are being introduced at one end and manipulated according to rules written in English, and other symbols are going out at the other end. The whole point of the original example was to argue that such symbol manipulation by itself couldn't be sufficient for understanding Chinese in any literal sense because the man could write "squoggle squoggle" after "squiggle squiggle" without understanding anything in Chinese. And it doesn't meet that argument to postulate subsystems within the man, because the subsystems are no better off than the man was in the first place; they still don't have anything even remotely like what the English-speaking man (or subsystem) has. Indeed, in the case as described, the Chinese subsystem is simply a part of the English subsystem, a part that engages in meaningless symbol manipulation according to rules in English.

Let us ask ourselves what is supposed to motivate the systems reply in the first place; that is, what *independent* grounds are there supposed to be for saying that the agent must have a subsystem within him that literally understands stories in Chinese? As far as I can tell the only grounds are that in the example I have the same input and output as native Chinese speakers and a program that goes from one to the other. But the whole point of the examples has been to try to show that that couldn't be sufficient for understanding, in the sense in which I understand stories in English, because a person, and hence the set of systems that go to make up a person, could have the right combination of input, output, and program and still not understand anything in the relevant literal sense in which I understand English. The only motivation for saying there *must* be a subsystem in me that understands Chinese is that I have a program and I can pass the Turing test; I can fool native Chinese speakers. But precisely one of the points at issue is the adequacy of the Turing test. The example shows that there could be two "systems," both of which pass the Turing test, but only one of which understands; and it is no argument against this point to say that since they both pass the Turing test they must both understand, since this claim fails to meet the argument that the system in me that understands English has a great deal more than the system that merely processes Chinese. In short, the systems reply simply begs the question by insisting without argument that the system must understand Chinese.

Furthermore, the systems reply would appear to lead to consequences that are independently absurd. If we are to conclude that there must be cognition in me on the grounds that I have a certain sort of input and output and a program in between, then it looks like all sorts of noncognitive subsystems are going to turn out to be cognitive. For example, there is a level of description at which my stomach does information processing, and it instantiates any number of computer programs, but I take it we do not want to say that it has any understanding [cf. Pylyshyn: "Computation and Cognition" *BBS* 3(1) 1980]. But if we accept the systems reply, then it is hard to see how we avoid saying that stomach, heart, liver, and so on, are all understanding subsystems, since there is no principled way to distinguish the motivation for saying the Chinese subsystem understands from saying that the stomach understands. It is, by the way, not an answer to this point to say that the Chinese system has information as input and output and the stomach has food and food products as input and output since from the point of view of the agent, from my point of view, there is no information in either the food or the Chinese—the Chinese is just so many meaningless squiggles. The information in the Chinese case is solely in the eyes of the programmers and the interpreters, and there is nothing to prevent them from treating the input and output of my digestive organs as information if they so desire.

This last point bears on some independent problems in strong AI, and it is worth digressing for a moment to explain it. If strong AI is to be a branch of psychology, then it must be able to dis-tinguish those systems that are genuinely mental from those that are not. It must be able to distinguish the princples on which the mind works from those on which nonmental systems work; otherwise it will offer us no explanations of what is specifically mental about the mental. And the mental–nonmental distinction cannot be just in the eye of the beholder but it must be intrinsic to the systems; otherwise it would be up to any beholder to treat people as nonmental and, for example, hurricanes as mental if he likes. But quite often in the AI literature the distinction is blurred in ways that would in the long run prove diastrous to the claim that AI is a cognitive inquiry. McCarthy, for example, writes, "Machines as simple as thermostats can be said to have beliefs, and having beliefs seems to be a characteristic of most machines capable of problem solving performance" (McCarthy 1979). Anyone who thinks strong AI has a chance as a theory of the mind ought to ponder the implications of that remark. We are asked to accept it as a discovery of strong AI that the hunk of metal on the wall that we use to regulate the temperature has beliefs in exactly the same sense that we, our spouses, and our children have beliefs, and furthermore that "most" of the other machines in the room—telephone, tape recorder, adding machine, electric light switch,—also have beliefs in this literal sense. It is not the aim of this article to argue against McCarthy's point, so I will simply assert the following without argument. The study of the mind starts with such facts as that humans have beliefs, while thermostats, telephones, and adding machines don't. If you get a theory that denies this point you have produced a counterexample to the theory and the theory is false. One gets the impression that people in AI who write this sort of thing think they can get away with it because they don't really take it seriously, and they don't think anyone else will either. I propose for a moment at least, to take it seriously. Think hard for one minute about what would be necessary to establish that that hunk of metal on the wall over there had real beliefs, beliefs with direction of fit, propositional content, and conditions of satisfaction; beliefs that had the possibility of being strong beliefs or weak beliefs; nervous, anxious, or secure beliefs; dogmatic, rational, or superstitious beliefs; blind faiths or hesitant cogitations; any kind of beliefs. The thermostat is not a candidate. Neither is stomach, liver, adding machine, or telephone. However, since we are taking the idea seriously, notice that its truth would be fatal to strong AI's claim to be a science of the mind. For now the mind is everywhere. What we wanted to know is what distinguishes the mind from thermostats and livers. And if McCarthy were right, strong AI wouldn't have a hope of telling us that.

II. The Robot Reply (Yale). "Suppose we wrote a different kind of program from Schank's program. Suppose we put a computer inside a robot, and this computer would not just take in formal symbols as input and give out formal symbols as output, but rather would actually operate the robot in such a way that the robot does something very much like perceiving, walking, moving about, hammering nails, eating, drinking—anything you like. The robot would, for example, have a television camera attached to it that enabled it to 'see,' it would have arms and legs that enabled it to 'act,' and all of this would be controlled by its computer 'brain.' Such a robot would, unlike Schank's computer, have genuine understanding and other mental states."

The first thing to notice about the robot reply is that it tacitly concedes that cognition is not solely a matter of formal symbol manipulation, since this reply adds a set of causal relation with the outside world [cf. Fodor: "Methodological Solipsism" *BBS* 3(1) 1980]. But the answer to the robot reply is that the addition of such "perceptual" and "motor" capacities adds nothing by way of understanding, in particular, or intentionality, in general, to Schank's original program. To see this, notice that the same thought experiment applies to the robot case. Suppose that instead of the computer inside the robot, you put me inside the room and, as in the original Chinese case, you give me more Chinese symbols with more instructions in English for matching Chinese symbols to Chinese symbols and feeding back Chinese symbols to the outside. Suppose, unknown to me, some of the Chinese symbols that come to me come from a television camera attached to the robot and other Chinese symbols that I am giving out serve to make the motors inside the robot move the robot's legs or arms. It is important to emphasize that all I am doing is manipulating formal symbols: I know none of these other facts. I am receiving "information" from the robot's "perceptual" apparatus, and I am giving out "instructions" to its motor apparatus without knowing either of these facts. I am the robot's homunculus, but unlike the traditional homunculus, I don't know what's going on. I don't understand anything except the rules for symbol manipulation. Now in this case I want to say that the robot has no intentional states at all; it is simply moving about as a result of its electrical wiring and its program. And furthermore, by instantiating the program I have no intentional states of the relevant type. All I do is follow formal instructions about manipulating formal symbols.

III. The brain simulator reply (Berkeley and M.I.T.). "Suppose we design a program that doesn't represent information that we have about the world, such as the information in Schank's scripts, but simulates the actual sequence of neuron firings at the synapses of the brain of a native Chinese speaker when he understands stories in Chinese and gives answers to them. The machine takes in Chinese stories and questions about them as input, it simulates the formal structure of actual Chinese brains in processing these stories, and it gives out Chinese answers as outputs. We can even imagine that the machine operates, not with a single serial program, but with a whole set of programs operating in parallel, in the manner that actual human brains presumably operate when they process natural language. Now surely in such a case we would have to say that the machine understood the stories; and if we refuse to say that, wouldn't we also have to deny that native Chinese speakers understood the stories? At the level of the synapses, what would or could be different about the program of the computer and the program of the Chinese brain?"

Before countering this reply I want to digress to note that it is an odd reply for any partisan of artificial intelligence (or functionalism, etc.) to make: I thought the whole idea of strong AI is that we don't need to know how the brain works to know how the mind works. The basic hypothesis, or so I had supposed, was that there is a level of mental operations consisting of computational processes over formal elements that constitute the essence of the mental and can be realized in all sorts of different brain processes, in the same way that any computer program can be realized in different computer hardwares: on the assumptions of strong AI, the mind is to the brain as the program is to the hardware, and thus we can understand the mind without doing neurophysiology. If we had to know how the brain worked to do AI, we wouldn't bother with AI. However, even getting this close to the operation of the brain is still not sufficient to produce understanding. To see this, imagine that instead of a monolingual man in a room shuffling symbols we have the man operate an elaborate set of water pipes with valves connecting them. When the man receives the Chinese symbols, he looks up in the program, written in English, which valves he has to turn on and off. Each water connection corresponds to a synapse in the Chinese brain, and the whole system is rigged up so that after doing all the right firings, that is after turning on all the right faucets, the Chinese answers pop out at the output end of the series of pipes.

Now where is the understanding in this system? It takes Chinese as input, it simulates the formal structure of the synapses of the Chinese brain, and it gives Chinese as output. But the man certainly doesn't understand Chinese, and neither do the water pipes, and if we are tempted to adopt what I think is the absurd view that somehow the *conjunction* of man *and* water pipes understands, remember that in principle the man can internalize the formal structure of the water pipes and do all the "neuron firings" in his imagination. The problem with the brain simulator is that it is simulating the wrong things about the brain. As long as it simulates only the formal structure of the sequence of neuron firings at the synapses, it won't have simulated what matters about the brain, namely its causal properties, its ability to produce intentional states. And that the formal properties are not sufficient for the causal properties is shown by the water pipe example: we can have all the formal properties carved off from the relevant neurobiological causal properties.

IV. The combination reply (Berkeley and Stanford). "While each of the previous three replies might not be completely convincing by itself as a refutation of the Chinese room counterexample, if you take all three together they are collectively much more convincing and even decisive. Imagine a robot with a brain-shaped computer lodged in its cranial cavity, imagine the computer programmed with all the synapses of a human brain, imagine the whole behavior of the robot is indistinguishable from human behavior, and now think of the whole thing as a unified system and not just as a computer with inputs and outputs. Surely in such a case we would have to ascribe intentionality to the system."

I entirely agree that in such a case we would find it rational and indeed irresistible to accept the hypothesis that the robot had intentionality, as long as we knew nothing more about it. Indeed, besides appearance and behavior, the other elements of the combination are really irrelevant. If we could build a robot whose behavior was indistinguishable over a large range from human behavior, we would attribute intentionality to it, pending some reason not to. We wouldn't need to know in advance that its computer brain was a formal analogue of the human brain.

But I really don't see that this is any help to the claims of strong AI; and here's why: According to strong AI, instantiating a formal program with the right input and output is a sufficient condition of, indeed is constitutive of, intentionality. As Newell (1979) puts it, the essence of the mental is the operation of a physical symbol system. But the attributions of intentionality that we make to the robot in this example have nothing to do with formal programs. They are simply based on the assumption that if the robot looks and behaves sufficiently like us, then we would suppose, until proven otherwise, that it must have mental states like ours that cause and are expressed by its behavior and it must have an inner mechanism capable of producing such mental states. If we knew independently how to account for its behavior without such assumptions we would not attribute intentionality to it, especially if we knew it had a formal program. And this is precisely the point of my earlier reply to objection II.

Suppose we knew that the robot's behavior was entirely accounted for by the fact that a man inside it was receiving uninterpreted formal symbols from the robot's sensory receptors and sending out uninterpreted formal symbols to its motor mechanisms, and the man was doing this symbol manipulation in accordance with a bunch of rules. Furthermore, suppose the man knows none of these facts about the robot, all he knows is which operations to perform on which meaningless symbols. In such a case we would regard the robot as an ingenious mechanical dummy. The hypothesis that the dummy has a mind would now be unwarranted and unnecessary, for there is now no longer any reason to ascribe intentionality to the robot or to the system of which it is a part (except of course for the man's intentionality in manipulating the symbols). The formal symbol manipulations go on, the input and output are correctly matched, but the only real locus of intentionality is the man, and he doesn't know any of the relevant intentional states; he doesn't, for example, *see* what comes into the robot's eyes, he doesn't *intend* to move the robot's arm, and he doesn't *understand* any of the remarks made to or by the robot. Nor, for the reasons stated earlier, does the system of which man and robot are a part.

To see this point, contrast this case with cases in which we find it completely natural to ascribe intentionality to members of certain other primate species such as apes and monkeys and to domestic animals such as dogs. The reasons we find it natural are, roughly, two: we can't make sense of the animal's behavior without the ascription of intentionality, and we can see that the beasts are made of similar stuff to ourselves—that is an eye, that a nose, this is its skin, and so on. Given the coherence of the animal's behavior and the assumption of the same causal stuff underlying it, we assume both that the animal must have mental states underlying its behavior, and that the mental states must be produced by mechanisms made out of the stuff that is like our stuff. We would certainly make similar assumptions about the robot unless we had some reason not to, but as soon as we knew that the behavior was the result of a formal program, and that the actual causal properties of the physical substance were irrelevant we would abandon the assumption of intentionality. [See "Cognition and Consciousness in Nonhuman Species" *BBS* I(4) 1978.]

There are two other responses to my example that come up frequently (and so are worth discussing) but really miss the point.

V. The other minds reply (Yale). "How do you know that other people understand Chinese or anything else? Only by their behavior. Now the computer can pass the behavioral tests as well as they can (in principle), so if you are going to attribute cognition to other people you must in principle also attribute it to computers."

This objection really is only worth a short reply. The problem in this discussion is not about how I know that other people have cognitive states, but rather what it is that I am attributing to them when I attribute cognitive states to them. The thrust of the argument is that it couldn't be just computational processes and their output because the computational processes and their output can exist without the cognitive state. It is no answer to this argument to feign anesthesia. In "cognitive sciences" one presupposes the reality and knowability of the mental in the same way that in physical sciences one has to presuppose the reality and knowability of physical objects.

VI. The many mansions reply (Berkeley). "Your whole argument presupposes that AI is only about analogue and digital computers. But that just happens to be the present state of technology. Whatever these causal processes are that you say are essential for intentionality (assuming you are right), eventually we will be able to build devices that have these causal processes, and that will be artificial intelligence. So your arguments are in no way directed at the ability of artificial intelligence to produce and explain cognition."

I really have no objection to this reply save to say that it in effect trivializes the project of strong AI by redefining it as whatever artificially produces and explains cognition. The interest of the original claim made on behalf of artificial intelligence is that it was a precise, well defined thesis: mental processes are computational processes over formally defined elements. I have been concerned to challenge that thesis. If the claim is redefined so that it is no longer that thesis, my objections no longer apply because there is no longer a testable hypothesis for them to apply to.

Let us now return to the question I promised I would try to answer: granted that in my original example I understand the English and I do not understand the Chinese, and granted therefore that the machine doesn't understand either English or Chinese, still there must be something about me that makes it the case that I understand English and a corresponding something lacking in me that makes it the case that I fail to understand Chinese. Now why couldn't we give those somethings, whatever they are, to a machine?

I see no reason in principle why we couldn't give a machine the capacity to understand English or Chinese, since in an important sense our bodies with our brains are precisely such machines. But I do see very strong arguments for saying that we could not give such a thing to a machine where the operation of the machine is defined solely in terms of computational processes over formally defined elements; that is, where the operation of the machine is defined as an instantiation of a computer program. It is not because I am the instantiation of a computer program that I am able to understand English and have other forms of intentionality (I am, I suppose, the instantiation of any number of computer programs), but as far as we know it is because I am a certain sort of organism with a certain biological (i.e. chemical and physical) structure, and this structure, under certain conditions, is causally capable of producing perception, action, understanding, learning, and other intentional phenomena. And part of the point of the present argument is that only something that had those causal powers could have that intentionality. Perhaps other physical and chemical processes could produce exactly these effects; perhaps, for example, Martians also have intentionality but their brains are made of different stuff. That is an empirical question, rather like the question whether photosynthesis can be done by something with a chemistry different from that of chlorophyll.

But the main point of the present argument is that no purely formal model will ever be sufficient by itself for intentionality because the formal properties are not by themselves constitutive of intentionality, and they have by themselves no causal powers except the power, when instantiated, to produce the next stage of the formalism when the machine is running. And any other causal properties that particular realizations of the formal model have, are irrelevant to the formal model because we can always put the same formal model in a different realization where those causal properties are obviously absent. Even if, by some miracle, Chinese speakers exactly realize Schank's program, we can put the same program in English speakers, water pipes, or computers, none of which understand Chinese, the program notwithstanding.

What matters about brain operations is not the formal shadow cast by the sequence of synapses but rather the actual properties of the sequences. All the arguments for the strong version of artificial intelligence that I have seen insist on drawing an outline around the shadows cast by cognition and then claiming that the shadows are the real thing.

By way of concluding I want to try to state some of the general philosophical points implicit in the argument. For clarity I will try to do it in a question and answer fashion, and I begin with that old chestnut of a question:

"Could a machine think?"

The answer is, obviously, yes. We are precisely such machines.

"Yes, but could an artifact, a man-made machine, think?"

Assuming it is possible to produce artificially a machine with a nervous system, neurons with axons and dendrites, and all the rest of it, sufficiently like ours, again the answer to the question seems to be obviously, yes. If you can exactly duplicate the causes, you could duplicate the effects. And indeed it might be possible to produce consciousness, intentionality, and all the rest of it using some other sorts of chemical principles than those that human beings use. It is, as I said, an empirical question.

"OK, but could a digital computer think?"

If by "digital computer" we mean anything at all that has a level of description where it can correctly be described as the instantiation of a computer program, then again the answer is, of course, yes, since we are the instantiations of any number of computer programs, and we can think.

"But could something think, understand, and so on *solely* in virtue of being a computer with the right sort of program? Could instantiating a program, the right program of course, by itself be a sufficient condition of understanding?"

This I think is the right question to ask, though it is usually confused with one or more of the earlier questions, and the answer to it is no.

"Why not?"

Because the formal symbol manipulations by themselves don't have any intentionality; they are quite meaningless; they aren't even *symbol* manipulations, since the symbols don't symbolize anything. In the linguistic jargon, they have only a syntax but no semantics. Such intentionality as computers appear to have is solely in the minds of those who program them and those who use them, those who send in the input and those who interpret the output.

The aim of the Chinese room example was to try to show this by showing that as soon as we put

something into the system that really does have intentionality (a man), and we program him with the formal program, you can see that the formal program carries no additional intentionality. It adds nothing, for example, to a man's ability to understand Chinese.

Precisely that feature of AI that seemed so appealing—the distinction between the program and the realization—proves fatal to the claim that simulation could be duplication. The distinction between the program and its realization in the hardware seems to be parallel to the distinction between the level of mental operations and the level of brain operations. And if we could describe the level of mental operations as a formal program, then it seems we could describe what was essential about the mind without doing either introspective psychology or neurophysiology of the brain. But the equation, "mind is to brain as program is to hardware" breaks down at several points, among them the following three:

First, the distinction between program and realization has the consequence that the same program could have all sorts of crazy realizations that had no form of intentionality. Weizenbaum (1976, Ch. 2), for example, shows in detail how to construct a computer using a roll of toilet paper and a pile of small stones. Similarly, the Chinese story understanding program can be programmed into a sequence of water pipes, a set of wind machines, or a monolingual English speaker, none of which thereby acquires an understanding of Chinese. Stones, toilet paper, wind, and water pipes are the wrong kind of stuff to have intentionality in the first place—only something that has the same causal powers as brains can have intentionality—and though the English speaker has the right kind of stuff for intentionality you can easily see that he doesn't get any extra intentionality by memorizing the program, since memorizing it won't teach him Chinese.

Second, the program is purely formal, but the intentional states are not in that way formal. They are defined in terms of their content, not their form. The belief that it is raining, for example, is not defined as a certain formal shape, but as a certain mental content with conditions of satisfaction, a direction of fit (see Searle 1979), and the like. Indeed the belief as such hasn't even got a formal shape in this syntactic sense, since one and the same belief can be given an indefinite number of different syntactic expressions in different linguistic systems.

Third, as I mentioned before, mental states and events are literally a product of the operation of the brain, but the program is not in that way a product of the computer.

"Well if programs are in no way constitutive of mental processes, why have so many people believed the converse? That at least needs some explanation."

I don't really know the answer to that one. The idea that computer simulations could be the real thing ought to have seemed suspicious in the first place because the computer isn't confined to simulating mental operations, by any means. No one supposes that computer simulations of a five-alarm fire will burn the neighborhood down or that a computer simulation of a rainstorm will leave us all drenched. Why on earth would anyone suppose that a computer simulation of understanding actually understood anything? It is sometimes said that it would be frightfully hard to get computers to feel pain or fall in love, but love and pain are neither harder nor easier than cognition or anything else. For simulation, all you need is the right input and output and a program in the middle that transforms the former into the latter. That is all the computer has for anything it does. To confuse simulation with duplication is the same mistake, whether it is pain, love, cognition, fires, or rainstorms.

Still, there are several reasons why AI must have seemed—and to many people perhaps still does seem—in some way to reproduce and thereby explain mental phenomena, and I believe we will not succeed in removing these illusions until we have fully exposed the reasons that give rise to them.

First, and perhaps most important, is a confusion about the notion of "information processing": many people in cognitive science believe that the human brain, with its mind, does something called "information processing," and analogously the computer with its program does information processing; but fires and rainstorms, on the other hand, don't do information processing at all. Thus, though the computer can simulate the formal features of any process whatever, it stands in a special relation to the mind and brain because when the computer is properly programmed, ideally with the same program as the brain, the information processing is identical in the two cases, and this information processing is really the essence of the mental. But the trouble with this argument is that it rests on an ambiguity in the notion of "information." In the sense in which people "process information" when they reflect, say, on problems in arithmetic or when they read and answer questions about stories, the programmed computer does not do "information processing." Rather, what it does is manipulate formal symbols. The fact that the programmer and the interpreter of the computer output use the symbols to stand for objects in the world is totally beyond the scope of the computer. The computer, to repeat, has a syntax but no semantics. Thus, if you type into the computer "2 plus 2 equals?" it will type out "4." But it has no idea that "4" means 4 or that it means anything at all. And the point is not that it lacks some second-order information about the interpretation of its first-order symbols, but rather that its first-order symbols don't have any interpretations as far as the computer is concerned. All the computer has is more symbols. The introduction of the notion of "information processing" therefore produces a dilemma: either we construe the notion of "information processing" in such a way that it implies intentionality as part of the process or we don't. If the former, then the programmed computer does not do information processing, it only manipulates formal symbols. If the latter, then, though the computer does information processing, it is only doing so in the sense in which adding machines, typewriters, stomachs, thermostats, rainstorms, and hurricanes do information processing; namely, they have a level of description at which we can describe them as taking information in at one end, transforming it, and producing information as output. But in this case it is up to outside observers to interpret the input and output as information in the ordinary sense. And no similarity is established between the computer and the brain in terms of any similarity of information processing.

Second, in much of AI there is a residual behaviorism or operationalism. Since appropriately programmed computers can have input-output patterns similar to those of human beings, we are tempted to postulate mental states in the computer similar to human mental states. But once we see that it is both conceptually and empirically possible for a system to have human capacities in some realm without having any intentionality at all, we should be able to overcome this impulse. My desk adding machine has calculating capacities, but no intentionality, and in this paper I have tried to show that a system could have input and output capabilities that duplicated those of a native Chinese speaker and still not understand Chinese, regardless of how it was programmed. The Turing test is typical of the tradition in being unashamedly behavioristic and operationalistic, and I believe that if AI workers totally repudiated behaviorism and operationalism much of the confusion between simulation and duplication would be eliminated.

Third, this residual operationalism is joined to a residual form of dualism; indeed strong AI only makes sense given the dualistic assumption that, where the mind is concerned, the brain doesn't matter. In strong AI (and in functionalism, as well) what matters are programs, and programs are independent of their realization in machines; indeed, as far as AI is concerned, the same program could be realized by an electronic machine, a Cartesian mental substance, or a Hegelian world spirit. The single most surprising discovery that I have made in discussing these issues is that many AI workers are quite shocked by my idea that actual human mental phenomena might be dependent on actual physical–chemical properties of actual human brains. But if you think about it a minute you can see that I should not have been surprised; for unless you accept some form of dualism, the strong AI project hasn't got a chance. The project is to reproduce and explain the mental by designing programs, but unless the mind is not only conceptually but empirically independent of the brain you couldn't carry out the project, for the program is completely independent of any realization. Unless you believe that the mind is separable from the brain both conceptually and empirically—dualism in a strong form—you cannot hope to reproduce the mental by writing and running programs since programs must be independent of brains or any other particular forms of instantiation. If mental operations consist in computational operations on formal symbols, then it follows that they have no interesting connection with the brain; the only connection would be that the brain just happens to be one of the indefinitely many types of machines capable of instantiating the program. This form of dualism is not the traditional Cartesian variety that claims there are two sorts of *substances,* but it is Cartesian in the sense that it insists that what is specifically mental about the mind has no intrinsic connection with the actual properties of the brain. This underlying dualism is masked from us by the fact that AI literature contains frequent fulminations against "dualism"; what the authors seem to be unaware of is that their position presupposes a strong version of dualism.

"Could a machine think?" My own view is that *only* a machine could think, and indeed only very special kinds of machines, namely brains and machines that had the same causal powers as brains. And that is the main reason strong AI has had little to tell us about thinking, since it has nothing to tell us about machines. By its own definition, it is about programs, and programs are not machines. Whatever else intentionality is, it is a biological phenomenon, and it is as likely to be as causally

dependent on the specific biochemistry of its origins as lactation, photosynthesis, or any other biological phenomena. No one would suppose that we could produce milk and sugar by running a computer simulation of the formal sequences in lactation and photosynthesis, but where the mind is concerned many people are willing to believe in such a miracle because of a deep and abiding dualism: the mind they suppose is a matter of formal processes and is independent of quite specific material causes in the way that milk and sugar are not.

In defense of this dualism the hope is often expressed that the brain is a digital computer (early computers, by the way, were often called "electronic brains"). But that is no help. Of course the brain is a digital computer. Since everything is a digital computer, brains are too. The point is that the brain's causal capacity to produce intentionality cannot consist in its instantiating a computer program, since for any program you like it is possible for something to instantiate that program and still not have any mental states. Whatever it is that the brain does to produce intentionality, it cannot consist in instantiating a program since no program, by itself, is sufficient for intentionality.

ACKNOWLEDGMENTS

I am indebted to a rather large number of people for discussion of these matters and for their patient attempts to overcome my ignorance of artificial intelligence. I would especially like to thank Ned Block, Hubert Dreyfus, John Haugeland, Roger Schank, Robert Wilensky, and Terry Winograd.

NOTES

1. I am not, of course, saying that Schank himself is committed to these claims.

2. Also, "understanding" implies both the possession of mental (intentional) states and the truth (validity, success) of these states. For the purposes of this discussion we are concerned only with the possession of the states.

3. Intentionality is by definition that feature of certain mental states by which they are directed at or about objects and states of affairs in the world. Thus, beliefs, desires, and intentions are intentional states; undirected forms of anxiety and depression are not. For further discussion see Searle (1979c).

Open Peer Commentary

*   *   *   *   *

"Searle on What Only Brains Can Do"

J. A. FODOR

1. Searle is certainly right that instantiating the same program that the brain does is not, in and of itself, a sufficient condition for having those propositional attitudes characteristic of the organism that has the brain. If some people in AI think that it is, they're wrong. As for the Turing test, it has all the usual difficulties with predictions of "no difference"; you can't distinguish the truth of the prediction from the insensitivity of the test instrument.[1]

2. However, Searle's treatment of the "robot reply" is quite unconvincing. Given that there are the right kinds of causal linkages between the symbols that the device manipulates and things in the world—including the afferent and efferent transducers of the device—it is quite unclear that intuition rejects ascribing propositional attitudes to it. All that Searle's example shows is that the kind of causal linkage he imagines—one that is, in effect, mediated by a man sitting in the head of a robot—is, unsurprisingly, not the right kinds.

3. We don't know how to say what the right kinds of causal linkage are. This, also, is unsurprising since we don't know how to answer the closely related question as to what kinds of connection between a formula and the world determine the interpretation under which the formula is employed. We don't have an answer to this question for *any* symbolic system; a fortiori, not for mental representations. These questions are closely related because, given the mental representation view, it is natural to assume that what makes mental states intentional is primarily that they involve relations to semantically interpreted mental objects; again, relations of the right kind.

4. It seems to me that Searle has misunderstood the main point about the treatment of intentionality in representational theories of the mind; this is not surprising since proponents of the theory—especially in AI—have been notably unlucid in expounding it. For the record, then, the main point is this: intentional properties of propositional attitudes are viewed as inherited from semantic properties of mental representations (and not from the functional role of mental representations, unless "functional role" is construed broadly enough to include symbol-world relations). In effect, what is proposed is a reduction of the problem *what makes mental states intentional*

to the problem *what bestows semantic properties on (fixes the interpretation of) a symbol.* This reduction looks promising because we're going to have to answer the latter question anyhow (for example, in constructing theories of natural languages); and we need the notion of mental representation anyhow (for example, to provide appropriate domains for mental processes).

It may be worth adding that there is nothing new about this stragegy. Locke, for example, thought (a) that the intentional properties of mental states are inherited from the semantic (referential) properties of mental representations; (b) that mental processes are formal (associative); and (c) that the objects from which mental states inherit their intentionality are the same ones over which mental processes are defined: namely ideas. It's my view that no serious alternative to this treatment of propositional attitudes has ever been proposed.

5. To say that a computer (or a brain) performs formal operations on symbols is not the same thing as saying that it performs operations on formal (in the sense of "uninterpreted") symbols. This equivocation occurs repeatedly in Searle's paper, and causes considerable confusion. If there are mental representations they must, of course, be interpreted objects; it is because they are interpreted objects that mental states are intentional. But the brain might be a computer for all that.

6. This situation—needing a notion of causal connection, but not knowing which notion of causal connection is the right one—is entirely familiar in philosophy. It is, for example, extremely plausible that "a perceives b" can be true only where there is the right kind of causal connection between a and b. And we don't know what the right kind of causal connection is here either.

Demonstrating that some kinds of causal connection are the *wrong* kinds would not, of course, prejudice the claim. For example, suppose we interpolated a little man between a and b, whose function it is to report to a on the presence of b. We would then have (inter alia) a sort of causal link from a to b, but we wouldn't have the sort of causal link that is required for a to perceive b. It would, of course, be a fallacy to argue from the fact that this causal linkage fails to reconstruct perception to the conclusion that *no* causal linkage would succeed. Searle's argument against the "robot reply" is a fallacy of precisely that sort.

7. It is entirely reasonable (indeed it must be true) that the right kind of causal relation is the kind that holds between our brains and our transducer mechanisms (on the one hand) and between our brains and distal objects (on the other). It would not begin to follow that *only* our brains can bear such relations to transducers and distal objects; and it would also not follow that being the same sort of thing our brain is (in any biochemical sense of "same sort") is a necessary condition for being in that relation; and it would also not follow that formal manipulations of symbols are not among the links in such causal chains. And, even if our brains *are* the only sorts of things that can be in that relation, the fact that they are might quite possibly be of no particular interest; that would depend on *why* it's true.[2]

Searle gives no clue as to why he thinks the biochemistry is important for intentionality and, prima facie, the idea that what counts is how the organism is connected to the world seems far more plausible. After all, it's easy enough to imagine, in a rough and ready sort of way, how the fact that my thought is causally connected to a tree might bear on its being a thought about a tree. But it's hard to imagine how the fact that (to put it crudely) my thought is made out of hydrocarbons could matter, except on the unlikely hypothesis that only hydrocarbons can be causally connected to trees in the way that brains are.

8. The empirical evidence for believing that "manipulation of symbols" is involved in mental processes derives largely from the considerable success of work in linguistics, psychology, and AI that has been grounded in that assumption. Little of the relevant date concerns the simulation of behavior or the passing of Turing tests, though Searle writes as though all of it does. Searle gives no indication at all of how the facts that this work accounts for are to be explained if not on the mental-processes-are-formal-processes view. To claim that there is no argument that symbol manipulation is necessary for mental processing while systematically ignoring all the evidence that has been alleged in favor of the claim strikes me as an extremely curious strategy on Searle's part.

9. Some necessary conditions are more interesting than others. While connections to the world and symbol manipulations are both presumably necessary for intentional processes, there is no reason (so far) to believe that the former provide a theoretical domain for a science; whereas, there is considerable a posteriori reason to suppose that the latter do. If this is right, it provides some justification for AI practice, if not for AI rhetoric.

10. *Talking* involves performing certain formal operations on symbols: stringing words together. Yet, not everything that can string words together can talk. It does not follow from these banal observations that what we utter are uninterpreted sounds, or that we don't understand what we say, or that whoever talks talks nonsense, or that only hydrocarbons can assert—similarly, mutatis mutandis, if you substitute "thinking" for "talking."

NOTES

1. I assume, for simplicity, that there is only one program that the brain instantiates (which, of course, there isn't). Notice, by the way, that even passing the Turing test requires doing more than *just* manipulating symbols. A device that can't run a typewriter can't play the game.

2. For example, it might be that, in point of physical fact, only things that have the same simultaneous values of weight, density, and shade of gray that brains have can do the things that brains can. This would be surprising, but it's hard to see why a psychologist should care much. Not even if it turned out—still in point of physical fact—that brains are the only things that can have that weight, density, and color. If *that's* dualism, I imagine we can live with it.

from "Author's Response"

John Searle

Intrinsic Intentionality

I am pleased at the amount of interest my target article has aroused and grateful that such a high percentage of the commentaries are thoughtful and forcefully argued. In this response I am going to attempt to answer every major criticism directed at my argument. To do that, however, I need to make fully explicit some of the points that were implicit in the target article, as these points involve recurring themes in the commentaries.

Strong AI. One of the virtues of the commentaries is that they make clear the extreme character of the strong AI thesis. The thesis implies that of all known types of specifically biological processes, from mitosis and meiosis to photosynthesis, digestion, lactation, and the secretion of auxin, one and only one type is completely independent of the biochemistry of its origins, and that one is cognition. The reason it is independent is that cognition consists entirely of computational processes, and since those processes are purely formal, any substance whatever that is capable of instantiating the formalism is capable of cognition. Brains just happen to be one of the indefinite number of different types of computers capable of cognition, but computers made of water pipes, toilet paper and stones, electric wires—anything solid and enduring enough to carry the right program—will necessarily have thoughts, feelings, and the rest of the forms of intentionality, because that is all that intentionality consists in: instantiating the right programs. The point of strong AI is not that if we built a computer big enough or complex enough to carry the actual programs that brains presumably instantiate we would get intentionality as a by-product (contra **Dennett**), but rather that there isn't anything to intentionality other than instantiating the right program.

Now I find the thesis of strong AI incredible in every sense of the word. But it is not enough to find a thesis incredible, one has to have an argument, and I offer an argument that is very simple: instantiating a program could not be constitutive of intentionality, because it would be possible for an agent to instantiate the program and still not have the right kind of intentionality. That is the point of the Chinese room example. Much of what follows will concern the force of that argument.

* * * * *

Intrinsic intentionality and observer-relative ascriptions of intentionality. Why then do people feel inclined to say that, in some sense at least, thermostats have beliefs? I think that in order to understand what is going on when people make such claims we need to distinguish carefully between cases of what I will call *intrinsic intentionality,* which are cases of actual mental states, and what I will call *observer-relative ascriptions of intentionality,* which are ways that people have of speaking about entities figuring in our activities but lacking intrinsic intentionality. We can illustrate this distinction with examples that are quite uncontroversial. If I say that I am hungry or that

Carter believes he can win the election, the form of intentionality in question is intrinsic. I am discussing, truly or falsely, certain psychological facts about me and Carter. But if I say the word "Carter" refers to the present president, or the sentence "Es regnet" means it's raining, I am not ascribing any mental states to the word "Carter" or the sentence "Es regnet." These are ascriptions of intentionality made to entities that lack any mental states, but in which the ascription is a manner of speaking about the intentionality of the observers. It is a way of saying that people *use* the name Carter to refer, or that when people say literally "Es regnet" they *mean* it's raining.

Observer-relative ascriptions of intentionality are always dependent on the intrinsic intentionality of the observers. There are not two kinds of intentional mental states; there is only one kind, those that have intrinsic intentionality; but there are ascriptions of intentionality in which the ascription does not ascribe intrinsic intentionality to the subject of the ascription. Now I believe that a great deal of the present dispute rests on a failure to appreciate this distinction. When **McCarthy** stoutly maintains that thermostats have beliefs, he is confusing observer-relative ascriptions of intentionality with ascriptions of intrinsic intentionality. To see this point, ask yourself why we make these attributions to thermostats and the like at all. It is not because we suppose they have a mental life very much like our own; on the contrary, we know that they have no mental life at all. Rather, it is because we have designed them (our intentionality), to serve certain of our purposes (more of our intentionality), to perform the sort of functions that we perform on the basis of our intentionality. I believe it is equally clear that our ascription of intentionality to cars, computers, and adding machines is observer relative.

Functionalism, by the way, is an entire system erected on the failure to see this distinction. Functional attributions are always observer relative. There is no such thing as an intrinsic function, in the way that there are intrinsic intentional states.

* * * * *

Fodor agrees with my central thesis that instantiating a program is not a sufficient condition of intentionality. He thinks, however, that if we got the right causal links between the formal symbols and things in the world that would be sufficient. Now there is an obvious objection to this variant of the robot reply that I have made several times: the same thought experiment as before applies to this case. That is, no matter what outside causal impacts there are on the formal tokens, these are not by themselves sufficient to give the tokens any intentional content. No matter what caused the tokens, the agent still doesn't understand Chinese. Let the egg foo yung symbol be causally connected to egg foo yung in any way you like, that connection by itself will never enable the agent to interpret the symbol as meaning egg foo yung. To do that he would have to have, for example, some *awareness* of the causal relation between the symbol and the referent; but now we are no longer explaining intentionality in terms of symbols and causes but in terms of symbols, causes, and intentionality, and we have abandoned both strong AI and the robot reply. Fodor's only answer to this is to say that it shows we haven't yet got the right kind of causal linkage. But what is the right kind, since the above argument applies to any kind? He says he can't tell us, but it is there all the same. Well I can tell him what it is: it is any form of causation sufficient to produce intentional content in the agent, sufficient to produce, for example, a visual experience, or a memory, or a belief, or a semantic interpretation of some word.

Fodor's variant of the robot reply is therefore confronted with a dilemma. If the causal linkages are just matters of fact about the relations between the symbols and the outside world, they will never by themselves give any interpretation to the symbols; they will carry by themselves no intentional content. If, on the other hand, the causal impact is sufficient to produce intentionality in the agent, it can only be because there is something more to the system than the *fact* of the causal impact and the *symbol,* namely the intentional content that the impact produces in the agent. Either the man in the room doesn't learn the meaning of the symbol from the causal impact, in which case the causal impact adds nothing to the interpretation, or the causal impact teaches him the meaning of the word, in which case the cause is relevant only because it produces a form of intentionality that is something in addition to itself and the symbol. In neither case is symbol, or cause and symbol, constitutive of intentionality.

This is not the place to discuss the general role of formal processes in mental processes, but I cannot resist calling attention to one massive use-mention confusion implicit in **Fodor's** account. From the fact that, for example, syntactical rules concern formal objects, it does not follow that they are formal rules. Like other rules affecting human behavior they are defined by their content, not

their form. It just so happens that in this case their content concerns forms.

In what is perhaps his crucial point, **Fodor** suggests that we should think of the brain or the computer as performing formal operations only on *interpreted* and not just on *formal* symbols. But who does the interpreting? And what is an interpretation? If he is saying that for intentionality there must be intentional content in addition to the formal symbols, then I of course agree. Indeed, two of the main points of my argument are that in our own case we have the "interpretation," that is, we have intrinsic intentionality, and that the computer program could never by itself be sufficient for that. In the case of the computer we make observer-relative ascriptions of intentionality, but that should not be mistaken for the real thing since the computer program by itself has no intrinsic intentionality.

REFERENCES

Fodor, J. A. (1980) Methodological solipsism considered as a research strategy in cognitive psychology. *The Behavioral and Brain Sciences* 3·1

McCarthy, J. (1979) Ascribing mental qualities to machines. In: *Philosophical perspectives in artificial intelligence,* ed. M. Ringle. Atlantic Highlands, N.J.: Humanities Press.

Newell, A. (1979) Physical symbol systems. Lecture at the La Jolla Conference on Cognitive Science.

Newell, A. & Simon, H. A. (1963) GPS, a program that simulates human thought. In: *Computers and thought,* ed. A. Feigenbaum & V. Feldman, pp. 279–93. New York: McGraw Hill.

Pylyshyn, Z. W. (1980a) Computation and cognition: issues in the foundations of cognitive science. *Behavioral and Brain Sciences* 3.

Schank, R. C. & Abelson, R. P. (1977) *Scripts, plans, goals, and understanding.* Hillsdale, N.J.: Lawrence Erlbaum Press.

Searle, J. R. (1979a) Intentionality and the use of language. In: *Meaning and use,* ed. A. Margalit. Dordrecht: Reidel.

——— (1979c) What is an intentional state? *Mind* 88·74–92.

Weizenbaum, J. (1965) Eliza—a computer program for the study of natural language communication between man and machine. *Communication of the Association for Computing Machinery* 9:36–45.

——— (1976) *Computer power and human reason.* San Francisco: W. H. Freeman.

Winograd, T. (1973) A procedural model of language understanding. In: *Computer models of thought and language,* ed. R. Schank & K. Colby. San Francisco: W. H. Freeman.

Afterthoughts: Yin and Yang in the Chinese Room

J. A. FODOR

Here's a two person, zero sum game that philosophers like to play.

Yin says 'Being A is sufficient for being B; whatever is A is ipso facto B.'

'Not so,' Yang replies. 'For consider *a*. *a* is A and not B, so *a* shows that being A is not sufficient for being B after all.'

There is now a variety of strategies that Yin can play. For example:

   i. Yin can argue that (contrary to appearances perhaps) *a* really is B after all, and hence does not offer a counterexample to the claim that being A is sufficient for being B. Or,
   ii. Yin can argue that, although *a* is A and not B, still there is some set of further conditions C such that if *a* were A and C, *then a* would be B. Or,
   iii. Yin can argue that *a* is *irrelevant* to whether being A is sufficient for being B because, *a* isn't A. If it's true that *a* isn't A, then, of course, *a*'s (putative) failure to be B is not an argument against the claim that being A is sufficient for being B.

Notice that playing strategy iii is, in a certain sense, less heroic than playing i or ii. Unlike i and ii, iii undertakes to dismiss *a* as a counterexample to $A \rightarrow B$ without undertaking to adduce evidence that $A \rightarrow B$ is true. Strategy iii is unlike strategies i and ii in that it declines to take *a* very seriously.

All the replies I've seen to Searle's Chinese room argument are of the first two types. Either they bite the bullet and argue, in the spirit of i, that Searle's setup really is an intentional system (either because—contrary to appearances—the guy in the room actually does understand Chinese; or because—still contrary to appearances—the guy *together with the room* actually does understand Chinese . . . etc.); or they argue that Searle's setup *would be* an intentional system under further conditions (e.g. the room or the guy is causally connected to the world 'in the right sort of way' . . . etc.).

Such arguments now strike me as supererogatory. Whatever their merits may be, if all you want to do is draw the fangs of Searle's example, it sufficcs to play strategy iii. I.e. to argue that it doesn't matter whether Searle's setup is an intentional sys-

tem, because Searle's setup is not, in the intended sense, a Turing machine.

Strictly speaking, of course, a Turing machine is anything that satisfies a Turing machine table. And a Turing machine table is a specification of a (typically infinite) set of sequences of machine states. For present purposes, the program for Turing machine M is a set of instructions of (approximately) the form: 'if you're in state A, then you go into state B; if you're in state B, then you go into state W; if you're in state W, then you go into state A; . . . .' etc. Anything that (does or would) exhibit the state sequences that the table specifies is, by stipulation, an *instantiation* of M, and all instantiations of M are, by stipulation, *strongly equivalent* to one another.

Notice that these conditions constrain the sequences of states that instantiations of M (do or would) go through; but they do *not* otherwise constrain the relations among the states. For example, they do not require that the states of an instantiation of M should be spatio-temporally adjacent. If M is defined as the machine that goes from state A to state B, and from state B to state W, then the discontinuous "system" that is in state A on 25 June 1800 in Kansas, and state B on 12 December 2075 in Haifa, and in state W on 13 December 2075 on Alpha Centuri, is ipso facto an instantiation of M. A fortiori, the requirements for instantiating M do not constrain the causal relations among a machine's states. The table requires that state B succeed state A, but it does *not* require that state A cause (or even be a member of the same causal chain as) state B. Given the technical notion of instantiation, some very odd objects count as instantiations of Turing machines.

It is because of this loophole in the characterization of instantiation that Searle's setup counts as strongly equivalent to the mind of a Chinese speaker. The program for the mind is given by the machine table that the guy in the room follows. The instructions specify operations on symbols (to a first approximation, they're of the form 'if you have symbol S1 in the input box, put symbol S2 in the output box') and the function of the guy is to carry out the instructions by moving the symbols around. Since, strictly speaking, anything that effects the right sequences of transformations of symbols is an instantiation of the mind program, Searle's setup counts as strongly equivalent to the

Chinese speaker's mind. (And so too does the 'system' which consists of a tokening of S1 in Tibet followed by a tokening of S2 on Alpha Centuri . . . etc.)

People who were wont to claim that the brain is intentional in virtue of instantiating some (specified) Turing machine didn't, of course, have these funny sorts of instantiations in mind. The cleverness of Searle's example is that it exploits this loophole. Correspondingly, however, the short way with Searle's example is simply to plug the loophole it exploits. The idea would be to define a notion of instantiation such that, when a machine table requires that a token of state-type Y succeeds a token of the state-type X, nothing counts as an instantiation of the table unless it's tokening of X is the effective (immediate, proximal) cause of it's tokening of Y. One could have fun working out the required notion of effective (immediate, proximal) cause more precisely, but I won't fuss with that here. Because, however it is construed, it would surely rule out systems in which the mechanism by which S1 tokens bring about S2 tokens involves a little man who applies the rule 'if you see an S1, write down an S2'.

So, under the revised reading of 'instantiates', even though the program the guy in the room follows is the same program that a Chinese speaker's brain follows, Searle's setup does not instantiate the machine that the brain instantiates. A fortiori, Searle's setup is not strongly equivalent to the Chinese speaker's brain. So, *Searle's setup is irrelevant to the claim that strong equivalence to a Chinese speaker's brain is ipso facto sufficient for speaking Chinese*. And this is so *whether or not* Searle's setup is an intentional system.

None of this shows that strong equivalence to an intentional system *is* sufficient for intentionality. My own view is that it's not. Semantic evaluability is a matter of mind/world connections, so a computer that's strongly equivalent to my brain is in my intentional states only if it's hooked up to the world in something like the way my brain is. However, I don't think that it is *obvious* that this is so (as I do think that it is obvious that Searle's setup doesn't understand Chinese). And, more to the point, you can't use Searle's setup to *show* that it is so. The mistake everybody makes is to suppose that Searle's setup provides an *interesting* problem for "Strong AI"; i.e. a problem that has to be met by playing strategy i or ii. On the contrary, strategy iii will do: Searle's setup is *irrelevant* to the claim that strong equivalence to a mind is a sufficient condition for intentionality because, given the sense of 'strong equivalence' that's intended by people who make this sort of claim, Searle's setup *isn't* strongly equivalent to a mind.

So Yin wins.

Yin and Yang Strike Out

JOHN R. SEARLE

Of all the zillions of criticisms of the Chinese Room argument, Fodor's is perhaps the most desperate. He claims that precisely because the man in the Chinese room sets out to implement the steps in the computer program, he is not implementing the steps in the computer program. He offers no argument for this extraordinary claim. He says that "when a machine table requires that a token of state type y succeeds a token of the state type x, nothing counts as an instantiation of the table unless its tokening of x is the effective (immediate proximal) cause of its tokening of y." Then he says, assuming we accept this condition, it would rule out systems in which the mechanism by which S1's tokens brings about S2's tokens involves a little man who applies the rule, "if you see an S1, write down an S2". But why? It seems to me clear as day that this is an ideal case which fits Fodor's requirement. That is, even if we accept his requirement that there must be a (immediate proximal) causal connection between the tokenings, it does not violate that condition to suppose that the causal connection is brought about through the (immediate proximal) conscious agency of someone going through the steps. To suppose that the idea of implementing a computer program, by definition, rules out the possibility of the conscious implementation of the steps of the program is, frankly, preposterous. It would have the result that Alan Turing didn't know what a Turing machine was, since precisely some of his examples of Turing machines involved conscious agents going through the steps of the program.[1]

To see the falsity of Fodor's claim, you can simply imagine the following thought experiment. Suppose that we found that the quickest and most efficient way to make computers work was by utilizing tiny creatures imported from Mars who were the size of a few molecules and who implemented the program by consciously going through all the steps in the symbol manipulation. That is, they simply applied such rules as, "when you see an S1, write down an S2". We can suppose that they find it enormous fun to do this, so they enjoy the work and are willing to work for no pay, and that they compute faster than any known electronic circuits. They are better, cheaper, and easier to program than silicon chips. Now, it would not be even remotely plausible to say that in this eventuality they were not actually going through the steps of the programs.

To bring the discussion down to the realm of reality, however, it is worth pointing out that there is something very ironic in eliminating conscious agents from the possibility of implementing computer algorithms. When the first calculators were invented, precisely what was considered so wonderful about their invention was that they made it unnecessary for clerks to have to implement the algorithms. Instead of clerks sitting on stools with green eyeshades adding up columns of figures according to the algorithm for addition, and thus instantiating the machine table, we simply built a machine which implemented the same table. Now,

on Fodor's arbitrary definition, it turns out that the clerks were never implementing that table in the first place.

In any case, even if we adopted this desperate maneuver, it is quite irrelevant to the point of the Chinese Room argument. The point of the argument, as I stressed in the abstract of the original paper and in several subsequent writings, is simply that since the program is purely formal or syntactical, the program by itself could not be constitutive of nor sufficient for the mental content or semantic content of actual human minds. One way to think of the Chinese Room Argument can be represented as a three-step proof:

1. Programs are formal (syntactical).
2. Minds have contents (semantic contents).
3. Syntax is not identical nor sufficient by itself for semantics.

From these we can derive:

Programs are not sufficient for nor identical with minds; i.e. strong AI is false.

Now where does Fodor think he is challenging this argument?

NOTE

1. This was pointed out to me by Paul Kube.

56

Hilary Putnam

"Computational Psychology and Interpretation Theory"

I once got into an argument after dinner with my friend Zenon Pylyshyn. The argument concerned the following assertion which Pylyshyn made: 'cognitive psychology is impossible if there is not a well-defined notion of *sameness of content* for mental representations'. It occurred to me later that the reasons I have for rejecting this assertion tic in closely with Donald Davidson's well-known interests in both meaning theory and the philosophy of mind. Accordingly, with Zenon's permission and (I hope) forgiveness, I have decided to make my arguments against his assertion the subject of this paper.

Mental Representation

Let us consider what goes on in the mind when we think 'there is a tree over there', or any other common thought about ordinary physical things. On one model, the computer model of the mind, the mind has a 'program', or set of rules, analogous to the rules governing a computing machine, and thought involves the manipulation of words and other signs (not all of this manipulation 'conscious', in the sense of being able to be verbalized by the computer). This model, however, is almost vacuous as it stands (in spite of the heat it generates among those who do not like to think that a mere device, such as a computing machine, could possibly serve as a model for something as special as the human mind). It is vacuous because the program, or system of rules for mental functioning, has not been specified; and it is this program that constitutes the psychological theory. Merely saying that the correct psychological theory, whatever it

may be, can be represented as a program (or something analogous to a program) for a computer (or something analogous to a computer) is almost empty; for virtually any system that can be described by a set of *laws* can at least be *simulated* by a computer. Anything from Freudian depth psychology to Skinnerian behaviorism can be represented as a kind of computer program.

Today, however, computer scientists working in 'artificial intelligence', and cognitive psychologists thinking about reference, semantic representation, language use, and so on, have a little more specific hypothesis in mind than the almost empty hypothesis that the mind can be modelled by a digital computer. (Even that hypothesis is not wholly empty because it does imply *something*: the causal structure of mental processes; it implies that they take place according to deterministic or probabilistic rules of sequencing according to a finite program.) The further hypothesis to which workers on computing machines and cognitive psychologists have been converging is this: that the mind thinks with the aid of *representations*. There seem to be two different ideas, actually, which are both involved in talk of 'representations' today.

The first idea, based on experience with trying to program computers to simulate intelligent behavior is that thinking involves not just the manipulation of arbitrary objects or symbols, but requires the manipulation of symbols that have a very specific structure, the structure of a *formalized language*. The experience of computer people was that the most interesting and successful programs in 'artificial intelligence' *typically* turned out to involve giving the computing machine something like a formalized language and a set of

From *Philosophical Papers: Realism and Reason*, vol. III. New York: Cambridge University Press, 1983, pp. 139–54. Copyright © 1983 by Cambridge University Press. Reprinted with permission of the publisher and Hilary Putnam.

rules for manipulating that formalized language ('reasoning' in the language, so to speak).

The second idea associated with the term 'representation' is that the human mind thinks (in part) by constructing some kind of a 'model' of its environment: a 'model of the world'. This 'model' need not, of course, literally *resemble* the world. It is enough that there should be some kind of *systematic relation* between items in the representational system and items 'out there', so that what is going on 'out there' can be read off from its representational system by the mind.

Once a reference definition has been given for a formalized language, a set of sentences in that language can serve as a 'representational system' or 'model of the world'.

Suppose, for example, we wish to represent the fact that the city of Paris is bigger than the city of Vienna. If we have a predicate, say *F*, which represents the relation *bigger than* (i.e., if the open sentence which we write in the formal notation as *'Fxy'* is correlated to the relation which holds between any two things if and only if they are both cities and the first is larger—in, say, population—than the second), and if we have 'individual constants' or proper names, say, *a* and *b*, which represent the cities of Paris and Vienna (i.e., '*a*' is correlated to Paris and '*b*' is correlated to Vienna by the reference definition for the language), then we can represent the fact that Paris is a bigger city than Vienna by just including in our list of accepted sentences (our 'theory of the world') the sentence *'Fab'*. In a similar way, any state of affairs, however complex, that can be expressed using the predicates, proper names, and logical devices of the formal language can be asserted to obtain by including in the 'theory of the world' the formula that represents that state of affairs.

When our 'representational system' is itself a *theory,* and when our method of employing our representational system involves *making formal deductions,* we see that *one and the same object*— the formalized language, including the rules for deduction—can be the formalized language that computer scientists have been led to postulate as the brain or mind's (the difference does not appear particularly significant, from this perspective) medium of computation, and, simultaneously, the medium of representation. *The mind uses a formalized language* (or something significantly like a formalized language) *both as medium of computation and medium of representation.* This may be called the working hypothesis of cognitive psychology today.

Part of this working hypothesis seems to me certainly correct. I believe that we cannot account at all for the functioning of thought and language without regarding at least some mental items as representations. When I think (correctly) 'there is a tree in front of me', the occurrence of the word 'tree' in the sentence I speak in my mind is a *meaningful* occurrence and one of the items in the *extension* of that occurrence of the word 'tree' is the very tree in front of me. Moreover, the open sentence '*x* is in front of me' is correlated (in the correct semantics for my language) with the relational property of being in front of me, and the entire sentence 'there is a tree in front of me' is, by virtue of these and similar facts, one which is *true* if and only if there is a tree in front of me.

Where there is room for psychologists to differ is over *how many* mental items are representations, how useful it is to postulate a large and complex *unconscious* system of representations in order to explain conscious thought and intelligent action, etc.

The Verificationist Semantics of 'Mentalese'

So far what I have said is in line with the thinking of Pylyshyn and other 'propositionalist' cognitive psychologists. For the sake of the argument, we shall assume all this is right. Of course, the actual story may be much more complicated. The mind may employ more than *one* formalized language (or, rather, formalized-language-analog). Different parts of the brain may compute in different 'media'. And both sentence-analogs and image-analogs may be used in the actual computational procedures, along with things that are neither. But let us assume the best case for Pylyshyn's view: a mind which does *all* its computing in *one* formalized language.

In what does the mind's *understanding* of its *own* medium of computation consist? It will do no good to say, as Fodor (1975) has, that we should not apply the word 'understand' to 'mentalese' itself. ('Mentalese' is a name for the hypothetical formalized-language-analog in the brain.) For 'mentalese' and 'formalized-language-in-the-brain' are *metaphors.* They may be scientifically useful and rich metaphors; but *as* metaphors they are inseparable from the notion of *understanding.* Something cannot literally be a language unless it can be *understood;* and something cannot be a language-*analog* unless there is a suitable *understanding-analog.* If some representations in the brain are sentence-analogs and predicate-analogs, then what is the corresponding *understanding-analog*?

The answer, I suggest, is this: the brain's 'understanding' of its own 'medium of computation and representation' consists in its possession of a *verificationist semantics* for the medium, i.e. of a computable predicate[1] which can represent acceptability, or warranted assertibility, or credibility. Idealizing, we treat the language as interpreted (in part) *via* a set of rules which assign *degrees of confirmation* (i.e., subjective probabilities) to the sentence-analogs relative to experiential inputs and relative also to other sentence-analogs. Such rules must be computable; and their 'possession' by the mind/brain/machine consists in its being 'wired' to follow them, or having come to follow them as a result of learning. (I do *not* assume that mentalese must be *innate*, or that it must be disjoint from the natural language the speaker has acquired.)

But why a verificationist semantics? Why not a meaning theory in Davidson's sense?

Obviously, if we interpret mentalese as a 'system of representation' we do ascribe extensions to predicate-analogs and truth conditions to sentence-analogs. But the 'meaning theory' which represents a particular interpretation of mentalese is not *psychology*. In fact, if we formulate it as Davidson might, its only primitive notion is 'true', and 'true' is not psychological notion. To spell this out: the meaning theory yields such theorems ('T sentences') as (pretend that mentalese is English): '"Snow is white" is true in mentalese if and only if snow is white'. This contains no psychological vocabulary at all.

We might try to say 'well, the understanding consists in the brain's *knowing* the T-sentences of the meaning theory'. But the notion of *knowing* cannot be a *primitive* notion in sub-personal cognitive psychology.[2]

Suppose we try to say: the mind understands *without using representations* what it is for snow to be white, and it knows the representation 'snow is white' is true if and only if that state of affairs holds. Not only does this treat the mind as something that 'knows' things, instead of *analyzing knowing into more elementary and less intentional processes*, but it violates the fundamental assumption of cognitive psychology, that understanding what states of affairs are, thinking about them, etc., *cannot be done without representations*. At bottom, we would be stuck with the myth of comparing representations directly with unconceptualized reality.

On the other hand, if we say, 'the brain's/mind's *use* of the sentence "Snow is white" (or the corresponding sentence-analog) is such as to warrant the interpretation that "Snow is white" is true in mentalese if and only if snow is white, *and this is what it means to say that the brain (implicitly) "knows" the T-sentence'*, then we do not give any theory of what that 'use' consists in. This is what a *verificationist* semantics gives (and, as far as I can see, what *only* a verificationist semantics gives). I suggest, then, that verificationist semantics is the natural semantics for functionalist (or 'cognitive') psychology. Such a semantics has a notion of 'belief' (or 'degree of belief') which is what makes it *cognitive;* at the same time it is a *computable* semantics, which is what makes it functionalist.

Of course, we want the semantics to connect with *action*, and this means that the model must incorporate a *utility function* as well as a degree of confirmation function. This function, too, must be computable (or, strictly speaking, semi-computable). This idealization is, of course, severe: we are assuming that the belief–analog (represented by the degree-of-confirmation function) and the preference-analog (represented by the utility function) are both *fully consistent*. The actual (neurologically realized) analogs of both belief *and* preference (or belief-representations and preference-representations) may well be *inconsistent*, as long as there are procedures for resolving the inconsistencies when practical decisions have to be made. In a terminology used by Reichenbach in another context, consistency may be '*de faciendo* and not *de facto*'. What significance this has for philosophy of mind, I shall discuss briefly at the end of this paper.

For now, the problem is this: if the *brain's* semantics for its medium of representation is verificationist and not truth-conditional, then what happens to the notion of the 'content' of a mental representation?

Two Ruritanian Children

Imagine that there is a country somewhere on earth called Ruritania. In this country let us imagine that there are small differences between the dialects which are spoken in the north and in the south. One of these differences is that the word 'grug' means silver in the northern dialect and aluminum in the southern dialect. Imagine two children, Oscar and Elmer, who grow up in Ruritania. They are as alike in genetic constitution and environment as you please, except that Oscar grows up in the south of Ruritania and Elmer grows up in the north of Ruritania. Imagine that in the north of Ruritania, for some reason, pots and pans are normally made of silver, whereas in the south of Ruritania pots and pans are normally made of aluminum. So northern children grow up knowing that pots and pans are normally made of 'grug', and southern children grow up knowing that pots and pans are normally made of 'grug'.

We may suppose that Oscar and Elmer have the same 'mental representation' of 'grug', that they have the same *beliefs* in connection with grug, etc. Of course some of these beliefs will differ in meaning even if they are identical in verbal and mental representation. For example, when Oscar believes 'my mother has grug pots and pans' and when Elmer believes 'my mother has grug pots and pans' the indexical word 'my' refers to different persons, and hence the term 'my mother' refers to different mothers. But unless such small differences in collateral information are already enough to constitute a difference in the *content* of the mental representation (in which case it would seem that the ordinary distinction between the meaning of a sign and collateral information that we have in connection with the sign has been wholly abandoned),[3] then it would seem that we should say that the content of the mental representation of 'grug' is exactly the same for Oscar and for Elmer at this stage in their lives.

I do not mean to suggest that the *word* 'grug' has the same meaning in Oscar's idiolect as it does in Elmer's idiolect at this stage; I've argued elsewhere (Putnam, 1975*a*) that the difference in reference in the two communities should be regarded as infecting the speech of the individual speakers. To spell this out: when Oscar tries to determine what *is* grug he will ultimately have to rely on 'experts'. These experts need not necessarily be scientists, he may simply ask his parents (who may in turn consult store owners or even scientists). But the point is that since the extension of 'grug' is in fact different in the two communities, and since, on the theory of meaning that I have defended in other places, difference in extension constitutes difference of meaning, and since extension is fixed collectively and not individually, it ends up that the *meaning* of the word 'grug' in the idiolects of Oscar and Elmer is not the same even though there is nothing 'psychological', nothing 'in their heads', which constitutes the difference in meaning. *Meanings aren't in the head.* There is a difference in the meaning of the word 'grug' in this case; but it is in the *reference* of the word, as objectively fixed by the practices of the community, and not in the conceptions of grug entertained by Oscar and Elmer.

But the concept of content that Pylyshyn is interested in and that Chomsky[4] has expressed an interest in is one that would factor out such objective differences in extension. What Pylyshyn is looking for is a notion of the content of a mental representation in which 'water' on earth and 'water' on Twin Earth would be said to have the same content for speakers who had identical conceptions of 'water' even though it might be the case that 'water' on earth referred to H_2O and 'water' on Twin Earth referred to XYZ. And what I have said

so far is that *on any such notion of content it would seem that 'grug' in Oscar's mind would have the same content as 'grug' in Elmer's mind.*

Not only would the words have the same content; any mental signs or predicate-analogs that the brain might use in its computations and that corresponded to the verbal item 'grug' would have the same content at this stage. But if the word 'grug', and the mental representations that stand behind the word 'grug' on a theory of the kind Pylyshyn advocates, have the same content at this stage, then *when do they come to differ in content?* By the time Oscar and Elmer have become adults, have learned foreign languages, and so on, they certainly will not have the same conception of grug. Oscar will know that *grug* is the metal called 'aluminum' in English (I assume that everybody in Ruritania learns English as a second language in High School), and Elmer will know that the metal called *grug* in his part of Ruritania is the metal called 'silver' in English. Each of them will know many facts which serve to distinguish silver from aluminum, and 'grug' in the south Ruritanian sense from 'grug' in the north Ruritanian sense.

However, on a verificationist model of the kind described in the first section of this paper there is no stage at which the word 'grug' or the corresponding mental representation in the mind of Oscar (or in the mind of Elmer) is ever treated as changing its reference. *Internally* to treat a sign as changing its reference is to treat it as, in effect, a different sign. This never happens; in the internal point of view all that happens is that Oscar acquires more information about grug. At one time he knew only that pots and pans are made of grug; that grug is a metal; and that grug has a certain color. Later he learned additional facts about grug (e.g., what it is called in English). When the use of a word is modified by the continual acquisition of collateral information, without it being supposed that at any stage the word is being committed to a new extension, all that happens (in the verificationist model) is that the degree of confirmation of various sentences containing the word changes. Moreover this change in the degree of confirmation of various sentences containing the word is a *continuous* change; it is continuous because it is brought about merely by the conditionalization of prior probabilities to added information. What this simple example shows is that there is nothing in a functionalist model of the use of a language (or even of a system of internal representations) which automatically gives us a decision as to when we should say that a representation has changed its 'content'. We can have a complete description of the use of mental signs without thereby having a criterion which distinguishes changes in the content of mental signs from changes in collateral information. So we have a problem with synonomy *for mental signs*.

Possible Solutions

In 'The meaning of "meaning"' I proposed to decide whether or not words of a certain kind (natural kind words) are synonymous by looking at two things: the extension and the correlated *stereotype*. By the *stereotype* I meant a certain set of beliefs, or idealized beliefs, which all speakers are expected to have in connection with the word. For example, if all speakers are expected to believe that a tiger is striped (or that idealized tigers are striped) then stripes are part of the 'stereotype' of a tiger. Can the idea of a stereotype be extended to mental representations, and can *sameness of stereotype* provide us with a criterion for the synonomy of mental representations? To explore this, let me again imagine an Oscar, only this time let me imagine that Oscar lives in an experimental research station very near the north pole. Perhaps this is a community of scientists and engineers experimenting with finding oil in extreme arctic conditions. I shall imagine that in this community, for some reason, there are no green plants, but that there are artificial plants and even artificial grass which people have introduced in order to make the place look more hospitable.

Now consider the word 'grass' in the idiolect of Oscar and in the idiolect of an ordinary American child, whom we shall call Elmer. If we take the stereotype of grass to be simply the perceptual prototype, then the stereotype of grass may be exactly the same in Oscar's mind as in Elmer's mind; but Oscar does not know that grass is in any sense a living or growing thing. I think we would regard it as wrong in such a case to suppose that the mental representation, or *the word* 'grass', had the same content in Oscar's mind as in Elmer's mind.

Perhaps we should require that in addition to having the same perceptual prototype for 'grass', Oscar and Elmer should have the same 'markers': for example, they should both believe that 'grass is a plant'. But this simply raises what I shall call the *infection problem*. If they do believe that grass is a plant, how similar do their notions of a *plant* have to be in order for their belief that *grass is a plant* to be relevantly the same belief? I think that in actual *interpretation* our policy is not to let infection go very far; i.e., for the purposes of deciding that an Oscar and an Elmer have the same notion of grass we may require that they both believe that grass is a plant *without* requiring that their notion of a plant be exactly the same. But this is already

to accept the stance that interpretation is an essentially informal and interest-relative matter.

If we try for a notion of *exact sameness of content of mental representation*, which is what Pylyshyn is arguing for, then the infection problem becomes an infinite regress problem. Suppose, for example, that Oscar and Elmer are two children who both live in the United States; who both know that grass is a plant; but that Elmer knows that plants can be microscopic, whereas Oscar's notion of a plant involves being of visible size, being green, etc. Then the problem of distinguishing what is a difference in the content of the representations and what is a difference in collateral information re-arises again at the level of the marker 'plant'.

The point is that while discovering whether or not stereotypes are the same is good methodology for translation, it is nothing like an *algorithm*. Stereotypes themselves are beliefs expressed in *words*. Once we have accepted translations, however tentative, for some words or representations, then stereotype theory may give us a handle on how to translate other words or representations; but it cannot serve to *define* a notion of sameness of content for words or mental representations.

Nor can *sameness of perceptual prototype*, another notion that we have mentioned. We have seen that even if two words are associated with the same perceptual prototypes they may differ in meaning; for the meaning of the word is not just a function of associated perceptual prototypes, but also of various more or less abstract beliefs that one has in connection with the word ('grass is a plant'). Not only would it be wrong to say that two words (or two mental representations) have the same content when they are associated with the same perceptual prototypes; it would be wrong to take sameness of perceptual prototype as even a *necessary* condition for sameness of content of mental representations. For two speakers may have exactly the same meaning for the word 'bachelor', i.e., male adult human of marriageable age who has never been married, and have quite different perceptual prototypes associated with the word. On any intuitive notion of semantic content, to count every difference in perceptual prototype as a difference in semantic content would be just as unnatural as to count every difference in collateral information as a difference in semantic content.

Chomsky's response to my 'The meaning of "meaning"' was to suggest that one might be able to save the Fregean notion of an 'intension' by giving up the principle that 'intension determines extension'. On Chomsky's proposal, as applied to my Twin Earth example, we should say that the word 'water' has the same *intension* on earth and on Twin Earth even though it has a different *extension* on earth than on Twin Earth. In terms of what has just been said, however, it would seem that this is the wrong way to go. For if we go the way I went in 'The meaning of "meaning"', and take the extension of a term as one of the components of its 'meaning vector', then we have a clear reason for saying that 'grug' has a different meaning in north Ruritanian and in south Ruritanian. Since the word 'grug' clearly has a different reference in the two dialects of Ruritanian, it also has a different meaning. Once we decide to put the reference (or rather the difference in reference) aside, and to ask whether 'grug' has the same 'content' in the minds of Oscar and Elmer, we have embarked upon an impossible task. Far from making it easier for ourselves to decide whether the representations are synonymous, we have made it impossible. In fact, the first approximation we have to a principle for deciding whether words have the same meaning or not in actual translation practice is to look at the extensions. 'Factoring out' differences in extension will only make a principled decision on when there has been a change in meaning totally impossible.

On the other hand, if we do decide to take extension as a factor in determining synonymy, either of words or of mental representations, then we still will not arrive at anything like an algorithm. For, just as determining the stereotype involves determining the meanings of other words, so determining the extension of a term always involves determining the extension of other terms. That words should not be regarded as the same in content if they have different extensions is a useful principle in translation after we already have the enterprise of interpretation underway. But until we have started interpreting a language we don't have any idea what the extension of a term is.

How then do we ever get started in interpretation? The answer that I would defend is one which has been vigorously urged by Donald Davidson and by Quine. (David Wiggins has pointed out that the germ of this view can already be found in Vico.) This is the view that *interpretation is essentially a holistic enterprise*. To interpret a language (and it makes no difference whether the language be a public language or 'mentalese', assuming the existence of 'mentalese') involves finding a translation scheme, an 'analytical hypothesis', which is capable of being learned, capable of yielding ready equivalents in our home language to the expressions being translated, and, most important, which is such that when we interpret the speakers of the alien language as meaning what the translation scheme says they mean we are able to 'understand'

their purposes, beliefs, and behavior. As Vico put it, in interpretation we seek to maximize the *humanity* of the beings being translated. If this is right then the only criteria that we actually have for the 'content' of any signs, or sign-analogs, are our intuitive criteria of successful interpretation; and to *formalize* these would involve formalizing our entire conception of what it is to be human, of what it is to be intelligible in human terms (see Putnam, 1976).

This discussion is not meant to suggest that interpretation theory is something incapable of study. Interpretation is something that can be studied in many ways and from many perspectives. But it is meant to suggest that, contrary to Pylyshyn's suggestion, the theory of interpretation and cognitive psychology deal with quite different projects and that to a large extent success in one of these projects is independent of success in the other. What the example I have developed shows is that it may be possible to give a complete functionalist psychology, including a complete verificationist semantics for mentalese, without in any way solving the problem of interpretation, or even the problem of reference-preserving translation (assignment of extensions). To have a description of how a system of representations works in functionalist terms is one thing; to have an *interpretation* of that system of representations is quite another thing.

The difference between functionalist psychology and interpretation theory is in part due to this: functionalist psychology treats the human mind as a computer. It seeks to state the rules of computation. The rules of computation have the property that although their interactions may be complicated and global, their action at any particular time is local. The machine, as it might be, moves a digit from one address to another address in obedience to a particular instruction, or to finitely many instructions, and on the basis of a finite amount of data. Interpretation is never local in this sense. A translation scheme, however well it works on a finite amount of corpus, may always have to be modified on the basis of additonal text.

Let me illustrate this point by means of what may seem to be a digression. Some years ago Hartry Field (1972) advocated the view that *reference* is a physicalistic relation between sign-uses and things (including properties). When he commented on my paper 'Language and reality' (Putnam, 1975b) at Chapel Hill some years ago, Field spelled this out a little further with some examples. Considering the case of a Newtonian scientist who used the term 'gravitation', Field suggested that the decision we should make as to which objects or properties this term refers to should be based on finding which objects the scientist had better be referring to as a matter of objective fact, if his theory as a whole is to be a rationally acceptable approximation to the truth. The reason I mention this is that, although the notion of interpretation involved here is as different from Pylyshyn's notion of finding 'content' as could possibly be imagined, the same considerations turn up. It turns out that the 'physicalistic relation' that Field is looking for is one whose very definition will involve *interpreting the language as a whole,* and not just individual signs (since what constitutes an interpretation of a theory that makes the theory rationally acceptable depends on looking at the *whole* theory), and is a relation whose very definition involves an analysis of rationality in its normative sense. Whether any relation whose definition involves these elements is properly called 'physicalistic' I shall not inquire; but the point is that *every* project for analyzing the notion of *interpretation* sooner or later involves recognizing that the analysis of the notion of interpretation is inseparable from the analysis of either the normative notion of rationality, or from some such notion as Vico's 'humanity'.

To expect anything like complete success at stating in a completely rigorous and formal way what the correct procedures are in interpretation would obviously be utopian. This may not, in itself, seem like a terribly important point. After all, complete success at stating the laws of physics may well be a utopian project; certainly complete success at describing the functional organization of a human brain is a utopian project. But physics is possible, even though complete success eludes us, because the laws of physics can be successively approximated; and functional psychology is possible because (we hope) the functional organization of the human brain can be partly described and approximated. Similarly one might hope that one could obtain partial success in describing the practices and procedures of interpretation.

I have no doubt that this is true; indeed I have no doubt that each of these subjects can be studied at more than one level (physics, after all, is not just elementary particle theory; it is also magnetohydrodynamics, solid state physics, and many things besides) and in connection with many different projects requiring many different notions of precision and many different vocabularies. The important point is that the kind of partial success that is realistically foreseeable in cognitive psychology and the kind of partial successes that is realistically foreseeable in interpretation theory are quite different.

In one sense, I hope the present paper is a contribution to interpetation theory. The interesting successes that we are likely to have in interpretation theory are more likely to be philosophical discussions than technical 'results'. But even if we confine attention to the sorts of contributions to interpretation theory that are likely to come from computer science and related areas, then, as Marvin Minsky (1975) has pointed out, these successes are likely to be by their very nature partial. When we mechanize interpretation, Minsky points out, what we typically do is *restrict* it to a definite set of texts which are on a specific subject matter and which share a common vocabulary, a common set of projects, and a common set of empirical or other assumptions. The reason that partial successes in interpretation theory are always so limited is that any global success, any program for interpretation of sentences in a variable language, a variable theory, on variable topics and with variable presuppositions, would involve an analysis of the notion of humanity, or of the notion (which in my view is closely related) of rationality. The function of limiting interpretation to a specific frame is to avoid having to tackle the totally utopian project of algorithmic analysis of these notions.

The kind of partial success we are likely to have in cognitive psychology, however, is quite different. Here what we might hope for are the identification of the kinds of physical states that realize various functional roles. If the hypothesis that the brain computes in something analogous to a formalized language is correct then we might hope to identify such things as predicate-analogs and sentence-analogs in the brain, or to say something about the computation rules for manipulating these. I think that anyone who has a clear idea of what these two kinds of partial success amount to, and who does not allow himself to be carried away by utterly utopian dreams of a complete mathematical analysis of what it is to be human (or what it is to be rational), will see at once that they are independent projects and neither really presupposes the other at all.

Nelson Goodman (1978) has advocated 'pluralism' as opposed to 'monism'. In this terminology, the view that we should aim for a single science of cognitive psychology which solves the problems of syntax and semantics together and at one stroke (and which solves the problems of semantics both in the sense of verificationist semantics and in the sense of interpretation) is a species of monism. In opposition to it I suggest that we should let a hundred flowers blossom, that we should let them blossom in their separate ways, in their separate seasons, and even in their separate gardens.

Relevance to Davidson's Philosophy of Mind

I think that the points that I have made have a certain 'Davidsonian' quality. It may be appropriate in this place to bring out more explicitly how this is so. In 'Mental events', Davidson (1970) put forward the thesis of 'anomalous monism'. This is the thesis that there are token–token identities between physical events and mental events (i.e., events described in the vocabulary of belief and desire), but no type–type identities. The argument that he gives for the non-existence of type–type identities has been widely misunderstood. To many it has seemed like a 'howler'; Davidson has been charged with arguing for the non-existence of type–type identities from the mere fact that mental concepts and physical concepts owe allegiance to different criteria. (Such an argument would be fallacious since it would block all type–type identities, even the identity 'water is H_2O', or 'light is electromagnetic radiation'. For certainly, before the reduction, 'water' and 'H_2O' owed allegiance to different criteria, as did 'light' and 'electromagnetic radiation'.) This is simply a misreading, however; Davidson does have an argument, and it is both a subtle and an interesting one.

Davidson is very familiar with the work of Amos Tversky (see Tversky & Kahneman, 1975, 1982). Thus he is extremely aware that *preferences* cannot be read off from even *sincere verbal reports*. As Tversky's very careful empirical research shows, people's sincere verbal reports of their own preferences are totally incoherent. If we acted on the maxim of ascribing to people all of the preferences they say (sincerely) they have then we would be unable to interpret their behavior at all, for *expressed* preferences are totally contradictory (e.g., they violate the logical property of the transitivity of preference very badly). Now, and perhaps this is the step that Davidson should have spelled out a little more explicitly, there is no reason to think that the availability of a 'cerebroscope' which enabled us to directly read off the subject's 'mentalese' could make things any better. Sincere verbal reports presumably correspond to mental representations that are present in the subject's brain. There is no reason to believe that the patient's 'mentalese' representations are any more consistent than his sincere verbal reports. If we could *read* the 'mentalese' we would undoubtedly find coded in the brain itself such reports as 'I prefer A to B', 'I prefer B to C', 'I prefer C to A', on

certain occasions. What we do when we discover such reports in a discourse is look at the subject's total behavior and try to decide on the basis of his total behavior, and also on the basis of further linguistic material, further 'corpus', what is the most reasonable *reconstruction* of the patient's behavior and talk. A reasonable reconstruction accounts for the subject's behavior, or for most of his behavior, in terms of preferences which may be a subset of those he avows or which may even be slightly different from any that he avows, and accounts for those expressed preferences which we decide the patient does not really have as being confusions of various kinds. We may decide that some of the patient's expressed preferences were the product of suggestion in the particular context, for example.

Of course, someone may say that at a deeper level than even the patient's mentalese there must be a level of what we might call Platonic mentalese which records in the form of neurologically salient representations in a hidden code what the subject's *true* preferences are. But there is absolutely no reason to believe this. People may just be computers which are wired so that most of the time what they end up doing admits of some rational explanation or other; it need not be the case that the rational explanation which is the best *rational reconstruction* of the behavior is itself actually physically coded in their brains somewhere.

In short, Davidson's point is that what is true of public language is almost certainly going to be true of any 'mental representations' or salient neurological states which stand causally *behind* public language. Just as we have to say that a person's true preferences are not exactly the same as the preferences he *avows*, so we will have to say that a person's 'true preferences' (i.e., the ones it would be best to ascribe to him in rationally reconstructing his behavior) are not the same as the one's coded in his brain representations. Belief-desire explanation belongs to the level of what I've been calling *interpretation theory*. It is as holistic and interest relative as all interpretation. Psychologists often speak as though there were *concepts* in the *brain*. The point of my argument (and, I think, of Davidson's) is that there may be *sentence-analogs* and *predicate-analogs* in the brain, but not concepts. 'Mental representations' require interpretation just as much as any other signs do.

NOTES

1. Strictly speaking a *semi-computable* (*partial* recursive) predicate: in *psychology*, as opposed to idealized inductive logic, we cannot require that degrees of belief be always *defined*. Let me emphasize also that in a psychological model

not all learning is a matter of *induction* even in the wide sense in which inductive logicians use that term. We learn many things just by being *told* them or *shown* them: believing things that other people tell us or show us (to some extent) must be incorporated into the 'degree of confirmation' function whether or not one thinks this is good 'inductive logic'.

2. The reason is that, as both Fodor and Dennett have emphasized, cognitive psychology is *computational* psychology. It is alright to have 'homunculi' who make inferences, etc., as part of one's explanations provided the homunculi are eventually 'discharged' (as Dennett puts it), i.e., explained away as computer algorithms. But this means 'knowing' must eventually be 'discharged'.

3. The reason that we cannot count every difference in the collateral information we have as difference in the meaning of a *word*, is that to do so abandons the distinction between our 'concepts' and what beliefs we have that contain those concepts, and just this distinction is the *basis* of the intuitive notions of meaning, synonymy, analyticity, etc. To give up the meaning/belief distinction amounts to agreeing with Quine that we may as well give up the notion of *meaning* altogether. The same goes for the distinction between the 'content' of our mental representations and our beliefs involving them; this is nothing but a *picture*, a picture of 'words in the head'. Pictures are not always a *mistake;* they can be useful models. But if the picture of 'mental representations' and their 'content' is to have any use, then 'content' must remain stable under *some* changes of *belief.*

4. Chomsky wrote me a long letter after the appearance of 'The meaning of "meaning"' defending this way out. Fodor (1979) defends the same program.

REFERENCES

Davidson, D., 1967. 'Truth and meaning', *Synthese,* XVII, 304–23.

———— 1970. 'Mental events', in L. Foster and J. Swanson (eds.) *Experience and Theory,* London, 79–101.

Field, H., 1972a. 'Tarski's theory of truth', *Journal of Philosophy,* LXIX, 347–75.

———— 1972b. 'Theory change and the indeterminacy of reference', *Journal of Philosophy,* LXX, 462–81.

Fodor, J., 1975. *The Language of Thought,* New York.

———— 1979. 'Methodological solipsism considered as a research strategy in cognitive psychology', *The Behavioral and Brain Sciences,* 63–109.

Goodman, N., 1978. *Ways of Worldmaking,* Indianapolis.

Minsky, M., 1975. 'A framework for representing knowledge', published as part of his *The Psychology of Computer Vision,* New York.

Putnam, H., 1975a. 'The meaning of "meaning"', reprinted in Putnam (1975e), 215–71.

———— 1975b. 'Language and Reality', in Putnam (1975e), 272–90.

———— 1975e. *Mind, Language and Reality: Philosophical Papers, Volume 2,* Cambridge.

———— 1976. 'Realism and reason', reprinted in Putnam (1978), 123–38.

———— 1978. *Meaning and the Moral Sciences,* London.

Tversky, A. and Kahneman, D., 1982. *Judgment under Uncertainty,* Cambridge.

———— 1975. 'Judgment under uncertainty: heuristics and biases', *Science,* 185, 1124–31.

B. Individualism

57

Tyler Burge

"Individualism and the Mental"

Since Hegel's *Phenomenology of Spirit,* a broad, inarticulate division of emphasis between the individual and his social environment has marked philosophical discussions of mind. On one hand, there is the traditional concern with the individual subject of mental states and events. In the elderly Cartesian tradition, the spotlight is on what exists or transpires "in" the individual—his secret cogitations, his innate cognitive structures, his private perceptions and introspections, his grasping of ideas, concepts, or forms. More evidentially oriented movements, such as behaviorism and its liberalized progeny, have highlighted the individual's publicly observable behavior—his input–output relations and the dispositions, states, or events that mediate them. But both Cartesian and behaviorist viewpoints tend to feature the individual subject. On the other hand, there is the Hegelian preoccupation with the role of social institutions in shaping the individual and the content of his thought. This tradition has dominated the continent since Hegel. But it has found echoes in English-speaking philosophy during this century in the form of a concentration on language. Much philosophical work on language and mind has been in the interests of Cartesian or behaviorist viewpoints that I shall term "individualistic." But many of Wittgenstein's remarks about mental representation point up a social orientation that is discernible from his flirtations with behaviorism. And more recent work on the theory of reference has provided glimpses of the role of social cooperation in determining what an individual thinks.

In many respects, of course, these emphases within philosophy—individualistic and social— are compatible. To an extent, they may be regarded simply as different currents in the turbulent stream of ideas that has washed the intellectual landscape during the last hundred and some odd years. But the role of the social environment has received considerably less clear-headed philosophical attention (though perhaps not less philosophical attention) than the role of the states, occurrences, or acts in, on, or by the individual. Philosophical discussions of social factors have tended to be obscure, evocative, metaphorical, or platitudinous, or to be bent on establishing some large thesis about the course of history and the destiny of man. There remains much room for sharp delineation. I shall offer some considerations that stress social factors in descriptions of an individual's mental phenomena. These considerations call into question individualistic presuppositions of several traditional and modern treatments of mind. I shall conclude with some remarks about mental models.

I. Terminological Matters

Our ordinary mentalistic discourse divides broadly into two sorts of idiom. One typically makes reference to mental states or events in terms of sentential expressions. The other does not. A clear case of the first kind of idiom is 'Alfred thinks that his friends' sofa is ugly'. A clear case of the second sort is 'Alfred is in pain'. Thoughts, beliefs, intentions, and so forth are typically specified in terms of subordinate sentential clauses, that-clauses, which may be judged as true or false. Pains, feels, tickles, and so forth have no special semantical relation to sentences or to truth or falsity. There are intentional idioms that fall in the second category on this characterization, but that share important

From *Midwest Studies in Philosophy,* vol. IV, Peter A. French, Theodore E. Uehling, Jr., and Howard K. Wettstein, eds. Minneapolis: University of Minnesota Press, 1979, pp. 73–121. Reprinted with permission of the publisher and Tyler Burge.

semantical features with expressions in the first—idioms like 'Al worships Buicks'. But I shall not sort these out here. I shall discuss only the former kind of mentalistic idiom. The extension of the discussion to other intentional idioms will not be difficult.

In an ordinary sense, the noun phrases that embed sentential expressions in mentalistic idioms provide the *content* of the mental state or event. We shall call that-clauses and their grammatical variants *"content clauses."* Thus the expression 'that sofas are more comfortable than pews' provides the content of Alfred's belief that sofas are more comfortable than pews. My phrase 'provides the content' represents an attempt at remaining neutral, at least for present purposes, among various semantical and metaphysical accounts of precisely how that-clauses function and precisely what, if anything, contents are.

Although the notion of content is, for present purposes, ontologically neutral, I do think of it as holding a place in a systematic *theory* of mentalistic language. The question of when to count contents different, and when the same, is answerable to theoretical restrictions. It is often remarked that in a given context we may ascribe to a person two that-clauses that are only loosely equivalent and count them as attributions of the "same attitude." We may say that Al's intention to climb Mt. McKinley and his intention to climb the highest mountain in the United States are the "same intention." (I intend the terms for the mountain to occur obliquely here. See later discussion.) This sort of point extends even to content clauses with extensionally non-equivalent counterpart notions. For contextually relevant purposes, we might count a thought that the glass contains some water as "the same thought" as a thought that the glass contains some thirst-quenching liquid, particularly if we have no reason to attribute either content as opposed to the other, and distinctions between them are contextually irrelevant. Nevertheless, in both these examples, every systematic theory I know of would want to represent the semantical contribution of the content-clauses in distinguishable ways—as "providing different contents."

One reason for doing so is that the person himself is capable of having different attitudes described by the different content-clauses, even if these differences are irrelevant in a particular context. (Al might have developed the intention to climb the highest mountain before developing the intention to climb Mt. McKinley—regardless of whether he, in fact, did so.) A second reason is that the counterpart components of the that-clauses allude to distinguishable elements in people's cognitive lives. 'Mt. McKinley' and 'the highest mountain the the U.S.' serve, or might serve, to indicate cognitively different notions. This is a vague, informal way of generalizing Frege's point: the thought that Mt. McKinley is the highest mountain in the U.S. is potentially interesting or informative. The thought that Mt. McKinley is Mt. McKinley is not. Thus when we say in a given context that attribution of different contents is attribution of the "same attitude," we use 'same attitude' in a way similar to the way we use 'same car' when we say that people who drive Fords (or green 1970 Ford Mavericks) drive the "same car." For contextual purposes different cars are counted as "amounting to the same."

Although this use of 'content' is theoretical, it is not I think theoretically controversial. In cases where we shall be counting contents different, the cases will be uncontentious: On any systematic theory, differences in the *extension*—the actual denotation, referent, or application—of counterpart expressions in that-clauses will be semantically represented, and will, in our terms, make for differences in content. I shall be avoiding the more controversial, but interesting, questions about the general conditions under which sentences in that clauses can be expected to provide the same content.

I should also warn of some subsidiary terms. I shall be (and have been) using the term *'notion'* to apply to components or elements of contents. Just as whole that-clauses provide the content of a person's attitude, semantically relevant components of that-clauses will be taken to indicate notions that enter into the attitude (or the attitude's content). This term is supposed to be just as ontologically neutral as its fellow. When I talk of understanding or mastering the notion of contract, I am not relying on any special epistemic or ontological theory, except insofar as the earlier-mentioned theoretical restrictions on the notion of content are inherited by the notion of notion. The expression, *'understanding (mastering) a notion'* is to be construed more or less intuitively. Understanding the notion of contract comes roughly to knowing what a contract is. One can master the notion of contract without mastering the term 'contract'—at the very least if one speaks some language other than English that has a term roughly synonymous with 'contract'. (An analogous point holds for my use of 'mastering a content'.) Talk of notions is roughly similar to talk of concepts in an informal sense. 'Notion' has the advantage of being easier to separate from traditional theoretical commitments.

I speak of *attributing* an attitude, content, or notion, and of *ascribing* a that-clause or other piece of language. Ascriptions are the linguistic analogs of attributions. This use of 'ascribe' is non-standard, but convenient and easily assimilated.

There are semantical complexities involving the behavior of expressions in content clauses, most of which we can skirt. But some must be touched on. Basic to the subject is the observation that expressions in content clauses are often not intersubstitutable with extensionally equivalent expressions in such a way as to maintain the truth value of the containing sentence. Thus from the facts that water is H_2O and that Bertrand thought that water is not fit to drink, it does not follow that Bertrand thought that H_2O is not fit to drink. When an expression like 'water' functions in a content clause so that it is not freely exchangeable with all extensionally equivalent expressions, we shall say that it has *oblique occurrence*. Roughly speaking, the reason why 'water' and 'H_2O' are not interchangeable in our report of Bertrand's thought is that 'water' plays a role in characterizing a different mental act or state from that which 'H_2O' would play a role in characterizing. In this context at least, thinking that water is not fit to drink is different from thinking that H_2O is not fit to drink.

By contrast, there are non-oblique occurrences of expressions in content clauses. One might say that some water—say, the water in the glass over there—is thought by Bertrand to be impure; or that Bertrand thought that *that* water is impure. And one might intend to make no distinction that would be lost by replacing 'water' with 'H_2O'—or 'that water' with 'that H_2O' or 'that common liquid', or any other expression extensionally equivalent with 'that water'. We might allow these exchanges even though Bertrand had never heard of, say, H_2O. In such purely nonoblique occurrences, 'water' plays *no role* in providing the *content* of Bertrand's thought, *on our use of 'content'*, or (in any narrow sense) in characterizing Bertrand or his mental state. Nor is the water part of Bertrand's thought content. We speak of Bertrand *thinking his content of* the water. At its nonoblique occurrence, the term 'that water' simply isolates, in one of many equally good ways, a portion of wet stuff to which Bertrand or his thought is related or applied. In certain cases, it may also mark a context in which Bertrand's thought is applied. But it is expressions at oblique occurences within content clauses that primarily do the job of providing the content of mental states or events, and in characterizing the person.

Mentalistic discourse containing obliquely occurring expressions has traditionally been called *intentional discourse*. The historical reasons for this nomenclature are complex and partly confused. But roughly speaking, grammatical contexts involving oblique occurences have been fixed upon as specially relevant to the representational character (sometimes called "intentionality") of mental states and events. Clearly oblique occurrences in mentalistic discourse have something to do with characterizing a person's epistemic perspective—how things seem to him, or in an informal sense, how they are represented to him. So without endorsing all the commitments of this tradition, I shall take over its terminology.

The crucial point in the preceding discussion is the assumption that obliquely occurring expressions in content clauses are a primary means of identifying a person's intentional mental states or events. A further point is worth remarking here. It is normal to suppose that those content clauses correctly ascribable to a person that are not in general intersubstitutable *salva veritate*—and certainly those that involve extensionally non-equivalent counterpart expressions—identify different mental states or events.

I have cited contextual exceptions to this normal supposition, at least in a manner of speaking. We sometimes count distinctions in content irrelevant for purposes of a given attribution, particularly where our evidence for the precise content of a person or animal's attitude is skimpy. Different contents may contextually identify (what amount to) the "same attitude." I have indicated that even in these contexts, I think it best, strictly speaking, to construe distinct contents as describing different mental states or events that are merely equivalent for the purposes at hand. I believe that this view is widely accepted. But nothing I say will depend on it. For any distinct contents, there will be imaginable contexts of attribution in which, even in the loosest, most informal ways of speaking, those contents would be said to describe different mental states or events. This is virtually a consequence of the theoretical role of contents, discussed earlier. Since our discussion will have an "in principle" character, I shall take these contexts to be the relevant ones. Most of the cases we discuss will involve *extensional* differences between obliquely occurring counterpart expressions in that-clauses. In such cases, it is particularly natural and normal to take different contents as identifying different mental states or events.

II.   A Thought Experiment

IIa.   First Case

We now turn to a three-step thought experiment. Suppose first that:

> A given person has a large number of attitudes commonly attributed with content clauses containing 'ar-

thritis' in oblique occurrence. For example, he thinks (correctly) that he has had arthritis for years, that his arthritis in his wrists and fingers is more painful than his arthritis in his ankles, that it is better to have arthritis than cancer of the liver, that stiffening joints is a symptom of arthritis, that certain sorts of aches are characteristic of arthritis, that there are various kinds of arthritis, and so forth. In short, he has a wide range of such attitudes. In addition to these unsurprising attitudes, he thinks falsely that he has developed arthritis in the thigh.

Generally competent in English, rational and intelligent, the patient reports to his doctor his fear that his arthritis has now lodged in his thigh. The doctor replies by telling him that this cannot be so, since arthritis is specifically an inflammation of joints. Any dictionary could have told him the same. The patient is surprised, but relinquishes his view and goes on to ask what might be wrong with his thigh.

The second step of the thought experiment consists of a counterfactual supposition. We are to conceive of a situation in which the patient proceeds from birth through the same course of physical events that he actually does, right to and including the time at which he first reports his fear to his doctor. Precisely the same things (non-intentionally described) happen to him. He has the same physiological history, the same diseases, the same internal physical occurrences. He goes through the same motions, engages in the same behavior, has the same sensory intake (physiologically described). His dispositions to respond to stimuli are explained in physical theory as the effects of the same proximate causes. All of this extends to his interaction with linguistic expressions. He says and hears the same words (word forms) at the same time he actually does. He develops the disposition to assent to 'Arthritis can occur in the thigh' and 'I have arthritis in the thigh' as a result of the same physically described proximate causes. Such dispositions might have arisen in a number of ways. But we can suppose that in both actual and counterfactual situations, he acquires the word 'arthritis' from casual conversation or reading, and never hearing anything to prejudice him for or against applying it in the way that he does, he applies the word to an ailment in his thigh (or to ailments in the limbs of others) which seems to produce pains or other symptoms roughly similar to the disease in his hands and ankles. In both actual and counterfactual cases, the disposition is never reinforced or extinguished up until the time when he expresses himself to his doctor. We further imagine that the patient's non-intentional, phenomenal experience is the same. He has the same pains, visual fields, images, and internal ver-

bal rehearsals. The *counterfactuality* in the supposition touches only the patient's social environment. In actual fact, 'arthritis', as used in his community, does not apply to ailments outside joints. Indeed, it fails to do so by a standard, non-technical dictionary definition. But in our imagined case, physicians, lexicographers, and informed laymen apply 'arthritis' not only to arthritis but to various other rheumatoid ailments. The standard use of the term is to be conceived to encompass the patient's actual misuse. We could imagine either that arthritis had not been singled out as a family of diseases, or that some other term besides 'arthritis' were applied, though not commonly by laymen, specifically to arthritis. We may also suppose that this difference and those necessarily associated with it are the only differences between the counterfactual situation and the actual one. (Other people besides the patient will, of course, behave differently.) To summarize the second step:

> The person might have had the same physical history and non-intentional mental phenomena while the word 'arthritis' was conventionally applied, and defined to apply, to various rheumatoid ailments, including the one in the person's thigh, as well as to arthritis.

The final step is an interpretation of the counterfactual case, or an addition to it as so far described. It is reasonable to suppose that:

> In the counterfactual situation, the patient lacks some—probably all—of the attitudes commonly attributed with content clauses containing 'arthritis' in oblique occurrence. He lacks the occurrent thoughts or beliefs that he has arthritis in the thigh, that he has had arthritis for years, that stiffening joints and various sorts of aches are symptoms of arthritis, that his father had arthritis, and so on.

We suppose that in the counterfactual case we cannot correctly ascribe any content clause containing an oblique occurrence of the term 'arthritis'. It is hard to see how the patient could have picked up the notion of arthritis. The word 'arthritis' in the counterfactual community does not mean *arthritis*. It does not apply only to inflammations of joints. We suppose that no other word in the patient's repertoire means *arthritis*. 'Arthritis', in the counterfactual situation, differs both in dictionary definition and in extension from 'arthritis' as we use it. Our ascriptions of content clauses to the patient (and ascriptions within his community) would not constitute attributions of the same contents we actually attribute. For counterpart expressions in the content clauses that are actually and counterfactually ascribable are not even extensionally equivalent. However we describe the patient's attitudes in the counterfactual situation, it will not be with a term or phrase extensionally equivalent with 'arthritis'. So the patient's counterfactual attitude contents differ from his actual ones.

The upshot of these reflections is that the patient's mental contents differ while his entire physical and non-intentional mental histories, considered in isolation from their social context, remain the same. (We could have supposed that he dropped dead at the time he first expressed his fear to the doctor.) The differences seem to stem from differences "outside" the patient considered as an isolated physical organism, causal mechanism, or seat of consciousness. The difference in his mental contents is attributable to differences in his social environment. In sum, the patient's internal qualitative experiences, his physiological states and events, his behaviorally described stimuli and responses, his dispositions to behave, and whatever sequences of states (non-intentionally described) mediated his input and output—all these remain constant, while his attitude contents differ, even in the extensions of counterpart notions. As we observed at the outset, such differences are ordinarily taken to spell differences in mental states and events.

IIb.   Further Exemplifications

The argument has an extremely wide application. It does not depend, for example, on the kind of word 'arthritis' is. We could have used an artifact term, an ordinary natural kind word, a color adjective, a social role term, a term for a historical style, an abstract noun, an action verb, a physical movement verb, or any of various other sorts of words. I prefer to leave open precisely how far one can generalize the argument. But I think it has a very wide scope. The argument can get under way in any case where it is intuitively possible to attribute a mental state or event whose content involves a notion that the subject incompletely understands. As will become clear, this possibility is the key to the thought experiment. I want to give a more concrete sense of the possibility before going further.

It is useful to reflect on the number and variety of intuitively clear cases in which it is normal to attribute a content that the subject incompletely understands. One need only thumb through a dictionary for an hour or so to develop a sense of the extent to which one's beliefs are infected by incomplete understanding.[1] The phenomenon is rampant in our pluralistic age.

a. Most cases of incomplete understanding that support the thought experiment will be fairly id-

iosyncratic. There is a reason for this. Common linguistic errors, if entrenched, tend to become common usage. But a generally competent speaker is bound to have numerous words in his repertoire, possibly even common words, that he somewhat misconstrues. Many of these misconstruals will not be such as to deflect ordinary ascriptions of that-clauses involving the incompletely mastered term in oblique occurrence. For example, one can imagine a generally competent, rational adult having a large number of attitudes involving the notion of sofa—including beliefs that *those* (some sofas) are sofas, that some sofas are beige, that his neighbors have a new sofa, that he would rather sit in a sofa for an hour than on a church pew. In addition, he might think that sufficiently broad (but single-seat) overstuffed armchairs are sofas. With care, one can develop a thought experiment parallel to the one in secton IIa, in which at least some of the person's attitude contents (particularly, in this case, contents of occurrent mental events) differ, while his physical history, dispositions to behavior, and phenomenal experience—non–intentionally and asocially described—remain the same.

b. Although most relevant misconstruals are fairly idiosyncratic, there do seem to be certain types of error which are relatively common—but not so common and uniform as to suggest that the relevant terms take on new sense. Much of our vocabulary is taken over from others who, being specialists, understand our terms better than we do.[2] The use of scientific terms by laymen is a rich source of cases. As the arthritis example illustrates, the thought experiment does not depend on specially technical terms. I shall leave it to the imagination of the reader to spin out further examples of this sort.

c. One need not look to the laymen's acquisitions from science for examples. People used to buying beef brisket in stores or ordering it in restaurants (and conversant with it in a general way) probably often develop mistaken beliefs (or uncertainties) about just what brisket is. For example, one might think that brisket is a cut from the flank or rump, or that it includes not only the lower part of the chest but also the upper part, or that it is specifically a cut of beef and not of, say, pork. No one hesitates to ascribe to such people content-clauses with 'brisket' in oblique occurrence. For example, a person may believe that he is eating brisket under these circumstances (where 'brisket' occurs in oblique position); or he may think that brisket tends to be tougher than loin. Some of these attitudes may be false; many will be true. We can imagine a counterfactual case in which the person's physical history, his dispositions, and his non-intentional mental life, are all the same, but in which 'brisket' is commonly applied in a different way—perhaps in precisely the way the person thinks it applies. For example, it might apply only to beef and to the upper and lower parts of the chest. In such a case, as in the sofa and arthritis cases, it would seem that the person would (or might) lack some or all of the propositional attitudes that are actually attributed with content clauses involving 'brisket' in oblique position.

d. Someone only generally versed in music history, or superficially acquainted with a few drawings of musical instruments, might naturally but mistakenly come to think that clavichords included harpsichords without legs. He may have many other beliefs involving the notion of clavichord, and many of these may be true. Again, with some care, a relevant thought experiment can be generated.

e. A fairly common mistake among lawyers' clients is to think that one cannot have a contract with someone unless there has been a written agreement. The client might be clear in intending 'contract' (in the relevant sense) to apply to agreements, not to pieces of paper. Yet he may take it as part of the meaning of the word, or the essence of law, that a piece of formal writing is a necessary condition for establishing a contract. His only experiences with contracts might have involved formal documents, and he undergeneralizes. It is not terribly important here whether one says that the client misunderstands the term's meaning, or alternatively that the client makes a mistake about the essence of contracts. In either case, he misconceives what a contract is; yet ascriptions involving the term in oblique position are made anyway.

It is worth emphasizing here that I intend the misconception to involve the subject's attaching counterfactual consequences to his mistaken belief about contracts. Let me elaborate this a bit. A common dictionary definition of 'contract' is 'legally binding agreement'. As I am imagining the case, the client does not explicitly define 'contract' to himself in this way (though he might use this phrase in explicating the term). And he is not merely making a mistake about what the law happens to enforce. If asked why unwritten agreements are not contracts, he is likely to say something like, 'They just aren't' or 'It is part of the nature of the law and legal practice that they have no force'. He is not disposed without prodding to answer, 'It would be possible but impractical to give unwritten agreements legal force'. He might concede this. But he would add that such agreements would not be contracts. He regards a docu-

ment as inseparable from contractual obligation, regardless of whether he takes this to be a matter of meaning or a metaphysical essentialist truth about contracts.

Needless to say, these niceties are philosopher's distinctions. They are not something an ordinary man is likely to have strong opinions about. My point is that the thought experiment is independent of these distinctions. It does not depend on misunderstandings of dictionary meaning. One might say that the client understood the term's dictionary meaning, but misunderstood its essential application in the law—misconceived the nature of contracts. The thought experiment still flies. In a counterfactual case in which the law enforces both written and unwritten agreements and in which the subject's behavior and so forth are the same, but in which 'contract' *means* 'legally binding agreement based on written document', we would not attribute to him a mistaken belief that a contract requires written agreement, although the lawyer might have to point out that there are other legally binding agreements that do not require documents. Similarly, the client's other propositional attitudes would no longer involve the notion of contract, but another more restricted notion.

f. People sometimes make mistakes about color ranges. They may correctly apply a color term to a certain color, but also mistakenly apply it to shades of a neighboring color. When asked to explain the color term, they cite the standard cases (for 'red', the color of blood, fire engines, and so forth). But they apply the term somewhat beyond its conventionally established range—beyond the reach of its vague borders. They think that fire engines, including *that* one, are red. They observe that red roses are covering the trellis. But they also think that *those* things are a shade of red (whereas they are not). Second looks do not change their opinion. But they give in when other speakers confidently correct them in unison.

This case extends the point of the contract example. The error is linguistic or conceptual in something like the way that the shopper's mistake involving the notion of brisket is. It is not an ordinary empirical error. But one may reasonably doubt that the subjects misunderstand the dictionary meaning of the color term. Holding their non-intentional phenomenal experience, physical history, and behavioral dispositions constant, we can imagine that 'red' were applied as they mistakenly apply it. In such cases, we would no longer ascribe content-clauses involving the term 'red' in oblique position. The attribution of the correct beliefs about fire engines and roses would be no less affected than the attribution of the beliefs that, in the actual case, display the misapplication. Cases bearing out the latter point are common in anthropological reports on communities whose color terms do not match ours. Attributions of content typically allow for the differences in conventionally established color ranges.

Here is not the place to refine our rough distinctions among the various kinds of misconceptions that serve the thought experiment. Our philosophical purposes do not depend on how these distinctions are drawn. Still, it is important to see what an array of conceptual errors is common among us. And it is important to note that such errors do not always or automatically prevent attribution of mental content provided by the very terms that are incompletely understood or misapplied. The thought experiment is nourished by this aspect of common practice.

IIc.   Expansion and Delineation of the Thought Experiment

As I have tried to suggest in the preceding examples, the relevant attributions in the first step of the thought experiment need not display the subject's error. They may be attributions of a true content. We can begin with a propositional attitude that involved the misconceived notion, but in a true, unproblematic application of it: for example, the patient's belief that he, like his father, developed arthritis in the ankles and wrists at age 58 (where 'arthritis' occurs obliquely).

One need not even rely on an underlying *misconception* in the thought experiment. One may pick a case in which the subject only partially understands an expression. He may apply it firmly and correctly in a range of cases, but be unclear or agnostic about certain of its applications or implications which, in fact, are fully established in common practice. Most of the examples we gave previously can be reinterpreted in this way. To take a new one, imagine that our protagonist is unsure whether his father has mortgages on the car and house, or just one on the house. He is a little uncertain about exactly how the loan and collateral must be arranged in order for there to be a mortgage, and he is not clear about whether one may have mortgages on anything other than houses. He is sure, however, that Uncle Harry paid off his mortgage. Imagine our man constant in the ways previously indicated and that 'mortgage' commonly applied only to mortgages on houses. But imagine banking practices themselves to be the same. Then the subject's uncertainty would plausibly not involve the notion of mortgage. Nor would his other propositional attitudes be cor-

rectly attributed with the term 'mortgage' in oblique position. Partial understanding is as good as misunderstanding for our purposes.

On the other hand, the thought experiment does appear to depend on the possibility of someone's having a propositional attitude despite an incomplete mastery of some notion in its content. To see why this appears to be so, let us try to run through a thought experiment, attempting to avoid any imputation of incomplete understanding. Suppose the subject thinks falsely that all swans are white. One can certainly hold the features of swans and the subject's non-intentional phenomenal experience, physical history, and non-intentional dispositions constant, and imagine that 'swan' meant 'white swan' (and perhaps some other term, unfamiliar to the subject, meant what 'swan' means). Could one reasonably interpret the subject as having different attitude contents without at some point invoking a misconception? The questions to be asked here are about the subject's dispositions. For example, in the actual case, if he were shown a black swan and told that he was wrong, would he fairly naturally concede his mistake? Or would he respond, "I'm doubtful that that's a swan," until we brought in dictionaries, encyclopedias, and other native speakers to correct his usage? In the latter case, his understanding of 'swan' would be deviant. Suppose then that in the actual situation he would respond normally to the counterexample. Then there is reason to say that he understands the notion of swan correctly; and his error is not conceptual or linguistic, but empirical in an ordinary and narrow sense. (Of course, the line we are drawing here is pretty fuzzy.) When one comes to the counterfactual stage of the thought experiment, the subject has the same dispositions to respond pliably to the presentation of a black specimen. But such a response would suggest a misunderstanding of the term 'swan' as counterfactually used. For in the counterfactual community, what they call "swans" could not fail to be white. The mere presentation of a black swan would be irrelevant to the definitional truth 'All swans are white'. I have not set this case up as an example of the thought experiment's going through. Rather I have used it to support the conjecture that *if* the thought experiment is to work, one must at some stage find the subject believing (or having some attitude characterized by) a content, despite an incomplete understanding or misapplication. An ordinary empirical error appears not to be sufficient.

It would be a mistake, however, to think that incomplete understanding, in the sense that the argument requires, is in general an unusual or even deviant phenomenon. *What I have called "partial* understanding" is common or even normal in the case of a large number of expressions in our vocabularies. 'Arthritis' is a case in point. Even if by the grace of circumstance a person does not fall into views that run counter to the term's meaning or application, it would not be the least deviant or "socially unacceptable" to have no clear attitude that would block such views. 'Brisket', 'contract', 'recession', 'sonata', 'deer', 'elm' (to borrow a well-known example), 'pre-amplifier', 'carburetor', 'gothic', 'fermentation', probably provide analogous cases. Continuing the list is largely a matter of patience. The sort of "incomplete understanding" required by the thought experiment includes quite ordinary, nondeviant phenomena.

It is worth remarking that the thought experiment as originally presented might be run in reverse. The idea would be to start with an ordinary belief or thought involving no incomplete understanding. Then we find the incomplete understanding in the second step. For example, properly understanding 'arthritis', a patient may think (correctly) that he has arthritis. He happens to have heard of arthritis only occurring in joints, and he correctly believes that that is where arthritis always occurs. Holding his physical history, dispositions, and pain constant, we imagine that 'arthritis' commonly applies to rheumatoid ailments of all sorts. Arthritis has not been singled out for special mention. If the patient were told by a doctor 'You also have arthritis in the thigh', the patient would be disposed (as he is in the actual case) to respond, 'Really? I didn't know that one could have arthritis except in joints'. The doctor would answer, 'No, arthritis occurs in muscles, tendons, bursas, and elsewhere'. The patient would stand corrected. The notion that the doctor and patient would be operating with in such a case would not be that of arthritis.

My reasons for not having originally set out the thought experiment in this way are largely heuristic. As will be seen, discussion of the thought experiment will tend to center on the step involving incomplete understanding. And I wanted to encourage you, dear reader, to imagine actual cases of incomplete understanding in your own linguistic community. Ordinary intuitions in the domestic case are perhaps less subject to premature warping in the interests of theory. Cases involving not only mental content attribution, but also translation of a foreign tongue are more vulnerable to intrusion of side issues.

A secondary reason for not beginning with this "reversed" version of the thought experiment is that I find it doubtful whether the thought experiment always works in symmetric fashion. There may be special intuitive problems in certain cases—perhaps, for example, cases involving perceptual natural kinds. We may give special interpretations to individuals' misconceptions in imagined foreign communities, when those misconceptions seem to match our conceptions. In other words, there may be some systematic intuitive bias in favor of at least certain of our notions for purposes of interpreting the misconceptions of imagined foreigners. I do not want to explore the point here. I think that any such bias is not always crucial, and that the thought experiment frequently works "symmetrically." We have to take account of a person's community in interpreting his words and describing his attitudes—and this holds in the foreign case as well as in the domestic case.

The reversal of the thought experiment brings home the important point that *even those propositional attitudes not infected by incomplete understanding* depend for their content on social factors that are independent of the individual, asocially and non-intentionally described. For if the social environment had been appropriately different, the contents of those attitudes would have been different.

Even *apart* from reversals of the thought experiment, it is plausible (in the light of its original versions) that our well-understood propositional attitudes depend partly for their content on social factors independent of the individual, asocially and non-intentionally construed. For each of us can reason as follows. Take a set of attitudes that involve a given notion and whose contents are well-understood by me. It is only contingent that I understand that notion as well as I do. Now holding my community's practices constant, imagine that I understand the given notion incompletely, but that the deficient understanding is such that it does not prevent my having attitude contents involving that notion. In fact, imagine that I am in the situation envisaged in the first step of one of the original thought experiments. In such a case, a proper subset of the original set of my actual attitude contents would, or might, remain the same—intuitively, at least those of my actual attitudes whose justification or point is untouched by my imagined deficient understanding. (In the arthritis case, an example would be a true belief that many old people have arthritis.) These attitude contents remain constant despite the fact that my understanding, inference patterns, behavior, dispositions, and so on would in important ways be different and partly inappropriate to applications of the given notion. What is it that enables these unaffected contents to remain applications of the relevant notion? It is not *just* that my understanding, inference patterns, behavior, and so forth are enough like my actual understanding, inference patterns, behavior, and so forth. For if communal practice had *also* varied so as to apply the relevant notion as I am imagining I misapply it, then my attitude contents would not involve the relevant notion at all. This argument suggests that communal practice is a factor (in addition to my understanding, inference patterns, and perhaps behavior, physical activity, and other features) in fixing the contents of my attitudes, even in cases where I fully understand the content.

IId. Independence from Factive-Verb and Indexical-Reference Paradigms

The thought experiment does not play on psychological "success" verbs or "factive" verbs—verbs like 'know', 'regret', 'realize', 'remember', 'foresee', 'perceive'. This point is important for our purposes because such verbs suggest an easy and clearcut distinction between the contribution of the individual subject and the objective, "veridical" contribution of the environment to making the verbs applicable. (Actually the matter becomes more complicated on reflection, but we shall stay with the simplest cases.) When a person knows that snow is common in Greenland, his knowledge obviously depends on more than the way the person is. It depends on there actually being a lot of snow in Greenland. His mental state (belief that snow is common in Greenland) must be successful in a certain way (true). By changing the environment, one could change the truth value of the content, so that the subject could no longer be said to know the content. It is part of the burden of our argument that even intentional mental states of the individual like beliefs, which carry no implication of veridicality or success, cannot be understood by focusing purely on the individual's acts, dispositions, and "inner" goings on.

The thought experiment also does not rest on the phenomenon of indexicality, or on *de re* attitudes, in any direct way. When Alfred refers to an apple, saying to himself "That is wholesome," what he refers to depends not just on the content of what he says or thinks, but on what apple is before him. Without altering the meaning of Alfred's utterance, the nature of his perceptual experiences, or his physical acts or dispositions, we could conceive an exchange of the actual apple for another one that is indistinguishable to Alfred. We would thereby conceive him as referring to something different and even as saying something with a different truth value.

This rather obvious point about indexicality has come to be seen as providing a model for understanding a certain range of mental states or

events—*de re* attitudes. The precise characterization of this range is no simple philosophical task. But the clearest cases involve non-obliquely occurring terms in content clauses. When we say that Bertrand thinks of some water that it would not slake his thirst (where 'water' occurs in purely non-oblique position), we attribute a *de re* belief to Bertrand. We assume that Bertrand has something like an indexical relation to the water. The fact that Bertrand believes something of some water, rather than of a portion of some other liquid that is indistinguishable to him, depends partly on the fact that it is water to which Bertrand is contextually, "indexically" related. For intuitively we could have exchanged the liquids without changing Bertrand and thereby changed what Bertrand believed his belief content *of*—and even whether his belief was true of it.[3] It is easy to interpret such cases by holding that the subject's mental states and contents (with allowances for brute differences in the contexts in which he applies those contents) remain the same. The differences in the situations do not pertain in any fundamental way to the subject's mind or the nature of his mental content, but to how his mind or content is related to the world.

I think this interpretation of standard indexical and *de re* caes is broadly correct, although it involves oversimplifications and demands refinements. But what I want to emphasize here is that it is inapplicable to the cases our thought experiment fixes upon.

It seems to me clear that the thought experiment need not rely on *de re* attitudes at all. The subject need not have entered into special *en rapport* or quasi-indexical relations with objects that the misunderstood term applies to in order for the argument to work. We can appeal to attitudes that would usually be regarded as paradigmatic cases of *de dicto,* non-indexical, *non-de-re,* mental attitudes or events. The primary mistake in the contract example is one such, but we could choose others to suit the reader's taste. To insist that such attitudes must all be indexically infected or *de re* would, I think, be to trivialize and emasculate these notions, making nearly all attitudes *de re*. All *de dicto* attitudes presuppose *de re* attitudes. But it does not follow that indexical or *de re* elements survive in every attitude. (Cf. notes 2 and 3.)

I shall not, however, argue this point here. The claim that is crucial is not that our argument does not fix on *de re* attitudes. It is, rather, that the social differences between the actual and counterfactual situations affect the *content* of the subject's attitudes. That is, the difference affects standard cases of obliquely occurring, cognitive-content-conveying expressions in content clauses. For example, still with his misunderstanding, the subject might think that this (referring to his disease in his hands) is arthritis. Or he might think *de re* of the disease in his ankle (or of the disease in his thigh) that his arthritis is painful. It does not really matter whether the relevant attitude is *de re* or purely *de dicto*. What is crucial to our argument is that the occurrence of 'arthritis' is oblique and contributes to a characterization of the subject's mental content. One might even hold, implausibly I think, that all the subject's attitudes involving the notion of arthritis are *de re*, that 'arthritis' in that-clauses *indexically* picks out the property of being arthritis, or something like that. The fact remains that the term occurs obliquely in the relevant cases and serves in characterizing the *dicta* or contents of the subject's attitudes. The thought experiment exploits this fact.

Approaches to the mental that I shall later criticize as excessively individualistic tend to assimilate environmental aspects of mental phenomena to either the factive-verb or indexical-reference paradigm. (Cf. note 2.) This sort of assimilation suggests that one might maintain a relatively clear-cut distinction between extra-mental and mental aspects of mentalistic attributions. And it may encourage the idea that the distinctively mental aspects can be understood fundamentally in terms of the individual's abilities, dispositions, states, and so forth, considered in isolation from his social surroundings. Our argument undermines this latter suggestion. Social context infects even the distinctively mental features of mentalistic attributions. No man's intentional mental phenomena are insular. Every man is a piece of the social continent, a part of the social main.

III. Reinterpretations

IIIa. Methodology

I find that most people unspoiled by conventional philosophical training regard the three steps of the thought experiment as painfully obvious. Such folk tend to chafe over my filling in details or elaborating on strategy. I think this naivete appropriate. But for sophisticates the three steps require defense.

Before launching a defense, I want to make a few remarks about its methodology. My objective is to better understand our common mentalistic notions. Although such notions are subject to revision and refinement, I take it as evident that there is philosophical interest in theorizing about them as they now are. I assume that a primary way of achieving theoretical understanding is to concentrate on our *discourse* about mentalistic no-

tions. Now it is, of course, never obvious at the outset how much idealization, regimentation, or special interpretation is necessary in order to adequately understand ordinary discourse. Phenomena such as ambiguity, ellipsis, indexicality, idioms, and a host of others certainly demand some regimentation or special interpretation for purposes of linguistic theory. Moreover, more global considerations—such as simplicity in accounting for structural relations—often have effects on the cast of one's theory. For all that, there is a methodological bias in favor of taking natural discourse literally, other things being equal. For example, unless there are clear reasons for construing discourse as ambiguous, elliptical or involving special idioms, we should not so construe it. Literal interpretation is *ceteris paribus* preferred. My defense of the thought experiment, as I have interpreted it, partly rests on this principle.

This relatively non-theoretical interpretation of the thought experiment should be extended to the gloss on it that I provided in Section IIc. The notions of misconception, incomplete understanding, conceptual or linguistic error, and ordinary empirical error are to be taken as carrying little theoretical weight. I assume that these notions mark defensible, common-sense distinctions. But I need not take a position on available philosophical interpretations of these distinctions. In fact, I do not believe that understanding, in our examples, can be explicated as independent of empirical knowledge, or that the conceptual errors of our subjects are best seen as "purely" mistakes about concepts and as involving no "admixture" of error about "the world." With Quine, I find such talk about purity and mixture devoid of illumination or explanatory power. But my views on this matter neither entail nor are entailed by the premises of the arguments I give (cf. e.g., IIId). Those arguments seem to me to remain plausible under any of the relevant philosophical interpretations of the conceptual-ordinary empirical distinction.

I have presented the experiment as appealing to ordinary intuition. I believe that common practice in the attribution of propositional attitudes is fairly represented by the various steps. This point is not really open to dispute. Usage may be divided in a few of the cases in which I have seen it as united. But broadly speaking, it seems to me undeniable that the individual steps of the thought experiment are acceptable to ordinary speakers in a wide variety of examples. The issue open to possible dispute is whether the steps should be taken in the literal way in which I have taken them, and thus whether the conclusion I have drawn from those steps is justified. In the remainder of Section III, I shall try to vindicate the literal interpretation of our examples. I do this by criticizing, in order of increasing generality or abstractness, a series of attempts to reinterpret the thought experiment's first step. Ultimately, I suggest (IIId and IV) that these attempts derive from characteristicaly philosophical models that have little or no independent justification. A thoroughgoing review of these models would be out of bounds, but the present paper is intended to show that they are deficient as accounts of our actual practice of mentalistic attribution.

I shall have little further to say in defense of the second and third steps of the thought experiment. Both rest on their intuitive plausibility, not on some particular theory. The third step, for example, certainly does not depend on a view that contents are merely sentences the subject is disposed to utter, interpreted as his community interprets them. It is compatible with several philosophical accounts of mental contents, including those that appeal to more abstract entities such as Fregean thoughts or Russellian propositions, and those that seek to deny that content-clauses indicate any *thing* that might be called a content. I also do not claim that the fact that our subject lacks the relevant beliefs in the third step follows from the facts I have described. The point is that it is plausible, and certainly possible, that he would lack those beliefs.

The exact interpretation of the second step is relevant to a number of causal or functional theories of mental phenomena that I shall discuss in Section IV. The intuitive idea of the step is that none of the different physical, non-intentionally described causal chains set going by the differences in communal practice need affect our subjects in any way that would be relevant to an account of their mental contents. Differences in the behavior of other members of the community will, to be sure, affect the gravitational forces exerted on the subject. But I assume that these differences are irrelevant to macro-explanations of our subjects' physical movements and inner processes. They do not relevantly affect ordinary non–intentional physical explanations of how the subject acquires or is disposed to use the symbols in his repertoire. Of course, the social origins of a person's symbols do differ between actual and counterfactual cases. I shall return to this point in Sections IV and V. The remainder of Section III will be devoted to the first step of the thought experiment.

IIIb.   Incomplete Understanding and Standard Cases of Reinterpretation

The first step, as I have interpreted it, is the most likely to encounter opposition. In fact, there is a line of resistance that is second nature to linguistically oriented philosophers. According to this line, we should deny that, say, the patient really believed or thought that arthritis can occur outside of joints because he misunderstood the word 'arthritis'. More generally, we should deny that a subject could have any attitudes whose contents he incompletely understands.

What a person understands is indeed one of the chief factors that bear on what thoughts he can express in using words. If there were not deep and important connections between propositional attitudes and understanding, one could hardly expect one's attributions of mental content to facilitate reliable predictions of what a person will do, say, or think. But our examples provide reason to believe that these connections are not simple entailments to the effect that having a propositional attitude strictly implies full understanding of its content.

There are, of course, numerous situations in which we normally reinterpret or discount a person's words in deciding what he thinks. Philosophers often invoke such cases to bolster their animus against such attributions as the ones we made to our subjects: "If a foreigner were to mouth the words 'arthritis may occur in the thigh' or 'my father had arthritis', not understanding what he uttered in the slightest, we would not say that he believed that arthritis may occur in the thigh, or that his father had arthritis. So why should we impute the belief to the patient?" Why, indeed? or rather, why do we?

The question is a good one. We do want a general account of these cases. But the implied argument against our attribution is anemic. We tacitly and routinely distinguish between the cases I described and those in which a foreigner (or anyone) utters something without any comprehension. The best way to understand mentalistic notions is to recognize such differences in standard practice and try to account for them. One can hardly justify the assumption that full understanding of a content is in general a necessary condition for believing the content by appealing to some cases that tend to support the assumption in order to reject others that conflict with it.

It is a good method of discovery, I think, to note the sorts of cases philosophers tend to gravitate toward when they defend the view that the first step in the thought experiment should receive special interpretation. By reflecting on the differences between these cases and the cases we have cited, one should learn something about principles controlling mentalistic attribution.

I have already mentioned foreigners without command of the language. A child's imitation of our words and early attempts to use them provide similar examples. In these cases, mastery of the language and responsibility to its precepts have not been developed; and mental content attribution based on the meaning of words uttered tends to be precluded.

There are cases involving regional dialects. A person's deviance or ignorance judged by the standards of the larger community may count as normality or full mastery when evaluated from the regional perspective. Clearly, the regional standards tend to be the relevant ones for attributing content when the speaker's training or intentions are regionally oriented. The conditions for such orientation are complex, and I shall touch on them again in Section V. But there is no warrant in actual practice for treating each person's idiolect as always analogous to dialects whose words we automatically reinterpret—for purposes of mental content attribution—when usage is different. People are frequently held, and hold themselves, to the standards of their community when misuse or misunderstanding are at issue. One should distinguish these cases, which seem to depend on a certain *responsibility* to communal practice, from cases of automatic reinterpretation.

Tongue slips and Spoonerisms form another class of example where reinterpretation of a person's words is common and appropriate in arriving at an attribution of mental content. In these cases, we tend to exempt the speaker even from commitment to a homophonically formulated assertion content, as well as to the relevant mental content. The speaker's own behavior usually follows this line, often correcting himself when what he uttered is repeated back to him.

Malapropisms form a more complex class of examples. I shall not try to map it in detail. But in a fairly broad range of cases, we reinterpret a person's words at least in attributing mental content. If Archie says, 'Lead the way and we will precede', we routinely reinterpret the words in describing his expectations. Many of these cases seem to depend on the presumption that there are simple, superficial (for example, phonological) interference or exchange mechanisms that account for the linguistic deviance.

There are also examples of quite radical misunderstandings that sometimes generate reinterpretation. If a generally competent and reasonable speaker thinks that 'orangutan' applies to a fruit drink, we would be reluctant, and it would unquestionably be misleading, to take his words as revealing that he thinks he has been drinking orangutans for breakfast for the last few weeks. Such total misunderstanding often *seems* to block literalistic mental content attribution, at least in

cases where we are not directly characterizing his mistake. (Contrary to philosophical lore, I am not convinced that such a man cannot correctly and literally be attributed a belief that an orangutan is a kind of fruit drink. But I shall not deal with the point here.)

There are also some cases that do not seem generally to prevent mental content attribution on the basis of literal interpretation of the subject's words in quite the same way as the others, but which deserve some mention. For almost any content except for those that directly display the subject's incomplete understanding, there will be many contexts in which it would be misleading to attribute that content to the subject without further comment. Suppose I am advising you about your legal liabilities in a situation where you have entered into what may be an unwritten contract. You ask me what Al would think. It would be misleading for me to reply that Al would think that you do not have a contract (or even do not have any legal problems), if I know that Al thinks a contract must be based on a formal document. Your evaluation of Al's thought would be crucially affected by his inadequate understanding. In such cases, it is incumbent on us to cite the subject's eccentricity: "(He would think that you do not have a contract, but then) he thinks that there is no such thing as a verbally based contract."

Incidentally, the same sort of example can be constructed using attitudes that are abnormal, but that do not hinge on misunderstanding of any one notion. If Al had thought that only traffic laws and laws against violent crimes are ever prosecuted, it would be misleading for me to tell you that Al would think that you have no legal problems.

Both sorts of cases illustrate that in reporting a single attitude content, we typically suggest (implicate, perhaps) that the subject has a range of other attitudes that are normally associated with it. Some of these may provide reasons for it. In both sorts of cases, it is usually important to keep track of, and often to make explicit, the nature and extent of the subject's deviance. Otherwise, predictions and evaluations of his thought and action, based on normal background assumptions, will go awry. When the deviance is huge, attributions demand reinterpretation of the subject's words. Radical misunderstanding and mental instability are cases in point. But frequently, common practice seems to allow us to cancel the misleading suggestions by making explicit the subject's deviance, retaining literal interpretation of his words in our mentalistic attributions all the while.

All of the foregoing phenomena are relevant to accounting for standard practice. But they are no more salient than cases of straightforward belief attribution where the subject incompletely understands some notion in the attributed belief content. I think any impulse to say that common practice is *simply* inconsistent should be resisted (indeed, scorned). We cannot expect such practice to follow general principles rigorously. But even our brief discussion of the matter should have suggested the beginnings of generalizations about differences between cases where reinterpretation is standard and cases where it is not. A person's overall linguistic competence, his allegiance and responsibility to communal standards, the degree, source, and type of misunderstanding, the purposes of the report—all affect the issue. From a theoretical point of view, it would be a mistake to try to assimilate the cases in one direction or another. We do not want to credit a two-year-old who memorizes 'e $=$ mc^2' with belief in relativity theory. But the patient's attitudes involving the notion of arthritis should not be assimilated to the foreigner's uncomprehending pronunciations.

For purposes of defending the thought experiment and the arguments I draw from it, I can afford to be flexible about exactly how to generalize about these various phenomena. The thought experiment depends only on there being some cases in which a person's incomplete understanding does not force reinterpretation of his expressions in describing his mental contents. Such cases appear to be legion.

IIIc. Four Methods of Reinterpreting the Thought Experiment

I now want to criticize attempts to argue that even in cases where we ordinarily do ascribe content clauses despite the subject's incomplete understanding of expressions in those clauses, such ascriptions should not be taken literally. In order to overturn our interpretation of the thought experiment's first step, one must argue that none of the cases I have cited is appropriately taken in the literal manner. One must handle (apparent) attributions of unproblematically true contents involving incompletely mastered notions, as well as attributions of contents that display the misconceptions or partial understandings. I do not doubt that one can erect logically coherent and metaphysically traditional reinterpretations of all these cases. What I doubt is that such reinterpretations taken *in toto* can present a plausible view, and that taken individually they have any claim to superiority over the literal interpretations—either as accounts of the language of ordinary mentalistic ascription, or as accounts of the evidence on which mental attributions are commonly based.

Four types of reinterpretation have some currency. I shall be rather short with the first two, the first of which I have already warned against in Section IId. Sometimes relevant mentalistic ascriptions are reinterpreted as attributions of *de re* attitudes *of* entities not denoted by the misconstrued expressions. For example, the subject's belief that he has arthritis in the thigh might be interpreted as a belief *of* the non-arthritic rheumatoid ailment that it is in the thigh. The subject will probably have such a belief in this case. But it hardly accounts for the relevant attributions. In particular, it ignores the oblique occurrence of 'arthritis' in the original ascription. Such occurrences bear on a characterization of the subject's viewpoint. The subject thinks of the disease in his thigh (and of his arthritis) in a certain way. He thinks of each disease that it is arthritis. Other terms for arthritis (or for the actual trouble in his thigh) may not enable us to describe his attitude content nearly as well. The appeal to *de re* attitudes in this way is not adequate to the task of reinterpreting these ascriptions so as to explain away the difference between actual and counterfactual situations. It simply overlooks what needs explication.

A second method of reinterpretation, which Descartes proposed (cf. Section IV) and which crops up occasionally, is to claim that in cases of incomplete understanding, the subject's attitude or content is indefinite. It is surely true that in cases where a person is extremely confused, we are sometimes at a loss in describing his attitudes. Perhaps in such cases, the subject's mental content *is* indefinite. But in the cases I have cited, common practice lends virtually no support to the contention that the subject's mental contents are indefinite. The subject and his fellows typically know and agree on precisely *how to confirm or infirm* his beliefs—both in the cases where they are unproblematically true (or just empirically false) and in the cases where they display the misconception. Ordinary attributions typically specify the mental content without qualifications or hesitations.

In cases of partial understanding—say, in the mortgage example—it may indeed be unclear, short of extensive questioning, just how much mastery the subject has. But even this sort of unclarity does not appear to prevent, under ordinary circumstances, straightforward attributions utilizing 'mortgage' in oblique position. The subject is uncertain whether his father has two mortgages; he knows that his uncle has paid off the mortgage on his house. The contents are unhesitatingly attributed and admit of unproblematic testing for truth value, despite the subject's partial understanding. There is thus little *prima facie* ground for the appeal to indefiniteness. The appeal appears to derive from a prior assumption that attribution of a content entails attribution of full understanding. Lacking an easy means of attributing something other than the misunderstood content, one is tempted to say that there *is* no definite content. But this is unnecessarily mysterious. It reflects on the prior assumption, which so far has no independent support.

The other two methods of reinterpretation are often invoked in tandem. One is to attribute a notion that just captures the misconception, thus replacing contents that are apparently false on account of the misconception, by true contents. For example, the subject's belief (true or false) that that is a sofa would be replaced by, or reinterpreted as, a (true) belief that that is a *chofa,* where 'chofa' is introduced to apply not only to sofas, but also to the armchairs the subject thinks are sofas. The other method is to count the error of the subject as purely metalinguistic. Thus the patient's apparent belief that he had arthritis in the thigh would be reinterpreted as a belief that 'arthritis' applied to something (or some disease) in his thigh. The two methods can be applied simultaneously, attempting to account for an ordinary content attribution in terms of a reinterpreted object–level content together with a metalinguistic error. It is important to remember that in order to overturn the thought experiment, these methods must not only establish that the subject held the particular attitudes that they advocate attributing; they must also justify a *denial* of the ordinary attributions literally interpreted.

The method of invoking object-level notions that precisely capture (and that replace) the subject's apparent misconception has little to be said for it as a natural and generally applicable account of the language of mentalistic ascriptions. We do not ordinarily seek out true object-level attitude contents to attribute to victims of errors based on incomplete understanding. For example, when we find that a person has been involved in a misconception in examples like ours, we do not regularly reinterpret those ascriptions that involved the misunderstood term, but were intuitively unaffected by the error. An attribution to someone of a true belief that he is eating brisket, or that he has just signed a contract, or that Uncle Harry has paid off his mortgage, is not typically reformulated when it is learned that the subject had not fully understood what brisket (or a contract, or a mortgage) is. A similar point applies when we know about the error at the time of the attribution—at least if we avoid misleading the audience in cases where the error is crucial to the issue at hand. Moreover, we shall frequently see the subject as sharing beliefs with others who understand the relevant notions better. In counting beliefs as shared, we do not require, in every case, that the subjects "fully understand" the notions in those belief contents, or understand them in just the same way. Differences in understanding are frequently located as differences over other belief contents. We agree that you have signed a contract, but disagree over whether someone else could have made a contract by means of a verbal agreement.

There are reasons why ordinary practice does not follow the method of object-level reinterpretation. In many cases, particularly those involving partial understanding, finding a reinterpretation in accord with the method would be entirely nontrivial. It is not even clear that we have agreed upon means of pursuing such inquiries in all cases. Consider the arthritic patient. Suppose we are to reinterpret the attribution of his erroneous belief that he has arthritis in the thigh. We make up a term 'tharthritis' that covers arthritis and whatever it is he has in his thigh. The appropriate restrictions on the application of this term and of the patient's supposed notion are unclear. Is just any problem in the thigh that the patient wants to call 'arthritis' to count as tharthritis? Are other ailments covered? What would decide? The problem is that there are no recognized standards governing the application of the new term. In such cases, the method is patently *ad hoc.*

The method's willingness to invoke new terminology whenever conceptual error or partial understanding occurs is *ad hoc* in another sense. It proliferates terminology without evident theoretical reward. We do not engender better understanding of the patient by inventing a new word and saying that he thought (correctly) that tharthritis can occur outside joints. It is simpler and equally informative to construe him as thinking that arthritis may occur outside joints. When we are making other attributions that do not directly display the error, we must simply bear the deviant belief in mind, so as not to assume that all of the patient's inferences involving the notion would be normal.

The method of object-level reinterpretation often fails to give a plausible account of the evidence on which we base mental attributions. When caught in the sorts of errors we have been discussing, the subject does not normally respond by saying that his views had been misunderstood. The patient does not say (or think) that he had thought he had some-category-of-disease-like-arthritis-and-including-arthritis-but-also-capable-of-occurring-outside-of-joints in the thigh *instead* of the error commonly attributed. This sort of response would be disingenuous. Whatever other beliefs he had, the subject thought that he had arthritis in the thigh. In such cases, the subject will ordinarily give no evidence of having maintained a true object-level belief. In examples like ours, he typically admits his mistake, changes his views, and leaves it at that. Thus the subject's own behavioral dispositions and inferences often fail to support the method.

The method may be seen to be implausible as an account of the relevant evidence in another way. The patient knows that he has had arthritis in the ankle and wrists for some time. Now with his new pains in the thigh, he fears and believes that he has got arthritis in the thigh, that his arthritis is spreading. Suppose we reinterpret all of these attitude attributions in accord with the method. We use our recently coined term 'tharthritis' to cover (somehow) arthritis and whatever it is he has in the thigh. On this new interpretation, the patient is right in thinking that he has tharthritis in the ankle and wrists. His belief that it has lodged in the thigh is true. His fear is realized. But these attributions are out of keeping with the way we do and should view his actual beliefs and fears. His belief is not true, and his fear is not realized. He will be relieved when he is told that one cannot have arthritis in the thigh. His relief is bound up with a network of assumptions that he makes about his arthritis: that it is a kind of disease, that there are debilitating consequences of its occurring in multiple locations, and so on. When told that arthritis cannot occur in the thigh, the patient does not decide that his fears were realized, but that perhaps he should not have had those fears. He does not think: Well, my tharthritis *has* lodged in the thigh; but judging from the fact that what the doctor called "arthritis" cannot occur in the thigh, tharthritis may not be a single kind of disease; and I suppose I need not worry about the effects of its occurring in various locations, since evidently the tharthritis in my thigh is physiologically unrelated to the tharthritis in my joints. There will rarely if ever be an empirical basis for such a description of the subject's inferences. The patient's behavior (including his reports, or thinkings-out-loud) in this sort of case will normally not indicate any such pattern of inferences at all. But this is the description that the object-level reinterpretation method appears to recommend.

On the standard attributions, the patient retains his assumptions about the relation between arthritis, kinds of disease, spreading, and so on. And he concludes that his arthritis is not appearing in new locations—at any rate, not in his thigh. These attributions will typically be supported by the subject's behavior. The object-level reinterpre-

tation method postulates inferences that are more complicated and different in focus from the inferences that the evidence supports. The method's presentation in such a case would seem to be an *ad hoc* fiction, not a description with objective validity.

None of the foregoing is meant to deny that frequently when a person incompletely understands an attitude content he has some other attitude content that more or less captures his understanding. For example, in the contract example, the client will probably have the belief that if one breaks *a legally binding agreement based on formal documents,* then one may get into trouble. There are also cases in which it is reasonable to say that, at least in a sense, a person has a notion that is expressed by his dispositions to classify things in a certain way—even if there is no conventional term in the person's repertoire that neatly corresponds to that "way." The sofa case may be one such. Certain animals as well as people may have non-verbal notions of this sort. On the other hand, the fact that such attributions are justifiable *per se* yields no reason to deny that the subject (also) has object-level attitudes whose contents involve the relevant incompletely understood notion.

Whereas the third method purports to account for the subject's thinking at the object level, the fourth aims at accounting for his error. The error is construed as purely a metalinguistic mistake. The relevant false content is seen to involve notions that denote or apply to linguistic expressions. In examples relevant to our thought experiment, we ordinarily attribute a metalinguistic as well as an object-level attitude to the subject, at least in the case of non-occurrent propositional attitudes. For example, the patient probably believes that 'arthritis' applies in English to the ailment in his thigh. He believes that his father had a disease called "arthritis." And so on. Accepting these metalinguistic attributions, of course, does nothing *per se* toward making plausible a denial that the subjects in our examples have the counterpart object-level attitudes.

Like the third method, the metalinguistic reinterpretation method has no *prima facie* support as an account of the language of mentalistic ascriptions. When we encounter the subject's incomplete understanding in examples like ours, we do not decide that all the mental contents which we had been attributing to him with the misunderstood notion must have been purely metalinguistic in form. We also count people who incompletely understand terms in ascribed content clauses as sharing true and unproblematic object-level attitudes with others who understand the relevant terms better. For example, the lawyer and his client may share a wish that the client had not signed the contract to buy the house without reading the small print. A claim that these people share *only* attitudes with metalinguistic contents would have no support in linguistic practice.

The point about shared attitudes goes further. If the metalinguistic reinterpretation account is to be believed, we cannot say that a relevant English speaker shares a view (for example) that many old people have arthritis, with *anyone* who does not use the English word 'arthritis'. For the foreigner does not have the word 'arthritis' to hold beliefs about, though he does have attitudes involving the notion arthritis. And the attribution to the English speaker is to be interpreted metalinguistically, making reference to the word, so as not to involve attribution of the notion arthritis. This result is highly implausible. Ascriptions of such that-clauses as the above, regardless of the subject's language, serve to provide single descriptions and explanations of similar patterns of behavior, inference, and communication. To hold that we cannot accurately ascribe single content-clauses to English speakers and foreigners in such cases would not only accord badly with linguistic practice. It would substantially weaken the descriptive and explanatory power of our common attributions. In countless cases, unifying accounts of linguistically disparate but cognitively and behaviorally similar phenomena would be sacrificed.

The method is implausible in other cases as an account of standard evidence on which mental attributions are based. Take the patient who fears that his arthritis is spreading. According to the metalinguistic reinterpretation method, the patient's reasoning should be described as follows. He thinks that the word 'arthritis' applies to a single disease in him, that the disease in him called "arthritis" is debilitating if it spreads, that 'arthritis' applies to the disease in his wrists and ankles. He fears that the disease called "arthritis" has lodged in his thigh, and so on. Of course, it is often difficult to find evidential grounds for attributing an object-level attitude *as opposed* to its metalinguistic counterpart. As I noted, when a person holds one attitude, he often holds the other. But there are types of evidence, in certain contexts, for making such discriminations, particularly contexts in which *occurrent* mental events are at issue. The subject may maintain that his reasoning did not fix upon words. He may be brought up short by a metalinguistic formulation of his just-completed ruminations, and may insist that he was not interested in labels. In such cases, especially if the reasoning is not concerned with linguistic issues in any informal or antecedently plausible sense, attribution of an object-level thought content is supported by the relevant evidence, and metalinguistic attribution is not. To insist that the occurrent mental event really involved a metalinguistic content would be a piece of *ad hoc* special pleading, undermined by the evidence we actually use for deciding whether a thought was metalinguistic.

In fact, there appears to be a general presumption that a person is reasoning at the object level, other things being equal. The basis for this presumption is that metalinguistic reasoning requires a certain self-consciousness about one's words and social institutions. This sort of sophistication emerged rather late in human history. (Cf. any history of linguistics.) Semantical notions were a product of this sophistication.

Occurrent propositional attitudes prevent the overall reinterpretation strategy from providing a plausible total account which would block our thought experiment. For such occurrent mental events as the patient's thought that his arthritis is especially painful in the knee this morning are, or can be imagined to be, clear cases of object-level attitudes. And such thoughts may enter into or connect up with pieces of reasoning—say the reasoning leading to relief that the arthritis had not lodged in the thigh—which cannot be plausibly accounted for in terms of object-level reinterpretation. The other reinterpretation methods (those that appeal to *de re* contents and to indefiniteness) are non-starters. In such examples, the literally interpreted ascriptions appear to be straightforwardly superior accounts of the evidence that is normally construed to be relevant. Here one need not appeal to the principle that literal interpretation is, other things equal, preferable to reinterpretation. Other things are not equal.

At this point, certain philosophers may be disposed to point out that what a person says and how he behaves do not infallibly determine what his attitude contents are. Despite the apparent evidence, the subject's attitude contents may in all cases I cited be metalinguistic, and may fail to involve the incompletely understood notion. It is certainly true that how a person acts and what he says, even sincerely, do not determine his mental contents. I myself have mentioned a number of cases that support the point. (Cf. IIIb.) But the point is often used in a sloppy and irresponsible manner. It is incumbent on someone making it (and applying it to cases like ours) to indicate considerations that override the linguistic and behavioral evidence. In Section IIId, I shall consider intuitive or *a priori* philosophical arguments to this end. But first I wish to complete our evaluation of the metalinguistic reinterpretation method as an account of the language of mentalistic ascription in our examples.

In this century philosophers have developed the habit of insisting on metalinguistic reinterpretation for any content attribution that directly *displays* the subject's incomplete understanding. These cases constitute but a small number of the attributions that serve the thought experiment. One could grant these reinterpretations and still maintain our overall viewpoint. But even as applied to these cases, the method seems dubious. I doubt that any evidentially supported account of the language of these attributions will show them in general to be attributions of metalinguistic contents—contents that involve denotative reference to linguistic expressions.

The ascription 'He believes that broad overstuffed armchairs are sofas', as ordinarily used, does not in general *mean* "He believes that broad, overstuffed armchairs are covered by the expression 'sofas'" (or something like that). There are clear grammatical and semantical differences between

  (i) broad, overstuffed armchairs are covered by the expression 'sofas'

and

  (ii) broad, overstuffed armchairs are sofas.

When the two are embedded in belief contexts, they produce grammatically and semantically distinct sentences.

As noted, ordinary usage approves ascriptions like

  (iii) He believes that broad, overstuffed armchairs are sofas.

It would be wildly *ad hoc* and incredible from the point of view of linguistic theory to claim that there is *no* reading of (iii) that embeds (ii). But there is no evidence from speaker behavior that *true* ascriptions of (iii) always (or perhaps even *ever*) derive from embedding (i) rather than (ii). In fact, I know of no clear evidence that (iii) is ambiguous between embedding (i) and (ii), or that (ii) is ambiguous, with one reading identical to that of (i). People do not in general seem to regard ascriptions like (iii) as elliptical. More important, in most cases no amount of nonphilosophical badgering will lead them to withdraw (iii), under some interpretation, *in favor of* an ascription that clearly embeds (i). At least in the cases of *non-occurrent* propositional attitudes, they will tend to agree to a clearly metalinguistic ascription—a belief sentence explicitly embedding something like (i)—in cases where they make an ascription like (iii). But this is evidence that they regard ascriptions that embed (i) and (ii) as both true. It hardly tells against counting belief ascriptions that embed (ii) as true,

or against taking (iii) in the obvious, literal manner. In sum, there appears to be no ordinary empirical pressure on a theory of natural language to represent true ascriptions like (iii) as *not* embedding sentences like (ii). And other things being equal, literal readings are correct readings. Thus it is strongly plausible to assume that ordinary usage routinely accepts as true and justified even ascriptions like (iii), literally interpreted as embedding sentences like (ii).

There are various contexts in which we may be indifferent over whether to attribute a metalinguistic attitude or the corresponding object-level attitude. I have emphasized that frequently, though not always, we may attribute both. Or we might count the different contents as describing what contextually "amount to the same attitude." (Cf. Section I.) Even this latter locution remains compatible with the thought experiment, as long as both contents are *equally attributable* in describing "the attitude." In the counterfactual step of the thought experiment, the metalinguistic content (say, that broad, overstuffed armchairs are called "sofas") will still be attributable. But in these circumstances it contextually "amounts to the same attitude" as an object-level attitude whose content is in no sense equivalent to, or "the same as," the original object-level content. For they have different truth values. Thus, assuming that the object-level and metalinguistic contents are equally attributable, it remains informally plausible that the person's attitudes are different between actual and counterfactual steps in the thought experiment. This contextual conflation of object-level and metalinguistic contents is not, however, generally acceptable even in describing non-occurrent attitudes, much less occurrent ones. There are contexts in which the subject himself may give evidence of making the distinction.

IIId. *Philosophical Arguments for Reinterpretation*

I have so far argued that the reinterpretation strategies that I have cited do not provide a plausible account of evidence relevant to a theory of the language of mentalistic ascriptions or to descriptions of mental phenomena themselves. I now want to consider characteristically philosophical arguments for revising ordinary discourse or for giving it a nonliteral reading, arguments that rely purely on intuitive or *a priori* considerations. I have encountered three such arguments, or argument sketches.[4]

One holds that the content clauses we ascribed must be reinterpreted so as to make reference to words because they clearly concern linguistic matters—or are about language. Even if this argument were sound, it would not affect the thought experiment decisively. For most of the mental contents that vary between actual and counterfactual situations are not in any intuitive sense "linguistic." The belief that certain armchairs are sofas is intuitively linguistic. But beliefs that some sofas are beige, that Kirkpatrick is playing a clavichord, and that Milton had severe arthritis in his hands are not.

But the argument is unpersuasive even as applied to the contents that, in an intuitive sense, do concern linguistic matters. A belief that broad, overstuffed armchairs are sofas is linguistic (or "about" language) in the same senses as an "analytically" true belief that no armchairs are sofas. But the linguistic nature of the latter belief does not make its logical form metalinguistic. So citing the linguistic nature of the former belief does not suffice to show it metalinguistic. No semantically relevant component of either content applies to or denotes linguistic expressions.

Both the "analytically" true and the "analytically" false attitudes are linguistic in the sense that they are tested by consulting a dictionary or native linguistic intuitions, rather than by ordinary empirical investigation. We do not scrutinize pieces of furniture to test these beliefs. The pragmatic focus of expressions of these attitudes will be on usage, concepts, or meaning. But it is simply a mistake to think that these facts entail, or even suggest, that the relevant contents are metalinguistic in form. Many contents with object-level logical forms have primarily linguistic or conceptual implications.

A second argument holds that charitable interpretation requires that we not attribute to rational people beliefs like the belief that one may have arthritis in the thigh. Here again, the argument obviously does not touch most of the attitudes that may launch the thought experiment; for many are straightforwardly true, or false on ordinary empirical grounds. Even so, it is not a good argument. There is nothing irrational or stupid about the linguistic or conceptual errors we attribute to our subjects. The errors are perfectly understandable as results of linguistic misinformation.

In fact, the argument makes sense only against the background of the very assumption that I have been questioning. A belief that arthritis may occur in the thigh appears to be inexplicable or uncharitably attributed only if it is assumed that the subject must fully understand the notions in his attitude contents.

A third intuitive or *a priori* argument is perhaps the most interesting. Sometimes it is insisted that we should not attribute contents involving incompletely understood notions because *the indi-*

vidual must mean something different by the misunderstood word than what we non-deviant speakers mean by it. Note again that it would not be enough to use this argument from deviant speaker meaning to show that the subject has notions that are not properly expressed in the way he thinks they are. In some sense of 'expressed', this is surely often the case. To be relevant, the argument must arrive at a negative conclusion: that the subject cannot have the attitudes that seem commonly to be attributed.

The expression 'the individual meant something different by his words' can be interpreted in more than one way. On one group of interpretations, the expression says little more than that the speaker incompletely understood his words: The patient thought 'arthritis' meant something that included diseases that occur outside of joints. The client would have misexplained the meaning, use, or application of 'contract'. The subject applied 'sofa' to things that, unknown to him, are not sofas. A second group of interpretations emphasizes that not only does the speaker misconstrue or misapply his words, but he had *in mind* something that the words do not denote or express. The subject sometimes had in mind certain armchairs when he used 'sofa.' The client regarded the notion of legal agreement based on written documents as approximately interchangeable with what is expressed by 'contract', and thus had such a notion in mind when he used 'contract'. A person with a problem about the range of red might sometimes have in mind a mental image of a non-red color when he used 'red'.

The italicized premise of the argument is, of course, always true in our examples under the first group of interpretations, and often true under the second. But interpreted in these ways, the argument is a *non sequitur*. It does not follow from the assumption that the subject thought that a word means something that it does not (or misapplies the word, or is disposed to misexplain its meaning) that the word cannot be used in literally describing his mental contents. It does not follow from the assumption that a person has in mind something that a word does not denote or express that the word cannot occur obliquely (and be interpreted literally) in that-clauses that provide some of his mental contents. As I have pointed out in Section IIIb, there is a range of cases in which we commonly reinterpret a person's incompletely understood words for purposes of mental-content attribution. But the present argument needs to show that deviant speaker-meaning always forces such reinterpretation.

In many of our examples, the idea that the subject has some deviant notion *in mind* has no intuitively clear application. (Consider the arthritis and mortgage examples.) But even where this expression does seem to apply, the argument does not support the relevant conclusion. At best it shows that a notion deviantly associated with a word plays a role in the subject's attitudes. For example, someone who has in mind the notion of an agreement based on written documents when he says, "I have just entered into a contract," may be correctly said to believe that he has just entered into an agreement based on written documents. It does not follow from this that he *lacks* a belief or thought that he has just entered into a contract. In fact, in our view, the client's having the deviant notion in mind is a *likely consequence* of the fact that he believes that contracts are impossible without a written document.

Of course, given the first, more liberal set of interpretations of 'means something different', the fact that in our examples the subject means something different by his words (or at least applies them differently) is *implied* by certain of his beliefs. It is implied by a belief that he has arthritis in the thigh. A qualified version of the converse implication also holds. Given appropriate background assumptions, the fact that the subject has certain deviant (object-level) beliefs is implied by his meaning something different by his words. So far, no argument has shown that we cannot accept these implications and retain the literal interpretation of common mentalistic ascriptions.

The argument from deviant speaker-meaning downplays an intuitive feature that can be expected to be present in many of our examples. The subject's willingness to submit his statement and belief to the arbitration of an authority suggests a willingness to have his words taken in the normal way—regardless of mistaken associations with the word. Typically, the subject will regard recourse to a dictionary, and to the rest of us, as at once a check on his usage and his belief. When the verdict goes against him, he will not usually plead that we have simply misunderstood his views. This sort of behavior suggests that (given the sorts of background assumptions that common practice uses to distinguish our examples from those of foreigners, radical misunderstandings, and so forth) we can say that in a sense our man meant by 'arthritis' *arthritis*—where 'arthritis' occurs, of course, obliquely. We can say this despite the fact that his incomplete understanding leads us, in one of the senses explicated earlier, to say that he meant something different by 'arthritis'.

If one tries to turn the argument from deviant speaker-meaning into a valid argument, one arrives at an assumption that seems to guide all three of the philosophical arguments I have discussed.

The assumption is that what a person thinks his words mean, how he takes them, fully determines what attitudes he can express in using them: the contents of his mental states and events are strictly limited to notions, however idiosyncratic, that he understands; a person cannot think with notions he incompletely understands. But supplemented with this assumption, the argument begs the question at issue.

The least controversial justification of the assumption would be an appeal to standard practice in mentalistic attributions. But standard practice is what brought the assumption into question in the first place. Of course, usage is not sacred if good reasons for revising it can be given. But none have been.

The assumption is loosely derived, I think, from the old model according to which a person must be directly acquainted with, or must immediately apprehend, the contents of his thoughts. None of the objections explicitly invoke this model—and many of their proponents would reject it. But I think that all the objections derive some of their appeal from philosophical habits that have been molded by it. I shall discuss this model further in Section IV.

One may, of course, quite self-consciously neglect certain aspects of common mentalistic notions in the interests of a revised or idealized version of them. One such idealization could limit itself to just those attitudes involving "full understanding" (for some suitably specified notion of understanding). This limitation is less clearcut than one might suppose, since the notion of understanding itself tends to be used according to misleading stereotypes. Still, oversimplified models, idealizations, of mentalistic notions are defensible, as long as the character and purpose of the oversimplifications are clear. In my opinion, limiting oneself to "fully understood" attitudes provides no significant advantage in finding elegant and illuminating formal semantical theories of natural language. Such a strategy has perhaps a better claim in psychology, though even there its propriety is controversial. (Cf. Section IV.) More to the point, I think that models that neglect the relevant social factors in mentalistic attributions are not likely to provide long-run philosophical illumination of our actual mentalistic notions. But this view hardly admits of detailed support here and now.

Our argument in the preceding pages may, at a minimum, be seen as inveighing against a long-standing philosophical habit of denying that it *is* an oversimplification to make "full understanding" of a content a necessary condition for having a propositional attitude with that content. The oversimplification does not constitute neglect of some quirk of ordinary usage. Misunderstanding and partial understanding are pervasive and inevitable phenomena, and attributions of content despite them are an integral part of common practice.

I shall not here elaborate a philosophical theory of the social aspects of mentalistic phenomena, though in Section V I shall suggest lines such a theory might take. One of the most surprising and exciting aspects of the thought experiment is that its most literal intepretation provides a perspective on the mental that has received little serious development in the philosophical tradition. The perspective surely invites exploration.

IV.   Applications

I want to turn now to a discussion of how our argument bears on philosophical approaches to the mental that may be termed *individualistic*. I mean this term to be somewhat vague. But roughly, I intend to apply it to philosophical treatments that seek to see a person's intentional mental phenomena ultimately and purely in terms of what happens to the person, what occurs within him, and how he responds to his physical environment, without any essential reference to the social context in which he or the interpreter of his mental phenomena are situated. How I apply the term 'individualistic' will perhaps become clearer by reference to the particular cases that I shall discuss.

a. As I have already intimated, the argument of the preceding sections affects the traditional intro- (or extro-) spectionist treatments of the mind, those of Plato, Descartes, Russell, and numerous others. These treatments are based on a model that likens the relation between a person and the contents of his thought to seeing, where seeing is taken to be a kind of direct, immediate experience. On the most radical and unqualified versions of the model, a person's inspection of the contents of his thought is infallible: the notion of incompletely understanding them has no application at all.

The model tends to encourage individualistic treatments of the mental. For it suggests that what a person thinks depends on what occurs or "appears" within his mind. Demythologized, what a person thinks depends on the power and extent of his comprehension and on his internal dispositions toward the comprehended contents. The model is expressed in perhaps its crudest and least qualified form in a well-known passage by Russell:

> Whenever a relation of supposing or judging occurs, the terms to which the supposing or judging mind is related by the relation of supposing or judging must be terms with which the mind in question is acquainted. . . . It seems to me that the truth of this principle is evident as soon as the principle is understood.[5]

Acquaintance is (for Russell) direct, infallible, non-propositional, non-perspectival knowledge. "Terms" like concepts, ideas, attributes, forms, meanings, or senses are entities that occur in judgments more or less immediately before the mind on a close analogy to the way sensations are supposed to.

The model is more qualified and complicated in the writings of Descartes. In particular, he emphasizes the possibility that one might perceive the contents of one's mind unclearly or indistinctly. He is even high-handed enough to write, "Some people throughout their lives perceive nothing so correctly as to be capable of judging it properly."[6] This sort of remark appears to be a concession to the points made in Sections I and II about the possibility of a subject's badly understanding his mental contents. But the concession is distorted by the underlying introspection model. On Descartes' view, the person's faculty of understanding, properly so-called, makes no errors. Failure to grasp one's mental contents results from either blind prejudice or interference by "mere" bodily sensations and corporeal imagery. The implication is that with sufficiently careful reflection on the part of the individual subject, these obstacles to perfect understanding can be cleared. That is, one need only be careful or properly guided in one's introspections to achieve full understanding of the content of one's intentional mental phenomena. Much that Descartes says suggests that where the subject fails to achieve such understanding, no definite content can be attributed to him. In such cases, his "thinking" consists of unspecifiable or indeterminate imagery; attribution of definite conceptual content is precluded. These implications are reinforced in Descartes' appeal to self-evident, indubitable truths:

> There are some so evident and at the same time so simple that we cannot think of them without believing them to be true. . . . For we cannot doubt them unless we think of them; and we cannot think of them without at the same time believing them to be true, i.e. we can never doubt them.[7]

The self-evidence derives from the mere understanding of the truths, and fully understanding them is a precondition for thinking them at all. It is this last requirement that we have been questioning.

In the Empiricist tradition Descartes' qualifications on the direct experience model—particularly those involving the interfering effects of sensations and imagery—tend to fall away. What one thinks comes to be taken as a sort of impression (whether more imagistic or more intellectual) on or directly grasped by the individual's mind. The tendency to make full comprehension on the part of the subject a necessary condition for attributing a mental content to him appears both in philosophers who take the content to be a Platonic abstraction and in those who place it, in some sense, inside the individual's mind. This is certainly the direction in which the model pulls, with its picture of immediate accessibility to the individual. Thus Descartes' original concessions to cases of incomplete understanding became lost as his model became entrenched. What Wölfflin said of painters is true of philosophers: they learn more from studying each other than from reflecting on anything else.

The history of the model makes an intricate subject. My remarks are meant merely to provide a suggestive caricature of it. It should be clear, however, that in broad outline the model mixes poorly with the thought experiment of Section II, particularly its first step. The thought experiment indicates that certain "linguistic truths" that have often been held to be indubitable can be thought yet doubted. And it shows that a person's thought *content* is not fixed by what goes on in him, or by what is accessible to him simply by careful reflection. The reason for this last point about "accessibility" need not be that the content lies too deep in the unconscious recesses of the subject's psyche. Contents are sometimes "inaccessible" to introspection simply because much mentalistic attribution does not presuppose that the subject has fully mastered the content of his thought.

In a certain sense, the metaphysical model has fixed on some features of our use of mentalistic notions to the exclusion of others. For example, the model fastens on the facts that we are pretty good at identifying our own beliefs and thoughts, and we have at least a *prima facie* authority in reporting a wide range of them. It also underlines the point that for certain contents we tend to count understanding as a sufficient condition for acknowledging their truth. (It is debatable, of course, how well it explains or illumines these observations.) The model also highlights the truism that a certain measure of understanding is required of a subject if we are to attribute intentional phenomena on the basis of what he utters. As we have noted, chance or purely rote utterances provide no ground for mental content attributions; certain verbal pathologies are discounted. The model extrapolates from these observations to the claim

that a person can never fail to understand the content of his beliefs or thoughts, or that the remedy for such failure lies within his own resources of reflection (whether autonomous and conscious, or unconscious and guided). It is this extrapolation that requires one to pass over the equally patent practice of attributing attitudes where the subject incompletely understands expressions that provide the content of those attitudes. Insistence on metalinguistic reinterpretation and talk about the indefiniteness of attitude contents in cases of incomplete understanding seem to be rearguard defenses of a vastly overextended model.

The Cartesian–Russellian model has few strict adherents among prominent linguistic philosophers. But although it has been widely rejected or politely talked around, claims that it bore and nurtured are commonplace, even among its opponents. As we have seen in the objections to the first step of the argument of Section II, these claims purport to restrict the contents we can attribute to a person on the basis of his use of language. The restrictions simply mimic those of Descartes. Freed of the picturesque but vulnerable model that formed them, the claims have assumed the power of dogma. Their structures, however, misrepresent ordinary mentalistic notions.

b. This century's most conspicuous attempt to replace the traditional Cartesian model has been the behaviorist movement and its heirs. I take it as obvious that the argument of Section II provides yet another reason to reject the most radical version of behaviorism—"philosophical," "logical," or "analytical" behaviorism. This is the view that mentalistic attributions can be "analytically" defined, or given strict meaning equivalences, purely in non-mental, behavioral terms. No analysis resting purely on the individual's dispositions to behavior can give an "analytic" definition of a mental content attribution because we can conceive of the behavioral definiens applying while the mentalistic definiendum does not. But a new argument for this conclusion is hardly needed since "philosophical" behaviorists are, in effect, extinct.

There is, however, an heir of behaviorism that I want to discuss at somewhat greater length. The approach sometimes goes by the name "functionalism," although that term is applied to numerous slogans and projects, often vaguely formulated. Even views that seem to me to be affected by our argument are frequently stated so sketchily that one may be in considerable doubt about what is being proposed. So my remarks should be taken less as an attempt to refute the theses of particular authors than as an attack on a way of thinking that seems to inform a cluster of viewpoints. The quotations I give in footnotes are meant to be suggestive, if not always definitive, of the way of thinking the argument tells against.[8]

The views affected by the argument of Section II attempts to give something like a philosophical "account" of the mental. The details and strategy—even the notion of "account"—vary from author to author. But a recurrent theme is that mental notions are to be seen ultimately in terms of the individual subject's input, output, and inner dispositions and states, where these latter are characterized purely in terms of how they lead to or from output, input, or other inner states similarly characterized. Mental notions are to be explicated or identified in functional, non-mentalistic, non-intentional terminology. Proponents of this sort of idea are rarely very specific about what terms may be used in describing input and output, or even what sorts of terms count as "functional" expressions. But the impression usually given is that input and output are to be specified in terms (acceptable to a behaviorist) of irritations of the subject's surfaces and movements of his body. On some versions, neurophysiological terms are allowed. More recently, there have been liberalized appeals to causal input and output relations with particular, specified physical objects, stuffs, or magnitudes. Functional terms include terms like 'causes', 'leads to with probability n', and the like. For our purposes, the details do not matter much, as long as an approach allows no mentalistic or other intentional terms (such as 'means' or that–clauses) into its vocabulary, and as long as it applies to individuals taken one by one.

A difference between this approach and that of philosophical behaviorism is that a whole array of dispositional or functional states—causally or probabilistically interrelated—may enter into the "account" of a single mental attribution. The array must be ultimately secured to input and output, but the internal states need not be so secured one by one. The view is thus not immediately vulnerable to claims against simplistic behaviorisms, that a *given* stimulus–response pattern may have different contents in different social contexts. Such claims, which hardly need a defender, have been tranquilly accepted on this view. The view's hope is that differences in content depend on functional differences in the individual's larger functional structure. From this viewpoint, analytical behaviorism erred primarily in its failure to recognize the interlocking or wholistic character of mental attributions and in its oversimplification of theoretical explanation.

As I said, the notion of an account of the mental varies from author to author. Some authors take over the old-fashioned ideal of an "analysis" from philosophical behaviorism and aim at a definition of the meaning of mentalistic vocabulary, or a definitional elimination of it. Others see their account as indicating a series of scientific hypotheses that identify mental states with causal or functional states, or roles, in the individual. These authors reject behaviorism's goal of providing meaning equivalences, as well as its restrictive methods. The hypotheses are supposed to be type or property identities and are nowadays often thought to hold necessarily, even if they do not give meaning relations. Moreover, these hypotheses are offered not merely as speculation about the future of psychology, but as providing a philosophically illuminating account of our ordinary notion of the mental. Thus if the view systematically failed to make plausible type identities between functional states and mental states, ordinarily construed, then by its own lights it would have failed to give a philosophical "account" of the mental. I have crudely over–schematized the methodological differences among the authors in this tradition. But the differences fall roughly within the polar notions of *account* that I have described, I think our discussion will survive the oversimplifications.[9]

Any attempt to give an account of specific beliefs and thoughts along the lines I have indicated will come up short. For we may fix the input, output, and total array of dispositional or functional states of our subject, as long as these are non-intentionally described and are limited to what is relevant to accounting for his activity taken in isolation from that of his fellows. But we can still conceive of his mental contents as varying. Functionally equivalent people—on any plausible notion of functional equivalence that has been sketched—may have non-equivalent mental-state and event contents, indicated by obliquely non-equivalent content clauses. Our argument indicates a systematic inadequacy in attempts of the sort I described.

Proponents of functionalist accounts have seen them as revealing the true nature of characteristic marks of the mental and as resolving traditional philosophical issues about such marks. In the case of beliefs, desires, and thoughts, the most salient mark is intentionality—the ill-specified information-bearing, representational feature that seems to invest these mental states and events.[10] In our terminology, accounting for intentionality largely amounts to accounting for the content of mental states and events. (There is also, of course, the application of content in *de re* cases. But we put this aside here.) Such content is clearly part of what the functional roles of our subjects' states fail to determine.

It is worth re-emphasizing here that the problem is unaffected by suggestions that we specify input and output in terms of causal relations to particular objects or stuffs in the subject's physical environment. Such specifications may be thought to help with some examples based on indexicality or psychological success verbs, and perhaps in certain arguments concerning natural kind terms (though even in these cases I think that one will be forced to appeal to intentional language). (Cf. note 2.) But this sort of suggestion has no easy application to our argument. For the relevant causal relations between the subject and the physical environment to which his terms apply—where such relations are non-intentionally specified—were among the elements held constant while the subject's beliefs and thoughts varied.

The functionalist approaches I have cited seem to provide yet another case in which mental contents are not plausibly accounted for in non-intentional terms. They are certainly not explicable in terms of causally or functionally specified states and events of the *individual* subject. The intentional or semantical role of mental states and events is not a function merely of their functionally specified roles in the individual. The failure of these accounts of intentional mental states and events derives from an underestimation of socially dependent features of cognitive phenomena.

Before extending the application of our argument, I want to briefly canvass some ways of being influenced by it, ways that might appeal to someone fixed on the functionalist ideal. One response might be to draw a strict distinction between mental states, ordinarily so-called, and psychological states. One could then claim that the latter are the true subject matter of the science of psychology and may be identified with functional states functionally specified, after all. Thus one might claim that the subject was in the same psychological (functional) states in both the actual and the imagined situations, although he had different beliefs and thoughts ordinarily so-called.

There are two observations that need to be entered about this position. The first is that it frankly jettisons much of the philosophical interest of functionalist accounts. The failure to cope with mental contents is a case in point. The second observation is that it is far from clear that such a distinction between the psychological and the mental is or will be sanctioned by psychology itself. Functionalist accounts arose as philosophical interpretations of developments in psychology influenced by computer theory. The interpretations have been guided by philosophical interests, such as

throwing light on the mind–body problem and accounting for mentalistic features in non-mentalistic terms. But the theories of cognitive psychologists, including those who place great weight on the computer analogy, are not ordinarily purified of mentalistic or intentional terminology. Indeed, intentional terminology plays a central role in much contemporary theorizing. (This is also true of theories that appeal to "sub-personal" states or processes. The "sub-personal" states themselves are often characterized intentionally.) Purifying a theory of mentalistic and intentional features in favor of functional or causal features is more clearly demanded by the goals of philosophers than by the needs of psychology. Thus it is at least an open question whether functional approaches of the sort we have discussed give a satisfactory account of *psychological* states and events. It is not evident that psychology will ever be methodologically "pure" (or theoretically purifiable by some definitional device) in the way these approaches demand. *This* goal of functionalists may be simply a meta-psychological mistake.

To put the point another way, it is not clear that functional states, characterized purely in functional, non-intentional terms (and non-intentional descriptions of input and output) are the natural subject matter of psychology. Psychology would, I think, be an unusual theory if it restricted itself (or could be definitionally restricted) to specifying abstract causal or functional structures in purely causal or functional terms, together with vocabulary from other disciplines. Of course, it *may* be that functional states, functionally specified, form a psychological natural kind. And it is certainly not to be assumed that psychology will respect ordinary terminology in its individuation of types of psychological states and events. Psychology must run its own course. But the assumption that psychological terminology will be ultimately non-intentional and purely functional seems without strong support. More important from our viewpoint, if psychology did take the individualistic route suggested by the approaches we have cited, then its power to illumine the everyday phenomena alluded to in mentalistic discourse would be correspondingly limited.

These remarks suggest a second sort of functionalist response to the argument of Section II, one that attempts to take the community rather than the individual as the object of functional analysis. One might, for example, seek to explain an individual's responsibility to communal standards in terms of his having the right kind of interaction with other individuals who collectively had functional structures appropriate to those standards. Spelling out the relevant notions of interaction and appropriateness is, of course, anything but trivial. (Cf. Section V.) Doing so in purely functional, non-intentional terms would be yet a further step. Until such a treatment is developed and illustrated in some detail, there is little point in discussing it. I shall only conjecture that, if it is to remain non-intentional, such a treatment is likely to be so abstract—at least in our present state of psychological and sociological ignorance—that it will be unilluminating from a philosophical point of view. Some of the approaches we have been discussing already more than flirt with this difficulty.

c. Individualistic assumptions about the mental have infected theorizing about the relation between mind and meaning. An example is the Gricean project of accounting for conventional or linguistic meaning in terms of certain complex intentions and beliefs of individuals.[11] The Gricean program analyzes conventional meaning in terms of subtle "mutual knowledge," or beliefs and intentions about each others' beliefs and intentions, on the part of most or all members of a community. Seen as a quasi-definitional enterprise, the program presupposes that the notion of an individual's believing or intending something is always "conceptually" independent of the conventional meaning of symbols used to express that something. Insofar as 'conceptually' has any intuitive content, this seems not to be the case. Our subject's belief or intention contents can be conceived to vary simply by varying conventions in the community around him. The content of individuals' beliefs seems sometimes to depend partly on social conventions in their environment. It is true that our subjects are actually rather abnormal members of their community, at least with respect to their use and understanding of a given word. But normality here is judged against the standards set by communal conventions. So stipulating that the individuals whose mental states are used in defining conventional meaning be relevantly normal will not avoid the circularity that I have indicated. I see no way to do so. This charge of circularity has frequently been raised on intuitive grounds. Our argument gives the intuitions substance. Explicating convention in terms of belief and intention may provide various sorts of insight. But it is not defining a communal notion in terms of individualistic notions. Nor is it reducing, in any deep sense, the semantical, or the intentional generally, to the psychological.

d. Individualistic assumptions have also set the tone for much discussion of the ontology of the mental. This subject is too large to receive detailed consideration here. It is complicated by a variety of crosscurrents among different projects, methodologics, and theses. I shall only explore how our argument affects a certain line of thinking closely allied to the functionalist approaches already discussed. These approaches have frequently been seen as resuscitating an old argument for the materialist identity theory. The argument is three-staged. First, one gives a philosophical "account" of each mentalistic locution, an account that is *prima facie* netural as regards ontology. For example, a belief or a thought that sofas are comfortable is supposed to be accounted for as one functionally specified state or event within an array of others—all of which are secured to input and output. Second, the relevant functionally specified states or events are expected to be empirically correlated or correlatable with physiological states or events in a person (states or events that have those functions). The empirical basis for believing in these correlations is claimed to be provided by present or future physical science. The nature of the supposed correlations is differently described in different theories. But the most prevalent views expect only that the correlations will hold for each organism and person (perhaps at a given time) taken one by one. For example, the functionally specified event type that is identified with a thought that sofas are comfortable may be realized in one person by an instance (or "token") of one physiological event type, and in another person by an instance of another physiological event type. Third, the ("token") mental state or event in the person is held to be identical with the relevant ("token") physiological state or event, on general grounds of explanatory simplicity and scientific method. Sometimes, this third stage is submerged by building uniqueness of occupancy of functional role into the first stage.[12]

I am skeptical about this sort of argument at every stage. But I shall doubt only the first stage here. The argument we gave in Section II directly undermines the attempt to carry out the first stage by recourse to the sort of functionalist approaches that we discussed earlier. Sameness of functional role, individualistically specified, is compatible with difference of content. I know of no better non-intentional account of mentalistic locutions. If a materialist argument of this genre is to arrive, it will require a longer first step.

I shall not try to say whether there is a philosophically interesting sense in which intentional mental phenomena are physical or material. But I do want to note some considerations against materialist *identity* theories.

State-like phenomena (say, beliefs) raise different problems from event-like phenomena (say, occurrent thoughts). Even among identity theorists, it is sometimes questioned whether an identity theory is the appropriate goal for materialism in the case of states. Since I shall confine myself to identity theories, I shall concentrate on event-like phenomena. But our considerations will also bear on views that hope to establish some sort of token identity theory for mental states like beliefs.

One other preliminary. I want to remain neutral about how best to describe the relation between the apparent event-like feature of occurrent thoughts and the apparent relational feature (their relation to a content). One might think of there being an event, the token thought event, that is in a certain relation to a content (indicated by the that-clause). One might think of the event as consisting—as not being anything "over and above"—the relevant relation's holding at a certain time between a person and a content. Or one might prefer some other account. From the viewpoint of an identity theory, the first way of seeing the matter is most advantageous. So I shall fit my exposition to that point of view.

Our ordinary method of identifying occurrent thought events and differentiating between them is to make reference to the person or organism to whom the thought occurs, the time of its occurrence, and the content of the thought. If person, time, and content are the same, we would normally count the thought event the same. If any one of these parameters differs in descriptions of thought events (subject to qualifications about duration), then the events or occurrences described are different. Of course, we can differentiate between events using descriptions that do not home in on these particular parameters. But these parameters are dominant. (It is worth noting that differentiations in terms of causes and effects usually tend to rely on the content of mental events or states at some point, since mental states or events are often among the causes or effects of a given mental event, and these causes or effects will usually be identified partly in terms of their content.) The important point for our purposes is that in ordinary practice, sameness of thought content (or at least some sort of strong equivalence of content) is taken as a necessary condition for sameness of thought occurrence.

Now one might codify and generalize this point by holding that no occurrence of a thought (that is, no token thought event) could have a different (or extensionally non-equivalent) content and be the very same token event. If this premise is accepted, then our argument of Section II can be deployed to show that a person's thought event is not *identical* with any event in him that is described by physiology, biology, chemistry, or physics. For let *b* be any given event described in terms of one of the physical sciences that occurs in the subject

while he thinks the relevant thought. Let '*b*' be such that it denotes the same physical event occurring in the subject in our counterfactual situation. (If you want, let '*b*' be rigid in Kripke's sense, though so strong a stipulation is not needed.) The second step of our argument in Section II makes it plausible that *b* need not be affected by counterfactual differences in the communal use of the word 'arthritis'. Actually, the subject thinks that his ankles are stiff from arthritis, while *b* occurs. But we can conceive of the subject's *lacking* a thought event that his ankles are stiff from arthritis, while *b* occurs. Thus in view of our initial premise, *b* is not identical with the subject's occurrent thought.[13]

Identity theorists will want to reject the first premise—the premise that no event with a different content could be identical with a given thought event. On such a view, the given thought event that his ankles are stiff from arthritis might well have been a thought that his ankles are stiff from tharthritis, yet be precisely the same token thought event. Such a view is intuitively very implausible. I know of only one reasonably spelled-out basis of support for this view. Such a basis would be provided by showing that mentalistic phenomena are causal or functional states, in one of the strong senses discussed earlier, and that mental events are physical tokens or realizations of those states. If 'that thought that his ankles are stiff from arthritis' could be accounted for in terms like 'that event with such and such a causal or functional role' (where 'such and such' does not itself involve intentional terminology), and if independently identified physical events systematically filled these roles (or realized these states), we could perhaps see a given thought event as having a different role—and hence content—in different possible situations. Given such a view, the functional specification could perhaps be seen as revealing the contingency of the intentional specification as applied to mental event tokens. Just as we can imagine a given physiological event that actually plays the role of causing the little finger to move two inches, as playing the role of causing the little finger to move three inches (assuming compensatory differences in its physiological environment), so we could perhaps imagine a given thought as having a different functional role from its actual one—and hence, assuming the functionalist account, as having a different content. But the relevant sort of functionalist account of intentional phenomena has not been made good.[14]

The recent prosperity of materialist-functionalist ways of thinking has been so great that it is often taken for granted that a given thought event might have been a thought with a different, obliquely non-equivalent content. Any old event, on this view, could have a different content, a different significance, if its surrounding context were changed. But in the case of occurrent thoughts—and intentional mental events generally—it is hardly obvious, or even initially plausible, that anything is more essential to the identity of the event than the content itself. Materialist identity theories have schooled the imagination to picture the content of a mental event as varying while the event remains fixed. But whether such imaginings are possible fact or just philosophical fancy is a separate question.[15]

At any rate, functionalist accounts have not provided adequate specification of what it is to be a thought that ____, for particular fillings of the blank. So a specification of a given thought event in functionalist terms does not reveal the contingency of the usual, undisputed intentional specifications.

Well, *is* it possible for a thought event to have had a different content from the one it has and be the very same event? It seems to me natural and certainly traditional to assume that this is not possible. Rarely, however, have materialists seen the identity theory as natural or intuitive. Materialists are generally revisionist about intuitions. What is clear is that we currently do identify and distinguish thought events primarily in terms of the person who has them, the rough times of their occurrence, and their contents. And we do assume that a thought event with a different content is a different thought event (insofar as we distinguish at all between the thinking event and the person's being related to a thought content at a time). I think these facts give the premise *prima facie* support and the argument against the identity theory some interest. I do not claim that we have "*a priori*" certainty that no account of intentional phenomena will reveal intentional language to be only contingently applicable to belief states or thought events. I am only dubious.

One might nurture faith or hope that some more socially oriented functionalist specification could be found. But no such specification is ready to hand. And I see no good reason to think that one must be found. Even if such a specification were found, it is far from clear that it would deflect the argument against the identity theory just considered. The "functional" states envisaged would depend not merely on what the individual does and what inner causal states lead to his activity—non-intentionally specified—but also on what his fellows do. The analogy between functional states and physiological states in causing the individual's internal and external activity was the chief support for the view that a given token mental event might

have been a token of a different content. But the envisaged socially defined "functional states" bear no intuitive analogy to physiological states or other physical causal states within the individual's body. Their function is not simply that of responding to environmental influences and causing the individual's activity. It is therefore not clear (short of *assuming* an identity theory) that any event that is a token of one of the envisaged socially defined "functional states" could have been a token of a different one. The event might be essentially identified in terms of its social role. There is as yet no reason to identify it in terms of physically described events in the individual's body. Thus it is not clear that such a socially oriented functional account of thought contents would yield grounds to believe that the usual intentional specifications of mental events are merely contingent. It is, I think, even less clear that an appropriate socially oriented functional account is viable.

Identity theories, of course, do not exhaust the resources of materialism. To take one example, our argument does not speak directly to a materialism based on composition rather than identity. On such a view, the same physical material might compose different thoughts in different circumstances. I shall say nothing evaluative about this sort of view. I have also been silent about other arguments for a token identity theory—such as those based on philosophical accounts of the notions of causality or explanation. Indeed, my primary interest has not been ontology at all. It has been to identify and question individualistic assumptions in materialist as well as Cartesian approaches to the mental.

V.   Models of the Mental

Traditional philosophical accounts of mind have offered metaphors that produce doctrine and carry conviction where argument and unaided intuition flag. Of course, any such broad reconstructions can be accused of missing the pied beauties of the natural article. But the problem with traditional philosophy of mind is more serious. The two overwhelmingly dominant metaphors of the mental—the infallible eye and the automatic mechanism—have encouraged systematic neglect of prominent features of a wide range of mental phenomena, broadly speaking, social features. Each metaphor has its attractions. Either can be elaborated or doctored to fit the facts that I have emphasized. But neither illumines those facts. And both have played some part in inducing philosophers to ignore them.

I think it optimistic indeed to hope that any

one picture, comparable to the traditional ones, will provide insight into all major aspects of mental phenomena. Even so, a function of philosophy is to sketch such pictures. The question arises whether one can make good the social debts of earlier accounts while retaining at least some of their conceptual integrity and pictorial charm. This is no place to start sketching. But some summary remarks may convey a sense of the direction in which our discussion has been tending.

The key feature of the examples of Section II was the fact that we attribute beliefs and thoughts to people even where they incompletely understand contents of those very beliefs and thoughts. This point about intentional mental phenomena is not everywhere applicable: non-linguistic animals do not seem to be candidates for misunderstanding the contents of their beliefs. But the point is certainly salient and must be encompassed in any picture of intentional mental phenomena. Crudely put, wherever the subject has attained a certain competence in large relevant parts of his language and has (implicitly) assumed a certain general commitment or responsibility to the communal conventions governing the language's symbols, the expressions the subject uses take on a certain inertia in determining attributions of mental content to him. In particular, the expressions the subject uses sometimes provide the content of his mental states or events even though he only partially understands, or even misunderstands, some of them. Global coherence and responsibility seem sometimes to override localized incompetence.

The detailed conditions under which this "inertial force" is exerted are complicated and doubtless more than a little vague. Clearly, the subject must maintain a minimal internal linguistic and rational coherence and a broad similarity to others' use of the language. But meeting this condition is hardly sufficient to establish the relevant responsibility. For the condition is met in the case of a person who speaks a regional dialect (where the same words are sometimes given different applications). The person's aberrations relative to the larger community may be normalities relative to the regional one. In such cases, of course, the regional conventions are dominant in determining what contents should be attributed. At this point, it is natural to appeal to etiological considerations. The speaker of the dialect developed his linguistic habits from interaction with others who were a party to distinctively regional conventions. The person is committed to using the words according to the conventions maintained by those from whom he learned the words. But the situation is more complicated than this observation suggests. A person born and bred in the parent community

might simply decide (unilaterally) to follow the usage of the regional dialect or even to fashion his own usage with regard to particular words, self-consciously opting out of the parent community's conventions in these particulars. In such a case, members of the parent community would not, and should not, attribute mental contents to him on the basis of homophonic construal of his words. Here the individual's intentions or attitudes toward communal conventions and communal conceptions seem more important than the causal antecedents of his transactions with a word—unless those intentions are simply included in the etiological story.

I shall not pursue these issues here. The problem of specifying the conditions under which a person has the relevant general competence in a language and a responsibility to its conventions is obviously complicated. The mixture of "causal" and intentional considerations relevant to dealing with it has obvious near analogs in other philosophical domains (etiological accounts of perception, knowledge, reference). I have no confidence that all of the details of the story would be philosophically interesting. What I want to stress is that to a fair degree, mentalistic attribution rests not on the subject's having mastered the contents of the attribution, and not on his having behavioral dispositions peculiarly relevant to those contents, but on his having a certain responsibility to communal conventions governing, and conceptions associated with, symbols that he is disposed to use. It is this feature that must be incorporated into an improved model of the mental.

I think it profitable to see the language of content attribution as constituting a complex *standard* by reference to which the subject's mental states and events are estimated, or an abstract grid on which they are plotted. Different people may vary widely in the degree to which they master the elements and relations within the standard, even as it applies to them all. This metaphor may be developed in several directions and with different models: applied geometry, measurement of magnitudes, evaluation by a monetary standard, and so forth. A model I shall illustrate briefly here borrows from musical analysis.

Given that a composer has fulfilled certain general conditions for establishing a musical key, his chordal structures are plotted by reference to the harmonic system of relations appropriate to the tonic key. There is vast scope for variation and novelty within the harmonic framework. The chords may depart widely from traditional "rules" or practices governing what count as interesting or "reasonable" chordal structures and progressions. And the composer may or may not grasp the harmonic implications and departures present in his composition. The composer may sometimes exhibit harmonic incompetence (and occasionally harmonic genius) by radically departing from those traditional rules. But the harmonic system of relations applies to the composition in any case. Once established, the tonic key and its associated harmonic framework are applied unless the composer takes pains to set up another tonic key or some atonal arrangement (thereby intentionally opting out of the original tonal framework), or writes down notes by something like a slip of the pen (suffering mechanical interference in his compositional intentions), or unintentionally breaks the harmonic rules in a massive and unprincipled manner (thereby indicating chaos or complete incompetence). The tonic key provides a standard for describing the composition. The application of the standard depends on the composer's maintaining a certain overall coherence and minimal competence in conforming to the standard's conventions. And there are conditions under which the standard would be replaced by another. But once applied, the harmonic framework—its formal interrelations, its applicability even to deviant, pointless progressions—is partly independent of the composer's degree of harmonic mastery.

One attractive aspect of the metaphor is that it has some application to the case of animals. In making sounds, animals do sometimes behave in such a way that a harmonic standard can be roughly applied to them, even though the standard, at least in any detail, is no part of what they have mastered. Since they do not master the standard (though they may master some of its elements), they are not candidates for partial understanding or misunderstanding. (Of course, this may be said of many people as regards the musical standard.) The standard applies to both animals and people. But the conditions for its application are sensitive in various ways to whether the subject himself has mastered it. Where the subject does use the standard (whether the language, or a system of key relationships), his uses take on special weight in applications of the standard to him.

One of the metaphor's chief virtues is that it encourages one to seek social explications for this special weight. The key to our attribution of mental contents in the face of incomplete mastery or misunderstanding lies largely in social functions associated with maintaining and applying the standard. In broad outline, the social advantages of the "special weight" are apparent. Symbolic expressions are the overwhelmingly dominant source of detailed information about what people think, intend, and so forth. Such detail is essential not only to much explanation and prediction, but also to

fulfilling many of our cooperative enterprises and to relying on one another for second-hand information. Words interpreted in conventionally established ways are familiar, palpable, and public. They are common coin, a relatively stable currency. These features are crucial to achieving the ends of mentalistic attribution just cited. They are also critical in maximizing interpersonal comparability. And they yield a bias toward taking others at their word and avoiding *ad hoc* reinterpretation, once overall agreement in usage and commitment to communal standards can be assumed.

This bias issues in the practice of expressing even many differences in understanding without reinterpreting the subject's words. Rather than reinterpret the subject's word 'arthritis' and give him a trivially true object-level belief and merely a false metalinguistic belief about how 'arthritis' is used by others, it is common practice, and correct, simply to take him at his word.

I hardly need re-emphasize that the situation is vastly more complicated than I have suggested in the foregoing paragraphs. Insincerity, tongue slips, certain malapropisms, subconscious blocks, mental instability all make the picture more complex. There are differences in our handling of different sorts of expressions, depending, for example, on how clear and fixed social conventions regarding the expressions are. There are differences in our practices with different subject matters. There are differences in our handling of different degrees of linguistic error. There are differences in the way meaning-, assertion-, and mental-contents are attributed. (Cf. note 4.) I do not propose ignoring these points. They are all parameters affecting the inertial force of "face value" construal. But I want to keep steadily in mind the philosophically neglected fact about social practice: Our attributions do not require that the subject always correctly or fully understand the content of his attitudes.

The point suggests fundamental misorientations in the two traditional pictures of the mental. The authority of a person's reports about his thoughts and beliefs (*modulo* sincerity, lack of subconscious interference, and so forth) does not issue from a special intellectual vision of the contents of those thoughts and beliefs. It extends even to some cases in which the subject incompletely understands those contents. And it depends partly on the social advantages of maintaining communally established standards of communication and mentalistic attribution. Likewise, the descriptive and explanatory role of mental discourse is not adequately modeled by complex non-intentional mechanisms or programs for the production of an individual's physical movement and behavior. Attributing intentional mentalistic phenomena to individuals serves not only to explain their behavior viewed in isolation but also to chart their activity (intentional, verbal, behavioral, physical) by complex comparison to others—and against socially established standards.[16] Both traditional metaphors make the mistake, among others, of treating intentional mental phenomena individualistically. New approaches must do better. The sense in which man is a social animal runs deeper than much mainstream philosophy of mind has acknowledged.[17]

NOTES

1. Our examples suggest points about learning that need exploration. It would seem naive to think that we first attain a mastery of expressions or notions we use and then tackle the subject matters we speak and think about in using those expressions or notions. In most cases, the processes overlap. But while the subject's understanding is still partial, we sometimes attribute mental contents in the very terms the subject has yet to master. Traditional views take mastering a word to consist in matching it with an already mastered (or innate) concept. But it would seem, rather, that many concepts (or mental content components) are like words in that they may be employed before they are mastered. In both cases, employment appears to be an integral part of the process of mastery.

2. A development of a similar theme may be found in Hilary Putnam's notion of a division of linguistic labour. Cf. "The Meaning of 'Meaning'," *Philosophical Papers* 2 (London, 1975) pp. 227 ff. Putnam's imaginative work is in other ways congenial with points I have developed. Some of his examples can be adapted in fairly obvious ways so as to give an argument with different premises, but a conclusion complementary to the one I arrive at in Section IIa:

Consider Alfred's belief contents involving the notion of water. Without changing Alfred's (or his fellows') non-intentional phenomenal experiences, internal physical occurrences, or dispositions to respond to stimuli on sensory surfaces, we can imagine that not water (H_2O), but a different liquid with different structure but similar macro-properties (and identical phenomenal properties) played the role in his environment that water does in ours. In such a case, we could ascribe no content clauses to Alfred with 'water' in oblique position. His belief contents would differ. The conclusion (with which I am in sympathy) is that mental contents are affected not only by the physical and qualitatively mental way the person is, but by the nature of his *physical environment.*

Putnam himself does not give quite this argument. He nowhere states the first and third steps, though he gives analogs of them for the meaning of 'water'. This is partly just a result of his concentration on meaning instead of propositional attitudes. But some of what he says even seems to oppose the argument's conclusion. He remarks in effect that the subject's *thoughts* remain constant between his actual and counterfactual cases (p. 224). In his own argument he explicates the difference between actual and counterfactual cases in terms of a difference in the extension of terms, not a difference in those aspects of their meaning that play a role in the cognitive life of the subject. And he tries to explicate his examples in terms of indexicality—a mistake, I think, and one that tends to divert attention from major implications of the examples he gives. (Cf. Section IId.) In my view, the examples do illustrate the fact that all attitudes involving natural kind notions, including *de dicto* attitudes, presuppose *de re* attitudes. But the examples do not show that natural kind linguistic expressions are in any ordinary sense indexical. Nor do they show that beliefs involving natural kind notions are always *de re*. Even if they did, the change from actual to counterfactual cases would affect oblique occurrences of natural kind terms in that-clauses—occurrences that are the key to attributions of cognitive content. (Cf. above and note 3.) In the cited paper and earlier ones, much of what Putnam says about psychological states (and implies about mental states) has a distinctly individualistic ring. Below in Section IV, I criticize viewpoints about mental phenomena influenced by and at least strongly suggested in his earlier work on functionalism. (Cf. note 9.)

On the other hand, Putnam's articulation of social and environmental aspects of the meaning of natural kind terms complements and supplements our viewpoint. For me, it has been a rich rewarder of reflection. More recent work of his seems to involve shifts in his viewpoint on psychological states. It may have somewhat more in common with our approach than the earlier work, but there is much that I do not understand about it.

The argument regarding the notion of water that I extracted from Putnam's paper is narrower in scope than our argument. The Putnam-derived argument seems to work only for natural kind terms and close relatives. And it may seem not to provide as direct a threat to certain versions of functionalism that I discuss in Section IV: At least a few philosophers would claim that one could accommodate the Putnamian argument in terms of *non*-intentional formulations of input-output relations (formulations that make reference to the specific nature of the physical environment). Our argument does not submit to this maneuver. In our thought experiment, the physical environment (sofas, arthritis, and so forth in our examples) and the subject's causal relations with it (at least as these are usually conceived) were held constant. The Putnamian argument, however, has fascinatingly different implications from our argument. I have not developed these comparisons and contrasts here because doing justice to Putnam's viewpoint would demand a distracting amount of space, as the ample girth of this footnote may suggest.

3. I have discussed *de re* mental phenomena in "Belief De Re," *The Journal of Philosophy* 74 (1977):338–62. There I argue that all attitudes with content presuppose *de re* attitudes. Our discussion here may be seen as bearing on the details of this presupposition. But for reasons I merely sketch in the next paragraph, I think it would be a superficial viewpoint that tried to utilize our present argument to support the view that nearly all intentional mental phenomena are covertly indexical or *de re*.

4. Cf. my "Belief and Synonymy," *The Journal of Philosophy* 75 (1978):119–38, Section III, where I concentrate on attribution of belief contents containing "one criterion" terms like 'vixen' or 'fortnight' which the subject misunderstands. The next several pages interweave some of the points in that paper. I think that a parallel thought experiment involving even these words is constructible, at least for a nar-

rowly restricted set of beliefs. We can imagine that the subject believes that some female foxes—say, those that are virgins—are not vixens. Or he could believe that a fortnight is a period of ten days. (I believed this for many years.) Holding his physical history, qualitative experience, and dispositions constant, we can conceive of his linguistic community defining these terms as he actually misunderstands them. In such a case, his belief contents would differ from his actual ones.

5. Bertrand Russell, *Mysticism and Logic* (London, 1959), p. 221. Although Russell's statement is unusually unqualified, its kinship to Descartes' and Plato's model is unmistakable. Cf. Plato, *Phaedrus*, 249b–c, *Phaedo*, 47b6–c4; Descartes, *Philosophical Works*, eds. Haldane and Ross 2 vols. (New York, 1955), *Rules for the Direction of the Mind*, section XII, Vol. I, pp. 41–42, 45; *Principles of Philosophy*, Part I, XXXII–XXXV. Vol. I, pp. 232–33; *Replies*, Vol. II, 52; Hume, *A Treatise of Human Nature*, I, 3,5; II, 2,6; Kant, *A Critique of Pure Reason*, A7–B11; Frege, *The Foundations of Arithmetic*, section 105; G. E. Moore, *Principia Ethica*, 86.

6. Descartes, *Principles of Philosophy*, XLV–XLI.

7. Descartes, *Philosophical Works*, Vol. II, *Replies*, p. 42.

8. Certain movements sometimes called "functionalist" are definitely not my present concern. Nothing I say is meant to oppose the claim that hypotheses in psychology do and should make reference to "sub-personal" states and processes in explaining human action and ordinary mental states and processes. My remarks may bear on precisely how such hypotheses are construed philosophically. But the hypotheses themselves must be judged primarily by their fruits. Similarly, I am not concerned with the claim that computers provide an illuminating perspective for viewing the mind. Again, our view may bear on the interpretation of the computer analogy, but I have no intention of questioning its general fruitfulness. On the other hand, insofar as functionalism is merely a slogan to the effect that "once you see how computers might be made to work, you realize such and such about the mind," I am inclined to let the cloud condense a little before weighing its contents.

9. A representative of the more nearly "analytical" form of functionalism is David Lewis, "Psychophysical and Theoretical Identifications," *Australasian Journal of Philosophy* 50 (1972):249–58: "Applied to common-sense psychology—folk science rather than professional science, but a theory nonetheless—we get the hypothesis . . . that a mental state M . . . is definable as the occupant of a certain causal role R—that is, as the state, of whatever sort, that is causally connected to specified ways to sensory stimuli, motor responses, and other mental states" (249–50). Actually, it should be noted that the argument of Section I applies to Lewis's position less directly than one might suppose. For reasons unconnected with matters at hand, Lewis intends his *definition* to apply to relational mentalistic predicates like 'thinks' but not to complex predicates that identify actual mental states or events, like 'thinks that snow is white'. Cf. *Ibid.*, p. 256, n13. This seems to me a puzzling halfway house for some of Lewis's philosophical purposes. But our argument appears to apply anyway, since Lewis is explicit in holding that physical facts about a person taken in isolation from his fellows "determine" all his specific intentional events and states. Cf. 'Radical Interpretation', *Synthese* 27 (1974):331ff. I cite Lewis's definitional approach because it has been the most influential recent piece of its genre, and many of those influenced by it have not excluded its application to specific intentional mental states and events. Other representatives of the definitional approach are J.J.C. Smart, "Further Thoughts on the Identity Theory," *Monist* 56 (1972):149–62; D. W. Armstrong, *A Materialist Theory of Mind* (London, 1968), pp. 90–91 and *passim;* Sidney Shoemaker, "Functionalism and Qualia," *Philosophical Studies* 27 (1975):306–7. A representative of the more frequently held "hypothesis" version of functionalism is Hilary Putnam, "The Mental Life of Some Machines," *Philosophical Papers* 2 (Cambridge, 1975), and "The Nature of Mental States," *Ibid.*, cf. p. 437: ". . . if the program of finding psychological laws that are not species specific . . . ever succeeds, then it will bring in its wake a delineation of the kind of functional organization that is necessary and sufficient for a given psychological state, as well as a precise definition of the notion 'psychological state'." In more recent work, Putnam's views on the relation between functional organization and psychological (and also mental) states and events have become more complicated. I make no claims about how the argument of Section II bears on them. Other representatives of the "hypothesis" approach are Gilbert Harman, "Three Levels of Meaning," *The Journal of Philosophy* 65 (1968); "An Introduction to 'Translation and Meaning'," *Words and Objections*, eds. D. Davidson and J. Hintikka (Reidel, 1969), p. 21; and *Thought* (Princeton, 1973), pp. 43–46, 56–65, for example, p. 45: ". . . mental states and processes are to be functionally defined (by a psychological theory). They are constituted by their function or role in the relevant programme", Jerry Fodor, *The Language of Thought* (New York, 1975), Chapter I; Armstrong, *A Materialist Theory of Mind*, p. 84. An attempt to articulate the common core of the different types of functionalist "account" occurs in Ned Block and Jerry Fodor's "What Psychological States Are Not," *Philosophical Review* 81 (1972), p. 173: ". . . functionalism in the broad sense of that doctrine which holds that type identity conditions for psychological states refer only to their relations to inputs, outputs and one another."

10. Often functionalists give mental contents only cursory discussion, if any at all. But claims that a functional account explains intentionality by accounting for all specific intentional states and events in non-intentional, functional language occur in the following: Daniel Dennett, *Content and Consciousness* (London, 1969), Chapter II and *passim;* Harman, *Thought*, for example, p. 60: "To specify the meaning of a sentence used in communication is partly to specify the belief or other mental state expressed; and the representative character of that state is determined by its functional role"; Fodor, *The Language of Thought*, Chapter I and II, for example, p. 75: "The way that information is stored, computed . . . or otherwise processed by the organism explains its cognitive states and in particular, its propositional attitudes"; Smart, "Further Thoughts on the Identity Theory"; Hartry Field, "Mental Representation," *Erkenntnis* 13 (1978): 9–61. I shall confine discussion to the issue of intentionality. But it seems to me that the individualistic cast of functionalist accounts renders them inadequate in their handling of another major traditional issue about intentional mental states and events—first-person authority.

11. H. P. Grice, "Meaning," *Philosophical Review* 66 (1957):377–88; "Utterer's Meaning, Sentence-Meaning, and Word-Meaning," *Foundations of Language* 4 (1968):225–42; Stephen Schiffer, *Meaning* (Oxford, 1972), cf. especially pp.

13, 50, 63ff; Jonathan Bennett, "The Meaning-Nominalist Strategy," *Foundations of Language* 10 (1974):141–68. Another example of an individualistic theory of meaning is the claim to explicate all kinds of meaning ultimately in psychological terms, and these latter in functionalist terms. See, for example Harman, "Three Levels of Meaning," note 9. This project seems to rest on the functionalist approaches just criticized.

12. Perhaps the first reasonably clear modern statement of the strategy occurs in J. J. C. Smart, "Sensations and Brain Processes," *Philosophical Review* 68 (1959):141–56. This article treats qualitative experiences; but Smart is explicit in applying it to specific intentional states and events in "Further Thoughts on the Identity Theory." Cf. also David Lewis, "An Argument for the Identity Theory," *The Journal of Philosophy* 63 (1966):17–25; "Psychophysical and Theoretical Identifications"; Armstrong, *A Materialist Theory of Mind, passim;* Harman, *Thought,* pp. 42–43; Fodor, *The Language of Thought,* Introduction.

13. The argument is basically Cartesian in style, (cf. *Meditations* II), though the criticism of functionalism, which is essential to its success, is not in any obvious sense Cartesian. (Cf. note 14.) Also the conclusion gives no special support to Cartesian ontology. The terminology of rigidity is derived from Saul Kripke, "Naming and Necessity," *Semantics of Natural Language,* eds., Davidson and Harman (Dordrecht, 1972), though as mentioned above, a notion of rigidity is not essential for the argument. Kripke has done much to clarify the force of the Cartesian sort of argument. He gives such an argument aimed at showing the non-identity of sensations with brain processes. The argument as presented seems to suffer from a failure to criticize materialistic accounts of sensation language and from not indicating clearly how token physical events and token sensation events that are *prima facie* candidates for identification could have occurred independently. For criticism of Kripke's argument, see Fred Feldman, "Kripke on the Identity Theory," *The Journal of Philosophy* 71 (1974):665–76; William G. Lycan, "Kripke and the Materialists," *Ibid.,* pp. 677–89; Richard Boyd, "What Physicalism Does Not Entail," *Readings in the Philosophy of Psychology,* ed. N. Block (forthcoming); Colin McGinn, "Anomalous Monism and Kripke's Cartesian Intuitions," *Analysis* 37 (1977):78–80. It seems to me, however, that these issues are not closed.

14. It is important to note that our argument against functionalist specifications of mentalistic phenomena did not depend on the assumption that no occurrent thought could have a different content from the one it has and be the very same occurrence or event. If it did, the subsequent argument against the identity theory would, in effect, beg the question. The strategy of the latter argument is rather to presuppose an independent argument that undermines non-intentional functionalist specifications of what it is to be *a* thought that (say) sofas are comfortable; then to take as plausible and undefeated the assumption that no occurrent thought could have a different (obliquely non-equivalent) content and be the same occurrence or event; and, finally, to use this assumption with the modal considerations appealed to earlier, to arrive at the non-identity of an occurrent thought event with any event specified by physical theory (the natural sciences) that occurs within the individual.

Perhaps it is worth saying that the metaphorical claim that mental events are identified by their *role* in some "inference-action language game" (to use a phrase of Sellars's) does not provide a plausible ground for rejecting the initial premise of the argument against the identity theory. For even if one did not reject the "role-game" idea as unsupported metaphor, one could agree with the claim on the understanding that the roles are largely the intentional contents themselves and the same event in *this* sort of "game" could not have a different role. A possible view in the philosophy of mathematics is that numbers are identified by their role in a progression and such roles are essential to their identity. The point of this comparison is just that appeal to the role metaphor, even if accepted, does not settle the question of whether an intentional mental event or state could have had a different content.

15. There are *prima facie* viable philosophical accounts that take sentences (whether tokens or types) as truth bearers. One might hope to extend such accounts to mental contents. On such treatments, contents are not things over and above sentences. They simply *are* sentences interpreted in a certain context, treated in a certain way. Given a different context of linguistic interpretation, the content of the same sentence might be different. One could imagine mental events to be analogous to the sentences on this account. Indeed, some philosophers have thought of intentional mental events as being inner, physical sentence (or symbol) tokens—a sort of brain writing. Here again, there is a picture according to which the same thought event might have had a different content. But here again the question is whether there is any reason to think it is a true picture. There is the prior question of whether sentences can reasonably be treated as contents. (I think sentence types probably can be; but the view has hardly been established, and defending it against sophisticated objections is treacherous.) Even if this question is answered affirmatively, it is far from obvious that the analogy between sentences and contents, on the one hand, and thought events and contents, on the other, is a good one. Sentences (types or tokens) are commonly identified independently of their associated contents (as evidenced by inter- and intra-linguistic ambiguity). It is *relatively* uncontroversial that sentences can be identified by syntactical, morphemic, or perceptual criteria that are in principle specifiable independently of what particular content the sentence has. The philosophical question about sentences and contents is whether discourse about contents can be reasonably interpreted as having an ontology of nothing more than sentences (and intentional agents). The philosophical question about mental events and contents is "What is the nature of the events?" "Regardless of what contents are, could the very same thought event have a different content?" The analogous question for sentences—instead of thought events—has an uncontroversial affirmative answer. Of course, we know that when and where non-intentionally identifiable physical events have contents, the same physical event could have had a different content. But it can hardly be *assumed* for purposes of arguing a position on the mind-body problem that mental events are non-intentionally identifiable physical events.

16. In emphasizing social and pragmatic features in mentalistic attributions, I do not intend to suggest that mental attributions are any the less objective, descriptive, or on the ontological up and up. There are substantial arguments in the literature that might lead one to make such inferences. But my present remarks are free of such implications. Someone

might want to insist that from a "purely objective viewpoint" one can describe "the phenomena" equally well in accord with common practice, literally interpreted, or in accord with various reinterpretation strategies. Then our arguments would, perhaps, show only that it is "objectively indeterminate" whether functionalism and the identity theory are true. I would be inclined to question the application of the expressions that are scare-quoted.

17. I am grateful to participants at a pair of talks given at the University of London in the spring of 1978, and to Richard Rorty for discussions earlier. I am also indebted to Robert Adams and Rogers Albritton whose criticisms forced numerous improvements. I appreciatively acknowledge support of the John Simon Guggenheim Foundation.

58

Brian Loar

"Social Content and Psychological Content"

By *psychological content* I shall mean whatever individuates beliefs and other propositional attitudes in commonsense psychological explanation, so that they explanatorily interact with each other and with other factors such as perception in familiar ways. In discussions of what appropriately individuates propositional attitudes there occurs the following kind of argument. Some thesis about psychological content is proposed, about, say, what constitutes it in general or constitutes some aspect of it. The reply is made that the thesis fails to capture the correct individuation conditions because correct ascriptions of attitudes using *that-clauses* count them the same when the proposed thesis distinguishes them or vice versa. Here are some examples.

1. There is the idea that the perceptual ability to discriminate objects of a given kind, cats say, may constitute a concept of that kind of object. Think of "concept" here as meaning a certain abstraction from the individuation conditions of certain beliefs and other attitudes, about cats, say. Then the capacity to have certain beliefs about cats, beliefs that have certain psychological contents, would involve the ability perceptually to discriminate cats. Variants of this idea have seemed natural to empiricists and recently to certain functionalists: what better criterion for having certain ordinary concepts than the ability systematically to pick out their instances?

But there is a problem when we consider how apparently we individuate beliefs, as Stephen Stich points out. "Suppose I tell a blind person and a sighted person that there is a cat in the next room, and they believe my report. It seems natural to say that they both come to have the same belief: the belief that there is a cat in the next room. Our intuitions remain the same if we change the example by replacing the merely blind subject with a person like Helen Keller whose perceptual deficiencies are staggering."[1] On these grounds Stich regards as false any theory that implies that the sighted and the blind person's beliefs have distinct contents.

The premise appears correct, for "believes that there is a cat in the next room" does seem univocally assertible of both the sighted person and Helen Keller. For if each were sincerely to assert "there is a cat in the next room" their words conventionally would *mean* the same; and so by ordinary criteria the belief ascription would be true of each on an *oblique* or *de dicto* univocal reading. (The sameness of belief ascription is not then merely a function of a common *de re* reference to the kind *cat*.)

2. There is the very general thesis that the psychological content of a person's attitudes consists in their conceptual or cognitive-functional roles, thus presupposing that our commonsense system of psychological explanation individuates attitudes along non-social, individualistic lines. Tyler Burge has mounted an imposing counter-argument.[2] He has two objections: that the individualist conceptual role theory counts beliefs as different which common sense counts the same; and that the conceptual role theory counts beliefs as the same which common sense counts different. Both objections rest on the following well-known example of Burge's.

Suppose that a person who is otherwise a normal English speaker believes that he has arthritis in his thigh, and that he also has many true beliefs about arthritis, for example, that he has it in his wrists and ankles. When a doctor tells him that arthritis cannot occur in the thigh ("arthritis means an ailment of the joints") he is surprised but takes the doctor's word for it. Now consider that earlier belief which he would have expressed as "I have arthritis in my ankles." On the conceptual role theory, that belief should count as distinct from the doctor's belief that his patient has arthritis in his ankles. For the two have, or had, crucially different ideas about what "arthritis" means, and consequently the two beliefs have (should on a conceptual role theory be counted as having) crucially different conceptual links to other beliefs. But as Burge argues, common sense ascribes the same belief to both: the belief that the patient has arthritis in his ankles. Thus sameness of conceptual role is not *necessary* for sameness of psychological content.[3] Now it seems clear that Burge is right that the belief ascription applies both to the doctor and to the patient in his uncorrected state on a univocal reading, one that is, moreover, oblique or *de dicto*.

That sameness of conceptual role is not *sufficient* for sameness of content is argued as follows. Suppose the patient (whom we'll now call Bert) had lived in a world much like this one, but one in which doctors apply "arthritis" not to a disease specifically of joints but to a broader class of rheumatoid ailments including one that can occur in thighs. Suppose that Bert's history in that world had from an individualistic point of view been identical with what it is in the real world, and that therefore before visiting the doctor Bert had had a belief he would have expressed as "I have arthritis in my thigh." As we see things, would that have been a belief that he had *arthritis* in his thigh? Burge says no, and again I believe he is right. In that world Bert may have had a belief that he had *tharthritis* (as we may choose to say) in his thigh, for there "arthritis" does not mean what it means among us. So in the actual and the counterfactual situations, the individualistic facts about the conceptual roles of Bert's beliefs are the same, but distinct belief ascriptions are true of him. Burge draws the strong conclusion that the content of a person's beliefs depends in part on social facts that are independent of his cognitive make-up, social facts of which he may not be aware.

Stich's point and the first of Burge's points have a common structure: it is said to be false that discriminative abilities are partially constitutive of psychological contents, and that individual conceptual roles are constitutive of psychological contents, because those theses would count beliefs as distinct to which the same *de dicto* or oblique ascription univocally applies.

3. Metalinguistic contents have often been invoked for beliefs that normally would not be expressed metalinguistically. Thus suppose a person asserts "there are elms in Spain" but knows of no non-metalinguistic distinguishing features of elms among trees or of Spain among countries. It could be said that the content of this person's belief involves the conception of elms as "those trees which among us are called 'elms'" and of Spain as "that country which among us is called 'Spain'."

One objection (there are others I shall not discuss) is the following. Suppose an Italian who would assert "Ci sono olmi in Spagna" is in the same situation as our English speaker; he does not know elms ("olmi") from other trees or Spain ("Spagna") from other countries. To be consistent we then say that his beliefs involve metalinguistic reference to those Italian nouns. But of course if everything else is normal we should rather say that the two speakers believe the same thing, namely that there are elms in Spain. This holds of them *de dicto* and univocally. They have the same belief, while the metalinguistic analysis counts them as having distinct beliefs. Once again, I find the premise about the oblique or *de dicto* ascription correct, not open to an unforced denial; it would be misguided to insist that we must throw out the univocal that-clause and substitute a pair of metalinguistic that-clauses in order to describe those beliefs correctly.

The question then to be addressed is the relation between *de dicto* or oblique ascriptions of beliefs and their psychological contents, between such ascriptions and their individuation in commonsense psychological explanation. I shall argue that psychological content is not in general identical with what is captured by oblique that-clauses, that commonsense constraints on individuation induce only a loose fit between contents and that-clauses, and that this does not make contents ineffable or even especially elusive. Let me emphasize that the topic is not some theoretical refinement of commonsense psychology, but ordinary everyday psychological explanation.

Behind the three arguments—against recognitional concept theories, conceptual role theories, and metalinguistic concept analyses—lies something like the following assumption:

(*) Sameness of *de dicto* or oblique ascription implies sameness of psychological content.

Perhaps there are facts about the occurrence of indexicals and demonstratives which would generally be perceived nowadays as counterexamples to (*) in its unqualified form. But it is pretty evident, I think, that the above arguments presuppose a version of (*) restricted to general terms (including also proper names; cf. "Spain"). So we have something like:

(A) Sameness of the *de dicto* or oblique occurrence of a general term in two belief ascriptions implies, if everything else is the same, sameness of the psychological content of the two beliefs thus ascribed.

My reply to the above arguments involves denying (A): sameness of the general terms in a pair of belief ascriptions does not (even though all else is equal) ensure that the ascribed beliefs are individuated as the same belief in commonsense psychological explanation.

I shall also argue the falsity of the converse of (A), viz.

(B) Differences in *de dicto* or oblique ascription imply differences in psychological content.

This is important again in connection with Burge's anti-individualism, for it seems to be required for his argument that sameness in the conceptual roles of thoughts is not sufficient for their sameness in psychological content.

A variant of a well-known example of Kripke's may serve to introduce the reason for rejecting (A). In the original example[4] Pierre grew up monolingual in France, where he had heard of a pretty city called "Londres"; he was moreover disposed to assert "Londres est jolie." Subsequently he was taken to live in London, not knowing it to be the Londres he had heard of; the part he lived in was unattractive and he was disposed to assert "London is not pretty." Our ordinary principles of belief ascription lead us then to say, as Kripke points out, both that Pierre believes that London is pretty and that Pierre believes that London is not pretty. These ascriptions are true on an oblique reading[5] and "London" is univocal as we use it.

Now Pierre might have been more fortunate; he might have been taken to an attractive part of London and thus been happy to assert "London is pretty," still unaware that this was the Londres he had heard of. The upshot is interesting: "Pierre believes that London is pretty" is true by virtue of the earlier facts about Pierre, and it is true by virtue of the later facts. And its double truth is on a univocal oblique reading. The point does not depend on translation; parallel cases arise in which someone mistakenly thinks a name names two things, and ascribes the same predicate twice.

But how many beliefs does Pierre have? In other words, how many belief-types are involved, as that is individuated by commonsense psychology? Clearly there are two beliefs, and they are as distinct as my beliefs that Paris is pretty and that Rio is pretty. Those beliefs would interact differently with other beliefs in ordinary psychological explanation. Perhaps in France Pierre came to believe that were he ever to live in "Londres" he would live in the same city as Oscar Wilde, and he retains this belief. But he does not draw from the conjunction of this belief and his later beliefs the conclusion that he now lives in a pretty city also inhabited by Oscar Wilde; and this is not because he has not bothered to put them together.

These beliefs not only are individuated by commonsense psychology as distinct in their psychological roles; it also seems quite appropriate to regard them as distinct in *content*. The differences in their interactive properties flow from differences in how Pierre conceives things, in how he takes the world to be, in what he regards the facts as being— that is, differences in some semantic or intentional dimension. And yet one and the same oblique belief description is true of Pierre univocally by virtue of these beliefs that are distinct in their psychological content.

Let us now look at some beliefs involving general terms. Suppose that Paul, an English speaker, has been raised by a French nanny in a sheltered way. She speaks English with Paul, but amuses herself by referring to the cats around them as "chats" (she says "shahs," pronouncing the "s") and never as "cats." Paul acquires thereby a perfectly good recognitional acquaintance with cats and many beliefs about them, but he does not know that in English they are properly called "cats." Suppose he forms the belief he would express as "All chats have tails"; it seems we are then justified in asserting that Paul believes that all cats have tails, on an oblique reading.[6] As it happens, he occasionally sees his parents, who speak of animals called "cats." Because no cats are ever present, nor any pictures of cats, Paul does not realize that cats are his familiar "chats." Now Paul's parents tell him various things about cats, in particular that they all have tails. On this basis it is again true of Paul that he believes that all cats have tails. And it seems clear that Paul has two beliefs, with distinct psychological contents. For they interact potentially with other beliefs in different ways despite their common univocal ascription.

Had Paul's parents told him of Manx cats, it would have been true that Paul believes that all cats have tails and believes that not all cats have tails, on oblique unequivocal readings. But we should say that those beliefs are not inconsistent in their psychological contents,[7] and this means that these oblique ascriptions do not individuate Paul's beliefs in a way that reflects their psychological relations.

Stephen Stich's reply to the general thesis that recognitional abilities may be crucial to the individuation of beliefs was that Helen Keller and a sighted person both may believe that there is a cat in the next room. Now suppose that Paul had had a slightly different phonological history. His nanny used the English "cat," but somehow Paul got the idea that there are two different meanings of "cat," each referring to a distinct kind of animal (cf. "crab"), the kind he recognizes at a glance and the kind his parents speak of. This idea is so entrenched that when his nanny and his parents, on one of their rare joint appearances, both say "there's a cat in the next room," Paul believes that there are two animals in the next room and is interested to see finally one of the unfamiliar "cats." Now Helen Keller has conveniently dropped by, and she overhears Paul's parents' remark. It seems that she thereby acquires only one belief that there's a cat in the next room, but that Paul has two such beliefs, distinct as types in their psychological individuation. Helen Keller's belief is then identical in type with at most one of Paul's beliefs. And so it is left open that the content of the other belief is constituted in part by Paul's ability to recognize cats. Naturally (A) is thereby falsified.

Now consider again Tyler Burge's first thesis, that two beliefs may differ in their conceptual roles (by virtue of different understandings of some concept) and nevertheless have the same content. Suppose that when Paul leaves home he lives in France for a while, learns about a rheumatoid ailment called "arthrite," and comes to believe that he has it both in his thigh and in his ankles. He would be surprised to learn that you can't have "arthrite" in your thigh. As it happens Paul has a perfectly good understanding of the English "arthritis," which he does not realize is renderable in French as "arthrite" (perhaps he never sees them written down). He is unfortunately given to hypochondria, and comes to believe that he has two problems with his ankles, in his words "arthrite" and "arthritis." It seems that "believes that he has arthritis in his ankles" is doubly but univocally true of Paul, by virtue of beliefs with distinct psychological contents. Had he been less inclined to hypochondria his English belief could have instead been that he does not have arthritis in his ankles. Now that belief would clearly have been psychologically consistent with his French belief that he has arthritis in his ankles, but not with his *actual* English belief. The latter two therefore must be distinct in psychological content—unless, that is, you want to deny that the relevant sort of consistency is consistency in content.[8]

So Burge's observation that "believes that Bert has arthritis in his ankles" is true of the doctor and Bert on an oblique univocal reading, which I have agreed is correct, does not imply that their beliefs

have the same content as that is individuated in commonsense psychological explanation.

I shall not go into the third argument, the one against metalinguistic analyses. But it should by now be clear that it does not follow from the fact that "believes that there are elms in Spain" is univocally true of those English and Italian speakers that their beliefs are not metalinguistic with regard to their respective languages and therefore distinct in their psychological contents.

It may be useful to distinguish two theses in what I have been arguing, namely, a thesis about how beliefs are *individuated* in commonsense psychological explanation, and a thesis about *content*, the former being more minimal than the latter.

Commonsense psychological explanation appeals to various elementary *structures* in the relations among beliefs, wants and so on. There are motivational structures: x's believing something, x's believing something else to the effect that given the first thing doing A would have a certain result, and x's desire for that result may explain x's doing A. There are inferential structures: x's believing something and x's believing something else to the effect that the first thing is sufficient for a certain further thing may explain x's believing that further thing. There are structures of irrationality: x's believing something, x's desire for a certain thing and x's belief to the effect that the first thing could rule out the second may conjointly explain x's compartmentalizing or suppressing the first belief. And so on.[9]

These structures apply to beliefs and desires only as they are appropriately individuated. The simple cases I have been discussing can be spun out in obvious ways to show that the appropriate individuation conditions are not captured by oblique readings of ordinary belief ascriptions. For example, imagine Paul's English belief that he has arthritis in his ankles interacting with a French belief of his that if he has arthritis in his ankles he should apply heat: not much happens as a result. The correct individuation transcends, in some crucial respects at least, what ordinary ascriptions capture. And I am speaking always of commonsense explanation.

As for psychological *content*, if it is not captured by that-clauses, what constitutes it? Are we entitled to regard my alleged underlying psychological individuation as determining a kind of content? I shall return to this question.

Let us take up the second strong Burgean thesis. Suppose "arthritis" had meant *tharthritis*: even if Bert's non-socially-described ruminations remained the same it would not have been true that Bert believed that he had arthritis in his ankles and thigh. *Therefore* sameness of individualist conceptual role is not sufficient for sameness of psychological content.

Now Burge's premise, that our old belief ascription would not then be true of Bert, is correct; and it is an important discovery that belief ascriptions are thus sensitive to social facts which may not be reflected in believers' own versions of things. But the further thesis, that content as it is individuated in psychological explanation depends on independent social factors, is I think not correct.

The anti-individualist conclusion depends on (B), that differences in oblique ascription imply differences in psychological content. But the intuitions which in the cases of Paul and Pierre led us to reject (A) ought also to bring us to reject (B). We should hold that despite their different ascriptions Bert's belief that he has arthritis in his ankles and his belief that he has tharthritis in his ankles have the same psychological content, because they have the same potential for explanatory interaction with other beliefs; what intuitively appeared to determine that potential in the case of Paul and Pierre was how they, as it were, personally conceived things. But let me give some new arguments directed specifically against (B) and the Burgean thesis that sameness of individualist conceptual role is not sufficient for sameness of psychological content.

That (B) is false is already accepted by whoever takes a certain widespread view of Twin Earth cases. Although those Twin Earthling thoughts which they express using "water" are, as the story goes,[10] like ours in their personal conceptual roles, we cannot ascribe to them the thought that, say, they bathe in water. Twin Earthlings have referential contact not with H_2O but with a chemically distinct if phenomenally indistinguishable substance, and so we cannot translate their "water" into English as "water" and hence cannot assert of them anything of the form "believes that ... water...." Conceding these facts about belief *ascriptions,* many have found it intuitive, indeed have taken it to be the point of Twin Earth cases, that Twin Earthlings' thoughts have the same content as ours as that is individuated in psychological explanation, the same "narrow content."

Such intuitions appear to be vindicated by two rather different thought experiments. (1) Suppose Bert is a full member of two English-speaking communities that differ linguistically in small ways of which he is unaware. The first is ours, where "arthritis" means arthritis; but in the second "arthritis" means tharthritis. Let the individual facts about Bert be as in Burge's case. How are we to describe him? If there is no reason to choose just one of the languages as his language, then apparently the best thing for us to say is that Bert believes that he has arthritis in his ankles and believes that he has tharthritis in his ankles. But in explaining Bert psychologically the natural thing to say is that he has just one belief, one way of conceiving what is wrong with his ankles. Similarly, we may imagine a commuter between Earth and Twin Earth who is biworldly in his language without knowing of these systematic referential differences between English and Twin English. He would assert "Water quenches thirst." Again it seems that two belief ascriptions are in order, but that they should be seen as merely different extrinsic descriptions of what is, as regards psychological explanation, the commuter's one way of conceiving things.

2. Here is a different thought experiment. One is given a diary and told that it is by either an Earthling or a Twin Earthling but not which. An entry says: "No swimming today; we think the water is too rough." This reports a psychological explanation, one that loses nothing from our ignorance of the diary's provenance, that is, from our ignorance of whether it would be correct, in reporting that thought obliquely in a that-clause, to use "water" or "twin-water." It is not that we switch rapidly back and forth between two explanations, one in terms of water and the other in terms of twin-water; all we have to have been told is that the diary was written in one of a class of worlds that resemble Earth in the relevant respects. Or, again, suppose that I do not know whether in Bert's linguistic community "arthritis" means arthritis or tharthritis, but that I know all the relevant individualist facts about Bert. I read in his diary: "I fear I have arthritis, and so today I have made an appointment with a specialist." It is difficult to accept that we do not fully understand the psychological explanation given here, despite our not being in a position to produce the correct that-clause. We understand the diarists' explanations because we know how they conceive things.

What is there to be said against these intuitions in favor of "narrow content"? Two objections could be thought to have force. The first is that so-called narrow content cannot capture an *intentional* property; for the two beliefs in the Burge case and those in the Twin Earth case do not share *truth conditions.* "Content" should mean intentionality, and intentionality is a certain *directedness* of thoughts onto things, properties, states of affairs, in short, truth conditions and the components of truth conditions. The second objection is that there is no appropriate way to *specify* the common content in those pairs of beliefs; and thus the notion of narrow content is just hand-waving.

I shall not say in response to either objection that there *are* that-clauses which do not contain "water" or "arthritis" and which capture the common content of those pairs of beliefs. I am quite prepared to concede that that-clauses are so generally shot through with social and causal presuppositions that narrow content cannot in general be captured thus.

There is a kind of reply to the objection concerning intentionality and truth conditions which I believe is important but shall not develop at length here. Put sketchily the idea is this: the conceptual roles of thoughts are distinct from their truth conditions, and in more than one sense do not determine truth-conditions (except perhaps for certain demonstrative judgments involving perceptual discriminative concepts).[11] But commonsense psychological explanation of the sort we have intuitively appealed to in discussing Paul and Pierre individuates attitudes according to their conceptual roles, the specification of truth conditions having some further function—on which more anon. How can there be *content* without truth conditions? This is, I think, not merely a terminological question, for it involves intuitions about the apparent intentionality of one's own thoughts as judged from a first-person perspective. The point is that the conceptual roles of one's thoughts determine *how* one *conceives* things, and it is difficult to see how one can consider how one oneself conceives things without that in some sense involving what one's thoughts are "about." And that is appropriately called content, by a Principle of the Transparency of Content: if something from an unconfused perspective appears to be content then it is a kind of content. As I say, this is sketchy, but I mention it to register that the defender of "narrow content" has more than one line of defense: it would not matter that narrow content does not determine truth conditions if there is a kind of content that does not involve truth conditions.

Furthermore the demand for a narrow or individualist account of intentionality, in the sense of the outward directedness of thoughts onto states of affairs, is not unanswerable. Consider Bert's diary again. I do not know whether Bert's use of "arthritis" involves a misconception because I do not know the social facts about it. But I do know this: how the world *would* be if Bert's conceptions are or were not misconceptions. How Bert thinks of things—as that is described from an individualist perspective—appears to determine a set of possible worlds, namely, those in which Bert's thoughts are or would be true if they are or were not misconceptions. Call that set of worlds the *realization conditions* of Bert's beliefs. If my ability to explain Bert psychologically presupposes a grasp of something "intentional," something like truth condi-

tions, then it would seem that my grasp of the realization conditions of Bert's beliefs is sufficient. The diary thought experiment supports this.

Realization conditions are of course not truth conditions in our official sense. The truth conditions of a belief depend on some that-clause which correctly ascribes it, and as Burge has shown that is not in general determined by individualist facts. Thus I am not saying that the *real* truth conditions of thoughts are their realization conditions. I am not proposing a redefinition of anything. Rather I am saying that if psychological explanation involves a mapping of thoughts onto possible states of affairs, then realization conditions are there for the taking. There is nothing recondite in the idea; our commonsense understanding of others delivers the realization conditions of their beliefs without our having a name for them.[12]

An adjustment to this suggestion is needed. Suppose I find a diary with the entry: "Hot and sunny today; phoned Maria to invite her to the beach." Now, the date has been torn off the page. Still I appear to understand the diarist's explanation of his/her phoning Maria, despite not knowing the truth conditions (in one sense) of the thought expressed by "hot and sunny today." Is there not, however, a sense in which I do know the truth conditions? Suppose on Tuesday one thinks "it is hot and sunny today," and on Friday one thinks "it is hot and sunny today." They have the same truth conditions in the sense of conditions of truth in abstraction from context. Call them *context-indeterminate,* by contrast with the context-determinate truth conditions that determine sets of possible worlds. Then if understanding the psychological explanation given in the diary requires in some sense knowing truth conditions, they need merely be context-indeterminate.

To put this together with the former point, we may say this: if psychological explanation involves intentionality, then *context-indeterminate realization conditions* are all the intentionality required.[13]

There is still the objection that we cannot in general *specify* the narrow content of thoughts. Now if this means merely that narrow content is not in general captured by ordinary that-clauses, it is difficult to see why it is an objection. We have perfectly sound intuitions about when to distinguish the beliefs of Paul, Pierre, and Bert, despite the fact that that-clauses do not make the right distinctions. If we then lack specifications of narrow content, in the sense in which we have specifications of wide, social content, that must mean that psychological explanation does not require such specifications. We get along perfectly well without them; we individuate beliefs and understand their realization conditions without an official system of generating such specifications. Narrow contents are not ineffable; we get at them in context via various devices. (a) We use that-clauses with one eye on the background facts: different narrow contents are implied by "Paul believes that cats have tails" in the "chat" context and in the "cat" context. (b) We report a person's words, or approximations thereto, together with other utterances which help us to interpret his words: Bert says "I have arthritis in my ankles," but he also says "I have arthritis in my thigh." The second helps one to understand the narrow content expressed by the first. (c) We ascribe narrow content by producing words that have the same narrow content for us. Imagine a Twin Earthling whose language is Twin German; it may help to render one of his beliefs as "I bathe in water" even though there is no water there and those are not the words he would utter. Not that we have much opportunity for interpreting Twin Earthlings, but interpretation by approximately matching narrow contents is one of our fundamental techniques in psychological explanation.

It now seems to me somewhat extraordinary that we should have thought that psychological states are captured by a neat set of content-specifications. But what then are that-clauses for? Of course they play a central role in psychological explanation, given suitable background information; but we have been misconceiving that role in thinking that they define precisely the individuation conditions of psychological states. That-clauses on their oblique readings are sensitive, either directly or indirectly via translation, to how beliefs would linguistically be expressed, and that is, as the examples of Paul and Pierre show, only loosely related to psychological content. Now, as Burge's cases show, that-clauses capture how a belief would be expressed by exhibiting something that is equivalent in *social content* (as we might say) to what the subject would utter, given his deference to the usage of his linguistic community. This enables that-clauses to capture certain extra-psychological relations of propositional attitudes to independent states of affairs, what we may think of as their *socially determined truth conditions*. The fundamental usefulness of this is that we may then describe people as conveyors of more or less determinate information, which remains constant even when the psychological contents of their states vary. That-clauses enable us to impose a grid of socially regularized information on the vagaries of individual psychology. Presumably the system of propositional attitude ascription is part of a larger framework of *restraints*, even, on the centrifugal tendencies of the thoughts of each of us.

NOTES

1. Stephen P. Stich, *From Folk Psychology to Cognitive Science: The Case Against Belief* (Cambridge, Mass.: MIT Press/Bradford Books, 1983), 66–67.

2. Tyler Burge, "Individualism and the Mental," in *Midwest Studies in Philosophy, Vol. IV: Studies in Metaphysics,* ed. Peter French, *et al.* (Minneapolis: University of Minnesota Press, 1979), 73–122.

3. It is fair to say that many have taken this to be the message of Burge's paper, that is, that beliefs are not individuated in commonsense explanation by their conceptual roles. Of course Burge's direct point is about the presuppositions of *ascriptions* of beliefs. But because of the widespread supposition that the significance of this point lies in the stronger point, I am taking the stronger point to be the consequential burden of Burge's paper. He writes: "It is expressions at oblique occurrences within content clauses that primarily do the job of providing the content of mental states or events, and in characterizing the person" (*op. cit., 76*). And again he writes of "the idea that the distinctively mental aspects can be understood fundamentally in terms of the individual's abilities, dispositions, states, and so forth, considered in isolation from his social surroundings" as follows: "our argument undermines this latter suggestion. Social context infects even the distinctively mental features of mentalistic attributions. No man's intentional mental phenomena are insular" (*op. cit., 87*). More recently, Burge has argued for an apparently less stringent position, namely, that even though there *might* be a level of scientific psychology which is individualist, (a) there are important examples of scientific psychology which cannot be construed individualistically, (b) such non-individualist explanation is legitimate as regards scientific methodology, and (c) commonsense psychological explanation is non-individualist. In this paper I am concerned to argue that Burge's observations about belief ascriptions may be accepted while denying (c).

4. Saul Kripke, "A Puzzle about Belief," in *Meaning and Use,* ed. Avishai Margalit (Dordrecht: Reidel, 1979), 239–83.

5. This assumes that when we ascribe beliefs obliquely to speakers of other languages, the correct way to do so is (roughly) to translate how they would be expressed.

6. How else to represent the belief obliquely than by translating "chats" as "cats"? Keep in mind that the point does not depend on translation.

7. In "Names in Thought," *Philosophical Studies* 51 (1987): 169–85, I discuss the significance of the phenomenon in connection with Saul Kripke's "puzzle about belief."

8. Perhaps it is some sort of "formal" consistency. But then beliefs would not be individuated in commonsense psychological explanation by their *content,* which seems implausible.

9. The circumlocutory wording is meant to avoid propositional variables which appear to presuppose that-clauses. For a way of understanding these structures of rationality and irrationality, see sections 4 and 6 of my accompanying paper "A New Kind of Content."

10. Hilary Putnam, "The Meaning of 'Meaning'," in *Mind, Language and Reality: Philosophical Papers, Vol. 2* (Cambridge: Cambridge University Press, 1975), 215–71.

11. See Brian Loar, "Must Beliefs be Sentences?" in *PSA 1982: Proceedings of the 1982 Biennial Meeting of the Philos-*

ophy of Science Association, ed. Peter D. Asquith and Thomas Nickles (East Lansing, Michigan: Philosophy of Science Association, 1983), 627–42.

12. This is perhaps similar to what David Lewis proposes in "What Puzzling Pierre Does Not Believe," *Australasian Journal of Philosophy* 59 (1981): 283–89.

As several people have pointed out to me, my "context-independent realization conditions" are quite similar, including their detachment from that-clauses, to Daniel Dennett's *notional worlds* (see "Beyond Belief," in *Thought and Object,* ed. Andrew Woodfield (Oxford: Clarendon Press, 1982), 1–95). I discuss the relation between my account, as that is elaborated in section 6 of "A New Kind of Content," and Dennett's theory in footnote 6 of that paper.

13. Jerry Fodor has recently proposed that narrow content be construed in terms of functions from contexts to sets of possible worlds (in a paper given at UCLA, Spring 1985). And in correspondence he has suggested that this would preclude the need for the realization conditions I propose here.

But I do not think that Kaplanesque characters will in fact do the job of capturing the narrow content of general terms, or not unless I am missing something. The reason is that, if you treat natural kind terms as if they are pure indexicals whose semantic values are determined by context, then "water" and "alcohol" would count as having the same narrow content—viz. that function which maps a natural kind term onto a natural kind in accordance with certain causal facts in its history of use. A Kaplanesque "character," a function of that kind, may well individuate the narrow content of a very special feature of thought such as the first-person pronoun, for it can be argued that self-ascription is the only aspect of narrow content whose reference-function always maps the belief onto the believer. But in the narrow individuation of beliefs involving "water" and "alcohol" we want their contributions to be different, in accordance with their conceptual roles. That combination of indexicality and substantive conceptual content is what context-indeterminate realization conditions are supposed to capture.

59

Robert Stalnaker

"On What's in the Head"

"Cut the pie any way you like, 'meanings' just ain't in the head!"[1] So Hilary Putnam taught us some years ago. He made the point with some compelling examples all fitting a now familiar pattern: first we are asked to imagine a counterfactual person exactly like some actual person with respect to all purely internal psychological and physical properties, but situated in a counterfactual environment which differs from ours in some subtle way. For example, where we have aluminum, they have a metal that resembles aluminum superficially, but that has a different chemical structure. We are then invited to note that despite the intrinsic similarities of the two doppelganger, their utterances have different semantic properties. When the earthling says "Aluminum is used in the construction of airplanes," she says something that differs in content from what her twin says when she utters the same sounds. Since what is in the heads of the two is the same, while what they mean when they use certain words is different, the meanings of those words must depend on something other than what is in those heads. Tyler Burge developed this kind of example in more detail and extended the point in several ways.[2] First he argued that it is not just meaning and other semantical properties, but also intentional psychological properties that are shown to depend on external conditions: beliefs, desires, hopes and fears ain't in the head either. Second, he argued that social conditions—facts about the linguistic practices of members of the agent's community—were among the external conditions on which intentional mental states depend. Third, he emphasized that the dependence on external conditions was a pervasive phenomenon, one not restricted to some narrow range of concepts and expressions. It applies not just to de

re attitudes or to attitudes expressed with proper names, indexical expressions and natural kind terms, but to de dicto attitudes and to all kinds of concepts and expressions. Burge called the thesis he was attacking—the thesis that intentional mental states are intrinsic properties of the individuals who are in those states—*individualism.*

In retrospect, it seems that we should not have been surprised by the conclusions of Putnam and Burge. Isn't it obvious that semantic properties, and intentional properties generally, are *relational* properties: properties defined in terms of relations between a speaker or agent and what he or she talks or thinks about. And isn't it obvious that relations depend, in all but degenerate cases, on more than the intrinsic properties of one of the things related. This, it seems, is not just a consequence of some new and controversial theory of reference, but should follow from any account of representation that holds that we can talk and think, not just about our own inner states, but also about things and properties outside of ourselves. But the conclusions were surprising, and they remain controversial. One reason is that the anti-individualistic thesis seems to have some paradoxical consequences. If what we mean or think is not in the head, it would seem that we cannot know, or at least cannot be authoritative about, what we mean or think.[3] Another reason is that this thesis seems to be incompatible with the explanatory role that intentional mental states are thought to play. We explain why people behave the way they do in terms of what they believe and want. In fact, it is often assumed that belief and desire states are to be defined in terms of the behavior they dispose the agents in those states to engage in. But how can such states be causally relevant if they are rela-

From *Philosophical Perspectives, 3: Philosophy of Mind and Action Theory* (1989): 287–316. Reprinted with permission of the editor and Robert Stalnaker.

tional states—states that depend on things outside of the agent?

One response to the anti-individualist thesis is to grant it, but to deny its significance. If our ordinary concepts of belief, desire, and meaning are relational concepts that individuate mental states in a non-individualistic way, this only shows that our ordinary concepts are inappropriate for the purpose of the explanation of behavior. But, this response suggests, the revisions needed to render intentional concepts individualistic are not very radical. What such a revision must do is to factor out the "organismic contribution" to an intentional mental state—that component of the state that is dependent or supervenient on the internal states of the agent.

The revisionist response makes a negative and a positive claim. The negative claim is that no systematic explanatory theory of behavior will be tenable unless it is individualistic. The positive claim is that although ordinary intentional psychological concepts are not individualistic as they stand, they can be revised in a way that renders them individualistic while preserving the basic structure of intentional explanation. Jerry Fodor has defended both claims; Daniel Dennett has proposed ways to defend the positive thesis, and Stephen Stich and P. M. and P. S. Churchland have defended the negative thesis while rejecting the positive claim. In this paper, I want to explore both parts of the revisionist doctrine, beginning with the positive side. After trying to get clear about what is required in general to define an individualistic analogue of a relational concept, I will look at two proposals for defining narrow content—a kind of content that is intended to render intentional states purely internal. Then I will turn to the negative side of the case, discussing a number of formulations of the negative thesis and a number of arguments in its defense. I will be arguing, first, that it is harder than some have assumed to define narrow content, and second that ordinary wide content is less mysterious than some have assumed.

A number of quite different issues are involved in the revisionist doctrine: some are relatively abstract questions concerning concept formation, methodology, and the distinction between intrinsic and relational properties; others are more specific questions concerning the nature of intentional concepts and the psychological mechanisms that underlie their application. To help separate these different issues from each other, I will begin by exploring an analogy: I will look at a very simple causal-relational concept—a concept that should be relatively transparent and uncontroversial—and consider what is involved in the attempt to define a narrow or purely intrinsic version of it. Then

I will look back at the intentional concepts themselves and at the proposals for carving out narrow content.

Consider the concept of a *footprint*. This is a causal–relational concept: something is a footprint in virtue of the way it was caused. One might make the point that a footprint is not intrinsic to the sand or mud in which it is located by telling a Twin–Earth story: imagine a beach on Twin–Earth which is, at a certain moment on July 4, 1985, exactly like Jones Beach in every intrinsic detail. The difference is that the counterpart on Twin-Earth of a certain footprint on Jones Beach was caused, not by a foot, but by the way the waves happened to fall some hours earlier. So something on Twin-Earth that is intrinsically indistinguishable from a footprint is not a footprint. A philosopher with a gift for coining slogans might sum up the lesson of this thought experiment this way: *Cut the pie any way you like, footprints just ain't in the sand!*

The revisionist replies that this may be true of our ordinary folk concept of a footprint, but explanatory science is interested only in states that *are* intrinsic to the sand. So let us define a new concept that individuates the relevant state of the sand in a way that is independent of its causal history and environment: let us say that a *narrow footprint* is a foot-shaped indentation, whatever its cause. Can't we, in this way, isolate that component of the state of containing a footprint that is intrinsic to the medium that is in that state? The anti-individualist will note that the new concept is still a relational one. Footprints in the new sense no longer depend on the *particular* cause of the indentation, but they still depend on general facts that are extrinsic to the sand. An elaboration of the Twin-Earth story makes the point: suppose that on Twin-Earth feet have a different normal shape. If this is true, the indentation in the sand there will not only fail to be an ordinary footprint because of its different causal history, it will also fail to be a *narrow* footprint because normal footprints are differently shaped there, and so the indentation on the beach is not even shaped like a foot.

This pattern of conceptual revision—replacing a dependence on a specific causal interaction with dependence on a general regularity in the environment—is exemplified in less artificial cases. It seems reasonable to say that in defining dispositional properties, for example, we begin with a kind of causal interaction (a substance dissolves, or an object is observed). We then use suitably hedged counterfactuals to get at a stable property of one of the things involved in the interaction—a property that the thing has independently of the fact that the interaction took place. A sugar cube is soluble if it would dissolve if put in water (under normal conditions). An object is observable if it would be observed if a normal observer were suitably placed. Some such dispositional properties (such as solubility in water) may be purely intrinsic, but others will not be. Whether something is observable may depend on the capacities of normal observers, perhaps also on the lighting conditions that in fact obtain, or at least on the lighting conditions that normally obtain. The concept of belief may be this kind of narrowed version of the concept of knowledge, replacing a dependence on more specific causal relations between the fact known and a state of the knower with more general patterns of causal relations between facts and internal states.

One might further narrow our revised concept of footprint by taking the phrase "foot-shaped indentation" in a reference-fixing way. That is, by a narrow footprint we mean an indentation that is shaped the way feet are *actually* shaped. So whatever shape feet have on Twin-Earth, the counterpart on Twin-Earth of the footprint on Jones Beach is still a narrow footprint. Now, it seems, we have succeeded in isolating a purely internal state of the sand.

The pattern of concept formation now looks like this: we begin with a concept that classifies states of a thing in terms of a relational property—specifically, in terms of the way those states are caused. We then focus on the intrinsic properties of the states the concept picks out, classifying them in a new way: as states that share those intrinsic properties. This pattern too seems to be exemplified in less artificial cases. Consider, for example, the concepts of *mass* and *weight*. Weight is the quantity that is closer to the surface—more directly observed and measured. But it is a relational concept: what you weigh depends on the gravitational field you are in. Mass is the quantity that a body has, independently of its gravitational field, that explains why it weighs what it does in different gravitational fields. Even at an initial stage of inquiry when we may not know very much about the relevant intrinsic properties, we can still use this strategy of concept formation to point at the properties, whatever they are, that play a certain role in the explanation of a thing's behavior.[4]

Our definition of narrow footprint may make use of a sound strategy of concept formation, but the success of this kind of definition will always depend on a substantive presupposition: that the things picked out by the relational property are similar to each other in an appropriate way. The substantive presupposition will never be plausible unless one idealizes a bit: there are deformed feet, and distorting conditions that may give rise to

footprints of an unusual shape. These will certainly be footprints, but if our definition of narrow footprint is to succeed, they, and other indentations shaped like them, must be excluded. By foot-shaped indentations we mean indentations that have the *normal* or *characteristic* shape that feet make under *normal* conditions. This kind of qualification is a familiar part of characterizations of dispositional properties: a thing is soluble in water if it would dissolve if put in water *under normal conditions.* The point of the qualification is to insure that what is defined is a stable property that we can generalize about. It might be that a thing would not dissolve if put in water in a particular situation because of anomalous environmental conditions even though the thing is intrinsically similar to soluble things. But we don't want to say that the thing loses its solubility under the abnormal external conditions. The qualification allows us to say that the thing remains soluble even though, in this case, it would not dissolve if put in water.

Even given such qualifications, a definition of this kind may fail. If the concept of footprint we begin with is the concept of a print made by a human bare foot, then the concept of a narrow footprint is perhaps well defined, since there is a relatively well defined shape that prints have, in normal cases, when they are made by such feet. But suppose we start with a more general notion: by "footprint" we mean a print made by a foot of some animal or other. This concept includes prints made by cloven hooves, webbed feet, and the paws of dogs as well as human feet, and it is not clear that these footprints have any one characteristic shape at all. If they do not, then our concept will collapse when we try to abstract away from the causal origin of the indentations we want to pick out. Or at best we will be left with a wildly disjunctive concept that will be of no interest.[5]

The moral of the story is that the narrowing of causal-relational concepts exemplifies a legitimate pattern of concept formation, but not a pattern that will in all cases yield a well-defined purely internal property. First, the pattern may succeed in eliminating a dependence of a property on specific interactions with other things, while leaving a dependence on general facts about the environment. Second, whether the pattern succeeds at all will depend on substantive presuppositions about the intrinsic similarities of things that share the causal-relational property. To evaluate the positive part of the revisionist thesis we need to see just what the presuppositions are in the case of intentional mental concepts, and to consider whether we have good reason to accept them.

The defense of the positive part of the revisionist thesis requires more than just the definition of narrow analogues for particular belief properties such as the property of believing that aluminum is used in the construction of airplanes; what is needed is a narrow analogue of belief in general. Like ordinary belief, narrow belief must be expressed as a relation between the believer and some kind of *content*. This is essential since the project is to explain mental states as internal states *while preserving the structure of intentional explanations*. The strategy is to change the notion of content in a way that makes belief states purely internal. But however content is explained, how is it possible for belief to be both a relation between a person and a content and also a purely internal state? To answer this we need to distinguish two ways in which a concept can be relational. Consider again the quantities weight and mass: a Twin-Earth thought experiment will show that weight is a relational property. William weighs three hundred pounds, but his twin on the less massive Twin-Earth weighs less. Mass, in contrast, is intrinsic: Twin–William is equally massive. But both weight and mass are relational in another sense: they are both *semantically* relational concepts. There is a relation—weight (or mass) in pounds—that William bears to the number three hundred and that Wilma bears to one hundred and two. Both weight and mass are concepts expressed by using a relational *predicate* together with a number to pick out a property. It is the fact that the family of properties—weight or mass properties—has a certain structure that makes it possible for them to be expressed in this way. But this is compatible with the properties being intrinsic in the sense that whether a thing has one of them is not contingent on anything external to the thing. The revisionist project requires a concept of belief that is semantically relational, but that expresses belief properties that are ontologically intrinsic; it proposes to accomplish this by changing or restricting the contents that are used to pick out the properties. Belief is to be narrowed by narrowing content.

So how is narrow content to be explained? The first answer I will consider is Jerry Fodor's.[6] Let me sketch, first Fodor's diagnosis of the problem—his explanation of the fact that content, in the ordinary wide sense, is not in the head—and then say how he proposes to revise the notion of content to get it back into the head where it belongs. The problem, Fodor says, derives from the following constraint on the identity conditions for content: beliefs that are true under different conditions have different contents. It is because the Earthling's thought or statement, "Aluminum is used in the construction of airplanes" could be true in possible circumstances in which her twin's corresponding statement or thought is false that we are required to conclude that the two have different content. Narrow contents cannot differ in this way, but if narrow content is not constrained by truth conditions, how can it be a notion of content at all? The solution, Fodor proposes, is not to give up the connection between content and truth conditions, but rather to relativize this connection to context. Narrow content will be something that determines the truth conditions of a belief or utterance as a function of the external environment of the believer or speaker. The model for this account of narrow content is David Kaplan's account of the semantics for demonstratives and indexicals. Kaplan makes a distinction between *meaning* (or what he calls *character*) and *content,* and this distinction provides the model for Fodor's distinction between narrow and wide content. According to Kaplan's account, when Daniels and O'Leary both say "I am bald," they say something with the same *character,* but with different *content.* Daniels's statement says that Daniels is bald, whereas O'Leary's says that O'Leary is. Character is explained as a function from context to content. The pronoun "I" has a constant character: it always refers to the speaker. But because different speakers use that pronoun, the same sentences containing it may be used to say different things. In general, the character of a sentence of the form "I am F" will be a function taking a context in which x is the speaker into the proposition that is true if and only if x has the property expressed by "F." Narrow content, on Fodor's account of it, is a generalization of character in Kaplan's sense, where the context includes any fact external to the believer that is relevant to the determination of wide content.[7]

Fodor suggests that once we are clear about the general nature of narrow content, "it's quite easy to see how the required principles of individuation should be formulated."[8] Here is his explanation of the "extensional identity criterion" for narrow content:

> There is presumably something about the relation between Twin-Earth and Twin-me in virtue of which his 'water'–thoughts are about XYZ even though my water-thoughts are not. Call this condition that's satisfied by [Twin-Me, Twin–Earth] condition C. . . . Similarly, there must be something about the relation between me and Earth in virtue of which my water-thoughts are about H_2O even though my Twin's 'water'-thoughts are not. Call this condition that is satisfied by [me, Earth] condition C'. . . . Short of a miracle, it must be true that if an organism shares the neurophysiological constitution of my Twin *and satisfies C,* it follows that its thoughts and my Twin's thoughts share their truth conditions. . . . But now we have an extensional identity criterion for mental con-

tents: two thought contents are identical only if they effect the same mapping of thoughts and contexts onto truth conditions.[9]

This argument tells us what kind of thing narrow content should be: a mapping from context into truth conditions; and it shows that *if* we succeeded in specifying such a mapping, it would have the right properties: it would be *narrow* (intrinsic) and it would be like *content* in the crucial way: it would determine the semantic or intentional properties of the thought (relative to context). But the argument tells us less than it seems about how such mappings are to be specified, and it obscures the fact that it is a substantive hypothesis that the internal states of believers contain thoughts that determine such mappings.

It is surely right that if the context (C or C′) includes all information external to the believer that may be relevant to the determination of truth conditions, then context, together with the internal states of the believer, will determine truth conditions. That is only to say that truth conditions are determined by the conditions that are relevant to determining them. But pointing this out does not tell us what function from context to content narrow content is supposed to be, or explain how it is that the relevant function is determined by what is in the believer's head. If the abstract procedure outlined in the argument could, by itself, show how to narrow content, then it could be used to define a narrow analogue of any relational property.

Consider this parody of Fodor's characterization of the criterion for narrow content: Take the property of being exactly three miles from a burning barn. Suppose I have this property, even though my counterpart who is located at exactly the same place in a certain counterfactual situation does not. He, let us suppose, is instead exactly three miles from a snow-covered chicken coop. Now there is presumably something about the relation between my counterpart and his world in virtue of which he is three miles from a snow-covered chicken coop even though I am not. Call this condition C. Similarly, there is something about the relation between me and my world in virtue of which I am three miles from a burning barn, even though my counterpart is not. Call it C′. Whatever these conditions are, we *do* know this: short of a miracle, it must be true that anyone in the location that both I and my counterpart are in in our respective worlds would be three miles from a snow-covered chicken coop if condition C obtained, and three miles from a burning barn if instead C′ obtained. But this does not help us identify a specific function that takes condition C′ into the property of being three miles from a snow-covered chicken coop and also takes C into the property of being three miles from a burning barn—a function that is supposed to represent the contribution that an individual's location makes to the relational property. There are many such functions, and no reason to identify any of them with the contribution that my intrinsic location makes to the specific relational property. My counterpart cannot reasonably say, "I did my part toward being three miles from a burning barn by going to a place where, if conditions C′ had obtained instead of C, I would have been three miles from a burning barn." *Every* location is such that for some external conditions, if those conditions obtain, then anything in that location is three miles from a burning barn.

The exclusive focus on Twin-Earth situations makes it look easier than it is to factor out the contribution that the external environment makes to the possession of some relational property. In a Twin-Earth story, we are asked to consider a possible situation in which an individual shares *every* intrinsic property with its actual counterpart. So if the actual individual has the relational property in question, we can be sure that its Twin-Earth counterpart will have whatever property is supposed to be the purely intrinsic component of that relational property. But the story does not help us to identify the relevant intrinsic property. If we were to consider, not *Twin*-Earths, but say, *Cousin*-Earth stories in which an individual resembles its counterpart in some but not all internal ways, it would be clearer that this strategy for defining intrinsic properties in terms of relations may leave many questions unanswered. Suppose, for example, that Cousin-Earth contains both H_2O and XYZ. In this world the two substances are easily distinguished. Their superficial properties are somewhat different from the superficial properties that H_2O has on Earth, and that XYZ has on Twin-Earth, and also somewhat different from each other. But both substances are somewhat like water in fact is. Suppose also that Cousin-English has different (non–scientific) words for the two substances, neither one of which is spelled or pronounced like "water," but that otherwise Cousin-English is a lot like English. Now suppose my counterpart on Cousin-Earth believes that salt is soluble in water, but does not believe that salt is soluble in the other stuff. Does his belief have the same narrow content as my belief that salt is soluble in water (and so the same narrow content as my Twin's belief that salt is soluble in the other stuff)? Fodor's abstract account, by itself, gives no guidance about how to answer this question.[10]

There are several disanalogies between Kaplan's notion of character and Fodor's proposed account of narrow content—disanalogies that suggest that Fodor's project is much more ambitious, and much more speculative. First, Kaplan's notion of context is not designed to include everything external to the individual, and the character of an utterance is not something determined by the purely internal properties of the speaker. As a result, characters are not required to have the counterfactual power that narrow contents must have. That the pronoun "I" has the character it has is a fact about a social practice—the practice of speaking English. The functions from context to content that Kaplan calls characters are not intended to tell us what speakers would be saying if they were speaking some other language. Kaplan's notion need not tell us this since the aim of his theory is not to isolate the purely internal component of what determines the content of speech acts, but simply to explain how some languages in fact work. The practice of speech is more efficient if speakers can exploit information about the environment—information available to all the participants in a conversation—in communicating. So languages make this possible by including rules that make what is said a function of that kind of information. That a language contains such rules (rather than, say, just lots of unsystematic ambiguity) is a substantive hypothesis, though in this case an obviously correct one. That our minds contain much more general systematic procedures for determining content as a function of context in a more general sense is a much more ambitious and speculative hypothesis.

Second, because Kaplan's theory is a theory of speech rather than a theory of thought we can identify, more or less independently of theory, the objects that the theory is interpreting: the objects that *have* character and content. A speech act can be described in terms of its content (O'Leary said that salt is soluble in water), but it also may be described in more neutral ways (O'Leary uttered the sentence, or the sounds, "Salt is soluble in water"). But in the case of thought it is much less clear what it is that has a particular content, or narrow content. As with a speech act, we can describe a particular belief in terms of its content (O'Leary believes that salt is soluble in water), but in this case there is no easily identifiable mental state, describable independently of its content, that constitutes that person's having that belief. Of course a psychological theory might turn up such a mental state or object. It might be that what it is to believe that salt is soluble in water is to be storing in a certain location a mental sentence that says that salt is soluble in water. If this were true, then we could identify the thing that has the content independently of the content that it has. But it also might be that states of belief are more holistic. Suppose a

total belief state were a complex cluster of dispositions to behave in various ways under various conditions. One might be able to use particular belief contents such as the belief that salt is soluble in water to describe such a state without it being possible to match up those contents with particular dispositions in the cluster. On this kind of account, the question "what makes it true (given the facts about the external context) that O'Leary believes that salt is soluble in water?" will be answered by describing how O'Leary is disposed to behave under various conditions. But the same behavioral dispositions that constitute O'Leary's total belief state will also make it true that he believes various other nonequivalent propositions. Compare: the question "what makes it true (given the facts about the external context) that O'Leary is three miles from a burning barn?" will be answered by describing O'Leary's location. But this same location will also make it true that O'Leary has various other nonequivalent relational properties (being more than two thousand miles from Los Angeles, being closer to Istanbul than to New Delhi, etc.). Even if we could find a narrow, purely internal characterization of the belief state as a whole, it wouldn't follow that we could find narrow analogues of the (relational) facts about the belief state that are expressed by ordinary attributions of belief.[11]

Fodor's abstract account of narrow content is motivated by a particular picture of belief and other mental states, a picture that he has made explicit and vigorously defended. Beliefs are internal sentences stored in the mind. The particular contents of those sentences depend on the believer's environment, but the sentences themselves can be identified as sentences, and as *beliefs,* independently of the particular environmental conditions that determine their interpretation. The sentences are beliefs in virtue of their internal functional role—the way they are affected by sensory inputs, interact with other internal states, and determine behavioral outputs. Their semantic properties will depend in part on what is going on outside—beyond the periphery—but the way they depend on what is going on outside is determined by the purely internal state. This is a very attractive picture, but it is not inevitable: it has strong, highly speculative, empirical presuppositions. Fodor's abstract account of narrow content as a function from context (in a very broad sense) to truth-conditional content may seem plausible given this picture, but it does not contribute much to defending the picture, or to explaining how it is to be developed. It does not, by itself, tell us how to identify narrow contents, and it does not give us reason to believe that internal states determine functions of this kind that will do any explanatory work. No general a priori argument will show that this is the way that things must be.

Is there a way to define narrow content that does not depend on the language of thought picture? Daniel Dennett, after criticizing the sententialist approach, makes some suggestions about how we might isolate what he calls the "organismic contribution" to the content of belief in a way that is neutral as to how that contribution is represented in the believer.[12] He calls his approach *"notional attitude psychology,"* and contrasts it both with *propositional attitude psychology,* which describes attitudes in terms of the ordinary wide conception of content, and *sentential attitude psychology,* which takes the contents of attitudes to be syntactic objects—sentences of an inner language. The contents of notional attitudes are explained in terms of a kind of possible world, which Dennett calls a "notional world." "A notional world should be viewed as a sort of *fictional* world devised by a theorist, a third-party observer, in order to characterize the narrow-psychological states of a subject."[13] Notional worlds are supposed to be defined so that, "although my *Doppelganger* and I live in different real worlds—Twin-Earth and Earth—we have the *same* notional world."[14] The set of notional worlds that define the narrow contents of a person's beliefs is something like the worlds that *are* the way that the person takes the real world to be.

Notional worlds, it seems, are just the possible worlds that have been used to characterize ordinary wide contents in *propositional* attitude psychology. Possible worlds—at least all but one of them—are also fictional worlds in the sense that they are not actual. So how are notional attitudes different from propositional attitudes, characterized in this way? What difference explains why the contents of notional attitudes are narrow, while the contents of propositional attitudes are wide? The difference will not be found in the nature of the worlds themselves, or in the nature of the contents, which in both cases are just sets of worlds. So far as I can see, narrow contents, on Dennett's account, are just propositions. The difference between notional and propositional content is to be found in the different answers that the two theories give to the question, "in virtue of what facts do a believer's beliefs have the (notional or propositional) contents that they have?" According to propositional attitude psychology, the contents of an organism's attitudes are picked out as a function of relations between the organism and its actual environment. Just what relations do the job is a difficult and controversial question, but the Twin-Earth thought experiments show that the content

of a belief, as ordinarily conceived, is not a function of purely internal properties of the believer. The task of narrow, notional attitude psychology is to explain how purely internal properties of an organism can be used to pick out a set of possible worlds—a perhaps different set that will characterize the organism's attitudes in a way that is different from the way it is characterized by an ordinary propositional attitude attribution. The idea is roughly this: O'Leary believes (correctly) that there is water in the basement. The proposition he believes is true in the actual world, but false in the counterfactual world where there is no water, but only XYZ in the basement. There is, however, a different proposition that does not distinguish the actual world from this counterfactual world—a proposition that we might roughly describe as the proposition that there is some water-like stuff in the basement. The first proposition is the wide content of O'Leary's belief; the aim of Dennett's project is to define narrow content so that the second of these propositions is the narrow content.

One can contrast Fodor's strategy with Dennett's in the following very abstract way: Fodor proposes to revise and narrow the folk concept of belief by changing the *kind* of thing that is the content of belief. Narrow contents are not propositions; they are functions from context to propositions. But for Dennett, in contrast, narrow contents are the same kind of thing as wide contents: both are propositions—functions from possible worlds (= notional worlds) into truth values. What is changed in the move to narrow content is the relation between a believer and a proposition in virtue of which that proposition correctly describes the believer's beliefs. To accomplish that change, Dennett needs to tell us just how the purely internal properties of indivduals determine the narrow propositional content of their beliefs.

Here is Dennett's strategy for answering this question: suppose we know about an organism everything there is to know about its capacities and dispositions, but nothing about how it got that way: nothing about its historical properties, or about the environment that it came from. The problem is to say how to go from this limited information about the organism to a characterization of its notional world. "Our task," Dennett says,"is like the problem posed when we are shown some novel or antique gadget, and asked: what is it for?" We can't know, Dennett supposes, what it was actually designed for, but we could try to figure out, from its internal properties, what functions it is ideally suited to perform. *"We try to imagine a setting* in which . . . it would *excellently* perform some imaginably useful function."[15] In the same way, to find an organism's notional world—the world according to it—we try to imagine "the environment (or a class of environments) for which the organism as currently constituted is best fitted."[16] Propositions true in those possible environments will be the narrow contents of the organism's beliefs.

On the face of it, this doesn't look like what we want at all. Possible worlds picked out in this way look more like worlds in which the organism's needs or wants are satisfied than like worlds in which its beliefs are true. The antelope, for example, is aware of lions in its environment, and equipped to detect and escape from them. But it is not clear that it is better fitted for a lion-filled environment than for one that is lion-free. The antelope would have some useless defense mechanisms in certain lion-free environments, but it might still do a better job of "surviving and flourishing and reproducing its kind"[17] in such an environment. But, Dennett says, we are not supposed to understand "ideal environments" in a straightforward way: "By 'ideal environment' I do not mean the best of all possible worlds for this organism. . . . It might be a downright nasty world, but at least the organism is prepared to cope with its nastiness."[18] So ideal environments, in the intended sense, are environments for which the organism is prepared to cope. This is better: we do try to cope with the world as we believe it to be, and so worlds that are that way are presumably among the ones that our behavior is best fitted to cope with. But something essential still seems to be left out. Many features of organisms that help them cope with their environments seem intuitively to have nothing to do with their beliefs, and the fact that we have some feature that *would* help us cope with some counterfactual environment is surely not sufficient to say that such a counterfactual possibility is compatible with the world as we take it to be.

Consider the porcupine whose quills protect it from predators. It is best fitted, in Dennett's sense, for an environment containing animals that would attack and eat it if it weren't for the quills, and this will be true even if the porcupine's *only* defense mechanism is this passive one that does not require the porcupine to perceive or respond in any way to the presence of such predators. If the porcupine goes through life oblivious to the potential predators that its quills protect it against, it would surely be unreasonable to populate its notional world—the world according to it—with them.

The dangers that the porcupine's quills protect it from are real ones. The problem gets even worse if one considers, as Dennett's procedure requires, merely possible dangers that some actual feature we have might help to guard against. For example,

consider a possible world containing fierce and powerful beasts that would love to eat human beings if it weren't for the fact that these beasts are repelled by the distinctive smell that humans in fact give off. We humans, as we actually are, are ideally fitted to cope with such predators, but I don't think worlds containing them can be used to characterize our beliefs.

It seems to me right that states of belief are states that help the believer to cope with an environment, and that the contents of those states are essentially connected with the kind of environment they help the believer to cope with. But to be a belief state, a feature of an organism must contribute in a particular way to the fitness of the organism to cope with its environment. At the very least, a belief state must involve the reception of information from the environment, and a role for this information in the determination of the behavior of the organism. While Dennett's general account of his procedure for identifying narrow content is not restricted to this kind of case, the examples he uses focus on it, and we can consider how his strategy fares if we apply it only to states of an organism that help it cope by receiving and storing information in a form that makes it available to help determine the organism's behavior.

Understood in this way, Dennett's procedure is a variation of one kind of naturalistic account of wide content that has been proposed. According to this kind of account, a representational system is a system that is capable of being in a range of alternative internal states that tend to be causally dependent on the environment in a systematic way. Suppose that an organism is capable of being in internal states, $S_1, S_2, \ldots, S_n$, and that which of these states it is in normally depends on which of a corresponding range of alternative states the environment is in. Normally, for each i, the organism is in state S_i if (and because) the environment is in state E_i. Whenever a structure of causal dependencies of this kind obtains, it is appropriate to say that the organism *represents* the environment as being in state E_i in virtue of the fact that it is in state S_i, and that the organism's states contain *information* about the environment. Suppose further that the states of the organism are, or determine, behavioral dispositions, and that for each i, the behavior that state S_i disposes the organism to engage in is behavior that would be appropriate (given its needs or wants) in environment E_i. Then those representational states will be of the right general kind to be belief states.

This account of representation is like Dennett's account of narrow content in that it identifies content with a set of possible states of the environment. This account, like Dennett's, treats the descriptions of the relevant environments as the theorist's way of classifying internal states: the descriptions are not attributed to the organism. And like Dennett's, it does not distinguish information from misinformation. If the organism is in state S_i, then it represents the world as being in state E_i, whatever state the environment is actually in. But the notion of content that results from the causal account of representation will be a notion of *wide* content since the structure of causal relations in virtue of which the internal states are representational states will depend not just on the internal structure of the organism, but on general features of the environment. If the environment were radically different in certain ways, then the same states of the organism might tend to be sensitive to different features of the environment, or might not be sensitive to the environment at all. Content ascriptions, on this kind of account, are descriptions of internal states, but they describe them in terms of the organism's capacity to distinguish between a limited range of alternative possibilities, a range of possibilities that is constrained by certain facts about the organism's actual environment.

But even if our ordinary concept of content depends on facts about the actual environment in this way, might we apply this sort of procedure without relying on such facts? If we knew enough about the purely internal dispositional properties of a believer, might we be able to determine, from this information alone, a set of possible environments meeting this condition: if the believer were in such an environment it would tend to behave in ways that are appropriate (that tend to satisfy its needs better than alternative actions available in that environment), and it would do so *because* it is in such an environment? Dennett claims that if the believers were sophisticated enough we could, and that the resulting notion of content would be just the notion of narrow content we want.

> Highly adaptive organisms like ourselves . . . have internal structure and dispositional traits so rich in information about the environment in which they grew up that we could in principle say: this organism is best fitted to an environment in which there is a city called Boston, in which the organism spent its youth, in the company of organisms named . . . and so forth. We would not be able to distinguish Boston from Twin-Earth Boston, of course, but except for such virtually indistinguishable variations on a theme, our exercise in notional world formation would end in a unique solution.[19]

I see no basis for this optimism. I suspect that the attempt to recover information about a virtual environment without making any assumptions at all about the actual environment is just too uncon-

strained to work. Imagine a purely internal description of the movements that I am disposed to make under various internal conditions, as I walk down the streets of Boston going places to satisfy my wants and needs, a description that makes no reference to what is going on either specifically or in general beyond my skin. How could anything about *Boston,* or about Boston–like cities, be recovered from such a description? With a little imagination, one should be able to tell all kinds of wild fairy tales about environments in which the movements I am disposed to make are appropriate, but that are not anything like the way the world seems to me. The world beyond myself *could* be wired up so that the actions whose actual appropriateness depends on facts about Boston instead depended for their appropriateness on some totally different set of facts, say facts about the social organization of termite colonies. If the organism's internal structure and dispositional traits are rich and complex, then we will have to tell a long fairy tale. The world described by such a tale will perhaps have to share an abstract structure of some kind with the worlds that define the ordinary wide content of the organism's beliefs, but I don't see why they would have to share any content.

In normal everyday ascriptions of content we usually ignore not only fairy tale possibilities, but all possibilities except those that differ from the actual world only in very limited ways. When I say that O'Leary believes there is water in his basement, I may be saying only that O'Leary's conception of the world distinguishes the possibility that there is water in the basement from the possibility that his basement is dry. What this means, on the causal–informational account of representation, is that O'Leary is in a state that he would normally be in only if there were water in his basement. Further, that state is one that would normally cause O'Leary to behave in ways that would better serve his needs and wants if there were water in his basement than if the basement were dry: it disposes him to get out the mop, or call the plumber. But does O'Leary really believe that the liquid on his basement floor is *water?* Well, he certainly knows, or assumes, that it is not gasoline or olive oil. If it were any of a range of familiar alternative liquids, O'Leary's states and behavior would normally be different. But what about the possibility that it is a substance just like water in its superficial properties, but different from water in its underlying chemical structure? Does O'Leary's internal state contain information that distinguishes the actual situation from this one? Is there anything about him that would dispose him to behave differently (under normal conditions) if that situation were actual? In the usual context, that possibility is not relevant. When we claim that O'Leary thinks there is water in the basement, we are not claiming that he has ruled out the possibility that the stuff down there is really not water, but XYZ. We can, however, raise the question, and in this way change the range of relevant alternatives. The question will then shift, focussing on O'Leary's knowledge and beliefs about the chemical composition of water. If O'Leary is innocent of even the most elementary knowledge of chemistry, then nothing in his mind or behavioral dispositions will distinguish Earth from Twin-Earth, but that won't make it wrong to say, in a normal context in which Twin-Earth possibilities are ignored, that O'Leary believes that the stuff on his basement floor is water. That ascription of content distinguishes, in the right way, the relevant alternative possibilities that are compatible with O'Leary's conception of the world from the relevant possibilities that are not.

The revisionist may argue that it is this context-dependence of ordinary wide content ascriptions that makes them inappropriate for the purposes of theoretical explanation in cognitive science. Dennett's project might be seen as an attempt to eliminate the context-dependence by defining content relative to an absolutely neutral context that is free of all presuppositions about the external environment. But on the casual-informational account of representation, informational content is *essentially* relative to a range of alternative possibilities that are determined by general facts about the casual structure of the world in which the organism functions. It is internal states of the representor, on this kind of account, that contain information (or misinformation), but the system of causal relationships in virtue of which those internal states contain information cannot itself be something internal to the representor. The theorist, in describing the internal states of a representor in terms of informational content, has some choice in the range of alternatives relative to which content is defined. It may even be that for any possibility we can describe, there is a context in which we can ask whether the representor's beliefs distinguish that possibility from certain others. But this does not imply that there is an absolutely neutral context, a context free of all presuppositions about the environment, relative to which content ascriptions make sense.

In his attempt to characterize narrow content, Dennett has tied one hand behind his back. He proposes to extract a kind of content from facts about the believer while ignoring certain information that is available and that is used to determine ordinary wide content—information about the believer's historical properties and relation to the actual environment. I have argued that no reasonable notion of content will result from this procedure; one might also question the point of the exercise. Why bother? Why shouldn't an explanatory theory make use of historical and environmental information in defining content? To answer this we need to look at the other half of the revisionist's project: the arguments for the negative thesis.

The negative side of the revisionist doctrine has been formulated in various ways and given various labels: *methodological solipsims,*[20] *individualism,*[21] *the principle of autonomy.*[22] These different theses are sometimes distinguished from each other, but the general idea of all of them is that the states and properties that are described and expressed in an explanatory psychological theory should be intrinsic states and properties of the organism whose behavior is being explained. A number of similar arguments for this thesis have been advanced; they go roughly like this: an explanatory theory of human behavior, or of the behavior of anything else for that matter, should concern itself only with properties that are relevant to the causal powers of the thing whose behavior is being explained. Things that are intrinsically indistinguishable are indistinguishable with respect to causal powers, and so should not be distinguished by an explanatory theory. The Putnam–Burge thought experiments help to bring this point out: it is clear that people on Earth and their doppelganger on Twin–Earth will behave in exactly the same ways when put into the same environments. No tenable theory will explain their behavior in different ways, and so no tenable theory needs concepts that distinguish them.[23]

Before turning to this argument, we need to look more closely at the theses it is intended to support. First, here is Fodor's formulation of what he calls *individualism:* "Methodological individualism is the doctrine that psychological states are individuated *with respect to their causal powers.*"[24] This doctrine is, Fodor says, a special case of a completely general methodological principle that all scientific taxonomies should conform to, a principle that can be defended on a priori metaphysical grounds. He emphasizes that individualism, in his sense, does not by itself rule out the individuation of mental states by relational properties.

Relational properties can count taxonomically whenever they affect causal powers. Thus, 'being a planet' is a relational property par excellence, but it's one that individualism permits to operate in astronomical taxonomy. For whether you are a planet affects your trajectory and your trajectory determines what you can bump into; so whether you're a planet affects your causal powers.[25]

There is a shift in this characterization of individualism from a stronger to a weaker claim: it is one thing to individuate by causal powers, another to individuate by what *affects* causal powers. The fact that a planet is a planet is a fact about the configuration of its environment. This configuration plays a role in causing the planet to have the causal powers it has, for example its velocity. But the environmental facts do not *constitute* causal powers. Does individualism really require only that mental states be individuated by what causally affects causal powers? If so, then individualism in Fodor's sense is a much weaker doctrine than the individualism that Burge has argued against. On this interpretation, individuation by ordinary wide content will be compatible with Fodor's individualism since, for example, the fact that it is *water* in O'Leary's basement—or at least the fact that there is water in his environment generally—surely plays a role in putting him into the internal state that disposes him to behave as he does. Of course as the Twin-Earth story shows, there are alternative causal histories that could have put O'Leary into the same internal state, but an analogous claim will be true for the planets. Imagine a Twin-Earth that is not a planet but is in a field of forces exactly like the one the Earth is in.

The defense of the negative thesis by Fodor and others trades on a conflation of the weaker and the stronger thesis. If the thesis is to have any bite—if it is to be a thesis that rules out the individuation of psychological states by ordinary wide content—it must be the stronger thesis. But the arguments and examples used to support individualism often count only against the weaker thesis. Fodor, for example, illustrates his version of individualism and defends its plausibility with an example of a causally irrelevant relational property: call a particle an h-particle if a certain coin is heads up, and a t-particle if the coin is tails up. No plausible theory, Fodor argues, will use this distinction to explain the behavior of particles. No one will disagree with this; it should be clear and uncontroversial that facts that are causally irrelevant to the internal states of a particle or an organism should play no role in characterizing its theoretically important physical or psychological states. But it does not follow from this that such states must be purely internal.

The same shift between a weaker and a stronger version of the negative thesis is evident in other discussions. Consider, for example Stephen Stich's principle of autonomy: "The basic idea of the principle is that the states and processes that ought to be of concern to the psychologist are those that supervene on the current, internal, physical states of the organism." This is clearly the strong thesis, restricting the psychologist to purely internal states. But causal language creeps into Stich's subsequent discussion of the principle: historical and environmental facts, he says, will be irrelevant to psychological theory except when they "make a difference" to the organism's internal state; such facts "will be psychologically relevant only when they *influence* an organism's current, internal, physical state." The facts about distant causal histories of a term that determine its reference are said to be psychologically irrelevant because they need not "leave their trace" on the current internal state of the subject using the term.[26]

Stich argues for his principle of autonomy with what he calls the *replacement argument:* "Suppose that someone were to succeed in building an exact physical replica of me—a living human body whose current internal physical states at a given moment were identical to mine at that moment. . . . The replica, being an exact physical copy, would behave just as I would in all circumstances. . . . But now, the argument continues, since psychology is the science which aspires to explain behavior, any states or processes or properties which are not shared by Stich and his identically behaving replica must surely be irrelevant to psychology."[27] Stich illustrates his point with an example of an industrial robot. Suppose we describe the robot by saying that it is successfully performing its millionth weld. This is, in Stich's terminology, a nonautonomous behavioral description. An exact physical replica behaving in a way that is, in a reasonable sense, exactly the same, might not satisfy it. The description is a "conceptual hybrid" of an autonomous description—"successfully performing a weld"[28]—and a purely historical description—"having performed 999,999 other welds". "If we are seeking a set of generalizations to explain robot behavior, it would be perverse to expect them to explain the latter fact or the hybrid into which it enters."[29]

The argument and the example seem compelling, I think, only if we assume that the historical property is causally irrelevant to the current state of the robot. But if we keep in mind that those first 999,999 welds must surely have taken their toll, then it may not seem so perverse to look for generalizations that explain the fact that the robot satisfies the hybrid description. Suppose that, because of metal fatigue, robots of this kind almost always break down soon after about nine hundred thousand welds. If the robot failed to break down, we might ask for an explanation: how was this particular robot able to perform its millionth weld? We might call robots "old" after their nine hundred thousandth weld, and generalize about the behavior of old robots. We certainly generalize about the behavior of human beings on the basis of historical properties such as age and experience.

If we replace our robots with new ones after 900,000 welds, they won't break down as often, but, Stich might point out, this is because real replacements won't be the exact replicas required by the replacement argument. If the new robots were really physically exactly like the ones they replace, then of course they would be similarly unreliable. If an eighty year old woman were physically exactly like a seven year old child, then she would behave like a seven year old child, falsifying biological and psychological generalizations about eighty year old women. But this counterfactual possibility does not, by itself, threaten the truth, or even the explanatory power, of such generalizations.

There may be a sense in which certain nonautonomous properties are causally irrelevant. Consider a simple causal chain: A causes B, which in turn causes C. Suppose that B is sufficient, in the circumstances, for C: that is, B would have caused C even if it had been caused by something other than A. So this causal chain contrasts with a more complex one where A is doing some additional work, perhaps not only causing B but also causing other things that enable B to cause C. To rule out this contrasting case, we might say that A is causally irrelevant to the fact that B causes C. But in another sense, A is causally relevant to this fact, since without A, B would not have happened, and so would not have caused C. Suppose we have a pair of alternative causal chains: alternative inputs A_1 or A_2 will cause a device to be in one of two alternative internal states, B_1 or B_2, which in turn will cause the device to produce outputs C_1 or C_2. If we ask why the internal state B_1 produces output C_1, it is not relevant to mention A_1. But if we ask why the device produces output C_1, it would be correct and informative to say, because it is in the B-state caused by A_1. It is one thing to explain why a particular internal state has the causal powers it has; it is another to explain why something is in an internal state that has those causal powers.

Does the internal state of the device contain *information* about how it came to be in that state? If there are alternative causes of B_1, then the fact that the device is in state B_1 does not distinguish them: the device does not 'know' that A_1 causes B_1, as contrasted with a counterfactual possibility in which A_2 causes B_1. But since it is A_1 that in fact causes the device to be in state B_1, and since the

device would not have been in that state if A_1 hadn't happened, it 'knows', in virtue of being in state B_1, that A_1 happened.

In light of these distinctions, consider the following argument in defense of methodological solipsism from a paper by P. M. and P. S. Churchland:

> A neuron cannot know the distant causal ancestry . . . of its input. . . . An activated neuron causes a creature to withdraw into its shell not because such activation represents the presence of a predator—though it may indeed represent this—but because that neuron is connected to the withdrawal muscles, and because its activation is of the kind that causes them to contract. *The 'semantic' content of the state, if any, is causally irrelevant.*[30]

One cannot explain why the neuron's being activated causes the creature to withdraw by citing the fact that the activation represents the presence of a predator. But this does not prevent us from explaining why the creature withdraws by citing the presence of a predator, or by citing the fact that the creature is in a state that represents the presence of a predator. The semantic content is causally relevant to the behavior of the creature since if the creature had not been in a state with that semantic content, it would not have withdrawn into its shell. Can a neuron know the distant causal ancestry of its input? It cannot distinguish the situation in which its activation is caused by the presence of a predator from the situation in which it is caused by something else. But if in fact the neuron was activated by the presence of a predator, and would not have been activated if a predator had not been present, then it 'knows', in virtue of being activated, that a predator is present.

The critic of wide content might respond to these general considerations as follows: even if a theory *can* generalize about properties and states that are individuated by their causes, wouldn't it be better, methodologically, to try to find a theory that individuates them more narrowly? Won't generalizations in terms of the internal properties be deeper and more accurate? Generalizations about the causal powers or behavioral dispositions of old robots, creatures that are representing the presence of a predator, or footprints will inevitably have exceptions; to the extent that they are true, they must hold in virtue of internal properties of those things, and we won't understand why the generalizations hold until we are clear about the relevant internal properties.

It is right that *one* explanatory task is the task of characterizing the mechanisms that underlie certain causal regularities. We want to know how the creature represents the presence of a predator, and how that representation causes it to withdraw into its shell. But there are at least three reasons why we may still want to generalize about causal and historical properties. First, we need to refer to such properties, and to generalizations about them, in order to pose the explanatory questions about the mechanisms. The creature has certain capacities: it can recognize predators and protect itself from them. The reason we are interested in the neurophysiological processes in the creature is that they explain how it is able to do such things. Second, we may not know enough to be able to generalize in terms of internal properties. Suppose our device is a black box and that all we know about the states B_1 and B_2 is that they are the states caused (or normally caused) by A_1 and A_2, respectively. Often we know something about the mechanisms that explain why a device has certain capacities or incapacities, but not enough to describe them in purely autonomous terms. We may have to wait for the completion of science before we are able to describe things in purely internal terms, if there are such terms. As Fodor said in another context, and in defense of the opposite conclusion, "No doubt it's all right to have a research strategy that says 'wait a while', but who wants to wait *forever?*"[31] Third, there may be generalizations that can be stated only in terms of non-individualistic states and properties. Different mechanisms explain how different creatures recognize predators, but we may still be able to generalize about the recognition of predators. Suppose there are lots of black boxes that take inputs A_1 and A_2 into outputs C_1 and C_2, but that they do it in different ways. It is, of course, the idea of functionalism that it is possible and useful to generalize about causal roles independently of the specific mechanisms by which those causal roles are realized. Functional theories are theories that characterize the internal states of individuals in nonautonomous terms in order to generalize at a certain level of abstraction. It is not a mysterious coincidence that such generalizations hold. There may be general causal pressures, such as evolutionary pressures, that tend to favor situations in which A causes C but that leave open the question of the means or intervening process by which this is accomplished. In such a case there may be two different questions about why A causes C. If the question is about the mechanism, one cites B. If it is about the general pattern, then one cites the general pressures. Why do chameleons change color to match their background? Because this provides camouflage and in this way helps them survive, or because certain chemical processes take place in the chameleon's skin.

Any psychological theory, folk or scientifc, that understands mental states in terms of intentional states is a theory that sees a person or other organism as a receiver and user of information. The real lesson of Twin-Earth is that the fact that we are receivers and users of information is a fact, not just about us, but about the way we relate to our environments. In different environments, the internal states that in fact carry certain information would carry different information, or would not carry information at all. Ironically, the Twin-Earth stories that make this point so vividly also serve to obscure its significance in at least two ways: they make the dependence of intentional states on the environment seem, first, easier to avoid, and second, more mysterious, than it is. In the special case of Twin-Earth, it is easy to match up O'Leary's beliefs with corresponding beliefs of his twin, and to identify the narrow content with what these corresponding beliefs have in common. It is less easy to say, in general, how to factor out the purely internal component of a belief. I have argued that it is a highly speculative substantive hypothesis that there is any narrow notion of content that can be used to individuate intentional states autonomously. The special case of Twin-Earth also makes the dependence of intentional states on environment seem stranger than it is. Since the internal states of O'Leary's twin are exactly the same as O'Leary's, there is a sense in which the environmental differences between the two worlds make no difference to the internal states of the two twins, and so one is tempted to conclude that the environmental facts on which intentional states depend are therefore causally irrelevant. But the fact that a state might have had different causes does not show that the causes it does have are causally irrelevant.

Is O'Leary's belief that there is water in his basement an internal state of O'Leary? Is it in his head? Of course it is, in the same way that the mosquito bite on his nose is on his nose, and the footprint in the sand is in the sand. We can appeal to that belief to explain the fact that he is looking for the mop, just as we can appeal to the mosquito bite to explain why he is scratching his nose. We commonly individuate states and properties in terms of the way things interact with their environments, and use them to explain why things behave as they do. It is not easy to see how we could get along without doing this, or why we should try.[32]

NOTES

1. Hilary Putnam, "The Meaning of 'Meaning'", in Keith Gunderson (ed.), *Language, Mind and Knowledge* (Minneapolis, University of Minnesota Press), 1975, 144.

2. Tyler Burge, "Individualism and the Mental," in P. French *et al.* eds., *Midwest Studies in Philosophy, 4, Studies in Epistemology* (Minneapolis, University of Minnesota Press), 1979.

3. It is not clear that this is right. What does follow is that the intrinsic state of the head is not authoritative: that is, it does not follow from the head's being in the intrinsic state it is in that it has certain beliefs. But unless we assume the kind of individualism that is being denied, this does not imply that we are not authoritative.

4. There is a rough but useful analogy between this strategy of concept formation and a popular account of the way natural kind terms acquire their content. According to that account, one kind of property—a cluster of superficial properties—determines a set of things—say a set of animals—and then this extension is used to determine a different type of property-structural or explanatory or essential properties. The relevant properties of this type are the ones shared by the things in the extension.

5. One might argue that concepts, such as the general concept of footprint, that collapse when we try to abstract away from causal origins are just the concepts that are of no interest to science. But this need not be true. It is conceivable, for example, that there be ecological generalizations about the role of footprints in the behavior of certain kinds of predators and their prey even if there were no interesting generalizations about the shapes of the relevant footprints. If there can be functional theories at all, then there can be theories that generalize about causal roles in abstraction from the intrinsic properties of the states that realize those roles.

6. Jerry A. Fodor, *Psychosemantics: The Problem of Meaning in the Philosophy of Mind* (Cambridge, MA: Bradford Books, The MIT Press, 1987), ch. 2.

7. An explanation of narrow content based on this analogy was developed in some detail in Stephen White, "Partial Character and the Language of Thought," *Pacific Philosophical Quarterly, 63* (1982), 347–365.

8. Fodor, *Psychosemantics,* 30.

9. *Ibid.,* 48.

10. The point of my Cousin–Earth story is not just that narrow content may in some cases be indeterminate. That, I would argue and many would agree, is true of wide content as well. The point is that once we go beyond the Twin–Earth scenario, it becomes clear that we have been told nothing at all about how to identify narrow content. That there is such a thing to be identified is a substantive hypothesis.

11. The point is that it doesn't follow that one could find *interesting* purely internal analogues of the relational properties of belief states that are expressed by ordinary attributions of belief—internal properties that might be expected to play a role in an explanatory theory of behavior. One could always, by brute force, define some sort of internal property. Consider the location analogy: there is a set of absolute locations that are (in fact, at a certain moment) three miles from a burning barn. The property of being in one of those locations is (assuming, as we have been for purposes of the analogy, absolute space) independent of the external environment, and it is distinct from the property of being in one of the locations in the set that is in fact at least two thousand miles from Los Angeles. But such properties will have no interest; at other times or in counterfactual situations where barns are burning at different places, there will be no point in distinguishing the locations where, at this time and in this situation, a barn is burning three miles away.

12. Daniel C. Dennett, "Beyond Belief," in Andrew Woodfield (ed.), *Thought and Object: Essays on Intentionality* (Oxford: Clarendon Press, 1982), 1–95.

13. *Ibid.,* 38.

14. *Ibid.*

15. *Ibid.,* 41.

16. *Ibid.,* 42.

17. *Ibid.,* 41.

18. *Ibid.,* 42.

19. *Ibid.,* 43.

20. This term is first used for this doctrine by Hilary Putnam in "The Meaning of 'Meaning'" (see note #1). Jerry Fodor defends the doctrine in "Methodological Solipsism as a Research Strategy in Cognitive Science," in *Representations* (Cambridge, MA: Bradford Books, The MIT Press, 1981).

21. This is Burge's term. Fodor distinguishes methodological solipsism from individualism in chapter 2 of *Psychosemantics,* though I think it is not clear that Fodor and Burge are using the term in the same sense.

22. This is Stephen Stich's term. Stich distinguishes the principle of autonomy from methodological solipsism. See Stich, *From Folk Psychology to Cognitive Science* (Cambridge, MA: Bradford Books, The MIT Press), 1983.

23. Fodor's chapter 2 of *Psychosemantics* contains a clear development of this argument. See also Stich's replacement argument in Stich, 165ff.

24. Fodor, *Psychosemantics,* 42. Fodor's emphasis.

25. *Ibid.,* 43.

26. Stich, 164–165.

27. *Ibid.,* 167.

28. Paul Teller has pointed out that "successfully performing a weld" is not really an autonomous description, since its application depends on a social and technological context. With a little imagination, one could tell a twin earth story in which what twin robot was doing did not count as performing a weld.

29. Stich, 168.

30. Patricia S. Churchland and Paul M. Churchland "Stalking the Wild Epistemic Engine," *Nous, 17* (1983), 5–18. Emphasis mine.

31. Fodor, "Methodolgical Solipsism . . ." *Re-Presentations,* 248.

32. Many people provided me with helpful comments on an earlier version of this papper. I want to thank Kathleen Akins, Ned Block, Richard Boyd, Dan Dennett, Hartry Field, Sydney Shoemaker, Paul Teller, J. D. Trout, and Paul Weirich.

C. Scientific Versus Folk Psychology

60

Stephen P. Stich

"Autonomous Psychology and the Belief–Desire Thesis"

A venerable view, still very much alive, holds that human action is to be explained at least in part in terms of beliefs and desires. Those who advocate the view expect that the psychological theory which explains human behavior will invoke the concepts of belief and desire in a substantive way. I will call this expectation *the belief-desire thesis*. Though there would surely be a quibble or a caveat here and there, the thesis would be endorsed by an exceptionally heterogeneous collection of psychologists and philosophers ranging from Freud and Hume, to Thomas Szasz and Richard Brandt. Indeed, a number of philosophers have contended that the thesis, or something like it, is embedded in our ordinary, workaday concept of action.[1] If they are right, and I think they are, then insofar as we use the concept of action we are *all* committed to the belief–desire thesis. My purpose in this paper is to explore the tension between the belief–desire thesis and a widely held assumption about the nature of explanatory psychological theories, an assumption that serves as a fundamental regulative principle for much of contemporary psychological theorizing. This assumption, which for want of a better term I will call the *principle of psychological autonomy,* will be the focus of the first of the sections below. In the second section I will elaborate a bit on how the belief–desire thesis is to be interpreted, and try to extract from it a principle that will serve as a premise in the argument to follow. In the third section I will set out an argument to the effect that large numbers of belief–desire explanations of action, indeed perhaps the bulk of such explanations, are incompatible with the principle of autonomy. Finally, in the last section, I will fend off a possible objection to my argument. In the process, I will try to make clear just why the

argument works and what price we should have to pay if we were resolved to avoid its consequences.

I. The Principle of Psychological Autonomy

Perhaps the most vivid way of explaining the principle I have in mind is by invoking a type of science fiction example that has cropped up with some frequency in recent philosophical literature. Imagine that technology were available which would enable us to duplicate people. That is, we can build living human beings who are atom for atom and molecule for molecule replicas of some given human being.[2] Now suppose that we have before us a human being (or, for that matter, any sort of animal) and his exact replica. What the principle of autonomy claims is that these two humans will be psychologically identical, that any psychological property instantiated by one of these subjects will also be instantiated by the other.

Actually, a bit of hedging is needed to mark the boundaries of this claim to psychological identity. First, let me note that the organisms claimed to be psychologically identical include any pair of organisms, existing at the same time or at different times, who happen to be atom for atom replicas of each other. Moreover, it is inessential that one organism should have been built to be a replica of the other. Even if the replication is entirely accidental, the two organisms will still be psychologically identical.

A caveat of another sort is needed to clarify just what I mean by calling two organisms "psychologically identical." For consider the following objection: "The original organisms and his replica do not share *all* of their psychological properties. The

From *The Monist* LXI, 4 (October 1978):573–91. Reprinted with permission of the editor and Stephen P. Stich.

original may, for example, remember seeing the Watergate hearings on television, but the replica remembers no such thing. He may think he remembers it, or have an identical "memory trace"; but if he was not created until long after the Watergate hearings, then he did not see the hearings on television, and thus he could not remember seeing them." The point being urged by my imagined critic is a reasonable one. There are many sorts of properties plausibly labeled "psychological" that might be instantiated by a person and not by his replica. Remembering that p is one example, knowing that p and seeing that p are others. These properties have a sort of "hybrid" character. They seem to be analyzable into a "purely psychologial" property (like seeming to remember that p, or believing that p (along with one or more non-psychological properties and relations (like p being true, or the memory trace being caused in a certain way by the fact that p). But to insist that "hybrid" psychological properties are not psychological properties at all would be at best a rather high handed attempt at stipulative definition. Still, there is something a bit odd about these hybrid psychological properties, a fact which reflects itself in the intuitive distinction between "hybrids" and their underlying "purely psychological" components. What is odd about the hybrids, I think, is that we do not expect them to play any role in an explanatory psychological theory. Rather, we expect a psychological theory which aims at explaining behavior to invoke only the "purely psychological" properties which are shared by a subject and its replicas. Thus, for example, we are inclined to insist it is Jones' *belief* that there is no greatest prime number that plays a role in the explanation of his answering the exam question. He may, in fact, have *known* that there is no greatest prime number. But even if he did not know it, if, for example, the source of his information had himself only been guessing, Jones' behavior would have been unaffected. What knowledge adds to belief is psychologically irrelevant. Similarly the difference between really remembering that p and merely seeming to remember that p makes no difference to the subject's behavior. In claiming that physical replicas are psychologically identical, the principle of psychological autonomy is to be understood as restricting itself to the properties that can play a role in explanatory psychological theory. Indeed, the principle is best viewed as a claim about what sorts of properties and relations may play a role in explanatory psychological theory. If the principle is to be observed, then the only properties and relations that may legitimately play a role in explanatory psychological theories are the properties and relations that a subject and its replica will share.

There is another way to explain the principle of psychological autonomy that does not appeal to the fanciful idea of a replica. In a recent paper Jaegwon Kim has explicated and explored the notion of one class of properties *supervening* upon another class of properties.[3] Suppose S and W are two classes of properties, and that $S^\#$ and $W^\#$ are the sets of all properties constructible from the properties in S and W respectively. Then, following Kim, we will say that the family S of properties supervenes on the family W of properties (with respect to a domain D of objects) just in case, necessarily, any two objects in D which share all properties in $W^\#$ will also share all properties in $S^\#$. A bit less formally, one class of properties supervenes on another if the presence or absence of properties in the former class is completely determined by the presence or absence of properties in the latter.[4] Now the principle of psychological autonomy states that the properties and relations to be invoked in an explanatory psychological theory must be supervenient upon the *current, internal physical* properties and relations of organisms (i.e., just those properties that an organism shares with all of its replicas).

Perhaps the best way to focus more sharply on what the autonomy principle states is to look at what it rules out. First, of course, if explanatory psychological properties and relations must supervene on *physical* properties, then at least some forms of dualism are false. The dualist who claims that there are psychological (or mental) properties which are not nomologically correlated with physical properties, but which nonetheless must be invoked in an explanation of the organism's behavior, is denying that explanatory psychological states supervene upon physical states. However, the autonomy principle is not inimical to all forms of dualism. Those dualists, for example, who hold that mental and physical properties are nomologically correlated need have no quarrel with the doctrine of autonomy. However, the principle of autonomy is significantly stronger than the mere insistence that psychological states supervene on physical states.[5] For autonomy requires in addition that certain physical properties and relations are psychologically irrelevant in the sense that organisms which differ *only* with respect to those properties and relations are psychologically identical.[6] In specifying that only "current" physical properties are psychologically relevant, the autonomy principle decrees irrelevant all those properties that deal with the history of the organism, both past and future. It is entirely possible, for example, for two organisms to have quite different physical histories and yet, at a specific pair of moments, to be replicas of one another. But this sort of difference, according to the autonomy principle, can make no difference from the point of view of explanatory psychology. Thus remembering that p (as contrasted with having a memory trace that p) cannot be an explanatory psychological state. For the difference between a person who remembers that p and a person who only seems to remember that p is not dependent on their current physical state, but only on the history of these states. Similarly, in specifying that only *internal* properties and relations are relevant to explanatory psychological properties, the autonomy principle decrees that relations between an organism and its external environment are irrelevant to its current (explanatory) psychological state. The restriction also entails that properties and relations of external objects cannot be relevant to the organism's current (explanatory) psychological state. Thus neither my seeing that Jones is falling nor my knowing that Ouagadougou is the capital of Upper Volta can play a role in an explanatory psychological theory, since the former depends in part on my relation to Jones, and the latter depends in part on the relation between Ouagadougou and Upper Volta.

Before we leave our discussion of the principle of psychological autonomy, let us reflect briefly on the status of the principle. On Kim's view, the belief that one set of properties supervenes on another "is largely, and often, a combination of metaphysical convictions and methodological considerations."[7] The description seems particularly apt for the principle of psychological autonomy. The autonomy principle serves a sort of regulative role in modern psychology, directing us to restrict the concepts we invoke in our explanatory theories in a very special way. When we act in accordance with the regulative stipulation of the principle we are giving witness to the tacit conviction that the best explanation of behavior will include a theory invoking properties supervenient upon the organism's current, internal physical state.[8] As Kim urges, this conviction is supported in part by the past success of theories which cleave to the principle's restrictions, and in part by some very fundamental metaphysical convictions. I think there is much to be learned in trying to pick apart the various metaphysical views that support the autonomy principle, for some of them have implications in areas quite removed from psychology. But that is a project for a different paper.

II.   The Belief–Desire Thesis

The belief–desire thesis maintains that human action is to be explained, at least in part, in terms of beliefs and desires. To sharpen the thesis we need to say more about the intended sense of *explain,* and more about what it would be to explain action *in terms of beliefs and desires.* But before trying to pin down either of these notions, it will be useful to set out an example of the sort of informal belief–desire explanations that we commonly offer for our own actions and the actions of others.

> Jones is watching television; from time to time he looks nervously at a lottery ticket grasped firmly in his hand. Suddenly he jumps up and rushes toward the phone. Why? It was because the T.V. announcer has just announced the winning lottery number, and it is the number on Jones' ticket. Jones believes that he has won the lottery. He also believes that to collect his winnings he must contact the lottery commission promptly. And, needless to say, he very much wants to collect his winnings.

Many theorists acknowledge that explanations like the one offered of Jones rushing toward the phone are often true (albeit incomplete) explanations of action. But this concession alone does not commit the theorist to the belief–desire thesis as I will interpret it here. There is considerable controversy over how we are to understand the 'because' in "Jones rushed for the phone because he believed he had won the lottery and he wanted. . . ." Some writers are inclined to read the 'because' literally, as claiming that Jones' belief and his desire were the *causes* (or among the causes) of his action. Others offer a variety of non-causal accounts of the relation between beliefs and desires on the one hand and actions on the other.[9] However, it is the former, "literal," reading that is required by the belief–desire thesis as I am constructing it.

To say that Jones's belief that he had won the lottery was among the causes of his rushing toward the phone is to say of one specific event that it had among its causes one specific state. There is much debate over how such "singular causal statements" are to be analyzed. Some philosophers hold that for a state or event S to be among the causes of an event E, there must be a law which somehow relates S and E. Other philosophers propose other accounts. Even among those who agree that singular causal statements must be subsumed by a law, there is a debate over how this notion of subsumption is to be understood. At the heart of this controversy is the issue of how much difference there can be between the properties invoked in the law and those invoked in the description of the event if the event is to be an instance of the law.[10] Given our current purposes, there is no need to take a stand on this quite general metaphysical issue. But we will have to take a stand on a special case of the relation between beliefs, desires, and the psychological laws that subsume them. The belief–desire thesis, as I am viewing it, takes seriously the idea of developing a psychological theory couched in terms of beliefs and desires. Thus, in addition to holding that Jones's action was caused by his belief that he had won the lottery and his desire to collect his winnings, it also holds that this singular causal statement is true in virtue of being subsumed by laws which specify nomological relations among beliefs, desires and action.[11]

There is one further point that needs to be made about my construal of the belief–desire thesis. If the thesis is right, then action is to be explained at least in part by appeal to laws detailing how beliefs, desires and other psychological states effect action. But how are we to recognize such laws? It is, after all, plainly not enough for a theory simply to invoke the terms 'belief' and 'desire' in its laws. If it were, then it would be possible to convert any theory into a belief–desire theory by the simple expedient of replacing a pair of its theoretical terms with the terms 'belief' and 'desire'. The point I am laboring is that the belief–desire thesis must be construed as the claim that psychological theory will be couched in terms of beliefs and desires *as we ordinarily conceive of them.* Thus to spell out the belief–desire thesis in detail would require that we explicate our intuitive concepts of belief and desire. Fortunately, we need not embark on that project here.[12] To fuel the arguments I will develop in the following section, I will need only a single, intuitively plausible, premise about beliefs.

As a backdrop for the premise that I need, let me introduce some handy terminology. I believe that Ouagadougou is the capital of Upper Volta, and if you share my interest in atlases then it is likely that you have the same belief. Of course, there is also a perfectly coherent sense in which your belief is not the same as mine, since you could come to believe that Bobo Dioulasso is the capital of Upper Volta, while my belief remains unchanged. The point here is the obvious one that beliefs, like sentences, admit of a type–token distinction. I am inclined to view belief tokens as states of a person. And I take a state to be the instantiation of a property by an object during a time interval. Two belief states (or belief tokens) are of the same type if they are instantiations of the same property and they are of different types if they are instantiations of different properties.[13] In the example at hand, the property that both you and I instantiate is *believing that Ouagadougou is the capital of Upper Volta.*

Now the premise I need for my argument concerns the identity conditions for belief properties. Cast in its most intuitive form, the premise is simply that if a particular belief of yours is true and a particular belief of mine is false, then they are not

the same belief. A bit more precisely: If a belief token of one subject differs in truth value from a belief token of another subject, then the tokens are not of the same type. Given our recent account of belief states, this is equivalent to a sufficient condition for the non-identity of belief properties: If an instantiation of belief property p_1 differs in truth value from an instantiation of belief property p_2, then p_1 and p_2 are different properties. This premise hardly constitutes an analysis of our notion of sameness of belief, since we surely do not hold belief tokens to be of the same type if they merely have the same truth value. But no matter. There is no need here to explicate our intuitive notion of belief identity in any detail. What the premise does provide is a necessary condition on any state counting as a belief. If a pair of states can be type identical (i.e., can be instantiations of the same property) while differing in truth value, then the states are not beliefs as we ordinarily conceive of them.

Before putting my premise to work, it might be helpful to note how the premise can be derived from a quite traditional philosophical account of the nature of beliefs. According to this account, belief is a relation between a person and a proposition. Two persons have the same belief (instantiate the same belief property) if they are belief-related to the same proposition. And, finally, propositions are taken to be the vehicles of truth, so propositions with different truth values cannot be identical. Given this account of belief, it follows straightforwardly that belief tokens differing in truth value differ in type. But the entailment is not mutual, so those who, like me, have some suspicions about the account of belief as a relation between a person and a proposition are free to explore other accounts of belief without abandoning the intuitively sanctioned premise that differences in truth value entail difference in belief.

III. The Tension Between Autonomy and the Belief–Desire Thesis

In this section I want to argue that a certain tension exists between the principle of psychological autonomy and the belief–desire thesis. The tension is not, strictly speaking a logical incompatibility. Rather, there is an incompatibility between the autonomy principle and some assumptions that are naturally and all but universally shared by advocates of the belief–desire thesis. The additional assumptions are that singular causal statements like the ones extractable from our little story about Jones and the lottery ticket are often true. Moreover, they are true because they are subsumed by laws which invoke the very properties which are invoked in the characterization of the beliefs and desires. A bit less abstractly, what I am assuming is that statements like "Jones's belief that he had won the lottery was among the causes of his rushing toward the phone" are often true; and that they are true in virtue of being subsumed by laws invoking properties like *believing that he had just won the lottery*. The burden of my argument is that if we accept the principle of autonomy, then these assumptions must be rejected. More specifically, I will argue that if the autonomy principle is accepted then there are large numbers of belief properties that cannot play a role in an explanatory psychological theory. My strategy will be to examine four different cases, each representative of a large class. In each case we will consider a pair of subjects who, according to the autonomy principle, instantiate all the same explanatory psychological properties, but who have different beliefs. So if we accept the principle of psychological autonomy, then it follows that the belief properties our subjects instantiate cannot be explanatory psychological properties. After running through the examples, I will reflect briefly on the implications of the argument for the belief–desire thesis.

Case I: Self-Referential Beliefs[14]

Suppose, as we did earlier, that we have the technology for creating atom for atom replicas of people. Suppose, further, that a replica for me has just been created. I believe that I have tasted a bottle of Chateau d'Yquem, 1962. Were you to ask me whether I had ever tasted a d'Yquem, '62, I would likely reply, "Yes, I have." An advocate of the belief–desire thesis would urge, plausibly enough, that my belief is among the causes of my utterance. Now if you were to ask my replica whether he had ever tasted a d'Yquem, 1962, he would likely also reply, "Yes, I have." And surely a belief–desire theorist will also count my replica's belief among the causes of *his* utterance. But the belief which is a cause of my replica's utterance must be of a different type from the one which is a cause of my utterance. For his belief is false; he has just been created and has never tasted a d'Yquem, nor any other wine. So by the premise we set out in Section II, the belief property he instantiates is different from the one I instantiate. Yet since we are replicas, the autonomy principle entails that we share all our explanatory psychological properties. It follows that the property of believing that I have tasted a Chateau d'Yquem, 1962, cannot be one which plays a role in an explanatory psychological theory. In an obvious way, the example can be

generalized to almost all beliefs about oneself. If we adhere to the principle of autonomy, then beliefs about ourselves can play no role in the explanation of our behavior.

Case 2: Beliefs About One's Spatial and Temporal Location

Imagine, to vary the science fiction example, that cryogenics, the art of freezing people, has been perfected to the point at which a person can be frozen, stored, then defrosted, and at the end of the ordeal be atom for atom identical with the way he was at the beginning of the freezing process. Now suppose that I submit myself to cryogenic preservation this afternoon, and, after being frozen, I am transported to Iceland where I am stored for a century or two, then defrosted. I now believe that it is the 20th century and that there are many strawberry farms nearby. It would be easy enough to tell stories which would incline the belief–desire theorists to say that each of these beliefs is serving as a cause of my actions. I will leave the details to the reader's imagination. On being defrosted, however, I would presumably still believe that it is the 20th century and that there are many strawberry farms nearby. Since my current beliefs are both true and my future beliefs both false, they are not belief tokens of the same type, and do not instantitate the same belief property. But by hypothesis, I am, on defrosting, a replica of my current self. Thus the explanatory psychological properties that I instantiate cannot have changed. So the belief property I instantiate when I now believe that it is the 20th century cannot play any role in an explanatory psychological theory. As in the previous case, the example generalizes to a large number of other beliefs involving a subject's temporal and spatial location.

Case 3: Beliefs About Other People

In several recent papers, Hilary Putnam has made interesting use of the following fanciful hypothesis.[15] Suppose that in some distant corner of the universe there is a planet very much like our own. Indeed, it is so much like our own that there is a person there who is my doppelganger. He is atom for atom identical with me and has led an entirely parallel life history. Like me, my doppelganger teaches in a philosophy department, and like me has heard a number of lectures on the subject of proper names delivered by a man called 'Saul Kripke.' However, his planet is not a complete physical replica of mine. For the philosopher called 'Saul Kripke' on that planet, though strikingly similar to the one called by the same name on our planet, was actually born in a state they call 'South Dakota,' which is to the north of a state they call 'Nebraska.' By contrast, our Saul Kripke was born in Nebraska—our Nebraska, of course, not theirs. But for reasons which need not be gone into here, many people on this distant planet, including my doppelganger, hold a belief which they express by saying 'Saul Kripke was born in Nebraska.' Now I also hold a belief which I express by saying 'Saul Kripke was born in Nebraska.' However, the belief I express with those words is very different from the belief my doppelganger expresses using the same words, so different, in fact, that his belief is false while mine is true. Yet since we are dopplegangers the autonomy principle dictates that we instantiate all the same explanatory psychological properties. Thus the belief property I instantiate in virtue of believing that Saul Kripke was born in Nebraska cannot be a property invoked in an explanatory psychological theory.

Case 4: Natural Kind Predicates

In Putnam's doppelganger planet stories, a crucial difference between our planet and the distant one is that on our planet the substance which we call 'water,' which fills our lakes, etc. is in fact H_2O, while on the other planet the substance they call 'water' which fills their lakes, etc. is in fact some complex chemical whose chemical formula we may abbreviate XYZ. Now imagine that we are in the year 1700, and that some ancestor of mine hears a story from a source he takes to be beyond reproach to the effect that when lizards are dipped in water, they disolve. The story, let us further suppose, is false, a fact which my ancestor might discover to his dismay when attempting to dissolve a lizard. For the belief–desire theorist, the unsuccessful attempt has as one of its causes the belief that lizards dissolve in water. Now suppose that my ancestor has a doppelganger on the far off planet who is told an identical sounding story by an equally trustworthy raconteur. However, as it happens that story is true, for there are lizards that do dissove in XYZ, though none will dissolve in H_2O. The pattern should by now be familiar. My ancestor's belief is false, his doppelganger's is true. Thus the belief tokens instantiate different belief properties. But since ex-hypothesis the people holding the beliefs are physically identical, the belief properties they instantiate cannot function in an explanatory psychological theory.[16]

This completes my presentation of cases. Obviously, the sorts of examples we have looked at are not the only ones susceptible to the sort of argument I have been using. But let us now reflect for a moment on just what these arguments show. To begin, we should note that they do *not* show the belief–desire thesis is false. The thesis, as I have construed it here, holds that there are psychological laws which invoke various belief and desire properties and which have a substantive role to play in the explanation of behavior. Nothing we have said here would suffice to show that there are no such laws. At best, what we have shown is that, if we accept the principle of psychological autonomy, then a large class of belief properties cannot be invoked in an explanatory psychological theory. This, in turn, entails that many intuitively sanctioned singular causal statements which specify a belief as a cause of an action cannot be straightforwardly subsumed by a law. And it is just here, I think, that our argument may serve to undermine the belief–desire thesis. For the plausibility of the thesis rests, in large measure, on the plausibility of these singular causal statements. Indeed, I think the belief–desire thesis can be profitably viewed as the speculation that these intuitively sanctioned singular causal statements can be cashed out in a serious psychological theory couched in terms of beliefs and desires. In showing that large numbers of these singular causal statements cannot be cashed out in this way, we make the speculation embodied in the belief–desire thesis appear idle and unmotivated. In the section that follows, I will consider a way in which an advocate of the belief–desire thesis might try to deflect the impact of our arguments, and indicate the burden that this escape route imposes on the belief–desire theorist.

IV. A Way Out and Its Costs

Perhaps the most tempting way to contain the damage done by the arguments of the previous section is to grant the conclusions while denying their relevance to the belief–desire thesis. I imagine a critic's objection going something like this: "Granted, if we accept the autonomy principle, then certain belief properties cannot be used in explanatory theories. But this does nothing to diminish the plausibility of the belief–desire thesis, because the properties you have shown incompatible with autonomy are the *wrong kind* of belief properties. All of the examples you consider are cases of *de re* beliefs, none of them are *de dicto* beliefs. But those theorists who take seriously the idea of constructing a belief–desire psychological theory have in mind a theory invoking de dicto beliefs and desires. De re beliefs are a sort of hybrid; a person has a de re belief if he has a suitable underlying de dicto belief, *and* if he is related to specific objects in a certain way. But it is only the underlying de dicto belief that will play a role in psychological explanation. Thus your arguments do not cast any serious doubt on the belief–desire thesis."[17]

Before assessing this attempt to protect the belief–desire thesis, a few remarks on the de dicto/de re distinction are in order. In the recent philosophical discussion of de re and de dicto beliefs, the focus has been on the logical relations among various sorts of belief attributions. Writers concerned with the issue have generally invoked a substitution criterion to mark the boundary between de dicto and de re belief attributions. Roughly, a belief attribution of the form

S believes that p

is de re if any name or other referring expression within p can be replaced with a co-designating term without risk of change of truth value; otherwise the attribution is de dicto.[18]

But now given this way of drawing the de re/de dicto distinction, my imagined critic is simply wrong in suggesting that all of the examples used in my arguments are cases of de re belief. Indeed, just the opposite is true; I intend all of the belief attribution in my examples to be understood in the de dicto sense, and all my arguments work quite as well when they are read in this way. Thus, for example, in Case 3 I attribute to myself the belief that Saul Kripke was born in Nebraska. But I intend this to be understood in such a way that

Stich believes 'ϕ' was born in Nebraska

might well be false if 'ϕ' were replaced by a term which, quite unbeknownst to me, in fact denotes Saul Kripke.

There is, however, another way the critic could press his attack that sidesteps my rejoinder. Recently, a number of writers have challenged the substitutional account of the de dicto/de re distinction. The basic idea underlying their challenge is that the term 'de re' should be used for all belief attributions which intend to ascribe a "real" relation of some sort between the believer and the object of his belief. The notion of a real relation is contrasted with the sort of relation that obtains between a person and an object when the object happens to satisfy some description that the person has in mind.[19] Burge, for example, holds that "a *de dicto* belief is a belief in which the believer is related only to a completely expressed proposition *(dictum),*" in contrast to a de re belief which is "a belief whose correct ascription places the believer in an appropriate, *nonconceptual, contextual relation* to the objects the belief is about."[20] Thus, if

Brown believes that the most prosperous Oriental rug dealer in Los Angeles is an Armenian, and if he believes it simply because he believes all prosperous Oriental rug dealers are Armenian, but has no idea who the man may be, then his belief is de dicto. By contrast, if Brown is an intimate of the gentleman, he may have the de re belief that the most prosperous Oriental rug dealer in Los Angeles is an Armenian. The sentence

Brown believes that the most prosperous Oriental rug dealer in Los Angeles is an Armenian.

is thus ambiguous, since it may be used either in the de re sense to assert that Brown and the rug dealer stand in some "appropriate, nonconceptual, contextual relation" or in the de dicto sense which asserts merely that Brown endorses the propositon that the most prosperous rug dealer in Los Angeles (whoever he may be) is an Armenian.

The problem with the substitutional account of the de dicto/de re distinction is that it classifies as de dicto many belief attributions which impute a "real" relation between the believer and the object of his belief. In many belief attributions the names or definite descriptions that occur in the content sentence do a sort of double duty. First, they serve the function commonly served by names and descriptions; they indicate (or refer to) an object, in this case the object to which the believer is said to be related. The names or descriptions in the content sentence *also* may serve to indicate how the believer conceives of the object, or how he might characterize it. When a name or description serving both roles is replaced by a codesignating expression which does *not* indicate how the believer conceives of the object, then the altered attribution (interpreted in the "double duty" sense) will be false. Thus the substitutional account classifies the original attribution as de dicto, despite its imputation of a "real" relation between believer and object.[21]

Now if the de dicto/de re distinction is drawn by classifying as de re all those belief attributions which impute a "real" relation between believer and object, then the critic conjured in the first paragraph of this section is likely right in his contention that all of my arguments invoke examples of de re beliefs. Indeed, the strategy of my arguments is to cite an example of a de re (i.e., "real relation") belief, then construct a second example in which the second believer is a physical replica of the first, but has no "real relation" to the object of the first believer's belief. However, to grant this much is not to grant that the critic has succeeded in blunting the point of my arguments.

Let me begin my rejoinder with a fussy point.

The critic's contentions were two: first, that my examples all invoked de re belief properties; second, that de re belief properties are hybrids and are analyzable into de dicto belief properties. The fussy point is that even if both the critic's contentions are granted, the critic would not quite have met my arguments head on. The missing premise is that de dicto belief properties (construed now according to the "real relation" criterion) are in fact compatible with the principle of psychological autonomy. This premise may be true, but the notion of a "real" relation, on which the current account of de dicto belief properties depends, is sufficiently obscure that it is hard to tell. Fortunately, there is a simple way to finesse the problem. Let us introduce the term *autonomous beliefs* for those beliefs that a subject must share with all his replicas; and let us use the term *non-autonomous* for those beliefs which a subject need not share with his replica.[22] More generally, we can call any property which an organism must share with its replicas an *autonomous property*. We can now reconstrue the critic's claims as follows:

1) All the examples considered in Section III invoke non-autonomous belief properties.

2) Non-autonomous belief properties are hybrids, analyzable into an underlying autonomous belief property (which can play a role in psychological explanation) plus some further relation(s) between the believer and the object of his belief.

On the first point I naturally have no quarrel, since a principal purpose of this paper is to show that a large class of belief properties are non-autonomous. On the second claim, however, I would balk, for I am skeptical that the proposed analysis can in fact be carried off. I must hasten to add that I know of no *argument* sufficient to show that the analysis is impossible. But, of course, my critic has no argument either. Behind my skepticism is the fact that no such analysis has ever been carried off. Moreover, the required analysis is considerably more demanding than the analysis of de re belief in terms of de dicto belief, when the distinction between the two is drawn by the substitutional criterion. For the class of autonomous beliefs is significantly smaller than the class of de dicto beliefs (characterized substitutionally).[23] And the most impressive attempts to reduce de re beliefs to de dicto plainly will not be of much help for the analysis my critic proposes.[24] But enough. I have already conceded that I cannot prove my critic's project is impossible. What I do hope to have established is that the critic's burden is the burden of the belief–desire theorist. If the reduction of non-autonomous beliefs to autonomous beliefs cannot be carried off, then there is small prospect that a psychological theory couched in terms of beliefs and desires will succeed in explaining any substantial part of human behavior.

A final point. It might be argued that, however difficult the analysis of non-autonomous beliefs to autonomous ones may be, it must be possible to carry it off. For, the argument continues, a subject's non-autonomous beliefs are determined in part by the autonomous psychological properties he instantiates and in part by his various relations to the objects of the world. Were either of these components suitably altered, the subject's non-autonomous beliefs would be altered as well. And since non-autonomous beliefs are jointly determined by autonomous psychological properties and by other relations, there must be some analysis, however complex, which specifies how this joint determination works. Now this last claim is not one I would want to challenge. I am quite prepared to grant that non-autonomous beliefs admit of some analysis in terms of autonomous psychological properties plus other relations. But what seems much more doubtful to me is that the autonomous properties invoked in the analysis would be *belief properties*. To see the reasons for my doubt, let us reflect on the picture suggested by the examples in Section III. In each case we had a pair of subjects who shared all their autonomous properties though their non-autonomous beliefs differed in truth value. The difference in truth value, in turn, was rooted in a difference in reference; the beliefs were simply about different persons, places or times. In short, the beliefs represented different states of affairs. If the non-autonomous belief properties of these examples are to be analyzed into autonomous psychological properties plus various historical or external relations, then it is plausible to suppose that the autonomous psychological properties do not determine a truth value, an appropriate reference or a represented state of affairs. So the state of exhibiting one (or more) of these autonomous properties itself has no truth value, is not referential, and does not represent anything. And this, I would urge, is more than enough reason to say that it is not a belief at all. None of this amounts to an *argument* that non-autonomous beliefs are not analyzable into autonomous ones. Those who seek such an analysis are still free to maintain that there will be at least one autonomous belief among the autonomous properties in the analysans of each non-autonomous belief property. But in the absence of an argument for this claim, I think few will find it particularly plausible. The ball is in the belief–desire theorists's court.[25,26]

APPENDIX

A bit more needs to be said about the premise urged at the end of Section II. The premise, it will be recalled, was this:

> If a belief token of one subject differs in truth value from a belief token of another subject, then the tokens are not of the same type.

A number of helpful critics have pointed out to me that we actually have a variety of intuitively sanctioned ways to decide when two belief tokens are of the same type. Moreover, some of these patently violate my premise. Thus, for example, if Jones and Smith each believes that he will win the next presidential election, there would be no intuitive oddness to the claim that Jones and Smith have the same belief. Though, of course, if Jones' belief is true, Smith's belief is false. It would be equally natural in this case to say that Jones and Smith have different beliefs. So I cannot rest my premise on our intuitive judgements; the intuitions will not bear the weight.

I think the best way of defending the premise is to make clear how it is related to a certain view (actually a category of views) about what beliefs are. The views I have in mind all share two features in common:

(i) they take belief to be a relation between a believer and a type of abstract object;
(ii) they take the abstract objects to be representational—that is, the abstract objects are taken to picture the world as being a certain way, or to claim that some state of affairs obtains. Thus the object, along with the actual state of the believer's world, determine a truth value.

For example, certain theorists take belief to be a relation between a person and a proposition; a proposition, in turn, determines a truth value for every possible world—truth for those worlds in which it is true and falsity for those worlds in which it is false. A person's belief is true if the proposition is true in his or her world. Rather more old fashioned is the theory which holds belief to be a relation between a person and an image or a mental picture. The belief is true if and only if the mental picture correctly depicts the believer's world.

Now on views such as these which take belief to be a relation between a person and an abstract object, the most natural way of determining when a pair of belief tokens are of the same type is by appeal to the abstract objects. A pair of subjects' belief tokens are of the same type when the subjects are related to the same abstract object. Thus

when subjects are in the same possible world, their belief tokens are of the same type only if they are identical in truth value. And this, in effect, was the premise advanced in Section II. The thesis of this paper is best taken to be that the principle of psychological autonomy is in conflict with the belief–desire thesis, *when beliefs are construed as in (i) and (ii)*.

Let me add a final observation. A number of recent theorists have taken belief to be a relation between a person and a sentence or sentence-like object. For example, in *The Language of Thought* (Crowell, 1975) Jerry Fodor holds that belief is a relation between a person and a sentence in "the language of thought." It is interesting to ask whether a theory like Fodor's is at odds with the principle of psychological autonomy. The answer, I think, turns on whether the sentences in the language of thought are taken to have truth values, and whether their referring expressions are taken to determine a referent in a given world, independent of the head in which they happen to be inscribed. If sentences in the language of thought are taken to be analogous to Quine's eternal sentences, true or false in a given world regardless of who utters them or where they may be inscribed, then Fodor's view will satisfy (i) and (ii) and will run head on into the principle of psychological autonomy. For Fodor, I suspect, this would be argument enough to show that the sentences in the language of thought are not eternal.

NOTES

1. The clearest and most detailed elaboration for this view that I know of is to be found in Goldman (1970). The view is also argued in Brandt and Kim (1963) and Davidson (1963). However, Davidson does not advocate the belief–desire thesis as it will be construed below. Cf. n11.

2. Cf. Putnam (1973) and (1975).

3. Kim. (1978).

4. Kim's account of supervenience is intentionally noncommittal on the sort of necessity invoked in the definition. Different notions of necessity will yield different, though parallel, concepts of supervenience.

5. This weaker principle is discussed at some length in Kim (forthcoming, a).

6. Note, however, that physical properties that are irrelevant in this sense may nonetheless be *causally* related to those physical properties upon which psychological properties supervene. Thus they may be "psychologically relevant" in the sense that they may play a role in the explanation of how the organism comes to have some psychological property.

7. Kim (1978).

8. It has been my experience that psychologists who agree on little else readily endorse the autonomy principle. Indeed, I have yet to find a psychologist who did not take the principle to be obviously true. Some of these same psychologists also

favored the sort of belief–desire explanations of action that I will later argue are at odds with the autonomy principle. None, however, were aware of the incompatibility, and a number of them vigorously resisted the contention that the incompatibility is there.

9. For a critique of these views, cf. Goldman (1970), Chapter 3; Alston (1976b).

10. For discussion of these matters, see Kim (1973). Kim defends the view that the property invoked in the description must be identical with the one invoked in the law. For a much more liberal view see Davidson (1967).

11. Thus Davidson is not an advocate of the belief–desire thesis as I am construing it. For on his view, though beliefs and desires may be among the causes of actions, the general laws supporting the causal claims are not themselves couched in terms of beliefs and desires. Cf. Davidson (1970). But Davidson's view, though not without interest, is plainly idiosyncratic. Generally, philosophers who hold that beliefs and desires are among the causes of behavior also think that there are psychological laws to be found (most likely probabilistic ones) which are stated in terms of beliefs and desires. Cf., for example, Hempel (1965), pp. 463–87; Alston (1967,a) and (1967,b); Goldman (1970), chaps. 3 and 4.

We should also note that much of recent psychology can be viewed as a quest for psychological laws couched in terms of beliefs and/or desires. There is, for example, an enormous and varied literature on problem solving (cf. Newell & Simon [1972]) and on informal inference (cf. Nisbett & Ross [forthcoming]) which explores the mechanisms and environmental determinants of belief formation. Also, much of the literature on motivation is concerned with uncovering the laws governing the formation and strength of desires. Cf. Atkinson (1964).

12. For an attempt to explicate our informal concepts of belief and desire in some detail, see Stich (in preparation).

13. For more on this way of viewing states and events, cf. Kim (1969) and (1976). I think that most everything I say in this paper can be said as well, though not as briefly, without presupposing this account of states and events.

14. The examples in Case 1 and Case 2, along with my thinking on these matters, have been influenced by a pair of important papers by Castañeda (1966) and (1967).

15. Putnam (1973) and (1975).

16. We should note that this example and others invoking natural kind words work only if the extension of my ancestor's word 'water' is different from the extension of the word 'water' as used by my ancestor's doppelganger. I am inclined to agree with Putnam that the extensions are different. But the matter is controversial. For some support of Putnam's view, cf. Kripke (1972) and Teller (forthcoming); for an opposing view cf. Zemach (1976). Incidentally, one critic has expressed doubt that my doppelganger and I could be physically identical if the stuff called 'water' on the far off planet is actually XYZ. Those who find the point troubling are urged to construct a parallel example using kinds of material not generally occurring within people.

17. The idea that de dicto beliefs are psychologically more basic is widespread. For a particularly clear example, cf. Armstrong (1973), pp. 25–31. Of the various attempts to analyze de re beliefs in terms of de dicto beliefs, perhaps the best known are to be found in Kaplan (1968) and Chisholm (1976).

18. The substitutional account of the de re/de dicto dis-

tinction has a curious consequence that has been little noted. Though most belief sentences of the form

S believes that Fa

can be used to make either de re or de dicto attributions, the substitutional account entails that some can only be used to make de re attributions. Consider, for example,

(i) Quine believes that the Queen of England is a turtle.

The claim of course, is false. Indeed, it is *so* false that it could not be used to make a de dicto belief attribution. For in all likelihood, there is *no* name or definite description ϕ denoting Elizabeth II such that

Quine believes that ϕ is a turtle

is true. Thus 'Quine believes that the Queen of England is a turtle' is false and cannot be turned into a truth by the replacement of 'the Queen of England' by a codesignating expression. So on the substitutional account, this sentence can be used to make only de re attributions. A parallel problem besets Quine's well known substitutional account of a *purely referential position* (Quine [1960], pp. 142 ff.). In (i), the position occupied by 'the Queen of England' can only be regarded as purely referential.

19. For more on the distinction between "real" relations and mere "satisfaction" relations, cf. Kim (forthcoming).

20. Burge (1977), pp. 345 and 346; last emphasis added.

21. For more on this "double duty" view of the role of names and descriptions in content sentences, cf. Loar (1972).

22. Of course when the notion of a "real relation" has been suitably sharpened it might well turn out that the autonomous/non-autonomous distinction coincides with the "real relation" version of the de dicto/de re distinction.

23. For example, when I say, "I believe that Kripke was born in Nebraska," I am attributing to myself a belief which is substitutionally de dicto, but not autonomous.

24. Kaplan's strategy, for example, will be of no help, since his analysans are, for the most part, non-autonomous substitutionally de dicto belief sentences. Cf. Kaplan (1968) and Burge (1977), pp. 350, ff.

25. I am indebted to Robert Cummins, Jaegwon Kim, William Alston, and John Bennett for their helpful comments on the topics discussed in this paper.

26. After completing this paper, I was delighted to discover a very similar view in Perry (1979). Fodor (forthcoming) defends a version of the principle of psychological autonomy.

REFERENCES

Alston, W. P. (1967, a). "Motives and Motivation," *The Encyclopedia of Philosophy*. New York, 1967.

———— (1967, b). "Wants, Actions and Causal Explanations," in H. N. Castañeda, ed., *Intentionality, Minds and Perception*. Detroit, 1967.

Armstrong, D. M. (1973). *Belief, Truth and Knowledge*. Cambridge, 1973.

Atkinson, J. W. (1964). *An Introduction to Motivation*. New York, 1964.

Brandt, R. B. and Jaegwon Kim (1963). "Wants as Explanations of Actions," *The Journal of Philosophy*, LX, 1963.

Burge, T. (1977). "Belief De Re," *The Journal of Philosophy*, LXXIV, 1977.

Castañeda, H. N. (1966). "'He': A Study in the Logic of Self-Consciousness," *Ratio,* 8, 1966.

——— (1967). "Indicators and Quasi Indicators," *American Philosophical Quarterly,* 4, 1967.

Chisholm, R. (1976). *Person & Object.* LaSalle, Ill., 1976.

Davidson, D. (1963). "Actions, Reasons and Causes," *The Journal of Philosophy,* LX, 1963.

——— (1967). "Causal Relations," *Journal of Philosophy,* LXIV, 1967.

——— (1970). "Mental Events," in L. Foster & J. W. Swanson, eds., *Experience And Theory.* Amherst, 1970.

Fodor, J. (forthcoming). "Methodological Solipsism Considered as a Research Strategy in Cognitive Psychology," to appear in *The Behavioral and Brain Sciences,* vol. 3, no. 7.

Goldman, A. (1970). *A Theory of Human Action.* Englewood Cliffs, 1970.

Hempel, C. G. (1965). *Aspects of Scientific Explanation.* New York, 1965.

Kaplan, D. (1968). "Quantifying In," *Synthese,* 19, 1968.

Kim, J. (1969). "Events and Their Descriptions: Some Considerations," in *Essays in Honor of C. G. Hempel,* ed. by N. Rescher, et al., Dordrecht, Holland, 1969.

——— (1973). "Causation, Nomic Subsumption and the Concept of Event," *Journal of Philosophy,* LXX, 1973.

——— (1976). "Events As Property-Exemplifications," in M. Brand & D. Walton, eds., *Action Theory.* Dordrecht Holland, 1976.

——— (1978). "Supervenience and Nomological Incommensurables." *American Philosophical Quarterly,* 15, 2, April 1978.

——— (forthcoming). "Perception & Reference Without Causality" [*The Journal of Philosophy* LXXIV, 10 (October 1977): 606–620].

Kripke, S. (1972). "Naming and Necessity," in D. Davidson & G. Harman, eds., *Semantics of Natural Language.* Dordrecht, Holland, 1972.

Loar, B. (1972). "Reference and Propositional Attitudes," *Philosophical Review,* LXXX, 1972.

Newell, A. and H. A. Simon (1972). *Human Problem Solving.* Englewood Cliffs, 1972.

Nisbett, R. and L. Ross (forthcoming) [*Human Inference: Strategies and Shortcomings of Social Judgment.* Englewood-Cliffs, 1980].

Putnam, H. (1973). "Meaning and Reference," *The Journal of Philosophy,* LXX, 1973.

——— (1975). "The Meaning of Meaning," in K. Gunderson, ed., *Language, Mind and Knowledge.* Minneapolis, 1975.

Perry, J. (1979). "The Problem of The Essential Indexical," to appear in NOUS, Vol. XIII.

Quine, W.V.O. (1960). *Word and Object.* Cambridge, 1960.

Stich, S. (in preparation) [*From Folk Psychology to Cognitive Science: The Case Against Belief* (Cambridge, MA: MIT Press/Bradford Books, 1983].

Teller, P. (forthcoming). "Indicative Introduction."

Zemach, E. (1976). "Putnam's Theory on the Reference of Substance Terms," *The Journal of Philosophy,* LXXXIII, 1976.

61

Paul M. Churchland

"Eliminative Materialism and the Propositional Attitudes"*

Eliminative materialism is the thesis that our common-sense conception of psychological phenomena constitutes a radically false theory, a theory so fundamentally defective that both the principles and the ontology of that theory will eventually be displaced, rather than smoothly reduced, by completed neuroscience. Our mutual understanding and even our introspection may then be reconstituted within the conceptual framework of completed neuroscience, a theory we may expect to be more powerful by far than the common-sense psychology it displaces, and more substantially integrated within physical science generally. My purpose in this paper is to explore these projections, especially as they bear on (1) the principal elements of common-sense psychology: the propositional attitudes (beliefs, desires, etc.), and (2) the conception of rationality in which these elements figure.

This focus represents a change in the fortunes of materialism. Twenty years ago, emotions, qualia, and "raw feels" were held to be the principal stumbling blocks for the materialist program. With these barriers dissolving,[1] the locus of opposition has shifted. Now it is the realm of the intentional, the realm of the propositional attitude, that is most commonly held up as being both irreducible to and ineliminable in favor of anything from within a materialist framework. Whether and why this is so, we must examine.

Such an examination will make little sense, however, unless it is first appreciated that the relevant network of common-sense concepts does indeed constitute an empirical theory, with all the functions, virtues, *and perils* entailed by that status. I shall therefore begin with a brief sketch of this view and a summary rehearsal of its rationale. The resistance it encounters still surprises me. After all, common sense has yielded up many theories. Recall the view that space has a preferred direction in which all things fall; that weight is an intrinsic feature of a body; that a force-free moving object will promptly return to rest; that the sphere of the heavens turns daily; and so on. These examples are clear, perhaps, but people seem willing to concede a theoretical component within common sense only if (1) the theory and the common sense involved are safely located in antiquity, and (2) the relevant theory is now so clearly false that its speculative nature is inescapable. Theories are indeed easier to discern under these circumstances. But the vision of hindsight is always 20/20. Let us aspire to some foresight for a change.

I. Why Folk Psychology Is a Theory

Seeing our common-sense conceptual framework for mental phenomena as a theory brings a simple and unifying organization to most of the major topics in the philosophy of mind, including the explanation and prediction of behavior, the semantics of mental predicates, action theory, the other-minds problem, the intentionality of mental states, the nature of introspection, and the mind-body problem. Any view that can pull this lot together deserves careful consideration.

*An earlier draft of this paper was presented at the University of Ottawa, and to the *Brain, Mind, and Person* colloquium at SUNY/Oswego. My thanks for the suggestions and criticisms that have informed the present version.

From *The Journal of Philosophy* LXXVIII, 2 (February 1981): 67–90. Reprinted with permission of the editors and Paul M. Churchland.

Let us begin with the explanation of human (and animal) behavior. The fact is that the average person is able to explain, and even predict, the behavior of other persons with a facility and success that is remarkable. Such explanations and predictions standardly make reference to the desires, beliefs, fears, intentions, perceptions, and so forth, to which the agents are presumed subject. But explanations presuppose laws—rough and ready ones, at least—that connect the explanatory conditions with the behavior explained. The same is true for the making of predictions, and for the justification of subjunctive and counterfactual conditional concerning behavior. Reassuringly, a rich network of common-sense laws can indeed be reconstructed from this quotidean commerce of explanation and anticipation; its principles are familiar homilies; and their sundry functions are transparent. Each of us understands others, as well as we do, because we share a tacit command of an integrated body of lore concerning the lawlike relations holding among external circumstances, internal states, and overt behavior. Given its nature and functions, this body of lore may quite aptly be called "folk psychology."[2]

This approach entails that the semantics of the terms in our familiar mentalistic vocabularly is to be understood in the same manner as the semantics of theoretical terms generally: the meaning of any theoretical term is fixed or constituted by the network of laws in which it figures. (This position is quite distinct from logical behaviorism. We deny that the relevant laws are analytic, and it is the lawlike connections generally that carry the semantic weight, not just the connections with overt behavior. But this view does account for what little plausibility logical behaviorism did enjoy.)

More importantly, the recognition that folk psychology is a theory provides a simple and decisive solution to an old skeptical problem, the problem of other minds. The problematic conviction that another individual is the subject of certain mental states is not inferred deductively from his behavior, nor is it inferred by inductive analogy from the perilously isolated instance of one's own case. Rather, that conviction is a singular *explanatory hypothesis* of a perfectly straightforward kind. Its function, in conjunction with the background laws of folk psychology, is to provide explanations/predictions/understanding of the individual's continuing behavior, and it is credible to the degree that it is successful in this regard over competing hypotheses. In the main, such hypotheses are successful, and so the belief that others enjoy the internal states comprehended by folk psychology is a reasonable belief.

Knowledge of other minds thus has no essential dependence on knowledge of one's own mind. Applying the principles of our folk psychology to our behavior, a Martian could justly ascribe to us the familiar run of mental states, even though his own psychology were very different from ours. He would not, therefore, be "generalizing from his own case."

As well, introspective judgments about one's own case turn out not to have any special status or integrity anyway. On the present view, an introspective judgment is just an instance of an acquired habit of conceptual response to one's internal states, and the integrity of any particular response is always contingent on the integrity of the acquired conceptual framework (theory) in which the response is framed. Accordingly, one's *introspective* certainty that one's mind is the seat of beliefs and desires may be as badly misplaced as was the classical mans's *visual* certainty that the star-flecked sphere of the heavens turns daily.

Another conundrum is the intentionality of mental states. The "propositional attitudes," as Russell called them, form the systematic core of folk psychology; and their uniqueness and anomalous logical properties have inspired some to see here a fundamental contrast with anything that mere physical phenomena might conceivably display. The key to this matter lies again in the theoretical nature of folk psychology. The intentionality of mental states here emerges not as a mystery of nature, but as a structural feature of the concepts of folk psychology. Ironically, those same structural features reveal the very close affinity that folk psychology bears to theories in the physical sciences. Let me try to explain.

Consider the large variety of what might be called "numerical attitudes" appearing in the conceptual framework of physical science: '. . . has a $mass_{kg}$ of n', '. . . has a velocity of n', '. . . has a $temperature_K$ of n', and so forth. These expressions are predicate-forming expressions: when one substitutes a singular term for a number into the place held by 'n', a determinate predicate results. More interestingly, the relations between the various "numerical attitudes" that result are precisely the relations between the numbers "contained" in those attitudes. More interesting still, the argument place that takes the singular terms for numbers is open to quantification. All this permits the expression of generalizations concerning the lawlike relations that hold between the various numerical attitudes in nature. Such laws involve quantification over numbers, and they exploit the mathematical relations holding in that domain.

Thus, for example,

(1) (x) (f) (m) $[((x$ has a mass of $m)$ & $(x$ suffers a net force of $f))$ ⊃ $(x$ accelerates at $f/m)]$

Consider now the large variety of propositional attitudes: '. . . believes that p', '. . . desires that p', '. . . fears that p', '. . . is happy that p', etc. These expressions are predicate–forming expressions also. When one substitutes a singular term for a proposition into the place held by 'p', a determinate predicate results, e.g., '. . . believes that Tom is tall.' (Sentences do not generally function as singular terms, but it is difficult to escape the idea that when a sentence occurs in the place held by 'p', it is there functioning as or like a singular term. On this, more below.) More interestingly, the relations between the resulting propositional attitudes are characteristically the relations that hold between the propositions "contained" in them, relations such as entailment, equivalence, and mutual inconsistency. More interesting still, the argument place that takes the singular terms for propositions is open to quantification. All this permits the expression of generalizations concerning the lawlike relations that hold among propositional attitudes. Such laws involve quantification over propositions, and they exploit various relations holding in that domain. Thus, for example,

(2) (x) (p) $[(x$ fears that $p)$ ⊃ $(x$ desires that $\sim p)]$

(3) (x) (p) $[(x$ hopes that $p)$ & $(x$ discovers that $p))$ ⊃ $(x$ is pleased that $p)]$

(4) (x) (p) (q) $[((x$ believes that $p)$ & $(x$ believes that (if p then $q)))$ ⊃ (barring confusion, distraction, etc., x believes that $q)]$

(5) (x) (p) (q) $[((x$ desires that $p)$ & $(x$ believes that (if q then $p))$
& $(x$ is able to bring it about that $q))$
⊃ (barring conflicting desires or preferred strategies, x brings it about that $q)]^3$

Not only is folk psychology a theory, it is so obviously a theory that it must be held a major mystery why it has taken until the last half of the twentieth century for philosophers to realize it. The structural features of folk psychology parallel perfectly those of mathematical physics; the only difference lies in the respective domain of abstract entities they exploit—numbers in the case of physics, and propositions in the case of psychology.

Finally, the realization that folk psychology is a theory puts a new light on the mind–body problem. The issue becomes a matter of how the ontology of one theory (folk psychology) is, or is not, going to be related to the ontology of another theory (completed neuroscience); and the major

philosophical positions on the mind–body problem emerge as so many different anticipations of what future research will reveal about the intertheoretic status and integrity of folk psychology.

The identity theorist optimistically expects that folk psychology will be smoothly *reduced* by completed neuroscience, and its ontology preserved by dint of transtheoretic identities. The dualist expects that it will prove irreducible to completed neuroscience, by dint of being a nonredundant description of an autonomous, nonphysical domain of natural phenomena. The functionalist also expects that it will prove irreducible, but on the quite different grounds that the internal economy characterized by folk psychology is not, in the last analysis, a law-governed economy of natural states, but an abstract organization of functional states, an organization instantiable in a variety of quite different material substrates. It is therefore irreducible to the principles peculiar to any of them.

Finally, the eliminative materialist is also pessimistic about the prospects for reduction, but his reason is that folk psychology is a radically inadequate account of our internal activities, too confused and too defective to win survival through intertheoretic reduction. On his view it will simply be displaced by a better theory of those activities.

Which of these fates is the real destiny of folk psychology, we shall attempt to divine presently. For now, the point to keep in mind is that we shall be exploring the fate of a theory, a systematic, corrigible, speculative *theory*.

II. Why Folk Psychology Might (Really) Be False

Given that folk psychology is an empirical theory, it is at least an abstract possibility that its principles are radically false and that its ontology is an illusion. With the exception of eliminative materialism, however, none of the major positions takes this possibility seriously. None of them doubts the basic integrity or truth of folk psychology (hereafter, "FP"), and all of them anticipate a future in which its laws and categories are conserved. This conservatism is not without some foundation. After all, FP does enjoy a substantial amount of explanatory and predictive success. And what better grounds than this for confidence in the integrity of its categories?

What better grounds indeed? Even so, the presumption in FP's favor is spurious, born of innocence and tunnel vision. A more searching examination reveals a different picture. First, we must reckon not only with FP's successes, but with its explanatory failures, and with their extent and seriousness. Second, we must consider the long-term history of FP, its growth, fertility, and currrent promise of future development. And third, we must consider what sorts of theories are *likely* to be true of the etiology of our behavior, given what else we have learned about ourselves in recent history. That is, we must evaluate FP with regard to its coherence and continuity with fertile and well-established theories in adjacent and overlapping domains—with evolutionary theory, biology, and neuroscience, for example—because active coherence with the rest of what we presume to know is perhaps the final measure of any hypothesis.

A serious inventory of this sort reveals a very troubled situation, one which would evoke open skepticism in the case of any theory less familiar and dear to us. Let me sketch some relevant detail. When one centers one's attention not on what FP can explain, but on what it cannot explain or fails even to address, one discovers that there is a very great deal. As examples of central and important mental phenomena that remain largely or wholly mysterious within the framework of FP, consider the nature and dynamics of mental illness, the faculty of creative imagination, or the ground of intelligence differences between individuals. Consider our utter ignorance of the nature and psychological functions of sleep, that curious state in which a third of one's life is spent. Reflect on the common ability to catch an outfield fly ball on the run, or hit a moving car with a snowball. Consider the internal construction of a 3-D visual image from subtle differences in the 2-D array of stimulations in our respective retinas. Consider the rich variety of perceptual illusions, visual and otherwise. Or consider the miracle of memory, with its lightning capacity for relevant retrieval. On these and many other mental phenomena, FP shed negligible light.

One particularly outstanding mystery is the nature of the learning process itself, especially where it involves large–scale conceptual change, and especially as it appears in its pre-linguistic or entirely nonlinguistic form (as in infants and animals), which is by far the most common form in nature. FP is faced with special difficulties here, since its conception of learning as the manipulation and storage of propositional attitudes founders on the fact that how to formulate, manipulate, and store a rich fabric of propositional attitudes is itself something that is learned, and is only one among many acquired cognitive skills. FP would thus appear constitutionally incapable of even addressing this most basic of mysteries.[4]

Failures on such a large scale do not (yet) show that FP is a false theory, but they do move that prospect well into the range of real possibility, and they do show decisively that FP is *at best* a highly superficial theory, a partial and unpenetrating gloss on a deeper and more complex reality. Having reached this opinion, we may be forgiven for exploring the possibility that FP provides a positively misleading sketch of our internal kinematics and dynamics, one whose success is owed more to selective application and forced interpretation on our part than to genuine theoretical insight on FP's part.

A look at the history of FP does little to allay such fears, once raised. The story is one of retreat, infertility, and decadence. The presumed domain of FP used to be much larger than it is now. In primitive cultures, the behavior of most of the elements of nature were understood in intentional terms. The wind could know anger, the moon jealousy, the river generosity, the sea fury, and so forth. These were not metaphors. Sacrifices were made and auguries undertaken to placate or divine the changing passions of the gods. Despite its sterility, this animistic approach to nature has dominated our history, and it is only in the last two or three thousand years that we have restricted FP's literal application to the domain of the higher animals.

Even in this preferred domain, however, both the content and the success of FP have not advanced sensibly in two or three thousand years. The FP of the Greeks is essentially the FP we use today, and we are negligibly better at explaining human behavior in its terms than was Sophocles. This is a very long period of stagnation and infertility for any theory to display, especially when faced with such an enormous backlog of anomalies and mysteries in its own explanatory domain. Perfect theories, perhaps, have no need to evolve. But FP is profoundly imperfect. Its failure to develop its resources and extend its range of success is therefore darkly curious, and one must query the integrity of its basic categories. To use Imre Lakatos' terms, FP is a stagnant or degenerating research program, and has been for millennia.

Explanatory success to date is of course not the only dimension in which a theory can display virtue or promise. A troubled or stagnant theory may merit patience and solicitude on other grounds; for example, on grounds that it is the only theory or theoretical approach that fits well with other theories about adjacent subject matters, or the only one that promises to reduce to or be explained by some established background theory whose domain encompasses the domain of the theory at issue. In sum, it may rate credence because it holds promise of theoretical integration. How does FP rate in this dimension?

It is just here, perhaps, that FP fares poorest of all. If we approach *homo sapiens* from the perspective of natural history and the physical sciences, we can tell a coherent story of his constitution, development, and behavioral capacities which encompasses particle physics, atomic and molecular theory, organic chemistry, evolutionary theory, biology, physiology, and materialistic neuroscience. That story, though still radically incomplete, is already extremely powerful, outperforming FP at many points even in its own domain. And it is deliberately and self-consciously coherent with the rest of our developing world picture. In short, the greatest theoretical synthesis in the history of the human race is currently in our hands, and parts of it already provide searching descriptions and explanations of human sensory input, neural activity, and motor control

But FP is no part of this growing synthesis. Its intentional categories stand magnificently alone, without visible prospect of reduction to that larger corpus. A successful reduction cannot be ruled out, in my view, but FP's explanatory impotence and long stagnation inspire little faith that its categories will find themselves neatly reflected in the framework of neuroscience. On the contrary, one is reminded of how alchemy must have looked as elemental chemistry was taking form, how Aristotelean cosmology must have looked as classical mechanics was being articulated, or how the vitalist conception of life must have looked as organic chemistry marched forward.

In sketching a fair summary of this situation, we must make a special effort to abstract from the fact that FP is a central part of our current *lebenswelt,* and serves as the principal vehicle of our interpersonal commerce. For these facts provide FP with a conceptual inertia that goes far beyond its purely theoretical virtues. Restricting ourselves to this latter dimension, what we must say is that FP suffers explanatory failures on an epic scale, that it has been stagnant for at least twenty-five centuries, and that its categories appear (so far) to be incommensurable with or orthogonal to the categories of the background physical science whose long-term claim to explain human behavior seems undeniable. Any theory that meets this description must be allowed a serious candidate for outright elimination.

We can of course insist on no stronger conclusion at this stage. Nor is it my concern to do so. We are here exploring a possibility, and the facts demand no more, and no less, than it be taken seriously. The distinguishing feature of the eliminative materialist is that he takes it very seriously indeed.

III. Arguments Against Elimination

Thus the basic rationale of eliminative materialism: FP is a theory, and quite probably a false one; let us attempt, therefore to transcend it.

The rationale is clear and simple, but many find it uncompelling. It will be objected that FP is not, strictly speaking, an *empirical* theory; that it is not false, or at least not refutable by empirical considerations; and that it ought not or cannot be transcended in the fashion of a defunct empirical theory. In what follows we shall examine these objections as they flow from the most popular and best-founded of the competing positions in the philosophy of mind: functionalism.

An antipathy toward eliminative materialism arises from two distinct threads running through contemporary functionalism. The first thread concerns the *normative* character of FP, or at least of that central core of FP which treats of the propositional attitudes. FP, some will say, is a characterization of an ideal, or at least praiseworthy mode of internal activity. It outlines not only what it is to have and process beliefs and desires, but also (and inevitably) what it is to be rational in their administration. The ideal laid down by FP may be imperfectly achieved by empirical humans, but this does not impugn FP as a normative characterization. Nor need such failures seriously impugn FP even as a descriptive characterization, for it remains true that our activities can be both usefully and accurately understood as rational *except for* the occasional lapse due to noise, interference, or other breakdown, which defects empirical research may eventually unravel. Accordingly, though neuroscience may usefully augment it, FP has no pressing need to be displaced, even as a descriptive theory; nor could it be replaced, qua normative characterization, by any descriptive theory of neural mechanisms, since rationality is defined over propositional attitudes like beliefs and desires. FP, therefore, is here to stay.

Daniel Dennett has defended a view along these lines.[5] And the view just outlined gives voice to a theme of the property dualists as well. Karl Popper and Joseph Margolis both cite the normative nature of mental and linguistic activity as a bar to their penetration or elimination by any descriptive/materialist theory.[6] I hope to deflate the appeal of such moves below.

The second thread concerns the *abstract* nature of FP. The central claim of functionalism is that the principles of FP characterize our internal states in a fashion that makes no reference to their intrinsic nature or physical constitution. Rather, they are characterized in terms of the network of causal relations they bear to one another, and to sensory circumstances and overt behavior. Given its abstract specification, that internal economy may therefore be realized in a nomically heterogeneous variety of physical systems. All of them may differ, even radically, in their physical constitution, and yet at another level, they will all share the same nature. This view, says Fodor, "is compatible with very strong claims about the ineliminability of mental language from behavioral theories."[7] Given the real possibility of multiple instantiations in heterogeneous physical substrates, we cannot eliminate the functional characterization in favor of any theory peculiar to one such substrate. That would preclude our being able to describe the (abstract) organization that any one instantiation shares with all the other. A functional characterization of our internal states is therefore here to stay.

This second theme, like the first, assigns a faintly stipulative character to FP, as if the onus were on the empirical systems to instantiate faithfully the organization that FP specifies, instead of the onus being on FP to describe faithfully the internal activities of a naturally distinct class of empirical systems. This impression is enhanced by the standard examples used to illustrate the claims of functionalism—mousetraps, valve-lifters, arithmetical calculators, computers, robots, and the like. These are artifacts, constructed to fill a preconceived bill. In such cases, a failure of fit between the physical system and the relevant functional characterization impugns only the former, not the latter. The functional characterization is thus removed from empirical criticism in a way that is most unlike the case of an empirical theory. One prominent functionalist—Hilary Putnam—has argued outright that FP is not a corrigible theory at all.[8] Plainly, if FP is construed on these models, as regularly it is, the question of its empirical integrity is unlikely ever to pose itself, let alone receive a critical answer.

Although fair to some functionalists, the preceding is not entirely fair to Fodor. On his view the aim of psychology is to find the *best* functional characterization of ourselves, and what that is remains an empirical question. As well, his argument for the ineliminability of mental vocabulary from psychology does not pick out current FP in particular as ineliminable. It need claim only that *some* abstract functional characterization must be retained, some articulation or refinement of FP perhaps.

His estimate of eliminative materialism remains low, however. First, it is plain that Fodor thinks there is nothing fundamentally or interestingly wrong with FP. On the contrary, FP's central conception of cognitive activity—as consisting in the manipulation of propositional attitudes—turns up as the central element in Fodor's own theory on the nature of thought *(The Language of Thought, op. cit.)*. And second, there remains the point that, whatever tidying up FP may or may not require, it cannot be displaced by any naturalistic theory of our physical substrate, since it is the abstract functional features of his internal states that make a person, not the chemistry of his substrate.

All of this is appealing. But almost none of it, I think, is right. Functionalism has too long enjoyed its reputation as a daring and *avant garde* position. It needs to be revealed for the short-sighted and reactionary position it is.

IV. The Conservative Nature of Functionalism

A valuable perspective on functionalism can be gained from the following story. To being with, recall the alchemists' theory of inanimate matter. We have here a long and variegated tradition, of course, not a single theory, but our purposes will be served by a gloss.

The alchemists conceived the "inanimate" as entirely continuous with animated matter, in that the sensible and behavioral properties of the various substances are owed to the ensoulment of baser matter by various spirits or essences. These nonmaterial aspects were held to undergo development, just as we find growth and development in the various souls of plants, animals, and humans. The alchemists's peculiar skill lay in knowing how to seed, nourish, and bring to maturity the desired spirits enmattered in the appropriate combinations.

On one orthodoxy, the four fundamental spirits (for "inanimate" matter) were named "mercury," "sulphur," "yellow arsenic," and "sal ammoniac." Each of these spirits was held responsible for a rough but characteristic syndrome of sensible, combinatorial, and causal properties. The spirit mercury, for example, was held responsible for certain features typical of metallic substances—their shininess, liquefiability, and so forth. Sulphur was held responsible for certain residual features typical of metals, and for those displayed by the ores from which running metal could be distilled. Any given metallic substance was a critical orchestration principally of these two spirits. A similar story held for the other two spirits, and among the four of them a certain domain of physical features and transformations was rendered intelligible and controllable.

The degree of control was always limited, of course. Or better, such prediction and control as the alchemists possessed was owed more to the manipulative lore acquired as an apprentice to a master, than to any genuine insight supplied by the theory. The theory followed, more than it dictated, practice. But the theory did supply some rhyme to the practice, and in the absence of a developed alternative it was sufficiently compelling to sustain a long and stubborn tradition.

The tradition had become faded and fragmented by the time the elemental chemistry of Lavoisier and Dalton arose to replace it for good. But let us suppose that it had hung on a little longer—perhaps because the four-spirit orthodoxy had become a thumb-worn part of everyman's common sense—and let us examine the nature of the conflict between the two theories and some possible avenues of resolution.

No doubt the simplest line of resolution, and the one which historically took place, is outright displacement. The dualistic interpretation of the four essences—as immaterial spirits—will appear both feckless and unnecessary given the power of the corpuscularian taxonomy of atomic chemistry. And a reduction of the old taxonomy to the new will appear impossible, given the extent to which the comparatively toothless old theory cross-classifies things relative to the new. Elimination would thus appear the only alternative—*unless* some cunning and determined defender of the alchemical vision has the wit to suggest the following defense.

Being "ensouled by mercury," or "sulphur," or either of the other two so-called spirits, is actually a *functional* state. The first, for example, is defined by the disposition to reflect light, to liquefy under heat, to unite with other matter in the same state, and so forth. And each of these four states is related to the others, in that the syndrome for each varies as a function of which of the other three states is also instantiated in the same substrate. Thus the level of description comprehended by the alchemical vocabulary is abstract: various material substances, suitably "ensouled," can display the features of a metal, for example, or even of gold specifically. For it is the total syndrome of occurrent and causal properties which matters, not the corpuscularian details of the substrate. Alchemy, it is concluded, comprehends a level of organization in reality distinct from and irreducible to the organization found at the level of corpuscularian chemistry.

This view might have had considerable appeal.

After all, it spares alchemists the burden of defending immaterial souls that come and go; it frees them from having to meet the very strong demands of a naturalistic reduction; and it spares them the shock and confusion of outright elimination. Alchemical theory emerges as basically all right! Nor need they appear too obviously stubborn or dogmatic in this. Alchemy as it stands, they concede, may need substantial tidying up, and experience must be our guide. But we need not fear its naturalistic displacement, they remind us, since it is the particular orchestration of the syndromes of occurrent and causal properties which makes a piece of matter gold, not the idiosyncratic details of its corpuscularian substrate. A further circumstance would have made this claim even more plausible. For the fact is, the alchemists *did* know how to make gold, in this relevantly weakened sense of 'gold', and they could do so in a variety of ways. Their "gold" was never as perfect, alas, as the "gold" nurtured in nature's womb, but what mortal can expect to match the skills of nature herself?

What this story shows is that it is at least possible for the constellation of moves, claims, and defenses characteristic of functionalism to constitute an outrage against reason and truth, and to do so with a plausibility that is frightening. Alchemy is a terrible theory, well-deserving of its complete elimination, and the defense of it just explored is reactionary, obfuscatory, retrograde, and wrong. But in historical context, that defense might have seemed wholly sensible, even to reasonable people.

The alchemical example is a deliberately transparent case of what might well be called "the functionalist strategem," and other cases are easy to imagine. A cracking good defense of the phlogiston theory of combustion can also be constructed along these lines. Construe being highly phlogisticated and being dephlogisticated as functional states defined by certain syndromes of causal dispositions; point to the great variety of natural substrates capable of combustion and calxification; claim an irreducible functional integrity for what has proved to lack any natural integrity; and bury the remaining defects under a pledge to contrive improvements. A similar recipe will provide new life for the four humors of medieval medicine, for the vital essence or archeus of pre-modern biology, and so forth.

If its application in these other cases is any guide, the functionalist strategem is a smokescreen for the preservation of error and confusion. Whence derives our assurance that in contemporary journals the same charade is not being played out on behalf of FP? The parallel with the case of alchemy is in all other respects distressingly complete, right down to the parallel between the search for artificial gold and the search for artificial intelligence!

Let me not be misunderstood on this last point. Both aims are worthy aims: thanks to nuclear physics, artificial (but real) gold is finally within our means, if only in submicroscopic quantities; and artificial (but real) intelligence eventually will be. But just as the careful orchestration of superficial syndromes was the wrong way to produce genuine gold, so may the careful orchestrations of superficial syndromes be the wrong way to produce genuine intelligence. Just as with gold, what may be required is that our science penetrate to the underlying *natural* kind that gives rise to the total syndrome directly.

In summary, when confronted with the explanatory impotence, stagnant history, and systematic isolation of the intentional idioms of FP, it is not an adequate or responsive defense to insist that those idioms are abstract, functional, and irreducible in character. For one thing, this same defense could have been mounted with comparable plausibility no matter *what* haywire network of internal states our folklore had ascribed to us. And for another, the defense assumes essentially what is at issue: it assumes that it is the intentional idioms of FP, plus or minus a bit, that express the *important* features shared by all cognitive systems. But they may not. Certainly it is wrong to assume that they do, and then argue against the possibility of a materialistic displacement on grounds that it must descibe matters at a level that is different from the important level. This just begs the questions in favor of the older framework.

Finally, it is very important to point out that eliminative materialism is strictly *consistent* with the claim that the essence of a cognitive system resides in the abstract functional organization of its internal states. The eliminative materialist is not committed to the idea that the correct account of cognition *must* be a naturalistic account, though he may be forgiven for exploring the possibility. What he does hold is that the correct account of cognition, whether functionalistic or naturalistic, will bear about as much resemblance to FP as modern chemistry bears to four-spirit alchemy.

Let us now try to deal with the argument, against eliminative materialism, from the normative dimension of FP. This can be dealt with rather swiftly, I believe.

First, the fact that the regularities ascribed by the intentional core of FP are predicated on certain logical relations among propositions is not by itself grounds for claiming anything essentially normative about FP. To draw a relevant parallel, the fact that the regularities ascribed by the classical gas

law are predicated on arithmetical relations between numbers does not imply anything essentially normative about the classical gas law. And logical relations between propositions are as much an objective matter of abstract fact as are arithmetical relations between numbers. In this respect, the law

(4) $(x)(p)(q)$ [((x believes that p) & (x believes that (if p then q))) $\supset$ (barring confusion, distraction, etc., x believes that q)]

is entirely on a par with the classical gas law

(6) $(x)(P)(V)(\mu)$ [((x has a pressure P) & (x has a volume V) & (x has a quantity μ)) $\supset$ (barring very high pressure or density, x has a temperature of $PV/\mu R$)]

A normative dimension enters only because we happen to *value* most of the patterns ascribed by FP. But we do not value all of them. Consider

(7) $(x)(p)$ [((x desires wtih all his heart that p) & (x learns that $\sim p$)) $\supset$ (barring unusual strength of character, x is shattered that $\sim p$)]

Moreover, and as with normative convictions generally, fresh insight may motivate major changes in what we value.

Second, the laws of FP ascribe to us only a very minimal and truncated rationality, not an ideal rationality as some have suggested. The rationality characterized by the set of all FP laws falls well short of an ideal rationality. This is not surprising. We have no clear or finished conception of ideal rationality anyway; certainly the ordinary man does not. Accordingly, it is just not plausible to suppose that the explanatory failures from which FP suffers are owed primarily to human failure to live up to the ideal standard it provides. Quite to the contrary, the conception of rationality it provides appear limping and superficial, especially when compared with the dialectical complexity of our scientific history, or with the ratiocinative virtuosity displayed by any child.

Third, even if our current conception of rationality—and more generally, of cognitive virtue—is largely constituted within the sentential/propositional framework of FP, there is no guarantee that this framework is adequate to the deeper and more accurate account of cognitive virtue which is clearly needed. Even if we concede the categorial integrity of FP, at least as applied to language-using humans, it remains far from clear that the basic parameters of intellectual virtue are to be found at the categorial level comprehended by the propositional attitudes. After all, language use is something that is learned, by a brain already capable of vigorous cognitive activity; language use is acquired as only one among a great variety of learned manipulative skills; and it is mastered by a brain that evolution has shaped for a great many functions, language use being only the very latest and perhaps the least of them. Against the background of these facts, language use appears as an extremely peripheral activity, as a racially idiosyncratic mode of social interaction which is mastered thanks to the versatility and power of a more basic mode of activity. Why accept then, a theory of cognitive activity that models its elements on the elements of human language? And why assume that the fundamental parameters of intellectual virtue are or can be defined over the elements at this superficial level?

A serious advance in our appreciation of cognitive virtue would thus seem to *require* that we go beyond FP, that we transcend the poverty of FP's conception of rationality by transcending its propositional kinematics entirely, by developing a deeper and more general kinematics of cognitive activity, and by distinguishing within this new framework which of the kinematically possible modes of activity are to be valued and encouraged (as more efficient, reliable, productive, or whatever). Eliminative materialism thus does not imply the end of our normative concerns. It implies only that they will have to be reconstituted at a more revealing level of understanding, the level that a matured neuroscience will provide.

What a theoretically informed future might hold in store for us, we shall now turn to explore. Not because we can foresee matters with any special clarity, but because it is important to try to break the grip on our imagination held by the propositional kinematics of FP. As far as the present section is concerned, we may summarize our conclusions as follows. FP is nothing more and nothing less than a culturally entrenched theory of how we and the higher animals work. It has no special features that make it empirically invulnerable, no unique functions that make it irreplaceable, no special status of any kind whatsoever. We shall turn a skeptical ear then, to any special pleading on its behalf.

V. Beyond Folk Psychology

What might the elimination of FP actually involve—not just the comparatively straightforward idioms for sensation, but the entire apparatus of propsositional attitudes? That depends heavily on what neuroscience might discover, and on our determination to capitalize on it. Here follow three scenarios in which the operative conception of

cognitive activity is progressively divorced from the forms and categories that characterize natural language. If the reader will indulge the lack of actual substance, I shall try to sketch some plausible form.

First suppose that research into the structure and activity of the brain, both fine-grained and global, finally does yield a new kinematics and correlative dynamics for what is now thought of as cognitive activity. The theory is uniform for all terrestrial brains, not just human brains, and it makes suitable conceptual contact with both evolutionary biology and non-equilibrium thermodynamics. It ascribes to us, at any given time, a set or configuration of complex states, which are specified within the theory as figurative "solids" within a four- or five-dimensional phase space. The laws of the theory govern the interaction, motion, and transformation of these "solid" states within that space, and also their relations to whatever sensory and motor transducers the system possesses. As with celestial mechanics, the exact specification of the "solids" involved and the exhaustive accounting of all dynamically relevant adjacent "solids" is not practically possible, for many reasons, but here also it turns out that the obvious approximations we fall back on yield excellent explanations/predictions of internal change and external behavior, at least in the short term. Regarding long-term activity, the theory provides powerful and unifed accounts of the learning process, the nature of mental illness, and variations in character and intelligence across the animal kingdom as well as across individual humans.

Moreover, it provides a straightforward account of "knowledge," as traditionally conceived. According to the new theory, any declarative sentence to which a speaker would give confident assent is merely a one-dimensional *projection*—through the compound lens of Wernicke's and Broca's areas onto the idiosyncratic surface of the speaker's language—a one-dimensional projection of a four- or five-dimensional "solid" that is an element in his true kinematical state. (Recall the shadows on the wall of Plato's cave.) Being projections of that inner reality, such sentences do carry significant information regarding it and are thus fit to function as elements in a communication system. On the other hand, being *sub*dimensional projections, they reflect but a narrow part of the reality projected. They are therefore *un*fit to represent the deeper reality in all its kinematically, dynamically, and even normatively relevant respects. That is to say, a system of propositional attitudes, such as FP, must inevitably fail to capture what is going on here, though it may reflect just enough superficial structure to sustain an alchemylike tradition among folk who lack any better theory. From the perspective of the newer theory, however, it is plain that there simply are no law–governed states of the kind FP postulates. The real laws governing our internal activities are defined over different and much more complex kinematical states and configurations, as are the normative criteria for developmental integrity and intellectual virtue.

A theoretical outcome of the kind just described may fairly be counted as a case of elimination of one theoretical ontology in favor of another, but the success here imagined for systematic neuroscience need not have any sensible effect on common practice. Old ways die hard, and in the absence of some practical necessity, they may not die at all. Even so, it is not inconceivable that some segment of the population, or all of it, should become intimately familiar with the vocabulary required to characterize our kinematical states, learn the laws governing their interactions and behavioral projections, acquire a facility in their first–person ascription, and displace the use of FP altogether, even in the marketplace. The demise of FP's ontology would then be complete.

We may now explore a second and rather more radical possibility. Everyone is familiar with Chomsky's thesis that the human mind or brain contains innately and uniquely the abstract structures for learning and using specifically human natural languages. A competing hypothesis is that our brain does indeed contain innate structures, but that those structures have as their original and still primary function the organization of perceptual experience, the administration of linguistic categories being an acquired and additional function for which evolution has only incidentally suited them.[9] This hypothesis has the advantage of not requiring the evolutionary saltation that Chomsky's view would seem to require, and there are other advantages as well. But these matters need not concern us here. Suppose, for our purposes, that this competing view is true, and consider the following story.

Research into the neural structures that fund the organization and processing of perceptual information reveals that they are capable of administering a great variety of complex tasks, some of them showing a complexity far in excess of that shown by natural langauge. Natural languages, it turns out, exploit only a very elementary portion of the available machinery, the bulk of which serves far more complex activities beyond the ken of the propositional conceptions of FP. The detailed unraveling of what that machinery is and of the capacities it has makes it plain that a form of language far more sophisticated than "natural"

language, though decidedly "alien" in its syntactic and semantic structures, could also be learned and used by our innate systems. Such a novel system of communication, it is quickly realized, could raise the efficiency of information exchange between brains by an order of magnitude, and would enhance epistemic evaluation by a comparable amount, since it would reflect the underlying structure of our cognitive activities in greater detail than does natural language.

Guided by our new understanding of those internal structures, we manage to construct a new system of verbal communication entirely distinct from natural language, with a new and more powerful combinatorial grammar over novel elements forming novel combinations with exotic properties. The compounded strings of this alternative system—call them "übersatzen"—are not evaluated as true or false, nor are the relations between them remotely analogous to the relations of entailment, etc., that hold between sentences. They display a different organization and manifest different virtues.

Once constructed, this "language" proves to be learnable; it has the power projected; and in two generations it has swept the planet. Everyone uses the new system. The syntactic forms and semantic categories of so-called "natural" language disappear entirely. And with them disappear the propositional attitudes of FP, displaced by a more revealing scheme in which (of course) "übersatzenal attitudes" play the leading role. FP again suffers elimination.

This second story, note, illustrates a theme with endless variations. There are possible as many different "folk psychologies" as there are possible differently structured communication systems to serve as models for them.

A third and even stranger possiblity can be outlined as follows. We know that there is considerable lateralization of function between the two cerebral hemispheres, and that the two hemispheres make use of the information they get from each other by way of the great cerebral commissure—the corpus callosum—a giant cable of neurons connecting them. Patients whose commisure has been surgically severed display a variety of behavioral deficits that indicate a loss of access by one hemisphere to information it used to get from the other. However, in people with callosal agenesis (a congenital defect in which the connecting cable is simply absent), there is little or no behavioral deficit, suggesting that the two hemispheres have learned to exploit the information carried in other less direct pathways connecting them through the subcortical regions. This suggests that, even in the normal case, a developing hemisphere *learns* to make use of the information the cerebral commissure deposits at its doorstep. What we have then, in the case of a normal human, is two physically distinct cognitive systems (both capable of independent function) responding in a systematic and learned fashion to exchanged information. And what is especially interesting about this case is the sheer amount of information exchanged. The cable of the commissure consists of ≈ 200 million-neurons,[10] and even if we assume that each of these fibres is capable of one of only two possible states each second (a most conservative estimate), we are looking at a channel whose information capacity is $> 2 \times 10^8$ binary bits/second. Compare this to the < 500 bits/second capacity of spoken English.

Now, if two distinct hemispheres can learn to communicate on so impressive a scale, why shouldn't two distinct brains learn to do it also? This would require an artificial "commissure" of some kind, but let us suppose that we can fashion a workable transducer for implantation at some site in the brain that research reveals to be suitable, a transducer to convert a symphony of neural activity into (say) microwaves radiated from an aerial in the forehead, and to perform the reverse function of converting received microwaves back into neural activation. Connecting it up need not be an insuperable problem. We simply trick the normal processes of dendritic arborization into growing their own myriad connections with the active microsurface of the transducer.

Once the channel is opened between two or more people, they can learn *(learn)* to exchange information and coordinate their behavior with the same intimacy and virtuosity displayed by your own cerebral hemispheres. Think what this might do for hockey teams, and ballet companies, and research teams! If the entire population were thus fitted out, spoken language of any of any kind might well disappear completely, a victim of the "why crawl when you can fly?" principle. Libraries become filled not with books, but with long recordings of exemplary bouts of neural activity. These constitute a growing cultural heritage, an evolving "Third World," to use Karl Popper's terms. But they do not consist of sentences or arguments.

How will such people understand and conceive of other individuals? To this question I can only answer, "In roughly the same fashion that your right hemisphere 'understands' and 'conceives of' your left hemisphere—intimately and efficiently, but not propositionally!"

These speculations, I hope, will evoke the required sense of untapped possibilities, and I shall in any case bring them to a close here. Their function is to make some inroads into the aura of inconceivability that commonly surrounds the idea

that we might reject FP. The felt conceptual strain even finds expression in an argument to the effect that the thesis of eliminative materialism is incoherent since it denies the very conditions presupposed by the assumption that it is meaningful. I shall close with a brief discussion of this very popular move.

As I have received it, the reductio proceeds by pointing out that the statement of eliminative materialism is just a meaningless string of marks or noises, unless that string is the expression of a certain *belief,* and a certain *intention* to communicate, and a *knowlege* of the grammar of the language, and so forth. But if the statement of eliminative materialism is true, then there are no such states to express. The statement at issue would then be a meaningless string of marks or noises. It would therefore *not* be true. Therefore it is not true. Q.E.D.

The difficulty with any nonformal reductio is that the conclusion against the initial assumption is always no better than the material assumptions invoked to reach the incoherent conclusion. In this case the additional assumptions involve a certain theory of meaning, one that presupposes the integrity of FP. But formally speaking, one can as well infer, from the incoherent result, that this theory of meaning is what must be rejected. Given the independent critique of FP leveled earlier, this would even seem the preferred option. But in any case, one cannot simply assume that particular theory of meaning without begging the question at issue, namely, the integrity of FP.

The question-begging nature of this move is most graphically illustrated by the following analogue, which I owe to Patricia Churchland.[11] The issue here, placed in the seventeenth century, is whether there exists such a substance as *vital spirit.* At the time, this substance was held, without significant awareness of real alternatives, to be that which distinguished the animate from the inanimate. Given the monopoly enjoyed by this conception, given the degree to which it was integrated with many of our other conceptions, and given the magnitude of the revisions any serious alternative conception would require, the following refutation of any anti-vitalist claim would be found instantly plausible.

> The anti-vitalist says that there is no such thing as vital spirit. But this claim is self-refuting. The speaker can expect to be taken seriously only if his claim cannot. For if the claim is true, then the speaker does not have vital spirit and must be *dead.* But if he is dead, then his statement is a meaningless string of noises, devoid of reason and truth.

The question-begging nature of this argument does not, I assume, require elaboration. To those moved by the earlier argument, I commend the parallel for examination.

The thesis of this paper may be summarized as follows. The propositional attitudes of folk psychology do not constitute an unbreachable barrier to the advancing tide of neuroscience. On the contrary, the principled displacement of folk psychology is not only richly possible, it represents one of the most intriguing theoretical displacements we can currently imagine.

NOTES

1. See Paul Feyerabend, "Materialism and the Mind-Body Problem," *Review* of *Metaphysics*, XVII.1, 65 (September 1963):49–66; Richard Rorty, "Mind–Body Identity, Privacy, and Categories," *ibid.*, XIX.1, 73 (September 1965): 24–54; and my *Scientific Realism and the Plasticity of Mind* (New York: Cambridge, 1979).

2. We shall examine a handful of these laws presently. For a more comprehensive sampling of the laws of folk psychology, see my *Scientific Realism and Plasticity of Mind, op. cit.*, ch. 4. For a detailed examination of the folk principles that underwrite action explanations in particular, see my "The Logical Character of Action Explanations," *Philosophical Review*, LXXIX, 2 (April 1970): 214–236.

3. Staying within an objectual interpretation of the quantifiers, perhaps the simplest way to make systematic sense of expressions like ⌜*x* believes that *p̄*⌝ and closed sentences formed therefrom is just to construe whatever occurs in the nested position held by '*p*', '*q*', etc. as there having the function of a singular term. Accordingly, the standard connectives, as they occur between terms in that nested position, must be construed as there functioning as operators that form compound singular terms from other singular terms, and not as sentence operators. The compound singular terms so formed denote the appropriate compound propositions. Substitutional quantification will of course underwrite a different interpretation, and there are other approaches as well. Especially appealing is the prosentential approach of Dorothy Grover, Joseph Camp, and Nuel Belnap, "A Prosentential Theory of Truth," *Philosophical Studies*, XXVII, 2 (February 1975): 73–125. But the resolution of these issues is not vital to the present discussion.

4. A possible response here is to insist that the cognitive activity of animals and infants is linguaformal in its elements, structures, and processing right from birth. J. A. Fodor, in *The Language of Thought* (New York: Crowell 1975), has erected a positive theory of thought on the assumption that the innate forms of cognitive activity have precisely the form here denied. For a critique of Fodor's view, see Patricia Churchland, "Fodor on Language Learning," *Synthese*, XXXVIII, 1 (May 1978): 149–159.

5. Most explicitly in "Three Kinds of Intentional Psychology" (forthcoming), but this theme of Dennett's goes all the way back to his "Intentional Systems," *Journal of Philosophy* LXVIII, 4 (Feb. 25, 1971): 87–106; reprinted in his *Brainstorms* (Montgomery, Vt.: Bradford Books, 1978).

6. Popper, *Objective Knowledge* (New York: Oxford, 1972); with J. Eccles, *The Self and Its Brain* (New York: Springer Verlag, 1978). Margolis, *Persons and Minds* (Boston: Reidel, 1978).

7. *Psychological Explanation* (New York: Random House, 1968), p. 116.

8. "Robots: Machines or Artificially Created Life?", *Journal of Philosophy* LXI, 21 (Nov. 12, 1964): 668–691, pp. 675, 681 ff.

9. Richard Gregory defends such a view in "The Grammar of Vision," *Listener*, LXXXIII, 2133 (February 1970): 242–246; reprinted in his *Concepts and Mechanisms of Perception* (London: Duckworth, 1975), pp. 622–629.

10. M. S. Gazzaniga and J. E. LeDoux, *The Integrated Mind* (New York: Plenum Press, 1975).

11. "Is Determinism Self-Refuting?", *Mind*, forthcoming [XC, 357 (January 1981): 99–101].

62

Daniel C. Dennett

"Three Kinds of Intentional Psychology"[1]

1

Suppose you and I both believe that cats eat fish. Exactly what feature must we share for this to be true of us? More generally, recalling Socrates' favourite style of question, what must be in common between things truly ascribed an *intentional* predicate— such as 'wants to visit China' or 'expects noodles for supper'?[2] As Socrates points out, in the *Meno* and elsewhere, such questions are ambiguous or vague in their intent. One can be asking on the one hand for something rather like a definition, or on the other hand for something rather like a theory. (Socrates of course preferred the former sort of answer.) What do all magnets have in common? First answer: they all attract iron. Second answer: they all have such-and-such a microphysical property (a property that explains their capacity to attract iron). In one sense people knew what magnets were—they were things that attracted iron— long before science told them what magnets were. A child learns what the word 'magnet' means not, typically, by learning an explicit definition, but by learning the 'folk physics' of magnets, in which the ordinary term 'magnet' is embedded or implicitly defined as a theoretical term.[3]

Sometimes terms are embedded in more powerful theories, and sometimes they are embedded by explicit definition. What do all chemical elements with the same valence have in common? First answer: they are disposed to combine with other elements in the same integral ratios. Second answer: they all have such-and-such a microphysical property (a property which explains their capacity so to combine). The theory of valences in chemistry was well in hand before its microphysical explanation was known. In one sense chemists knew what valences were before physicists told them.

So what appears in Plato to be a contrast between giving a definition and giving a theory can be viewed as just a special case of the contrast between giving one theoretical answer and giving another, more 'reductive' theoretical answer. Fodor (1975) draws the same contrast between 'conceptual' and 'causal' answers to such questions, and argues that Ryle (1949) champions conceptual answers at the expense of causal answers, wrongly supposing them to be in conflict. There is justice in Fodor's charge against Ryle, for there are certainly many passages in which Ryle seems to propose his conceptual answers as a bulwark against the possibility of *any* causal, scientific, psychological answers, but there is a better view of Ryle's (or perhaps at best a view he ought to have held) that deserves rehabilitation. Ryle's 'logical behaviourism' is composed of his steadfastly conceptual answers to the Socratic questions about matters mental. If Ryle thought these answers ruled out psychology, ruled out causal (or reductive) answers to the Socratic questions, he was wrong, but if he thought only that the conceptual answers to the questions were not to be given by a microreductive psychology, he was on firmer ground. It is one thing to give a causal explanation of some phenomenon and quite another to cite the cause of a phenomenon in the analysis of the concept of it.

Some concepts have what might be called an essential causal element.[4] For instance, the concept of a genuine Winston Churchill *autograph* has it that how the trail of ink was in fact caused is essential to its status as an autograph. Photocopies, forgeries, inadvertently indistinguishable signatures—but perhaps not carbon copies—are ruled

From *Reduction, Time and Reality: Studies in the Philosophy of the Natural Sciences*, Richard Healey, ed. pp. 37–60. Copyright © 1975 by Cambridge University Press. Reprinted with permission of the publisher and Daniel C. Dennett.

out. These considerations are part of the *conceptual* answer to the Socratic question about autographs.

Now some, including Fodor, have held that such concepts as the concept of intelligent action also have an essential causal element; behaviour that appeared to be intelligent might be shown not to be by being shown to have the wrong sort of cause. Against such positions Ryle can argue that even if it is true that every instance of intelligent behaviour is caused (and hence has a causal explanation), exactly *how* it is caused is inessential to its being intelligent—something that could be true even if all intelligent behaviour exhibited in fact some common pattern of causation. That is, Ryle can plausibly claim that no account in causal terms could capture the class of intelligent actions except *per accidens*. In aid of such a position—for which there is much to be said in spite of the current infatuation with causal theories—Ryle can make claims of the sort Fodor disparages ('it's not the mental activity that makes the clowning clever because what makes the clowning clever is such facts as that it took place out where the children can see it') without committing the error of supposing causal and conceptual answers are incompatible.[5]

Ryle's logical behaviourism was in fact tainted by a groundless anti-scientific bias, but it need not have been. Note that the introduction of the concept of valence in chemistry was a bit of *logical chemical behaviourism:* to have valence *n* was 'by definition' to be disposed to behave in such-and-such ways under such-and-such conditions, *however* that disposition to behave might someday be explained by physics. In this particular instance the relation between the chemical theory and the physical theory is now well charted and understood—even if in the throes of ideology people sometimes misdescribe it—and the explanation of those dispositional combinatorial properties by physics is a prime example of the sort of success in science that inspires reductionist doctrines. Chemistry has been shown to reduce, in some sense, to physics, and this is clearly a Good Thing, the sort of thing we should try for more of.

Such progress invites the prospect of a parallel development in psychology. First we will answer the question 'What do all believers–that–*p* have in common?' the first way, the 'conceptual' way, and then see if we can go on to 'reduce' the theory that emerges in our first answer to something else—neurophysiology most likely. Many theorists seem to take it for granted that *some* such reduction is both possible and desirable, and perhaps even inevitable, even while recent critics of reductionism, such as Putnam and Fodor, have warned us of the excesses of 'classical' reductionist creeds. No one today hopes to conduct the psychology of the future in the vocabulary of the neurophysiologist, let alone that of the physicist, and principled ways of relaxing the classical 'rules' of reduction have been proposed. The issue, then, is *what kind* of theoretical bonds can we expect—or ought we to hope—to find uniting psychological claims about beliefs, desires, and so forth with the claims of neurophysiologists, biologists and other physical scientists?

Since the terms 'belief' and 'desire' and their kin are parts of ordinary language, like 'magnet', rather than technical terms like 'valence', we must first look to 'folk psychology' to see what kind of things we are being asked to explain. *What do we learn beliefs are when we learn how to use the words 'believe' and 'belief'?* The first point to make is that we do not really learn what beliefs are when we learn how to use these words.[6] Certainly no one *tells us* what beliefs are, or if someone does, or if we happen to speculate on the topic on our own, the answer we come to, wise or foolish, will figure only weakly in our habits of thought about what people believe. We learn to *use* folk psychology—as a vernacular social technology, a craft—but we don't learn it self-consciously as a theory—we learn no meta-theory with the theory—and in this regard our knowledge of folk psychology is like our knowledge of the grammar of our native tongue. This fact does not make our knowledge of folk psychology entirely unlike human knowledge of explicit academic theories, however; one could probably be a good practising chemist and yet find it embarrassingly difficult to produce a satisfactory textbook definition of a metal or an ion.

There are no introductory textbooks of folk psychology (although Ryle's *The Concept of Mind* might be pressed into service), but many explorations of the field have been undertaken by ordinary language philosophers (under slightly different intentions), and more recently by more theoretically minded philosophers of mind, and from all this work an account of folk psychology—part truism and the rest controversy—can be gleaned. What are beliefs? *Roughly,* folk psychology has it that *beliefs* are information-bearing states of people that arise from perceptions, and which, together with appropriately related *desires,* lead to intelligent *action.* That much is relatively uncontroversial, but does folk psychology also have it that non-human animals have beliefs? If so, what is the role of language in belief? Are beliefs constructed of parts? If so, what are the parts? Ideas? Concepts? Words? Pictures? Are beliefs like speech acts or maps or instruction manuals or sentences? Is it implicit in folk psychology that beliefs enter into causal relations, or that they don't? How do decisions and intentions intervene between belief–desire complexes and actions? Are beliefs introspectible, and if so, what authority do the believer's pronouncements have?

All these questions deserve answers, but one must bear in mind that there are different reasons for being interested in the details of folk psychology. One reason is that it exists as a phenomenon, like a religion or a language or a dress code, to be studied with the techniques and attitudes of anthropology. It may be a myth, but it is a myth we live in, so it is an 'important' phenomenon in nature. A different reason is that it seems to be a *true* theory, by and large, and hence is a candidate— like the folk physics of magnets and unlike the folk science of astrology—for incorporation into science. These different reasons generate different but overlapping investigations. The anthropological question should include in its account of folk psychology whatever folk actually include in their theory, however misguided, incoherent, gratuitous some of it may be.[7] The proto-scientific quest, on the other hand, as an attempt to prepare folk theory for subsequent incorporation into or reduction to the rest of science, should be critical, and should *eliminate* all that is false or ill-founded, however well-entrenched in popular doctrine. (Thales thought that lodestones had souls, we are told. Even if most people agreed, this would be something to eliminate from the folk physics of magnets prior to 'reduction'.) One way of distinguishing the good from the bad, the essential from the gratuitous, in folk theory is to see what must be included in the theory to account for whatever predictive or explanatory success it seems to have in ordinary use. In this way we can criticize as we analyse, and it is even open to us in the end to discard folk psychology if it turns out to be a bad theory, and with it the presumed theoretical entities named therein. If we discard folk psychology as a theory, we would have to replace it with another theory, which while it did violence to many ordinary intuitions would explain the predictive power of the residual folk craft.

We use folk psychology all the time, to explain and predict each other's behaviour; we attribute beliefs and desires to each other with confidence— and quite unself-consciously—and spend a substantial portion of our waking lives formulating the world—not excluding ourselves—in these terms. Folk psychology is about as pervasive a part of our second nature as is our folk physics of middle-sized objects. How good is folk psychology? If we concentrate on its weaknesses we will notice that we often are unable to make sense of particular bits of human behaviour (our own included) in terms of belief and desire, even in retrospect; we

often cannot predict accurately or reliably what a person will do or when; we often can find no resources within the theory for settling disagreements about particular attributions of belief or desire. If we concentrate on its strengths we find first that there are large areas in which it is extraordinarily reliable in its predictive power. Every time we venture out on a highway, for example, we stake our lives on the reliability of our general expectations about the perceptual beliefs, normal desires and decision proclivities of the other motorists. Second, we find that it is a theory of great generative power and efficiency. For instance, watching a film with a highly original and unstereotypical plot, we see the hero smile at the villain and we all swiftly and effortlessly arrive at the same complex theoretical diagnosis: 'Aha!' we conclude (but perhaps not consciously), 'he wants her to think he doesn't know she intends to defraud his brother!' Third, we find that even small children pick up facility with the theory at a time when they have a very limited experience of human activity from which to induce a theory. Fourth, we find that we all use folk psychology knowing next to nothing about what actually happens inside people's skulls. 'Use your head' we are told, and we know some people are brainier than others, but our capacity to use folk psychology is quite unaffected by ignorance about brain processes—or even by large-scale misinformation about brain processes.

As many philosophers have observed, a feature of folk psychology that sets it apart from both folk physics and the academic physical sciences is the fact that explanations of actions citing beliefs and desires normally not only describe the provenance of the actions, but at the same time defend them as reasonable under the circumstances. They are reason-giving explanations, which make an ineliminable allusion to the rationality of the agent. Primarily for this reason, but also because of the pattern of strengths and weaknesses just described, I suggest that folk psychology might best be viewed as a rationalistic calculus of interpretation and prediction—an idealizing, abstract, instrumentalistic interpretation-method that has evolved because it works, and works because we have evolved. We approach each other as *intentional systems*,[8] that is, as entities whose behaviour can be predicted by the method of attributing beliefs, desires and rational acumen according to the following rough and ready principles:[9]

(1) A system's beliefs are those it *ought to have,* given its perceptual capacities, its epistemic needs, and its biography. Thus, in general, its beliefs are both true and relevant to its

life, and when false beliefs are attributed, special stories must be told to explain how the error resulted from the presence of features in the environment that are deceptive relative to the perceptual capacities of the system.

(2) A system's desires are those it *ought to have,* given its biological needs and the most practicable means of satisfying them. Thus intentional systems desire survival and procreation, and hence desire food, security, health, sex, wealth, power, influence, and so forth, and also whatever local arrangements tend (in their eyes—given their beliefs) to further these ends in appropriate measure. Again, 'abnormal' desires are attributable if special stories can be told.

(3) A system's behaviour will consist of those acts that *it would be rational* for an agent with those beliefs and desires to perform.

In (1) and (2) 'ought to have' means 'would have if it were *ideally* ensconced in its environmental niche'. Thus all dangers and vicissitudes in its environment it will *recognize as such* (i.e. *believe* to be dangers) and all the benefits—relative to its needs, of course—it will *desire.* When a fact about its surroundings is particularly relevant to its current projects (which themselves will be the projects such a being ought to have in order to get ahead in its world) it will *know* that fact, and act accordingly. And so forth and so on. This gives us the notion of an ideal epistemic and conative operator or agent, relativized to a set of needs for survival and procreation and to the environment(s) in which its ancestors have evolved and to which it is adapted. But this notion is still too crude and overstated. For instance, a being may come to have an epistemic need that its perceptual apparatus cannot provide for (suddenly all the green food is poisonous but alas it is colourblind), hence the relativity to perceptual capacities. Moreover, it may or may not have had the occasion to learn from experience about something, so its beliefs are also relative to its biography in this way: it will have learned what it ought to have learned, *viz.* what it had been given evidence for in a form compatible with its cognitive apparatus—providing the evidence was 'relevant' to its project then.

But this is still too crude, for we understand that evolution does not give us a best of all possible worlds, but only a passable jury-rig, so we should look for design shortcuts that in specifiably abnormal circumstances yield false perceptual beliefs, etc. (We are not immune to illusions—which we would be if our perceptual systems were *perfect.*)

To offset the design shortcuts we should also expect design bonuses: circumstances in which the 'cheap' way for nature to design a cognitive system has the side benefit of giving good, reliable results even outside the environment in which the system evolved. Our eyes are well adapted for giving us true beliefs on Mars as well as on Earth—because the cheap solution for our Earth-evolving eyes happens to be a more general solution.[10]

I propose that we can continue the mode of thinking just illustrated *all the way in*—not just for eye-design, but for deliberation-design and belief-design and strategy-concocter-design. In using this optimistic set of assumptions (nature has built us to do things right; look for systems to believe the truth and love the good) we impute no occult powers to epistemic needs, perceptual capacities and biography, but only the powers common sense already imputes to evolution and learning.

In short, we treat each other as if we were rational agents, and this myth—for surely we are not all that rational—works very well because we are *pretty* rational. This single assumption, in combination with home truths about our needs, capacities and typical circumstances, generates both an intentional interpretation of us as believers and desirers and actual predictions of behaviour in great profusion. I am claiming, then, that folk psychology can best be viewed as a sort of logical behaviourism: *what it means* to say that someone believes that *p*, is that that person is disposed to behave in certain ways under certain conditions. What ways under what conditions? The ways it would be rational to behave, given the person's other beliefs and desires. The answer looks in danger of being circular, but consider: an account of what it is for an element to have a particular valence will similarly make ineliminable reference to the valences of other elements. What one is given with valence-talk is a whole system of interlocking attributions, which is saved from vacuity by yielding independently testable predictions.

I have just described in outline a *method* of predicting and explaining the behaviour of people and other intelligent creatures. Let me distinguish two questions about it: (1) is it something we could do and (2) is it something we in fact do? I think the answer to (1) is obviously yes, which is not to say the method will always yield good results. That much one can ascertain by reflection and thought experiment. Moreover, one can recognize that the method is familiar. Although we don't usually use the method self-consciously, we do use it self-consciously on those occasions when we are perplexed by a person's behaviour, and then it often yields satisfactory results. Moreover, the ease and naturalness with which we resort to this self-conscious and deliberate form of problem-solving provide some support for the claim that what we are doing on those occasions is not *switching methods* but simply becoming self-conscious and explicit about what we ordinarily accomplish tacitly or unconsciously.

No other view of folk psychology, I think, can explain the fact that we do so well predicting each other's behaviour on such slender and peripheral evidence; treating each other as intentional systems works (to the extent that it does) because we really are well designed by evolution and hence we *approximate* to the ideal version of ourselves exploited to yield the predictions. But not only does evolution not guarantee that we will always do what is rational; it guarantees that we won't. If we are designed by evolution, then we are almost certainly nothing more than a bag of tricks, patched together by a *satisficing*[11] Nature, and no better than our ancestors had to be to get by. Moreover, the demands of nature and the demands of a logic course are not the same. Sometimes—even *normally* in certain circumstances—it pays to jump to conclusions swiftly (and even to forget that you've done so), so by most philosophical measures of rationality (logical consistency, refraining from invalid inference) there has probably been some positive evolutionary pressure in favour of 'irrational' methods.[12]

How rational are we? Recent research in social and cognitive psychology suggests we are *minimally* rational, appallingly ready to leap to conclusions or be swayed by logically irrelevant features of situations,[13] but this jaundiced view is an illusion engendered by the fact that these psychologists are deliberately trying to produce situations that provoke irrational responses—inducing pathology in a system by putting strain on it—and succeeding, being good psychologists. No one would hire a psychologist to prove that people will choose a paid vacation to a week in jail if offered an informed choice. At lease not in the better psychology departments. A more optimistic impression of our rationality is engendered by a review of the difficulties encountered in artificial intelligence research. Even the most sophisticated AI programmes stumble blindly into misinterpretations and misunderstandings that even small children reliably evade without a second thought.[14] From this vantage point we seem marvellously rational.

However rational we are, it is the myth of our rational agenthood that structures and organizes our attributions of belief and desire to others, and that regulates our own deliberations and investigations. We aspire to rationality, and without the myth of our rationality the concepts of belief and desire would be uprooted. Folk psychology, then,

is *idealized* in that it produces its predictions and explanations by calculating in a normative system; it predicts what we *will* believe, desire, and do, by determining what we *ought* to believe, desire, and do.[15]

Folk psychology is *abstract* in that the beliefs and desires it attributes are not—or need not be—presumed to be intervening distinguishable states of an internal behaviour-causing system. (The point will be enlarged upon later.) The role of the concept of belief is like the role of the concept of a centre of gravity, and the calculations that yield the predictions are more like the calculations one performs with a parallelogram of forces than like the calculations one performs with a blueprint of internal levers and cogs.

Folk psychology is thus *instrumentalistic* in a way the most ardent realist should permit: people really do have beliefs and desires, on my version of folk psychology, just the way they really have centres of gravity and the earth has an Equator.[16] Reichenbach distinguished between two sorts of referents for theoretical terms: *illata*—posited theoretical entities—and *abstracta*—calculation-bound entities or logical constructs,[17] Beliefs and desires of folk psychology (but not all mental events and states) are *abstracta*.

This view of folk psychology emerges more clearly in contrast to a diametrically opposed view, each of whose tenets has been held by some philosopher, and at least most of which have been espoused by Fodor:

> Beliefs and desires, just like pains, thoughts, sensations and other episodes, are taken by folk psychology to be real, intervening, internal states or events, in causal interaction, subsumed under covering laws of causal stripe. Folk psychology is not an idealized, rationalistic calculus but a naturalistic, empirical, descriptive theory, imputing causal regularities discovered by extensive induction over experience. To suppose two people share a belief is to suppose them to be ultimately in some structurally similar internal condition, e.g. for them to have the same words of Mentalese written in the functionally relevant places in their brains.

I want to deflect this head-on collision of analyses by taking two steps. First, I am prepared to grant a measure of the claims made by the opposition. *Of course* we don't all sit in the dark in our studies like mad Leibnizians rationalistically excogitating behavioural predictions from pure, idealized concepts of our neighbours, nor do we derive all our readiness to attribute desires from a careful generation of them from the ultimate goal of survival. We may observe that some folks seem to desire cigarettes, or pain, or notoriety (we observe this by hearing them tell us, seeing what they choose, etc.)

and without any conviction that these people, given their circumstances, ought to have these desires, we attribute them anyway. So rationalistic generation of attributions is augmented and even corrected on occasion by empirical generalizations about belief and desire that guide our attributions and are learned more or less inductively. For instance, small children believe in Santa Claus, people are inclined to believe the more self-serving of two interpretations of an event in which they are involved (unless they are depressed), and people can be made to want things they don't need by making them believe that glamorous people like those things. And so forth in familiar profusion. This folklore does not consist in *laws*—even probabilistic laws—but some of it is being turned into science of a sort, e.g. theories of 'hot cognition' and cognitive dissonance. I grant the existence of all this naturalistic generalization, and its role in the normal calculations of folk psychologists—i.e. all of us. People do rely on their own parochial group of neighbours when framing intentional interpretations. That is why people have so much difficulty understanding foreigners—their own beliefs and desires, and those of their neighbours, than they would if they followed my principles of attribution slavishly. Of course this is a perfectly reasonable shortcut for people to take, even when it often leads to bad results. We are in this matter, as in most, satisficers, not optimizers, when it comes to information gathering and theory construction. I would insist, however, that all this empirically obtained lore is laid over a fundamental generative and normative framework that has the features I have described.

My second step away from the conflict I have set up is to recall that the issue is not what folk psychology as found in the field truly is, but what it is at its best, what deserves to be taken seriously and incorporated into science. It is not particularly to the point to argue against me that folk psychology is *in fact* committed to beliefs and desires as distinguishable, causally interacting *illata;* what must be shown is that it ought to be. The latter claim I will deal with in due course. The former claim I *could* concede without embarrassement to my overall project, but I do not concede it, for it seems to me that the evidence is quite strong that our ordinary notion of belief has next to nothing of the concrete in it. Jacques shoots his uncle dead in Trafalgar Square and is apprehended on the spot by Sherlock; Tom reads about it in the *Guardian* and Boris learns of it in *Pravda.* Now Jacques, Sherlock, Tom and Boris have had remarkably *different* experiences—to say nothing of their earlier biographies and future prospects—but there is one thing they share: they all believe that a Frenchman

has committed murder in Trafalgar Square. They did not all *say* this, not even 'to themselves'; *that proposition* did not, we can suppose, 'occur to' any of them, and even if it had, it would have had entirely different import for Jacques, Sherlock, Tom and Boris. Yet they all believe that a Frenchman committed murder in Trafalgar Square. This is a shared property that is, as it were, visible only from one very limited point of view—the point of view of folk psychology. Ordinary folk psychologists have no difficulty imputing such useful but elusive commonalities to people. If they then insist that in doing so they are postulating a similarly structured object, as it were, in each head, this is a gratuitious bit of misplaced concreteness, a regrettable lapse in ideology.

But in any case there is no doubt that folk psychology is a mixed bag, like folk productions generally, and there is no reason in the end not to grant that it is much more complex, variegated (and in danger of incoherence) than my sketch has made it out to be. The *ordinary* notion of belief no doubt does place beliefs somewhere midway between being *illata* and being *abstracta.* What this suggests to me is that the concept of belief found in ordinary understanding, i.e. in folk psychology, is unappealing as a scientific concept. I am reminded of Anaxagoras' strange precursor to atomism: the theory of seeds. There is a portion of everything in everything, he is reputed to have claimed. Every object consists of an infinity of seeds, of all possible varieties. How do you make bread out of flour, yeast and water? Flour contains bread seeds in abundance (but flour seeds predominate—that's what makes it flour), and so do yeast and water, and when these ingredients are mixed together, the bread seeds form a new majority, so bread is what you get. Bread nourishes by containing flesh and blood and bone seeds in addition to its majority of bread seeds. Not good theoretical entities, these seeds, for as a sort of bastardized cross between properties and proper parts they have a penchant for generating vicious regresses, and their identity conditions are problematic to say the least.

Beliefs are rather like that. There seems no comfortable way of avoiding the claim that we have an infinity of beliefs, and common intuition does not give us a stable answer to such puzzles as whether the belief that 3 is greater than 2 is none other than the belief that 2 is less than 3. The obvious response to the challenge of an infinity of beliefs with slippery identity conditions is to suppose these beliefs are not all 'stored separately'; many—in fact *most* if we are really talking about infinity—will be stored *implicitly* in virtue of the *explicit* storage of a few (or a few million)—the *core be-*

liefs.[18] The core beliefs will be 'stored separately', and they look like promising *illata* in contrast to the *virtual* or *implicit* beliefs which look like paradigmatic *abstracta*. But although this might turn out to be the way our brains are organized, I suspect things will be more complicated than this: there is no reason to suppose the core *elements,* the concrete, salient, separately stored representation-tokens (and there must be some such elements in any complex information processing system), will explicitly represent (or *be*) a subset of our *beliefs* at all. That is, if you were to sit down and write out a list of a thousand or so of your paradigmatic beliefs, *all* of them could turn out to be virtual, only implicitly stored or represented, and what was explicitly stored would be information (e.g. about memory addresses, procedures for problem-solving, or recognition, etc.) that was entirely unfamiliar. It would be folly to prejudge this empirical issue by insisting that our core representations of information (whichever they turn out to be) are beliefs *par excellence,* for when the facts are in our intuitions may instead support the contrary view: the least controversial self-attributions of belief may pick out beliefs that from the vantage point of developed cognitive theory are invariably virtual.[19]

In such an eventuality what could we say about the *causal* roles we assign ordinarily to beliefs (e.g. 'Her belief that John knew her secret caused her to blush')? We could say that whatever the core elements were in virtue of which she virtually believed that John knew her secret, they, the core elements, played a direct causal role (somehow) in triggering the blushing response. We would be wise, as this example shows, not to tamper with our *ordinary* catalogue of beliefs (virtual though they might all turn out to be), for these are predictable, readily understandable, manipulable regularities in psychological phenomena in spite of their apparent neutrality with regard to the explicit/implicit (or core/virtual) distinction. What Jacques, Sherlock, Boris and Tom have in common is probably only a virtual belief 'derived' from largely different explicit stores of information in each of them, but virtual or not, it is their sharing of *this* belief that would explain (or permit us to predict) in some imagined circumstances their all taking the same action when given the same new information. ('And now for one million dollars, Tom [Jacques, Sherlock, Boris], answer our jackpot question correctly: has a French citizen ever committed a major crime in London?')

At the same time we want to cling to the equally ordinary notion that beliefs can cause not only actions, but blushes, verbal slips, heart attacks and the like. Much of the debate over whether or not intentional explanations are causal explana-

tions can be bypassed by noting how the core elements, *whatever they may be,* can be cited as playing the causal role, while belief remains virtual. 'Had Tom not believed that p and wanted that q, he would not have done A.' Is this a causal explanation? It is tantamount to this: Tom was in some one of an indefinitely large number of structurally different states of type B that have in common just that each one of them licenses attribution of belief that p and desire that q in virtue of its normal relations with many other states of Tom, and this state, whichever one it was, was causally sufficient, given the 'background conditions' of course, to initiate the intention to perform A, and thereupon A was performed, and had he not been in one of those indefinitely many type B states, he would not have done A. One can call this a causal explanation because it talks about causes, but it is surely as unspecific and unhelpful as a causal explanation can get. It commits itself to there being some causal explanation or other falling within a very broad area (i.e. the intentional interpretation is held to be supervenient on Tom's bodily condition), but its true informativeness and utility in actual prediction lie, not surprisingly, in its assertion that Tom, however his body is currently structured, has a particular set of these elusive intentional properties, beliefs and desires.

The ordinary notion of belief is pulled in two directions. If we want to have *good* theoretical entities, good *illata,* or good logical constructs, good *abstracta,* we will have to jettison some of the ordinary freight of the concepts of belief and desire. So I propose a divorce. Since we seem to have both notions wedded in folk psychology, let's split them apart and create two new theories: one strictly abstract, idealizing, holistic, instrumentalistic—pure intentional system theory—and the other a concrete, micro-theoretical science of the actual realization of those intentional systems—what I will call sub–personal cognitive psychology. By exploring their differences and interrelations, we should be able to tell whether any plausible 'reductions' are in the offing.

2

The first new theory, intentional system theory, is envisaged as a close kin of—and overlapping with—such already existing disciplines as decision theory and game theory, which are similarly abstract, normative and couched in intentional language. It borrows the ordinary terms, 'belief' and 'desire' but gives them a technical meaning within the theory. It is a sort of holistic logical behaviourism because it deals with the prediction and explanation from belief–desire profiles of the actions of whole systems (either alone in environments or in interaction with other intentional systems), but treats the individual realizations of the systems as black boxes. The *subject* of all the intentional attributions is the whole system (the person, the animal, or even the corporation or nation)[20] rather than any of its parts, and individual beliefs and desires are not attributable in isolation, independently of other belief and desire attributions. The latter point distinguishes intentional system theory most clearly from Ryle's logical behaviourism, which took on the impossible burden of characterizing individual beliefs (and other mental states) as particular individual dispositions to outward behaviour.

The theory deals with the 'production' of new beliefs and desires from old, *via* an interaction among old beliefs and desires, features in the environment, and the system's actions, and this creates the illusion that the theory contains naturalistic descriptions of internal processing in the systems the theory is about, when in fact the processing is all in the manipulation of the theory, and consists in updating the intentional characterization of the whole system according to the rules of attribution. An analogous illusion of process would befall a naive student who, when confronted with a parallelogram of forces, supposed that it pictured a mechanical linkage of rods and pivots of some kind instead of being simply a graphic way of representing and plotting the effect of several simultaneously acting forces.

Richard Jeffey (1970), in developing his concept of probability kinematics, has usefully drawn attention to an analogy with the distinction in physics between kinematics and dynamics. In kinematics,

> you talk about the propagation of motions throughout a system in terms of such constraints as rigidity and manner of linkage. It is the physics of position and time, in terms of which you can talk about velocity and acceleration, but not about force and mass. When you talk about forces—*causes* of accelerations—you are in the realm of dynamics (172).

Kinematics provides a simplified and idealized level of abstraction appropriate for many purposes—e.g. for the *initial* design development of a gearbox—but when one must deal with more concrete details of systems—e.g. when the gearbox designer must worry about friction, bending, energetic efficiency and the like—one must switch to dynamics for more detailed and reliable predictions, at the cost of increased complexity and diminished generality. Similarly one can approach the study of belief (and desire and so forth) at a highly abstract level, ignoring problems of realization and simply setting out what the normative demands on the design of a believer are. For instance, one can ask such questions as 'What must a system's epistemic capabilites and propensities be for it to survive in environment A?'[21] or 'What must this system already know in order for it to be able to learn B?' or 'What intentions must this system have in order to mean something by saying something?'[22]

Intentional system theory deals just with the performance specifications of believers while remaining silent on how the systems are to be implemented. In fact this neutrality with regard to implementation is the most useful feature of intentional characterizations. Consider, for instance, the role of intentional characterizations in evolutionary biology. If we are to explain the evolution of complex behavioural capabilities or cognitve talents by natural selection, we must note that it is the intentionally characterized capacity (e.g. the capacity to acquire a belief, a desire, to perform an intentional action) that has survival value, however it happens to be realized as a result of mutation. If a particularly noxious insect makes its appearance in an environment, the birds and bats with a survival advantage will be those that come to believe this insect is not good to eat. In view of the vast differences in neural structure, genetic background and perceptual capacity between birds and bats, it is highly unlikely that this useful trait they may come to share has a common description at any level more concrete or less abstract than intentional system theory. It is not only that the intentional predicate is a projectible predicate in evolutionary theory; since it is more general than its species-specific counterpart predicates (which characterize the successful mutation just in birds, or just in bats), it is preferable. So from the point of view of evolutionary biology, we would not want to 'reduce' all intentional characterizations even if we knew in particular instances what the physiological implementation was.

This level of generality is essential if we want a theory to have anything meaningful and defensible to say about such topics as intelligence in general (as opposed, say, to just human or even terrestrial or natural intelligence), or such grand topics as meaning or reference or representation. Suppose, to pursue a familiar philosophical theme, we are invaded by Martians, and the question arises: do they have beliefs and desires? Are they that much *like us?* According to intentional system theory, if these Martians are smart enough to get here, then they most certainly have beliefs and desires—in the technical sense proprietary to the theory—no matter what their internal structure, and no matter how our folk-psychological intuitions rebel at the thought.

This principled blindness of intentional system theory to internal structure seems to invite the retort:[23] but there has to be *some* explanation of the *success* of intentional prediction of the behaviour of systems. It isn't just magic. It isn't a mere coincidence that one can generate all these *abstracta*, manipulate them *via* some version of practical reasoning, and come up with an action prediction that has a good chance of being true. There must be some way in which the internal processes of the system mirror the complexities of the intentional interpretation, or its success would be a miracle.

Of course. This is all quite true and important. Nothing without a great deal of structural and processing complexity could conceivably realize an intentional system of any interest, and the complexity of the realization will surely bear a striking resemblance to the complexiy of the instrumentalistic interpretation. Similarly, the success of valence theory in chemistry is no coincidence, and people were entirely right to expect that deep microphysical similarities would be discovered between elements with the same valence, and that the structural similarities found would explain the dispositional similarities. But since people and animals are unlike atoms and molecules not only in being the products of a complex evolutionary history, but also in being the products of their individual learning histories, there is no reason to suppose that individual (human) believers that *p*— like individual (carbon) atoms with valence 4— regulate their dispositions with *exactly* the same machinery. Discovering the constraints on design and implementation variation, and demonstrating how particular species and individuals in fact succeed in realizing intentional systems is the job for the third theory: sub-personal cognitive psychology.

3

The task of sub-personal cognitive psychology is to explain something that at first glance seems utterly mysterious and inexplicable. The brain, as intentional system theory and evolutionary biology show us, is a *semantic engine;* its task is to discover what its multifarious inputs *mean,* to discriminate them by their significance and 'act accordingly'.[24] That's what brains *are for.* But the brain, as physiology or plain common sense shows us, is just a *syntactic engine;* all it can do is discriminate its inputs by their structural, temporal, and physical features, and let its entirely mechanical activities be governed by these 'syntactic' features of its inputs. That's all brains *can do.* Now how does the brain manage to get semantics from syntax? How could *any* entity (how could a genius, or an angel, or God) get the semantics of a system from nothing but its syntax? It couldn't. The syntax of a system doesn't determine its semantics. By what alchemy, then, does the brain extract semantically reliable results from syntactically driven operations? It cannot be designed to do an impossible task, but it could be designed to *approximate* the impossible task, to *mimic* the behaviour of the impossible object (the semantic engine) by capitalizing on close (close enough) fortuitous correspondences between structural regularities—of the environment and of its own internal states and operations—and semantic types.

The basic idea is familiar. An animal needs to know when it has satisfied the goal of finding and ingesting food, but it settles for a friction-in-the-throat-followed-by-stretched-stomach detector, a mechanical switch turned on by a relatively simple mechanical condition that *normally* co-occurs with the satisfaction of the animal's 'real' goal. It's not fancy, and can easily be exploited to trick the animal into either eating when it shouldn't or leaving off eating when it shouldn't, but it does well enough by the animal in its normal environment. Or suppose I am monitoring telegraph transmissions and have been asked to intercept all *death threats* (but only death threats in English—to make it 'easy'). I'd like to build a machine to save me the trouble of interpreting semantically every message sent, but how could this be done? No machine could be designed to do the job perfectly, for that would require defining the semantic category *death threat in English* as some tremendously complex feature of strings of alphabetic symbols, and there is utterly no reason to suppose this could be done in a principled way. (If somehow by brute-force inspection and subsequent enumeration we could list all and only the English death threats of, say, less than a thousand characters, we could easily enough build a filter to detect them, but we are looking for a principled, projectible, extendable method.) A really crude device could be made to discriminate all messages containing the symbol strings

...I will kill you ...

or

... you .. die ... unless ...

or

...(for some finite disjunction of likely patterns to be found in English death threats).

This device would have some utility, and further refinements could screen the material that passed this first filter, and so on. An unpromising beginning for constructing a sentence understander, but if you want to get semantics out of syntax (whether the syntax of messages in a natural language or the syntax of afferent neuron impulses), variations on this basic strategy are your only hope.[25] You must put together a bag of tricks and hope nature will be kind enough to let your device get by. Of course some tricks are elegant, and appeal to deep principles of organization, but in the end all one can hope to produce (all natural selection can have produced) are systems that *seem* to discriminate meanings by actually discriminating things (tokens of no doubt wildly disjunctive types) that co-vary reliably with meanings.[26] Evolution has designed our brains not only to do this but to evolve and follow strategies of self-improvement in this activity during their individual lifetimes.[27]

It is the task of sub-personal cognitive psychology to propose and test models of such activity—of pattern recognition or stimulus generalization, concept learning, expectation, learning, goal-directed behaviour, problem-solving—that not only produce a simulacrum of genuine content-sensitivity, but that do this in ways demonstrably like the way people's brains do it, exhibiting the same powers and the same vulnerabilities to deception, overload and confusion. It is here that we will find our good theoretical entities, our useful *illata,* and while some of them may well resemble the familiar entities of folk psychology—beliefs, desires, judgments, decisions—many will certainly not.[28] The only similarity we can be sure of discovering in the *illata* of sub-personal cognitive psychology is the intentionality of their labels.[29] They will be characterized as events with content, bearing information, signalling this and ordering that.

In order to give the *illata* these labels, in order to maintain any intentional interpretation of their operation at all, the theorist must always keep glancing outside the system, to see what normally produces the configuration he is describing, what effects the system's responses normally have on the environment, and what benefit normally accrues to the whole system from this activity. In other words the cognitive psychologist cannot ignore the fact that it is the realization of an intentional system he is studying on pain of abandoning semantic interpretation and hence psychology. On the other hand, progress in sub-personal cognitive psychology will blur the boundaries between it and intentional system theory, knitting them together much as chemistry and physics have been knit together.

The alternative of ignoring the external world and its relations to the internal machinery (what Putnam has called psychology in the narrow sense, or methodological solipsism, and Keith Gunderson lampoons as black world glass box perspectivalism)[30] is not really psychology at all, but just at best abstract neurophysiology—pure internal syntax with no hope of a semantic interpretation. Psychology 'reduced' to neurophysiology in this fashion would not be psychology, for it would not be able to provide an explanation of the regularities it

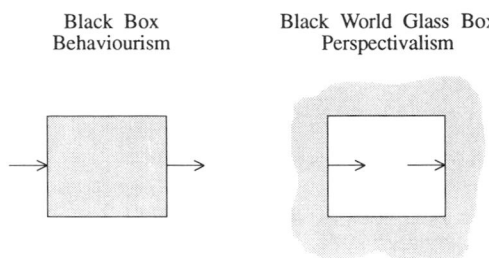

Black Box
Behaviourism

Black World Glass Box
Perspectivalism

is psychology's particular job to explain: the reliability with which 'intelligent' organisms can cope with their environments and thus prolong their lives. Psychology can, and should, work towards an account of the physiological foundations of psychological processes, not by eliminating psychological or intentional characterizations of those processes, but by exhibiting how the brain implements the intentionally characterized performance specifications of sub-personal theories.[31]

Friedman, discussing the current perplexity in cognitive psychology, suggests that the problem

> is the direction of reduction. Contemporary psychology tries to explain *individual* cognitive activity independently from *social* cognitive activity, and then tries to give a *micro* reduction of social cognitive activity—that is, the use of a public language–in terms of a prior theory of individual cognitive activity. The opposing suggestion is that we first look for a theory of social activity, and then try to give a *macro* reduction of individual cognitive activity—the activity of applying concepts, making judgments, and so forth—in terms of our prior social theory.[32]

With the idea of macro-reduction in psychology I largely agree, except that Friedman's identification of the macro level as explicitly *social* is only part of the story. The cognitive capacities of non-language-using animals (and Robinson Crusoes, if there are any) must also be accounted for, and not just in terms of an analogy with the practices of us language users. The macro level *up* to which we should relate micro-processes in the brain in order to understand them as psychological is more broadly the level of organism-environment interaction, development and evolution. That level includes social interaction as a particularly important part,[33] but still a proper part.

There is no way to capture the semantic properties of things (word tokens, diagrams, nerve impulses, brain states) by a micro-reduction. Semantic properties are not just relational but, you might say, superrelational, for the relation a particular vehicle of content, or token, must bear in order to have content is not just a relation it bears to other similar things (e.g. other tokens, or parts of tokens, or sets of tokens, or causes of tokens) but a relation between the token and the whole life—and counter-factual life[34]—of the organism it 'serves' *and* that organism's requirements for survival *and* its evolutionary ancestry.

4

Our three psychologies—folk psychology, intentional system theory, and sub-personal cognitive psychology—what then might reduce to what? Certainly the one-step micro-reduction of folk psychology to physiology alluded to in the slogans of the early identity theorists will never be found—and should never be missed, even by staunch friends of materialism and scientific unity. A prospect worth exploring, though, is that folk psychology (more precisely, the part of folk psychology worth caring about) reduces—conceptually—to intentional system theory. What this would amount to can best be brought out by contrasting this proposed conceptual reduction with more familiar alternatives: 'type–type identity theory' and 'Turing machine functionalism'. According to type–type identity theory, for every mentalistic term or predicate '*M*', there is some predicate '*P*' *expressible in the vocabulary of the physical sciences* such that a creature is *M* if and only if it is *P*. In symbols:

(1) (x) (Mx ≡ Px)

This is reductionism with a vengeance, taking on the burden of replacing, in principle, all mentalistic predicates with co-extensive predicates composed truth-functionally from the predicates of physics. It is now widely agreed to be hopelessly too strong a demand. Believing that cats eat fish is, intuitively, a *functional* state that might be variously implemented physically, so there is no reason to suppose the commonality referred to on the left-hand side of (1) can be reliably picked out by any predicate, however complex, of physics. What

is needed to express the predicate on the right-hand side is, it seems, a physically neutral language for speaking of functions and functional states, and the obvious candidates are the languages used to describe automata—for instance, Turing machine language.

The Turing machine functionalist then proposes

(2) (x) (Mx ≡ x realizes some Turing machine k in logical state A)

In other words, for two things both to believe that cats eat fish they need not be physically similar in any specifiable way, but they must both be in a 'functional' condition specifiable in principle in the most general functional language; they must share a Turing machine description according to which they are both in some particular logical state. This is still a reductionist doctrine, for it proposes to identify each mental type with a functional type picked out in the language of automata theory. But this is still too strong, for there is not more reason to suppose Jacques, Sherlock, Boris and Tom 'have the same programme' in *any* relaxed and abstract sense, considering the differences in their nature and nurture, than that their brains have some crucially identical physico-chemical feature. We must weaken the requirements for the right-hand side of our formula still further.

Consider

(3) (x) (x believes that p ≡ x can be predictively attributed the belief that p)

This appears to be blatantly circular and uninformative, with the language on the right simply mirroring the language on the left. But all we need to make an informative answer of this formula is a systematic way of making the attributions alluded to on the right-hand side. Consider the parallel case of Turing machines. What do two different realizations or embodiments of a Turing machine have in common when they are in the same logical state? Just this: there is a system of description such that according to it both are described as being realizations of some particular Turing machine, and according to this description, which is predictive of the operation of both entities, both are in the same state of that Turing machine's machine table. One doesn't *reduce* Turing machine talk to some more fundamental idiom; one *legitimizes* Turing machine talk by providing it with rules of attribution and exhibiting its predictive powers. If we can similarly legitimize 'mentalistic' talk, we will have no need of a reduction, and that is the point of the concept of an intentional system. Intentional systems are supposed to play a role in the legitimization of mentalistic predicates parallel to the role played by the abstract notion of a Turing machine in setting down rules for the interpretation of artifacts as computational automata. I fear my concept is woefully informal and unsystematic compared with Turing's, but then the domain it attempts to systematize—our everyday attributions in mentalistic or intentional language—is itself something of a mess, at least compared with the clearly defined field of recursive function theory, the domain of Turing machines.

The analogy between the theoretical roles of Turing machines and intentional systems is more than superficial. Consider that warhorse in the philosophy of mind, Brentano's Thesis that intentionality is the mark of the mental: all mental phenomena exhibit intentionality and no physical phenomena exhibit intentionality. This has been traditionally taken to be an *irreducibility* thesis: the mental, in virtue of its intentionality, cannot be reduced to the physical. But given the concept of an intentional system, we can construe the first half of Brentano's Thesis—all mental phenomena are intentional—as a *reductionist* thesis of sorts, parallel to Church's Thesis in the foundation of mathematics.

According to Church's Thesis, every 'effective' procedure in mathematics is recursive, that is, Turing-computable. Church's Thesis is not provable, since it hinges on the intuitive and informal notion of an effective procedure, but it is generally accepted, and it provides a very useful reduction of a fuzzy-but-useful mathematical notion to a crisply defined notion of apparently equal scope and greater power. Analogously, the claim that every mental phenomenon alluded to in folk psychology is *intentional-system-characterizable* would, if true, provide a reduction of the mental as ordinarily understood–a domain whose boundaries are at best fixed by mutual acknowledgment and shared intuition–to a clearly defined domain of entities, whose principles of organization are familiar, relatively formal and systematic, and entirely general.[35]

This reductive claim, like Church's Thesis, cannot be proven, but could be made compelling by piecemeal progress on particular (and particularly difficult) cases—a project I set myself elsewhere (in *Brainstorms*). The final reductive task would be to show not how the terms of intentional system theory are eliminable in favour of physiological terms via sub-personal cognitive psychology, but almost the reverse: to show how a system described in physiological terms could warrant an interpretation as a realized intentional system.

NOTES

1. I am grateful to the Thyssen Philosophy Group, the Bristol Fulbright Workshop, Elliot Sober and Bo Dahlbom for extensive comments and suggestions on an earlier draft of this paper.

2. Other 'mental' predicates, especially those invoking episodic and allegedly *qualia*-laden entities—pains, sensations, images—raise complications of their own which I will not consider here, for I have dealt with them at length elsewhere, especially in *Brainstorms* (1978). I will concentrate here on the foundational concepts of belief and desire, and will often speak just of belief, implying, except where I note it, that parallel considerations apply to desire.

3. The child need learn only a portion of this folk physics, as Putnam argues in his discussion of the 'division of linguistic labour' (1975).

4. Cf. Fodor 1975: 7n.

5. This paragraph corrects a misrepresentation of both Fodor's and Ryle's positions in my critical notice of Fodor's book in *Mind*, 1977, reprinted in *Brainstorms*, pp. 90–108.

6. I think it is just worth noting that philosophers' use of 'believe' as the standard and general ordinary language term is a considerable distortion. We *seldom* talk about what people *believe*; we talk about what they *think* and what they *know*.

7. If the anthropologist marks part of the catalogue of folk theory as false, as an inaccurate or unsound account of the folk craft, he may speak of *false consciousness* or *ideology;* the role of such false theory in constituting a feature of the anthropological phenomenon is not diminished by its falseness.

8. See my 'Intentional Systems' (1971).

9. For a more elaborate version of similar pinciples, see Lewis 1974.

10. Cf. Sober (unpublished) for useful pioneering exploration of these topics.

11. The term is Herbert Simon's (e.g. 1969).

12. While in general true beliefs have to be more useful than false beliefs (and hence a system ought to have true beliefs), in special circumstances it may be better to have a few false beliefs. For instance it might be better for beast B to have some false beliefs about whom B can beat up and whom B can't. Ranking B's likely antagonists from ferocious to pushover, we certainly want B to believe it can't beat up all the ferocious ones, and can beat up all the obvious pushovers, but it is better (because it 'costs less' in discrimination tasks and protects against random perturbations such as bad days and lucky blows) for B to extend 'I can't beat up x' to cover even some beasts it can in fact beat up. *Erring on the side of prudence* is a well recognized good strategy, and so Nature can be expected to have valued it on occasion when it came up. An alternative strategy in this instance would be to abide by the rule: avoid conflict with penumbral cases. But one might have to 'pay more' to implement that strategy than to implement the strategy designed to produce, and rely on, some false beliefs.

13. See, e.g. Tversky and Kahneman 1974; and Nisbett and Ross 1978.

14. Roger Schank's (1977; Schank and Abelson 1977) efforts to get a computer to 'understand' simple but normally gappy stories is a good illustration.

15. It tests its predictions in two ways: action predictions it tests directly by looking to see what the agent does; belief and desire predictions are tested indirectly by employing the predicted attributions in further predictions of eventual action. As usual, the Duhemian thesis holds: belief and desire attributions are under-determined by the available data.

16. Michael Friedman's 'Theoretical Explanation' [*Reduction, Time and Reality,* edited by Richard Healey, (Cambridge: Cambridge University Press, 1981), pp. 1–16] provides an excellent analysis of the role of instrumentalistic thinking within realistic science. Scheffler (1963) provides a useful distinction between *instrumentalism* and *fictionalism.* In his terms I am characterizing folk psychology as instrumentalistic, not fictionalistic.

17. Reichenbach 1938: 211–12. 'Our observations of concrete things confer a certain probability on the existence of *illata*—nothing more . . . Second, there are inferences to *abstracta.* These inferences are . . . equivalences, not probability inferences. Consequently, the existence of abstracta is reducible to the existence of concreta. There is, therefore, no problem of their objective existence; their status depends on a convention.'

18. See my 'Brain Writing and Mind Reading', 1975. See also Fodor 1975, and Field 1978.

19. See Field 1978: 55, n. 12 on 'minor concessions' to such instrumentalistic treatments of belief.

20. See my 'Conditions of Personhood' (1976).

21. Cf. Campbell 1973, and his William James lectures (Harvard U.P., forthcoming).

22. The questions of this variety are familiar, of course, to philosophers, but are now becoming equally familiar to researchers in artificial intelligence.

23. From Ned Block and Jerry Fodor, *inter alia,* in conversation.

24. More accurately if less picturesquely, the brain's task is to come to produce internal mediating responses that reliably vary in concert with variation in the actual environmental significance (the natural and non-natural meanings, in Grice's (1957) sense) of their distal causes and independently of meaning-irrelevant variations in their proximal causes, and moreover to respond to its own mediating responses in ways that systematically tend to improve the creature's prospects in its environment if the mediating responses are varying as they ought to vary.

25. One might think that while *in principle* one cannot derive the semantics of a system from nothing but its syntax, *in practice* one might be able to cheat a little and exploit syntactic features that don't *imply* a semantical interpretation, but strongly suggest one. For instance, faced with the task of deciphering isolated documents in an entirely unknown and alien language, one might note that while the symbol that *looks like* a duck doesn't *have* to mean 'duck', there is a good chance that it does, especially if the symbol that looks like a wolf seems to be eating the symbol that looks like a duck, and not *vice versa.* Call this *hoping for hieroglyphics* and note the form it has taken in psychological theories from Locke to the present: we will be able to tell which mental representations

are which (which idea is the idea of *dog* and which of *cat*) because the former will look like a dog and the latter like a cat. This is all very well as a crutch for us observers on the ouside, trying to assign content to the events in some brain, but it is of no use to the brain . . . because brains don't know what dogs look like! Or better, this cannot be the brain's fundamental method of eking semantic classes out of raw syntax, for any brain (or brain part) that could be said—in an extended sense—to know what dogs look like would be a brain (or brain part) that had already solved its problem, that was already (a simulacrum of) a semantic engine. But this is still misleading, for brains in any event do not *assign* content to their own events in the way observers might: brains *fix* the content of their internal events in the act of reacting as they do. There are good reasons for positing *mental images* of one sort or another in cognitive theories (see 'Two Approaches to Mental Images' in *Brainstorms* pp. 174–89) but hoping for hieroglyphics isn't one of them, though I suspect it is covertly influential.

26. I take this point to be closely related to Davidson's reasons for claiming there can be no psycho-physical laws, but I am unsure that Davidson wants to draw the same conclusions from it that I do. See Davidson 1970.

27. This claim is defended in my 'Why the law of effect will not go away' (1974).

28. See, for instance, Stephen Stich's (1978) concept of subdoxastic states.

29. See my 'Reply to Arbib and Gunderson', in *Brainstorms*, pp. 23–38.

30. In his reply to Fodor's 'Methodological Solipsism as a Research Strategy in Psychology' at the Cincinnati Colloquium on Philosophy of Psychology, February 1978.

31. I treat methodological solipsism in (much) more detail in 'Beyond Belief', in Andrew Woodfield, ed. *Thought and Object.*

32. Michael Friedman, 'Theoretical Explanation,' this volume, pp. 15–16 [see fn. 16].

33. See Tyler Burge 1979.

34. What I mean is this: counterfactuals enter because content is in part a matter of the *normal* or *designed* role of a vehicle whether or not it ever gets to play that role. Cf. Sober (unpublished).

35. Ned Block (1978) presents arguments supposed to show how the various possible functionalist theories of mind all slide into the sins of 'chauvinism' (improperly excluding Martians from the class of possible mind havers) or 'liberalism' (improperly including various contraptions, imagined human puppets, and so forth among the mind-havers). My view embraces the broadest liberalism, gladly paying the price of a few recalcitrant intuitions for the generality gained.

REFERENCES

Block, N. 1978. 'Troubles with functionalism.' *Perception and Cognition: Issues in the Foundations of Psychology,* ed. C. Wade Savage, pp. 261–326. Minnesota Studies in Philosophy of Science, vol. IX. Minneapolis: Minnesota University Press.

Burge, T. 1979. 'Individualism and the mental.' *Midwest Studies in Philosophy,* vol. IV, pp. 73–121.

Campbell, D. 1973. 'Evolutionary epistemology.' *The Philos-*

ophy of Karl Popper, ed. Paul A. Schilpp. La Salle, Illinois: Open Court.

Davidson, D. 1970. 'Mental events.' *Experience and Theory,* ed. L. Foster and J. Swanson, pp. 79–102. Amherst: University of Massachusetts Press.

Dennett, D. C. 1971. 'Intentional systems.' *Journal of Philosophy* 68, 87–106. Reprinted (with other essays on intentional systems) in *Brainstorms,* pp. 3–22.

Dennett, D. C. 1974. 'Why the law of effect will not go away.' *Journal of the Theory of Social Behaviour* 5, 169–187. Reprinted in *Brainstorms,* pp. 71–89.

Dennett, D. C. 1975. 'Brain writing and mind reading.' *Language, Mind and Knowledge,* ed. K. Gunderson. Minnesota Studies in Philosophy of Science, vol. VII. Minneapolis: Minnesota University Press. Reprinted in *Brainstorm,* pp. 39–50.

Dennett, D. C. 1976. 'Conditions of personhood.' *The Identities of Persons,* ed. A. Rorty. Reprinted in *Brainstorms,* pp. 267–85.

Dennett, D. C. 1978. *Brainstorms.* Montgomery, Vermont: Bradford Books; Hassocks, Sussex: Harvester Press.

Field, H. 1978. 'Mental representation.' *Erkenntnis* 13, 9–61.

Fodor, J. 1975. *The Language of Thought.* Hassocks, Sussex: Harvester Press; Scranton, Pa. Crowell.

Grice, H. P. 1957. 'Meaning.' *Philosophical Reivew* 66, 377–88.

Jeffrey, R. 1970. 'Dracula meets Wolfman: acceptance vs. partial belief.' *Induction, Acceptance and Rational Belief,* ed. Marshall Swain. Dordrecht: Reidel.

Lewis, D. 1974. 'Radical interpretation.' *Synthèse* 23, 331–44.

Nisbett, R. E. and Ross, L. D. 1978. *Human Inference: Strategy and Shortcomings.* Englewood Cliffs, N.J.: Prentice Hall.

Putnam, H. 1975. 'The meaning of "meaning".' *Mind, Language and Reality (Philosophical Papers,* vol. II), pp. 215–71. Cambridge: Cambridge University Press.

Reichenbach, H. 1938. *Experience and Prediction.* Chicago: University of Chicago Press.

Ryle, G. 1949. *The Concept of Mind.* London: Hutchinson.

Schank, R. 1977. 'Sam—a story understander.' Research Report 43, Yale University Dept of Computer Science.

Schank, R. and Abelson, R. 1977. *Scripts, Plans, Goals and Understanding.* Hillside, N.J.: Erlbaum.

Scheffler, I. 1963. *The Anatomy of Inquiry.* New York: Knopf.

Simon, H. 1969. *The Sciences of the Artificial.* Cambridge, Mass.: M.I.T. Press.

Sober, E. (unpublished) 'The descent of Mind.'

Stich, S. 1978. 'Belief and subdoxastic states.' *Philosophy of Science* 45, 499–518.

Tversky, A. and Kahneman, D. 1974. 'Judgement under uncertainty: heuristics and biases.' *Science* 185, 1124–31.

Woodfield, A., ed., forthcoming. *Thought and Object.* Oxford: Oxford University Press.

Postscript: "Reflections: Instrumentalism Reconsidered"

"Three Kinds of Intentional Psychology," though written before "True Believers,"* follows it in expository order, since it presupposes somewhat more familiarity with my basic position and deals in more detail with some of the problems. In these Reflections I will concentrate on the problem of my so-called *instrumentalism,* which has occasioned much debate; but before presenting and defending my variety of instrumentalism and distinguishing it from its neighboring alternatives, I will comment briefly on four other themes in "Three Kinds" which cast their shadows ahead into other chapters and other controversies.

(1) What is the rationality presupposed by adoption of the intentional stance? The brief and allusive remarks here are supplemented in detail in the next chapter, "Making Sense of Ourselves."

(2) "The syntax of a system doesn't determine

*["True Believers" occurs as chapter 2 of *The Intentional Stance* (Cambridge, MA: MIT/Bradford, 1987); it is also reprinted in this volume. When not otherwise indicated, chapters and reflections are from *The Intentional Stance.*]

its semantics. By what alchemy, then, does the brain extract semantically reliable results from syntactically driven operations?" This way of putting the issue was echoed by Searle (1980b)—"The computer, to repeat, has a syntax but no semantics,"—and again in (1982):

Actually Dennett couln't have shown how to get from the syntax to the semantics, from form to mental content, because his brand of behaviourism makes it impossible for him to accept the existence of semantics or mental contents literally construed. (p. 57)

This passage makes clear one of Searle's fundamental disagreements with me: while we agree that a computer is a syntactic engine, and hence can only approximate the performance of a semantic engine, he thinks an organic brain is a mechanism that somehow eludes this limitation on computers. He concludes his 1980b paper thus: "Whatever it is that the brain does to produce intentionality, it cannot consist in instantiating a program since no program, by itself, is sufficient for intentionality." Searle and I agree that brains are machines, but he thinks they are very special machines:

> "Could a machine think?" My own view is that *only* a machine could think, and indeed only very special kinds of machines, namely brains and machines that had the same causal powers as brains. (1980b, p. 424)

To me, these conjured causal powers of brains are just the sort of alchemy I was warning against in my rhetorical question. A machine is a machine, and there is nothing about the construction or materials of any subvariety that could permit it to transcend the limits of mechanism and eke out "real semantics" over and above its merely syntactical churning. I pursue this disagreement with Searle in more detail in Chapters 8 and 9.

(3) The suggestion that we can "reduce" the intuitive notion of mentality to the concept of an intentional system, modeled on Turing's reduction of effectiveness to Turing-computability, was first made explicit by me in the Introduction to *Brainstorms*. Searle (1980b) has called this style of thinking about the mind operationalism—a supposedly dirty word in these post-positivist times. But not to me. I make explicit my fundamental sympathy with Turing's vision, and even its reputedly shocking operationalism, in "Can Machines Think?" (1985a).

(4) The distinction between "core" beliefs and virtual or implicit beliefs is treated with more care and detail in "Styles of Mental Representation," but my main point about the distinction was already made in this essay, and in some quarters it has still not sunk in: even if considerations of compositionality or generativity drive us to the conclusion that the brain *has* to be organized into a modest, explicit set of core elements from which "the rest" is generated somehow as needed (Dennett 1975), no reason at all has thereby been given to suppose that any of the core elements will be beliefs rather than some as yet unnamed and unimagined neural data structures of vastly different properties. Those who want to be "realists about beliefs"—in opposition to my instrumentalism, for instance—often respond to my arguments about the inexhaustible supply of beliefs by saying they are realists about the core beliefs only. Some intuit that only the core beliefs are properly speaking beliefs at all (e.g., Goldman 1986, pp. 201–2). What makes them so sure there are any core *beliefs*? I am as staunch a realist as anyone about those core information-storing elements in the brain, whatever they turn out to be, to which our intentional interpretations are anchored. I just doubt (along with the Churchlands, P. M. 1981, 1984; P. S. 1980, 1986) that those elements, once individuated, will be recognizable as the beliefs we

purport to distinguish in folk psychology. In the reflections following chapter 6, I explain why I do not draw the Churchlands' moral from this shared doubt.

Instrumentalism

> I propose to say that someone is a *Realist* about propositional attitudes iff (a) he holds that there are mental states whose occurrences and interactions cause behaviour and do so, moreover, in ways that respect (at least to an approximation) the generalizations of common-sense belief/desire psychology; and (b) he holds that these same causally efficacious mental states are also semantically evaluable. (Fodor 1985, p. 78)

As I said on page 37,* I am a sort of realist, but I am not Fodor's Realist with a capital *R* since I expect that the actual internal states that cause behaviour will not be functionally individuated, even to an approximation, the way belief/desire psychology carves things up. I have let myself be called an instrumentalist for a half-dozen years (so it is my own fault), but I am not at all happy with the guilt-by-association I have thereby acquired. For instance:

> *First Anti-Realist option:* You could take an *instrumentalist* view of intentional explanation.... The great virtue of instrumentalism—here as elsewhere—is that you get all the goodness and suffer none of the pain: you get to use propositional-attitude psychology to make behavioural predictions; you get to "accept" all the intentional explanations that it is convenient to accept; but you don't have to answer hard questions about what the attitudes *are*. (Fodor 1985, p. 79)

Classical instrumentalism was an all-embracing view, a complete rejection of realism; one was instrumentalistic not only about centers of gravity and parallelograms of forces and the Equator, but also about electrons, cells, planets—everything but what could be observed with the naked senses. This embracing instrumentalism did excuse its adherents, as Fodor says, from having to answer certain hard ontological questions, but I have not ducked these interesting questions about beliefs and the other propositional attitudes. From the outset I have maintained a contrast between my realism about brains and their various neurophysiological parts, states, and processes and my "instrumentalism" about the belief-states that appear as *abstracta* when one attempts to interpret all those real phenomena by adopting the intentional

---

*[first page of the reflections to "True Believers," in *The Intentional Stance*]

stance. The distinction I meant to draw is familiar enough and (I think) uncontroversial in other contexts. As Friedman (1981) notes:

> The reduction/representation distinction is not a mere philosopher's invention; it plays a genuine role in scientific practice. Scientists themselves distinguish between aspects of theoretical structure that are intended to be taken literally and aspects that serve a purely representational function. No one believes, for example, that the so-called "state spaces" of mechanics—phase space in classical mechanics and Hilbert space in quantum mechanics—are part of the furniture of the physical world. (p. 4)

My attempt to endorse and exploit this distinction as a variety of *selective* instumentalism was evidently a tactical error, given the confusion it has caused. I should have forsworn the term and just said something like this: My *ism* is whatever *ism* serious realists adopt with regard to centers of gravity and the like, since I think beliefs (and some other mental items drawn from folk psychology) are *like that*—in being *abstracta* rather than part of the "furniture of the physical world" and in being attributed in statements that are *true* only if we exempt them from a certain familiar standard of literality.

Some instrumentalists have endorsed *fictionalsim*, the view that certain theoretical statements are *useful falsehoods*, and others have maintained that the theoretical claims in question *were neither true nor false* but mere instruments of calculation. I defend neither of these varieties of instrumentalism; as I said when first I used the term above: "people really do have beliefs and desires, on my version of folk psychology, just as they really have centers of gravity." Do I then grant that attributions of belief and desire under the adoption of the intentional stance can be *true*? Yes, but you will misunderstand me unless you grant that the following are also true:

(1) The gravitational attraction between the earth and the moon is a force that acts between two points: the two bodies' centers of gravity.

(2) Hand calculators add, subtract, multiply, and divide.

(3) A Vax 11/780 is a universal turing machine.

(4) SHAKEY (the "seeing" robot described in Dennett 1982b) makes line drawings even when its CRT is turned off.

It is arguable that each of these is a useful, oversimplifying falsehood; I would rather say that each is a truth one must understand *with a grain of salt.* I have no official, canonical translation of that familiar phrase, but I also do not see the need for one. I would rather make my view as clear and convincing as I can be explaining why I think all belief talk has the same status (*veritas cum grano salis,* to put it technically) as (1–4). The status derives from the uses we find for the intentional stance.

One can view the intentional stance as a limiting case of the design stance: one predicts by taking on just one assumption about the design of the system in question: whatever the design is, it is optimal. This assumption can be seen at work whenever, in the midst of the design stance proper, a designer or design investigator inserts a frank homunculus (an intentional system as subsystem) in order to bridge a gap of ignorance. The theorist says, in effect, "I don't know how to design this subsystem yet, but I know what it's supposed to do, so let's just pretend there is a demon there who wants nothing more than to do that task and knows just how to do it." One can then go on to design the surrounding system with the simplifying assumption that this component is "perfect." One asks oneself how the rest of the system must work, given that this component will do its duty.

Occasionally such a design effort in AI proceeds by literally installing a human module *pro tempore* in order to explore design alternatives in the rest of the system. When the HWIM speech-recognition system was being developed at Bolt Beranek and Newman (Woods and Makhoul 1974), the role of the phonological analysis module, which was supposed to generate hypotheses about the likely phonemic analysis of segments of the acoustic input, was temporarily played by human phonologists looking at segments of spectrograms of utterances. Another human being, playing the role of the control module, could communicate with the phonology demon and the rest of the system, asking questions and posing hypotheses for evaluation.

Once it was determined what the rest of the system had to "know" in order to give the phonologist module the help it needed, that part of the system was designed (discharging, *inter alia,* the control demon) and then the phonologists themselves could be replaced by a machine: a subsystem that used the same input (spectrograms—but not visually encoded, of course) to generate the same sorts of queries and hypotheses. During the design testing phase the phonologists tried hard not to use all the extra knowledge they had—about likely words, grammatical constraints, etc.—since they were mimicking *stupid* homunculi, specialists who only knew and cared about acoustics and phonemes.

Until such time as an effort is made to replace the phonologist subsystem with a machine, one is committed to virtually none of the sorts of design assumptions *about the working of that subsystem* that are genuinely explanatory. But in the meantime one may make great progress on the design of the other subsystems it must interact with and the design of the supersystem composed of all the subsystems.

The first purported chess-playing automaton was a late-eighteenth-century hoax: Baron Wolfgang von Kempelen's wooden mannequin, which did indeed pick up and move the chess pieces, thereby playing a decent game. It was years before the secret of its operation was revealed: a human midget chess master was hidden in the clockwork under the chess table and could see the moves through the translucent squares—a literal homunculus (Raphael 1976). Notice that the success or failure of the intentional stance as a predictor is so neutral with regard to design that it does not distinguish von Kempelen's midget-in-the-works design from, say, Berliner's Hitech, a current chess program of considerable power (Berliner and Ebeling 1986). Both work; both work well; both must have a design that is a fair approximation of optimality, so long as what we mean by optimality at this point focuses narrowly on the task of playing chess and ignores all other design considerations (e.g., the care and feeding of the midget versus the cost of electricity—but try to find a usable electrical outlet in the eighteenth centruy!). Whatever their internal differences, both systems are intentional systems in good standing, though one of them has a subsystem, a homunculus, that is itself as unproblematic an intentional system as one could find.

Intentional system theory is almost literally a black box theory, which makes it *behavioristic* to philosophers like Searle and Nagel, but hardly behavioristic in Skinner's sense. On the contrary, intentional system theory is an attempt to provide what Chomsky, no behaviorist, calls a competence model, in contrast to a performance model. Before we ask ourselves how mechanisms are designed, we must get clear about what the mechanisms are supposed to (be able to) do. This strategic vision has been developed further by Marr (1982) in his methodological reflections on his work on vision. He distinguishes three levels of analysis. The highest level, which he misleadingly calls *computational,* is in fact not at all concerned with computational processes but strictly (and more abstractly) with the question of what function the system in question is serving—or, more formally, with what fucntion in the mathematical sense it must (somehow or other) "compute" (cf. Newell 1982; Dennett 1986c, forthcoming e). At this computational level one attempts to specify formally and rigorously the system's proper competence (Millikan

1984 would call it the system's proper function). For instance, one fills in the details in the formula

> "given an element in the set of *x's* as input, it yields an element in the set of *y's* as output according to the following formal rules . . ."

while remaining silent or neutral about the implementation or performance details of whatever resides in the competent black box. Marr's second level is the *algorithmic* level, which does specify the computational processes but remains as neutral as possible about the physical mechanisms implementing them, which are described at the *hardware* level.

Marr claims that until we get a clear and precise understanding of the activity of a system at its highest, "computational" level, we cannot properly address detailed questions at the lower levels or interpret such data as we may already have about processes implementing those lower levels. This echoes Chomsky's long insistence that the diachronic process of language learning cannot be insightfuly investigated until one is clear about the end-state mature competence toward which it is moving. Like Chomsky's point, it is better viewed as a strategic maxim than as an epistemological principle. After all, it is not impossible to stumble upon an insight into a larger picture while attempting to ask yourself what turn out to be subsidiary and somewhat myopically posed questions.

Marr's more telling strategic point is that if you have a seriously mistaken view about what the computational-level description of your system is (as all earlier theories of vision did, in his view), your attempts to theorize at lower levels will be confounded by spurious artifactual puzzles. What Marr underestimates, however, is the extent to which computational level (or intentional stance) descriptions can also mislead the theorist who forgets just how idealized they are (Ramachandran 1985a, b).

The fact about competence models that provokes my "instrumentalism" is that the decomposition of one's competence model into parts, phases, states, steps, or whatever *need* shed no light at all on the decomposition of actual mechanical parts, phases, states, or steps of the system being modeled—even when the competence model is, as a competence model, excellent.[1]

Consider what we can say about the competences of two very different sorts of entities, a hand calculator and a Newfie-joke-getter. A Newfie-joke-getter is a person who laughs when told the following Newfie joke. (In Canada, the ethnic slur jokes are about "Newfies"—Newfoundlanders—and my favorite was told to me some years ago by Zenon Pylyshyn. Anyone familiar with Pylyshyn's position on mental imagery will wonder if it was foolhardy of him to divulge this particular phenomenon to me.)

A man went to visit his friend the Newfie and found him with both ears bandaged. "What happened?" asked the man, and the Newfie replied, "I was ironing my shirt when the telephone rang."—"That explains one ear, but what about the other?"—"Well, I had to call a doctor!"

If you "got" the joke, you are in the class of Newfie-joke-getters. How can we characterize the competence required to get the joke? Notice that the text is radically enthymematic—gappy. It never mentions answering the telephone or putting the iron to the ear or the similarity in shape, or heft, of an iron and a telphone receiver. Those details you fill in for yourself, and you have to have the requisite knowledge, the know-how, to do it. We could try to list all the "things you needed to know" to get the joke (Charniak 1974). These "things" are propositions, presumably, and we would create quite a long list if we worked at it. Had you not known any particular one of these "things," you would not have got the point of the joke. Your behavior on this occasion (supposing you laughed, smiled, snorted, or groaned) is almost proof positive that your intentional characterization includes, in the list of beliefs, all these items.

At the same time, no one has much of an idea what a good processing theory of your comprehension of the story would look like. Most readers, probably, would say that what happened as they were reading the joke was that they formed a visual image of some sort in their mind's eye—first of the Newfie reaching for the phone and then of him raising both hands at once—as soon as they read the bit about the phone ringing. It is easy enough to tell a sincere and plausible introspective story of this sort, but if we asked a number of readers to share their recalled phenomenology with us, it would not surprise us if there were considerable variation around the central, essential themes. And even if someone denied experiencing any imagery at all but still laughed heartily (and there are definitely such people in my sampling experience), we would suppose that a story of *unconscious* processing—having otherwise much the same content—must be true of the individual. It isn't magic, after all, and there must be an information-sensitive process in each individual that takes them from the seen words to the chuckle.

The story to be told about the actual process in different individuals will not be told by intentional system theory. Among the propositions one has to believe to get the joke is the proposition that people usually answer the telephone when it rings. An-

other is that answering the telephone typically involves lifting a telephone receiver with one hand and bringing it into contact with one's ear. I will not bore you with a recitation of other required beliefs. Not only do these beliefs not "come to mind" in the form of verbal judgements (which might seriously distract one from paying attention to the words of the story), but it is also highly implausible to suppose that each and every one of them is consulted, independently, by a computational mechanism designed to knit up the lacunae in the story by a deductive generation process. And yet the information expressed in those sentences has to be somehow in the heads of those who get the joke. We can predict and explain some phenomena at this level. For instance, I predict that that in this day of wash-and-wear clothes, there is a generation of children growing up that includes many who really do not know what the action of ironing a shirt looks like; these sheltered individuals will be baffled by the joke because they lack some essential beliefs.

The list of beliefs give us a good general idea of the information that must be in the head, but if we view it as a list of axioms from which a derivational procedure deduces the "point of the joke," we may have the sketch of a performance model, but it is a particularly ill-favored performance model. So even though it is far from idle to catalogue the minimal set of beliefs of the canonical Newfie-joke-getter, that intentional stance characterization, for all its predictive and even explanatory power, sheds virtually no light on the underlying mechanisms.

Now consider a familiar competence model of a hand calculator. Suppose I use my ability to do pencil-and-paper arithmetic to predict the behavior of my pocket calculator (philosophers often like to make life difficult for themselves). The formalism of arithmetic makes for an exemplary "computational level" model: rigorous and precise to a fault, it provides rules for predicting exactly which output the black box will yield for any input. These rules transform the input ("26 × 329") through a series of phases ("six times nine is fifty-four, put down the four, carry the five . . .") until eventually an output is yielded, which (if we've done the computation right) is borne out by the behavior of the calculator. But do the component stages of the process by which I calculated my prediction mirror any component stages in the process by which the calculator produced its predicted result? Some do and some don't. Those that do on one occasion need not on another; the "fit," when it exists, can be accidental. There are indefinitely many ways of engineering a calculator to fit our competence model, and only some of them "bear a strong resemblance" to the details of the competence model calculations.

There isn't just one arithmetical competence model for my hand calculator, of course. Arithmetic ignores finitude, but my calculator doesn't. In its finite way, it uses a process that involves approximation and either truncation (two-thirds comes out .6666) or round-off (two-thirds comes out .6667). A prediction and experiment will determine which. Arithmetic says that 10, divided by 3, times 3 is 10, and that 20, divided by 3, times 3, is 20, but my calculator says that the first answer is 9.9999999, and the second is 19.999999. Discovering this mismatch between perfection and reality gives us a powerful clue about the actual machinery of the calculator.

Here I can use the initial competence model to generate hypotheses the falsification of which sheds light on the actual organization of the machinery. This permits a refinement of the competence model itself—in the direction of turning it into a performance model. To ask which of the many possible algorithms for approximate arithmetic is used by the calculator is to descend to the algorithmic level. If, when we descend to the algorithmic level, we lose a few of the familiar categories of the computational level (perhaps nothing counts as the step where you "put down the four and carry the five"), this will not diminish the practical utility of using the pure competence model as a predictor or as an ideal, a specifier of what the system ought to do, but it will certainly prevent us from discovering the (material) identity of what appear, from that perspective, to be the components and phases of the process.[2]

Moving away from an oversimple ideal toward greater realism is not always a wise tactic. It depends on what you want; sometimes quick-and-dirty prediction is more valuable than an extension of one's fine-grained scientific understanding even in science. The fact that an object can be reliably expected to approximate optimality (or rationality) may be a deeper and more valuable fact than any obtainable from a standpoint of greater realism and detail.

I have always stressed the actual predictive power of the pure intentional stance. I have claimed, for instance, that one can use the intentional stance to predict the behavior of an unknown chess opponent (human or artifact), and this sometimes provokes the objection (e.g., Fodor 1981a, chapter 4) that what makes chess an interesting game is precisely that one's opponent's moves are *not* predictable from the intentional stance. If they were, the game would be boring.

This objection sets the standards for prediction too high. First of all, there are those situations during the endgame when we speak of "forced moves" and these are predictable from the intentional stance (and only from the intentional stance) with virtual 100 percent reliability. (One's only serious source of doubt is whether or when one's opponent is going to resign rather than take the next forced move.) Forced moves are forced only in the sense of being "dictated by reason." An irrational opponent (human or artifact) might self-defeatingly fail to make a forced move, and for that matter a rational opponent (again, human or artifact) might have a higher ulterior motive than avoiding defeat at chess.

What about the opponent's moves in the middle game? These are seldom reliably predictable down to uniqueness (and as the critics claim, that is what makes chess interesting), but it is a rare situation when the thirty or forty *legal* moves available to the opponent can't be cut down by the intentional stance to an unordered short list of half a dozen most likely moves on which one could bet very successfully if given even money on all legal moves. This is a tremendous predictive advantage plucked from thin air in the face of almost total ignorance of the intervening mechanisms, thanks to the power of the intentional stance.

This is how chess programs themselves are designed to economize. Instead of devoting equal attention to all possible continuations of the game, a chess program at some point will concentrate on those branches of the decision tree on which its opponent makes (what the program calculates to be) *its* best response. It makes no difference to the chess program whether its opponent is human or artifact; it simply calculates on the assumption that any opponent worth playing will try to make the best moves it can. Bold "blunders" can thus be ways of surprising—upsetting the expectations of—a program that economizes too optimistically about its opponents. Ought the program be redesigned to keep on the lookout for patterns of such "suboptimal" choice in its opponents—as a step in the direction of greater realism, a more fine-grained understanding of its individual opponents? Perhaps. It all depends on the costs of maintaining, and accessing, such detail while under the pressure of the time clock. Probably the risks of being tricked by deliberate "blunders" are so low that they are a tolerable cost of the speed and efficiency of using the less realistic optimality assumption.

Fodor (1981b) misses this when he suggests that the rationality assumption would actually prevent a chess player from planning a threat.

So, if I am assuming Black's rationality, I am assuming, inter alia, that Black notices the threat. Whereas, what I hope and predict is precisely that the threat will go unmarked. Nor, in so predicting, have I abandoned the intentional stance. On the contrary, I may rationally predict Black's lapse precisely *because* of what I know or believe about Black's intentional states: in particular, about what he is and is not likely to notice. (p. 108)

What is Black not likely to notice? I can tell you without even knowing who Black is. Being approximately rational, Black is not likely to notice threats that would take a great deal of time and effort to discover and is extremely likely to notice obvious threats. If Black is, as Fodor supposes, rather unlikely to notice the threat, it must be because the threat is somewhat distant in the search tree and hence may well fall outside Black's more or less optimal focus of attention.

So even when we are planning to exploit another rational agent's foibles, we make use of the rationality assumption to guide our efforts (see Dennett 1976, reprinted in *Brainstorms*). Since the general power of the intentional stance is thus not explained by any knowledge we might happen to have about mechanisms in the objects we thereby comprehend, I continue to resist the brand of realism that concludes from the stance's everyday success that there must be belief-like and desire-like states in all such objects. Bechtel (1985) has suggested, constructively, that this still does not bar me from a variety of realism. I could reconstrue my instrumentalism as realism about certain abstract relational properties: properties that relate an organism (or artifact) to its environment in certain indirect ways. Millikan (1984) has a positive account in the same vein. So far as I can see, this is indeed a viable ontological option for me, but as chapter 5 will show, the properties one would end up being a realist about are hardly worth the effort.[3]

NOTES

1. Bechtel (1985) observes, "Dennett seems to reduce the question of instrumentalism *versus* realism to an empirical issue about how the human cognitive system is structured—if there turns out to be a reasonable mapping of intentional idioms onto processing states, then realism will be vindicated, while instrumentalism will be justified if there is no such mapping." (p. 479)

2. Please note that *our* capacity to "do arithmetic" without succumbing directly to round-off or truncation error does not at all show that we are not mechanisms or not finite! Perhaps we are just bigger and fancier finite mechanisms. There are computer systems (such as MACSYMA) that are adept at algebraic manipulations and have alternative ways of representing irrational numbers, for instance.

3. I considered a similar tactical move in Chapter 1 of

Content and Consciousness, where the option was a similarly convoluted identity theory, and I decided against it: "Hasn't one lost the point of *identity* theory once one begins treating whole sentences as names in effect of situations or states of affairs which are then proclaimed identical with other situations or states of affairs?" (p.18n)

BIBLIOGRAPHY

Bechtel, W. (1985). "Realism, Reason, and the Intentional Stance," *Cognitive Science,* 9, pp. 473–97.

Berliner, H. and Ebling, C. (1986). "The SUPREM Architecture: a new Intelligent Paradigm," *Artificial Intelligence,* 28, pp. 3–8.

Charniak, E. (1974). "Toward a Model of Children's Story Comprehension," unpublished doctoral dissertation, MIT, and MIT AI Lab Report 266.

Churchland, P. M. (1981). "Eliminative Materialism and the Propositional Attitudes," *Journal of Philosophy, 78,* pp. 67–90.

Churchland, P. M. (1984). *Matter and Consciousness: A Contemporary Introduction to the Philosophy of Mind.* Cambridge, MA: The MIT Press/A Bradford Book.

Churchland, P. S. (1980). "Language, Thought, and Information Processing," *Nous,* 14, pp. 147–70.

Churchland, P. S. (1986). *Neurophilosophy: Toward a Unified Theory of Mind/Brain.* Cambridge, MA: The MIT Press/A Bradford Book.

Dennett, D. C. (1969). *Content and Consciousness.* London: Routledge and Kegan Paul.

Dennett, D. C. (1975). "Brain Writing and Mind Reading," in K. Gunderson, ed., *Language, Mind, and Meaning.* Minnesota Studies in Philosophy of Science, VII. Minneapolis: University of Minnesota Press.

Dennett, D. C. (1976). "Conditions of Personhood," in A. Rorty, ed., *The Identities of Persons.* Berkeley: University of California Press. (Reprinted in Dennett 1978a.)

Dennett, D. C. (1978a). *Brainstorms: Philosophical Essays on Mind and Psychology.* Montgomery, VT: Bradford Books.

Dennett, D. C. (1982b). "How to Study Human Consciousness Empirically: or, Nothing Comes to Mind," *Synthese,* 53, pp. 159–80.

Dennett, D. C. (1985a). "Can Machines Think?" in M. Shafto, ed., *How We Know.* San Francisco: Harper and Row.

Dennett, D. C. (1986c). "Is There an Autonomous 'Knowledge Level'?" (commentary on Newell, same volume), in Z. Pylyshyn and W. Demopoulos, eds., *Meaning and Cognitive Structure: Issues in the Computational Theory of Mind,* Norwood, NJ: Ablex.

Dennett, D. C. (forthcoming e). "The Moral first Aid Manual" 1986 Tanner Lecture, University of Michigan.

Fodor, J. (1981a). *Representations.* Cambridge, MA: The MIT Press/A Bradford Book.

Fodor, J. (1981b). "Three Cheers for Propositional Attitudes," in Fodor 1981a.

Fodor, J. (1985). "Fodor's Guide to Mental Representation," *Mind,* XCIV, pp. 76–100.

Friedman, M. (1981). "Theoretical Explantion," in R. Healy, ed., *Reduction, Time and Reality.* Cambridge: Cambridge University Press, pp. 2–31.

Goldman, A. (1986). *Epistemology and Cognition.* Cambridge, MA: Harvard University Press.

Marr, D. (1982). *Vision.* San Francisco: W. H. Freeman and Company, 1982.

Millikan, R. (1984). *Language, Thought and Other Biological Categories.* Cambridge, MA: The MIT Press/A Bradford Book.

Newell, A. (1982). "The Knowledge Level," *Artificial Intelligence,* 18, pp. 81–132.

Ramachandran, V. S. (1985a). "Apparent Motion of Subjective Surfaces," *Perception,* 14, pp. 127–34.

Ramachandran, V. S. (1985b). Guest editorial in *Perception,* 14, pp. 97–103.

Raphael, B. (1976). *The Thinking Computer: Mind Inside Matter.* San Francisco: Freeman.

Searle, J. (1980b). "Minds, Brains, and Programs," *Behavioral and Brain Sciences,* 3, pp. 417–58.

Searle, J. (1982). "The Myth of the Computer: An Exchange," *The New York Review of Books,* June 24, pp. 56–57.

Woods, W. A. and Makhoul, J. (1974). "Mechanical Inference Problems in Continuous Speech Understanding," *Artificial Intelligence,* 5, pp. 73–91.

Bibliography

ABBREVIATIONS

Journals

A (Analysis)
AJP (Australasian Journal of Philosophy)
APA (Proceedings and Addresses of the American Philosophical Association)
APQ (American Philosophical Quarterly)
BBS (The Behavioral and Brain Sciences)
CJP (Canadian Journal of Philosophy)
D (Dialectica)
E (Erkenntnis)
I (Inquiry)
JP (The Journal of Philosophy)
M (Mind)
Midwest (Midwest Studies in Philosophy)
ML (Mind and Language)
Mon (The Monist)
MSPS (Minnesota Studies in the Philosophy of Science)
N (Nous)
ND (Notre Dame Journal of Formal Logic)
P (Philosophy)
PAS (Proceedings of the Aristotelian Society)
PBA (Proceedings of the British Academy)
PPQ (Pacific Philosophical Quarterly)
PPR (Philosophy and Phenomenological Research)
PQ (Philosophical Quarterly)
PR (The Philosophical Review)
PS (Philosophical Studies)
PSci (Philosophy of Science)
RM (The Review of Metaphysics)
S (Synthese)
SR (Social Research)

Publishers

BB (Oxford: Basil Blackwell)
CA (Berkeley and Los Angeles: University of California Press)
CUP (Cambridge: Cambridge University Press)
Harvard (Cambridge, Mass.: Harvard University Press)
Minn (Minneapolis: University of Minnesota Press)
MIT (Cambridge, Mass.: MIT Press/Bradford Books)
OUP (Oxford: Oxford University Press)
PUP (Princeton: Princeton University Press)
RKP (London: Routledge & Kegan Paul)
Yale (New Haven: Yale University Press).

I. PROBLEMS ABOUT MIND

A. Mind as Consciousness

Broad, C. D. The Mind and its Place in Nature. RKP, 1925.

Kenny, Anthony. "Cartesian Privacy." In Wittgenstein: The Philosophical Investigations, ed. George Pitcher. New York: Doubleday, 1966, pp. 352–70.

Mackie, J. L. Problems from Locke. OUP, 1976.

Malcolm, Norman. "Descartes's Proof That His Essence Is Thinking." PR LXXIV, 3 (July 1965): 315–38.

McGinn, Colin. The Character of Mind. OUP, 1982.

Richardson, Robert C. "The 'Scandal' of Cartesian Interactionism." M XC, 1 (January 1982): 20–37.

Rorty, Amélie O., ed. Essays on Descartes' Meditations. CA, 1986.

Spinoza, Ethics. In The Collected Works of Spinoza, I. Ed. and tr. Edwin Curley. PUP, 1985, pp. 408–617.

Wilson, Margaret D. "Superadded Properties: The Limits of Mechanism in Locke." APQ XVI, 2 (April 1979): 143–50.

B. Mind and Nature

Aristotle. de Anima: Books II, III. Tr. D. W. Hamlyn. OUP, 1968.

Brentano, Franz. The Psychology of Aristotle. Ed. and tr. Rolf George. CA, 1977.

Gregory, Richard L., ed., with the assistance of O. L. Zangwill. The Oxford Companion to the Mind. OUP, 1987.

Hampshire, Stuart. "Critical Notice of The Concept of Mind, by Gilbert Ryle." M LIX, 234 (April 1950): 237–55.

Hardie, W.F.R. "Concepts of Consciousness in Aristotle." M LXXXV, 339 (July 1976): 388–411.

Kosman, L. A. "Perceiving that We Perceive: On the Soul III, 2." PR LXXXIV, 4 (October 1975): 499–519.

La Mettrie, Julien Offray de. Man a Machine. La Salle, IL: Open Court, 1912.

Russell, Bertrand. The Analysis of Mind. London: George Allen & Unwin, 1921.

Sellars, Wilfrid. "Aristotelian Philosophies of Mind." In Philosophy for the Future, ed. Roy Wood Sellars, V. J. McGill, and Marvin Farber. New York: The Macmillan Company, 1949, pp. 544–70.

Smith, Peter, and O. R. Jones. The Philosophy of Mind. CUP, 1986.

Wilkes, Kathleen V. Physicalism. RKP, 1978.

Wood, Oscar P., and George Pitcher, eds. Ryle. New York: Doubleday, 1970.

II. SELF AND OTHER

A. Knowing Other Minds

Albritton, Rogers. "On Wittgenstein's Use of the Term 'Criterion'." JP LVI, 22 (October 22, 1959): 845–57.

————. "Postscript (1966)." In Wittgenstein: The Philosophical Investigations, ed. George Pitcher. New York: Doubleday, 1966, pp. 247–50.

Ayer, A. J. "One's Knowledge of Other Minds." Theoria XIX (1953): 1–20. Rpt. in his Philosophical Essays. London: Macmillan and Co. Ltd., 1954, pp. 191–214.

Buck, R. C. "Non–Other Minds." In Analytical Philosophy I, ed. R. J. Butler. BB, 1962, pp. 187–210.

Cook, John W. "Human Beings." In Studies in the Philosophy of Wittgenstein, ed. Peter Winch. RKP, 1969, pp. 117–51.

————. "Wittgenstein on Privacy." PR LXXIV, 3 (July 1965): 281–314.

Kripke, Saul A. Wittgenstein on Rules and Private Languages. Harvard, 1982.

Long, Douglas C. "The Philosophical Concept of a Human Body." PR LXXIII, 3 (July 1964): 321–37.

Malcolm, Norman. "Wittgenstein's Philosophical Investigations." PR LXIII, 4 (October 1954): 530–59.

Pitcher, George. *Wittgenstein: The Philosophical Investigations.* New York: Doubleday, 1966.

Rorty, Richard. "Verificationism and Transcendental Arguments." *N* V, 1 (February 1971): 3–14.

———. "Wittgenstein, Privileged Access, and Incommunicability." *APQ* VII, 3 (July 1970): 192–205.

Teichman, Jenny. "Wittgenstein on Persons and Human Beings." In *Understanding Wittgenstein,* ed. Godfrey Vesey. Ithaca: Cornell University Press, 1976, pp. 133–48.

Thomson, J. F. "The Argument from Analogy and Our Knowledge of Other Minds." *M* LX, 239 (March 1951): 336–50.

Thomson, Judith Jarvis. "Privates Languages." *APQ* I, 1 (January 1964): 20–31.

Wittgenstein, Ludwig. *Philosophical Investigations.* Ed. G. E. M. Anscombe and R. Rhees; tr. G.E.M. Anscombe. BB, 1953.

Wright, Crispin. "Kripke's Account of the Argument against Private Language." *JP* LXXXI, 12 (December 1984): 759–78.

Ziff, Paul. "About Behaviorism," *A* XVIII, 6 (June 1958): 132–36.

———. "The Simplicity of Other Minds." *JP* XLII, 20 (October 21, 1965): 575–84.

B. Privileged Access

Alston, William. "Varieties of Privileged Access." *APQ* VIII, 3 (July 1971): 223–41.

Aune, Bruce. "On the Complexity of Avowals." In *Philosophy in America,* ed. Max Black. Ithaca: Cornell University Press, 1965, pp. 35–57.

Ayer, A. J. "Privacy." *PBA* XLV (1959): 43–65. Rpt. in his *The Concept of a Person.* London: Macmillan and Co. Ltd., 1963, pp. 52–81.

Davidson, Donald. "First Person Authority." *D* XXXVIII, 2/3 (1984): 101–11.

Gasking, Douglas. "Avowals." In *Analytical Philosophy* I, ed. R. J. Butler. BB, 1962, pp. 154–69.

Malcolm, Norman. "The Privacy of Experience." In *Epistemology: New Essays in the Theory of Knowledge,* ed. Avrum Stroll. New York: Harper & Row, 1967, pp. 129–58.

McDowell, John. "Criteria, Defeasibility, and Knowledge." *PBA* LXVIII (1982), pp. 455–79.

Myers, Gerald E. "Introspection and Self-Knowledge." *APQ* XXIII, 2 (April 1986): 199–207.

Nisbett, Richard E., and Timothy DeCamp Wilson. "Telling More Than We Can Know: Verbal Reports on Mental Processes." *Psychological Review* LXXXIV, 3 (May 1977): 231–59.

Shoemaker, Sydney. "Self-Reference and Self-Awareness." *JP* LXV, 19 (October 3, 1968): 555–67. Rpt. in a revised version in his *Identity, Cause, and Mind.* CUP, 1984, pp. 6–18.

C. The Theory Approach

Aune, Bruce. "The Problem of Other Minds." *PR* LXX, 3 (July 1961): 320–39.

Castañeda, Hector-Neri. "Consciousness and Behavior: Their Basic Connections." In *Intentionality, Minds, and Perception,* ed. Hector-Neri Castañeda. Detroit: Wayne State University Press, 1966, pp. 121–58.

Parsons, Kathryn Pyne. "Mistaking Sensations." *PR* LXXIX, 2 (April 1970): 201–13.

III. MIND AND BODY

A. The Topic-Neutral Approach

Armstrong, D. M. *A Materialist Theory of the Mind.* New York: Humanities Press, 1968.

Baier, Kurt. "Pains," *AJP* XL, 1 (May 1962): 1–23.

———. "Smart on Sensations." *AJP* XL, 1 (May 1962): 57–68.

Bradley, M. C. "Sensations, Brain-Processes and Colours." *AJP* XLI, 3 (December 1963): 385–93.

Brandt, Richard, and Jaegwon Kim. "The Logic of the Identity Theory." *JP* LXIV, 17 (September 7, 1967): 515–38.

Coder, David. "The Fundamental Error of Central State Materialsim." *APQ* X, 4 (October 1973): 289–98.

Cornman, James W. *Materialism and Sensations.* Yale, 1971.

Feigl, Herbert. *The "Mental" and the "Physical,"* The Essay and a Postscript. Minn., 1967.

Goldberg, Bruce. "The Correspondence Hypothesis." *PR* LXXVII, 4 (October 1968): 438–54.

Hill, Christopher S. "In Defense of Type Materialism." *S* LIX, 3 (June 1984): 295–320.

Kim, Jaegwon. "On the Psycho-Physical Identity Theory." *APQ* III, 3 (July 1966): 227–35.

Levin, Janet. "Physicalism and the Subjectivity of Secondary Qualities." *AJP* LXV, 4 (December 1987): 400–411.

Levin, Michael E. *Metaphysics and the Mind-Body Problem.* OUP, 1979.

Nagel, Thomas. "Physicalism." *PR* LXXIV, 3 (July 1965): 339–56.

Place, U. T. "Is Consciousness a Brain Process?" *British Journal of Psychology* XLVII, Part 1 (February 1956): 44–50.

Rosenthal, David M. "Mentality and Neutrality." *JP,* LXXIII, 13 (July 15, 1976): 386–415.

Shaffer, Jerome A. *Philosophy of Mind.* Englewood Cliffs, N.J.: Prentice-Hall, Inc., 1968.

Smart, J.J.C. "Further Thoughts on the Identity Theory." *Mon* LVI, 2 (April 1972): 149–62.

———. "Materialism." *JP* LX, 22 (October 24, 1963): 651–62.

———. "Reports of Immediate Experiences." *S* XXII, 3/4 (May 1971): 346–59.

B. Functionalist Approaches

Anderson, Alan Ross, ed. *Minds and Machines.* Englewood Cliffs, N.J.: Prentice-Hall, Inc., 1964.

Armstrong, D. M., *The Nature of Mind.* Ithaca, N.Y.: Cornell University Press, 1980.

Bealer, George. "Mind and Anti-Mind: Why Thinking Has No Functional Definition." *Midwest* IX (1984): 283–328.

Bennett, Jonathan. *Linguistic Behaviour.* CUP, 1976.

Block, Ned. "Psychologism and Behaviorism." *PR* XC, 1 (January 1981): 5–43.

———, and Jerry A. Fodor. "What Psychological States Are Not." *PR* LXXXI, 2 (April 1972): 159–81.

Cummins, Robert. "Functional Analysis." *JP* LXXII, 20 (November 20, 1975): 741–65. Rpt., in a revised version, in Ned Block, ed., *Readings in Philosophy of Psychology* I. Harvard, 1980.

Davis, Lawrence H. "Functionalism and Absent Qualia." *PS* XLI, 2 (March 1982): 231–49.

Dennett, Daniel C. *Content and Consciousness*. RKP, 1969.

Fodor, Jerry A. "Explanations in Psychology." In *Philosophy in America*, ed. Max Black. Ithaca, N.Y.: Cornell University Press, 1965, pp. 161–79.

———. *Psychological Explanation*. New York: Random House, Inc., 1968.

———. "The Mind-Body Problem." *Scientific American* CCXLIV, 1 (January 1981): 114–23.

Goldberg, Bruce. "Mechanism and Meaning." In *Knowledge and Mind: Philosophical Essays*, ed. Carl Ginet and Sydney Shoemaker. New York: Oxford University Press, 1983, pp. 191–210.

Gunderson, Keith. "Asymmetries and Mind-Body Perplexities." *MSPS* IV, ed. Michael Radner and Stephen Winokur. Minn, 1970, pp. 273–309.

———. *Mentality and Machines*. 2nd ed. Minn, 1985.

Kalke, William. "What's Wrong with Fodor and Putnam's Functionalism." *N* III, 1 (February 1969): 83–93.

Levin, Janet. "Functionalism and the Argument from Conceivability." *CJP* Supplementary Volume 11 (1985): 85–104.

Lewis, David. "An Argument for the Identity Thesis." *JP* LXIII, 1 (January 6, 1966): 17–25. Rpt. with additional material in *Materialism and the Mind-Body Problem*, ed. David M. Rosenthal. Indianapolis, IN: Hackett Publishing Co., 1987, 162–71.

———. "Counterparts of Persons and Their Bodies." *JP* LXVIII, 7 (April 8, 1971): 203–11.

Lycan, William G. "Form, Function, and Feel." *JP* LXXVIII, 1 (January 1981): 24–50.

von Neumann, John. *The Computer and the Brain*. Yale, 1958.

Owens, Joseph. "Functionalism and Propositional Attitudes." *N* XVII, 4 (November 1983): 529–49.

Putnam, Hilary. *Mind, Language and Reality: Philosophical Papers, Volume 2*. CUP, 1975.

———. "Minds and Machines." Rpt. in *Minds and Machines*, ed. Alan Ross Anderson. Englewood Cliffs, N.J.: Prentice-Hall, Inc., 1964, pp. 72–97.

———. "The Mental Life of Some Machines." In *Intentionality, Minds, and Perception*, ed. Hector-Neri Castañeda. Detroit, MI: Wayne State University Press, 1966, pp. 177–200.

Rorty, Richard. "Functionalism, Machines, and Incorrigibility." *JP* LXIX, 8 (April 20, 1972): 203–20.

Rosenthal, David M. "Armstrong's Causal Theory of Mind." In *Profiles: David Armstrong*, ed. Radu J. Bogdan. Dordrecht: D. Reidel Publishing Co., 1984, pp. 79–120.

Schiffer, Stephen. "Functionalism and Belief." In *The Representation of Knowledge and Belief*, ed. Myles Brand and Robert M. Harnish. Tucson: The University of Arizona Press, 1986, pp. 127–159.

Shoemaker, Sydney. "Some Varieties of Functionalism." *Philosophical Topics* XII, 1 (Spring 1981): 93–119.

Turing, A. M. "Computing Machinery and Intelligence." *M* LIX, 236 (October 1950): 433–60.

Wilkes, Kathleen V. "Functionalism, Psychology, and the Philosophy of Mind." *Philosophical Topics* XII, 1 (Spring 1981): 147–67.

Ziff, Paul. "The Feelings of Robots." *A* XIX, 3 (January 1959): 64–68.

Zuboff, Arnold. "The Story of a Brain." In *The Mind's I*, ed. Douglas R. Hofstadter and Daniel C. Dennett. New York: Bantam Books, 1981.

C. The Mental–Physical Contrast

Antony, Louise. "Anomalous Monism and the Problem of Explanatory Force." *PR* XCVIII, 2 (April 1989): 153–87.

Bealer, George. "The Logical Status of Mind." *Midwest* X (1985): 231–74.

Boyd, Richard. "Materialism without Reductionism: What Physicalism Does Not Entail." In *Readings in Philosophy of Psychology*, vol. I, ed. Ned Block. Harvard, 1980. pp. 67–106.

Collins, Arthur W. *The Nature of Mental Things*. Notre Dame, IN: University of Notre Dame Press, 1987.

Davidson, Donald. "Psychology as Philosophy." In *Philosophy of Psychology*, ed. S. C. Brown. London: The Macmillan Press Ltd., 1974, pp. 41–52.

———. "The Material Mind." Rpt. in his *Actions and Events*. OUP, 1980, pp. 245–59.

Feldman, Fred. "Kripke on the Identity Theory." *JP* LXXI, 18 (October 24): 665–76.

Goldberg, Bruce. "A Problem with Anomalous Monism." *PS* XXXII, 2 (August 1977): 175–80.

Goldman, Alvin I. "The Compatibility of Mechanism and Purpose." *PR* LXXVIII, 4 (October 1969): 468–82.

Hart, W. D. *The Engines of the Soul*. CUP, 1988.

Haugeland, John. "Ontological Supervenience." *The Southern Journal of Philosophy* XXII, Supplement, Spindel Conference 1983: The Concept of Supervenience in Contemporary Philosophy: 1–12.

———. "Weak Supervenience." *APQ* XIX, 1 (January 1982): 93–104.

Hellman, Geoffrey, and Frank Wilson Thompson. "Physicalism: Ontology, Determination, and Reduction." *JP* LXXII, 17 (October 2, 1975): 551–64.

———. "Physicalist Materialism." *N* XI, 4 (November 1977): 309–45.

Horgan, Terence. "Supervenient Qualia." *PR* XCVI, 4 (October 1987): 491–520.

Kim, Jaegwon. "Causality, Identity, and Supervenience in the Mind–Body Problem." *Midwest* IV (1979): 31–49.

———. "Psychophysical Supervenience." *PS* XLI, 1 (January 1982): 51–70.

———. "Supervenience and Supervenient Causation." *The Southern Journal of Philosophy* XXII, Supplement: 45–56.

Kripke, Saul A. "Identity and Necessity." In *Identity and Individuation*, ed. Milton K. Munitz. New York: NYU Press, 1971, pp. 135–64.

LePore, Ernest, and Barry Loewer. "Mind Matters." *JP* LXXXIV, 11 (November 1987): 630–42.

Lycan, William G. "Kripke and the Materialists." *JP* LXXI, 18 (October 24): 677–89.

Mackie, J. L. "Mind, Brain, and Causation." *Midwest* IV (1979): 19–29.

Malcolm, Norman. "Explaining Behavior." *PR* LXXVI, 1 (January 1967): 97–104.

———. "The Conceivability of Mechanism." *PR* LXXVI, 1 (January 1968): 45–72.

———. "Wittgenstein on the Nature of Mind." *APQ* Monograph Series, No. 4: *Studies in the Theory of Knowledge*. BB, 1970, pp. 9–29.

Margolis, Joseph. *Philosophy of Psychology.* Englewood Cliffs, N.J.: Prentice-Hall, Inc., 1984.

Maxwell, Grover. "Rigid Designators and Mind-Brain Identity." *MSPS* IX, ed. C. Wade Savage. Minn, 1978, pp. 365–403.

McGinn, Colin. "Anomalous Monism and Kripke's Cartesian Intuitions." *A* XXXVII, 2 (January 1977): 78–80.

Nagel, Thomas. "Panpsychism." In his *Mortal Questions.* CUP, 1979, pp. 181–95.

Robinson, Howard. *Matter and Sense.* CUP, 1982.

Shaffer, Jerome. "Persons and Their Bodies." *PR* LXXV, 1 (January 1966): 59–77.

Sosa, Ernest. "Mind–Body Interaction and Supervenient Causation." *Midwest* IX (1984): 271–81.

Stanton, William. "Supervenience and Psychophysical Law in Anamolous Monism." *PPQ* LXIV, 1 (January 1983): 72–89.

Taylor, Charles. "Mind–Body Identity, a Side Issue?" *PR* LXXVI, 2 (April 1967): 201–13.

———. *The Explanation of Behaviour,* RKP, 1964.

D. Eliminative Materialism

Feyerabend, Paul. "Materialism and the Mind-Body Problem." *RM* XVII, 1 (September 1963): 49–66.

Rorty, Richard. "Contemporary Philosophy of Mind." *S* LIII, 2 (November 1982): 323–48.

———. "Incorrigibility as the Mark of the Mental." *JP* LXVII, 12 (June 25, 1970): 399–424.

———. "Mind-Body Identity, Privacy, and Categories." *RM* XIX, 1 (September 1965): 24–54.

Rosenthal, David M. "Keeping Matter in Mind." *Midwest* V (1980): 295–322.

IV. THE NATURE OF MIND

A. Thinking

Armstrong, D. M. *Belief, Truth and Knowledge.* CUP, 1973.

Bach, Kent. "Thought and Object: *De re* Representations and Relations." In *The Representation of Knowledge and Belief,* ed. Myles Brand and Robert M. Harnish. Tucson: The University of Arizona Press, 1986. pp. 187–218.

Boër, Stephen E., and William G. Lycan. *Knowing Who.* MIT, 1986.

Brentano, Franz. *Psychology from an Empirical Standpoint,* ed. Oskar Kraus, English edition ed. Linda L. McAlister and tr. Antos C. Rancurello, D. B. Terrell, and Linda L. McAlister. RKP, 1973.

Burdick, Howard. "A Logical Form for the Propositional Attitudes." *S* LII, 3 (September 1982): 185–230.

Burge, Tyler. "Belief and Synonymy." *JP* LXXV, 3 (March 1976): 119–38.

———. "Belief *De Re*." *JP* LXXIV, 6 (June 1977): 338–62.

———. "Russell's Problem and Intentional Identity." In *Agent, Language, and the Structure of the World: Essays Presented to Hector-Neri Castañeda, with his Replies,* ed. James E. Tomberlin. Indianapolis, IN: Hackett Publishing Co., 1983, pp. 79–110.

Castañeda, Hector-Neri. "Indicators and Quasi-Indicators." *APQ* IV, 2 (April 1967): 85–100.

———. "On the Logic of Attributions of Self-Knowledge to Others." *JP* LXV, 15 (August 8, 1968): 439–56.

———. "Perception, Belief, and the Structure of Physical Objects and Consciousness." *S* XXXV, 3 (July 1977): 285–351.

Chisholm, Roderick M. "Beyond Being and Nonbeing." *PS* XXIV, 4 (July 1973): 245–57.

———. "Homeless Objects." *Revue Internationale de Philosophie,* XXII, 2–3 (1973): 207–23.

———. "On Some Psychological Concepts and the 'Logic' of Intentionality." In *Intentionality, Minds, and Perception,* ed. Hector-Neri Castañeda. Detroit, MI: Wayne State University Press, 1966, pp. 11–35.

———. "Sentences about Believing." *PAS,* LVI (1955–56): 124–48.

———, and Wilfrid Sellars. "Chisholm–Sellars Correspondence on Intentionality." *MSPS* II, ed. Herbert Feigl, Michael Scriven, and Grover Maxwell. Minn, 1958, pp. 521–39.

Chomsky, Noam, *Language and Mind.* Enl. ed. New York: Harcourt Brace Jovanovich, 1972.

———. *Rules and Representations.* New York: Columbia University Press, 1980.

Church, Alonzo. "On Carnap's Analysis of Statements of Assertion and Belief." *A* X, 5 (April 1950): 97–99.

Danto, Arthur C. "Beliefs as Sentential States of Persons." In *Language, Belief, and Metaphysics,* ed. Howard E. Kiefer and Milton K. Munitz. Albany: State University of New York Press, 1970: 122–40.

Davidson, Donald. "Belief and the Basis of Meaning," *S* XXVII, 3/4 (July/August 1974): 309–323.

———. "On Saying That." In *Words and Objections,* ed. Donald Davidson and Jaakko Hintikka. Dordrecht: D. Reidel Publishing Company, 1969, pp. 158–74.

———. "On the Very Idea of a Conceptual Scheme." *APA* XLVII (November 1974): 5–20.

———. "Radical Interpretation." *D* XXVII, 3–4 (1973): 313–28.

de Sousa, Ronald. "How To Give a Piece of Your Mind: or, The Logic of Belief and Assent." *RM* XXV, 1 (September 1971): 52–79.

Dennett, Daniel C. "Beyond Belief." In *Thought and Object,* ed. Andrew Woodfield, OUP, 1982, pp. 1–95.

———. "Intentional Systems." *JP* LXVIII, 4 (February 25, 1971): 87–106.

———. *The Intentional Stance,* MIT, 1987.

Devitt, Michael, "Thoughts and Their Ascription." *Midwest* IX (1984): 385–420.

Dretske, Fred. "Aspects of Cognitive Representation." In *The Representation of Knowledge and Belief,* ed. Myles Brand and Robert M. Harnish. Tucson: Univ of Arizona Press, 1986, pp. 101–15.

Dretske, Fred I. *Knowledge and the Flow of Information.* MIT, 1981.

———. "Misrepresentation." In *Belief: Form, Content and Function,* ed. Radu J. Bogdan. OUP, 1986. pp. 16–36.

Field, Hartry H. "Mental Representation." *E* XIII, 1 (July 1978): 9–61. Rpt., with postscript, in Ned Block, ed., *Readings in Philosophy of Psychology* II. Harvard, 1981, pp. 78–114.

Fodor, Jerry A., "Fodor's Guide to Mental Representation," *M* XCIV, 373 (January 1985): 76–100.

———. *Representations.* MIT, 1981.

———. "Semantics, Wisconsin Style." *S* LIX, 3 (June 1984): 231–50.

————. *The Language of Thought.* New York: Thomas Y. Crowell, 1975; paperback ed.: Harvard, 1979.

————. "Why Paramecia Don't Have Mental Representations." *Midwest* X (1986): 3–23.

————. "Why There Still Has to Be a Language of Thought." Appendix to *Psychosemantics.* MIT, 1987.

Geach, P. T. "Intentional Identity." *JP* LXIV, 20 (October 26, 1967): 627–32.

————. *Mental Acts,* RKP, 1957.

Grice, H. P. "Meaning." *PR* LXVI, 3 (July 1957): 377–88.

Harman, Gilbert. "Conceptual Role Semantics," *ND* XXIII, 2 (April 1982): 242–56.

————. "Is There Mental Representation?" *MSPS* IX, ed. C. Wade Savage. Minn, 1978, pp. 57–64.

————. *Thought.* PUP, 1973.

Kaplan, David. "Opacity." In *The Philosophy of W. V. Quine,* ed. Lewis Edwin Hahn and Paul Arthur Schilpp. La Salle, IL: Open Court, 1986, pp. 229–94.

————. "Quantifying In." In *Words and Objections,* ed. Donald Davidson and Jaakko Hintikka. Dordrecht: D. Reidel Publishing Company, 1969, pp. 206–42.

Kripke, Saul A. "A Puzzle About Belief." In *Meaning and Use,* ed. Avishai Margalit. Dordrecht: D. Reidel Publishing Company, 1979, pp. 239–83.

Levine, Joseph. "Demonstrating in Mentalese." *Pacific Philosophical Quarterly* LXIX, 3 (September 1988): 222–40.

Lewis, David. "Attitudes *De Dicto* and *De Se.*" *PR* LXXXVIII, 4 (October 1979): 513–43.

————. "Radical Interpretation." *S* XXVII, 3/4 (July/August 1974): 331–44.

Loar, Brian. *Mind and Meaning.* CUP, 1981.

Lycan, William G. "Toward a Homuncular Theory of Believing." *Cognition and Brain Theory* IV, 2 (Spring 1981): 139–59.

Maloney, J. Christopher. "The Mundane Mental Language: How To Do Words With Things." *S* LIX, 3 (June 1984): 251–94.

Marcus, Ruth Barcan, "Rationality and Believing the Impossible." *JP* LXXX, 6 (June 1983): 321–38.

Markie, Peter J. "Multiple Propositions and 'De Se' Attitudes." *PPR* XLVIII, 4 (June 1988): 573–600.

Marras, Ausonio. "Sellars on Thought and Language." *N* VII, 2 (May 1973): 152–63.

Matthews, Robert J. "Troubles with Representationalism." *SR,* LI, 4 (Winter 1984): 1065–97.

McGinn, Colin. "Charity, Interpretation, and Belief." *JP* LXXIV, 9 (September 1977): 521–35.

————. "The Structure of Content." In *Thought and Object,* ed. Andrew Woodfield. OUP, 1982, pp. 207–58.

Millikan, Ruth Garrett. *Language, Thought, and Other Biological Categories.* MIT, 1984.

Peacocke, Christopher. *Thoughts: An Essay on Content.* BB, 1986.

Perry, John. "The Problem of the Essential Indexical." *N* XIII, 1 (March 1979): 3–21.

Putnam, Hilary. "Meaning Holism." In *The Philosophy of W. V. Quine,* ed. Lewis Edwin Hahn and Paul Arthur Schilpp. La Salle, IL: Open Court, 1986, pp. 405–26.

Rosenthal, David M. "Intentionality." *Midwest* X (1986): 151–84.

————. "Talking about Thinking." *PS* 24, 5 (September 1973): 283–313.

Samet, Jerry. "Troubles with Fodor's Nativism." *Midwest* X (1986): 575–94.

Scheffler, Isreal. "An Inscriptional Approach to Indirect Quotation." *A* XIV, 4 (March 1954): 83–90.

Schiffer, Stephen. *The Remnants of Meaning.* MIT, 1987.

Schwartz, Robert. "'The' Problems of Representation." *SR,* LI, 4 (Winter 1984): 1047–64.

Searle, John R. *Intentionality.* CUP, 1983.

————. "What Is an Intentional State?" *M* LXXXVIII, 349 (January 1979): 74–92.

Sellars, Wilfrid. "Empiricism and the Philosophy of Mind." In his *Science, Perception and Reality.* RKP, 1963, pp. 127–96.

————. "Language as Thought and as Communication." *PPR* XXIX, 4 (June 1969): 506–27.

————. "Notes on Intentionality." *JP* LXI, 21 (November 12, 1964): 655–65.

————. *Science and Metaphysics.* RKP, 1968.

————. *Science, Perception and Reality.* RKP, 1963.

Sosa, Ernest. "Propositional Attitudes *de Dicto* and *de Re.*" *JP* LXVII, 21 (November 5, 1970): 883–96.

Stalnaker, Robert. "Belief Attribution and Context." In *Contents of Thought,* ed. Robert Grimm and Daniel Merrill. Tucson: University of Arizona Press, 1988, pp. 140–56.

————. *Inquiry.* MIT, 1984.

————. "Propositions." In *Issues in the Philosophy of Language: Proceedings of the 1972 Oberlin Colloquium in Philosophy,* ed. Alfred F. MacKay and Daniel D. Merrill. Yale, 1976, pp. 79–91.

————. "Semantics for Belief." *Philosophical Topics* XV, 1 (Spring 1987): 177–90.

Sterelny, Kim. "Mental Representation: What Language is Brainese?" *PS* XLIII, 3 (May 1983): 365–82.

Stich, Stephen P. "Are Belief Predicates Systematically Ambiguous?" In *Belief: Form, Content and Function,* ed. Radu J. Bogdan. OUP, 1986, pp. 119–47.

————. "Beliefs and Subdoxastic States." *PSci* XLV, 4 (December 1978): 499–518.

Unger, Peter. "Propositional Verbs and Knowledge." *JP* LIX, 11 (June 1, 1972): 301–12.

Vendler, Zeno. *Res Cogitans.* Ithaca, N.Y.: Cornell University Press, 1972.

Woodfield, Andrew, ed. *Thought and Object.* OUP, 1982.

B. Sensing

Anscombe, G.E.M. "The Intentionality of Sensation: A Grammatical Feature." In *Analytical Philosophy* II, ed. R. J. Butler. BB, 1968, pp. 158–80.

————. "The Subjectivity of Sensation." *Ajatus* XXXVI (1976): 3–18. Rpt. in her *Metaphysics and the Philosophy of Mind.* Minn, 1981, pp. 44–56.

Armstrong, D. M., *Bodily Sensations.* RKP, 1962.

————. *The Nature of Mind.* Ithaca, N.Y.: Cornell University Press, 1980.

Audi, Robert. "The Ontological Status of Mental Images." *I* XXI, 3 (Autumn 1978): 348–61.

Block, Ned. "Are Absent Qualia Impossible?" *PR* LXXXIX, 2 (April 1980): 257–74.

————. "Mental Pictures and Cognitive Science." *PR* XCII, 4 (October 1983): 499–541.

————, ed. *Imagery.* MIT, 1981.

Chisholm, Roderick M. *Perceiving: A Philosophical Study.* Ithaca, N.Y.: Cornell University Press, 1957.

Clark, Romane. "Objects of Consciousness: The Non-Relational Theory of Sensing." *Philosophical Perspectives,* I: *Metaphysics* (1987): 481–500.

———. "Sensuous Judgments." *N* VII, 1 (March 1973): 45–56.

Clarke, Thompson. "Seeing Surfaces and Physical Objects." In *Philosophy in America,* ed. Max Black. Ithaca, N.Y.: Cornell University Press, 1965, pp. 98–114.

Delaney, C. F. "Sellars' Grain Argument." *AJP* L, 1 (May 1972): 14–16.

Dennett, Daniel C. "Quining Qualia." In *Consciousness in Contemporary Science,* ed. A. J. Marcel and E. Bisiach. OUP, 1988, pp. 42–77.

———. "Two Approaches to Mental Images." In his *Brainstorms.* MIT, 1978, pp. 174–89.

Fodor, Jerry A. *The Modularity of Mind.* MIT, 1963.

Gibson, James J. *The Ecological Approach to Visual Perception.* Boston: Houghton Mifflin, 1979.

Gregory, R. L. *Eye and Brain: The Psychology of Seeing.* 3rd ed. New York: McGraw-Hill, 1978.

Grice, H. P. "Some Remarks about the Senses." In *Analytical Philosophy* I, ed. R. J. Butler. BB, 1962, pp. 133–53.

Hardin, C. L. *Color for Philosophers.* Indianapolis, IN: Hackett Publishing Co., 1988.

Harrison, Bernard. *Form and Content.* BB, 1973.

Jackson, Frank. "Epiphenomenal Qualia." *PQ* XXXII, 127 (April 1982): 127–36.

———. *Perception.* CUP, 1977.

Kitcher, Patricia. "Phenomenal Qualities." *APQ* XVI, 2 (April 1979): 123–30.

Kosslyn, Stephen Michael. *Image and Mind.* Harvard, 1980.

Kraut, Robert. "Sensory States and Sensory Objects." *N* XVI, 2 (May 1982): 277–93.

Leon, Mark. "Character, Content, and the Ontology of Experience." *AJP* LXV, 4 (December 1987): 337–99.

Levin, Janet. "Could Love Be Like a Heatwave?: Physicalism and the Subjective Character of Experience." *PS* XLIX, 2 (March 1986): 245–61.

Lewis, David. "What Experience Teaches." In *Mind and Cognition: A Reader,* ed. William Lycan. BB, 1989.

Loar, Brian. "Phenomenal States." *Philosophical Perspectives,* IV: *Action Theory and Philosophy of Mind* (1990): 81–108.

McDowell, John. "Values and Secondary Qualities." In *Morality and Objectivity: A Tribute to J. L. Mackie,* ed. Ted Honderich. RKP, 1985, pp. 110–29.

Melzack, Ronald. *The Puzzle of Pain.* New York: Basic Books, 1973.

———, and Patrick D. Wall. *The Challenge of Pain.* New York: Basic Books, 1982.

Nemirow, Larry. "Physicalism and the Cognitive Role of Acquaintance." In *Mind and Cognition: A Reader,* ed. William Lycan. BB, 1989.

O'Shaughnessy, Brian. "Secondary Qualities." *PPQ* LXVII, 3 (July 1986): 153–71.

Peacocke, Christopher. "Consciousness and Other Minds." *PAS,* Supplementary Volume LVIII (1984): 97–117.

———. *Sense and Content.* OUP, 1983.

Pitcher, George. *A Theory of Perception.* PUP, 1971.

———. "Minds and Ideas in Berkeley." *APQ* VI, 3 (July 1969): 198–207.

———. "Pain Perception." *PR* LXXIX, 3 (July 1970): 368–93.

———. "The Awfulness of Pain." *JP* LXVII, 14 (July 23, 1970): 481–92.

Richardson, R. C., and G. Muilenberg. "Sellars and Sense Impressions." *E* XVII. 2 (March 1982): 171–211.

Rock, Irvin. *The Logic of Perception.* MIT, 1983.

Rosenthal, David M. Review of *Perception: A Representative Theory,* by Frank Jackson. *JP* LXXXII, 1 (January 1985): 28–41.

Sanford, David H. "Illusions and Sense-Data." *Midwest* VI (1981): 371–85.

Schwartz, Robert A. "Imagery—There's More to It Than Meets the Eye." Rpt. in *Imagery,* ed. Ned Block. MIT, 1981, pp. 109–29.

Sellars, Wilfrid. "Empiricism and the Philosophy of Mind." In his *Science, Perception and Reality.* RKP, 1963, pp. 127–96.

———. *Foundations for a Metaphysics of Pure Process.* The Carus Lectures. *Mon* LXIV, 1 (January 1981): 3–90.

———. *Science and Metaphysics.* RKP, 1968.

———. *Science, Perception and Reality.* RKP, 1963.

———. "Sensa or Sensing: Reflections on the Ontology of Perception." *PS* XLI, 1 (January 1982): 83–111.

———. "Some Reflections on Perceptual Consciousness." In Ronald Bruzina and Bruce Wilshire, eds., *Crosscurrents in Phenomenology.* The Hague: Martinus Nijhoff, 1977, pp. 169–85.

———. "The Adverbial Theory of the Objects of Sensation." *Metaphilosophy* VI, 2 (April 1975): 144–60.

———. "The Identity Approach to the Mind–Body Problem." *RM* XVIII, 3 (March 1965): 430–51.

Shepard, Roger N., and Lynn A. Cooper. *Mental Images and Their Transformations.* MIT, 1982.

Shoemaker, Sydney. "The Inverted Spectrum." *JP* LXXIX, 7 (July 1982): 357–81.

Smith, Michael A. "Peacocke on Red and Red'." *S* LXVIII, 3 (September 1986): 559–76.

Sterelny, Kim. "The Imagery Debate." *PSci* LIII, 4 (December 1986): 560–83.

Strawson, Galen. "Red and 'Red'." *S* LXXVIII, 2 (February 1989): 193–232.

Tye, Michael. *The Metaphysics of Mind,* CUP, 1989.

———. "The Adverbial Approach to Visual Experience." *PR* XCIII, 2 (April 1984): 195–225.

———. "The Subjective Qualities of Experience." *M* XCV, 377 (January 1986): 1–17.

von Eckart, Barbara. "Mental Images and Their Explanations." *PS* LIII, 3 (May 1988): 441–60.

Warner, Richard. "A Challenge to Physicalism." *AJP* LXIV, 3 (September 1986): 249–65.

White, Stephen L. "Curse of the Qualia." *S* LXVIII, 2 (August 1986): 333–68.

Wilson, Mark. "What Is This Thing Called Pain?—The Philosophy of Science Behind the Contemporary Debate." *PPQ* LXVI, 3/4 (July/October 1985): 227–67.

C. Consciousness, Self, and Personhood

Albritton, Rogers. "Freedom of Will and Freedom of Action." *APA* LIX, 2 (November 1985): 239–51.

Anscombe, G.E.M. *Intention.* 2nd ed. BB, 1963.

Armstrong, D. M., and Normal Malcolm. *Consciousness and Causality.* BB, 1984.

Austin, J. L. "A Plea for Excuses." *PAS* LVII (1956–57): 1–30.

Baier, Annette. "Mind and Change of Mind." *Midwest* IV (1979): 157–76.

———. *Postures of Mind*. Minn, 1985.

Bennett, Jonathan. *Rationality*, RKP 1964.

Berofsky, Bernard, "Purposive Action." *APQ* VII, 4 (October 1970): 311–20.

Carter, W. R. "Once and Future Persons." *APQ* XVII, 1 (January 1980): 61–66.

Charlton, William. "Knowing What We Think." *PQ* XXXVI, 143 (April 1986): 196–211.

Churchland, Patricia Smith. "Consciousness: The Transmutation of a Concept." *PPQ* LXIV, 1 (January 1983): 80–95.

Cognition and Consciousness in Nonhuman Species. Special issue of *BBS* (including articles by David Premack and Guy Woodruff, Donald R. Griffin, and E. Sue Savage-Rumbaugh, Duane M. Rumbaugh, and Sally Boysen) I, 4 (December 1978).

Davidson, Donald. *Actions and Events*, OUP, 1980.

———. "Actions, Reasons, and Causes." *JP* LX, 23 (November 7, 1963): 685–700.

———. "Paradoxes of Irrationality." In *Philosophical Essays on Freud*, ed. Richard Wollheim and James Hopkins. CUP, 1982, pp. 289–305.

———. "Rational Animals." *D* XXXVI, 4 (1982): 317–27.

Davis, Wayne. "Expression of Emotion." *APQ* XXV, 4 (October 1988): 279–91.

de Sousa, Ronald. *The Rationality of Emotion*. MIT, 1987.

Dennett, Daniel C. *Brainstorms*. MIT, 1978.

———. "Conditions of Personhood." In *The Identities of Persons*, ed. Amélie Oksenberg Rorty. CA, 1976, pp. 175–96.

———. *Elbow Room: The Varieties of Free Will Worth Wanting*. MIT, 1984.

———. "How to Study Consciousness Empirically: Or, Nothing Comes to Mind." *S* LIII, 2 (November 1982): 159–80.

———. "Toward A Cognitive Theory of Consciousness." *MSPS* IX, ed. C. Wade Savage. Minn, 1978, pp. 201–28.

Dretske, Fred. *Explaining Behavior: Reasons in a World of Causes*. MIT, 1988.

Frankfurt, Harry G. *The Importance of What We Care About*. CUP, 1988.

Freud, Sigmund. *The Complete Psychological Works of Sigmund Freud*. 24 vols. Tr. and ed. James Strachey. London: The Hogarth Press, 1966–74; esp. "The Unconscious," XIV: 166–215; "Some Elementary Lessons in Psycho-Analysis," XXIII: 279–86; *An Outline of Psycho-Analysis*, XXIII: 141–208; and *The Ego and the Id*, XIX: 3–68.

Gazzaniga, Michael S. *The Social Brain: Discovering the Networks of the Mind*. New York: Basic Books, 1985.

———, and Joseph E. LeDoux. *The Integrated Mind*. New York: Plenum Press, 1978.

Glover, Jonathan. *The Philosophy and Psychology of Personal Identity*. London: Penguin Press, 1988.

Goldman, Alvin I. *A Theory of Human Action*. Englewood Cliffs, N.J: Prentice-Hall, Inc., 1970.

Gordon, Robert M. *The Structure of Emotions: Investigations in Cognitive Philosophy*. CUP, 1987.

Griffin, Donald R. *The Question of Animal Awareness*. Rev. and enl. ed. New York: Rockefeller University Press, 1981.

Hampshire, Stuart. "Feeling and Expression." In his *Freedom of Mind and Other Essays*. PUP, 1971, pp. 143–59.

———. *Freedom of the Individual*. Expanded ed. PUP, 1975.

Hofstadter, Douglas R., and Daniel C. Dennett, eds. *The Mind's I*. New York: Bantam Books, 1981.

Humphrey, Nicholas. *Consciousness Regained*. OUP, 1983.

Jackendoff, Ray. *Consciousness and the Computational Mind*. MIT, 1987.

Jeffrey, Richard. "Animal Interpretation." In *Actions and Events: Perspectives on the Philosophy of Donald Davidson*, ed. Ernest LePore and Brain McLaughlin. BB, 1985, pp. 481–87.

Johnston, Mark. "Human Beings." *JP* LXXXIV, 2 (February 1987): 59–83.

Kenny, Anthony. *Action, Emotion and Will*. RKP, 1963.

Kraut, Robert. "Love *De Re*." *Midwest* X (1986): 413–30.

Lewis, David. "Survival and Identity." In *The Identities of Persons*, ed. Amélie Oksenberg Rorty. CA, 1976, pp. 17–40.

Long, Douglas C. "The Bodies of Persons." *JP* LXXI, 10 (May 30, 1974): 291–301.

Lycan, William. *Consciousness*. MIT, 1987.

Lyons, William. *Emotion*. CUP, 1980.

———. *The Disappearance of Introspection*. MIT, 1986.

MacIntyre, A. C. *The Unconscious*. RKP, 1958.

Mackie, J. L. "The Transcendental 'I'." In *Philosophical Subjects: Essays Presented to P. F. Strawson*, ed. Zak van Straaten. OUP, 1980, pp. 48–61.

Marcel, A. J., and E. Bisiach, eds. *Consciousness in Contemporary Science*. OUP, 1988.

Marks, Charles. *Commissurotomy, Consciousness, and the Unity of Mind*. MIT, 1981.

Matthews, Gareth B. "Animals and the Unity of Psychology." *P* LIII, 206 (October 1978): 437–54.

McDowell, John. "Singular Thought and Inner Space." In *Subject, Thought, and Context*, ed. Philip Pettit and John McDowell. OUP, 1986, pp. 137–68.

McGinn, Colin. *The Subjective View*. OUP, 1983.

McMullen, Carolyn. "'Knowing What It's Like' and the Essential Indexical." *PS* XLVIII, 2 (September 1985): 211–33.

Melden, A. I. *Free Action*. RKP, 1961.

Mellor, D. H. "Conscious Belief." *PAS*, LXXXVIII (1977–78), 87–101.

———. "Consciousness and Degrees of Beliefs." *Prospects for Pragmatism*, ed. D. H. Mellor. CUP, 1980, pp. 139–73.

Myers, Gerald E. "Feelings into Words." *JP* LX, 26 (December 19, 1963): 801–11.

Nagel, Thomas. *The View From Nowhere*. New York: Oxford University Press, 1986; esp. chaps. 1–7.

Nelson, John O. "Do Animals Propositionally Know? Do They Propositionally Believe?" *APQ* XX, 2 (April 1983): 149–60.

O'Shaughnessy, Brian. *The Will: A Dual Aspect Theory*. 2 vols. CUP, 1980.

Parfit, Derek. "Personal Identity." *PR* LXXX, 1 (January 1971): 3–27.

———. *Reasons and Persons*. OUP, 1984; Part Three: "Personal Identity."

Perry, John. *Personal Identity*. CA, 1975.

Rey, Georges. "A Question about Consciousness." In *Per-*

spectives on Mind, ed. H. R. Otto and J. A. Tuedio. Dordrecht: D. Reidel Publishing Company, 1986.

Rorty, Amélie Oksenberg, *Mind in Action.* Boston: Beacon Press, 1988.

————, ed. *Explaining Emotions.* CA, 1980.

————, *The Identities of Persons.* CA, 1976.

Rosenthal, David M. "Emotions and the Self." In *Emotion: Philosophical Studies,* ed. Gerald E. Myers and K. D. Irani. New York: Haven Publications, 1983, pp. 164–91.

Routley, Richard. "Alleged Problems in Attributing Beliefs, and Intentionality, to Animals." *I* XXIV, 4 (December 1981): 385–417.

Searle, John R. *What's Wrong With the Philosophy of Mind.* Forthcoming.

Shaffer, Jerome A. "An Assessment of Emotion." *APQ* XX, 2 (April 1983): 161–74.

Shoemaker, Sydney. "Introspection and the Self." *Midwest* X (1986): 101–20.

————. *Self-Knowledge and Self-Identity.* Ithaca: Cornell University Press, 1963.

————, and Richard Swinburne. *Personal Identity.* BB, 1984.

Solomon, Robert C. "On Emotions as Judgments." *APQ* XXV, 2 (April 1988): 183–92.

Solomon, Robert C. *The Passions.* New York: Anchor Press/Doubleday, 1977.

Springer, Sally P., and Georg Deutsch. *Left Brain, Right Brain.* San Francisco: W. H. Freeman and Co., 1981.

Thalberg, Irving. *Perception, Emotion and Action.* BB, 1977.

Tversky, Amos. "Cognitive Illusions in Judgment and Choice." In *The Kaleidoscope of Knowledge,* ed. Edna Ullmann-Margalit. Dordrecht: D. Reidel Publishing Company, 1986, pp. 75–87.

Unger, Peter. "Consciousness and Self-Identity." *Midwest* X (1986): 63–100.

Van Gulick, Robert. "A Functionalist Plea for Self-Consciousness." *PR* XCVII, 2 (April 1988): 149–81.

Vendler, Zeno. *The Matter of Minds.* OUP, 1984.

Warner, Richard. "Enjoyment." *PR* LXXXIX, 4 (October 1980): 507–26.

White, Stephen L. "Metapsychological Relativism and the Self." *JP* LXXXVI, 6 (June 1989): 298–323.

Wiggins, David. *Sameness and Substance.* Harvard, 1980.

Wilkes, Kathleen V. "Consciousness and Commissurotomy." *P* LIII, 204 (April 1978): 185–99.

————. "Is Consciousness Important?" *British Journal for the Philosophy of Science* XXXV, 3 (September 1984): 223–43.

————. *Real People: Personal Identity without Thought Experiments.* OUP, 1988.

Williams, Bernard. *Problems of the Self.* CUP, 1973.

————. "The Self and the Future." *PR* LXXIX, 2 (April 1970): 161–80.

Wilson, J.R.S. *Emotion and Object.* CUP, 1972.

Wollheim, Richard. *The Thread of Life,* Harvard, 1984.

————, and James Hopkins, eds. *Philosophical Essays on Freud.* CUP, 1982.

V. PSYCHOLOGICAL EXPLANATION

A. The Computational Approach

Anderson, John R. *The Architecture of Cognition.* Harvard, 1983.

Block, Ned. "Advertisement for a Semantics for Psychology." *Midwest* X (1986): 615–78.

Boden, Margaret A. *Minds and Mechanisms: Philosophical Psychology and Computational Models.* Ithaca, N.Y.: Cornell University Press, 1981.

Boër, Stephen E., and William G. Lycan. *Knowing Who.* MIT, 1986.

Cummins, Robert. *Meaning and Mental Representation.* MIT, 1989.

Dennett, Daniel C. "Cognitive Wheels: the Frame Problem of AI." In *Minds, Machines and Evolution,* ed. Christopher Hookway. CUP, 1984, pp. 129–51.

————. "The Logical Geography of Computational Approaches: A View from the East Pole." *The Representation of Knowledge and Belief,* ed. Myles Brand and Robert M. Harnish. Tucson: The University of Arizona Press, 1986, pp. 59–79.

Dreyfus, Hubert L. *What Computers Can't Do.* Rev. ed. New York: Harper & Row, 1979.

Flanagan, Owen J., Jr. *The Science of Mind.* MIT, 1984.

Fodor, Jerry A. "A Theory of Content." In his *A Theory of Content and Other Essays.* MIT, 1990.

————. *Psychosemantics.* MIT, 1987.

————, and Zenon Pylyshyn. "Connectionism and Cognitive Architecture: A Critical Analysis." *Cognition* XXVIII, 1/2 (March 1988): 3–71. Special issue rpt. as *Connections and Symbols,* ed. Steven Pinker and Jacques Mehler. MIT, 1988.

Harman, Gilbert. "(Nonsolipsistic) Conceptual Role Semantics." In *New Directions in Semantics,* ed. Ernest LePore. New York: Academic Press, 1987, pp. 55–81.

Haugeland, John. "The Nature and Plausibility of Cognitivism" (with commentaries and responses). *DDS* I, 2 (June 1981): 215–60.

————, ed. *Mind Design.* MIT, 1981.

Horgan, Terence, and John Tienson, eds. *Connectionism and the Philosophy of Mind, Southern Journal of Philosophy,* XXVI, Supplement (1987).

Jackson, Frank, and Philip Pettit. "Functionalism and Broad Content." *M* XCVII, 387 (July 1988): 381–400.

Johnson-Laird, Philip N. *Mental Models.* Harvard, 1983.

————. *The Computer and the Mind: An Introduction to Cognitive Science.* Harvard, 1988.

————, and P. C. Wason, eds. *Thinking: Readings in Cognitive Science.* CUP, 1977.

Marr, David. *Vision.* San Francisco: W. H. Freeman and Company, 1982.

Mellor, D. H. "What Is Computational Psychology?" *PAS,* Supplementary Volume LVIII (1984): 37–53.

Newell, Allen, and Herbert Simon. *Human Problem Solving.* Englewood Cliffs, N.J.: Prentice-Hall, Inc., 1972.

Peacocke, Christopher. "Explanation in Computational Psychology: Language, Perception, and Level 1.5." *ML* I, 2 (Summer 1986): 101–23.

Putnam, Hilary. *Representation and Reality.* MIT, 1988.

Pylyshyn, Zenon W. *Computation and Cognition.* MIT, 1984.

Schank, Roger C., and Robert P. Abelson. *Scripts, Plans, Goals, and Understanding.* Hillsdale, N.J.: Laurence Erlbaum Press, 1977.

Searle, John R. *Minds, Brains, and Science.* Harvard, 1984.

Smolensky, Paul. "On the Proper Treatment of Connectionism" (with commentaries and response). *BBS* XI, 1 (March 1988): 1–74.

B. Individualism

Bilgrami, Akeel. "An Externalist Account of Psychological Content." *Philosophical Topics* XV, 1 (Spring 1987): 191–226.

Burge, Tyler. "Individualism and Psychology," *PR* XCV, 1 (January 1986): 3–45.

———. "Individualism and Self-Knowledge." *JP* LXXXV, 11 (November 1988): 649–63.

———. "Intellectual Norms and Foundations of Mind." *JP* LXXXIII, 12 (December 1986): 697–720.

———. "Other Bodies." In *Thought and Object,* ed. Andrew Woodfield. OUP, 1982, pp. 97–120.

Davidson, Donald. "Knowing One's Own Mind." *APA* LX, 3 (January 1987): 441–58.

Fodor, Jerry A. "Cognitive Science and the Twin-Earth Problem." *ND* XXIII, 2 (April 1982): 98–118.

Jacob, Pierre. "Thoughts and Belief Ascriptions." *Mind and Language,* II, 4 (Winter 1987): 301–25.

Kitcher, Patricia. "Narrow Taxonomy and Wide Functionalism." *PSci* LII, 1 (March 1985): 78–97.

Loar, Brian. "Subjective Intentionality." *Philosophical Topics* XV, 1 (Spring 1987): 89–124.

McDowell, John. "*De Re* Senses." In *Frege: Tradition and Influence,* ed. Crispin Wright. BB, 1984, pp. 98–109.

McGinn, Colin. *Mental Content.* BB, 1989.

Owens, Joseph. "In Defense of a Different Doppelganger." *PR* XCVI, 4 (October 1987): 521–54.

Putnam, Hilary. "The Meaning of 'Meaning'." In *MSPS* VII, ed. Keith Gunderson. Minn, 1975, pp. 131–93.

White, Stephen. "Partial Content and the Language of Thought." *PPQ* LXIII, 4 (October 1982): 347–65.

C. Scientific versus Folk Psychology

Baker, Lynn Rudder. *Saving Belief.* PUP, 1987.

Churchland, Patricia Smith. "A Perspective on Mind–Brain Research." *JP* LXXVII, 4 (April 1980): 185–207.

———. *Neurophilosophy: Toward a Unified Science of the Mind/Brain.* MIT, 1986.

———, and Paul Churchland. "Stalking the Wild Epistemic Engine." *N* XVII, 1 (March 1983): 5–18.

Churchland, Paul M. *A Neurocomputational Perspective: The Nature of Mind and the Structure of Science.* MIT, 1989.

———. *Matter and Consciousness.* Rev. ed. MIT, 1988.

———. "Reduction, Qualia, and the Direct Introspection of Brain States," *JP* LXXXII, 1 (January 1985): 8–28.

———. *Scientific Realism and the Plasticity of Mind,* CUP, 1979.

———, and Patricia Smith Churchland. "Functionalism, Qualia, and Intentionality." *Philosophical Topics* XII, 1 (Spring 1981): 121–45.

Cummins, Robert. *The Nature of Psychological Explanation.* MIT, 1983.

Garfield, Jay L. *Belief in Psychology: A Study in the Ontology of Mind.* MIT, 1988.

Gordon, Robert M. "Folk Psychology as Simulation." *ML* I, 2 (Summer 1986): 158–71.

Horgan, Terence, and James Woodword, "Folk Psychology is Here to Stay." *PR* XCIV, 2 (April 1985): 197–225.

Kitcher, Patricia. "In Defense of Intentional Psychology." *JP* LXXI, 2 (February 1984): 89–106.

Kosslyn, Stephen M., and Gary Hatfield. "Representation Without Symbol System." *SR,* LI, 4 (Winter 1984): 1019–45.

Millikan, Ruth Garrett. "Thoughts Without Laws: Cognitive Science With Content." *PR* XCV, 1 (January 1986): 47–80.

Morton, Adam. *Frames of Mind.* OUP, 1980.

Papineau, David. *Reality and Representation.* BB, 1987.

Rorty, Richard. "Wittgensteinian Philosophy and Empirical Psychology." *PS* XXXI, 3 (March 1977): 151–72.

Stich, Stephen P., "Do Animals Have Beliefs?" *AJP,* 57, 1 (March 1979): 15–28.

———. *From Folk Psychology to Cognitive Science.* MIT, 1983.

———. "On the Ascription of Content." In *Thought and Object,* ed. Andrew Woodfield. OUP, 1982, pp. 163–206.

von Eckart, Barbara. "Cognitive Psychology and Principled Skepticism." *JP* LXXXI, 2 (February 1984): 67–88.